D1291634

The Complete Works of
WASHINGTON
IRVING

Richard Dilworth Rust
General Editor

LETTERS

Volume I

Washington Irving

1809

WASHINGTON IRVING

LETTERS

Volume I 1802-1823

Edited by
Ralph M. Aderman, Herbert L. Kleinfield
and Jenifer S. Banks

Twayne Publishers
Boston
1978

Published by Twayne Publishers

A Division of G. K. Hall & Co.

Copyright © 1978 by

G. K. Hall & Co.

All rights reserved

The Complete Works of Washington Irving

Volume XXIII

CENTER FOR EDITIONS OF
AMERICAN AUTHORS

AN APPROVED TEXT

MODERN LANGUAGE
ASSOCIATION OF AMERICA

®

Library of Congress Cataloging in Publication Data

Irving, Washington, 1783–1859.
Letters.

(His The complete works of Washington Irving ; v. 23–   )
Includes index.
CONTENTS: v. 1.   1802–1823.
1.   Irving, Washington, 1783–1859—Correspondence.
2.   Authors, American—19th century—Correspondence.
I. Aderman, Ralph M.   II.   Kleinfield, H. L.
III.   Banks, Jenifer S.
PS2081.A4   1978   818'.2'09 ₍B₎   78–13933
ISBN 0–8057–8522–1

CONTENTS

LETTERS, 1802–1823

ILLUSTRATION

FRONTISPIECE

An 1809 Portrait of Washington Irving by
John Wesley Jarvis.
Reproduction courtesy of Sleepy Hollow Restorations

ACKNOWLEDGMENTS

In the long and complex task of their work with these letters, the editors have contracted so many debts and obligations, as well as valuable assistance and friendship, that some approximation of full acknowledgment has bounded beyond their reach. Librarians, collectors, curators, earlier and contemporary scholars, autograph dealers, colleagues and friends have played their parts in our little drama; and whether minor or major, each has been truly valued. For all those who had a part—whether in contributing, answering queries, offering opinions, supplying funds and other forms of support, expressing interest and encouragement—this edition of the letters is collectively the work of all. Although holding the leading roles, the editors would never have accomplished their aims without this marvelous supporting cast. If some of their names do not appear here, the editors meekly plead limitations of printing space, weaknesses of memory, method, massive materials, and the inexorability of time. If their list of acknowledgments falls short, the burden of the hearts overflows.

The editors' primary debt is to the heirs of Washington Irving who, in the persons of Mrs. A. Duer Irving, of Wilmington, Delaware, and the late Washington Irving, of Providence, Rhode Island, graciously permitted the printing of materials never before published. Of great importance, too, were grants from the American Philosophical Society, which made possible a survey of Irving manuscripts out of which plans for this edition could be formed. Sleepy Hollow Restorations, whose interest in Washington Irving includes, but exceeds, this edition, has been helpful in many ways. The Center for Editions of American Authors of the Modern Language Association, through its grant from the National Endowment for the Humanities (National Foundation on the Arts and Humanities) furnished funds for research assistance, travel, staff, and free working time for the editors. The American Council of Learned Societies also assisted with grants-in-aid. The research funds of the Graduate School of the University of Wisconsin—Milwaukee and of C. W. Post Centre, Long Island University, provided the editors with additional support.

The editors had the benefit of materials and assistance from curators, collectors, owners, librarians and their staffs both throughout the United States and also in Spain, France, Scotland, and England. Their chief debtors along with their staffs include Dr. Donald Gallup, Curator of

American Literature, Beinecke Library, Yale University; Dr. James Henderson, Director of Research Libraries, New York Public Library; C. Waller Barrett and the Barrett Collection, University of Virginia; Edmund Berkeley, Jr., Curator of Manuscripts, University of Virginia; the late William A. Jackson, and Dr. William H. Bond, Houghton Library, Harvard University; Roger Baumann, former Curator, and Kenneth Lohf, Curator, Special Collections, Columbia University; the late Sir John Murray and Mr. John G. Murray, London, England; Dr. Oliver Wendell Holmes, Director, National Historical Publications Commission.

Other university collections, those of state historical societies, collectors, and descendants contributed materials in smaller numbers but of no less importance than those already mentioned. The source of each letter is duly noted in a designated place throughout the work. The editors' appreciation is noted here in addition.

In the preparation of final copy certain individuals have given unstintingly of their time and effort. Foremost among these are the late Professor Henry A. Pochmann, original creative force behind the entire Irving edition and its first Senior Editor; Mrs. Betty Husting, Executive Assistant to Professor Kleinfield; Susan Sandler, who tirelessly gathered annotations for many letters; and Professor James F. Beard for helpful editorial advice. Professors Walter A. Reichart, Lewis Leary, Richard D. Rust, and C. Hugh Holman also read the manuscript and gave wise counsel concerning problems connected with transcribing Irving's erratic handwriting. For invaluable aid in transcribing and translating Irving's letters in Spanish the editors wish to acknowledge the generous assistance of Professors Pierre Ullman and Gerard Flynn of the Department of Spanish and Portuguese of the University of Wisconsin—Milwaukee and of Professors Frank Duffey, William McKnight, Pablo Casado, and Lawrence Sharpe of the Department of Romance Languages of the University of North Carolina at Chapel Hill. In addition, Professor Aderman wishes to thank Mrs. Joanne Michalak, William Baurecht, Thomas Buchholz, Katherine Glowes, Jenifer Banks, Mrs. Sally Wasielewski, Betty Ann Trampe, Constantin Popescu, Sister Jane Eschweiler, and Dean Werner, graduate students at the University of Wisconsin—Milwaukee who have worked diligently in preparing copy and in collecting material for the annotations. Alice Aderman and Jeanne Kleinfield continually provided the essential emotional and intellectual sustenance without which few works of scholarship like this can live.

R. M. A.

H. L. K.

J. S. B.

GENERAL INTRODUCTION
TO LETTERS

Today the name of Washington Irving is associated in the popular mind with Rip Van Winkle, Ichabod Crane, and Sleepy Hollow and perhaps with a burlesque treatment of the early settlers of New York. He is remembered for his easy, felicitous style of expression, and literary historians have acclaimed him as the father of the American short story. Despite these achievements, Irving is not a popular writer today, though probably his reputation is equal to that of fellow Knickerbockers like James Fenimore Cooper and William Cullen Bryant and greater than that of James Kirke Paulding, Nathaniel P. Willis, and Fitz-Greene Halleck. In contrast, Irving's nineteenth-century reputation enabled him to live comfortably from his writing after 1820 and to establish himself as the first successful professional author in the United States. The innumerable collected editions of his works testify to their widespread attractiveness to the common reader. Although his genial sentimentality, his avoidance of controversy, his romantic coloring of history and biography, and his shunning of metaphysics and serious philosophical issues probably contributed much to his contemporaneous popularity, they are doubtless the reasons why many readers today pass him by.

Yet Washington Irving deserves a second glance today because he is such a typical representative of the middle-class mentality of nineteenth-century America. In his concerns and in his writings Irving mirrored the attitudes of a large proportion of his contemporaries. They desired entertainment, and Irving provided it in his tales and sketches. In a sentimental age when the people wanted their emotions stirred up, Irving obliged with stories like "The Broken Heart" or "The Wife." At a time when the robust humor of the Southwestern and Western frontiers was beginning to attract attention, Irving countered it with his own genial comic observations which appealed to more conventional minds. Thus by reflecting popular tastes, he collected the tribute which readers paid him when they bought his books in great quantities.

These public productions, however, represent only one side of Washington Irving the writer. Another facet is to be found in the private or semiprivate utterances in his letters. Living in an age which depended heavily on the written word for communication, Irving was an inveterate and prolific letter-writer. Since he lived before the convenience of the telephone and felt inhibited by the limitations imposed by the telegraph,

Irving used letters as a major means of expressing his ideas. In society
he enjoyed nothing more than a pleasant chat in an intimate circle of
friends. Often when such meetings were not possible, he carried on the
same kind of discourse in solo fashion by setting down his observations
on paper and sending them off to his friends. The reader today can
readily recapture the warmth and geniality conveyed in letters to such
different personalities as Henry Brevoort, Mary Fairlie, Charles Leslie,
Thomas Storrow, relatives like his sisters Catharine and Sarah and his
nieces who lived with him at Sunnyside in his later years, John P. Kennedy, Mary Kennedy, and Mrs. O'Shea. Irving also used letters in his
negotiations with and directions to his publishers and in his instructions
to his literary agent in England, Colonel Thomas Aspinwall. In these
communications, because circumstances dictated it, Irving wrote more
directly and forcefully so that his position would not be misunderstood
or misinterpreted.

As an official in the diplomatic service Irving learned to write letters
reporting delicate political, social, or economic issues to his superiors in
Washington. In them he was precise and specific, conveying the full range
of facts and implications from which a high-level decision could be
made. As a diplomat Irving also corresponded with his counterparts in
other governments, and his communications to them are couched in the
formal language which diplomatic convention required. Irving was able
to adapt and utilize the particular style and mode of expression in his
diplomatic correspondence which would achieve maximum effectiveness.

Since Irving's correspondence spans the first six decades of the nineteenth century, it provides an interesting record of one alert observer's
reactions to many, though not all, of the issues and concerns of the day.
While it is true that Irving was not directly involved in most of the significant events of the time, still his occasional comments and asides
enlighten the reader as much as the studied responses of more active
participants. Despite his seeming diffidence, Irving was usually aware
of what was happening around him.

THE EARLY YEARS (TO 1815)

Although Washington Irving throughout his lifetime was associated with
New York and the Hudson River valley, the bulk of his earliest correspondence sets forth his responses to Europe. Like many young men of
the late eighteenth and early nineteenth centuries, Irving took the Grand
Tour of Europe as a climax to his student years. Though largely self-
taught, he had reached the point where exposure to the rich culture and
traditions of Western Europe would give him the necessary finish desirable for the son of a New York merchant. Moreover, Irving, the youngest

of the nine children of William Irving, was petted and fussed over by the other members of his family who were especially concerned about his delicate health. Since the sea voyage and an extended tour were considered effective remedies in such cases, Washington was sent off to Bordeaux on May 19, 1804, about six weeks after reaching his twenty-first birthday.

His physical condition at the time of sailing was precarious, and Captain Shaler of *The Rising States* observed candidly as the young invalid was helped onto the deck, "There's a chap who will go overboard before we get across." This prediction, however, proved false; and Irving, despite a brief period of seasickness and fevers at night, regained his strength during the calm passage of thirty-six days. After a delay for the routine quarantine he stepped ashore after forty-two days, ready to begin an adventure which would last for nineteen months, carry him through France, Italy, Switzerland, Belgium, Holland, and England, and provide him with social perspective that he would later apply vigorously in his satiric examination of New York life and manners in *Salmagundi*.

Since one of the conditions for family support of his trip was a full account of his observations and experiences, Irving was soon engaged in writing letters to his brother William and in keeping a journal of his activities. The two types of writing provide a very full picture of the young American's wanderings in Europe. Sometimes he composed the account for his notebook first, and on other occasions he wrote a letter and copied out the essential details before mailing it. Frequently, in an effort to make his reports more complete, he would embellish them with quotations or adaptations from the guidebooks and travel narratives he was consulting. As a result, his reports combine factual details about the architecture and other cultural landmarks with the intelligent responses of a sensitive observer.

Irving spent about six weeks in Bordeaux before proceeding on his travels. Part of his time was occupied with the study of French, particularly in developing his proficiency in comprehending the spoken language. Among other activities were his visits to the churches, his attendance at the Grand Theatre to see several performances by Pierre Lafon, his socializing with Jean Ferrière, former mayor of Bordeaux, and with Americans like William Lee and Dr. John G. Ellison, then residing in the French city. In his letters Irving conveys the excitement and exhilaration which gripped him as he wandered about the streets and promenades of the busy port.

As he prepared to leave, Irving experienced a difficulty which was to be repeated frequently during his trip—passport trouble. The uncertainties caused by the effects of the Napoleonic Wars and the lack of standardized procedures for issuing travel documents and the unwillingness of officials to take responsibility for them brought delays for the traveler. Finally on August 5 he started his leisurely course across southern France toward Marseilles, a trip which occupied the next two weeks. At Toulouse he fell in with Dr. Henry or Henory, an American physician well acquainted with French customs, who was to render the inexperienced Irving valuable assistance during his journey through Montpellier, Nîmes, Avignon, and Marseilles. After a stay of two and one-half weeks at Marseilles Irving and Dr. Henry proceeded to Nice, via Fréjus and Cannes. When Irving applied for a passport for Genoa, he learned to his astonishment that his passport was the type given to suspected persons and that he would have to await authorization from Paris before another could be issued. For five weeks Irving was exasperated by the incompetence and evasions of the bureaucrats in Nice, and only after the United States minister in Paris, Robert R. Livingston, in response to Irving's own plea, personally intervened with the appropriate officials was the frustrated traveler able to set off for Genoa, still fuming about his bad treatment.

In Genoa Irving thoroughly relaxed and enjoyed himself, probably for the first time in Europe. He moved in with Thomas Hall Storm, an old New York friend then serving as United States vice-consul in Genoa, and for two months partook of amusements and social activities involving some of the English-speaking residents of the city. Among these were the James Birds, the Joseph Walshes, and Lord and Lady Shaftesbury and their charming daughter. Standing out vividly in Irving's mind were a trip into a romantic mountain setting in the company of several beautiful ladies, his witnessing the execution of a fabled bandit, Giuseppe Musso, "the Great Devil of Genoa," and attendance at a private theatrical at Madame Brignoli's. When the opportunity to sail to Sicily in an American vessel presented itself shortly before Christmas, Irving eagerly seized it, because he had no desire to become involved with the lines of troops which were cordoning off the plague-ridden sections of the Italian peninsula.

The sea voyage to Messina nevertheless provided Irving with an exciting adventure with privateers, an encounter which he related with great relish in his letters home. After some tense moments the pirates departed with several kegs of brandy and some quicksilver, the only valuables on the vessel. During the remainder of the trip Irving read travel accounts concerning Sicily and Italy in anticipation of the days ahead, copied extensive notes from them into his journal, and worked intermittently on a letter which eventually ran to forty-eight pages, giving a detailed description of his activities in Genoa. Irving's Sicilian excursions were delayed for two and a half weeks by a quarantine imposed upon all vessels entering the harbor of Messina.

After regaining his freedom, Irving met with some American naval officers stationed in the area, and the social intercourse seemed to restore his genial disposition. Shortly afterward he took a schooner to Syracuse, where he visited the Ear of Dionysus, the catacombs, the fountain of Arethusa, and other local tourist attractions, all of which he duly noted in his journal. Then in company with officers from several American warships at Syracuse Irving went on horseback along the coast to Catania, took a side trip up the slope of Mount Etna, and then overland to Palermo in the northwestern part of the island. From here he took a ship to Naples, where he arrived on March 7, 1805. After a few days of desultory sightseeing Irving met Joseph C. Cabell and John Mercer, young Virginians then traveling in Europe, with whom he went to see Vesuvius, Herculaneum, and the other ruins in the area. These agreeable companions intensified his pleasure in exploring Naples and its environs.

From Naples the travelers leisurely made their way toward Rome, just in time for the activities of Holy Week. They busied themselves with sightseeing, examining the Villa Borghese, the Farnese Palace, the museum of the Vatican, the Barberini Palace, and numerous churches and Roman ruins, including the Coliseum, the Baths of Diocletian, and the Pantheon. Coupled with these daytime activities were visits with Baron Karl von Humboldt, Count Khevenhüller, Countess Carador, Chevalier Giustiniani, and several other American visitors, plus attendance at several religious services during Holy Week. The rather staccato entries in his journal suggest something of Irving's hectic pace in Rome.

In company with Joseph Cabell, Irving left Rome on April 11, traveling to Foligno, then veering northeastward to Ancona and Rimini and the Adriatic seacoast, thereby skirting Tuscany, which was then suffering from an epidemic of malignant fevers. Although Irving was thus forced to omit Florence from his itinerary, he hoped to compensate in part for it by reaching Paris in time for the botany lectures at the Jardin des Plantes in May. From Rimini Irving and Cabell turned inland along the Lombardy plain and headed toward Milan via Forli, Bologna, Modena, Parma, Piacenza, and Lodi, arriving there at 9:00 P.M. on April 29. During their brief visit in Milan they attended an operatic performance at La Scala, examined the cathedral, and hurried through two galleries of paintings. By this time Irving was sated from his exposure to Italian art. As he observed in his journal, "I have been kept in constant employment and my mental powers in continual exercise since my arrival at Naples by a succession of fine paintings statues buildings and curiosities and I have hardly room left for another picture or bust."

The next leg of the journey provided Irving and Cabell with a respite from art and led them through breathtaking mountain scenery, which appealed strongly to Irving's romantic nature. Moving from Milan to

Sesto Calende, across Lago Maggiore, through Intra, Locarno, and
Bellinzona, the two Americans soon reached St. Gotthard's pass over a
narrow, winding road bordered by towering masses of snow. From
there they descended into the village of Andermatt in the canton of
Uri and progressed next to Altdorf, the village made famous by William
Tell's feat of shooting the apple off his son's head with a crossbow.
Braving the cold rain, they pushed on to Lucerne, where they were
detained by bad weather before going on to Zurich and Basel. In Basel
they visited the library and an art collection containing works by Rubens,
Holbein, and Breughel. On May 19 the travelers set out for Paris by
diligence, arriving there after a five and one-half day trip.

Irving's stay in Paris lasted from May 24 to September 24, an interval of four months filled with exercises in self-improvement, theatergoing,
and socializing, if the brevity of the journal entries and the scarcity of
letters are a true indication. For this period only four letters have been
located, but they confirm that Irving had set up a rigorous schedule
for himself, including lectures on natural history at the Jardin des
Plantes and French lessons to improve his competence in the language. His enthusiastic reaction to Paris is seen in his observation to
his brother Peter on July 15: "Of all the places that I have seen in
Europe Paris is the most fascinating, and I am well satisfied that for
pleasure and amusements it must leave London far behind. The favorableness of the climate, the brilliancy of the theatres, operas, &c., the
beauty of the public walks, the gaiety, good-humor, and universal
politeness of the people, the perfect liberty of private conduct, are calculated to enchant a stranger, and to render him contented and happy
with every thing about him." Then he quickly adds that "America
has still the stronghold of my heart." But since he was living on a
rather Spartan allowance, he was unable to indulge in reckless spending
to gratify his senses. Nonetheless, the summer in Paris was probably
the high point of Irving's European visit and prepared him for later
visits to the French capital a decade and a half later.

Irving started for London at the beginning of autumn, taking a route
through Brussels to Rotterdam, where he caught a sailing packet for
Gravesend. At Rotterdam and again at Gravesend the ship was delayed
until the proper clearance papers could be secured. In fact, Irving's
passport for entering was delayed almost four days because of the
indifferent handling of his papers. Even though the time lost was
trifling in comparison with his experience at Nice, the delay disturbed
him so much that he felt wary and suspicious during much of his three-
month stay in London. As might be expected, he hurried to the theater
and reacted favorably to the acting of Charles Kemble and Mrs. Siddons.
But the smoke and fog of London in November distressed him, so that

he left the city in mid-December for a brief excursion to Oxford, Bath, and Bristol. After more socializing in London upon his return, Irving went to Gravesend, where he boarded the *Remittance*, which sailed for New York on January 23, 1806. When it reached its destination on March 24, sixty-four days later, Irving's *Wander-* and *Lehrejahre* were finished, and he had to think about preparing himself for the future.

Almost immediately upon his return to New York, Irving plunged into the social whirl. With his health restored, he was ready to drink and sing and flirt, and soon a group of congenial spirits, calling themselves the "Lads of Kilkenny," was roistering at Dyde's and other drinking establishments in Manhattan, as well as at Gouverneur Kemble's country home near Newark, later celebrated as Cockloft Hall in *Salmagundi*. Such escapades were offset, however, by his serious application to the reading of the law, from which his European trip had providentially extricated him two years earlier. Soon he had to take the bar examination, an ordeal for which he was poorly prepared. But with the indulgence of his examiners he was permitted to pass and so hung out his shingle as a partner of his brother John. Fortunately for the legal profession, Washington's interests lay in other directions, and he did not exercise his legal talents to any appreciable extent.

The long letters and voluminous journals which Irving had composed during his European travels had shown him that he could easily set down his ideas and impressions on paper in a graceful and interesting manner with a minimum of effort. Consequently he readily agreed to enter into a project of writing humorous social satire with his brother William and with William's brother-in-law, James Kirke Paulding, his long-time friend, now a clerk at the United States Loan Office, who for some years past had entertained the young ladies with his witty verses and his humorous sallies in the newspapers. Thus *Salmagundi* was born, and for twelve months and through twenty numbers, beginning on January 24, 1807, the polite society of New York was amused and scandalized by the outrageous castigation of its behavior by Launcelot Langstaff, Anthony Evergreen, and William Wizard in the fashion of the *Spectator* papers of the previous century. The verse was supplied by William Irving in the guise of Pindar Cockloft, and its topical references added to the titillations at the tea tables. In the third issue appeared Mustapha Rub-a-dub Keli Khan, a Tripolitan captive in New York, whose observations and comments about American life and institutions provided another angle for social satire. Using the device of the outlander as Goldsmith had done in *The Citizen of the World*, the Salmagundians ridiculed the windy, wordy proceedings in Congress, poked fun at elections, and needled women for their vanity and their interest in the "dancing mania." Travel writing, too, was satirized in the spoofs involv-

ing "The Stranger" in New Jersey, Philadelphia, and New York. Interspersed among these selections were reviews of musical and dramatic
performances, historical accounts, character sketches, and burlesques
of political behavior. The material thus provided a potpourri by which
the fledgling authors could exercise their talents and show their versa-
tility. Still such a constant outpouring was a drain upon their energy
and their ingenuity; so when a disagreement over their remuneration
arose with David Longworth, the publisher, the Irvings and Paulding
abruptly discontinued *Salmagundi*.

Washington Irving, however, did not allow his pen to remain idle
for long. Joining with his brother Peter, the former editor of the Burrite
Morning Chronicle who had just returned from a year in Europe,
Washington decided to burlesque Dr. Samuel Mitchill's *Picture of
New-York* by using some of the satiric techniques which had been so
successful in *Salmagundi*. The project was interrupted while the brothers
attempted to thwart the Embargo by bringing money from Montreal to
pay for merchandise sent to Canada illegally. Before they could resume
the burlesque, which had now developed into a mock heroic history of
New York, further distractions intervened, with the result that Peter left
hurriedly for Liverpool to assist there with the hard-pressed importing
business of the family.

With the departure of Peter, Washington turned his attention again
to the mock history, altering the original plan and focussing specifically
on the Dutch period. Again he was distracted, this time by the failing
health of Matilda Hoffman, the attractive daughter of his former legal
mentor, Josiah Ogden Hoffman. During his study of the law Irving was
treated as a member of the Hoffman family, and out of this intimacy he
developed a deep attachment for Matilda. When she died of tuberculosis on April 26, 1809, Irving was completely crushed. In an effort to
regain control of himself he retired to Kinderhook and immersed himself
in his comic history of New York. Throughout the summer and early fall
he worked away, encouraged and assisted by his former collaborator,
James Kirke Paulding. Finally, after a series of publicity stunts which
paralleled those of Madison Avenue today, *Knickerbocker's History of
New York* was launched on December 6, 1809. The book caught the
public fancy and sold well, bringing the author about $3000 for his efforts.

The letters in the period following the publication of the history
indicate that Irving was trying to find employment more dependable than
authorship. Even though he had influential friends working in his behalf,
he failed to get a clerkship in one of the New York courts. Finally, after
other frustrating experiences, he was offered a one-fifth partnership in
the importing firm of P. & E. Irving Co. His responsibilities were slight;
and as long as business prospered, he was provided with a modest

income and leisure to pursue his literary interests. In the future this business connection would change the course of Irving's life, for because of it he would be drawn to England and a world of new experiences.

In the meantime the political and economic tensions between England and the United States worsened, and the young partner was sent to Washington early in 1811 to lobby for legislation which would benefit the New York merchants with English connections. As happened so frequently with Irving, his social activities in the capital dominated his time, and soon he wrote to his friend Henry Brevoort, describing a reception at the White House and proudly announcing his friendship with Mrs. Madison and several members of Congress, including Henry Clay and John Randolph.

Upon his return to New York, Irving resumed his social activities with many of his long-time friends—Paulding, Brevoort, Gouverneur and Peter Kemble—and began revising *Knickerbocker's History*, which retained its popularity both at home and abroad. This revision was published in June, 1812, and from the resulting attention caused by it Irving was offered the editorship of a Philadelphia magazine, the *Analectic*, published by Moses Thomas. Since he was still trying to find himself, Irving agreed to accept the position, with the understanding that it was not a full-time commitment. Enlisting the aid of Paulding, he made the *Analectic* a vehicle for patriotic and nationalistic sentiments. Among the regular features was the "Naval Chronicle" devoted to reporting the exploits of American warships and to laudatory biographies of Navy officers like Stephen Decatur, Oliver Hazard Perry, David Porter, and James Lawrence. Many of the reviews of American writers included strong nationalistic overtones; for example, Paulding's *Lay of the Scottish Fiddle* was highly praised for its staunch defense of American principles and its harsh satiric treatment of the British.

As the British campaign against the Americans reached its peak with the burning of Washington in late August, 1814, Irving enlisted in the New York State militia and spent the remainder of the year serving as aide-de-camp to the commander, Governor Daniel Tompkins. Although Irving's duties were not onerous and never involved him in any danger, he felt that he was contributing to the defense of his country. His brief diversion into military service convinced him, among other things, that he was not temperamentally suited for the steady responsibilities of magazine editing, so he resigned from the *Analectic* with a feeling of relief.

YEARS AS EXPATRIATE, 1815–1832

Still restless after his military adventure, Irving welcomed Commodore Stephen Decatur's suggestion that he accompany the American fleet to

Algiers. When Napoleon's return from Elba delayed the sailing, Irving switched to a commercial vessel bound for Liverpool. There he joined his brother Peter in the family importing business, taking time out only for a short trip to Birmingham to see his sister and brother-in-law, Sarah and Henry Van Wart, and then on to London to see the convening of Parliament and to partake of the excitement caused by Napoleon's defeat at Waterloo. Soon he returned to Liverpool to assume responsibility for the business during Peter's illness. Apart from occasional visits to Birmingham and London and an excursion or two into the English and Welsh countryside, Irving spent the next two years in the little office in James Street near Goree Wharf, trying to breathe life into the faltering business. By mid-1817 the situation was hopeless, so he began to think about writing as a means of supporting himself. In addition to asking Brevoort to send him copies of two Indian sketches published in the *Analectic,* Irving was taking notes and drafting sketches in anticipation of his English literary debut. Finally he set off for London in pursuit of literary inspiration. While there, he met Thomas Campbell, the poet, and James Ogilvie, an orator whom he had known in New York. Hoping also to act as entrepreneur for the republication of English writings in America, Irving had dinner with John Murray and commenced his long and profitable association with the "Prince of Booksellers."

The meeting at Murray's, where Irving met George Canning and Isaac D'Israeli, stimulated him to make other literary acquaintances; and since London in August did not hold out many other prospects, Irving decided to head northward to Scotland, where he could meet people like Walter Scott and Francis Jeffrey. As he sailed in the smack *Lively* for Berwick, the American, with a copy of *Marmion* in his hand, compared Scott's descriptions of the coast with the scenes that passed before his eyes. Exhilarated by the experience, Irving proceeded by coach to Edinburgh, where he paid his respects to Jeffrey and other Edinburgh notables. Even so, he was anxious to meet Scott, whose poetry was well known in New York and whose interest in legend, folklore, and local history accorded with Irving's own.

The details of Irving's warm reception at Abbotsford have been told many times, best of all by Irving himself, and need not be repeated here. He was welcomed by Scott as one of the family and invited to stay and join him on an excursion to Dryburgh Abbey and on tramps through the hills along the River Tweed. He was entertained by the border songs sung by Sophia, the eldest daughter, and by romantic tales narrated by Scott himself. Moreover, Scott convinced him to study German so that he could discover for himself the folk stories of the Black Forest. These suggestions reinforced Irving's own predilection to use such materials for literary purposes, and he returned to Liverpool, eager to carry out his plans.

In Liverpool, however, there was still the distraction of dissolving the family business through bankruptcy, a dreary affair which dragged on through the spring of 1818 before it was concluded. In the meantime Irving had decided to remain abroad a while longer and pursue his writing. As he observed to his brother William, "I feel that my future career must depend very much upon myself, and therefore every step I take at present, is done with proper consideration. In protracting my stay in Europe I certainly do not contemplate pleasure, for I look forward to a life of loneliness and of parsimonious and almost painful economy." What little income he now had was derived from a contract with Moses Thomas, the Philadelphia bookseller, to supply him with new English works to be printed for the American trade.

By August, 1818, Irving had gone to London, determined to move ahead with his literary plans. Among his new acquaintances were Washington Allston, Gilbert Stuart Newton, and Charles Leslie, with whom he developed an intimacy that made his life much more enjoyable during the next few years of his self-imposed exile. Allston and Leslie prepared illustrations for the new edition of *Knickerbocker's History of New York* which Thomas was publishing in Philadelphia, and so their ties were strengthened. Meanwhile, William Irving, ever solicitous of his younger brother's welfare, had arranged a clerkship for him with the Navy Board in Washington. But Irving declined the position, saying that he preferred to remain in England and gamble on the literary project he had under way.

By March 3, 1819, he had completed and sent off to Ebenezer in New York the set of essays which was to comprise the first number of *The Sketch Book*. Though somewhat diffident about them, Irving justified them as representing the kind of activity for which he was best fitted. The enthusiastic reception of the first number vindicated his faith in himself and spurred him forward in his creative efforts. By the end of the year he had sent off to New York the materials for six numbers and had arranged for the publication in volume form of the first four by John Miller, the English bookseller to whom he turned after John Murray had declined to publish them. Just as the English numbers were starting to attract readers, Miller went bankrupt. Providentially for Irving, Walter Scott, who was then in London to receive his baronetcy, intervened with Murray, and the printing and distribution of the work continued, with a second volume added as soon as Irving had composed the essays for it. Murray's taking over of the publication of *The Sketch Book* marked the beginning of an association which was to be mutually profitable, even though in later years it was marked by recrimination and misunderstanding.

With the book safely behind him and selling well, Washington Irving decided to visit Paris in the company of his brother Peter. They stopped in Le Havre to check on the possibility of investing in a steamboat company then being started by Edward Church and Reuben Beasley, with the idea that the profits from it could be used to support Peter. However, the Irving brothers in New York objected to Washington's using his money for this purpose and refused to honor his bank drafts on them. As a result, he had to make financial arrangements for the venture through Henry Brevoort until he could get control of his own funds in America. The hagglings and complaints related to this venture filled many of the letters that Irving wrote at this time.

In Paris Irving met Thomas Moore, the Irish poet, who was to be one of his closest friends in the months ahead. Though his rather active social life also involved George Canning, Sydney Smith, Lord John Russell, John Howard Payne, and many other congenial spirits in the English-speaking colony, Irving did not entirely neglect his literary enterprises. Already he was thinking of a sequel to *The Sketch Book* which would draw more extensively on English customs and manners as they related to an old-fashioned English squire and his manorial life. In July, 1821, Irving announced to Murray, "I have a mass of writings by me, rather desultory," which he hoped soon to get into order. *Bracebridge Hall* was taking shape. A few days later he returned to London and settled down to work on his manuscript. In September, during a visit to the Van Warts in Birmingham, he became ill and was forced to remain there for almost four months, thus delaying the completion of *Bracebridge Hall*. With considerable exertion he finished the writing and sent it off to New York to secure the American copyright. From Murray he received a thousand guineas for the book which appeared on May 23, 1822. That the reading public received it warmly in America can be seen in his observation to Brevoort: "It seems to give satisfaction here and I am nearly killed with kindness." The fatigue of seeing *Bracebridge Hall* through the press brought a recurrence of the lameness and swelling in the ankles which he had experienced in Birmingham. In an effort to gain relief from his complaint and to escape the distractions of the social whirl Irving decided to go to Aix-la-Chapelle, where he could take the waters.

This excursion into the German-speaking area of Europe was to last an entire year, to expose Irving to a different mode of life, and to provide him with materials which he proposed to incorporate into a German version of *The Sketch Book*. He was constantly on the lookout for anecdotes and legends which would appeal to his novelty-seeking readers.

As he gradually relaxed at the spas in Aix-la-Chapelle, Wiesbaden, and Mainz, his lameness and skin irritation lessened; and he found himself enjoying the spectacular scenery of the Black Forest as he pushed eastward toward Munich and Vienna. The Tyrolean Alps filled him with awe, and he responded to them with emotions as strong as those which had gripped him in the Swiss Alps seventeen years earlier. Though Irving found Vienna a perplexing city, he soon succumbed to its pursuits of pleasure. After several weeks there he departed for Dresden, which he considered "a more quiet and intellectual city, . . . a place of taste, intellect, and literary feeling." In Dresden he was to spend the winter and to pursue the study of German in its pure Saxon form.

The months in Dresden were filled with a bewildering variety of social activities for Irving. He was soon drawn into the parties and dinners of the English-speaking colony where his gracious manner charmed the ladies and impressed the men. He was introduced to King Friedrich August of Saxony and to his brothers, Princes Anton and Max, all of whom seemed pleased to have a man of letters of Irving's stature at the court for the winter. He entered enthusiastically into a project with Colonel Barham Livius to translate Weber's *Der Freischütz* into English, and later he worked on an English version of Weber's *Abu Hassan,* an adaptation of a tale in the *Arabian Nights.* Although these efforts added little to his literary reputation, they kept Irving's creative impulses alive.

Probably the most important aspect of Irving's Dresden residence was his association with the Foster family. Mrs. John Foster, her daughters Emily and Flora, aged eighteen and sixteen, and three younger sons soon became Irving's closest friends, and his relationship with Emily deepened into a love which was not returned with equal ardor by the young lady. His journal entries and letters reveal his constant attendance upon the family, an intimacy which was heightened by the preparation and performance of several amateur theatricals, including Fielding's *Life and Death of Tom Thumb,* Arthur Murphy's *Three Weeks After Marriage,* and Mrs. Centlivre's *The Wonder.* With his deep involvement in drama in Dresden it is easy to understand why Irving was willing to collaborate with John Howard Payne later in Paris. But despite his obvious pleasure in the company of the Foster family, especially Emily, he was restless and unsettled. Perhaps his involvement was taking too serious a turn, one that deflected him from his projected literary goals. So on May 20, 1823, in company with Lieutenant John Cockburn, he set out on a tour of Silesia and Bohemia.

Because of unexpected events this journey took more time than the two men had planned. In Prague Cockburn was stricken with scarlet fever and immobilized for several weeks. En route to the city Irving had complained about fever and pains in his face, and it is possible that he had a milder case of the same illness. Irving used his enforced leisure in Prague for sightseeing, letter-writing, theatergoing, or work on his own literary projects, as well as for recovering from his strenuous social involvements in Dresden. Finally on June 23, Irving and Cockburn left Prague, arriving at Dresden after four days of steady driving.

Irving now determined to leave Dresden and return to Paris, where he could concentrate on his writing. After rounds of leave-taking during the next two weeks he departed from the Saxon capital in the company of the Fosters, who were returning to England. Even though his love for Emily had not been reciprocated, his affection for the family was undiminished, and he savored their company on their trek through Meissen, Leipzig, the Harz, Thuringia, and into Hesse. At Kassel, Irving had intended to leave the Fosters and travel up the Rhine River toward Paris, but he changed his mind and accompanied them to Rotterdam, where they caught a boat for England. Saddened by their departure, Irving soberly headed for Paris by way of Antwerp and Brussels.

After settling there, Irving hoped to resume his writing, picking up and completing some of the projects he had worked on sporadically amid the distractions of his social life in Germany. Almost immediately, however, Irving found himself actively involved in the dramatic undertakings of John Howard Payne as collaborator and play doctor. Undoubtedly this involvement appealed to Irving, for it enabled him to dust off and polish up his translation of *The Wild Huntsman* and *Abu Hassan* as well. Throughout the fall of 1823 he continued his tinkering; at one point, stimulated by his exposure to Oriental subjects, he considered adapting some Arabian tales which Murray had passed along to him. But this venture ultimately came to naught as the pressing concerns of Payne overshadowed his own. Early in 1824, he revised *Salmagundi* for a new edition to be published in Paris by Galignani. This attention to his own writing brought him back to his second sequel to *The Sketch Book*; and spurred on by Murray's generous offer for the manuscript, he settled down to steady work on it. A trip to London completed the arrangements with Murray for immediate publication of *Tales of a Traveller*, and during the next ten weeks Irving combined visits with relatives and English friends and chores connected with the book— reading and revising proof and padding out various episodes to swell the two volumes to the required size.

On August 25, 1824, the new work appeared in two octavo volumes; and English readers, anticipating the charming stories and gracious style of *The Sketch Book*, bought it in great quantities. But they were disappointed in the quality of the new tales, and their feeling was supported by the critics, who remarked upon the derivative nature of the material and the occasional indelicate suggestions in some of the stories.

Irving himself, though acknowledging the unsystematic and hurried composition of parts of the material, felt that the book contained some of his best writing. When the verdicts of the English critics reached him in Paris, he became discouraged and depressed.

In an effort to find distraction and to raise his spirits, and perhaps in anticipation of a future course of action, Irving began a serious, concentrated study of Spanish in December, 1824. He purchased a Spanish grammar and a dictionary from Galignani, engaged a teacher of Spanish, and immersed himself in the details of Spanish language, literature, and history during the remainder of his residence in Paris. Although his social involvements for this period remained undiminished, Irving's main attention was directed toward acquiring competence in Spanish.

By August, Irving's confidence in himself had begun to return. A few weeks earlier he had brushed aside as impossible Constable's proposal for writing a life of George Washington. Although he did not seriously consider such an undertaking at that time, the germ was planted in his mind; and he would return to it for the final literary project of his career. Now, however, he proposed to his brother Peter that they go to Bordeaux to see the vintage in that famed wine-making region. For Irving it would be a return to the spot where he first touched foot on European soil. The visit to Bordeaux proved to be a pleasant interlude in which the brothers observed the wine-making process and socialized with congenial friends. Moreover, the creative impulses began to stir in Washington, and he worked steadily on what, in his journals, he called his "American Essays." Precisely what these writings dealt with is not known, for they apparently have not been preserved. Irving's concentration on them during his stay in Bordeaux suggests that he had thrown off his despair and self-pity and had once more started to write with confidence, even though the results must not have ultimately pleased him.

While in this mood of self-assurance Irving wrote to Alexander H. Everett, United States minister to Spain, reminding him of an earlier promise to attach Irving to the American Embassy in Spain to facilitate his movements in that country. In his favorable reply Everett suggested that Washington might like to translate into English a new work on Columbus by Martín Fernández de Navarette, a Spanish historian. This collection of materials included many documents which threw new light on Columbus and his activities. In his acceptance Irving enthusiastically outlined his plans, which included his making a proposal to Murray for publication of such a book. Apparently Irving felt sufficiently competent in Spanish to undertake confidently the translation. After arriving in Madrid and examining Navarette's account, Irving decided that he would start afresh. Navarette's version was too incoherent and prosaic to suit Irving's taste; and besides, he had discovered in talking to Obadiah

Rich, the American consul and a collector of Spanish books and manuscripts, that there were other materials in the Spanish archives which could add to the drama of Columbus's exploits.

By April, 1826, Irving had settled down to a regular routine of studying the books and documents in Rich's library and foraging among other collections in Madrid. With Peter's help, he took notes and started to organize the materials for his biography of Columbus. In his reading Irving also encountered a vast body of historical material relating to the reconquest of Granada by Ferdinand and Isabella, the patrons of Columbus. Led on by his fascination with the vicissitudes of Granada, he soon found himself caught up in the history of the Moorish conquest of Spain in an earlier period. His investigations of Moorish history occupied most of his attention from midsummer to mid-autumn of 1826. However, by Christmas of that year Irving optimistically informed Murray that the manuscript of *Columbus* was nearly ready. Actually Irving overestimated his completion date by seven months. By the end of July, 1827, he informed Murray that he had finished most of the book and that he expected to receive 3000 guineas for it, an amount which Murray was willing to pay for outright control of the work.

Somewhat to Irving's surprise, Murray accepted the proposal but then failed to communicate with the author in Madrid about the details needed to complete the book for the press. Finally in December, 1827, after seeing in a London newspaper an announcement of its impending publication, Irving wrote to Murray, chided him for his dereliction, and suggested that he might consult with Obadiah Rich, then in London, about unresolved questions concerning the manuscript. The tone of Irving's comments suggests that he was perturbed by Murray's seeming indifference, and in the months ahead the relations between author and publisher became increasingly strained, partly because of Murray's realization that Irving's books were not selling as well as both men had hoped.

For the time being, however, Irving turned his attention elsewhere. His friendship with Prince Dmitri Dolgorouki, the Russian diplomat, flourished, as did his association with Madame D'Oubril, wife of the Russian minister in Madrid, and with her niece, Antoinette Bollviller. David Wilkie, the Scottish painter whom Irving had known in Paris, was now working in Madrid, and he too became one of the American's intimates. But life was not all socializing; Irving was deep in his researches dealing with the Moors in Spain, and he had also determined to mine the Spanish archives for details about the conquest of Mexico, the latter a project which he later abandoned to W. H. Prescott. Still he was restless, eager for new scenes and new experiences.

On March 1, 1828, in the company of Stoffregen, secretary of the

Russian Legation, and Gessler, the Russian consul general, Irving set out for Andalusia, traveling by way of Cordoba to Granada. In Granada he was exhilarated by the scenery. As he observed to his friend Storrow, "Granada ... is a most picturesque and beautiful city, situated in one of the loveliest landscapes that I have ever seen. The Alhambra differs in many respects from the picture that had been formed by imagination; yet it equals my expectations, high as they were wrought." The profound impact upon Irving of the beauty, history, and legend of Granada led to his return to the city a year later, and out of these experiences came *The Alhambra*, an engaging excursion into Spanish Gothicism.

The travelers then proceeded southward through the savage grandeur of the Sierra Nevada Mountains and over the fertile vegas to Malaga, a Mediterranean port basking in lush tropical splendor. The luxuriant settings evoked pages of florid descriptions in his letters to relatives and friends. Irving had fallen in love with southern Spain and determined to spend some time there, combining enjoyment of the setting with his researches in the archives of Seville. Before reaching that city, however, Irving enriched his impressions with delightful visits to Gibraltar and Cadiz. When he reached Seville in mid-April, he found Wilkie waiting for him. Together they ranged through the city, studying the paintings of Murillo and Zurbarán, with Irving benefiting from Wilkie's expert comments.

When Irving went to the Archives of the Indias to gather material for his history of the Moorish conquest of Spain, he found that he could not gain access to them until he had received royal permission. While waiting for A. H. Everett, the United States minister in Madrid, to procure the necessary documents, Irving revised his life of Columbus, incorporating into it corrections and suggestions mentioned in the reviews. Careful checking revealed that Navarette had consulted and utilized so fully the materials in Seville relating to Columbus that Irving had to be satisfied in his revision with corrections of fact, addition of a few details, and improvements in style.

The oppressive heat of Seville drove Irving and John Nalder Hall, a consumptive young Englishman whom he had fallen in with, to the Cadiz area, where they rented a house at Puerto de Santa María in the heart of the Spanish sherry country. There Irving settled down to work on *The Conquest of Granada* and by the end of August had completed most of the manuscript. Six weeks later he told his brother Ebenezer, acting as his literary agent in New York, that the new work would make about a thousand pages printed in the format of *The Sketch Book*. Meanwhile, Irving had made the acquaintance of Johann Nicholas Böhl von Faber, an erudite German scholar who was managing the Duff

Gordon winery at Puerto de Santa María. From him Irving borrowed historical works in Spanish for materials to be used in his study of the companions of Columbus. A short time later Irving was to meet Böhl's daughter Cecile, the Marchioness de Arco Hermosa, who subsequently became famous for her novels written under the name of Fernán Caballero.

Suggestions from London and New York impelled Irving to abridge his life of Columbus upon his return to Seville in early November. Working furiously, he completed the condensation in a few weeks and sent it off to his publishers. As he continued his researches in the Archives of the Indias, he began also to work up some of the notes and other Spanish materials into tales and impressionistic essays, some of them on the *Sketch Book* pattern. The pressure of this intense activity brought on a recurrence of the skin ailment which he had suffered in England eight years previously. However, the pleasant climate of Seville and the welcome word of the publication of *The Conquest of Granada* enabled him to overcome his difficulties.

In March, 1829, Prince Dolgorouki informed Irving that he was planning to visit Seville. This news greatly excited the American, who, after his rigorous efforts with the pen, longed for the witty and urbane conversation which the cosmopolitan Russian prince could provide. Furthermore, Dolgorouki agreed to accompany Irving to Granada on May 1 for a leisurely visit to the Alhambra in the spring. When they arrived at the seat of the Moorish kings, the governor of the Alhambra offered them the use of his apartment there, a gesture which greatly pleased Irving. After the departure of the prince and of Irving's nephew Edgar, who had appeared unannounced, Irving settled down to enjoy the atmosphere of the Moorish palace and to revise and expand his material on Spanish history and legend. As he observed to Peter, "I have nothing but the sound of water, the humming of bees, and the singing of nightingales to interrupt the profound silence of my abode; and at night, stroll until midnight about the galleries overlooking the landscape, which are now delicious at night from the brightness of the moon. I am determined to linger here until I get some writings under way connected with the place, and that shall bear the stamp of real intimacy with the charming scenes described."

But Irving's idyllic, indolent existence was shattered with the receipt of news that he had been appointed secretary to the American Legation in London, a position arranged for by his brothers and by his old friend Paulding, who exerted considerable influence in Jacksonian circles. Although somewhat shocked by the action which had been taken without his assent, Irving readily accepted the post because he believed that service to his country might help to quiet the frequent comments that he had deserted his native land permanently. With his usual good luck, Irving met a young Englishman named Ralph Sneyd as he was about to leave Granada, and the two men set out on July 28, 1829, on the long journey to London.

When Irving reached London in mid-September, he immediately plunged into his duties as secretary to the American mission, assisting the new minister, Louis McLane, in the establishment of the office routine. Although his work in the Legation occupied most of his attention, Irving soon reestablished friendly relations with Charles Leslie and Gilbert Stuart Newton, his intimates of earlier years. He sent Thomas Moore's *Life of Byron* in manuscript off to Ebenezer Irving in New York with an urgent plea for suitable arrangements for its publication. In similar fashion he assisted the aged William Godwin, who was trying to find an American publisher for his novel, *Cloudsley*. Despite the hectic pace, Irving still had time to think about a literary project to which he would not be able to devote his full attention for many years. This was the biography of Washington.

With Irving's return to England he began to receive further recognition for his literary achievements. In April, 1830, the Royal Society of Literature awarded him a fifty-guinea gold medal for literary work of eminent merit. At almost the same time Oxford University proposed him for an honorary LL.D. degree, but the ceremony was postponed until June, 1831, because of the serious illness of the king.

During the summer of 1830 Irving broke away from the routine of the Legation by making a trip to Paris, where he saw the elevation of Louis Philippe to the French throne. On that journey Irving took with him the final pages of *The Voyages of the Companions of Columbus*, which he polished and had ready for Murray upon his return to London. Later he went to Birmingham to visit his sister and her family and to work on some of the Spanish tales and sketches. This literary activity he continued after his return to London, his goal being the completion of the manuscript during the forthcoming winter. But another literary distraction intervened; he agreed to revise the American edition of Alexander Slidell's *A Year In Spain* and to read the proofs as Murray put it through the press. The chore extended through the spring of 1831 and delayed Irving's own projects.

By June, McLane had decided to resign from the ministership in London and join Andrew Jackson's cabinet as secretary of the treasury, leaving Irving in charge of the Legation during a very tumultuous period. The debates on the English Reform Bill created additional problems for Irving, and soon he was chafing under the added burden. Part of the difficulty was that though he was the *chargé d'affaires*, he still remained on the secretary's salary, an arrangement not at all to his liking. He made it clear to his superiors in Washington that he intended to resign as soon as McLane's successor, Martin Van Buren, arrived in London. By August 30, Irving was already thinking of his release from the harassments of the Legation and of his early return to New York.

His departure was delayed, however, because he wished to take a holiday in the Midlands and to finish the manuscript of *The Alhambra*. But the burdensome distractions of his official position left their mark on his creative powers, and he found it difficult to resume his writing. As he observed to Peter on November 6: "The restlessness and uncertainty in which I have been kept, have disordered my mind and feelings too much for imaginative writing, and I now doubt whether I could get the *Alhambra* ready in time for Christmas." Furthermore, the unsettled state of British affairs appeared to keep people from reading, and the publishers were reluctant to bring out new books.

Irving's dealings with John Murray at this time compounded his frustration because Murray did not respond as quickly to Irving's letters as the American thought he should. Finally, Irving's continued pressure prompted a tart reply from the publisher which revealed his disenchantment with Irving's recent books. *Columbus* and *The Conquest of Granada* had not sold well, resulting in a loss of 2250 pounds for Murray, who reminded Irving of his earlier statement that he did not wish the publisher to lose any money from any work of his. Irving's answer was firm and persuasive; he emphasized that the sales of the books would continue for some time, that he had charged Murray nothing for the abridgement of *Columbus* nor for editing Slidell's *A Year in Spain* nor for two articles contributed to the *Quarterly Review*, and that the forthcoming *Alhambra* would also arouse interest in the earlier Spanish works. He concluded, "If you would give me & my works a fair chance I have no doubt you would find both of us to work well in the long run, but you must not always expect to clear the price of a farm by the first years crop." At about the same time Irving offered the publisher his partially completed manuscript of *Mahomet*, but Murray remained inflexible. Through the agency of Colonel Thomas Aspinwall, Irving eventually sold the two volumes of *The Alhambra* to Colburn and Bentley for 1000 guineas, while putting *Mahomet* in storage.

Even before he had completed these arrangements, Irving had received a letter from Gulian Verplanck in New York, asking him to act as intermediary with John Murray concerning the collection of William Cullen Bryant's poems. When Murray indicated his antipathy toward poetry in general, Irving retrieved the volume, placed it with J. Andrews with a dedication to Samuel Rogers, and saw it through the press before he left for America. Because he altered a line in "The Song of

Marion's Men" to avoid offending the British, Irving was severely criticized by some American readers, though not by Bryant himself.

In the period before his departure Irving toured the English countryside with Martin Van Buren, the minister-designate, to acquaint him with English customs, manor houses, and castles. They visited Newstead Abbey, Lord Byron's ancestral home, where Irving's antiquarian propensities asserted themselves, as they had three years earlier at the Alhambra. As a result, he lingered in the mansion for two weeks, savoring its historical, literary, and religious associations, and gathering impressions which he would later use in his essay on Newstead Abbey in *The Crayon Miscellany*.

But the time had come for his departure for home. He said farewell to his relatives in Birmingham and to Van Buren, who by now had learned of the Senate's rejection of him as minister at the Court of St. James. Irving then hurried over to Le Havre to say good-bye to his ailing brother Peter, whom he would not see again for three years. After seventeen years Irving turned his face westward and set out for his native land with mixed feelings of sadness and anticipation.

YEARS OF PUBLIC ACCLAIM IN AMERICA, 1832–1842

On May 21, after a stormy trip of forty days, Irving reached New York, where he was greeted warmly by his friends and admirers. Their enthusiasm resulted in a public dinner at the City Hotel on May 30, with three hundred of the leading citizens paying their respects to their compatriot who had returned as a famous literary figure. This enthusiastic reception helped to offset some of the earlier charges that Irving had deserted his country for the romantic blandishments of Europe. In his remarks Irving emphasized his desire to remain in America for the rest of his days, and the statement brought a loud outburst of applause from the listeners.

From New York Irving hastened after a few days to Washington to visit Louis McLane, his superior in the Legation in London. McLane, as Jackson's secretary of the treasury, was bothered by the problems relating to the renewal of the charter of the Bank of the United States. But Irving was not primarily interested in politics at this point; he soon renewed his acquaintance with Henry Clay, heard of his vicissitudes, and concluded that official life in Washington must be harassing and dismal in the extreme. After declining public banquets in his honor in Baltimore and Philadelphia, he returned to New York for a brief interval before he started up the Hudson River in the company of James Paulding, Charles J. Latrobe, and Count de Pourtalès. The latter two had crossed the Atlantic with Irving, and they now joined him for a visit to Gouverneur Kemble, who was casting cannon for the government in his West Point Foundry at Cold Spring, across the river from the Military Academy.

This pleasant visit was followed by a swing into New England covering Boston, the White Mountains, and the Connecticut River valley. After a short stay at Ebenezer's cottage at Tarrytown Irving headed north for Saratoga Springs, where he rejoined Latrobe and Pourtalès for a trip through western New York state. In the course of this excursion they met Henry Ellsworth, one of the commissioners of Indian Affairs, who suggested that they join him on a journey to the Pawnee country in the Indian Territory on the prairies beyond the Mississippi. Finding the idea attractive, Irving and his friends accompanied Ellsworth on Lake Erie to Ashtabula, across Ohio to Cincinnati, down the Ohio River to St. Louis, overland to Independence, Missouri, and on to Fort Gibson, Arkansas, where they soon found themselves among the Indians.

The novelty of the setting appealed to Irving's romantic nature, and he carefully recorded his observations in his notebooks. For him a new phase in his literary career was emerging. He would treat native American scenery and inhabitants and early exploits of exploration and settlement in the West with the same vigor and purity of style that he had used in *The Sketch Book, Bracebridge Hall, Tales of a Traveller, The Alhambra*, and the Spanish histories and biographies and would thus open up new vistas for a waiting body of readers. In the next five years he utilized aspects of the American West in such works as *A Tour on the Prairies, Astoria*, and *The Adventures of Captain Bonneville, U. S. A.*, which showed his doubting countrymen that his long stay in Europe was but a necessary preparation for a romantic literary treatment of his own beloved United States.

Irving's adventures in Indian country exposed him to white trappers and frontiersmen as well as to half-breeds and red men. In some phases of his European travels Irving had encountered primitive conditions among unsophisticated people living close to nature, so he was not surprised at finding the same things on the prairies. Now forty-nine years old, Irving did not possess the vigor and stamina of some of the younger men in the party, but he carried on with a minimum of complaint. Although the rough country and the natural obstacles caused some difficulties, the members of the group made their way in the period between October 9 and November 9 around a circuit along the Arkansas and Cimarron Rivers and skirted the branches of the Canadian River on their return to Fort Gibson. There Irving caught the steamboat which took him down the Arkansas River to the Mississippi and thence to New Orleans.

After viewing the cultural mixture which made up New Orleans,

Irving journeyed by mail stage to Mobile, Alabama, and then on to Columbia, South Carolina, where he called upon his former traveling companion in England and Scotland, William C. Preston, now a leader of the nullifiers. Although Irving did not agree with Preston's political views, he did not allow their differences to interfere with their reminiscing. After a pleasant day he continued his journey to Washington, where he joined McLane's circle for several weeks of fraternizing during the holiday season and listening to the debates in Congress on the tariff and the nullification issues. In retrospect, as he considered his western trip, Irving reached a decision which he communicated to Peter: "It is absolutely my intention to make our country my home for the residue of my days; and the more I see of it, the more I am convinced, that I can live here with more enjoyment than in Europe."

In the spring and summer of 1834 Irving continued his leisurely reacquaintance with his own country. Before returning to New York, he stopped off in Baltimore for three weeks, meeting John Pendleton Kennedy, who was to be a close friend for the next quarter of a century. After a few weeks in New York Irving again headed south and visited Fredericksburg, Charlottesville, and the Blue Ridge Mountains. He dined with President Jackson in Washington and was delighted with the old general's salty remarks concerning an attempt on his life. A few weeks later the two men met again in New York during Jackson's northern visit. Irving continued his desultory wandering, with a stay at Saratoga Springs to take the baths and a visit to Martin Van Buren at Kinderhook which ended with the two men taking a carriage trip to Poughkeepsie and the Catskill Mountains and stopping at many Dutch places along the way. By early autumn Irving had gone again to Washington to encourage McLane during the political turmoil which still engulfed Jackson and his Cabinet.

Upon his return to New York Irving began to reflect upon a suitable literary subject, much to the relief of his concerned relatives and friends who thought he had frittered away too much time in fruitless wandering and socializing. Although Irving still had undeveloped European materials in his notebooks, he felt the need to deal with an American subject. Further spurs to literary productivity were his losses on investments and his failure to have an abridgement of *Columbus* adopted as a school textbook. Thus, amid the distractions caused by living among Ebenezer's large family and by frequent social interruptions, Irving began to work up the impressions gleaned on his trans-Mississippi trip of 1832. By November 24, 1834, he could report to Peter: "I have written a little narrative of my tour from Fort Gibson on the Pawnee hunting grounds. It makes about three hundred and fifty pages of my usual writing; but I feel reluctant to let it go before the public...."

what I have written is extremely simple, and by no means striking in its details." Despite Irving's diffidence, *A Tour on the Prairies* appeared as part of "The Crayon Miscellany," with Murray bringing it out in March, 1835, followed by the Carey, Lea & Blanchard edition in the following month.

Once started, Irving steadily continued his literary outpourings in subsequent months. *Abbotsford and Newstead Abbey*, the second number of "The Crayon Miscellany," was issued in English and American editions on May 1 and on May 30, 1835, respectively. By rummaging through his portfolios and notebooks he produced a third number entitled *Legends of the Conquest of Spain*, which appeared in the autumn of 1835. In characteristic fashion he turned out three volumes of impressionistic material in less than a year's time.

Even while completing "The Crayon Miscellany," Irving was launched on his next literary venture. He had been approached by John Jacob Astor in the summer of 1834 to write a history of Astor's fur-trading establishment at the mouth of the Columbia River from letters, documents, and personal reminiscences of some of the survivors. The task of reducing the mass of historical material to manageable form seemed too large for Irving while he was occupied with the Crayon essays, so he arranged with Astor for Pierre Munro Irving, his nephew, to be employed to put the details into coherent form. Then, as Irving noted, "I might be able to dress it up advantageously, and with little labor, for the press." Arrangements were made for Pierre to live in with Astor as he shaped the documents into an orderly narrative, and by August, 1835, Irving himself had moved into Astor's house at Hellgate to revise and polish Pierre's draft. Within a month Washington could report to Peter that he had "written more than a volume, and have got within half a dozen chapters of the end of my work—an achievement which I did not expect to do for months." By October 8 he had completed his first draft, with only polishing and adding of personal details from interviews remaining. The writing was delayed by the failure of one of the participants in the fur-trading venture to appear, so Irving was unable to finish the manuscript before February, 1836. After the conclusion of satisfactory negotiations for his fees Irving saw the simultaneous publication of *Astoria* in America and England in October, 1836, and read the favorable critical reactions on both sides of the Atlantic.

However, Irving's writing did not occupy his full attention during this period. In the spring of 1835 he had purchased a ten-acre tract of land along the Hudson River near Tarrytown, and immediately he arranged with an architect to remodel and expand the cottage on the property. Since the changes and additions were extensive, the work progressed slowly. But by late November he could report to Peter that the building was enclosed and the work on the interior could continue in heated comfort. The completed building, Irving suggested, would be a suitable place for him and his brother Ebenezer to live out their days. Work on "The Roost," as Irving was to call it, dragged on through the summer of 1836, and he was not able to occupy it until October, the same time that *Astoria* appeared.

Other concerns weighed on Irving's mind during 1836. His investments (or speculations) in Indian lands proved to be spectacularly unsuccessful, and a loan to a friend remained unpaid when the funds were lost in a speculative venture. His invalid brother Peter, still in Europe trying to improve his physical condition, had decided to return to New York, and his voyage was a source of great concern to his family. But Peter arrived without difficulty and joined the others waiting to occupy Washington's new home on the Hudson.

In 1836 Irving also began his third volume on the American West. While at Hellgate in September, 1835, he had met Captain Benjamin Bonneville, who had just returned from three and one-half years of wandering in the Rocky Mountains and other western wilderness areas. After receiving Bonneville's assistance on some maps for *Astoria,* Irving became interested in a narrative which the explorer was writing and, during a visit to Washington in March, offered him a thousand dollars for his manuscripts and maps. This material Irving worked on intermittently during the next nine months before delivering it to his Philadelphia publishers, Carey, Lea & Blanchard. Immediately he contacted Colonel Thomas Aspinwall, his literary agent in London, who negotiated the sale of *The Adventures of Captain Bonneville* to Richard Bentley for a sum of 900 pounds, or 400 pounds more than Bentley had paid for *Astoria*. This additional amount suggests that, despite the precarious financial state of the times, Irving's western writings were attracting English readers with something close to his earlier drawing power.

With the successful completion of *Bonneville* Irving turned his attention to financial, personal, and family matters. Despite the tight money situation and his dubious investments in western lands, Irving added to his Hudson River property by purchasing adjoining acreage. He felt that Van Buren's subtreasury scheme might alleviate some of the distress by bringing control and order into the financial picture. But on these matters Irving was speaking as an interested party whose own livelihood was affected, not as an expert.

Irving's literary successes subjected him to further public importunings for which he had no sympathy. A group of admirers from Tammany Hall nominated him as mayor of New York City, but he quickly and firmly declined the honor. At about the same time President Van Buren offered him the secretaryship of the Navy Department, a post which Irving refused on the grounds that he was "too sensitive to endure the bitter personal hostility, and the slanders and misrepresentations of the press, which beset high station in this country." Instead, he suggested his old friend James K. Paulding for the position.

Besides these matters, Irving suffered the loss of his brother John Treat, who worked himself to death in his judgeship. To strengthen the family ties, Irving insisted that Ebenezer's girls move into the house at Tarrytown with him, but another misfortune befell him on June 27, 1838, with the death of Peter, the brother with whom he had been closely associated since his Jonathan Oldstyle essays in the *Morning Chronicle*. In Europe, even during the periods of Peter's precarious health, Washington could turn to him for encouragement, moral support, and sensitive criticism. The loss was great; the womenfolk with whom he was surrounded could merely divert him but not fill the void left by Peter's passing.

Partially to distract himself and partially to add to his lean purse, Irving started another literary project, the history of the Spanish conquest of Mexico, which had first suggested itself when he was researching in the archives of Madrid and Seville. But soon he abandoned it to William Hickling Prescott, a scholar who had recently completed a *History of the Reign of Ferdinand and Isabella* and whom Irving considered better qualified to carry out the task. Shortly after relinquishing his claim to this material, Irving agreed to be a regular contributor to the *Knickerbocker Magazine* at a stipend of $2000 per year. Most of the pieces were rifled from his notebooks or miscellaneous sheets written at earlier times. The arrangement was mutually satisfactory, bringing Irving extra income and adding luster to the pages of the magazine.

Other literary enterprises included a life of Oliver Goldsmith to accompany two volumes of selections for Harper's Family Library. Once again, Irving refurbished earlier materials prepared in 1825 for Galignani's edition of Goldsmith's writings. He also wrote a sentimental sketch of Margaret Davidson, the precocious poetess who died at sixteen, to accompany an edition of her verses. Irving's attitude toward them is evident in his observation that "Her poetical effusions are surprising, and the spirit they breathe is heavenly." Although these writings added little to his literary stature, they did keep his name before the reading public at a slack period in his career.

By the summer of 1841, amid the usual social distractions that came with warm weather, Irving had begun the preliminary investigations on a project that had interested him for many years—a biography of George Washington. As yet, he had not settled down to a regular regimen, but he was collecting relevant materials, including some hard-to-find books which T. W. Storrow sent him from Paris. By the end of the year he was writing steadily on Washington, and he could report that he was "now in a complete state of literary activity." However this happy condition did not continue for long.

YEARS OF INTERNATIONAL DIPLOMACY, 1842–1846

Irving's name and reputation made him an attractive target for various offers and inducements, most of which he could reject without hesitation. When in February, 1842, Daniel Webster, the secretary of state, asked Irving to become envoy extraordinary and minister plenipotentiary to the Spanish Court in Madrid, he hesitated only briefly before accepting the appointment as "the crowning glory" of his career. Remembering his stay in Spain fifteen years earlier, Irving apparently believed that the post would not be burdensome and that he would have ample time to continue with the life of Washington. Within a few days the appointment was approved by the Senate, and the direction of Irving's life had changed once more.

The period following his acceptance was a busy one. He had to select a staff to accompany him, a task complicated by the refusal of Joseph G. Cogswell to be his secretary of the Legation. Irving then settled upon Alexander Hamilton, Jr., grandson of the great Federalist statesman, for the post, with J. Carson Brevoort, son of his long-time friend, selected as one of the attachés. In mid-March he went to Washington for briefing and instruction and soon found himself lionized on every hand. Upon his return to New York his well-wishers tried to inflict another public dinner upon him. This one, however, Irving refused, using the shortness of time and excessive obligations as his excuses. On April 10, 1842, scarcely two months after his nomination, Irving sailed again for Europe.

As a result of unforseen circumstances, he landed at Bristol instead of Liverpool and so went to London before he visited his sister in Birmingham. While in London, he was presented to Queen Victoria at her levee. For most of the month of May he was occupied with social engagements, renewing old acquaintances, and occasionally finding himself in the limelight, though he intensely disliked being the center of attention. Finally he hurried across the English Channel, stopping briefly in Le Havre to see his old friend, Reuben Beasley, before proceeding to Paris to visit his niece, Sarah Storrow, who a short time before had been living with him at Sunnyside. His presence in Paris required some diplomatic calls in company with Lewis Cass, the American minister, and purchasing supplies and furnishings for his residence in Madrid delayed his departure from Paris until July 11. He proceeded by carriage to Bordeaux, where he renewed his friendship with the Guestiers and the Johnsons. Finally on July 25 he arrived in Madrid and established himself temporarily in the house occupied by Aaron Vail, the former chargé.

Soon after reaching the Spanish capital Irving met the minister of foreign affairs, Count Almodovar, and arranged for an appointment to present his credentials to General Baldomero Espartero, regent of Queen Isabella II. The reigning monarch was the twelve-year-old daughter of King Ferdinand, who before his death had issued a "pragmatic sanction" rescinding the Salic law excluding the succession of females to the Spanish throne. Consequently during the period before Isabella reached her majority the country was ruled by the regent, Espartero, to whom Irving submitted his letter of credence. After a brief formal interview with Espartero the two men and their staffs went to the Royal Palace, where the new minister was introduced to the little queen. Irving's comment to his sister conveys his strong personal sympathy for the child: "I could not but regard her with deep interest, knowing what important concerns depended upon the life of this fragile little being, and to what a stormy and precarious career she might be destined. Her solitary position, also, separated from all her kindred except her little sister, a mere effigy of royalty in the hands of statesmen, and surrounded by the formalities and ceremonials of state, which spread sterility around the occupant of the throne."

In a very short time Irving grew familiar with the tangled background of recent Spanish politics, and he summarized the details in a letter to his sister, Catharine Paris, on September 2, 1842. It soon became apparent to him that the leisure he had counted on for writing would not be available to him. In fact, the manner in which Irving conducted himself was watched closely by various factions at the Spanish court, so he had to move with great deliberation and circumspection. Furthermore, the complexity of issues required that he write long, detailed despatches to the secretary of state, analyzing the problems and the possible effects upon American foreign policy. After a thorough report on various schemes and plots affecting the Spanish court Irving succinctly assessed the situation: "All this would be mere diplomatic gossip of little interest, did not every thing connected with the minority and marriage of the young Queen bear upon the vital politics of the nation and affect the future destinies of Spain; and were not the whole policy of the country a game of trick and hazard." One can readily understand why Daniel Webster, according to report, would put aside whatever he was working upon to read one of Irving's diplomatic despatches.

Although these events provided spice and excitement for the American minister, they distracted him from his avowed project of continuing his life of George Washington. The drama unfolding in Madrid in the months after Irving's arrival stimulated his imagination, and he wrote long descriptions of happenings to his relatives. In a sense the ongoing action preempted his attention and became a substitute for the historical scholarship which he had planned. A further complication arose with the violent outbreak of a skin inflammation similar to the one which had afflicted him twenty years earlier after an overzealous application of the pen and lack of exercise. As at that time, Irving had to abandon all endeavors as a creative professional writer for the remainder of his tour of duty as a diplomat. The flow of diplomatic correspondence and family letters continued undiminished, though these efforts probably took their toll by heightening Irving's discomfort. The gloomy political circumstances also weighed heavily upon the ailing diplomat, as is evident in a comment on June 27, 1843, to his niece in Paris: "I never expect to see Spain enjoy tranquility and a settled form of Government during the time I may have to witness some sanguinary scenes of popular commotion."

By mid-July Irving found his prophecy coming true, with Madrid under siege and in a state of political confusion which posed problems for diplomats who were supposed to deal with the government in power. In the resulting turmoil Irving tried to maintain a moderate position between the extremes represented by the French and British ministers, a position designed to protect the young queen and her sister. Espartero, the regent, was overthrown, and in his place was installed General Ramón María Narváez. As a consequence, Irving faced a problem. Did his government recognize the regime of Narváez? Since it would take months to receive formal instructions from Washington, Irving approached the matter pragmatically and, with the agreement and support of the Mexican minister, extended the recognition of the United States to the *de facto* government of Narváez which now had effective control of most of the country.

With political conditions relatively stable under Narváez, Irving, at the suggestion of his physician, left Madrid in early September for a holiday in France. After visiting his friends in Bordeaux for a few days, he went on to Versailles, where Sarah Storrow, his niece, and her family maintained an apartment. Traveling had inflamed his skin ailment, and Irving remained housebound for several weeks there and in Paris. By December he was back at his post in Madrid, still suffering from his malady and still annoyed at his inability to move ahead with his literary project.

During the winter Irving carefully watched the shifting current of Spanish politics and dutifully reported the colorful events to the state department and to his relatives. He delighted in describing the pageantry and ceremonies connected with the activities of the court and, as his health improved, found himself drawn into the social activities of the diplomats. Affairs at the Legation were complicated by the departure of Alexander Hamilton, Jr., who had remained after Carson Brevoort's leaving and had managed the mission during Irving's absence in Paris. However, the new secretary, Joseph Livingston, son of Justice Brockholst Livingston, proved to be a capable replacement. As a result, Irving was able to leave the Legation in his care and join the court in Barcelona in July, in accordance with the custom that the diplomatic corps follow the queen and her counselors wherever they went. After three weeks of indolent socializing in the pleasant surroundings of Barcelona, Irving left by coastal steamer for Marseilles, the first leg of his holiday trip to Paris, Le Havre, London, and Birmingham. His visit to the Van Warts reassured him about the health of his sister, and after a sojourn of three weeks he returned to Paris. There he took curative baths and visited Louis Philippe, the king of France, in company with William King and Henry Wheaton, American ministers to France and Prussia.

By mid-November, 1844, Irving had returned to Madrid and was immediately caught up in the social activities of the diplomatic corps and the Spanish Court. Amid the gaiety which prevailed during the winter Irving watched the court intrigues involving Maria Christina, the queen mother, who was attempting to restore the powers of the church. Narváez, through constitutional reforms, had sold off confiscated church lands, and now the queen mother was plotting to undermine the constitution and the power of Narváez. Despite his fascination with these maneuverings, Irving was tiring of the frenetic pace and longing for the quiet routine of Sunnyside. In September, 1845, he announced to Sarah Storrow that he had moved his residence to an apartment in the dwelling of the Brazilian minister, in anticipation of his resigning his post the following spring.

But unforeseen developments changed Irving's plans. On a vacation visit to Paris in the autumn of 1845 he became involved in the negotiations connected with the settlement of the Oregon boundary question. Louis McLane, with whom Irving had worked in the London Legation in 1830, was again American minister to England, and he invited his former secretary to assist in the delicate discussions with British officials. Since Irving knew many of these government officers personally, he was able to win their confidence and help to effect a settlement satisfactory to both parties. While in Paris, Irving submitted his resignation as minister to Spain, expressing a desire to return to his home and friends. Such action could not be taken, however, until the United States government had appointed his successor, so Irving returned to Madrid on March 6, 1846.

Upon his arrival Irving discovered that more political upheavals had occurred during his absence, resulting eventually in the overthrow of Narváez and the triumph of the supporters of the queen mother. In his despatches Irving reported fully on Spanish politics, even though he was anxiously awaiting word of the appointment of his successor. Affairs at the Legation were poorly organized, and Irving frequently had to copy his own despatches and letters in the absence of a secretary, a situation which heightened his desire to leave the post as quickly as possible. Finally he learned that Romulus M. Saunders was to replace him, and from then until late July, when Saunders was officially received, Irving grudgingly carried out the responsibilities of his office which were further complicated by the war with Mexico.

Finally the transfer of the Legation to the new minister was made, and Irving could depart with a feeling of relief. Even though he was not trained for diplomacy and fully expected to use much of the time in Madrid for his own purposes, Irving succeeded at his post. By nature levelheaded and by temperament genial and gracious, he won the confidence and respect of the Spanish Court and the succession of regents and ministers from 1842 to 1846. Approaching problems realistically and pragmatically, he made a favorable impression upon everyone with his sensible, sympathetic attitudes during a very difficult period. He paid for this success by forfeiting his own plans for working on the biography of Washington, but in the last analysis the good will which he created seems worth his personal sacrifice.

THE GOLDEN YEARS, 1846–1859

Stopping in France and England en route, Irving reached New York on September 18, 1846, and proceeded to Sunnyside the next day. Almost immediately upon his return he began to plan for an addition to his cottage and to harvest more income from his literary properties, partly in anticipation of his forthcoming remodeling expenses. An examination of his writings convinced him that the time was right for a revised edition of them, together with additions from unpublished materials. In July, 1848, he made an agreement with George P. Putnam to publish a uniform edition of his writing with whatever revisions he wished to make. In the case of *Knickerbocker's History of New York* these changes were quite extensive. In the next few months he worked assiduously at the editorial modifications, and by the end of the year Putnam had published four of the works, with very good sales.

In 1849 Irving continued the revising of his earlier works and expanded his *Life of Oliver Goldsmith* beyond its 1840 format. From time to time he turned briefly to the Washington project, but he decided also to resurrect and finish *Mahomet and His Successors,* with the result that his Moorish study reached the bookstores early in the spring of

1850. By summer the last of his revisions appeared, and he was free to concentrate on Washington.

The energy which Irving expended in the preparation of the new edition of his writings benefited him in several ways. Once again he was before the reading public, introducing his writings in many instances in a new format. The response of readers was enthusiastic, so that both author and publisher profited handsomely. Furthermore, he was reassured that he still had the knack of captivating readers and so was encouraged to move along with the life of Washington.

The remainder of 1850 was marked by periods of indisposition and by frequent social activities in New York and visits to old friends. The writing moved ahead slowly; he was diverted by his family and by leisurely excursions to places with sentimental associations, like Saratoga Springs. The biography required further researching in the public records, so he made his way to Washington early in 1853, stopping at New York for dinners, balls, and opera performances and at Baltimore to visit J. P. Kennedy and his family. In Washington he was carried away from his main purpose by further social activities, which included a trip to Mount Vernon, attendance at the president's levee and a ball, and installation as an honorary member of the Smithsonian Institution. Despite these distractions, he continued his study of documents in the state department, gathering materials and facts for his book. Writing to Pierre M. Irving, he observed, "I cannot say that I find much that is new among the manuscripts of Washington, Sparks having published the most interesting; but it is important to get facts from the fountain head, not at second hand through his publications." After the inauguration of Franklin Pierce as president Irving returned to Sunnyside.

Irving labored steadily for two months, then abandoned his writing and headed south again to see the Kennedys in Baltimore, to examine other manuscripts relating to Washington, and to visit several spots associated with the first president. Following a trip to Berkeley Springs for the waters, he returned to Sunnyside, but he was unable to resume his writing. A stay at Saratoga Springs was equally ineffectual, the confusion of the resort only adding to his distress. So he rambled through upstate New York, returning to some of the spots he had first seen fifty years earlier and visiting the Thousand Islands, the Finger Lakes, and Niagara Falls. Still unsettled upon his return to Tarrytown, he left almost immediately for another visit to the Kennedys. This restlessness continued throughout the fall and winter, with Irving's conviction growing that he had written himself out. Most of 1854 was also literarily unproductive, with Irving frequently on the move. But, even so, he was shaping the biographical materials into a pattern. In February, 1855, when Putnam brought out *Wolfert's Roost*, a collection chiefly of sketches and stories published earlier, he won fresh praise from critics who admired his elegant diction, gentle humor, and graceful style.

About two months later the first volume of *The Life of Washington* appeared, carrying Washington's career up to the Revolutionary War. Its favorable reception encouraged him to move along with Volume II; and by late September it was in press, with Irving revising the proof sheets extensively. Even with these changes it appeared in December, 1855, the third volume from the seventy-two-year-old Irving's hand to be published that year. Again the critical response to the biography was favorable, and Irving was encouraged to push ahead with the third volume. By April 24, 1856, he could report to Sarah Storrow that two-thirds of that segment was in type, noting, in addition, that "It is a toilsome task, though a very interesting, and, I may say, delightful one. It expands and grows more voluminous as I write, but the way it is received by the public cheers me on. . . . I must say I am sometimes surprised at my own capacity for labor at my advanced time of life—when I used to think a man must be good for nothing." He persisted in his efforts, and the third volume, which carried the story of Washington's activities up to the winter of 1779, appeared in July, 1856.

A distraction intervened at this point and evoked a flood of memories from thirty-three years earlier. Irving received a letter from Emily Foster, now Mrs. Fuller, to whom he had paid court in Dresden. She described the delighted reactions of her five children to hearing *The Alhambra*, *The Sketch Book*, and *Bracebridge Hall* read aloud. For her, Irving's words brought back a vivid recollection of his smile, his mannerisms, and his sense of humor. In his heartfelt response Irving alluded to the happy days in Dresden and to his home at Sunnyside, one room of which was graced with a head of Herodias which Emily had copied for him in the Dresden gallery.

As he continued to work on the biography, Irving complained frequently of pains in his head. Later he was bothered with a vexatious catarrh which caused considerable discomfort and a temporary deafness. He found also that he became short of breath from mild physical exertion. But he persisted in his writing and revising and had finished the rough draft of the fourth volume by the end of 1857. Despite the development of a pronounced asthmatic condition, Irving worked away at the concluding volume, amusing himself occasionally with social activities in New York and Sunnyside. Progress on the manuscript was slow because of nervous restlessness, frequent drowsiness, and worrying about his capability to complete the project. Irving's concern continued into the autumn, with additional complications in his health which prevented concentrated work on the book. P. M. Irving's notations in his diary suggest a steady decline in his uncle's physical condition marked by increasing difficulty in breathing and excessive nervousness which the medication could not check. By January 19, 1859, Pierre had started sending the manuscript to the printer, even though it was not entirely finished, and checked the proof sheets to spare his uncle from that tiresome chore while he was concluding the composition. Two months later the proofreading was completed, and in April the last volume of *The Life of Washington* was issued. At last the study which Irving had had in mind for more than thirty years was ended, standing as a testimonial to his strength of mind and his unswerving resolution.

The ailing writer, however, was not physically able to enjoy the accolades bestowed upon the book, his labored breathing and coughing causing him frequent distress. The summer wore on, with occasional days of improvement in his condition, but the nervousness, asthma, and sleeplessness gradually increased in intensity. Visits from friends like J. P. Kennedy and N. P. Willis helped him to take his mind away from his own misery, but he was now no longer able to enjoy himself by the exercise of his pen. It was a matter of waiting for the suffering to be ended by death.

The waiting and suffering continued for another month, during which his anxious relatives parried off solicitous friends and inquisitive strangers. The end finally came as he was preparing to retire on November 28, 1859. Seized with a heart attack, he fell to the floor and died instantaneously, freed from the pain and misery that had been his constant companion during his last days.

Throughout his active writing career extending over fifty-seven years Washington Irving had used his imagination and his skill of felicitous expression to convey to his readers the rich sense of the past, the wry humor of the ridiculous and the absurd, the warm sentiment of human relationships, and his sensitive impressions of human nature and the world around him. For Irving writing was not so much a task imposed by necessity as an integral part of his existence, without which he could not live in a complete, meaningful fashion. Even though his published works were often produced in a desultory, sporadic fashion, the intervals between them were filled with another kind of writing—his letters, which in their unstudied spontaneity, freshness, and vigor, reveal the breadth and humanity of Washington Irving the man.

EDITORIAL PLAN
TO LETTERS

Although Irving's letters are scattered over the eastern United States and Western Europe, several institutions have brought together a large number of them. The New York Public Library, with its Seligman, Hellman, and Berg collections, is especially rich; and these, together with other holdings, form the largest body of Irving correspondence held by a single repository. Another valuable group is to be found in the Clifton Waller Barrett Collection of the Alderman Library of the University of Virginia. At Tarrytown, Sleepy Hollow Restorations has assembled an important collection of letters along with photocopies of items held elsewhere. Other noteworthy concentrations of Irving's letters repose in the libraries at Yale, Harvard, and Columbia Universities, in the Historical Society of Pennsylvania, and in the archives of John Murray, Irving's chief British publisher. The National Archives in Washington contain Irving's official diplomatic communications, as well as letterbook copies of his despatches and letters written as minister to Spain. A few letters remain in the hands of private collectors but the bulk of those extant are preserved in institutional libraries. Others are widely scattered, as may be observed by consulting the notes that identify the location or source of each letter printed.

This edition, arranged in chronological order, is the first comprehensive collection in print of all letters of Washington Irving presently known and available, both published and hitherto unpublished. But a considerable number of letters have escaped detection, although they have been identified through a systematic search of dealers' and auctioneers' catalogs, as well as by evidence found in journals and other letters, or from other sources. They are enumerated in an appendix to the final volume in order to supply the broadest possible record of Irving's letter-writing available at the time of this publication. It is hoped that this checklist will eventually lead to the discovery of additional holograph material. Letters that came to the editors' attention too late to be presented in their proper place in these volumes are printed in an appendix at the end of the final volume, in a chronological ordering of their own.

Since the present edition is not designed to include surviving letters written to Irving, no exhaustive effort was made to locate or list all of them. Many of them are not directly related to Irving's letters, and the contents of many may be inferred from what Irving wrote. Those having a special bearing on Irving's letters to these correspondents are quoted or summarized in appropriate notes, and all of them are listed, with location when known, in a separate calendar at the end of the final volume in the hope that the utility of the collection may be enhanced.

The great bulk, at least eighty-five percent, of the letters here presented has been taken from the original manuscripts. Although transcriptions of holographs are derived from photocopies, they were checked for accuracy by four or more readers, and all transcriptions were read (often twice) against the holographs. In the absence of holographs, letters derived from a printed source were collated against any other existing printed versions and explanatory notes added wherever warranted.[1] This is not to claim absolute authenticity for resulting text, but represents the best that can be done with the evidence at hand. Equally difficult are the cases where the only available text is a copy made by someone other than Irving (known or unknown), presumably from a holograph no longer extant.[2] Here again the editors can only reproduce what is before them, while noting whatever facts they have regarding the transmission of the text, and hoping that the original letter may yet come to light.

Fragments of letters, whether derived from manuscript or printed sources, are incorporated in sequence, unless they are mere scraps of little meaning or significance, in which case they are relegated to an appendix at the end of the last volume, where they appear in sequence with notations on whatever information may be available and desirable regarding their authenticity, for many of these scraplike fragments are derived from biographical and other secondary works, some from cata-

---

1. A comparison of Pierre M. Irving's four-volume *Life and Letters of Washington Irving* (1862–1864) with the three-volume edition (copyrighted 1869) reveals numerous instances of the biographer's effort to refine his earlier work. The second edition omits many letters of the first edition (or extracts them), and further bowdlerizes those remaining. The two editions of George S. Hellman's *Letters of Washington Irving to Henry Brevoort* (1915 and 1918), on the other hand, reveal few alterations. In both cases, first and later printings were collated for variants, editorial decisions were made in accord with Irving's known practice or other available evidence, and explanatory notes were added wherever indicated. These are the only two bodies of Irving letters in book form that went into second editions or settings. Other letters lacking holographs that are not in these two collections but that exist in printed forms differing from each other (some of them appearing in periodicals) are similarly treated.

2. For example, the letterbook copies of Irving's diplomatic correspondence for which original holographs are not available.

logs of book dealers or autograph dealers, as well as from auction catalogs.

The circumstances under which Irving wrote determine the varying conditions of the existing holograph letters, as much as the writing materials at his disposal or the conditions under which they were stored during the long lapse of years since they were written. During his first trip to Europe in 1804 to 1806, Irving drew upon entries in his journals and frequently copied them precisely into letters to his friends and relatives in New York.[3] During periods of protracted residence in one place—whether in New York, London, Paris, Madrid, at Sunnyside, or elsewhere—he often wrote leisurely and carefully, but there is sometimes a marked falling-off in precision as a letter stretched out under his hand. Generally his business letters and official diplomatic or consular despatches were written with greater care than personal letters. At other times, especially between stints of travel, or when pressed for time, he wrote in a careless, almost illegible scrawl, with whatever pen, ink, or grade of paper came to hand. Often he used a thin or low grade of paper and a blunt pen which caused the ink to bleed through the paper. On a few occasions when he resorted to writing with pencil, the result made the work of the twentieth-century editor doubly difficult. Letters may be presumed to have been written in ink except where there is a note to the contrary. Variations in the inks used are often no longer precisely distinguishable and are not recorded unless an unusual circumstance makes a description desirable, in which case a notation is made in the notes. Similarly, the paper used covers a great variety of grades, from good to bad, laid and wove, white and tinted, lined and unlined, with and without watermarks, and of various shapes and sizes; in short, he appears to have used whatever was available. Description of kinds of paper is not attempted except in a few exceptional cases where it has textual significance.

While the editors have made every effort to record what Irving wrote, the condition of some manuscript pages and the anomalous readings occasioned by Irving's erratic handwriting produced so many problems which the eye cannot resolve that recourse was had to a set of ground rules, the chief of which is that when a word, character, spacing, construction, or mark of punctuation is in doubt, presenting equally defensible alternatives, the reading is rendered in conformity with the con-

3. This parallelism between the journals and letters has been indicated in Nathalia Wright's edition of *Journals and Notebooks*, Vol. I, of the present edition. Parallel passages of this kind will be noted in successive volumes of the journals and letters as they appear.

textual requirement (if ascertainable), insofar as it accords with Irving's practice (if known) or with accepted usage in his day. In short, the aim has been to produce a reliable text, short of an absolutely literal transcription, which is manifestly impossible, as the sequel will demonstrate.

It does not follow that Irving's errors and inconsistencies are eliminated. Indeed, the aim of the editors, which is to present Irving as faithfully as possible, precludes this possibility. To correct his miscues and normalize his idiosyncrasies would destroy the distinctive texture of his writing. So it is that the two primary objectives of the editors—fidelity to Irving's text and utility for the reader—are constant but not always compatible aims, causing the editors to tread a very narrow line between what is ideally desirable and what is practically possible or permissible.

Despite the variety of difficulties, the editors have made a conscientious and considered effort to render faithfully the text as Irving wrote it— his oversights, inconsistencies, and often his errors included. No effort was made to correct or "improve" the holograph version, unless the error or flaw is clearly unintentional, and failure to emend would lead to misreading or misconstruction of Irving's meaning. In all such cases, editorial alterations made are signaled by square brackets or explained in the notes. No alteration is made silently. Hence any odd or erroneous idiom or phraseology, error in punctuation or spelling, or omission or transposition of letters or words in the text are to be presumed to be Irving's.

This policy of reproducing the holograph as accurately as possible perpetuates various inconsistencies, sometimes on the same page, even in the same paragraph, occasionally in the same sentence. Thus the same sentence may spell out a numeral and subsequently use the arabic form, or it may use "and" as well as the ampersand for both "and" and "et cetera," in the latter case usually "&c" without a period. Words normally written as one are often separated ("every thing"), and others commonly separated or hyphenated are joined ("forgetmenots"). Irving's contractions follow no recognizable pattern, but do not often lead to obscurity or misinterpretation; when they do, missing elements are added in brackets or clarified in the notes. Similarly, his misuse or neglect of the apostrophe is not corrected unless it leads to misconstruction, in which case editorial emendations are bracketed and noted. His superscripts are uniformly brought down to the line. Often he omitted the period following a superscript but signalized the contraction or abbreviation by adding one or more dots under the superscript, by underscoring it, or by adding a dash after it. These signals are all rendered as a period, thus honoring his intention, while ridding the page of eccentric mannerisms very difficult to reproduce on the printed page.

Irving's erratic terminal punctuation presents special problems. Often he used a dash, rather than a period, at the end of the sentence. This sometimes seems to have happened inadvertently because he failed to lift his pen cleanly from the paper and so elongated an intended period to look like a dash; at other times he clearly meant to write a dash. In all cases his dashes at the ends of sentences are respected as deliberate terminal punctuation. His sentence beginnings and endings are rendered as he wrote them, with or without period (or dash) if the succeeding sentence in the same paragraph begins with a capital letter, except in cases where the next sentence begins with "I" or a proper noun, in which case a bracketed period is added as a necessary signal for the reader. When the following sentence begins with a small letter, preceded by a period (or dash), it is so rendered. Only when it begins with a small letter and Irving failed to supply a period (or dash) is a bracketed period (sometimes a semicolon) added. No missing period is added at the end of the paragraph.

Similarly, his internal punctuation is respected; any necessary marks of punctuation added or changed for clarity are bracketed or footnoted (usually the former). When doubt exists among his uses internally of commas, colons, semicolons, or dashes, the questionable marks are rendered in accord with the demands of the context, compatible with Irving's general practice or the usage common in his time. His occasional use of the colon instead of a period to denote an abbreviation (usually in connection with titles of books) is respected. If, as is true in a few instances, he used what seems to be a period for a comma, or what seems to be a comma for a period, and the error is corrected, it is so noted. Commas, parentheses, dashes, and quotation marks missing from intended pairs are added in square brackets. Missing sets of quotation marks are added (in brackets) when their omission would result in misreading. Quotation marks when used by Irving at the beginning of successive lines of a quoted passage (verse or prose) are omitted.

Carets, which Irving sometimes used to indicate inserted matter, are transcribed as arrows in accordance with the system of editorial symbols explained in the table below. His abbreviations stand as he left them unless clarity demands amplifications or corrections, which are then bracketed or noted, normally the former. His occasional use of the long form of "s," "ʃ," usually when the letter is doubled, is not reproduced.

Irving often wrote participial forms normally ending in *ed* without the penultimate *e,* and without an apostrophe indicating an elision or a period designating an abbreviation. These are rendered as he wrote them: i.e., "servd" rather than "serv'd" or "serv^{d}" or "serv[e]d." In a very few cases where the elision involves more than the *e* or some other single letter, and misreading is likely to result, missing elements in brackets are added.

Certain misspellings occur so frequently as to become routine and not worth noting or correcting, unless they convey false information, in which case a note is added. Names of passing acquaintances, even of friends and long-term associates, may vary from page to page. In the interest of unencumbered text these are allowed to stand, but where the proper form is ascertainable, the correct form is given in a note keyed to the first occurrence, and also in the index.

Loosely associated with the problem of handling proper names is the problem of distinguishing between capital and lowercase forms of initial letters of his words—not only of nouns but of all parts of speech. Often the formation of a letter is not sufficiently distinctive nor its size in relation to adjacent letters sufficiently marked to indicate clearly which Irving intended. He commonly wrote the initial letter of a word beginning with a consonant with an upward sweep which often raises it higher than the letters which follow it. This upward flourish is especially noticeable when the initial letter *y* appears at the beginning of a new line. When conformation of the letter in question is not sufficiently distinctive and the context indicates a lowercase form, the letter is rendered lowercase. Conversely, if the content calls for a capital, and the letter rises only slightly above adjacent high-rise lowercase letters, it is capitalized; it need not reach the height of high-rise letters which follow it. A more objective procedure, based on a mechanical measurement of differences in height, introduces a new body of inconsistencies and a maze of contradictions and indefensible readings or renditions, and invariably increases the incidence of error. Throughout, the editors have followed the principle that where Irving seems to use capital letters for lowercase words, the transcriptions of those letters have been rendered to accord with knowledge of his customary practice and the customary orthographical practice of his time, by transcribing as capitals only those letters which are clearly so—all intermediate forms being rendered in lowercase.

The height of initial letters in Irving's complimentary closings is also often troublesome. They can vary from an apparent "yrs Truly," "yours Very truly," "Very truly Yrs," or almost any other combination of initial lowercase or capital letters. These and other such doubtful cases are rendered as "Yrs truly," "Yours very truly," or "Very truly yrs," only the initial letter in the first word in the closing capitalized in accord with Irving's usual practice and the common usage of his time. Less formal closings, such as "ever your devoted friend," are transcribed in conformity to the demands of the text, as ascertained. When doubt rises between what the eye measures and what knowledge of Irving, his handwriting and habits of expression suggests, then Irving is given the benefit of that doubt.

Another problem which occasionally presents itself is that of Irving's ending a paragraph at the bottom of a page with a short line containing very few words. He would then on the following page begin a new paragraph on a new subject with little or no ascertainable indentation of the first line of that paragraph. Rather than submit to a policy of strict measurement, the editors in such instances have honored Irving's intention by indenting the first line of the new paragraph.

Occasionally Irving would so crowd what he had to say on the last page of a letter that he left little space for a complimentary closing and signature, writing, for example, "Truly your friend Washington Irving" on, or so nearly on, the last line of the text that it is often impossible to determine whether he intended a new line or new lines. In such instances, the complimentary close and the signature have been given each a line to itself in accordance with his customary practice.

In short, though mindful of Irving's request to his brother Peter, in a long letter of July 7–25, 1804, that "If you find anything . . . in the letters I may write that you thing[k] proper to publish, I beg that you will arrange and finish it *handsomely*," the editors have avoided complete compliance with that request, thinking it useful and instructive to present as exactly as possible what Irving wrote, sometimes in informal haste without care for niceties of spelling or punctuation, or even consistent capitalization of proper nouns, and sometimes in handwriting filled with orthographic peculiarities which are rendered in his favor when consistent with the guidelines already mentioned. The editors will try to present him as handsomely as modern textual principles allow.

In those letters where a covering sheet has been preserved, postal markings and other information which it contains have been recorded. Lines or elements of postal markings are separated one from the other with a horizontal line; when two or more discrete postal markings appear, each is separated from the other by a double horizontal line.

Lacunae in the manuscript and torn places in a page that remove a word or passage are explained in the notes. If the missing element can be conjectured, it is supplied in brackets and noted if necessary. Doubtful or alternate readings are indicated by the appropriate editorial symbol and the needed explanation is supplied in the notes. Erasures and cancellations in the holographs, when recoverable, are inclosed in angle brackets. Unrecovered cancellations are marked "⟨[*unrecovered*]⟩." Some cancellations have obviously been made by persons other than Irving— some of them almost certainly by Pierre M. Irving, in the interest of what the nephew-biographer considered propriety. When one or more letters are canceled or written over (i.e., traced over), the substitution appears immediately after the canceled matter, without intervening space; for example "the⟨ir⟩re" and "3⟨7⟩8." Cancellations which are identical with the substitution, canceled fragments of characters which are illegible, obvious slips of the pen, and meaningless false starts (which often occur at the ends of lines and indicate merely that Irving ran out of space and elected to begin the word anew on the next line but neglected to strike the false start made at the end of the preceding line) are not reproduced. There are many instances of this kind, even in the letters which he seems to have written with more than usual leisure or care.

Most of the marks in the margins and at the beginning and end of passages (usually in pencil)—crosses, *x*'s, checks, arrows, vertical and horizontal lines, encirclings, parentheses, and slashes—are the work of earlier owners or editors of the manuscripts, including Pierre M. Irving, while preparing his uncle's biography. Only those demonstrably Irving's are reproduced. Irving's catchwords, placed at the bottom of a page and repeated as the first word of the next page, are not reproduced. On rare occasions Irving numbered the pages of his letters; but since the significance of these numbers is slight and, having no relevance to the present edition, they are not reproduced.

No effort is made to reproduce Irving's irregular spacings between characters, words, sentences, or paragraphs—unless the space has a special significance, e.g., to indicate a change of subject matter or to begin a new sequence.

Quotations, allusions, and literary, historical, or biographical references are identified wherever possible. Such identifications are made at their first occurrence only. Quotations of poetry in the text are printed in reduced type size when they are known to be from other authors. Quotations are to be presumed Irving's unless otherwise indicated, and accordingly are printed in the same type as the text.

Irving's infrequent notes, usually at the bottom of the manuscript page or along the side, are reproduced in the notes and labeled as his.

Many of the foregoing forms and procedures in preparing the text of Irving's letters stem from peculiarities of his handwriting, and consequently do not differ materially from those adopted for the editing of his journals and notebooks and therefore are not dealt with in the same detail with which they are explained by Nathalia Wright in Volume I of the Twayne edition of the journals, where they can be consulted on pages xix–xxvi. But the inherent differences in genre between journals and letters accentuate certain aspects of form and procedure sufficiently unique or peculiar to the letters as to require special treatment by the editors, and consequently need particularization and explanation.

Basic to these procedures is the numbering of the letters in simple chronological order throughout the four volumes, which correspond roughly to periods in Irving's life. A single introductory essay discussing the relation of the letters to his literary career has been adopted as the most suitable way for the reader to see them in context; there is no introductory note for successive volumes after the first, but a chronological table of Irving's activities corresponding to the period covered in each volume is provided for the reader's orientation. Each volume also has a table of editorial symbols, abbreviations, and short-title forms used, as well as a self-contained index, the last volume having a cumulative index instead.

Each letter is assigned an arabic number in accord with its position in the entire sequence. This numeral, printed flush to the left margin, is followed by the name of the addressee, printed in its accepted spelling, unless the notation "To ———" appears in its place. This entire line is set in italics to serve as a caption and provide ready identification.

The transcription itself begins, in accord with Irving's normal practice, with the local or street address (if given), name of the city or place, and date on the first line. The year (or other element of the date), if not given, is added in brackets, whenever ascertainable. These elements, in whatever order, are reproduced as Irving wrote them, punctuation included, except that their location on the page (which in the holograph may appear anywhere, left to right) ends flush with the right margin, with slashes added if they occupy more than one line in the original. If Irving wrote the date at the end of the letter, it is so printed, but it is also added in brackets in the usual place at the head of the letter, so that this necessary index for cross-referencing can be found readily.

In cases of misdating, the correction is made in brackets immediately following the erroneous date, and the letter is placed in its proper chronological order. Incomplete or missing dates are supplied in brackets if they can be ascertained from postmarks, internal evidence, biographical information, perpetual calendar, or other sources. The evidence for dates supplied by the editors is explained in the notes. A letter that is dated ["Fall, 1823,"] and for which no closer dating can be made, appears at the end of November, 1823; one simply dated "1812" appears at the close of that year. Letters that cannot be dated conjecturally appear in alphabetical order according to the recipient's name at the end of the final volume immediately following the appendix which contains letters received too late to be incorporated in the regular chronological sequence. Following the undated letters are printed those for which both date and addressee are unknown.

The inside address, in whatever manner Irving wrote it, follows his text except that it is printed flush left, with slashes if separate lines need to be indicated. Immediately following is the salutation, again flush left. Following the body of the letter, the complimentary close, usually occupying several lines in the holograph, is printed in one line, flush right, with slashes if lineation needs to be indicated. The signature follows, also flush right. If, instead of placing the inside address at the beginning of the letter, Irving wrote it at the bottom of the first page or at the end of the letter, it is positioned at the end, on one line, flush left, with slashes, if needed; and if the date appears at the end, instead of the beginning, it is so placed, again flush left. The recording of postmarkings has been explained above.

The introductory and concluding elements appear in the originals in so confusing a variety of forms and locations that they defy exact reproduction on the printed page. Hence a degree of regularization is adopted as a simple, sensible means to bring order and uniformity into Irving's calligraphic vagaries, without doing violence to his general ordering of these parts or to his intended meaning. Included in this category is the regularization of salutations for letters derived from secondary sources, such as George S. Hellman's edition of the Irving-Brevoort correspondence and Pierre M. Irving's biography of Irving, where capital letters throughout or a combination of large and small capitals are used. These are all rendered uniformly in capital and lowercase letters in accord with Irving's own practice, thus: "My dear Brother," not "MY DEAR BROTHER" or "My dear Brother."

The first unnumbered note presents significant information on the address leaf or envelope, if available, in the following order: name of addressee, address, postmark or docketing, followed by any other details, such as the name of the ship or carrier, regular mail, ambassador's pouch, or whatever the means of conveyance, as well as endorsements and postmarkings including date on which letters were received or answered, etc. These details vary widely from letter to letter, and any omissions are to be understood as indicating that they are missing from the original. However, the numbers indicating the cost of postage or carriage are not reproduced, nor are extraneous words or symbols added by owners or readers of the letter.

The second unnumbered paragraph gives the ownership and location of the manuscript or text from which the transcription was made, and details about previous publication, transmission, and provenance of the text, and other pertinent data. For letters transcribed from a printed version, only the copy-text (usually the first printed) version is cited, unless unusual circumstances obtain (e.g., variations in two or more printed forms), in which case a description or explanatory note is added.

A third unnumbered note gives biographical details about the recipient. This biographical note, usually more detailed than notes identifying persons merely mentioned in the letters, is attached to the first letter addressed to him by Irving. Earlier or later casual mentions of the addressee are cross-referenced to this main biographical notation.

Numbered notes following each letter identify persons, places, events, allusions, quotations, or circumstances necessary for an understanding of the letter. Facts found in the encyclopedias and biographical dictionaries are not ordinarily documented in the notes.

A list of abbreviations and of short titles for books cited three or more times as sources of information in the notes and a list of editorial symbols are supplied at the beginning of each volume.

Cross references are made by recipient and date, rather than by letter number, and should be understood to include both text and relevant notes.

The first three volumes are separately indexed; the last volume provides a cumulative index, as well as an index of recipients and a catalog of sources.

CHRONOLOGICAL TABLE
1783 – 1823

1783   April 3, born in New York City, youngest child of William and Sarah Irving.

1787–1789   Attended Mrs. Ann Kilmaster's school.

1789–1799   Attended Benjamin Romaine's school.

1799–1804   Read law with Henry Masterson, Brockhulst Livingston, and Josiah Ogden Hoffman.

1800   Made trip up Hudson, visited sisters in Johnstown, N. Y.

1802   July, visited sisters in Johnstown, N. Y.

1802–1803   November 15–April 23, wrote "Letters of Jonathan Oldstyle, Gent." for New York *Morning Chronicle.*

1803   Summer, visited Ballston, Saratoga Springs, Ogdensburg, and Montreal.

1804   March–April, contributed essays and sketches to *The Corrector,* edited by Peter Irving; May 19, sailed for Bordeaux; July 1–August 3, Bordeaux; August 4–October 20, Bordeaux to Genoa; October 20–December 23, Genoa; December 23–January 24, 1805, Genoa to Messina.

1805   January 24–March 5, Sicily; March 6–April 14, Palermo to Naples and Rome; April 14–May 24, Rome to Paris, via Switzerland; May 24–September 22, Paris; September 22–October 8, Paris to London; October 8–January 17, 1806, London.

1806   Sailed for New York; March 24, arrived in New York; November 21, passed bar examination.

1807   January 24, began contributions to *Salmagundi* (through January 25, 1808); May–June, attended trial of Aaron Burr in Richmond, Virginia.

1808   Began research for *Knickerbocker's History*; May, visited Montreal with brother Peter.

1809   April 26, Matilda Hoffman died; December 6, *Knicker-bocker's History* published.

1810   Summer, became partner with brothers Ebenezer and Peter in hardware firm operating in New York and Liverpool.

1811   January 9–March 7, acted as agent in Washington for family hardware firm.

1812   November–December, lobbied in Washington on behalf of New York merchants; December, became editor of *Analectic Magazine* (until January, 1815).

1814   September–December, commissioned lieutenant-colonel in New York state militia, served as aide-de-camp to General Daniel D. Tompkins.

1815   May 25, departed for Liverpool to assist brother Peter in operation of hardware business; July–August, toured Wales with James Renwick.

1816   Managed business in Liverpool, with occasional visits to the Van Warts in Birmingham.

1817   May, received news of death of mother on April 9; worked on *The Sketch Book*; August, visited London, met John Murray; August 25, landed in Scotland, visited Francis Jeffrey and Dugald Stewart in Edinburgh; August 30–September 3, visited Walter Scott at Abbotsford; September 3–22, visited Edinburgh and Scottish Highlands with William Preston.

1818   March 4, Irving hardware firm declared bankrupt; studied German and wrote more essays for *The Sketch Book*.

1819   March 3, April 1, May 13, August 2, October 28, December 29, sent off parts of *The Sketch Book* to New York.

1820   February 21, one volume of *The Sketch Book* published at author's expense by John Miller in London; June 28, sent off last part of *The Sketch Book* to New York; August 16, sold copyright of *The Sketch Book* to John Murray for 250 guineas; August 17, left London for Paris with brother Peter; December 20, met Thomas Moore.

1821   Worked on *Bracebridge Hall* in Paris; July 11, returned to London, prepared *Bracebridge Hall* for press.

1822   May 21 and 23, *Bracebridge Hall* published in United States and England, respectively; August 1, began travels in Germany; October 10–17, Munich; October 18–21, Salzburg; October 23, reached Vienna; November 18–22, left Vienna and traveled through Moravia and Bohemia; October 22–26, Prague; November 28–May 20, 1823, Dresden.

1823 May 20–June 24, left Dresden via Silesia for Prague; June 26, returned to Dresden; July 12, left Dresden and accompanied Foster family to Rotterdam; July 31, left Rotterdam for Paris via Brussels.

EDITORIAL SYMBOLS AND ABBREVIATIONS

EDITORIAL SYMBOLS

[roman]	Editorial additions.
[*italic*]	Editorial explanations.
⟨ ⟩	Restorations of canceled matter.
? ? or [?]	Doubtful or alternate readings. The former are used within angle brackets. The latter is used for a single doubtful word, and appears immediately after the word or character in question, with no intervening space.
[*unrecovered*]	Unrecovered word. When more than one word is involved, the fact is indicated (*"three unrecovered words"* or *"two unrecovered lines"*).
↑↓	Interlinear insertions, above or below the line.

Editorial situations not covered by these symbols are explained in the notes.

ABBREVIATIONS AND SHORT TITLES

Bayle, *Old Taverns of NY*: W. Harrison Bayle, *Old Taverns of New York*. New York, 1915.

Columbia: Columbia University Library.

Flagg, *Washington Allston*: Jared B. Flagg, *The Life and Letters of Washington Allston*. New York, 1892.

Genest, *Some Account of the English Stage*: John Genest, *Some Account of the English Stage from the Restoration in 1660 to 1830*. 10 vols. New York, 1964.

Guernsey, *Chronicles of NYC*: R. S. Guernsey, *Chronicles of Greater New York City during the War of 1812–15*. 2 vols. New York, 1911.

Harvard: Harvard University Library.

Horsman, *War of 1812*: Reginald Horsman, *The War of 1812*. New York, 1969.

HSP: Historical Society of Pennsylvania.

Huntington: Henry E. Huntington Library and Art Gallery.

Ireland, *NY Stage*: J. W. Ireland, *Records of the New York Stage*. 3 vols. New York, 1966.

J&N, I: Washington Irving, *Journals and Notebooks. Vol. I, 1803–1806*. Edited by Nathalia Wright. Madison, Wisc., 1969.

J&N, III: Washington Irving, *Journals and Notebooks. Vol. III, 1819–1827.* Edited by Walter A. Reichart. Madison, Wisc., 1970.

July, *Verplanck*: Robert W. July, *The Essential New Yorker: Gulian Crommelin Verplanck.* Durham, N.C., 1951.

Langfeld & Blackburn, *WI Bibliography*: William R. Langfeld and Philip C. Blackburn, *Washington Irving: A Bibliography.* New York, 1933.

LBI: *Letters of Henry Brevoort to Washington Irving.* Edited by George S. Hellman. 2 vols. New York, 1916.

LC: Library of Congress.

Leslie, *Autobiographical Recollections: Autobiographical Recollections by the late Charles Robert Leslie, R. A.* Edited by Tom Taylor. Boston, 1860.

Letters of J. K. Paulding: The Letters of James Kirke Paulding. Edited by Ralph M. Aderman. Madison, Wisc., 1962.

LIB: *Letters of Washington Irving to Henry Brevoort.* Edited by George S. Hellman. 2 vols. New York, 1915.

Maclay, *History of U.S. Navy*: E. S. Maclay, *A History of the United States Navy from 1775 to 1893.* 2 vols. New York, 1894.

MHS: Massachusetts Historical Society.

NYEP: New York *Evening Post.*

NYHS: New-York Historical Society.

NYPL: New York Public Library.

Odell, *NY Stage*: G. C. D. Odell, *Annals of the New York Stage.* 15 vols. New York, 1927–1949.

PMI: Pierre M. Irving; and Pierre M. Irving, *The Life and Letters of Washington Irving.* 4 vols. New York, 1862–1864.

Porter, *Astor*: Kenneth W. Porter, *John Jacob Astor, Business Man.* 2 vols. New York, 1966.

PRO: Public Records Office, London.

Reichart, *WI and Germany*: Walter A. Reichart, *Washington Irving and Germany.* Ann Arbor, Mich., 1957.

Scoville, *Old Merchants of NYC*: J. A. Scoville (used pseudonym of Walter Barrett), *The Old Merchants of New York City.* 5 vols. New York, 1885.

SHR: Sleepy Hollow Restorations, Tarrytown, New York.

STW: Stanley T. Williams, *The Life of Washington Irving.* 2 vols. New York, 1935.

Thiers, *History of the Consulate*: Adolphe Thiers, *History of the Consulate and the Empire of France under Napoleon.* 12 vols. Philadelphia, 1893–1894.

Va.–Barrett: Clifton Waller Barrett Collection of American Literature, University of Virginia.

Wheeler, *Ogden Family*: William Ogden Wheeler, *The Ogden Family in America*. Philadelphia, 1907.

WI: Washington Irving.

WI to Renwicks: *Letters from Washington Irving to Mrs. William Renwick, and to her Son, James Renwick*. n.p., n.d.

WIHM: Ben Harris McClary, *Washington Irving and the House of Murray: Geoffrey Crayon Charms the British, 1817–1856*. Knoxville, Tenn., 1969.

Willson, AAE: Beckles Willson, *America's Ambassadors to England, 1795–1928*. London, 1928.

Wilson, *NY, Old and New*: Rufus Rockwell Wilson, *New York: Old and New*. 2 vols. London, 1903.

WIS: *Washington Irving and the Storrows. Letters from England and the Continent. 1821–1828*. Edited Stanley T. Williams. Cambridge, Mass., 1933.

Yale: Yale University Library.

Young, *WI-Bordeaux*: John-Perry Young, *Washington Irving à Bordeaux*. Niagara Falls, Ontario, 1946.

LETTERS, 1803-1823

Volume I

1. To Mr. & Mrs. William Irving, Sr.

Johnstown, July 2, 1802.

My dear Parents:

We had a very quick passage to Albany, where we arrived at three o'clock on Thursday morning. I was unwell almost the whole time, and could not sleep either night. We left Albany about an hour after we arrived there, in a wagon, and reached Johnstown[1] between ten and eleven in the evening. The roads were fine, being turnpike almost the whole way; but I was so weak that it was several days before I got over the fatigue. I have had a little better appetite since I have been up here, though I have been troubled with the pain in my breast almost constantly, and still have a cough at night.[2] I am unable to take any exercise worth mentioning, and doze away my time pretty much as I did in New York; however, I hope soon to get in a better trim.

PUBLISHED: PMI, I, 45.

William Irving (1731–1807) and Sarah Sanders Irving (1738–1817), the parents of WI (1783–1859) and ten other children, had come to America from England in 1763. See STW, II, 251–54 and the genealogical table inserted between pp. 254 and 255.

1. WI, in poor health, had left New York City to visit his sister Ann (1770–1808), who had married Richard Dodge (1762–1832), and his sister Catharine (1774–1849), who had married Daniel Paris. Both families lived in Johnstown. See PMI, I, 38–39, 45.

2. WI's ailment was a tubercular disorder which caused a weakness of the lungs. See PMI, I, 45.

2. To John Furman

Johnstown July 26th. 1802

Dear John

It was with the greatest concern that I heard just before my departure from town of the death of your Brother[1]—it must indeed have been a severe shock to you all—however, poor fellow, he has left a world full of care and trouble and which from the profession he had adopted would doubtless have abounded with hardships and distresses.

3

I was extremely sorry that I could not see you before I left the City as there were two or three things I wished to talk to you about but which have since slipped my memory.

The journey from New York to this place[2] is delightful—the variety and beauty of the prospects is enchanting and I was continually regretting my inability to take drawings of them; however, I hope that the next time I visit these parts I shall have made sufficient progress to succeed in some degree. I beg you will not neglect the Drawing School[3]— I expect when I return to New York to find you quite expert with the pencil. Drawing is a delightful as well as Gentlemanly accomplishment. The command it gives a person over his time is inconceivable—It has the power of amusing in sickness—rendering home agreeable—and beguiling many a weary hour of its heaviness—the time which would otherwise be wasted in tri⟨ff⟩fling[4] pursuits or perhaps bad company is here employed in a useful and pleasing science that tends to correct the taste and enliven the imagination—though but little attended to by the gentlemen in this age of puppy-ism it will ever hold its rank among the most elegant of the arts and prove a strong recommendation of the possessor to the company of all persons of taste and genius. But I ask your pardon for entering into this detail convinced that you must be as fully sensible of its merit & advantages as myself, but I hope the strong desire I feel for your pursu⟨e⟩ing it will plead my excuse.

I have been unwell almost all the time I have been up here. I am too weak to take any exercise and too low spirited half the time to enjoy company. My chief amusements are reading drawing and writing letters— the two latter I have to do more sparingly than I could wish on account of the pain in my breast. I have nothing particular to communicate at present that would be in the least interesting. I shall go shortly to the Springs[5] and will write to you from there if any private opportunity presents—do write to me immediately about every thing and every body— every tri⟨ff⟩fle[6] of news from New York is interesting—tell me how all the girls do both in the City and country—tell Charles and Stewart to write away and not wait for answers,—I shall do the same. Make my warmest remembrances to all your family and

believe me—my dear fellow— / Your friend
Washington Irving

Mr John Furman

Addressed: Mr. John Furman

Manuscript: Yale. Published: PMI, I, 46 (in part).

This letter is a copy, not in WI's hand.
John S. Furman (b. May 16, 1784) was the son of Gabriel (1756–1844) and

Sarah Wall Furman (1759–1828). John's sister, Abigail Spicer Furman (1779–1864), married John Treat Irving (1778–1838) on April 27, 1806. See the *Furman-Irving Family Records* photostated from the Tyler-Furman-Irving Bible and deposited in NYHS. The Furmans, who lived at New Rochelle, eighteen miles from the Irving residence on Manhattan Island, often entertained members of the Irving family. See PMI, I, 45–46.

1. William Spicer Furman (b. 1781), who was a mate on the ship *Industry*, had died at Port au Prince, West Indies on June 6, 1802. See the *Furman-Irving Family Records* in the NYHS.

2. See WI's letter of July 2, 1802, to his parents for other details about his trip.

3. WI had studied drawing with Alexander Robertson (1772–1841). Presumably John Furman also studied with him. See Burton Albert, Jr., "Alexander Robertson: Irving's Drawing Teacher," *American Notes & Queries* 9 (June, 1971), 148–50.

4. Over *ff* is written *f* in another hand.

5. WI visited Ballston Springs with Daniel Paris, his brother-in-law. See PMI, I, 46.

6. Here, as earlier, the letter *f* is written over *ff*, presumably in another hand.

3.   *To Amos Eaton*

N York Decr. 15th. 1802.

My dear fellow

I have no doubt you are quite surprized, and can hardly beleive your eyes on seeing my name at the end of this Letter. however, it is a thing which I hope from frequent repetition you will in time get accustomed to

I am pleased to hear from Wilson[1] that you do not forget me,[2] when surrounded by your books, which are such far better company—but that you have desired to be remembered to me.

Things go on much in the old track except that I have turnd Editor in good earnest. My brother[3] left town some days ago for the City of Washington & will be absent some time. I am invested with *Editorial Authority* during his absence, but I assure you I "feel the weight of Honor bear heavy upon me." I have mounted a Horse I hardly know how to manage & it requires all my attention to keep him from throwing, or running away with, me.

I feel in a curious situation, manager of a paper, with the principles of which mine do not much accord, obliged to use strict attention & constant application—to be economic and almost parsimonious of my time—things to which I have never been accustomed. I have been used to wander over the fields of fancy & Belles letters and occasionally to tread the graver paths of History & science—but as to the rugged & intricate mazes of Politics, I always avoided them. however, I begin to enter into the "order of the day"[4] more and more and my eyes gradually open upon a new world—the world of politics.

I have undertaken my present employment cheerfully—convinced that it will be of the utmost benefit to me. It will render me more solidly studious, will enable me from constant ⟨[blotted word unrecovered]⟩ practice to be quick at arranging & expressing my ideas on paper, initiate me into the politics of the day and moderate in some degree that flow of spirits with which, I thank God, he has blessd me.

I have not been able to attend the office these some days past[5] ⟨& able to open a law book⟩ George[6] and Beebe,[7] however have visited me at the chronicle office several times—George is boiling as usual—Never was a poor devil of a dog more worried by a Kettle tied to his tail than Honest George is by the Jew.[8] poor George—an honester hearted, cleverer fellow I never knew—Our other fellow student Beebe is ⟨also?⟩ not behind him in worth.

I have not had much time lately to study Law, but I intend to stick to it earnestly as soon as I am more master of my time, as yet I have only swallowed it as we do medicine very quick, without tasting—but I hope in time to get more accustomed to the draught and that it may even become palatable—

I have left off, as much as possible the company of the Ladies merely that I may attend more diligently to my studies—and tho to me nothing is more delightful than the conversation of a charming and accomplished girl, nothing more facinating than an expressive female countenance glowing with modesty yet I am determined to sacrifice all to the Law—Law and Galantry I find, are incompatable to a fellow who like me is half an enthusiast ⟨and⟩ whose head and heart are ever in a fever and who can never be in company with a fine girl half an hour without falling in love—Such is my resolution—Heaven grant me fortitude to keep it!

I was going to say I envied you your studious solitude—but I should have told a falsehood—I never was made to live alone. I always wish to have a few friends around me and having not many I like to have them choice—but I envy you your situation suiting as it does your habits and disposition—and yet after all I cannot call it envy—for envy never can joy in anothers welfare—as I do in yours most heartily—

But Law—Law worries me prodigously in spite of all my resolutions—Oh if I could but have my wishes gratified (& god knows they are moderate enough) how far behind me I'd leave this wrangling driving unmerciful profession—a little independency—a snug handsome little wife (who I have in my eye & in my heart)[9] & an honest friend or two—& a fig for all the world besides—but here am I building castles & picturing distant scenes that never will be realized—however tho my head often rambles—my heart thank heaven is ever at home—in which be assured you have a place

Your friend
Washington Irving

direct to No 208 Bd. Way.

ADDRESSED: Amos Eaton Esqr. / to be left at the Post office / *Catskill.* POSTMARKED: NEW-YORK / DEC 15 DOCKETED: Washington Irving / Dec. 15h 1802

MANUSCRIPT: HSP; also an abridged copy in another hand in HSP.

Amos Eaton (1776–1842), a graduate of Williams College (1799) who was admitted to the New York bar in 1802, turned his attention to the sciences and became a professor at Rensselaer Institute from 1824 to 1842.

1. Probably George Wilson, a student in Josiah Ogden Hoffman's law office.
2. WI had visited his sisters Ann Dodge and Catharine Paris at Johnstown in the summer of 1802. On this trip taken to improve his health WI met Amos Eaton. See PMI, I, 45–47.
3. Peter Irving (1772–1838) was a physician who had recently assumed the editorship of the New York *Morning Chronicle.* A note in the margin in another hand elaborates: "His brother is edidor [*sic*] of the Cronicle [*sic*] Express—I now take that paper—it is democratic and Washinton [*sic*] is Federal."
4. WI may be putting quotations marks around a cliché.
5. A note in the margin in another hand explains: "He is student to Mr. Hoffman."
6. The name "Wilson," in another hand, is inserted in square brackets after "George."
7. Alexander Beebee received several letters from WI during his European tour. Beebee was a fellow student of law in Judge Hoffman's office.
8. After "Jew‡" has been added a footnote, possibly in WI's hand: "This Jew is one Zantr[?] a haughty ignorant fellow-student. He conducts you to the [*illegible word*], Sally, your [?reward?]."
9. After "heart" an asterisk referred to a marginal note: "Keep this a secret— he confides in me. It is Matilda Hoffman." This note, probably written by Eaton later, seems improbable, as Matilda Hoffman (b. November 8, 1791) was only eleven years old at this time.

4. *To William Irving, Jr.*

Ship Rising States, Mouth of the Gironne, at Quarantine/26th. June 1804.

Dear Brother.[1]

By the date of this Letter you will perceive that I am at length arrived in France and have safely pass↑e↓d *the dangers of the Deep.* We Anchored here yesterday after a passage of thirty six days and were ordered, (by a French guard ship stationed at the mouth of the river) to quarantine for four days.[2] This measure is observed towards all American Vessels. The day we sail from here up to Bordeaux is counted among the days of Quarantine so that we shall weigh anchor the day after to morrow. The boat of the guard ship is to bring us fresh provisions, sallads, fruits &c from a small ⟨town⟩ ↑village↓ opposite the Quarantine grounds, so that we are very well off.

My health is much better than when I left New York[.] I was but slightly sea sick for about a day and an half on first coming out. The rest of the voyage I was tolerably well except fevers that often troubled me at Night. We were seventeen in the cabin beside the Master & Mates and as I cannot speak very highly of the cleanliness of some of my fellow passengers you may suppose our nights were not over comfortable. I have often passed the greatest part of the night walking the Deck.

Our passage was what the sailors term, "a lady's Voyage," gentle and mild. We were tantalized however with baffling winds, particularly after entering the Bay of Biscay where the wind came directly ahead. The first land we made therefore was Cape Penas[3] on the coast of spain, (on the twentieth of the month.) I cannot express the sensations I felt on first catching a Glimpse of European Land. I gazed on the land almost the whole day; I clim[bed] [MS torn] to the mast head and endeavored to distinguish the houses and farms. The coast however did not appear capable of[4] much cultivation. Immense mountains of barren rock raised their heads high above the clouds, Their summits were covered with snow and it was half way down their sides, that the verdure first made its appearance. ⟨In scatterd⟩ They presented a grand and, to me, a novel spectacle. After ⟨losing⟩ standing on another tack and losing sight of this coast, we were for several days fagging about in the bay out of sight of land and worried with head winds and calms till we made Cordovan light House[5] and at last cast anchor in the river.

We spoke but one homeward bound ship in our passage which ⟨ves⟩ was the Independance[6] bound to New York. We spoke her about 60 leagues from Cordovan light house and she promised to report us. I expect you have heard of us by her. It was impossible to get a letter on board of her or I should have done it.

We have had fresh provisions throughout the voyage. Our cook was very indifferent so that we had to officiate in that capacity by turns. It would have amused you to see how busy I was on my cooking day, and how industriously I went to work stuffing fowls and making plumb pudding at both which I assure you I have proved myself no mean hand. It was a serious undertaking to prepare a dinner for so many mouths.

Some of my fellow passengers were disagreeable beasts enough, but there were three or four quite agreeable. Among the latter is a **Mr** Durand,[7] formerly a ↑sea↓ captain in the french service, now an American citizen. He was mentioned to me by Mr Juhel[8] and Mr Durand[9] of N York as a man in whom I might place confidence. From what I have seen of him I consider him as an upright worthy fellow. He has promised to point out to me such a place of residence in Bordeaux as I described to him. A respectable house where a stranger would not be exposed to extortion or Imposition—There ⟨was⟩ ↑is↓ also on board a Mr Bancel,[10] a young man who lately taught french in New York. He has been extremely obliging and has taken much pains to acquaint me with the french language. I have great reason to be satisfied with the progress I have made. I can ask for any thing I want beside a variety of casual questions, I begin to understand what is said to me, and can read and understand tolerably well any simple french book.

I should have made greater proficiency had not↑several of↓the passengers talked english fluently so that I was not obliged to resort to french to make myself understood. I have studied the grammer attentively and written exercises, in short I want but a week or two's practice in Bourdeaux to be enabled to travel through france ⟨and⟩ without an interpreter.

I was never more mistaken than in the opinion I had formed of the Captain of our Vessel.[11] I have found him a manly clever fellow possesd of a good understanding and much information. He is also ⟨very⟩ good humored and pleasant and a great part of my time has passed very agreeably in his company.

Remember me most affectionately to all the family. My heart warms towards you all the farther I am off. And I often lay in my birth or walk the deck for an hour or two thinking of home and fancying how you are all employing yourselves, till the tears stand in my eyes. I can see mother, frequently, ⟨hunting⟩ poring over the marine lists to see if any mention is made of our vessel; and on sundays particularly I picture you all grouped in your back parlour conjecturing how far I am on my voyage. If sally & nancy[12] are in town give them my affectionate remembrances[.] I should have left a letter for them but was too much hurried and agitated when I left the city—to write one. I regret very much I did not see Mr Cutting[13] before I sailed, I wished to assure him of the high sense I had of his very friendly attentions; present him with my warmest acknowledgements. remember[14] me particularly to the Hoffmans the Johnsons to Hicks to Robinson[15] to a hundred others I cannot find room to mention and whom I had not time to see in consequence of the ships sailing so early in the morning. This Letter is to be sent on board the Guard ship with a request that they will put it on board the first american Vessel that goes past. I shall write more particularly when I get to Bordeaux. I conclude with desiring you to mention me *most* particularly to father[16] and mother and assure them I will write them from Bourdeaux. Your⟨s⟩ affectionate brot[her] [*MS torn*]

W I.

amongst[17] the rest dont forget the Swartwouts and beg Sam to write me by every opportunity.

The[18] only News I have yet heard is that Bonaparte[19] is declared Emperor of the Gauls. Moreau[20] is banished two years to his estate in the country. Georges[21] is shot Pichegru[22] has hung himself in prison & preparations are still making for the Invasion.[23]

ADDRESSED: Mr. Wm. Irving Junr. / Merchant / New York, DOCKETED: Letter from Washington Irving Esqr. / Dated, Ship Rising States, Mouth of the G⟨a⟩ironne, at Quarantine / 26th. June 1804
MANUSCRIPT: Yale.

1. Most of the letters preserved from WI's first visit to Europe are addressed to his oldest brother William (August 15, 1766–November 9, 1821), who provided the funds for the trip and required detailed reports, both in letters and notebooks, from the young traveler.

2. In his journal entry of July 1, WI accurately reported that the quarantine lasted three days. Although the organization differs somewhat, the phraseology of many parts of this letter is echoed in the journal entry for July 1.

3. Cape Peñas is about 12 miles northwest of Gijon along the northern coast of Spain.

4. "Of" is written in the lower right corner of MS page 1 underneath "capable," as though it were intended to be a catchword, but it is not repeated at the beginning of the next manuscript page.

5. Located near Pointe de Grave on an island in the mouth of the Gironde River. The first lighthouse on this site was built in the ninth century by Louis the Pious.

6. The *Independence* reached New York on August 8, 1804. See NYEP, August 8, 1804.

7. I. B. Durand of 114 Pearl Street is listed as a merchant in the *New York City Directory* for 1805. He is probably the same person as James B. Durand (1772–1830), the confusion arising from a misreading of the first initial. See NYEP death notices (typescript at NYHS).

8. John Juhel is listed in the *New York City Directory* for 1804 as a merchant at 160 Greenwich Street. Scoville (*Old Merchants of NYC*, I, 324–337; V, 45) speaks of John Jukel (d. March, 1817), a Frenchman in the wine-importing trade with a store at 160 Greenwich. Perhaps Scoville's hazy recollection of the name was not entirely accurate.

9. Scoville (*Old Merchants of NYC*, I, 24) says that Jonathan Goodhue of Goodhue & Co. "took in a partner named C. Durand, but he did not remain with them many years." It is not clear from the context whether or not this partnership was formed as early as 1804.

10. Victor Bancel began a boarding school in New York City about 1801. After the decline of L'Ecole Economique "of G. Hyde de Neuville and General Victor Moreau," Bancel "secured its 'good will.'" Apparently Bancel returned to New York to continue teaching French. See Scoville, *Old Merchants of NYC*, I, 338–40.

11. Captain Nathaniel Shaler, commanding *The Rising States*, had commented when WI boarded the ship on May 19 that "There's a chap who will go overboard before we get across" (PMI, I, 63).

12. Apparently WI is referring to his sisters, Sarah Irving Van Wart and Ann Irving Dodge.

13. This may be Francis B. Cutting, a New York attorney who was the grandson of the Reverend Leonard Cutting, who had operated a famous grammar school at Hempstead, Long Island. See Scoville, *Old Merchants of NYC*, II, 220.

14. This word is the first in a passage written along the left margin of the third MS page of this three page MS letter.

15. WI may be referring to a son of Morris Robinson, cashier of the United States Branch Bank. One of Morris Robinson's daughters married Alexander Slidell Mackenzie, whose *A Year in Spain* WI edited for John Murray in 1830–1831. See Scoville, *Old Merchants of NYC*, II, 260, 367.

16. This word is the first of two sentences written along the right margin of the second MS page.

17. This word begins a postscript written along the right margin of the second MS page, to the left of the passage beginning "father and mother...." An asterisk following "a hundred others" three sentences earlier keys it to "others."

18. This paragraph is written along the right margin of the second MS page as an interpolation.

19. Napoleon Bonaparte (1769–1821), proclaimed Emperor by the *sénatus consulte* on May 18, 1804, ruthlessly crushed conspirators and continued his plans for invading England.

20. Jean-Victor-Marie Moreau (1763–1813), a French general who had opposed Napoleon and was sentenced to two years in prison, fled to America where he lived from 1804 to June, 1813. Moreau then returned to Europe to fight against Napoleon, but he died in Bohemia on September 2, 1813, from the complications resulting from a battle wound.

21. Georges Cadoudal (1771–1804), often called Georges, a French Royalist who was executed in late June, 1804.

22. Charles Pichegru (1761–1804), a French general found strangled in his cell in April, 1804.

23. By this time Napoleon had assembled hundreds of ships between Brest and Antwerp and had encamped his "Grande Armée" at Boulogne, but he could not invade the British Isles because he did not control the sea. Skirmishes in 1805 led ultimately to the battle of Trafalgar, resulting in the defeat of the French fleet and freedom on the seas for the British.

5. *To William Irving, Jr.*

Bordeaux. July 1st. 1804.

My dear Brother

I wrote you by the ship John from the Quarantine Ground, in the mouth of the Gironne; as that letter may not possibly come to hand I will just mention that we got out of the Hook the evening of the day we saild from New York, that we had a pleasant tho' rather tedious passage, ⟨of⟩ owing to calms & head winds, that the first ⟨earth⟩↑land↓we made was Cape Penas on the coast of Spain and that on the twenty fifth of June we came to anchor in Verdun Roads, mouth of the Gironne after a passage of thirty six days.

We remaind at Quarantine till the twenty eighth in compliance with a rule observed towards all american vessels. We were then examined with respect to our passports by the Guard ship, a soldier was put on board to prevent our landing till we arrived at Bordeaux, and to attend us to the municipality &c at that place, to have our names professions &c registered & our passports examined & signed. Such are a few of the precautions innumerable that are observed at this day in France.

Our sail up the ⟨Gironne⟩↑River↓ was delightful. At first the river was wide and the Banks poor and uninteresting. ⟨but After⟩ The river Geronne is formed by the junction of the Dordonne and the Garonne, after entering the latter, the prospects are vastly superior. You then begin to have an idea of

"The vine cover'd hills and gay vallies of France."[1]

The country is highly cultivated. ⟨The hills⟩ Hill and dale is one continued vineyard which presents a rich & most luxurient green; the trees are beautiful and ⟨well trimmed⟩ picturesque and kept in excellent order The country is diversified by villages, and chateaus, and along the Banks are scattered small cottages embosomed in trees and often overrun with vines. They reminded me[2] of those retreats of contentment and felicity so ⟨f⟩ often sung by our pastoral poets, and had but the Garonne have parted with its muddy character and "rolled a silver ⟨[unrecovered]⟩ wave"[3] I should have pronounced them the very habitations for our rural rhymsters.[4] About ten or twelve miles below Bourdeaux the banks of the river on one side became perpendicular, and we observed square holes cut in them that appeared like the mouths of caverns These we were told were ⟨the⟩ entrances to the Quarries from whence they cut the stone used for building at Bourdeaux.[5] These quarries are said to run eight and nine miles under ground; we wished to go ashore and enter one of them, but the *Militaire* would not consent to it, and we did not attempt to bribe him.

⟨?On our way?⟩ The chateaus cottages &c in the country are all built of stone. Among the former, one was pointed out to me by one of my fellow passengers (an old gentleman who had left Bordeaux eighteen years since) as worthy of notice. He informed me that for many years while he resided in France it was called "*Le chateau de Diable*"[6] from an opinion the country people had, that it was haunted, and that no body could be prevailed upon to live in it. Since the revolution however, the fear of his Satannick[7] majesty has ceased to prevail as much as formerly; they have turned him out of this country seat at least; for I perceived that it was inhabited.

On yesterday morning (Saturday the 30 July)[8] we arrived and disembarked at this port after having been exactly six weeks on ship board. I had began to be considerably of a sailor before ⟨we⟩I[9] left the ship. ⟨?Our?⟩ My[10] round jacket and loose trousers were extreemely convenient. I could lay[11] down any wheres[12] without fear of spoiling my clothes. I was quite expert at climbing to the mast head and going out on the main top sail yard.

I was thoughtless enough to forget my Surtout when I left New York, and should have suffered for the want of it had not the captain have lent me a comfortable great coat during the Voyage. I also forgot a bottle of Lavender water which Mrs Johnson[13] made for me. It would have been very grateful at sea as our cabin was crowded.

July 2d. 1804

I was interrupted in my letter yesterday; and I must now finish it in a great hurry as there is a Vessel to set sail for New York in an hour. I shall not therefore be as particular as I intended, but my next shall be very minute. Every thing is novel and interesting to me. The heavy gothic looking buildings. The ancient churches the manners of the people—it really appears like another world. There are few handsome streets, the whole city is cut up into lanes alleys &c and the houses on each side extremely high. The buildings are many of them extremely ancient. They are all built of stone and↑the better order↓decorated with sculpture. The weather is excessively hot, owing in a great degree to the reflection of the sun from the pavements which are of light colored lime stone the same as the buildings The heat of the weather will oblige me to leave the place soon and go to some pleasant situation in the country near Montpelier.

This morning I met Leffingwell[14] of the house of Leffingwell & Dudley of New York. You cannot conceive how glad I was to see him. He is an old acquaintance & a very clever fellow. He is here on business. I went with him to the consul Lee[15] to get my protection & to deliver my letter of introduction. My reception was very friendly and I shall dine with Mr Lee to morrow. As yet I have staid at the Hotel Franklin where Capt Shaler[16] and myself had a room together, but to day I ⟨shall⟩ expect to go in a french family. I have only delivered ⟨the⟩↑one of my↓ letters as yet, but intend to deliver the rest to day.

My ideas are not collected sufficient to give you a rational letter, ⟨but⟩ you must expect my next to be more satisfactory

I am much hurried ⟨so that⟩ & forget every thing I wished to say

Give my love to father mother and all the family and the warmest remembrances to my friends. Another vessel sails in a day or two by which I will write

Your affectionate Brother
W I.

P. S. Bonaparte ⟨w⟩has assumed the title of Emperor of france and it is expected will be crownd on the 14 inst Georges is shot. Moreau ⟨ha⟩ it is said has sat out for spain with an intention of embarking for America. Thus wags the world.

DOCKETED: Bourdeaux July 1 & 7–1804 (written vertically along left margin of MS page 1)

MANUSCRIPT: Rutgers University Library; PUBLISHED: *Journal of the Rutgers University Library* 9 (December, 1945), 6–8; PMI, I, 65, 66 (in part).

1. Not identified.

2. This word is written as a catchword underneath "reminded" in the lower right corner of the page but not repeated on page 2.

3. From Alexander Pope's *Windsor Forest* (1713), a fusion and confusion of lines 335 and 344.

4. The phrasing of several passages in the letter are echoed in the journal for July 1, although the order and details differ.

5. On the right bank of the Garonne, south of Bordeaux, are "yellow cliffs pierced to form cellars, in which is deposited the wine grown above them; and, for a considerable extent near Gauriac, they are excavated in quarries of building stone." See *Handbook for Travellers in France* (London, 1844), p. 274.

6. Either WI or his informant attributed this legend to the wrong house, for the actual Chateau du Diable was in Bordeaux, in the Saint-Seurin quarter. It was a small manor reached by a drawbridge from the Rue Judaïque. According to local superstition, one could, at night, hear groans, chains clanking, and shrieks. An inhabitant of Saint-Seurin, named Desarnaud, rented the manor and moved in. Disappointed by the skeptical lodger, legend says, the ghosts decided to leave the place. See *Guide de la France Mysterieuse* (Paris, 1964), p. 157.

7. The second *n* and the *k* have been crossed out by someone else.

8. In another hand the *ly* of July is crossed out and *ne* written above it.

9. "I" is written over "we."

10. "My" is written over "Our."

11. In another hand *ay* is crossed out and *ie* written above it.

12. The *s* has been crossed through by someone else.

13. Mrs. Elizabeth Johnson (d. June 16, 1830), an English-born actress best known for her roles in high comedy, often appeared at the Park Theater in New York. At this point is a penciled asterisk in another hand, with a note: "The then celebrated actress."

14. Daniel Leffingwell (1773–1804) and WI almost drowned in the Garonne River at Bordeaux when they tried to reach a ship arriving from New York. Later on December 8, 1804, upon his return to the United States, Leffingwell committed suicide after attending the Park Theater and seeing T. A. Cooper perform in the role of Hamlet. See PMI, I, 66–68, and NYEP, December 10, 1804.

15. American consul at Bordeaux, William Lee (1772–1840) served as commercial agent there from 1801 to 1816. See *J&N*, I, 93.

16. Captain of the ship on which WI sailed from New York to Bordeaux.

6. To Cadwallader D. Colden

Bourdeaux July 5th.1804

Dear Sir

You will excuse the liberty a stranger takes of addressing in this manner, when you are informed that it is prompted by sentiments of esteem and regard. It was mentioned to me by your friend Mr Jonathan Jones[1] of this place that you have not received any letters from your connections in New York for some time past and that you are extremely anxious to hear of their situations. As I am just arrived from New York and have had the pleasure of an intimacy at Mr J O Hoffmans and with others of your friends I promised Mr Jones to write you such particulars as occur to my reccollection

Mrs Colden[2] had arrived in New York a short time before I left it ⟨and⟩ with your son David;[3] they were both in good health and resided at Ogden Hoffmans. She was in high expectation of your speedy arrival and was making preparations for your reception She shewd me a few days before I saild a Letter she had just received from you dated ↑I think↓ at Montpelier wherein you mentiond your intended rout through Italy ⟨and⟩ Switzerland &c from which I concluded your return would not be so soon as she expected. I requested her often to write by me, but could not prevail. She said the writing a Letter, or indulging in the idea of the possibility of its finding you in Europe would render her low spirited; indeed it was a point on which none of her friends would venture to urge her, so that I think it improbable that you will recieve any more letters from her during your stay in France. The evening before my departure I was in company with her at Mr Hoffmans, she intended the next morning with the assistance of Eliza Fenno[4] and Mary Prevost[5] to commence arranging the House against you should arrive and she appeared to dwell with pleasure on the idea of such an employment. David has grown considerably in your absence and is a fine spirited boy.

Your business I believe goes on very well. M Graham[6] is extremely attentive and industrious and Cooper[7] has observed much application to the duties of the office. There are very few offices in town where such order and regularity ⟨is⟩ are maintaind.

Your Letters have been recieved with tolerable regularity. They circulate rapidly thro the hands of your friends, and the favorable accounts of your health give the warmest satisfaction. They have also written frequently in return and it is surprizing their letters have not come to hand.

Mr Ogden Hoffman and his family are in perfect health, and Mrs Hoffman it is expected will shortly make an addition to the family.[8]

Mr Hoffmans business is in a flourishing state, and his professional reputation daily encreasing.

Hoffman and Seton[9] are doing a vast deal of business. The Setons are all in their common state of health except that Charlotte[10] has been reduced very low with a ⟨consump plia [?]⟩ consumptive complaint in consequence of a cold, but has almost completely recovered. They received some time since Accounts of Mr Wm Setons death at Leghorn[11] The rest of your friends with whom I am acquainted are as far as I reccollect in good health.

The political occurrences of note in New York have probably reached you before this. There has been a warmly contested election for governor. The Clintonians held up Morgan Lewis[12] and the Burrites & Federalists united in support of Burr[13] in opposition. Before I left the city it was pretty well ascertained that Lewis would have a majority of near seven thousand. Gov. ⟨[unrecovered]⟩ Clinton[14] is the Democratic candidate for Vice President at next election.

I shall remain at Bordeaux for a mo[nth] [MS torn] longer, after which I shall pursue a similar ro[ute to] [MS torn] the one you have passed, ⟨with⟩ and chiefly for a similar o[b]ject [MS torn] the restoration of my health. If there are any inquiries you wish to make of me concerning your family or friends I shall be extremely happy to answer them as far as my knowledge extends

with sentiments of the warmest respect/I have the hon. to be/Sir Yrs &c
Cadwallader D Colden Esq.   Washington Irving

Please to present my remembrances to Mr Schiefflin[15]

ADDRESSED: Cadwallader D. Colden Esquire / Chez Messrs. Delessert & Co. / à
   Paris DOCKETED: Washington Irving. / Bordeaux 5th. July 1804 / Recd. at
   Paris 13
MANUSCRIPT: Yale.

Cadwallader D. Colden (1769–1834) was the brother of Mary Colden (1770–1797), first wife of Josiah Ogden Hoffman (1766–1837). Colden, the grandson of the Loyalist lieutenant-governor of the province of New York, was a lawyer who was active in public affairs. See Edwin R. Purple, *Genealogical Notes of the Colden Family in America* (New York, 1873), p. 21.

1. Jonathan Jones (1748–1835) was an American merchant residing in Bordeaux at 29 Allées de Tourny. See Young, *WI-Bordeaux*, p. 21.

2. The former Maria Provost (d. May 10, 1837), daughter of the Right Reverend Samuel Provost, married Colden on April 8, 1793. See Purple, *Colden Family in America*, p. 22.

3. David Cadwallader Colden (1797–1850) was Colden's only child.

4. Eliza Fenno (d. 1817) was the sister of Mrs. J. O. Hoffman. On October 2, 1811, Eliza married Gulian C. Verplanck (1786–1870), who had been a student in Hoffman's law office. See July, *Verplanck*, pp. 26–28, 50–51.

5. Presumably a relative of Mrs. C. D. Colden. WI has probably misspelled the surname.

6. Possibly John, the son of Isabella Marshall Graham (1742–1814), who had worked with Elizabeth Ann Bayley Seton (1774–1821) in founding the Society for the Relief of Poor Widows with Small Children. The death of Mrs. Seton's husband is alluded to later in the letter.

7. Probably a relative of Colden's. His sister Catherine married Thomas Cooper of Rhinebeck, New York. See Purple, *Colden Family in America*, p. 21.

8. The Hoffman family genealogies do not record a birth for Mr. and Mrs. J. O. Hoffman in 1804.

9. In 1795 Martin Hoffman (1763–1829) and George Seton had founded an auction and commission house at 67 Wall Street. Hoffman had married Mary Frances Seton, daughter of Harriet Colden, on May 14, 1802. See W. W. Hoffman, *Eleven Generations of Hoffmans in New York: Descendants of Martin Hoffman, 1657–1957* (New York, 1957), p. 12.

10. Charlotte Seton (1786–1852) was the daughter of William Seton (1746–1798) and his second wife, Anna Marie Curzon, and the half-sister of William Magee Seton.

11. William Magee Seton (1768–1803) went to Italy for his health in 1803 with his wife Elizabeth Ann Bayley (see note 6 above) and their five children. He died in Pisa in December, 1803.

12. Morgan Lewis (1754–1844), at first supported by De Witt Clinton, won the election for governor on the Republican ticket by defeating Aaron Burr.

13. Aaron Burr (1756–1836), suspecting that Alexander Hamilton had opposed his election, forced the duel which led to Hamilton's death on July 11, 1804.

14. George Clinton (1739–1812) replaced Burr on the Republican ticket in February, 1804, and was elected to the vice-presidency for Jefferson's second term in a landslide victory which gave the two candidates 162 of the 176 votes cast. See *Encyclopedia of American History*, ed. Richard B. Morris (New York, 1953), p. 134.

15. Henry Hamilton Schieffelin (1783–1865) was later associated with the wholesale drug business started by Jacob Schieffelin in 1794. See *King's Handbook of New York City* (Boston, 1893), p. 911; *Schieffelin Genealogy* (1934), chart.

7. To Peter Irving

Bordeaux July 7th. 1804

My dear Brother

I have now been a Week in Bordeaux and my ideas begin to collect again, for I assure you they have been quite in a state of derangement since my arrival, from the novelty of my situation My letters of introduction have procured me the most hospitable attentions. I was introduced shortly after my arrival to a Dr Ellison[1] resident of this place. He was a fellow student of yours under Dr Romayne[2] since which time he has been in different parts of Europe and at length settled himself in Bordeaux, I am told he is shortly to be married to a lady of this city. He is a very gentlemanly, clever fellow, and highly respected here. To his friendship I am indebted for the very agreeable situation in, which I am placed. I am in the family of a Monsr. Ferrier,[3] an old gentleman who sometime since was one of the ⟨P⟩ richest and most respectable merchants in Bordeaux and for sometime Mayor of the city, but a succession of misfortunes ⟨and⟩ have stripped him of most of his property. He has still enough to support him in an easy genteel style; His house is handsomely furnished and his table both plentiful and elegant. The family consists of the old gentleman the old lady and myself with three servants.[4] They are a most amiable old couple, highly estimated and visited by the first people of Bordeaux. The french that they speak is free from the barbarous gascon accent and dialect that prevails in this part of France, and as they do not speak english I am obliged to talk entirely in french, which makes me improve more rapidly in the language than I otherwise would. It is merely as a favor and in consequence of the reccommendation of Dr Ellison that I ⟨got⟩↑was↓ admitted in this family, for they do not take boarders. I am universally congratulated on my good fortune.

⟨My⟩ I am gradually growing accustomed to the looks of Bordeaux. Its narrow streets and high buildings no longer appear singular. There is a strength and solidity about the houses that gives them an air of dignity which we do not find in our ⟨aery⟩ light American buildings The houses ⟨are⟩ inside & out are of a kind of lime stone, excepting that their rooms are sometimes panneld, with ⟨[unrecovered]⟩ board floors. But generally the floors are of stone marble or tyle. The houses are commonly ⟨four⟩↑three↓ stories high, ⟨with⟩ The windows ⟨of⟩↑in↓ the casement style with handsome Iron raild balconies. The doors are folding and very large and eight or ten feet within the entrance a folding ⟨iron ba⟩ gate of open worked iron extends across the passage. In the middle of the houses is a square court open from top to bottom of the house with galleries running round it in the upper stories. ⟨The⟩ From this court the interior rooms of the houses receive ⟨the⟩ both light and air. You cannot conceive how cool and agreeable these houses are in Summer, and I am told they are very warm in winter when carpets are spread over the paved floors.

There are some remains of antiquity at this place, particularly the Palais Galien[5] which stands near my lodging. It is the remains of a roman ampitheatre built of Brick and stone, ⟨dur⟩ under the reign of the Emperor Galien, towards the middle of the third century. Since the revolution the land on which it stands was sold in common with other national property and the purchasers began demolishing the building to make way for streets and houses. Fortunately however a ⟨man⟩ ↑gentleman↓ of taste[6] arrived from paris in quality of Prêfet of this department, and rescued the precious remain of antiquity from entire demolition. The municipality have received a charge to look to its preservation so that there are hopes of its still remaining for a considerable space of time. Nothing however ⟨of its former⟩ stands but part of the bare walls and one of the grand entrances. Here and there on the inside are mutilated capitals of ⟨Corinthian⟩↑Tuscan↓ Columns which appear to have been ⟨built⟩ of the same kind of stone which they use in Bordeaux for building at present. I regard this ancient pile with peculiar reverence[.] two or three times I have strolld home at night thro its silent ruins and as I passd under the dark arches of the grand entrance I have almost fancied I could see an old roman stalking amidst the gloom.[7]

By thy bye this old building has not served merely for a place of amusement to the romans. As I was poring over an old book printed in 1619 and entitled ⟨co⟩ *Chronique Bourdeloise* I ⟨came across⟩↑found↓ an account of several ↑joviall↓ meetings held by some *bon vivants* of the infernal regions, ⟨who held here⟩ in the Palais Galien[.] they also held some kind of a court there,[8] I could not understand the french well enough perfectly to understand what kind of a one it was, but I believe it bore some resemblance to what we term in english a *Dover Court*.[9] The same book mentions the execution of a man for Sorcery, who before his death, confessed to have been at some of these diabolic festivals. Since the revolution, however, nothing of the kind has been known, the devil having abandoned his old habitations and entered into the heads and hearts of the *great men of the land*.[10]

There are also several Ancient churches of which I have only seen the interior of two which were ⟨in⟩ of inferior order, but extremely antique in their appearance. There is a party of us intend in a day or two, to visit the ⟨ch⟩ cathedral and several of the superior churches as also the Chateau Trompette ⟨An⟩a castle built in the reign of Lewis the fourteenth.[11]

The Grand Theatre[12] is a magnificent building & said to be the finest of of its kind in ⟨Europe⟩↑France↓. The interior however, is not painted to suit my taste, and the painting is much soild & faded. I have been twice to see La Fond[13] one of the two first tragedians in France. He was performing a few nights at this place and has ⟨be?⟩ I believe returned to paris. ⟨The characters he performed were [*unrecovered*] and Oedipe? to life?⟩ Tho I could not understand the language, yet I was delighted with the actor. His figure is tall and majestic, his face uncommonly expressive and his voice full and sonorous. The other actors are miserable enough as is generally allowd. The french actors are very violent in their gesticulations and their attitudes are often to[o][14] straind & unnatural. The scenery is very handsome & well executed, The dresses superb with great attention to *costume*.

There are two or three other Theatres of inferior merits, one of them called the theatre Francaise[15] is nearly as large as our theatre[16] but the actors are miserable. One of the low theatres has a Jack Pudding[17] on a stage in front of the house, to draw the multitude by his tricks and jokes.

July 8

At one Oclock I am to accompany Mr Bosc[18] (the gentleman to whom my letter of credit is directed) to his country seat a little ways[19] out of town, to dine & spend the afternoon there.

Mr Bosc has promised to take charge of my Letters to and from New York when I am travelling so that you will direct all my letters under cover to his firm in Bordeaux Messr. J. J. Bosc & Co rue du Pont— St Jean. I have established an exchange of papers for you with I Berner & Co ship Chandlers. Berner was formerly clerk to Constantine the broker who reccommended him to me as a person who would be eager to make such an exchange. He has promised to send the Journal du Commerce of Paris and a paper of Bordeaux with any ⟨little⟩ political or commercial handbill &c that occurs in return for the Morning Chronicle & such other american papers as you can spare. You will take care to be punctual as he has been repeatedly disappointed in similar arrangements. His direction is I Berner & Co No 96 Chartron Bordeaux. The french papers are very barren concerning public affairs. The motions of government are not so public here as in England or with us and it is merely by vague rumors we learn what is going forward in respect to affairs of the nation. Moreau has departed for some port of the continent to sail for america but what port I cannot learn. The Emperor it is expected will be crownd sometime this month,[20] but whether by the hands of the pope or by the cardinal T⟨ir⟩esch[?] uncle to the Emperor, I am uncertain. In fact I hear less of the war and of the public concerns of France, here, than I did in New York

July 9th.

The people in Bordeaux exercise a liberty of speech that at first surprized me. They make no scruple of talking very freely among themselves concerning the First Consul and reprobating his conduct. This I am told is not noticed by the police as long as it is done in private but should they express their sentiments publicly and endeavor to instill them in the minds of others they would certainly involve themselves in trouble. In New York we have an opinion that France is in a state of Agitation and confusion in consequence of the war and the preparations for the invasion. ⟨In this?⟩ As yet I have seen nothing of the kind. Every thing ↑apparently↓ goes on with smoothness and regularity. No armed forces are seen parading the streets no drums or cannons to be heard. All is order and tranquility and did I not know to the contrary I should think them in peace with all the world. The merchants are the chief sufferers

⟨in my opinion⟩ as I see their Vessels laid up in the river totally dismantled
of their rigging ↑and they universally complain of want of business↓.
The American shipping crowd the port and enjoy a fine harvest during
the contests of ⟨the⟩ Europe. It is only from seeing ⟨military⟩ soldiers
posted at the public places that I reccollect I am under a military
government. A stranger while he acts peaceably may walk the streets
continually and frequent every place of curiosity business or amusement apparantly[21] unnoticed and unknown, but let him once behave
improper and he will soon find his every movement is markd and known.

To this strictness of the Police may be ascribed the personal security
and public tranquility of france. The Roads and highways of the
country are patrolled by troops of Gens d'armes who visit the different
Taverns & houses and acquaint themselves with the manner of living
of the inhabitants and their modes of subsistance[.][22] the cities swarm
with spies in every direction In consequence the streets & lanes may
be traversed ⟨or⟩ & the roads & highways travelled night & day without
any danger of depredation or insult. Were this not the case every thing
might be apprehended from the number of poor people and beggars
with which this country abounds.[23] The streets swarm with fruit
women, tumblers, shoe blacks and savoyards with their musical instruments and now and then you have a grand concert ⟨of vo⟩ both vocal
& instrumental from half a dozen ⟨po⟩ Italian peasant women with
fiddles & tamborines. The streets are entirely free from broils & boxing
matches.[24] A drunken man is very rarely seen, and generally happens
to be some american who has been *enjoying* himself. Our country men
have got a name for drunkenness among this temperate people and often
when there is any disturbance at a public place of amusement it is
common for the french to say—"pho its only some drunken american or
other." This vice which they consider inexcusable among themselves,
they excuse in an american, they say "it is the custom of his country."

July 10th.

An Embargo has been laid on the Vessels in the port for some days
past, to facilitate the passage of a number of Gunboats down the River.
⟨This⟩ Yesterday it was taken off and a Schooner sails this morning for
New York which occasions me to finish my letter abruptly.[25]

The excellent situation I am in has determined me to remain about a
month longer at this place and to take a French master immediately. By
this plan I shall escape some of the hot weather which prevails in this
season in the South of France, and also be enabled to travel with more
satisfaction from a better acquaintance with the language. As I have
nearly got through the routine of dinners which my letters brought upon
me, I shall become quite domestic. M. Ferriere's house is in a retired

part of the city where I shall not be liable to noise or interruption. The
fashions here are very similar to those of New York, so that I have not
been obliged to purchase many articles of clothes, my other expences
independent of board have been very trifling.[26]

Amid the scenes of novelty that surround me, my thoughts often recur
towards home with the most lively emotions. The idea that I am ⟨far in a⟩
far from home, deprived of frequent communications with my friends, "a
stranger and a sojourner in the land"[27] often throws a damp upon my
spirits which I find it difficult to shake off. This I hope will wear away
in time as I become more[28] accustomed to the manners of the people
and more acquainted with their language, should it not, I am affraid it
will induce me to shorten the term of my absence. Those who have
never been far from home, have no idea with what fondness the imagination dwells upon the little spot of earth where our family and friends
are collected and from which we are far distant. I have laid in bed
and thought of you all for hours and you are nightly the subject of
my dreams.

My health is vastly improved. ⟨for the better.⟩ I am convinced that
a little travelling will be sufficient to restore it perfectly. The climate
and manner of living ⟨of⟩↑in↓ this country agrees[29] most excellently with
my constitution. The weather is not so hot as it was on my first arrival.
The heat here has not that oppressive and ennervating quality that it has
in New York, and the evenings are cool and delightful

There ⟨are several⟩ is a beautiful walk in the centre of one of the
Public streets with ↑three rows of↓ high trees ⟨on each side⟩ and stone
benches ⟨to sit on⟩ under them called the Rue Tourney[30]—There is also
a superb public garden calld the "Champ de Mars"[31] very extensive and
enclosed with Iron railing; before the revolution it was laid out with
flower beds paterres &c ⟨but since, it⟩ & was open to none but well
dressd persons, but since, it has become common to all ranks, and no
flowers are cultivatd[32] It contains several delightful shady walks and
groves. My chief amusement in the evening is walking in these places
and observing the various forms and faces around me. In the morning
I rise early and study; I then go down in the garden (we have a very
pretty one in rear of the house) where I find the old gentleman seated
under a favorite Fig tree reading the paper. After I have read the news
and the old gentleman has examined the state of his plants & flowers,
which form his chief objects of amusement we take our breakfast
sociably together. You cannot concieve how agreeably and tranquilly
we live. The old people are the pictures of health and good nature,
and I do not believe there was ever a sour word passed between them.
Mr Ferriere has for a long time wished for the seeds of ⟨plants⟩ some
plants from New York but has been repeatedly disappointed in his

endeavors to procure them, inclosed you will find a list of the seeds he most wishes for with a request to father to send them. I wish you would deliver it to Brother William and desire him when he has time to attend to it. If they are put in a small box and delivered to some captain sailing for this port, they will come safe to hand.

Remember me most affectionately to father mother and all the family. I have been too much engaged since my arrival to write to them all individually but this must serve for a family Letter. I wish you would let the letters I write to you & william & in fact to all of the family, be kept together with care and not scatterd about negligently as I shall wish to see them at some future period.

Remember me to Hicks,[33] the Swartwouts[34] Robertson[35] &c & request them to write frequently[.] you will also remember me to Mr Hoffman[36] and his family particularly. You will tell him that I was shewn by Mr Jonathan Jones[37] of this place a letter lately received by him from Mr Colden dated at paris. Mr Colden's health was much improved but he was extremely anxious respecting his connexions in new York, not having received any intelligence concerning them for a long time. He talked of shortening his tour in consequence & probably returning to embark at this place for new York. I took the liberty of writing him what particulars I reccollected concerning Mrs Colden and the rest of his family and friends and I hope it will have some effect in lessening his uneasiness.

July 11th.

The Vessel sailed yesterday sooner than I expected which prevented me from getting this letter on board her; I shall therefore continue it till the next opportunity.

You will find my letters, in some places contradictory; they are brief journals of my daily observations and ideas, collected from what I see and hear; and I often find, one day, some mistaken opinion I have formed or some misinformation I have recieved the day preceding. ⟨I merely promise to give⟩ You will therefore make all due allowances in this particular.

In a former part of this letter I mentioned that the people of Bordeaux exercise a liberty of speech in private which they dare not use in public, I am since informed that they make no hesitation of speaking their sentiments in the coffee houses ⟨or⟩ & other public places[.] this however I presume is only partially the case ↑and that this liberty is allowd them only as long as their sentiments are favorable to the Government.↓ certain it is however, the Emperor is no favorite among the Bordeaulaise. Some of the people of this place, merchants of respectability with whom I am acquainted, have spoken of him to me with the greatest contempt. I have seen verses of the most pointed and inflammatory kind which are written against him and circulated about in manuscript. At the theatre, when any sentence occurs that may be applied to him it is loudly applauded. The other evening in one of their celebrated Tragedies, speaking of an Usurper & a Tyrant, it was said "He is our conqueror, not our King."[38] This sentence I am told was extravagantly applauded for near ten minutes. The people of this city (which you know is a very commercial place) are extremely anxious for peace; which makes them the more bitter against the "powers that be."[39]

July 12th.

Yesterday afternoon, I spent most agreeably in viewing one of the finest peices of Gothic architecture said to be in France. This was the Church of St. André, the cathederal of Bordeaux.[40] It was built by the English when in possession of this city in the eleventh or twelvth century. The style of Architecture is said to be extremely similar to that of Westminster Abbey in London and bears about it an air of indescribable dignity and solemnity. The first view of it brought strongly to my reccollection the words of our invaluable poet

"How reverend is the face of this tall pile" &c[41]

It is a vast building entirely of stone decorated with all that profusion of carved work and minute ornament that characterizes the Gothic style. When inside, the lofty ⟨arched⟩ ceilings ↑of arched work↓ the vast pillars the windows of painted glass had a *tout ensemble* that produced emotions of awe and veneration. The effects of the revolution are descernable in this building. The unhallowd hands of tasteless barbarians have stripped the paintings from the walls, have torn the images of the saints from the niches ⟨in⟩ of which they had retained peaceable possession for centuries and have decapitated several of the ⟨apostles⟩↑cardinals↓ who are ranged over the grand Portal. Still however they could not injure the beauty of the main architecture, the undertaking would have required too much labor and time for the patience of a mob. The church has been cleaned, is undergoing repairs in several places[,] has again become the "house of prayer"[42] and promises to stand for centuries if left unmolested by sacriligious hands. Our Company consisted of five and we procured the old sexton of the place to shew us the way to the top of one of the Grand towers, of which there are two. Our ascent was quite ⟨[*unrecovered*]⟩ to me⟩ ↑intricate↓, and reminded me of some of those winding and perplexed passages thro which some of the heroes of modern romances wander when prowling about the interior of an old castle. In some places we had to ascend ⟨winding⟩ stone stair cases

that wound up a round tower of about six feet diameter and dimly
lighted by narrow appertures in the wall. We then had to pass through
narrow passages made in the wall of the church having now and then
on one side small ⟨holes that⟩ square holes that looked into the interior
of the building & on the other side similar ones that gave us a peep into
the city. In one place our route entered the church and formed a narrow
gallery almost ⟨at the top of⟩ ↑as high as↓ the cieling or roof from
whence we could see the people far below us at their prayers. In another
place we had to walk on a kind of stone cornice that ran round ↑part of↓
the outside of the edifice. After a great deal of this winding and twisting
through intricate passages we at last arrived on the highest *accessable*
part of one of the steeples. The view from this place was vast and interesting. Beneath us lay the city presenting a singular *melange* of architecture of different orders and periods. Beyond it the beautiful harbour in
form of a crescent, crowded with the ships of *my country,* and all around
in the distance, a level country covered with Vineyards, diversified by
chateaus and enlivened by the waters of the Garonne. From the ⟨?square?⟩
eminence on which we stood there ran up a spire of about an hundred
and twenty or thirty feet high. we could stand on the inside and see to
the very top of it as there was no stairs or any wooden work to intercept
the view. It is built entirely of stone with windows to the very top and
what surprized me was that the walls were not a foot in thickness. This
gave it a dangerous appearance particularly as I opserved cracks in
several places secured by bars of iron After we had remaind here for
some time and witnessed a beautiful sunset we set out to retrace the
labyrinth by which we had ascended, and got safe down again without
any bruises or dislocations.[43] I shall visit this church again before I leave
Bordeaux, for I have not examined in any satisfactory manner its construction & architecture. There are two churches in this city still more
ancient,[44] tho not equal to this in size or workmanship[.] I have not
seen them yet.

13th.

The Ship John Morgan arrived here three or four days since and I have
been extremely disappointed in not receiving letters by her. Do write
often to me, you cannot think how earnestly I desire to hear from you
all. Your best way will be to direct to me as I have before mentioned,
to the care of Messrs J J Bosc & Co, but if any Vessel should be sailing
to Genoa or Leghorn soon you may also ⟨send⟩ ↑write↓ to me by that
opportunity directed either to the house of ⟨Felechi at Leghorn⟩↑Messrs
Philip & Anthy. Felechi at Leghorn↓⟨Mr Hoffman will give you the
direction⟩ or to the House of ↑Kuhn↓ Green & Co Genoa.
There has been some talk here for these few days past of the invasions

having commenced, but it has subsided. The papers are mute on the subject, indeed they have little to say except about the intended Dresses of the Empereur & Empress at the Coronation, (which is to take place the 18 Brumaire) and similar subjects of abject adulation. A paper in paris entitled the *Publiciste* lately inserted an extract from a foreign paper, containing ⟨extra⟩ conjectures of Bonapartes designs with respect to the Papal territory. The paper was immediately stopped, and it was with great difficulty that it was permitted to commence again after two days cessation on condition of changing its Editor.[45]

A great part of the *Beau Monde* of Bordeaux have gone to take the waters of Bagneres,[46] a town situated among the Pyrenees, and famous for its medicinal springs. To this desertion of the fashionable world it is probably owing that there ⟨are qui such⟩ are so few handsome female faces in this place at present, I assure you I have hardly seen a lady since my arrival whose countenance accorded with my ideas of beauty. Large mouths & small eyes are very fashionable and they twist and oil their h⟨ea⟩air profusely.[47] There are two young ladies here however with whom I am delighted. They are the daughters of Mr Jonathan Jones ↑an american &↓ one of the first merchants of the place, and who has been very attentive to me in consequence of a letter I had for him. His daughters speak english tolerably well and though they are brought up in the french style, (as Mrs Jones[48] is a french lady) yet they ⟨bear a great⟩ have very much the appearance and manners of the American ladies, one of them is quite a handsome girl.

July 15th.

This morning I went with several others to visit the church of St Michel.[49] After viewing the cathedral of St André there is nothing in the Architecture of this church capable of exciting admiration. It is a gothic building not quite so old as St André but also built by the English. We ascended the steeple, which stands at a little distance from the main body of the church, and enjoyed a fine prospect from the top of it. The spire which was of stone & very high, was blown down in a storm about thirty years since.[50] I could not learn if it did much damage in the neighborhood In a vaulted appartment under this tower, are several bodies of persons who have been dead a long time. They have been taken out of the family vaults of the church to make room for fresh corps's. What is singular, the Skeletons remain entire and are covered with the skin as dry as parchment. They were ranged about the walls without order and many had fallen to the floor and were trodden to peices. The fellow who bore the light and acted as *cicerone* handled and toss them about without ceremony. It reminded me forcibly of the grave diggers scene in hamlet. Here was a true picture of the equality to which death reduces us. Persons of all ranks & discriptions crowded promiscuously together. In one place the body of a Belle leaned against that of a Beggar and in another a chevalier of St Louis was the intimate neighbor of a common Porter![51]

Sunday is considered in france as a day of relaxation and pleasure. The Principal people in Bordeaux go out of town and spend the day at their county[52] houses which ↑are↓ generally two or three miles from the city. The lower classes shut up their shops (except such as are very eager to make money, and such as keep confectionaries &c) and amuse themselves in the walks and public gardens.

The churches are again reopened, but the people do not attend them with any of the fervor that prevailed before the revolution. In the evening every place of amusement endeavors to entrap a portion of the multitude, and their choice is bewildered between stage dancing, plays, horse ri⟨g⟩ding, juggling & fireworks.

17th

The dealers in fashions & delicacies, such as milliners confectioners &c display a very pretty taste in the arrangements and decorations of their shops. The principal streets have a gay ⟨fo⟩ look, from this circumstance, and a stranger is often tempted to purchase what he does not want from the pretty and inviting manner in which the merchandize is exposed to view. The ⟨french⟩ trades people are also great adepts in the art of persuasion, and, with a trifling knowledge of the English language, and an infinite share of adroitness & insinuation, will often manage to make some of our simple Country men, buy a thousand things they have no occasion for.

I was highly amused the other day with an instance of the kind. I went to the Exchange[53] with an honest American captain and as the hour of business had not commenced we amused ourselves with walking in ⟨the lobby⟩[54] in a wide lobby that runs round ⟨a⟩ the change room, on each side of which are ranged *Boutiques* or stalls, of petty merchants, jewellers, confectioners &c The Captain stopped before one of these, to price a very small hand organ, ⟨which⟩ as he was thinking of purchasing one to teach a canary bird to whistle. The Boutique was kept by a pretty little black eyed woman who could prattle a little broken english. Finding the captain was not inclined to buy she prevaled upon him to accompany her to a small ware Room she had in the neighborhood where she would shew him some very fine instruments. As we were going the captain turned to me with a knowing wink & whispered, 'Now youl see how she'll palaver a body & try to come alongside of the L'argent, but the devil a sous do I lay out for her fiddles & music mills.[']

The little woman however, knew how to manage her cards, she playd
hail columbia yankee doodle got her husband to play on the forte piano,
helped us to wine in short I cannot repeat half her manouvres but by
the help of music & wine & flattery & a pretty face the honest captain
was so bewildered that before he got out of the ware room he had
bought a large, lumbering hand organ for 400 livres[55] (about a third
more than it was worth) which he declared he did not know what the
devil to do with after he had got it.[56]

20th.

The commencement of the revolution must have been fatal to many
fine specimens of the arts In this city there are still traces of the barbarism
that prevaild. The churches stripped of many of their paintings, the
saints broken to peices or decapitated, and ⟨th⟩ two or three fine bronze
statues of their kings, melted down and coind into money. ⟨To preserve⟩
The men of taste and understanding in many of the cities made use of
⟨an⟩ ↑a successful↓ artifice to preserve several of the finest monuments
of the arts from ⟨their⟩ the fury of the populace, which was directed
against every thing that reminded them of Royalty or nobility. On the
public statues, columns &c they caused to be written "Fellow citizens,
this is *your* property, let it not be destroyed"

Had the same mania prevaild in antient times in the revolutions that
took place, had they then extended their rage ⟨even⟩ to the very effigies
of ⟨Man &⟩ Gods & men, what would have become of the fine reliques
that now ⟨form⟩ excite the admiration of the world. Their temples would
have been demolished, their appolos their Herculus's their venus's
shatterd to atoms and as Laocoon was a priest, perhaps like the modern
saints, his head would have experienced a slight disunion from his body.

The French look back to the days of Robespierre & his contemporaries
with horror, and perhaps it is the fear of similar scenes ⟨that⟩ with those
that then prevaild, that prevents them from makeing some desperate
struggle to shake off the Tyrant that oppresses them.

25th.

I hasten to finish this letter to profit by an opportunity that occurs
in half an hour. I have been prevented from writing ⟨in this⟩ any thing
in this letter for these three or four days as I have been pretty steadily
employed in writing to others[.] I shall, however, go about a similar
family epistle as soon as this is closed, and direct it either to you or
william. This letter has been written at different times and in different
humors, but generally in a careless, hasty manner which must serve as
an excuse for its "manifold imperfections." If you find any thing in it,
or in any other letters I may write, that you thing[57] proper to publish,

I beg you will arrange and finish it *handsomely*. It would put a great restraint upon my letter writing if I was obliged to finish every sentence in a manner fit for publication[.] I shall conclude with again assuring you that my health is much improved. I have also got over the homesickness in a great measure, that oppressd my spirits ⟨a⟩ some time since.

I shall rest here till the Vintage commences. as I wish to acquire the language as much as possible before I set out. & I could not have a better situation than I am in at present. It is a perfect little palace where I reside and every thing around me is agreeable ⟨The⟩ I could not be accomodated in any decent hotel in Bordeaux at as cheap a rate as I pay where I am

You mention in a hasty addition to a letter of Hicks'[58] that you have no time to write punctually[.] I am perfectly sensible how much your time must be occupied, and, tho a letter ⟨wil⟩ from ⟨all⟩ you will always be received by me with the liveliest pleasure, yet I cannot complain if I receive one but seldom.

With every wish for your prosperity and happiness I am my dear brother

Yours affectionately
W I.

DOCKETED: Bourdeaux July 7 1804 (written along the left edge of page 1 of MS). MANUSCRIPT: Rutgers University Library. PUBLISHED: PMI, I, 139 (in part); *Journal of Rutgers University Library* 9 (December, 1945), 9–22.

Peter Irving studied medicine but turned to journalism and writing in the early years of the nineteenth century, serving as editor of the Burrite *Morning Chronicle* and the *Corrector,* to which WI contributed essays. After WI joined Peter in Liverpool in 1815 in a futile attempt to save the family business, the two brothers frequently traveled around Europe together.

The recipient of the letter is identified by PMI on a slip of paper: "To Peter Irving—New York / Bordeaux—July 7th—1804"

1. John Gabriel Ellison (b. 1773) was practicing medicine in the Faubourg des Chartrons, Rue du Couvent 23. Young, *WI-Bordeaux,* p. 40.

2. Nicholas Romayne (1756–1817), a doctor from Edinburgh with whom Peter had studied medicine.

3. Jean Ferrière (1741–1813) lived at 99 Rue la Trésorerie in a commodious house with a library which WI frequently used. See Young, *WI-Bordeaux,* p. 40.

4. The children of the Ferrières were grown up and no longer living at home. Mme. Ferrière was Marie O'Quin, of Irish extraction. See Young, *WI-Bordeaux,* pp. 49–50.

5. Named for P. Licinius Valerianus Gallienus, the Roman emperor (253–268). WI probably obtained his historical background for the Palais Galien from Pierre Bernadau, *Annales Politiques, Littéraires et Statistiques de Bordeaux* (Bordeaux, 1803), pp. 147–48. See *J&N,* I, 35.

6. Comte Antoine Claire Thibaudeau (1765–1854), whom Napoleon made

prefect of the Gironde in 1800, ordered the Palais Galien preserved in 1801 (Bernaudau, *Annales*, p. 148). See *J&N*, I, 35.

7. After "gloom" WI placed asterisks connected by a dash to locate the following paragraph in the text, also marked by asterisks, which he wrote as an afterthought on a separate sheet of paper.

8. *Chronique bourdeloise, composée cy-devant en latin par Gabriel de Lurbe ... et par luy do nouveau augmentée et traduite en francois ... A* Bourdeaus, impr. de S. Millanges, 1619. Irving probably found the story of the sorcerers in Bernadau's *Antiquities Bourdelaises* (Bordeaux, 1797), which was in Ferrière's library. See *J&N*, I, 35–36.

9. WI encountered this idea in Thomas Fuller's *The History of the Worthies of England* (London, 1840), II, 124: "There is a village in Essex, not far from Harwich, called Dover-court, formerly famous for a rood burnt in the reign of king Henry the Eighth. But I take it here to be taken for some tumultuous court kept at Dover, the confluence of many blustering seamen, who are not easily ordered into awful attention. The proverb is applied to such irregular conferences, wherein the people are all tongues and no ears, parallel to the Latin proverb 'Cyclopum Respublica.' "

10. In pencil at the bottom of the page and in another hand are the words "See Journal—page 5—" The foregoing paragraph is on a separate sheet of paper.

11. The Chateau Trompette was a fifteenth-century fortress built downstream from the Place Richelieu. The Grand Théâtre was built into one of the slopes of the fortification. See Young, *WI-Bordeaux*, p. 163.

12. Built by Victor Louis between 1773 and 1780.

13. Pierre Lafon (1775–1846) was one of the great French tragedians of his day, a rival of François Joseph Talma. Lafon began his stage career in Bordeaux and died there in 1846. WI probably attended performances of Voltaire's *Oedipe* (1718) on July 3 and La Harpe's *Philoctète* (1783) on July 5. See Young, *WI-Bordeaux*, pp. 311–12.

14. A second *o* has been added in another hand.

15. Located in a triangle between Rues Montesquieu, Condillac, and Fénelon, it seated 1200 people. Other theaters in Bordeaux in 1804, besides the Grand and the Française, were the Molière, the Gaîté, and the Union. See *Bordeaux, Aperçu Historique Sol, Population, Industrie, Commerce, Administration. Publié par La Municipalité Bordelaise.* (Paris, 1892), III, 352; Young, *WI-Bordeaux*, pp. 305–7.

16. Probably WI is referring to the Park Theater, located on City Hall Park between Ann and Beekman Streets and seating 1200 people. See STW, I, 37, and Martha J. Lamb, *History of the City of New York* (New York, 1877), II, 557.

17. A clown.

18. Jean Jacques Bosc (1757–1840) was a Bordeaux banker and later a deputy of the Département of the Gironde. See *J&N*, I, 512, n. 84.

19. The final *s* has two diagonal lines through it, in different ink.

20. Actually Napoleon was not crowned until December 2 at Notre Dame in Paris, at which time he declared war on England.

21. In pencil the second *a* has been crossed out and an *e* inserted in another hand.

22. In pencil the *a* has been crossed out and an *e* inserted in another hand.

23. The journal entry for July 9 is almost identical to the similar passage in the letter to this point. Because it has numerous corrections and changes not found in the journal, it seems reasonable to assume that WI copied the letter into the journal.

24. Beginning with this sentence and going to the end of the paragraph, WI copied the letter almost verbatim into the journal.

25. WI omitted this paragraph from the journal.

26. This paragraph is considerably expanded in the journal.

27. From Marcus Aurelius, *Meditations*, II, 17. See also King James translation of the Bible, Gen. 23:4 and Ps. 39:2.

28. At this point WI changed the journal entry for July 10, completing the sentence and adding one more.

29. The final *s* has a diagonal line through it, in different ink.

30. Allées de Tourny.

31. Louis Urbain Aubert, Marquis de Tourny (1695–1760), intendant of Guyenne, constructed the park between 1746 and 1756.

32. The preceding five sentences appear in a somewhat different version earlier in the journal.

33. Elias Hicks, a friend of WI's in New York.

34. Samuel Swartwout (1783–1856), an associate of Aaron Burr whom WI had met through his journalistic activities on the *Morning Chronicle*.

35. Alexander Robertson, a Scottish born artist who was WI's drawing instructor. For other details, see WI to John Furman, July 26, 1802.

36. Josiah Ogden Hoffman, in whose law office WI worked and studied.

37. Jonathan Jones, an American merchant with influential New York connections, who lived at 29 Allées de Tourny. See Young, *WI-Bordeaux*, pp. 53–57.

38. Not identified.

39. Rom. 13:1.

40. WI is in error here. Although the English controlled Bordeaux from 1154 to 1453, they did not build the church. For other details, see Young, *WI-Bordeaux*, pp. 179–80.

41. William Congreve, *The Mourning Bride*, II, i, 8.

42. Found in the King James version of the Bible: Isa. 56:7; Matt. 21:13; Mark 11:17; Luke 19:46.

43. Except for slight verbal changes, this paragraph is similar to the passage in WI's journals.

44. The older churches are St. Michel (begun in 1160) and St. Seurin (begun in 1175).

45. The gist of the two preceding sentences appears in different form in the journal entry for July 13. WI's source for these details was probably an article in the July 11 issue of the Bordeaux newspaper, *Echo du Commerce de Bordeaux*. See Young, *WI-Bordeaux*, p. 211.

46. Bagnères-de-Bigorre, a town southeast of Lourdes and 12 miles south of Tarbes.

47. The first sentence of this paragraph is similar to the journal entry, but those following express the same ideas in different constructions.

48. Mrs. Jones was Jeanne Texier (1765–1829), the mother of Suzanne (aged 18 in 1804), Sally (aged 15), and Jacques (aged 9). See Young, *WI-Bordeaux*, pp. 57–59.

49. Built between the fourteenth and sixteenth centuries and located south of the center of the city between Rue des Allemandiers and Rue des Faures.

50. Damaged by a hurricane in 1786, the spire was rebuilt in the 1860's.

51. Except for minor variations, this paragraph is the same as the passage in WI's journal.

52. WI probably intended to write "country."

53. Located on the Place de la Bourse.
54. While canceling "the lobby," WI forgot to erase the preceding "in."
55. About $74.00 at the going rate of exchange.
56. The paragraphs under date of July 17 roughly approximate those in the journal for the same day.
57. WI probably intended to write "think."
58. This letter has not been located.

8. *To Andrew Quoz?*

Bordeaux, July 20th. 1804.

My dear fellow

Your letter by the Brig Washington[1] came to hand this morning in company with four other letters from my friends,[2] and I need not mention how my heart danced at receiving them. The least syllable of news from home is invaluable to me, and I have already read those letters over so often that I believe I know them by heart. I was at first "greviously afflicted" with the mention made of your illness but the information that you had again crawled forth into day administered the balm of consolation to my anxious bosom.

I cannot pretend to give you any detail of my adventures or account of the wonders of the vasty deep which I have seen, for these I must refer you to my family letter or letters. I shall only say that the sea has much degenerated since ancient days, for then one could hardly sail out of sight of land without ⟨coming⟩ meeting Neptune and his suite in full gallop, whereas I have passd across the wide atlantic without seeing even a mermaid Tis true we were one blustring night visited by Castor & Pollux, at our mast head,[3] and once or twice had a shoal of ⟨porpoises⟩ ↑Grampuses↓ in ⟨our⟩ company, but as to the former, their Godships have of late fallen very much into disrepute and as to the latter they are at best but *queer fish* of which ↑⟨God knows⟩↓ we had enough aboard already—

As to Bordeaux, it is a pleasant, mercantile, dusty place enough, the people have a curious desire to make money, and their conversation chiefly runs upon wine cotton and coffee. As these have formed very little of my study, you may suppose I am but poorly calculated to support one of their commercial conversations, so I suppose I am put down as a well meaning young man with a great lack of knowledge & information.

As to the fair part of the community, I cannot say that they have as yet displayed charms sufficient to make me forget the *sweet creatures* I have left behind. However they are not to be blamed in this particular for they are by no means backward in displaying what charms they have. A sun beam falling on one of the Bordeaux bells, renders her perfectly transparent, and a slight zephyr betrays the contour of every limb, & the working of every muscle. In New York, formerly, ladies were allowed by the rules of modesty to shew the foot, as a greater freedom of manners ⟨crept⟩ gaind ground they gradually raisd the drapery till it reveald the ancle where they at present make a pause, The Ladies of france however have ↑more↓ rapidly progressd in refinement, and without transgressing the rules of fashionable propriety, they generously display to the very garter. But I will say this for them, whatever part of the body is forbid to be exhibited, is very scrupulously and modestly shrouded from view by an *impenetrable* veil of *fine muslin*.

With such fascinating objects around me, think what a warfare there is between the flesh and the spirit, and what dreadful conflicts I have with the "divinity that stirs within me"[4] You cant imagine how many narrow escapes I have every day from falling in love How often in walking the street, do I see a fair nymph before me tripping along in airy movements. Her form of the greatest symetry, while the zephyrs are continually betraying

> "—The alluring line of grace
> That leads they eye a wanton chase
> And lets the fancy rove"[5]

I hurry after her to catch a nearer view, to feast my eyes with the bright vision before it disappears. The sound of my steps call her attention, she turns her face towards me—the charm is broken, ⟨Her charm⟩ ↑⟨affli?⟩↓ and all my admiration & enthusiasm is disapated. I see a wide mouth, small black eyes, cheeks highly rouged and hair greased with antient oil and twisted from the forehead to the chin till it resembles the head dress of a Medusa! For fear however that I should leave you in a "damning error"[6] concerning the fair of Bordeaux I must inform you that there are some handsome beings among them. Yes, there are some, handsome & amiable, and for their sake we will not curse this sodom & Gomorrah.

The Grand Theatre is a superb building. The outside particularly the front, is a masterpeice of workmanship and bears a most majestic appearance. I have been twice at that theatre to See La Fond[7] one of the most celebrated french Tragedians, and a competitor of *Talma's* though the latter is generally recconed superior. La Fond is a young man and is not a Veteran, like Talma.[8] He possesses a handsome & commanding figure, his motions are graceful and his countenance extremely expressive His voice is ⟨good⟩ well toned, but his lungs are rather weak. This occasions him to fall off some times in his latter scenes, when he becomes fatigued with violent exertion and his voice grows hoarse. He is however a noble fellow, and made me regret severely my ignorance of the language, which prevented my enjoying the excellence of his performance. The rest are poor machines, and as to actresses, they cannot shew such a woman as Mrs Johnson[9] at ⟨either⟩ ↑any↓ of the theatres in Bordeaux.

As they were both tragedies that I saw, I have not had an opportunity of viewing any variety of their scenery. The same scene continuing throughout both ⟨scenes⟩ tragedies. It was the inside of a Palace and superbly executed. We complain very much in new York of a want of light in the theatre. The ↑audience part↓ grand theatre is much larger than ours and yet it is only lighted by a chandalier suspended from the dome, nor is the stage so well illuminated as ours.

The other theatre of importance is the Thatre Francaise It is about two thirds as large as our New York Theatre but by no means comparable to it for scenery or performers.[10]

The other ↑public↓ amusements of Bordeaux at this season of the year are a garden called *Wauxhall*[11] which is only open on *Sundays* when they give fireworks, and the Circus of Franconi,[12] similar to Ricketts's establishment in New York.[13] At present I frequent none of them. The Grand theatre attracted me while La fond was there; but he has been ordered to return to paris to supply the place of Talma who has permission to make a professional visit to Petersburgh.

I was much pleased with the file of papers you sent me, I have been reading the *French news* they contained. You will smile at my saying this but I assure you, you know more about the concerns of france than they generally do in this place. The French gazettes contain nothing but fulsome adulation of Bonaparte and details of his Equipages his parades his levees and his robes imperial. No authentic information is obtainable, of the national concerns, the plans the maneuvres & the intentions of the heads of department. We are obliged to be satisfied with vague rumors that *some body* or another direct from paris has spread about, for they dare not trust any thing of the kind to letter. This is a tormenting situation to be placed in. Residing in a Country where events the most striking and interesting are daily taking place where an undertaking vast, and that involves the interests of the whole world in a greater or less degree, is pending, one naturally desires to know what is going on and to observe the chain of circumstances that lead to these important effects. But the proceedings of the executive are silent and mysterious and a seal is imposed upon the lips of those who have it in their power to betray. ⟨the secret⟩ The gazettes are all awed into silence and dare not hazard a conjecture.

The people see the rights and privileges for which they have been fighting, for which they have sacraficed National tranquility, domestic felicity and friendly endearments, gradually stripped from them by a creature of their own creating. The imposing grandeur of the former Monarchy is risumed with tenfold extravagance. A new order of Nobility is springing up. Another court is established, surpassing in splendor & profligacy ⟨[those?]⟩ ↑that↓ of the former monarchy. Amidst the whole Bonaparte stalks about, the grand puppet of the scene, surrounded by guards and barriers to seperate him from the people he governs—and even in the midst of his guards & barriers, I am told that the hero of Marengo trembles.[14] But enough of this. I will leave this unfortunate man, who amidst all his riches & honors, I sincerely pity and turn to objects less splendid but far more interesting.

My *Mistress*[15] you say is still *growing in grace,* heaven grant her an *Accouchement* as ⟨gentle as⟩ pleasant as the Virgin Marys, (who if I reccollect right sat out on a Journey a day or two afterwards) Often do I trace in my fancy her sweet & gentle features, and at this very moment the "light of her countenance"[16] is beaming upon me with one of her usual smiles that a seraph or a *crying* cherubim might envy: Eliza[17] you discribe as still going on "conquering and to conquer."[18] As to Lord Squirt[19] he may have had a little ⟨singing⟩ ↑singe-ing↓ from the rays of her beauty in *former times,* but when I left town, the youth seemed to have his heart safe in ⟨[?side of?]⟩ its locker and occupied .by no one but his own sweet self. Remember me affectionately to the whole family, and tell them I shall never forget the happy, *happy hours* I have passed in their company. ⟨The accomplish⟩ As to Matilda[20] I hope among other accomplishments she will attend particularly to drawing. And I promise to bring here some *genuine* sketches of Italian scenery on my return.

Remember me particularly to Robertson, the happy Robertson He who riots amidst a profusion of beauty. Whose attentions are sought after by the ⟨[*two or three words unrecovered*]⟩ fairest of the fair and whose chamber might even vie with the haram of the Grand Turk. Tell him an intinerant diciple of his wandering amidst the Medusas of a foreign land, wishes him every felicity that can be bestowed on a mind of sensibility by the smiles of the fair. As you are of one household this letter must serve for you both. ⟨[*unrecovered*]⟩

I beg you will write to me, how Mrs. J. acquitted herself in *Breeches* and ⟨with⟩ whether she *figured* off to much advantage.[21] Remember me to her and her spouse when next you visit them, and present them with my best wishes for their prosperity.

I was quite surprized, shortly after my arrival to meet Leffingwell in the street. The last time I had seen him, you reccollect was shortly after our account of the Philharmonic Concert at which he was marvelously troubled. He had however quite forgot it and appeard ⟨quite⟩ overjoyed to see me. He is here with a Ship of which he is part owner, and is detained by government, for having touched at the English port of

Gibraltar. Leffingwell's head seems ⟨quite⟩ ↑entirely↓ turned with french manners, and I expect when he returns to new York he will be quite what the french term an *Incroyable.*

Tender "the homage of my high respects" to the Rodmans,[22] and tell them I shall endeavor to procure some picture or mummy or monster or Egyptian obelisk for their friend the Baron.[23]

I have had some serious attacks of home sickness while here, but they have wore off, and I again look forward with enthusiasm to the route before me. I am impatient to be moving, and only stay here a little while to acquire the language sufficiently to preserve me from imposition on the road. In about a fortnight I shall set off, and then, welcome the fruitful plains and salubrious climate of Languedoc.

As I have a number of Letters to write I shall make a finis to this one. I therefore entreat you earnestly, as you value the preservation of my friendship and the salvation of your soul, to write frequently and *particularly,* you must not expect such frequent answers For I have much to employ my time and many to write to, but I shall always seize my pen with pleasure to scribble to you my ideas.

Remember me to all my friends an believe me/Your friend.

W I

MANUSCRIPT: Yale. PUBLISHED: New York *Morning Chronicle*, October 11, 1804 (in part); STW, I, 48–52.

Professor Stanley T. Williams suggests that the recipient of this letter was probably Quoz. Andrew Quoz was a *nom de plume* used by a contributor to the *Morning Chronicle* at the time WI was writing as Jonathan Oldstyle. Professor Williams speculates that Quoz may have been Peter Irving, James K. Paulding, or Henry Brevoort. See STW, I, 392. Leonard Beach attributes the Quoz items to Elias Hicks (1771–1845), a business man, militia officer, and journalist who had been involved in dramatic criticism with Peter Irving in 1796. See Stanley T. Williams's introduction to the *Letters of Jonathan Oldstyle* (New York, 1941), pp. xiii–xiv. However, it seems unlikely that WI would write a separate letter to Hicks four days after this one if Hicks were Quoz. Until further evidence is located, the identity of Quoz must remain obscured.

1. The *Washington* under Captain Procter sailed from Bordeaux on October 20, 1804 and arrived in Boston on January 17, 1805, apparently on its return voyage following the arrival to which WI refers.

2. These may include Alexander Beebee, Sam Swartwout, and Elias Hicks.

3. Castor and Pollux, twin heroes of mythology, also known as the Dioscuri, who according to one legend were patrons of mariners and responsible for the atmospheric phenomenon called St. Elmo's fire.

4. A variation of Joseph Addison, *Cato*, V, i, 7.

5. John Logan, "Ode to Women," in *The Works of the British Poets*, ed. Robert Anderson (London, 1795), XI, 1037.

6. The source of this quotation has not been identified. The expression was probably a common one in WI's circle.

7. Pierre Lafon. WI mentions him in his journal entry for July 7, 1804. Miss Wright suggests the performances by Lafon which WI saw were on July 3 in Voltaire's *Oedipe* (1718) and on July 5 in La Harpe's *Philoctète* (1783). See *J&N*, I, 36, n. 20.

8. François Joseph Talma (1763–1828) was considered to be the greatest tragedian of this time.

9. Mrs. Elizabeth Johnson, a favorite actress at the Park Theatre.

10. An allusion to the Park Theatre, the chief theatre in New York at this time. In the *Letters of Jonathan Oldstyle*, published in the *Morning Chronicle*, WI severely criticized the theatre, its audiences, and its productions.

11. Probably this is WI's name for le Jardin Public, which he was associating with the Vauxhall Garden, a summer amusement place operating in New York City since 1799. See Odell, *NY Stage*, II, 69, 97, 124, 145, 184.

12. Antonio Franconi (1737–1836) founded a circus in the mid-eighteenth century specializing in equestrian acts. Members of the family continued the circus for almost one hundred years.

13. WI had many opportunities to see Ricketts's equestrian performers when they appeared in New York from August to November, 1793; November, 1794, to April, 1795; September, 1795; May and June, 1796; September, 1796; the spring of 1797; December, 1798. See Odell, *NY Stage*, I, 336–37, 396–97, 419–20, 441–43; II, 64.

14. A village in the Italian Piedmont where on June 14, 1800, the French under Napoleon defeated the Austrians.

15. This presumably was WI's familiar epithet for Maria Fenno Hoffman (Mrs. Josiah Ogden). See STW, I, 392.

16. Probably a variant of Ps. 4:6.

17. Eliza Ogden (1782–1837), the cousin of J. O. Hoffman, who had been a member of the party visiting northern New York the previous summer.

18. See Rev. 14:8.

19. An admirer of Eliza Ogden?

20. Matilda Hoffman (1791–1808), the daughter of J. O. Hoffman by his first wife, Mary Colden.

21. Mrs. Johnson had appeared in the male role of Young Norval in John Horne's tragedy *Douglas* (1765) in June, 1804, at the Park Theatre. See Odell, *NY Stage*, II, 205–6.

22. Probably a reference to the children of Daniel Rodman (d. 1799), friends of WI's. STW, I, 392.

23. Probably Henry Van Wart (1783–1873), who married Sarah Irving (1780–1849). In later letters WI frequently refers to Van Wart as the "Baron" or "Baron Van Tromp."

9. To Alexander Beebee

Dated. Bordeaux 22c. July 1804.

"I felt heavy hearted at leaving the city[1] as you may suppose; but the feverish moments of my departure were when I lost sight of the boat in which were my brothers who had accompanied me aboard, and when the steeples of the city faded from my view. It seemed, as if I had left the world behind me, and was cast among strangers, without a friend, without a protector, sick, solitary and unregarded. I looked around me; saw none but strange faces, heard nothing but a language I could not understand, and felt *"alone amidst a crowd."*[2] I passed a melancholy, lonesome day, turned into my birth at night sick at heart, and laid for hours thinking of the friends I had left behind. It appeared as if I had given up a life of ease and tranquil↑l↓ity,[3] for one of bustle and vexation. I had undertaken to make my way in a strange country, without knowing the language, open to knavery and imposition. where I could not expect to remain long enough in one place to form any interesting connections, or gain the friendship of a single bosom, a solitary wanderer doom'd

>—"to traverse realms ⟨unknown alone⟩ unknown
>And find no spot of all the world my own."[4]

Had this unhappy mood held possession of me long. I do not know if I should not have been a meal for the sharks before I had made half the passage but thanks to the "fountain of health and good spirits,"[5] he has given me enough of the latter to brighten up my dullest moments and to dispel the clouds of care & sorrow before they have quite darkened my horison. My home sickness wore of[f][6] by degrees; I again looked forward with enthusiasm to the classic scenes I was to enjoy, the land of romance and inspiration that I was to tread, and though new york and its inhabitants often occupied my thoughts, and constantly my dreams, yet there was no longer anything painful in the ideas they awakened. The captain proved to me a most entertaining and agreeable companion. I became acquainted with my fellow passengers and had high entertainment in quizzing some of them who savoured a little of the *queer things* of this world. I have thus given you a slight account of my emot⟨t⟩ions on first leaving home. I have felt a few similar ones since I have been in this place, but they soon wore away & I hope I shall in a little while become enough of *a citizen of the world*[7] to feel at home wherever I happen to be.

Your discription of the family of "O man & o Voman" was a high finished picture and had a striking effect on my imagination. In my *"minds eye"* I saw the *"flannell fumes" arise*, "the *"mighty vapours roll"*! I absolutely held my nose in one part of the tale, the potent steams seemed to have even crossed the atlantic and to have envel⟨l⟩oped my "olfactory organ" in clouds of *honest downright stench*!! How the sweet creatures will weather this hot season I cannot imagine, methinks the atmospheres that surround them must have nearly become *tangi⟨a⟩ble*, and *"feasible* to feeling as to smell."

———

I have read over your letter repeatedly with the highest pleasure; a few lines from New York are a treasure to me, and coming from you, have additional value. You cannot imagine with what fondness I dwell on the idea, that while in a foreign land, among strangers, solitary and almost unknown, I have friends at home who sometimes think of me with interest, who sometimes accompany me (in imagination) in my wanderings, and waft kind wishes for my welfare and happiness. This perhaps may savor of self flattery. Be it so—I should be a miserable dog if I did not indulge in it.

You seem to have a⟨n⟩ high idea of the superior attractions of the french ladies. they are I confess admirably calculated to

"Set fire to the head and set fire to the tail"[8]

but as to the *heart* I must be a little better acquainted with the language and discover their mental accomplishments, before I will suffer *that* to be affected. as yet I do not feel in much danger

"The wanton look, the leering eye
Bid loves devotion not be seen
Where constancy is never nigh."[9]

For fine girls, one need not quit New York, I'll assure you the girls of Bordeaux in my opinion are not to be compared to them for beauty. Many a wishful thought do I send to the fascinating little creatures I have left behind me, and full often do I wish it was in my power to spend the evening in their company.

"Ye daughters of *Manhattan* isle
Where e'er I go, where 'eer[10] I stray,
Oh charity's sweet children smile
To cheer a pilgrim on his way."[11]

This is the first prayer that I've made in Bordeaux, and even that is extracted from an old song, however, when next you see sam swartwout tell him to transmit it to my female acquaintances as a proof how much I remember them in my prayers.

There are several excellent institutions in Bordeaux called circles. These consist of a number of Gentlemen who hire the second floor of a house which is fitted up into a reading room, Billiard room, card room &c. The reading room is furnished with the different gazettes and periodical publications of Bordeaux and paris. all gambling is absolutely prohibited. in the evening the rooms are handsomely illuminated with chandaliers. The expense is defrayed out of the funds of the society to which each member subscribes an annual sum. Strangers from foreign parts are allowed to be introduced into these circles by a member for the space of two months, gratis. I have been introduced into two of them, one of which is rendered more agreeable by consisting of ladies as well as gentlemen. They are very agreeable places to resort to read the news, chat, play at cards or billiards, and hear what is going on in the world.

MANUSCRIPT: Yale. PUBLISHED: PMI, I, 63–64 (in part).

Alexander Beebee, from inferences in WI's letters, was a fellow student in J. O. Hoffman's law office. The holograph, not in WI's handwriting, reads "Extract of a Letter from Washington Irving esq. to Mr. Alex. Beebee. / Dated Bourdeaux 22 c. July 1804."

1. WI's allusion to his departure from New York on May 19.
2. Possibly a variant of Isa. 5:8: "alone in the midst of the earth."
3. The second *l* in "tranquillity" was added by a different hand than the copyist's.
4. "The Traveller," in *The Collected Works of Oliver Goldsmith*, ed. Arthur Friedman (Oxford, 1966), IV, 250, lines 29–30.
5. It is possible that many of the phrases quoted subsequently in this letter were taken from Beebee's letter to WI.
6. Bracketed letter has been added. The copyist may have inadvertently omitted the *f*.
7. WI may have underscored this passage to suggest the association with Goldsmith. See WI's letter to his brother of August 14, 1804, note 2.
8. From David Garrick, "Jupiter and Mercury. A Fable," a poem written as a retort to Goldsmith's portrait of Garrick in *Retaliation*. See *The Poetical Works of David Garrick* (1785), II, 533, line 12.
9. Not identified.
10. The apostrophe for "e'er" in the holograph is clearly misplaced.
11. This verse was not included by William R. Langfeld in "The Poems of Washington Irving," *Bulletin of the New York Public Library* 34 (November, 1930), 763–79.

10.   To Elias Hicks

July 24th [1804][1]

Friend of my life, which, didst not thou prolong

The world had wanted many an idle song[.][2] I am just made happy by the reception of more intelligence from you by the Sophrona.[3] You number one of your letters No 4, tho I have received but one preceding, which was by the Washington.[4] My sensibility has been much affected by the melancholy picture you draw of the 'dessartation' suffered by you and my very particular friend *Bobson*.[5] Methinks I see you seated opposite each other solitary and forlorn, smoking segars and sipping a glass of brandy and water,

> Deserted in your utmost need
> By those your former bounty fed,[6]

Geordy, charley, Figsby[7] and myself, all gone, all fled[.] I even hear your over loaded bosoms, "sighing like black smiths bellows"[8]—but avaunt ye grizly illusions, let us look forward to brighter days, days when once more united we shall ↑again↓ enjoy the jovial circle in that happy chamber in dey Street,[9] "where the wicked cease from troubling and the lazy are at rest"[10]

You talk of a tea party with Mrs K[11] in wall street, but in spight of the deepest study and reflection, I cannot imagine who Mrs K— is. As to the promise you made her of publishing my first letter, I give my solemn veto flatly against it. If I should think any thing I was writing would be published, it would put such a constraint upon my letters that they would become ⟨an⟩ intolerable tasks to me. They are at present the hasty sketches of ⟨what⟩ the ideas that arise, and as they are merely intended for a friends eye, I take no pains either to polish or correct them.

As to news, as I before observed, this is no place to learn any. The papers are miserable tools of government as you will see by those you receive. They dare ↑not↓ say any thing of themselves, and their paltry paragraphs always commence with *on dit* (they say) which answers to the mode in which some of our American gazettes launch out —*a correspondent informs.* One of these unfortunate papers having been rather free with his *on dit's*, was laid hold of by the official paper at paris entitled the *Moniteur*[12] and poor *on dit* got such a hetcheling that I fear he will not dare to shew his head in any newspaper for a month to come.

⟨The message from⟩
The remembrance from the "fair Eliza"[13] was received with delight and I beg you will kiss her *beautious hand* for me in return.

Your directions with respect to settling a correspondence with Mr Jonathan Jones shall be attended to. The old gentleman has treated me very politely in consequence of a letter I had to him, and I have the satisfaction of giving you the agreeable information that he has two daughters, the finest girls I have seen in Bordeaux

> With all due respect I am Sir/your humble servant
> **W I.**

P.S. I have written a letter to Mr Hoffman, which, if he is out of town I wish you would tell Mrs Hoffman to open, as it contains a letter I received from Mr Colden,[14] and which I wish Mrs Colden to see

ADDRESSED: Major Hicks / office M Chronicle / New York
MANUSCRIPT: Yale; copy of paragraph 3 (misdated July 20), Yale.

Major Hicks is probably Elias Hicks, Peter Irving's journalistic associate. Since WI addressed Hicks in care of the *Morning Chronicle*, Hicks was presumably assisting Peter Irving in the editing of that newspaper. See *Letters of Jonathan Oldstyle*, ed. Stanley T. Williams, p. xiv, note. An extract of this letter, apparently copied by PMI, misdated July 20, 1804, addressed to "My dear fellow," and conjectured to be to "Quoz," is made up of the third paragraph describing the censorship of the French press.

1. This date is verified by WI's allusion to *Le Moniteur* in the third paragraph.

2. Perhaps a veiled reference to Edmund Spenser's "Prothalamion," which has the refrain "Sweet *Themmes*, run softly, till I end my Song."

3. A search of the shipping news in the NYEP between May 25 and June 30, 1804 has disclosed no information about the *Sophrona*.

4. The *Washington* cleared New York on June 7, 1804. See NYEP, June 7, 1804.

5. Presumably a diminutive form of Robertson. For other details, see note 9.

6. John Dryden, *Alexander's Feast*, lines 80–81. WI has changed the possessive pronouns from third to second person.

7. Presumably these are nicknames for WI's chums, members of the "jovial circle" mentioned later in the sentence.

8. WI may have had in mind the familiar speech from *As You Like It* (II, vii, 147–49):

> And then the lover,
> Sighing like a furnace, with a woeful ballad
> Made to his mistress' eyebrow.

9. According to *Longworth's New York City Directory* for 1804, Alexander Robertson, the younger brother of Archibald Robertson (1765–1835), who was WI's instructor in drawing, maintained his own drawing academy at 17 Dey Street. The *Directory* also shows that most of the residents of Dey Street were merchants, but WI's earlier reference to "Bobson" and his quotation from *Alexander's Feast* suggest that the "happy chamber in dey Street" was a meeting place frequented by his intimate friends. Thus Alexander Robertson's academy is a likely reference.

10. Job 3:17.

11. The *Directory* for 1804 shows that Thomas Knox, merchant, lived at 46 Wall Street; and William Keese, attorney at law, at 11 Wall, having resided at 17 Wall the previous year.

12. WI refers to an article on the front page of the *Gazette Nationale ou Le Moniteur Universel* for 21 Messidor an 12 de la République (July 10, 1804).

13. Probably Eliza Ogden, who had been one of the party with WI on the trip to northern New York and Canada in the summer of 1803. See Wheeler, *Ogden Family*, p. 111.

14. The letters to Hoffman and from Colden have not been located.

11. To William Irving, Jr.

No

3   Bordeaux, August 1st. 1804.

   1 Sheet

My dear Brother

I received last evening your letter of the 30th of last month ↑June↓[1] inclosing one from James Paulding,[2] they came by the way of Nantes. I find by your letter that you expected I ⟨sho⟩ would have left Bordeaux before this time, and so I should were it not for reasons which I have mintioned in my other letters to the family. I shall set off the day after to morrow in the Dilligence for Toulouse[3] where I shall stop for two or three days to view the place and then take the Canal of Languedoc (if it is still open) for Montpelier. At the latter place I shall not make long stay as the ⟨season⟩ ↑time of year↓ is too hot for that climate to be of service, and as I beleive that travelling will be perfectly sufficient to restore me completely. I shall therefore set out after a short stay at Montpelier, for Marseilles, and after I have seen that place sufficiently, I shall take a passage either there or at Toulon for Genoa. I had anticipated much pleasure from travelling in the South of France in the gay season of the Vintage but I shall have, most reluctantly, to abandon the expectation, as the Vintage will not commence till some time in September, and I cannot spare time to wait so long.

Your information of the success of Peters paper[4] has given me the most lively satisfaction, which was increased by the intelligence concerning the Cit. I hope the latter may put his threats in execution and for once in his life do a good thing by chance, in tearing the veil from the characters of his despicable employers.[5]

I shall do all that lays in my power to promote the interest of Peters paper wherever I go. I have established two correspondences for him in this city of which I have wrote him word.

I am happy to hear that Nancys[6] health is so far recruited as you mention, I hope she will make use of constant exercise ⟨which⟩↑as it↓ is of the first importance to a constitution like hers. I regret exceedingly that I was not able to See the party from Johnstown before my departure. I wished much to shake dodge[7] by the hand and have a little chat with him.

Of Bordeaux &c I have wrote considerable in a letter to Peter[8] to which I refer you; little has occurred to me since that is worthy of mention[.] I have found the people of this place as hospitable and agreeable as could be expected, considering that our tastes and occupations are widely different. They are very mercantile in their conversations as well as their employments, of course there was but little amusement to be derived from their society.

I shall have several letters of Introduction given me for other places, and have had letters of credit offered to me very freely, but have declined them. A Mr Brown⁹ Merchant of this City, to whom I was introduced by Leffingwell of New York,¹⁰ has shown me very particular attentions, and is an exceeding clever fellow. I dine with him to morrow, when he intends giving me directions about travelling &c and also letters of introduction, one of which will be to a friend of his in Tolouse who is an old traveller and can give me a great deal of ⟨necessary⟩ advice that will be useful to me in my tour.

While in Bordeaux I have looked to Capt Shaler¹¹ as a man in whom I could place confidence and whose advice was worthy of attention. He is a worthy upright fellow, of a good understanding and much information. At first acquaintance he does not appear so but a little observation will discover his good qualities He has been at Bordeaux before, and is ↑known &↓ highly respected by those persons to whom I have been introduced. I shall now, launch out into the world with no pilot but my own discretion. I'll assure you the undertaking is almost awful to me, however I am confident that had I not the self pride nature has given me,—the love and respect I bear my family and the high opinion I have of the ⟨trust⟩↑confidence↓ they have reposed in me would be sufficient to make me call up all my prudence and circumspection. In the tour I am about commencing, I am to depend upon my own judgement and often to resort to my own resourses for assistance and expedient, it will therefore call forth the powers of my mind, oblige me to rely upon my own exertions and I hope tend to forming that manliness and independence of character which it has ever been my ambition to acquire.

I ⟨mentioned⟩↑expressd↓ in a letter to peter¹² a request that he would present you ⟨an⟩ a note inclosed from M Ferriere the old Gentleman with whom I reside, mentioning the names of some Seeds he wished procured for him. I forgot to put the note in Peters letter, I now inclose it to you with ⟨[unrecovered]⟩ the hope that you will attend to it. The old Gentleman has treated me like one of his children, I have before mintioned to you that he was once a man of great fortune and respectability, but the revolution stripped him of most of it and he narrowly escaped the Gullotine. His cheif amusement in his old days is to cultivate flowers, and he displays a noble example of ⟨tranquil⟩ resignation and contentment. He took me the other morning ⟨with⟩ to two of the principal artists of Bordeaux, with whom he is acquainted. One of them, an Architect named blochard has lately returned from Italy and shewed me a number of sketches & drawings he had made of the Palaces, ruins &c of that interesting country The other artist, a Painter, was very attentive and polite in displaying his gallery, port folios &c[.] among his paintings he had a considerable number of beautiful views that I shall see in my route.

In the afternoon I took a walk with the old gentleman in the country, as he is acquainted with many of the persons who own seats in the Vicinity of the City,[13] we had free admission into their gardens. The walk however seemd often to furnish ⟨the old Gentleman⟩↑him↓ subjects of melancholy reflection. The lands formerly owned by his old friends and companions had changed proprietors in the revolution and their present owners had suffered some of them to be neglected. The old gentleman shook his head at every turn & kept repeating partly to himself, "times are changd! times are changed!" In one part of our walk he pointed out to me a handsome house which formerly belonged to a particular friend, he said he had passed many happy hours there, that it ⟨of⟩ used to be very often his evening resort, to see the master of the house and his wife, a charming woman, But *times were changed* his friend had been gullotined & his wife had died of a broken heart, ⟨and⟩ the estate had been confiscated and the house was at present a Tavern. The relation brought tears into the eyes of the Good old man[.] he however suppressed them, and added the revolution had cost him dear, but thank god there were still a few friends his family and a little property left to comfort his old age and enable him to pass his ⟨few⟩ remaining days in tranquillity. Indeed, notwithstanding his misfortunes, he is a man to be envied He has sevral sons that are well situated in business and highly respected in this city. His wife is one of the finest & most amiable old ladies I ever knew and he possesses one of the happiest dispositions imaginable. I have perhaps fatigued you with an uninteresting account of a person you do no[t][14] know but it is natural to talk much of those we regard, and I shall seldom, I expect, encounter a character in my travels more worthy of notice

August 3d.

I was yesterday employed in taking a farewell look at Bordeaux and have been at several churches that I had not visited before. Many of them are undergoing repairs to fit them ↑again↓ for places of worship It is provoking to see many fine specimens of Gothic Architecture, monuments of the arts in ages long since passed away, defaced by the stupid rage of a misguided mob.[15] In one place I saw the ruins of what had once been a handsome church[.] the steeple was still standing by itself, and threatens one day or other to revenge itself on the heads of those who have accomplished its ruin.[16]

In the afternoon I visited the church and convent of the Chartreuse.[17] The bretheren had long since been driven from this habitation which

has been converted into a hospital for negroes. The church however
is still in a good state It is small but very handsome. The Altar and the
surrounding place is the most superb I have seen in Bordeaux. The walls
of this church are painted in arches, Columns, Galleries &c, the painting
is well executed and makes the place look much larger than it really
is. Over the altar is a picture of a singular construction. It represents
clouds with surrounding cherubims, the centre is open, and by the lights
being admitted behind in a peculiar manner, the picture appears to grow
more luminous the nearer you approach. This is said to be an emblem of
the Deity. I confess I could not perceive that it was a ⟨y⟩ very striking
one. The lateness of the hour prevented my examining the church &c as
much as I wished.

Yesterday evening Mr Colden arrived in this place and I have a note
requesting to see me at his lodgings, where I shall go after breakfast.

4th.

I was prevented from leaving this place Yesterday by a delay in getting
my passport. I had ↑on the 2d.↓ to dance attendance on some *dogs in
office* and was told I must make a ⟨demand⟩↑request↓ in writing to Mr.
le Commissaire Général,[18] having done this I was told I might call at
eleven the next morning and they would *see about it*. I represented that
I should wish to leave the place the next day and that it would inconvenience me much to be disappointed—"*tant pis* Monsieur"—was the
reply and with this I was obliged to be satisfied. The next morning at
eleven I attended, had a discription of my person & visage taken down
and was desired to call at three. The dilligence was to set off at four so
rather than fatigue myself into a fever I determined to stay till the next
dilligence set off. However this is one of the petty vexations a man must
make up his mind to bear in travelling. On these you write your
signature[.] a duplicate is also made out which you sign. likewise & which
is forwarded to paris. ⟨At Every⟩ Thus every passport you take is sent
on to the fountain head of the Police by which means they know your
movements &c. and by ⟨regul⟩ comparing your discriptions the[19] the
signatures you make they can immediately ⟨detect s⟩ discover if any
other person is travelling with your passport. In the interior and on the
frontiers they are far more strict than at Bordeaux.[20] The latter being
a very commercial city it is supposed that most who come are employed
in mercantile concerns. Since I have been here I have remained under the
protection of my American paper and of a protection given to me by the
Consul tho the right way was to have given the latter to the municipality
and to have taken a ticket of safety. In other places I shall be more
particular, it was not necessary here as I had numbers to testify ⟨for⟩
↑to↓ my being an american, if there had been occasion. By mistake they

have put me down in my passport as an American Merchant,—(negociant americaine) I shall retain that title as it is a very convenient one to travel under.

I passed yesterday morning & evening with Mr. Colden who has just returned from Paris, having made the Tour of Italy & Switzerland. I was highly pleased with his ⟨conf⟩ conversation which fully answered the high opinion I had formed of him—His health appears much improved and he possesses better spirits than formerly. Harry Schiefflin of New York accompanied him in his tour; he is a good hearted clever fellow but not as "deep as a well." He says he finds himself somewhat older than when he sat out, but very little wiser, two thousand dollars out of pocket and not two thousand cents ↑worth↓ of wisdom in. When he first arrived at Bordeaux from New. York,[21] he was much surprized and entertained with the novelties around him—the oxen drawing by their horns the carts with long bodies *the handles of the spoons turnd a different way from ours.*" In Italy he got ["]completely sick of Antiquities and would not go a hundred yards to see the best of them." by all this you will perceive that ⟨the⟩ honest Harry is ⟨not⟩ rather of the Lithgow order of travellers,[22] who saw "lumps of ruins" and in fact described every thing *by the lump,* but at the same time had no particle of affectation of science or connoisseurship about him; but confessd candidly his notions of things.

From Colden & Schiefflin I have got considerable advice & instructions that will be very servicible on my route. I shall set off positively tomorrow afternoon, I have procured my passport for Marseilles, and taken a place in the dilligence for Toulouse. It will seem like parting from a home to leave this place, I am so happily situated here. But enough; I am spinning out a letter about hum drum matters, and am in rather too much of a hum drum sleepy humor to make it interesting so I will finish at once—

Your plan of writing but one letter from the family by every opportunity, I highly approve, but let the letter be very particular & long. I have written so many letters at one time lately, that I am sure they will hardly any of them bear reading. Hereafter you must be contented with one letter at a time to the family and you will be sure of having it more particular & correct than if I had to write to a dozen. My friends must look but now & then for a letter. I shall not have so much time to spare in any place as I have had in Bordeaux and when I have a little leisure I am fatigued or I have considerable of the *vis inertiae* or I wish to read or study french or something or another which occasions me to hurry ⟨off⟩ when I write a letter. Take this then for granted that if I do not write to you all frequently, it is not thro carelessness, forgetfulness or want of affection, but merely because writing so much would encroach both upon my time & health. I wish continually to note down every thing I see, to impart to you all, whatever is curious or interesting and to make you partakers in every enjoyment, if I write many letters I shall defeat this wish, by being general in my observations, as I have rather been already.

Give my love to the old people, with my fervent wishes for fathers restoration to health, my affectionate remembrances to the family individually both in New York and ⟨also⟩at²³ Johnstown, and my best wishes to those who think it worth while to enquire after me

Your Affectionate Brother
WI.

PS This will be handed you by Capt Shaler; to whom I refer you for many little particulars that I have not written, requesting at the same time you will treat him with the attention that his gentlemanlike treatment to me, and his many amiable qualities eminently deserve

APPENDIX

The identity of "Cit." has not been uncovered. WI is apparently alluding to the following letter signed by "A Citizen" in the *Morning Chronicle*, April 26, 1804:

Citizens of New York:

This is the last moment in which you can resist the efforts of a powerful and selfish aristocracy. At this moment all depends on yourselves. The election is in your own power. Do not then suffer any paltry inclemency of weather to detain you from the polls.

When I contemplate the number of inhabitants in this city who disdain to bow at the foot of a proud and overbearing individual. When I consider the number of rational citizens, who reflect on consequences, and whose judgments can anticipate the consequences which will result from the establishment of an aristocracy, I feel convinced of the safety of my country.

Yet I dread lest a listlessness to passing occurrences and a fatal security may passively suffer the industrious efforts of a malignant faction to succeed. The moment is of a nature so critical, that inactivity becomes a crime.

Reflect, my countrymen, on the evils you have to dread, and which it is your duty as men and citizens to avert. The people endeavoring to elevate themselves into situations of importance, have given a specimen of the measures they will pursue to maintain themselves in power. Offices which is [*sic*] not engrossed by themselves, will be distributed among their minions.

They will serve as a convenient species of bribery, and will of course be only lavished upon the worthless. We may expect to see the bench of justice itself filled from among the most contemptible of the community.

The property of the individuals will be no further protected, than as may suit the convenience, or promote the interests of arbitrary and mercenary tyrants. The gale of political vengeance will overturn BANKS and carry ruin into our merchants counting rooms and warehouses, without decency, humanity, or remorse. A political tribunal, intolerant as ever disgraced a country, will be constituted by the board of Bank Directors. The Manhattan Bank is already in their power. The Merchants Bank is already overthrown, others will be destroyed or *seized*, as best suits their convenience, & every mercantile man or tradesman, will be frowned on, and persecuted, who will not crawl in the dust at the feet of these people. That this will be the event admits not the hesitation of a doubt. It has already been carried into partial execution.

Character will no longer be considered the sacred property of the individual. New victims will be daily singled out for slander and detraction. It is true the men who will direct these proceedings are screened from punishment by their notorious cowardice, which will point them to such expedients, and the employment of such instruments, as will effect the purposes of infamy, yet secure their own persons from resentment. The world has for two years beheld the shameful, the dishonorable, the unceasing and relentless attacks of these men, on the reputations of those who differ from them in political sentiment. A generous indignation has been awakened in all classes of people. Should not this indignation express itself at this moment of election, and prostrate the tyrants, I tremble for the consequences that must follow. Slander and defamation will become organized into a system—reputation will be regarded as a fair point of attack; and the characters of citizens, the tranquility of families, the feelings of individuals will daily be tortured, to gratify the malevolent passions, or to answer electioneering views of a merciless faction.

These are not fancied evils presented to the public by the enthusiastic ravings of a visionary. They are substantiated by occurrences recent and notorious. If my prophetic warning should be disregarded, they will not merely resemble those of Cassandra by the neglect by which they are treated, but also by the lamentable exactness with which they will be realized.

Once more, before the day is yet passed, let me intreat and conjure every citizen to reflect seriously on the importance and critical nature of the moment: this is the last day of the election. I know that our prospects are sanguine and flattering, yet the exertions of our enemies, backed by the unprincipled and base arts they employ may still defeat our hopes. Let every man consider it a sacred duty to be active on this occasion—let him reflect on the unavailing regret he will feel should the faction triumph through any remissness and over security on our part. Let every man lay his hand upon his heart and vote as his duty to himself, his fellow citizens and his country dictate.

A CITIZEN

Aaron Burr and DeWitt Clinton were rivals for control of the Republican party. Clinton refused to appoint any Burr men to office. In 1802, Clinton, whose family owned the Manhattan Bank, was elected to the United States Senate, but resigned a year later to be appointed mayor of New York. The more the Republicans attacked Burr, the more desirable he appeared to the Federalists. Burr received the Federalist nomination for governor in 1804. The Clintonians selected Morgan Lewis. "The campaign descended to depths of scurrility not seen since the time of the Revolution. The Republicans exposed Burr's questionable private life, while the Burrites accused the Livingstons & Clintons of packing state offices with their relatives." Hamilton wouldn't back Burr, who lost the election by over 9,000 votes. After the election, the Republicans were in control of the legislature and the Council of Appointment. See David M. Ellis, James A. Frost, Harold C. Syrett, and Harry J. Carman, A History of New York State (Ithaca, 1957), pp. 135–36.

BURR'S TICKET
Burr—Governor
Oliver Phelps, Lieutenant-Governor

Cornelius C. Roosevelt
William Benning   } Senators
Dr. John Smith (of South Hampton)

Marinus Willett
Isaac Kibbe
James Manning
Leonard Lispenard
Theodosius Fowler   } Assembly
William P. Van Ness
Coertlant Van Beuren
Peter Irving
John Swartwout

ADDRESSED: Mr William Irving Junr— / Pearl Street / *New York* / Pr Capt. Shaler
   DOCKETED: Letter from Washington Irving Esqr. / Dated Bordeaux. *Aug. 1st.—*
   @ 5th. / 1804
MANUSCRIPT: Yale.

Many details in this letter are similar in substance and phrasing to WI's Journal
entries for August 2 and 3, 1804.

1. "June" in pencil, apparently added later.
2. A portion of this letter from Paulding to WI, dated June 28, 1804, from
New York, is printed in *Letters of J. K. Paulding,* pp. 25–26, in the abridged form
taken from Paulding, *Literary Life of J. K. Paulding,* pp. 33–34.
3. Toulouse is 159 miles from Bordeaux.
4. Peter Irving edited the *Morning Chronicle,* a Burrite newspaper in New
York, from October, 1802, to December, 1805.
5. See the Appendix to Letter 11.
6. WI's familiar name for his sister Ann Sarah, who married Richard Dodge
on February 14, 1788. See STW, II, genealogical chart. The Dodges lived in
Johnstown, New York.
7. Richard Dodge, the husband of Ann Sarah Irving.
8. Probably WI's letter of July 7–25, 1804.
9. Brown Brothers & Co., a banking and exchange business, of major importance
in the mid-nineteenth century, originated as a dry goods business on Pine Street.
In Liverpool the firm was William and James Brown & Co. See Scoville, *Old Merchants of NYC,* I, 186–87. They had branches in Mobile and New Orleans, but
there is no mention of a Bordeaux branch.
10. Leffingwell of New York. Daniel Leffingwell, a New York merchant and
insurance broker, member of the firm of Leffingwell and Dudley, whom WI first
met in Bordeaux on July 2, 1804. See *J&N,* I, 54, n. 73.
11. Captain Shaler had sailed on July 24, 1804, for his return to New York. See
the entry from *Echo du Commerce de Bordeaux,* 23 Messidor Au XII (July 12,
1804) quoted in Young, *WI-Bordeaux,* p. 16.
12. See WI's letter of July 7–25, 1804, to Peter Irving. Young, *WI-Bordeaux,*
pp. 40–53.

13. In the upper left corner of the MS beginning with this word, MS page 5, is written "2 Sheet," corresponding to "1 Sheet" on MS page 1. These notations do not appear to be in WI's hand.

14. WI omitted the *t*.

15. WI is alluding to the attacks on religious buildings which occurred during the French Revolution.

16. Perhaps this was St. Projet, built during the seventeenth and eighteenth centuries. See *J&N*, I, 49, n. 60.

17. St. Bruno was built in the seventeenth-century Italian style. WI alludes to the Negroes who fled from St. Domingue in the Revolution of 1791, going first to Philadelphia and then to Bordeaux. The interior paintings giving the illusion of larger size were done by the Italian painter Jean-Antoine Berinzago (1701–1781). The painting over the altar is one of the Assumption by Philippe de Champagne (1602–1674). See Young, *WI-Bordeaux*, pp. 198–201.

18. The Commissaire Général de Police of Bordeaux was Pierre Pierre. To get a seat on the coach, WI had to have his passport properly approved by the police. See Young, *WI-Bordeaux*, p. 19.

19. WI probably intended to write "thro."

20. As WI was to discover at Nice.

21. The figure "3" appears in the upper left corner of the MS, MS page 9.

22. WI here alludes to William Lithgow (1582–1645?), who spent most of his life traveling around Europe and the Mediterranean area. His best-known book is *The Totall Discourse, of the Rare Adventures, and painefull Peregrinations of long nineteen yeares travayles, from Scotland to the most famous kingdomes in Europe, Asia, and Africa* (London, 1632).

23. "At" is written over "also."

12. To William Irving, Jr.

Bordeaux Aug 5th. 1804,—

My dear Brother,

I have been talking with Scheifflen this morning, and examining his Book of expences since he has been in Europe. He has spent, during a year that has passd since his arrival $1700.[1] I shall however travel more economically than he has done[.] for instance he went from here to Marseilles in a carriage purchased by him & Mr Colden. I shall go in the Dilligence from here to Toulouse, and then take [the c?]anal [MS torn] of Languedoc to Montpelier if it is still [open?] [MS torn], from Montpelier[2] I shall again take the dilligence

In Italy unless I can find a fellow traveller I shall have to hire voiturinos, for myself, as there are no diligences in that country. This will make it more expensive than if I were to travel in company. Upon the whole I conclude with the money I have I can make an economical tour and be back to paris some time late in next spring or in the beginning of summer, but I do not think I shall have sufficient to enable me to visit England. You mention that I need not mind one or two hundred dollars more. If you think proper to advance more I wish you would give the credit on the house of Bosc & Co At any rate it would be a dernier resort in case of difficulty or misfortune You will write me word on this subject and what you think of my going to England—If I should go to the latter place it would be but for a short visit.

Tho it would grieve me to put you to any additional expence, yet I should also be sorry not to finish my tour so as to give *you* satisfaction as well as myself[.] I shall I assure you, most cheerfully coincide with your opinion whatever it may be, and beg you will make no ⟨de⟩ scruple or have any delicacy about expressing it Be confident of this, that the most rigid economy, consistent with the deportment of a Gentleman shall be observed by me. I mention the additional credit, as a resort in case of emergency—& in [cons]equence [*MS torn*] of your first hinting at it— Tho I hope there will [be] [*MS torn*] no necessity for my using it, and I will endeavor to make the credit I have already—cover all my expences

I refer you to Scheifflen for particulars which may determine your opinion whether more will be necessary and how much. But I beg you will not mention to him that I told you the amount of his expences, nor that you will mention it to others, as he did not seem to wish it known

I conclude with again assuring you that the above is left entirely to your judgement. ⟨Whate⟩ I shall be perfectly contented with any arrangement you may form and shall be governed by your decision in respect to visiting England. I wish you would write a duplicate to your answer to this and have it left with Mr Bosc till I write for it from paris. The other you will direct him to send after me by post so that I may have some chance of finding one or the other.

Yours most affectionately
WI.

P.S. By the time I have travelled a little in Italy I shall be more able to estimate my expences and regulate my ⟨stay?⟩ time at the principal cities accordingly. I again assure you of my observing the strictest economy.—This letter you ⟨will⟩ need not shew to any one, it is merely meant for your self.

I return you three Louis' which are of those I brought from New York. They are said to be of base fabrication As the sum would be ⟨a⟩ considerable to my slender finances, I have given them to Shaler to hand them to you, and he has ⟨given⟩ ↑advanced↓ me thirteen dollars on them which you will refund. You will be able I suppose to pass them again to the Bank that gave them to you.

ADDRESSED: Mr William Irving Junr— / Pearl Street / New York. / p Capt Shaler
    DOCKETED: Letter from Washington Irving Esqr. / *Bordeaux 5th. Aug.* / *1804*
MANUSCRIPT: Yale; also copy in another hand.

1. In his journal WI noted that Schieffelin had spent $2000 and had received "not two thousand cents worth of improvement." *J&N*, I, 51.

2. WI here repeats details given in his letter of August 1. He actually left Bordeaux on the afternoon of August 5. See his letter of August 14.

13. *To William Irving, Jr.*

Montpelier, August 14th. 1804

My dear Brother

You perceive by my date that I am at length arrived at the *Grand market of Constitutions*[1] though rather at a wrong season, as this is not the time of the *fair*. The weather is too warm to act as a restorative or to brace up weak nerves, and the salutary breezes that waft health & spirits, have not yet began to blow. My frame however, I thank heaven is not in so very delicate a state as to depend upon these nice pecularities of climate. The Exercise & change of air I have undergone have acted ⟨in a manner more⟩ more beneficially than I expected, and the change of scene has ⟨served to⟩ ↑had a↓ salutary effect in interesting my imagination and arousing my feelings from the lassitude in which they lingred when I left new York. I now begin ⟨to⟩ again to feel myself alive, the firm elastic tread announces that my nerves are resuming a healthful tone and the liveliness of my feelings assure me that my mind is recovering from the languor & imbecility in⟨to⟩ which it had ⟨sunk⟩ participated with my body. Exercise I am every day more convinced is alone necessary to give me health & spirits, and, from the restoration I have already experienced, I promise to return to you, as hearty as ever I was in my life. That I am delighted & astonished with the objects around me, I need not tell you, and if I could but detach my thoughts from my native place I should be a happy fellow. But that is impossible. Amid the scenes of novelty, of gaiety & splendor thro which I am passing how often do my thoughts return to home with the fondest emotions. I am continually more and more sensible that I am not *Citizen of the World* enough to form a Traveller.[2] One little spot of earth attracts my tenderest feelings. There my earliest attachments my warmest friendships and ⟨ferm⟩ most fervent affections are reposed, and to that spot my heart is bound by ties too strong ever to be broken or impaired. I daily feel the truth of the observation *"it is not meet that man should be alone."*[3] I want a friend to whom I can impart my ⟨ideas⟩ sensations with whom I can exchange my ideas and to whom I can look for support and sympathy. When admiring a grand prospect or a magnificent piece of workmanship, how do I wish that I had some one with me to participate in the enjoyment and to whom I might communicate my feelings.

When in motion, occupied by a succession of objects my mind is interested in the things around me and my imagination amused. But when I set down in my chamber ⟨alone⟩ ↑solitary↓, far from home and apparantly alone in the world my thoughts instantly recur to New York. I picture you all to myself, long to be among you and almost sicken at heart ⟨for not⟩ at the prospect of being so long deprived of domestic endearments. These low spirited fits however I shake off *by force*, I anticipate the day when I shall again embrace you all, when, having known what it is to be away from home & to experience a temporary deprivation of family & friends, I shall know more fully how to enjoy them With these reflections, and a chapter or two of Sternes Sentimental journey,[4] I again resume the cheerful heart and ⟨that?⟩ lively countenance cry *vive la joie* and endeavor to make myself as merry as the gay creature's around me. If all this will not do, I sit down and read over all the letters I have received from home, which give me the comfortable assurance that though far away there are some bosoms that think of me with kindness. *Allons donc* to the business before us.

To give you a particular discription of my journey to this place would require much writing and be very fatiguing[.] I trust to your good nature therefore to be satisfied with a brief sketch[.][5] I set out in the Dilligence from Bordeaux on the afternoon of the 5th. The company presented that jumble of character that is generally met with in these machines. A little opera Singer with her Father & Mother who were returning ⟨fr⟩ to Tolouse after a short visit at Bordeaux, A young officer going to see his mother in Languedoc and a French gentleman who spoke english tolerably well & had just returned from a voyage round the world. In ⟨front⟩ the Cabriolet, (a seat in front of the Dilligence) was a little Doctor of Medicine originally of Pennsylvania but who has been for many years ⟨a⟩ travelling about Europe.[6] The latter proved a most amusing character having much talk and a great deal of whim & excentricity. On the evening of the seventh we arrived in Toulouse.[7] Our journey was thro a country the most luxurient & enchanting imaginable Vineyards & cornfields, towns castles & cottages were mingled on every side. The first afternoon our ride was thro a road sandy & heavy, the surrounding country low & not very interesting, we rode all that night and before day break crossed to the other side of the Garonne.[8] as the morning dawned I seemed as if transported into the very country of romance. We had just passed thro a small town,[9] and to our right near the road was the ruins of an old castle standing on the banks of the Garonne with the River washing its base. The first ruddy gleams of morning cast on its mouldering towers, had a most picturesque effect. It had formerly been the residence of a nobleman but now, deserted

& neglected, was tumbling to ruins The surrounding landscape was serene & beautiful. A rich valley where nature had been profusely fertile, with the garonne wandering thro its groves & vineyards

In another part of the route, the road ascended among the heights of Moissac, here I got out and walked up the hill to enjoy the magnificent prospect around me. To the right, on a neighboring eminence stood the ruins of a castle[.] the Hill on which it situated swept gradually down into the delightful valley from which we were ascending. The Hills were covered with vineyards, which even crept up the trees that bordered the road and hung in gay festoons from their branches loaded with their delicious fruit. Cottages shewed their white walls in contrast to the beautiful green of the vineyards, a number of peasant girls mounted on mules descending from the heights ⟨added⟩ formed picturesque objects in the scene. The View from the Top of the hill however surpasses discription. delightful valleys presented themselves on every side. The eye embraced a vast extent of country, ⟨of the⟩ a ⟨be⟩ charming vale thro which the garonne wandered now lost among the groves that fringed its banks & now breaking upon the view glittering with the beams of the morning sun. The country beyond the ⟨had a most⟩ river seemed like a perfect Fairy land. Groves vineyards, lawns & cornfields, interspersed with Towns villages &c and all softened by distance into the most perfect harmony formed a lándscape that might charm a soul of insensibility. They reminded me of that beautiful discription of Watts

> "Sweet fields beyond the swelling flood
>   Stand dressed in living green
> So to the jews Old Canaan stood
>   While Jordan rolld between.
> There everlasting spring abides
> And never withering flowers—"[10]

We continued riding for some time among the hills the most charming views continually presenting themselves till we came within sight of the little town of Moissac.[11] This was situated in a small valley far below us, as we wound down the hill the town was seen in different directions and its old towers & battlements had a picturesque appearance. ⟨Amid the surrounding⟩ ⟨Before it⟩ The other side of it a small river[12] rolled rapidly along beyond which one of the vast & luxurient plains of Languedoc terminated the expansive prospect.

I have here given you two or three specimens of the scenery that was continually before me. A repetition of similar views would probably be tiresome to you.

Whenever the Dilligence stopped in any of the towns to change horses &c, we generally strolled thro the streets talking to ⟨the⟩ every one we met. We found the women very frequently seated at the doors at work & they were always ready to enter into conversation. The ⟨peop⟩ lower class throughout this part of france speak a villainous jargon termed *Patois* composed of a jumble of Italian french & spanish, so that I find it difficult to understand them though I can make them understand me very readily In one of our strolls in the town of Tonneins[13] we entered a house where a number of girls were quilting. They gave me a needle & set me to work. My bad french seemed to give them much ⟨fond⟩ amusement, as I talked continually They asked me several questions, as I could not understand them I made them any answer that came in my head which caused a great deal of laughter among them. At last the little Doctor told them that I was an *English prisoner* that the young french officer (who was with us) had in custody. Their merriment immediately gave place to pity. "Ah! le pauvre garçon!" said one to another, "he is merry however in all his trouble." And what will they do with him said a young woman to the *Voyager*, "Oh nothing of consequence" replied he "perhaps shoot him or cut off his head." The honest souls seemed quite distressd for me and when I mentioned that I was thirsty a bottle of wine was immediately placed before me nor could I prevail upon them to take a recompence. In short, I departed loaded with their good wishes & benedictions & I suppose furnished a theme of conversation throughout the village.

I rested at Toulouse but one day as I found nothing in the place very deserving of curiosity. It is built of Brick. The Streets are narrow & winding. It has a handsome bridge[14] over the Garonne & several pleasant walks in the environs. The theatre[15] is old & shabby & the Scenery miserable. The Young french officer was very polite in shewing me the town, he had much of the gentleman in his Deportment & manners.

On the ninth I took passage on board a post boat of the canal of Languedoc[16] and in three days and an half arrived at Beziers.[17] The boat was dragged by two horses, which are changed occasionally. It is rather a tedious conveyance from the frequency of the locks, and as I adopted it chiefly thro curiosity I should very willingly have quitted it after the first day. Still however I was amused and interested with the charming country through which it passed, winding continually among the plains of Languedoc so celebrated for their fertility and beauty. The evenings were heavenly. At one place where we arrived in the afternoon with an intention of passing the night, I took a promenade to enjoy the ⟨evening⟩ sun set. It was a small town called Trebes,[18] the walls (formerly built by the gauls[)] were in ruins. The evening was one of those mild lovely ones common in this delightful region. The sun sunk slowly behind the distant hills shedding rays of the mildest glory on the surrounding country. His rich yellow gleams seemed to repose on the antient towers & battlements of Trebes. The mountains in the distance were tinged with the softest blues & purples and the mistiness of evening blended the valleys into the utmost harmony of tone softening every harsh & discordent feature or color of the landscape & producing a tout ensemble the most mild & enchanting. In the post boat I found the little Doctor & a young midshipman who had came by the same dilligence & was going to join his ship at Toulon. The Doctor was a continual fund of amusement to me, from his whimsical remarks & frequent jokes.

The peasantry throughout the country that I have passed did not by any means answer the expectations I had formed They are a co⟨u⟩arse rugged set of beings. Some of the men have exceeding sunburnt complexions and black hair which makes them resemble in some degree our Indians. The women share the sturdy labors of the men. I have seen them throughout the journey threshing wheat & working in the fields They are of course, brown, rough & masculine. Many of them are most disgusting viragos and nothing can stop their volubility and clamor when they once get agoing. I was walking along the side of the canal one day and gatherd some figs ↑from a tree↓ that grew on the banks. I was immediately attacked by one of these termagants who demanded money for what I had taken & scolded most horridly. I stood & listened to her very patiently and whenever she stopped to take breath shrugged up my shoulders & said *nong tong paw*. She at last had to give up the point & left me cursing me for *un miserable anglois*

At Beziers the Doctor engaged a Berlin[19] to take the young midshipman & myself to Montpelier. He is an excellent hand to deal with these people & made the owner of the Berlin take exactly half of what he at first demanded. The Doctor afterwards took a place in the same carriage as far as Meze[20] a small ⟨sea port⟩ ↑town on the coast↓ of the Mediteranian. We set out in the afternoon & slept at Pezenas.[21] The next morning just after sunrise we gained an eminence and for the first time I saw the Mediterranian. A vast extent of country lay before me presenting a perfect paradise, and beyond it the ocean terminated the scene, smooth & unruffled with numbers of fishing boats reposing on its bosom. We breakfasted at Meze, a small town beautifully situated on the coast and here we parted with the Doctor who intendd taking a fishing boat to Cette,[22] a small sea port below Montpelier[23] where he had business.

It was with regret that I parted with th⟨is⟩e little man, as he had proved one of the most excentric amusing character I had met with in france. He had a great flow of spirits much drollery and continual talk. He had the happy faculty of making himself at home every where and getting acquainted with any body in five minutes. He was continually creating whimsical scenes & incidents throughout the journey. Among all his vagaries however, he displayed considerable wit and much information and has given me many pieces of advice very serviceable in travelling. While in company with him he continually saved me from imposition & extortion.[24]

In the evening I arrived in this place. Montpellier has a ⟨romantic⟩ handsome appearance from without. The walls tho old have a decent look. There are two or three fine promenades. One in particular called ⟨the⟩ "La Place de Peyrou"[25] is superb. It is a grand terrace surrounded by stone ballustrades. In the centre is an ⟨be⟩ elegant temple with a fish pond before it and within a basin of the most limpid water This is supplied by a noble aqueduct built of white stone ↑with two rows of arches↓ like one bridge on another which brings water from an eminence at a great distance. From this Terrace the Prospect is enchanting—fine valleys terminated on one side by mountains, on the other by the Mediterranean. On a clear day you may from this place see the Alps to the eastward; and to the south west the Pyrenean mountains, both at vast distances. As this is not the exact time of the year when the air of Montpelier is most servicable, there is no occasion for my resting here longer than sufficient to see the place. I shall therefore take my departure the day after tomorrow. from here I go to nismes,[26] where I shall rest two or three days to see the roman antiquities[27] in that place from thence to avignon[28] where I must make a pilgrimage to the fountain of Petrarch & Laura at Vaucluse[.][29] from Avignon I repair to Marseilles,[30] where I shall spend some time to rest myself & breath a little.

15th.

I was surprized last evening on returning from walking, to find the little Doctor at the hotel. He had dispatched his business at Cette and intends going on to Nice where he will stay some time for his health. I find he is travelling chiefly on account of an infirm constitution. I shall travel in company with him and by that means be protected from extortion [sin?]ce [MS torn] he is a more important character than I at first supposed. [He?] [MS torn] has introduced me to a gentleman of his acquaintance who [serves?] [MS torn] as American consul[31] in this place. The latter is originally of Ireland, but a naturalized citizen of the United States. He received us in the most frank open & hospitable manner imaginable, insisted on our dining with us to day & promised to give me letters to Nismes. The Doctor has engaged a voiture to take us to Nismes tomorrow. He has an admirable manner of working these people who let carriages & has got the carriage at a much cheaper rate than I could travel even in the Dilligence. I have been attended, in viewing the town by a Young gentleman, who lives with Mr Walsh the consul & who ⟨is very⟩ speaks english very well.

Upon the whole, I ⟨may sa⟩ assure you that I have travelled with more ease, pleasure & cheapness than I expected and have been subjected to very trifling imposition. I can make myself understood with the greatest facility for any thing I have occasion to demand or enquire, even among those who speak patois, and among those who talk better french, I can make shift to support something of a conversation That this ↑letter↓ will not prove sufficiently minute and satisfactory I have much apprehension. I assure you I am not satisfied with it myself[.] I want to describe every thing, to relate every incident, to pour out my whole heart and lay open every feeling before you, but the task is too laborious, and would employ more time than I have to spare. If I could write as fast as I think you should have letters of perfect volumes, as it is, you must be contented with this and take it as best I can afford in present circumstances. I would not have you think however, that I consider it as a *task* to write to you. Heaven knows it is one of my pleasantest employments, and as it is impossible to see you face to face I fancy myself talking to you all the while I write The letter⟨s⟩ writing however takes up the time that sh[ould] [MS torn] be employed in minuting down notes, which will when [I?] [MS torn] return serve to give you a more particular Idea of [my?] [MS torn] Tour than I can transmit by letter. You must not exp[ect] [MS torn] however, anything very satisfactory from my journal. It is hastily scribbled whenever I can seize a moment of leisure and is perhaps but a dull matter of fact detail of uninteresting affairs. It is but at particular places such as cheif towns, where I open my trunk, that I can write in it, for if I was to be continually taking it out wherever I stopped, it would create suspicions and perhaps involve me in trouble.

Regard this letter ⟨therefore⟩ I entreat you, with "christian charity" and "pardon its many errors & imperfections."

Give my tenderest remembrances to all the family and tell them this letter is intended for the whole of them[.] I hope by this time father is in good health.[32] Where you all are, heaven knows, perhaps scatterd about the country in consequence of the fever,[33] but wherever this finds you may it find you enjoying the pure pleasures of domestic endearments, the smiles of fortune & the enjoyments of health[.] remember me to all my friends.

Yours Affect WI.

Nismes. 17th.

I neglected to put this letter in the post office at Montpellier on the fifteenth, and I left there the next morning before the office was open. The last afternoon at that place was spent most pleasantly. Walsh is one of those open hearted hospitable fellows that makes you at home in an instant He is not Consul, as I mentioned, but applications[34] are making to get him the office. The day that I dined with him was the grand religious fete of the Assumption. They are not allowed to celebrate it by processions in the streets as ⟨there are⟩ a great part of the Inhabitants of Montpellier are protestants, and those processions are forbidden to be held in any City where there are a number of that persuasion In the evening I was attracted by a crowd in one of the streets, & the sound of music. It was a company of bakers, & their sweethearts celebrating the holiday. The men were dressd in pink jackets, white pantaloons, sashes round [their?] [MS torn] waists and cocked hats with enormous bunches of co[ck] [MS torn] feathers, the girls in yellow bodices, ↑of [net?]↓, & White pettic[oats] [MS torn] little yellow hats stuck on one side of the head in a [unrecovered] [MS torn] pretty style, they held garlands of flowers in their hands and were dancing to the music of two or three savoyards. This was a pretty little sample of that vivacity & gaiety of heart that distinguished the french but which I am told is much impared since the revolution. The troubles in which the country has been involved and the internal inquietuds which they have suffered have thrown a degree of reserve into the manners of the people, unknown among them before. To me however, who did not know them before this change, they seem extremely affable and communicative and will enter into discourse without any hesitation—

I have not room to say any thing of this place or of the valuable roman antiquities[35] which it contains. When I arrived here in the evening they were holding the Fair of St. Roque[36] & we drove thro a square alive ⟨of⟩ with people displaying merchandize, eatables, puppet shews &c and were almost stunnd with the sound of two penny trumpets childrens whistles ⟨&⟩ the drums & bells of the shewmen, & the clack of the french women. The fair is over today, but the whistles & trumpets are in the hands of every brat of the place & make the town resound from one end to the other.

W I

P.S.[37] Walsh is a correspondent of the house of Kuhn Green & Co at Genoa. he tells me Mr & Mrs Kuhn[38] have gone to Gibraltar but that Hall Storm[39] remains at Genoa to carry on the business & that he receives letters from him every week. I have the pleasant certainty therefore of seeing that clever fellow after I quit Marseilles.

APPENDIX

WI may be referring to a passage from Laurence Sterne such as the following (see Laurence Sterne, A Sentimental Journey Through France and Italy [New York, 1930], p. 76):

Madame,

Je suis penetré de la douleur la plus vive, et reduit en même temps au désespoir par ce retour imprévû du Corporal qui rend notre entrevue de ce soir la chose du monde la plus impossible.

> Mais vive la joie! et toute la mienne sera de penser à vous.
> L'amour n'est *rien* sans sentiment.
> Et le sentiment est encore *moins* sans amour.
> On dit qu'on ne doit jamais se désesperer.

On dit aussi que Monsieur le Corporal monte la garde Mercredi: alors ce sera mon tour.

> *Chacun à son tour.*
> En attendant—Vive l'amour! et vive la bagatelle!
> Je suis, Madame,

Avec toutes les sentiments les plus respectueux et les plus tendres, tout à vous,
Jaques Roque.

ADDRESSED: Mr William Irving Junr / Care of the office of the Morning Chronicle / New York / United States of America / Care of / Messrs J J Bosc & Co / Negociants / Bordeaux. DOCKETED: Letter from Washington Irving Esqr. / Dated Montpelier and Nismes / *14th. & 17th. Augt. 1804.*

MANUSCRIPT: Yale.

Numerous parts of this letter are similar in idea and phrasing to sections of WI's journal for the same period.

1. Montpellier had long been renowned as a seat of learning, its schools of law and medicine having been founded in the twelfth century, its university toward the close of the thirteenth.

2. Possibly an allusion to Oliver Goldsmith's "Chinese Letters," no. 119, papers printed in the *Public Ledger* in 1760 and first published in book form in 1762 as *The Citizen of the World,* and also to Goldsmith's long philosophical poem, *The Traveller* (1764) in which an English wanderer comments upon scenery, climate, national characteristics, etc., much in the manner WI adopts in both his journals and his letters of this period.

3. Gen. 2:18.

4. See Appendix to this letter.

5. At this point WI has an asterisk directing the reader to the left margin, where he has written vertically: "I have taken hasty notes, which at [*MS torn*] future day will give you a more minute account."

6. Dr. Henory (or Henry) formerly of Lancaster, Pennsylvania. (See J&N, I. for August 8, 1804, p. 56; PMI, I, 69–81, passim.) Although a pleasant companion who helped the inexperienced WI on numerous occasions, Henory was later found to be a swindler.

7. Toulouse is about 159 miles from Bordeaux.

8. According to WI's journal (I, 55), this was Langon, about 26 miles from Bordeaux.

9. Probably St. Macaire (See WI's "Traveling Notes, 1804" for August 6). Part of the ruins of the chateau were still standing when WI passed through the town. For other details, see J&N, I, 55, n. 78.

10. From Isaac Watts, *Hymns and Spiritual Songs* (1707) (London, 1789),

p. 215. WI quotes from Book II, hymn 66, the third stanza, to which he adds the first two lines of the second stanza.

11. A town 102 miles from Bordeaux.

12. The Tarn.

13. In recalling this episode, WI backs up in his account to a town 60 miles from Bordeaux.

14. The Pont Neuf was built across the Garonne between 1552 and 1614.

15. The Salle Saint-Martial was called the Théâtre de la Liberté when it opened in 1793. For other details, see J&N, I, 60, n. 89.

16. The Canal du Languedoc or Canal du Midi was built by Paul Requet between 1666 and 1681 to connect the Atlantic Ocean and the Mediterranean Sea. It extends 148 miles from the edge of Toulouse to Agde, a port near Béziers.

17. A city about 100 miles from Toulouse.

18. About 61 miles from Toulouse, Trèbes dates back to the time of the Gauls.

19. A four-wheeled two-seated covered carriage with a protected seat in the rear. It was fashionable in Berlin in the late seventeenth and eighteenth centuries.

20. A town about 27 miles northeast of Béziers.

21. Pezenas is about 23 miles from Béziers.

22. Cette or Sète is on the opposite side of the Etang de Thau, a salt lagoon, which is the eastern terminus of the Canal du Midi. Cette is about six miles by water from Mèze.

23. Montpellier is about 18 miles from Cette and about 23 miles from Mèze.

24. WI was later to change his opinion of Dr. Henory. See WI's letter to William Irving, December 20, 1804.

25. The Peyrou, dating from the seventeenth and eighteenth centuries, is entered through a triumphal arch built in 1691 by Augustin Charles d'Aviler in honor of Louis XIV. Two stone groups by Injalbert which represent Love overcoming Strength are found alongside the great railing. The reservoir at the end of the Peyrou contains water brought in by the St. Clément Aqueduct from a distance of 8½ miles. The arches are more than one-half mile long and 70 feet high.

26. Nîmes is about 30 miles northeast of Montpellier.

27. The Amphitheater dating from the first or second centuries A.D., the Maison Carrée dedicated to Caius and Lucius Caesar between 1 and 14 A.D., the Temple of Diana, and the Thermae are the important Roman ruins in Nîmes.

28. Avignon is about 23 miles from Nîmes.

29. Vaucluse is about 19 miles from Avignon; the fountain, or spring, to which Petrarch retired in 1337, is about one-half mile from the village of Vaucluse.

30. Marseilles is about 76 miles from Avignon.

31. Peter Walsh (b. 1779?) was a business man in Montpellier who acted as American agent there. See J&N, I, 67, n. 109.

32. William Irving, Sr., was 73 years old at this time.

33. The yellow fever was active in the New York area during the summer of 1804. For other comments about it, see WI's letter to William Irving, Jr., August 27, 1804.

34. Walsh was never appointed to a consular post in Montpellier. See J&N, I, 67, n. 109.

35. WI described the antiquities of Nîmes in detail in his journal entry for August 17. See J&N, I, 69–72.

36. A citizen of Montpellier, St. Roch (or Roque) (ca. 1350–ca. 1378–1379) ministered to the plague-stricken, especially in Italy. He is regarded as a protector against pestilence and skin diseases. His feast day is August 16.

37. This postscript begins at the bottom of MS page 10 and runs vertically along the right margin of this page, then vertically along the left margin of MS page 11.

38. Peter Kuhn, oldest child of Peter Kuhn (1751–1826), married Ann Storm, daughter of Thomas Storm of New York, at Gibraltar, December 18, 1802. Peter Kuhn was consul at Genoa in 1808. Eliza Kuhn, fourth child of Peter Kuhn (1751–1826), married Hugh Green, Esquire, at Gibraltar, May 12, 1803. See Robert Winder Johnson, *The Ancestry of Rosalie Morris Johnson* (Philadelphia, 1905), p. 120. Presumably the two husbands formed the banking firm of Kuhn, Green & Co.

39. Hall Storm, a New York acquaintance of WI's and the brother-in-law of Mr. Kuhn, was United States vice-consul in Genoa at this time. See PMI, I, 81; and *Peter Irving's Journals*, ed. Leonard B. Beach, Theodore Hornberger, and Wyllis E. Wright (New York, 1943), p. 16, n. 13.

14. To Alexander Beebee

Marseilles, August 24th. 1804.

My dear Fellow

An opportunity occurs tomorrow morning by the way of Cadiz, and I sieze it with avidity to scribble a few lines to my friends. As the time is short and there are several to share it with you, you must excuse this letter if you do not find it sufficiently satisfactory.

I left Bordeaux the fifth of this month and arrived here the evening of the twenty first. The Journey has been delightful, and as I ⟨took⟩↑made↓ it by easy stages, stopping at every ⟨pl⟩ town worthy of notice, I have experienced the most beneficial effects from it. Languedoc, so ⟨fa⟩ celebrated for its delightful climate and the beauty and fertility of its plains has more than equalled my expectations. It presents a continual variety of rich and enchanting scenery ⟨and tho'⟩ There is nothing of the wild and sublime to be seen, ⟨the⟩ but the opposite species of landscape prevails in the utmost perfection. Valleys, highly cultivated and profusely luxurient in vineyards corn fields &c ⟨[unrecovered]⟩ [MS torn] diversified by towns and cottages, and enlivened by the windings of beautiful rivers Hills covered with olives almonds &c and often top'd with a castle mouldring to ruins, and sometimes the distant mountain melting into the horison and bounding the view with tints of the softest and richest hues, formed specimens of the tranquil and gentle order of landscape, superior to any I had ever beheld. In the peasantry I was miserably disappointed. Instead of finding a gay happy set of beings, with minds and dispositions as harmonious as the country around them I beheld, rough squalid looking creatures, blackened by exercise in the sun, and with little of that urbanity of manner ⟨ha⟩ and gaiety of heart that I had anticipated The women share in common the labors of the men, and acquire a masculine appearance and deportment which to a person who looks for nothing but gentleness & delicacy in the sex, is extremely disgusting. When irritated which is frequently the case, they are intolerable termagents and possess the language of Billingsgate, in all its variety of idiom & expression.

At Montpelli[er][1] I staid but two or three days to see the place [Ther]e[2] was no American company there and the weather was to[o][3] hot for the climate to be of service. The climate of Montpellier is said to have altered much of late years, the spring and summer are extremely variable and autumn is the only season when it is advisable for a sick person to reside there. From Montpellier it was an easy days journey to Nismes, ⟨on the road for the first time I had a full view of the [*two words unrecovered*]⟩ a town of great antiquity and which boasts several roman remains. The historians of this town pretend to make it 580 years older than Rome, I shall not ⟨pretend to⟩ contradict them, certain it is however, that this place has been of much greater dimension and importance antiently than at present. The principal antiquities are a grand ampitheatre in tolerable preservation, having several ranges of seats still remaining, The Maison Carrée a temple built in honor of Caius & Lucius Caesar, adopted sons of Augustus This temple still remains very little damaged and is a beautiful and highly finished piece of workmanship of the corinthian order, The temple of Diana in ruins, The *tour magne* supposed to have formerly been a pharos, a roman gateway &c &c You may figure to yourself the reverence and veneration with which I wanderd thro edifices built by a people whose very name inspires interest & admiration, with which I seated myself on the very places where they had reposed. They did not then indulge in the luxury of stuffd seats &c which modern ⟨luxury⟩ ↑refinement↓ has introduced. Their seats were oblong stones placed in ranges above each other without any place to lean. The seats of which I am speaking are those of the Ampitheatre.

From Nismes I sat off for Avignon in high and enthusiastic anticipations of the refined pleasures I was to experience in visiting the tomb of Laura and drinking from the fountain that was the favorite retreat of Petrarch. Avignon is delightfully situated on the banks of the Rhone and commands charming and romantic views, it is celebrated for being the native place of Laura and the chief residence of Petrarch. I expected to find the tomb of the former preserved and guarded with the utmost veneration, as reflecting celebrity on the place and attracting the particular curiosity of Strangers. when I enquired for it, I was told that the church in which it was erected had been demolished in time of the revolution and that the tomb had shared its fate.[4] Never did I curse the revolution, its authors and its consequences, more than at that instant; this is a cruel instance of the indiscriminating fury of the wretched rabble who predominated in that period of devastation, when the arts and sciences ⟨seemed to be⟩ were arrested and their ⟨bes⟩ choicest specimens defaced & distroyed. At the Church de Nôtre Dame de Dons,[5] I saw in the portico a painting of St George on Horseback piercing the dragon with his lance and before him a lady kneeling in an attitude of supplication. This is said to be intended for a representation of Petrarch & Laura the ↑likeness of the↓ former being hidden in the countenance of St. George and the Lady being a faithful copy of the face and person of Laura. The painting is very antient and the countenances and a great part of the figures are obliterated by time.[6] The interior of the church was exquisitely ornamented with carvings & relief, but ⟨they⟩ it has been ruined in the revolution.

About five leagues from Avignon is Vaucluse the place where Petrarch retired to indulge his unfortunate ⟨attatch⟩ attachment and to endeavor to seek solace in its wild and romantic solitudes.

Avignon was termed ⟨from⟩ by Rabelais the ↑Isle sonnante↓ from the continual ringing of bells that prevailed there The churches are still in great numbers but much injured in time of the revolution and the bells ⟨w⟩ have been melted down to make coin. ↑Some of↓ the churches are undergoing repairs but it will be impossible for them to replace the beautiful carvings, the fine paintings and Gothic ornaments that are destroyed. From Avignon to Marseilles the road offers nothing interesting. It is chiefly over ⟨h⟩ rocky hills where the soil is too poor & scanty to encourage cultivation

Marseilles you will reccollect was one of the hot beds of Liberty and Equality in time of the revolution. It was here they composed the famous Marseilles Hymn,[7] and it was from this place they sent the detestable rabble of Poissards (fish women) who committed the most shocking scenes of cruelty & fanaticism in Paris.[8] As to Marseilles itself, you may be sure it participated in the happy effects of revolutionary enthusiasm. As "charity always begins at home"[9] the populace first went to work to set their own city to rights before they undertook the good of others. They accordingly, with ⟨powser⟩ admirable industry and dispatch demolished ⟨all t⟩ almost all the churches and public monuments in the city, so that its most valuable curiosities are destroyed and there is little left to attract the attention of the antiquarian. It must be a mortifying thing for these miserable fanatics to look back from their present situation ⟨t⟩ on their shameful conduct when frantic in the cause of Liberty & the rights of man, They sported with the lives, the fortunes and the rights of thousands.

↑That part of Marseilles which is termed↓ the *new city* ⟨as it is called⟩ is very handsome, the streets are regular, paved like ours in New York, and kept tolerably clean. The Quay is well paved and it is amusing to walk on it and see the different beings that are assembled there.

The Turks The Italians Spaniards &c &c The town is not by any means so busy as before the present war. The Merchants ⟨throught⟩ throughout france are forbid to send out ships which causes a great stagnation of commerce This is peculiarly felt at Marseilles as she has not so much of the trade from America and from the ports of Holland Sweden or as the cities on the Atlantic.

There are two american ships here at present. I have found several Americans in the place, which renders it very agreeable to me. Isaac Ogden,[10] to whom I had a letter, had sailed for America before I arrived and I suppose ⟨has⟩ ↑will↓ reach⟨ed⟩ New York some time before this letter comes to hand. There is a young fellow here from Boston of the name of Appleton[11] who came out in a vessel which he has sent to Naples[.] he waits her return, when he intends going to ⟨Cadiz & par⟩ London. I believe he acts as Supercargo. He is a very clever worthy fellow, of extremely amiable manners and good sense.

⟨Marseilles is much handsomer in my opinion than Bordeaux. The new part of the city is well built the streets straight⟩

I had expected to find this place exceeding hot but have been agreeably disappointed. The Sea breezes have prevailed during my stay hitherto, and have rendred the city cool & pleasant. I shall remain here about a fortnight, as I like the city and have found agreeable company to make the time seem short. I intended to go from here to Genoa by water, but there are so many English Vessels cruising off the port and along the coast, that a passage would be tedious and disagreeable and liable to interruption. I shall therefore go from here to Nice and take a boat at that place for Genoa.

I have got into a very comfortable hotel here, and after having sufferd in every nerve from the noise of Postillions, the hurry of Inns and all the other little miseries of travelling you may imagine how grateful it must be to repose for a short time in peace. In travelling in france it is absolutely necessary to be quarrelling all the while to keep from being imposed upon. The postillions porters ⟨&c &c⟩ and every raggamuffin that you have to deal with ⟨is⟩ are exhorbitant in their demands and you can never settle with them without a dispute. As I was not well skilled in french, and absolutely unable to understand the miserable jargon that prevails in this part of France called *patois* ⟨you w⟩ I for some time came off but poorly in those contests, where the most voluble gaind the day. I however at length adopted ⟨two⟩ ↑an↓ expedient⟨s⟩ which I found answerd surprisingly well. I gave them just what I thought right, if they demanded more, I said *nong tong paw* and if ever they began to let loose their tongue, I started at the same time in english and rattled away most furiously[.] by this means I was on a par with them and often won the victory.

A french scold is a match for the very devil; they may say what they will of the billingsgate fish women, but I would make any bet on the head of a poissard of marseilles against the arrantest scold in Billingsgate. I saw two of these wretches quarrelling on the Quay yesterday morning. Their tongues run incessantly and they almost screamd with passion, curses imprecations, scurrility of the lowest kind were bandied from one to the other, one of them however had the strongest lungs and bid fair to conquer, when her breathless antagonist as a dernier resort, put her thumb in her mouth in a peculiar manner and made a most hideous gesture, this it seems is a peculiar insult of the most aggravating kind and the other immediately slapped her in the face, a serious contest might have ensued had not a soldier parted the two furies. This reminds me of an anecdote of I believe one of the termagants of Billingsgate who was furiously assailing and unfortunate tailor and calling him *crack louse,* the enraged tailor threw her in the river, as long as her head was above water she ⟨1⟩ continued repeating the insulting epithet and ⟨sh⟩ when drowning with her head under, she stretched her hands above the surface and imitated the killing of that kind of vermin.

I have nearly filled up the limits I gave myself when I set out, and it seems to me I have written nothing but a humdrum string of nonsense, but take it in friendship, I am in a poor humor for writing at present and am much hurried. remember me to George Dibblie,[12] & the other lads. I have received a letter from Dibblie for which I am much indebted to him. I have so many to write to whenever there is an opportunity that he must pardon me for not having answerd it

I conclude with assuring you that amid all the wonders the luxuries & pleasures of Europe I am continually thinking of home and of the relations the friends and the sweet girls that I have left behind me[13] Your friend.

W I.

MANUSCRIPT: Va.–Barrett.

1. The bracketed letters have been added because the ink has apparently faded.
2. A water stain covers most of the word.
3. WI omitted the bracketed letter.
4. Laura was buried in the chapel of the Church of the Cordeliers, which was wrecked during the French Revolution. After their removal to Paris during the Revolution Laura's remains were lost.
5. WI has "Dons" for "Doms." The Romanesque cathedral was built mainly in the twelfth century on foundations dating from the fourth century.
6. This fresco was executed by Simone Martini (1283–1344), who spent the last five years of his life in Avignon, during which time he also painted a portrait of Laura. See E. Bénézit, *Dictionnaire critique et documentaire des Peintres, Sculpteurs, Dessinateurs et Graveurs* (n.p., 1952), V, 815.

7. Actually Claude Joseph Rouget de Lisle (1760–1835) composed both the words and music, under the title of "Chant de guerre pour l'armée du Rhin," while on garrison duty in Strasbourg.

8. In late July, 1792, about 600 volunteers from Marseilles arrived in Paris to support the conspirators demanding the abdication of the king.

9. See Sir Thomas Browne, *Religio Medici*, pt. II, par. 4.

10. Isaac Ogden (1783–1868) was a first cousin of Henry N. Ogden, who was "Supercargo" of the Lads of Kilkenny.

11. Brother of Thomas Appleton (1763–1840), who had served as American consul at Leghorn. See STW, I, 392.

12. Dibblie was apparently one of WI's fellow students in Hoffman's law office.

13. WI here seems to be anticipating the idea expressed in John Howard Payne's "Home, Sweet Home."

15.   To William Irving, Jr.

Marseilles August 2⟨6⟩7th. 1804

My dear Brother

I wrote you from Montpellier by the way of Bordeaux, which letter you will have no doubt received before this comes to hand. An opportunity occurs at present by an American Vessel which sails for Cadiz, one of the owners of which has promised to put this Letter on board of the first Vessel that leaves that port for America. I am determined to let slip no opportunity however vague, by which I can scribble a few lines to you.

After staying two days at Nismes to view its roman antiquities, I sat off for Avignon full of enthusiasm at the thoughts of visiting the tomb of the *belle Laura*, of wandring amid the wild retreats and romantic solitudes of Vaucluse immortalized by Petrarch, and seeing ⟨the very⟩ his favorite fountain[1] by whose streams he so often indulged in tender melancholy.

Our road for a great part of the way passed along the summits of a chain of Hills, that presented nothing very pleasing or inviting to the eye. Towards sunset we began to descend, and the view that broke upon us awakened my admiration more than any I have seen in france. Below us lay the town of Villeneuve an old Convent of Chartreuse[2] formerly of great magnificence, situated on an Eminence high above the rest of the town, was glowing with the rich beams of the setting sun[.] at a distance was seen the antient towers and battlements of Avignon half embowerd in the trees that are planted round it, and delightfully situated on the banks of the Rhone. The Valley in which they lay was one of those charming scenes of Luxurient fertility that distinguish this part of France. The rhone wandered thro it in the most irregular manner, forming beautiful Islands, and was discernable from the heights where I was, for a vast distance. Nature seemed to have formed this landscape in one of her happiest moods and to have intended it for the land of Love & contentment. The Sun was setting among clouds, ⟨and⟩ here and there ⟨threw⟩↑throwing↓ a partial gleam of radiance on the valley & lighting up a distant mountain, whilst others were half lost in the harmonizing mists of evening. Such was the first view I had of Avignon, immortalized in the classic world for having been the residence of Petrarch & Laura.[3]

It seemed as if I was in the very country of romance, & enthusiasm[.] every ⟨comf⟩ common place⟨d⟩ Idea & feeling was discarded, like Sterne I felt *at peace with all the world*[4] and was almost ready to hail every man as a brother,—when, at the ferry where we had to cross the rhone, a violent altercation between two peasant women, jarrd every ⟨string⟩ ↑nerve↓ and ⟨put⟩ threw every feeling into discord & confusion. There is nothing so intolerable to me as a termagant; but a french one surpasses every thing of the tormenting kind.

I had therefore run a very narrow risque of entering Avignon completely out of tune, had not another little incident restored me to harmony & good humor. When we landed on the opposite side of the rhone we were under the walls of avignon.[5] ⟨Near to⟩ To approach the Gate we passed by a very high perpendicular cliff adjacent to the cidatel, and overlooking the shore, ⟨on an old ba⟩ on the battlements of an old tower ↑or wall↓ perchd on the Summit of the cliff, were seated two soldiers, They were enjoying the sunset and playing on a french horn & clarinet. Thier romantic situation their picturesque appearance and the sweetness of the music, mellowd by distance, had the most soothing effect and seemed to correspond with the scenery around.

These are foolish little details perhaps, but I promised sometimes to give you an account of such sensations as ⟨are⟩ were awakened by peculiar situations so you must bear with me if they appear trifling.

The next morning I rose early, and enquired for the church of the Cordeliers[6] that contained the tomb of the *"belle Laura"*[.] judge my surprise, my disappointment & my indignation when I was told that the church, tomb and all were utterly demolished in the time of the revolution. Never did the revolution, its authors & its consequences receive a more hearty & sincere execration than at that moment. Through out the whole of my journey I had found reason to exclaim against it for depriving me of some valuable curiosity or celebrated monument, but this was the severest disappointment it had yet occasioned. In the church of *Notre dame de Dons*[7] I saw the remains of a painting on the walls of the Portico, of St. George killing the Dragon & a Lady kneeling before him in a supplicating posture The knight is said to have been a likeness of Petrarch and the lady of Laura, but both are so much obliterated by time that the countenances are no longer to be distinguished. The inside of this church was formerly superbly ornamented with sculpture, paintings & reliefs and had excited the admiration of the first artists; it is ⟨however⟩ entirely ruined by the revolutionary miscreants and the ornaments strewed in fragments about the floor.

I had calculated much upon visiting Vaucluse but had most reluctantly to abandon the idea. It would have taken me two days to go there & return to avignon. My passport mentioned that I was to go *directly* to Marseilles, which I was told was something particular. I had been continually mistaken on the road for an Englishman and there were one or two spies of the police keeping a strict eye on me while at avignon. To have sat off for Vaucluse might therefore have occasioned an arrest, and as I could not understand the Patois which is spoken throughout these parts, I might have been involved in vexatious difficulties, so that I had to deny myself the gratification. One of these spies paid me a visit, *incog*, I however discovered him by a ribbon he wore under his coat, and as I was not in the best of humors I gave him a reception so dry and ungracious that I believe he was glad to make his *congé*

He talked a little english, and introduced himself by asking in a careless manner if I was from England, I said I was from america, "from what part, if he might take the liberty to ask" "from *North* America" The⟨g⟩ dry laconic manner in which this was given rather disconcerted him, he soon recovered—"Perhaps monsieur experienced some vexations in travelling, from resembling so much an Anglois" "No— not much—tho I was sometimes subjected to impertinent intrusions" "—Hem—hah—Monsieur, *sans doute* took care always to be provided with good passports" no answer—"Because monsieur must know the police was very strict in the interior, and had a sharp look out on every stranger." "Yes monsieur" said I turning pretty short upon him ["]I know very well the strictness of your police, the constant watch they keep on the Actions of Strangers, and the Spies with which an unfortunate devil of a traveller is continually surrounded Above all despicable scoundrels I despise a Spy most superlatively a wretch that intrudes himself into the company of an unwary traveller, endeavors to pry into his affairs & and gain his confidence only to betray him, such creatures should be flogged out of society and their employers meet with the contempt they merit for using such ungenerous means." The poor chap shrugged his shoulders bit his nails, shifted his seat and when I had finished replied that all that I had said was ⟨y⟩ very true, the police were very wrong, their regulations very vexatious, that he had thought proper as I was a stranger to give me a hint or two, hoped I might have a good journey and wished me a good day. I heard him *diable-ing* to himself all the way down stairs and meeting the master of the hotel at the foot, ⟨he exclaim⟩ exclaimed in a half loud tone "Je crois il est véritablement un Anglois" In the evening the master of the hotel acquired my passport to shew to the police, it was returned to me without any further trouble and I was permitted to resume my Journey without interruption.

Marseilles is a very handsome city, excepting the old town as it is called, which is filthy & confined. The new part is well built of white stone, the streets [are? ha]ndsomely [MS torn] paved and clean. The Houses are [u]niform [MS torn] in a great degree & decorated with ba[lconies?] [MS torn] of Iron work. This City was visited by the [fever?] [MS torn] in 1720 which is said to have destroyed about sixty [thousand?] [MS torn] persons.[8] In an Antichamber of the town hall I saw two paintings representing two of the streets in time of the pestilence.[9] They display scenes of the most abject misery. They have now fountains erected in ⟨the highe⟩ different parts of the place ↑from↓ which the water runs in streams thro the streets and contributes much to their cleanliness. I had expected to have found it very hot at Marseilles, but am agreeably disappointed; the frequency of the sea breezes renders it more cool even than Bordeaux. It is very pleasant to make excursions from this place on the Mediterra[nean] [MS torn] in boats, & ⟨the custom⟩↑it↓ is also very fashionable. T[he] [MS torn] Quay is an amusing place to walk, to see the different dresses &c of the people assembled there. Turks, Spaniards, Jews, Italians &c form a motley collection.

You no doubt reccollect the part this place took in the revolution, their detestable mob of fish women that was sent to paris, their celebrated him[10] that was chanted with enthusiasm by the miserable fanatics. Their own city bears evident marks of the industry with which they sat about reforming the morals of the Nation and abolishing the foolish restraints of religion under which they had before existed. The churches convents &c were ⟨total⟩ almost totally demolished & they have scarcely left a public building to attract the cu[riosity] [MS torn] of the traveller.

I have received the most hospitable attentions from Mr Schwartz,[11] settled at this place in con[sequence of a?] [MS torn] letter from his partner Abm Ogden[12] of New Yor[k. Mr Sch]wartz [MS torn] has also promised to give me letter to his [re?]lations [MS torn] in Italy. There is also a young gen[tlem]an [MS torn] [he]re [MS torn] from Boston of the Name of Appleton, he has charge of a Ship which he has sent on to Naples & waits her return. He is a worthy amiable young fellow of pleasing manners & excellent understanding. His Brother is American Consul at Leghorn & he will give me a letter to him when I leave this place. I shall set off in about ten days or a fortnight for Genoa, by the way of Nice. It is difficult to get there by water as there are several

english cruisers about and Genoa is blockaded by them. I will be able
to take a boat at Nice. My situation in Marseilles is very agreeable & I
am delighted with the place. Next [w]eek [*MS torn*] commences the
Grand Fair of St Lazarus[13] in this city, which will be very curious &
amusing. It lasts several days. They are already building stalls and shops
for it on the principal *courses.* (public walks.) ⟨of the⟩

There is some talk of preparations for war between France & Russia,[14]
how true it is I cannot ascertain, the papers as usual say nothing, and
we are informed merely by vague rumors. For my part I care but little
how much they fight so that they do not interfere with the rout I have
laid down. The invasion is I believe the same as it was a twelve month
since—*mu[ch]* [*MS torn*] *talked* of.

This letter is very hurried, which y[ou may] [*MS torn*] take as an
excuse for its deficiencies. I can [not tell?] [*MS torn*] you how anxious
I am to hear news from New [York. I] [*MS torn*] am very apprehensive
of the fevers visiting [us here and often?] [*MS torn*] dream of your
being all scatterd [*one or two words missing*] [*MS torn*] distresses &c
⟨till⟩ & it fairly gives me the horrors [*one or two words missing*] [*MS
torn*] I awake. Remember me to father Mother [and?] [*MS torn*] all the
family. If I had time I would writ[e to?] [*MS torn*] them severally & to
some of my friends, but the[y? must?] [*MS torn*] make allowances for a
person who has much to see in a little time and has not much liesure to
⟨[*unrecovered*]⟩ devote to writing. If you see the Johnsons remind them of
me. Tell Hicks to be particular in carr[y]ing[15] a load of remembrances to
my most valued friends in Wall St. and youself can bear as heavy a
pacquet as you please to the Rodmans. I am in much haste having to dress
immediately to go & eat roast beef & plumb pudding á la mode Anglais.
Yours most Affectionately

W I.

ADDRESSED: Mr Wm Irving Junr. / New York DOCKETED: Marseilles Aug 26. 1804 /
    Opened by the British Court of Admiralty / at Halifax, forwarded by /
    Your Obt St / *Wm. Allen*
MANUSCRIPT: Yale.   PUBLISHED: PMI, I, 75–77 (in part).

The last half of this MS is badly torn. The docket is in a different hand than
those on other letters to William Irving and may not be his notation.

Numerous details in this letter parallel those in WI's journal for August 19
and 20, 1804.

1. A reference to the source of the Sorgue River, immortalized by Petrarch,
and a symbol to him of the mystic forces of nature.

2. The Chartreuse du Val de Bénédiction was established by Pope Innocent VI
in 1356.

3. Francesco Petrarca (1304–1374) visited Avignon in 1326 and saw Laura
(1308–1348) in a nunnery-church.

4. See Laurence Sterne, *A Sentimental Journey Through France and Italy* (New York, 1899), p. 8.

5. The walls of Avignon were started by Pope Clement VI in 1358 and finished in 1368 by Urban V.

6. This church in the Franciscan convent was built in 1390.

7. WI wrote "Dons" for "Doms."

8. A more recent estimate states that 40,000 of the 75,000 inhabitants died in the plague.

9. The santé or quarantine office contained numerous paintings relating to the plague, including David's *St. Roch Praying for the Plague-Stricken* (1780), and Gerard's *Bishop Belsunce during the Great Plague.*

10. WI is referring to the *Marseillaise,* a song called *Hymn to the Army of the Rhine,* when it was composed by Rouget de Lisle in 1792.

11. WI describes Schwartz in his letter to William Irving, September 20, 1804.

12. Presumably Abraham Ogden (1775–1846), a brother of Thomas Ludlow Ogden. See Wheeler, *Ogden Family,* p. 189.

13. St. Lazarus of Bethany purportedly was martyred in Marseilles. Although his feast day falls on December 17, a fair in his honor is held in Marseilles for several days beginning on August 31.

14. These rumors were probably strengthened by the reports that Great Britain was actively seeking an alliance with Russia against France.

15. WI omitted the *y* when he wrote the word.

16. To Peter Irving

[Marseilles, September 5, 1804]

...Of the character of the French in general, I will not tell you the opinion I have formed, it is not sufficiently unprejudiced and matured, and if I were to give it strongly and candidly, you might perhaps class me among the *Smellfungis*[1] of this world. Of the women, however, I assert my prerogative to speak.[2] I have ever been the fervent admirer of their sex, and hold myself entitled to make such observations on them as the laws of propriety will justify. In the first place then I assure you, there is a most lamentable scarcity of *naturally* pretty faces, but then there is the consoling certainty that a superabundant quantity of paint and washes may at all times be obtained. If the ladies of France have not handsome faces given them by nature, they have the art of improving them vastly, and setting nature at defiance. Beside[s], they never grow old; you stare perhaps, but I assure you it is a fact.—An old lady would be a *rara avis* in the fashionable world; there are to be sure, *girls* of all ages from thirteen to three-score, but never an old lady to be seen.

Tho' the French ladies have not that modesty, that delicacy, that sentiment, that *je ne scai quoi*, which is common to our American females, and which "thou knowest my soul loveth,"[3] yet they make up for it in the eyes of their admirers, by their ease, their gaiety, and sociability. As to their *ease*, I allow it to them in its greatest latitude, they are easy even in their *virtue*, but as to their gaiety, I insist upon it our American women have full as much though more tempered by modesty, and a strict sense of propriety. By this time I suppose you have convicted me of being prejudiced in favor of the females of my own country, I confess the truth of the charge, they have commanded my most enthusiastic regards, and whatever comparisons I made with foreign beauties, tends to the advantage of the former.

Among the men, for I must say something of them, I have experienced much *politeness;* they make you a world of compliments on being introduced to them, a vast number of protestations of their felicity on being acquainted with you, desire you to call on them frequently, and consider their house your own, (which means nothing) and at parting give you the embrace and kiss of fraternity. As to their compliments, &c. I take them as things of course, and pay them in their own coin, but as to the kiss of fraternity my heart does not sufficiently abound with *brotherly* love, to endure it; so I always content myself with the honest shake of the hand, and tell them its the custom of my country.

I am now dancing attendance on the Police, for a passport, to go N——— [Nice], I had intended departing tomorrow, but I fear I shall not obtain my papers in time. These petty magistrates, "dressed in a little brief authority,"[4] are very fond of exercising the power delegated to them, and of making a stranger feel their importance, by detaining him two, three, and four days, for a thing that might be done in an hour at farthest.

On Sunday last Blanchard[5] made an ascension in a Balloon, from an eminence in the suburbs of the city. You will recollect this same genius, so famous for his aerial flights, made an attempt in New York some years since, in company with the celebrated little Baker, the *curiosity* of the museum; and how a violent tornado, "one hundred feet in diameter," swept off the balloon and the house in which it was suspended. On the present "beautiful occasion" he was rather more fortunate. He sold the profits of the day to some worthy gentlemen of the police, by which the latter suffered a loss of two or three thousand francs, for though all the good folks of Marseilles were willing to see the Balloon, a very small proportion were inclined to give thirty sous to be admitted into the enclosure from which it ascended. At the time appointed Mr. Blanchard took his flight—he varied a little from his advertisement, which announced that he would be accompanied by his wife in the voyage, and that they would be carried *to the stars* in a very large balloon, with two smaller ones attached to it. He was content however to go up *solus;* in a small balloon not above two thirds filled, and after ascending to an inconsiderable height, he landed safely about a mile from the place where he started, whereupon the honest folks who had assembled to see the wonder, forthwith decreed him to be a f———, and gave him over to *le diable.*[6]

Of news I can give you none. I again repeat it, you know more in America of the concerns of France and her political situation, than her own citizens. Preble[7] has gone to bombard Tripoli, the king of Naples having lent him several gun boats.[8] The Tripolitans, I am told, dread Americans more than any other nation. At the time that our tars burnt the Philadelphia,[9] they were almost frantic; shrieking [,] running about, and using the most violent gesticulations, regarding the Americans as a troop of devils let loose among them, and thinking they intended to come and attack them at their homes.

PUBLISHED: New York *Morning Chronicle,* January 10, 1805

WI had written this letter to his brother Peter, who was editor of the *Morning Chronicle.* Peter printed excerpts which he thought would be of interest to his readers.

1. The printed text has *i* for *u.* Smellfungus, taken from Laurence Sterne's *A Sentimental Journey,* denoted a discontented person, a grumbler or faultfinder. "The learned Smellfungi travelled from London to Paris ... he set out with spleen or jaundice, and every object he pass'd by was discoloured or distorted" (Philadelphia, 1770), p. 27. In *Salmagundi* WI also employed the term. "Let the grumbling smellfungi ... rail at the extravagance of the age" (*Salmagundi,* No. I, [New York, 1807], p. 18).

2. For other comments about the women of Bordeaux, see WI's letter of July 22, 1804, to Alexander Beebee, and his journal entry for July 29, 1804 (*J&N,* I, 48).

3. Probably a variation of *Richard III,* IV, iv, 255.

4. *Measure for Measure,* II, ii, 118.

5. Jean Pierre Blanchard (1750–1809), who was the first to make successful balloon ascensions in England, France, and the United States. Details of Blanchard's failure in New York have not been ascertained.

6. The preceding paragraph follows the journal entry for September 3, 1804, where the word left blank is given as "foutre." See *J&N,* I, 80–81.

7. Edward Preble (1761–1807) was in command of the American squadron during the Tripolitan War. Preble's force assaulted Tripoli on August 3, 1804, and four times subsequently but failed to destroy or capture the city.

8. The king of the Two Sicilies lent Preble six gunboats and two mortar boats with which to make his attack.

9. In a daring raid into the harbor of Tripoli on February 15, 1804, Stephen Decatur with eighty-one men in the four-gun ketch *Intrepid* surprised the Tripolitan crew guarding the captured American frigate *Philadelphia* and burned it.

17. To Stephen Cathalan, Jr.

Nice, September 15th. 1804.

Sir

From the embarrassing situation[1] in which I find myself placed in this City I am obliged to call upon you in your official capacity to render me such services as will effectually extricate me from my difficulties. You will reccollect the nature of the passport with which I came on to your City—that it placed me under the surveillance of the municipality till the decision of the Grand Judge[2] was known. You will reccollect also that you testified officially on the back of that passport that I was an American citizen, to the effect that the Police satisfied of my identity might grant me a free passport such as is usually given to my Country-men. Depending therefore upon the influence that you said you had, both private & official with the Commissary General[3] I took the passport they gave me without hesitation. On arriving ⟨then⟩ at this place I was surprized to find the passport as defective as the one with which I arrived at Marseilles, and that I should be obliged to remain here till a better passport or an Order from the Grand Judge should arrive, permitting me to depart. The Secretary General,[4] who behaved much like a Gentleman, assured me that had you given me a passport they would have had no hesitation in permitting me to proceed. He had[5] been good enough to write to the Commissary General of Your city inclosing my passport & requiring another that would enable me to depart.

I beg therefore you will await upon Monsieur Le Commissaire in your official character and endeavor to represent my case in such a manner as will speedily expedite my departure. Mr Schwartz[6] I have no doubt will render any [frie]ndly [*word partly blotted*] assistance that may be requisite.

If there is no other method of releasing me speedily I request you will reclaim me in due form of office, and relieve me from a dependance on the police and from the attendant embarrassments so humiliating to a free citizen of the United States of America

I am Sir &c /Your humble servt.

Washington Irving

Stephen Cathalin Esqr.

ADDRESSED: Á Monsieur / Monsieur E Cathalin / Consul des Etats Unis / d'Amerique / *Marseilles* POSTMARKED: 85 / Nice DOCKETED: 1804 / Nice Septr. 15 —. / Washington Irving / R. the 19 / A the 20th. Dit
MANUSCRIPT: HSP.

Stephen (or Étienne) Cathalan, Jr. (d. 1819), a merchant of Marseilles, had represented the United States there since 1790, first as vice-consul and then, after the disruption of diplomatic relations between the United States and France, as commercial agent, and finally as consul. The spelling of the name in the official records differs from WI's version. See *J&N*, I, 81, n. 152.

1. As WI indicates in his journal (*J&N*, I, 94), he had been accused of being an English spy and taken by a policeman to the adjoint of the mayor of Nice.

2. Grand Juge de France from 1802 to 1813 was Claude Ambroise Régnier (1736–1814).

3. M. Permion, the Commissaire Général de Police de Marseilles, replied on September 19, 1804, to Cathalan's letter of the preceding day that the question of WI's passport did not fall within his jurisdiction. See *J&N*, I, 93, n. 185.

4. M. Grivel was Secrétaire Général de la Mairie in Marseilles until September 21, 1804. See *J&N*, I, 92, n. 183.

5. WI probably intended to write "has."

6. In his letter to William Irving, September 20 to October 27, 1804, WI tells of Schwartz's efforts to expedite WI's case with French officials in Marseilles.

18. *To Alexander Beebee*

Nice, Septr. 18th. 1804.

"Health to my friend and many happy days!"[1]

When I reccollect the many Jovial hours we have passed together, when, ⟨to jest and laugh⟩ the ready joke and hearty laugh testified the freedom from care and gaiety of heart we were blest with, I cannot but wish most fervently you was with me to participate in my dull moments and lighten the weight of them by your company. I am, to use our office slang—completely *fotchd up*

I have came on to this place ⟨y⟩ very *gingerly* and with all the facility imaginable, and now that I am on the very frontier of France and have but to step into a felucca and be wafted in ⟨almost⟩ a few hours to the classic shore of Italy, I am all at once stopped in my carreer and obliged to "rest from my labors"[2] till Messieurs the police think proper to let me proceed.

All this however is greek to you without further explanation so I will endeavor to throw a little light upon the subject.

The passport ⟨with⟩ which I procured at Bordeaux— to Marseilles mentioned that *I was to go direct to that place and on my arrival to deliver myself up immediately to the municipality and rest under their "surveillance" without quitting the city till the decision of the Grand Judge*[3] *at Paris was known.* The Same kind of passport was given me at Marseilles for Nice, and I, ignorant of the forms & customs of the police, supposed it such as was usually given to americans and accepted it without hesitation. You may judge my surprize then, when on applying at this place for a passport to Genoa the Secretary General[4] told me it was not in his power to permit me to leave france, ⟨and that I must rest here till a better pass⟩—that I had brought on such a passport as is usually given to *suspected persons* and that I must remain here till a better passport came on, or a permission for me to depart, or till I was reclaimed by one of our consuls as an American citizen. ⟨The⟩Why the Police of Bordeaux should have given me such a vile passport I cannot concieve. They had me under the[ir][5] eye while in their city, all my actions, my conversations, my friendships and pursuits were open and unconceald and I defy them to find ⟨in any of⟩ throughout, any just cause for suspicion. Why should I take any interest for or against their government; you who know me well, know that I am little concernd about it, and it is not likely I should be meddling either in word or deed in a matter so productive of trouble. Is this the manner an American Citizen is to be treated by a people who pretend an amity for his country. To be interrupted in the peaceable pursuit of his lawful affairs, subjected to detention & examination of police officers to have the freedom of going from place to place denied him—and all for what?—because the police of the place where he first landed ⟨refused⟩ were pleased to indulge silly suspicions of him which they would not take the trouble to satisfy. I cannot speak of this subject without warmth. I am here solitary and low spirited absolutely among strangers, for, as I did not expect to make any stay at Nice I brought on no letters of introduction.[6] The equinoctial is coming on and a dreary time I shall have of it, for even in fair weather, Nice with all its beauty of situation and romantic prospects, appears as a prison, so intolerable to a *free american* is any inovation on his personal liberty.

The Secretary General told me he felt for my situation and if it was in his power, would have forwarded me with pleasure, as it was, he would do his utmost and would write immediately to the Commissary General of Marseilles[7] inclosing my passport from that place and desiring another ↑that↓ would enable me to depart. As I did not put much faith in the influence of his letter I have written to my friends in Marseilles & to our consul there to represent my case to the Com: Genl. & endeavor to get the passport, but if there was no other way,—for the Consul of that city to reclaim me as a citizen of the U. S. I have also written to my friends & our consul in Bordeaux[8] to the same purport requesting a passport or reclamation from that place. Lastly, I have written to ⟨H⟩ my old friend Hall Storm[9] who is settled at Genoa to use his interest with our consul there to have me reclaimed, and have sent the letter by Dr Henory an american Gentleman who has travelled with me most of the way from Bordeaux, has proved himself in this affair warmly my friend, and has promised to use his utmost exertions in my cause at Genoa. From this latter place I look for the most speedy release ⟨but⟩ and I think it will be hard, if among so many ⟨recla⟩ applications I do not get some effectual assistance. The Secretary general of this place has behaved much like a gentleman to me. He told me that to make my situation as easy as possible he would give me a letter of surety which granted me the liberty of the city without danger of molestation

In spight however of his letter of surety I was disturbed the next evening from a nap I was taking in consequence of being indisposed, by a police officer who entered my chamber without ceremony and demanded my papers to came before the mayor.[10] I delivered them up without hesitation and changing my dress, waited upon the mayor. I found he spoke english, and I experienced a very polite reception from him. He professed regret for my circumstances and in the course of our conversation I discovered that some scoundrel of a Spy had denounced me as an Englishman which had occasioned the demand for my papers. The Mayor assured me of his being convinced of ⟨my⟩ the identity of my citizenship but at the same time he was responsible to superior power & could not let me depart without authority; but I might rest satisfied that my tranquility should not again be disturbed. I expressed my sense of his politeness and retired[.] since that time I have remained undisturbed, and wait the result of my applications to our Consuls

Having thus got thro with a long detail, which I should suppress, were I writing to any other than a friend who I hope takes an interest in my concerns I shall now endeavor to talk a little of other matters.

19th.

I was going on last evening, my dear fellow, to give you an account of the different objects & incidents that particularly awakened my attention since my former letter, but it would have been a very dull, *smellfungus like* story—for my heart was sad & heavy. "Beshrew the sombre pencil!" cried I ⟨ner⟩ using nearly the words of Sterne, "why should I sit here painting the evils of my situation in so hard and deadly a coloring"[11] why should I worry my friend wth a recital of my chagrins, my ill humors and my little embarrassments? I threw down my pen and determined not to take it up again till the harmony of my feelings would enable me to write in a more amusing and agreeable manner. I arose this morning with a mind easy & cheerful. I dressed myself and walked on the public terrace that[12]

the ⟨title subject I th⟩ title was Cupid & ↑Psyche↓[13] The female dancers shew their persons without any modesty and reserve[.] they are dressed in a flesh colored habit that is fitted exactly to the shape and looks like the skin. Over this they have a transparent dress of muslin that reaches a little below the knee thro which their figures are perfectly visible. Their dancing surprized me, as I had never before seen any thing of the kind that could be ⟨in the⟩ compared to it. the Beauty of their steps their agility and their elegant attitudes delighted me. In dancing the females will sometimes ⟨stand on the points of⟩ turn round on one toe with the greatest rapidity for several times till their light muslin robe flies up and discovers their whole person, and they will finish by a fine attitude. I confess my american notions of delicacy & propriety are not sufficiently conquerd for me to view this shameless exposure of their persons without sentiments bordering on disgust, and I could have been happy to have given them another petticoat or a thicker robe to cover their *nakedness*. But these spectacles ⟨at⟩ which one of our american girls would hardly dare to look at thro her fan are here contemplated by the ladies ⟨as⟩ with the utmost indifference. As to the men they all profess much gallantry and libertinism and often accuse themselves of being far more extravagant in this respect than I am convinced they really are. The keeping of a Mistress is considered a matter of course & of consequence, nothing ill is thought of it. This is not confined to batchelors, the married men must also have their *concubines*. When I first arrived at Bordeaux I understood hardly a word of the language, I was of course advised immediately to apply myself to *the study*. I told my advisers that I had taken a French master—"very good, very good," was the reply "but you must take a french *mistress* also." An old gentleman of much respectability, to whom I was introduced gave me similar counsel. "What! my good sir," cried I "Is this the advice you give to a poor devil who is travelling for his health and who has a constitution to *get* instead of to *spend?*" "Phoo. Phoo." replied the old genius "I have a girl myself and she dont hurt my constitution—I only *play* with her"—!!! This conduct in an old man which would excite contempt among us, is so common here that it is not remarked. Old debauchees with one foot in the grave will squander immense sums on prostitutes who have the art of awakening faint sparks of that fire which age and libertinism have nearly quenched. As to the advice that has been so liberally bestowed upon me, I have been too headstrong to attend to it, and have endeavored to keep the morals I brought with me from america as untainted as possible from foreign profligacy. The Women are not behind hand with the men in amorous indulgencies. The married ladies particularly, are easily assailable, indeed they are often *themselves the assailants*, and will throw out a lure with the most consummate address. Their husbands are *complaisant* to a proverb.[14] You have heard no doubt much of ⟨the⟩ *french politeness* and I'll assure you if politeness consists in bows and scrapes and compliments and professions of friendship & rapture at seeing you and proffers of service &c &c &c they are the most polite people under the sun,—But if politeness consists more in *actions than words & promises,* ⟨they⟩ I must confess they are very deficient in it. I have had several letters of introduction to french men. They were "enchanted to see me" "would be proud and happy of my acquaintance," "I knew the way to their houses and they hoped I would consider myself at home and call frequently"—Now all this means exactly *nothing*, ten chances to one if they would do me the *honor* to return my visit, and as to an invitation to dinner, 'twould be a folly to expect it. I speak with regard to french *merchants* for ↑at the sea ports of france↓ it [is]¹⁵ chiefly to that class of society ⟨we can get⟩ ↑our↓ letters from america are directed. A French merchant generally speaking is a mercenary selfish being, who only pays you attentions when he expects to get something in return. My most agreeable acquaintances in France have been among American merchants settled in the French towns, (who I have generally found happy to see their fellow countrymen & to make their stay agreeable.) and with americans who were in france either on temporary business, or pleasure. You cannot imagine how

—"the heart opens in a foreign land;
And with a brother's warmth, a brother's smile,
The stranger greets each native of his isle.["]¹⁶

But whenever I have found a french family hospitable and entertaining, I never failed to cultivate their acquaintance.

I am just summoned to dinner, so I'll endeavor to get you out of Marseilles and then leave you for the day; if I go on at this rate I do not know when I shall bring you to Nice, or whether I shall not drop you on the road among the Alps. There are several public walks in and about Marseilles (as is the case in all the french towns) planted with two or three rows of large trees and ornamented with marble fountains. There are a vast number of caffés in this city ⟨so it⟩ and many of them I expect must starve for want of custom. A french caffé is very different from our Coffee houses in America. They consist of ⟨a large⟩ ↑a↓ room open to the street decorated very handsomely with paintings, looking glasses, ⟨f⟩ very beautiful ⟨fan⟩ landscape hanging paper, marble tables &c and some times they have one or more private rooms for billiards, cards &c At these caffés you are served with coffee, chocolate, punch lemonade liqueuers &c &c at a moments warning, and they have generally the latest paris papers for you to read while you are eating or drinking. I very often take my dish of coffee or chocolate ⟨of⟩ at one of these places in a morning ⟨then⟩ ↑in↓ preference to the hotel as I have the advantage of the papers. You are served with a cup & saucer & a small dish of sugar & a roll or bread; the waiter ⟨pours⟩ fills ⟨into⟩ your cup and then carries away the coffee pot. If you take another dish you pay more. The charge however is moderate, generally about ten or twelve sous and the custom very accomodating & agreeable.—I shall lose my dinner if I do not stop—

⟨sh⟩ so I shall only add that Marseilles is remarkable in latter days from the circumstance that Bonapartes mother and sisters once used to *wash silk stockings there*, for a living and his mother was one time pelted in one of the streets for some article of conduct ↑⟨that⟩↓ I could not learn.[17] I left there the morning of the tenth in a voiture, ⟨with⟩ in company with Dr Henory and took a kind of cross road that was to join the main road from Aix to Nice in the evening—adieu for the present.

20th.

I shall go on to give you a brief—but *very brief* account of our Journey from Marseilles to Nice for there ⟨w⟩ is nothing interesting to mention about it. The towns through which we past were very disagreeable from the manure heaped up against every house to fertilize the adjacent country. Provence in general is very sterile without the assistance of manure—tho in some parts the soil is good and yields in abundance. The accomodations at the inns in General on this road are miserable, the travelling not being by any means so great as ⟨i⟩on the other side of Aix. This road was much infested with robbers a year or two back, we passed thro two or three towns that had been absolute hordes of Banditti. Our Voiturin ⟨shewe⟩ particularized several places where the road wound among the mountains, as having been the scenes of frequent depredations. One place in particular where the road was stoney and where the steep ascents & descents of the mountain rendered it impossible for either carriage or horseman to proceed without he mentioned that the robbers would sometimes make their appearance in troops of twenty and thirty at a time. Latterly however, the excellent regulations of the police ⟨with⟩ have effectually put a stop to them. They have been ferretted out by the *Gens d⟨e⟩'Arms* (Soldiers in the service of the police troops of whom scour the roads to apprehend robbers &c) & gullotined by dozens at a time so that the⟨y⟩ road at present is perfectly safe. On the third day we dined at Frejus a little town on the shore of the Mediterranean formerly of some trade & importance, but at present in a ruinous condition. It is remarkable for being the place where Bonaparte & his suite landed on his sudden return from Egypt.[18] There are at ⟨this place⟩ ↑Frejus↓ the remains of a roman ampitheatre, a roman Aqueduct & the roman walls that formerly surrounded the town.[19] That afternoon we ascended the mountain of Estrelles[20] one of the maritime Alps—and slept at a solitary house romantically situated among the heights. The next evening we arrived at Nice. and so much for the present as I have to write a letter to my brother. Writing is my mornings employment. I rise early, take a walk on the promenade along the sea shore, take my dish of chocolate at a caffé where I read the papers then return home & write till dinner and after dinner take a walk in the country. In the evening I walk again on the promenade by moon light & so passes my day, the mornings amusement is sometimes varied with reading or studying french.

22d

Last evening I recieved a letter from Mr Schwartz[21] of Marseilles which has quite enlivened me. He has exerted himself in my case & with the assistance of our Consul has made such representations that he expects the proper orders for my release will be sent on by the next post. Mr Schwartz is a partner of Mr Abm Ogden[22] of New York who gave me letters to him. I have experienced the most friendly and Gentlemanlike treatment from him and have been charmed with his acquaintance

This morning also I recieved a letter from Dr Henory the gentleman who has been my fellow traveller thro france & who exerted himself very earnestly in my cause here. His letter was dated the 20th. at Monaco a little sea port about three leagues from here, where he was obliged to put in on the 17th. (the day he left Nice) on account of the swell at sea & the same cause has detained him there ever since suffering from bad inns & extortionate landlords. The felucca men are the cursedest cowards that ever saild on salt water, they are affraid of the least rolling of the sea. This detention of the Doctor will prevent my recieving assistance from Genoa very soon but I hope the papers will come on from Marseilles & render it unnecessary.

24th.

Yesterday was the first day of the thirteenth year of the *republic* of France, of course it was necessary to celebrate it with some rejoicing as we do our fourth of July in America. ⟨A fête⟩ Every thing of the kind grows stale with this fickle nation, as soon as the novelty is worn away. Their public fétes are daily becoming more and more neglected and they wait for a new set to be formed. The birth day of the Emperor, the anniversary of his coronation &c &c will soon supplant the anniversary of the demolition of the Bastile, of the oath of federation & the anniversary of the republick—They in their turns perhaps will give way to others & so on to the end of the Chapter. As it was necessary however to give some celebrity to the day, there were some cannons fired, some people shut up their shops & kept holiday, the house of the municipality was magnificently illuminated with two paper lanthorns in each window and one of the public walks had pots of tar or turpentine placed on posts at certain distances, by the light of which some of the peasantry & soldeir danced waltz's & cotillions—and so passed this glorious and never to be forgotten anniversary!

25th.

The Post from Marseilles arrived yesterday but brought me no letters nor passport so that I must content myself with a little longer delay. *"Hope deferred maketh the heart sick,"*[23] this I believe is said somewheres in the writings of *Solomon* and I can readily testify to the justness of the remark. I am this morning vastly below par but lest I should communicate the vapours to you I'll break off abruptly——

26th.

"Vive la Joie!— Vive la Joie!["] I have just received two or three letters that raise me to the highest pinnacle of transport! One from Hall Storm at Genoa, warm as my heart could wish, inclosing a reclamation from our Consul[24] there — and urging me to haste to him with the utmost speed—that his house, himself & every thing he has is at my service. He had recieved my letter the day before & had hardly eat or slept since but had immediately proceeded with all possible dispatch to forward my liberation—In consequence of an affidavit from him & Dr. Henory of the identity of my Citizen ship &c a reclamation was instantly made & instantly forwarded. In the same packet came a letter from Dr H informing me of the hearty reception he had met from Storm in consequence of ⟨my⟩ ↑a↓ letter of introduction from me & speaking in the highest terms of Storms exertions on my behalf & the friendship he had testified. I have also recieved a letter from our consul at Marseilles inclosing one to the Prefet of this place[25] representing my situation & urging the Prefet to give me a passport. You now see the change in my affairs. I have but to wait on the municipality this morning—obtain a passport & Huzza for Italy & my friend Storm. I dont know really which I most desire to see.

Evening

All that I have to do is "Curse the police and go to bed." I have presented my reclamation and the letter from our consul at Marseilles and am now ⟨that⟩ told that I must still wait some days till an answer is recieved to a letter that has been written to the Commissary General of Marseilles.[26] What business I have to do with this letter I cant imagine[.] I was told by the Secretary General[27] that as soon as a reclamation should arrive I should be forwarded with pleasure and now that I have produced a reclamation supported also by a letter from our Consul at Marseilles— I am still detained. However I should reccollect the promise was made by a *french man* When these continual chagrins will cease tormenting me I cannot tell, but really they prey upon me worse than a fever—

Good night

October 4th.

"To morrow and tomorrow and tomorrow."[28]

So drags on the time with me, one day an exact ditto of the preceding except that yesterday and the day before it rained furiously—which afforded an *agreeable variety*. I am still wasting my time ⟨there to agreeable⟩ here waiting for I know not what, for I have been so abused with lies and empty promises by the municipality that I have no longer faith in what they tell me. In the midst of my vexations the other day when I was dancing attendance on the police I could not help laughing when the Idea occurd how much my situation resembled the poor ⟨del frec⟩ frenchmans who was bandied about in our office[29] from one to another— you reccollect his complaint—"I go to Misser Wilson—Misser Wilson say go to Misser Macomb—I go to Misser Macomb—Misser Macomb say go to Misser Zuntz—I go to Misser Zuntz—Misser Zuntz say go to Misser Cuttin—I go to Misser Cuttin—Misser Cuttin say *Goddam!*"——much in the same manner have I been devild about except that my situation is rather more grevious. As the answer that I recieved that I must wait four or five days was delivered by one of the under Clerks (for it was impossible for me to obtain a sight of the Sec. Genl.) I called upon the french merchant[30] to whom I had brought a letter of Introduction, and begged him to endeavor to see the Prefet or Secretary & obtain a proper & true reply. I was mortified at being obliged to apply for assistance to a man who had shewn me so little attention—but as I knew he was acquainted with the prefet—and that his wealth gave him some importance & influence, I made an *offset* of the probable benefits of his services against the humiliation of desiring them and in this manner made some sort of a compromise with my Pride. Accordingly—I recieved a reply that had more truth in it, tho less encouraging than the one I had recieved by the Clerk. I was told that a letter would immediately be ⟨wa⟩ wrote to the Commissary General of Marseilles & desiring him to send to Nice the passport with which I came on from Bordeaux—That as soon as this passport was recieved at Nice it would be sent on to Paris and submitted to the Grand Judge and I must await here his decision—Here then was a delicious prospect of *at least* a months detainment. I ⟨was⟩ had been at Nice two weeks, amused by their lies and now they were going to commence my affair exactly as they ought to have done on my first arrival You see how the rights of Individuals are respected here. I cannot express to you how I have been worried, enraged—fevered by the uncertaint⟨ies⟩y in which I have been kept and by repeated disappointments. I now wait for a reply to a letter I wrote to our consul at Bordeaux. It must arrive either to day or the day after tomorrow.[31] If that affords me any assistance— good—I shall make at any rate one strong attempt to procure a passport, ⟨either⟩ by giving securities, if that will not answer, I shall endeavor to make my escape without one ⟨tho'⟩ at the risque of arrestation & imprisonment, for I really cannot support confinement here much longer.

Genoa Oct 27th.

You see my dear fellow that at length I am released from all my troubles and safely arrived in Italy. I was bantered about by the police till the fifteenth or sixteenth when I recieved a passport from our Minister at Paris.[32] That soon procured me my Liberty. From there I sat sail in a Felucca and after coasting along the Italian Shore for three days & an half putting into the chief towns at night we at length arrived at Genoa — Here I have been engaged ever since with my friend Storm talking visiting & rambling about so that I have had no time to continue my letter methodically. The post goes off before day light and I am now writing by candlelight so that you will excuse the hurried manner in which the Letter is finished. I am delighted with Genoa. It is all splendor & magnificence. Churches Palaces &c &c dazzle the eye with the riches of architecture & the choice productions of the arts. The Italian women are Beautiful and leave the french quite in the background. They have generally fine figures and black eyes most languishingly powerful.[33] I have recieved another letter from friend Diddler[34] and will write to him by the first opportunity. He tells me Squirt has gone to Washington to petition the appointment of Secretary of the french Embassy!!! He is really an *aspiring* genius, but I am affraid the young mans diffidence will hinder his advancement in this world.

Remember me to all the Lads in the office and tell Old King Cole[35] to keep up his spirits ⟨in⟩ ↑with↓ the joyful consolation that there is *another & a better world."*[36] My dear fellow I anticipate the day when I shall once more enlist with you under Boss's banners and attack old Coke & Littleton with renewed vigor. How does my sweet Misse[37] & what has she brought forth to bless her honest spouse. How does my young Missies[38] & has Ann[39] returned from Canada. I regret a thousand times that your jaunt to Newark prevented my recieving a letter from you in the last pacquet. Tell me every thing you see hear & know and tell Sam Swartwout that he must not expect another line from me while I am in Europe.

Your friend
W I.

Manuscript: Va.–Barrett.

In another hand to the left of the dateline is written "Washington Irving's Letter." In this letter WI uses many of the same details and phrases found in his journal entries from September 10 to October 27, 1804, and in his letter to William Irving, September 20 to October 27, 1804.

1. Not identified.

2. Variation of Rev. 14:13.

3. Claude Ambroise Régnier, prominent attorney and jurist. See WI to Stephen Cathalan, Jr. September 15, 1804, note 2 and J&N, I, 92, n. 184.

4. M. Grivel was followed by Jean Baptiste Masseille. See J&N, I, 92, n. 183. Perhaps the change of officials coinciding with WI's arrival in Nice is responsible for some of his difficulties and delays in obtaining a new passport. See WI to Stephen Cathalan, Jr., September 15, 1804, note 4.

5. WI inadvertently wrote "they."

6. In a journal entry for September 17, 1804, WI indicates that he had a letter to Mr. Guide, a merchant of Nice. WI is probably referring to Jean Baptiste Guide, Ile 85, Maison No. 1. See J&N, I, 95, n. 191.

7. A M. Permion served as the Commissaire Général de Police in Marseilles at this time. See J&N, I, 93, n. 185.

8. William Lee was United States commercial agent in Bordeaux from 1801 to 1816. Although WI calls him "consul," Lee's official title was "commercial agent." For a discussion of the ramifications of the term, see A Yankee Jeffersonian: Selections from the Diary and Letters of William Lee of Massachusetts, ed. Mary Lee Mann (Cambridge, 1958), p. 263.

9. Thomas Hall Storm, formerly a friend of WI's in New York, now a business man in Genoa. In 1805 he was appointed United States vice-consul there. See PMI, I, 81, and J&N, I, 93, n. 187.

10. The mayor of Nice was Louis Chalcédoine Romey, who held the post from April 20, 1804, to May 2, 1808. See J&N, I, 94, n. 188.

11. Sterne wrote, "Beshrew the sombre pencil! said I vauntingly—for I envy not its power, which paints the evils of life with so hard and deadly a colouring." "The Passport—The Hotel at Paris," in Laurence Sterne, A Sentimental Journey Through France and Italy, p. 240.

12. Pages 5 to 8 of the holograph letter are missing. They may have been destroyed because of the intimate nature of WI's comments.

13. This may be Pierre Gardel's Psyché, a ballet in three acts, first given at the Opera in 1790, in which his wife Marie-Elisabeth danced. Annales Dramatiques, ou Dictionnaire Générale des Théâtres (1808–1812), (Geneva, 1967), VII, 522. Other possibilities include Psyché (1670), a tragicomic ballet in free verse by Molière, Quinault, and Corneille, with music by Lully (Annales Dramatiques, VII, 521) and L'Histoire des Amours de Cupidon & de Psiché, Spectacle à machines en cinq Actes, de l'invention de M. Bazin Ingénieur, musique de Blaise, représenté sur un modele de Théâtre au Palais de Luxembourg (Louis La Valliere, Ballets, Opera, et Autres Ouvrages Lyriques ... [Paris, 1760], pp. 233–34).

14. In his comments to a friend of his own age WI is very candid and explicit about sexual matters and other suggestive details which members of the family reading his letters to his brother William might consider indecorous. See his journal entry for September 8, 1804, in which he describes a performance witnessed at a Marseilles theater.

15. When WI canceled "we can get" later in the sentence, he apparently failed to observe that the altered construction required "is" following "it."

16. Samuel Rogers, *The Pleasures of Memory*, 6th ed. (London, 1794), pt. II, lines 194–96.

17. Documented accounts have not been found to verify WI's statements.

18. Fréjus is approximately 100 miles northeast of Marseilles. Napoleon landed at the town on October 8, 1799. See *J&N*, I, 89.

19. The amphitheater, with a seating capacity of 9100, was built in the time of Septimius Severus (193–211). Behind it, to the north, are the ruins of the ancient city walls. The aqueduct, which had arches 60 feet high, brought water to the town from the Seaguole River, about 25 miles away.

20. The Estérel interposes between Fréjus and Cannes; Mont Vinaigre, the highest point, is about 2000 feet high.

21. WI had met Schwartz in Marseilles, where he represented the interests of Ogden and Schwartz, a New York firm. WI describes Schwartz more fully in his letter to William Irving, September 20–October 27, 1804.

22. Abraham Ogden, Jr., New York merchant and brother of T. L. Ogden. See Wheeler, *Ogden Family*, p. 190; *J&N*, I, 475, n. 35.

23. Prov. 13:12.

24. The United States consul in Genoa at this time was Frederic Hyde Wollaston. See *J&N*, I, 163, n. 369.

25. Marc Joseph de Gratet Dubouchage served as prefect of the Département des Alpes-Maritimes at this time. See *J&N*, I, 99, n. 202.

26. M. Permion. See *J&N*, I, 93.

27. Jean Baptiste Masseille. See *J&N*, I, 92.

28. *Macbeth*, II, v, 19.

29. Presumably a reference to the law office of Josiah Ogden Hoffman, where WI and Beebee had been reading the law.

30. WI contradicts what he said earlier in the letter. See note 5.

31. In his journal under the date of October 8, WI notes that he had received a letter from William Lee. This letter has not been located.

32. Robert R. Livingston (1746–1813), who served in Paris from 1801 to 1804.

33. WI describes his first impressions of Genoa and its inhabitants more fully in his letter to William Irving, September 20–October 27, 1804, and in his journal under the entry for October 25.

34. This may be the George Dibblie mentioned in his letter of August 24, 1804.

35. This is probably a jocular reference to Josiah Ogden Hoffman.

36. Variant of *As You Like It*, I, ii, 295.

37. An allusion to Mrs. Hoffman.

38. Probably a reference to Matilda and Ann Hoffman.

39. Ann Hoffman.

19.   To William Irving, Jr.

Nice, Septr. 20th. 1804.

Dear Brother,

I wrote two letters to the family from Marseilles one of which I forwarded by the way of Cadiz, the other by a Mr Shaw[1] of New York who intended embarking at Bordeaux. A day or two before I left Marseilles a Vessel arrived in Sixty days from New York, she brought, however, neither letters ⟨o⟩nor newspapers, which was quite a disappointment to me, and as she had to perform quarantine, I was not able to go on board of her. After spending near three weeks at Marseilles very agreeably I left it in company with Dr Henory for this place. We took a cross road, that was to strike into the main road from Aix to nice, in the evening. The country thro which we passed in the morning was sterile & cultivated by the assistance of manure. This road was very much infested by robbers about eighteen months or two years since. We passed thro ⟨some⟩ ↑two or three↓ towns that had been absolutely hordes of banditti[.] they had began, the fauxbourgs or suburbs by plundring the houses of the richer inhabitants after which they committed continual depredations on travellers till the road was almost abandoned Tho' gulotined by dozens, they were not effectually checked till the present system of police & the *gendarmerie* was established They now content themselves, since they cannot rob, to *cheat* the traveller as much as lies in their power. Throughout the inns on this road, dirt, noise and insolence reigned without controul After making a miserable dinner at one of those inns we ascended the mountains and found the road so rugged & stoney that we were glad to descend from the carriage and walk, tho the sun was very hot. In one part of the mountains we passed a long piece of road that wound among rocks & precipices and where the carriage could hardly get along. Here our driver told us, had been many robberies & murders committed, the robbers sometimes appearing in troops of twenty or thirty at a time and this road was so bad that it was impossible for either carriage or horseman to escape. At present however, there was nothing of the kind known, the Gens darmes having scoured this road completely and put a stop to these robberies. I have no doubt but the Voiturin's have often had a good understanding with the robbers and have let them know when they were to pass with a good frieght of passengers. In the evening we slept at Tourves[2] on the main road—a miserable inn. The town was loathesome ⟨from⟩ in common with the other small towns in provence from the custom of piling manure up against their houses which they use to fertilize the country. These piles of manure occasion the most abominable smells throughout the villages, which, together with ⟨d⟩ the dirt of the houses, destroy all idea of comfort to a traveller unaccustomed to them. Fortunately for me, I am seasoned in some degree to these disagreeables, from my Canada journey of last summer.[3] When I enter one of these inns to put up for the night I have but to draw a comparison between it and Some of the log hovels where my fellow travellers and myself were huddled into after a fatiguing day's journey thro the woods and the inn appears a palace. For my part I endeavor to take things as they come, with cheerfulness and when I cannot get a ⟨repast⟩ ↑dinner↓ to suit my taste I endeavor to get a taste to suit my dinner.

I have made a hearty meal of cucumbers and onions off of a *dirty* table in a *filthy* log hut on *black river* and I have made as hearty a one ↑in a vile french auberge↓ of a stale fowl ⟨in⟩ that I verily believe had mounted guard on the table ⟨a⟩ half a score of times; in fact the latter was done rather out of compassion to the next traveller who might pass, as I was fearful his nose might be keener than his appetite and the *wild flavor* of the fowl might spoil his dinner. There is nothing I dread more than to be taken for one of the *Smellfungii*[4] of this world. ⟨When⟩ I therefore endeavor to be pleased with every thing about me and ⟨I⟩ with the Masters, Mistresses & servants of the inns, particularly when I percieve they have "all the dispositions in the world" to serve me — As Sterne says—"It is enough for heaven and ⟨also would[?]⟩ ↑ought to↓ be enough for me"[5]—I find, indeed, an advantage in this, I am attended with more cheerfulness and promptness, and generally before those who are most apt to find fault and curse the waiters.

In the morning (11th) we sat out at day break, the country was much more fertile and picturesque than the preceding day. In some places I saw this years fourth crop of oats in great forwardness. Wine is very cheap from the great quantities of vineyards & the abundant vintages. They sell the last years wine in this part of the country for *one sous* a bottle exclusive of the bottle itself. The wine is of a good wholesome quality and excellent for table drink. Grapes 10 sous pr Cwt.—between Vidauban & Frejus,[6] Figs are sold 9 livres pr Cwt. & 10 livres if they pack them up. By this you may judge of the plenty of the land. In riding along we had it in our power to regale ourselves whenever we pleased with the fine grapes & figs that ⟨gre⟩ were in abundance along the road. In the afternoon we passed where they were gathering the Vintage. They do not, however, celebrate it with the mirth & rejoicing here as they do in other parts of france. The song, the dance, the inspiring sound of the pipe & tabor and the hospitable feast, are the usual attendants of this happy season in some of the provinces, "when nature is pouring her abundance into every ones lap *and every eye is lifted up*"—["]when music beats time to *labour* and her children are rejoicing as they carry in their clusters."[7]

There it is really "a joyous riot of the affections"[8] but here it seems ranked with the other employments of threshing—plowing &c. In fact the peasants throughout the south of france have a stupidity and heaviness of looks and manners that I had not expected to find ↑among a↓ people so celebrated for gaiety. If you wish for something of an idea of their persons Ill refer you to the figures in the landscapes that hang up in your parlour for there is a great similarity between them with respect to dress & beauty of proportion. For aught I know, they may be very good hearted worthy people, ↑but↓ as they talk that barbarous jargon the *patois* I could not understand them sufficiently to converse. A traveller is too apt to form his opinion of the ↑lower↓ people from those whom he employs, as guides postillions—servants, waiters, &c &c, who are the most extortionate insatiable wretches in existence. They will generally complain, when you make them a present for any little service they have rendered, of the smallness of the gratuity, and I do not reccollect of ever having been thanked *but once* by any of these fellows, and that was, when, for want of small change in my pocket, I gave ↑a man↓ about six times as much as he deserved for shewing me the inside of a church at Avignon

In the evening we put up at Vidauban and as the Inn seemed to have considerable company we took care to look out for rooms immediately. This precaution was well timed for just before supper the hostess came in with a countenance somewhat perplexed and told me the Engineer General of the Department[9] had just arrived with his lady—that he was a *grand* man and ought to be well accomodated—that he patronized her inn, and wished to have my room as it was the best in the inn and he had slept in it before and liked it that therefore she supposed "*Monsieur* would have the *bonté* to give up his room to Monsieur L'Engineer Generale" As I was somewhat piqued at this second hand cavalier request of Monsieur le Eng: Gen: I ⟨replied to the madame?⟩ that I was an A⟨m⟩the⟨r⟩ni⟨c⟩an[10] gentleman and of course I considered myself *equal at least* to any engineer general in France nor would I give up my room if he were to come with all his engines & lay siege to it but ↑would↓ that I [*unrecovered*] to hesitate not[11] if thus [*unrecovered*] part of my room[?] t⟨he⟩o ⟨these⟩ engineers *lady*⟩ The landlady retired much chagrined with my ⟨message⟩ ↑answer↓ but I heard nothing more from the *grand* man and was suffered to retain my room without any farther interruption

(12th) we sat out in the morning and had a fatiguing hilly road to traverse. In one part of our road the Voiturin pointed to a mountain at some distance and told us we should ascend that in the afternoon, we could see the road here and there as it wound up the mountain, and its height & steepness promised a most fatiguing toil for so warm a day. We dined at Frejus a small town pleasantly situated on the Sea Coast, it was formerly a place of some trade and importance but it is now in decay and ruinous. ⟨There are here the⟩ ↑It is enriched with the↓ remains of a Roman theatre & Aqueduct and some reliques of the Roman wall that formerly surrounded the Village. It was here that Bonaparte & ⟨his *suite*⟩ landed when he returned from Egypt without performing quarantine[12] (a thing punishable with death to any person coming from the levant) he staid but long enough to have his baggage brought on shore & to obtain post horses & then set off for Paris. ⟨From Frejus we⟩ After leaving Frejus we rode for some time ⟨along⟩ within sight of the Mediterranean and then began to ascend the mountain of Estrelles, one of the maritime alps & the same we had seen in the morning. As the ascent was steep and laborious we got out and walked. The road wound in different directions, humoring the ascents & declivities, and every now and then we caught an extensive & delightful prospect. The Sea calm and unruffled the Steeples of Frejus rising on its shore and on the other side a wide valley variegated with different plantations trees &c & bounded by the mountains.

In one of the highest parts of the road we over took two old women who solicited charity. They had been on a pilgrimage to a hermitage among the mountains and were now returning to their native homes near Milan in Italy. I was astonished to see two such antient beings who seemed almost too infirm to support their own weight undertaking such a long toilsome journey on foot.

The Sunset was rich and charming, & the evening delightfully serene. The pure breeze of the mountains, loaded with perfumes from the aromatic herbs & shrubs that abound ⟨on every side⟩, was refreshing & invigorating. After riding ⟨along⟩ for some distance, often along the brink of Precipices we arrived about dusk at a house where the Voiturin told us we must put up for the night as the next town was a considerable distance off and the road thro the mountains too dangerous to think of passing it in the dark. I did not ⟨at all⟩ like the looks of the house. It was large & solitary over hung by ⟨a par?⟩ part of the mountain and em- bowerd in large trees. Before the door ⟨were seated⟩ some fellows were seated on a bench drinking wine. They looked as rough as the mountains that surrounded us. On entering the inn we desired the hostess to shew us to our rooms. She took a candle & we followed her up stairs to one end of the building where she opened the doors of two rooms in one of which were three & in the other two beds. The rooms would serve as perfect representations of the residence of Poverty & sloth. Dirty, without furniture except one broken chair each, no glass in the win- dows, in short every thing had ⟨of⟩ an appearance the most deplorable & forlorn particularly to weary travellers who had need of comfortable accomodations to recover from fatigue. We demanded if these were all they had in the house[.] the hostess replied in a sulky tone that these were all that they had *furnished* and that she was sure they were good enough. We were obliged therefore to content ourselves & after a miserable supper retired to one of the rooms the door of which we fastned as secure as possible

I confess I did not feel well at ease in this lodging. The wild &

solitary situation of the house ⟨&⟩ the rough manners of the people & their apparent poverty were sufficient to awaken disagreeable sensations, particularly as I knew that about 18 months or two years since this road was very dangerous on account of the numerous robbers that infested it. In spight, however, of these uneasy reflections, of a hard bed and a host of hungry fleas I soon fell asleep and when ⟨I was⟩ awakened in the morning by the drivers knocking at the Door I had the pleasure to find that I was neither *robbd nor murdered.* We resumed our road thro the wild & romantic Scenery of the mountains, now and then ⟨shooting?⟩ catching a glympse of a distant valley. The mountains were covered with Pines, laurels, Box, myrtle, cypress, tamarisc &c & fragrant shrubs and herbs as Hysop thyme lavendar &c. At last we came once more in sight of the Mediterranean and after long and rugged descents we gained the Valleys and passing thro the little village of Cannes we continued riding ⟨alon⟩ within a little distance of the shore, having on the otherside Vineyards & Plantations of figs & olives in luxurient abundance and behind them the alps grandly terminating the prospect. These mountains ↑near the coast↓ are by no means to be compared to those of the same chain that are in the interior, particularly in Switzerland, either for Size height of singularity, they are by no means lofty enough to have snow on the top; but when I passed over them I could feel a considerable change in the atmosphere. The air feeling more pure and refreshing than in the valleys.

⟨At dinner⟩ We arrived in time to dine at Antibes[13] a small Sea port well fortified & garrisoned and formerly the frontier town of france. In the evening we arrived at Nice.[14] Thus having happily accomplished my Journey thro the *South of France* I felicitated myself with the idea that nothing remained but to step into a Felucca & be gently wafted to the classic shore of Italy! Little did I think of being *persuaded* by the police to defer my departure & take time to enjoy the climate & prospects of Nice.

The next morning (14th) I waited on the municipality to deliver my passport & request another one for Genoa. Monsr. Le Secretaire Generale perused my passport, and told me it was not in his power to grant me permission to depart. That my passport was such as is given to suspected persons and that I must rest here contented till a better passport was sent on, or a permission from the Grand Judge at Paris authorizing my departure. This speech absolutely struck me dumb. The Doctor however, who was with me & could talk french infinitely more fluently than ⟨me⟩ ↑I↓, took up my cause. He represented to the Secretary General my situation,—young inexperienced, for the first time seperated from my family, in a foreign land and ignorant of the language a vile passport had been given to me and I ignorant of the forms of the police had taken it as one of the same kind that was generally given to my countrymen. That now I would be detained among strangers, not understanding their language, out of health, solitary (as his affairs obliged him to set off immediately for Italy) In short I cannot repeat one half of the distresses the calamities & the bugbears that the doctor summoned to his assistance to render his harangue as moving as possible. The Secretary General assured him that he felt for my situation but it was absolutely out of his power to allow me to proceed—that he was amenable to superior authority and dared not indulge his inclination and that *something suspicious* in my deportment or affairs must certainly have occasiond this precaution in the municipality of Bordeaux. The Doctor assured him that it was a mistake, He had traveled with me all along and would swear, would pledge his person, his property his all, for my ·being a Citizen of the United States and that nothing had occured either in my deportment or conversation that merited suspicion. In short he manifested the most friendly zeal & earnestness in my cause and said every thing he could think of to obtain my passport. It was all in vain, The Secretary repeated it was out of his power to grant it, or ⟨wi⟩ he would with the sincerest pleasure, but that he would write to the Commissary General of Police at Marseilles ⟨in re⟩ inclosing my passport and requesting another that should enable me to proceed, in the mean time he would give me a letter of surety that granted me the liberty of the place without being subject to molestation from police officers. Having recieved this we withdrew thanking him for the politeness he had shewn. By the doctors advice I immediately wrote to Mr Schwartz & our Consul at Marseilles, requesting them to represent my case to the Com: Genl. and endeavor to have a good passport sent on immediately or if there was no other way,—to reclaim as an American Citizen. I have written to Dr Ellison[15] & our consul Mr Lee at Bordeaux requesting them to take the same measures there and as Dr Henory ⟨departs⟩ ↑was to depart↓ from here for Genoa ⟨the Day after tomorrow⟩ ↑in two days↓ I ⟨have written⟩ ↑wrote↓ by him to Hall Storm[16] to get our consul there to reclaim me[.] Dr Henory has promised to do all in his power to forward the business in that quarter so that I think it will be hard if there does not come relief from one quarter or another.

    The next day (15th) I was laying down after dinner & had ⟨fell⟩ ↑fallen↓ asleep, being rather indisposed, when I was suddenly awakened by the noise of some persons entering my chamber & found an officer of the police & the Doctor standing before me. He had come to demand my papers to carry before the Mayor for particular reasons, the Dr told me not to disturb myself, that he would accompany the man and learn what was the cause of this visit. In about half an hour I heard the Doctor coming up stairs humming a tune ↑in a voice↓ something like

that of Tom Pipes[17]—between a *screech* & *a whistle*[.] he enterd my
room with a furious countenance, flung himself into a chair & stopping
all at once in the middle of his tune began to curse the police ⟨furio⟩
in a most voluble manner ⟨&⟩ nor could I get a word of intelligence out
of him till he had consigned them all to purgatory. He then let me know
that we had been dogged about by some scoundrel of a spy who had
denounced me as an Englishman which had occasioned the demand of
my papers. He told me he had been before the adjoint of the mayor[18]
who spoke english and was very polite—That he had represented my
situation to him, and had told him, that he would bring me before him,
and if he did not at once see by my countenance that I was an *honest man*
incapable of deceit, he would himself pledge both his property and
person, that I would prove so in the end. I accordingly accompanied the
doctor before the adjoint. The latter recieved me very politely—as he
spoke english I simply stated the circumstances of my case, but he told
me it was unnecessary, he was convinced of ⟨my⟩ the folly of those
suspicions that had been indulged against me and assured me that while
I remained in Nice my tranquillity should not be again disturbed. Having
received my papers we withdrew. On the 17th. The Doctor sat off in a
Felucca for Genoa, and tho I was sorry to part with a man whose company was so amusing and who had proved himself sincerely my friend,
yet I could not but be pleased on one account as it would facilitate my
own departure, for I look chiefly to Genoa for effectual assistance. As
I did not expect to make any stay at Nice I did not procure letters of
introduction here, I have made out however, to pass the time by writing
reading &c. I am at the Hotel des Etrangers, kept by a Swiss[19] who has
all the characteristic honesty and goodness of heart of his nation. He
has two sons ⟨whom he⟩ one or other of whom he sends with me as a
guide when I walk into the country—to shew me the gardens &c[.]
I could not be in a house where more pains would be taken to oblige.
I am often cursed & blackguarded in my walks in the town by the low
soldiery who take me for an Englishman, indeed half the people of
france that are not well informed (over)[20] hardly know ⟨but where⟩
but ⟨w⟩↑t↓hat America appends[?] [*MS torn*] to England and that we
are ⟨as nearly⟩ in the same relation to them as Scotland or Ireland
Others again place it in quite a different quarter of the globe. I was
dining one day at a Table dehote where there were two or three french
men who were curious in enquiring about America. One wanted to know
if it was not a great *wine* country & whether my *province* (for he thought
the United States a mere province) did not lie in the neighborhood of
Turkey. Another time I was accosted by a French officer—"Vous etes
Anglois, monsieur"—"Pardonnez moi monsieur, Je suis des Etats Unis"—
"Eh bien—*c'est la même chose*"."

21st. September.

This afternoon I recieved a letter from Mr. Schwartz informing me that he had waited on the Commissary General of Marseilles immediately on recieving my letter. That the Com: Genl. had requested the application might be made by our Consul Mr Cathalan in his official capacity. This was accordingly done, and ⟨w⟩he expected that the proper papers giving me liberty to proceed to Italy would be sent on by the next Post. The thoughts of a speedy liberation has quite enlivened my spirits. I have written a letter of thanks to Mr S. for his very friendly behaviour. Indeed I had anticipated as much from the high opinion I had formed of him. He is the partner of Mr Abm Ogden of New York who gave me letters of introduction to him in consequence of which I experienced the most hospitable & friendly attentions from him during my stay in Marseilles He has much the countenance of Fay,[21] except that he has an older look, being about thirty. A complete gentleman in his deportment, of the most amiable manners and cultivated taste & understanding. You may smile at this eulogium & think it more the result of grateful sensations than of impartial observation, but I assure you it is well deserved & there is no gentleman I have seen in Europe that has pleased me so much.

22d.

I have recieved a letter this morning from Dr Henory dated the 20th. at Monaco a little town about three leagues hence. They put in there the first day of their voyage ⟨& have⟩ on account of the rolling of the sea & have been detained there ever since by the same cause. The Felucca men are the veriest cowards that ever ventured on salt water. The poor Doctor writes that he is quite sick, has been obliged to keep his bed one day & is suffering from bad accomodations, dirt & extortion. He says he is more vexed at this delay on my account than on his own and has written to me that I might not be surprized at not recieving the relief from Genoa so soon as I expected. I hope however that the papers from Marseilles will render the good Doctors exertions superfluous.

24th.

Yesterday was the thirteenth anniversary of the French *republic* and the commencement of a New Year according to their present calendar. It was necessary therefore to celebrate it with some rejoicing as we do our fourth of July. These national fêtes are seldom kept up with vigor for any length of time among a people so fickle as the French. They now wait for a *new batch* of public-days, such as the birth day of the Emperor—the anniversary of the Coronation &c But in the present instance, as the fête was not absolutely abolished it was requisite *for decency's sake* to give it some celebrity. There was therefore some firing of cannon, some shutting of shops & shewing of holliday aprons. The ↑house of the↓ Municipality was superbly illuminated in the evening by a couple of paper lanthorns in each window and one of the public walks was brilliantly lighted up by half a dozen tar buckets & pots of turpentine elevated on posts at equal distances by the light of which the soldiry & country people amused themselves with dancing. The day passed off with decency & decorum nor did I observe any of that amusement going forward, so fashionable among our *mobility* on similar occasions of boxing or cudgeling. The quarrels among the lower class in this country are generally settled by the *tongue* and he that has the Strongest lungs carries the day. I never saw a contest of fisty-cuffs in france but once and that was between two porters at Bordeaux and they managed it in such a clumsy manner as plainly shewed they were no adepts in the business. Three or four american sailors were standing by to enjoy the *fun*, but they got out of patience at the ⟨an⟩ combattants scratching and pulling hair, & went off damning them for a set of *brutes* that did not know how to box *like men.*

As the Catholic religion is rapidly regaining its former situation in france from the Countenance shewn it by the Emperor I expect the festivals of that religion will be again reestablished, and such is the fluctuating & capricious character of the French that it is ⟨not⟩ a chance if they ⟨are⟩ ↑will↓ not ↑be↓ celebrated with more enthusiasm than ever. ⟨Since⟩

There is continually some object or another presenting itself which evidences the changes that have repeatedly taken place in this country within a few Years. The Numerous churches ⟨testify⟩ & convents testify to what a height religious bigotry had arrived, their ruinous state and conversions into magazines of Hay—Manufactures of salt petre &c shew the effects of that persecution and fury that privailed against religion ⟨within⟩ a short time since. & the reparations they are at present undergoing shew that it is once more taken into favor. In ⟨po⟩ my pocket I have near a dozen coins all made within ⟨a dozen⟩ ↑12 or 15↓ years & all with different impressions. One in the reign of Louis the sixteenth, ⟨th⟩ another of the same King after the ⟨f⟩ oath was taken several during the reign of terror, & the glorious times of equality, one of Bonaparte as premier consul & lastly one of him as Emperor

In the numerous small towns thro which I have passed I have seen over many of the doors the traces of the words Liberty, *Equality*, indivisibility &c &c. They were all carefully erased except the words *Liberty & French republic*, how much longer these last ⟨two will⟩ will be sufferd to remain to excite the Smile of travellers I cant say. Whether they will still retain the Calender of the Republic—or institute a new one commencing at the Coronation, or return to the old one & write "the year of our lord" is equally uncertain.[22]

These trifling things serve as mementos of important events and in that one word *egalité* I read what has been the death warrant for thousands. Of the present *free happy & flourishing* situation of the people of ⟨the⟩ france I say nothing, they are *doubtless* contented with the present form of Government as the *unanimous* shouts of Vive L'Empereur whenever he makes his appearance in public, sufficiently testify— ⟨?Indeed?⟩ Leaving this subject, therefore, to those who are more concernd in it, I shall talk of something else less political in its nature.

You may ⟨wh⟩ wish to know something of Nice where I am vegetating so agreeably. It is situated in a small valley bounded on one side by the sea & on the others by the Alps Maritime which rise gradually at first in handsome hills covered with vineyards, olives, gardens of oranges & lemons diversified by white Country seats, behind which the alps rise more lofty & majestic in the distance All the valley & the hills are highly cultivated and have a beautiful appearance. As most of the trees are evergreens they flourish perpetually. Indeed properly speaking they have no winter here, as the climate is So mild in that season that the fruits &c thrive equaly as well as in Summer. It is delightful to walk into the country, & visit the Gardens. The Oranges are not yet ripe—but there ⟨are⟩ is abundance of grapes, figs, pomegranates &c[.] Nice is but a small place containing about ten or twelve thousand inhabitants The houses are neat & built of stone & the streets are narrow. There are some pleasant walks about the town, particularly one ⟨a⟩ on a raised terrace along the sea shore. The weather is warm at present but in the evening & the morning early the air is pure & bracing. There are great numbers of musquitoes gnats &c—but the general use of musquito curtains to the beds prevents their being very troublesome. The chief employments of the inhabitants are making oil, wine, cordage &c. They talk here a jargon of french & italian that it is impossible for me to understand, the better sort talk french also. Nice formerly was an Italian town[23] & is situated in Piedmont but at present it ⟨is th⟩ appertains to ⟨the french⟩ France and is the chief place of the department of the Alpes Maritimes. In time of peace there is a vast concourse of English invalids that crowd here to benefit by the climate during the winter which must render it very lively & fashionable. At present the only public amusement is a wretchedly performd play in a miserable theatre[24] twice or three times a week. Had I ⟨any person here⟩ an agreeable companion here to talk to, the time would pass very pleasantly, for I am delighted with the Situation of Nice & the surrounding country, but it is impossible to be perfectly contented alone. I am left often to much to my own reflections which return to home & make me wish to be with you at least for a day or two.

I have read in the paris papers that the fever has again made its appearance in ⟨the⟩ New York & that those who have fallen victims to it have been carried off in forty eight hours with the black vomit.[25] This account has given me the greatest uneasiness and I am impatient to get to Genoa ⟨h⟩ in hopes of finding letters forwarded to me there. The last letter I recieved from you was dated the thirtieth of June & I have heard nothing from or of you all since I left Bordeaux. I endeavor however to keep my spirits in as lively a mood as possible, and by dint of writing, reading, walking &c, I prevent the time from lagging heavily. The letters I have recieved from New York are continual sources of pleasure to me, I read one or two of them whenever I feel lonesome, and they generally act as a relief. Tell Jack[26] that his first letter has repeatedly set me a laughing in my dullest moments, ⟨his⟩ I beg he will write me some more of the same kind & that he will be particular in letting me know the anecdotes and occurrences in the *little world* of our acquaintance. My health is so much restored that I can hardly call myself any longer a valetudinarian but as to getting much flesh on my ribs, I believe ⟨it is not⟩ *the nature of the beast* will not allow of it. Adieu for the present.

26th Septr.

I have just recieved two or three letters—to express to you the revolution of feelings they occasioned is impossible They were put into my hands by the maitre dHotel just as I returned from one of my solitary morning rambles on the sea shore where I had been wishfully contemplating the ocean and wishing myself on its bosom in full sail to Italy. The first packet was from my indefatigable friend Dr Henory inclosing a letter from Hall storm and a reclamation from our Consul and all within twenty four hours after his arrival. As to the letter from Storm it breathes all th⟨at⟩e warmth and openness of heart that distinguishes that worthy fellow. He declares he has ⟨not⟩ hardly slept a wink all night at the thoughts of one of the *members of the tabernacle* being so near him, *and one too,* than whom⟨e⟩ there is none he would be more happy to see. He says I have but to keep up my spirits till I get to him *and then* we'll shew his *dry boned* majesty such *life* that he'll be glad to give up the chase of me—whip ⟨off⟩ ↑in↓ & cry *off off— wrong scent!*[27] As to my situation at Nice he expresses the utmost regret at my solitary detainment, ill health &c[.] however he says "My dear fellow you know the offer of *my Uncle Toby* to poor sick Le Fevre[28]— with the same honesty of soul I tender ⟨you⟩ the *same in every respect* to you. ——— I shall try to procure ↑for↓ you a letter of credit on some one there (at nice) in case you may have ⟨any⟩ wants as I know there is nothing sets a traveller ↑so much↓ at ease as good credits & Introductions."

I have here given you an extract or two from his letter to shew you with what warmth and sincerity this dear fellow enters into my interests. I know not ⟨whether⟩ ↑which↓ I wish to proceed most for, to see Italy or to see hall. The letter from Dr Henory speaks in the highest terms of Storms friendly reception of him in consequence of an introductory letter from me, and of the zeal Hall shewed in my concerns. In consequence of their united exertions & certificates a reclamation was immediately procured & sent on as promptly. I have also recieved a pacquet from our Consul at Marseilles inclosing a letter to the Prefet of Nice representing my case and urging him to give me a passport for Italy. Thus you see the prospect is opened. I have but to go to the Municipality get a passport &c & then away to Italy and Hall Storm!———

evening

Such were the enlivening ideas of this morning, and with a light heart I danced attendance on the Secretary general five or six times in the course of the day. At last I had the good fortune to have my paper either carried before him or the Prefet by one of the head clerks & after waiting in sanguine expectation of a passports being ordered me I was greeted with the cheering intelligence that I must rest here still for four or five days till they recieved an answer ⟨from⟩ to a letter that had been written to the Commissary General of Marseilles. What this answer is, or of what importance it is I neither know nor care, it is sufficient for me to know that I am in their power & that it is needless to complain *patience par for[ce]* [*MS torn*] is my motto. ⟨It is⟩ I was promised that I should be forwarded with pleasure when a reclamation arrived from Genoa and now that I have a reclamation supported by a letter from our Consul at Marseilles, I am still detained and shall be obliged to dance attendance on these scoundrels I do not know how much longer; I have felt what it is to have to deal with *Dogs in office* & can say with Swift

> "Ye Gods if there's a man I ought to hate
> *Attendance* and dependance be his fate."[29]

October 14th.

Upwards of two weeks have elapsed since the above was written, the time in that interval has dragged on without any thing particular to vary its monotony. I have been made the sport of promises and evasions by the Police who pretend that they are unable to give me a passport notwithstanding the reclamation &c. That they must [have] authority from Paris—tho they have not taken the trouble to write to Paris. Fortunately however I wrote to Mr Lee our Consul at Bordeaux when I was first detained—he immediately wrote to our Minister at Paris[30] in my favor—in consequence of which I received a very polite Letter from Robt L Livingston Esqr.[31] Son in Law of the minister informing me that the minister had recieved the ⟨d⟩ account of my situation from Mr Lee & immediately had sent a passport to the grand Judge for his signature and that it would most probably come on by the same mail, at farthest by the mail ensuing. He also mentioned his having recd. a letter from Mr Cutting[32] which I had forwarded from Bordeaux which mentiond me particularly to him and added that he hoped to see me in Paris & render me every service in his power. Two or three couriers have elapsed since the receipt of this letter but the promised passport has not arrived.

This morning I went to see mass performed in the cathederal[33] in presence of the Prefet Secretary Genl &c & the troops of the Garison. The Cathederal is ⟨ornament⟩ much ornamented in the interior with reliefs, frescos &c[.] it formerly boasted some excellent paintings but they have been taken away & inferior ones substituted The Music of the regiment played in different intervals of the Service. The Soldiers were marshalled in the centre of the church with their muskets shouldered[.] at a certain Signal of the drum they all presented arms & knelt down, after remaining on one knee for about a minute the[y] rose & shoulderd their arms on another Signal—The word of command was then given & they wheeld round & marched out of church. It is something of a novelty to see Soldiers *pray by the word of command.*

15th.

After the many efforts I have made & the trouble I have given to friends, consuls &c ⟨it is⟩ I have had my business effected from a Quarter I least expected. My honest Swiss landlord who is endowed with all the native goodness of heart that characterizes his countrymen has often expressed ⟨sh[?]⟩ much concern for my embarrassments and has repeatedly asked me to let him go to the prefeture and represent my case—not placing much confidence in the utility of his efforts I constantly declined them. Yesterday however when he saw how much I was chagrined at not recieving a passport by the Post he could restrain himself no longer but marched of[f] to see the Secretary General without letting me know a word of the matter. The Simple eloquence of my landlord dictated by the honest warmth of his feelings seems to have touched the Secretary General for he promised he would immediately see the Prefet and use all his influence in my favor. To day my landlord told me what he had done and begged me to go with him to see the Secretary—assuring me the Secretary was *un brave homme—un bon garçon,* to please him I consented tho without any expectation of reaping any benefit. What was my surprize then when the secretary immediately informed me that I might depart for Genoa as soon as I pleased, that a written permission would be given me on my leaving my passports &c with the municipality of Nice and giving my *parole d'honneur* that I would remain at Genoa till the permission arrived from Paris for me to proceed. Honest Laurent (my Landlord) was if possible more overjoyed than myself and exhibited a disinterestedness and native worth rarely to be found in people of his profession in france, who I have generally observed to be solicitous to make the most out of ⟨their⟩ travellers and to detain them as long as possible.

                                             Genoa Octr. 27th.

I have scarcely time my dear brother to finish the detail of my movements and bring them up to the present day. On the 17th. I received my passport from our Minister at paris accompanied with a very polite letter from R L Livingston his Son in law. This passport is good *for a year* (in general the minister I am told does not give them for more than six months) As a Felucca was to sail the next morning for Genoa I had no time to lose & immediately waited on the Secry. General for his Signature to the back of the passport that being necessary for me to enable me to procure the requisite papers &c at the Health office. When I saw the Secy he was just commencing a speech *"that the Prefet had not recieved any letter by the courier concerning me—that he was embarrassed about the propriety of granting me permission to proceed to Genoa &c"* By which I perceived that if my passport had not arrived so opportunely I should again have been put off with a contemptible evasion. He was going on mentioning how much the prefet was embarrassed—how much he felt for my situation &c when I told him as drily as possible that I was very happy to have it in my power to relieve the Prefet from his *embarrassments* and spare his *sensibility* from any further suffering. I then pulld out my passport and told the Secy. that tho they had thought proper to slight the reclamation of an American Consul yet I expected they would pay more respect to the passport of ⟨the⟩ our Minister.

He immediately began to bow & scrape and protest how happy he was to find I was relieved and how willing he was to do every thing to oblige me[.] I told him very cooly that I did not ask their signature to my passport as a matter of obligation but that I demanded it as a *right* that I had sufficiently tried the *generosity* of the police of Nice before and knew well what expectations might be indulged from it. Having arranged all my affairs with the police health office &c I sat sail early the next morning for Genoa In the Felucca were four or five french officers from the same Hotel with myself and three others from some other Hotel with a young German who spoke English perfectly.

Of my voyage from Nice to this place I cannot be very particular for I have not my note book at hand.[34] We coasted along continually near the shore for fear of the small english privateers that infest this coast. The Shore was a continual chain of high mountains rocky and sterile; yet by the industry of the inhabitants cultivated often to the very tops with olives oranges & vineyards. ⟨Along the foot of them we passed⟩ Towns & villages were built at little distances from each other along the Skirts of the mountains, and often a Small village was seen perched on the peak of some rocky height that seemed only accessable to the eagle. Convents Castles & villas were scattered among the mountains often in the most romantic & picturesque ⟨appearance⟩ situations and the white walls of the edifices had a pretty appearance amid the deep green foliage with which they were surrounded. In the evenings we put in to ⟨som⟩ one or other of the large towns, and even there were but miserably Accomodated.[35] ⟨The first night we put up⟩ The first day we passed the frontiers of France and put up in the Evening at St Remo[36] a town in the Genoese Republic. I could immediately percieve the difference in the looks of the people and in the appearance of the objects around me. Monks & priests swarmed in every street. The churches were in good condition unstripd of their paintings & statues

The next day we continued our voyage continually coasting along— sometimes sailing & sometimes rowed. The voyage was really delightful. In the day the sun was rather hot but the evenings were delicious. A fine moonlight enabled us to distinguish the objects from the shore. The sound of some convent bell from among the mountains would now & then salute our ears and immediately the rowers would ⟨sw[?]⟩ rest on their oars pull off their caps—and offer up their prayers. In one place near *Albenga*[37] we had receded for some distance from the shore when a small vessel that lay under the shore fired a gun a head of us. Our Padrone immediately displayed his flag and hailed the vessel It appears they thought from the number of us that were on board that we were ⟨one of⟩ a small english privateer for he fired another ball at us which *whizzd* over our heads and drove half of the french officers into the little hold of the felucca. Our Padrone repeated his cries to the vessel & waved his flag[.] they did not repeat the fire. about nine or ten leagues before I reached ⟨Legh⟩ Genoa we passed a small village [of which the name is in my memorandum book but which I do not reccollect at this moment][38] remarkable for being the ⟨birth⟩ native place of Christopher Columbus.[39] The same day ↑(20th)↓ we arrived about two O'Clock at Genoa having been ⟨about⟩ three days & an half on the passage and in course of the voyage seen the principal places of the Ligurian or Genoese republic. On arriving in this city I hardly gave myself time to change my clothes before I called on Storm. My reception was the most honest open

hearted & warm that could be wished. Since that time we have been
continually together; we have had so much to talk about that I have not
been able to examine the curiosities of the city attentively. Genoa has
acquired the title of *Superb*[40] and it deserves the appelation The palaces
are magnificent. There are two streets called the *Strada Nuovo* & *Strada
Balbi* that are said to be superior to any in the world for ↑the↓ grandeur
of the buildings. They are a continued string of Palaces the Architecture
executed by the best italian artists[41] The exterior decorated profusely
with carvings fresco-paintings & marbles and the interior with fine paintings gildings & sumptuous furniture. The churches are also superb. I
have been astonish'd at the riches that seem to have been lavished to
ornament them The cielings Walls &c ↑are↓ painted in fresco by excellent artists representing Scripture passages, and hung with fine
oil paintings—the Pavements, Pillars altars &c &c formed of the ⟨fin⟩
most costly marbles & finely sculptured. I have not time to enter into
any detail of them[42] and indeed it would be confused & uninteresting
for I could not give you any ↑correct↓ idea of their splendor. The streets
of Genoa are very narrow, some of them not above six or seven feet
wide even The two principal ones that I have mentiond above are
⟨of⟩ quite narrow. This prevents the fine buildings to be seen to advantage. ⟨In⟩ Those two principal streets are the great resort to see and
be seen like broad way in New York. The Italian Ladies far surpass the
French ⟨ones⟩ in my opinion for Beauty. The[y] are ⟨beau⟩ extremely
well made ⟨and⟩ have charming countenances and fine black eyes with
which they know the art of languishing most bewitchingly. They are
much given to intrigue and very warm in their attachments. Mr & Mrs
Kuhn[43] are not at Genoa at present ⟨f⟩ but they are on their return here
from Gibraltar. At present they are detained at Leghorn by a Quarantine.
Mrs ⟨Storm⟩ Kuhn has expressed her hopes of arriving here before I
depart and making my stay agreeable by some little parties &c.

⟨I was out wit⟩ Rode out in a carriage the other day to visit Sestri
a country place on the Midditeranean about six miles from Genoa where
the nobility have their country seats. I was in company with Storm and
an english gentleman.[44] ⟨We were entertained by them⟩ When we
arrived at Sestri we call'd at the House of Mrs Bird[45] whose husband
was formerly British Consul at Genoa. Here we found besides the family
of Mrs B. a Mrs Walsh[46] another english lady and her daughters who
were spending the warm weather at the country house of Mrs B. I
was introduced to them all round and in a few minutes found myself
quite at home. We prevaild on the girls to accompany us in our visit
to a garden laid out in the english taste. Here we rambled all the morning amidst *shady bowers* and *purling rivulets* and *cool grottos* and
refreshing fountains and all the other pretty affairs that we read of in

pastoral romances—for I really believe they were all assembled in the space of a few acres. We then returned to Mrs Birds to dinner which passd away most merrily after which we danced to the Harpsichord till quite late in the evening. Never before in Europe have I passed a day so happily—it reminded me of the many happy ones I have passed in America & I could hardly persuade myself that I was not among a number of my female acquaintance on the other side of the Ocean. The Miss Birds are very accomplished girls & one of them extremely handsome.

Last evening I was introduced by Hall Storm to the family of Lord Shaftesbury[47] one of the richest noblemen of England who is detained here a prisoner of war. We found his Lordship seated with Lady Shaftesbury[48] & Lady Barbara[49] his daughter a beautiful girl of sixteen. They were extremely polite & agreeable. His Lordship has had the misfortune to tumble from his horse some ti[m]e [*MS torn*] since and crackd his most noble noddle and it has not completely arranged itself since. He launched out most profusely in praise of America and americans and I believe really thought himself in the house of Lords from the length of his Harangue. Her ladyship ⟨was⟩ having her head sound & more under command entertained us far more agreeably and indeed is quite a pleasing woman.

I have not had time since I have been here to study the Italian but I intend to commence it the first opportunity—that is, as soon as I ⟨can⟩ have nothing more to see or talk about. The chief part of the nobility & Beau monde are in the country—Storm has an extensive acquaintance amongst them and intends to introduce me to as many as possible. As soon as the Doge[50] comes to town I am to be presented to him—I am already acquainted with his nephew who has promised to take us tomorrow evening to an entertainment given by a lady of fashion in the Country.

I have recieved your letter dated the seventh or eighth of July[51] and your account of the persecution [of][52] the friends of Col Burr[53] has fairly made my blood boil in my veins. Tho ⟨at first⟩ an Admirer of Genl Hamilton & a partizan ⟨of⟩ ↑with↓ him in politics I have ever felt a high sense of the merits of B——— and an indignation at seeing him persecuted. Whatever may have been the circumstances of the duel I am satisfied they have been honorable on both sides and the affair should have been treated with delicacy & suffered to sink into silence. The manner in which it has been prosecuted is a melancholy proof to what a rancorous height political animosities are attaining in our country. They threaten the subversion of our government and are regarded with astonishment by the people of Europe who think we ought to be the most happy & contented ⟨people⟩ ↑nation↓ in existance

For my part, from what little I have seen of Europe I shall, I think, never complain ⟨of⟩ against government when I return to america. My fellow countrymen do not know the blessings they enjoy; they are trifling with their felicity and are in fact *themselves* their worst enemies. I sicken when I think of our political broils, slanders & enmities and I think when I again find myself in New York I shall never meddle any more in politicks.[54] Be assured my dear Brother if you could once see the oppressions the extortions, the political wrongs and tyrannies that are daily practised on this side the ocean you would wonder that you could have found any cause of complaint in america. I have been troubled often with fits of *Homesickness* but they have now worn away and tho I often—*often* think of you all, yet it is without pain and I look forward to the day of our reunion as a happy period without lamenting the time that must elapse before it arrives.

From here I shall proceed to ⟨Gen⟩ Leghorn and from there most probably thro florence & rome to Naples where I intend to be in the height of the Carnaval

You mentioned in your letter your expectation that I would go to paris to see the Coronation.[55] If you consider a little you will find it would have deranged all my plans and perhaps have put it out of my power to visit Italy. Besides, paris will be crowded at that time and every thing vastly expensive. I considered the mater maturely and convinced myself of its impractability before I abandoned it.

And now I must as usual conclude with a host of remembrances. ⟨as usual⟩ By this time if you have been obliged to fly the city & the fever, I expect you have once more returned to your home and are quietly settled with your family. Give my love to them all. Remember me to the old people most affectionately & tell the old Gentleman that I read the book he gave me ten times oftener now than I did when I used to hear it read for me and that I hope I profit by the perusal.[56] Give my love also to Sally[57] and to my Brothers—and to all my friends my sincere remembrances ⟨Wh If you write to me⟩

When you write to me from this time Direct your letters to be detained in the hands of J J Bosc & Co[58] till I write for them from Paris or else-where[.] otherwise they may travel after me thro Italy & france perhaps lost, and if recieved the postage will be enormous[59]

P. S. There has been some talk of the yellow fevers prevailing at Leghorn and I now learn that it has encreased to a very alarming degree. Rigorous Quarantines are put on all vessels coming from that port and the communication stopped also by Land. This perhaps may occasion me to alter my route[;] however I shall stay here a month longer[60] & by that time I am in hopes it may subside, tho much apprehensions are entertained of its continuance. Storm intends writing something to Peter for his paper about genoa[61]—Tell Hicks[62] whenever there is an opportunity to send papers either by the way of Leghorn Marseilles Gibraltar or Cadiz to Kuhn & Co ↑Merchts Genoa↓ and continue to send them now & then—Storm has promised to write particulars from time to time about any thing that occurs in the Mediterranean.

My health is growing stronger & stronger every day. I do not know when I have felt myself so strong & brisk and I even begin to acquire a little tinge of health in my countenance. I am here with Storm in his *palace* and we keep house very merrily together. One wing of it is still retained by the proprietor an old Italian princess[.] I have almost a mind to make a *speck*[63] of her for she is immensely rich. What would you say to an old Princess Huncamunca[64] returning with me to America

Write to me the state of our Theatre[65] & how all my *old friends* in the green room make out. I expect that several of my friends will be offended at my not writing but I assure you it is an ⟨ha⟩ awful undertaking to write a letter when travelling you have so much to say and so little time to say it in—and such vast expectations are formed by your correspondents.

As to Sam Swartwout I have discharged him from my list of scribblers for I have recieved but twelve lines from him since I left New York.

I must conclude in haste assuring you that I am still with sincerity

Your affectionate Brother

W I.

P. S. tell Hicks the names of the correspondents of Kuhn & Co[66] are—at Giberaltar Kuhn Green & Co—at Cadiz, Strange & Co[67]—at Marseilles Gabriac & Cushing—& at Leghorn John Lewis Cailler[.] in every case they must be directed to *Kuhn & Co* to the care of the others.

When you write to Johnstown remember me very particularly—your mention of the state of Nancys health[68] has given me much uneasiness—her constitution would most undoubtedly have been benefited by a Sea voyage & if she could have passed the Winter in a mild climate I have no doubt she would be completely restored.

You do not tell me how you make out in business and how Jack[69] & Brom [70] &c succeed.

DOCKETED: Nice Sept 20–1804–fr W. I. (on page 1 of MS).

MANUSCRIPT: Yale (28 pp. MS); and Va.–Barrett (2 pp. MS). PUBLISHED: PMI, I, 78–86, 91–92 (in part).

In this letter WI also uses many of the same details and phrases found in his journal entries from September 10 to October 27, 1804, and in his letter to Alexander Beebee, September 18 to October 27, 1804.

1. The identity of Mr. Shaw has not been positively established. The most likely candidate is James W. Shaw, a wine merchant at 5 Wall Street, who might

have been arranging for wine purchases in Bordeaux. Other possibilities include John Shaw, a merchant at 15 Pearl Street; John C. Shaw, a merchant at 44 Beaver Street; or Robert Shaw, 106 Beekman Street. See *New York City Directory* for 1804.

2. A town about 26 miles east southeast of Aix-en-Provence.

3. WI is alluding to his trip to northern New York and Canada taken during August and September of 1803 in the company of Mr. and Mrs. Josiah Ogden Hoffman, Mr. and Mrs. Ludlow Ogden, Ann Hoffman, and Eliza Ogden. See STW, I, 28–34; *J&N*, I, 3–30.

4. WI, who had been reading Sterne's *A Sentimental Journey Through France and Italy*, alludes to "the learned Smellfungus" (Tobias Smollett) who "travelled from Boulogne to Paris—from Paris to Rome—and so on—but he set out with spleen and jaundice, and every object he pass'd by was discoloured or distorted—He wrote an account of them, but 'twas nothing but the account of his miserable feelings." See *A Sentimental Journey Through France and Italy*, pp. 98–99.

5. *A Sentimental Journey*, p. 111. Sterne makes this observation after his interview with La Fleur, his servant.

6. Fréjus is a town on the seacoast, 22 miles south of Cannes. Vidauban is approximately 18 miles west of Fréjus and 24 miles east of Tourves.

7. *A Sentimental Journey*, p. 379.

8. *Ibid.*, p. 395.

9. Jean Antoine Fabre (1748–1834), a highly respected hydraulic engineer, was Ingénieur en Chef des Ponts et Chaussées of the Department of Var at this time. His wife was Marie Charlotte Eléonore Gautier du Poët (1765–1805). See *J&N*, I, 88, n. 173.

10. In his corresponding journal entry for September 11, 1804, WI calls himself an American gentleman. See *J&N*, I, 89.

11. Parts of the following phrase are illegible. Since the letter parallels the journal at this point, the passage probably reads "I would have no objection to give a part of my room to the engineers *lady*." See *J&N*, I, 89.

12. Upon his return from Egypt, Napoleon landed at Fréjus on October 8, 1799. The local inhabitants ignored the quarantine regulations, shouting, "We prefer the plague to the Austrians" (Louis Antoine Fauvelet de Bourrienne, *Memoirs of Napoleon Bonaparte*, ed. R. W. Phipps [New York, 1889], I, 239–40).

13. Antibes is about 23 miles from Fréjus.

14. Nice is about 13 miles northeast of Antibes.

15. Dr. John G. Ellison, American physician whom WI met in Bordeaux.

16. Thomas Hall Storm, the son of Thomas Storm (1749–1843) and Elizabeth Graham (d. 1832), was born in 1781 and died unmarried. He became United States vice-consul in Genoa in 1805. See R. W. Storm, *Old Dirck's Book* (n.p., 1949).

17. In *The Adventures of Peregrine Pickle* (1751) by Tobias Smollett, Tom Pipes accompanied Peregrine Pickle in his travels. In addition to blowing his whistle frequently, Tom had a very unusual (or unnatural) voice.

18. François de Orestis and Louis Millonis were adjoints of the mayor of Nice at this time. See *J&N*, I, 94, n. 190.

19. Presumably this is Laurent Stir, Ile 17, Maison No. 14. See *J&N*, I, 95, n. 192.

20. The word "over" is at the bottom of the page in the center after "informed," the remaining half of the line being blank.

21. Probably Joseph Dewey Fay (1779–1825), an attorney at 31 William Street, who had studied law in the office of Alexander Hamilton and was the father of Theodore Sedgwick Fay, a minor New York author, whom WI later assisted.

22. The French Republican calendar was started with the autumnal equinox on September 22, 1792, to correspond with the beginning of the French Republic. When Napoleon restored the Catholic religion in 1805, the senatus-consulte provided for the return to the Gregorian calendar, effective January 1, 1806.

23. Nice, a city founded by the Phocaeans about 4,000 years ago, was the scene and subject of strife for much of modern history. After passing back and forth between Savoy and France, it became the property of Sardinia until captured by the armies of the French Republic in 1792.

24. This theater in the town was located on the site of the present Opera of Nice on the Boulevard du Midi, now the Quai des États-Unis. No record of the play seen by WI has been located. See J&N, I, 98, n. 198.

25. A dispatch from New York dated July 18 appeared in the Gazette Nationale ou Le Moniteur Universel for 11 Fructidor, An 12 (August 29, 1804). It reported that yellow fever had appeared on Long Island but had not yet reached New York City. Since subsequent issues of Le Moniteur do not give further details, WI apparently found them in another newspaper from Paris.

26. Probably John Treat Irving, WI's brother.

27. This allusion has not been identified.

28. Laurence Sterne, The Life and Opinions of Tristram Shandy, Gentleman, ed. James A. Work (New York, 1940), vol. VI, chap. X, p. 426.

29. WI made the wrong attribution of authorship. The quotation is from Abraham Cowley's "Of Liberty." See Essays, Plays and Sundry Verses, ed. A. R. Waller (Cambridge, 1906), p. 387. See J&N, I, 99, n. 20.

30. Robert R. Livingston.

31. Robert L. Livingston (1775–1843), who married Margaret Maria Livingston on July 10, 1799, served as Robert R. Livingston's secretary in Paris. See Edwin Brockholst Livingston, The Livingstons of Livingston Manor (n.p., 1910), p. 557; J&N, I, 102, n. 210.

32. Probably William Cutting, who had married Gertrude Livingston and through his Livingston connections had become associated with Robert Fulton in his steamboat venture. In T. A. Cutting, Cutting Kin (Campbell, Calif., 1939), William Cutting is designated as a lawyer and business associate of Robert Fulton, who had a son named Fulton Cutting.

33. St. Réparate in the older part of the town was constructed in 1650. Its interior exhibits many of the characteristics of Italian churches.

34. In his journal WI vividly describes the seasickness of several of the passengers and mentions sailing past Monaco, Ventimiglia, and Bordighera on the way to San Remo. See J&N, I, 104–5.

35. WI describes the hotel at San Remo as being "dark and dirty and miserably off for attendance." See J&N, I, 105–6.

36. San Remo is about 32 miles by land from Nice and 68 miles from Genoa.

37. Albenga is about 32 miles from San Remo.

38. The passage "of which . . . this moment" is in square brackets in the MS, apparently added later by another hand.

39. Cogoleto, about 16 miles from Genoa.

40. "Its situation, rising above the sea in a wide semicircle, and its numerous palaces justly entitle it to the epithet of 'La Superba'" (Karl Baedeker, Northern Italy, 14th ed. [Leipzig, 1913], p. 99).

41. These include the Palazzo Durazzo-Pallavici, the Palazzo Balbi-Senarega, the Palazzo dell'Universita, and the Palazzo Reale. Among the famous architects

who designed these buildings are Bartolomeo Beanco, Andrea Tagliafico, Pier Antonio Corradi, Francesco Cantoni, Giovanni Angelo Falconi, and Carlo Fontana.

42. In his journal entry for October 25, WI briefly describes Sant' Ambrogio, the Cathedral of San Lorenzo, Santissima Annunziata del Vastato, and the Santa Maria di Carignano. See J&N, 1, 112–15.

43. See letter to William Irving, August 14, 1804, note 38.

44. In his journal for October 26 WI identifies him as Edward Caffarena, who in 1805 was appointed United States vice-consul in Genoa. See J&N, I, 117, n. 249.

45. Mrs. James Bird was the daughter of John William Brame, the British consul in Genoa. Her husband performed most of the consular duties during Brame's incapacity. See J&N, I, 117, n. 252.

46. Probably the wife of Joseph Walsh, who was recommended to the United States consulship in Genoa by Frederic Hyde Wollaston, who retired in 1805. See J&N, I, 118, n. 253.

47. Anthony Ashley Cooper (1761–1811), the fifth earl of Shaftesbury.

48. Barbara Webb, daughter of Sir John Webb, who married Lord Shaftesbury in 1786.

49. Barbara Cooper (1788–1844), who married the Honorable William Francis Spencer Ponsonby in 1814.

50. Girolamo Durazzo (1739–1809) was the last to hold the position of Doge. In 1805 after Genoa was annexed to France, the office was abolished. See J&N, I, 135, n. 302.

51. This letter has not been located.

52. This word was added by the editors of the Twayne edition.

53. Aaron Burr fought a duel with Alexander Hamilton (1755–1804) on the heights of Weehawken on July 11, 1804, causing a wound from which Hamilton died on the following day. The public outrage which followed was directed both at the practice of dueling and at Burr.

54. WI is apparently alluding to his journalistic contributions to The Corrector, edited by Peter Irving. See The Contributions of Washington Irving to "The Corrector," ed. Martin Roth (Minneapolis, 1968).

55. Napoleon was crowned at Notre Dame on December 2, 1804.

56. Apparently a reference to Deacon Irving's Bible reading to his family.

57. Sarah Irving, WI's sister nearest in age to him, who married Henry Van Wart in 1804. For this reason WI probably singles her out for special mention.

58. WI's agents in Bordeaux.

59. At this point the Yale manuscript ends, without a signature. The manuscript of the postscript is in Va.–Barrett.

60. WI left Genoa for Messina on December 23, 1804 where he arrived on January 5, 1805. See J&N, I, 141–62.

61. No such article has been found in the Morning Chronicle.

62. Probably Elias Hicks, to whom WI had written on July 24, 1804.

63. Speculation.

64. Princess Hunca-munca, a character in Henry Fielding's Tom Thumb. A Tragedy (1730); in 1731 the play was revised as The Tragedy of Tragedies; or, the Life and Death of Tom Thumb the Great.

65. The Park Theatre on Broadway.

66. See WI's letter to William Irving, Jr., August 14, 1804, note 38.

67. The New York Morning Chronicle, April 5, 1805, reports receipt of a letter from "the respectable house of Strange & Co. of Cadiz dated February 15. . . ."

68. Johnstown, New York, was the residence of Mrs. Richard Dodge, WI's sister Ann.

69. Probably John Treat Irving, WI's brother.

70. Brom was probably Ebenezer Irving (1776–1868), another brother.

20. *To John Furman*

Genoa October 24th 1804

My dear fellow

On my arrival at this place I found among other letters that were waiting for me at my Bankers,[1] one from you dated the 7th of July.[2] The letter was as acceptable as it was unexpected, for in truth John you was the last fellow in New York from whom I expected to receive one—not that I doubted your friendship for me, such an idea would give me the greatest pain, but from a knowledge of your *natural indolence,* that deplorable *vis inertia* with which you are so plentifully endowed. This excuse (though I confess it is a *miserable* one) is the best I can offer for not having written to you from Europe. I have had two or three attentive corresponents[3] (besides my brothers) who were *entitled* to my scribbling moments and the writing to those to whom I was in a manner in *duty bound* to give histories of my *adventures* &c completely engrossed the few leisure hours I had to spare from the examination of towns, cities, curiosities &c. It is I assure you a laborious task to undertake giving descriptions of the scenes through which I pass in travelling, and I detest the long tedious details into which it continually leads me. This however is expected from me by those to whom I write, so that a letter is often an aweful undertaking in my eyes—I will therefore refer you to my letters to my brother for accounts of my journeyings and will only scribble to you any thing that comes uppermost, whether description, narration or reflection—* * * * * *[4] the effects of that enervating indisposition that rendered me for some time before I left New York, languid, irritable, spiritless, a burthen to my friends and to myself. My good fellow I know you well, I think I know your soul to its inmost recess, for it ever appeared to me open and unreserved. If then I could be so intimately acquainted with your heart and not admire its good qualities, if I could so long be the companion of your amusements and your pursuits and not have a friendship for you sincere and unreserved, I should show the most cold hearted insensibility to intrinsic merit and honest worth. I would not thus sound your praises to your face and adopt a language that one who did not know us both might take for flattery, did not your suspicions of my friendship call ⟨up⟩on me to vindicate it. I am not afraid to talk to you in this manner for I wish you to have a good opinion of yourself; the diffidence you have of your own merits is the greatest enemy you have to encounter and if Frey[5] as you say has taught you to think better of yourself than ever, trust me he has done you the most friendly office in his power. I wish to heavens John I had you with me travelling through Europe, there is nothing more calculated to call forth a mans powers and make him acquainted with his own resources than to have to make his way thro' strangers in a strange land where he must depend ↑entirely↓[6] on his own discretion his own exertions and circumspection to get along. Where different manners people and languages continually demand his attention, keep his mind forever active, his faculties forever awake, Where he learns to act and think as a man, a thing very difficult to acquire at home where we have been used to be treated like boys and cannot for a long time divest ourselves of boyish manners, ideas and propensities.

You may easily suppose I am delighted with the wonders, the amusements and the curiosities of Europe. I confess I am dazz⟨d⟩led, astonished, enraptured but as yet not *ensnared,* the affections of my tenderest attachments still attract my thoughts and secret wishes to America, and those are the true bonds that ever bind us to a country. How often amid the gayest scenes do I lose sight of every thing around me, transport myself to New York, and mingle in fancy among my friends. I look in vain in Europe for those warm friendships that honesty and openess of heart and manners that I have left behind me in America and for which French politeness is a miserable substitute. I turn with disgust from the profligacy and immorality of the *Old World* and reflect with delight on the *comparitive* purity of American Morals. In short, my dear John, I hope to return to you untainted with the vices of Europe, and if neither wiser nor better at least I hope I shall not be worse than when I set out. By the date of the letter you will see I have set foot on the far famed shore of Italy. My journey through the south of France has been delightful. I have seen nature in her sweetest and most luxuriant dress. The enchanting plains of Languedoc cultivated with the most parsimonious care shewed the gay assemblage of vineyards, cornfields and Olives interspersed with flourishing towns and villages. The country fertile to the utmost seemed a continual garden.

The route through provence afforded a more varied scene. The sterile mountain contrasted with the smiling valley, the road now winding thorugh the rocky Alps, perfumed with the odours of a thousand aromatic herbs that grew among the crevices of the mountains, and now descending into the vales of the most romantic and luxuriant appearance—

At Nice I was detained near five weeks on suspicion of being an Englishman. This was rather fatiguing as I had not expected to stay there above two days and was not provided with letters of reccommendation. I was therefore solitary and friendless—The charming situation of

Nice, however, and the romantically beautiful walks in its neighbourhood rendered my detention less distressing than it otherwise would have been. At length a passport was sent me from our Minister at Paris and I was permitted to proceed. From Nice I came to Genoa in a Felucca, coasting along continually near the land for fear of the Privateers that infest the Mediterranian. The shore was a continued chain of high rocky mountains being part of the chain that runs through Italy called the Appenines. In spite of their apparent sterility they were often cultivated to the top with olives, vineyards &c and along the shore we were presented with a succession of villages, towns, Castles, Convents, Seats &c. In the evenings we put in to one or other of the large towns ↑to pass the night↓[7] and generally met with some objects worthy of curiosity. After sailing along in this manner for three days and a half enjoying the most romantic and picturesque views we at length arrived at the celebrated city of Genoa. Here I have found my old friend Hall Storm who has established a house here in company with his brother in law Mr Kuhn.[8] You who have never been from home in a land of strangers and for some time without friends cannot conceive the joy the rapture of meeting with a favourite companion in a distant part of the world. We have been continually engaged since my arrival in talking over old affairs—friendship &c and discussing past scenes of fun and frolick in which we have mutually been engaged. In fact I have had no time to examine the curiosities of Genoa, for though we have wandered through the streets, churches and palaces we were so much taken up with New York that I scarce noticed any thing around me.

26th

I was called off from my letter the day before yesterday to go and look at the palace of the famous Doria.[9] This is the oldest palace in Genoa and situated in the Strada Nuovo, or as the English term it *the Street of palaces*. It is said there is not in all Europe—in all the world—two streets that can equal the Strada Nuovo and Strada Balbe for magnificence of Architecture. They present a continual string of sumptuous palaces decorated on the exterior with marbles, carvings, paintings in Fresco &c and are built by the best Italian Architects. Their interiors correspond in richness of Architecture and in exquisite productions of the Arts. From the grandeur of her palaces and churches this City has acquired ↑with justice↓[10] the name of *Genoa the Superb*. The palace Doria which we went to examine exhibits a striking picture of the transitory nature of human grandeur. In vast halls, its long suits of sumptuous apartments silent deserted and neglected where once the luxurious banquet and midnight revel were celebrated afford a melancholly lesson and testify that the great family of the Doria's is extinct.

The Churches of Genoa have dazzled me with their solemn magnificence. The most costly marbles, gildings, paintings &c are lavished on
them. You will spare me however a description of them, as you may read
one in almost any account of Italy—and after all the descriptions you will
have no correct idea of the originals.[11] But leaving churches—palaces
&c &c to themselves (for my head is really so confused that I cannot
write systematically ⟨about⟩ ↑of↓ them) I will give you a description of
a jaunt that strongly reminded me of some of our excursions to the
Island,[12] both in regard to the pleasures of it and the disasters on returning. I sat off the day before yesterday in the morning with Storm and a
Mr Caffriana[13] an *English Italian* for Sestri, a small country place on the
Mediterranian shore about six miles from Genoa where several of the
Beau-Monde of Genoa have their country seats. It was our intention
to visit some palaces and gardens. We however concluded to pay a visit
to a Mrs Bird, an English lady whose husband was British Consul in
Genoa formerly. Here we found a charming collection of English girls, the
daughters of Mrs Bird and of Mrs Walsh an English lady who is on a
long visit to Mrs Bird. The girls were in high spirits and seemed delighted
to receive a visit from English beaux as they termed us. We prevailed
upon them to accompany us to ramble in one of the gardens that was
laid out in the English taste with Grotto's, temples hermitages, wilder-
nesses &c. After wandering about in this delightful place all the morning
we returned to Mrs Birds where the girls entertained us with singing
and playing on the Harpsichord till dinner. The dinner hour was laughed
merrily away and as soon as it was over we some how or other fell a
dancing to the Harpsichord and jigged away till quite late in the
evening when Storm and myself recollected an engagement we had in
town which we did not dare to neglect. We had therefore to tear ourselves away after having passed by far the happiest day I have spent
in Europe and which by the company the amusements &c strongly
reminded me of the many happy ⟨happy⟩ ↑hours↓[14] I have spent in
America. As we had but a one horsed carriage to drag three of us to
town beside the driver you may suppose our progress did not equal our
wishes; it had begun to rain furiously—we were mired—our horse
stumbled &c &c so that before we reached Genoa the carriage gate was
shut and if we had persisted in proceeding home we would have been
obliged to walk a mile in the rain. We therefore stopped at a little
theatre in the Suburbs of St Pietra d'Arena[15] till the rain subsided which
was near an hour, and then marched home in the dark, often to our knees
in mud and water and arrived too late for any thing but bed. I have
written this account to show you it is possible now and then to stumble
over scenes in Europe similar to those we witness in America, and this
one has brought to my mind many of our marvellous expeditions wherein

we acquitted ourselves so gallantly. I have been considering ever since if I am not somewhat smitten with one of the Miss Birds—a beautiful girl—I have not as yet determined the matter.

Last evening we visited Lord & Lady Shaftesbury who are detained here prisoners of War. *My lord*[16] is one of the richest Noblemen of England. He had the misfortune some time since to fall from his horse by which his most noble pericranium was a little cracked and is not the most sound at this day. I believe he fancied himself in the House of Lords for he harangued us most unmercifully and whirled about from Europe to America and from America to Africa in the space of a single sentence. Her Ladyship was more reasonable and very agreeable.

The Italian ladies far surpass the French in personal charms. They have generally fine figures and handsome features with languishing black eyes full of expression. Their character for intrigue is not unmerited, though the idea that to slight them is often fatal, is as far as I can learn, completely erroneous. Their dress is formed after the french fashion except that they universally wear a veil of white lace or muslin that covers the head and shoulders and falls down before almost to the feet. This when worn by a lady of handsome features and figure has in my opinion, a charming effect; and I have seen some that could have served as fine models for a Madonna.

I have been scribbling I know not What. My ideas are in a state of chaos and I have so many things to see and do that I am in an absolute perplexity. I have to write two or three other letters before the post goes out so that you must be contented with what I have already written and look upon it rather as an apology for a letter—it is not fit to be submitted to the inspection of any but a friend—and even then the friend must be indulgent.

I thank you a thousand times my dear fellow for the information you give me about our circle of acquaintance—it is the only news I have heard of them for a long time, for nobody takes the trouble to give me an account of those little occurrences that I am so anxious to learn. You say you know many things you would have communicated to me by word of mouth but which were too trif⟨f⟩ling to write in a letter. Have I not told you a thousand and a thousand times that nothing is too trifling that relates to my friends or that calls past scenes to recollection. Never be afraid of being too minute when you write to me. Give me every article either amusing or interesting about every body What they say—what they do—how they are—how they look &c &c &c. Heavens you might write sheets full and I would read every article with the utmost eagerness. How does your father, your Mother, your Sister, your Aunts, the Blackwells the Bartows the Swartwouts, the Shuters, Wallaces, Hallets, Salmans,[17] with all the other belles and beaux that ⟨you⟩we know and

that we do not know; let me know all their pursuits amusements &c
&c with all the amours deaths and marriages that occur and I beg of
you let me know what Jack, Brom &c are doing, for though my own
brothers I know less of their maneuvres than of any of my acquaintances
since I left New York. Tell me of every ball, dance, tea party, with every
good thing that is said, every scandal that is broached and every quarrel
that is settled either by words ⟨or⟩ blows or fire arms. I think I have
now given you sufficient hints to enable you to write in volumes and I
hope never to see your letters again commence with "you know not
what to write about.["] I tell you solemnly and *peremptorily* write
about *every thing.* Never leave your letter till the ship is just sailing but
write a little at it about ten minutes each day and I'll warrant you'll soon
be able to swell a packet. Whatever you write to me from this time, and
whatever any of my friends write to me must be directed to my correspondent in Bordeaux[18] *to rest with him* till I write for them from
Paris, otherwise they will dance after Me through Europe and I shall
risque losing them entirely, or if they come to hand I shall have to pay
for their postage *in gold.*

I suppose by this time you have returned to the City in case you
have had to fly ⟨it⟩ from the fever or to retreat during the hot weather.
Heavens how anxious I am to hear how all my friends have weathered
out the summer. Whether they have been "scattered about on the face
of the earth"[19] or permitted to retain quiet possession of their homes
and houses. Write to me how you are pleased with your fathers purchase
at Haerlem[20] and whether there is an agreeable neighbourhood there. An
old gentleman of Bo⟨u⟩rdeaux[21] promised to send out some choice fruit
trees for your father. I do not know whether he will be able ⟨to⟩ *or
careful* to execute his promise and I would not advise you to calculate
much upon it. I shall collect a few of the stones of such fruit as I think
will be worth planting, though I assure you that as far as I have experienced all the fruits that I have eaten in Europe that will thrive in
America, are far superiour in the latter. I have eaten no peaches, cher-
ries or apples by any means to be compared to ours and the pears are,
if any thing, rather superior with us. The plumbs are finer in France
⟨and⟩ about Bordeaux and there is a greater variety, but their chief
advantage over us is in being able to raise grapes, figs, oranges and
lemons, for as to the other kinds of fruit we generally have the
superiority.

How often have I wished myself seated among your family at table,
or ranging about the fields and the *grove* at New Rochelle, and your
mentioning the *little loaves and ⟨the⟩ clams* reminded me strongly of the
"times that are past."[22] However we shall on some future day attack
them with fresh vigour and the birds and beasts of Haerlem shall

tremble at the *noise* of our fire arms. Remember me most particularly to your family and tell your father I have not as yet become a *Coxcomb* though I have travelled through a country that abounds with them. That my manners are much the same as when I left New York though I have continually mingled among people whose manners were entirely different *and* that from what I have seen of Europe I have formed the opinion, and it every day grows stronger, that America is the happiest country in the world and that my fellow countrymen are blind to the blessings heaped upon them. Give my warmest remembrances to my friends at the Island. I have had from Jack[23] an account of the melanchol⟨l⟩y manner in which he commenced the summer campaign in which he was driven *sundry times* into the docks and finally shipwrecked on Long Island. I expect that many similar disasters have taken place in the course of the summer.

Remember me *more over* to the Wallas's[24] and to the *Kitten* who I was in hopes would have become more tame as hot weather advanced. In short give my love, respect, admiration, astonishment and esteem to every body that takes the trouble of enquiring after me, and believe that I am dear John

Sincerely your *friend*
W.I.

Manuscript: Yale.   Published: PMI, I, 87 (in part).

The MS is not in WI's hand; it is possibly in the handwriting of PMI.
John Furman was a fellow student of WI's when he read law in the office of Judge Hoffman.

1. WI's bankers were apparently Kuhn, Green and Company, whose offices in Genoa were managed by Peter Kuhn, Jr. of Philadelphia, Hall Storm's brother-in-law and American consul in Genoa from 1805 to 1807. See *J&N*, I, 92, 549; *Peter Irving's Journals*, p. 16; letter of WI to William Irving, Jr., August 14, 1804.

2. This letter has not been located.

3. The copyist omitted the *d* in this word.

4. These asterisks have been supplied by the copyist and indicate an omission.

5. Frey has not been identified.

6. This insertion is in a hand other than that of the person who copied this letter.

7. This insertion is also in a hand other than that of the person who copied this letter.

8. See note 1 above.

9. Andrea Doria (1468–1560) freed Genoa from the French and established a republic. In 1522 the city presented Doria with a palace overlooking the harbor. About 1529 it was remodeled and made more comfortable and convenient for him, incorporating the designs of Fra Giovanni Angelo Montorsoli (1507–1563) and the decorations of Perin del Vaga (1499–1547).

10. Someone other than the copier of the letter inserted these words.

11. WI briefly describes the churches of Sant'Ambrogio, San Lorenzo, Santissima Annunziata del Vastato, and Santa Maria di Carignano in his journal on October 25, 1804. See J&N, I, 113–14.

12. A possible reference to Long Island where a branch of the Furman family had settled as early as 1645.

13. Edward Caffarena was appointed United States vice-consul in Genoa in 1805. From 1809 to 1819 he was responsible for the United States consular records there. See J&N, I, 117, n. 249.

14. Another insertion by someone other than the copier.

15. San Pier d'Arena, about 2½ miles west of Genoa, had no public theater until 1833, so WI and Caffarena must have stopped at a private theater. See J&N, I, 119, n. 256.

16. For other details about Lord Shaftesbury see WI's letter of September 20, 1804. In his journal WI noted that Shaftesbury had an annual income of £40,000 (J&N, I, 119–20).

17. These are families of the merchant class in New York with whom WI associated.

18. J. J. Bosc & Co.

19. Probably a variant of Gen. 11:4.

20. In July 1804, Gabriel Furman purchased a parcel of about ten acres in Harlem from William Lawrence (Gabriel Furman, Sr., Papers, NYHS).

21. Possibly Jean Ferrière, with whom WI lived in Bordeaux. WI refers to him several times in his journal as "the old gentleman."

22. Possibly a variant of "tyms that have ben past," from Thomas Wyatt's "You that in Love Find Lucke and Habundaunce."

23. Probably Jack Nicholson, one of the Lads of Kilkenny who joined the United States Navy.

24. Probably a variant spelling of the family mentioned earlier. See note 17.

21. To William Irving, Jr.

Genoa Novr. 30th. 1804.

My dear Brother,

I dispatched a long letter to you the beginning of this month[1] by the way of Leghorn together with two or three other voluminous ones to my friends. They contain a sketch of my journey from Marseilles ⟨here⟩ to this city by the way of Nice together with my five weeks detention at the latter place. I hope they have arrived safe to hand and relieved you from any anxiety on my account. I have now been in Genoa ⟨Seven⟩ ↑Six↓[2] Weeks and so far from being tired of it I every day feel more and more delighted with my situation & unwilling to part. I cannot speak with sufficient warmth of the ⟨f⟩ reception I have met with from Storm. We have scarcely been out of each others sight all the time I have been here, and he has introduced me to the first society of Genoa from whom I have received the most flattering attentions. One of the great draw backs upon a travellers pleasures is the reflection that whenever he has found an agreeable resting place or friendly circle of acquaintance or any pleasurable connection in which his heart has become engaged he must soon tear himself away from those enjoyments and again mingle among strangers,—⟨solitary and⟩ where the chance is ten to one if he finds one on whom he can implicitly [*MS torn*][3] or regard. This unpleasant reflection I feel most forcibly at present as I am looking forward to my departure (which will take place in a few days) with a heavy heart. The yellow fever which prevails at Leghorn has completely disconcerted me in the plans I had laid out for my route. It is impossible to describe to you the dread they have in Italy of that malady. Cordonè's (I.E. lines of soldiers) are formed in different parts of the Country to prevent ⟨communication⟩ persons from passing from the infected to the healthy parts without performing quarantine. Any person who breaks thro the Cordonè, and all who should assist any person in so doing whether father, brother child or any other relation, is punishable with death & may be shot immediately. At Leghorn & pisa the quarantines are very long and ⟨it is imp⟩ all Tuscany is surrounded by Cordonès which it is impossible to pass without performing quarantines of two or three weeks.

Thus you see my road is entirely shut up thro that part of Italy—for I should be exposed to innumerable difficulties & embarrassments was I to attempt to pass thro tuscany particularly as I am almost entirely ignorant of the italian language. A⟨n⟩ ship from Philadelphia[4] is now in this port the captain[5] of which had orders to sail for Sicily—If ⟨had⟩ he goes I shall take a passage with him and make a short tour in that very interesting island & from Messina pass over to Naples — If he does not sail as from circumstances I am apprehensive he will not, I shall accept an offer made me by a Danish Gentleman who ⟨is⟩ I have met in company several times in Genoa—who goes from here to Milan and from thence by way of Lodi—Ancona (on the Adriatic) and perugia to Rome, ⟨of⟩ avoiding all Tuscany for fear of quarantines. He has engaged a Carriage open in front but of a peculiar construction well adapted for travelling and calculated to accomodate two persons—and he wishes me to take one seat. This I shall certainly do if I do not go in the American ship—as it will lessen my expences and I shall have the advantage of agreeable company. He ⟨Se a⟩ is a Gentleman that has travelled much both in europe & *America* and speaks english as perfectly as myself. He appears to possess much information & taste & agreeable manners and has brought excellent letters of reccommendation to Genoa. I shall make some stay at Rome and then proceed to Naples where I wish to be in the Height of Carnaval.[6]

I am much concernd to hear that there has been a violent & distructive hurricane on the American coast[7]—I hope it will not occasion much distress in New York among my mercantile friends. I have not been able to learn the time it happend but am apprehensive it must have occurrd near about the time Colden & schiefflin were on the coast, they intended to sail from Bordeaux about the commencement of August.

I wrote you about that time a private letter which I ⟨am apprehensive⟩ fear has miscarried You mentiond to me ⟨that some thing about⟩ that I need not mind exceeding my present finances a little if there was occasion. I then wrote that I expected I should be able to accomplish my tour thro [*word missing*] [*MS torn*] to paris with the sum I have credit for, ⟨This I⟩ but that if you intended I should go to England for a short visit you must send me out something more. This I now repeat from the experience I have already had of the expences of travelling which have nearly doubled in Europe in a few years. I assure you I am strictly economic almost parsimonious—but I find that money will slip away faster than I had anticipated. If you think proper that I should return from some port in france write me word and I will most cheerfully comply. I do not wish ⟨to⟩ you to listen to your generosity so as to ⟨b⟩ injure yourself and I assure you I would rather forego the pleasure of seeing any part of Europe than run my family to expences they cannot afford. Did I not know that the advantages I already possess of travelling are granted me with the most pleasurable sensations I never should have accepted them, but I well know the delight my brothers experience in contributing to the happiness of each other.

Whenever you write me from this time direct your letters to remain with Mr Bosc till I write for them from Paris. If you think proper I should go to England Send me letters of introduction—Newspapers &c &c directed to the New England Coffee house London.[8]

I write in the greatest hurry which must apologize for the want of amusement & information ↑of↓ this letter, besides it goes thro france by the way of Bordeaux & is subject to being opened—

My love to father Mother & all my friends &c

[William Irv]ing [*MS torn*] Junr.   Yours affectionately
                                                                      WI

MANUSCRIPT: Yale. PUBLISHED: PMI, I, 88 (in part).

1. This letter has not been located.
2. The "seven" has been canceled and "six" written above it in another hand, probably PMI's. The printed version in PMI, I, 88, has "six."
3. Three or four words are missing because the corner of the sheet is torn away.
4. The *Matilda*, which had arrived in Genoa on September 29, 1804. See *J&N*, I, 140, n. 319.
5. Matthew Strong.
6. This is probably the celebration before the start of Lent. In 1805 Easter occurred on April 14.
7. This storm took place in the vicinity of Charleston, South Carolina. It

began about 11:00 P.M. on September 7 and continued until 1:00 P.M. on September 9. Several ships sank in the hurricane, and many others were damaged, including *The Rising States,* on which WI had sailed to Bordeaux. The NYEP for September 24, 1804, quotes extensively from the Charleston *Courier* of September 10. In the shipping news of the same issue of the NYEP is a report of the arrival of the brig *Thetis,* Captain Dockindorff, from Bordeaux in fifty-two days. Perhaps this is the vessel on which Colden and Schieffelin sailed from Bordeaux.

8. When WI reached London on October 8, 1805, he stayed first at the New York Coffee House before finding other quarters. This hostelry on Threadneedle Street is first mentioned in the *Daily Post* in 1720. By accepting and receiving correspondence privately, the proprietor of the New England Coffee House, along with many others at the time, was violating a post office regulation against the private handling of letters. See Bryant Lillywhite, *London Coffee Houses* (London, 1963), pp. 387–90.

22. To William Irving, Jr.

Genoa Decr. 20th. 1804

Dear Brother

I yesterday received your Letter No 6 containing extracts from No 5[1] and return you a thousand thanks for the length & minuteness of it. You cannot imagine how enlivening it was to me, and with what a greedy eye I read over every line three or four times

For the generous extension of my credit I can say nothing, my heart is full.[2] I shall now pursue my route with an easy mind, untroubled by those economic fears which have hitherto attended me and ⟨often⟩ continually damped my schemes of pleasure and improvement that were ⟨attende⟩ productive of a little extraordinary expence. Nothing I am convinced makes the heart so *light* as to have the pocket *heavy* — Every additional hundred adds an inch to our height, sets us more "upon our Centre" and infuses a spirit & independence that makes us carry ourselves like men and look every one boldly in the face. I shall let the credit remain with J J Bosc & Co subject to my ⟨draughts⟩ ↑Drafts↓, which I do not expect to make till I return to Paris next Spring. I have drawn out of the hands of My Banker here 1000 Livres of Genoa (about 155 Dollars) for my expences and between five & six hundred dollars which I have lodg'd in the hands of Kuhn & Co. for the remainder I shall take a circular letter of credit from my banker to his correspondents in Messina Palermo, Naples, rome, florence &c at which places I can draw for what money I want & those houses will honor my Bills

part of your Letter was written on the 25th. of Octr. which was *five days after I arrived in Genoa,* and here it found me still. It is a most fortunate thing that I recd. your letters before my departure as they will influence me much in my route. You will be pleased to hear that your wish that I should visit Sicily will be fully gratified, and in a manner most convenient & agreeable to myself. I set sail tomorrow in The Ship Matilda of Philadelphia bound for Messina in Sicily where she takes in a cargo of wines for America. The Ship was formerly a Charleston Packet & has excellent accomodations. The Captain is an honest worthy old gentleman of the name of Strong.[3] He is highly delighted with the thoughts of my going, has laid in excellent stores, prepared the best birth and says he intends to make my passage as comfortable as possible. Had not this opportunity have offerd I would have been obliged to make a long round about tour by the way of Milan Bologna—Ancona &c &c to rome, as all Tuscany is surrounded by *cordoneès* (lines of soldiers) where I should be detained, Quarantined, smoaked & vinegard and perhaps after all not have been sufferd to pass.

Travelling at this particular season is very uncomfortable and the said route would have been in many places very dreary. I shall now be spared the necessity of travelling the same ground twice and can pursue a straight course thro Italy in the spring when every thing will be charming. Tho' Genoa is ⟨not⟩ one of the coldest places in Italy yet I have felt very little of winter. The Snow has fallen on the Mountains & hills adjacent but the town is free from frost. I am perfectly free from cold ↑& cough↓ which used to harrass me in New York in the winter and never I think enjoyed better health & spirits. I shall now speed away to a still happier clime and become in some degree "companion of the spring"[4] The time is excellent to visit Sicily. In summer & during all the warm weather there, the musquitoes gnats &c are very troublesome and added to the heat of the climate they render living almost insupportable. But now the weather is mild & pleasant and the insects have disappeard.

I have been round today to bid farewell to my Genoese friends, and a painful task it was I assure you. The very particular attentions I have received here have rendered my stay delightful. I really felt as if at home surrounded by my friends. Tho my acquaintances were very numerous I particularly confined my visits to three places Lady Shaftesbury's, Madame Gabriac's and Mrs Bird's (the lady of the English Consul). From Lady Shaftesbury I have experienced the most unreserved and cordial friendship, I visited her house every night, dined there frequently & suppd whenever I chose. She has offerd me letters to her friends in England but the suddeness of the ships departure prevents her writing them while I am in Genoa but she will send them to me before I leave Italy unless I see her ⟨g⟩ again myself. ⟨Lord Shaftesbury as I have observed⟩ She has likewise solicited letters for me from some of the Nobility here to their friends in Florence Rome & Naples and gives me a Letter herself to an ↑Italian↓ Nobleman of the first distinction in rome and to an English Captain, prisoner of war in the same City Writing also to the same persons private letters by post in my favor. You cannot think how warmly she has interested herself for me.

His lordship,[5] who I mentiond in a former letter as being an original is a man of an excellent heart and has likewise shewn himself most particularly my friend—Lady Barbara, their daughter, is a Lovely girl of fifteen, full of Spirits ⟨of⟩ & of the best heart in the world. How many happy hours have I passed with this charming family. No restraint nor frigid cerimony is observed in their house; twas all one whether we read or wrote or danced or sung or playd blind mans buff or battle dore & shuttle cock, there were always some company present to join in the sport and every one was at liberty to follow his own inclination

Madame Gabriac's[6] was another favorite visiting place. She is a lady of the first rank and one of the two houses where the Doge & cardinal[7] visit. I have been in company with them several times there. Madame Gabriac talks english extremely well. she is a dear good soul, ever fond of a Joke & ready to laugh—always in good humor and possessd of much wit & brilliancy of understanding

We were always sure of a merry evening in her company when she would discuss the fashionable intelligence of Genoa with a whim & humor peculiar to herself. She expressd the greatest regret at my departure and furnishes me with a Letter of introduction to her friend the Marchesa Moranda[8] at Florence, a Lady of whom I have heard much talk both for beauty & understanding. Madame G ⟨has⟩ will also give me letters for her friends in paris who are of the first rank. Thus you see I shall have a series of acquaintance thro Europe that it is exceeding difficult for an American to make, as our letters are generally to Merchants in the sea ports who are ⟨gene⟩ most commonly a tasteless interested set of beings. Perhaps No American has ever traveld ↑in this country↓ with similar advantages, and surely if travelling is necessary to polish the manners this is the society the most conducive to that end. Neither is this kind of acquaintance so expensive as you might imagine Their pleasures are all among themselves & generally at their own expense, and I have found the Nobility of Genoa by far the cheapest society I ever was in. I dined to day at Mrs Birds at Sestri, to bid her family farewell. I believe I have spoken before to you of this charming woman and her lovely daughters. We have spent several delightful days in their Company at Sestr⟨y⟩i and recd. the most hospitable attentions. All my friends have pressd me most earnestly to return to genoa in the spring and I believe I shall consult my own inclinations and do so for a little while, it will make but a trifling deviation from my route. I shall then see Mr & Mr[s] Kuhn who are at present at Florence performing quarantine. They have written for me to stay at Genoa & pass the winter with them but that you know was impossible. The attentions I have recd. from Storm are of the warmest and most endearing kind. Tis to him I owe all my acquaintance in Genoa and the other ⟨set in⟩ polite acquaintances I shall make in Italy. He is one of the worthiest fellows that god ever created.

I had nearly forgotten to mention to you that I was presented to the Doge on his Levee night by his Nephew Sigr Serra[9] and had a very polite reception.

The letter which you mention Mr Colden was so very kind as to write to me at Toulouse, never came to hand as I stayd but one day in that city. There Seems to have been a fatality attending Coldens letters which generally prevented their arrival at their place of destination. As to his advice that I should have proceeded directly to Paris I differ from him in opinion. I should have arrived at that City without understanding the Language & of course unable to enjoy satisfactorily the amusements and curiosities of that grand repository of the Arts & sciences. I was too weak in health to bear the continual hurry I should have been in nor had I any Letters of introduction there except for our Minister & his son in Law.[10] These and several other reasons would have persuaded me to have continued the route I have pursued and which has given me perfect satisfaction[.] I passed thro the delicious scenes of Gascony & Languedoc in a charming season when all nature was Luxuriant & *riant* when the fruits were ripe & exquisite—and I took the Journey by such easy stages as not to be sensible in any great degree of the heat of the weather.

Your Letters No 4 & 5[11] have not reached me, perhaps No 6 had a quicker passage & has outstripped them as I recd. it in less than two months after it was written.

I mentiond in some of my former Letters a Dr Henory with whom I travelld in some part of my journey. I am sorry to say he was a swindling little scoundrel. For my part I was always on my guard so that he never took me in nor did he attempt it, but I gave him a letter of introduction to Storm from Nice and he made a cunning endeavor to work Some hundred Livres out of S—— but the latter smoakd him and sent him pack-ing. I have since heard that he took in Cathalan our Consul at Marseilles. Thus the world goes—knaves & rogues at every turn. The little Dr was an odd, whimsical, excentric amusing ⟨little⟩ chap and afforded me often high entertainment and I was really paind to find him so worthless a character, but above all poor devils I most sincerely pity a swindler[.] he has a restless life of it continual alarms shifts evasions & appre-hensions.

It is with the greatest uneasiness I hear of the continued precarious-ness of Sister Dodge's[12] health. I wish to heavens I had her with me in these mild climates where her feeble frame would soon recruit. The rude shocks of⟨of⟩[13] the boisterous winters she has to encounter are too violent for a delicate constitution that is at the mercy of every breeze. For myself I am another being. Health has new strung my limbs and endowd me with an elasticity of spirits that gilds every scene with sunshine & heightens every enjoyment. I am now ⟨g⟩ hasting to those scenes of romance & poetic fiction which the ancients so much delighted in and even thought them worthy of being the favorite haunts of *Gods*. Sicily you know is ⟨the⟩ one of the particular spots of Mythologic events and ⟨has is sung⟩ has been sung into eternal celebrity. Every step will seem to me to be on enchanted ground—every breeze seem to waft romance & inspiration.

Give my warm congratulations to Mr & Mrs Paris ⟨for⟩ on the pleasing encrease of their family.[14] Heaven smiles upon their labors and *enriches* them with a *numerous offspring* verily verily ↑as says the Revd Dr Rodgers↓[15] ["]the works of the righteous shall prosper" *"John the sixteenth & twenty seventh verse"*[16]

You have delighted me with the mention you ⟨have⟩ made of a visit to the Hoffmans—God bless them all—I love the whole of them "from the crown of their heads to the soles of their feet"[17] and have passd the happiest moments of my life in their company When you see them again give my *most affectionate* remembrances to them and assure them that I look forward to a meeting with them as one of the most delightful events providence has in store for me.

I am sorry from my heart for Johnsons[18] sufferings—and hope before this time he has experienced a resurrection from his Sepulchre of flannel & blankets—Thus it is "the righteous must sometimes suffer as well as the wicked."[19] however tell him he must *"just take the world as it chooses to go*[.]*"*[20] for my part I would almost willingly take his place to have so charming a nurse[21]—The latter you say sends her love to me—I repay her in the same coin *ten fold*. I am pleased to hear that the theatre is new painted.[22] I have seen several theatres in Europe but none that could equal ours for the ⟨stage⟩ scenery machinery & every thing belonging to the stage departments. This letter has to travel round by the way of Bordeaux so that it must be short, ⟨p⟩ When on board the Matilda I shall write you a *long letter* about every thing & forward it by the same vessel. My *best love* to father & mother & all family & friends

P S. Do not hesitate [to] [*MS torn*] write often[.] I shall arrange circumstances so as to a[*MS torn*]ve your letters safely—you see as yet I have been very fortunate in their reception

Tell Dunlap[23] if I can be of any service to him in England he may command me to the extent of his wishes and I shall be peculiarly happy in executing his commands. You know I am a friend to the theatre

I am finishing this letter in the morning—the wind is fair the day lovely & every thing appears to befriend me—I have to haste & pack up my trunk so that I must tear myself away from the pleasure of writing to you. In a little while I shall be once more on the ocean—I am a friend to that element for it has hitherto used me well and I shall feel quite at home on ship board

You see I set off in high glee tho I expect to have a serious heart ache when I lose sight of Genoa

Heaven bless you my Dear Brother
W I.

Give my most particular remembrances to such of my friends as appear interested in my wellfare—I think of them all but to mention their name[s would] [MS torn] take more time than I can sp[are] [MS torn]

Your old friend T H Storm pays his best respects to yourself family & friends[24]

ADDRESSED: Wm. Irving Junr. Esq / New York / United States of Am / via Bordeaux   DOCKETED: Genoa Dec 20 1804

MANUSCRIPT: Yale. PUBLISHED: PMI, I, 88–91, 92 (in part).

The docket is written in the same hand as that of August 27, 1804, and differs from those on the first two letters to William Irving.

1. These letters have not been located.
2. WI had discussed his unexpectedly heavy travel expenses in his letter of November 30, 1804.
3. Matthew Strong.
4. From John Logan's poem, "To the Cuckoo."
5. Lord Shaftesbury.
6. Marie Elizabeth Célésia, Marquise de Gabriac, was the daughter of the Genoese diplomat Pierre Paul Célésia and wife of the Marquis de Gabriac of Languedoc. See J&N, I, 121.
7. Girolamo Durazzo. See WI to William Irving Jr., September 20, 1804, note 50. Guiseppe Spina (1756–1828) was made cardinal and archbishop of Genoa in 1802. He resigned the archbishopric in 1819.
8. Marchesa Morandà may be the wife of a chemist who supported the French Revolution. See J&N, I, 121.
9. Gian Battista Serra (1768–1855).
10. Robert R. Livingston and Robert L. Livingston respectively.
11. These letters have not been located.
12. Ann Sarah Irving, who had married Richard Dodge on February 14, 1788.
13. The repeated "of" is smudged out.
14. Catharine Rodgers Irving, who was married to Daniel Paris, gave birth to Margaret on September 3 (5?), 1804. Margaret died on September 30, 1821.
15. The Reverend John Rodgers (1727–1811), a liberal Presbyterian minister who became pastor of the Wall Street Presbyterian Church in 1765. He is characterized as "a courtly personage, of gentle and conciliatory manners, but 'uncompromising in matter' " who gave "more encouragement to rebellion, by his

treasonable harangues from the pulpit, than any other republican preacher, perhaps, on the continent" (Martha J. Lamb, *History of the City of New York* [New York, 1877], I, 751; II, 275–76).

16. WI here is apparently parodying the manner of Dr. Rodgers. The passages alluded to do not appear in any of the books of John.

17. Shakespeare, *Much Ado About Nothing*, III, ii, 9–10. The same phrases occur in Beaumont & Fletcher's *Honest Man's Fortune*, II, i, La-poope's speech; and in Middleton's *A Mad World, My Masters*, I, i, 84–85; but it is probable that WI had the Shakespearean passage in mind.

18. John Johnson (1759–1819), an English actor who performed at the Park Theater, specializing in character parts of old men. He served briefly as co-manager of the Park Theater with Joseph Tyler, in March, 1805, after the failure of William Dunlap.

19. This quotation may be WI's version of Gen. 18:25: "That be far from thee to do after this manner, to slay the righteous with the wicked: and that the righteous should be as the wicked, that be far from thee: Shall not the Judge of all the earth do right?"

20. This may be a variation of "take things as they come" (John Heywood, *Proverbs*, pt. I, chap. 4 [1546]) or "take the world as it is, not as it ought to be" (German proverb).

21. A reference to Mrs. Elizabeth Johnson, actress-wife of the ailing John Johnson mentioned above.

22. William Dunlap alludes to this refurbishing: "On the 22d of October, 1804, the theatre of New-York was opened with the Clandestine Marriage, and Village Lawyer,—the theatre having been materially improved" (*A History of the American Theatre* [New York, 1832], p. 324). In the same paragraph Dunlap lists Mr. and Mrs. Johnson as members of the company at the Park Theater.

23. William Dunlap (1766–1820), who had managed the Park Theater since 1798, was having financial difficulties which forced him to close it early in 1805.

24. This sentence is not in WI's handwriting. It was probably added by Storm.

23. *To William Irving, Jr.*

Ship Matilda, Decr. 25th. 1804

My Dear Brother

I promised in my last letter (dated about the 20th inst. & forwarded via Bordeaux) to write you from on board ship and I now set down to devote Christmas day to your correspondence. Having brought my Journal up to the present date I shall give you a few extracts from it.[1]

Christmas day opens on me with a *Sombre* aspect. A head wind, ⟨and⟩ rain & broken sea making a furious noise without, and the honest Captain snoring pretty nearly as loud ⟨at⟩ in his birth at my elbow.[2] However my mind is tranquil—my heart contented and I have arisen before it is well day light to enjoy the pleasure of conversing with you. How joyfully would I transport myself to New York and pass the hollidays among my friends. May they be *merry* times with you all and in your gay moments when you⟨r⟩ toast your *distant friends* may I be rememberd among the rest.

In my last letter from Genoa I mentiond that I was on the point of Embarking with a fine wind & charming weather. I was disappointed in the expectation. The wind blew too strong for the Vessel to warp out of the Harbor and we were detaind till the 23d. when we set sail at two o'clock with a brisk gale and soon left *Sweet Genoa* and all its friendly inhabitants behind us. The Wind died away before evening and the next day it sprung up ahead where it has continued ever since keeping us baffling about opposite Leghorn. ⟨& the adjacent coast of⟩

In Genoa, as I mentiond in my former letters my time passed most delightfully having been introduced by Storm to a most agreeable circle of Acquaintance.

It is painful to witness the depressed state of the Genoese nobility. Deprived of their titles and stripped of part (& sometimes the whole) of their fortunes they are completely under the harrow,[3] fear to shew out with what is left and make as little display as possible. They have no handsome Carriages, their Servants are without livery and themselves dress as plainly as possible.

Madame Brignolli[4] (formerly Marchesa) is one of the greatest fortunes remaining among the nobles and at the head of the Brignolli family. She is a Woman of fine person & features & very elegant manners. During the Summer Months she resides at her palace at Voltri a small town about ten miles to the west of Genoa on the Mediterranean shore. ⟨During⟩ Here she has a private theatre where she gives plays once a week and has very brilliant audiences. On the Seventh of Novr. I set off with Storm to attend one of the performances. We were accommodated with seats in the carriage of Madame Gennistou[5] sister to Madame Gabriac.[6] This lady was one of the maids of honor to the late Queen of France[7] and was witness to many of the scenes of blood that took place in paris at the commencement of the revolution. She was present in the room when the head of the princess Lamballe[8] was struck off by the sanguinary mob. The horrid scene had such an effect on her as to produce a derangement of mind from which she was a long time recovering It has subsided into a melancholy that has become habitual

We found at Madame Brignoli's a number of the *Beau Monde* of Genoa collected in the billiard room and amusing themselves with that game till the commencement of the play. After remaining here about an hour we were summoned to the theatre. This is fitted up with much taste & judgement & at great expence, in one wing of the palace. A place in front of the stage in what we call the pit, is seperated from the other parts of the theatre for the reception of Madame Brignoli's Visitors— the rest of the theatre consisting of the back part of the pit and a gallery is free for the Country people. The play was Voltaires tragedy of Zaira[9] translated into italian. Zaira was performed by a Madame Reverollé[10] and was her first attempt at Theatrics. She is a lady of considerable talents and much beauty[.] she was therefore sure to please. The Hero of the peice was represented by Stephano Brignolli[11] the eldest Son of Madame B. about 18 years old, tall and well made His performance was graceful and energetic, his voice full & manly tho hardly of sufficient extent and flexibility.

As I could not understand the language I was unable to judge how he acquitted himself in the dialogue—but from the repeated *bravo's* and *bravissimo's* he appeared to give great satisfaction. The other characters were sustained tolerably well. Madame ↑B↓ filled one of the female parts with much grace & dignity but had not sufficient scope to display her Dramatic powers. After the play we partook of an elegant Supper served up in a room that was decorated to represent a Grotto. The walls were entirely covered with porcelaine[12] in imitation of shells or scales, and marine productions were distributed in some parts with great taste.

The *toute ensemble* was very brilliant and must have required a vast expence. After supper word was brought us that the rain that had fallen all the evening, together with the floods from the mountains, had swollen a small river that we had to cross in our way to town, to such a degree that it was dangerous to pass it in the dark. We were therefore obliged to rest contented at Madame B's till morning. To pass away the time we adjourned to another room and danced, between the dances some ladies & Gentlemen performed on different instruments & sung. In spight of every endeavor to prevent it, we began to be fatigued and heavy before day break. Storm, having in his usual, careless, excentric whimsical manner for some time endeavord to p⟨u⟩ersuade a young lady to let him lay his head in her lap at length fell asleep on a Sopha and three or four more of the Company soon followed his example. At length the morning dawned and we sat off for home as weary a looking set as ever was seen at the breaking up of a City ball. We nodded to one another very sociably the whole ride and now & then a jolt of the Carriage sent all our sleepy heads together.

Nov 13.[13]

Yesterday Storm & myself rode out to Sestri to Mrs. Bird's (the lady of the English Consul) with an intention of rambling upon the mountains. We found that Lady and her charming daughters is[14] their usual good spirits and they readily consented to accompany us in clambering up the heights—and to guide us to such places as commanded the most beautiful prospects. The ascent of the mountains was steep & rugged

but we were amply repaid by the variety of views that continually
opened upon us. The deep Gullies between the mountains were well
cultivated and interspersed with white cottages and thro the mountain vistas we caught fine glimpses of the sea shore and the pleasantly
situated village of Sestri. One of the highest spots afforded us a distant
view of Genoa, its steeples and towers having a picturesque effect in
the landscape. Turning to the other side we had spread beneath
us a long stretch of the sea shore, enlivened with villages & palaces
and industriously cultivated while behind, the grey appenines as a
contrast to the scene gradually rose from the coast into vast heights
of barren rock. While we rested at this place enjoying the variegated
prospects that surrounded us we were surprized by the sound of
some uncouth instrument & looking round we saw a strange, ragged
figure emerge from a cluster of bushy trees & approach us. He was
short & sturdy. His countenance, brown & full, but good humord and
his black eyes had a peculiar archness of expression. His clothes were
of the *rain bow* order and might well have vied with Josephs garment
of many colors and an old wo↑o↓llen cap graced his crown. His instrument was merely a piece of reed open at both ends with three
slits that ran ⟨nearly⟩ about half its length, and by blowing on this
and humoring the slit part with his hand he produced a sufficient
variety of notes to perform a few rude rustic airs. He advanced
towards us with his cap under his arm—played two or three of his
tunes and then handed us very good humoredly his instrument to
examine. We gave him a few sous tho he had not requested them. He
made no acknowledgments but laughed & appeard mightily pleased—
pulld some mushrooms out of his Cap and began to eat them raw. He
told the ladies his name & said he knew where they lived & would
come to their palace & play on his reed under their windows. We afterwards learned from some peasants that he was foolish, but an in-
nofensive good humord fellow that rambled about the neighborhood
of sestri and was supported by the peasants.

   Advancing a little further up the mountain we stopped at a peasants
Cottage built of Stone in form of a square tower & of a picturesque
appearance, ⟨Here the⟩ being half embowerd in large Chestnut trees.
Here the ladies told us they had once taken shelter when a sudden
shower of rain had surprized them in one of their rambles & they had
been so much delighted with the inhabitants of the Cottage as to
be induced frequently to visit them. The good folks saw us as we
approachd and came out to meet us. The family consisted of an old
man and his wife, three daughters & two sons. The old people were a
healthy contented looking couple and the girls were the handsomest
looking female peasants that I have seen in Italy—or I may say in

Europe. The youngest in particular had a blooming complexion, fine black eyes a beautiful set of teeth and when she smiled, two of the prettiest dimples imaginable; her light brown hair was turnd up behind & confined in a silk net as is the fashion of the Country—and before, it curled in natural ringlets about her temples & forehead. Her name was as pretty as herself, and↑one↓of those which we call romantic, tho' a very common one in Italy—it was Angelina. (I E *little angel*)

The inhabitants of the Cottage Crouded around us, seeming much pleased with our visit and delighted to see the ladies. After stopping with them a little while we sat off to ascend higher up and the pretty Angelina accompanied us to shew us to a pleasant spot. The place where she led us was a small plain that formed a kind of terrace on the top of one of the heights, and commanded extensive and charming views.

We remaind here a long while before we were satisfied with admiring the country around us and in the mean while Angelina employed herself in gathering wild flowers which she made up in to boquets and presented to the ladies. We asked her a number of Questions and there was a simplicity and artlessness in her replies that delighted us

She told us she was eighteen years of age and tho within six miles of Genoa she had only been there twice in her life. Mr Wilson[15] (a scotch Gentleman in company with us) asked her if she had not any sweetheart yet—She blush'd & smiled but replied with-out hesitation that "Jacimo loved her and she loved Jacimo likewise—and that they were to be married in about a year." We asked her who Jacimo was, and she answerd that he lived in Sestri, and came to see her very often and she saw him every sunday when she went to church to Sestri—that he was a charming young man—a *very charming young man.* (uno amabillissimo Giovonotto,) We could not help smiling at the warmth and sweetness with which she utterd the last words, I believe she perceived it, and tho apparantly accustomed to speak her thoughts without reserve—she thought she had expressd them rather feelingly on this occasion for she cast her eyes to the ground & blushd still deeper. In short—there was a gentleness a simplicity a *naïveté* in this *child of nature* inexpressibly interesting and as you wish me to be minute & particular I thought you could not but be pleased with a discription of her. Tho dressd in the common habilliments of the country, there was a neatness & *propreté* about her seldom to be found among the peasants except on Sundays & hollidays.

We returned to the Cottage to dispatch some bread & butter we had brought with us by way of luncheon. The good people were very anxious to please. They produced a pitcher of milk to eat with our bread—and were very assiduous in attending on us. Good humor and

content seemed to reign in this happy family and for the first time I realized in Europe, the many poetic Discriptions I have read of rustic felicity—
   (This account of the pretty cottager I beg you to communicate to
James Paulding. When at Bordeaux I recd. a letter from him[16] in which
among other solemn charges he enjoind me if ever I met 'in some
valley in the "hollow breast of Appenine" a fair flower blooming
ungatherd & unknown' that I should rescue her from oblivion by
describing her to him. I hope I have acquitted myself in this particular
to his satisfaction. I should have e'er this have written James a long
letter—but consider how many I have to write to, how much to see,
how much to study (having two languages to acquire) but notwithstanding time is so very precious ⟨t⟩with me, I shall one of those
days set down and afflict him with an epistle of a most grevious
magnitude containing divers marvellous details and pithy observations)

Novr. 14th.[17]

At eleven Oclock today took place the execution of a Notorious
Robber who has for some time past made a great noise in Europe and
was known by the name of *The great Devil of Genoa*[18] (Il grande
Diavolo). As this was a fellow of no little Celebrity I have been
curious in collecting some particulars concerning him. His real name
was Joseph Musso. he was a Genoese by birth, of obscure parentage
and followed the occupations of a common laborer or peasant till the
time the Germans besieged Genoa. He then enlisted under the
German Standard, served as a guide and by his bravery acquired
some inferior commission. When the German Army withdrew from
the country he remained behind but being outlawed he did not dare
to appear in his native city. His military life had inured him to toils &
dangers & gave a warlike turn to his disposition. His fortunes were
desperate—Every door to an honest subsistence in his own country was
shut against him. ⟨and⟩ Since then the world ⟨allowed⟩ afforded "no
law to make him rich"[19] he determined to set it at defiance and sacrifice
his honesty to his necessities. He soon found companions equally
desperate with himself and formed a band that in a short time became
notorious and dreaded for its intrepid exploits. He swore eternal
enmity to the French and particularly to Bonaparte. The appenines
in the neighborhood of Genoa afforded safe retreats for his gang from
whence they frequently descended to lay travellers under contribution & plunder convoys of Merchandize. A favorite scene of his attacks
was at the Boquetto[20]—a rugged pass over a mountain on the road to
Milan between twenty & thirty Miles from Genoa and the only pass
by which a carriage can leave the ligurian territories. Here from the
steepness & roughness of the mountain it is impossible for either

carriage or horseman to proceed faster than a slow walk[.] they were therefore unable to escape by flight—and robberies were incessant on this spot. He shewed, however, great discrimination in his deprada- tions, ⟨leaving it⟩ generally robbing the rich & leaving the poor un- molested & even relieving the⟨m⟩ir necessities with part of his spoils. The poor peasantry frequently experienced the effects of his bounty and he was careful to cultivate a good understanding with all the peasantry in his neighborhood. He was therefore very secure from being betrayd by them even when they knew his lurking places and large rewards were offerd for his apprehension. His depredations were not entirely confined to the neighborhood of Genoa, but extended to other parts of Italy, to France Germany spain & portugal and he has been condemnd to death and prices offerd for his head by different courts in those different countries. His band seldom consisted of above eighteen or twenty but they were all men of desperate courage, & their mode of life had inured them to dangers and hardships. The name of *The Great Devil* (given him in consequence of his daring exploits) soon became universally dreaded. Troops of soldiers were sent out to take or destroy him but he invariably escaped from their toils. At one time he and his comerades were surrounded on top of a mountain but they cut thro their enemies & effected their escape. His bodily strength & agility was astonishing—running with the greatest swiftness among the roughest places of the mountains and bounding among the rocks & precipices like a goat. Another time a body of soldiers surrounded a small hut in which he was sleeping, he leaped out of a window, fought his way through them and got off unhurt though a volley of musketry was fired after him. The common people believed that he carried about a charm with him that renderd all attempts against his life ineffectual. His relations and friends in Genoa gave him notice of every thing that was carrying on so that he knew when to profit by convoys of Merchandize or to escape parties that were sent out in pursuit of him. At one time when a body of soldiers were searching for him in the mountains he was sailing off the harbor in a small boat—Another time an officer of Police was sent to insinuate him- self into his band and act as a spy. Musso had full information of the matter and when the man presented himself to him & offerd his services as a man who was unfortunate & ill treated by the world Musso turnd to some of his gang who were present orderd them to "lead forth that man and shoot him"—the command was instantly obeyd.

There were several instances of his detaining persons of consequence or property, in the mountains, till they sent to their friends for the ransom he demanded—any one however that came to trade with him for his spoils might rely on his *Honor* & safely bring any sum of money for the purpose. He had once captured a rich convoy of Merchandize belonging to a Genoese merchant. The latter sent his brother to treat for their redemption. Musso gave him a meeting, having his guards stationd at a little distance to prevent surprise. The Merchant offerd him a price very inferior to the value of the Goods "Do you think" Says Musso "Your brother would have sold them at so miserable a rate!—They have become mine by capture and I cannot think of *sacrificing* my Goods at so inferior a price." The Merchant passed the night tranquilly in Mussos tent, confiding ↑in↓ his assurance of Safety and in the morning took his leave unmolested altho' he had a large sum of gold by him to make the purchase. He afterwards returnd with the sum Musso demanded.

It would be tiresome to enter into a detail of his different exploits during several years that he followed this kind of life, his robberies were innumerable and sometimes accompanied with murders, tho I do not know that he ever committed the latter wantonly. After the many regular attempts that had vainly been made to apprehend him, the business was effected by a mere accident. He had sailed from Gibraltar to Trieste a port in Germany to the eastward of Venice. While performing Quarantine there, he had a violent quarrel with the master and swore that the latter should not live ⟨f⟩ long after they landed. Intimidated by this menace and by the looks & manner of the person who made it the Captain as soon as he landed applied to the proper authorities for protection ⟨against a⟩ The Magistrate applied to the Genoese Consul to become responsible for his Countryman. The Consul was struck with the name & immediately suspected from the description ↑given↓ that it might be the notorious robber, of whom (in common with all genoese authorities) he had been put on his guard. He went on board of the Vessel & was confirmed in his suspicions. He had him instantly thrown into prison and wrote word of the affair to Genoa. A company of soldiers were directly dispatched who brought him to Genoa where he was closely confined in the Tower. After an imprisonment of three months he was ⟨condemned⟩ convicted and sentenced to be shot. ⟨He was brought to⟩ A Gentleman of my acquaintance happened to be present when he was brought to the ⟨pr⟩ chapel of the prison to recieve his sentence. He said Musso came skipping down stairs two steps at a time with a soldier each side of him, smoaking his pipe very cooly. When the priest read his sentence he shewed no Signs of agitation but replied carelessly "*è bene* (very well) you might as well have sentenced me at first & spared these three months imprisonment." He was then going off but stopped and turning briskly round—"Stop" says he "you have forgot to tell me when I am to be shot"[.] the priest replied on Monday—"Well" says

Musso "this is friday night—Saturday—one—Sunday two—Monday three (counting his fingers)—three days *è bene*" He was again going off very unconcernedly—but added "I suppose I may see my Sister & relations before I am shot" He was told that could not be granted "Then." replied he "they will have to drag me to the place of execution for my own feet shall not carry me there." He was however allowed to see his relations next day and sunday being St Martins[21] when all the Genoese eat Raviolli (a favorite dish of paste & meat) he was served with ⟨an ex⟩ a dish of the kind cooked in the best manner. It is a Custom at Genoa always to give the condemnd a bottle of good wine before their execution and they searchd all Genoa for a bottle of the finest, which was furnished by an old genoese princess of my acquaintance.

This morning all the lower class of Genoa was in commotion to see him suffer his sentence. He ⟨had⟩↑having↓ a number of relations in Genoa and the peasantry being highly prepossessed in his favor from the liberality with which he had often distributed his plunder among them, ⟨T⟩the police were apprehensive an attempt might be made to rescue him. A large body of soldiers were therefore orderd out to attend him to the place of Execution. The Streets, Windows &c were thronged with spectators to catch a sight of him as he passd. Having in common with the multitude a great curiosity to see this singular man I stationd myself near the gate of the City at which he was to go out & had a tolerable view of him as he went by. He appeared to be about five feet eight inches stout & well set of a dark complexion with strong but good features & immense black eye brows. He was twenty six years of age. Two priests attended him to whom he appeared to listen very attentively & he held a small cross between his hands. He was shot on the ⟨small⟩ banks of a small river[22] that runs without the town and sufferd his sentence in a manly decent manner.

perhaps I have been too minute & tiresome in my account of this man—I can only say, I am complying with the repeated requests I have recieved to be particular even in trifles. He is a fellow that has made some noise in Europe—an *anticipated* account of his apprehension was published some time ago in England[23] while he was still ranging the mountains and an afterpiece written of which he was the hero. In a better cause he might have distinguished himself to advantage—but even as a chief of banditti his courage & genius commanded admiration. In fact which in a moral sense is the most criminal the Great Devil of Genoa who eases a few rich individuals of their superfluities *or*[24] the Great Emperor of France who lays whole nations under contribution and entails poverty & wretchedness on thousands!—

Novr. 16.[25]

Yesterday Storm and myself dined at Lord Shaftesburys There were but three or four Visitors at table beside ourselves. His lordship expresses the greatest esteem for the Americans and the highest opinion of our Country. With Lady Shaftesbury I am particularly delighted— there is something in her looks & manners that reminds of Mrs Hoffman and yet there are no two women that, taken generally, are more different. Whatever the cause is, I know not, but I rarely see Lady S——— without thinking of Mrs. H. & I am ever delighted with any thing that reminds me of an amiable & far distant friend. After dinner in the evening more company came in and violins having been pro- vided we had a very pleasant little dance. Ices & iced lemonades are handed about during the dances and the italians do not hesitate to take them when in a state of the highest perspiration. A great amusement of the Genoese is playing at different games such as *My ladys toilet— passing the key* &c but a very favorite one is the *tableau* (I E picture). This ⟨we⟩I have seen played frequently at Lady Shaftes- burys, it requires a good memory and much historical reading to play it well. One person is sent out of the room—the rest dispose themselves in a group so as to represent some transaction in history such as the death of Cato—Brutus's sentence on his sons &c The person is then calld in who guesses what historical incident it is intended to represent. I have rarely seen them fail in guessing and one or two who were *improvisatori* (I E persons endowd with a native talent of making verses extempore) even sung the subject in verses by no means con- temptible.

December[26]

Of the different palaces & churches I have examined together with their paintings &c I forbear to give you a discription. It would but be a dry and uninteresting detail and after all you would not be able to form any correct idea of the things described. The palaces are as open to your inspection as the churches—you need only enter the hall where some servants are always in waiting and on signifying your wish to look at the appartments, one of them will immediately atten[d] [MS torn] you sometimes with a catalogue of the paintings in his hand open all the rooms and display every thing worthy of observa- [tion.] [MS torn] For this you pay him a trifling gratuity. I was rather delica[te] [MS torn] at first in entering so unceremoniously into private houses, b[ut] [MS torn] I soon found out that it was a very common thing, and practise[d] [MS torn] by every traveller. In fact in these countries as long as you have money in your pocket you may go any wheres. The family gen[erally] [MS torn] reside in appartments of the

Palace, that are less splendid—and k[eep] [*MS torn*] the others for shew
& company. The best rooms in the pala[ces] [*MS torn*] are on the
second story. The first story being used for nothin[g] [*MS torn*] but
store rooms & sometimes servants appartments. From the[se] [*MS torn*]
you enter most commonly into a large Hall, paved with m[arble]
[*MS torn*] & ornamented with marble pillars, but the whole is
misera[bly] [*MS torn*] dirty being never cleaned—for the Italians never
think of [cleaning] [*MS torn*] the halls staircases & corridors of their
houses. In this hall y[ou very] [*MS torn*] often find a cobler seated with
his stall and his old mend[ed] [*MS torn*] shoes & boots hung up at
the grating of the windows. This has caused a great mistake in the
⟨discriptions⟩↑accounts↓ of some travellers [who?] [*MS torn*] mention
that the owners of some of the finest palaces in italy a[re] [*MS torn*]
coblers &c whereas these geniuses are sufferd to have their stall[s]
[*MS torn*] in the halls from favor or long custom. From the Halls you
ascend to the second stor⟨y⟩ies by noble marble stairs. As genoa is
⟨over⟩situated along the f⟨oo⟩eet of hills they have to make the most
of their ground. This is the reason why the streets are so uncommonly
narrow. The houses are very high and a number of families live in
each house one above another to the very garret.

Tho' the Catholic religion has received a great shock in Genoa since
the french have had possession of it, yet it still retains much of its
former pomp & ceremony. There were formerly a vast number of
convents in and about the city, most of which have been stripped of
their property—abandond by their inhabitants and ruined by the mob.
Some few still remain but in a state of great poverty. Religious processions are no longer frequent in the streets but are generally confined to their churches except on particular occasions. The other
morning I attended Lady Shaftesbury & Lady Barbara to the church of
Notre dama De Vigne[27] to hear a grand concert that was to be given
in honor of some saint.

The church is one of the smaller ones of Genoa but well built and
richly ornamented with paintings gildings &c. The Cielings were hung
with festoons of red & blue Silk and the Marble columns coverd with
Crimson Damask. I was surprised that a people of so much judgement
& taste ⟨of⟩↑as↓ the Italians should be guilty of such a glaring absurdity.
As if the beautiful proportions of finely painted cielings of their church
could recieve any improvement by being disguised & disfiguerd by
gaudy strips of silk. or a noble pillar of fine marble needed a red jacket
to embellish it. They might with equal reason dress up their most
beautiful Statues in silks & sattins. The Orchestra was very numerous
and the vocal parts chiefly by Dilletánti (amateurs). The church music

of the Italians is extremely appropriate. It has a simplicity and grandeur best calculated to produce the sublime in Music and [we]ll [*MS torn*] suited to the dignity of the place and the solemnity of the occasion. In the churches here there are no fixed seats as in ours in America— These would injure the beauty of the building[.] rush bottomd chairs are kept in a corner of the church and brought to you by women to whom you pay two or three sous

A great annoyance in the churches, are the numerous beggars that swarm around you, and I never before, knew any so importunate. I have been amused at seeing them attack — an honest Catholic while at his prayers, the honest man however, had his thoughts too intently fixed on *things above* and continued his *ave marias* with tenfold devotion—nothing however would discourage his assailant who kept on worrying him for half an hour till he was fairly driven out of his strong hold of prayer & meditation and had to be charitable in his own defence. I have remarked in my former letters the numbers of beggars that I met with in france but they are nothing to compare with the multitudes that swarm in genoa[.] yet I am told that in some other Italian cities they are still more numerous. The demands upon your charity is incessant when walking the streets—and from objects of real want and misery. I almost fear I shall become callous to scenes of wretchedness from having them so continually before my eyes. Indeed the Italians seem to be completely so—for, at the very moment they are addressing their prayers to heaven for a continuance of the good things of this world—they can shut their ears to the earnest entreaties of a miserable half naked being at their elbow who desires but a sous or two to keep him from starving.

There certainly is something very solemn & imposing in the ceremonies of the Roman church. Unwilling as we may be to acknowledge it—it must be confessd that forms & ceremonies & situations & places, have a powerful effect on our feelings in matters of religion. To enter a supurb & solemnly constructed edifice

> Whose Ancient pillars rear their marble heads
> To bear aloft its archd & pondrous roof—[28]

gives us a dignified idea of the being to whom it is erected. Its long & ⟨dimly lighted⟩ ↑lofty↓ aisles & ⟨marbled⟩ ↑dimly lighted↓ chapels adorned with paintings & statues pointing out some Action or attribute of the Deity have an impressive appearance & the gloomy grandeur of the whole ⟨strikes⟩ ↑inspires↓ us with reverence & respect.

> "Looking tranquility it strikes an awe!"[29]

Then the Service itself has such an air of pomp & sublimity that I always feel more filled with an exalted idea of the deity than at any other time.—The Superb altars magnificently decorated & illuminated—the Solemn movements of the priests & the humble prostration of the Congregation The full chant of the choir, and the pealing sound of the organ swelling thro the arched aisles & dying away in soft gradations—the incense arising in fragrant columns before the Grand altar as if ascending to the "heaven of heavens"[30] a grateful offering of homage—has altogether an effect on my feelings irresistibly solemn.

Do not fear that I am turning Catholic—I only shew you how easily the imagination of an indifferent spectator may be heated by form & shew. In matters of religion it is the most assailable part of the man—and ⟨who⟩ were I attempting to introduce a new Doctrine my attempts should chiefly be directed against the imagination.

The roman church multiplies its saints to such a degree that a poor Catholic I should imagine must be often puzzled in his choice which to apply to, to plead his cause at the high tribunal of heaven—Several of them are of particular eminence and like our Great Lawyers—engross the ⟨greatest⟩ ↑chief↓ part of the business. Every Saint ⟨I beli⟩ however "*has his day*"[31] ⟨and⟩ which is religiously kept by his particular admirers. This reminds me of a story of an honest scotchman who boarded in a Catholic family. He was once told that he must fast the next day as it was *all saints day*[.] to this he made no objection thinking it the least mark of respect he could shew to so holy a body—a few days after he was told he must fast again—'And wha must I fast for noo" cries he "For St. Andrew" was the reply "Hoot awa mon" says Sawney "I fast for no St Andrew[.] why the Deel did he keep oot o' the way whan I fasted for *a the Saints* in a droove?"

———

Since the revolution much more liberty & freedom has introduced itself into the customs & manners of the Genoese. They now permit their daughters to frequent balls & public places a thing not known of before the revolution. Young ladies of respectability, however, are not permitted to walk out or visit without the company of their father, mother, gouvernante, or some other Sage personage and such a sight as a young gentleman gallanting a young lady along the street would really (to use a cant phraze) *astonish the natives*. It is only *married* ladies that are entitled to free egress & regress & unrestraind liberty of conduct. I was talking on this subject to a Lady of my acquaintance the other evening. and mentioning the vast difference of American manners in this respect. That our most respectable young ladies walked the streets entirely alone, or in the company of young gentlemen that they visited in the same manner—That young gentlemen attended them home in the evenings—in short that there were no suspicious restraints laid on their intimacy—The good lady ⟨was⟩ listend attentively to my account and was exceedingly surprized—but said "it was a mark of the simplicity and ⟨goodness⟩ honesty of our manners, but that it would never do in Italy & france—in both which countries the young ladies are kept under great restraint—"you are a happy set of beings" said she "in America, you still possess innocence of thought—which has long since been banishd from this Country."

To these restraints we may ascribe the tacit compliance with which italian ladies enter into the matrimonial estate when their affections have no interest in the union. They merely consider it as a priviliged state in which they can indulge themselves with greater freedom. The Italian husband perhaps conscious of this very often becomes jealous of his wife nor does he generally take much pains to hide any distrust that enters into his bosom. So much the worse for him. The lady seeing that implicit confidence is not placed in her virtue thinks there is no longer any advantage in observing those vows, when they will not credit her for an *inclination* to keep them Sacred and this among others may be one reason of the Notorious unfaithfulness of Italian Wives.

The News of the Coronation of Bonaparte[32] arrived lately at Genoa. You may well suppose, that he is no favorite in this City, whose fortunes he has almost ruined—whose citizens he has nearly impoverishd.[33] Still however there was a necessity to rejoice in compliment to the tyrant—and like many other places that are groaning under his oppressions—put on a show of joy while the heart is aching. The Govt. have therefore been for some time talking of giving a ball in honor of the *benefactor* of their Country. This has been deferred repeatedly and I was somewhat surprized at the delay till I was told by Madame G⟨abriac⟩—who enjoys the Confidence of the doge—that the government was really *too poor to give a ball!*" "and it would be a hard thing" added she ["]to have to run in debt in rejoicing at the success of the very man who has *drained our purses!*"

The French Minister[34] intends giving a splendid ball on the occasion, and indeed he can well afford it, as he takes care to pay himself well for his public services. He is in fact a little tyrant at Genoa being both feard & hated throughout the republic. He is one of the miscreants that played a principal part in france during the *reign of Terror* and gave the casting vote for the death of the King. He was the best friend Bonaparte had in the Commencement of his Carreer and it was thro his influence that ↑Bonaparte↓ was first put in Command. He is a man of strong passions & a Vindictive spirit—It is thought that Bonaparte merely retains him in favor thro fear and that one day or other he will meet with his deserts from his former Protegée At present he privately controls the doge & senate nor dare individuals displease him. Madame G⟨abriac⟩ expressd great reluctance to go to his ball—"but" said she "I do not *dare* refuse."

The Genoese were antiently renowned for their craftiness & want of ⟨faith⟩ ↑honesty;—↓ —and *Ligurian faith* was proverbial among the romans. The present generation seem to ⟨have descended legitimately from their ancestors⟩ ↑be their legitimate descendents↓ if we may judge from the dealing of their tradespeople. It is a saying in Italy that "It takes six Christians to cheat a Jew & six Jews to cheat a genoese but a *Genoese Jew* is a match for the Devil himself.[35] The Sumptuary Laws that formerly restricted the dress of the people in certain respects— no longer exist. The Genoese men are not however very remarkable for finery of dress. They follow the french fashions—particularly the women. There is notwithstanding—one article of female Dress which has been handed down from generation to generation & is still re- tained by all ages, ranks & fortunes. This is a kind of veil formd of an oblong piece of Lace, Cambrick, Muslin or Callicoe—which is thrown over the head & shoulders & falls down in front—It sets off a pretty face, I think, to great advantage. I have seen a pair of languish- ing blue eyes from under such a veil—give the countenance all the air of a beautiful madonna.

The Arsenal[36] which was formerly an object of curiosity ⟨is⟩ has been stripped of most of its contents at the time when the french committed such outrages in Genoa. The⟨y⟩ ↑mob↓ ran about the streets with old helmets on their heads—several of which were elevated on liberty poles and being painted up—served for liberty caps—others fell into the hands of some thrifty *knights of the needle* who put feet to them and converted them into chaffing dishes to heat their gooses[37] In which ignoble employment I saw many of them retained in the streets of Genoa to this day. I have seen none but helmets of inferior quality probably intended for common soldiers—and in the enterance to the National palace I saw several suits of armor hanging against the wall Had any opportunity presented ↑to forward it↓ I would have pur- chased one of the Taylors chaffing dishes & have sent it to you as a curiosity. Many of them may have seen service in the holy wars as the Genoese were very conspicuous in the times of the Crusades and still bear the *red cross* as the arms & standard of the republic.

I have given you such extracts from my Journal as I think will be

most amusing, and I expect by this time you are almost tired of it—
so I will bid it farewell and bring you up to the present moment in
which I am writing after which we will prosecute the voyage very
sociably together. I told you in the commencement of the letter that
we left Genoa with a fine breeze—The town gradually receded from
my view—Sestri and its environs—the favorite scene of many a romantic
ramble likewise faded in the distance and before evening the whole
was indistinguishable. The next morning (24th.) We found ourselves
quite becalmed—The Weather mild and delightful and the sky without
a cloud excepting a few morning ones that hung about the horison
and were gradually lighted up with ruddy tinges. In a little time the
sun emerged in full splendor from the Ocean—his beams diffused a
blaze of refulgence thro the clouds of indiscribable richness—The curl-
ing tops of the waves seemed tipp'd with gold and the snowy summits
of Corsica & the opposite shore of Italy brightned with reflection of
his rays—⟨So enchanting a scene⟩ Had those happy days continued
when the Deities made themselves visible to man and now and then
paid him a sociable visit—we might perhaps have been entertained
by the *raree shew* of Neptune & Ampithrite and all their gay train of
Nerieds & Dolphins—Such a morning would have been the very
time for them to have taken a *drive* round their dominions and examine
that all was safe after the late Stormy Weather. But those days of
romance are over—The Gods are tired of us heavy mortals and no
longer admit us to their intimacy. In these dull *matter of fact* times
our only consolation is to wander about the haunts they once frequented and endeavor to make up by imagination the want of the
reality. There is a poetic charm that diffuses itself into our ↑ideas↓
(if I may so express myself) in contemplating this classic part of the
world. Our imagination becomes tinctured with romance and we look
around us with an enthusiastic eye that heightens every scene, ⟨and w⟩
We can scarcely behold objects in their true light from the fiction and
illusion that envellopes them. Tis like beholding a delightful landscape from an eminence on a beautiful sunset. A delicious mistiness
is spread over the scene that softens the harshness of particular objects
& prevents our examining their forms too distinctly—A glow is thrown
over the whole that by blending & softening & enriching gives the
prospect a mellowness a sweetness a loveliness of coloring not absolutely its own but derived by the illusive light that is shed upon it.
I do not know whether I make my ideas well understood.—Those
sensations must be felt, to be well comprehended—but they are
delicious in the extreme.

———

I began this letter on christmas day—it is now the evening of the twenty eighth, all this while have we been beating about in nearly the same place among some small Islands that lie between Corsica and the Tuscan shore. We have been constantly worried with calms & baffling winds and frequent showers of rain. The weather, however, is remarkably temperate, and ⟨I have felt⟩ I have not found it uncomfortably cold since we saild from Genoa. The ship was formerly a charlestown packet and has consequently very good accomodations, but is by no means a fast sailer. There are three other passengers— Genoese Captains of Vessels who talk french very well, they sleep in the Steerage and leave me the Cabin to myself. The Captain is an honest worthy old soul of a religious turn (tho he never talks of religion) and violently smitten with an affection for Lunar observations. The old gentleman has likewise an invincible propensity to *familiarize* the names of people—its always *Tom* Truxton—*Kit* Columbus & *Jack* Styles—with him—and he cannot tell you the name of the author of a book without *Jacking or Gilling* him He is extremely obliging & good humord and strives to render my situation as agreeable as possible.

We have passed the small islands of Gorgona and Capraia[38] which are chiefly inhabited by fishermen—and are now endeavoring to weather the Island of Elba.[39]

This Island was antiently called by the Greeks Æ'thalia and by the romans Ilva—The principal town is Porto Ferraio[40] antiently termed Portus Argoris from ⟨the⟩ Argos the ship of Jason, which it is said passed into the Medditerranean and Homer mentions that Jupeter protected the Vessel in its passage by Scylla & Charybdes.[41] Virgil mentions that Æneas received a supply of 3000 men from the island of Ilva.[42] It is situated in latitude 42 deg 50 min ⟨&⟩ is of a triangular form and nearly 100 miles in circumference.[43] On the West side is a high mountain called Della Calamita from the load stone (calamita in italian) found frequently in its neighborhood.[44] Some travellers have asserted that[45] the attraction of the load stone is felt at some distance from the Island particularly in the straights of Piombino— but this the Genoese Captains who were onboard assured me was not the case.

Tho the island is generally rocky and the soil very scanty & shallow yet it produces ⟨ve⟩ excellent fruit and fine ↑white↓ wine that goes to the Leghorn Market. It also contains a mine of Iron[46] that supplies all Italy. Small as the island is it was formerly divided between three neighboring potentates viz. The prince of Piombino—The Grand Duke of Tuscany and the King of Naples, at length it was ceded to France in whose hands it still remains. It is situated opposite the tuscan state from which it is divided by the straights of Piombino.

I have now brought you up to the present moment, so as it is late I will make no "reflections upon what has been said"[47] but *turn in* comfortably for the night. I agree most heartily with honest Sancho Pança in blessing th⟨at⟩e man who first invented "that self same thing calld sleep"—not because it "covers me all over like a cloak"[48] but because ⟨it⟩ I ↑am↓ transported in a moment across the countless waves that roll between me & America ⟨and⟩ ↑&↓ placed ⟨me⟩ again in the delightful society of my friends. Scarce a night passes but ⟨what⟩ I visit New-York in my dreams, and to reccollect them in the morning is one of my ⟨great⟩ sweetest enjoyments.

29th.

Early this morning the Wind sprung up at the northwest, the Clouds had dissapeared and the Sun rise was clear and beautiful. After several days of Calms, head winds & rain such weather is really inspiring. We have at length to our great satisfaction, cleared the Island of Elba and are now passing between it and the Island of Planosa.[49]

The latter is a low flat of about a league in extent in Lat. 42.34— It was called by the Romans *Planasia* and is celebrated by the exile and death of Caesar Agrippa. This Caesar was the son of Julia and Marcus Agrippa and Grandson of Augustus (Julia being Augustus' daughter by his first wife Scribonia whom he afterwards repudiated) Livia the second wife of Augustus, ruined Caesar in the affections of his Grandfather, by different intrigues—Who confiscated his estate and banished him to the Island of Planasia—About eight years after Augustus Secretly ⟨p⟩ made him a visit—which Livia hearing of dreaded that he would be recalld—to prevent which she hastned the death of the Old King and sent some of her creatures to kill the young prince—The latter made a brave resistance and fell coverd with wounds.[50] Planosa at present is uninhabited—It yeilds a little grain and is cultivated by people from Elba who ⟨come⟩ ↑cross↓ over at the proper seasons to sew & reap. It is a place of shelter and Ambuscade for small privateers that infest these parts and lay in wait here to sally out on vessels as they pass. Those little privateers are of the kind that seamen term *pickaroons*. They are unprincipled in their depredations plundering from any nation. One of the Genoese Captains assured me that they were worse than the Algerines or tripolitans as the latter nations only capture & make prisoners whereas these villains often accompany their depredations with cruelty & murder and have even been known to plunder the ship sink her and kill the crew to prevent discovery & punishment. They may be termed the *Banditti of the Ocean*, having very seldom any commission or Authority.

I was sitting in the Cabin yesterday writing very tranquilly when word was brought that a sail was seen coming off towards us from the Island. The Genoese Captain after regarding it thro a Spy Glass, turned pale and said it was one of those privateers of which he had been speaking to me. A moment after she fired a Gun upon which we hoisted the American flag. Another gun was fired the ball of which passed between the main & formasts and we immediately brought to. We went ⟨an⟩ to work directly to conceal any trifling articles of value that we had. As to myself I put my letters of credit in my inside coat pocket, and gave two Spanish Doubloons (which was all the cash I had) one to the Cabin boy and the other to a little genoese lad to take care of for me—as it was not very probable that they would be searched. By this time the privateer had come within hail. She was quite small—about the size of one of our Staten Island ferry boats[51]— with latine sails and ⟨a⟩ ↑two↓ small guns in ⟨each⟩ ↑the↓ bow. (As for us we had not even a pisto⟨n⟩l on board.) They were under French colours and hailing us ordered the Captain to Come on board with his papers — He accordingly went and after Some time returned accompanied by several of the privateers men. One of them appeared to have command over the rest, he was a tall stout fellow shabbily drest, without any coat and his shirt sleeves rolld up to his elbows displaying a formidably muscular pair of Arms. His crew would have shamed Falstaffs ragged regiment[52] in their habilliments while their countenances displayed the strongest lines of villainy & rapacity. They carried rusty Cutlasses in their hands and pistols & stillettos (a kind of dagger) were stuck in their belts & waistbands. After the leader had given orders to shorten sail, he demanded the passports & bills of health of the passengers &c and made several enquiries concerning the cargo. These we answerd by means of one of his men who spoke a little english and another who talked french and to whom I translated our Replies. He then told the Captain & myself that we must go on board of the privateer as the Commander wanted to make some enquiries and that I could act as interpreter. As we were going over the side the genoese Captain stopped me privately and with tears in his eyes entreated me not to leave the ship as he believed they only intended to seperate us all, that they might cut our throats the more easily. I represented to him how useless & impolitic it would be to dispute their orders as it would only enrage them—that we were completely in their power and they could as easily dispatch us on board the ship as in the privateer—we having no arms to defend ourselves. The poor man shook his head and said he hoped *the Virgin would protect me.* When we arrived

on board the privateer I own my heart almost faild me—a more villainous looking crew I never beheld. Their dark complexions, rough
beards and fierce black eyes scowling under enormous bushy eye
brows gave a character of the greatest ferocity to their countenances.
They were as rudely accouterd as their comerades that had boarded
us, and like them, armed with cutlasses, stillettos & pistols. They seemed
to regard us with the most malignant looks, and I thought I could
percieve a malignant smile upon their Countenances as if triumphing
over us who had fallen so easily into their hands. Their Captain after
reading over our papers &c and asking us several questions about the
vessel & cargo, said he only stopped us to know if we had the regular
bills of health—telling us some confused contradictory story of his
being employed by the health office of Leghorn. After a while he told
us we might return on board with which we cheerfully complied but
our pleasure was dampned when we found that he retained all our
papers. On arriving on board we ⟨found⟩ understood that they had been
rummaging the ship and had ordered them to stand for the shore
that the Vessel might be *brought to anchor:* When our sails were almost
all in, a signal was given upon which the privateer fired a Gun gave
three cheers and hoisted *English Colours.* The Captain or leader then
turnd round with a grin that we were a *good prize.* We told him to
reccollect we were Americans—He said it was all one—every thing
was a good prize that came from Genoa as the port was blockaded.
We replied that there had been no ⟨Vessels⟩ English frigates off of the
port for six months back, consequently they could not pretend but
that the blockade had ceased. He said we would find the contrary
when we arrived at Malta where he intended to carry us. We ⟨were
then force⟩ thought it most advisable to be silent, confident that if
we were carried to Malta they could do nothing with us. The Genoese
Captain said he was convinced from their behaviour that they had no
intention of carrying us there but that they were merely a band of
pirates without commission & bent upon plundering.

    They then commenced overhauling the ship in hopes of finding
money—The leader and one of his comerades who spoke a little english
began with the cabin ordering the others to remain on Deck to keep
guard. They first came across my portmanteau which I opened for
them and the Captain rummaged it completely without finding any
money which appeared to be his main object. The⟨y⟩ one who spoke
english was employed in reading my papers—perhaps hoping to find
bills of exchange—but as they were chiefly Letters of Introduction he
soon grew tired & turning to his companion said it was unprofitable
business, ⟨as⟩ that I had letters for all Italy & france but they were
nothing but reccomendations. *Eh bien* replied the other—we may as

well let his things alone for the present—*C'est un homme qui court tout le monde* (Tis' a man ⟨ramblin Who⟩ who is rambling all over the world) Among other letters ↑of introduction↓ they came across two for Malta one to Sir Isaac Ball[53] the Governor and another to a principal English merchant[54]—after this they treated me with much more respect and the Captain told me I might put up my things again in the portmanteau. I huddled them in carelessly as I expected never again to have the use of them and locking the trunk offerd the key to the Captain—he however told me to keep it myself as he had no present occasion for it. By this time his myrmidons on Deck had lost all patience & came crowding into the cabin demanding permission to search the vessel—The leader spoke somthing to them and immediately they went to work, ravenous as wolves, ransacking every hole & corner. They were extremely disappointed at finding so little aboard to pillage— The vessel having an intention of lading with wine at Messina had no cargo on board but five or six pipes of Brandy some few tons of paper a little verdigrease & two boxes of Quicksilver. The latter they hoisted out of the run with triumph thinking them filled with money but were highly chagrined at discovering their real contents.

After several hours spent in this manner the *Commander in Chief* came off from the island in a boat. This fellow I believe was *commodore* of the squadron for I ⟨fo⟩ learnt that there were two more small privateers in a harbor of the Island. He was as ragged as the rest tho rather a good looking fellow in the countenance. After looking over our papers and consulting with his comerades I suppose they found out it would be impolitic to be very hard upon us, as we had not sufficient on board to encourage them in running any risk and they well knew they could not justify themselves in taking an American Vessel. They therefore returned our papers and told us that tho ⟨we⟩ the ship was a *lawful prize* yet they would be *generous* & permit us to proceed— That they did not wish to use any *force* but would be much obliged to us for some provisions, as they were almost out. We of course had to comply with their *request* and they took about half the provisions that we had on board—and would have taken more but we told them that we had but laid in sufficient for our passage to Messina and if ⟨they took any⟩ we had much longer passage we would have even with what we had left—to go on short allowance.

They likewise took some articles of ship furniture and one of the under vagabonds stole a watch & some clothes out of the trunks of the Genoese passengers. It is impossible to describe the chagrin and rage of the common fellows at being restraind from plundering—they swore the ship was a *good prize* & I almost expected ↑to see them↓ ⟨to⟩ rise against their leaders for contradicting them. The Captains then gave us a *receipt* for what they had taken—requesting the British Consul at Messina[55] to pay for the same & about sun down to our great joy they bid us *adieu* having been on board since 11 Oclock in the morning. You may be sure we felt delighted at escaping so well from the hands of a set of miscreants who have very seldom any idea of moderation or humanity. For my own part they ⟨had⟩ did not take⟨n⟩ the least article from me. The wind was fair and we spread every sail in hopes of leaving this nest of pirates behind us, but the wind fell before dark and we lay becalmd all night. You may imagine how unpleasant was our situation—under strong apprehension that some of the gang—inflamed with the liquors ⟨that⟩ they had taken from us, might come off in the night unknown to their leaders, and commit their depredations without fear or restraint. In spight of my uneasiness I was so fatigued that I laid down in my clothes and soon fell asleep, but ⟨was⟩ my rest was broken & disturbed by horrid dreams. The assassin-like figures of the ruffians were continually before me and two or three times I started out of bed with the horrid idea that their stillettos were raised against my bosom.

Happily for us a favorable wind sprung up early this morning and we had the satisfaction of leaving the island far behind us before ⟨day break⟩ sun rise. Had we been becalmed another day in th⟨is⟩e neighborhood it is most likely we should have enjoyed a repetition of their visit. The crew of this privateer was composed of Italians Maltese portuguese, Ragusees &c but I did not see an englishman among them ⟨whole⟩.[56]

31st.

We have had our usual weather—head winds and calms for th⟨is⟩ese twenty four hours past, but have cleared the small islands ⟨in⟩ ↑among↓ which we have been beating about for some days. We have likewise lost sight of the Corsican shore which in fact we were anxious to do as the Genoese Captains say it is infested with small privateers. The inhabitants are rude & hardly civilized and make no scruple (especially the fishermen) of coming off to any vessel that is becalmd in sight of the shore and plundering her. This part of the Mediterranean is what is sometimes called the *Etrurian* or *Tuscan* or *Tyrhennian* Sea.

January 1st. 1805.[57]

Thus commences a new Year with me—for the first time seperate from my family & friends—When I picture to myself the social festivity that reigns among you on this day, the cheerfulness the good humor & hospitality that prevails around ⟨hom⟩ I sigh at being unable to participate in those enjoyments & feel an unusual lonesomeness and depression of spirit. I am perhaps wrong & selfish in yeilding to such emotions. My friends are all enjoying themselves and I should be pleased with the idea of their felicity—"I wander, but they are at rest." and surely I may flatter myself that in the midst of their hilarity they will bestow some thought on me, and wonder ⟨in wh⟩ where I am wandering or in what part of the world I am spending this festive day—With me it passes much the same as Christmas—writing & reading in the cabin—We have commenced the year with a pleasant favorable wind and our ship sails gaily before it.

The Weather continues remarkably mild. Tho' it is now the middle of Winter I frequently get out of bed in the middle of the night and walk the deck for some time with no other covering but my great coat— without feeling in the least degree uncomfortable—we have no fire in the cabin nor have we felt any want of it the whole passage.

Friday evening Jany. 4th

After forty eight hours of fair wind we came in sight of the Lipari[58] Islands this morning a little after Sunrise. They rise boldly out of the sea to a great height and are visible afar off[.] Strombolo[59] particularly may be seen about twenty leagues. In the afternoon we could plainly see the Smoke arising from its crater, which is on the ⟨South⟩ ↑North↓ west side of the mountain.

Æolus has certainly given us a most gracious reception into his Dominions—. The Storms are pent up in their caverns and each unruly wind safe tied up in his respective *leather bag,* a pleasant breeze only is commissioned to waft us safely thro his Empire and conduct us to our destined port. The sun has descended ⟨into⟩ ↑in↓ all the boasted splendors of an Italian Sky—the horison brilliantly transparent with just clouds enough to recieve his parting rays and enrich the prospect with a variety of colors. I have seen many fine sunsets at Sea—but none so truly *magnificent.* The Moon has succeeded with her "meek eyed train" but having "scarce yet filld her horns"[60] she sheds but a pale light upon the waters—to use a pretty *della Cruscan* phraze—a *silver shower of radiance!*[61]

Now could any one wish a more delightful time to enter into the regions of Æolia? ⟨Is⟩ ↑Are↓ not the very weather and prospect, themselves, enough to enliven the feelings and captivate the imagination without the idea that one is passing among the very haunts of fable and romantic fiction? ——— Strombolo just begins to shew his fires. His explosions are sudden and of short duration, with ⟨an⟩ intervals generally of from ten to fifteen minutes. We are yet too ⟨far⟩ distant for them to appear of much magnitude but the light ⟨as⟩ is very brilliant and red. Brydone[62] mentions that several of the islands besides Strombolo, emited smoke, particularly Volcano & Volcanello. This is no longer the case ⟨the⟩ all except Strombolo being, I am informed, totally extinguished. The Genoese Captains mentiond to me that in bad weather ⟨and ↑also in↓ a southerly wind⟩ this Volcano is particularly boisterous, exploding red hot stones &c with a great noise, and that it also makes a load roaring when the southwind blows.

12. at night

We have now got to the southward of Strombolo so that his crater is no longer discernable ⟨being set⟩ the summit of the mountain being between us. The Explosions of this Volcano did not quite answer the expectations I had formed from the discriptions given by Brydone[63] and other Travellers, either in their magnitude or the height to which they are thrown; but they vary according to the weather and are sometimes formidable indeed.

The Island is high and rocky, and the crater is situated near the summit of the highest part. The island is mostly barren—yeilding a few grapes—yet it contains a number of inhabitants who reside ⟨on the⟩ chiefly in a village on the skirts of the island. The largest and most fertile of the Islands is Lipara and here Virgil fixes the abode of Æolus.[64] His sway extended over all these islands which were termed Æolia and feigned to be the empire of the winds. Both Virgil and Homer mention them more than once and the former if I reccollect right in the first part of the Æne⟨a⟩id represents the winds as shut up in their caverns round which they roam in search of a place to escape— roaring & howling at their imprisonment.[65] This fable is partly founded, I concieve, on the noise made by the internal fires which antiently burned in each of the islands. Homer, who, it appears ⟨was⟩ ↑did↓ not care to tax his talent of invention in this particular, ⟨merely neither⟩ simply ties up each wind in a *leather bag* or skin[66]—for which he has been censurd by different critics—as descending from his usual dig- nity—for my part I think he rather deserves commendation as having attentively consulted the convenience of his heroes—⟨for⟩ ↑as↓ he afterwards makes Æolus present them to Ulysses, ⟨and⟩ in which case it was mighty accommodating to have them in such handy packages. The gift however proved an unfortunate one—⟨f⟩ The Curiosity of Ulysses companions got the better of their prudence and when out at sea they opened the bags to take a peep at their contents. The winds burst forth from their narrow prisons, a dreadful storm was the conse- quence and they were all shipwreckd & drowned except Ulysses who drifted thro the straits of Messina on a mast or plank.[67]

One of the Islands antiently called Hiera (at present Volcano) is also described by Virgil as one of Vulcans forges where he made the thunderbolts of Jupiter and wrought the armor of Æneas.[68] Indeed the whole of these islands were frequently called by the antients *Vulcania.*

Vulcano is recorded to have been the production of a violent convulsion of the earth in time of the Roman Republic—it is likewise the opinion of many that all these islands have been produced in a similar manner and afterwards encreased in Size from the discharges of their own craters. Volcano formerly was formidable in its Eruptions—I find in Buonfiglio[69] ⟨an ita⟩ a sicilian historian an account of one that ⟨haf⟩ commenced about the year 1595 and continued for two years to make vast explosions of fire & red hot stones of a great size attended with terrible noises and earthquakes. When the northwind prevaild the ashes was carried in clouds into sicily & calabria, laying waste & desolate the Country.

As to the Fable of Æolus—Buonfiglio quotes Diodorus & other Historians to assist him in clearing it up.[70] Liparus (or Liparo) son of a King of Italy after a long war with his Brothers retired to these islands then desert & woody. He chose them for his residence and gave them his name. When very old he gave his daughter in marriage to Æolus presenting with her as a marriage portion the dominion of these Islands. Eolus was reputed a mighty honest, good sort of a man, and exceeding hospitable. He was also wondrous *weather wise* and could fortel the changes of the wind very correctly (doubtless prognosticating from the appearance, ↑Smoke↓ and motions of the volcano's—as the seamen in these seas do to this day) he is likewise said to have taught the use of sails—these were surely enough in all conscience to entitle a man to rank among the gods, in those rude times, when *deityships* were as common as enrolements in the *Legion of honor*[71] are at present in france—at least the antients thought so, and without more ado dubbd him *King of the winds.* Ulysses was received by him and treated with much honor, he departed well instructed in the art of navigation, from whence, Homer sung that Æolus has given him the winds. This is one of the ways in which they explain this fiction, and indeed many of the antient fables are traced to their sources by historians in the same manner and it is well if they can find as plausible foundation always as at present. It was supposed that there was a communication by subterraneous caverns from Mount Ætna to those islands.—At present they appertain to the King of Naples to whom they yield a considerable revenue; producing abundance of Alum, Nitre &c and excellent figs, raisins currants and other fruits. They likewise are celebrated for producing the rich sweet wine termed Malvasie.[72]

5th. At day break this morning we found ourselves within a few miles of the Straits of Messina and near to the Calabrian coast. The sun rise presented to us one of the most charming scenes I ever beheld. To our left extended the Calabrian mountains, their summits still partially envelloped in the mists of morning, the sun ha⟨d⟩ving just risen from behind them and breaking in full splendor from among the clouds. Immediately before us was the celebrated Straits[73] immortal in history and song; to the right Sicily gradually swept up into verdant mountains, skirted with delightful little plains. The whole country was lively and blooming as if in the midst of spring and villages, towns and cottages heightned the beauty of the prospect.

Our favorable breeze still continued and we glided on gently to the mouth of the Strait. About a mile without the enterance is situated *Scylla*, the rock which poets and historians were once so fond of cloathing with imaginary terrors. It is at the foot of one of the high Calabrian mountains and advances boldly into the sea forming a small promontory. ⟨of a⟩ From the points of view from whence I saw it, which were at a considerable distance, it had something the appearance of a large square tower. On the top of it is a small fortress and on part of the promontory is built the town of Sciglio which is the Italian name of the rock. The whole is very picturesque and would form a charming subject for the pencil.

The fable of this rock[74] is briefly that Scylla, daughter of Phorcus, a beautiful nymph, concieved a violent passion for Glaucus one of the deities of the Ocean—Circe the enchantress who also loved Glaucus, became jealous of her and exerted her spells over the fountain in which Scylla bathed, so that when she next entered it she was changed into ⟨hi⟩ a hideous monster with the upper parts of a Wolf and the tail of a Dolphin. Struck with terror at this horrid metamorphosis the Nymph threw herself into the sea where the poets say she remained the terror & peril of Mariners, surrounded by dogs who kept up a continual howling and yelling. These dogs are ⟨propa⟩ probably th⟨e⟩ree or four smaller rocks that I perceived at the foot of the large one, and their howling is the noise made by the current from the Straits—breaking & dashing against them. The danger that the ancients so often mention ↑from Scylla↓ was owing to the Current setting upon it and carrying vessels thither—but at present there appears to be no danger of the kind. This may be accounted for by the gradual enlargement of the Strait, which has rendered the current less rapid and decreased the violence of Charybdes. The latter is situated on the sicilian shore in front of Messina, and in avoiding it the vessels sometimes got too far on the Calabrian side—so as to be hurried by the current to Scylla. Many of the antient historians are of opinion that Sicily was formerly joind to the opposite shore of Calabria and that they have been seperated by some violent convulsion of the earth, or the gradual working of the waters of the strait.

Charybdes, that tremendous gulph in 'days of yore' has long since ceased to be an object of dread and horror, ⟨and⟩ I have not however, as yet been able to obtain a good sight of it

Opposite to Scylla, on the sicilian shore is ⟨Cape⟩ the Faro point[75] formerly termed the Promontory of Pylorus or Pelorus. Some ascribe the origin of this name to Pelorus Hannibals pilot whom he slew here, on suspicion of treachery, but finding afterwards his mistake, he appeased the manes of Pelorus by erecting a monument to his memory. By others it is said to be named after the pilot of Ulysses who was drowned here.[76] This is one of the three grand promontories of Sicily. At the point of the cape they have a light house. The straits at this place is about a mile across but immediately widens. Before we entered we saw Strombolo at a distance, make a great explosion, infinitely superior to any that we saw last night. The smoke arose in a vast pillar to the clouds and then spread around in volumes. This the genoese captains assured me was a sign of approaching bad weather.

As we drew near the enterance of the Straights the prospect became more and more beautiful. Sicily presented a rich picture of cultivation & firtility and at a great distance we could percieve Ætna rearing itself far above the other mountains,[77] covered with snow and the summit shrowded in thick clouds. Calabria had likewise an appearance the most picturesque & luxurient. It is a part of what was termed Great Greece, antiently ⟨so⟩ much renowned for its abundance At present it is over-run with woods, its inhabitants miserable, oppressd, barbarous and indolent, they are unwilling to cultivate the earth as they know the produce would be wrested from them[78]—they are therefore starving in a land, that with a little industry and attention would flow with "milk & honey"[79]

> "But what avails her unexhausted stores,
> Her blooming mountains & her sunny shores,
> With all the gifts that heaven & earth impart
> The smiles of nature & the charms of art.
> While proud oppression in her valleys reigns
> And Tyrrany usurps her happy plains."[80]

Advancing on our course we opened a Hill that had hitherto inter-cepted the view—and Messina broke upon our sight. ——

It is about ten miles from the mouth of the Faro (or Strait) ⟨It⟩ built at the foot of the mountains, in a half moon round ⟨the⟩ part of the harbor facing the east. The Churches, palaces &c being many of them built on rising grounds, shew one above another to great advantage, and their steeples & towers make a handsome appearance. ⟨On⟩ The summits of the heights around the city are occupied by forts, Convents and Castles, and the ⟨Key⟩ promontory or mole in front of the Harbor is fortified by a noble Cidital and several batt⟨e⟩aries.

If you can figure to yourself the City, with its beauty of situation and picturesque Architecture—its grand harbor, the Straits that extend before it and gradually widen into the ocean, Specled with numerous sails—the opposite Calabrian coast, boldly rising into mountains cloathed with wood and their bases adorned with smiling fields, vineyards Villages &c if you can figure to your imagination any thing like the scene and over the whole cast the enlivening beams of the morning sun, brightening every object and dancing on the tremulous waves of the Ocean, you may then form an idea how charming must be the approach to this city and how enchanting the scene that presented itself as our Vessel gently glided to the port.

Never perhaps did nature assist more in forming a safe and beautiful Harbor than at Messina. A narrow slip of land runs out from the foot of the mountains at the south end of the town and making a Curve compleatly encloses the Harbor like a huge bason, leaving only an entrance from the North between the end of this slip or promontory and the mainland. This neck of land has very much the shape of a Sickle, which was observed by the antients who for that reason ⟨term⟩ called the City Zancla. In their fables they ascribe its form to the sickle of Saturn which they say fell upon this spot.[81] It is well fortified by a strong cidital and several Batteries, tho at present they are not sufficiently garrisoned. The harbor is as safe as a mill pond. The middle of it is extremely deep and requires a great length of cable to anchor but near the shores it suddenly shallows into a commodious depth.

I forgot to mention to you that the before mentioned promontory of Pelorus was one of the antient haunts of the Sirens from whence they exerted their fatal allurements upon mariners.[82] When we passed it we only saw a few fisherwomen—these may perhaps be their descendants for they were *amphibious* looking animals. Their attractions however did not appear sufficiently powerful to oblige us to use Ulysses precautions for our safety. They, honest souls, were sufficiently employed in mending their husbands nets and seemed to have given up all idea of *catching men*, contenting themselves with the more profitable occupation of *catching Fish*.

On arriving at Messina we had to encounter one of the greatest torments of these seas, infinitely more hideous than Pelorus, Scylla or charybdes with all their terrors. This was no other than the Health

office. Here we made our report & had our bills of health & other
papers of the Ship examined, after they had been well fumigated,
and roasted almost to cinders. The people in these countries carry
their ⟨dread and⟩ precautions against the fever to a most ridiculous
length. They Quarantine vessels from every port, tho never so healthy,
and tho we came direct from Genoa where there has been no infectious malady known for years, yet they appear as apprehensive of us
as if we were direct from a city reeking with infection. I had a hearty
laugh at the whimsical manouvres of one of the men at the health
office. A small window was opened and he was sent to the door to ⟨th⟩
tell our Captain that he must talk thro this window to the people
within. The Captain not understanding italian thought he was told to
come in the house and was accordingly advancing up the Stoop when
the fellow half frightned to death, sprung to the other end of it and
halloo'd to him to keep back. The Captain stopped short in astonishment. The fellow made several attempts to pull shut the iron ⟨d⟩
wicket or door of the stoop but as the captain stood close by it he was
violently apprehensive ⟨of catching⟩ and as often as his fingers almost
reached the rails of the door he started back as if the iron rails were
red hot. He at length succeeded in[83] succeeded in jerking it shut and
darted into the house trembling at the risk he had run of catching the
fever from our honest captain who for rotundity of body and rosyness
of complexion seemed the picture of health itself.

10th.

We are safely moored at Quarantine in front of the Lazarretto which
is built on the promontory facing the town. They have doomed us to
this species of imprisonment for *twenty one* days, notwithstanding we
come from a healthy port, are all hearty and have scarcely any Cargo
on board. Our Quarantine is longer than it otherwise would have
been, in consequence of our having been boarded by the ⟨p⟨y⟩irates⟩
↑pirates↓ off planosa, but they are unreasonable in these matters and
seldom think of putting a vessel in Quarantine for less than a fortnight.
At the Lazaretto is a large square surrounded by the hospital, ⟨Ware⟩
store house &c &c where we are allowed to exercise ourselves, guards
generally attending with pikes or bayonets on the ends of sticks to
take care that ⟨we⟩ ↑the crews of different vessels↓ do not touch each
other.
Here I generally find a collection of curious uncouth figures for we
have vessels of different nations in Quarantine—Ragusees, Napolitans,
Greeks, venetians &c The present *Cock of the walk* appears to be a rich
old Greek, with a great turban, enormous trowsers that tuck in at the
knees and a pipe two or three Yards in length, he is generally attended

by four long bearded Capuchins who are quarantined with him and appear to be his travelling companions. at any rate they pay him humble court, doubtless much to the good of his soul and the edification of his pocket. They make a mighty handsome groupe as you may well suppose.

Arrivals are very frequent and we daily see vessels either entering the port or passing thro the straits which gives life and variety to the scene. This appears to be a great place of resort for the English force in the mediterranean; at present there are several transports here, taking in wine for Nelsons fleet—and there are generally more or less ⟨armed⟩ British frigates in the harbor.

The Same day that we arrived, there entered also the United States Schooner Nautilus[84] from Syracuse. I have already become quite intimate with the officers, and have had several conversations with them. As we are an *infectious* vessel we are not allowed to communicate with them except at a proper distance. Dent (the Captain)[85] is a philadelphian and appears to be a very clever gentlemanlike fellow. He expects to return to Syracuse in a few days and has invited me to take a passage with him which I of course shall do — it will shorten my Quarantine and I can return hither by land from Syracuse and then proceed to Palermo. The Lieutenant of the Schooner is Mr George Washington Reed,[86] son of Governor Reed[87] of Philadelphia and a very worthy fellow; He has been extremely polite and attentive to me. At Syracuse there are several of our Vessels so that I shall be quite among my fellow countrymen and most probably find some old acquaintances. Our Navy uniform has latterly undegone a few alterations and is very handsome & becoming.[88] The officers are genteel good looking fellows and the Vessels much admired. The Nautilus is a remarkable fine sailer and beautifully built.

Our captain has been repeatedly told that he should take two ↑health office↓ guards on board the ship ⟨on the part of the health office⟩. He however does not trouble himself about their commands and we remain without any—contrary to all regulations. For my part I find this extremely convenient as I can range the harbor in our boat and Visit the Nautilus without restraint. The guards from shore stamp & swear & brawl after me incessantly, if they had not a great respect for the Americans here I expect I should be used like the other persons whom I see now and then ordered back to their vessels. Indeed one of the boats did attempt a thing of the kind the other day and gave us chase having a guard in it armed as usual with a bayonet on the end of a stick; as we did not regard that kind of fire arms, we laughed at him and ⟨im⟩ advised him to keep his distance—he thought proper to take our advice as he saw four stout american sailors in our boat ready to *pat him* and his companions *on the head* with their long oars. I have in consequence received two or three severe reprimands from the health office which I pretended not to understand and took no notice of.

1⟨5⟩4th. The weather has been variable since our arrival, frequent showers of rain have fallen but not a day has passed that did not afford some hours of sunshine and the air has been always temperate and agreeable. For two or three days past I could have worn light summer cloathing without inconvenience and in general the fine weather is like that of our pleasant days in the month of May. There has some snow fallen on the tops of the mountains but it soon disappeared, nor was the cold felt in the lower places. The skirts of the mountains are green & flourishing and I observe the ground plowed and cultivated like in spring or summer. Fruit is exceeding cheap & good. for a basket of fine oranges, figs raisins & nuts I paid but a shilling sterling. The oranges are from Calabria, very large & delicious[.] for a dozen I paid about *Seven* Cents. These too are prices paid at Quarantine where you are sure to pay much more than the common price. Tho I compared the ⟨days to⟩ w⟨ar⟩eather here to our fine spring days, you must not imagine our evenings are as cold as spring evenings with you. Here they ↑are↓ mild & delightful. It is really romantic to sit on the deck and enjoy the effects of a brilliant moonlight, lighting up the surrounding scenery—dancing on the rapid waters of the straits and the more tranquil waves of the Harbor, and *sleeping in gentle radiance* on the towers ⟨and⟩ of Messina. All is tranquility and repose except now and then the silence is interrupted by the sound of a Vesper Bell the watch word of the Guards, or the full chorus's from some of the ships in Quarantine whose crews every evening chant a hymn to the Virgin. This music is simple solemn & affecting and peculiarly in unison with the scene. The other evening I was highly delighted when after having set on deck a long time indulging in those delicious reveries such scen[e]s are calculated to inspire, I was aroused by a strain of soft sicilian music that came from a distance but from whence I could not percieve. The silence of the night assisted the sounds which were so sweet yet so clear & distinct in their modulations that they seemed almost ærial. By turns they swelled into a full body of harmony and then melted away in liquid cadence. It ⟨seeme⟩ appeard almost like a choir of Æreal beings that were traversing the air—and being in the Country of romance I was almost tempted to yield to its sway and indulge the fancy that they were so.—I fear I tire you with discriptions. I wish to make you partaker in all my pleasures and those that are imparted to me by surrounding scenery are generally the greatest. My feelings are very often as much influenced by the prospects that surround me as others are by the weather and a lovely landscape has always an enlivening effect on my spirits.

I expect you will say I have grown quite *romantic*—and I confess I fear the *climate* of this country has had some effect upon me in that particular—But I have told you before I am in the *very country* of Romance—I breath the *air* of it—and you must not expect to have me rational and commonplaced till I once more return to the regions of plain fact & circumstance—good night.

15.th. I have learned since my arrival here that the blockade of Genoa was renewed for another year from the 14th. Octr last, we were fortunate therefore, in not encountering any ↑regular↓ British Cruser as we should certainly have been sent in to Malta. ⟨Wh⟩ A privateer arrived here a few days since under English Colors that had been on a Cruise and among. other prizes has captured one American Vessel bound for Genoa—The Brig Favorite of Philadelphia[89]— She was sent in to Malta & condemned but the Captain appealed to the Court of admiralty in Great Britain and from particular circumstances there is some prospect of his Succeeding. The crew of this privateer is a most delectable gang of Maltese italians &c and but four or five englishmen on board. Yesterday they had a high altercation at the Lazaretto several of the sailors having mutinied against the Lieutenant. The latter stripped to *box* the whole of them, but they were not accustomed to that mode of fighting, and one of them drew his knife and if not prevented would have stabbed the Lieutenant.

The Captain I believe was affraid to trust himself any longer among such a set of Cut throats so he sent them ashore this morning *bag* & baggage—and I dont believe Noahs ark itself could have furnished a more motley debarkation. I am surprized the english are not more jealous of the honor of their flag ⟨that⟩ than to suffer it to sanction the depredations of such unprincipled ruffians. At present it is the rallying standard for all the pirates in the mediterranean and perhaps there is no flag in the world under which greater enormities are committed.

This day we have been (to use an inquisitorial term) *put to the question* by the health office, to know whether we really had any yellow fever among us. For this purpose ⟨we⟩ a chaffing dish with charcoal and a couple of pacquets of drugs were sent on board. We were orderd down into the hold of the ship and the hatches nearly all closed. A fire was made in the chaffing dish and the drugs thrown thereon which occasioned a thick smoke of a most villainous smell. Here we were, huddled round the infernal pot of *incense* like a group of conjurers—inhaling the suffocating steams of a melange of vile drugs for a quarter of an hour after which we were permitted to evacuate the hold, ⟨the⟩ a most ghastly looking set of animals. This

is a sage expedient of the health Physician to know if any person
on board has the fever lurking in his veins as they say this fumiga-
tion would immediately make it break out. Afterwards we were summoned to the Lazerretto where we had our necks and bosoms examined
by the Doctor which he did *very narrowly* at ten or twelve feet
distance. We then had to whack our arms together like labourers do
in cold weather to warm themselves—after which we were permitted
to return on board. We shall have to undergo a repetition of these
pleasant operations before we are released from Quarantine, perhaps
with *additions & variations* for they seem as fond of trying experiments
upon us, as Philosophical professors at College, do upon unlucky rats
that fall in their ⟨power⟩ clutches.

25th. After another smoaking & examination we were released from
⟨Pratique the⟩↑Quarantine↓ Yesterday morning—I went immediately
on board of the Nautilus which it was expected would have got under
way the same evening for Syracuse but the Schooner has been detained in consequence of the timber's not arriving—which she is to
take on board for the repairs of the presidents[90] mast. I have therefore had time to take a look at Messina which by no means answers
the expectation I had formed from the outside appearance of it. The
dreadful earthquake of 1783 has reduced many parts of it, to heaps
of ruins and disfigurd the principal places & buildings[91]—as I mentiond before—that noble range of ⟨me⟨bu⟩⟩ buildings mentiond by
Brydone,[92] extending in front of the Quay the whole length of the
City—are completely destroyd not one of them remaining habitable—
But I will treat more particularly of Messina in my next letter—tho I
cannot promise you much from it, for there is hardly any thing
worth seeing and as to the company I have rather avoided mingling
in it in consequence of an unfortunate accident that occurd a few
days since. Two of the Officers of the Nautilus having dined in company were walking in one of the streets rather intoxicated, ⟨af⟩ in the
evening. Hearing an altercation between [*MS torn*] Some Sicilians
and a man that spoke english ⟨th⟩ one of the officers went to assist
the latter thinking him to be one of the Nautilus's men. He accordingly orderd him on board which the other refused saying he
was an englishman—What followed is not clearly ascertained, it is
certain, however, that the englishman was stabbed and died ⟨of⟩ next
morning. He was mate to an english transport and bore a very ill
character while living. The Young officer[93] that is charged with having
killd him is a young fellow of large fortune—great talents in his profession and of a very amiable character—he was completely intoxicated when this unfortunate affair took place and could not reccollect
any thing of it distinctly the next morning. The english in this place

have made a great stir about it. The two officers have been demanded by the Governor of ⟨the⟩ Messina[94] but Captain Dent (commander of the Nautilus) has refused to give them up—but has pledged himself that they shall be delivered into the hands of the Commodore at Syracuse[95] with a full statement of the affair. The english were urging the Governor to have the forts mannd and the Schr. stopped from leaving the port till the officers were given up. The Governor, however, is well disposed towards the Americans and has not hearkened to these instigations. I calld upon him this morning in company with Capt Dent & Mr Broadbent[96] (an english man our navy agent at messina) He gave me a very polite reception and conversed with me some time in english. He mentioned his regrets at the unfortunate affair that had taken place—his approbation of the conduct of Captain Dent and in fact shewed every disposition to be accommodating. Where this business will end I cannot foresee but I apprehend it will make some noise. At present it operates much against my pleasure in this place, as the society to which my letters introduce me are chiefly english and a circumstance of this nature throws a restraint over our intimacy. When so far from home it is impossible to avoid being extremely national

I wave giving you any further particulars on this point[.] it is a delicate subject and very probably you may have official accounts before this arrives—

I am on board of the Nautilus waiting still for the timber to set sail— the accomodations are very good—were I on shore I should be in a state of sufferance from the filth and other miseries of a Sicilian hotel. Dent is a very clever fellow and treats me like an old friend—it seems already as if I had known him as many years as I have days.

———

And now I will finish this discourse for the present promising faithfully to give you the rest (god willing) on another opportunity—Want of time is all that prevents me from drawing out this letter to a still more unreasonable length.

I need not desire *you* to write me frequently & particularly for you shew every disposition to do so; but I wish you would tell some of the rest of my family & friends that I am famishing for want of intelligence about the little world of my Acquaintance Was it in your power to give it me I am confident it would not be withheld but the difference of our Ages & situations made us move in different circles—Tell Jack Hicks swartwout &c That I wish them every felicity that can be derived from the smiles of beauty & the endearments of friendship—I envy them not the intellectual banquets they enjoy but only crave *a few of the crumbs from* their tables. As to Swartwout I have closed for the present my correspondence with him, a heavy balance remaining in my favor—twelve hasty lines are all that I have received from him since I left New York.

I acknowledged in a fo[rmer letter][97] [*MS torn*] receipt of your most acceptable letter of the mon[th] [*MS torn*] and I now mention it again—The Account you g[ave of my] [*MS torn*] friends was exquisitely grateful and I have [read it ov]er [*MS torn*] so often that I believe I have it by heart. [*MS torn*] few particulars of the famil⟨y⟩ies of the Hoffmans & Rodmans and I beg you will always let me have all you know about those families that are so very dear to me. Present them my most heartfelt remembrances.

By the time you recieve this I expect my worthy friend Johnson and his amiable spouse[98] will have nearly finished the seasons Campain. I hope he has not acted the invalid and limped thro the service— present him my compliments of condolence or congratulation as the case may require. To Mrs J I send kind wishes for her health & happiness—she promised to write me a letter to Miss A DeCamp[99] in England and I beg leave to ⟨re⟩ put her in mind of it.

To Father and Mother give my sincere love my earnest prayer that they may experience every comfort & enjoyment necessary to their age—remember me likewise affectionately to the rest of the family, and give a word or two for me to each friend that is kind enough to ask after me

I send you this letter "with all its imperfections on its head[.]"[100] receive it in brotherly kindness & Christian Charity.

Sincerely yours

W I

Manuscript: Yale. Published: PMI, I, 93–103 (in part).

1. WI's journal entries for the period from December 25, 1804, to January 25, 1805, are almost identical to the contents of this letter.

2. WI apparently shared a cabin with Captain Matthew Strong of the *Matilda*. In his journal for December 21, 1804, he notes that "There are two or three passengers besides myself.—Genoese captains who speak french very well. . . . They sleep in the steerage—so that I have the cabin to myself. The Captain is a worthy honest old gentleman who is always in good humor and strives to the utmost to render everything agreeable to me." See *J&N*, I, 143–44. It would seem, from WI's letter, that arrangements had been changed, with Captain Strong and WI now sharing quarters.

3. The Genoese nobility were the victims of Napoleon's rise to power. The city had been besieged in 1800 and in 1802, when the rest of the Ligurian Republic was brought under French rule. In 1805 it was annexed to France.

4. Anna Maria Gasparda Vincenze Pieri, Marchesa Brignole Sale (1765–1815). For other details, see *J&N*, I, 121–22, n. 262.

5. Marie Geronima Célésia, Comtesse de Ginestous. See *J&N*, I, 122, n. 263.

6. Marie Elizabeth Célésia, Marquise de Gabriac. See *J&N*, I, 121, n. 260.

7. Marie Antoinette (1755–1793), who was executed on October 16, 1793.

8. Marie Thérèse Louise of Savoy-Carignano, Princess de Lamballe (1749–1792), a close associate of Marie Antoinette, who was beheaded on September 3, 1792. See J&N, I, 122, n. 264.

9. Probably the translation by Francese da Giovambatista Richeri, published in Genoa in 1748.

10. Probably Anna Cicopero, Marchesa Rivarola. See J&N, I, 123, n. 265.

11. Antonio Brignole Sale (1786–1863). Is is not clear why WI calls him Stephano.

12. The first syllable of this word, "por," appears as a catchword at the bottom of the MS page and is repeated at the beginning of the next MS page. WI's use of catchwords in various parts of this letter suggests that he was copying from his journal.

13. WI copied the date from his journal entry into his letter, as well as most of the entry.

14. WI probably intended to write "in."

15. Andrew Wilson (1780–1848), a Scottish landscape painter who lived in Genoa from 1803 to 1806, during which time he was made a member of the Ligurian Academy. Returning to the British Isles, he taught and painted until 1826, when he took his family with him to Genoa where he resided for the next twenty years.

16. This letter has not been located.

17. WI follows the entry in his journal for this date.

18. As WI indicates, his name was Giuseppe Musso (1779?–1804). See J&N, I, 127, n. 279.

19. Variant of Romeo and Juliet, V, i, 75.

20. Passo la Bocchetta.

21. November 12 is the feast day of St. Martin, a Tuscan who became pope in 649. Pope Martin I was seized by Emperor Constans II, tried and condemned at Constantinople, and sent to the Chersonesi in the Crimea, where he died of starvation on September 16, 655. The feast day of St. Martin of Tours (ca. 316–397) occurs on November 11.

22. The Bisagno River runs through the southeastern section of Genoa.

23. The Great Devil; or, The Robber of Genoa by Charles Dibden, was produced at Sadlers Wells in 1801. Although the melodramatic plot has no resemblance to the career of Joseph Musso, as WI relates it, this may be the play to which he refers.

24. This word appears in the lower right corner of the thirteenth MS page, underneath "superfluities." WI intended "or" to be a catchword but forgot to pick it up on the first line of the following MS page.

25. In this paragraph WI greatly expands the journal entry for November 16.

26. WI copied several sections from his journal into the following paragraphs of his letter. He neglected to add a specific date.

27. Santa Maria delle Vigne, which dates from the thirteenth century, was restored in the baroque style about 1586.

28. William Congreve, The Mourning Bride (1697), II, iii, 9–10.

29. The Mourning Bride, II, iii, 12.

30. See J&N, I, 139, n. 315.

31. WI here seems to be altering "Every dog has his day." See Cervantes, Don Quixote, I, iii, 6.

32. Napoleon was crowned at Notre Dame de Paris on December 2, 1804.

33. See note 3 above.

34. Antoine Christophe Saliceti (1757–1809), French Minister to Genoa from 1803 to 1805. For other details, see *J&N*, I, 136, n. 306.

35. WI probably heard this saying from his friends in Genoa. It may be an expansion of the Italian proverb, "It takes nine Jews to equal one Genoese" (quoted in H. L. Mencken, *New Dictionary of Quotations* [New York, 1942], p. 450); or a variation of the Turkish proverb, "It takes ten Jews to make one Greek, and ten Greeks to make an Armenian" (quoted by Louis Golding in *The Jewish Problem* [Harmondsworth, England, 1939], p. 39).

36. The convent of the Sisters of St. Domenico was used as the land arsenal, while the navy yard served as the sea arsenal. See *J&N*, I, 115, n. 244.

37. Goose was a name for a tailor's smoothing-iron, whose handle resembled a goose's neck. The plural form was "gooses."

38. These islands, respectively, are about 22 and 45 miles from Leghorn.

39. Elba is about 5½ miles southwest of Piombino.

40. Located on the north coast of the island and so named because of its shipments of iron ore.

41. According to the *Odyssey* (bk. XII), it was Hera who protected the *Argo* as it passed Scylla and Charybdis.

42. According to the *Aeneid* (bk. X, line 173), Aeneas received 300 men from Ilva. WI apparently miscopied from Henry Swinburne, *Travels in the Two Sicilies* (London, 1783, 1785), I, 30.

43. Elba has an area of 86 square miles. WI probably drew details about the latitude and circumference from Swinburne, I, 31.

44. Monte Calamita is on the east side of the island, not the west, as WI says. The slope of the mountain produces the fruit and wine he alludes to in the next paragraph. In his description Swinburne (I, 32) locates Monte della Calamita at the southeast cape; he also mentions the lodestones.

45. This word appears as a catchword in the lower right corner below "asserted" but was not picked up at the beginning of the first line on the following MS page.

46. Details about the "celebrated iron mine" and its ore are given in Swinburne, I, 36–40.

47. Not identified.

48. Cervantes, *Don Quixote*, pt. II, chap. 68.

49. Pianosa lies about 7½ miles southwest of Elba.

50. For these historical details WI drew upon Swinburne, II, 43–44.

51. In his journal WI compares the pirate vessel to a North River ferry boat. See *J&N*, I, 148.

52. See *Henry IV*, Part I, IV, ii, 11–47.

53. The governor of Malta at this time was Sir Alexander John Ball (1759–1809).

54. Not identified. Forty English merchants were in Valetta, Malta in 1809. See *J&N*, I, 150, n. 336.

55. James Tough was the British consul at Messina.

56. When WI canceled "whole," he added an *m* to "the" to complete the thought.

57. "Janu" appears at the bottom of the MS page and is repeated in "January" where WI wrote the date of the new year at the top of the page.

58. A group of seventeen islands lying 20 to 50 miles off the northeast coast of Sicily.

59. Stromboli, the legendary home of Aeolus, is the site of one of the few active volcanoes in Europe.

60. A variation of Edward Young, *Night Thoughts*, "Night I," line 214.

61. The Della Cruscan poets, a group of eighteenth-century Englishmen living mostly in Florence, often used extravagant language. They derived their name from the Accademia della Crusca, which was started in the sixteenth century in Florence to advance linguistic purity. The words which WI quotes resemble those in Robert Merry's "The Adieu and the Recall to Love," *The British Album* (London, 1790), I, 2. See *J&N*, I, 154–55, n. 343.

62. WI drew upon Patrick Brydone (1736–1818), whose *Tour through Sicily and Italy*, 3d ed. (London, 1773), provided many of the factual details which WI incorporated in his letter. See I, 28.

63. Brydone, I, 28–30.

64. Lipari has an area of about 13½ square miles. See Brydone, I, 37.

65. *Aeneid*, I, 52–59; *Odyssey*, X, 1ff. "Hic vasto rex Aeolus antro / luctantes ventos tempestatesque sonoras / imperio premit ac vinclis et carcere frenat" (Brydone, I, 37–38).

66. See *Odyssey*, X, 18–26.

67. See *Odyssey*, X, 42–53. See Brydone, I, 44.

68. See *Aeneid*, VIII, 416–32; Brydone, I, 38–40.

69. Giuseppe Buonfiglio Constanzo, *Prima Parte [e Secunda] Parte dell' Historia Siciliana* (Venice, 1604).

70. Diodorus Siculus (second half of first century B.C.) compiled a work of forty books, *Bibliotheke*, a universal history from mythological beginnings to Caesar's time, using an analytical rather than chronological arrangement. Brydone (I, 38) also mentioned Diodorus.

71. Bonaparte created the Legion of Honor in 1802.

72. Malvasia di Lipari is a sweet, strong Italian wine, the most important vineyards of which are on Salina Island.

73. The distance between the shores of the straits varies in width from 1¾ to 8 miles.

74. See Ovid, *Metamorphoses*, XIII–XIV.

75. The words "the Faro point" are written in a different ink and were presumably added later.

76. See *Odyssey*, XII, 483–84; Brydone, I, 44.

77. Mount Etna rises to 10,810 feet.

78. For similar descriptions see Brydone, I, 46.

79. See Exod. 3:18, 17; Jer. 11:15; 32:22; Ezek. 20:6, 15.

80. Joseph Addison, "A Letter from Italy, to the Right Honourable Lord Halifax" (1701), lines 107–12.

81. WI seems to be following Brydone (I, 53) here.

82. See *Odyssey*, XII, 200–239.

83. The word "in" appears at the bottom of the MS page under the word "succeeded" as a catchword, and WI then absentmindedly repeated the preceding word as well, thus accounting for the appearance of "succeeded" twice in the text.

84. A twelve-gun schooner in Commodore Edward Preble's squadron operating on the Mediterranean against the Barbary pirates. After the bombardment of Tripoli the *Nautilus* left for Syracuse with four other American ships. See Maclay, *History of U. S. Navy*, I, 270–99.

85. John Herbert Dent (1782–1823) entered the United States Navy in 1798 and rose to the rank of captain in 1811.

86. Reed (1780–1813) was commissioned a lieutenant in 1803.

87. Joseph Reed (1741–1785) was a lawyer who served in the Continental Army with Washington and as a member of the Continental Congress from Pennsyl-

vania and as president of the Supreme Executive Council of Pennsylvania from
1778 to 1781.

88. The changes resulted from an order of August 27, 1802, by Robert Smith,
secretary of the navy, which stipulated that navy officers were to wear blue coats
lined with blue cloth, blue collars and cuffs, gold-lace decorations, white breeches
and vest, and cocked hat. See James C. Tily, *The Uniforms of the United States
Navy* (New York, 1964), pp. 60, 63.

89. The brig *Favorite* of Philadelphia, John Dove, master, Messrs. James Van-
nuxem and John Charles, owners, bound for Genoa, was captured November 8–9,
1804, by the private ship of war, *Old Maid*, Clement Worts, commander, and taken
to Malta. See *Original Printed Records of American Vessels Captured by British
Men-of-War and Privateers, 1803–1811* (New York, 1926), item no. 166.

90. The *President,* the 44-gun flagship of the United States Mediterranean
force under the command of Captain Samuel Barron, had been built in New York
in the 1790's. See Maclay, *History of U.S. Navy*, I, 158, 297–98.

91. For example, the Norman-style cathedral, begun in 1098, was so completely demolished in the earthquake of 1783 that very little of the original struc-
ture remained afterward. The frequently recurring earthquakes in Messina result
from the city's being on a line of contact between the formations joining Etna
and Vesuvius.

92. Probably derived from Brydone, I, 49.

93. Lieutenant Charles G. Ridgely (1784–1848) who was subsequently tried by
a Sicilian military court and acquitted. For other details, see *J&N*, I, 175, n. 11.

94. Cavaliere Giovanni Guillichini. See *J&N*, I, 175. n. 12.

95. Commodore Samuel Barron.

96. John Broadbent (d. 1826) served as United States consul in Messina from
1805 to 1826. See *J&N*, I, 163, n. 367.

97. At this point in the letter, on MS page 47, there is a piece about two inches
square torn away. Other missing words are indicated in the text of the letter.

98. Mr. and Mrs. John Johnson, actors at the Park Theatre, to whom WI had
alluded in earlier letters, for example, on July 1, 1804.

99. Marie Therese De Camp (1774–1838), who married the English actor,
Charles Kemble, on July 2, 1806. Her oldest child was Frances Anne Kemble,
well known as an actress in the United States.

100. A variation of *Hamlet*, I, v, 79.

24. *To Andrew Quoz*

Ship Matilda, at Sea, Jany. 1st.180⟨4⟩5.

Dear Andrew

I wrote you sometime since by the way of Leghorn[1] but as the fever
at that time occasiond some confusion in that city I am apprehensive
my letter may be detained or neglected. The uncertainty of letters
getting safe to America from the Mediterranean ports[2] has prevented
my writing as frequently as I otherwise should have done. The surest
conveyance from Genoa was to send them quite to Bordeaux, I however,
forwarded two large pacquets from thence to Leghorn to be sent
by the first ship that saild for America.

I have been considerably afflicted my Dear Quoz at not recieving a line from you since I left Bordeaux—while there, I confess I was much obliged to you for the frequency of your correspondence—but since that, there has been a deplorable falling off. Our long and unimpaired amity, my venerable friend, should have assured you that nothing could have given me greater "comfort & rejoicing" than frequent communications from you, especially when in these *outlandish* parts 'a pilgrim & a sojourner in the land.'[3]

You see I ⟨have⟩ am once more venturing my *life & fortunes* on the "vasty deep"[4] speeding away to sicily that Island of fable & Romance. ⟨where⟩ Accustomed to our *honest* American Hills & dales where *stubborn fact* presides and checks the imagination in its wandrings you may concieve with what enthusiasm I haste to those "poetic fields"[5] where fiction has shed its charms o'er every scene, where

"—not a mountain rears its head unsung.
Renownd in verse each shady thicket grows
And every stream in heavenly numbers flows."[6]

Another year has opened upon us, but ah, my worthy friend, how different the commencement from that of the year that has elapsed. Then, assembled around the *Council fire* with you, & Bobson & Charley and Figsby & Pop and the rest of our numerous Corps of *Amateurs & Litterati*[7] we sipped the inspiring *Cherry bounce* and haild the coming year with jovial countenances—But now, seated soberly in the Cabin the hours pass gravely by—unmarked by any pleasure but that of writing to you and bringing you present in my imagination.

Happy—happy Quoz! permitted on this jocund day to rove among the fair ones of your acquaintance—and "snatch immortal blessings from their lips"[8] I cannot but envy your felicity—I who "not destind such delights to share"[9] must solace myself with the ⟨dull⟩ melancholy pleasure of recalling past enjoyments and the fond hope that amid all your amusements you may now & then bestow a thought upon your far distant friend. On my part be assured you shall not be forgotten and to day, when, after a New-Years dinner of *Pork & pease soup* I toast the fair damsels and honest fellows of America a bumper of the best wine I have, shall form a deep potation to your health & happiness.

For a brief account of travelling incidents &c I refer you to my *family letters* wherein I am as particular as leisure and opportunity will permit, as you of course, will have the perusal of them[10] I need not enter into details which have already been given there.

I gave you in some of my former letters a few vague opinions that I had formed of the ⟨French⟩ fair inhabitants of France—tho' I could by no means pretend to the justice of them. The very imperfect knowledge I had of the french language prevented me from conversing with them freely, so that I never had an opportunity to judge of them impartially—When I return in France I shall be able to speak more about them. I have found far more handsome women in ⟨Gen⟩ proportion in Genoa than in any other city that I have visited in Europe. They have charming figures, beautiful features and fine black eyes that sparkle with animation or languish most bewitchingly. They are said to be as *kind* too as they are *fair,* and a lover is very rarely known to hang himself in dispair at their cruelty. I have heard it frequently observed that a french woman is much given to gallantry, but an italian woman, to love. They indeed seem remarkably susceptible of the tender passion and their attachments are generally sincere and fervent *while they last.* They have also had the character of being equally violent in revenging the unfaithfulness & slights of a lover, but I believe they do not deserve it as much as is supposed, especially of late years.

Great restraints are still observed over the conduct ·of young unmarried ladies—tho they are latterly allowed to appear frequently at Balls &c yet they are never seen from home except under the guardian eye of some sage Cerberus. The innocent familiarities that prevail between young people of both sexes in America & England is unknown in this, Country and to press the *ruby lips* of a fair damsel would be a howling abomination. Such favors are only bestowed by the *married* ladies—*in private.* To kiss the *hand* of a married woman, however, is a fashionable & gallant mode of salutation.

Much has been said likewise about the jealousy of italian husbands, whether they are as much so *as is reported,* I have not been able to discover, but I am well convinced they have abundant [cause][11] for their suspicions. In fact, ⟨my⟩ friend Quoz—though to a single man the italian women are a mighty agreeable accomodating set of beings, yet, were I what is called a *marrying man* I would as soon put my neck into a hempen noose as into the hymenial one, with any of them. It is my misfortune, perhaps, to be forever drawing comparisons between the Women of Europe and the fair beings I have left behind me in America and the balance turns heavily in favor of the latter— Not but that I confess I have experienced a little wandering of the *head* among the fair ones of Italy and some transient attachments that are necessary to give a *flavor* to existence—but my *heart* still points towards new york as the quarter from whence it feels the most powerful attractions. Thus you see I have not yet lost my national prejudices, but I trust I am not illiberal in my ideas with respect to the people & places thro which I am passing. ⟨I hope to return h⟩ I am highly susceptible of delight from the novelties that continually present themselves—and hope I just retain enough of the *Amor patriae* to return to my own country with ⟨correct⟩↑liberal↓ ideas of the blessings & advantages of Europe but the firm conviction that there is no country so well suited to render me happy as America.

Jany. 20th I have had this letter laying by me a long time untouched for which I offer two excuses, first, that I am constantly employed in studying the italian language which frequently occupies me half the night, and second, that I have very little to write except what I give in my letter to William which as I have before mentioned you will of course peruse. To tell the truth friend Andrew, my writing to you is chiefly to prevent you from thinking I am neglectful of old friends. I expect some of my acquaintances will be offended at not receiving letters from me, not considering how difficult it is for a traveller to find the necessary time & opportunity for such long letters as they would expect. If you hear any complain I beg of you to inform them that it is not from want of inclination but to the absolute impossibility of my attending to different correspondences. ⟨I have⟩ I am now performing a pleasant Quarantine at Messina of twenty one days— we arrived here the fifth and of course have passed a good part of it—Twould make your heart bleed my dear Andrew to hear how your venerable friend has been besmoked and befunked by villainous fumigations.

I have been rammd into the hold with my unfortunate shipmates & stenchd & stifled with a chaffing dish of burning drugs & doctor stuff—I have been overhauld by Physicians, bullied by health officers and have even run a narrow chance of being shot & killd by a guard armed with a bayonet on the end of a broom stick—These friend Quoz are misfortunes worth lying down and crying over—yet I survive them all—I have thus far escaped in safety, in spight of Robbers by sea & ⟨Robbers⟩↑rascals↓ by land offices of Police & Offices of health— Storms, volcanoes, Scyl⟨a⟩la charybdes charcoal & assafoetida—Were I to tell you of all that I have seen & heard in these my perilous adventurings antres vast—desarts idle, anthropophagi[12]—long bearded Capuchins & whiskerd Greeks twould make you swear "twas strange twas passing strange"[13] but these shall all be reserved for future discourses around the Council fire—if ever I arrive there safe thro the rocks & quicksands of Europe.

I pray you resume your pen and let me know what is stirring in the little world in which we moved. Be particular I charge you with respect to the fair part of it as you know I am peculiarly anxious to have every intelligence ⟨concerning⟩↑respecting↓ them. I have heard nothing concerning the manner in which my gent[l]e mistress[14] fared amid the anticipated trials of the month of august and there is nothing that I have been more desirous to hear. The *fair Eliza*[15] also—I must positively have every article of news relative to her—I had even written her a letter—dont start friend Quoz,—it was not a love letter—thou knowest well the nature of my friendship for her—I had promised to send her a pair of Gloves from Italy inclosd in a nut Shell, but have not been able to find any ⟨of that⟩↑sufficiently↓ fine; I intended to use this as an excuse for sending her a letter but after I had wrote it my heart failed me, I was affraid of being too presumptious and so tore the letter up You will therefore mention to her that it is not thro negligence or forgetfulness that I have not sent the gloves but from the most unaccommodating reason—that they are not to be had—I intend however to make another search when I return to Italy.

By my last letter from America I find Ann[16] has returnd from Canada—write me an account of her, ⟨how⟩ and what effect the nunnery has had in altering & improving her—She promised to make a charming Girl when last I saw her

Lastly—Of the affairs of Day Street[17] and its inhabitants with their movements, looks & employments I demand a geographical historical & philosophical discription and general observations upon every thing else that passes either in the little or Great world. Thus I have given you directions for writing a letter at least four sheets long so that you need not complain that you do not know what to write about—As it is late at night and I am in an uncommon Stupid humor (as this letter plainly evinces) I will conclude with desiring my remembrances to Bobson and all other friends and assuring you that I am

with high respect/Your friend until Death

J O[18]

Mr Andrew Quoz.

DOCKETED: Wash: Irving / Jany. ⟨5⟩ 1. 1805
MANUSCRIPT: Yale.

1. This letter has not been located.
2. The British blockade of Mediterranean ports had successfully stopped much of the shipping. WI alludes to it in his letter to William Irving, December 25, 1804–January 25, 1805.
3. Probably a variant of Gen. 23:4.
4. *Henry IV*, Part I, III, i, 53.
5. Joseph Addison, "A Letter from Italy, to the Right Honourable Charles Lord Halifax" (1701), line 11.
6. Addison, "A Letter from Italy," lines 14–16.
7. WI may be referring to earlier meetings of the group of young writers

and men about town which became known as the Lads of Kilkenny after his return to New York. They often met at Gouverneur Kemble's house in Newark which was not as rustic as the allusion to "cabin" here suggests.

8. Not identified.

9. Oliver Goldsmith, "The Traveller," in *Collected Works of Oliver Goldsmith,* ed. Arthur Friedman (Oxford, 1966), IV, 249, line 23.

10. This statement supports the contention sometimes advanced that Andrew Quoz was WI's name for James Kirke Paulding (1778–1860), whose sister Julia had married William Irving. Paulding, as an intimate member of the family, would have easy access to WI's letters. Furthermore, Paulding was living with the William Irving family at this time.

11. WI omitted a word here. The sense seems to suggest "cause," which has been added in brackets.

12. WI's takeoff on *Othello,* I, iii, 140–44.

13. *Othello,* I, iii, 160.

14. This refers to Maria Fenno Hoffman, who had been expecting a child in August, 1804. See WI's letter of July 2, 1804.

15. Probably Eliza Ogden, who had made the trip into northern New York in August, 1803, with Mr. and Mrs. Josiah Ogden Hoffman.

16. Ann Hoffman.

17. See July 24, [1804], note 9.

18. With this singular signature, WI apparently designated himself as Jonathan Oldstyle.

25. *To William Irving, Jr.*

Rome, April 4th. 1805.

My dear Brother,

With the most painful self reproach I sit down to write you a few lines, conscious that I have both merited and recieved your censures for my long silence Still however I will venture an excuse and trust to your indulgence and the conviction that I hope you have—that I am never willingly negligent in my correspondence, to grant me a ready forgiveness. While ⟨I⟩ in Sicily I was so continually in motion that I had scarcely a moment to spare to write even if I had the conveniences necessary, but that Island is so wretchedly provided with the requisite accomodations for that purpose, that I had to give up my usual mode of writing a little to you every day or two. Travelling on mules—I was so excessively fatigued in the evenings that ⟨[*unrecovered*]⟩ immediate repose was necessary—and we had always a great deal to arrange before we could enjoy even that in comfort—thus being unable to treat of objects & incidents as they occurd they multiplied on me so rapidly that I found it would require a considerable time to write of them all as minutely as I had been accustomed to do in former letters Continually occupied as I was with present pursuits I felt the impossibility of the thing and shrunk from the attempt—a neglect of this kind always becomes more irreparable by delay[.] the task is daily accumulating. While ⟨I⟩ in Naples I had scarcely a moment to myself excepting for two or three days when confined by a Cold in my face and even then I was busied in bringing up my journal on sicily. Thus you see the ⟨th⟩ causes that have kept me silent. I have continually felt that uneasiness at mind that attends the neglect of a duty and have determined to relieve myself from it by this appeal to your indulgence. I find it is impossible to continue the same minuteness in my letters as formerly—especially now that I ⟨shall⟩ am continually in motion, Objects present themselves so rapidly and in such endless variety that they engross every moment in contemplating them attentively. It is only when at rest in any particular spot that I can be particular. At present I am completely engaged in examining the interesting remains of antient Rome and the more modern production of ⟨arts⟩ the arts which her palaces & churches afford. You may therefore easily suppose that I have little time to write. I shall give you a very brief account of my tour in sicily &c. I wrote you a long letter from Messina while in Quarantine in the ship Matilda of Philadelphia, and left it in the hands of the Captain to take to America. From Messina I sailed ↑31 Jany↓ to Syracuse in the Schooner Nautilus, one of the armd vessels ⟨we have stat⟩ stationd by our Government in the Mediterranean. The Captain Dent was a very clever young fellow of Philadelphia and the officers extremely agreeable. We sailed thro the Straights of Messina at the same time with the Fleet of Lord Nelson then in search of the French fleet—it was one of the noblest naval scenes I have ever beheld.[1] The ships are in the finest order and move most majestically. They are in such excellent dicipline that their manouvres are performed like a body of men. We entered the beautiful harbor of Syracuse about two Oclock on the second of February and I had the pleasure of seeing there at anchor several of our ships of War, viz the Frigates President, Essex, Constellation, & ⟨Constitution⟩ Congress and the Brig Vixen.

I remained at Syracuse about nine days, delighted with finding myself surrounded by fellow countrymen. Among the officers of the ships I found several of the finest young fellows I ever knew—"open & generous & bountiful & brave"[2] every ship was to me ⟨as⟩ a home and every officer a friend. Having satisfied myself with respect to the melancholy monuments of antient greatness that remain around Syracuse I left there with extreme regret on the 11th. Feby. in Company with Capt. Hall[3] Capt. of Marines on board of the president a young fellow of Charleston of great vivacity & spirits—Wynn[4] &

Wadsworth[5] of Connecticut pursers of the ⟨President⟩ Congress &
president, both excellent companions—particularly Wynn who is a
fellow of great whim & humour. ⟨We were mounted on⟩ Our destination was Catania[6] and we made a very respectable cavalcade[.] Hall,
myself and a servant we had with us were mounted on mules, Wynn
& wadsworth were seated in a Latiga a kind of Sedan chair that
accomodates two persons who sit facing each other—it is slung on
two poles that are borne by two mules one before & the other
behind—We had besides a numerous retinue of guides & Muleteers.
This is the only mode of travelling in this country for the roads are
meer footpaths that wind among rocks and along precipices where 'it
would be impossible for carriages to pass—We were well armed with
pistols swords & dirks to guard against the attacks of banditti with
which the island is said to abound[.] indeed the first day we passed
thro several solitary places where the mountains abounded in vast
gloomy caverns that seemed the very haunts of robbery & assassination.
In the evening we put up at Lentini,[7] a miserable village though a
very respectable one for Sicily. This was antiently the city Leontino
⟨the⟩ inhabited by the Listrigonians whom the antients stigmatized
as cannibals—The inhabitants of this city boasted that Hercules gave
them a lion for a standard[8]
    In the ⟨fo⟩ morning we left the village and passed thro beautiful
vallies ⟨for⟩ antiently termed the Listrigonian plains and celebrated
for their fertility There we saw the lake Bevero feigned to have
been made by Hercules, it abounds with fish & wild fowl. About
two Oclock we arrived at Catania
    This is a beautiful city chiefly built during the last century on the
ruins of the former one which had Æen almost entirely destroyed
by an eruption of Lava from Mount Ætna. It is an instance of great
religious faith in these people that they have the hardihood to rebuild
their city in the very spot where ⟨they have⟩ ↑it has↓ so often been
overwhelmed, but they blindly trust the protection of St. Agatha[9]
the patroness of the City.
    I ⟨was⟩ mentioned to one of the Cattanese my surprise that they
should rely any longer on her good services when she had shewed
them so evidently that she was not inclined to protect them[.] I
particularly alluded to the last flood of lava that laid the finest part
of the city in ruins. "Ah["] said he, ["]we had been very wicked,
very neglectful of the saint, so she sufferd the lava to run over
one part of the city that the *other* might see from what miseries she
had preserved it."
    The evening of our arrival there was a grand ceremony in the
⟨church⟩ ↑cathedral↓[10] & the figure of the saint was borne round the

interior of the church in solemn procession amidst the shouts shrieks prayers and benedictions of the populace, indeed they behaved like frantic people throwing their hats in the air and clapping their ⟨ands⟩ hands[11]—All this is to keep the saint in good humour for they fear, should she take another affront, that she might suffer the whole city to be overwhelmed. We were treated with great politeness and suffered even to enter into the sanctum sanctorum where the image of the saint is kept under strong doors & bolts of iron—Here they even let us examine & touch the image, (perhaps they did not know we were heretics) The saint is a good natured looking little woman, and covered with jewels and precious stones to an immense amount.

Our stay in Catania was rendered extremely agreeable by the attentions of the Chevalier Landolini[12] a Knight of Malta to whom we had brought letters. He introduced us to several of the Nobility by whom we were recieved with great politeness & attention and invited to all the parties that took place during our stay. The situation of Catania is very beautiful—⟨on one⟩ behind it the mountain rears its sublime and awful head, vomiting smoke and often envelloped in clouds—in ⟨the⟩ front is the Ocean forming a vast bay and to the right is the extensive plain of Catania with the river ⟨Gadeda?⟩ ↑Giaretta↓ wandering thro it. This stream ⟨was⟩ ↑is the↓ antient Simetus into which it is said Thalia was transformed[13] We ascended about half way up the mountain, but were prevented from attaining the summit by the vast quantity of snow in which it was enveloped. No guide would venture up it, and the attempt we were told would be hazardous in the extreme, and certainly fruitless. We mounted to the top of several of the small mountains thrown up on the sides of the great one by different eruptions, particularly Monte Rosso, (red mountain,) from which issued the last stream of lava that destroyed Catania.[14] The view from hence was superb, and almost unbounded, and we could trace the enormous flood of lava till it lost itself in the sea, about ten miles distant.

* * * At Catania our company divided. Wynn and Wadsworth returned to Syracuse, and Captain Hall and myself set out to cross the island to Palermo. We chose a route that lay directly through the centre of the island, because it was one that we had never seen described by travellers, and we were told it was very interesting. We were mounted as before on mules, armed ourselves well with pistols and swords, and had a servant with us, a courageous fellow, with at least half a dozen pistols stuck in his pockets and girdle. We were about five days accomplishing this journey.[15] I have no time to be particular in an account of it; indeed, it would be a detail of misery, poverty, wretched accommodation, and almost every incon-

venience a traveller could suffer. The peasants are in the most abject
state of want and wretchedness imaginable, they live in cabins worse
than our meanest log-huts—very often in caverns, in the sides of
mountains, amid filth and vermin. In such places were we forced
to accommodate ourselves; fortunately for us, we had carried a
mattress with us, upon which we slept at night. We had to pass one
night in a chapel for want of other accommodations. It would be
painful to you to read an account of the "variety of wretchedness"
we witnessed. We had supplied ourselves with provisions for the
route, and several times, when I have thrown a bone to a half-
famished dog or cat, it has been snatched away from the miserable
animal by the woman of the house, and given to her children! God
knows my mind never suffered so much as on this journey, when I
had such scenes of want and misery continually before me, without
the power of effectually relieving them.[16]

We arrived at Palermo about the 24th of February, and passed
several days there very agreeably. We had brought letters to Mr. Gibbs,[17]
American agent there, and to the Princess Camporeale from her sister
at Catania.[18] We, therefore, soon found acquaintance among the
nobility; and as it was the latter part of carnival, the gayest season
of the year, our time was completely occupied by amusements. As
the time for my departure from Palermo approached, I began to feel
extremely uneasy. The packet that sails constantly between that city
and Naples, and is always well armed, was unfortunately undergoing
repairs at Naples. No alternative offered than to venture across in one
of the small vessels that carry fruit to the continent. Reports were
in circulation of two or three Tripolitan cruisers hovering about the
Italian coast, and that they had taken two American ships; besides
these the Sicilian vessels are subject to capture from the cruisers of
every Barbary power....[19]

All that time I passed on shore in a wretched hovel, where I had
scarce any thing to eat, and where I had to sleep in my clothes and
great coat at night, for want of other covering. After these two days
of suffering, we made out to get to Palermo. There I passed another
day of uneasiness of mind till a favorable wind sprung up. We hoisted
sail and weighed anchor at night; the next morning we were out of
sight of Sicily, had a fine run all day, and in the course of the next
night entered the bay of Naples, where, to my great comfort, I saw
the flaming summit of Vesuvius, which was a joyful token that we
were out of danger.[20] I have been several times congratulated on my
good fortune, for three or four days after two Neapolitan vessels were
taken by Barbary cruisers, as they were crossing from Sicily.[21]

a[22] thing, of which I have long been convinced. To a man of fortune travelling for amusement or who has plenty of time to spare, it may be well enough to spend a couple of months in Rome, but to one whose object is improvement and who has to be economic of his time a much shorter term will suffice. Where[23] I to consult my inclination merely, I should be induced to lengthen my stay, and linger about a spot that brings to mind so many interesting incidents of history—so many exalted characters that I have been accustomed from infancy to admire and that presents a variety of information concerning a nation that has so much interested the world. But ⟨my⟩ the nature of my plans does not permit me to remain longer here than ⟨to observe the⟩ is necessary to acquire a correct idea of the place—its situation antient & modern and to examine the best specimens of sculpture painting & architecture it affords; this I think I have tolerably succeeded in doing and any farther stay would but be spent in gratifying an unprofitable curiosity at the expence of superior advantages. I am impatient to get to paris where I may rest a while from my wanderings, and spend a little ⟨while⟩ ↑time↓ in studying certain arts & sciences which it is impossible to attend to while in my present rambling unsettled state. ⟨Paris is at this 'day centre of⟩ There will commence in may a course of lectures at the Garden of plants in paris, on botany, chemistry and different other branches of science by the most experienced and learned men, and which are attended with no charge or expence to the student[.][24] I shall profit by them during my stay, which I expect will be longer at that ⟨place⟩ city than I originally contemplated. In fact there is no place in Europe where a young man who ⟨ad⟩ wishes to improve himself and is determined to act with prudence—can spend a certain space of time to more advantage than at Paris. The doors of knowledge are there thrown open and the different pursuits both useful and ornamental may be prosecuted with more facility and less expence than at any other city in the world Whatever be the motive whether from vanity, affectation or real taste the french have shewn a liberality of disposition towards the ⟨f⟩ arts and sciences, that does them honour. They have collected at Paris the chef d'ouvres of Painting & sculpture— their galleries, liberaries, museums are open to the Stranger free of any charge, nor is he assaild by a herd of beggarly servants ⟨that ass⟩ as in the palaces museums &c of Italy & England, whose demands ⟨are⟩ form in the aggregate one of the heaviest contributions on his purse. ⟨It is this article of⟩ It is the feeing of servants that makes a residence in Rome & Naples so very expensive to the traveller, nor is it solely confined to the vis[i]ting[25] galleries You cannot in Rome, go to a conversazione or visit a person of fashion but the next morning you have a servant at your door demanding a *buono mano* (a gratuity.)

I am induced likewise to hasten my departure as by that means I shall have for my fellow traveller ⟨the⟩ Mr Cabell,²⁶ the same who travelled with me from Naples. As our pursuits, finances ↑routes,↓ &c are much the same we are extremely well fitted in those respects to agree together[.] Mr C is likewise well acquainted in Paris where he has already passed some time and consequently will be of great assistance to me on arriving at that place. For his character I refer you to Schiefflen who was acquainted with him in Paris—with the general observation, that he is the most Estimable young man I have encountered in Europe. We shall proceed from hence to Bologna by the way of Loretto & Ancona—avoiding all Tuscany round which the Cordoné of troops still exists²⁷—From Bologna to Milan—from Milan I expect our route will continue to the Lake Maggiore, where we embark and ⟨sail⟩ traverse the lake from one end to the other—then along the course of the River Ticino to Mount St. Goatherd, ⟨fr⟩ across the mountain and by the way of the Lake of Lucerne to Zurich from Zurich to Basle and from thence make the best of our way to Paris. Thus we shall make a tour thro a very picturesque part of Switzerland entering it by one of the most sublime and romantic passes. Perhaps we may vary a little from the route I have laid down, to visit some remarkable places or beautiful scenes.

So much for my route—which I hope will meet with your approbation.

On my arrival at Naples I was made indiscribably happy by the receipt of a number of letters from New York consisting of five from you, one from Jack and one from my worthy and affectionate fellow student Beebee.²⁸ It was a complete deluge of domestic intelligence and afforded me several of the happiest hours I have spent in Europe. In consequence of your very judicious precaution of writing duplicates I have now recieved several letters that had been delayed and have a regular file of your epistles to number 9 dated 30th. Novr. which is the latest I have heard by letter from New York. I have stitchd them together and they form a little volume²⁹ which I read over repeatedly with delight. It was at Naples that I received your letter containing some lines which were written by Mrs Rodman³⁰— The good opinion of *such a woman* would be highly flattering to a fellow of less vanity than myself—but I assure you it was not merely my vanity that was aroused—while exiled in a manner from my country & home mingling among³¹

strangers to whom my very existence is unimportant, it is consoling to reflect that there are distant beings who think of me with less indifference, and to whom my welfare is interesting. The least token of remembrance from them is enlivening, and like a gleam of sunshine on my lonely feelings. But when the testimony of regard was so kind, so animated, breathing such a spirit of sympathy and friendship, and that too from a woman whom I have long admired as one of the most estimable of her sex, by heavens it was too exquisite. The tears rushed to my eyes like an infant's, and I could only bless her with all the fervor of my heart.

MANUSCRIPT: Va.–Barrett (incomplete). PUBLISHED: PMI, I, 113–16, 123–26, 127 (in part).

Only pages 1–4 and 9–10 of the holograph letter have been located. Other portions of the letter have been printed in PMI and are included in the text as indicated in the notes.

1. WI developed this point more fully in his journal entry for January 31, 1805. See J&N, I, 177–78.

2. Not identified.

3. John Hall was made a first lieutenant on August 2, 1798, captain on December 1, 1801, and major on June 8, 1804. See J&N, I, 188, n. 50.

4. Timothy Winn (d. 1836) was listed as a purser on the muster roll of the Congress for 1804–1805. See J&N, I, 195, n. 73.

5. Charles Wadsworth (d. 1809) was made purser on May 28, 1798. See J&N, I, 193, n. 66.

6. Catania is 47 miles from Syracuse.

7. Lentini is 29 miles northwest of Syracuse.

8. For his details about the Listrigonians and Hercules WI used Swinburne, Travels in the Two Sicilies, II, 313, 315, and Buonfiglio Constanzo, Prima . . . Parte dell'Historia Siciliana, 21, 46, 415. See J&N, I, 200, n. 91.

9. St. Agatha (d. ca. 250), martyred patroness of Catania whose intervention supposedly prevented an eruption of Mt. Etna the year after her burial.

10. The cathedral, which was started by Roger I in 1091, was almost completely destroyed by an earthquake in 1169. After being rebuilt, it was frequently damaged in subsequent earthquakes.

11. Special observances for St. Agatha which WI saw were held on February 12. See J&N, I, 202–3.

12. Pietro Landolina, Marchese di Trezzano and di Sant'Alfano, became a Knight of Malta in 1790. See J&N, I, 201, n. 97.

13. WI acquired this story from Patrick Brydone, A Tour Through Sicily and Malta . . . (London, 1774), I, 281. Page 4 of the holograph ends at this point. Collation of printed portions with the manuscript reveals that PMI sometimes omitted sentences from the holograph without the use of ellipses. The continuation of this passage is printed in PMI, I, 115–16.

14. The Monti Rossi were formed during the violent eruption of March 11, 1669. WI alludes to the earthquake and accompanying flow of lava on January 3, 1693, which completely destroyed Catania.

15. On February 19 WI and Hall left Catania with a servant and a muleteer on the overland journey to Palermo, which they reached on February 24. For details of their unpleasant experiences, see J&N, I, 210–16.

16. The passage printed in and here reproduced from PMI, 115–16 ends here.

17. Abram Gibbs served as United States consul in Palermo from 1805 to 1816. See *J&N*, I, 216, n. 149.

18. The Princess Camporeale was presumably Stephania Beccadelli, and her sister, Marianna Beccadelli Branciforte, was the Princess Gravina di Ramacca. See *J&N*, I, 218, n. 158.

19. This paragraph is printed in PMI, I, 123. The manuscript has not been located.

20. According to his journal, WI boarded a fruit boat bound for Naples in the evening of March 1. After false starts and delays the boat finally left Palermo on March 5 and arrived in Naples on March 7. See *J&N*, I, 221–23.

21. This paragraph is printed in PMI, I, 124. The manuscript has not been located; hence the hiatus between the preceding paragraph and the next passage taken from the fragmentary MS.

22. Page 9 of the holograph begins at this point.

23. WI intended to write "Were."

24. Le Museum d'Histoire Naturelle, which was founded in 1629 and of which le Jardin des Plantes was a part, preserved botanical and zoological specimens, provided research facilities for scientists, and conducted lectures and courses which presented the latest findings of its scientific investigators.

25. WI wrote "visting."

26. Joseph Carrington Cabell (1778–1856), a Virginia lawyer interested in agricultural innovations, traveled with WI from March to June, 1805. For details about their friendship, see Richard Beale Davis, "Washington Irving and Joseph C. Cabell," in *English Studies in Honor of James Southall Wilson*, ed. Fredson Bowers, University of Virginia Studies, no. 5 (Charlottesville, 1951), pp. 7–22.

27. In 1801 by the terms of the treaty of Lunéville, Tuscany, with the support of French troops, was established as the kingdom of Etruria for the Bourbon prince Louis and later for his son Charles Louis.

28. The manuscripts of these letters have not been located. Part of one of William Irving's letters is printed in PMI, I, 126–27.

29. This collection of William Irving's letters has not been located.

30. WI had mentioned Mrs. Rodman and her children in his letter of July 20, 1804. She died in New York on June 11, 1808.

31. Page 10 of the holograph ends here, but PMI's printed version (I, 127), which continues the text for several lines, is added at this point.

26. To William Irving, Jr.

Rome, April 12th. 1805

My dear Brother

I wrote you a letter which I finished and dispatched the day before yesterday by the way of Bordeaux, but hearing of an opportunity that presents for New York from Leghorn I improve it to send you a few lines which are scribbled in the midst of the hurry of preparation for a long Journey. I leave this City tomorrow in company with Mr Cabell[1] of Virginia, our ultimate destination is paris. The route we expect to take will be from hence to Bologna by the way of Loretto & Ancona, avoiding all Tuscany which is still surrounded by a *Cordon* of Troops. From Bologña [to]² Milan, then across the lake Maggiore—along the course of the river Tecina to Mount St Goatherd —across the mountain to the lake of Lucerne in Switzerland, over the lake to Lucerne from thence to Zurich—from Zurich to Basle and then by the best route, to Paris. Those are the general points we expect to strike tho we may make many deviations as circumstances may render necessary or advisable. It is a long fatiguing journey to contemplate but the beautiful scenery and interesting objects throughout make me anticipate it with delight. ⟨This⟩ The Season is highly favorable.

I have not spent the time generally allowed by Travellers for viewing rome, but I think I have taken as comprehensive a view of it as is consistent with my plans. I am eager to get to Paris where I can rest some time from my wanderings and pay attention to several branches of art & science into which I wish to get a little insight. I have been rambling about, restless and unsettled for nearly a year and shall be glad of a little repose. My mind is fatigued by being kept on the stretch so long by a continual succession of novelties and wonders in Nature & Art It requires relaxation, but that it can never enjoy while I am in motion—I fear, not while I am in Europe— Rome has almost exhausted me and I have hardly room for another city in my head.

On my arrival at Naples from Sicily I received a number of Letters from New York—five from you one from Jack³ and one from my worthy friend Beebee[.]⁴ I have now all your letters to number nine inclusive[.] the last date is 30th. Novr. Since which I have received no letters from my friends. I am impatient to hear farther from you all, but do not expect to do so till I arrive at Paris.

My health is perfectly restored, I never was in a better state of body and mind than at present. I [am]⁵ much the same, slender looking fellow as usual but have a degree of strength & activity that almost places me above fatigue For my part it is immaterial to me whether I grow ⟨stout as t⟩ stouter or not—as to growing *fat* I have decided absolutely against it—it is one of those unweildy tokens of health that I would willingly be excused the burden of.

I have been a witness of all the glories of *Holy Week*⁶ so much cried up by the italians as a miracle of religious pomp & ceremony—to me it has been the most empty parade I ever saw[.] the absence of the pope⁷ is much regretted[.] it is said his presence would have made the ceremonies much more imposing. Perhaps I am prejudiced against the Romish religion from having been a witness to the gross ignorance superstition and misery it has intailed upon the inhabitants of these countries—but their grand ceremonies are to me the most pompous farces imaginable—To describe them would but be fatiguing you with discriptions of ostentatious humility and the grossest absurdities. The chief parts of the business that pleased me were the *miserere* a fine piece of sad, melancholy music representing the passion of our Saviour. It is counted an exquisite piece of music by the italians and is sung by very fine voices. The illumination of the Cross in St Peters. This is a large Cross suspended in the centre of the church coverd with lamps. The effect of light and shade it produces among the arcades columns aisles & recesses of the church is inimitable —Here the best company of rome resort as to a promenade. This church is one of the finest objects of art which I have seen in Europe and well deserves to be ranked among the Wonders of the world—as I am no architect I can not pretend to give you a description of it, except that it is built with such fine judgement, that, though it abounds with the richest marbles, tombs, chapels &c no one part obtrudes itself to injure the majestic—striking effect of the whole.

Time will not allow me to be particular. Your future letters will be forwarded to the same address at Bordeaux and you may also safely write to me by the way of Nantz—Dieppe Antwerp, Amsterdam & Rotterdam directing my letters to the care of Mr. Luc Callaghan[8]— Banker Paris. I wish you would desire my acquaintances to write frequently to me—their letters will cost me but trifling postage which I will cheerfully pay There is nothing cheers me so much as frequen[t][9] letters from my friends.

You mention in one of your letters a wish that I should visit Scotland before I return—I am affraid the season when I shall be in England will be unfavorable for that purpose and I doubt much, after I have seen england whether scotland will afford me much instruction— I think it is better to see fewer countries & see them well—however I shall be guided by your future advice—by circumstances & by expences.

Remember me to father mother the family and all my friends, and I again beg you to request them to write often

Your affectionate Brother
WI.

ADDRESSED: Mr William Irving Junr. / New York / *United States of America*
    DOCKETED: Rome Apl 4 X 12 / 1805
MANUSCRIPT: Rutgers University Library. PUBLISHED: PMI, I, 139 (in part);
    Journal of the Rutgers University Library 9 (June, 1946), 39–41.

1. Joseph Carrington Cabell, with whom WI traveled to Paris and whom he saw again upon his return to New York. See Richard Beale Davis, "Washington

Irving and Joseph C. Cabell," in *English Studies in Honor of James Southall Wilson*, pp. 7–22.

2. The word is torn away by the seal.

3. Perhaps his brother John Treat.

4. These letters have not been located.

5. The word is torn away by the seal.

6. Easter occurred on April 14 in 1805.

7. Pope Pius VII (1800–1823) (Barnaba Chiaramontini, 1742–1823) had gone to Milan to confer with Napoleon, who had arrived on March 16 and was crowned king of Italy there on May 10, 1805.

8. Callaghan is listed as a second lieutenant in the national guard and as a merchant at 15 Rue Bleue in the *Almanach de 25,000 Adresses . . .* for 1817.

9. The last letter is obscured by a blot.

27. To Elias Hicks

Intra. Lago Maggiore—May 4th. 1805.

Seated in a comfortable Inn, in one of the picturesque little villages that grace the borders of this beautiful lake my mind softned by the lovely scenery around—occurs with fond reccollection to my far distant friends in America—I seize a moment of leisure that occurs—to address a few lines to my friend to assure him that "*the affections of our early youth and the intimacy of riper years,*"[1] are not obliterated from my heart. I should look back with infinite self reproof on the long long period I have sufferd to elapse in silence, did not the continual occupation both of mind and body which I have experienced in travelling, operate as a sufficient excuse. My *friend Andrew*[2] I have no doubt will regard my silence in a charitable light, convinced that it does not result from any deficiency of Friendship.

An Account of my Journey from Rome through the delightful scenes of Antient Umbria and the fertile plains of Lombardy would be too long for the few moments I have to write.[3] From Rome to Loretto the country was indescribably picturesque. The solitary, romantic passes of the appenines were finely contrasted by the chain of delicious valleys that extends through them. Nothing could be more delightful than after passing thro a long defile of the mountains—surrounded by rocks precipices & torrents, where nature put on her most wild & fantastic forms—to descend into a valley—blooming with all the graces of spring—variegated by Groves cornfields and ⟨vil⟩ meadows—enlivened by villages convents and cottages and waterd by the classic streams of the Tiber the Nar or the clitumnus—The charms of these valleys have been extolld both by the antients and moderns and among the latter Addison describes them in the following beautiful lines

"————umbrias ⟨blest⟩ ↑green↓ retreats
Where Western gales eternally preside
And all the seasons lavish all their pride
Blossoms & fruits & flowers ⟨promenade⟩ ↑together↓ rise
And the whole year in gay confusion lies."[4]

————I find I am already wandering from the original intention of this letter ⟨g⟩ and talking of Umbria instead of my voyage on Lake Maggiore. Of my travelling arrangements you are probably informed from my former letters—My fellow traveller is Mr Cabell of Virginia a gentleman of whose talents information & disposition I cannot speak too highly. We have for servant *honest* John ↑Josse↓ Vandermoere[5]—a native of Bruxelles, and one of the most faithful upright fellows I ever knew in his profession — He speaks french dutch & English and can make out to murder the italian tongue almost as badly as myself.

Having engaged a boat at the Village of Sesto[6] to take us to Magadino[7] at the other extremity of the lake we embarked yesterday morning after breakfast.[8] Our bark was small—coverd with a linen awning and rowed by four stout men. The morning was overcast but the weather mild and pleasant and the country around so beautiful that we did not feel the want of sunshine to enliven us. We gently moved along thro a succession of romantic scenery—on the transparent waters of the lake and about nine oclock landed at the Village of Arona[9] situated at the foot of the picturesque promontory of the same name. While the boatmen were taking their breakfast we visited the remarkable statue of St. Carlo Barromeo[10] situated on the summit of a neighboring hill that overlooks the lake—The walk was long and fatiguing. I would give you some account of this St. Carlo[11] were it not imposing too much on your patience. He is one of the numerous host of saints that Italy has produced and like the generality, was besainted either because he was of a powerful family or had been very charitable—to the church. If I reccollect right he even carried his goodness to Milan, so far as to found there another church, ⟨of which⟩ That city having not more than between *one and two hundred* churches already erected. His statue is proportiond to his services and sanctity—It is a huge figure of Bronze *Sixty feet high* and more remarkable for its size than for either grace of attitude or elegance of proportions, for the cardinals habit in which it is represented effectually excludes either. The statue stands on a proportionable pedestal of Granite and the whole is erected on a mound of earth to which you ascend by an avenue of handsome horsechestnuts. The admirers of St. Carlo are loud in their boastings of this statue which they say equals the famous Colossus of Rhodes;[12] I forget the proportions of the latter, but I apprehend the saint must yield the palm to his unsanctified rival. At any rate the statue is sufficiently enormous to gratify the ambition of any priest—When we approached it a flight of little birds were sporting about its head and shoulders having formed their nests in the ears & eylids and others in the plaits of the garment, secured by their elevated station from the attempts of the most aspiring urchin.

From the hill on which the statue stands is one of the most lovely prospects imaginable—The eye embraces a great extent of the lake winding among the mountains—in some places ruffled by gentle Zephyrs—in others smooth and tranquil—reflecting the churches cottages & groves that ornamented its borders or the white sails of the little barks that seemed to repose upon its surface. The surrounding mountains presented a variety of character—Some—rough and craggy rose abruptly from the waters edge—their sides were rocky & barren scantily coverd in different places with dwarf trees and scatterd shrubbery—Their snowy summits were lost in clouds that rolld half way down them. ⟨in⟩ Others rose in gentle gradations clothed with flourishing trees thro the thick foliage of which, were seen the white walls of cottages or the towering spires of chapels and convents. Their sides were cultivated and fertile and skirted by luxurient plains that extended to the borders of the lake varied by groves & meadows. Opposite to us on the right was the romantic Promontory of Anghiera[13] crowned by a picturesque castle, which with a small village below it, was reflected in the serene ⟨b⟩ waters of the lake. We could not resist our inclination to linger some time about this charming spot—so sending the boatman who accompanied us, to tell his companions when they had finished their breakfast to come with the boat to the foot of the mountain we threw ourselves on the grass to enjoy at leisure the enchanting prospect. The air was pure & salubrious—perfumed by numerous flowers that grew about the mountains. ⟨No⟩ The repose of the scene was only interrupted by the chirp of the Swallow as he skimmd over the tranquil lake below us and dipp'd his wings in its glassy surface—the full melody of the nightingale—robin & Lark or the distant song of some peasants at work on a neighboring hill. You have no doubt often experienced the effect of such scenes & situations ⟨of⟩ on the mind soothing it into the most voluptuous state of tranquility and pensiveness. Ogilvie expresses it most correctly

> "On the airy mount reclin'd
> What wishes sooth the musing mind
> How soft the velvet lap of spring
> How sweet the Zephyrs violet-wing"[14]

After re-embarking we continued our voyage keeping along the borders of the Lake—now passing by a neat village the white houses of which seemed almost to rise out of the water—and now skirting the base of a mountain whose summit was almost envelloped in clouds

Towards afternoon the Weather began to break away—the clouds rolld off to the snowy tops of the alps which they completely shrowded and the sun breaking[15] from among them enlivened the superb scenery—chequering the lake and mountains with broad masses of light & shade. About two o'clock we entered the ⟨charming⟩ bay of Marzozzo which presents an assemblage of the most romantic objects. The Bay is ⟨surrounded⟩↑bounded↓ by stupenduous hills the tops of which were coverd with snow and their sides broken in cliffs and precipices—On the borders of the water were situated small villages the white buildings of which had a beautiful effect contrasted to the green of the mountains at whose feet they stood.

The bosom of the bay was unruffled by the slightest breeze and from the Centre of it rose the celebrated Borromean (or as they have been termed *enchanted*) Islands.)[16] These are three inconsiderable little islands the largest not above a third of a mile in circumference—but ⟨eminently⟩ indescribably picturesque from their form and situation. Isola Bella (I.E. The beautiful Island) in particular has the most delicious appearance from a distance—No pains or expence have been spared to ornament it. It is coverd with orangeries—terraces of Lemon citron myrtle &c and an overhanging grove of vast Laurel trees—and thro the rich foliage are seen the walls of a magnificent palace. The whole is beautifully reflected in the transparent waters of the lake and forms a picture that almost realizes the discription of fairy abodes given by the poets—Were not the days of romance at an end I should have been tempted to mistake it for an Elysian isle formed among the silver waves by the wand of an Enchantress. It reminded me of the lines of Thompson

> "The landscape such inspiring perfect ease
> Where Indolence (for so the wizard hight)
> Close hid his castle mid embowering trees
> That half shut out the ⟨chequerd day and night⟩↑beams
>   of phoebus bright↓
> And made a kind of chequerd day and night."[17]

Numerous Travellers have been rapturous in their praises of this Island—among others Keysler[18] very quaintly compares it to ⟨[*unrecovered*]⟩ "a pyramid of sweetmeats, ornamented with green festoons and flowers." On approaching near to it the illusion ⟨vanished⟩↑dis-

appated↓ and its charms in a great measure vanished—The works of
art became too vis⟨a⟩ible and we were disappointed in finding it laid
out in all the preposterous ⟨style of⟩ formalities of clipped walks—
artificially trimd trees—stone terraces—heavy statues and dutch flower
beds. We were all thro the palace and gardens. The former is immensely large and magnificent and contains a few good paintings—
part of it is built over the lake the waves of which wash its base.
⟨From⟩ ⟨t⟩The windows and balconies command exquisite views of
the lake from different points. The garden is ⟨bui?⟩ raised on
arches and partly usurped from the lake—its soil is brought from the
neighboring shores. From the grand terrace of the garden you have
an extensive prospect of the surrounding scenery. The two other
Islands—one called Isola Madre—is ornamented with a palace & groves
—the other called Isola Piscatori (fishermans Island) is completely
covered by a small village of fishermans huts with the church in
the middle—the ⟨island⟩↑village↓ seems to rise out of the lake. All
these Islands belong to the Borromean family[19] who likewise own vast
tracts of land in the vicinity of the lake and are immensely rich.

We parted from Isola Bella early this morning in a heavy shower of
rain; our boat, however, was well coverd & dry—We rowed close under
Isola Madre which is far more picturesque on a near approach than its
more artificial neighbor. About ⟨eight⟩↑nine↓ oclock we arrived in this
village[20] situated in a most beautiful part of the lake where the scenery
reminds me of the highlands in the hudson. As the weather threatned
to be stormy all day we determined to remain here till tomorrow
morning—particularly as we were told that if we proceeded we should
have to sleep at Magadino where there is no decent hotel. To this
detention you are indebted for this letter, as there w⟨as⟩ere no objects
of curiosity to employ my attention. I am ever happy to avail myself
of such moments of leisure to scribble to my friends—but in travelling
it is not very often that they occur—and when I write generally I tres-
pass on the time that should be occupied in acquiring information. The
Weather has cleared off this afternoon and we have had a charming
ramble in the environs of the village and along the beautiful borders
of the Lake. Adieu for the present—as I have began the history of
my voyage on the Lake I will finish it—You shall have the rest after
my arrival at Magadino.

6th. Bellinzona—We left our Inn at Intra on the morning of the 5th.
without regret for we could find nothing fit to eat there—the few
articles they gave us were so ⟨fried⟩ stewd & fritterd in oil that we could
not relish them—We had sent John on a foraging party in the kitchen
& Larder but he returned with the melancholy intelligence "That there
was to be a grand feast the next day in honor of St Francis[21] and all

the *prog* was monopolized to satisfy the greedy stomachs of several fat
members of the church, who were to officiate at the solemn ceremony."

I will not fatigue you with the discriptions of the subsequent Scenery
of the Lake except generally remarking that the mountains became
grander as we proceeded—descending more abruptly to the waters
edge—in some places cultivated around the bases and speckled with
villages convents & cottages that had a very picturesque appearance—
in other places, they were rugged & sterile, torrents dashed down the
precipices and large masses of rock detached from the heights had
tumbled to the shore. The scenery had less of the beautiful in it than at
the commencement of the lake, but there was more of the Sublime.
It approached considerably to the character of the highland scenery
of the Hudson excepting that here the mountains were of greater
magnitude.

Paris June 19th. 1805.

Dear Hicks—

The above was scribbled ⟨while⟩ at two different places on my
journey where I happened to have a moment of leizure. You will
percieve it breaks off rather abruptly which if I reccollect right was
occasioned by the sudden ⟨of⟩ apparition of "mine host" at Bellinzona
with a smoaking fricassee. The pen immediately gave way to the knife
& fork[.] the letter was thrust among my other papers nor did it ever
make ⟨itself⟩ its appearance again till this morning when in tumbling
over my portfolio it popd unexpectedly upon me. *À la bonne heure* ⟨it
will save me the trouble of⟩ its a sheet & an half of writing—*clear gain*.
So Ill just add a few lines to it and send it off. If you please we'll
make no longer stay at Bellinzona but skip over Mount St Goatherd
to Altorf—from altorf along the Lake of the four Cantons to Lucerne
from Lucerne to Zurich from Zurich to Basle from basle thro franche
Comté Alsace & Champaine to Paris[22] and here behold me quietly seated
in my room in Hotel d' Angleterre, rue du Colombier, fau⟨s⟩bourg St
Martin.

And now, I suppose, you expect I am about to give you some idea
of Paris—if so you will be disappointed—I have not as yet acquired a
single clear idea about this enormous city myself except that there
is not a place on the globe where the sensual pleasures appetites &c &c
&c are more ↑thoroughly↓ studied and may be more completely gratified
The most languid mind the most sickly & vitiated palate cannot fail
of enjoyment among the infinite variety of amusement the endless
articles of luxury with which this metropolis abounds—Every desire,

wish, inclination—natural or artificial ⟨is⟩ seems to have been completely investigated—to have been followed up to its source traced
thro every turning twisting and ramification—and a thousand means
devised both to incite and satisfy it. Heaven—earth—seas, seem to
have been ransacked to furnish out this vast magazine of[23]

DOCKETED: Lago Maggiore May 4 1805 (*written along the right margin of the
last page of the letter*).
MANUSCRIPT: Rutgers University Library; extracts in another hand at Yale.   PUB-
LISHED: *Journal of the Rutgers University Library* 9 (June, 1946), 42–49.

Clara and Rudolf Kirk assume that the addressee is Andrew Hicks because of
the phrase "my friend Andrew" in the last sentence of the first paragraph. The
construction of the sentence, however, does not bear out this assumption. See
"Seven Letters of Washington Irving," *Journal of the Rutgers University Library*
9 (December, 1945), 15; 10 (December, 1946), 42. Probably "Andrew" refers to
"Andrew Quoz," who had contributed to the *Morning Chronicle* at the time WI
was writing the letters of Jonathan Oldstyle. Elias Hicks, an associate of Peter
Irving on the *Morning Chronicle*, is probably the recipient of this letter. See the
note from WI to Elias Hicks, July 24, [1804].

1. Not identified.
2. Probably an allusion to Andrew Quoz. See WI's letters to Quoz dated July
20, 1804, and January 1, 1805.
3. In his journal WI gives a detailed account of his observations from his
departure from Rome on April 14 to his arrival in Isola Bella on May 3. See
J&N, I, 296–355.
4. Joseph Addison, "A Letter from Italy," lines 64–68. See *The Miscellaneous
Works of Joseph Addison*, ed. A. C. Guthkelch (London, 1914), I, 55.
5. This Belgian servant, who remained with the party until they reached Paris,
was particularly useful in the bargaining for travel accommodations, meals, and
lodgings. See *J&N*, I, 354; PMI, I, 141.
6. Sesto Calende is about 36 miles from Milan at the southernmost point of
Lago Maggiore.
7. Magadino is at the northern end of Lago Maggiore, opposite Locarno.
8. WI's account of his journey in this letter is given in greater detail in his
journal for May 3–5, 1805. See *J&N*, I, 350–59.
9. Arona is about five miles from Sesto on the west bank of Lago Maggiore.
10. The bronze and copper statue of San Carlo, erected in 1697, is 75 feet
high with a 40 foot pedestal. WI gives the same description in his journal. See
J&N, I, 351.
11. Cardinal Carlo Borromeo (1538–1584), archbishop of Milan, who was canon-
ized in 1610, was born in a castle in Arona. WI took his details from William Coxe,
Travels in Switzerland, and in the Country of the Grissons (London, 1789), III, 327.
12. The Colossus of Rhodes was approximately 120 feet high.
13. Angera, on the eastern shore of Lago Maggiore, is separated from Arona
at one of the narrowest points in the lake.
14. James Ogilvie, "Ode to Evening," in *Poems on Several Subjects* (London,
1769), I, 101, lines 103–6.
15. WI inadvertently repeated "breaking."

16. The three islands of Isola Bella, Isola Superiore or dei Pescatore, and Isola Madre lie offshore from Stresa and Baveno. WI has another parenthesis at this point.

17. James Thomson, "The Castle of Indolence," canto I, stanza 7, lines 1–5, in *The Complete Poetical Works of James Thomson,* ed. J. Logie Robertson (London, 1908), p. 255.

18. John George Keysler, *Travels through Germany, Bohemia, Hungary, Switzerland, Italy, and Lorrain,* 3d ed. (London, 1760), I, 374.

19. Count Vitaliano Borromeo built a summer residence for himself on Isola Bella between 1650 and 1671 with formal gardens containing ten terraces. On Isola Madre the Borromeos also built a palace and laid out gardens more varied and spectacular than those on Isola Bella.

20. Intra is on the northwestern shore of Lago Maggiore, about three miles beyond Isola Madre.

21. In his journal WI records that John reported that the feast would honor St. Joseph. Since WI visited a shrine to St. Francis at Intra on May 5, his confusion of the names is understandable. See J&N, I, 357–58.

22. WI reached Paris on May 24. His journal entries between May 7 and May 24 record his impressions of the trip through Switzerland and France. See J&N, I, 364–419.

23. WI's letter breaks off at this point. A note added on the sheet by James Bankhead, with whom WI lived in Paris at the Hotel d'Angleterre from June 4 to September 22, explains the circumstances:

Sir

The above fragments were forgotten by our friend Irving, on his departure from Paris. (which was about a fortnight ago) and he has written me from Holland requesting that I would forward them to you. which I do with pleasure. Mr. Irving is in good health and spirits, and will I have no doubt, on his arrival in London, give you, as interesting and entertaining ⟨of his⟩ an account of his visit to Holland, as the above of Italy—In haste, I beg Sir that you will accept the assurances of ⟨respect⟩

respect & consideration from / yr. ob St.

Jas. Bankhead

Paris. October 10th. 1805

28. *To William Irving, Jr.*

Paris, May 31st.180⟨4⟩5

My dear Brother,

I was renderd extremely happy yesterday by the reception of your letters No. 12 & 13. which were sent on to me to paris by my very attentive friends the Bosc's[.] as to Nos. 10 & 11 I expect they are taking an improving tour in the South of Europe in company with others from my Acquaintances—they may perhaps follow the route I have taken and passing from Banker to Banker at length arrive to hand; I would be glad, however, ⟨if⟩↑should↓ you retain copies of them, ⟨to⟩ if you will give me the most interesting passages from them in your next letter

You find fault with my letters from Genoa as not being sufficiently particular, but I expect before this you have received my long letter from Messina which will be more satisfactory. In my tour thro Sicily Italy and Switzerland objects multiplied on me so rapidly each deserving such particular attention, that I found it impossible to continue ⟨my⟩ the same degree of particularity in my letters that I had formerly observed. Every moment was occupied either by observation study or reflection, and in sitting down to communicate information, I should have sacrificed an additional stock that might have been acquired. Even the hasty notes which I usually take in travelling, became troublesome & encroaching.

If then you feel disappointed at not receiving letters from me equally long as formerly, you must excuse their insufficiency, as resulting not from idleness but from ⟨my⟩ occupation, and a wish to profit as much as possible from the scenes thro which I am passing.

I wrote you from Rome[1] a short letter mentioning the route I intended to take. I have happily completed it and arrived in this city a few days since in excellent health & spirits. The journey tho long & fatiguing was the most interesting and delightful I have made in Europe. As I informed you in my letter from Rome, we took the Route by the way of Loretto and Ancona to Bologna, from thence to Milan, from Milan across the beautiful lake of Locarno (or as it is sometimes calld lake Maggiore) to Bellinzona thence over the Mount St Goatherd to Altorf—from Altorf across the lake of the four cantons (or Lake of Lucerne) to Lucerne, from thence to Zurich, from Zurich to Basle and from Basle thro the provinces of Alsace, franche Comté and champagne to Paris.[2]

The Scenery of Switzerland surpassed my expectations. The route we had chosen was particularly favorable to present us with every variety and gradation from the awful solitudes of the alps, where rocks pild on rocks lift their stupend⟨u⟩ous summits into the clouds, roaring with torrents and hung with *Avalanches,* to the gentle scenes of Lucerne Zurich and the Rhine where all is beauty tranquility & luxurience. Nor is the character of the swiss less singular than that of his native mountains. Like his country—he seems to stand alone in Europe, ⟨an exception to⟩ and to possess traits and qualities that are peculiar to himself. In him is still seen the proper dignity of man preserved, that independence of thought that frankness and candor that we may search for in vain among the surrounding nations. In him are still seen the sublime characteristics of a freeman nor have the misfortunes & subjugation of his country been able to destroy that energy of mind and firmness of manner that liberty alone produces. Honesty, long since driven from courts and palaces seems to have

taken up her residence among the wild mountains of Switzerland
and to have fixd her empire in the hearts of its ⟨simple⟩↑worthy↓ Inhabitants—After strugg⟨el⟩ling along thro the miserable inhabitants
of italy—continually encompassed by swarms of rogues & vagabonds
and irritated by the uniform system of imposition and peculation
that is observed in that country towards the traveller, ⟨with⟩ what
pleasurable sensations did we experience on finding ourselves among
the honest Swiss. We went thro the country—in a manner with our
purses open in our hands and I may safely say that during our whole
route thro that country, not one incident of the most trivial nature
occurred, to ⟨render our⟩ injure the harmony of our feelings or to
derogate from that high opinion we had formed of the national
character. No part of Europe has interested me so much as this little
spot. France speaks to the senses, Italy to the imagination, but Switzerland to the *heart*. My fellow traveller, Cabell, was so highly charmed
with the Country that he intends returning there and pass↑ing↓ a part
of the Summer among the mountains, pursuing at the same time
practical studies in botany & mineralogy—Did my time & plans permit
I should gladly have joined him in the expedition.

This letter is merely written to let you know where I am so that
you will excuse ⟨any⟩ its being very short. ⟨in so⟩ I have not yet recovered from that kind of delirium which every stranger experiences
on first arriving in paris—and my ideas are entirely unsettled. I am
at present in a hotel in the most gay and noisy part of the city, but
I have taken an ap⟨p⟩artment in the other part of the city on the
other side of the Seine where I shall be more retired.[3] I have begun
to attend a course of Lectures on natural history delivered early in the
morning at the Garden of plants.[4] They are gratis as well as most of
the lectures in paris. Tho I do not expect to make any important proficiency in ⟨this science⟩ these studies, yet they serve to improve me in
the language, and it is always well, to be acquiring information. I
shall take a french master as soon as I get settled. I daily find my
deficiency in the language more and more irksome, I wish to become
master of it. I have formed some american acquaintances here that
are both agreeable and highly advantageous. Mr Cabell has introduced
me to Mr McClure[5] one of our commissioners for the settlement of
claims. ⟨He is a man who⟩ ↑He↓ unites the pleasing qualifications &
manners of the gentleman to the solid information & talents of the man
of Science & literature. His conversation is extremely instructive and
he takes peculiar delight in imparting his knowledge & advice to
young men—The attentions I daily receive from him are very flattering—He lives in a retired but handsome style[.] I have likewise found
here Col. Mercer,[6] another of our Commissioners with whom I became

acquainted at Naples as I mentioned in a former letter. I then gave you my opinion of this gentleman who⟨m⟩ I expect will in a little while make a conspicuous figure in america—both he⟨m⟩ & Mr Cabell reside at the house of Mr McClure[.] Vanderlyn[7] is also here and I shall be a near neighbour of his when I remove to my new appartment. These gentlemen together with Mr Biddle[8] the Secretary of our Minister,[9] are as yet my most intimate acquaintances, I shall in a day or two be introduced to Mr Skipworth[10] and two or three other americans of merit. (There are a considerable number of Americans in paris but as most of them are either trifling or questionable characters I do not wish to become acquainted with them.) I give you this account of my acquaintances as I suppose you are anxious generally to know what company I am in, especially in such a City as Paris. Be assured my dear brother that the importance of being guarded in my intimacies is sufficiently impressed on my mind. Left to my own discretion I feel the great necessity of keeping a steady eye on my ⟨own⟩ conduct and of endeavoring to convince my friends that the confidence they reposed in me was not misplaced. That they have indulged considerable expectations of me I cannot pretend to be ignorant—but I candidly assure you it is more a subject of uneasiness than pleasure to me. I fear I shall disappoint their hopes. Travelling has made me better acquainted with myself, it has given me a humilliating conviction of my own insufficiency—of my own ignorance and how very much I have to learn, how very much to acquire. Still however I flatter myself that I have not let any opportunity of instruction pass by without endeavoring to profit by it, and on reviewing my conduct while in Europe, tho I here and there observe little follies that a young man surrounded by allurements cannot always avoid—yet it is with satisfaction I reflect that there is no action which I would seriously blush to acknowledge. To render myself worthy of the good opinion of my friends shall ⟨be my⟩ still be my chief study to ensure their approbation my constant effort and with all my soul I join in the prayer of the poet

> Raise me above the vulgar breath,
> Pursuit of fortune, fear of death,
>   And all in life thats mean;
> Still true to reason be my plan,
> And let my ⟨conduct⟩↑actions↓ speak the man,
> Thro' ev'ry varying scene.[11]

You mentiond in one of your former letters that you were collecting letters of introduction for me for England; I hope it has been attended to as I have no other letters for London excepting those that Mr.

Robertson wrote for me. As I did not return to Genoa I have not received the letters of introduction that Lady Shaftesbury offerd me for her friends, tho I might still have them on writing to her. I have no inclination however to be acquainted with the nobility in england, their company would be too expensive, and tho I am confident letters from Lady S——— would procure me the politest attentions, yet I am not sure but that an untitled american would be considerd among them as a very insignificant personage—I will never move in any circle where my society is merely tolerated. I have had a complete surfeit of nobility in Italy & Sicily. It makes my blood boil to see a star on the jacket or a ribband in the button hole, entitle a blockhead a puppy ⟨even⟩ a scoundrel to rank above the man of worth and merit, whose very countenance ought to awe him into insignificance. I mingled among them thro curiosity, and tho I had every reason to be satisfied with the attentions I received, yet⟨as⟩ I soon became completely fatigued with their empty uninstructive society. Thank heavens, we *order these matters* better *in America*[.] every day makes me more and more sensible of the peculiar blessings of my country—every government thro which I pass enables me to draw an advantageous comparison. My eyes are opened in respect to many things that were hid from me while in America—I regard objects in another point of view. I have experienced a great change ⟨of⟩ in my opinions ⟨respecting⟩ on several important subjects, and look back with surprise on former errors & prejudices. These are the grand advantages I have gaind by travelling and they are to me invaluable—I am enabled to take a view of my country—like an edifice, at a distance—The eye without resting on trifling particulars embraces the whole and is enabled to judge of the form, the proportions, the harmony & solidity and to admire the simplicity the strength & grandeur of the building In new york you are in a manner thrust in ⟨a dark corner⟩ a corner, darkend by petty factions and family contests and the observer is apt to be prejudiced against the fabrick by the obscure nook in which he is placed.

As to your wish that I should pass thro ⟨G⟩ part of Germany on my way to England, I have some doubts whether the route would be very advantageous—by a person who has performed it I am told it is very disagreeable, that however should not prevent my undertaking it, was there sufficient instruction to be obtained to balance the trouble & expence. I shall enquire more concerning that subject. I have thoughts of remaining in paris till some time in September as there is no place in Europe where a man has equal opportunities of improvement and at so little expence—It is a thing that does honor to the french, that their public gallaries, liberaries &c &c are open to the world, ⟨for⟩

without any rapacious keeper porter or servant as in Italy & england, to extort a gratuity from the visitor. Lectures on almost every art and science are given gratis. Gardens for the botanist, schools for the anatomist &c &c are provided and attended by the most learned men. The Stranger is even treated with more attention than the Citizen of paris. the latter is admitted into the Louvre but twice a week, but the stranger can gain admittance every day (except the day of cleaning) ⟨by⟩ upon shewing his passport.

I cannot fix exactly the time when I shall return to America—I should not like to venture across the Atlantic in the winter, neither should I wish to remain another year in Europe. Much as I am interested and amused by the scenes in which I am mingling my amor patriae still predominates and I feel I could never be content to reside out of America. I expect however, my return will be in next Spring as early as the season will permit.

As you express a wish to know something of my money matters, I have at present about 340 $ of my original credit left out of which I shall have to pay for a few articles of clothing that I have had made, for I arrived in paris with a ward robe much like Yoricks.[12] When those debts are settled I suppose I shall have about 270 or 80 $ left— my additional credit remains in the hands of Bosc untouched. Upon the whole I think I have managed pretty well considering I have made a larger tour than I originally contemplated. I found travelling in Italy far more expensive that I had expected.

I am obliged to finish this letter abruptly that it may go off with the post; I am eager to send you intelligence of my safe arrival here. Give my remembrances as usual and desire all my friends to write to me; letters may be sent me by the way of Nantz, Havre, Amsterdam &c delivering them with a careful charge to the captain and directed to me, to the care of Messrs. Rougemont & Scherer,[13] Bankers, Paris.

Give my love to all the family

Your Affectionate Brother
W I.

P S. I shall write again in a day or two when I get settled— I shall then give you accounts from time to time of difft. parts of my tour. P S After the first of August, direct all your letters to me to London.[14]

ADDRESSED: Mr William Irving Junr. / New York / United States of America
DOCKETED: Rome Apl 4 X 12 / 1805 [on separate fold] New / Wm / New York
MANUSCRIPT: Rutgers University Library PUBLISHED: Journal of the Rutgers University Library 9 (June, 1946), 49–55.

1. April 4, 1805.

2. WI left Rome on April 4, 1805 and arrived in Paris on the afternoon of May 24. For the detailed account of his journey see J&N, I, 296–419.

3. WI stayed at the Hotel de Richelieu on Rue de la Loi (now Rue de Richelieu) until June 4, when he moved into the Hotel d'Angleterre on Rue du Colombier, Faubourg St. Martin (now Rue Jacob in the Faubourg St. Germain). See *J&N*, I, 419, 425.

4. These lectures were given by the French botanist, René Louiche Desfontaines (1750–1833), at 7:00 A.M. on Mondays, Fridays, and Saturdays. See *J&N*, I, 424, n. 56. WI's notes on these lectures are printed in *J&N*, I, 558–64.

5. William Maclure (1763–1840), a Scot who had become a naturalized American citizen, was negotiating to settle the spoliation claims.

6. James Mercer (d. 1817), a member of the Virginia legislature in 1797, was appointed to the commission settling the claims against French privateers in connection with the purchase of Louisiana. The third commissioner was Isaac Cox Barnet of New Jersey. See George Dangerfield, *Chancellor Robert R. Livingston of New York, 1746–1813* (New York, 1960), p. 381.

7. John Vanderlyn (1775?–1852), an American painter who executed a crayon portrait of WI in August, 1805, was collecting casts for the American Academy of Fine Arts. He lived at the Hotel de Marigne [Marigny?] in the spring of 1804. See *J&N*, I, 425, n. 61.

8. Nicholas Biddle (1786–1844) had already distinguished himself as a scholar by the time he went to France in 1804.

9. General John Armstrong (1758–1843) was United States minister to France, succeeding Robert R. Livingston.

10. Fulwar Skipworth, the American consul general in Paris, also served as commercial agent of the United States. See Dangerfield, *Chancellor Robert R. Livingston* . . . , pp. 365, 380.

11. Mark Akenside, "Hymn to Science," in *The Poetical Works of Mark Akenside* (London, [1845]), p. 306, lines 73–78. We are indebted to Mr. Anthony W. Shipps of Indiana University for this identification.

12. Yorick, the jester in *Hamlet*, was probably dressed in motley. After his extensive travels WI found his wardrobe tattered and inappropriate for Paris.

13. "Rougemont" was also known as "Rougemont de Lowenberg." Later he and Scherer dissolved their partnership. See *J&N*, I, 420, n. 39.

14. This postscript is written in a large script vertically along the left margin of MS page 6.

29. *To Peter Irving*

Paris, July 15, 1805.

My dear Brother,

* * * In consequence of my acquaintance at the Minister's,[1] I have the reading of all the American papers which he receives, so that I have continually opportunities of informing myself how matters go on at home. . . . I am very agreeably situated in respect to lodgings. I have taken handsome apartments in company with Mr. Bankhead, late secretary to Mr. Monroe. They are in a genteel hotel in the Fauxbourg[2] St. Germain, near the Seine. Though retired from the gay, noisy part of the city, we have but to cross the Pont des Arts, and we are immediately among the amusements. This part of Paris is tranquil and reasonable, and almost all the Americans of my acquaintance reside here.

One of my most intimate acquaintances is Vanderlyn; he lives in my neighborhood. By-the-bye, I wish you would interest yourself with the Academy[3] about this worthy young fellow. He has been sent out here by the Academy to collect casts, &c., and has executed this commission with faithfulness, but he is extremely in want of money. The Academy gave him a credit on Leghorn, in the name of Wm. M. Seton,[4] but the death of that gentleman has rendered the letter useless. He has written repeatedly to the Academy, but has received no answer. His object was to go on to Italy, and he has been detained here merely for want of the means. Mr. McClure,[5] one of our commissioners, has generously patronized him, and advanced him money for the journey; he will therefore set off in about a fortnight. I trust the Academy will evince a spirit of generosity towards a young artist, whose talents and character do credit to our country. They are in a manner responsible, having already taken such marked notice of him. I beg you to attend to this request, and to write Vanderlyn word as *soon as possible*, of the disposition and intentions of the Academy towards him. The poor fellow seems to be quite low-spirited, and to think that the Academy has forgotten him!

By the papers I find that the Emperor is at Fontainebleau,[6] having travelled *incog.* from Genoa to that place in eighty hours! This is an instance of that promptness, decision, and rapidity that characterize his movements. You may well suppose I am impatient to see this wonderful man, whose life has been a continued series of actions, any one of which would be sufficient to immortalize him.

You expect, most probably, that I will say something of Paris, but I must beg you to excuse me. I have neither time nor inclination to begin so endless a subject. I should be at a loss how to commence, and I am almost afraid to own that I have not taken a single note since I have been in this metropolis. This, however, I find to be the case with all my acquaintances, so that I plead for some degree of indulgence on that score. The city is rapidly beautifying under the auspices of the Emperor; the Louvre, Tuileries, &c., are undergoing alterations and repairs. The people seem all gay and happy, and *vive la bagatelle!* is again the burden of their song.

Of all the places that I have seen in Europe Paris is the most fascinating, and I am well satisfied that for pleasure and amusements it must leave London far behind. The favorableness of the climate, the brilliancy of the theatres, operas, &c., the beauty of the public walks, the gaiety, good-humor, and universal politeness of the people, the perfect liberty of private conduct, are calculated to enchant a stranger, and to render him contented and happy with every thing about him. You will smile to see that Paris has obtained complete possession of my head, but I assure you that America has still the stronghold of my heart.

I am busily employed in studying the French language, and I hope before I leave France to have a pretty satisfactory acquaintance with it. I shall remain in Paris as late in the fall as possible, as there is no place where I can both amuse and instruct myself at less expense, and more effectually. * * *

When you see Mr. Hoffman present him my warmest remembrances, and tell him I long for the time when I shall be once more numbered among his disciples.

You will excuse the shortness and hastiness of this letter, for which I can only plead as an excuse that I am a *young man* and in *Paris*

Your affectionate brother,
W. I.

PUBLISHED: PMI, I, 148–50.

1. John Armstrong was the American Minister. See WI's letter of May 31, 1805, to William Irving.

2. WI apparently misspelled the word because he confused the first syllable with "faux" ("false"), which would be pronounced the same way. Since the original of this letter has not been located, the spelling of the printed version is retained. In the three-volume abridgment of PMI's *Life and Letters of WI* (ca. 1869) the word is spelled "Faubourg."

3. When the New York Academy of the Fine Arts was established on December 3, 1802, Dr. Peter Irving was elected secretary. See William Dunlap, *History of the Rise and Progress of the Arts of Design in the United States* (New York, 1965), II, 105.

4. William M. Seton, head of the firm of New York merchants, Seton, Maitland & Co., died of consumption at Pisa on December 27, 1803, and was buried in the English cemetery at Leghorn. See George Seton, *A History of the Family of Seton* (Edinburgh, 1896), pp. 305, 307.

5. The Academy sent Vanderlyn to Europe to purchase casts of ancient sculpture for its collection. While in Paris, Vanderlyn attracted the attention of William McClure of Philadelphia, who gave him money to study in Rome from 1805 to 1808. Dunlap, *History of the Rise and Progress of the Arts of Design . . .*, II, 159–60; E. P. Richardson, *Painting in America* (New York, 1956), p. 90.

6. Napoleon had left Genoa in disguise on the evening of July 8 with two post carriages and arrived in Fontainebleau eighty hours later. See Thiers, *History of the Consulate*, III, 369.

30. To Joseph C. Cabell

Paris July 31st. 1805.

Dear Cabell.

It is with pleasure I learn by your letters to Mr. Skipwith and Vanderlyn that you and Mr. McClure have arrived at Geneva in good health, and that the journey thus far has been agreable. I am also happy to relieve any anxiety you may have about your friends by forwarding to you the enclosed, which comes, I believe, from America.

I thank you for the kind wishes you express for my health and improvement. They are both in as flourishing a state as could be expected in a young man, who is no philosopher, and is for the first time turned adrift in the gay City of Paris. You expect perhaps by this time that I am able to talk about Tiges and fructifications and bulbous roots almost equal to Des Fontaines[1] himself. I am sorry to announce to you that my "Voyage dans L'Empire de Flora" was of as short duration as our late tour in Switzerland. I can hardly tell you how the matter fell thro. I began to find the hour very unseasonable,[2] as it completely interfered with other occupations, then it was so fatiguing to walk to Mr. Caille's[3] in the heat of the sun at Midday.— then either from the heat of the walk—the soporific flavor of the plants collected on the table—the heaviness of my own head, or the length of Mr. Cailles Lectures, I caught myself several times almost napping whilst he was laboring for my Edification.

I was several times prevented attending Lectures on account of particular business. In short in spite of all my efforts to persuade my self to the Contrary, I was troubled with a powerful conviction, that my botanical knowledge increased but slowly. Monsieur Caille I believe thought as much, and to enliven the hours of Lecture—perhaps to draw me there more effectually, he cheered our meetings with the Company of a pretty girl who I believe was his Mistress.

Now this you Know was the very Devil. I heard no word what my learned Professor said about Tiges and roots and fructifications. I was more taken up with the pretty eyes of the French girl than with the Petals and Stamens of the Flower; and was so completely employed in rendering myself amiable that I almost forgot friend Caille was in the room. Finding therefore how matters were going I determined to quit the undertaking effectively rather than continue on in so lame a manner. As soon as I had made this determination you cannot imagine how many excellent reasons came pouring in upon me, to show the wisdom of it. Like every body else on giving up a study, they have not capacity or industry to pursue. I saw clearly that it was very useless to me—very embarrassing—that it took up too much

valuable time,—in short that it was highly disadvantageous. However as I do not like to take any important step, without proper counsel, I resolved to advise with my philosophic friend *Mercer*, (tho I confess I had some previous ideas of his sentiments on the subject.) We discussed the matter coolly and candidly over a hearty dinner, and by the time we had finished our wine, we decided clearly that the study of Botany was totally useless and extremely disadvantageous, as it tended to fill my mind with weeds that would inevitably choke the seeds of useful Knowledge; and Mercer was firmly of opinion "que le ciel de Mademoiselle Milliere[4] vaut mieux que tous les fleurs dans le jardin des Plants." Our friend Mercer continued to enjoy the amusement of the Capitol as placidly as usual for some time after your departure. He seemed to participate in its pleasures in a truly philosophic manner, always sipping but never satiating himself. Amid the bustle, splendor, noise and gaiety of theatres, Operas—gardens and the Palais Royal he still kept on "The noiseless tenor of his way,"[5] ↑jostling no one, interfering in no body's way,↓ and tranquilly enjoying the scenes and objects before him with the nice palate of an Epicure. I felt my esteem for Mercer continually increasing, from the first moment that I became acquainted with him to the moment of our parting, and of all the transient friendships that I have made in Europe I know of none of which I ever felt more the immediate deprivation.
I shall remain in France untile the fall is far advanced—I do not Know but that I shall make a little tour in the Country some time in August.
Neighbour Vanderlyn talks of setting off on his travels in about five or six days. He⟨f⟩will find you among the Mountains. I have been twice out to the country seat of Mr. Skipwith & am charmed with his amiable family. He intends departing for America in about a month.
This I believe is all I have to communicate concerning your male friends, and as I have not the advantage of Knowing the fair ones who smiled on you here, I must be silent in respect in respect to them, excepting that the little handkerchief. girl says you are *un Philosophe,* and the washwoman that you are *un bon Enfant.*
Present my remembrances to Mr. McClure

yours sincerely
Washington Irving.

Docketed: Washington Irving. / July 31st. 1805 / (Copy.) / (Original among autographs.)
Manuscript: University of Virginia Library, Bremo Recess Papers.
This manuscript is a handwritten copy of WI's original, and it is not in his handwriting.

1. The copyist did not cross the *t*. WI is referring to René Louiche Desfontaines.

2. See WI to William Irving, Jr., May 31, 1805.

3. M. Caille was not on the faculty of the Museum D'Histoire Naturelle in 1805. See *Annales du Museum D'Histoire Naturelle* ... (Paris, 1805), VI, unpaged, for the list of the faculty at this time. Caille's lectures were perhaps in a different field, and WI may have been taking them as a part of his program for self-improvement in Paris.

4. Presumably the French girl with whom WI was flirting.

5. Thomas Gray, "Elegy Written in a Country Churchyard," stanza 19.

31. *To Alexander Beebee*

Paris. August 3d. 1805.

My dear Beebee,

I had been wondering for a long time what could occasion your silence. Letters after letters arrived from my friends but none from you. This would not have surprised me from most of my acquaintances but I have ever judged you one whose friendship would not be weakned by the temporary absence of its object. It is with extreme concern that I find I must ascribe this silence to a long and severe illness. Gladly my dear fellow[1] would I have been with you to administer those little attentions which I found so grateful from you in the course of my indisposition. ⟨B⟩ Long before this time however I trust you are once more blessd with the "vigorous joys of health"—inhaling the pure breezes of the country and tasting those honest unsophisticated pleasures that america alone affords.

A long time has elapsed since I last wrote you. I have been completely occupied in body & mind, passing thro the most celebrated places of Europe which are renowned by historic event and enrichd by the solemn ruins of antiquity My imagination has been on the full stretch ⟨t⟩ vainly striving to grasp the accumulating wonders.

Between two and three months has elapsed since my arrival in *Paris,* that grand centre to which are attracted the curiosities the luxuries & the pleasures of every quarter of the Globe. I have endeavored however to enjoy them as rationally as possible and to keep in mind that I am not travelling for mere pleasure. Paris, my friend, is the true Island of Calypso[2]—Here every art is tried every charm displayed to captivate the senses, to banish reflection and to bewilder the imagination with an ↑infinite↓ variety of pleasures Does the inclination languish, ⟨does⟩↑are↓ the ⟨senses?⟩↑appetites↓ palld, new incitements are studied new stimulants devised to awaken the capacities for enjoyment—Here ⟨no one sees⟩ the difficulty is not to find gratifications for the desires—but desires for the gratifications. Amid these intoxicating scenes of disapation & extravagance the reccollection of home acts as my watchful Mentor. I reccollect there are friends to whom I am responsible for the time I spend in Europe—But above all perhaps a *frugal purse* is the best guardian I have. Notwithstanding however its gaieties & allurements you will be surprized probably when I tell you that I begin to feel impatient to be again on the move. Yet so it is, the thoughts of home continually pursue me, they haunt my dreams and render me often restless and pensive. Whenever I recieve a pacquet of letters from my friends I am sure to be homesick for two or three days afterwards. While journeying I do not feel this sensation[.] I them[3] seem as if approaching towards home but when long at rest in a place it returns with double force. I remember with what rapture I mounted my Mule and turned my back upon Syracuse when I parted from thence for Catania. I had then attained to the extremity of my tour and seemed as if returning homewards.

In travelling the understanding is enlightened the mind strengthened the imagination expanded and delighted, yet the social affections— those sweetners of life lie almost dormant—except when awakened by the pleasing but melancholy reccollection of distant friends, of early attachments. The connections ⟨that⟩ formed in travelling are transitory & feeble & do not reach the heart. Friendship is justly observed to be a plant of slow growth[.] intimate acquaintance is necessary to give it root. *Civility & politeness* but ill supply the vacuum that the heart experiences.

> "Alas! my friend, how vain to roam
> And seek abroad the joys that home
> And home alone bestows:—
> The beam of mirth that lights the face
> The love that warms the fond embrace
> The bliss that ever grows."

Often in the course of my journeying have I remained for hours in a half melancholy mood picturing to my self ⟨to⟩ ↑the↓ probable employments and situations of my friends. I have fancied myself transported among their little circles[.] I have heard the social laugh[.] I have seen the smile of affection beaming on each countenance—I have awakend from my reverie and found myself alone, wandering about the earth perhaps forgotten by those very persons on whose attachments I grounded my hopes of happiness—perhaps remembered but as a sick spiritless fellow whose dull society was irksome. How painful are such sensations yet how impossible is it in such situations to suppress them—for my part I do not attempt it. I consider them not as resulting from a melancholy habit, for thank heavens I am quite free from one, but as the irregular vibrations of those social cords of my heart which unless they may be touched too Severely by adversity misfortune or disappointment, will ever afford me the purest felicities.

In your Letters you give me sweet hints about *the future*—"I pray thee do not mock me, fellow student"[4] rather be silent than flatter my feelings on that subject. Her lovely image has accompanied me in all my wanderings has smiled upon me in my slumbers and awakend the softest remembrances. You see then how dangerous it is to feed my imagination. What has a poor devil like myself to do with love— Let me return to America with a tranquil bosom if possible—let me *endeavor* to bury myself among the musty authors of the Law and prepare myself for that starving profession with which I am to struggle thro this world. I look forward with a heavy eye to the cheerless prospect before me and feel how unfortunate it is to be *proud and poor.*

Beebee, how is it my good fellow, that I always get into a sombre mood when writing to you. Surely our conversations did not use to partake of that cast, the laugh was ever ready to preside at our meetings—but somehow or other when I write to you I do not as with others attend so much to amuse you as to unbosom to you my feelings. I trust to your honest friendship and become a complete egotist, confident that you will "bear with a friends infirmities[.]"[5] I charge you however not to shew my foolish scribblings to any one else.

While I think of it mention to sam Swartwout to prepare a suitable answer to the long letter I ⟨am about writing⟩↑*intend to write*↓ him and tell John Furman that I have long waited for another letter from him but fear I must give up all farther hopes.

———

I am highly amused with the gay whimsical inhabitants of this country. Happy souls! whose grand care is to banish reflection and seize the joy of the moment without looking to the future. Never were people more easily amused and with more trifling objects; the old couple mingle in the sports of their grand children and it is difficult to say which enjoys them most. I love to mingle with the good folks—to participate in their pleasures to act ⟨as they do⟩ and if possible to think as they do. 'Tis this inclination that leads me frequently on sunday evenings to their public gardens, where the honest old citizens repair with their families to relax themselves after the occupations of the week—Of these gardens Hameau ↑de↓ Chantilly[6] is the Most pleasant. Here you are admitted for about a quarter of a dollar and may partake in all the varied amusements of the place without further pay. The garden is extensive and elegant. In one part of it is a large green and here you may see above an hundred at a time ↑of all ages & sexes↓ amusing themselves with Battle door & shuttle cock. In another place is a large *duck pond* on which the young gentry display their feats of boatmanship by paddling their Sweethearts about in little boats about the size of a butchers ⟨trough⟩ tray—engagements & rencontres frequently take place and it is rare that the adventrous navigators quit the pond without being tolerably spatterd & bedaubed. To these recreations you may join those of Swinging—riding wooden horses &c but above all the favorite ⟨french⟩ one of Dancing. A large place is appointed for the purpose under spacious trees—a good orchestra is provided and here they dance cotillions and waltzes the whole evening

In the course of the evening they have very elegant fireworks[.] the company repair in crowds to admire them and then return with eagerness to their favorite dance.

You would laugh to see me seated among the good humord souls, acting the frenchman. It is all one to me whom I address—I am sure of a civil reply and a good lesson in the language. As I have not the luck to be acquainted in any french family in paris I must endeavor to improve every means of informing myself concerning the people and their language. Fortunately they are remarkably polite to strangers and it is one advantage, that ⟨the⟩ on addressing a french woman, tho she should be ever so averse to conversing with you, yet she never replies so abruptly or sever⟨l⟩ely as to wound your feelings; but discourages you merely by a polite reserve. Tho I make a point wherever I am to endeavor to enter into conversation with the person next to me yet I never in france received the least rebuff[.] on the contrary I was always treated with politeness & attention. The name of *Stranger* seems to entitle a man to extraordinary privileges ⟨in⟩ here. The people are more civil and endeavor more to please you— The public edifices institutions and curiosities are open to your inspection without the least expence—when ↑even↓ the inhabitants are excluded from visiting them This is a Circumstance that does honor to the Country—it is worthy of universal imitation. How different is it in England where the foreigner is looked upon as an inferior being, where he is abused & insulted in the streets and regarded as a mark for the finger of scorn. The french are quick in their dispositions but their anger is over in an instant and their usual gaiety of heart and good disposition prevails immediately. Go into⟨sh[?]⟩a shop and tumble over the goods of the shop keeper for an hour[.] he'll skip about and hand down fresh articles continually descant on the beauties of each—how much it would become you (throwing in at the same time a little spice of flattery) he'll try every art to induce you to buy when after giving him a world of pains for nothing ⟨he smiles⟩ you take your leave—he smiles makes half a dozen bows and has *"the honor to Salute you"* (j'ai l'honneur de vous saluer) I always have an hours talk when I purchase any thing—for the sake of hearing their remarks and the ingenious manner that they have of setting off the merits & apologizing for the deffects of their merchandize. A frenchman can contradict you with the best grace imaginable and even at the same time make you think he is complementing you. he is never off his guard in politeness—nor does he ever seem at a loss for a happy turn when the argument is against him

Franklin when in paris had employed a barber to make him a wig for a visit of ceremony. The wig was brought home just before the visiting hour. Unfortunately the Doctor could not get it on his head—⟨The Doctor insted?⟩↑He↓ of course condemned it as too small, the Barber ⟨politely⟩ maintaind with great politeness that the wig was of the proper size. He stretchd it on his knee—he *diabled* it fifty times but all would not do—"The fact is my honest friend (says franklin) the wig is too small for my head" The poor barber ⟨?of?⟩ could not yield up the credit of his wig—"Pardonnez moi mon cher monsieur (replied he with a low bow) ce n'est pas que la peruque est trop ⟨large⟩↑petite↓ pour votre tête, c'est que votre tête est trop large pour la perruque" (Pardon me my dear sir—it is not that the *wig* is too *small* for your head it is that your *head* is *too large* for the wig.)[7]

Tho' this politeness of deportment renders france extremely agreeable to the stranger yet were I to become a resident I would willingly exchange half of it for a little plain sincerity. Of all the national characters that I have had opportunity to observe in Europe, I am most pleased with that of the Swiss. Open manly & candid they decieve with no false promises—never stoop to abject flattery are polite without being officious and independant without rudeness. In travelling thro switzerland I found even among their wild & wintry mountains an information a liberality & expansion of ideas that astonished me. The matter however is easily accounted for. They have long been blessed with the illuminating rays of liberty—They have been allowed a freedom of thought and a licenced tongue[.] they have remaind a little band of freemen surrounded by nations of slaves. No wonder is it that like americans they languish when away from home and sigh after those pure unadulterated enjoyments ↑&↓ that honest simplicity of manners peculiar to their Country. Any thing that awakens the recollection of their beloved country completely unmans them It is for this reason that in france & holland they will not permit the musicians in the swiss regiments to play a certain little air that is a great favorite in their mountains. When at the village of Altorf in the beautiful valley of Uri my landlady gave me several annecdotes of the love the swiss have for their native homes, and how they cannot bear to be removed from them even tho it is only to another part of switzerland. She told us she had once employed as a servant a mountaineer who had passed all his life in tending cattle on his native mountain. He had not remaind long in her family before he began to shew discontent & uneasiness. The sight of a Cow a goat or a sheep affected him strongly and even frequently melted him into tears recalling to his mind the flocks & herds that he had left behind but the little air which I have already mentiond and which is sung by the mountain peasants while tending their cattle—completely overpowerd him—He pined away for some time melancholy & homesick till at length he took a sudden resolution asked his dismission and hurried back to his native alps preferring the inhospitable regions and scanty fare of the mountains to all the pleasures and comforts of the valley. How beautifully does Goldsmith describe this *amor patriae* of the Swiss.

> "Dear is that shed to which his soul conforms
> And dear that hill that lifts him to the storms
> And as a child when scaring sounds molest
> Clings close and closer to the mothers breast,
> So the loud torrent and the whirlwinds roar
> But bind him to his native mountains more"[8]

I would prolong this letter but other occupations prevent me from writing any more for the present. Write to me as often as possible— next to seeing my friends nothing can give me greater pleasure than to hear from them.

Remember me to honest King Cole and let me know when his spouse presents him with a pair of twins. The Wilson family is in a fair way to encrease and multiply—Before this time I suppose you are emancipated from office duties but I hope you will still be able to furnish me with intelligence of Boss and his sweet family[9]—of Misser Cuttin—Squirt—Coke—Diddles[10] &c &c With the warmest wishes for your prosperity

I am sincerely/Your friend
W I

MANUSCRIPT: Va.–Barrett.

1. There is an ink blot on the page at this point.
2. Calypso's mythical island, where, according to Homer, Odysseus lingered for seven years, was Ogygia.
3. WI probably intended to write "then."
4. *Hamlet,* I, ii, 177.
5. *Julius Caesar,* IV, iii, 85.
6. About 25 miles north of Paris, Chantilly was well known for its gardens which contained "les cascades, le hameau et le parc de Sylvie." See *La Grande Encyclopédie,* X, 532.
7. No source has been found to document this anecdote, which may be apocryphal. Franklin preferred to wear his beaver hat as a symbol of his Republican sympathy and to maintain a public image. J. J. Jusserand describes Franklin's simplicity of manner by reprinting a contemporary image of the American. "He has," says Jusserand, "long worn a wig like everybody else, but he had now discarded it. 'This Quaker,' we read in a police note drawn up shortly after his arrival and published by Bigelow, 'wears the full costume of his sect. He has an agreeable physiognomy, spectacles always on his eyes; but little hair, a fur cap is always on his head . . .'" (J. J. Jusserand, "Franklin in France," in *Essays Offered to Herbert Putnam,* ed. William Warner Bishop and Andrew Keogh [New Haven, 1929], p. 229).
8. Oliver Goldsmith, *The Traveller,* lines 203–8. This passage is quoted by William Coxe in *Travels in Switzerland and in the Country of the Grissons,* I, 301.
9. Mr. and Mrs. Josiah Ogden Hoffman and their children.
10. Coke is probably an allusion to Sir Edward Coke's *Commentaries upon Littleton,* a standard textbook for young men reading the law. The other names are probably WI's cronies in Hoffman's law office. Misser Cuttin may be William Cutting, later a lawyer who was associated with Robert Fulton and married Gertrude Livingston in 1798. See T. A. Cutting, *Cutting Kin* (Campbell, Calif., 1939).

32. To Peter Irving

London, Octr. 20th. 1805.

My dear Brother,

By the date of this Letter you will percieve that I am safely arrived in the land of our forefathers, and have become an inhabitant of the famous & foggy city of London. Thus you see I shift from city to city and lay countries aside like books, after giving them a hasty perusal. Thank heavens my ramblings are nearly at an end and in a little while I shall once more return to my friends and sink again into tranquil domestic life. It may seem strange to you who have never wanderd far from home, but I assure you it is true that in a short time one gets tired of travelling even in the gay & polished countries of Europe.

Curiosity cannot be kept ever on the stretch; like the sensual appetites it in time becomes sated and no longer enjoys the food it formerly ⟨coveted in⟩ searched after with avidity. On entering a strange place at present I feel no ⟨longer⟩ ↑more↓ that interest that prompted me on first arriving in Europe to be perpetually on the hunt for curiosities & beauties. In fact the duty imposed upon me as a traveller to do so, is often irksome

On arriving at Naples I became acquainted with an American Gentleman[1] of talents who had made the tour of Italy. I was much diverted with the manner in which he addressed his Valet de place one morning as we were going out in search of Curiosities "Now my friend" said he "reccollect, I am tired of churches, convents, pal⟨l⟩aces, galleries of paintings, subterraneous passages & Great men, if you have any thing else to shew me,—*allons.*" at present I could almost feel inclined to make a similar speech myself. I own notwithstanding, that London is extremely interesting to me, as it offers both in buildings & inhabitants such a contrast to the cities on the continent, and then, it is so completely familiarized to me from having heard & read so much about it since my infancy, that every square street & lane appears like an old acquaintance.

I left paris on the 22d. Septr. in company with Mr Gorham[2] of Boston & Mr Massie[3] of Virginia and after a pleasing tour thro the Netherlands by the way of Brussells and Maestricht we arrived at Rotterdam on the thirtieth. We had made a stop of two days at Brussells which is one of the most beautiful cities I have seen in Europe—we staid another day at Maestricht, ⟨which is⟩ in order to visit a remarkable cavern in its neighborhood[4] but I will not fatigue you with a description of it. I was much interested by the change that I continually observed ⟨in⟩ as I proceeded, from the carelessly cultivated plains of france to those of the netherlands where the hand of labor appears to be never idle in the improvement of the soil, from the dirty comfortless habitations of the french peasantry to those of holland where cleanliness is almost a Vice—in fine from the light skip and gay thoughtless air of the frenchman, to the heavy tread and phlegmatic leaden features of the dutchman. How astonishing is it that a trifling space—a mere ideal line should occasion such ⟨exte⟩↑a↓ vast difference between two nations that neither the people—houses, manners language —tastes should resemble each other. The Italian & the turk are more similar than the parisien & the Hollander.

I had intended making a hasty tour in Holland but on arriving at Rotterdam I found an excellent packet about sailing for Gravesend. The passing & repassing of these packets is connived at by the french general who *commands* at Rotterdam as he pockets a part of the passage money of each passenger—The Vessel clears out for Embden under the Prussian flag. On my arrival at Rotterdam I heard a report that Prussia ⟨has either had or was about to declare⟩ either had declared or was about to declare in favor of france in consequence of which the owners were fearful of sending any more packets to England under Prussian colours. As I dreaded any accidental detention in the Phlegmatic cities of Holland I determined on availing ⟨of⟩ myself of the packet that was about sailing, as did likewise my companions. Indeed I did not regret much my not being able to see more of Holland, as the little I had already seen I was told was a faithful specimen of the rest—a monotonous uniformity prevailing over the whole country.

Leaving therefore the gentle Mynheers to smoak their pipes in peace, we embarked on the evening of the third of October, and on the morning of the fourth, sailed from the mouth of the Meuse—The next morning on *turning out* I had the first glimpse of Old England; we were just opposite Margate within four or five miles of the shore. We anchored the same evening in the ⟨River⟩ Thames opposite Gravesend. As we were direct from ⟨the⟩ an enemies country we were not permitted to land till ⟨pa⟩ permits should arrive from the Alien office at London⟨e⟩. I did not recieve mine till the morning of the eighth (suffering a detention of three days) when I went immediately on shore took a post chaise and arrived ↑in↓ the afternoon at London. Such is a concise sketch of my Journey.

The next day I waited on Mr Robertson[5] to whom I had a letter from his Brother. He recieved me in the most friendly manner but you can have no idea what was my chagrin & disappointment at finding that he had no letters ⟨from⟩ for me. You will reccollect you had ⟨arranged in⟩ proposed in one of[6]

DOCKETED: London Oct & Novem 1805 [in left margin of page 1 of MS].
MANUSCRIPT: Rutgers University Library. PUBLISHED: PMI, I, 152–55 (in part); *Journal of the Rutgers University Library* 10 (December, 1946), 56–58.

1. This was Joseph Cabell. See WI's letter of April 12, 1805, to William Irving.
2. John Gorham (1783–1829), chemist and physician, fellow of the American Academy of Arts and Sciences and author of a textbook, *The Elements of Chemical Science.*
3. Thomas Massie (1783–1864) was studying abroad in 1805. See *Encyclopedia of Virginia Biography* (New York, 1915), II, 201; *J&N*, I, 427–28. Upon Massie's return to America WI wrote a letter of introduction for him to Joseph Gratz, July 8, 1806.
4. This cavern was in the sandstone quarries of the Petersberg Mountain, which contain many fossil specimens and flints. See Karl Baedeker, *Belgium and Holland* (Leipzig, 1897), pp. 226–27.
5. Andrew Robertson (1772–1841), the brother of Alexander Robertson, who had been WI's drawing teacher in New York, was a protégé of Benjamin West and a popular painter of miniatures in England.
6. The MS ends at this point.

33. *To William Irving, Jr.*

London, Octr. 26th. 1805.

My Dear Brother,

You are curious perhaps to know what were my sensations on first
arriving in England; I would willingly gratify you with a minute account of them if it were possible—but in such a situation my ideas &
emotions are so confused, so various, so fugitive, that it is out of my
power to analyse them.

When at Anchor opposite Gravesend I regarded the shore with a
wishful eye. ⟨The⟩ I longed to reach it and mingle among people whose
language & manners would almost make me fancy myself at home.
I reflected that I was "bone of their bone & flesh of their flesh"¹ and
was but entering the land of my forefathers. With such ideas you will
suppose no doubt that on landing my heart expanded with the most
⟨pleasing sensations⟩ ↑friendly sentiments↓ and my feelings were ready
to fly out & hail each Englishman as a kinsman.—Quite the contrary—
never did I enter a country with my bosom filld with such *ungenerous—
uncharitable* sentiments. All that I had heard ⟨to⟩ or read to the disadvantage of the English character seemed to rush to mind—haughti-
ness, illiberal prejudice, reserve, rudeness, insolence, brutality, knavery
were the black traits that represented² themselves. I looked round me
with distrust and suspicion—my heart was completely closed up and
every frank generous feeling, had retired within it. I thought myself
surrounded by rogues & swindlers and felt that I was ⟨among⟩ a foreigner among people who regard all foreigners with contempt & enmity.

How different is this from what I felt on arriving at Paris. It was
there all confidence & affability. The gay good humoured air of the
inhabitants put me perfectly at my ease and I knew that being a
stranger I had a prescriptive right to their politeness and civilities; for
in France (to the honor of ⟨this⟩the nation be it spoken) the name of
Stranger is sacred and entitled to all possible respect and attention. I
even delighted in addressing the commonest people and making enquiries, and felt sure of receiving those "small sweet courtesies,"³ that
make the intercourse of man & man so agreeable. I had nothing to
apprehend from impertinence or slight—and the argus pride, which is
ever on the watch lest *self consequence* should be insulted,—seemed
to slumber during my whole stay in Paris. In London on the contrary
I almost feared to make the necessary enquiries about the situation
of streets & houses. I thought every one eyed me with hostility, and
perceived that I was a foreigner—and I expected every moment to
experience some rudeness or vulgarity. My hands were half the time
in my pockets to guard them from depredations, in short I was com-

pletely *on the alert*. These Ideas w⟨h⟩ere whimsical enough—they soon
wore off and in a day or two I found I might walk the streets of London
with as much confidence as those of Paris. Tho I have by no means
experienced the same degree of politeness, as at the latter place; yet,
I have not sufferd the slightest impertinence, and my pockets tho
very frequently exposed, have never been plundered.

On entering London I put up at the New York Coffee house[4] aside of
the Royal Exchange—the next day however I went out with my fellow
traveller Mr Gorham[5] to look for rooms. ⟨After examining⟩ We experienced considerable difficulty in suiting ourselves—either the rooms
were inconvenient—or the price was too high—or the people were not
sufficiently goodhumoured & attentive. I wonderd at the latter, as
they made a living by letting lodgings—but on leaving one house I
heard the mistress say to the servant girls "Im sure they're foreigners
from their dress;" the mystery now was out—I had on a light grey coat
⟨and⟩ white embroiderd vest and coloured small clothes when all
england was in mourning[6]—I determined without delay to call in the
assistance of a Taylor and make a complete ⟨revolution⟩ reformation
in my *dress* that article so important to be attended to in england.

At length I found ⟨room⟩ lodgings to my liking. The house is kept
by an Old Lady *dressd in black* of a venerable appearance—⟨and⟩ a
mighty good honest old soul. I have a parlour—bed room & cabinet on
the ground floor—tho the furniture is not quite so modern and fashionable as some I had seen—it was so clean, well polished and together
with the rooms had such a genteel, *respectable* comfortable appearance
that I made no hesitation in deciding in favor of the old Lady. The
house is admirably well situated for my views—it is in Norfolk Street
↑(No 35)↓—strand and not far from the City, so that tho not subject
to the bustle and confusion of the latter, I am not too far removed
from the Coffee houses—exchange & other places of resort—while the
Theatres are close at hand. The street ⟨I let⟩ I live in is broad clean
and airy and my rooms are very light, a great advantage in this foggy
climate during the gloomy months.

A[7] Stranger from the Continent must be struck with the difference
between the physical construction of the english and french—The⟨ir⟩y
are as opposite in this as in their moral characteristics. The french are
generally light but well made; the idea that they are a meagre half
starvd looking race of people is a vulgar error, they have not it is true
that superfluous fat that only disfigures and embarasses the human
form, but their limbs are well turnd and ⟨they⟩ display a union of
agility & strength. Their complexions are sallow and their eyes black
& lively. The English are athletic and rather inclining to corpulency

their limbs ⟨large⟩ heavy and ill made, the joints, particularly the knees ↑& ankles↓ large—this gives them more actual strength than the french, but they have not the agility of the latter. Their countenances are full & ruddy—their eyes generally grey or blue the nose almost universally turnd up a little. They are a ⟨full⟩ hear*ty, handsome, haughty* looking people of a gross well fed appearance and it seems as if roast beef & plumb pudding were continually staring you in the face. Easy in his circumstances and well assured of his personal security, the Englishman looks around him with proud independence. The proper importance which the constitution & laws of England give⟨s⟩ to ↑the↓ individual has an effect on his manners & deportment that cannot fail but ↑⟨to⟩↓[8] strike the observing stranger from the Continent. In the shop keepers & tradesmen, while I have ever experienced from them the profoundest respect & attention, I ⟨see⟩ remarked an independence of manners, ⟨and⟩ a degree of self respect and personal consequence that I have never before witnessed in Europe. The difference between the french & english women is not less striking than between the men. The ⟨former have the⟩ french women have the advantages of form to an eminent degree. Their figures are small and exquisitely proportiond and they take pains to set them off by a lightness of drapery, not inconsistent with the mildness of their climate. The english women tho deficient in the beauties of form, have charming countenances rather of a grave cast but expressive of sentiment & feeling. Their figures would not be bad if they took pains to dress & carry themselves properly but they load on garment over garment without taste and their clothes hang about them as if hung on pegs. They have now a fashion of wearing huge tippets of bear or foxskin, which, added to an habitual stoop in the shoulders gives them the appearance of having a hunch there, equal to a Dromedarys. When they walk it is a kind of hobbling uneven gait owing to their being continually crampd up in carriages or shackled with pattens. The french women are remarkable for the grace and vivacity of their movements—they can never be seen to greater advantage than on the promenade, excepting it is in the ball room. Their countenances are lively and with a pair of pretty eyes & good teeth (which they have very generally) a french woman can do every thing. She has an air of good humour & affability that draws you to her and encourages you to be sociable. The english woman— with a countenance of the most fascinating loveliness—possesses a dignified reserve that forbids familiarity and awes you into respect. She strikes you by her beauty—the french woman wins you by a thousand little graces and amiabilities—the former is a divinity you feel inclined to admire and worship—the latter to laugh and sport with; She enchants your imagination but the former enslaves your heart.—Here am I addressing a long dissertation upon *women* to a sober, steady *married man*—its a *whimsical* subject enough, and you perhaps (*like* the *wise* Solomon who never judged of any thing till after he had *indulged* in it to *satiety*,) will pronounce it "all vanity & vexation of spirit."⁹

———

29th.

Kemble¹⁰ is the "grand Colossus" of Tragedy in London and is considered as infallible by an english audience as the pope is by all true catholics. Yet I cannot subscribe to this opinion even tho' I should risk the damnation of the critic's for such an avowal. I have seen some peices of acting from Mr Kemble that from any other performer would have been termed very indifferent. But the good natured folks have got into the habit of thinking that he has some particular & sterling meaning in every thing he does. When therefore in a passage that requires energy & warmth—⟨as the ex⟩ he does not particularly exert himself— but suffers his *natural coldness of style* ↑to↓ prevail—the audience immediately discover that he is expressing *smotherd grief—calm despair* or *dignified firmness*. Kemble appears to me to be a very studied— artificial actor. His performances throughout—evince deep study and application joind to amazingly judicious conception. They are *correct* & *highly finished* paintings but much *labored.* Thus, therefore, when witnessing the exertions of his powers—tho my head is satisfied and even astonished—yet my heart is seldom affected[.] I am not led away to forget that it is Kemble ⟨before me⟩ ↑the actor↓ not Othello the moor. *Once,* I must own however, I was *completely overpowerd* by his acting. It was in the part of Zanga¹¹—he was great throughout—but his last scene with Alonzo was truly Sublime—I then, in *very truth,* forgot that it was a mere mimic scene before me, indeed Kemble seemed to have forgotten it himself, and for the moment ↑to have↓ fancied himself Zanga. When the delusion ⟨was over⟩ ↑ceased↓ I was enraptured. I was surprized at what had been my emotions—I could not have believed that Tragic representation could so far decieve the senses & the judgement. I felt willing to allow Kemble all the Laurels that had been awarded him. The next time I saw him, however, I was less satisfied. It was in the character of Othello. Here his performance was very unequal. In many parts he was cold & labored—in the tender scenes he wanted *mellowness.* (I think him very often wanting in this quality) it was only in particular scenes ⟨where great exertion was⟩ that he seemed to collect all his powers and exert them with effect. His speech to the senate was lofty & admirable—indeed in declamation he is excellent. The last time I saw him was in the part of Jaffier¹² and I again remarked that it was but in certain passages that he was strikingly fine—tho his correct and unceasing attention to the character was visible throughout.

Kemble treads the stage with peculiar grace and dignity His figure is tall & imposing—much such an one as Fennels.[13] His countenance is noble & expressive—in a word he has a most *majestic presence*. I must not forget to observe that the *Pierre*[14] to Kembles Jaffier was acted by Mr Hargrave[15]—and a *noisy swaggering bully* did he make of him—I would have given any thing to have had Cooper[16] or Fennell in the character—so you see a principal character may be miserably performed even on a London stage. Kembles grand disadvantage is his voice—it wants the deep rich bass ⟨not⟩ tones—and has not sufficient extent. Constant exercise has doubtless done a vast deal for it—and given it a degree of flexibility and softness ⟨that⟩ ↑which↓ it had not naturally. Some of its tones are touching and pathetic, but when violent exclamation is necessary it is evident from the movements of his head and mouth & chest that he is obliged to use great exertions. This circumstance was at first a considerable draw back ⟨from⟩[17] on the pleasure I received from his performances. I begin now to get recconciled to it and not to notice it so much which confirms me in the opinion I ⟨have⟩ originally entertained that it is necessary to become in some degree accustomed to Kembles manner before you can perfectly enjoy his acting. ⟨As⟩ To give you if possible a fuller idea of my ⟨opinion⟩ general opinion of Kemble I shall only say that tho at present I decidedly give him the preference yet were Cooper to be equally studious & pay equal attention to his profession I would transfer it to him without hesitation. It would be a long time however before C. would be equally *correct* in his performances. Perhaps he would never be so—his style is different and with a little correction—its warmth & richness would perhaps make up for the want of Kembles correctness & precision. Actors are like painters. they seldom combine all these qualities but excel in different styles.

Cooke:[18] is the next to Kemble in the tragic department—or rather his equal taking them in their different lines. Cookes range is rather confined—The artful designing Hypocrite is his *forte* and in Iago he is admirable. I never was more completely satisfied with a performance. His Richard I am told is equally good but I have not seen it. In Sir Pertinax Mac Sycophant[19] also, he is every thing that could be desired and gives the Scotch accent with peculiar richness. Notwithstanding that he has disgusted the audience several times in consequence of his bacchanalian festivities he is a vast favorite and is always haild with the warmest applause. Indeed I am told he performs ⟨much⟩ with peculiar spirit when inspired by the grape, he must at any rate be *mellow* on such occasion.

Were I to indulge with out reserve in my praises of Mrs Siddons[20] I am affraid[21] you would think them hyperbolical. What a wonderful woman! The very first time I saw her perform I was struck with admiration. It was in the part of Calista[22]—Her looks—her voice her gesture delighted me—She penetrated in a moment to my heart[.] she froze & melted it by turns—a glance of her eye—a start—an exclamation thrilld thro my whole frame. The more I see her the more I admire her— I hardly breathe while she is on the stage—she works up my feelings till I am like a meer child. And yet this woman is old and has lost all elegance of figure—think then what must be her powers that she can delight & astonish even in the characters of Calista & Belvidera.[23] In person Mrs S. is not unlike her sister Mrs Whitlock[24] for she has latterly rather outgrown in size the limits even of *en bon point*. I even think there is some similarity in their countenances tho that of Mrs S. is infinitely superior. It is in fact the very index of her mind and in its mutable transitions may be read those nice gradations of passion that language is inadequate to express. In dignity and grace she is no ways inferior to Kemble, and they never appear to better advantage than when acting together. What Mrs Siddons *may* have been when she had ⟨youth and figure⟩ the advantages of youth and form I cannot say—but it appears to me that her performance at present leaves room to wish for nothing more—Age has planted no visible wrinkles on her brow and it is only by the practice & experience of years that she has been enabled to attain to her present consummate excellence.[25]

MANUSCRIPT: Rutgers University Library. PUBLISHED: PMI, I, 155–59 (in part); *Journal of the Rutgers University Library* 10 (December, 1946), 21–27.

1. A variant of Gen. 2:23.
2. The *re* has been crossed out by another hand.
3. From Laurence Sterne, *A Sentimental Journey*, "The Pulse," p. 179.
4. Located at No. 7 Sweeting's Alley and frequented mostly by merchants. See Bryant Lillywhite, *London Coffee Houses*, pp. 408–9.
5. John Gorham of Boston who had traveled with WI from Paris.
6. For the brother of King George III, William Henry, duke of Gloucester, who had died on August 25, 1805.
7. The entire paragraph which follows has diagonal lines through it in pencil.
8. Above "but" "to" is written in pencil.
9. Eccles. 1:14.
10. Charles Kemble (1775–1854), noted English actor who later became manager of Covent Garden.
11. Character in Edward Young's *The Revenge* (1721), as is Alonzo. Alonzo is also a character in Richard Brinsley Sheridan's *Pizarro* (1799), which played at Covent Garden on October 8, 1805, with Mrs. Siddons in the role of Elvira. See Genest, *Some Account of the English Stage*, VII, 658. Although Genest does not list him, it is quite possible that Kemble played Alonzo; for when *Pizarro* opened at Drury Lane on May 24, 1799, Mrs. Siddons appeared as Elvira, John

Philip Kemble as Rolla, and Charles Kemble as Alonzo. See *The Plays and Poems of Richard Brinsley Sheridan*, ed. R. Crompton Rhodes (New York, 1929), III, 17. WI may have seen William Dunlap's adaptation of Kotzebue, *Pizarro in Peru, or, the Death of Rolla* in one of its performances at the Park Theater in the spring of 1800. See Arthur Hobson Quinn, *A History of the American Drama* (New York, 1951), pp. 98–99; Odell, *NY Stage*, II, 85–87.

12. Hero of Thomas Otway's *Venice Preserved* (1682).

13. James Fennell (1766–1816), English-born actor who went to the United States in 1793. WI may have seen him in recitations from Young's *The Revenge* on January 5, 1799, or playing the role of Zanga on April 23, 1799, or in November, 1800. Fennell played the part of Jaffier on July 10, 1799, and on January 20, 1804, and the role of Pierre from *Venice Preserved*, all of which WI may have seen in New York. See Odell, *NY Stage*, II, 64, 65, 100, 66, 192.

14. A character in Otway's *Venice Preserved*.

15. Hargrave was an Irish actor who played with Kemble and Cooke in *Richard III* on October 15. See Genest, *Some Account of the English Stage*, VII, 658. Since Genest's listings are incomplete, many of the performances which WI saw are not included.

16. Thomas Abthorpe Cooper (1776–1849), English-born actor who had come to America in 1796. WI was acquainted with Cooper and with Mary Fairlie, whom Cooper married on June 11, 1812.

17. WI smudged out "from" and wrote "on" beneath it as the catchword for the next page.

18. George Frederick Cooke (1756–1811), English actor who played frequently with the Kembles in Shakespearean roles. In 1803 he had been hissed off the stage for drunkenness.

19. A character in Charles Macklin's *The Man of the World* (1764), which played at Covent Garden on October 5, 1805. See Genest, VII, 658.

20. Sarah Siddons (1755–1831), member of the Kemble family of actors who became famous playing the roles of Shakespeare's heroines.

21. A line has been drawn through the second *f*.

22. The heroine of Nicholas Rowe's *The Fair Penitent* (1703).

23. The heroine of Thomas Otway's *Venice Preserved*.

24. Elizabeth Kemble Whitlock (1761–1836), sister of Mrs. Siddons and a well-known actress in her own right.

25. The MS ends at this point.

34. To Peter Irving

London, November 7, 1805

My dear Brother:

By the papers you will perceive that England is all alive with the news of Nelson's victory.[1] It could not have happened more opportunely, for the disastrous accounts from the continent had made poor John Bull quite heart-sick—nothing was heard from him but execrations of Mack's[2] conduct as cowardly and treacherous, and desponding anticipations of the future. It is the prevalent opinion here that Mack has been bribed, and they are vociferous in their abuse both of him and his purchasers.

Poor John, however, was so completely down-hearted and humble, that I began really to pity him, when suddenly the news of Nelson's triumph arrived, and the old fellow reared his broad rosy countenance higher than ever. To his honor, however, let me say, that I have universally remarked, that whenever speaking of the affair, his first mention was of "poor Nelson's death," with a tribute of feeling to his memory; but John, as I have before testified, is a "kind-hearted old soul" at bottom. Notwithstanding the brilliancy of this victory and its importance at so alarming a crisis, yet I can scarcely say which is greatest, joy at its achievement, or sorrow for Nelson's fall. Last evening the chief streets and buildings were illuminated, but the illumination was not universal. The song of triumph is repressed—among the lowest of the mob I can hear Nelson's eulogium passed from mouth to mouth; every one yields his voice to the national tribute of gratitude and affection.

PUBLISHED: PMI, I, 161–62.

1. On October 21, 1805, Lord Horatio Nelson (b. 1758) was killed at Trafalgar, during a battle against the French in which the British fleet was victorious.
2. On October 20, 1805, Baron General Karl Mack (1752–1828) was forced to surrender after he was outmaneuvered. He had amassed the Áustrian army at Ulm to stop Napoleon's advance. See Thiers, *History of the Consulate*, III, 464–76.

35. *To William Irving, Jr.*

[November? 1805?]

Whilst I am on the subject of tributes to departed worth, let me mention one which tho not to be compared to the preceding for grandeur or elegance—perhaps surpasses them all in *pathos*—I do not reccollect if I ever wrote you about it in any of my former letters.

When crossing the varied & enchanting Lake of Lucerne in Switzerland we stopped at the little village of Gersau[1] which is romantically situated on the borders of the lake in a small valley at the foot of the stupenduous Mount Rigi—the ⟨neat⟩ white washd houses of the village and its neat church & spire were reflected in the tranquil bosom of the water and from a little distance had a picturesque ⟨effect⟩ appearance that delighted us. While our boatmen ⟨M⟩ Were dining my fellow traveller Cabell, and myself rambled thro the village and into the church yard

The graves were marked with small crosses of carved wood many of them gilt and ornamented with little pictures of saints and sometimes coarse miniatures apparently of the deceased. ⟨Among⟩ ↑On surveying↓ these humble testimonies of affectionate remembrance I was much

affected on percieving that several of the crosses were hung with
wreaths of flowers and others were planted on the graves! These are
genuine tributes of simple, unadulterated nature, that surpass all the
splendor and parade of marble monuments. They speak to the heart
with a tenderness and pathos that the ↑labord efforts of the↓ chissel
⟨at the⟩ & pencil can never attain[2]

> Each village matron, village maid,
>   shall with chaste fingers chaplets tie
> Due honours to the rural dead,
>   And emblems of mortality.[3]

What a rich chapter would Sterne have made of such a subject and
how did I regret at the time that he had never seen it.[4]

November weather has commenced and we are completely enveloped in gloom & fog—heaven bless the people for it has curs'd the
climate. I had made a long stroll into the city the other morning ⟨but⟩
The sky was over cast and the gloom thickend so sensibly that I pushd
homeward, ⟨f⟩ thro fear of being caught in the rain when in hurrying
along cheapside I happend to cast up my eyes and beheld the sun in
full rotundity peeping from behind a chimney—but the poor fellow
was so "shorn of his beams,"[5] so obscure that it was by mere chance I
discerned[6] him. I consequent[ly][7] found that it was a *very fine day*
and all this gloom that had allarmed[8] me was nothing but a little *fog &*
coal smoak[9] Two or three nights ago the fog was so dense that altho
the City was lighted with its usua[l][10] number of lamps and all the
strand was illuminated by the ⟨innumerable⟩ shop windows yet it was
impossible to discern any object at the distance of ten feet and in
crossing the streets the risk of being run over by carriages was imminant.
It was a complete scene of confusion & bawling—I have not yet learnt
how many were killd ⟨th⟩ in the streets or how many have killd themselves in consequence of this uncommon fog—but for my part I swal-
lowd so much of it that my throat has been sore ever since and I am
troubled with continual ⟨after?⟩ coughing and sneezing

This is the third letter I have written you by the Bristol packet and
as the bag closes this afternoon I must conclude as usual with remembrances to my friend[s][11]

> Your affectionate brother
> **W I**

Washington Irving[12]
MANUSCRIPT: NYPL—Seligman collection.

This sheet, written on both sides, is part of a letter which WI wrote to a brother,
doubtless William, during his travels in 1805. The first side, which describes Gersau,

Switzerland and its cemetery, is similar to his journal entry for May 10, 1805. See *J&N*, I, 382. It is possible that WI was interrupted after completing one side of the sheet, for the verso, numbered 36 in the upper left corner, deals with his impressions of London in November. He often resumed letters at a later time, though no others at such a long interval. Or he may have recalled the cemetery scene at Gersau and copied his journal entry into a letter written in England.

1. Gersau was independently governed until 1817. See *J&N*, I, 382, n. 188.

2. WI alludes to the burying ground at Gersau in the last paragraph of "Rural Funerals" in *The Sketch Book*.

3. Not identified.

4. The recto ends here.

5. John Milton, *Paradise Lost*, I, 596.

6. Also written in pencil as "deserned" above the word in ink.

7. The word runs off the paper.

8. The second *l* is crossed out in pencil, possibly by WI.

9. The *a* is crossed out and *e* added in pencil, not by WI.

10. The word runs off the paper.

11. The word runs off the paper.

12. This signature on another kind of paper is pasted in the lower corner of the MS page.

36. *To Gouverneur Kemble*

NEW YORK, May 24, 1806

Since I cannot have the pleasure, my dear fellow, of conversing with you in any other manner, I am determined to have a sociable dish of chat with you every morning upon paper, though I am fearful you will find me very stupid company.

I have the pleasure of informing you that the easterly wind, which has so mortally depressed the Lads of Kilkenny[1] latterly, is undergoing a finishing drench, and I greet the rain that now pours in torrents, as it bids fair to restore us to sunshine and good humor.

The *pensive Petronius*[2] and myself smoked a sentimental or rather philosophic segar together yesterday afternoon, over the office fire. You would have been amused to have witnessed our melancholy confab. We had met together with the express determination to be miserable, and to indulge in all the luxury of spleen. We could not have chosen a more happy time and place. It was in the dusk of the afternoon, and the dirty windows, and green blinds, made our old-fashioned office look still more gloomy. We were lolling in crazy arm-chairs on each side of a grate, in which smoked a few handsful of vile sea-coal. Our deadly foe, the east wind, howled without, and our still more inveterate enemies, the ponderous fathers of the law, frowned upon us from their shelves in all the awful majesty of *Folio* grandeur.

The pensive Petronius and myself sat moralizing on the direful scene of abominations that this wicked world presents, complaining of the "various turns of fate below;" and with the experimental wisdom of two Solomons, determined that all was vanity and vexation of spirit. Our conversation was truly evangelic, and at "each dreary pause between"[3] we whiff'd our segars, watched the smoke as it ascended to the elegantly stuccoed ceiling, or tormented the unhappy fire with the remains of a shattered shovel, and an old iron poker. We pictured to ourselves how differently you were employed, perhaps sipping in inspiration and champagne; listening to the light joke; enjoying the union of mirth, melody, and sentiment, in a song, or basking in the sunshine of some fair Hunkamunka's[4] eyes.

After this sombre tête-à-tête, I found my mind wonderfully relieved; whether the spleen had evaporated in the clouds of tobacco smoke, or had passed off in the many sage, philosophic, and ill-humored reflections I had made, I can't say; but I began to feel my whole system renovated; my pulse beat more briskly; my blood seemed to circulate with greater vivacity, and to play about my heart with greater activity, causing it to dilate and throb, and glow in the most comfortable and enlivening manner; so I forthwith went into company in the evening, and enjoyed myself in a marvellously satisfactory degree.

* * * Present my particular remembrances to your sister,[5] and tell her she occupies three long sentences in my prayers, whether French or English; in return for which, I only beg that she will take particular notice of the different kinds of tea they drink in Philadelphia, their several effects; whether it is still the fashion there to give grand perspirations; whether the young ladies are still educated in the market place as the best means of preparing them *for the market;* whether Hyson, Gunpowder, or Cat-nip is the rage; and any other information that may be of service to me in my folio dissertation on tea. Write to me, if you have time; show this scrawl to nobody, but gallant it, as quick as possible, to the fire, and believe me,

Yours sincerely,
W. I.

PUBLISHED: PMI, I, 168–70.

Gouverneur Kemble (1786–1875), son of Peter Kemble, a New York merchant. He served as American consul at Cadiz in 1813 and, after studying Spanish methods of cannon casting, established the West Point Foundry at Cold Spring in 1818.

1. A group of young men who were also called the Nine Worthies and the Ancient Club, even though their number was frequently more than nine. Since most of the group except WI had nicknames, it has been suggested that WI provided the names for the others because some of these epithets appear in WI's letters. They include Henry Brevoort (Nuncle), Gouverneur Kemble (The Patroon), James K. Paulding (Billy Taylor), William Irving (The Membrane), Ebenezer

Irving (Captain Great-heart), Peter Irving (The Doctor), Henry Ogden (The Supercargo), David Porter (Sinbad), Richard McCall (Oorombates), David Longworth (The Dusky), and Captain Philipse (The Chieftain). Kemble's house in Newark, called Cockloft Hall in *Salmagundi,* was a gathering place for the Lads. See Paulding, *Literary Life of J. K. Paulding,* pp. 35–36; LBI, I, xx–xxi; Amos L. Herold, *James Kirke Paulding, Versatile American* (New York, 1926), pp. 28–29; and PMI, I, 164–68.

2. Probably one of the other young men reading law in the office of Josiah Ogden Hoffman.

3. William Collins, "The Passions, An Ode for Music," line 48. See *The Poems of William Collins,* ed. Edmund Blunden (London, 1929), p. 108.

4. The wife of Tom Thumb in Henry Fielding's *Tom Thumb* (1730).

5. Gertrude Kemble (1791–1841), who married James K. Paulding in 1818.

37. To Gouverneur Kemble

New York, May 26, 1806

Dear Kemble:

I have just received your most welcome lines of the 24th;[1] and being immediately sent out on an errand, I amused myself with reading them along the street; the consequence was, I stumbled twice into the gutter; overset an old market-woman, and plumped head and shoulders into the voluminous bosom of a fat negro wench, who was sweating and smoking in all the rankness of a summer heat. I was stopped two or three times by acquaintances to know what I was laughing so heartily at; and, by the time I had finished the letter, I had completely forgotten the errand I was sent on; so I had to return, make an awkward apology to *boss,*[2] and look like a nincompoop. * * *

I can give you no news, except that the weather is charming, and we are all once more in a state of existence. The lads of Kilkenny are completely scattered; and, to the riotous, roaring, rattle-brained orgies at Dyde's,[3] succeeds the placid, picnic, picturesque pleasures of the tea-table. We have resigned the feverish enjoyments of Madeira and Champagne, and returning with faith and loyalty to the standard of beauty, have quietly set down under petticoat-government. There's a touch of the poetic for you. Inspired by the sublimity of the subject, I find my ideas begin once more to rise from the melancholy slough into which they have been plunged. I am a new man, and am hasting with rapid strides towards perfection. In a month or two I shall become as modest, well-behaving, pretty-boy-kind of a fellow as ever graced a tea-party. God bless the women! I ascribe this reformation entirely to the influence of their charms.

You have appointed me your champion at the tea-parties, and I accept the office with enthusiasm; but you must let me know in what light you wish to be held up, whether as a true lad of Kilkenny, or a gentle prince prettyman; of this you will inform me by the next mail.

Having, as usual, scribbled three pages about nothing, I shall conclude with my sincere remembrances to your sister, my benediction to Jo Gratz,[4] and my compliments to his family.

Your friend,
W. I.

P. S.—If those chaps in Philadelphia don't treat you better, cut and run; and, foregad, we'll hear the cocks crow in New York for three mornings at least.

PUBLISHED: PMI, I, 170–72.

1. This letter has not been located.

2. This seems to be WI's familiar name for Josiah Ogden Hoffman, in whose law office he was studying.

3. Dyde's Hotel, built during WI's absence in Europe and located next to the Park Theater, was a popular place for eating and for public meetings. It had a ball room which would accommodate about 120 people. See Bayle, *Old Taverns of NY*, pp. 396–97; STW, I, 397.

4. Joseph Gratz (1785–1858), brother of Rebecca Gratz (1781–1869) and prominent citizen of Philadelphia. Miss Gratz, well known for her philanthropic and educational activities, is said to have been the model for Rebecca in *Ivanhoe*. Scott was apparently inspired in his characterization by WI's description of the beautiful and charming Philadelphia Jewess.

38. To John R. Murray

[July 4, 1806]

Dear Sir,

I understand that it is probable there will be a vacancy in the board of the Mechanics Bank[1] tomorrow—It is the wish of my Brother Williams friends to get him in the directorship; I hope you will excuse the liberty I take in asking you to be favourable to his election: provided you have no particular objection and are not inclined in favour of any other candidate—

I am Sir,/with great respect & esteem/Your Hbl St
Washington Irving

Mr Jno R Murray
Friday 4th July. [1806][2]

MANUSCRIPT: SHR.

John R. Murray was the son of John Murray (1737–1808), New York merchant and real estate investor. See Scoville, *Old Merchants of NYC*, I, 295.

1. The Merchants Bank here alluded to was probably a predecessor of the one given a state charter in 1810. See James W. Gilbert, *A History of Banking in*

America (1837) (New York, 1967), p. 58; and John Jay Knox, *The History of Banking in the United States* (New York, 1900), pp. 394, 428.

2. The date was determined by the perpetual calendar.

39. *To Joseph Gratz*

New York, July 8, 1806.

Dear Gratz:—

You will receive this letter from the hands of Dr. Massie of Virginia, who has just returned from a European tour and will stop for a short time in your city on his way home.

Having had the pleasure of travelling for some time with Dr. Massie in Europe, I can recommend him with confidence to your attentions and civilities as a gentleman from whose acquaintance you will derive great pleasure.

Yours sincerely,
Washington Irving

P.S. Your kind attentions to my friend Cabell have laid me under great obligation, which I shall be happy at any time to discharge.

PUBLISHED: *Canadian Magazine* 60 (January, 1923), 231.

For details about the Gratz-Irving relationship see Mildred Low, "A Lover of Good Company," *Canadian Magazine* 60 (January, 1923), 231.

40. *To Joseph Gratz*

New York July 8th. 1806

Dear Gratz

This letter will be handed you by my particular friend Mr Sam Swartwout whom I introduce to your special consideration and choice attentions as one of the true and loyal association, of the *Lads of Kilkenny*.[1] Another word in his favor or eulogy would be superlative so merely informing you that two of our tickets are blanks and that two are still in the wheel—I have the honor to salute you

respectfully &c

Mr Joseph Gratz.

Washington Irving

P. S. I will enquire concerning the *Silenus*[2] and give you the *earliest* intelligence concerning her departure. Remember me particularly to your family and present your Sister my Sincere congratulations on he[r][3] safe arrival, or if she should have had the misfortune to break a limb or ⟨an⟩ a neck—my most heartfelt condolements.

ADDRESSED: Mr Joseph Gratz / Market Street / Phila. / pr. Mr Swartwout / at the Indian Queen.
MANUSCRIPT: Va.–Barrett.

1. For other details about the Lads of Kilkenny see WI to Gouverneur Kemble, May 24, 1806.
2. A search of the shipping news in the NYEP during July, 1806, reveals no news about the *Silenus*.
3. WI omitted the bracketed letter.

41. To Henry Ogden

[New York, July, 1806]

I am so completely engrossed with law at present, that I have no time to go about and pick up intelligence. Examination comes on in about three weeks,[1] and I begin to feel the fever incident to occasions of the kind. I wish, while in Canton,[2] you would pick me up two or three queer little pretty things, that would cost nothing, and be acceptable to the girls; but above all, do not forget the Mandarin's dress. If you can conveniently, get two or three drawings of the most superlative tea put up in a little quizzical box for me, and packed up with mighty care and importance. I will have some high fun with it.[3]

PUBLISHED: PMI, I, 172.

Henry N. Ogden, who never married, was, along with Peter and David Ogden, the son of Nicholas Ogden (1753–1812) and Hannah Cuyler (1758–1816). One of the Lads of Kilkenny, he was called "The Supercargo." Like WI, he was fond of traveling. See Wheeler, *Ogden Family*, p. 107.

1. Although WI apparently planned to take his bar examination in August, he did not actually take it until November 21, 1806, with an undistinguished performance. See PMI, I, 173.
2. Ogden had recently embarked for China.
3. "The Mandarin's dress and the tea evidently point to some whimsical project, but whether any 'high fun' came of it I cannot say, though there is hint in his correspondence of Ogden's return 'laden with the riches of the East, some of which were intended for him,' and of a supper at the Kembles which followed, 'in true Chinese style, in which none were permitted to eat except with chopsticks'" (P. M. Irving's comment in PMI, I, 172).

42. *To Josiah Ogden Hoffman*

New York, Feb. 2, 1807.

Dear Sir

I am writing this letter from your parlor, and have the pleasure of informing you that the family, at this moment, are perfectly well; the girls all out in the sunshine; Mrs. H. sewing like a good housewife; little Charles[1] sleeping upstairs, and *little old fashion*[2] by my side, most studiously turning over the leaves of a family Bible. The only occurrences of *importance* that have taken place in the family, since Mrs. Hoffman wrote last, are, that Mr. Edgar[3] has sent to know if you took the house for the ensuing year, and Mrs. Hoffman has answered in the affirmative. Louis has received *sailing orders,* and I have beaten the old lady[4] most deplorably at cribbage. . . .

Having given you all the domestic intelligence that I am master of, I hope you will not think it impertinent if I speak a little of myself.

I learn with pleasure, that the council of appointment are decidedly Lewisite.[5] As there will, doubtless, be a liberal dispensation of loaves and fishes on the occasion, I would humbly put up my feeble voice in the general application. Will you be kind enough to speak a "word in season" for me. There will, doubtless, be numerous applicants of superior claims to myself, but none to whom a "crumb from the table" would be more acceptable. I can plead no services that I have rendered, for I have rather shunned than sought political notoriety. . . . I know that there are few offices to which I am eligible, either from age or legal information. My brother, John T. Irving,[6] is much older than myself, and from his knowledge of the law is capacitated to fill offices to which I cannot pretend; our interests are the same, as we shall share whatever falls to either of our lots. . . . I do not intend that you should give yourself any trouble on my account; your good word is all I solicit, should any thing present which you should think suitable to me. I am a little acquainted with Mr. Storm,[7] and am inclined to suppose he would be in my favor. . . .

PUBLISHED: PMI, I, 174–75.

In this printed version there is no punctuation after the salutation. Usually PMI printed a colon there, regardless of what WI may have used. The text in PMI is followed here.

1. Charles Fenno Hoffman (February 7, 1806–June 7, 1884) was the first child of Hoffman's marriage with Maria Fenno.

2. A reference to Mary Hoffman (June 15, 1796–September 7, 1818), Hoffman's third child of his marriage with Mary Colden.

3. Probably William Edgar, a wealthy merchant and director of the Bank of New York, with a store at 7 Wall Street. See Scoville, *Old Merchants of NYC,* I, 304–5; II, 250.

4. Probably Mrs. Nicholas Hoffman (d. 1823), J. O. Hoffman's mother, who is also mentioned in WI's letter of August 10, 1807.

5. The followers of Governor Morgan Lewis had allied themselves with the Federalists and gained control of the New York state legislature. The council of appointment made key appointments and controlled political patronage. See David M. Ellis, James A. Frost, Harold C. Syrett, and Harry J. Carman, *A History of New York State* (Ithaca, 1967), pp. 136–37.

6. Actually John Treat Irving was only about five years older than WI.

7. "A member of the Council of Appointment" (PMI, I, 175, n.). Thomas Storm, a New York city alderman in the 1790's and a state legislator afterward, was lieutenant governor under Morgan Lewis.

43. *To Mary Fairlie*

Philadelphia March 17. 1807[1]

Your charming letter[2] has just reached me, and the post shall not depart without an Answer, if it is only to testify my gratitude for the exquisite entertainment you have furnished me—I should have written you a Second letter without waiting for a reply to my first, but really I have been reduced to such an extremity of nervous affliction that I dared not run the hazard of being stupid—Oh my friend, how dreadfully I have been maltreated in this most facetious City. The good folk of this place have a most wicked determination of being all thought wits & *beaux esprits* and they are not content with being thought so ↑by↓ themselves, but they insist that every body else should be of the same opinion—now this in my humble opinion is the very d——l—as Chaucer says,[3] and ↑it↓ has produced a most violent attack of puns upon my nervous system. The Philadelphians do absolutely "live and move and have a being" entirely upon puns—and their wits are absolutely cut up in six penny bits and dealt out in small change—I cannot speak two sentences but ⟨w⟩that[4] I see a pun gathering in the faces of my hearers— I absolutely shudder with horror. think what miseries I suffer—Me to whom⟨a⟩ a pun is an abomination—is there any thing in the whole volume of the "miseries of human life" to equal it. I experienced the first attack of this ⟨unlucky⟩ forlorn wit on entering philadelphia—it was equal to a ⟨fit⟩ twinge of the gout, or a *stitch in the side*—I found it was repeated at every step[.] I could not turn a corner but ⟨w⟩that[5] a pun was hurled at my head—till, to complete my annoyance, two young devils of punsters, who began just to crow in the art like young bantams, pennd me up in a corner at a tea party and did so *bepun* [m]e[6] that I was reduced to absolute stupidity[.] I hastend home prodigiously indisposed, took to my bed and was only roused therefrom by the sound of the breakfast bell. I have sufferd more or less ever

since, but thank heaven it is a complaint of which few die, otherwise
I should be und[er?] [*hole in paper*] no small apprehension.

Your message to the "elegant ⟨Clymer⟩"[7] shall be faithfully remembered. Maria L——[8] has sent him a handkerchief of yours which she
happened accidentally to have with her—I expect to see him wearing
it in his bosom or on his hat or perhaps as a night cap. He still retains
a spark of faithful reccollection—and was particular⟨ly⟩ in his enquiries
of Brevoort, whether you was not in low spirits. He called on me two
or three times and I on him but we could not find each other at home—
by good fortune however I ⟨met⟩ overtook him yesterday as he was
treating his legs to an airing in Market street. as I hold those ponderous
supporters of his body in no inconsiderable estimation I was particular
in noting their appearance and am happy to say they are in a state
of tolerable prosperity though they have rather a pensive aspect—owing
I suppose to the weight of misery and Carcass they have to ⟨support⟩
und[*er*]*go* [*hole in paper*] ("⟨somewhat of⟩ ↑meaning↓ a villainous pun,"
for which god forgive me). The dear dog was very loving in his salutation,
and made several kind of *pulse feeling* questions—Were there not several
ladies coming on from New York?—*No!*—Mrs Crawford and Mrs John
Livingston[9] he believed had been expected—⟨were⟩ ↑did↓ they not
propose a visit to Philadelphia?—*No!* The reply was like a gullotine[.]
it chopped off his hopes & his question at one stroke and the unhappy
⟨clymer⟩ relapsed into stupidity—and thought of the moon! As I have
no such thing as malice in my composition and do love dearly to make
every body happy, I advised him to make new York a visit, he expressed
a wish to do so. I begged him to go on with me—he wanted to know how
soon I should go—this I could not tell, as my stay depends entirely on
my whim and my pocke[t] [*MS torn*][.] he seemed to listen to the
proposition with complacency, [*MS torn*] it shall go hard but you will
have him puffing and lumbering about your parlour in the course of
a Week or two. ⟨Clymer⟩ is reputed to be a very sensible, profound
young man but I scarce know how to depend on philadelphia judgement—Would you think it—do not discredit it I pray you—⟨Clymer also⟩
is discovered to be *interesting!*—nay more a *good dancer!!*—nay still
more the belle of New York!!! an ounce of civit, good apothecary—for
heavens sake advise a whole host of our hum drum—unadmired—no
body—cares—about—young gentlewomen to translate themselves forthwith to philadelphia—where they may be sure of figuring with great
eclat and exercising the small wits of all the poets & punsters with
which this city is running over.

In fact the yorkers are in great repute here—we cannot possibly
answer the demands upon our time and Maria L—— & myself have
serious thoughts of writing to New York for a cargo to ⟨ans⟩ stock the

market. You may suppose we feel our importance in no small degree and endeavor to keep up the dignity of New York by abusing every thing around us. I have met with Maria repeatedly in different parties; but can never find her at home. She is in excellent spirits and I never knew her more entertaining—she is a very special girl. I found myself seated between her & her cousin Miss Swift[10] last evening at Mrs Dallas,[11] They opened a most incessant fire upon me, and shewed me no quarter for the whole evening. This Miss Swift is a young lady of great capability and has abused me so much that I really begin to take her into prodigious favor. I walked home with them "by the light of the moon" felt quite romantic—sentimental and all that—and made an apostrophy to bright Cynthia in which I proved her to be a very pretty planet—almost as pretty as a New York lamp—They abused me for my poetic flight—whereupon I straightway fell into great dudgeon.

I have been introduced to Mrs Derby by her husband[12]—I wont speak ↑all↓ what I think of her—you would accuse me of hyperbole—but to say that I admire her would be too cold—too feeble[.] I think she would be a belle in heaven itself—I cannot refrain from gazing on her continually whenever I meet her, and were I an eastern visionary I should bow down and do her homage as one of the Houris, destined to perfect the bliss of true believers—This is all honest, sober fact, whatever you may think of it.

I approve of your plan of retirement and think it the most politic one a young lady could adopt—when there is a dearth of invitations—should you put your ⟨plan⟩ idea in execution concerning the gutter & the poplar I would reccommend Maria L———s little curse of a puppy dog—and a two peny trumpet—and then you might play sternes maria[13]—I will undertake to support the character of yorick and appear with a rueful countenance—waving a genuine bandana.

I should have described the palace in which I [write] [*MS torn*] to you—its spacious halls—its marble stair cases—but of [that?] [*MS torn*] anon—I occasionally of a morning—when troubled with [mournful?] [*MS torn*] moments—play the part of Mrs Macbeth—and hunt all over the house for ends of candles to write letters by—though I carry the taper in my hand instead of my night cap.

A whole host of Yorkers ⟨have⟩ arrived here last evening—headed by Dickey—who swears most manfully he will suffer matrimony—*with* benefit of clergy—they all departed last night excepting *Prince Pretty-man* hight Jacky Lawrence[14] who was left behind "like a lame duck out of a flock["][15]—as Milton says—I shall wait on Maria with your message—I believe she has anticipated your project as we have detected one of your handerkerchiefs in her possession—besides a pair of Ear rings—a comb—a breast pin &c which Miss Patterson[16] declares belong to different members of the family—Maria has confessed a pair of sleeves and I have strong suspicions of a Bonnet—she is in "superlative snuff"[17] here as Dryden observes.

You need not be under any apprehensions of my forgetting New York while you are in it (very like a compliment) but I have so many engagements on hand—am so ⟨fav⟩ intolerably admired and have still so much money in my pocket that I really can fix no time when I shall return to my New York insignificance.

I fear I shall ⟨lose⟩ ↑miss↓ the post—so though I have a world of matter more to communicate I must hastily conclude with my warmest remembrance to your family and a fervent request for an immediate answer—

Sincerely your friend
Washington Irving

P.S. As your Mama is so kindly solicitous about my health do not let her know any thing about my being so violently indisposed with this *pun* fever—particularly as I feel myself on the recovery ever since I have read that estimable work entitled 'Gods revenge against punning[']'[18]—

MANUSCRIPT: Yale. PUBLISHED: PMI, I, 180–83 (in part).

Mary Fairlie, a vivacious, quick-witted belle who served as the model for Sophy Sparkle in the *Salmagundi* papers being written at this time. She married Thomas A. Cooper, the actor, on June 11, 1812.

1. Except for the month, the date is in another hand than WI's because the corner of the MS containing the rest of the dateline has been torn off.

2. WI is replying to Mary Fairlie's letter of March 13, 1807, which was filled with gossip about their friends. (MS in NYPL—Personal Papers of WI.)

3. Chaucer does not use this exact phrase. In "The Pardoner's Tale" (line 480) is the line "Whiche been the verray develes officeres," but WI apparently is not alluding to that here. As in the supposed quotations from Milton and Dryden later and in other quoted passages in the letter, he is probably trying to impress Miss Fairlie with his wide reading and erudition.

4. A *t* has been substituted for the *w* by another hand.

5. A *t* has been substituted for the *w* by another hand.

6. WI wrote "be."

7. Clymer has not been identified; difficult to recover, the name is consistently canceled throughout the letter. Since the cancellations were made with a different pen, they appear to be later and probably made by PMI, who substitutes blanks for Clymer in his printed version.

8. WI is probably referring to Maria Livingston, whom Miss Fairlie alluded to in her letter as "Maria L_____n."

9. John R. Livingston was married to Mary McEvers, who died February 17, 1843. See Florence Van Rensselaer, comp., *The Livingston Family in America* (New York, 1949), p. 101.

10. Miss Swift is not positively identified. She may be the daughter of Joseph, who lived on South Front Street in Philadelphia in the 1790's. See *Heads of Families at the first Census of the United States Taken in the Year 1790: Pennsyl-*

vania (Baltimore, 1966), 219. Or she may have been the daughter of John White Swift (1750–1819), a Philadelphia merchant. See *Appleton's Cyclopaedia of American Biography*, V, 10.

11. Probably the wife of Alexander James Dallas (1759–1817), who served as Madison's secretary of the treasury.

12. Richard Crowninshield Derby (1777–1854), the youngest son of Elias Haskett Derby (1739–1799), who married Martha Coffin (d. 1832) in 1800. See Perley Derby, "Genealogy of the Derby Family," *Essex Institute Historical Collections* 3 (1861), 203, 287.

13. Probably an allusion to *Tristram Shandy*, vol. IX, chap. 24, in which the mad, sorrowing Maria is playing the flute. See Laurence Sterne, *The Life and Opinions of Tristram Shandy, Gentleman*, ed. James Aiken Work, pp. 629–31.

14. Possibly the brother of James Lawrence (1781–1813), the Navy officer killed in a battle with the British. Or he may be John L. Lawrence (b. 1785), the son of Major Jonathan Lawrence (b. 1737), who became prominent in legal circles in New York City. See Margherita A. Hamm, *Famous Families of New York* (New York, 1902), I, 237.

15. WI errs in attributing this quotation to Milton, for it does not appear in the Milton concordance.

16. Miss Patterson may be the daughter of John Patterson, who lived between Vine and Race Streets and the Delaware and Schuylkyl Rivers in the 1790's. See *1790 Census*, p. 215. The collector of customs in Philadelphia, Patterson married Catherine Livingston, the great-granddaughter of Robert Livingston. Or Miss Patterson may be the daughter of Robert Patterson (1743–1824), professor of mathematics at the University of Pennsylvania from 1779 to 1814. He had a son Robert (1787–1854).

17. This phrase is not attributed to Dryden in the concordance to his writings.

18. No such book has been located. Perhaps WI, with tongue in cheek, is playing on the title of John Reynolds's book, *The Triumph of Gods Revenge, against the Crying and Execrable Sin of Murther* (London, 1629).

44. To [Mary Fairlie?]

New York, April ⟨8⟩9th. 1807.

I do hate all apologies, excuses and explanations from the very bottom of my soul, and I would ⟨now⟩ most readily give a two dollar jersey bank bill[1] (though it is a fee from a client & therefore a *curiosity*) if I had my dear uncle Howard[2] at my elbow to apologize for my not answering your invaluable letter sooner. To shuffle off the disagreeable matter as soon as possible I do assure you that it was the flattering expectation of your daily arrival that prevented me from writing, and when that ⟨adv⟩ excuse could no longer hold good there came to pass one of the most indecent, outrageous and ungentlemanlike storms of Wind & snow & hail & all other mischevious deviltries of the elements that ever happened in the *memory of the oldest inhabitants,* several of whom I questioned very particularly on the subject. Now so it is, that next to apologies, compliments, puns and the devil, I do most vehemently & emphatically abominate bad weather, and whenever ⟨the⟩ dame Nature chooses to play the termagant and get in her tantrums, I consider myself fully privileged & authorized to be as stupid, silent and unsociable as I please, and surely when in such a state you could not have the conscience to require a letter at my hands. ⟨To day we⟩ Never trust me as a philosopher if this is not one of the most rantipole crazy headed, coquetish little snivelling planets in the whole system— always on extremes—hot or cold, wet or dry—Would that I could have the management of one of its volcanoes! fore george but I'd set fire to it and blow the world and all its inhabitants into quite another orbit—trust me we should profit marvelously by the exchange

All the foregoing ⟨th⟩ is meant for an apology—and a most excellent one it is, or I am very much mistaken—for I never ⟨made one⟩ in my whole life made one so much to the purpose before. You doubtless expect much intelligence concerning our beloved city—this centre of delights, this whirlpool of felicity—you wish for animated accounts of Balls, routs, ⟨&⟩ assemblies and all the fiddle faddle of fashionable life —in this you will be disappointed for three very substantial reasons— first because that one ball is so exactly similar to another that the only circumstance of news that can be ⟨given⟩↑imparted↓ concerning it is the name of the lady who gave it—your imagination can supply all the rest, with the most faithful correctness—Secondly—Because if I knew all the fashionable news in town I feel no ways disposed ↑at present↓ to take the trouble to retail it, and thirdly because I have kept the world at *such a distance* since my return, that I am quite out of the tide of circumstance & incident. Shew me any *woman* in the whole world that can produce half so much reason for her conduct and I will fall down and worship her as a prodigy

Madam Moreau[3] has returned the civilities of our citizens and citizen-esses in their own style, by giving them [a] [*MS torn*] most outrageous squeeze, suffocation and steam bath at her own house. As I was not present I can give you no account of it that[4] that it was most uncom-fortably delightful and all the company looked the next day as if they had been stewed down to mummies in a patent digester. The only *reason* I can alledge for my absence is that miserable worn out one of *"not being ⟨asked⟩ invited"*—You know that Madam and me are *not on terms* and never spoke to one another in the whole course of our lives. I must confess I once believed that I was on the very brink of an acquaintance with her, as she gave me a most gracious smile when I was turning her in a cotillion—I absolutely shuddered at the abyss of honour into which I was about to be plunged, when to my great relief I observed she gave exactly the same smile in exactly the same manner to every gentleman in the Cotillion.

My venerable uncle "the benevolent"[5] has returned home brim full and running over with Philadelphia—of which he talks incessantly; and in a manner so incoherent that I begin to fear the poor lads head or heart must be damaged—Now such conduct I take to be highly ⟨improper⟩ indecorous and unseemly—to praise Philadelphia in the very face of New York—Abominable! Why it is just as bad as entertaining a fair lady with ⟨the⟩ eulogiums on the charms of a cotemporary Belle—⟨which⟩↑and that↓ you know is one of the "deadly sins" which no penitence or atonement can expiate For my own part (excuse my modest egotism) I must say I have been remarkably circumspect and *genteel* in this particular. I have talked but little of philadelphia since my return and expressed my opinion of it only in private, under charges of the most inviolable secrecy—I long for ⟨retur⟩ your return, when I may make you my confident and pour into your friendly bosom the "Wondrous Love" I bear for that delectable City. It is my strong suspicion that poor uncles heart has been sadly peppered by the eyes of that mischevious damsel Miss Keaton[6]—"Oh this Love—this Love."[7] What a most wicked preposterous passion it is—What an arrant fool does it make of that self dubbed "Lord of the Creation"[8]—Witness my unhappy friend[9] who has ⟨lat⟩ of late fallen into very "melancholy and gentlemanlike" manners and has taken to a wig! Alas poor lad—⟨he⟩ since my return he has wasted more sighs than would turn a wind mill; and as to segars—I have placed another box to your account. You will certainly have to take compassion on him if it is out of a principle of sheer Economy.——

Enough for the present. I am striving to write a gay letter when I am almost as "melancholy & gentlemanlike" as poor *Wiggens* himself—Kiss the tip ends of the fingers of all your fair cousins for me—Would to heavens I were there to save you the trouble—One of *"the children"*[10] has wandered to philadelphia—be kind unto her I pray you—the poor little thing is young and inexperienced but I do assure you it is a very good child—very good indeed. Remember me to the Gratzs Pattersons[11] &c and believe me

Sincerely your friend
Washington Irving

Manuscript: Free Library of Philadelphia.

The style and tone of this letter are similar to those WI wrote to Mary Fairlie on March 17 and May 2, 1807. In them he also omits the salutation and deals with social trivia which would interest a girl like Mary Fairlie. The letter *could* be addressed to one of the "Lads of Kilkenny" visiting or now residing in Philadelphia.

1. States could not issue bills of credit but could charter private banks, which were to issue notes. Twenty-eight banks of this kind existed in 1800 and 89 in 1811. See William Graham Sumner, *A History of Banking in the United States* (New York,

1896), p. 70. A contemporary comment on the worthlessness of such paper currency is the following made in 1815: "Such was the state of the currency that, in New Jersey, I met with an instance where one dollar note I had taken in change, which was current on one side of a turnpike gate, would not pass at an hundred yards' distance on the other side." See E. S. Thomas, *Reminiscences of the Last Sixty-five Years, commencing with the Battle of Lexington* (Hartford, 1840), p. 84. The Bank of New Jersey was incorporated in 1804 and issued its first paper money in 1806.

2. WI is probably using a familiar title for a friend.

3. Madame Moreau, the wife of General Jean Victor Moreau, was the former Mlle. Hulot, a Creole friend of Napoleon and Josephine Bonaparte. She accompanied her husband to America after he was banished for his part in the Pichegru affair. See *La Grande Encyclopédie*, XXIV, 326.

4. WI probably intended to write "than."

5. Perhaps a playful reference to Henry Brevoort, who was called "Nuncle" by the Lads of Kilkenny.

6. The *Philadelphia Directory* for 1807 lists a Mary Keating who kept a boardinghouse at 130 South Fourth Street, but it is unlikely that this is the person WI refers to.

7. Not identified.

8. From Robert Burns, "The Twa Dogs" (line 45).

9. This is probably "poor Wiggins" mentioned in the next paragraph. Of the five Wigginses in the 1807 *New York City Directory* only Samuel Wiggins, who operated a dry goods store at 105 Chatham, seems like a possible candidate. The others are laborers or tradesmen below WI's social station. Or WI may be punning.

10. Possibly one of the older children of J. O. Hoffman.

11. General Robert Patterson lived at 13th and Locust Streets in Philadelphia. WI may have met him and his family on one of his visits.

45. *To Mary Fairlie*

New York, May 2d. 1807.

I thank you a thousand times for the wish you express that I should write to you, and this ⟨for three⟩ is the more satisfactory for three reasons[.] first because it satisfies me that I cannot have offended you in having already written without your authority—second, because it shews that my letters are acceptable and afford some amusement—third, because it gives me the delectable privilege of scribbling to you, which, an[d][1] please God, I shall exercise to my hearts content.

Well—no—thats a silly beginning for a sorrowful tale—Alas!—tis[2] much better—though too much on the peccavi—we have toiled through the purgatory of an Election and "may the day stand for aye accursed on the Kalender,"[3] for never were poor devils more intollerably beaten & discomfitted than my forlorn bretheren the federalists.[4] What makes me the more outrageous is that I got fairly drawn into the vortex and before the third day was expired I was as deep in mud & politics as

ever a moderate gentleman would wish to be—and I drank beer with
the multitude, and I talked handbill fashion with the demagogues, and
I shook hands with the mob—whom my heart abhorreth—Tis true for the
first two days I maintained my cooleness & indifference ⟨and⟩[.] the first
day I merely hunted for whim character & absurdity according to my
usual custom. the Second day being rainy I sat in the bar room at the
seventh ward & read a volume of Galatea[5] which I found on a shelf—
but before I had got through a hundred pages I had three or four
good feds sprawling around me on the floor and another with his eyes
half shut leaning on my shoulder in the most affectionate manner, and
spelling a page of the book as if it had been an electioneering handbill. But the third day—Ah—then came the tug of War—My patriotism
all at once blazed forth, and I determined ⟨like many⟩ to save my
Country! Oh my friend ↑I have been in↓ such holes & corners—such
filthy nooks and filthy corners, sweep offices & oyster cellars! ⟨as I have⟩
"I have been sworn brother to a leash of drawers, and can drink with
any tinker in his own language during my life."[6]—faugh! I shall not be
able to bear the smell of small beer or tobacco for a month to come,
and a negro is an abomination ⟨whic⟩ unto me. Not that I have any
disrespect for Negroes—on the contrary I hold them in particular estimation, for by some unaccountable freak they have all turned out for
the federalists to a man! poor devils! I almost pitied them—for we had
them up in an enormous drove in the middle of the day waiting round
the poll for a chance to vote. the Sun came out intollerably warm—
⟨the poor⟩ and being packed together like sheep in a pen, they absolutely fermented, and a cloud of vapour arose like frank incense to
the skies—had Jupiter (who was a good federalist) still been there,
he would have declared it was a sweet smelling savour. Truly this
serving ones country is a nauseous piece of business—and if patriotism
is such a dirty virtue—prythee no more of it—I was almost the whole
time at the seventh ward—as you know—that the most fertile ward in
mob-riot & incident—and I do assure you the scene was exquisitely ludi-
crous[7]—⟨There⟩ Such haranguing & puffing & strutting among all the
little great men of the day—Such shoals of unfledged heroes from the
lower wards, who had broke away from their mamas and run to
electioneer with a slice of bread & butter in their hands. Every carriage
that drove up disgorged a whole nursery of these pigmy wonders,
who all seemed to put on the brow of thought, the air of bustle &
business and the big talk of general committee men. There were the
Master Hamiltons and Master Fleming and little Master Gracie[8] on
top of a big horse and Master ⟨Jackey and⟩ Tommy and Master Dicky
& Master Harry not one of whom but had effectually t[u]rned[9] the
election and satisfied themselves and their mamas that they were smart

little men, and most important pillars to the federal party. The two young Kings[10] rode out to the seventh ward in the true hidalgo style on horseback, but on dismounting & mingling with the mob, they were immediately dubbed Prince of Wales an[d] [*MS torn*] duke of York, and the villainous Jacobins arou[nd] [*MS torn*] them bowed themselves to the ground—hoped their royal highnesses were well—applauded every thing they said though ever so silly—begged their royal highnesses to keep their royal persons perfectly cool and at every reply, they almost prostrated themselves in the mud with the most cervantic affectation of gravity—now you know there was no possibility of answering a quiz so preposterously respectfull—it completely discomfited poor Master Johnny & Charley—who were glad to get to their horses and make a most ignominious retreat. But it would have done your heart good to have seen Pierre every now and then encouraging his bretheren of the mob, from the window of the poll—I ⟨could only get⟩ could not get near enough to hear him, but could only distinguish his gestures or rather the waving of his capacious hand, which ever and anon he layed on his breast in the most graceful man[11]

MANUSCRIPT: Yale. PUBLISHED: PMI, I, 186–88 (in part).

The Beinecke Library at Yale has this letter cataloged as addressed to Mary Fairlie, an identification corroborated by PMI. See PMI, I, 186.

1. WI wrote "ant."

2. WI may have intended to put an apostrophe before "tis" and carelessly misplaced it over the *s*. Or the mark may be regarded as an elongated dot for the *i*, as it is construed in the present transcription.

3. WI's variant of *Macbeth*, IV, i, 134: "Let this pernicious hour stand always cursed on the calendar."

4. All of the Federalist candidates for state offices were defeated in the election. Among them was WI's legal mentor, Josiah Ogden Hoffman, who had run for the state assembly. See NYEP, May 2, 1807.

5. A novel by Cervantes (1585).

6. *Henry IV*, Part I, II, iv, 5–6, 18–19.

7. NYEP for May 1, 1807, reported demonstrations and marches in the seventh ward.

8. Probably the sons of Alexander Hamilton—Alexander (1786–1875) and James Alexander (1788–1878); the son of John B. Fleming, a merchant; and Robert Gracie (1799–1877), the son of Archibald Gracie.

9. WI wrote "twrned."

10. John Alsop King (1788–1867) and Charles King (1789–1867), sons of Rufus King, a pillar in the Federalist party.

11. The MS ends at this point.

46. *To Mary Fairlie*

Fredericksburgh (Virginia) May 13th. 1807.

"There is a tide in the affairs of men"[1]
and a pretty rapid one too sometimes, as witness myself all at once
hurried off by the stream to this part of the Union, without a previous
pro or con about the matter. You are doubtless surprized (if any
movement of mine interests you sufficiently to occasion surprise), at
my sudden transition from New York to Virginia without giving you
an inkling of such an intention in my last letter. To save you therefore, the trouble of wo[ndering] [*MS torn*] about the circumstance, &
of running through the [*unrecovered*] [*MS torn*] catalogue of certainties,
probabilities & possibilities with th[eir?] [*MS torn*] attendant hows &
whens & whys, I merely inform you, that I did not so much as dream of
this jaunt four and twenty hours before my departure⟨,⟩—that I am on
business, but having got into this part of the world I shall spend some
time in visiting my virginia friends,[2] tending Burrs trial[3] &c &c—&
lastly that I have been transported here thus rapidly, not in the Aereal
carr of an Enchanter, but in that deplorably matter of fact vehicle an
American Stagewaggon, which has about as little of romance, or
fiction, or classic charm about it as any modern carriage I am acquainted with. ⟨I shall⟩ This sudden journey has prevented my replying
sooner to your charming letter of the 30th April,[4] for which I return you
my most "hearty thanks as in duty bounden."[5] It has given me much
useful information, particularly concerning the Museum of Yale College;
to which on my return I intend to contribute a rind of Mammoth cheese,
and a lump of salt, *very similar* to that of which the presidents mountain
is composed[6]—both of th[em] [*MS torn*] I have picked up in the course
of my Journey—and (but between ourselves) a Taylor at Washington
has promised me a snip of red cloth cabbaged from the presidential
pants which will doub[t]less[7] be as precious a relique in the eyes of a
devout democrat, like yourself,[8] as St Agathas veil[9] in the estimation of
a Sicilian Catholic.

I sympathize sincerely with you my dear friend on the miserable state
of our country, where stubborn fact predominates, and a heroine like
yourself may travel from one end of the ⟨[*unrecovered*]⟩ union to the
other without being assailed by a single ruffian or robber—What a
charming incident t'would have made for the eleventh volume of my
Romance of Rattle snake hill,[10] to have described you carried of[f][11] by
a tremendous yankee giant, confined in a gloomy Log hut and condemned
[to eat?] [*MS torn*] Pork and Molasses!

[In re?]turn [*MS torn*] for your "intristing information" concerning
[Yale Col?]lege [*MS torn*] I must give you some account of the Cele-

brated Village of Elting in the ⟨Vall⟩ State of Delaware—celebrated throughout the world—the world, according to Yorick, being comprised in an extent of country ten miles in diameter.[12] This Village is romantically situated on ⟨an eminence⟩ a gentle elevation (alias hill) commanding a picturesque view of a valley clothed in an exhuberance of verdure and watered with a thousand rills and purling streams; ⟨this has⟩ ↑being↓ one of those "Umbrian vales" with which our country abounds and which are familarly denominated *Marshes*. The most conspicuous public buildings in Elting are a pillory and a whipping post, whether these betoken the provident forethought of the Magistrates, or the frequent delinquency of the people, I will not determine, though travellers like I charitably suppose the latter. The greatest man in this town is a little negro boy, who ⟨has⟩ was ⟨accide⟩ unjudiciously born without ⟨leg⟩ arms, yet he surpasses all his cotemporary urchins of the village in the elegant accomplishments of ball & chuck farthing[13]—he moreover exhibits pretty specimens of *penmanship* with a piece of *chalk* held between his toes—and I have no doubt writes a *legible*, *running* hand (meaning a brace of most flagitious puns, in return for several which you have ⟨most⟩ wickedly & mischeviously levelled at me in your letters)

At Baltimore I made a stay of two days, during whi[ch] [*MS torn*] I was *toted* about town and introduced to every body; in the course of which laborious occupation I encounterd several very imminent hazards from the beauteous damsels of the place, who have the same murderous thirst for conquest that characterizes their sex throughout the world. I particularly mention a Miss Dugan a very pretty good looking young woman. I had not been in her company long before her manners alarmed my suspicions & upon whispering to a gentleman next me I had them fully confirmed, in short I discovered that I had fallen in[to the?] [*MS torn*] clutches of a *declared Belle*—whereupon I siezed my h[at? and?] [*MS torn*] ⟨as foll⟩ retreated as rapidly as ever did his highness t[he? Duke of?] [*MS torn*] York. Of all beings in the world I do eschew a pro [fessed Belle] [*MS torn*] from my very soul—A merciless little Despot! w[ho is] [*MS torn*] absolute as a tyrant of Japan, and like him, expects [*unrecovered*] [*MS torn*] approach to crawl in the dust and kiss the toe of her [boot] [*MS torn*] who like an eastern Monarch has her Court an[d] [*MS torn*] her courtiers & her parisites, by whom she is so [*MS torn*] surrounded that a poor devil who ⟨she⟩ is too [*MS torn*] careless to speak any thing but the truth, stands no chance for either audience or promotion.

At Washington all was silent & forlorn and the only great personages I saw there were two Jackasses in a field, kicking at each other—Metempsychosis forever! thought I—here are the souls of two of our illustrious Congressmen transfused into the bodies of Kindred animals, and they are engaged in the presidential experiment of "trying which shall do each other the most harm."

In a word, (for my paper grows scanty & I am determined you should not pay double postage) behold me in Virginia, that land famous for grog drinking, horse racing and cockfighting; where every man is a colonel a captain or a Negro, the first title being conferred on every man who has killed a rattle snake—where indolence is the true (& often the only) mark of gentility, and where as Gouverneur Morris[14] ↑once↓ asserted, the only industrious animal is the Tumble Turf.[15] From the little I have seen a[nd] [MS torn] heard I anticipate a rich field of character and incident a[nd] [MS torn] notwithstanding the string of encomiums I have just enumerated I am prepared to judge of the people, with indulgence and regard for I have seen many bright traits in their character. I am now with my Friend Col Mercer[16] of Fredericksburgh—tomorrow I set off for Richmond & from thence almost immediately to Williamsburg to see Cabell who has lately married one of the finest & richest girls ⟨of⟩ in the state.[17] It is probable I shall not return to New York for five or six weeks perhaps more, by which time I hope I shall once more find you at home.[18] Though it will consequently be out of my power to give you any domestic news yet I hope ⟨yo⟩ I may still be favoured with your letters which you need only direct to NYork, from whence they will punctually be forwarded to me, and I do entr[eat] [MS torn] you to write frequently. ⟨In⟩ I have read of ⟨distant⟩ heroes & heroines of novels when seperated, looking at the moon at the same time & thus in a manner holding "sweet converse"[19] with each other; I leave to these lovesick gentlefolk all such lunatic speculations as mere matters of *moonshine*; but I will improve upon their idea, and while writing to you, will fancy you are at the same time scribbling an answer—theres a thought fo[r] [MS torn] you, worthy of Looney McTwolter ↑himself↓; but though I may rival pat in [unrecovered] [MS torn] bulls believe me I equal him in his sincerity when I style myself

Truly your friend
W I.

Present my particular remembrances to Mr & Mrs Derby,[20] and ⟨Mis⟩ *Your* friend Miss Mason—provided she's *not* a belle

ADDRESSED: Miss Mary Fairlie / Care of Richard Derby Esqr.— / Boston.
   POSTMARKED: Fredericksburgh[?] / May / 13
MANUSCRIPT: Yale. PUBLISHED: PMI, I, 189–90 (in part).

1. *Julius Caesar*, IV, iii, 218.
2. Joseph C. Cabell and Dr. Thomas Massie, whom WI had met in Europe.
3. Aaron Burr had been arrested in the Mississippi Territory on February 19, 1807, and brought to Richmond. On April 1 he was formally charged with treason and misdemeanor, then freed on bail until the start of the trial on May 22. See

David Robertson, *Reports of the Trials of Colonel Aaron Burr* ... (Philadelphia, 1808), I, 1–21.

4. This letter has not been located.

5. Probably a variation of the Prayer of Oblation in the *Book of Common Prayer*.

6. An allusion to a cheese weighing 1230 pounds, measuring over five feet in diameter and fifteen inches thick, which the Republican farmers of New England had presented to Thomas Jefferson on January 1, 1802. See Nathan Schachner, *Thomas Jefferson, A Biography* (New York, 1951), II, 700.

7. WI omitted the bracketed letter.

8. These remarks are typical of WI's anti-Jeffersonian sentiments at this time.

9. The veil of St. Agatha, who was martyred in Catania, Sicily during the Decian persecution of 251, is supposed to provide protection against the volcanic eruptions of Mount Etna.

10. This was apparently an imaginary literary work which WI discussed facetiously with Miss Fairlie.

11. WI omitted the final *f*.

12. Yorick defines the world "as no more of it, than a small circle described upon the circle of the great world, of four English miles, or thereabouts ..." (Laurence Sterne, *The Life and Opinions of Tristram Shandy, Gentleman*, p. 11).

13. A game in which players toss farthings at a mark, with the one whose coin has come the closest to the mark then permitted to throw all the farthings at a hole and to keep those which fall into it.

14. Gouverneur Morris (1752–1816), American minister to France from 1792 to 1794, often made comments contemptuous of democracy.

15. A beetle which makes balls out of dung and deposits its eggs in them.

16. Colonel John Mercer had been WI's traveling companion in Europe in the spring of 1805.

17. On January 1, 1807, Cabell had married Mary Walker Carter of Lancaster, Virginia. See R. B. Davis, "WI and Joseph C. Cabell," in *English Studies in Honor of James Southall Wilson*, p. 20, n. 18.

18. Miss Fairlie was visiting in Boston at this time.

19. John Milton, *Paradise Lost*, IX, 909.

20. Mr. and Mrs. Derby are probably Elias Haskett Derby and his wife, Lucy Brown. Derby was a prominent New England merchant.

47. *To Mrs. Josiah Ogden Hoffman*

Richmond, June 4, 1807.

I cannot express to you how much I feel indebted to your goodness, for the attention you have shown in writing to me, and I am the more sensible of your friendship, since you are the only one who takes the trouble of scribbling me a line. I am totally ignorant of all the events that are taking place in the little circle of my intimates, except those anecdotes which your letters contain. The sudden death of Mrs. Seton[1] I had learned by the public papers, and I need not tell you that it affected me deeply; for, in addition to that kind of selfish sorrow, which we all feel in losing a valued friend, I felt for the poignant distress it must occasion in those bosoms, whose tranquillity and happiness are dear to me.

You expected that the trial[2] was over at the time you were writing; but you can little conceive the talents for procrastination that have been exhibited in this affair. Day after day have we been disappointed by the non-arrival of the magnanimous Wilkinson;[3] day after day have fresh murmurs and complaints been uttered; and day after day are we told that the next mail will probably bring his noble self, or at least some accounts when he may be expected. We are now enjoying a kind of suspension of hostilities; the grand jury having been dismissed the day before yesterday for five or six days, that they might go home, see their wives, get their clothes washed, and flog their negroes. As yet we are not even on the threshold of a trial; and, if the great hero of the South does not arrive, it is a chance if we have any trial this term. I am told the Attorney-General[4] talks of moving the Court next Tuesday for a continuance and a special Court, by which means the present grand jury (the most enlightened, perhaps, that was ever assembled in this country)[5] will be discharged; the witnesses will be dismissed; many of whom live such a distance off that it is a chance if half of them will ever be again collected. The Government will be again subjected to immense expense, and Col. Burr, besides being harassed and detained for an additional space of time, will have to repeat the enormous expenditures which this trial has already caused him. I am very much mistaken, if the most underhand and ungenerous measures have not been observed towards him. He, however, retains his serenity and self-possession unshaken, and wears the same aspect in all times and situations. I am impatient for the arrival of this Wilkinson, that the whole matter may be put to rest; and I never was more mistaken in my calculations, if the whole will not have a most farcical termination as it respects the charges against Col. Burr....

PUBLISHED: PMI, I, 191–92.

1. See the NYEP, May 21, 1807: "Died . . . Yesterday, aged 83 Years, Mrs. Mary Seton, the lamented wife of Mr. James Seton."

"The friends of Mrs. Seton are particularly requested to attend her funeral on Fridry [sic] at 5 o'clock an [sic] the afternoon, from the house of Josiah Ogden Hoffman, corner of Broad way & Leonard Street."

2. The trial dragged on until October 20, when Burr was finally found not guilty of misdemeanor. A verdict of not guilty of treason had been returned on September 1.

3. Major General James Wilkinson (1757–1825) did not reach Richmond until June 10 and did not appear at the trial until June 15.

4. Caesar Augustus Rodney (1772–1824), who had been appointed by Jefferson in January, 1807.

5. The foreman of the grand jury was John Randolph (1773–1833).

48. To James K. Paulding

Richmond, June 22, 1807.

Dear James:

I have been expecting a few lines from you for some time past, and am sorry to find you stand upon ceremony. Had I the same leisure that I had when in New York, you should not want for scrawls as often as you choose, but here I have but few moments that are not occupied in attending the trial, and observing the character and company assembled here. I wish to know all the news about our work,[1] and any literary intelligence that may be in circulation. I am much disappointed at your having concluded the first volume at No. 10. Besides making an insignificant baby house volume, it ends so weakly at one of the weakest numbers of the whole. At least it is a number which is not highly satisfactory to me, perhaps because I wrote the greatest part of it myself, and that at hurried moments. I had intended concluding it in style, and commencing Vol. 2 with some eclat; "but let that pass." I have no doubt you had *three special reasons* for what you have done, and am content. What arrangement have you made with the Dusky[2] for the profits? I shall stand much in need of a little sum of money on my return. I shall endeavor to send you more matter for another number,[3] as soon as I can find time and humor to write it in; at present I have neither.

I can appoint no certain time for my return, as it depends entirely upon the trial. Wilkinson you will observe has arrived; the bets were against Burr that he would abscond, should W. come to Richmond; but he still maintains his ground, and still enters the Court every morning with the same serene and placid air that he would show were he brought there to plead another man's cause, and not his own.

The lawyers are continually entangling each other in law points, motions, and authorities, and have been so crusty to each other, that there is a constant sparring going on. Wilkinson is now before the grand jury, and has such a mighty mass of *words* to deliver himself of, that he claims at least two days more to discharge the wondrous cargo. The jury[4] are tired enough of his verbosity. The first interview between him and Burr was highly interesting, and I secured a good place to witness it. Burr was seated with his back to the entrance, facing the judge, and conversing with one of his counsel. Wilkinson strutted into Court, and took his stand in a parallel line with Burr on his right hand. Here he stood for a moment swelling like a turkey cock, and bracing himself up for the encounter of Burr's eye. The latter did not take any notice of him until the judge directed the clerk to swear Gen. Wilkinson; at the mention of the name Burr turned his head, looked him full in the face with one of his piercing regards, swept his eye over his whole person from head to foot, as if to scan its dimensions, and then coolly resumed his former position, and went on conversing with his counsel as tranquilly as ever. The whole look was over in an instant; but it was an admirable one. There was no appearance of study or constraint in it; no affectation of disdain or defiance; a slight expression of contempt played over his countenance, such as you would show on regarding any person to whom you were indifferent, but whom you considered mean and contemptible. Wilkinson did not remain in Court many minutes.

Do write me immediately. Answer me the questions I have already asked, and give me all the news you hear.

Love to Pindar[5] and family./Yours truly,

W. I.

Published: PMI, I, 193–95.

1. *Salmagundi,* the joint production of Paulding and Washington and William Irving, had created a great sensation in New York on account of its irreverent social satire. It had passed through ten numbers by May 16, 1807.

2. The epithet used by the Salmagundians for David Longworth, the publisher of the pamphlets. Longworth apparently appropriated most of the profits for himself, a reason given by the authors for discontinuing publication with the twentieth number on January 25, 1808.

3. The next issue appeared on July 2, while Irving was still in Richmond.

4. WI may be reporting something he heard from John Randolph, foreman of the grand jury. There is nothing in David Robertson's *Reports of the Trials of Colonel Aaron Burr . . .* to indicate this reaction, but these reports do not include testimony before the grand jury.

5. A reference to William Irving, who was responsible for the poetical effusions of Pindar Cockloft in *Salmagundi.*

49. To ———

[Richmond, summer, 1807]

I have been treated in the most polite and hospitable manner by the most distinguished persons of the place—those friendly to Colonel Burr and those opposed to him, and have intimate acquaintances among his bitterest enemies. I am absolutely enchanted with Richmond, and like it more and more every day. The society is polished, sociable, and extremely hospitable, and there is a great variety of distinguished characters assembled on this occasion, which gives a strong degree of interest to passing incidents.

Published: PMI, I, 196.

50. *To Gouverneur Kemble*

Richmond July 1, 1807

My dear Gouv,

I have a dozen times been on the point of writing to you since I have been here, but have as often been prevented by some fatality which has presided for a long time over my correspondence with you. I am determined to break the spell, and to scribble, though the affairs of the nation should stand still while I write. That I am charmed with Richmond I need not tell you, for you have been here, and if I may conclude from the warm expressions of regard I have heard bestowed on your memory, you were well received by the denizens of this puissant city. Nay certain young ladies have absolutely declared that you must return here, for they longed once more to enjoy the light of your countenance—though between ourselves I believe the little scoundrels only said so, to ingratiate themselves in my *favour*, knowing the friendship I entertained for you. Currie has behaved in the most praiseworthy manner and proved himself entitled to the honour of being a corresponding member of the Kilkenny club. Little Picket has returned from Baltimore; when the union is to take place is still a mystery; she is a fine lively little girl and holds you in great respect.

For myself I find I am declining ↑very much↓[1] in popularity from having resolutely and manfully resisted sundry temptations and invitations to tea parties—stews—balls and other infernal orgies which have from time to time been celebrated by the little enchantresses of this place. I tried my hand two or three times at an apology for my non attendance, but it would not do, my usual ill luck followed me; for once when I alleged[2] the writing of letters, it was plainly proved that I was seen smoking a cigar and lolling in the porch of the Eagle,[3] and another time when I plead a severe indisposition, I was pronounced guilty of having sat at a young ladies elbow the whole evening and listened to her piano—All which brought me into manifest disgrace and reduced me to great extremity—upon the which I forthwith summoned up my pride, girded up my loins, foreswore all apologies in future and declared that I should thenceforward consider an invitation as an insult since which time I have had but little to complain of on that score, and enjoy sovereign independence and a perfect command of my time & person.

If ⟨you⟩ ever ↑you↓ come to Richmond again, let me warn you against suffering the ladies to consider you as an interesting young man. Of all characters it is the most toilsome and irksome to support. Two or three took into their heads to think me so on my first arrival and to be most mightily pleased with me Mercy on us! what a time I had of it. I had to puff and blow up all these damned hot hills of a fiery day to escort them on their visits. I had to undergo the perspiring horrors of routs and tea parties—and I had to leave my beloved bed at sun rise to take a romantic walk along the canal[4]—I tried it a little while, but it would not do—I determined to return to my old habits and become as unsentimental as possible—so I made no visits at noon day—I forgot engagements at tea parties—I overslept myself of a morning and in less than a fortnight was given up as a young man of most incorrigible habits, to my great outward sorrow and contrition, but inward rejoicing of the spirit.

As to little B.[5] you have heard all about his case in the public papers— He bears his misfortunes without the least depression. His countenance and manner are still the same through every change. To day he is to be removed to the penitentiary as a place of more security than the private house ↑in↓ which he is ↑at present↓ confined. He was for two days lodged in the common jail—of all holes the most horrible and desolate.[6] He speaks of you with much feeling and regard.

Remember me to all & believe me,

Ever yours
W. I.

Manuscript: NYPL—Hellman Collection.

The manuscript letter is a copy, not in WI's hand.

Gouverneur Kemble was a member of the literary circle which called itself the Lads of Kilkenny. Many of their frolics were held at Kemble's summer home in Newark, the Cockloft Hall of *Salmagundi*. Like WI, Kemble never married. He established the West Point Foundry in Cold Spring, New York, and made a fortune casting guns for the United States Army.

1. The inserted portion is written in another hand.
2. A *d* has been struck out before the *g*.
3. The Eagle Tavern, in which WI had his room, "stood on Main Street, an east-west thoroughfare at the foot of Capitol Hill occupied chiefly by shops and other business establishments. A trifle less refined than the Swan Tavern at the top of the hill, it catered to a wide variety of guests, including sportsmen, legislators, and planters who came up to Richmond periodically for a brief respite from the monotony of their plantations. The hostelry was identified by a sign, eight feet by five, displaying a golden eagle . . . painted by the artist Thomas Sully who . . . got $50 for the eagle, not an insignificant sum according to 1800 standards of value" (Francis F. Beirne, *Shout Treason: The Trial of Aaron Burr* [New York, 1959], p. 31).
4. The basin of the James River and Kanawha Canal was only a block from the Eagle Tavern. The canal itself extended westward from this point, running parallel to the river.
5. Aaron Burr had close associations with the Irvings, especially Peter, whose newspaper, the *Morning Chronicle*, during his editorship had been a strong supporter of Burr. The trial in Richmond resulted from Burr's arrest on charges of fomenting treason west of the Alleghenies.
6. After his brief imprisonment in jail Burr was lodged in a room in a house

rented by Luther Martin across from the Swan Tavern. Because of protests of favored treatment the authorities took Burr to the penitentiary near by. See Beirne, *Shout Treason*, pp. 129–30.

51. To [Mary Fairlie?]

Washington City. July 7th. 1807.

The interval that has elapsed since last I wrote to you certainly ⟨demans⟩ requires some apology—but apologies I always consider as implying some restraint or ceremony or controul—and as I wish our correspondence to ⟨fr⟩ be perfectly free, pleasant, independent, voluntary, unconstrained, ⟨&⟩ unshackled &c &c I am determined, though I have some half a dozen excellent apologies at the end of my pen, yet they shall be passed over ⟨in solitary⟩ in silence, or taken for granted, as best suits your humour. I feel the more indebted to you for the letters I have received[1] in as much as they must have interfered with a thousand of those splendid engagements ⟨in⟩ ↑by↓ which you, as a declared belle must be necessarily engrossed. Trust me it is grateful to my feelings, and not a little flattering to my vanity, ⟨to⟩ the proud idea, that, when surrounded like the grand Lama or the immortal Josh by a crowd of humble adorers, you can still think upon such an insignificant personage as myself, and even steal away from the shrine at which you are worshiped, to bestow on me an hours conversation. ⟨Impressed with⟩ Inspired by such thoughts I open your letters with a kind of triumph; I consider them as testimonies of those brilliant moments which I have rescued from the ⟨happy⟩ buzzards that surround you—moments perhaps, for which some hapless Damon[2] sighed—of which he counted the tedious seconds with a stopwatch—fancied them puffd up into half hours ⟨and⟩ or any other portly dimensions—and curs'd the *giant minutes* as they pass'd!! Vainglorious mortal that I am! perhaps these same epistles on which I so much value myself are merely the effusions of some vacant hour; some interval between dressing & dinner—or dinner & a ball—perhaps the mere method by which you *delassitude* yourself after the fatigues of an evenings campaign, like the illustrious Jefferson who after toiling all day in deciding the fates of a nation, retires to his closet and amuses himself with impaling a tadpole.[3]_____ but let them be written when; where, or how they will be assured they will ever be received with delight and read with avidity.

I am now scribbling in the parlour of Mr Van Ness[4] at whose house I am on a visit—having, as you plainly percieve—torn myself from Richmond. I own the parting was painful for I had been treated there with the utmost kindness, and having become a kind of old inhabitant of

the place, was permitted to consult my own whims, inclinations &
caprices just as I chose—a privilege which a stranger has to surrender
on first arriving in a place. By some unlucky means or other, when I
first made my appearance in Richmond, I got the character, among
three or four novel read damsels of being an *interesting young man*—
Now of all characters in the world, believe me this is the most intolerable for any young man, who has a will of his own, to support—particularly in warm weather—The tender hearted fair ones think you
absolutely at their command—they conclude that you must of course
be fond of moonlight walks—and rides at day break, and red hot strolls
in the middle of the day (Farenheits Thermom. 98½ in the shade) and
"Melting hot—hissing hot" tea parties—and what is worse they expect
you to talk sentiment and act Romeo & Sir Charles & King pepin[5] all
the while_____'Twas too much for me—had I been in love with any
one of them I believe I could have played the dying swain, as eloquently and foolishly as most men, but not having the good luck to be
inspired by the tender passion I found the slavery insupportable—so
I forthwith set about ruining my character as speedily as possible—I
forgot to go to tea parties—I overslept myself of a morning—I protested
against the moon and derided that blessed planet most villainously—In a
word I was soon given up as a young man of mos[t] [*MS torn*] preposterous and incorrigible opinions and was left to do—e'en just [as]
[*MS torn*] I pleased—Yet believe me I did, notwithstanding, admire the
fair damsels of Richmond exceedingly—and to be candid at once, the
character of the whole sex, though it has ever ranked high in my estimation—is Still more exalted than ever. I have seen traits of female
goodness, while at Richmond, that have sunk deeply in my heart—not
displayed in one or two individuall instances but frequently and generally manifested. I allude to the case of Col Burr. Whatever may be
his innocence or guilt in respect to the charges alledged against him
(And god knows, I do not pretend to decide thereon) his situation is
such as should appeal eloquently to the feelings of every generous
bosom—Sorry am I to say, the reverse has been the ⟨case⟩ fact—fallen,
proscribed—prejudged, the cup of bitterness has been administered to
him with an unsparing hand—it has almost been considered as culpable
to evince towards him the least sympathy or support, and many a
hollow hearted caitiff have I seen, who basked in the sunshine of his
bounty when in power, who ⟨h⟩ now skulked from his side and even
mingled among the most clamorous of his enemies. The ladies alone
have felt, or at least had candor & independence sufficient, to express
those feelings which do honour to humanity. ⟨There is not, I believe⟩,
They have been uniform in their expressions of compassion for his
misfortunes and ⟨interest in⟩ a hope for his acquittal—not a lady I

believe in Richmond, whatever may be her husbands sentiments on the subject, but what would rejoice on seeing Col Burr at liberty—It may be said that Col Burr has ever been a favorite with the sex, but I am not inclined to account for it in so illiberal a manner—⟨I like⟩ it results from that merciful—that heavenly disposition implanted in the female bosom, which ever inclines in favour of the accused & the unfortunate—You will smile at this high strain in which I have indulged—believe me it is because I feel it—and I love your sex ten times better than ever. The last time I saw Burr was the day before I left Richmond—He was then in the Penetentiary—a kind of State Prison The only reason given for immuring him in his abode of Theieves—Cut throats & incendiaries was that it would save the United States *a couple of hundred dollars* (the charge of guarding him at his lodgings) & it would insure the security of his person. This building stands about a mile and a half from town—situated in a solitary place among the hills. It will prevent his counsel from being as much with him as they deemed necessary. I found great difficulty of gaining admission to him, for a few moments—Th[e] [*MS torn*] keeper had orders to admit none but his counsel & his Witnesses—Strange measures these! That it is not sufficient that a man against whom no certainty of crime is proved, should be confined by bolts & bars & massy walls in a criminal prison but he is likewise to be cut off from all intercourse with society, ⟨all⟩ deprived of all the kind offices of friendship—and made to suffer all the penalties & deprivations of a condemned criminal. I was permitted to enter *for a few moments*—as a special favour contrary to orders—Burr seemed in lower spirits than formerly[.] he was composed & collected as usual; but there was not the same cheerfulness that I have hitherto remarked—He said it was with difficulty his very servant was allowed occasionally to see him—he had a bad cold, which I supposed was occasioned by the dampness of his chamber ⟨& its having⟩ which had been lately white-washed. I bid ⟨?thef?⟩ him farewell with a heavy heart, and ↑he↓ expressed with peculiar warmth & feeling, his sense of the interest I had taken in his fate—I never felt in a more melancholy mood than when I rode from his solitary prison—such is the last interview I had with poor Burr—and I shall never forget it.

———I have written myself into a sorrowful kind of a mood so I will at once desist, begging you to recieve this letter with indulgence and ⟨ge⟩ regard with an eye of christia[n] [*MS torn*] charity its many imperfections. believe me truly & affectionately

Your friend
Washington Irvin[g] [*MS torn*]

MANUSCRIPT: Yale. PUBLISHED: PMI, I, 199–203.

1. These letters have not been located.
2. WI alludes to the story of Damon and Pythias, friends living in Syracuse

in the fourth century B.C. After Dionysius the tyrant had condemned Pythias to death, Pythias requested permission to return home to put his affairs in order, a request granted with the understanding that Damon would remain in his place to guarantee his return and be executed if Pythias did not reappear. When Pythias was delayed, Damon was about to be executed, only to be reprieved by the timely arrival of his friend. Impressed by this show of friendship, Dionysius pardoned them both. WI's allusion plays upon Damon's devotion and friendship.

3. Compare this example with some of the actions attributed to Jefferson in *Knickerbocker's History of New York*.

4. John P. Van Ness (1770–1846), originally from Columbia County, New York, was in Congress from 1801 to 1803, after which he served in the militia in the District of Columbia, his occupation when WI visited him.

5. WI is alluding to Shakespeare's Romeo; to Sir Charles Grandison, central figure in Samuel Richardson's *The History of Sir Charles Grandison* (1754); and to Pepin the Short (ca. 714–768), father of Charlemagne, who seized the throne of the Merovingian king, Childric III, in 751 and established the Carolingian line, of which Charlemagne was the most famous member.

52. *To Ann Hoffman*

New York, August 10th. 1807.

My dear child

I am unanimously appointed by the family a "Committee of Correspondence," and am requested [to .fur]nish [*MS torn*] you with all the in door and out door [events] [*MS torn*] to forward you all the pacquets of love, friend[ship] [*MS torn*] and ⟨affection⟩ remembrance that may be com[mit]ted [*MS torn*] to your charge, in short to say unto you [all] [*MS torn*] that is to be said, to tell you all that is to be [told] [*MS torn*]— and as much more as I please. The [reason] [*MS torn*] why I am elected to this important office is that some of the family happen to be sick, and some happen to be lazy—which latter reason is always an unanswerable one for not writing a letter. As influenza is the order of the day, and as the first question on the end of our tongues, & consequently uppermost in our minds, is ⟨a dema⟩ an enquiry after a bodys health, I shall endeavour to give you as accurate a return as ever was furnished by a health committee—Your good old Grandmama[1] was seized with a violent suspicion that she had the ⟨fever?⟩ influenza on Thursday ⟨last⟩ evening last—her suspicion gained ground on friday, but she still resolutely eat a hearty dinner in defiance of it, but by the evening she became so absolutely convinced that she was sick that she went to bed on sheer conviction of the fact and remained very greviously afflicted in head limbs and stomach all the next day—she is now ⟨on the⟩ once more on the eating list; and can even muster her forces at a moments warning to the dinner table. Your father—good man—took a week to prepare for a grand shooting expedition to Rockaway, and took the children down with him—I

suppose by way of spaniel [s———] [*MS torn*] I took charge of the house
during his absence [& all] [*MS torn*] had reigned very tranquilly for
two days whe[n the] [*MS torn*] poor man returned to town in a complete
fit [of the] [*MS torn*] influenza and a touch of the headach; ⟨which⟩
[it was] [*MS torn*] evident he had a pretty tolerable attack, for [he]
[*MS torn*] eat nothing and mentioned the name of Belial three or four
times in a minute—a gentleman he seldom makes mention of except
when out of sorts or in a fit of perplexity. He is likewise in a fair way to
recover though he still struts about in his picturesque robe de chambre
and his countenance retains a most unheard of longitude and a kind of
pea green complexion. Your Mama[2] hinted to me two or three times
that she had a great inclination to be sick, but upon my representing
the folly & inconvenience of the measure, she kindly altered her mind.
As to Matilda[3] her only complaint is Nothing—a malady that seizes
her under a thousand different forms, for whatever may be the matter
with her, I never heard her complain of any thing else. Gertrude Kemble
has had an attack likewise but I have not heard how she managed it[.]
Gouv ⟨likewise⟩ also came in for a share, but got over it by writing letters,
eating onion soup and wearing purple velvet slippers. Maria & Jane[4]
[*unrecovered*] [*MS torn*] both kept their rooms but were cured by a
[t]ea [*MS torn*] party at McCombs[5] and Mary Fairlie ⟨las⟩ staid at home
two days waiting for it, and actually began to wax unwell until I administered to her a pair of Chinese shoes which she declared relieved her
stomach immediately & she has not complained since. Nuncle[6] has been
woefully sick & Jim Paulding [has] [*MS torn*] run grumbling about
town for a week past—[for] [*MS torn*] myself—the only complaint I have
had, was that of being shut out one night by the family when I was
playing Master of the house during your fathers absence—I went up next
day to turn over a new leaf when I was appeased by finding them in the
sick state I have mentiond

I have thus given you a complete bill of health with the exception
of poor Charles Fenno[7]—who is quite unwell & rather unmanageable—I
shall start for Morristown in a coachee[8] tomorrow morning & bring him
& Eliza[9] to town ⟨for⟩ to pass some days—twill cheer his spirits—The
family all desire their love to you & Mr & Mrs Colden[10]—remember me
likewise to all the good family & to the Willets[11] In my next I shall give
you a history of the adventures of me & Larry[12]—or rather for politeness
sake Larry & Myself

Yours ever WI

ADDRESSED: Miss Ann Hoffman / at T Coldens Esqr / Coldenham / care of Mr
Jones / New Burgh
MANUSCRIPT: NYPL—WI Papers; Minnesota Historical Society (copy). PUBLISHED:
(copy at Minnesota Historical Society) St. Paul *Daily News*, Magazine Section,

April 18, 1920, pp. 1–2 (in part); *Notes While Preparing the Sketch Book,* ed. S. T. Williams (New Haven, 1927), pp. 32–35; S. T. Williams, "WI and Matilda Hoffman," *American Speech* 1 (June, 1926), 465–67; STW, I, 86–87 (in part).

This letter survives in three versions: the original MS in NYPL—WI Papers; a handwritten copy with the caption, "Letters of Washington Irving to my Grandmother Alice Anne [*sic*] Hoffman," in the Minnesota Historical Society; and a typescript copy with the notation, "The original I loaned to his biographer P. M. Irving upon condition that he would *return them,* which he has not done yet (1862)" (also in the Minnesota Historical Society).

The bracketed words have been supplied for a missing portion of the holograph. They are inserted in the body of the letter in keeping with the context of WI's thought and idiom. Aid in supplying these missing words was obtained from the handwritten copy of this letter in the Minnesota Historical Society.

Ann Hoffman (b. 1790) was the oldest daughter of Josiah Ogden Hoffman and his first wife, Mary Colden, who died on February 19, 1797 (STW, I, 401, n. 76). Ann had been one of the party with whom WI had traveled in 1803 to upstate New York and Canada. In 1809 she married Charles Nicholas, a Philadelphia bookseller. Their home in Philadelphia was a convenient stopping place for WI and other visitors from New York.

1. Sarah Ogden Hoffman, daughter of David Ogden and Gertrude Gouverneur, who had married Nicholas Hoffman on November 14, 1762. She was born in 1742 and died in 1823. See W. H. Hoffman, *Eleven Generations of Hoffmans . . . ,* p. 9.

2. The second Mrs. J. O. Hoffman, Maria Fenno.

3. Ann's sister (b. 1791).

4. Maria may be Maria Moore, who is mentioned in WI's letter to Brevoort, June 11, 1808. Jane may be Jane Watts, alluded to in Matilda Hoffman's letter to Ann Hoffman, August 29, 1807. See STW, I, 87–88, 401, n. 88.

5. Possibly John McComb (1763–1853), a prominent New York architect. The McComb family was apparently on friendly terms with the Irvings and Pauldings. See *Letters of J. K. Paulding,* pp. 23, 28.

6. "George" has been penciled in the blank in the transcription in the Minnesota Historical Society.

7. Charles Fenno Hoffman (1806–1884) was the stepbrother of Ann Hoffman.

8. A coachee was a carriagelike vehicle with high wheels, rolling side curtains instead of panels, and the front open with the top covering the driver as well as the passengers.

9. Probably Eliza Fenno.

10. The Thomas Coldens, with whom Ann was staying.

11. Probably Mr. and Mrs. Marinus Willet. Willet (1740–1830) had been a Revolutionary soldier and sheriff of New York. In 1807 he became mayor of New York.

12. Larry is the Hoffmans' saddle horse. See WI's letter of November 17, 1807, to Ann Hoffman.

53. *To Rebecca Gratz*

N York Nov. 4th. 1807.

I hardly need introduce the bearer, Mr Sully,[1] to you, as I trust you reccollect him perfectly. He proposes passing the winter in your city and as he will be a mere "stranger & sojourner in the land,"[2] I would solicit for him your good graces. He is a gentleman for whom I have a great regard, not merly ⟨of⟩ on account of his professional abilities, which are highly promising, but for his amiable character and engaging manners.

I think I cannot render him a favour for which he ought to be more grateful than in introducing him to the notice of your self and your connections. Mr Hoffmans family is all well, and you are often the subject of their conversation[3]—Remember me affectionately to all the family—excuse this liberty I have taken and believe me with the warmest friendship

ever yours—
Washington Irving[4]

ADDRESSED: Miss Rebecca Gratz / Philadelphia / Mr Sully. DOCKETED: Mr Irving / Nov 4th. 1807

MANUSCRIPT: HSP. PUBLISHED: *Century Magazine* 24, n.s. 2 (September, 1882), 681; William Vincent Byars, *B. and M. Gratz, Merchants in Philadelphia* (Jefferson City, Mo., 1916), p. 274.

1. Thomas Sully (1783–1872), English-born painter and miniaturist, settled permanently in Philadelphia in 1808 after periods of residence in Richmond, Norfolk, and New York.

2. WI's variation of Lev. 25:23.

3. This sentence is omitted from the version printed in Byars on page 274.

4. In the lower left corner of the sheet in another hand is written "addressed to Miss Rebecca Gratz."

54. *To William Meredith*

N York Nov. 4th. 1807

Dear Sir,

Permit me to introduce to you Mr Sully, a young artist of talents and a gentleman of the most amiable character & deportment. He intends passing the winter in your city and should you be able to render him any attentions or services, I shall consider them as encreasing the debt of friendship which I owe you. His attention at present is chiefly devoted to portraits and he has executed a number in this city which have been highly approved of.

Present my remembrances to Mrs Meredith

and believe me sir/With great respect/Yours &c
Washington Irving

ADDRESSED: Wm Meredith Esqr. / Counsellor at Law / Philadelphia / fwrd. pr /
    Mr Sully   DOCKETED: Washington Irvin. / Nov. 4. 1807
MANUSCRIPT: HSP.

William Meredith (1772–1844) was a banker, lawyer, and city solicitor in
Philadelphia. With his wife, Gertrude Gouverneur Ogden, he was a contributor to
the *Port Folio*.

55. *To Ann Hoffman*

New York Nov 17th 180⟨9⟩7

My good little girl
    In one of your late family epistles you have wronged me most cruelly
by the old proverb of "out of Sight out of mind,"[1] which was about as
well applied as old proverbs generally are. Now I do assure you in
Sober Sadness & on the indifferent word of an honest gentleman, that I
have been thinking of ⟨you⟩ writing to you these three months past which
I take ⟨it⟩ is a pretty tolerable proof of Constant recollection. How long
I might have lived on in the daily indulgence of this situation & the
daily neglect of its performance I Cannot Say, had I not beheld you
last night in my dreams, not in all the Smiling radiance of Venus when
She beamed upon the visions of ↑the↓[2] pious _____ [Aeneas][3] but
with an expression of bitter wrath or indignation or to use a Scriptural
quotation with a Countenance "fair as the Sun, clear as the moon, and
terrible as an army with banners"[4][.] I awoke in all the horrors of a
quandary, I raised my Self in my bed & Solemy[5] taking off my night
cap with my right hand & waving it gallently in the air, Swore never
to put it on again or to comb the feathers out of my hair until I had
written you an epistle. Now we are Still in a manner in the introduction
I cannot help hinting that I do not perceive any right you have to
expect a letter Seeing that you have never had the kindness to answer
the one I wrote Some time Since & which if I recollect right abounded
with interesting information. You can offer no reasonable excuse for
this neglect, Surely you cannot be So indifferent of your abilities as to
stand in fear of criticism. This would be doing injustice both to your
own talents & my friendship, for Surely you who can write with So
little hesitation to your own family, should at least have kindness enough
to believe that your letters would be received with equal pleasure &
equal indulgence by one who regards you with the Sincere affection
of a brother.[6] At any rate a letter should ever be exempt from critical
examination being not the Studied production of the head, but the free
will offering of the heart, and I would Sooner one Scrawl that had the
genuine Stamp of native feeling than a thousand elegant epistles abound-
ing in effected sentiment and well turned periods. But I am confident my

dear Anne your letters would never Stand in need of apology, just write what *you* feel, or rather *feel* what you write, (for the first would be too great a demand) & trust me I never shall complain through[7] your letters should be as unintelligible as the literary lore on a tea chest. The Substance of all this preamble is Simply *I wish you to write me,* and Since I am not to have the pleasure of Seeing you for So long a time, at least let me have the ⟨indemnification⟩↑gratification↓[8] of hearing from you occasionally, this will be an additional inducement for me to write often, for through[9] the mere idea that my letters could yeild you the least pleasure ought to be Sufficient. Yet the prospect of being re*paid* in kind would render me a much more attentive correspondent. Thus you see I am Selfish even in these little offices of friendship & must be induced to perform them by the hopes of a reward.

Your Singular determination to pass the winter in the country has occasioned me great regret & Surprise not that I thereby mean to insinuate anything derogatory to Coldenham,[10] or its inhabitants, or its woods or its vales, or the mountains, or the little negroes or the kittens or the old horse that travels Sometimes Side ways like a crab, Sometimes backwards like a bear, & Sometimes has to be led by his rider like an obedient & discreet Saddle horse, far be it from me to offend any being animate or inanimate, but Surely you are paying New York and its citizens a very Sorry compliment to absent yourself all Summer & all winter into the bargain. Well, well there is no accounting for the whims of a young gentlewoman in her teens, So I say no more on the Subject. Not but what there is a little of the bitterness of disappointment fermenting at the bottom of all this, in honest truth I had calculated on another sociable jog trot through the mountains with you & had hinted as much to friend Lary[11] in an airing I took with him Some time Since, the poor beast was So overjoyed at the thought that he pricked up his ears and frisked after Such a fashion that he had well nigh flung my companion the Baron[12] out of his Seat. Surely the brute is a good brute a very well disposed brute of most civil & excellent demeanour.

You have heard no doubt of Maggy Ashtons having married[13] a little limping round shouldered, blear eyed, fat Sided foreigner, a corpulent oily little knave, who looked for all the world like a pumpkin on Stilts. The marriage has caused the wonder of all that portion of the world, who have nothing to do but wonder at the follies of each other, for my part I can see nothing Surprising in it, I never yet knew a young gentlewoman who has gilted[14] Some half a Score of honest lovers, but what She either was condemned to a life of single bliss, or was brought to a melancholly & untimely matrimonial end like Maggie Ashton.

Take warning all ye flinty damsels who, making a business of breaking the hearts of Simple brainless Soft headed young gentlemen, who reduce so many brilliant youths, the hope of their families, the darlings of their Mothers, to a state of absolute Stupidity & insignificance, who turn So many block heads into poets, poets into madmen & madmen into idiots who cause So many aspiring agents & gallent young merchants to dash about, & then drive them by your frowns to despair & the limits. Take warning I repeat, ye most flinty hearted young women, by the melancholly marraige of Maggie Ashton, & beware of the innocent, though hazardous amusement of jilting! On Sunday last there was Somewhat of a family dinner at your fathers, at which your Uncle & Aunt[15] were present. Bass[16] as usual was very much at home & together with his brother Martin[17] was rather hard upon Uncle David,[18] you know Uncle David is a little of a witch & has long controversies at times with George upon various Abstract Subjects, such as whether a Spade is really a Spade or a Shovel, George maintains the former position & between ourselves I am inclined to think he has the best of the argument. Kimble (meaning Gouvy)[19] was of the party, but rather out of Spirits, not having recovered from the horrors of an invasion which was made on his territory about five weeks ago, by the lads of Kilkenny[20] who made a Sudden de↑s↓cent upon his empire at Newark where they remained two or three days, committed great devastation, & absolutely eat him out of doors. Petronius[21] is absent at Philadelphia, where he lives in clover at the expense of an uncle who had the weakness poor man to take him along, we understand he Suffers great extremity, his face having been completely conflagrated by drinking burgundy and eating tarapins & canvass backs[.] we have sent orders in case his nose Should catch fire to have it extinguished in the Delaware. The lads of Kilkenny are thrown into a wonderful turmoil by the singular & uncommon deportment of Jim Paulding,[22] I know you will think I am romancing when I assure you that he was absolutely detected in handing a young lady out of the coffee room in the theatre & that he even Saw her quite down Stairs into the box! A meeting of the club has been notified for this evening, when we are to take into consideration & properly to investigate this astonishing piece of gallantry in our honorable fellow member. Paulding is a fine boy,—as Bass Says, but this unparalleled instance of attention in him has excited the strongest suspicion. He has just entered my office & I am interrupted, farewell for the present[.] I will continue this letter tomorrow. Write to me I entreat you & beleive me as ever you affectionate friend

Washington Irving

To Miss Alice Anne Hoffman/Care Thomas Colden Esqr[23]/⟨Newburgh⟩ Coldenham[24]

MANUSCRIPT: Minnesota Historical Society. PUBLISHED: St. Paul *Daily News,*
Magazine Section, April 18, 1920, p. 2.

This manuscript is a handwritten copy of the original. The copyist, possibly
because of idiosyncrasy in his or her own handwriting, wrote each initial *s* and
c as a capital. It is impossible to determine whether or not this represents WI's
intention. The Minnesota Society also has a typescript which fills in the blank
after "pious" in the first paragraph with "Aeneas."

1. Thomas à Kempis, *Imitation of Christ* (ca. 1420), chap. 23.
2. This word is inserted above the line in pencil by another hand.
3. See the *Aeneid,* II, 799–806. The word "Aeneas" is supplied from the typescript mentioned in the opening note.
4. Eccles. 6:10.
5. Probably a miscopying of "solemnly."
6. WI's close association with the Hoffman family resulted from his studying
law in the office of J. O. Hoffman and from a long-standing acquaintance with the
second Mrs. Hoffman and her stepchildren.
7. Probably a miscopying of "though."
8. The cancellation and the addition have been made in pencil by another hand.
9. Probably a miscopying of "though."
10. The home of Ann's maternal grandparents at Montgomery, in Orange County,
New York.
11. The name of the Hoffmans' horse.
12. The Baron is probably WI's facetious name for his brother-in-law, Henry Van
Wart. Later WI regularly used this epithet for Van Wart.
13. The NYEP for September, October, and November, 1807, does not report
this marriage.
14. WI probably intended "jilted" here. It is not possible to ascertain whether
the error was his or the copyist's. The copyist who prepared the typescript wrote
"jilted," but may have corrected WI's MS on his own authority.
15. Probably Mr. and Mrs. Martin Hoffman.
16. Perhaps a nickname for Lindley Murray Hoffman (1793–1861), son of
Martin Hoffman.
17. Martin Hoffman (1795–1857), brother of Lindley Murray Hoffman.
18. This may be WI's facetious reference to David Murray Hoffman (1791–1878),
brother of Lindley and Martin Hoffman.
19. Apparently Gouverneur Kemble, but both copyists spell the name "Kimble."
20. This group of young men about town included, in addition to WI, Peter and
Ebenezer Irving, Gouverneur Kemble, James K. Paulding, Henry Brevoort, David
Porter, Richard McCall, and Henry Ogden. For other details, see STW, I, 398,
n. 22; and Amos L. Herold, *James Kirke Paulding,* pp. 28–29.
21. The name given to Peter Kemble, Jr. (1787–1813).
22. At this time Paulding was collaborating with WI on *Salmagundi.*
23. Thomas Colden, the great-uncle of Ann Hoffman.
24. The cancellation and addition have been made in pencil in another hand.

56.   *To Joseph Gratz*

New York, March 30th, 1808.

Dear Jos:—

We arrived here on Sunday between four and five, having experienced several minutes' delay on the road, to the great annoyance of Cooper,[1] who travels watch in hand.

I have had a world of inquiries made about me in Philadelphia, and have given as unsatisfactory answers as an honest gentleman could conscientiously give, inasmuch as I had no time like a man who has had a taste of his dinner and then hurries away with a prodigious appetite. The peep I took at your city[2] has made me impatient to pay it another visit, but when I shall be enabled to do so remains, with other great and important events of futurity, wrapped in impenetrable uncertainty.

I just returned in time for a sort of crazy party at Mary Fairlie's, where we went to take tea in a sociable humdrum manner, but scarcely a dozen of us had assembled together before a fiddler made his appearance. Had it been the D——l himself (not meaning to speak irreligiously) he could not have thrown us in a greater uproar. In a word there was dancing and romping and playing the fool until one o'clock, to the great discomposure of my gravity and decorum. A certain Capt. Smith of the Navy[3] was the nonpareil of the evening, and five ladies at least conceived the most deadly hatred and jealousy for each other on the spot— which they most palpably evinced by behaving to each other with the most vehement politeness, dearing and love-ing each other at every ten words. Among the number was your good friend, Eliza Patterson,[4] who seemed to bear the palm. This story is meant for Philadelphia circulation, therefore don't let it rest, I beg of you.

Jim[5] talks of writing you next month. He has become quite a tea-party hero, and I have no doubt will assist at all the conventions of petticoats in Philadelphia while he is there.

As to myself the ride to Philadelphia has quite renovated me, for to tell the truth I had fallen into very melancholy and gentlemanlike habits before I left home. At present I am again recovered into tolerable circulation, therefore I beg you without delay to bid Mr. Watson[6] to forward my new black coat, as I perceive I shall have many drawing-room demands to answer. To-morrow evening I am to attend a party at Mrs. Price's[7] and if my coat does not arrive in time I shall be in as great distress as ever was young lady when disappointed by her mantua-maker.

Write me immediately about my expected steed, the good Bayardo—for I am determined he shall have a true chevalier name. I hope you have sent him to pasture, and tell the people to let him feed low as it is necessary for his health and marvellously convenient for my pocket. To hear of his health will much rejoice me.

I am writing in the greatest hurry, which is the only excuse I can offer for this abominable scrawl. Remember me affectionately to all your good family and believe me,

Your friend,
W. Irving

PUBLISHED: *Canadian Magazine* 60 (January, 1923), 231.

For Joseph Gratz, see July 6, 1806.

1. Thomas Abthorpe Cooper, English-born actor and theater manager who was very popular in the United States.

2. Philadelphia.

3. Probably Theophilus Washington Smith (1784–1846) who had earlier studied law in the office of Aaron Burr.

4. Elizabeth Patterson (1785–1879) had married Jerome Bonaparte on December 24, 1803. When Napoleon refused to recognize the marriage or to permit her to set foot on European soil, Jerome had the marriage annulled, whereupon Napoleon provided her with an annual pension of 6,000 francs.

5. James Kirke Paulding, who had many friends in Philadelphia, including the Gratzes, in common with WI. Perhaps "writing" is a misreading of "visiting."

6. Perhaps a tailor in Philadelphia from whom WI had ordered a new coat.

7. Probably Mrs. Stephen Price, wife of the manager of the Park Theater.

57. *To Henry Brevoort*

Skeenesborough—May 9th. 1808

My Dear Brevoort—

Here have I been embargoed by confounded contrary winds for five days[1]—having arrived the day after you set sail—I feel extremely embarrassed how to proceed—The good folks at the ⟨?U S?⟩ line are so excessively strict that I dare not risk my silver across. I believe I shall sail for burlington tomorrow if the wind favours & deposit my silver there —either getting gold in exchange or receipts from the cashier—which I am told I can get cash at par for, in Montreal from merchants who wish to remit money to their agents in ⟨Montreal⟩ ↑Vermont↓. I have about 9,000$ with me—look about if you can secure me good Bills[2]—I am affraid this will turn out but a lame business all round—I have heard of ⟨your⟩↑nuncles[3]↓ getting through the trap—with the loss of ⟨your⟩↑his↓ *tail*; and as for myself, I expect to rival honest Primroses son Moses, in his great bargain of the green spectacles.[4]

I entreat you not to leave Montreal until my arrival—we must return together. My Brother Peter is with me—and we are both at the house of

Bully Rock, mine host of the Garter[5]—We have nearly read through the library of the good Dame Quickly[6]—who by the way is a great friend of yours—⟨and had she legs? [*unrecovered*]⟩ Enquire about, whether you can find any who will accept Drafts on the Burlington Bank at par— remember me to our friends & believe me

Ever yours
WI.

ADDRESSED: Mr Henry Brevoort / care of David Ogden Esqr / Montreal—
    DOCKETED: W Irving / *May 9. 1808*
MANUSCRIPT: NYPL—WI Papers. PUBLISHED: PMI, I, 215–16; LIB, I, 5–6.

1. Travel on the rivers was still carried on in sailboats which were frequently becalmed because of lack of wind.
2. Because of the governmental restrictions imposed by the Embargo, WI was trying to convert his funds at a favorable rate. It is quite probable that the Irving brothers were involved in an illegal venture. Illicit trade with Canada was quite common; it was a source of great concern to President Jefferson. See Lewis Martin Sears, *Jefferson and the Embargo* (1927) (New York, 1966), p. 64, and passim.
3. The name given to Brevoort by the Lads of Kilkenny. WI's specific allusion to the trap and the loss has not been uncovered.
4. Moses is sent to a fair to sell a pony and buy groceries. He sells the pony for £3 5s. 2d. and spends all of it on a gross of green spectacles with silver rims which turn out to be varnished-over copper. See Oliver Goldsmith, *The Vicar of Wakefield*, chap. 12.
5. WI has apparently been reading *The Merry Wives of Windsor*. *Bully rook* is used there (I, iii, 2) as a term for a jolly companion. WI also uses the same name for his landlord in Washington in a letter to Brevoort on January 13, 1811.
6. Another allusion to *The Merry Wives of Windsor*, where Mistress Quickly is the servant of Dr. Caius, a French physician. Probably WI is also associating the name with the hostess of the tavern in East-cheap in which Falstaff and his cronies caroused in *Henry IV*, Parts I and II.

58.   To Mrs. Josiah Ogden Hoffman

Albany, June 2, 1808.

My Dear Friend:

I have just arrived in Albany, and found two letters from you and Mr. Hoffman, so kind and so affectionate that I cannot express to you how grateful they were to my feelings. My journey has been tedious and unpleasant, but it is so far over, and past fatigues are soon forgotten.

On the road, as I was travelling in high spirits with the idea of home to inspire me, I had the shock of reading an account of my dear sister's death,[1] and never was a blow struck so near my heart before. Five years have nearly elapsed since I have seen her, and though such an absence might lessen the pang of eternal separation, still it is dreadfully severe. One more heart lies still and cold that ever beat towards me with the warmest affection, for she was the tenderest, best of sisters, and a woman of whom a brother might be proud. To add to my distress, I have to reproach myself that I drew my brother[2] into that wretched journey when he was on the way to Johnstown, where his presence might have cheered and comforted the last moments of my poor sister. But God knows I had no presentiment of the sad event that was to happen. * * *

To-morrow morning early I set off for Johnstown. Would to Heaven I had gone there a month ago. * * *

PUBLISHED: PMI, I, 217–18.

1. Ann Sarah Irving (February 14, 1770–May 10, 1808). She had six children, five of whom survived her. The youngest of these, Helen, married Pierre Munro Irving in 1836.

2. Peter Irving was on his way to Johnstown to visit the Dodges when Washington met him in Schenectady and persuaded him to make the trip to Montreal first. See PMI, I, 214–15.

59. *To Henry Brevoort*

New York, June 11th. 1808.

My dear Harry—

McKenzie[1] starts this afternoon and I ⟨now⟩ snatch ⟨one⟩ a moment from a crowd of avocations to scribble you a line, if it is merely to let you know how much, how very much I long to see you. The fates, who I ⟨at⟩ once for all curse for a set of perverse, ill natured old maids—have most obstinately persisted in keeping us asunder during our travels, and I have no other method of baffling their malice, that[2] to remain stock still in town until you return.[3] I entreat you & believe me I do it most earnestly, and in the fullness of my heart, to come back as soon as your ⟨smuggling⟩ honest occupations will permit, for I never was more impatient to shake you by the hand than I am at present. Our poor friend Mrs. R_____.[4] breathed her last this morning — I am now writing at the house of Mr H which is a melancholy mansion indeed. What between one melancholy event & another, and my own fickle spirits, I find myself sadly depressed, but I am certain your return would perfectly revive me. I g[ot][5] home the evening before last and foun[d our] friends much I believe as you left the[m. You know] that Mary Fairlie is down at Rockawa[y.] Louisa & Maria Moore[6] has[7] gone dow[n to] keep her company. Ann[8] is fair & be[autiful] as ever & full of fascination. you are [a] prodigious favourite of hers & seem to have [won] all the epaulettes &c &c in fact you are spoken of with a degree of affection by the whole family, ⟨that⟩ which I assure you has delighted me; for I wish all my friends to be thoroughly yours.

I shall not pretend to give you much news in this letter, for it is an even chance whether McKenzie meets with you or not—but shall close with again begging you to let me see you in N York as soon as possible—

I am my dear fellow/truly yours
W I.

P.S. Mr H sent a letter to me by you which you were to leave in Albany —I never received it & hope you will be careful to bring it with you.

ADDRESSED: Mr Henry Brevoort / Montreal. / Care of Mr McKenzie. DOCKETED: June 11–1808 / Washington Irving
MANUSCRIPT: NYPL—WI Papers. PUBLISHED: PMI, I, 218 (in part); LIB, I, 7–9.

1. Donald Mackenzie (1783–1851) was involved in the fur trade and in 1809 became the partner of John Jacob Astor in a project for establishing fur trading posts west of the Rocky Mountains.

2. WI probably intended to write "than."

3. In 1808 Brevoort, who was a cousin of Astor's wife, Sarah Todd, was working for Astor in connection with the fur trade, probably along the Canadian border with New York state.

4. Mrs. Harriet Rodman. The following notice appeared in the NYEP for June 11, 1808: "Died, early this morning, in the 20th year of her age, Mrs. Harriet Rodman. The relatives and friends are requested to attend her funeral tomorrow afternoon at 5 o'clock, from the house of Ogden Hoffman, Esq., No. 16 Wall St."

5. In this and subsequent bracketed passages the ink is obliterated by water damage.

6. The Moore sisters were the daughters of Dr. William Moore (1754–1824), a New York obstetrician, and the nieces of Bishop Benjamin Moore. Maria Teresa Moore married Henry C. DeRham, a merchant and importer of Swiss birth. Her brothers Benjamin and William became members of DeRham's firm. See Scoville, *Old Merchants of NYC*, I, 211, 328–29.

7. WI probably intended to write "have."

8. Ann Hoffman, daughter of Josiah Ogden Hoffman. See WI's letters to her of August 10 and November 17, 1807.

60. To Richard McCall[?]

New York. Novr. 18th. 1808[1]

My dear Mac—

As our friend the smuggler[2] sets off on one of his righteous & patriotic expeditions tomorrow, I shall trouble him to be my post boy—which is what I call "making much of a friend"[3] As I have been very free with my pen of late,[4] and have written myself completely blank, I shall not pretend to any thing like amusement; but shall give you all the information I can; which perhaps you will like better.

You left us in one of our gayest moods; when pleasure came over us like a freshet—(to ⟨you⟩ use a local figure) the torrent has passed by, and we are again as tranquil and monotonous as a mill pond. The club[5] is completely disorganized and dispersed. You have banished yourself "from Veronas walls"[6] for the love of filthy lucre—As to the Supercargo,[7] he has gone on a voyage of discovery, no one knows whither—No ⟨let⟩ tidings have reached us of his welfare & mishap—but, like a second La Peyrouse,[8] a dark & fearful mystery, hangs over his fate. His honour the Patroon,[9] ⟨has⟩ is displaying his royal person in Boston—⟨among⟩ Billy Taylor[10] is "romping with a lady fair"—The Heir apparent[11] is immersed in law, preparing for examination—Little Johnny Fig[12] is buried ⟨in pots⟩ among pots & kettles, or hid in a Brummagen Pepper Box— And as to Nuncle[13] he has ⟨[unrecovered]⟩ got the green sickness from eating sour grapes, and moreover, ↑has↓ taken to building of Book cases and studying Johnsons Dictionary. What is to become of the Club I know not; last evening we had a half starved meeting ⟨where⟩ at the Wig wam,[14] where Billy Taylor & Petronius[15] & little Fig and myself dozed away about two hours, in the smallest room, until we smoaked ourselves out. Nuncle was to have been there—But he unluckily stumbled over a tea party at Miss Hulls and could not think of exchanging his miserable gentility—for the happy vulgarity of Battins.[16] The fact is the rogue had stored himself with three numbers of the Rambler,[17] besides the whole life of Savage[18] and a few happy hits from Boswell[19]—and was in prodigious luck—until he ⟨unluckil⟩ unfortunately broke down at the foot of a tall word, and was not able to recover his legs the whole evening afterwards.

I suppose you have heard before this that Little Ann and Charles[20] have completely reconciled old differences, and are once more on their former footing—The little couple were exceedingly happy—and Charles seemed so well pleased with New York that there is no knowing when he would have quitted it had not his brother came on from Philadelphia & carried him home, willy, nilly. Since that time Ann has taken very much to Italian, Dancing and other abstruse studies, to calculate her for the Domestic State. But she has lately atcheeved a feat which has given her considerable celebrity at the Tea tables of the City—At the New Play of Adelgitha,[21] some few evenings since ⟨an⟩↑a false↓ alarm of fire was given in the house,[22] & threw the whole audience in confusion— The Ladies were all in a panic—and Ann who was ⟨the⟩ in box No 3— made a tremendous leap from the front of the next box on the stage— clearing the spikes of the orchestra &c—and landing with great decency and considerable grace. The actors, you may easily imagine were astonished by so brilliant a "first appearance"—But as the New performer seemed excessively frightened & embarrassed Cooper[23] advanced from the other side of the stage, led her to the prompter & directed him to conduct her to Mrs Prices[24] box—where the little heroine, had a most-tragic fainting fit—the alarm of the audience subsided—⟨and as soon as the⟩ and peace was soon restored. The ladies having got over their panic, immediately began to consider how they might turn the incident, to the best advantage—and several of those worthy, amiable fair ones, whom heaven in its mercy has sent into the world to do all the mischief they can—agreed nem. con. that Ann had jumped into Mr Coopers **Arms**— and that—considering the skill & caution with which she escaped being impaled alive on the spikes, or breaking her ⟨kne⟩ neck in the orchestra— she could not have been much frightened—Would it not be a benefit to society, that a few such charitable ladies were roasted alive in the next conflagration?

Mary F——[25] ⟨is studying⟩ has put herself under the care of a new Professor of Dancing, who has lately become quite the rage, in consequence of introducing an ⟨new⟩ improved style of kicking the heels— he makes his pupils walk like old Wyncoop the Tax gatherer[26]—Curtsey something in the style of Punchinello,[27] and fling their feet about in such a manner, that I would advise every discreet parent, who sends his daughter to the school, to provide her with a pair of small clothes. Mary and Ann have been pestering Petronius and myself with their abominable steps whenever we have been in their company of late. And some evenings since they insisted upon shewing us a new way of coming into a room, but be[28] disappointed them by displaying an old way of going out—and actually made a safe retreat to our own homes; since which I have foresworn & abandoned their society; until they shall have regained their *understanding* (meaning a pun) ⟨[*unrecovered—3¾ lines heavily inked out*]⟩ The Old Doctors family[29] are all thriving—The Fair Maria[30] speaks very kindly of you—Little Mrs Major[31] keeps house in her own room, where she is studying how to be domestic—I suppose she has a complete house in miniature fitted up there, with a kitchen, parlour, *nursery* &c

Little Swan is courting (to use a vulgar expression) "like a horse"— I never saw a little fellow labour more faithfully in his vocation. he is continually gallanting his Patagonian beauty to the theater; up & down broad way &c—and always puts me in mind of a little cock boat[32] towing an India man. Last evening he had two ladies in charge, ↑at the theatre,↓ and I know not what the little man would have done, had not *Jessy*[33] acted as his aid.

Remember me to Hallowell,[34] and tell him that in consequence of three of his rivals having resigned, two deserted—and one absolutely declared off—he stands ⟨in⟩ a great chance of being the foremost on the little Lionesses list—having none to contend with but Nuncle, who has lately revived an old attachment in consequence of a tender look in the theatre some evenings since

Make as masterly a speech as possible to honest McKay[35] on the state of his affairs—and tell him we hope to see him in New York, "with his true love in his hand."

Take care of our friend Sir Harry[36]—who is very much troubled with a swampiness of the head in consequence of drinking water instead of wine—I am constantly in fear of his going off in a dropsy—

McKay promised to get me a pair of Ladies Moccasons—ask him if he has thought of it since

fare well my dear Mac—I have written you a hum drum letter in a hum drum mood—I will endeavor to atone for it another time Remember me to David & all my friends in Montreal.

Yours truly
W Irving.

Manuscript: HSP.

This letter is probably addressed to Richard McCall (1780–1831) one of the Lads of Kilkenny (see STW, I, 404). McCall was later United States consul at Gibraltar and a partner in business there with Bernard Henry (STW, I, 483).

1. Under the dateline is written in another hand than WI's "from Washington Irving the Author."

2. This could be WI's term for his brother Peter, as the result of their efforts to smuggle American money into Canada in the late spring and early summer of 1808 (see STW, I, 99–100), but since WI refers to the "smuggler" as "our friend" (not "brother"), he probably meant Henry Brevoort, who was in Canada at about the same time as an employee of John Jacob Astor.

3. Probably WI's adaptation of "Make use of ev'ry friend," from Pope's *Essay on Criticism,* pt. II, line 13.

4. WI had been writing on a sequel to *Salmagundi,* which had ceased publication on January 25, 1808. This material he probably incorporated into *Knickerbocker's History of New York.* See PMI, I, 220.

5. The Lads of Kilkenny.

6. WI is thinking of Shakespeare, either "From Verona banished/ For practicing to steal a lady" (*Two Gentlemen of Verona,* IV, i, 147), or "Hence from Verona thou art banished" (*Romeo and Juliet,* III, iii, 15).

7. Henry Ogden.

8. Jean François de Galup, La Pérouse (1741–1788), an explorer who was last heard from in the Pacific Ocean, probably perished with his men in a shipwreck.

9. Gouverneur Kemble (1786–1875).

10. James Kirke Paulding.

11. Peter Kemble, Jr. (1787–1813).

12. Probably John Irwin. In 1809, according to Paulding, "Little John Irwin" went "to the D_____l or the West Indies" (*Letters of J. K. Paulding,* p. 28). WI mentions "Little Cousin John" in a letter to Brevoort March 15, 1816.

13. Henry Brevoort.

14. Probably the Tammany Wigwam in the Long Room of Abraham B. Martling's tavern located on the corner of George and Nassau Streets. This tavern was

a popular hangout, especially for political groups. See Bayles, *Old Taverns of NY*, pp. 375–76.

15. Either Peter Irving or Peter Kemble, Jr.

16. Probably an allusion to the tavern operated by John Batten at 37 Nassau Street. See Bayles, *Old Taverns of NY*, p. 449.

17. A periodical conducted and largely written by Samuel Johnson between March, 1749/50 and March, 1751/52.

18. Written by Samuel Johnson in 1744 and later incorporated into his *Lives of the Poets*.

19. James Boswell's *Life of Samuel Johnson* appeared in 1791.

20. Ann Hoffman and Charles J. Nicholas, to whom Irving frequently alludes in his letters.

21. M. G. Lewis's *Adelgitha, or The Fruits of a Single Error* was first acted at the Park Theater on November 14, 1808. See Odell, *NY Stage*, II, 312.

22. This false alarm was not reported in the NYEP.

23. Thomas Abthorpe Cooper, the actor who was playing Guiscard in *Adelgitha*.

24. Mrs. Stephen Price, the former Miss Warren, who had married the manager of the Park Theater.

25. Mary Fairlie.

26. Benjamin Wynkoop, a silversmith, who served as collector and assessor in New York at various times between 1703 and 1732. See STW, I, 404, n. 155.

27. A character from an old Italian puppet show.

28. Although WI wrote "be," he probably intended to write "we."

29. Dr. William Moore. See WI's letter of June 11, 1808.

30. Maria Moore.

31. Possibly a relative of Dr. William Moore.

32. A small boat, used as a tender for a larger vessel.

33. Possibly Jesse Merwin. See WI's letter to Wm. Van Ness, December 18, 1809.

34. WI is probably referring to one of the sons of James Hallowell, who was a partner in the fur company of McTavish, Fraser, & Simon. William and James Hallowell, Jr. were partners in McTavish, McGillivray, and Co., organized in 1806. See Marjorie Wilkins Campbell, *McGillivray, Lord of the Northwest* (Toronto, 1962), pp. 74, 137.

35. Probably a son of Alexander McKay, a veteran fur trader who joined with Astor to form the Pacific Fur Company in 1810. Young McKay was presumably about the same age as WI. See Porter, *Astor*, I, 181–82.

36. Probably Henry Brevoort.

61. To Henry Brevoort

Kinderhook, May 5th. 1809.

My dear fellow

As the servant is waiting to take this Letter, I have only time to scrawl you six hasty lines. My mind has been so languid since I have been here,[1] that I have not been able to do any thing at my *business*— I begin to feel more myself, and hope in a day or two to get at work again. In the mean time I wish Jim to attend particularly to what he has in his hands,[2] for I must depend more upon his revision than I would have done had my mind & spirits been in proper tone[.] I feel in no hurry to return to the noise and worry of the City—I wish you would write to me about any thing and every thing—and that your letters may be as little of a task as possible, I beg you to scrawl them as negligently and slovenly as I do this—so long as they contain the least particle of news about my friends they will be always interesting.

Remember me to all my friends

and believe me truly/Yours
W I.

You must not be vexed at the shortness & nothingness of this letter—it is the best I can write at present; for I am completely blank & spiritless.

ADDRESSED: Mr Henry Brevoort Junr. / care of Mr John Hyslop / John Street / New York. POSTMARKED: Kinderhook / May 7 DOCKETED: May 5. 1809 / W Irving MANUSCRIPT: NYPL—WI Papers.

1. After the death of Matilda Hoffman on April 27, 1809, WI retired to the country home of William P. Van Ness (1778–1826), politician, jurist, and former supporter of Aaron Burr.

2. Presumably WI is referring to a draft of *Knickerbocker's History of New York* which James Kirke Paulding was criticizing.

62. *To Henry Brevoort*

Kinderhook, May 11th 1809.

My dear Brevoort,

I wrote you a hasty letter a few days since, and as Mr. Van Ness is about visiting the City I will scrawl you a few more, since they will cost you no postage. I feel much heartier than when I left town, particularly within these two last days; and have been able to resume my pen this morning, ⟨though rather⟩ but not with much spirit—I am in hopes however, that I shall brighten up as I proceed. My time here, though I pass most of it by myself, slips off very pleasantly—and I find so little want of amusement to while it away, that for two days I have scarcely been out of the house. You wou⟨d⟩ld be highly pleased with a visit here—the house is spacious and judiciously planned and the surrounding country ⟨very⟩ affords ⟨va⟩ a variety of agreeable scenery.[1]

The only Country acquaintance I have made, is a schoolmaster who ⟨keeps a⟩ teaches the neighbouring children—a pleasant good natured fellow, with much native, unimproved shrewdness and considerable humour—as he is a kind of inmate at Van Ness's we have become very great friends, and I have found much entertainment in his conversation.[2]

Van Ness mentioned that he meant to invite you to return with him, if he does so, I wish you would accept his invitation. Perhaps the picture I have given of my situation may not be calculated to entice you from the city; for I own it bears the features of dull monotony—but I assure you the hours move along here with a calmness and serenity, that, if I may judge of your feelings from my own, would be infinitely more gratifying than all the hurry and noisy mirth of more dissipated scenes.

If you should come up enquire of Jim whether he has looked at any of those things I left with him, and if he has done with any of them bring them with you. Should he leave town for any time, I wish he would seal them up and leave them with my mother—

I wish you would procure me a bottle of that oil you used for your hair—the Nervous fever with which I have lately been troubled has occasiond mine to come out a little—and I would wish to try your prescription—let me have it by Mr Van Ness.

Write me if there is any news about the Orator[3]—the Iron man or any other topic of conversation—Does Cooper[4] go out to England?— How does King Stephen[5] make out? and all the other chit chat of the day—

I have just time to finish & fold up my letter—Remember me to my friends the Hyslops[6] &c

Yours most truly
W. I.

ADDRESSED: Mr Henry Brevoort / ⟨care of⟩ John Street / New York. /
   pr / Wm. P Van Ness Esq}   DOCKETED: May 11 1809 / W Irving
MANUSCRIPT: NYPL—Seligman Collection. PUBLISHED: LIB, I, 10–12.

1. Later the Van Ness estate became the home of Martin Van Buren.

2. This schoolmaster was Jesse Merwin (1784–1852), who served as the model for Ichabod Crane. On February 12, 1851, WI wrote to Merwin, recalling some of the incidents of his visit in 1809.

3. This is James Ogilvie (1774–1820), the English teacher of oratory, whom WI had met at Aaron Burr's trial in Richmond in 1807. For details about Ogilvie, see Richard Beale Davis, "James Ogilvie and Washington Irving," *Americana* 35 (July, 1941), 435–58; and Richard Beale Davis, "James Ogilvie, An Early American Teacher of Rhetoric," *Quarterly Journal of Speech* 28 (1942), 289–97.

4. Thomas Abthorpe Cooper.

5. Stephen Price (1783–1840) had bought a share of Cooper's interest in the Park Theater in the 1808–1809 season. Price's methods in the theater were often flamboyant. See Odell, *NY Stage*, II, 309.

6. Robert Hyslop (1787–1863) is first listed in the *New York Directory* in 1812 as an accountant. In 1813 he is listed as an auctioneer and in 1817 as a merchant. In 1818 he joined the auction house and commission business of Irving & Smith, which became Irving, Smith & Hyslop. Later he set up his own business of hardware importing, under the name of Robert Hyslop and Son. He was a vestryman of Trinity Church, and had nine children. Scoville, *Old Merchants of NYC*, II, 79; III, 50.

63. *To Mrs. Josiah Ogden Hoffman*

Kinderhook, May 19th. 1809.

Since last I wrote I have received your two letters, and feel most grateful for these marks of your attention. The first of them had Loitered for some time at Hudson, in consequence of being directed to the neighbourhood of that place, instead of Kinderhook. The accounts you give of all your healths, have relieved me from great anxiety—I am glad to hear that Ann and Mary have gone to the country;[1] I think the more you can keep Mary out of the city the better. If I conveniently can, I will visit them on my way down, but I do not think it will be in my power.

I am so ⟨p⟩ well pleased with the half Monastic life that I lead, that I cannot endure the thoughts of giving it up and returning to the City. By constantly exercising my mind, never suffering it to prey upon itself, and resolutely determining to be cheerful, I have in a manner worked myself into a very enviable state of serenity & self possession, which is promoted by the tranquility of every thing around me. In Mrs Van Ness[2] I have found a most valuable companion, she is a woman, who the utmost equanimity of disposition unites a highly intelligent and cultivated understanding—Her reading has been very extensive and well chosen. My honest acquaintance the Schoolmaster[3] also, who is possessed of a considerable portion of good sense and native humour, ⟨affords⟩ (and who, according to the custom of the country, passes part of the time at Mr Van Ness's in consequence of teaching his children) yields me occasionally ⟨conv⟩ an hour of very entertaining conversation— So time goes—If not in gaiety, at least in useful and agreeable occupation. We are apt to retain an impression in respect to a place, from the state of our feelings on last quitting it, and when I left New York, I emerged from such a scene of gloom and heart aching distress that in returning to it I should feel like a prisoner returning to his dungeon.

You need be under no apprehension of my walking in the night dews— I am so much on the contrary extreme that I do not go out enough—but there are now greater temptations to exercise

This has been a starveling spring—After a continual spell of harsh, ungenial weather, in which the trees seemed to shrink back & fear to put forth their blossoms, the temperature of the atmosphere has suddenly changed and all nature has burst forth into luxurience & song. There is a delightful meadow at a short distance from the house, through which runs one of the most beautiful brooks I ever saw—broad, fair & limpid; winding in a thousand wild mazes—bordered with spreading trees and tufted bushes, and making a number of picturesque little Islands. This meadow seems at present the general resort of all the singing birds in the neighbourhood, and is a charming place for a ramble. I shall therefore be more out of doors than I have hitherto been.

The servant is waiting to take this letter to the Post office so I have only time to beg you to remember me to Mr Hoffman Eliza & all my friends & believe me ever

truly your friend
W. I.

MANUSCRIPT: NYPL—WI Papers. PUBLISHED: PMI, I, 228 (in part); Waldron, *WI & Cotemporaries*, pp. 164–65.

1. Possibly Mrs. Hoffman, following Matilda's death, decided to send her stepdaughters to their maternal grandparents at Coldenham. In addition to its sorrowful associations, New York was agitated by rumors relating to the Embargo and British threats of violence.

2. Probably Mrs. John P. Van Ness (née Marcia Burns, 1782–1832), whose intelligence and cultivation matched WI's description. Residents of Washington, D.C., she and her husband may have been visiting the family home in Kinderhook at this time. WI was to visit the Van Nesses in Washington in 1811. See PMI, I, 263. Although WI was a close friend of William P. Van Ness, there is no evidence that Van Ness ever married. According to tradition, WI tutored children at the Van Ness home in Kinderhook at this time. Whose children is not clear. See Harold Donaldson Eberlein and Cortlandt Van Dyke Hubbard, *Historic Houses of the Hudson Valley* (New York, 1942), p. 124.

3. Jesse Merwin of Kinderhook.

64.   To Sarah Irving

Kinderhook, May 20th. 1809.

My dear Mother,

I am very glad to hear by the letters receive[1] from home[2] that you are all well; Mr Van Ness arrived here last night and handed me one from you, among several others. You do not mention whether you have procured another servant, I hope you have found a good one, that will suit you. You must make yourself as comfortable as possible, and spare no expense that you can afford, to make yourself easy and happy. Mr. Paris's letter[3] gives me great satisfaction, as I find they will be able to get the children to the sea shore, after which I feel very confident they will do well. If I should not be in town in time, some other of the family must endeavour to find a place for the sick folks—Staten Island, or perhaps Long Island, near Gravesend, will ⟨be⟩ present some convenient situation. If I reccollect right Henry Dodge once mentioned some place to me which I know to be very much such an one as was wanted.

Tell Ebenezer I thank him for his postscript and congratulate him and Eliza[4] on their little son[5]—This I believe is the twenty fifth of my regiment of nephews & neices. Ebenezer wishes me to think of a name for it—I can think of none other than that of its uncle Henry's[6]—It is a handsome manly name, and the little fellow cannot have a worthier namesake. We have no Henrys in the Irving part of the family so that his name will not be liable to be confounded with that of any cousin—

I received a large packet from Peter,[7] and promised myself a rich treat, but on opening it, I found enclosed a sealed pacquet to Miss Moore,[8] and nothing but a blank cover for poor me. I think, since he makes me his post boy, he might at least scribble me a line by way of postage. ⟨I shall send his⟩ Mr Van Ness informs me that some of the goods which he shipped, have arrived. I hope they will sell well, and turn out profitable for both William[9] and Himself. I have heard nothing particular about either William or Harrys[10] business—I am deeply interested in the welfare of all my brothers, and love to have daily accounts of every little change & turn in their affairs.

My situation here is so very agreeable that I cannot bear the thoughts of leaving it. Mrs Van Ness is a most amiable and valuable woman and what will recommend her the more to you, most truly and unaffectedly pious. I do not know when I have met with a woman who has so completely gained my esteem in so short a time. Every thing around me is comfortable—and the country at present is delightful. Mr Van Ness is extremely friendly. He has expected that I would pass the summer here, ⟨and it is only in [one word unrecovered]⟩ and would not listen to my mention, of returning to town. Business however will require me to return soon, but I have promised, if it is in my power, to come up here again in the course of the summer, and pursue my studies, in this tranquil retreat. I feel quite well, and hope to look so, when we meet— but my lanthorn visage would be just as lank as ever, if I were to eat up a team of oxen and drink all the buttermilk in the country. As the weather has become warm and pleasant I hope you amuse yourself by visiting your children, and taking every other means of making time pass away agreeably—Your mentioning in one of your letters that you was very lonesome, made me feel anxious to return, but I hope sally[11] visits you occasionally—and if caty[12] comes down soon, you will have company and bustle enough. I shall, however, return as soon as possible. At present I find it more to my comfort as [well] [MS obscured by seal] as advantage to remain here a little longer. I think of the City with disagreeable recollections [and,] [MS obscured by seal] I fear if I return there immediately, I shall only get out of spirits, and unable to do any thing.

Give my love to sally and her little ones, and to all the family—Tell William I hope he is turning iron into gold like another Midas—if you can reccollect the name—if not, youll find it somewhere in the Apocrypha.

I am my dear mother—/affectionately your son

Washington Irving

P. S. I wish you would have all the linen which I have left behind bleached.

ADDRESSED: Mrs Sarah Irving / No 157. Williams Street / New York. POSTMARKED: Kinderhook / May 23
MANUSCRIPT: SHR (collection of Mrs. W. W. Phelps).

1. WI inadvertently omitted the final *d*.

2. These letters have not been located.

3. This letter has not been located. Daniel Paris was WI's brother-in-law, the husband of his sister Catharine.

4. Elizabeth Kip (1784–1827) had married Ebenezer Irving on November 14, 1805.

5. Theodore Irving (1809–1880) was the third son of Ebenezer and Elizabeth Irving. His birthdate is given by STW (II, opposite 254) as March[?] 9, 1809; but in view of the fact that the child had not been named by the date of this letter, a more plausible birthdate may be May 9, 1809.

6. Probably an allusion to Henry Van Wart, who had married WI's sister Sarah in 1804.

7. WI refers to Peter Irving, his brother who had recently gone to Liverpool to attend to the family importing business.

8. Probably either Louisa or Maria Moore, friends who are mentioned in several of WI's letters of 1807 and 1808.

9. William Irving, WI's oldest brother.

10. Probably Henry Van Wart. See WI's letter of June 24, 1809, to William P. Van Ness, where he speaks of "Harry Van Wart."

11. Sally is probably Sarah Van Wart, presumably in New York on a visit from Birmingham, England, where she and her husband were living.

12. Catharine Paris lived at Johnstown, New York, near Schenectady.

65. To Henry Brevoort

Kinderhook May 20th. 1809.

My dear fellow—

Van Ness mentions that you sent me a pacquet by the Steam boat but it has never come to hand. He says it contained a recent work called letters from the Mountain[1]—but I am apprehensive that it contains some of my Mss.[2] You cannot think how uneasy I feel—Why did you not drop me a line in the post office at the same time to let me know a pacquet was coming—as to directing it to be left at Hudson, you might as well say *the bank of the river*—I know not where to look for it, or whether it has been put ashore at Hudson or carried to albany —Do write me immediately on the receipt of this—if it is only a single line to put me out of suspense—if you have not forwarded any of the Mss. do not do so unless you or Peter K[3] come up here — I would not have them sent by a chance conveyance.

I hope Jim[4] has nearly run through them. I fear he will be too minute

& either be very long about it or tire himself out before he has got half ways[.] I have almost finished—and in the course of a week hope to be released from my pen. I shall then drive with all possible dispatch to get completely done with the business and once more at liberty. ⟨to⟩ When I shall take up a regular course of study for the summer[.] I shall return in the course of a fortnight—though my good friend Van Ness had insisted upon my staying until September—I have promised if possible to return here—and I rather think this will be my summers retreat—It is exactly the kind of place I have long pictured to myself as an enviable summers seclusion.

I have received a long letter from my worthy friend Peter Kemble, to whom I feel more gratitude for this mark of affection than I can easily express. I wish you had ⟨return⟩ come up with Van Ness so as to return with me—You may yet take a trip here and accompany me down. If you come up & bring up the Mss ⟨in⟩ that are in Jims hands I will have occupation enough to keep me here some time longer — I wish you would do so. The country is heavenly—every thing is in bloom.

farewell—I am writing at almost midnight and scarce know what I scrawl—Do not fail to write me word immediately about the pacquet —& who you put it[5] in charge of. Write by the very first mail after you receive this otherwise it will make a difference of two or three days —Remember me to all & believe me

Yours most truly
W I.

P. S. I wish Jim to save a little of his attention & critical industry for the remainder which I have in hands. I have not been able to do it the justice I could wish from not being in full health & spirits—I have done little more than copy off from my original scrawls.

ADDRESSED: Mr Henry Brevoort Junr. / John Street. / New York. POSTMARKED: Kinderhook / May 23 DOCKETED: May 20. 1809 / W Irving
MANUSCRIPT: NYPL—WI Papers. PUBLISHED: LIB, I, 13–15

1. *Letters from the Mountains: Being the Real Correspondence of a Lady, between 1773 and 1807* by Mrs. Anne McVickar Grant. A second edition was published in London by Longman, Hurst, Rees & Orme in 1807.

2. Presumably a reference to some part of *Knickerbocker's History of New York*, upon which WI was working in Kinderhook.

3. Probably Peter Kemble, a member of the Lads of Kilkenny, who is mentioned later in the letter. In a letter of May 17, 1809, James Kirke Paulding writes that "Our Club has undergone a dispersion, to which that of the Tower of Babel was a mere breaking up of the Congregation of a village Church. . . . Peter Kemble [has gone] to Brunswick . . . and Washington Irving is somewhere in the Kaatskill mountains, catching running chubs—and wooing the villainous wood-nymphs. Thus poor Brevoort & unfortunate I—are left disconsolate and alone, like the dear Babes in the wood . . ." (*Letters of J. K. Paulding*, pp. 27–28).

4. James Kirke Paulding, who remained in New York at his clerkship in the United States Loan Office.

5. Although WI wrote "in," he probably intended "it."

66. *To William P. Van Ness*

New York, June 24th. 1809

My dear Sir,

I received your letter some days since and should have answered it sooner, but that I have had a very bad hand in consequence of the bite of a Spider received on the tenth of June in that memorable expedition of the Deacon[1] & myself against the crows.

As to your inquiries as to what I am doing in the city, I can simply answer *nothing*, except I can call it doing something to be crawling between heaven & earth, railing at hot weather & close houses, and reviling all inventors and builders of cities, from the mighty Nimrod,[2] down to his modern Successors, the founders of Harsimus, Hoboken, & Manhattanville.[3] I have been nervous, debilitated and out of spirits ever since my return—and I only wait to see my brotherinlaw and Sister[4] embark for Europe, and ⟨Jack⟩ to hear Jack[5] deliver ⟨an⟩ a fourth proof, thunder & turf oration to the Sovreign Swine on the fourth of of July—after which, I shall shake the dust off of my feet and abandon this city and its inhabitants for the Summer.

Whether I shall be able to accept your friendly invitation to return, or not, I cannot positively say—I ⟨have no⟩ am pressed to pass the hot weather in a retreat in the Neighbourhood of the City, and as it will be more convenient for the business I have in hand I am strongly tempted to comply. ⟨no⟩ As the deacon says, "I have *arrangements to make*," which must influence my movements—but were I to consult merely my inclinations they would lead me at once to the red Lane.

I have found all our friends well—Little Gill[6] has been making very suspicious advances towards the good graces of Miss F____[7] She has just gone on a visit ⟨up th⟩ to Mrs Dykemans in the vicinity of Peekskill —in the mean time the Little man,[8] who ⟨h⟩ is no less assiduous in his courtship of immortal Fame, is studying an Ogilvian oration[9] to be delivered before the Washington Society on the fourth of July[10]—thus he & Jack are the rival orators of the day.

We expect the Doctor[11] back in the fall, as Harry Van Wart goes out to take his place.

I have inquired at Ward & Goulds[12] for the rules of the Court.[13] com. pleas of Pennsylvania as you requested me, but they had not a copy in their store. If I can find it elsewhere I will procure & send it to you.

I congratulate you on the prospect of your getting in favour with these dispensers of infamy & renown the Newspaper Editors—If I can get your scrap of immortality reinserted in any of our papers I will—but where to apply is the question—Coleman[14] you know is federal—Cheetham[15] is as one of the profane—and as to the Public adv.[16] Jack tells [me] [*MS torn*] you have lately recieved a rub in that righteous [chron]icle [*MS torn*] as being a Clintonian—Ill see about it.—however

—I am writing in great hurry & am affraid I shall be too late for the Steam boat—

Remember me most particularly to Mrs Van Ness—Tell the Deacon to be of good heart, and the first morning he rises early, to gird up his loins and go down & secure my catterpillars nest, that I may have the young ones against I come up.

With my respects to the prime Minister—the chancellor, The Emperor, Old Dingman, The Duke of York and Miss Wickham[17] I am &c

Yours sincerely
W I.

ADDRESSED: Wm P Van Ness Esqr. / Kinderhook. DOCKETED: Washington Irving
(along left margin).
MANUSCRIPT: NYPL—Madigan Collection.

1. William Van Ness, Sr., uncle of WI's friends William P. and John P., was a deacon in the Claverack Dutch Reformed Church and "voorleser in the Church ... for 33 years. He begins the service by reading the scripture including the Commandments. Then he gives out a psalm and in an old fashioned though not unpleasing style of simple music leads the tune for his choir. . . . All this is in Dutch, of course . . ." (Franklin Ellis, *History of Columbia Country, New York* [Philadelphia, 1878], p. 245).

2. See Gen. 10:8–9.

3. An allusion to the Dutch settlers of New York in *Knickerbocker's History*.

4. Henry Van Wart and Sarah Irving, who were to settle permanently in Birmingham, England, where Van Wart engaged in business.

5. WI's brother, John Treat.

6. Gulian Crommelin Verplanck, who studied law with Josiah Ogden Hoffman and later married Mrs. Hoffman's sister, Eliza Fenno, was well acquainted with WI's circle.

7. Probably Eliza Fenno.

8. A reference to Verplanck, who was quite short.

9. An allusion to the rhetorical style of James Ogilvie, a Scotsman who taught elocution in Virginia from 1794 to 1808 and toured the eastern seaboard with lectures and declamations for several more years. Ogilvie's florid speeches, delivered in sepulchral tones while he wore a Roman toga, excited both admiration and ridicule. James K. Paulding's reaction is typical: "You must know I went the other night to hear an oration of Ogilvie, and when it was finished, stamping about in the crowd with the patroon, we encountered Mary Fairlie, and the Hoffman's, and Gertrude, who were waiting the dispersion of the multitude. I took Miss Fairlie under my arm, and we all sallied down to Hoffman's, where Ogilvie was expected to come. He came after a while in the dress of Oratory, to wit, black velvet edged with red, and a cloak of the same lined with Scarlet velvet.

After supper, finding his head a little too warm, the queer Caitiff, without any ceremony pulled off his wig in the face of the company, and began to rub his half bald pate most vociferously. I never in my life was much more astounded, and could not help blessing my stars that I was 'no orator, as Brutus is'—" (Paulding to Peter Kemble, Jr., Jan 8, 1809; letter owned by William Kemble, Bedford Hills, New York). Southerners like William C. Rives and Francis W. Gilmer were students of Ogilvie's. See Richard Beale Davis, "James Ogilvie, An Early American Teacher of Rhetoric," *Quarterly Journal of Speech* 28 (October, 1942), 282–97; Richard Beale Davis, *Intellectual Life in Jefferson's Virginia, 1790–1830* (Chapel Hill, 1964), pp. 40–42, 368–70.

10. Verplanck spoke to the Washington Benevolent Society on July 4, after their patriotic parade. See July, *Verplanck*, pp. 21–23.

11. Peter Irving, in England attending to the family business.

12. WI had apparently checked at two booksellers: M. & Wm. Ward, 4 City Hotel; and S. Gould, on the corner of Broad and Wall. See *Longworth's City Directory for 1809*, pp. 372, 190.

13. Sir George Cooke, *Rules, Orders, and Notices, in the Court of Common Pleas. . . .* This suggests that Van Ness was studying law or wanted the book for reference.

14. William Coleman (1766–1829), editor of the New York *Evening Post.*

15. James Cheetham (1772–1810), volatile editor of the *American Citizen,* who supported Republican policies.

16. The New York *Public Advertiser* was a daily newspaper published from 1807 to 1813.

17. Presumably allusions to some of WI's acquaintances at Kinderhook. Several families named Dingman lived in the area at this time.

67. *To Mrs. Josiah Ogden Hoffman*

[June? 1809]

My good friend,

I cannot tell you how much I feel obliged to you for your letters. There is always a kindness & affection in them which give a pleasure superior to any that the ⟨ha⟩ finest flushes of imagination or the happiest sallies of wit could ever impart. ⟨My stay↑will↓ here must soon⟩ I must soon leave this[1] & return once more to the City. ⟨but not through any satiety of the Country. It seems as if I could [*unrecovered*]⟩ but it will be necessity not inclination that will lead me. I feel so contented here, so quiet. Life seems to flow on so smoothly in the country—without even a ripple to disturb the current, that I could almost float with the stream and glide insensibly through existence. I verily believe those who live in retirement are unconscious of half the painful passions that the best of us who mingle with society are subject to—I am sure that when I am quietly settled in the country I forget half of my vexatious feelings. all those little exacerbations of the temper & repinings of the heart that are irresistibly produced by the ⟨?joinings?⟩ and crossings & jostlings of the world, are here unknown and a man seems to ⟨ju⟩ journey on thro life, in better humour with himself & in better humour with all around him.[2]

MANUSCRIPT: NYPL. PUBLISHED: PMI, I, 228–29 (in part).

This letter to Mrs. J. O. Hoffman is found in a rough draft in pencil in a MS notebook, *Notes for Knickerbocker 1807–1808.* PMI (I, 228) suggests that it was written after Mrs. Hoffman's letter of May 29, 1809.

1. The Van Ness home at Kinderhook.
2. The draft ends at this point.

68. *To Rebecca Gratz*

New York July 4th. 1809

My good friend,

The situation of poor little Eliza[1] ⟨is⟩so completely engrosses Mrs Hoffmans attentions & agitates her feelings that she is unable to answer a letter just received from you, and at her request I scrawl you a few hasty lines.

Yesterday afternoon the appearances were very favourable, and through the evening we entertained great hopes, but she has passed a bad night, and has been in constant fits this morning. She now lays in a state the most distressing—and scarce a hope remains of her recovery unless her spasms subside she cannot exist many hours. The rest of the family are well—Ann is still at Coldenham; & is expected in town the latter end of the week—

Present my warmest remembrances to all your family & believe me—
in great haste—/Your sincere friend
Washington Irving

ADDRESSED: Miss Rebecca Gratz / Philadelphia. POSTMARKED: NEW YORK / JUL / 4 DOCKETED: W Irving / July 4th. 1809
MANUSCRIPT: Va.—Barrett.

1. Possibly Eliza Fenno, Mrs. J. O. Hoffman's sister.

69. *To Peter Irving*

[New York, late summer, 1809]

* * * I am really at a loss what to write to you about. I have been so little abroad in the world since my return from Van Ness's that I know nothing how matters are going on. * * * My health has been feeble and my spirits depressed, so that I have found company very irksome, and have shunned it almost entirely. I propose setting out on an expedition to Canada with Brevoort on Saturday next, to be absent sixteen days.[1] There is a steamboat on the lake[2] which makes the journey

sure and pleasant. I trust the jaunt will perfectly renovate me. On my return I shall go to Mr. Hoffman's retreat at Hellgate,[3] and prepare *esta obra*[4] for a launch. * * *

We are all well. Irving and Smith[5] are highly satisfied with your assiduity. I refer you to Hal and Sally[6] for family particulars.

PUBLISHED: PMI, I, 232.

1. No details of this trip seem to be preserved.
2. Lake Champlain, on the route to Canada.
3. WI spent most of July and August at Ravenswood, J. O. Hoffman's farm near Hellgate.
4. This phrase (Spanish for "that work") was used by the Irving brothers to refer to *Knickerbocker's History*. See Peter Irving to WI, April 30, 1808, quoted in PMI, I, 214.
5. William Irving, Sr. and William Irving, Jr. founded the commission firm of Irving & Smith in 1803, with a store at 162 Pearl Street, and later at 145 Pearl Street. See Scoville, *Old Merchants of NYC*, II, 76, 79–80. Peter Irving was the English agent for the firm.
6. Mr. and Mrs. Henry Van Wart were about to depart for England. For a time Van Wart had worked for Irving and Smith. See PMI, I, 233.

70. *To Henry Brevoort*

Philadelphia Oct 23d 1809

My dear Brevoort,

I am so pressed for time that I have not been able to write to any of my friends in N York. I wish you would tell Mrs Hoffman—James & Peter that I shall write to each of them as soon as I can find leisure, and do let me know how you are all coming on and what you are doing in N York. Is the little orator[1] still faithful to his post? I am peculiarly anxious that he should persevere & succeed, and then he & his delectable Rib[2] might love or hate one another as much as they pleased for aught I'd care—I only chuckle to myself to think how the little man would be stumped, if he offerd to read one of his dull pieces of wit, or sport one of his Johnsonian contradictions after matrimony.

I have been delayed in putting my work[3] to press by some minute & curious facts which I found in a Mss in the Philad Library[4] & which has obliged me to make alterations in the first vol. but tomorrow I begin—by God.

I ⟨?heart?⟩ wish you would immediately forward me the inscription on old P. Stuyvesants Tomb stone[5]—and get Jim as well as yourself to ⟨?wr?⟩ prepare some squibs &c to attract attention to the work when it comes out.[6]

I am my good fellow/yours ever
W I.

P. S Ann & Charles are as loving and happy as two little robins in one nest.

ADDRESSED: Mr Henry Brevoort Junr. / at Mr John Hyslops / John Street / N York. POSTMARKED: PHI / 23 / OC
MANUSCRIPT: NYPL—Seligman Collection.

1. Gulian Verplanck had attracted attention by his oratory earlier in the year. See WI's letter to William P. Van Ness on June 24, 1809, where Verplanck's speechmaking is mentioned.

2. A reference to Eliza Fenno, whom Verplanck was courting at this time. They were married on October 2, 1811. See Robert W. July, *The Essential New Yorker: Gulian Crommelin Verplanck* (Durham, 1951), p. 28.

3. *Knickerbocker's History of New York*. The words "my work" have been underscored by another hand.

4. Probably an extract of David Pieterszoon De Vries's *Korte Historiael ende Journael aenteyckeninge van verscheyden Voyagiens in de vier deelen des Wereldts Ronde . . .* (Alckmaer, 1655), made by Du Simitière and placed in the Philadelphia Library Company after his death. WI in his footnotes to *Knickerbocker's History* refers to De Vries's "Reyze naer Nieuw Nederlandt onder het yaer 1640," which may be the title of the section WI drew upon. Since De Vries was available in the United States only in this manuscript version in 1809, WI presumably used him to embellish his account at the last minute and acknowledged his indebtedness in footnotes. See *Knickerbocker's History*, XXVI–XXVII, 195 n., 196 n.

5. WI alludes to the vault which is mentioned in the inscription on Stuyvesant's tombstone. See *Knickerbocker's History*, p. 453.

6. Brevoort and Paulding obliged by inserting notices concerning Diedrich Knickerbocker in the NYEP on October 26 and November 6, and, 16, 1809, before the appearance of the book on December 6, 1809. WI included these "squibs" in his 1848 revision of the work. See STW, I, 111–112, 409, n. 27.

71. To John Howard Payne

[October? 1809?]

My dear Payne,

I enclose you a few letters to some of my friends in philadelphia & Baltimore—they are chiefly literary gentlemen, for I did not make sufficient intimacy with any others, while on there, or rather have not kept up one since my return—to warrant my giving letters—These will procure you I trust valuable acquaintances, and if Gov Crawford[1] is in Phil. his lady & daughter will have it in their power to exert that friendship they have so often expressed for you—Write to me occasionally and do not wait for replies for I am a very irregular correspondent. If you wish to ⟨[unrecovered]⟩ have my opinion about any characters, write any inquiries you may chuse to make & I will answer them—with this proviso—that you never shew such letters to a soul.

With the best wishes for your success/I am yours sincerely
W I.

ADDRESSED: Mr John H Payne   DOCKETED: Washington Irving / on leaving New
    York / [In another hand]: 1809?
MANUSCRIPT: Columbia.

John Howard Payne (1791–1852), a precocious boy who edited the *Thespian
Mirror* in 1805–1806, made his debut as an actor in New York on February 24,
1809. During WI's residence abroad, he and Payne renewed their friendship in
England and France, with WI collaborating on some of his plays. This letter deals
with Payne's acting tour to Baltimore. See WI's letter of November 2, 1809, for
other details.

    1. Not identified. No state governor at this time seems appropriate.

72. *To John Howard Payne*

Philadelphia. Nov. 2d 1809.

My dear Payne,
    I received some few days since your letter from Baltimore, which was
forwarded to me from New York, and should have answered it before,
had not my time been completely occupied by different engagements.
I am very much gratified to hear through various channels, of your
success at Baltimore[1]—and I hope your Benefit has been a good one.[2]
I am sorry to find, however, that you are still persecuted by ⟨you⟩ newspaper friends; for I read a critique in a Baltimore paper on your
performance, that made my blood run cold.[3] The honest man absolutely
seemed to foam at the mouth with a delirium of rapture, and was in
danger of falling into a paroxysm of stark, staring nonsense. Now
though I trust you have too much good sense to be flattered and rendered
self satisfied, by these agonies & extasies of delight, yet the mischief is
that they disgust the cooler part of the community, and dispose them
to find fault where they otherwise would praise—and they likewise
raise expectations in the minds of people, who are not up to the cant &
fustian of news paper criticism, which it would be impossible for the
most consummate actor to satisfy.
    And now I am going to give you a piece of advice which I suspect
you wont much relish, and if you dont relish it I feel tolerably certain
you wont follow it—which is, to leave Baltimore as soon as possible. I
know you are very much caressed there & are surrounded by *friends,*
⟨an⟩ but that is one reason why you should decamp—You cannot excite
more attention—You cannot gain greater notoriety & applause; but you
may cease to be a novelty—curiosity may become satisfied—and the
public becoming familiar with you in private as well as in public, ⟨may⟩
will not have the same eagerness to see you perform, ⟨at⟩ on future
occasions. Theres very little flattery in this to be sure, but you will find
it invariably the truth—nor need a man be vexed with the world, nor

humbled in his own opinion when he perceives it. Were the Angel Gabriel to come down from heaven (and I speak with all reverence) and sojourn a year or two upon earth—though the multitude might all throng & stare at first, to behold an angel, yet in a little while he might walk the streets and excite no more attention or wonderment than Maria Moore[4]—Miss Keene or Susan Farmar.[5]

Your great object should be to visit different places—stay a short time at each, so as to excite without allaying curiosity and thus you may ⟨soon⟩ move in an extensive and agreeable orbit that shall embrace the chief Cities in the union. Every time you visit one, as the inhabitants know your stay will be short, they will be curious to see you, and you may fill your pockets from their Curiosity. Do you reccollect the comet that made its appearance about two years ago?[6] how much we stared at it the first week—how little the second? had it remained a third I warrant we would not have thought a whit more of it, than of the other honest, steady, little stars which we see every night in the year.

And now John let me conclude with one more short piece of advice —for I begin to draw near the hour of breakfast[7] and am mortal hungry —take care of the money you make[8] and dont squander it away idly, like a mere boy. Your present[9] sunshine may be but short, yet in that time, with assiduity & good management, you may lay up a little competence that shall ⟨make you independent of t⟩ place you out of the reach of bad weather all the rest of your life—should you do so, I shall think your theatrical enterprize a very well advised project—should you not—I shall consider it one of the most unfortunate ones that could ever have entered into your head.

I shall remain here about two weeks longer, and hope to see you before I return—in the mean ⟨time⟩ while take care of yourself and play any thing but the idler, the spendthrift & the little great man—I hope you are superior to all of these

Your friend.
Washington Irving.

ADDRESSED: Mr John H Payne / Care of Jonathan Meredith Esq. / Baltimore.
POSTMARKED: PHI 2 NO   DOCKETED: [Philadelph]ia [*MS torn*] Nov 2. 1809 / Washington Irving
MANUSCRIPT: Columbia.

1. After making his first appearance on the New York stage on February 24, 1809, Payne acted in Boston, Providence, and New York again before going to Baltimore in October, 1809. See Gabriel Harrison, *John Howard Payne,* ... *His Life and Writings* (Philadelphia, 1885), pp. 37–41.

2. William B. Wood tells of Payne's reception in Baltimore: "On my return to the United States, in October, 1809, I found Master Payne in the full tide of popular favor at Baltimore, where the enthusiasm for his acting was perhaps more intense than in any other city. I speak particularly of his first engagement, for such

a furor could not be expected to last. He appeared as Young Norval, Hamlet, Romeo, Tancred, Octavian, Frederic, Rolla, Achmet, and Zaphna, to large and brilliant audiences. His benefit proved a crowning triumph. On this memorable night, the receipts touched the extraordinary amount of $1160. It must here be remarked, that the house when filled at other times to its utmost capacity, had never yet produced $800. Where then, it may be asked, did we contrive to stow away $1160? This is the answer. Great numbers of tickets were paid for at high prices, and without intention of being used. One gentleman I know gave his check of $50 for a single ticket, besides paying liberally for the box occupied by his family. Many others paid sums varying from five to twenty dollars for single tickets, and the large gallery was filled with box tickets, failing to obtain seats below" (William B. Wood, *Personal Recollections of the Stage* [Philadelphia, 1855], pp. 127–28).

3. WI probably alludes to notices appearing in the Baltimore *Federal Republican and Commercial Gazette* for October 20 and 23, 1809. In the earlier story is a quotation from a Boston paper praising Payne as "a rare instance of intellectual precocity." The article concludes by printing a half column of verse written by Robert Treat Paine, Jr. which was read at John Howard Payne's first appearance as Young Norval in Boston. In a full column notice on October 23 the *Federal Republican and Commercial Gazette* speaks of Payne's "fascinating grace, his polished style, his harmonious voice, and the admirable tragick powers of his mind." Payne's "acting has never been surpassed on the American boards. . . . The style was entirely new, original, and peculiar to *our Roscius.* Genius like his disdains to imitate, and nature has been his only tutor." The review concludes with "Our Roscius never strikes the air with an empty, unmeaning, dying sound. His utterance is melodious, strong and critically exact. . . . Can we be mistaken, when we say the bosom of master Payne is the asylum of every noble and refined passion—that he displays in public, and in private, all the finer and polished feelings of the heart?" Before Payne appeared as Young Norval in John Home's *Douglas; Or, The Noble Shepherd* on October 20, *The Federal Gazette and Baltimore Daily Advertiser* of that date observed: ". . . of Master Paine as an individual, no encomium can be considered as squandered praise; and if worth, talents, and eru[d]ition, have weight to entitle an individual to an impartial and widely extended notice of professional exertion, it will not be adjudged favoritism to Master Paine. or enthusiasm in his friends, to say, that the intelligence of his opinions, the sweetness of his discourse, as well as his experience in matters of daily concern, the true modesty of his deportment, and his filial piety, forbid any fear, that a mere impulse of character, aided by artificial heat, has created a precocity of intellect, by which his companions have been fascinated, and his friends devoted to him. Such a youth has too just claims upon his fellow-citizens, to be neglected."

4. Maria Moore is mentioned in WI's letter to Henry Brevoort, June 11, 1808.

5. Susan Farmar is probably the daughter of Thomas Farmar of 8 Greenwich Street. See *Longworth's Directory* for 1809, p. 172.

6. The *Annual Register* for 1807 (p. 850) reports the appearance of a comet in Roxburghshire on October 12, 1807, but no published notice of it has been found in American newspapers or journals.

7. The page is torn, with the removal of the seal, but the word "breakfast" can be identified from a scrap of writing now pasted in the margin of the first page of the letter.

8. The page is torn. See note 7.

9. The page is torn. See note 7.

73. To William Coleman

[November 6, 1809]

To the Editor of the Evening Post:

Sir,

Having read in your paper of the 26th Oct. last[1] a paragraph respecting an old gentleman by the name of *Knickerbocker*, who was missing from his lodgings; if it would be any relief to his friends, or furnish them with any clue to discover where he is, you may inform them, that a person answering the description given was seen by the passengers of the Albany Stage early in the morning, about four or five weeks since, resting himself by the side of the road a little above Kingsbridge—He had in his hands a small bundle tied in a red bandana handkerchief; he appeared to be travelling northward, and was very much fatigued and exhausted.

Nov. 6, 1809.[2]

A TRAVELLER.

PUBLISHED: NYEP, November 6, 1809; PMI, I, 234–35; *Diedrich Knickerbocker's A History of New York,* ed. Stanley Williams and Tremaine McDowell (New York, 1927), p. xxv.

Since WI wrote to John Howard Payne from Philadelphia on November 2, 1809, it is unlikely that he was in New York on November 6. Probably the letter was written by James Kirke Paulding or Henry Brevoort, who were parties to the Knickerbocker hoax. The letter is included for the light it throws on WI's publicizing of the book.

1. On October 26 and the two succeeding days the following notice appeared in the NYEP:

DISTRESSING.

Left his lodgings some time since, and has not since been heard of, a small elderly gentleman, dressed in an old black coat and cocked hat, by the name of KNICKER-BOCKER. As there are some reasons for believing he is not entirely in his right mind, and as great anxiety is entertained about him, any information concerning him left either at the Columbian Hotel, Mulberry street, or at the Office of this paper will be thankfully received.

P. S. Printers of Newspapers would be aiding the cause of humanity, in giving an insertion to the above.

Oct. 26   3 t

2. Ten days later, on November 16, the following letter was printed in the NYEP:

To the Editor of the Evening Post

Sir,

You have been good enough to publish in your paper a paragraph about Mr. *Diedrich Knickerbocker,* who was missing so strangely from his lod[g]ings some time since. Nothing satisfactory has been heard of the old gentleman since; but a *very curious kind of a written book* has been found in his room in his own hand writing.—Now I wish you to notice him, if he is still alive, that if he does not return and pay off his bill for boarding and lodging, I shall have to dispose of his Book to satisfy me for the same.

I am sir, your humble servant,

SETH HANDASIDE

Landlord of the Independent Columbian Hotel Mulberry-street.

The New York directory for 1809 does not list either Seth Handaside or the Independent Columbian Hotel. Knowledgeable New Yorkers must have sensed that there was something unusual connected with Diedrich Knickerbocker and thus were eager to satisfy their curiosity when his *History of New York* appeared on December 6, 1809.

74. To William P. Van Ness

New York, Dec. 18, 1809.

My dear Sir:

A few days since, on returning from a long visit to Philadelphia, I found a letter from you[1] which had lain some time at my office. I should have answered it before, but the crowd of engagements that harass a man when he first arrives at home, prevented me from putting pen to paper. As to your portentous dream, which justly occasioned such anxious forebodings, I assure you it was better founded than these sage omens generally are: the only defect was, that you dreamed too late, and I was not absolutely drowned. The truth of the matter is, that I was upset in a small sail-boat two or three months ago, in the broad bay just above Corlaer's Hook; and after clinging to the boat about a quarter of an hour up to my chin in water, I was kindly picked up by a little fishing-skiff.[2] This is the *real* foundation of your dream; and henceforth you may consider yourself a match for the immortal Bunyan himself, in the art of dreaming.

"The old Governors" are at length ushered into the world;[3] and I am now an idle man: so if you have any disposition to royster a little, you will find me completely at your service, when you pay your promised visit to this city. You must come down completely the gentleman of leisure: leave your farm and its cares behind you: put your household under the ghostly superintendence of that evangelical sinner Jesse Marvin;[4] and determine to unbend and become one of us boys: and then I'll insure you some pleasant relaxation.

Our Theatre will remain open for some time yet,[5] and as our company[6] is very good at present, you will find it an amusing resort. We have two excellent new actors, Mr Simpson and Mrs. Mason,[7] who were sent out by the Doctor,[8] and have completely retrieved the credit of the Theatre.

How does my friend Partridge[9] and his Academy? Do the flesh and the spirit still keep up their hostilities within him? I long once more to visit your little empire: and am only deterred by the austerity of old Winter from gratifying my inclinations. But next year, when the country is once more in full dress, I shall certainly indulge in a few more rambles about the red lane.

Remember me with great regard and respect to Mrs. Van Ness; and let my friend Jesse know that I still recollect him with great consideration. I shall leave all discussion of domestic and literary[10] topics until I see you, which I hope will be in a few days. Recollect Christmas should always be spent in the city.

Ever yours,
Washington Irving.

W. P. Van Ness, Esq./Kinderhook, New-York.

PUBLISHED: *Knickerbocker Magazine* 55 (April, 1860), 439–40; and *The Athenaeum*, no. 3212 (May 18, 1889), 632.

The text of this letter is based on a printed version in *Knickerbocker Magazine*. Although the punctuation varies somewhat from WI's usual style and from that in the *Athenaeum* text, it is retained here in the absence of the manuscript of the letter. A statement accompanying the *Athenaeum* text indicates that the original letter was in the collection of Frederick McGuire of Washington at that time, but the manuscript has not been located.

1. This letter has not been located.

2. This incident occurred while WI was staying at J. O. Hoffman's summer place near Hellgate. The sailboat, called the *Tinker*, belonged to Henry Brevoort. See PMI, I, 233.

3. A reference to the publication of *Knickerbocker's History of New York* on December 6, 1809.

4. A misreading of "Merwin." See WI to Henry Brevoort, May 11, 1809, note 2.

5. The Park Theater opened the season on September 6, 1809, and closed on January 16, 1810, with a reopening on February 22, 1810. See Odell, *NY Stage*, II, 327, 336.

6. The acting company at the Park Theater for this season included Mr. and Mrs. William Twaits, Mr. and Mrs. Charles Young, Mr. and Mrs. David Poe, and Mrs. Oldmixon. See Odell, *NY Stage*, II, 327–28.

7. Edmund Simpson (1784–1848) first appeared at the Park Theater on October 25 as Harry Dornton in Thomas Holcroft's *The Road to Ruin*. Two days earlier Mrs. Mason (1780–1835) had made her American debut inauspiciously as Mrs. Beverley in *The Gamester* by James Shirley. See Odell, *NY Stage*, II, 330–32; Ireland, *New York Stage*, I, 261–63.

8. WI is probably alluding to the efforts of his brother Peter, often called "the Doctor," who was now living in England. Since Peter Irving had long had an interest in drama and particularly in the fortunes of the Park Theater, he probably seized the opportunity to improve the quality of acting there by persuading Mrs. Mason and Mr. Simpson to desert the boards in Dublin and Edinburgh for those in New York.

9. Partridge was apparently one of the teachers at Kinderhook.

10. The *Athenaeum* version has "other" instead of "literary."

75. *To Mrs. Josiah Ogden Hoffman*

Johnstown, Feb. 12, 1810.

My dear Friend:

I wrote Mr. Hoffman a hasty letter from Albany,[1] uncertain whether it would reach New York before his departure, and should have written him again, but that I concluded from what he told me before I left the city, that he would start for Albany[2] on Saturday last.[3] His presence has been anxiously looked for at Albany, and I am in hopes he will arrive there either this evening or to-morrow. I stayed three days there, and then left it for Johnstown; though I could have passed several days there with much satisfaction, in attending the profound discussions of the Senate and Assembly; and the movements of the crowd of office-hunters, who, like a cloud of locusts, have descended upon the city to devour every plant and herb, and every "green thing." The anxiety I felt, however, to see my sister induced me to hasten my departure, and one or two other considerations of trifling moment, concurred in urging me on. * * *

Your city is no doubt waiting with great solicitude to hear of the proceedings of the Council of Appointment.[4] The members have a difficult task allotted them, and one of great responsibility. It is impossible they should avoid disappointing many, and displeasing more, but the peculiar circumstances in which they are placed entitle them to every indulgence. I wish Mr. H. had started when I did; his presence would, I think, have been of infinite service.

I can give you nothing that will either interest you or yield you a moment's amusement. I have witnessed nothing since my departure but political wrangling and intriguing,[5] and this is unimportant to you; and my mind has been too much occupied by worldly cares and anxieties to be sufficiently at ease to write any thing worthy perusal. Add to this, I have been sick either from a cold, or the intolerable atmosphere of rooms heated by stoves, and have been disgusted by the servility, and duplicity, and rascality I have witnessed among the swarm of scrub politicians who crawl about the great metropolis of our State, like so many vermin about the head of the body politic; excuse the grossness of this figure, I entreat you.

I was much interested and pleased, while at Albany, with Dickinson,[6] a young miniature painter, who has resided there for some time past. He is an artist of highly promising talents, and of most amiable demeanor and engaging manners. I have endeavored to persuade him to leave this city of darkness and dulness and come to New York, and am strongly in hopes he will soon do so. He is not a mere mechanic in his art, but paints from his imagination. He has lately executed a figure of Hope,[7] which does great credit to his invention and execution, and bespeaks a most delicate and classic taste. He has promised to let me have it for a while to show it in New York. How I would glory in being a man of opulence, to take such young artists by the hand, and cherish their budding genius! A few acts of munificence of the kind done in a generous and liberal manner by some of our wealthy nabobs, would, I am satisfied, be more pleasing in the sight of Heaven, and more to the glory and advantage of their country, than building a dozen shingle church steeples, or buying a thousand venal votes at an election. * * *

I have just written to Peter Kemble, and strangely forgot to tell him (being a brother sportsman) that I had just returned from a couple of hours' bushbeating, having killed a brace of partridges and a black squirrel! Give my love to all, and believe me ever affectionately,

Your friend,
W. I.

PUBLISHED: PMI, I, 243–45.

1. This letter has not been located. WI was in Albany to seek appointment as a clerk in one of the courts of New York. Daniel Paris, WI's brother-in-law, who was on the Council of Appointments for New York, tried to promote his interest, but he was unsuccessful. See PMI, I, 242.

2. Hoffman, as recorder of the city of New York, had to make frequent trips to Albany. He, too, was ready to support WI's candidacy for a clerkship.

3. February 10.

4. The Council of Appointments was empowered by the state constitution of 1777 to make appointments to state positions.

5. WI alludes to the squabbling between the supporters of De Witt Clinton and members of Tammany Hall.

6. Anson Dickinson (1779–1852), a portrait painter and miniaturist, who was widely acclaimed for his skillful use of color. See William Dunlap, *The History of the Rise and Progress of the Arts of Design in the United States* (New York, 1965), II, 369–70.

7. Details concerning this work are lacking. One study of Dickinson's painting discusses *Hope* only in reference to WI's allusion to it in this letter. See Mary Helen Kidder, ed., *List of Miniatures Painted by Anson Dickinson, 1803–1851* (Hartford, 1937), pp. vii, ix.

76. *To Mrs. Josiah Ogden Hoffman*

Albany, Feb. 26, 1810.

My dear Friend:

I have just left Mr. Hoffman, who is suffering under a severe attack of the sick headache, and groaning in his bed most piteously. Since last I wrote you, I have relinquished all cares and thoughts about an appointment,[1] and am now merely remaining in Albany to witness the interesting scenes of intrigue and iniquity that are passing under my eye—to inform myself of the manner of transacting legislative business, with which I was before but little acquainted—to make myself acquainted with the great and little men of the State whom I find collected here, and lastly to enjoy the amusements and society of this great metropolis. I think I have most bountiful variety of occupation. You will smile, perhaps, when I tell you, that in spite of all my former prejudices and prepossessions, I like this queer little old-fashioned place more and more, the longer I remain in it.[2] I have somehow or another formed acquaintance with some of the good people, and several of the little Yffrouws, and have even made my way and intrenched myself strongly in the parlors of several genuine Dutch families, who had declared utter hostility to me. Several good old ladies, who had almost condemned my book to the flames, have taken me into high favor, and I have even had the hardihood to invade the territories of Mynheer Hans _____, and lay siege to his beauteous daughter, albeit that the high blood of all the burghers of the _____ family was boiling against me, and threatening me with annihilation.

So passes away the time. I shall remain here some days longer, and then go to Kinderhook. What time I shall return to New York I cannot tell. I have now no prospect ahead, nor scheme, nor air castle to engage my mind withal; so that it matters but little where I am, and perhaps I cannot be more agreeably or profitably employed than in Van Ness's library. I shall return to New York poorer than I set out, both in pocket and hopes, but rich in a great store of valuable and pleasing knowledge which I have acquired of the wickedness of my fellow-creatures. That, I believe, is the only kind of wealth I am doomed to acquire in the world, but it is a kind of which I am but little covetous. * * *

PUBLISHED: PMI, I, 245–46.

1. For other details about WI's aspirations to appointive office, see his letter of February 12, 1810.

2. WI is referring to his comic and often unflattering treatment of the Dutch in *Knickerbocker's History*.

77. *To Josiah Ogden Hoffman*

Philadelphia, June 5, 1810.

Dear Sir:

We[1] arrived safe in Philadelphia this morning, between eight and nine o'clock, and took the city by surprise, the inhabitants not having expected us until evening. All this is in consequence of my unparalleled generalship, which already begins to be talked of with great admiration throughout the country. I took a light coachee from Brighton to Brunswick[2] where we breakfasted, and finding it impossible to procure a four-horse carriage there, I changed carriage and horses and pushed on to Trenton,[3] where, while the Philistines were dining, I engaged a fresh carriage and horses for Philadelphia, and made out to reach Homesburgh[4] (about ten miles from Philadelphia) between seven and eight in the evening. I was anxious to get as far as possible, lest the weather might change or the children get unwell. The journey has been infinitely more comfortable and pleasant than I had anticipated. Yesterday was a fine day for travelling, and I never knew children travel so well. Charles has behaved like a very good boy, and George is one of the sprightliest little travellers I ever knew; he has furnished amusement during the whole ride, and what is still better, has gained unto himself a very rare and curious stock of knowledge; for besides the unknown tongue in which he usually converses, and which none but Mammy Caty[5] (who you know is at least one-half witch) can understand, he has picked up a considerable smattering of high Dutch since he entered the State of Pennsylvania, so that I regretted exceedingly, and that more than once during my travels, that the immortal Psalmanazar[6] was not present to discourse with him.

Little Julia has had an astonishing variety of complaints since our leaving New York, has had two doctors to attend her, has taken three score and ten doses of medicine, not to mention aniseed tea and peppermint cordial, and what is passing strange, is still alive, fat and hearty; a case only to be paralleled by that of the famous Spinster of Ratcliff Highway, who was cured of nineteen diseases in a fortnight, and every one of them mortal!

You cannot conceive what speculation our appearance made among the yeomanry of Jersey and Pennsylvania. Many of the excellent old Dutch farmers mistook us for a family of Yankee squatters, and were terribly alarmed, and the little community of Bustletown (who are very apt to be thrown into a panic) were in utter dismay at our approach, insomuch that when we entered one end of the town, I saw several old women in Pompadour and Birdseye gowns, with bandboxes under their arms, making their escape out of the other. However, I contrived to pacify them by letting them know it was the family of the Recorder of New York,[7] who, being an orthodox Bible man, always travelled into foreign lands, as did the Patriarchs of yore—that is to say, with his wife and his sons, and his daughters, his men-servants and his maid servants, and his cattle and the stranger that is within his gates, and every thing that is his, whereat they were exceeding glad and glorified God.[8]

We are all comfortably situated at Ann's,[9] who lives in a little palace. Mary[10] is much improved in her looks, and appears to be a great favorite with the family. Ann has taken her under her care, and is making her a hard student. She has already read seven pages in Rollin,[11] and the whole history of Camilla and Cecilia,[12] not to mention a considerable attack which she has made upon "the Castle of Inchvalley; a tale, alas, too true!"[13]

In the hurry of my writing the above (for I write as fast as we travelled) I forgot to mention to you that having safely arrived within the suburbs of Philadelphia, the old carriage in which we came from Trenton sank beneath its burden and gave up the ghost!

In other words, we broke down just after entering the city; but as it was merely a spring had given way, the whole party, man, woman, and child, were dug out of the ruins without any other mishap than that of overturning the medicine chest, and spilling fifteen phials, which were as full of plagues as those mentioned in the Revelations. I immediately perceived a change in little Julia for the better, and I make bold to conjecture that had a dozen more been demolished, she would have been the heartiest child in Philadelphia at this present writing. You cannot imagine the astonishment of all Philadelphia at seeing so many living beings extracted out of one little carriage.

Farewell, my good Sir. Remember me to the remnants and rags of your household that remain behind. Keep all marauders from breaking into my room and disturbing the pictures of my venerable ancestors, and believe me

Ever your friend,
W. I.

PUBLISHED: PMI, I, 248–51.

1. WI accompanied Mrs. J. O. Hoffman and her three young children—Charles Fenno, George Edward (1808–1884), and Julia (1810–1861).
2. Brighton, a town 53 miles north of Trenton, New Jersey.
3. A distance of about 26 miles.
4. A distance of about 28 miles from Trenton.
5. Presumably the nurse of the Hoffman children.
6. Psalmanazar (1679–1763) published the catechism in Formosan, a language which he invented.
7. J. O. Hoffman's official position.

8. Probably WI's adaptation of the phraseology of the Fourth Commandment. See Exod. 20:10 and Deut. 5:14.

9. Ann Hoffman. See WI's letter to her, August 10, 1807.

10. Mary (1796–1818), another daughter by Hoffman's first marriage, later married Philip Rhinelander.

11. Charles Rollin, *Histoire romaine depuis la fondation de Rome jusqu'à la bataille d'Actium* (Paris, 1748–1754).

12. Probably a reference to Fanny Burney's popular novels, *Cecilia, or Memoirs of an Heiress* (1782) and *Camilla, or a Picture of Youth* (1796).

13. *The Castle of Inchvalley* is a gothic novel by Stephen Cullen, published in three volumes in 1796. See Montague Summers, *A Gothic Bibliography* (New York, 1964), p. 263.

78. *To Mrs. Josiah Ogden Hoffman*

New York, June 23, 1810.

My dear Friend:

I have several times sat down and begun an answer to your letter, but as often have been interrupted, for the cottage[1] has been quite a scene of gaiety for these few days past. Brevoort has been there since the day before yesterday with his famous ship the Tinker, which has been much altered and reformed, so as to behave like a very steady, sober, upright little ship. We took the girls over to Hamilton's monument[2] yesterday, and made a very prosperous and delightful voyage.

I am rejoiced that Mr. Hoffman is about to bring you home with all your household. I long to see my little playmate, George, and once more to have my little god-daughter under my eye, for I am extremely apprehensive lest she should contract bad habits in these outlandish places. Charles is very correct in his opinion that you have rather too many babies with you, and I think when next you go abroad, you will do well to consult a little with him. * * * * *

As Mr. Hoffman will be the bearer of this letter, it would be totally superfluous for me to give you any particulars of domestic news, as he will be able to relate you the whole history of the cottage and its inhabitants at full length. I am happy, however, to inform you that I have obtained from Mr. Wilkes[3] the genuine and original name of the place, which is Rockdale cottage, which I am determined henceforth to call it, in solemn defiance of all the old gentlemen in the country, though ———— and ————[4] should be at the head of them. And what is better, I have found reason on my side, for as to calling it *Rose* cottage, the roses are almost gone already, whereas, an' it please God, we shall have rocks and dales enough all the year round, unless I am very much mistaken.

Greet Ann for me "by the name of most kind Hostess."[5] Tell Charles I will be able to write to him about the beginning of the week, as Mr. Campbell[6] is to spend part of to-morrow with me. * * *

PUBLISHED: PMI, I, 251–52.

1. Later in the letter WI calls it Rockdale. PMI suggests that the cottage was located along the east bank of the Hudson River on the upper part of Manhattan Island. See PMI, I, 251.

2. In 1806 the St. Andrews Society erected a monument to the memory of Alexander Hamilton on the duelling ground at Weehawken, New Jersey, where he was killed by Aaron Burr. According to a contemporaneous description, the monument "was an obelisk on a pedestal four feet square and was composed of four slabs of white marble, eight feet in length, surmounted by a flaming urn" (I. N. Phelps Stokes, *The Iconography of Manhattan Island* [New York, 1967], III, 877).

3. Probably John De Ponthieu Wilkes, a successful New York business man who had married Mary Seton.

4. These omissions were made by PMI.

5. *Macbeth*, II, i, 16.

6. Archibald Campbell, brother of Thomas Campbell, who supplied WI with details about the poet which were incorporated into a biographical sketch included with "*The Poetical Works of Thomas Campbell. Including several pieces from the original manuscript, never before published in this country. To which is prefixed a biographical sketch of the author, by a gentleman of New York.* Printed for Philip H. Nicklin & Co., Baltimore. Also for D. W. Farrand and Green, Albany; D. Mallory and Co., Boston; Lyman and Hall, Portland; and E. Earle, Philadelphia. Fry and Kammerer, Printers, 1810." Charles I. Nicholas (husband of Ann Hoffman) and his partner in the Philadelphia bookselling trade agreed to underwrite publication if WI contributed a new biographical sketch of Campbell. See PMI, I, 253.

79.   To Henry Brevoort

New York, Sept. 22d. 1810.

My dear fellow,

I engaged to write you a letter to Albany, and this is ⟨just⟩ scribbled in haste to keep my promise & *save my supper*. I had hoped before this to have had you in New York, but a letter I have just seen from you to Hyslop[1] informs me that you will not be here until some time next week.

We have received news that poor L'Herbert[2] is taken and carried into Plymouth—this I am affraid will knock up your french speculation.[3] I see by this mornings Papers that honest Sindbad[4] has arrived safe in port—I mean to visit him tomorrow if I am in town. I am so much pressed for time that I cannot enter into a narrative of all that has come to pass among our ⟨little⟩ friends since your departure, though I believe the catalogue of events would by no means be voluminous.

I passed eight or ten days delightfully at the Captain's Castle in the

Highlands.[5] He lives in a royal Bachelor style and is a true Lad of Kilkenny.

Charles & Ann are still here, but talk of leaving us tomorrow[.] ⟨We⟩ Our Theatre has opened with as Sorry a show of cattle as you could imagine. we have however,[6] had Wood[7] from Philadelphia to perform a few nights and he has acquitted himself admirably. I wish you had been here to get acquainted with him. He is a perfect gentleman in private life, and of the most amiable disposition & engaging manners. He has established a high reputation here.

Purser Hunt ⟨has⟩ and the fair Cleora,[8] it is discovered were married in April last—at the house of your fair friend *Moshes*[9]—I suppose of course you were in the secret. Old Jauncy[10] swears most horribly and so does his immaculate though ancient spinster of a Sister that the match shall be annulled, because Jancy was ⟨for⟩ frightened into it, by the handsome pursers threatening to blow out the small matter of brains he had in his head. Harry Barckley[11] endeavours to put on a bright face and laugh it off—but he cannot get further than a *gashly gum*.

The knowing ones are in fine order excepting little Sue who has had a sad inflammation in her eyes as a judgement from heaven on her for taking a jaunt on Long Island with that King of Beasts Dr Romaine[12] and his Buckram spouse.

As I have but just two minutes left to walk half a mile & pay half an hours visit to Ann & Charles Ill conclude by ⟨my best⟩ assurances of friendship & affection

Yours ever
W Irving.

ADDRESSED: Mr Henry Brevoort Junr. / care of Mr Gregory at the / City Hotel / Albany. DOCKETED: Sept 22. 1810 / W Irving
MANUSCRIPT: NYPL—Seligman Collection. PUBLISHED: LIB, I, 16–18.

1. See WI's letter to Henry Brevoort, May 11, 1809, note 7.

2. Probably John P. L'Herbette, in whose company Brevoort had traded for furs at Michilimackinac. See Porter, *Astor*, I, 59.

3. Brevoort, who was a nephew of John Jacob Astor, had involved himself in some of Astor's fur-trading activities in the St. Lawrence valley and the Great Lakes. The exact nature of Brevoort's French speculations is not known, but probably they were related to some aspect of fur trading if L'Herbette was involved.

4. David Porter (1780–1843), a naval officer who had participated in the Barbary Wars and was to distinguish himself as commander of the *Essex* in the War of 1812, was called "Sinbad" by his associates in the Lads of Kilkenny.

5. The home of Captain Frederick Philipse near Peekskill in the Highlands of the Hudson.

6. In 1810 the Park Theater opened on September 10 with a performance of *She Stoops to Conquer* featuring Vauxhall Bray as Tony Lumpkin and John Hogg as Hardcastle. Odell, *NY Stage*, II, 348; Ireland, *NY Stage*, I, 270.

7. William B. Wood (1779–1861) appeared in five performances at the Park

Theater between September 13 and 21, 1810. Odell, *NY Stage*, II, 349–50; Ireland, *NY Stage*, I, 270–71.

8. No marriage for Hunt and Cleora is listed in the NYEP marriage directory. In 1809, the *New York Directory* lists William Hunt, shipmaster (also 1813). In 1813, Henry Hunt, mariner; 1814, Joseph Hunt, mariner; 1816, Benjamin, Henry, Matthew, mariners.

9. In 1811 and 1813, William Mosher, shipwright, is listed in the *New York Directory*; in 1812 he is listed as mariner.

10. William Jauncy (1744–1828) graduated from Princeton in 1761. He was a governor of New York Hospital from 1797 to 1802, member of the Public School Society, and trustee for the Society for Promotion of Religion and Learning. No occupation is listed in the *New York Directory*. He never married and the heirs named in his will were friends, a niece, various relatives, but no Cleora.

11. Henry Barkley is listed in the *New York Directory* in 1810.

12. Dr. Nicholas Romayne (1756–1817), professor at the New York College of Physicians and Surgeons.

80.   *To John E. Hall*

New York, Septr. 26th. 1810.

Dear Hall,

I have received several very friendly letters[1] from you, from time to time, which I am ashamed to say, have remained unanswered. I can only plead as a miserable apology, my extreme antipathy to letter writing,[2] which prevails as much in matters of business, as of friendship or courtesy, so that I assure you I do not treat you worse than I do the rest of my friends. Your last letter ⟨fr⟩ by Master Payne[3] however, I will not allow myself to neglect, as it contains matters in which your own interests are concerned.

As to the proposal of commencing a literary journal,[4] though I think if such a thing were properly conducted it would be very profitable, yet I cannot ⟨allow⟩ reconcile it to myself to engage in any thing of the kind at least for the present. In fact I do not wish to meddle with my pen for a long while—I would rather devote a year or two at least to study— as there are several ⟨def⟩ branches of knowledge which ⟨I sh⟩ I am but little acquainted with at present, which are indispensible to popular writing. Indeed I feel conscious that my mind wants much improvement, and it is impossible to give it the regular cultivation that is necessary, ⟨if I⟩ unless I disengage myself from literary enterprises. While occupied by any work, however light, a mans reading must inevitably be desultory and interrupted and he is apt to read, more for this sake of the work in hands, than for the general improvement of his mind.

The affectionate solicitude and extreme liberality of my brothers, (who are engaged in commerce) have placed me beyond the necessity of

⟨writing⟩ using my pen as a means of support—and while they have admitted me to a share in the profits of regular business, I am left to the free indulgence of my own tastes & habits. Not being pressed therefore and hurried into ⟨publication⟩ a random exercise of my talents, such as they are, I wish to proceed as cautiously as possible; and if my caution does not enable me to write better, it will at least preserve me from the hazardous error of writing a great deal. I know it is one of the difficult things of this world, to check and keep down an itching propensity to scribble, which every man has, who has once appeared with any success in print—but this I am determined to do as much as lays in my power. This excellent determination I confess I broke through lately, in writing a queer and rather anomalous biography of Campbell[5]— and as a punishment therefore, I had the misery of seeing my delectable sketch most horribly misprinted, with outrages on grammar & good language that made my blood run cold, to look at them—but let these offences lay at the printers door, I swear myself innocent of them.

I received a long time since your subscription lists for the poems of poor Shaw[6]—they are somewhere in my ⟨[unrecovered]⟩ desk and I will look them up & procure what subscribers I can. I am however an indifferent hand for any thing of the kind, and indeed, as you must already have perceived, my activity & punctuality are not much [to] [*MS torn*] be relied on.

Little Payne has returned here, but as we are receiving supplies of new actors from Europe I question whether he will get an engagement, at least while their novelty lasts. I am affraid your ⟨have done your share in your city, to spoil⟩ ↑city has done its share in spoiling↓ this little fellow. Were he to remain in New York he might grow up to some good, for here he is not fondled and made a play thing of—but this wandering from town to town, and being the transient bawble and pigmy wonder of the young ladies and gentlemen, will make him good for nothing. He has very fine natural qualifications, if they could be properly cultivated

I am sir/yours truly
W Irving

P. S. I have heard your Law Journal extremely well spoken of here. Particularly by my friend Mr Hoffman who is the Recorder of our city and one of our best lawyers. He thinks it will encrease in credit & circulation. I hope you will ⟨[unrecovered]⟩ attend to it with spirit & accuracy, it will be a ⟨gre⟩ source of profit to you.

Addressed: John E Hall Esqr. / Baltimore   Postmarked: NEW-YORK / 27 / SEP
      Docketed: 26 Sept. / 1810 W. Irvine
Manuscript: University of Wisconsin—Milwaukee Library.   Published: STW, I, 120
      (in part).

John Elihu Hall (1783–1829), who was educated at Princeton and admitted to the bar in 1805, published the *American Law Journal* from 1808 to 1817. Later, from 1816 to 1827, he was to edit the *Port Folio*.

1. These letters have not been located.

2. WI was still despondent over the death of Matilda Hoffman.

3. John Howard Payne, widely acclaimed as the American Roscius, had been playing in theaters from Boston to Charleston.

4. This venture of Hall's apparently never materialized.

5. WI, who had selected some of Thomas Campbell's poems for American publication, added a brief biographical note on the poet. STW (I, 121) observes that it contains "some of Irving's most banal writing."

6. Dr. John Shaw (1778–1809), who had served with the United States Navy in the Mediterranean in 1798 and 1799, traveled extensively before settling in Baltimore, where he established his medical practice. He died from the aftereffects of chemical experiments. *Poems by the Late Doctor John Shaw*, with a biographical sketch by John E. Hall, appeared in 1810.

81. To _____

[September, 1810]

Dear Madam

I parted with you at Peekskill your debtor not only for a world of kindness and amiable attentions but for the enclosed sum which I borrowed to pay to my boatman & ⟨The Patroon⟩ which I forgot to return you. The latter I can readily repay[.] for the former I must still ⟨retain?⟩ remain your debtor unless you will consider my grateful sensibility & hearty acknowledgment as a sufficient discharge

MANUSCRIPT: Yale. PUBLISHED: *Yale University Library Gazette* 29 (July, 1949), 77.

82. To Mrs. Josiah Ogden Hoffman

Baltimore Jany 6th. 1811.

My dear friend

You may perceive I am travelling with great expedition toward the seat of Government, it being now not quite three weeks since I left New York.[1] In truth there are so many temptations laid in my way to induce me to loiter and, as the Yankees say, *tarry*, that were I not in some measure obliged to return home in a certain time I dont know when I should ⟨get there⟩ be with you again.

You have learnt before this, no doubt, how my host, like that of Hannibal[2] became corrupted and utterly seduced ⟨in⟩ by the capuan luxuries and pleasures of Philadelphia,[3] and how Brevoort, that recreant varlet absolutely deserted and and made a retrograde movement home-

wards. I determined however, to persevere in my expedition and resolutely made my way to this city, through "⟨flood⟩ ↑fog↓ and fire by lake⟨s⟩
and moorish fen" and struggled through more "sloughs of despond" than
did ever the invincible heroes of pilgrims progress.[4] I arrived here on
sunday afternoon, and will depart on Wednesday morning.

I suppose before this you have received the first number of Walsh's
Review, which will no doubt be for some time the topic of Literary
discussion.[5] Charles[6] furnished me with ⟨a number⟩ one to amuse me on
the road, but I have had no time to read it attentively. As far however
as I can judge from hastily looking through it, the work ⟨does great
credit⟩ bears great testimony of the fertility and diversity of Walshes
genius, and the elevated range of thought ↑in↓ which his mind delights
to move. Still however there are strong infusions of national partialities
and prejudices that tincture the whole course of his writings, and an
⟨ironic⟩ indignant vehemence of invective, that I am affraid will prevent
his work from having the full effect that his talents and the immaculate
honesty of his intentions should insure it. I became very intimate with
him at Philadelphia, and he has quite won my heart. He is very eloquent
in conversation, full of energy and feeling of the right kind, and of the
most amiable & ingenuous manners. ⟨It is⟩ He is very pale and emaciated,
but of a most interesting countenance, and ⟨it⟩ I could hardly help
smiling, though I felt both delight & admiration while he was zealously
engaged in ⟨conversation⟩ ↑discourse↓, to see so feeble and diminutive a
body, illumined and almost consumed, by so brilliant & fervid a mind.
He gave me letters to his family[7] in this city—with whom however, I was
previously acquainted. His sister is a charming and intelligent girl, of
highly cultivated mind.

I found an old acquaintance Jack Hall here, busily employed as usual
in unsuccessful literary labours. ⟨Had Jack⟩ I never met with a man
more determined and obstinate in a hopeless pursuit than Hall—Half
as much perseverence & industry in any other vocation, would have
insured him wealth & renown Had he been one tenth part as assiduous
in his attentions & wooings to any other ladies than the nine muses, he
⟨would⟩ ↑might↓ by this time have had as many wives as the grand Turk.
Jacks room is strewed with prospectus's of works, which he could never
publish for want of subscribers, and I firmly believe that after his
death his biographer will be enabled to make a couple of very tolerable
volumes of his works, consisting merely of prospectus's, title pages,
advertisements & proposals for publication of works that never saw the
day—

I have little to tell you of an amusing or interesting nature—besides
it is so thick & foggy a day ⟨and I can⟩ that I can scarcely see the pen
I am writing with—add to which I supped late last night with some of

the Merry-landers, and they so confounded—or as Lady Macbeth says *convinced* my brain[8] with apple toddy & whisky punch, that I am a mere animal this morning. I wrote to you from philadelphia and was in hopes of getting an answer but was disappointed. I hope I shall hear from you soon[;] you know what pleasure it gives me. Give my love to my little god daughter & see that she behaves like a worthy little gentlewoman. Remember me affectionately to all the family and to such of my friends as you see—not forgetting my good friend Mrs Renwick[9]

[*Closing and signature cut out*]

ADDRESSED: Mrs Ogden Hoffman / No 56 Greenwich St. / New York.   POSTMARKED:
    BALTIMORE MD / JAN 18
MANUSCRIPT: NYPL—WI Papers.

1. WI left New York on December 21, 1810, and arrived in Washington on January 9, 1811. Recently made a partner in the importing firm established by his brothers, Ebenezer and Peter, he was sent to Washington to observe the activities in Congress which affected their importing business and to report to Ebenezer. See PMI, I, 258–59.

2. During his Italian campaigns, Hannibal spent the winter of 216–217 at Capua, where, it was alleged, perhaps falsely, that luxurious quarters undermined the discipline of his troops. See *The Oxford Classical Dictionary* (Oxford, 1949), p. 404.

3. WI lingered with friends in Philadelphia during the holiday season, part of the time, as he suggests, in the company of Henry Brevoort.

4. He also alludes to the journey in his letter to Brevoort, January 13, 1811.

5. Robert Walsh (1784–1859), who had been a writer for the *Port Folio*, launched the *American Review of History and Politics and General Reporting of Literature and State Papers* in January, 1811. Filled primarily with articles written by Walsh, it continued through eight numbers, closing with the October, 1812, issue. Its purpose was the "propagation of sound political doctrines, and the direction and improvement of the literary traits of the American people."

6. Presumably Charles J. Nicholas, whom Ann Hoffman had married. See WI to Ann Hoffman, Aug. 10, 1807, and PMI, I, 250.

7. Robert Walsh, a merchant in Baltimore, was an immigrant from Ireland who married Elizabeth Steel, a Pennsylvania Quakeress.

8. In Act I, scene vii, lines 61–67, Lady Macbeth tells Macbeth: "When Duncan is asleep— / Whereto the rather shall his day's hard journey / Soundly invite him—his two chamberlains / Will I with wine and wassail so convince, / That memory, the warder of the brain, / Shall be a fume, and the receipt of reason / A limbec only. . . ."

9. Mrs. William Renwick (1774–1850) was Jean Jeffrey, the daughter of a Scotch Presbyterian minister in Lochmaben, Scotland. Robert Burns, who frequently visited there, wrote two poems to her: "The Blue-eyed Lassie" and "When first I saw my Jeanie's face." She married William Renwick at Lochmaben in 1791, and came to New York soon afterward. See *WI to the Renwicks*.

83. To Ebenezer Irving

[Washington, January 9, 1811]

I arrived here this evening, after literally struggling through the mud and mire all the way from Baltimore. I must confess I am not one of the most expeditious travellers in the world; but it was impossible to withstand the extremely friendly and hospitable attentions of the good people of Philadelphia and Baltimore; at any rate, I am a mere mortal on these occasions, and yield myself up, like a lamb to the slaughter.[1]

Congress has been sitting with closed doors for two or three days, engaged, as it is supposed, in the Florida business.[2] I have not been able to learn any thing of matters as yet, but I mean to be as deep in the mysteries of the cabinet as that "entire chrysolite"[3] of wisdom, * * * notwithstanding that he rode post, as I am well informed, from New York to Washington, with his finger beside his nose, and nodding and winking all the way to every man, woman, and child he saw.

PUBLISHED: PMI, I, 259.

1. WI elaborates upon his activities en route in his letter of January 13, 1811, to Henry Brevoort.
2. The House of Representatives met in closed session on January 5, 7, and 8; the Senate, on January 3, 7, 8, and 9, 1811. See *Annals of Congress*, 11th Cong., 3d sess., pp. 507–8, 87–88.
3. WI's variation on *Othello*, V, ii, 145.

84. To Henry Brevoort

City of Washington, Jany 1⟨2⟩3th. 1811

Dear Brevoort,

I have been constantly intending to write to you, but you know the hurry and confusion of the life I at present lead, and the distraction of thought which it occasions, and which is totally hostile to letter writing. The letter however which you have been so good as to write me[1] demands a return of some kind or another, so I answer it, partly through a sense of duty & partly in hopes of inducing you to write another. My Journey to Baltimore was terrible & sublime—as full of adventurous matter and direful peril as one of Walter Scotts pantomimic, melodramatic, romantic tales. I was three days on the road & slept one night in a Log house—Yet some how or another I lived through it all— and lived merrily into the bargain, for which I thank a large stock of good humour which I put up before my departure from N York, as travelling stores to last me throughout my expedition. In a word, I left home determined to be pleased with every thing, or if not pleased, to be amused, if I may be allowed the distinction, and I have hitherto kept to my determination. To beguile the ruggedness & tediousness of the road between Phila. & Baltimore I had an old ackwaintance in the Stage with me—Lieut Gibbon[2] of the Navy—whom I was well acquainted with in Richmond—& who is a true gentleman sailor & a very amiable pleasant fellow—He entertained me for two whole days with a minute and ⟨?moreover?⟩ agreeably related narration of the Exploits of our little navy in the Mediterranean & particularly of the captivity of our officers in Tripoli—he having been one of the prisoners I had a full and very entertaining account of all their misfortunes—plots—attempts at escape—pastimes, exercises &c &c—with a very familiar picture of Tripoli & its inhabitants. All this was told with the simple frankness of a sailor & the ⟨agreeable⟩ liberal spirit of a gentleman. He passed but one night in Baltimore but I have met him several times in company in Washington, where he is quite a favourite.

I remained two days in Baltimore where I was very well treated and was just getting into very agreeable Society when the desire to get to Washington induced me to set off abruptly—deferring all enjoyment of Baltimore until my return. While there I dined with honest Coale[3]— (whose sister[4] By the bye, verifies the assertion of Mrs. Hopkinson,[5] that she is handsomer than her picture)[6] At his table I found Jarvis,[7] who is in great vogue in Baltimore—painting all the people of note & fashion, and universally passing for a great wit, a fellow of infinite jest;[8]—in short—"the agreeable rattle."[9] I was likewise waited on by Mr. Tezier, the french gentleman who has translated my history of N.Y. He is a very pleasant, gentlemanly fellow, and we were very civil to each other as you may suppose. He tells me he has sent his translation to Paris, where I suspect they will understand & relish it about as much as they would a Scotch haggis & a singed sheepshead.

The ride from Baltimore to Washington was still worse than the former one—but I had two or three odd geniuses for fellow passangers & made out to amuse myself very well. I arrived at the Inn about dusk and, understanding that Mrs Madison[10] was to have her levee or drawing room that very evening, I swore by all my gods, I would be there—But how? was the question. I had got away down into George town, & the persons to whom my letters of introduction were directed lived all upon Capitol Hill about three miles off—while the presidents house was exactly half way. Here was a nonplus, enough to startle any man of less enterprizing spirit—but I had sworn to be there—and I determined to keep my oath, & like Caleb Quotem,[11] to "have a place at the Review." So I mounted with a stout heart to my room, resolved to put on my pease blossoms & ⟨stock⟩ silk stockings, gird up my loins—sally forth on my expedition & like a vagabond Knight errant, trust to providence for

Success and whole bones. Just as I descended from my attic chamber, full of this valourous spirit I was met by my landlord, with whom ⟨by the way⟩ & the head waiter by the bye, I had held a private cabinet council on the subject. Bully Rock[12] informed ⟨tho⟩ me that there ⟨were a number⟩ was a party of gentlemen just going from the house, one of whom Mr Fontaine Maury[13] of N York had offered his services to introduce me to "the Sublime porte[.]"[14] I cut one of my best opera flourishes, skipped into the Dressing room, ⟨put m⟩ popped my head into the hands of a sanguinary Jacobinical barber, who carried havoc & desolation into the lower regions of my face, mowed down all the beard on one of my cheeks and laid the other ↑in↓ blood, like a conquered province—and thus like a second Banquo, with "twenty mortal murthers on my head,"[15] in a few minutes I emerged from dirt & darkness into the blazing splendour of Mrs Madison's Drawing room. Here I was most graciously received—found a crowded collection of great & little men of ugly old women, and beautiful young ones—and in ten minutes was hand and glove with half the people in the assemblage. Mrs Madison is a fine, portly, buxom dame—who has a smile & a pleasant word for every body—Her sisters, Mrs Cutts & Mrs Washington[16] are like the two Merry Wives of Windsor—but as to Jemmy Madison[17]—ah! poor Jemmy! he is but a withered little apple-John[18]—But of this no more—perish the thought that would militate against sacred things—Mortals avaunt! touch not the lords anointed!

Since that memorable evening I have been in a constant round of banquetting ⟨and⟩ revelling & dancing—the Congress has been sitting with closed doors so that I have not seen much of the wisdom of the Nation, but I have had enough matter for observation & entertainment to last me a handful of months—I only want a chosen fellow like yourself to help me wonder admire and laugh—as it is I must endeavour to do these things as well as I can by myself.

I am delightfully moored, "head & stern" in the family of John P. Van Ness[19]—Brother of William P. He is an old friend of mine & insisted on my coming to his house the morning after my arrival. The family is very agreeable—Mrs Van Ness[20] is a pretty & pleasant woman, & quite gay—then there are two pretty girls ⟨in the⟩ likewise—one a Miss Smith,[21] clean from Long Island, her father being Member of Congress—she is a fine blooming country lass, and a great Belle here—You see I am in clover—happy dog!—close Jacob!—& all that.

The other evening at the City assembly I was suddenly introduced to my cousin the congressman from Scaghtikoke[22]—and we forthwith became two most loving friends. He is a goodhumoured fellow & withal a very decent country member—He was so overjoyed at ⟨being⟩ the happy commencement of our family compact, that he begged to introduce me to his friend Mr Simmons.[23] This is a Son of old Simmons of N York of corpulent memory by dint of steady attention to business—an honest character & a faithful fagging at the heels of Congress he has risen to some post of considerable emolument & respectability. Honest Simmons shook me heartily by the hand—professed himself always happy to see any body that came from New York—"Some how or another it was *natteral* to him—being the place where he was *first* born.["]

Mat Davis is here, and "my brother George"[24] into the bargain—Mat is endeavouring to obtain a deposit in the Mechanics bank in case the U.S. Bank does not obtain a charter. Mat is as deep as usual—shakes his head & winks through his spectacles at every body he meets. He swore to me the other day—that he had not told any body what his opinion was whether the Bank *ought* to have a charter or not—nobody in Washington knew what his opinion was—not one—nobody—he defied any one to say what it was—["]any body—damn the one—no sir—nobody knows,"—and if he had added nobody cares I believe honest mat would have been exactly in the right. Then theres his Brother George—damn that fellow—knows eight or nine languages—yes Sir nine languages—Arabic—Spanish—Greek—Ital—and theres his wife[25] now—She & Mrs Madison are always together—Mrs Madison has taken a great fancy to her little daughter—only think sir, that little child is only six years old and talks the italian like a book by God—little devil learnt it all from in[26] Italian servant—damned clever fellow—lived with my Brother George ten years—George says he would not part with him for all tripoli" &c &c &c

I wish you would let me hear from you again[. I shall] [*MS torn*] remain some days yet at this place & when I [leave] [*MS torn*] my letters will be taken care of by Van Ness.

I received a letter from Mrs Hoffman the day before yesterday & would have answered it, but have not time—this letter will do for her as well as yourself—It is now almost one oclock at night—I must to bed—remember me to all the lads & lasses Gertrude Miss Wilkes[27] and the Bonny lasses in Greenwich street, whose fair hands I kiss

I am my dear fellow/Yours ever
W I.

ADDRESSED: Mr Henry Brevoort Jr. / New York. POSTMARKED: WASH CITY / JAN 14
    DOCKETED: [Jan 13. 1811] / W Irving.
MANUSCRIPT: NYPL—Seligman Collection.   PUBLISHED: PMI, I, 260–65 (in part);
    LIB, I, 19–28.

1. This letter has not been located.

2. James Gibbon became a midshipman in 1799 and was made a lieutenant in 1807. In December, 1811, during a fire at the Richmond Theater, he led his mother out of the burning building, then returned to rescue his fiancée, but died with her in his arms when a stairway collapsed. See PMI, I, 265.

3. Edward Johnson Coale (1776–1832) was a Baltimore lawyer and book-

seller whose shop was across the street from the post office. See *Maryland Historical Magazine* 39 (June, 1944), 98; 40 (June, 1945), 123.

4. Probably Anna Maria Coale (1779–1813). See *Maryland Historical Magazine* 41 (March, 1946), 16.

5. Probably Coale's aunt. His mother was Anne Hopkinson, and this lady may be the wife of his mother's brother.

6. The version of this letter printed in PMI, I, 260–65, omits the passage in parentheses.

7. John Wesley Jarvis (1781–1839) was a popular portrait painter who sometimes associated with WI and his friends.

8. See *Hamlet*, V, i, 204.

9. In act III of *She Stoops to Conquer* Sir Charles Marlow observes, "At the Ladies Club in town I'm called their agreeable Rattle" (*Collected Works of Oliver Goldsmith*, ed. Arthur Friedman [Oxford, 1966], V, 172).

10. Dolley Payne Madison (1768–1849) was famous as a Washington hostess while her husband was secretary of state (1801–1809) and president (1809–1817).

11. Caleb Quotem was a parish clerk and jack of all trades in George Colman's play, *The Review* (1800).

12. WI sometimes called landlords or hotel keepers Bully Rock (see letter of May 9, 1808).

13. Fontaine Maury was the son of the Reverend James Maury and Mary Walker and was from either Washington or Virginia. He married Betsy Brooke.

14. WI facetiously uses the name given to the Ottoman court at Constantinople to suggest the quality of Mrs. Madison's reception.

15. See *Macbeth*, III, iv, 81.

16. Anna Payne Cutts was the wife of Richard Cutts, congressman from Maine; and Lucy Payne Washington was the wife of George Steptoe Washington, nephew of the first president.

17. President James Madison (1750/51–1836) was a small man of unimpressive appearance.

18. The term "apple-john" was given to an apple which matured about St. John's Day (December 27). According to tradition, apple-johns will keep for two years and are best when shrivelled. See *Brewer's Dictionary of Phrase and Fable*, p. 43. Falstaff says, "I am withered like an old apple-john" (*Henry IV*, Part I, III, iii, 4).

19. John P. Van Ness (1770–1846), congressman from New York (1801–1803) remained in Washington in various official positions. WI had stayed with the family of William P. Van Ness in Kinderhook after the death of Matilda Hoffman in 1809. See letter of May 11, 1809, and STW, I, 108.

20. Mrs. Van Ness was Marcia Burns, daughter of David Burns of Washington, D.C. She married Van Ness on May 22, 1802, in Washington.

21. Miss Smith was the daughter of John Smith (1752–1816) of Mastic, Long Island, senator from New York.

22. Herman Knickerbocker (1779–1855) from Schaghticoke, New York, who served as a Federalist congressman from March, 1809 to March, 1811, was unrelated to WI. He is acknowledged as WI's model for Diedrich Knickerbocker.

23. WI is probably referring to George Abel Simmons (1791–1857), later a New York assemblyman and from 1853 to 1857 a member of Congress.

24. Matthew Livingston Davis (1773–1850), an associate and biographer of Aaron Burr and later the Grand Sachem of the Tammany Society, was active in journalism and politics throughout his life. At about this time he was connected

with Davis & Strong, a South American trading firm. George Davis (1778–1818) was a surgeon in the United States Navy who served intermittently between 1802 and 1810 as American consul in Tunis and during this time acted as mediator for several governments in their dealings with the Barbary States. As early as January 2, 1810, Matthew L. Davis was soliciting the assistance of William P. Van Ness, General John Armstrong, and William Paulding to procure for George Davis the appointment as health physician for the port of New York. See the obituary of George Davis in the NYEP, August 19, 1818; and the letter of Matthew L. Davis to William P. Van Ness, January 2, 1810 (MS in NYHS).

25. Mrs. George Davis (1784–1856). See her death notice in NYEP, April 26, 1856.

26. WI probably intended to write "an," but there is a dot over the vowel.

27. Charlotte Wilkes was the daughter of Charles Wilkes. She married Sir Francis Jeffrey on October 23, 1813. On June 24, 1813, Brevoort wrote to WI to "try to make a match between him [Jeffrey] and Miss Wilkes; possibly the affair may not be beyond the control of the fates" (LBI, I, 96). She was the cousin of Admiral Charles Wilkes (1798–1877).

85.   To Mrs. Josiah Ogden Hoffman

[Washington, January, 1811]

When you see my good friend Mrs. Renwick, tell her I feel great compunction at having deprived her of her Tartan pladdie all the winter; but if it will be any gratification to her, she may be assured it has been of signal comfort to me, and has occasionally served as a mantle to some of the prettiest girls in Washington.

PUBLISHED: PMI, I, 266.

86.   To Henry Brevoort

Washington, Feby 7th. 1811.

Dear Brevoort,

I am ashamed at not having answered your letter[1] before, but indeed I am too much occupied & indeed distracted here, by the multiplicity of objects before me, to write with any degree of coherency.

I wish with all my heart you had come on with me, for my time has passed delightfully. I have become acquainted with almost every body here, and find the most complete medley of character I ever mingled amongst. As I do not Suffer party feelings to bias my mind I have ⟨me?⟩ associated with both parties—and have found worthy and intelligent men in both—with honest hearts, enlightened minds, generous feelings and bitter prejudices. A free communication of this kind tends more than any thing else to divest a mans mind of party bigotry—⟨and⟩ to make him regardless of those jaundiced representations of persons & things, which he is too apt to have held up to him by ⟨the th⟩ party writers— and to beget in him that candid, tolerant, good natured ⟨opinion of⟩ habit of thinking, which I think every man that values his own comfort and utility should strive to cultivate.

You would be amused, were you to arrive here just ⟨know⟩ now—to see the odd, & heterogeneous circle of acquaintance I have formed. One day I am dining with a knot of honest, furious federalists, who are damning all their opponents as a set of consummate scoundrels, pandars of Bonaparte, &c &c, The next day I dine perhaps with some of the very men I have heard thus anathematized, and find them equally honest, warm & indignant—and if I take their word for it, I had been dining the day before with some of the greatest knaves in the nation—men absolutely paid & suborned by the British government. Among my great cronies is General Turreau[2]—who, notwithstanding he is represented abroad as a perfect sanguinary ferocious bloodhound, I have found an exceeding pleasant jocose companion, and a man of shrewdness, ⟨and⟩ information & taste. Latrobe[3] (who is excessively abused here as an extravagant spendthrift of the public money &c) is very civil to me[.] I have been ⟨[unrecovered]⟩ two or three entertainments ⟨there⟩ at his house, & dine there today with a choice party of intelligent & agreeable men—⟨among⟩

To shew you the mode of life I lead I give you my engagements for this week—On Monday ⟨at the Bar⟩ I dined with the Mess of Officers at the Barracks—in the evening a Ball at Van Nesses. On Tuesday with my cousin Knickerbacker[4] & several merry Federalists—On Wednesday I dined with General Turreau who had a very pleasant party of Frenchmen & democrats—in the evening at Mrs Madisons Levee, which was brilliant & crowded with interesting men & fine women—on thursday a dinner at Latrobe's—on Friday a dinner at the Secretary of the Navys[5] and in the evening a ball at the Mayors[6]—Saturday as yet is unengaged. at all these parties you meet with so many intelligent people, that your mind is continually & delightfully exercised.

The Supreme Court has likewise within a day or two brought a crowd of new Strangers to the city. Jo Ingersoll,[7] Clement Biddle[8]—Clymer,[9] Goodloe Harper[10] & several others have arrived—and one of your old flames Miss Keaton ⟨wh⟩ with whom Ingersoll is so much in love, as report says. There you see, my good fellow, how much you lost by turning back. This place would Suit you to a fraction, as you could find company Suitable to every varying mood of mind—and men capable of conversing and giving you information on any Subject you wish to be informed. I may compare a place like this, to a huge library where a man may turn to any department of ⟨?Business?⟩ knowledge he pleases, and find an author at hand into which he may dip until his curiosity is satisfied.

What are you all doing at N York—I have not received a letter from there in an age—do give me all the little chit chat of the town, and I give you leave to pen it as slovenly as you please—I send you this letter as a ⟨specimen⟩ proof how carelessly a man may write to his friends. I have written to my brothers repeatedly, but have received no answers— I am tired of this kind of correspondence where the writing is all on my side—& I wish you would tell them so. I am rejoiced to hear you have shifted your quarters,[11] and I make no doubt but you will be happier by the change. How do the Wilkeses—I am truly grieved to hear that my good friend Mr Wilkes[12] has been one of the sufferers in these hard ·times. How do the knowing ones—their brave McPherson[13] (the *interesting young man* who wore regimentals, played on the flute & wrote bad poetry) is here as evidence in the case of Wilkinson[14]—I hope you visit them and do not suffer them to feel abandoned. How does Gertrude—Peter, Billy Taylor[15]—Gilpin—old Konkapot—curl[16]—The King of Clouts[17] &c &c &c write me three lines concerning each of them I charge you ⟨did you but⟩—had you but seen how eagerly I devoured your last letter—how I ⟨[unrecovered]⟩ read it over & over & chuckled & laughed over it, I am sure you would have set down immediately & wrote me another. I find by the papers & various other ways, that a new council is formed & the feds are all to be swung off at Tyburn Hill— Boss[18] & the Mayor,[19] it is said, are very contrite & sue for mercy—but in vain—"they die at sun rise—"

Has Boss taken his flight to Philadelphia from the top of a steeple— As to Gill,[20] he is like a little fat dunghill cock, that cant fly across the water—the Hudson I fear will be impassable to him this winter.

How are you likely to make out in respect to the Man that failed—I hope you feel yourself safe, among the breakers. I understand there are two new Performers[21] arrived—what kind of animals are they—Write to me immediately I beg of you—Give my love to Mrs Hoffman and the Kembles & all my other friends—not forgetting the lads Tell my brothers that when I recieve ⟨a letter⟩↑an answer↓ to any one of the letters I have written I will begin to write again—but if I do before damme.

God bless you my dear fellow/Yours ever

W I.

PS. Your opinion of Walshes review meets mine exactly. I am much disappointed in it, on a fair reading I even think his letters concerning france & england[22] much tinctured with prejudice—the whole however shows great literary powers—

ADDRESSED: Mr Henry Brevoort Junr. / New York.   POSTMARKED: WASH [–?] / FEB / 7   DOCKETED: [Feb 7?] 1811 / W Irving
MANUSCRIPT: NYPL—Seligman Collection.   PUBLISHED: LIB, I, 25–35; PMI, I, 267–70 (in part).

1. Brevoort had written to WI on January 19, including comments on Walsh's new magazine and several New York newspaper articles, together with other bits of gossip. See LBI, I, 3–10.

2. Louis Marie Turreau de Garambouville, Baron de Tineres (1756–1816), who fought under Count Rochambeau in the Revolutionary War, served as minister to the United States from 1804 to 1811 and tried to promulgate an American foreign policy favorable to France.

3. Benjamin H. Latrobe (1764–1820), English-born architect who was surveyor of public buildings in Washington. On his Western tour in 1832 Irving was accompanied by Latrobe's nephew, Charles Joseph (1801–1875).

4. See WI to Henry Brevoort, January 13, 1811, note 23.

5. Paul Hamilton (1762–1816) of South Carolina served as Madison's secretary of the navy.

6. The mayor of Washington, D.C. from 1802 to 1812 was Robert Brent (1763–1819).

7. Joseph Reed Ingersoll (1786–1868), Philadelphia-born lawyer who later served in Congress (1835–1837, 1843–1849) and as minister to England in 1852. He married Ann Wilcocks of Philadelphia on September 22, 1813. She died on May 28, 1831, aged forty-nine.

8. Clement Biddle (1740–1814), a Revolutionary soldier now a Philadelphia merchant.

9. George Clymer (1739–1813), a signer of the Declaration of Independence and a prosperous Philadelphia mechant.

10. Robert Goodloe Harper (1765–1825), a congressman from ·South Carolina with strong social connections.

11. In a letter to WI dated January 19, 1811, Brevoort writes that he is moving and will share a room with Nick Ogden at Mrs. Rumsey's boarding house on Broadway. See LBI, I, 7–8.

12. Either John de Ponthieu Wilkes (1755–1818) or his brother Charles Wilkes (1764–1833). John was a prominent banker (founder-member of the Bank of New York) and notary. He married Mary Seton and had five children: Charles W., Henry, Edmund, Eliza, and John. (Irving mentions Eliza and John in other letters.) Charles Wilkes was president of the Bank of New York and a founder of the New-York Historical Society. The parties at his Greenwich Village home and at his country home in Bloomingdale were social events. He married Mary Pixton, whose daughter by her first marriage (to John Rogers) married William Rhinelander. They had four children: Horace, Fanny, Charlotte, and John. (Charlotte is the Miss Wilkes WI mentions in his letter to Brevoort, January 13, 1811.) See Charles D. Wilkes, *The Wilkes Chronology* (Vevey, Switzerland, 1959).

13. Robert Hector McPherson fought in the Canadian campaign on the St. Lawrence in 1813 and 1814 under the command of Wilkinson; he was made a lieutenant colonel for "distinguished gallantry in battle" and for "severe and honorable wounds sustained by him" in 1814. He was honorably discharged on the same day as Wilkinson, June 15, 1815, and died January 1, 1817. F. Heitman, *Historical Register and Dictionary of the United States Army* (Washington, D.C., 1903), I, 681.

14. General James W. Wilkinson (1757–1825), who had had a notorious role in the Aaron Burr conspiracy and trial (see WI's letters of July, 1807), was undergoing congressional investigation of his alleged corruption. In July, 1811, President Madison ordered a court-martial. Its verdict, on December 25, of "not guilty" was so worded that the president approved it "with regret." Wilkinson was restored to

command. His ineptitude in the Canadian campaign led to another military investigation in 1813, the third of his career. As a result of the inquiry, he was relieved from duty and not reinstated in the service. See *D.A.B.*, XX, 225–26.

15. WI's intimates in New York: Gertrude Paulding, Peter Kemble, and Billy Taylor, WI's name for James Kirke Paulding.

16. PMI (I, 269) transcribes this as "old Konkapot, Curl," in which case WI is referring to two intimates. "Konkapot" seems to be a coinage used whimsically for one of the Lads of Kilkenny. In a letter from Edinburgh, Brevoort writes to WI on March 1, 1813: "Here are shops and libraries stored with treasures of the learned, yet are they less attractive than those of the recondite Curl and eke the critical Johnny Forbes" (LBI, I, 71). Curl was apparently engaged in bookselling or library work. His name does not appear in the *New York City Directory*. Brevoort had alluded to him in a letter of January 19, 1811. See LBI, I, 3.

17. George Frederick Cooke (1756–1811).

18. Brevoort to WI, February 14, 1811: "Boss is still in existence, but considers himself as one among the dead; I am told however this evening that the Council are at a stand owing to a meeting that took place lately at Martlings, at which, Clinton was denounced, & a committee dispatched to Albany with a copy—" (LBI, I, 18–19).

19. DeWitt Clinton.

20. WI's familiar name for Gulian Verplanck. See his letter of June 24, 1809, for a similar example.

21. WI probably refers to actors who made their first appearances in New York at this time. Odell observes, "On January 18th [1811], Knox, 'from the Theatre Royal, Edinburgh,' made his debut as the Stranger, to the Mrs. Haller of Mrs. Mason. He played Lieutenant Worthington, in the Poor Gentleman, on the 21st, though then a far more important first appearance was carried through in the introduction as Frederick of James Pritchard, 'from the Theatres, Aberdeen and Liverpool.' Knox quickly left the scene in New York, but Pritchard was prominent in our theatricals up to the time of his early death in 1823" (Odell, *NY Stage*, II, 364).

22. The first issue of *The American Review of History and Politics*, edited by Robert Walsh of Philadelphia, appeared in January, 1811, with "Letters on France and England" on pages 110–65.

87. *To William Irving, Jr.*

Washington, Feb. 9, 1811.

My dear Brother:

I am very much obliged to you for your kind letter of the 5th.[1] I had begun to feel quite impatient at not hearing from home, and to think that the news I occasionally scribbled from here might be of little importance. * * *

Your opinion with respect to the matter I hinted at has decided me, should any thing of the kind be proposed. I have heard, however, nothing further on the subject,[2] and do not suffer it to occupy my thoughts much. I should only look upon it as an advantageous opportunity of acquiring information and materials for literary purposes, as I do not feel much ambition or talents for political life. Should I not be placed in the situation alluded to, I shall pursue a plan I had some time since contemplated, of studying for a while, and then travelling about the country for the purpose of observing the manners and characters of the various parts of it, with a view to writing a work, which, if I have any acquaintance with my own talents, will be far more profitable and reputable than any thing I have yet written. Of this, however, you will not speak to others. But whatever I may write in future I am determined on one thing — to dismiss from my mind all party prejudice and feeling as much as possible, and to endeavor to contemplate every subject with a candid and good-natured eye.

Give my love to all the family. I shall endeavor to write Jack a line or two by this opportunity.

Affectionately, your brother,
W. I.

Published: PMI, I, 270–71.

1. This letter has not been located.
2. According to PMI (I, 270), WI was being considered for the secretaryship of the American Legation to France. PMI believed that the appointment was not made because Joel Barlow, the minister-designate, felt that WI had adversely criticized his epic, the *Columbiad*, but this point has not been corroborated by other documentation.

88.   *To William Irving, Jr.*

Washington, Feb. 16, 1811.

* * * The discussion of the Bank question[1] is going on vigorously in the Senate. Giles[2] made a very ingenious speech both for and against it. He was opposed to the Bank, but the enemies of the Bank thought he had done their cause more harm than any that had spoken on the opposite side. It seems Giles was compelled to take the side he did by the instructions of his constituents, but like an elephant he trampled down his own army. I was very much pleased with his speaking; he is a close reasoner, and very perspicuous. Clay,[3] from Kentucky, spoke against the Bank. He is one of the finest fellows I have seen here, and one of the finest orators in the Senate, though I believe the youngest man in it. The galleries, however, were so much crowded with ladies and gentlemen, and such expectations had been expressed concerning his speech, that he was completely frightened and acquitted himself very little to his own satisfaction. When his speech is printed, I will send it to you; he is a man I have great personal regard for. * * *

As to the appointment of which I spoke to you,[4] I do not indulge any sanguine hopes about it, and don't trouble myself on that score. I find that it has been the custom to leave the choice to the minister himself, in which case I have no chance. The Secretary of State[5] was the first person who suggested the idea, and he is very solicitous for it; indeed, I have experienced great civility from him while here. The President, on its being mentioned to him, said some very handsome things of me, and I make no doubt will express a wish in my favor on the subject, more especially as Mrs. Madison is a sworn friend of mine, and indeed all the ladies of the household and myself great cronies. I shall let the thing take its chance. I have made no application, neither shall I make any; and if I go away from Washington with nothing but the great good will that has been expressed and manifested towards me, I shall thank God for all his mercies, and think I have made a very advantageous visit.

PUBLISHED: PMI, I, 271–72.

1. A bill for renewing the charter of the Bank of the United States was introduced by Senator William A. Crawford of Georgia on February 5, 1811. See *Annals of Congress*, 11th Cong., 3d sess., p. 122.
2. William B. Giles (1762–1830) of Virginia, who served in the Senate from 1803 to 1815, spoke on the Bank bill on Thursday, February 14, 1811. See *Annals of Congress*, 11th Cong., 3d sess., pp. 175–207.
3. Henry Clay (1777–1852) represented Kentucky in the Senate at this time. He made his speech on the Bank question on February 15, 1811. See *Annals of Congress*, 11th Cong., 3d sess., pp. 210–39.
4. For other allusions to this appointment, see WI's letter of February 9, 1811.
5. Robert Smith (1757–1842) of Maryland.

89. *To William Irving, Jr.*

[Washington, February 20, 1811]

The non-intercourse question will come before the House either to-morrow or next day, and the discussion will be extremely animated. * * * Jack Randolph has been keeping himself up for the non-intercourse question, and I expect will attack it with all his forces. There is no speaker in either house that excites such universal attention as Jack Randolph. But they listen to him more to be delighted by his eloquence and entertained by his ingenuity and eccentricity, than to be convinced by sound doctrine and close argument.

PUBLISHED: PMI, I, 273.

90. To William P. Van Ness

Washington City. Feby. 20th. 1811.

My dear Sir,

I am writing late in the evening, in great haste, at your Brothers[1] request, who is too unwell to write to you himself. The Bank question was decided this afternoon, in the Senate. The members were equally divided and the Vice president[2] gave the casting vote, *against it.*

We are looking with anxiety, to your proceedings in our State,[3] particularly in Albany; where you seem to be in a delectable state of turmoil and confusion. I wish you would let us know what Armstrong[4] is manouvering about, whether he and Spencer[5] are great confidants, and whether he seems to be on full understanding with the Clintonians. For my part—I thank the Gods that I have attained to that desireable state of mind, in which I can contemplate their party feuds without caring two straws which side gets the worst of it—my only wish being, that they may give each other a sound drubbing. As to talking of patriotism & principle, I've seen enough both of general & state politics to convince me they are mere words of Battle—"Banners hung on the outer walls,"[6] for the rabble to fight by—the knowing leaders laugh at them in their sleeves—for being gulled by such painted rags.

I have not heard what course you are taking—what your prospects are —or whether the Clintonians are still lulling you with deceitful professions — if they do not come to something decisive at once — some fair sharing of purse & office I would break with them outright and go over to the Martling men,[7] who⟨m?⟩ I am convinced only want a few experienced officers to enable them to overturn the whole clintonian host.

I have been passing my time very pleasantly here in your Brothers family. My reception here has been very flattering, and I am on the best of terms with the presidents family, the heads of department &c &c

I am with great regard/Your sincere friend

Washington Irving.

ADDRESSED: William P Van Ness Esqr. / Albany / State N York   POSTMARKED:
WASH-CITY / FEB 20   DOCKETED: Washington Irving / 20 Feby 1811
MANUSCRIPT: Va.–Barrett. PUBLISHED: Adrian H. Joline, *Meditations of An Autograph Collector* (New York, 1902), p. 147 (in part).

1. John P. Van Ness, with whom WI was staying.
2. George Clinton of New York, the vice-president, broke the 17–17 tie by voting in favor of striking out the first section of the bill chartering the National Bank. This action was equivalent to rejecting the bill. See *Annals of Congress,* 11th Cong., 3d sess., pp. 346–47.
3. The Republicans, having swept the state electors in New York, began to replace the Federalist appointees with Clintonians. See D. S. Alexander, *A Political History of New York,* I, 179.

4. John Armstrong (1758–1843), American minister to France from 1804 to 1810, was thought to favor the Clinton faction, but later he supported President Madison.

5. Ambrose Spencer (1765–1848), a justice of the New York Supreme Court, was a supporter of the Clintonians at this time. Later he broke with Clinton over policies concerning the War of 1812.

6. A misquotation of *Macbeth*, V, v, 1.

7. A group composed mainly of members of the Tammany Society who opposed the fusion of Burrites and Clintonians. See Alexander, *A Political History of New York*, I, 152, 172.

91. To Henry Brevoort

Washington, March 5th. 1811.

Dear Brevoort,

Your letter sometime since concerning the modern feast of the Centaurs and Lapythae was truly heroic & historical, and I defy Dan Homer himself to present a more hideous battle than that of the host of the puissant "King of Clouts."[1] I received a letter yesterday from Peter the great[2] who informs me of your recent trip to Phila. I wonder much that you did not intimate something to me of such a movement, we might have calculated so as to meet there.

I shall leave this city the day after tomorrow, ⟨having a little business to⟩ I should have gone tomorrow but the stage⟨s⟩ ↑books↓ were ⟨eng⟩ full. You cannot imagine how forlorn this desert City appears to me, now the great tide of casual population has rolled away. The three or four last days have been quite melancholy. Having formed a great number of intimate and agreeable acquaintances, I have been continually taking leave of persons for whom I had contracted a regard, and who are dispersing to various parts of this immense country, without much chance of our ever meeting one another again. I think nothing would tempt me to remain again in Washington until the breaking up of congress; ⟨at least⟩ unless I might start off with the first of the tide. I have been detained by business at the comptrollers office, which after all has terminated unprofitably. I now begin to feel extremely anxious to be once more at home, and do not think I shall stop ⟨much⟩ long by the way. I must, however, reconnoitre ⟨at⟩ a little on our old seat of war at Philadelphia and at least find out what you have been about in your late secret expedition to those parts.

If you have not settled yourself permanently in lodgings at Mrs Rumseys,[3] I think you had better look out for a situation where the company will be more congenial to your taste & habits—as far as I reccollect Mrs R's boarders are more to be admired for their talents at eating & drinking than anything else—as you are a man ⟨born of woman?> of very immoveable disposition when you once locate yourself, it behoves you to be a little choosie of the spot where you determine to take root.

I beg you "as you are friend, scholar & soldier"[4] to give me this poor request, that you would write to me immediately, a full and satisfactory letter, touching affairs in New York, and also touching your late expedition to Phila. ⟨wh⟩ in which expedition I am told you played Squire to the Ex Recorder.[5] Do not fail to write, my good lad, for you cannot concieve how earnestly I covet another letter from you—direct to the care of Charles I Nicholas. And let me find the letter at Phila. when I arrive there. Let me know how you come on with the lads. Peter has hinted that he did not think the majestic Hen[6] would ever find favour in your eyes ⟨however she owns ?rather singular?⟩ but peter is a varlet and I cannot give my faith to his assertion ⟨?What a woman—? ay friend? that it should be suffered to extinguish her other charms⟩[7] No—no—my dear Brevoort—the mind—the mind! is what you must consult—and then thank heaven the divine Hen rises superior to "common ordinary mortals"[8] —as my favourite poet says—

I am writing most execrably flat—and to tell the truth am in a deplorable humdrum mood this morning—but *allons*—a few cracks of the whip & whirls of the wheel will change the scene—and a few more will bring me once more among my cronies—

Give my love to all at Mrs Hoffmans, the Kembles &c &c &c and so God Bless you all.

                                                           W Irving.

P.S. About the time you receive this, I expect "my cousin" Knickerbacker will arrive in N Y. I wish you would call at the city Hotel & look for him and give him some attention among you. he is a right honest sound hearted pleasant fellow.

ADDRESSED: Mr Henry Brevoort Jr. / New York   POSTMARKED: WASH [*unrecovered*] / MAY / 15   DOCKETED: March 5. 1811
MANUSCRIPT: NYPL—Seligman Collection.   PUBLISHED: PMI, I, 273–74 (in part); LIB, I, 36–39 (complete).

1. The drinking and brawling of the Centaurs and Lapythae were matched at a party given in early February, 1811, by George Frederick Cooke, "the King of the Clouts." Brevoort described it in a letter to WI on February 14, 1811. See LBI, I, 113–18. For other details about Cooke's drinking see Odell, *NY Stage,* II, 358, 362.

2. Peter Kemble.

3. Harriet Rumsay of 13 Broadway is listed in Longworth's *New York Directory* for 1811, p. 252.

4. A variation of *Hamlet,* I, v, 141.

5. Joseph Ogden Hoffman.

6. This person is also mentioned in WI's letter of January 2, 1813.

7. This cancellation and that immediately preceding it were scratched over in a different ink, apparently at a later time and by another hand than WI's.

8. Possibly an echo of Puck in *Midsummer Night's Dream*.

92. *To Dolley Madison*

Baltimore, March 10th. 1811.

Madam,

The very friendly attentions I received from you while at Washington encourage⟨s⟩ me to take the liberty of introducing to your acquaintance Mr Jarvis, a native of our state, a young artist,[1] to serve him, and a consciousness that you feel a pleasure in yielding that countenance to men of talents, whi[ch] [*MS torn*] your situation renders peculiarly gratifying, have mad[e] [*MS torn*] me thus particular in his recommendation.

I have the honor to be Madam/With great respect—/Your friend

Washington Irving

Mrs Madison.

MANUSCRIPT: Va.–Barrett.

Only the top fold of the letter, with writing on both sides, has been located.

1. The remainder of the sheet below the fold is missing.

93. *To Henry Brevoort*

Philadelphia, March 16th 1811

My dear fellow—

I arrived in this city the day before yesterday, and was delighted to find a letter from you waiting for me on Charles'[1] mantelpiece. I thank you for this mark of attention, and for the budget of amusing & interesting news you have furnished me with. I stopped but ⟨flo⟩ four days at Baltimore on my return, one of which I was confined at home by indisposition—The people of Baltimore are exceedingly social and very hospitable to strangers, and I saw that if I let myself once get into the stream I should not be able to get out again under a fortnight at least— So being resolved to push homewards as expeditiously as was reasonably possible, I resisted the world the flesh & the devil at Baltimore, and after three days & nights stout carousal and a fourth's sickness, sorrow & repentance, I girded up my loins and hurried off from that sensual city. By the Bye that little "Hydra & chimera dire"[2] Jarvis, is in prodigious great circulation at Baltimore—The gentlemen have all voted him a ⟨wa⟩ rare wag and most brilliant wit, and the ladies pronounce him one of the queerest, ugliest, most agreeable little creatures in the world.

The consequence is, that there is not a ball, tea party, concert, supper or any other private regale, but what Jarvis is the most conspicuous personage—and as to a dinner, they can no more do without him, than they could without Friar John at the roystering revels of the renowned Pantagruel.[3] He is overwhelmed with business & pleasure, his pictures admired & extolled to the skies, and his jokes industriously repeated & laughed at. I had not been in Baltimore an hour before I heard one of his Bon mots—Being very much importuned to go to church he resolutely refused observing that it was the same thing whether he went or staid at home—"If I don't go, said he, the Minister says Ill be d⟨a⟩——d—and—Ill be d——d if I do go—" This profane sally seemed to tickle the Baltimoreans exceedingly. ⟨Ran⟩ Jack Randolph[4] was at Baltimore for a day or two after my arrival. He sat to Jarvis for a likeness for one of the Ridgeleys[5] and consented that I should have a copy—I am in hopes of receiving it before I leave philadelphia & of bringing it home with me.

I found our friends here all in good health & spirits excepting the little Doctor, who seems to be very much depressed by his late misfortunes. I called at the Rawles[6] and had a long conversation with the old lady, who was extremely friendly & agreeable—I am to dine there on Tuesday next. She mentioned your having been in town without calling there, and I apologized as well I could—Am I forever to be thus embarrassed with your confounded negligence & backwardness!

I was out visiting with Ann[7] Yesterday, and met that little assemblage of smiles and fascinations Mary Jackson. She was bounding with youth, & health and innocence & good humour. She had a pretty straw hat tied under her chin with a pink ribband, and looked like some little woodland nymph, just lured out by Spring and fine weather—God bless her light heart, and grant that it may never know care or sorrow! its enough to cure spleen & melancholy only to look at her.

Your familiar pictures of home make me extremely desirous again to be there—It will be impossible however to get away from the kind attentions of our friends in this city until some time next week, perhaps towards the latter end—When I shall once more return to sober life, satisfied with having ⟨made⟩ secured three months of sunshine in this valley of shadows and darkness.[8]—In this space of time I have seen considerable of the world but I am sadly affraid I have not grown wiser thereby, inasmuch as ⟨I⟩ it has generally been asserted by the sages of every age that wisdom consists in a knowledge of the wickedness of mankind, and the wiser a man grows the more discontented he becomes with those around him—Whereas, woe is me! I return in infinitely better humour with the world than I ever was before—and with a most melancholy good opinion & good will for the great mass of my fellow creatures!

I rejoice to hear of the approaching nuptials of our redoubtable Highland chieftain,[9] and hope you are preparing a grand Epithalamium for
the joyful occasion. Remember me affectionately to the Hoffmans
Kembles &c—And kiss the hands of the fair ladies in Greenwich St.

yours ever.

W Irving.

ADDRESSED: Mr Henry Brevoort Jun. / at Mrs Rumsey's— / New York   POSTMARKED:
     PHI / 16 / MR   DOCKETED: March 16 1811 / W Irving
MANUSCRIPT: NYPL—Seligman Collection. PUBLISHED: PMI, I, 274-75 (in part);
     LIB, I, 40-45 (in part).

1. Charles Nicholas, son-in-law of Josiah Ogden Hoffman.
2. *Paradise Lost*, II, 628.
3. In the works of Rabelais, Pantagruel, son of Gargantua and last of the
giants, was often accompanied by Friar John of Seville, who was known for his
quick handling of matins and vigils and for his prowess as a brawling fighter.
4. John Randolph, a colorful Virginia orator and statesman who opposed
the embargo, a fact which interested hardware importers like the Irvings.
5. The Ridgeley family of Maryland was prominent socially and politically.
Captain Charles Ridgeley (1784-1848), an American Navy officer, built "Hampton," thirteen miles from Baltimore. His nephew, Charles Carnan Ridgeley was
governor of Maryland from 1815 to 1818. See Swepson Earle, *The Chesapeake Bay
Country* (Baltimore, 1924), pp. 235-36.
6. William Rawle (1759-1836), a Quaker lawyer advocating abolition, was a
leader in civic affairs in Philadelphia. The "old lady" is probably his mother, Mrs.
Rebecca Warner Rawle Shoemaker, who lived until 1819. See William Brooke
Rawle, "Laurel Hill and Some Colonial Dames Who Once Lived There," *Pennsylvania Magazine of History and Biography* 35 (1911), 388-89, 412.
7. Ann Hoffman Nicholas.
8. The remainder of this paragraph is omitted from Hellman's printed version.
9. Captain Frederick Philipse (1755-1829), whose first marriage ended with
the death of his wife, Mary Marston, in childbirth on October 14, 1779. Captain
Philipse was married a second time to Maria Kemble, niece of General Gage. The
editors are indebted to Miss Patricia E. Smith, librarian of Sleepy Hollow Restorations, Tarrytown, New York, for supplying details about Captain Philipse and his
marriages.

94. *To Henry Brevoort*

Phila. March 18th 1811.

Dear Brevoort,

I write this letter merely to introduce to you Mr Wm Rogers[1] of
Rhode Island; who will be a fellow lodger of yours. ⟨We⟩ I have seen
considerable of him at Washington, Baltimore &c and am much pleased
with him. Make him acquainted with Peter, Jim &c—and at Mrs
Hoffmans, the Lads or wherever you may visiting—I am sure you will

be pleased with him—ask him to ride Amy Dardens horse for you a little—I shall be with you in a few days, and then we will look out for Gouv[2] and prepare for the captains Hymeneals.[3]

Yours ever
W I.

ADDRESSED: Mr Henry Brevoort Junr / New York— / Mr William Rogers. DOCKETED: March 18, 1811 / W Irving
MANUSCRIPT: NYPL—WI Papers. PUBLISHED: LIB, I, 44.

    1. Possibly the son of William Rogers (1751–1824), who was a professor at the University of Pennsylvania at this time.
    2. Gouverneur Kemble, one of the Lads of Kilkenny, who established the West Point Foundry at Cold Spring and later served in Congress from 1837 to 1841.
    3. A reference to the impending marriage of Captain Frederick Philipse.

95. To Henry Brevoort

[Washington, April 2, 1811]

We arrived in this city yesterday afternoon, after a very expeditious journey of fifty-two hours from New York. We were extremely fortunate in meeting with no delays. The moment we arrived in Philadelphia, the packet was about starting for Newcastle, so that we were in full sail in about twenty minutes in company with Van Ness[1] and Mr. Harison, (house of Ogden & Harison,)[2] who were sent on the part of the consignees. The next morning at half-past six we arrived at Baltimore, breakfasted, and set off at eight in an extra stage, and reached Washington about half-past four in the afternoon. The attack has been commenced on Gallatin[3] this morning by Harison and Van Ness. Brother William and myself remain behind as a corps de reserve. Pindar[4] is in fine health and spirits after his journey, and is quite pleased with this vast city—which, indeed, makes a very pleasing rural appearance this fine sun-shiny day. I have been whirled here with such rapidity, that I can scarcely realize the transition; it is quite contrary to my loitering *hospitable* mode of travelling. I have seen nobody on my route but the elegant Jarvis, whom I found sleeping on a sopha bed in his painting room, like a sleeping Venus, and his beautiful dog couched at his feet. I aroused the varlet, and bid him on pain of death to have the likeness of Randolph[5] done on my return; he breakfasted with us, and entertained us with several jokes, which had passed the ordeal of Baltimore dinner tables.

Harison and Van Ness have just returned, and with complete success. The Magdalen and the Hercules[6] will both be allowed to enter with flying colors.

Van Ness is on the point of starting off; he is half crazy with joy. I must conclude this letter. Brother William and myself will leave this place in two days. Remember me to all, and believe me ever,

Yours truly,
W. Irving

Write to me at Philadelphia.

PUBLISHED: PMI, I, 276–77.

1. John Van Ness, long-time friend of the Irving family.
2. Located at 55 Pine Street, this firm was a partnership of Andrew Ogden and J. Harrison.
3. Albert Gallatin (1761–1849), Madison's secretary of the treasury, had informed collectors of revenue that trade with Great Britain would stop on February 2, 1811. This order was reinforced by the Non-Intercourse Act of March 2, 1811, which dealt a heavy blow to importers like the Irvings and Ogdens.
4. William Irving contributed poetry to *Salmagundi* under the name of Pindar Cockloft.
5. See WI's letter of March 16, 1811, for other details.
6. The NYEP for April 11, 1811, reported that the *Hercules* out of Liverpool, carrying dry_goods and hardware for about thirty-five New York firms including P. and E. Irving, was boarded by a British frigate and two seamen were impressed. The *Hercules* ultimately reached New York and was cleared for Liverpool on May 23, 1811. The NYEP does not mention the *Magdalen*.

96. To Henry Brevoort

Phila. April 11th. 1811.

Dear Brevoort,

I have neglected answering your letter from an expectation that I should have been home home[1] before this; but I have suffered day after day to slip by, and here I still am, in much the same mood as you are when in bed of a fine genial morning endeavouring to prolong the indolent enjoyment, to indulge in another doze, and renew those delicious half waking dreams that give one an idea of a musselmans paradise

I have for a few months past led such a pleasant life that I almost shrink from awaking from it, into the common place round of regular existence—"but this eternal blazon must not be" (shakespeare)[2] so in two or three days Ill gird up my loins, take staff in hand and return to the land of my fathers.[3] To tell the truth I have been induced to stay a day or two longer than I otherwise would have done to have the gratification of seeing Cooke in Kitely & Lear[4] the first he plays to night the other on Wednesday. The old fellow is in great repute here and draws excellent houses. I stopped in accidentally at the theatre a few evenings since when he was playing Macbeth; not expecting to receive any pleasure, for you reccollect he performed it very indifferently in New York.[5] I entered just at the time when he was meditating the murder, and I remained to the end of the play in a state of admiration & delight. The old boy absolutely out did himself—his dagger scene, his entrance to Duncans chamber & his horror after the commission of the deed completed a dramatic action that I shall never forget as long as I live—it was sublime. I place the performance of that evening among the highest pieces of acting I have ever witnessed—you know how I had before considered cooper[6] as much superior to him in Macbeth—but on this occasion the character made more impression on me than when played by cooper or even Kemble.[7] The more I see of Cooke the more I admire his style of acting—he is very unequal, from his irregular habits and nervous affections—but when he is in proper mood there is a truth and of course a simplicity in his performance, that throws all rant, stage trick & stage effect completely in the back ground. Were he to remain here a sufficient time for the public to perceive & dwell upon his merits and the true character of his playing, he would produce a new taste in acting. ⟨I regard his playing⟩ One of his best performances ⟨when in⟩ may be compared to a masterpiece of ancient ⟨sculpture⟩ statuary; where ⟨the⟩ you have the human figure destitute of ⟨ornament⟩ idle ⟨&⟩ ornament depending upon the truth of Anatomical proportion and arrangement, the accuracy of character and gracefulness of com-position—in short a simple display of nature—

Such a production requires the eye of taste & knowledge to perceive its eminent excellencies—whereas ⟨any⟩ ↑a↓ vulgar spectator ⟨is delighted with an inferior⟩ will turn from it to be enraptured with some ⟨inferior⟩ bungling workmanship, loaded with finery, & drapery and all the garish ornaments in which unskillfulness takes refuge.

Sully has finished a very fine & correct portrait of cooke[8]—and has begun a full length picture of him in the character of Richard—This he is to receive 300$ for from the gentlemen of Phila. who ⟨have⟩ opened a subscription for the purpose, which was filled up [in an] [*MS torn*] hour—The picture is to be placed in the academy of arts.[9]

I rode out yesterday to see your country seat in the neighbourhood of this city. It is in a state of great neglect & very much out of order—I would advise you to sell it without delay.

Walshes 2d. number will be out in two or three days—I have seen it, but have not had time to read more than a few pages of a masterly review of Hamiltons works.[10] I think the number will do him credit.

Give my love to all who love me and remember me kindly to the rest—

Yours truly

W I.

ADDRESSED: Mr Henry Brevoort Jun / New York   POSTMARKED: PHI / [11?] / AP
    DOCKETED: Ap. 11. 1811 / W. Irving
MANUSCRIPT: NYPL—Seligman Collection.   PUBLISHED: PMI, I, 277–79 (in part);
    LIB, I, 45–49.

1. WI repeated "home" at the beginning of the line.
2. *Hamlet*, I, v, 21.
3. See 2 Kings 4:29.
4. WI's chronology does not agree with the schedule of Cooke's performances
recorded by William Wood. According to Wood, Cooke played Macbeth on April
11, Kitely in *Every Man in His Humor* on April 15, and Lear on April 17. See
William B. Wood, *Personal Recollections of the Stage*, p. 133; Reese D. James, *Old
Drury of Philadelphia* (Philadelphia, 1932), pp. 86–87.
5. WI is alluding to Cooke's portrayal of Macbeth on December 10, 1810 at
the Park Theater. See Odell, *NY Stage*, II, 360.
6. Thomas Apthorpe Cooper, who married Mary Fairlie on June 11, 1812.
7. John Philip Kemble (1751–1823), whom WI had seen in London in 1805.
See *J&N*, I, 457.
8. This portrait is called "one of the most important of Sully's works." See
Helen W. Henderson, *The Pennsylvania Academy of the Fine Arts and Other
Collections of Philadelphia* (Boston, 1911), pp. 107–8.
9. The painting of Cooke is part of the permanent collection of the Pennsylvania Academy of Fine Arts.
10. The review of *The Works of Alexander Hamilton* published by Williams and
Whiting in three volumes appeared in the *American Review of History and
Politics* 1 (April, 1811), 201–58.

97. To Henry Brevoort

New York May 15th 1811

Dear Brevoort

The *Great Mandarian*[1] has just informed me that there will be an
opportunity to forward a letter to you on Friday, so my dear boy, though
busied almost unto death, yet I will endeavour to indite a little epistle
which may follow you even unto your savage haunts, and be as welcome
to your fainting spirits, as was a cup of water to Hagar[2] of yore, when
drooping in the wilderness. Since you left us I have been a mere animal;
working among hardware and cutlery. We have been moving the store,[3]
and I (my pen weeps at the very thought of it) have had, in this time
of hurry and confusion, to lend all the assistance in my power, and bind
my indolent and restive habits to the plodding routine of traffic. But
this is only a temporary sacr⟨a⟩ifice. Shut your eyes, oh ye blessed Muses,
lest ye afterwards look upon me with scorn! By all the Martyrs of Grub
Street I'd sooner live in a garret and starve into the bargain, than follow
so sordid dusty, soul-killing a way of life; though certain it would make
me as rich as old Croesus, or John Jacob Astor[4] himself. I am in quiet

possession of your room, and am very much pleased with my situation—
Mine host and his wife[5] are a very obliging, agreeable couple. I hope
you will be induced to take up your quarters with us when you return,
you need not fear *shocking the feelings* of Mrs Rumsey,[6] as she expects it.

Charles and Ann arrived here last evening. They are bothe hearty and
their little girl[7] more beautiful than ever.

May 16.th. I was interrupted in this letter yesterday. Last evening I was
at a tea party at Mrs Hoffman's—rather a stupid one. The piano was out
of tune and they had not been able to get it put in order, so we were
disappointed, in the musical treat we had promised ourselves—Charles
sang one or two songs without accompaniment. Your Sister was there.
She came in town the evening before, to go to the play with Mrs Renwick
at whose house she is on a visit of two or three days. She is quite a
favourite with the Bonny widow.[8]

I have scarcely seen any thing of the Lads since your departure—
business and an amazing want of inclination has kept me from their
thres⟨h⟩hold. Jim,[9] that sly poacher, however, prowls about there, and
vitrifies his heart by the furnace of their charms. I accompanied him
there on Sunday evening last, and found the *Lads* and Miss Knox[10] with
them—⟨She⟩ ↑Sue↓[11] was in great spirits, and played the Sparkler with
such great success as to silence the whole of us excepting Jim—who was
the *agreeable rattle of the evening*. God defend me from such vivacity
as hers in future. Such smart speeches without point or meaning such
bubble and squeak[12] nonsense. I'd as leave stand by a frying pan for an
hour and listen to the cooking of apple fritters. After two hours dead
silence of suffering on my part I made out to drag him off, and did not
stop running until I was a mile from the house—I have not been able
to go there since—but I hope the humour will return again. All this
entre nous.

The Heir Apparent is in close siege of the little Heiress near the park;
with the whole influence of Pistareen John's family opposed to him.[13]
Peter has been obliged to lay by his buckram dignity and bow to
Belial, or what is the same thing—to shake hands with Alex Stewart.
Whether he will carry his point or not is a matter of ↑very↓ great doubt
to me, as Peter is very much given to play truant from his post, and run
after sundry little damsels about the City. Little Miss Gouvernier,[14] the
little Mac⟨c⟩ombs[15] of Belleville &c &c have at different times seduced
him from his allegiance—and in two days philandering he has lost the
headway of a fortnights courtship.

The noble captain[16] was married shortly after your departure, and
immediately fled with his turtle dove to the groves. I have bet a coat
with John King[17] that he would have occasion for a nirsery within two
years, and I feel no apprehension of losing.

Mrs Colden[18] has lately been to Philadelphia with Alice Ann[19] and the fair Angelica & her sisters.[20] Mrs C returned a few days since and left Angelica and Julia there, where I am told they are making sad havoc among the Beaux. Mrs C gave a tea party on her return, by way no doubt of a rejoicing. I was there, and made my entry in the back room, where I found Peter in full blast of gallantry & eloquence, with a fan in one hand and Nosegay in the other, declaiming in a true Will Honeycomb style to a knot of little blossoms; one of whom I soon found was little Miss Beach. Among the other turtles who were pairing at this convocation was old Satan[21] and Mary Fairlie. It would have amused you to see Cooper playing softness and suavity. The ⟨H⟩ Divine Kitty was likewise there, but I bethought me of the smoky chimney, and kept at a wary distance.

May 17th The arrival of Ann & Charles has been the signal for a host of little rascally tea parties; there was one at the Douglas's[22] last evening— but I swore off and went to the theatre. Your sister Margaret w⟨as⟩ent there under the protection of Mrs Renwick. I can't stomach these omnipresent Douglass's—They break in every where, with such a troop of retainers and moss troopers[23] at their heels that I should be fearful of relapsing into barbarism in their society. And then there is Cousin Betsy—rigged out in fine blue silks with diamond necklaces—breastpins— broaches—ear ring bobbs and three score rings on each finger, that I never see her without thinking of some of the eminent pawnbrokers ladies I have seen in London.

Sam Swartwout arrived from England a few days since, as rugged and hearty as ever I saw him,

Cooke and Cooper have been playing together for several nights.[24] The old fellows Iago was admirable and threw Othello in the back ground in my opinion. He has however been sick and been bled and reduced most confoundedly so that the second time he played Iago he was comparitively languid. Cooper has not used him quite fairly I think. He got up Alexander the great[25] that he might rant about in fine clothes and old Cooke be sunk in the inferior⟨er⟩ part of Glylus. The old Boy however in the two or three passages where he had a chance came out nobly, and received great applause. As to Cooper he was so highly begilt and be tinselled, that the finery outdazzled itself, and he looked not unlike a pyramid of macaroons, bedizzened with sugar candy.

Last night nothing would serve Cooper but he must have the play of the Fair Penintent,[26] though several remonstrated ↑with↓ him and numerous parties of ladies declined going. Cooper, however, was bent upon playing up to old Cooke in Lothario. Here he was sadly disappointed. His Lothario has become a terrible, formal, heavy fine gentleman and in the scene between him and Horatio old Cooke completely bore away the

palm, receiving applause at every speech, while Cooper was not cheered
by a single clap. On Monday, they play Pierre & Jaffier,[27] on Wednesday
Cooke plays King John[28] for his benefit to Coopers Faulconbridge—On
Friday they conclude by a repetition of Othello—and then adieu to the
Theatre.

We received long letters from little Johnny ⟨a few⟩Fig[29] a few days
since. He has been a *Cacao planter* in Trinadad and writes in great
spirits—by his account he is likely to do very well. A gentleman of property has befriended him, and advances all the funds—purchases the
plantation, negroes &c and John is to receive half the profits for his
attention and labour in superintending and managing it.

I am languishing to return to my books and my pen, but this moving of
merchandize and the attendant hurry was completely broken in upon my
time and habits. I hope however to begin next week well, and once started,
I feel certain I shall go on prosperously. Had I any choice I would go
into the country and bury myself among the groves for the whole summer;
but I rather think I shall pass the greatest part of it in the City. I rode
out to Mrs Renwicks place yesterday and rambled over the scenes of last
summers pastimes. but some how or another my mind was so bewildered
and poisoned by worldly thoughts and cares, that the sweet face of nature
had not its usual effect upon my feelings—I'm weary of company and dissipation—I have gone through such a variety this last winter, that I am
perfectly sated for the present, and feel no disposition to visit or mingle
in any scene of amusement. I'd give any thing to be accompanying you
through the sublime solitudes of our savage country. I feel as if I could
sit for hours and muse deliriously on the borders of one of our vast lakes
or on the summit of one of our solitary promontor⟨ie⟩ys[30] in the Highlands
as I did last summer—or in fact any where where I had not to listen
to the tedious common place of fashionable society—and had some of the
grand scenes of nature to occupy my mind. I have been mingling in
company for some days past, without any soul or spirit—a mere vacant
carcass of a man—sunk in apathy and indifference. Not that I feel any
thing like gloom or ill humour—it is a languor of the mind—or rather my
mind is tired of being mocked with trif⟨f⟩les ⟨of⟩& mere amusement, and
craves food, occupation, and its own society. This makes me restless and
unsatisfied though surrounded with pleasure—As I know the malady,
however, I feel no fear of speedily curing it.

McGillivray[31] and the honest, hard favoured Emas Cameron arrived
here a few days since and the former will probably hand you this letter.
I have I believe written pretty nearly all I have to say—and this letter
is made up of ↑such trifling chit chat &↓[32] such trif⟨f⟩ling topics that
I should be ashamed to send it to any body but yourself. You may see
from the tenor of it, in how slip slop a manner I have been passing my

time. But this is transient and temporary prodigality of life and talent—
I will make up for it all when I return to busy occupation.

I expected to have heard, from you before this, but I find nobody
has had a line from you but *Dashwood* so I ⟨wo⟩shan't complain.

God bless you my dear fellow and keep you sound, prosperous and
happy.

Affectionately yours
W Irving.

MANUSCRIPT: Yale. PUBLISHED: *Irvingiana* (New York, 1860), p. ix (in part).
This letter, a copy in an unidentified hand, has a heading by P. M. Irving "To
Henry Brevoort Ford by Mr McGillivray."

1. The context suggests that WI may be referring facetiously here to John Jacob
Astor, by whom Brevoort was employed in Mackinac at this time.

2. See Gen. 16:7.

3. In the *New York City Directories* for 1811 and 1812, P. & E. Irving Co.
is located at 135 Pearl Street. The firm is not listed in 1810, though William
Irving had a mercantile establishment at 153 Pearl Street. Perhaps WI was helping
to move the merchandise of P. & E. Irving Co. into separate quarters.

4. Astor had amassed a fortune of $250,000 in the fur trade with Canada
by 1800. In the next decade he successfully expanded his enterprises to include
the upper Mississippi Valley and the Pacific Northwest.

5. WI and Brevoort had shared quarters in the boarding house of Mr. and
Mrs. Albert Ryckman at 18 Broadway before Brevoort's departure into the wilder-
ness on fur-trading business. For other details, see WI's letter to Mrs. Ryckman,
February 13, 1815.

6. See WI's letter to Henry Brevoort, March 5, 1811.

7. Matilda, daughter of Charles Nicholas and Alice Ann Hoffman. See Eugene
A. Hoffman, *Genealogy of the Hoffman Family—Descendants of Martin Hoffman*
(New York, 1899), p. 277.

8. Margaret Ann Brevoort (1794–1868), who married James Renwick (1792–
1863) on October 10, 1816. Jean Jeffrey Renwick (1774–1850), to whom Robert
Burns had addressed his poems, "The Blue-eyed Lassie" and "When First I Saw
Fair Jeanie's Face," had married William Renwick in 1791 and moved to New
York a few years later. See Helen H. McIver, comp., *Genealogy of the Jaffrey-
Jeffrey Family*, (n.p., 1925), p. 3.

9. James Kirke Paulding.

10. Possibly the daughter of Thomas Knox, a New York merchant. See Scoville,
Old Merchants of NYC, III, 24; *New York Directory* for 1811.

11. "Sue" is written in PMI's handwriting.

12. Bubble and squeak is an English dish consisting of cold boiled potatoes and
greens fried together, sometimes with pieces of cold meat added. The potatoes and
greens first "bubble" in water when they are boiled and then hiss or "squeak"
in the frying pan.

13. Probably this is Peter Kemble, Jr., alluded to in the next sentence. Being
"Jr." might make him the heir apparent. The "little Heiress" is perhaps the
daughter of Alex Stewart mentioned in the next sentence. There are four Alexander
Stewarts listed in *Longworth's Directory* for 1811; the best choice seems to be
Alexander Stewart, a ship chandler with a store at 68 Wall Street. Pistareen John

is perhaps an allusion to Prester John, the fabulous Christian king and priest, supposed to have ruled in the heart of Asia in the twelfth century. Since WI refers to John Jacob Astor as the "Great Mandarian" in the beginning of the letter, perhaps he is continuing his Asiatic theme and means Astor here also.

14. Probably Louisa Augusta Gouverneur, daughter of Nicholas and Hester (Kortwright) Gouverneur. Louisa was allegedly engaged to C. C. Cambreling in 1819 (see LBI, I, 115) but married David Johnston Ver Planck (b. 1789) in June, 1823. David Ver Planck was a prominent New York politician and was at one time editor of the New York *American*.

15. The Macombs were a large family who lived in Belleville, New Jersey. Apparently members of the clan lived there on-and-off for indefinite periods of time, as *The Macomb Family Record* notes many births occurring there in the late 1700's and early 1800's, although the parents in question may have had their permanent residence elsewhere. Some Macombs WI might have known were Alexander (1782–1841) and Catharine Macomb, cousins who married in 1803 and produced a large family. The "little Macombs" WI refers to are probably sisters and cousins of Catharine and Alexander.

16. Captain Frederick Philipse.

17. John Alsop King, son of Rufus King and later congressman and governor of New York.

18. Mrs. Colden, the former Maria Provost (d. May 10, 1837), whose sister-in-law was the first wife of Josiah Ogden Hoffman.

19. Alice Ann Hoffman was now married to Charles Nicholas. See note 6.

20. John Robert (1755–1851) and Eliza McEvers Livingston had the following daughters: Angelica, d. 1815, unmarried; Serena, married Colonel Charles Croghan; Eliza, married Captain Benjamin Page; Margaret, married Captain Lowndes Brown. John R. Livingston's brother, Edward L., had a daughter named Julia, b. 1794. See F. Van Rensselaer, *The Livingston Family in America*. WI discusses Angelica's death in a letter to Brevoort, March 15, 1816.

21. Thomas Apthorpe Cooper, who was courting Mary Fairlie at this time.

22. The *New York Directory* for 1810 lists Isaac S. Douglass, merchant, who was a member of the New York City Council, and James Douglass, merchant.

23. A term then in vogue denoting freebooters.

24. Cooke and Cooper had played together in Philadelphia in late April before coming to New York. Between May 6 and 24 they appeared together nine times, three of which were in *Othello*. See Reese D. James, *Old Drury of Philadelphia*. p. 88; Odell, *NY Stage*, II, 369.

25. *Alexander the Great* was performed on May 15.

26. *The Fair Penitent* appeared May 17, not May 14, as WI claims.

27. *Venice Preserved* was presented on May 20, with Cooke playing Pierre and Cooper playing Jaffier.

28. Cooke's benefit on May 22 was *Henry IV*, Part I, not *King John*. Cooke played Falstaff, Cooper played Hotspur. *Othello* was performed on May 24.

29. Johnny Fig may be John Irwin, who had gone to the West Indies in 1809. See *Letters of J. K. Paulding*, p. 28.

30. The copyist changed the word to the incorrect spelling.

31. William McGillivray (1764–1825), who signed an agreement with John Jacob Astor concerning the division of territory between McGillivray's North West Company and Astor's American Fur Company. See Marjorie Wilkins Campbell, *McGillivray, Lord of the Northwest* (Toronto, 1962), p. 162.

32. This insertion is in the hand of PMI.

98. *To Henry Brevoort*

New York, June 8th. 1811.

Dear Brevoort,

L'Herbette has just informed me of an opportunity which departs today, of writing to you—I am half inclind not to use it, as you remained several days at Montreal without writing me a line, though Judge Ogdens family[1] ⟨Prender?⟩ afforded a certain & speedy conveyance. I wrote you a long letter by McGillivray which I suppose you have received. Nothing of particular moment has happened Since the writing of that epistle excepting the arrival of the most noble Patroon, ⟨h⟩who has once more resumed his Sway over the club.[2] Gouv has had a long and boisterous voyage in an old leaky hulk of a british ship, with a mutinous crew and a nincompoop captain—⟨?before?⟩ He & Ben Seaman[3] were so tired of their ship that they quit her about 150 miles from land & got on board a coaster by which ⟨they were⟩ after being tossed about 4 days they were landed at *folly landing* in Virginia[4] & got home in a week more; ⟨p⟩ having by this *short cut*, arrived here in little more than 8 days *after* the ship, which made the light house in 20 hours after they quit her. Gouv has now been home three or four days, and has already become so regular, and domestic, and has fallen so exactly into his old habits, that it begins to seem as if he had never been away from us—I never knew a fellow so little changed by European travelling. His looks too are much the same, excepting that he is a little sun burnt, but he is still as spare and gaunt as a greyhound—Since his return we have treated Peter,[5] the late Prince Regent, with great contempt, and take all possible occasions to flout him and piss upon him.[6] I am convinced there is nothing on earth so truly *dispiseable*, as a great man shorn of his power. Peter[7] however consoles himself by courting all the little girls in town, who are under Sixteen; for you must know this old lecher has become so dainty and sickly in his palate, that nothing will go down with him but your squab pidgeons and your first weeks green pease. He[8] has likewise become a notable leerer at buxom chamber maids and servant girls, and there is not a little bitch of a house maid that runs *proud* about the streets, but what peter has had the nosing of her—not that the little villain tups them all, but he is one of your little gluttons whose eyes are greedier than his belly, and where he honestly rodgers one, he dishonours a dozen with his lascivious looks. When he sits at the parlour window and snuffs up the gale as any little "piece of beef" goes by, he reminds me most powerfully of the old duke of Queensbury whom I used to see, wheeled out in his easy chair, to the porch before his door, that he might ogle the wenches as they passed by—But peter is a "Dam rascal" and theres an end of it.

As to the Lads, I have seen them but once or twice since that memorable evening of which I wrote you—I passed an evening with them about a week ago at Miss Wilke's's, and as they did not attempt to ⟨b⟩ sparkle, they did very well. But I am weary of gossipping, and have almost entirely ⟨do⟩ left off visiting for some time past; it will become amusing again by next fall. I do want most deploreably to apply my mind to something that will arrouse and animate it; for at present it is very indolent & relaxed; and I find it extremely difficult to shake off the lethargy that enthrals it. This makes me restless and dissatisfied with myself, and I am convinced I shall not feel comfortable & contented until my mind is fully employed—⟨[unrecovered]⟩ Pleasure is but a transient stimulus, and leaves the mind more enfeebled than before; give me rugged toil, fierce disputation, wrangling controversy, harrassing research, give me any thing that calls forth the energies of the mind; but for heavens ⟨sh⟩ sake shield me from those calms, those tranquil slumbrings, those ennervating triflings, those syren blandishmints that I have for some time indulged in, ⟨and⟩ which lull the mind into complete inaction, which benumb its powers, and cost it such painful & humiliating struggles to regain its activity and independence.

I am ashamed to say that I have not been out to your fathers since your departure. I have however frequently seen Margaret[9] at Mrs Renwicks, with whom she is a great favourite; and who is a friend worthy of her cultivating. Your family I believe are all well; I suppose L'Herbette will give you particular accounts of them.

Cooke & Cooper played here several nights to very good houses and are now performing at Baltimore[10]—Since their Departure ⟨the⟩ King Rusher[11] kindly gave Dwyer[12] six nights engagement; during which time he played as might be expected to empty boxes, and will probably clear 50 Dolls by his engagt. Write to me by the first opportunity & believe me ever

Yours truly
W Irving

ADDRESSED: Mr Henry Brevoort Junr. / Michilimackinac   DOCKETED: New York Jun 8. 1811 / Washington Irving
MANUSCRIPT: The Carl H. Pforzheimer Library; abridged copy, not in WI's hand, at Yale. PUBLISHED: LIB, I, 196–200.

1. Isaac Ogden, the son of David Ogden, was a Loyalist during the Revolution who fled to Canada in 1783. In 1794 he moved with his wife and nine children to Montreal, where he served as judge of the Puisne Court. See Archie Binns, *Peter Skene Ogden: Fur Trader* (Portland, Ore., 1967), pp. 3–10.

2. The Patroon was the name given to Gouverneur Kemble by the Lads of Kilkenny.

3. The *New York Directory* for 1811 (p. 258) lists B. Seaman, merchant, Liberty near Greenwich, and Benjamin R. Seaman, 296 Pearl.

4. Folly's Landing was a port of entry for Accomac County; it was located on Folly Creek, which runs into Metomkin Bay of the coastal side of Virginia's Eastern Shore.

5. Peter Kemble was the younger brother of Gouverneur.

6. George Hellman (LBI, I, 197) omits the last four words of the sentence, and the Yale copy has "hiss upon him."

7. The Yale copy, beginning with "Peter," omits the rest of the paragraph.

8. Hellman (LBI, I, 197) omits from "He has likewise ..." through "piece of beef goes by."

9. Margaret was the sister of Henry Brevoort.

10. Cooke appeared seven times in Baltimore between May 31 and June 10, appearing in *Richard III, Othello, The Man of the World, Venice Preserved, The Merchant of Venice,* and *Henry IV,* Part I. Cooper also played Hamlet. See James, *Old Drury of Philadelphia,* pp. 91–92.

11. This is probably a reference to Stephen Price, manager of the Park Theater, whom WI often called "King Stephen." Why Price is called "Rusher" here is not clear.

12. John H. Dwyer (d. 1843) was an Irish-born actor who first appeared at the Park Theater on March 14, 1810. During this engagement he appeared six times between May 27 and June 7, 1811. See Odell, *NY Stage,* II, 337, 369–70. Hellman (LBI, I, 200) transcribes Dwyer as "Duryea."

99. *To James Renwick*

New York, Septr. 10th. 1811.

My good lad,

There is nobody in this world that loves more to bestow a favour than myself—when it costs nothing & may as well be bestowed as let alone. So having a morning totally at my disposal and nothing else to do, I have determined to write you a letter, to let you see how much trouble I am willing to put myself to on account of the friendship I bear you.

You may remember the time you passed by in the steam boat, as I was standing on the rocks in the highlands—and I never felt more disposed in all my life to do a mischivious prank, than I did then, to catch up ⟨one of⟩ the Rock⟨s⟩ I was standing on, and like another Polyphemus,[1] hurl it upon your vessel, even though I should throw myself along with it—for it grieved my very soul to see these upstart, copperhead skippers, with their opposition boat, running away with all poor Fultons well earned profits.[2] I passed a fortnight very agreeably among those noble solitudes. There is something ennobling and elevating in being shut up among the stupendous mountains, a man rises into a fine swelling style of thinking. His mind seems to reflect the sublime objects around him, and his ideas become by degrees very grand and mountainous—at least such I found to be my case and I had not been up there above a week before I conceived every thing on a huge shadowy scale, and I verily

believe the smallest idea that sprung up in my brain was equal in alti-
tude to Anthonys nose and at least as broad as Dunderbarrack.[3] This may
account for one or two attacks I had of the headache—a very unusual
complaint with me, and caused no doubt by the gigantic reflections
↑with which my pericranium was↓ ⟨that was⟩ continually in labour—
⟨However I therefore can determine wheth⟩ Just at the time you passed
by me I was in the very act of making a great & curious discovery—I had
⟨been studying⟩ finished my dinner and having refreshed & moistened
my thinking faculties with a flaggon of the captain's excellent Madeira,
I all at once found myself in a wonderful fine mood to sally out and
pursue my philosophical studies of the surrounding country—There is
no time so favourable to your true philosophical theorizing, as just after
an exceedingly good dinner—Well, sir, I repaired down to the rock where
you saw me and began to con over in my mind the theory of Dr Mitchell
and others concerning the origin of that river[4]—These worthy gentlemen
you know hold it for certain that the Hudson was formerly a huge lake,
but that at last the mountains of the Highlands, either from old age,
or some other natural cause, all at once becoming very incontinent of
their water, suffered it all to escape them, when it forthwith made its
due course to the ocean—that convenient chamber utensil, which all the
river gods make such barefaced use of. While I was meditating upon
this wonderful breaking up of the waters, it occurred to me and I have
since ascertained it to be a fact, that Gibbet Island, Ellisons Island
& all the little Islands in our harbour,[5] were all little fragments of the
highlands that floated down on this sudden inundation, some of which
run aground opposite Communipaw—and others floated out to sea,
where they foundered and were never heard of more. And what is ⟨more⟩
strongly in favour of this opinion is, that an old Dutchman gave me his
word, that ⟨near⟩ pollipois Island,[6] which you know lies at the mouth of
the Highlands, had drifted at least two miles down the river since he was
a boy—Nay I am told old Peche Praun Van Zandt[7] reccollects when he
was a little shaver, that he was once swimming at Gibbet Island, and
taking a deep dive, when he came up he found himself on the other
side of it having passed quite under the Island—As I am about publishing a new Edition of the Hist of New York[8] I shall certainly impart
these interesting discoveries to the world—in the mean time, you may as
well consult Dr Kemp[9] as to the probability of them, for I like always
to be on the safe side in what I assert.

Since my return I have passed my time very pleasantly, now and
then making a little excursion on this best of Islands—but I believe the
shortest way to give you an account of Domestic matters will be to
detail the history of my last Sundays campaign. Just before Sundown I
took me a hack and rode out alone, in the true Bank Director Style, as

far as little Margarets,[10] where I discharged my equipage and stayed to tea—Margaret has behaved herself very tolerably of late, romps very little, does not tear above three frocks in a week, has not lamed more than six young gentlemen in the last fortnight, and in a word is considered a very promising little good for nothing gentlewoman—I assure you I am not exaggerating.

From Margarets I went to a tea party at Mr. Turnbulls.[11] By the bye, I lately found out in the course of my reading, that the Turnbulls derive their name from a gallant gentleman, who rescued Robert the Bruce[12] from the attack of a furious animal of the kind, & who was therefore rewarded by the name in commemoration of his exploit. As I am always grateful for any good turn done to my ⟨an⟩ poor dear ancestors, I have ever since felt a kindness for the Turn-bull family. This tea party I discovered was given in compliment to Mr & Mrs Gallatin,[13] and a number of young gentlemen and ladies were assembled to regale the man, whom the president delighteth to honour. I found your mother in close discussion with Mrs Gallatin, just behind the fire place. It is always politic to appear on familiar terms with people who are rising in the world, so as I percieved how matters stood, I accosted your mother in a very sociable manner, and I will do her the justice to say, she received me with all the kindness and condescension I could possibly expect, considering what a vast accession of dignity & importance she had derived from ⟨the recent th⟩ her confidential conversations with Mrs Gallatin. I must say however, that these communications with the heads of Departments have had some unfortunate effects upon the worthy lady— She has been closetted two or three times with Mrs Gallatin since when she has now and then fallen into a deep reverie and altogether has lost her usual frank unreserved manner, and become very thoughtful and mysterious. I have been endeavouring, but in vain, to gather from her looks and ⟨actions⟩ conversation what is likely to be the result of our present ⟨a⟩ situation with England, she has dropped several hints about the necessity of being cautious in what one sa⟨id⟩ys in the present distracted state of affairs. ⟨and I am told often⟩ It was but the day before yesterday I asked her at table whether she would choose English or American cheese, when with one of the most gracious, but at the same time mysterious & baffling smiles in the world, she observed that it was a delicate matter to decide—she wished to shew no national partialities—so she took some of each. I observe however, with great satisfaction, that she has come completely round on the affair of the little Belt,[14] ever since she had that close conversation with Mrs Gallatin in the chimney corner, while the young folks were dancing; for a few evenings since happening to stumble on this accursed Victory of ours, she be-rated me so soundly, that like poor Rodgers[15] (according to Admiral Sawyers[16].

account) after three quarter of an hours fighting I was fain to sheer off with a broken heart and absolutely went supperless to bed—whereas, mirabile dictu! she now begins to fight most valourously on the side of Rodgers, and thinks, with little Parson Berrian,[17] that "Bingham[18] will certainly be hanged" Such, my dear Boy, are some of the wonderful ⟨effects⟩ changes in your good lady Mother, ever since she has become one of the heads of departments—nor must I forget to mention that she begins to shew a great disposition to patronize—↑which you know is↓ one of the invariable attendants upon power and greatness She has of late been pleased to speak very kindly of Fulton, and in fact told me that she meant to take him under her care. Nay she hinted, though somewhat obscurely, that she meant to get her friend Mr Gallatin to grapple all the new Steam boats, as Gulliver did the fleet of Lilliput;[19] and tow them all round to Washington. This however, you need not repeat, as I am noways desirous it should be either told in Gath, or published in the streets of Askalon,[20] for there is no knowing what the Albanians might do, were they to get an inkling of the matter.

Tho' I am very much opposed to petticoat government in either church or state, yet I confess (so selfish a being am I) that I cannot but witness with pleasure the growing influence of your mother in the Cabinet—I believe the good woman wishes me well, and who knows but she may speak a good word for me to the Secretary of the Treasury, and then as Dennis Brulgruddery[21] says, "he may give me a big bag of money!"

But to return to Capt Turnbulls—the company after some time fell to dancing, by way of amusing Giaffer the Grand Vizier,[22] and you would have been astonished to see how zealous the young folks were to reccommend themselves to his notice by feats of activity. Maria Laight[23] did wonders—she was the Sturdiest little sylph on the floor and found such favour in the eyes of the Vizier, that had not the calif been limited in his wives, I verily believe he would have carried her to Washington for little Haroun Alraschids Seraglio. For my part I took no part in the dance—it is true Mrs Kemp[24] & myself did once talk a little about dancing a cotillion, but it was only in the course of a little flirtation that took place between us, of which you of course will not mention a word to the Doctor.

—I set out to give you an account of my Sundays campaign and here I have written a volume & am still busy with saturday evening—so the only way will be at once to break up capt Turnbulls party and get to Lindesfern[25] where I went & passed the night. In the morning I bestirred myself by times and having arrayed myself in goodly garments, and had my coat particularly well brushed, I girded up my loins and prepared to walk to church, being determined not to be troubled with the poney, who I grieve to say, shews great impatience when carried to church, and makes no scruple of sneezing in the window, during divine worship. As to your mother and Mrs Kemp they ⟨chose to⟩ preferred to stay at home and romp with the children—and when I reproved them for their want of zeal, your mother had the malice to insinuate that I went to church purely to see the little beauty of the Sugar house[26]—But I forgave her in my heart, and prayed most fervently that she might be endued with the spirit of charity. After a long walk to church I had the mortification to find there was no service in consequence of Mr Jarvis[27] being absent for his health, and all the other clergy remaining in town to talk over and mourn the decision of the vestry against their Beloved Brother Cave Jones.[28] I was returning home very disconsolate on account of not being able to go to church, say my prayers, and see little Sugar plumb—when ⟨I⟩ in the midst of my musing I stumbled over something, which on getting up & rubbing my eyes I found to be a little presbyterian church, where a young apostle by the name of Gunn[29] (an old acquaintance of mine) kept up a constant firing upon the world, the flesh & the devil. I was seized with a great curiosity to see how Master Gunn, who I had not known since he was as big as a pocket pistol, discharged his duties—wherefore, looking around to see that I was not observed, I slyly slipped into the little Tabernacle. Here however I found a great many stray sheep of our own flock assembled, so that I plucked up heart, inasmuch as if it did get to the ears of the Bishop[30] that I had been in the congregations of the unbelievers, I could at least plead my being there in good company—The subject of the worthy parsons text was a moral & physical account of the Devil—and I never heard any poor fellow rated so soundly—he called him all manner of hard names, and in short, having got him cooped up in that little box of a church, he put me in mind of a rat in a trap or a snake in a cage which some unlucky urchin worries without mercy—the poor devil having no chance of escape or room to turn. My worthy friend old Mr Rhinelander[31] who happened to be present at this Devil baiting— observed to me that the Presbyterian Devil must be ⟨much⟩ a much sadder fellow than the devil of our church, for he never heard such a black character given of him before. For my part I dont wonder that these poor parsons get now and then out of humour with the fellow—Passing their whole lives in a state of constant warfare with him, and finding that in spite of all the excellent sermons they have preached, he is still as strong as ever, they must at length fall into down right personal hatred to him, much as the English at present do in respect to Bonaparte— among whom, every yeoman, independent of his national antipathy has a large stock of private pique and ill will to that most rascally little conqueror.

Well sir—having waited at the door after church—seen all the pretty girls come out—talked with the old folks about the sermon & agreed that the Parson was a very zealous, valiant little man that hated the Devil as he did poison, I prevailed on Phil Rhinelander[32] to accompany me home—this you will perceive was in the true style of Ally Croaker,[33] whom I look upon to have been one of the most accomplished generals that ever engaged in the wars of the heart. Arriving rather suddenly & unexpectedly at the chateau, we took the family by surprise—Your mother—excellent lady!—was napping most sweetly over a huge family bible indulging no doubt in some dream like the pious Bunyan[.] Mrs Kemp in another corner, was in the same plight over a book of poetry— I had the satisfaction to see however, that though her eyes were shut, her spectacles were broad awake and earnestly intent upon the book— which I suppose answerd the same end.

Before Dinner we strolled down to the river, where, from the uncommon fatigue I had endured I fell into a profound sleep on the grass—this your mother ⟨wa⟩very kindly excused to Rhinelander as the effect of my romantic disposition—and I have no doubt it has been accordingly reported—After a very agreeable dinner, ⟨I⟩ in which we vainly tried to draw some cabinet secrets from your mother, Aleck Fleming[34] & myself in the Gig escorted Rhinelander home—where I passed an hour or two very delectably; diligently employed in admiring a young lady,[35]—who shall be nameless—I am not a man to boast of success, or to reckon my chickens before they're hatched—but you shall have the baking of the sugar moulds— Ive said it & thats enough. To be sure, I must confess that I was more engaged in talking with the old Gentleman than with his daughter; and I dont know but what I cast more earnist looks at a comet which has lately made its appearance in a full bottomd wig, than I did at the little Star by my side, but Aleck, who acted as my Squire made up for all my deficiencies, by earnest attentions to the ladies; though I am half inclined to suspect the varlet played traitor to my cause & said a sneaking word or two for himself.

The next morning, lest I should be fatigued with walking I was kindly put on top of a huge Coach Horse—Daniel[36] led him out in the lane, where all the family, "large & Small, little & tall, merry men all" were assembled to see me off and overwhelm me with prayers & good wishes— I almost wished them all to Jericho—However Daniel turned the mighty chargers head toward town, started him off & let him go—& go he did— by the mass I thought I should have died before I got to the top of the lane—my heart was jolted up into my throat, and had I not kept my teeth close clinched I truly believe it would have bounced out at my mouth—This, thought I, is killing a man with kindness—however, I moderated my gallant grey into a shambling walk, and made out to reach town in little more than an hour—⟨sweating⟩ ⟨when?⟩ envying every humble pedestrian I saw—and sweating so intolerably that I mistook the weather & thought it was amazing sultry; and it was not until I had gone home changed my clothes & put on nankeens, that I was absolutely frozen out of my mistake—for it was, in sober sadness, the most wintry morning we've had this season—And so, my good lad, ends the history of my Sundays campaign.

Having written so long a letter already, I cannot in conscience think of adding any more, and must therefore suffer a world of news to remain untold. Little Cave Jones has been regularly denounced by the vestry. This was to have been expected—There were too many parsons busy in his affair to expect forgiveness. It is proverbial that ⟨the⟩ your amazingly virtuous women, never forgive one of their own Sex, who has unfortunately made a slip—and I think the same may be said of parsons in respect to ⟨their⟩ the frail among their bretheren — As I am fond of tracing things to their causes, I took some trouble to account for this inflexible and outrageous abhorrence to the frail of the ministry —and I am led to ascribe it to the kind of petticoat garments in which our clergy are arrayed—which no doubt invest⟨s⟩ them with a host of petticoat qualities—the aforesaid one among the number This, together with their constant flirtations and gossippings among the old "Saint errants" makes them in time lose their fine, generous masculine attributes, and to become very old womanish kind of animals. I know it is difficult for a parson to withstand all the baits & lures that the old dowagers throw out for him—Independent of the power which these old ⟨angels⟩ Matrons undoubtedly possess over the church, they are so surrounded by comforts & dainties; they have always such store of delicate cakes & sweetmeats & snug junkettings—things which your Liquorish toothed parsons do mightily delight in—that it is no wonder the poor clergymen are assiduous in their attentions. As to the old Ladies, they en[c]ourage[37] their attentions—for what think you?—for religions sake?—No such thing my good boy—from a mere lingering spirit of vanity & coquetry, which still exists even among the wrinkles & ⟨greedy⟩ grey hairs of age. When a woman begins to grow old and ugly—or rather when she thinks she does(⟨–⟩for she is generally a long while in finding it out ⟨–⟩) & when she no longer can flatter herself with the hopes of conquest—she then begins to turn her eyes to things above—that is to say to the parsons in the pulpits—and like a stool pidgeon endeavour to draw them down into her net—Trust me no young Belle can feel more pride in being surrounded by Beaux than one of these old saints does in being surrounded by parsons—and the more they have attending on them the more do they become a ⟨kind of⟩ in a manner Belles of the Sanctuary. And this let me tell you occasions not a little jealousy and ⟨hard⟩ heart burning & pulling of caps among them—but hold—Ill not say another word. I know I am treading on dangerous ground—Of all petticoats in the world I'd rather meddle with any other than those of a parson—His stormy virtue outblusters that of the veriest prude & brimstone—Therefore keep what I have said close within your breast my dear boy & s[ay not] [*MS torn*] a word of it to any [body?] [*MS torn*]—Heaven defend me from incurring the *tender mercies* of the righteous—

Give my sincere respects & regards to your worthy mentor,[38] who I hope & trust will bring you safe and much advanced in knowledge & virtue, to Ithaca—where I am happy to say every thing goes on much better than it did in Ithaca of yore—

I am, my exceeding good boy,

Yours ever
W Irving

ADDRESSED: Mr James Renwick
MANUSCRIPT: Columbia. PUBLISHED: *WI to the Renwicks*, pp. 5–15.

1. Poylphemus was a Cyclops, a one-eyed giant who imprisoned Odysseus in Sicily and ate six of his companions.

2. Robert Fulton and Robert Livingston were granted exclusive rights by the New York legislature in 1798 to operate steamboats on the Hudson River. However, Colonel John Stevens and his son, John Cox Stevens, challenged and broke their monopoly. See Archibald Douglas Turnbull, *John Stevens, An American Record* (New York, 1928), chap. XII, passim.

3. Anthony's Nose (elevation 900 feet) and Dunderbarrack (elevation 865 feet), now called Dunderberg, lie opposite from each other, on the east and west banks respectively of the Hudson River, above Peekskill at the southern edge of the Highlands of the Hudson. Anthony's Nose was named after the most prominent facial feature of Anthony Corlear, Peter Stuyvesant's trumpeter, whom WI had celebrated in *Knickerbocker's History of New York*. See Wallace Bruce, *The Hudson* (New York, 1907), pp. 82–84; *Knickerbocker's History*, bk. VI, chap. 3.

4. Dr. Samuel Latham Mitchill (1764–1831) had suggested the importance of water in the formation of the earth. See Courtney Robert Hall, *A Scientist in the Early Republic, Samuel Latham Mitchill* (New York, 1967), pp. 71–72. WI alludes to Dr. Mitchill's theory of the Hudson as a lake in a footnote in Book II, chapter 4 of the 1812 edition of *Knickerbocker's History* and also in Book VI, chapter 3.

5. Gibbet Island, the former name of Ellis Island, was so called because a pirate named Anderson was hanged there in 1765. Ellison's Island may be a variant for Ellis Island. The other little islands would probably include Bedlow's Island.

6. Pollipois or Pollopel Island was located at the northern gateway to the Highlands of the Hudson, near the east bank of the river, six miles above West Point. See Bruce, *The Hudson*, pp. 101–2.

7. Probably related to Wynant Van Zandt, II (1730–1814), or perhaps this was a familiar name for him. Another possibility: Peter P. Van Zandt, who died in August, 1812, aged 82. See Scoville, *Old Merchants of NYC*, IV, 92.

8. The exact date has not been determined, but it was some time during the

last half of September. The revised volume was reviewed in the *Port Folio* for October, 1812, which was published on October 6. See the NYEP, October 6, 1812.

9. John Kemp (1763-1812) was professor of natural philosophy at Columbia College.

10. WI is referring to Margaret Brevoort, mentioned in earlier letters. She later married James Renwick.

11. Probably Colonel George Turnbull, who lived on Broad Street and owned considerable real estate in lower Manhattan. One of his daughters married either Henry or Edmund Wilkes. See Scoville, *Old Merchants of NYC*, II, 314.

12. Robert Bruce (1274-1329) was a leader in the struggle for Scottish independence.

13. Albert Gallatin (1761-1849) was Madison's secretary of the treasury. He had married Hannah Nicholson (1766-1849), daughter of Commodore James Nicholson, in 1793.

14. The United States frigate *President* fired upon the British corvette *Little Belt* after she refused to identify herself. Five of her crew were killed and twenty-three wounded.

15. Captain John Rodgers (1771-1838) was in command of the *President* when she attacked the *Little Belt*. See C. O. Paullin, *Commodore John Rodgers* (Annapolis, 1967), pp. 223-41.

16. Rear Admiral Herbert Sawyer (d. 1833) was commander-in-chief of the British vessels along the coast of North America in 1811. See C. O. Paullin, *Commodore John Rodgers*, p. 235.

17. The Reverend William Berrian (1787-1862) was the assistant minister of Trinity Episcopal Church at this time.

18. Arthur Batt Bingham was captain of the *Little Belt*, a corvette of twenty guns. See C. O. Paullin, *Commodore John Rodgers*, p. 223.

19. See *Gulliver's Travels*, bk. I, chap. 5.

20. See 2 Sam. 1:20.

21. Dennis Brulgruddery was a character in *John Bull* (1803) by George Colman the younger (1762-1836). WI probably saw John Harwood perform in the role at the Park Theater in the fall of 1803 or after his return from Europe in the spring of 1806. See Odell, *NY Stage*, II, 188-89, 259, 266.

22. Giaffer was the companion of Caliph Haroun-al-Raschid, whose adventures are recounted in the *Arabian Nights*. WI is probably referring facetiously to Albert Gallatin here.

23. Maria Laight is probably the daughter of William Laight (1749-1802), a merchant who helped to found the Tontine Coffee House. See Bayles, *Old Taverns of NY*, p. 356; and John A. Stevens, Jr., "Biographical Sketches," in *Colonial Records of the New York Chamber of Commerce, 1768-1784* (1867), pp. 141-42.

24. Mrs. Kemp was the sister of William Renwick (1769-1808), James's father.

25. Lindisferne was the name given to the country home where Mrs. Kemp and Mrs. Renwick were staying. It was located in Bloomingdale, the area west of what is now Central Park between 68th and 81st Streets. See Stokes, *The Iconography of Manhattan Island*, III, 773.

26. This was an epithet applied to Mary Hobart Rhinelander (1795-1846), who married Robert Renwick (1793-1875), James's younger brother, on December 16, 1815. See *WI to the Renwicks*, pp. 10 n., 34 n. William Rhinelander's Sugar House was located on the west side of Rose Street near Duane. See Stokes, *The Iconography of Manhattan Island*, III, 963.

27. Samuel Farmar Jarvis (1780-1851) was in charge of St. Michael's Church,

Bloomingdale. See Morgan Dix, *A History of the Parish of Trinity Church in the City of New York* (New York, 1898–1906, 1950), III, 48–49.

28. The Reverend Cave Jones (d. 1829), an assistant minister of Trinity Church, opposed the nomination of the Reverend John Henry Hobart as assistant bishop in a pamphlet called *A Solemn Appeal to the Church*, but Hobart was elected on May 29, 1811. Although Jones was subsequently dismissed from his post, he protested the action for the next two years. See Dix, *A History of . . . Trinity Church*, II, 209–27.

29. Alexander Gunn (1784–1829) entered the ministry of the United Presbyterian Church in 1807. In 1808 he became pastor of a Reformed Dutch Church at 68th Street and Bloomingdale Road (now Broadway). See William Sprague, *Annals of the American Pulpit* (New York, 1869), IX, 166.

30. Bishop Benjamin Moore (1748–1816) had served in the place of the incapacitated Bishop Samuel Provoost since 1801.

31. William Rhinelander (1753–1825). See MS genealogy of the Rhinelander family in NYHS.

32. Philip Rhinelander (1787–1830) married Mary Colden Hoffman (1796–1818) on December 22, 1814.

33. "Ally Croker" was an Irish song popular from the mid-eighteenth century onward. Alicia Croker, the sister of the high sheriff of Limerick Breck-Hunt County in 1735, married Charles Langley of County Kilkenny. See Thomas Croker, *Popular Songs of Ireland* (London, 1886), p. 238. "Ally Croker" is referred to in Boswell's *Life of Johnson*, in Goldsmith's *She Stoops to Conquer*, and in Maria Edgeworth's *Belinda*.

34. Aleck Fleming is probably Alexander Fleming, who received a B.A. from Columbia College in 1809. He is listed in the *New York Directory* for 1821 as a merchant.

35. It is not clear to which of Rhinelander's daughters WI is referring—Eliza (1789–1873) or Mary. See note 26.

36. Probably the stableman.

37. WI omitted the *c* in writing this word.

38. John Kemp was probably regarded as James Renwick's mentor. See note 9.

100. To William Irving, Jr.

[October(?), 1811]

I don't know whether I mentioned to you that Salmagundi has been reviewed in the London Monthly Review,[1] and much more favorably than I had expected. The faults they point out are such as I had long been sensible of, and they seem particularly to attack the quotations and the Latin interwoven in the poetry, which certainly does halt most abominably in the reading. On the whole, however, I think we came off very handsomely, and I only hope the other critics may be as merciful.

PUBLISHED: PMI, I, 213.

1. This edition of *Salmagundi*, with an introduction and notes by John Lambert, was printed in London for J. M. Richardson. It was given a six-page notice in the

London Monthly Review Enlarged 65 (August, 1811). For a digest of the contents of this review see William B. Cairns, *British Criticisms of American Writings, 1783–1815* (Madison, Wisc., 1918), pp. 84–86.

101. To David B. Warden

New York, March 7th. 1812.[1]

Dear Sir,

This letter will be handed you by Mr Henry Brevoort Jr. whom I reccommend to your particular attentions. He is one of the dearest friends I have, with whom I have been for years on terms of the closest & most confidential intimacy. I am satisfied that I do you both a service, by this introduction; since, from the similarity of your tastes, and the natural bent of your minds,[2] I know of no men more likely to find gratification in each others society.

I am sure I have already said more than enough to procure your kind offices for my friend, and will only add, that I beg you will ever consider me at your commands, to render you all services in my power.

with sincere regard/Yours truly
Washington Irving

David B Warden Esqr.

MANUSCRIPT: Maryland Historical Society.

David B. Warden (1772–1845), an Irishman who became a naturalized American citizen in 1804, accompanied General John Armstrong, United States minister to France, to Paris in the same year as his private secretary. He held the post of United States consul at Paris from 1810 to 1814, after which he continued to live in France. WI may have met Warden in Paris in 1805.

1. In another hand, probably Warden's is written "Washington Irving—" above the dateline and "introducing Mr. Brevorrt" below it.

2. Warden was a collector of Americana and an enthusiastic supporter of the United States. Collections of his books dealing with America were later sold to Harvard College and the New York State Library. As WI suggests, Brevoort's interests were similar.

102. To Henry Brevoort

New York, March 17th. 1812.

Dear Brevoort,

I write this Letter in haste, merely to apprise you of the developement of Henrys[1] real character and schemes, which has come to light since your departure. Perhaps he may have told his own story to you, *in his own way*, but from the full disclosures he has made to our Government,

& which have been published, there is but one opinion here, which is, that Henry is an unprincipled and dangerous character. ⟨Your friends will feel⟩ By his own account he has been prowling about this country as a British spy, & was employed by Govr Craig[2] in 1809 to visit the Eastern States, ascertain the state of politics, and ⟨the⟩ if there was any disposition to rise in opposition to the General Govt. in case of a continuance of the Embargo; and if so, to offer the assistance of the British. This righteous mission was rendered unnecessary by the arrangement of Erskine[3]— Henry has been disappointed in his hopes of recompense from the British Ministry, and partly out of revenge, and partly as it is said, on condition of a large douceur & ⟨personal⟩ assurance of personal protection, has revealed the whole affair to our Government. I do not pretend to enter into the particulars of the transaction, you will doubtless hear it at large from other quarters. I only write in haste and anxiety, to charge you at once to break off from this ⟨?churl?⟩ dangerous man. How far his true history may yet be known; or how far he may have completed th⟨is⟩e desperate [game][4] he is evidently playing — it is impossible even to conjecture; but he is evidently a man far gone in the dark paths of deception and perfidy; and now that the mask is pulled off, may become bold faced and ⟨unsparing in⟩ unhesitating in his enterprizes.

I have been to all the editors, and prevented your name from being mentioned as fellow passenger &c — &c Zachy Lewis[5] had already mentioned you as one of the bearers of dispatches, and Lang[6] was laying his finger beside his nose, and knowingly inserting the initial of your name — This, however, was before Henrys affair was known. Since then, though the papers have been full of him & his ↑mysterious↓ departure, they have faithfully kept their words and not mentioned you. I feel extremely for the pain that this discovery will give you, ⟨and⟩ for it is always a horrible shock to the heart to find we have been placing confidence and friendship in ⟨one?⟩ a deceitful & worthless character.

I have not been very well since your departure, and am completely out of spirits, I do miss you terribly. I dined yesterday with a small party at Mrs Renwicks and was at a tea party in the evening, and yet passed one of the heaviest days I have toiled through this long time.

Your commission[7] has arrived from the Governor[8] and I will forward it to you by one of the present opportunities.

Your family are all well—/God Bless you my dear fellow/Yours Ever
                                                                         WI

ADDRESSED: à Mons: / Mons. Henry Brevoort Jr. / aux Soins de Mr. Jean M L'herbette / rue St Lazare No 5 / à Paris / pr N Dick [?]
    DOCKETED: March 17 1812 / W Irving
MANUSCRIPT: NYPL—Seligman Collection.   PUBLISHED: LIB, I, 54–57; PMI, I, 282 (in part).

1. John Henry, an Irishman who served in the United States Army between 1798 and 1802, went to Montreal in 1806. The disclosures relating to Henry as a British spy were communicated by President Madison to Congress on March 9 and 13, 1812. See *American State Papers: Foreign Relations,* III, no. 244, pp. 545–57. The NYEP, as well as other New York newspapers, covered various aspects of the case from March 12, 1812, onward. For other details see WI's letter of March 29, 1812.

2. Sir James Henry Craig (1748–1812), an English general who had been appointed governor general of Canada in 1807. He returned to England in 1811.

3. David Montagu Lord Erskine (1776–1855), appointed British minister plenipotentiary to the United States in 1806, had assured the United States Secretary of State Robert Smith that the Orders in Council of 1807 would cease to be operative after June 10, 1809. Erskine's assurance was disavowed by British Foreign Secretary George Canning but not before President Madison had proclaimed a resumption of legal trade with Great Britain.

4. WI probably inadvertently omitted the bracketed word.

5. Zachariah Lewis (1773–1840) was the editor of the New York *Commercial Advertiser* and of the New York *Spectator* from 1803 until 1820.

6. John Lang (1769–1836) was associated with the New York *Gazette* from March, 1797, until its demise in 1820. He was taken into partnership in 1797 by Archibald M'Lean, the publisher. When M'Lean died in 1798, Lang became sole proprietor. In 1801 Lang took John Turner into partnership, and in 1820 Lang's son Robert A. entered the firm. See Clarence Brigham, *History and Bibliography of American Newspapers, 1690–1800* (Worcester, 1947), I, 421.

7. The nature of this commission has not been ascertained.

8. Daniel D. Tompkins (1774–1825), governor of New York from 1807 to 1817.

103. To Henry Brevoort

New York, March 27th. 1812.

Dear Brevoort,

I have written you by two former opportunities[1] and lest the letters should have miscarried I again write to you, concerning your fellow traveller, Henry. He has made disclosures to our Government, confessing that he has been employed as a British Spy and Agent, to endeavour, in the Year 1808 to stir up Sedition in the eastern States & effect a dissolution of the Union. Being disappointed in his expectations of reward from the British Government he has betrayed the Secret to ours, and it is said has received a large reward. At any rate, his character is held infamous here, and you must by all means separate from him immediately. I have ⟨no⟩↑little↓ doubt however but you will have heard all the particulars before this letter reaches you and will have acted accordingly.

I have been so much occupied of late, partly by a severe indisposition of my good old mothers, (who has however recovered) and partly by my history,[2] that I have not had time to write you a letter worth reading. I will atone for it hereafter. I have concluded my bargain with Inskeep,

& am about publishing. I receive 1200$ at 6 months for an edition of
1500 copies. He takes all the expense of printing &c on himself.

I write in extreme haste for I fear my letter will be too late.

God bless you my dear fellow

Washtn Irvg

ADDRESSED: a Monsr. / Monsr. Henri Brevoort Junr. / aux-soins de M: Jean M
L'Herbette / rue St. Lazare / à Paris   POSTMARKED: Juin / 9 / 1812
DOCKETED: March 29, 1812
MANUSCRIPT: NYPL—WI Papers.   PUBLISHED: LIB, I, 58 (in part); PMI, I, 283
(in part).

To the right above the address in a different ink and not in WI's hand is an
unrecovered word, underscored, possibly "cendos." Below the address in what are
probably the same hand and ink is written: "[a]mericain Soire Mme Grenier / St
Lazare".

1. WI had written to Brevoort on March 17, 1812, and on another undetermined date. The latter letter has not been located.

2. A footnote, "revised edition of Knickerbocker," probably added by WI in
darker ink with a sharper pen, explains the allusion.

104.   To Henry Brevoort

New York, July 8th. 1812.

Dear Brevoort,

The unsettled state of the times, and the uncertainty of your movements almost discourages me from writing to you, lest my letter should
never come to hand—which, considering the great aversion I have to
letter writing and the great trouble it costs me to manufacture an
epistle, would be a vast deal of labour thrown away. But I will now
draw my bow at random and trust to providence that my shot may
reach you.

I am at present rusticating at a little snug retreat about six miles and
half from town,[1] on one of the hills just opposite Hellgate, and within
a stones throw of William Pauldings country seat. I am very pleasantly
lodged in a french family, with a wood around me and a beautiful
peep at the sound. Here I have settled myself for the Summer & part of
the fall to read, and, if it please heaven and the muse, to write. I have
a very pleasant neighbourhood—the Rhinelanders & Gracies[2] living within
ten minutes walk of me. I intend however, in the course of three or four
weeks, to voyage up the Hudson and see the fair nymphs of the Ferry
House.[3] These *exquisite creatures* left town about a fortnight since,
and took Miss Dallas[4] with them—She had been about three weeks in
N York, and had made great havoc round her. The Heir apparant,[5] that
liquorish young rogue, having just crawled out of the powthering tub,[6]
and being well primed with Mercury—was among the first to feel the

force of her charms; and followed faithfully in her train to the very last–⟨when⟩ not without suffering greatly from sundry long walks of hot days, which put him back very much in his complaint. The very day they left town he departed for the highlands, where he and the Captain[7] are toe to toe, drinking Madeira, ⟨talking⟩↑discussing↓ politics and morals, and both disputing very positively on the Same side of the question.

As to the captain he has taken me in for a coat, as I see no hopes of an Encrease to his family, and my bet with John King[8] will fall due ⟨this sp⟩ next spring–I have no chance for some months at least as the captain is so down about this war, that I do not believe he has animal spirits enough to go through the necessary operations.

I am extremely anxious to hear how you conducted in respect to Henry[.][9] I was very fearful that he might be able by some plausable story told in his plausible manner, to gloze over his conduct and interest your sympathy in his favour. In the United States there is but one sentiment respecting him; that of ⟨an⟩ the most thorough contempt. He is regarded as an unprincipled adventurer, with shewy but superficial talents and more cunning than wisdom. I hope the letters I wrote to you had their proper effect, in detaching you from him entirely and immediately.

I have not seen your parents for some time past. The distance I live from town makes it inconvenient for me to call there–particularly as I do not keep a horse, and have to depend upon chance conveyances to the city. I saw Margaret[10] lately at Mrs Renwicks. She informs me that Mess[?] John[11] has returned from Canada, having, according to David Ogden's[12] account, learnt all that it was possible for mortal man to learn in his situation. I mean to call in the course of a day or two and see how the young gentleman talks and looks after his travels.

The marriage has at last taken place between Mary F—— and Cooper.[13] They were married at his new house–Neither Mr nor Mrs F were present, nor any one excepting King Stephen[14] and his spouse– after the ceremony was performed Cooper attended her home and left her–and two or three days after they set off for Baltimore. ⟨Cooper has b⟩ The old Major[15] was worried into a kind of half consent. That is to say, if the girl could not be happy without it, why, he supposed it must take place. Cooper has been applying for a Lieut Colonelcy or a Majority in the army; but I believe has not succeeded. I was told yesterday that they had returned home again. Such is the end of a dismal courtship and the commencement I fear of an unhappy union.

I hinted in the former part of my letter that the heir apparant had been in the *powthering* tub; but I did not consider that ⟨you⟩ this misfortune had happened to him since your departure. ⟨This [*unrecovered*]⟩ I dont know but that part of the sin lies at your door, for I believe it was from one of your virgins that he received the blessing. I was for some time at a loss what to make of the little man's manouvres. [*unrecovered*] He would have a large tub of hot water brought into his room and then shut himself up for an hour with his man Toney, as if he was intent upon some infernal incantations. I happened to enter his room abruptly one morning, and caught him *in querpo*[16] in the middle of this machine up to his chin in hot water. I immediately concluded peter must be suffering under a fit of the Hypo. fancying himself a green turtle keeping up for a corporation feast, and that I was an Alderman come to inspect his condition. I expected every moment to see him dive to the bottom of his kraal. He has had a very long siege of it, and is now almost thoroughly recovered. He might have been well long since; but the little bellipotent knave cannot help toying occasionally with his bottle.

We had the magnanimous little Dr Earle here some short time since; and determined to shew him the glories of our Island. To which end we embarked six of us in a coach, like so many jolly captains of vessels, just landed, and took a days journey round the Island. We dined at Manhattan ville, and passed one of the merriest days I have spent for a long while. Indeed we have had three or four warm days work of late,.that reminded me very much of old times. The fourth of June we dined at Captain Philips and all got very much convinced by wine & wassel, what between the wine and the Song of Rule Britannia the captain got into a complete extacy—from thence we adjourned to Battins[17]—and finished the evening by Jims[18] singing under the Fair Julias window, an old song travestied and most horribly out of tune. A few days after Gouv Peter George Dallas[19] of Phila & myself dined on board the President[20] with the officers in the ward room—We had a most convivial time, but sat so late that we could not go on shore that night—and the next day we were kept on board by a perfect storm of wind & rain until evening. I believe the ward room wont forget the rouse we gave it for some time to come. The frigate is in excellent order. The officers are a set of very fine ⟨gallant⟩ young fellows, and I have no doubt if a proper opportunity presents will acquit themselves handsomely. But I look upon their fate as desperate, in a war with England

The little Taylor[21] ⟨was here⟩ has been here and passed some time since your departure. She is a delightful little creature, but alas, my dear Hal, she has not *the pewter*, as the sage peter says. As to beauty, what is it "but a flower!" Handsome is that handsome has,—is the modern maxim. Therefore, little Taylor, "though thy little finger be armed in a thimble," yet will I set thee at defiance. In a word, she is like an ortolan, too rare and costly a dainty for a poor man to afford; but were I a nabob, 'fore George, ortolans should be my only food.

As I rode into town the other day, I had nearly ran down the fair Maria M——re. I immediately thought of your sudden admiration for her, which seemd to spring up rather ⟨out of⟩ late in the season, like strawberries in the fall—when every other swain's passion had died ⟨of⟩ a natural & lingering death. The fair Maria (for almighty truth will out) begins in my eyes to look, as that venerable Trencherman Todd[22] would say—d——d stringy. She has been acting very much the part of the Dog in the manger—she cannot enjoy her own chastity but seems unwilling to let any body else do it. There certainly is a selfish pleasure in possessing a thing which is exclusively our own and which we see every body around us coveting—and this may be the reason why we sometimes behold very beautiful women maintaining resolute possession of their charms—and what makes me think this must be the reason, is that in proportion as these women grow old, and the world ceases to long after their treasures, they seem the more ready to part with them, until they at length seem ready to sacrafice them to the first bidder, and even to importune you to take them off their hands. This however I hope and believe will never be the case with the fair Maria, who, thanks to her cool temperament can still pass on "in maiden meditation, fancy free.["][23]

I forgot to mention that I received your letter written just after your arrival in Paris, and giving an account of your journey thither. I hope you may have found your other excursions in France equally agreeable. This war completely shuts up all my prospects of visiting Europe for some time to come; though I must confess I am so well pleased with home that I have no great desire at present to leave it. Travelling is a convenient alternative to resort to, when ⟨a⟩ we begin to grow sated with objects around us, and require to be stimulated by novelty and variety. I always keep it in view as a kind of succedaneum for matrimony, and promise myself, in case I am not fortunate enough to get happily married, to console myself by ranging a little about the world.

While I am in the country Jim garrisons my room in town and acts as guardian to the book cases. Jim has intimated a wish to commence another work and I have agreed to join with him provided he will prepare a number of essays.[24] I have commenced to do so myself, and unless he produces his share beforehand, I will dish mine up in some other form. I am in hope however, of drawing some out of him.

The Patroon[25] had very satisfactory intelligence from Uncle Nick[26] sometime since about their property in the Mediterranean. It has relieved his mind exceedingly; and for a week after, he was one of the most spirited, gay hearted beaux in the City. I dont think he is so ardent in his devoirs to the divine Julia as formerly—I suspect she has an alabaster heart in that fair bosom—not that I think the Patroon ever made any serious attacks upon it.

July 9th. In coming to town this morning I stopped at your fathers. The old gentleman took me all over his territories to shew me his subjects. Margaret has been rather unwell for a week past & looks pale; but is getting better. John too has taken cold and was indisposed, so that I did not see him—Your Mother, as you may suppose, is very anxious about the war, and wishes much that they would make peace so that you might return. The bear is in great spirits and is the wonder of the neighbouring swains. He does not seem however, to find favour in the eyes of the old man.

I have to conclude this letter abruptly in order to get it aboard the vessel—Your family all desired me to send as much love to you as my letter would carry—

Yours ever
W I

ADDRESSED: Mr Henry Brevoort Jr. / Care of Mr P Irving / Birmingham / England / via Halifax   DOCKETED: July 8. 1812

MANUSCRIPT: NYPL—Seligman Collection; partial copy made by PMI at Yale.

1. This was probably in the vicinity of J. O. Hoffman's country house where WI had stayed in the summer of 1809.

2. The farms of William Rhinelander and Alexander Gracie overlooked the East River near Hell Gate.

3. In *Knickerbocker's History of New York* (Book III, chapter 3), WI describes a "yellow brick, No. 23 Broad Street, with the gable end to the street, surmounted with an iron rod on which, until within three or four years, a little iron ferry boat officiated as weather cock." The identity of the girls is not known.

4. Miss Dallas is probably the daughter of Alexander J. Dallas, a Philadelphia attorney who later became Madison's secretary of the treasury.

5. Peter Kemble, Jr.

6. This was a sweating tub used for the treatment of venereal disease.

7. Captain Frederick Philipse, who had married the preceding fall.

8. John Alsop King (1788–1867), eldest son of Rufus King.

9. WI is referring to John Henry, Irish-born adventurer mentioned in his letters of March 17 and 27, 1812.

10. Brevoort's sister.

11. See note 9.

12. David Bayard Ogden (1775–1849), a socially prominent lawyer related to the Hoffman family.

13. Mary Fairlie and Thomas A. Cooper were married on June 11, 1812.

14. Stephen Price, manager of the Park Theater, at which Cooper was one of the leading stars.

15. Major James Fairlie, the father of Mary.

16. That is, naked.

17. John Battin ran a tavern and boardinghouse at 41 Nassau Street. For details concerning Battin, see Bayles, *Old Taverns of NY*, pp. 447–49; Wilson, *NY, Old and New*, II, 334.

18. James Kirke Paulding.

19. George M. Dallas (1792–1864), son of the distinguished public servant,

Alexander J. Dallas, was a graduate of Princeton who in 1813 accompanied Albert Gallatin on a mission to Russia.

20. The *President,* a 44-gun frigate under the command of Captain John Rodgers, had been on patrol to protect American ships from British attack. The ship had attracted widespread attention in May, 1811, when it put the British corvette, the *Little Belt,* out of action.

21. She may be a daughter of Jacob Tayler, who was later an alderman. Or she may be a granddaughter of Moses Taylor, a London merchant who settled in New York about 1736. See Lyman H. Weeks, ed., *Prominent Families of New York* (New York, 1897), p. 551.

22. Possibly John Payne Todd (1792–1852), Dolley Madison's son by her first marriage. WI probably met him in Washington in 1811.

23. *Midsummer Night's Dream,* II, i, 164.

24. This collaboration never reached fruition, although Paulding contributed extensively to the *Analectic Magazine* during WI's editorship.

25. Gouverneur Kemble.

26. Uncle Nick may be a reference to Nicholas Ogden.

105.   To Henry Clay

New York, Novr. 1st. 1812.

Dear Sir,

Permit me to introduce to your acquaintance Mr Abraham R Lawrence,[1] of this city. He is one of a committee appointed by the Importing Merchants of New York[2] to present a petition to Congress for relief from the bonds incurred under the Non importation Act. If I received a right impression from conversation I had with you last spring, I am strongly inclined to hope you will be in favour of our petiti[on] [*MS torn*] but at any rate, any advice and assistance that you can, consistently with your own opinions, and the disposition of your time, render to Mr Lawrence and his coadjutors I should esteem as a very particular obligation. I can moreover reccommend Mr L to your acquaintance on his own merits, as a gentleman of talents and information; well acquainted with the political affairs of this part of the union, and an active & influential supporter of your own side of the question

With my sincere remembrances to Mrs Clay

I am Sir/With great regard/ Your friend & Servt.

Washington Irving

Hon. Henry Clay

P.S. Should Mr Cheves, Lowndes & Calhoun[3] be of your household this sojourn I would thank you if you would make Mr L acquainted with them—

ADDRESSED: The Hon. / Henry Clay / Washington. / Mr Abm. R Laurence.
    DOCKETED: Mr. Irvings letter / of Intn to H Clay / not deld —

MANUSCRIPT: NYHS.

Henry Clay was a member of the House of Representatives and a staunch advocate of war with Great Britain.

1. Abraham R. Lawrence (b. 1780), fourth son of Jonathan Lawrence and Ruth Riker, was graduated from Columbia College in 1797. He was in the importing business from 1801 to 1811 with his cousin, John Lawrence, and in 1811 took his brother William into partnership. See Thomas Lawrence, *Historical Genealogy of the Lawrence Family* (New York, 1858), p. 109.

2. The committee consisted of Lawrence, John G. Coster, John Mason, and WI. See Lawrence, pp. 110–11.

3. Langdon Cheves (1776–1857), William Lowndes (1782–1822), John C. Calhoun (1782–1850), all members of Congress at this time from South Carolina.

106. To James Renwick

Washington, Novr. 24th. 1812.

Dear James,

I received your letter[1] some few days since but have been too much hurried and engrossed by business to be able to answer it sooner. It is with sincere sorrow that I hear of the death of Dr Kemp,[2] both on account of his own worth, and the important manner in which he was connected with your family. Any biographical sketch, which you prepare, I will be glad to receive for the first number:[3] you may inclose it to me directed to the care of Saml Ewing Esqr.[4] Phila. As I shall arrange ⟨the⟩ & ⟨publish⟩ print the first number in that city.

I am Sadly homesick, Sick of the business in which I am engaged and Sick of Washington.[5] I long once more to be at home among my friends, quiet in mind, and engaged in pursuits most congenial to my taste and habits. I think wealth acquired by this restlessness of body, anxiety of mind and sordid occupation of intellect, is dearly purchased indeed.

What will be the success of our mission is as yet quite uncertain; I trust that we ⟨shal⟩ will be ultimately relieved, but I anticipate great opposition and at any rate a strong and perhaps successful attempt to deprive us of the morsel of profits we may possibly be able to snatch from among the troubled waters. There is a narrow, pitiful spirit indulged towards us by many, that my gorge rises at. A disposition to extort money from the jeopardy and embarrassments into which the merchants have innocently fallen, from a reliance on the declarations of their Government.

But I loathe the subject and will not groan about it any longer.

I find by the papers that old Mrs Rogers[6] has at last literally laid down the burthen of existence. I hope the rest of Mr Gracies family are well, and beg when you see them and Charles Kings household[7] also, you will give them my sincerest remembrances.[8]

I am anxious to know how you make out in the Professors chair,[9] and whether the boys treat you with becoming reverence. You mention the matter very slightly in your letter, though you claim the tribute of homage from me, ex officio, a tribute which I am determined not to pay until I am satisfied that you make your rights respected.

I saw the Young Telemachus[10] and his knowing mentor (I. E. Bob and old Robin Gray)[11] on my arrival here. The former was dashing about upon a shambling pacing poney, and displaying the Equestrian graces of Rotten Row,[12] while the latter was lurking about the Galleries of Congress rolling his eyes warily from side to side, and dropping shrewd hints and surmises, with all the ⟨wary⟩ ↑portentous↓ demeanour of the "mysterious Beef eater." Finding that the young Telemachus was in great danger of falling in love with a little nymph from Ohio, who staid at Mrs Gallatin's, he suddenly hurried him off, and I have heard nothing of them since.

Mrs. Gallatin is the most stylish woman in the drawing room this Session. she dresses with more splendour than any other of the noblesse. "I dare be sworn, I think, that Albert is an honest man" but I could not help fancying that I saw two or three of my bonds trailing in her train. This however is between ourselves, dont let your good mother know a word of it.

I have to finish my letter hastily, for I must attend to business; so let this suffice to shew you that if I had time I would not want the disposition to write to you

Give my kindest regards to your mother and the family and believe me

truly your friend
Washington Irving

ADDRESSED: James Renwick Esqr. / Courtlandt Street / New York.   POSTMARKED: WASHN CITY / NOV / 24
MANUSCRIPT: Columbia.   PUBLISHED: WI to Renwicks, pp. 15–17; PMI, I, 286–87 (in part).

1. This letter has not been located.

2. Dr. John Kemp (b. 1763), professor at Columbia College, died on November 15, 1812. His first wife was Sarah Renwick (1771–1796), James Renwick's aunt and sister of his father, William Renwick.

3. WI assumed the editorship of the Analectic Magazine, beginning with the January, 1813, issue, but he published no sketch of Dr. Kemp.

4. Samuel Ewing (1776–1825), son of the provost of the University of Pennsylvania, was a Philadelphia friend of WI's. A decade earlier Ewing had been in love with Rebecca Gratz.

5. WI was again in Washington lobbying for remission of merchants' bonds forfeited under the provisions of the Non-Importation Act. The restrictions of this act were causing serious difficulties for the importing business of the Irving family.

6. Mrs. Esther Rogers was the mother of Mrs. Archibald Gracie. See PMI, I, 296.

7. Charles King (1789–1865) had married Eliza Gracie in 1810 and had become a partner in the mercantile firm of Archibald Gracie, her father.

8. Parentheses enclosing this paragraph appear to have been added by someone other than WI.

9. Renwick taught Dr. Kemp's classes at Columbia College during his illness and had now assumed full responsibility for them.

10. Young Telemachus was WI's facetious name for Robert Renwick (1793–1875).

11. "Auld Robin Gray" was a ballad written in 1772 by Lady Anne Lindsay (1750–1825) and set to an old Scotch melody. Although the song was very popular, Lady Anne did not acknowledge its authorship until 1823. See *DNB*, I, 1156–57. In WI's allusion "Bob" is Robert Renwick, accompanied by someone WI is parodying as Auld Robin Gray.

12. The riding path in Hyde Park frequented by English nobility and the socially elite.

107. To James Renwick

Washington, Decr. 8th. 1812.

My very good lad,

I am exceeding glad to hear, from your own self, which of course is the highest authority, what a prodigious fine fellow you have turned out to be. Your praises trumpeted forth by that *bang up* stentor, John Mason,[1] echoed through the nose of the worthy Dr Tillary,[2] while all the young ladies join in the chorus and laud you Secula Seculorum! God help thee, poor lad! dost thou take all this for sterling coin? I am half inclined to let thee remain in so vain glorious an error; but I hold him to be no true friend who suffers another to be happy without reason.

As to the praises of John Mason, I would not have you to count much on them, as they are founded on your disinterestedness—in other words you lecture for nothing, and Johnny Mason is too well versed in the proverbs to think of looking a gift horse in the mouth. As to the good Dr Tillary, he you say takes his cue from the account given of you by Mason, which of course speaks vastly in favour of his faith, but nothing of his judgement — and as to the ladies, (but this I speak under the most tremendous injunction of Secrecy) their praises are mere continental currency, — one hundred pounds for a dollar. I see how it is, you have been playing off your natural philosophy in the parlour, burning steel, making nitrous oxide, and worrying my old friend and favourite the jumping cat, by exhibiting her in an air pump,[3] to the great delight and wonderment of your good mother — and a number of ladies of her acquaintance. ⟨I expect on my return to see a perfect⟩

I suppose by this time a total revolution has taken place in your domestic circle. The young ladies tend lectures instead of dancing schools, read elementary works instead of novels and romances, and as to the statues of those two Scottish Grecians who whilom graced the mantle piece, clad in tartan plaids, they have had to make way for Sir Isaac

Newton and Ben Franklin — But jesting apart my dear James, I am really glad to hear, from various accounts, that you succeed so well in your perilous undertaking; and have no doubt, maugre the eulogiums of John Mason & the ladies, that you will do yourself great credit by this winters campaign. Still, however, let me beg you not to give ear to these "telltale women;"[4] nor attempt to make them wiser than they are. It is only spoiling them. I do adore their ignorance of divine philosophy, and beg you will suffer them still to believe that the sun travels daily around the earth, that the moon is made of green cheese, and that the antipodes crawl against the bottom of the earth on all fours, like flies against the ceiling.

⟨I could have wished⟩

I wish you had been here a few days since, to have heard Cheves open in our defence. He made one of the most eloquent speeches I have ever heard.[5] His views of the subject were so liberal and elevated, his sentiments so high minded, his illustrations so brilliant and such a manly generous spirit breathed throughout the whole, that I felt proud of our cause, since it was susceptible of such a vindication. The National Intelligencer of next thursday[6] will give a report of his speech; but it will be the mere body without the Soul. In the prosecution of the business I have in charge I have had opportunities of seeing a great deal of Cheves, and my opinion of him has been continually rising. I consider him one of the fittest men for public life ⟨of any⟩ that I have ever known. His natural talents are of a high order, he has bestowed the greatest pains in cultivating his mind his habits are industrious regular & persevering, his principles honourable & lofty, and his manners dignified, amiable and scrupulously delicate. With so fair a character, and such important requisites he cannot fail to rise to eminence. He has taken also a course of policy, which will certainly render him celebrated — He is the champion of Commerce. There is rapidly growing up and organizing two great parties in this country — which threaten to swallow up all others. The commercial & the agricultural. The latter ⟨have⟩ ↑has↓ the advantage of numbers, and its power and disposition is continually evinced in the debates & votes of Congress. To this class Cheves has given great offence, by his speech in our defence; ⟨where⟩ ↑wherein↓ he [has][7] vindicated the merchants from the overbearance of [the] agriculturalists. A great part of the democratic side [of the] house are much irritated by the generous warmth with [which] he assailed their popular measure of Non Importation &c and some have openly talked of denouncing him — but this they dare not do. Our Question has had a singular effect on the house in revealing this hostility of interests, and is making great dissensions in the democratic camp. We have strong talents on our side. I am in hopes of an able speech in our favour from Lowndes.

Phil Rhinelander & Paulding arrived here last evening — and informed me they had come on to ↑attend↓ my wedding.[8] I have determined therefore to give as much countenance to this report as possible and am ⟨determined⟩ resolved to become acquainted with the lady forthwith — that necessary preliminary not having as yet been attended to. Adieu, Domine felix!—remember me to your good lady mother, and ask her what is her opinion of the perpetual motion — if she has studied so far.

Yours truly
W I.

ADDRESSED: James Renwick Esqr. / Courtlandt Street / New York   POSTMARKED: WASHN. CITY / DEC / 8
MANUSCRIPT: Columbia.   PUBLISHED: *WI to the Renwicks*, pp. 17–19; PMI, I, 287–89 (in part).

1. Dr. John M. Mason (1770–1829) was a Presbyterian minister in New York and provost of Columbia College from 1811 to 1816.
2. Dr. James Tillery was a New York physician. See Scoville, *Old Merchants of NYC*, IV, 220–25.
3. WI alludes to some of Renwick's scientific experiments.
4. *Richard III*, IV, iv, 150.
5. Langdon Cheves, Chairman of the House Ways and Means Committee, spoke on December 4, 1812, in support of remission by the United States Treasury of the forfeiture on the bonds given by merchants according to the provisions of the Non-Importation Act. See *Annals of Congress*, 12th Cong., 2d sess., pp. 241–56. For other details concerning the remission of forfeitures, see *American State Papers: Finance*, II, no. 379, pp. 570–81; *The Memorial History of the City of New York*, ed. James Grant Wilson (New York, 1893), III, 260–61.
6. The *National Intelligencer* did not print Cheves's speech. On Saturday, December 5 it reported that "Mr. Cheves spoke at great length" against the Merchants' Bond Bill. On December 8 it printed the speech of Richard M. Johnson of Kentucky made on December 3, and on December 10 it printed the speech of Samuel L. Mitchill of New York, also made on December 3.
7. This and the words in the three subsequent bracketed passages are partially obscured by the seal on the letter.
8. WI's extensive socializing in Washington had apparently caused comment and speculation among his friends.

108. To David Longworth

Washington, Decr. 16th. 1812

Dear Sir,

I have been so much occupied and worried by the business I have to attend to here, that I have not been so punctual in executing your commission, as probably you expected, and as I certainly was disposed to be.

I find that it would be useless to apply at the War office for the list you require of the Army and Navy.[1] It has long been promised to Mr

Milligan a Bookseller of Georgetown, who I believe is befriended in this particular by Col Cushing, in consequence of an early application. He would have had it before this, but they are waiting until the grades are determined on, when the list will be put in his hands for publication.

You ask for a Gazzetteer of the seat of war, but I believe you are more likely to procure one in the large cities than in this place. As to a list of prizes you will find as accurate an one as is extant, in Niles Register.[2] If however either of the latter are to be procured here I will get them for you; but as far as I have enquired I give you the result—and believe it to be the fact. I hope you may succeed in your work though I much question whether undertakings of the kind will produce profit commensurate to the trouble.

I expect to be home in about eight days, when I will attend to the second edition of Salmagundi.[3]

Yours very truly
W Irving

Mr D Longworth.

Docketed: Washington Irving / December 16. 1812
Manuscript: Va.–Barrett.

1. David Longworth, who had published *Salmagundi*, brought out *The United States Kalendar and Army and Navy Register, for 1813, Corrected to the first of July*. Either WI succeeded in obtaining the list, or Longworth obtained it elsewhere.

2. Twenty-two prizes were itemized in the month preceding this letter. See *The Weekly Register* 3 (November 21, 1821), 192; (November 28, 1812), 207; (December 5, 1812), 224; (December 12, 1812), 239.

3. This edition was published in New York by Inskeep and Bradford and in Philadelphia by Bradford and Inskeep, with the title page deposited on June 3, 1812.

109. To James Renwick

Washington, Decr. 18th. 1812.

Dear James,

In one of your letters you desired to know when I would be in Philadelphia, and you proposed passing the Holydays there. I forgot to answer this question, nor would I have been able to have done it with certainty

I now expect to leave this city tomorrow. Our business is yet undecided, and will probably linger through several days more, but I consider the battle as won, & as there are enough here without me, to take care of our interests; and as it is very important I should be else where, I have made up my mind to depart.

I may possibly stop a day in Baltimore, ⟨to⟩ as I shall meet Gouverneur

Kemble there, and I wish to give him a farewell cheering — I shall then make the best of my way to Philadelphia, where I shall probably pass some days, but if possible I will pass *my* holydays in New York. I never wish to spend the merry ⟨S⟩ Christmass and jolly New Year, else where than in the gamesome city of the Manhattoes

My dear fellow you cannot imagine how I long to be once more at home — to doff this burden of care and business, and resume what the Portfolio calls my "elegant leisure."[1] By the bye, I have been "stayd with flaggons and comforted with apples"[2] by these editors and News paper writers, until I am sick of puffing. This Select Reviews has drawn upon me such an abundance of worthless complements, that I really stagger under the trash. Add to this, my publisher, who seems determined to make a comfortable penny out of me, has been advertizing, every day or two, some new addition and improvement, to be made to the Select reviews, of which I have known nothing until I saw the advertisements. At one time there is to be a series of portraits of our Naval Commanders with Biographical Sketches—at another a history of the events of our maratime war &c, on the plan of — the British Naval Chronicle! And here am I — poor I — while absent here, tied by the leg to the footstool of Congress, most ⟨fa⟩ wickedly made the editor of a vile farrago — a congregation of heterogenious articles, that have no possible affinity to one another—⟨It⟩ This motely collection, which is promised in my name, puts me in mind of a negros sign in New York of a fellow called Thomas Wilson — who was "Boot & shoe maker, washing ironing and fidler — N B. white washing up this Alley."[3]

I have written to Phila. that I would not consent to have such a fools cap put on my head — and if they ⟨did not chuse⟩ intended to interfere in the conduct of ⟨my⟩ the work I should decline having any thing to do with it. I think Job was a little out, when he ⟨exclaimed⟩ wished that his enemy had written a book[4] — had he wished him to be obliged to *print* one, he would have wished him a curse indeed! ⟨for these book-sellers are the greatest torments in creation.⟩

Rhinelander will remain here some days longer; he is much interested with the proceedings of Congress, and is a constant attendant in the Gallery. He has had a very favourable opportunity of judging of the talents of Congress; for our question has drawn out all the speakers.

I am very anxious to know whether Brevoort is expected out this winter, but have not been able to obtain information. I understand letters have been received from him in New York. By the letters which have arrived to our house, ⟨it app⟩ & which were written by my Brother [from] [*MS torn*] Liverpool, it appears that they were still on their [way?] [*MS torn*]

Tell your good lady mother that Mrs Madison has be[en?] [*MS torn*]

much indisposed, and at last wednesday evenings drawing room Mrs Gallatin presided in her place—I was not present, but those who were, assure me she filled Mrs Madisons chair to a miracle. You may likewise tell her that she may call ín her report about Madame Bonaparte[5] and myself as soon as she pleases, for it is all over with me in that quarter. I was last evening to have been introduced to her, and to have gone on a little *moonlight* party at Masons Island,[6] you may suppose what a favourable opportunity it was for sentiment & romance. As my unlucky stars would have it, I dined with a choice party at the Speakers,[7] drank wine, got gay, went home, fell asleep by the fire side, and forgot all about Madame Bonaparte until this morning — Do beg your mother for Gods sake to look out for some other lady for me — I am not particular about her being a princess, provided she has plenty of money — a pretty face and no understanding God bless you.

WI.

ADDRESSED: James Renwick Esqr. / Courtlandt Street / New Yor[k].
MANUSCRIPT: Columbia. PUBLISHED: *WI to the Renwicks*, pp. 20–22; PMI, I, 289–91 (in part); Waldron, *WI and Cotemporaries*, p. 180 (in part).

1. In a notice mentioning Moses Thomas's acquisition of the *Select Reviews* with WI as editor is the observation that "We cannot err in our anticipation that the acknowledged taste, and elegant leisure of the new editor, will enable him to render the Select Reviews still more attractive" (*Port Folio* 8 [December, 1812], 631).
2. Song of Sol. 2:5.
3. *Longworth's New York City Directory* for 1812 (p. 349) lists a Thomas Wilson, shoemaker, at 376 Greenwich.
4. WI seems to be wrenching the meaning of Job 19:23: "Oh that my words were now written! oh that they were printed in a book!" None of the references in Job relates to his comment.
5. Madame Jerome Bonaparte, née Elizabeth Patterson, was a Baltimore socialite whose marriage to Jerome Bonaparte was annulled by Napoleon.
6. Mason's Island, in the Potomac River opposite Georgetown, was an area of seventy acres. First called Annalorton Island, it was purchased by George Mason (1726–1792) in 1777 and inherited by General and Senator Steven Thompson Mason, who made it the seat of many noteworthy social gatherings. For a detailed description of the island and of a party held there in July, 1811, see Phillips P. Lee, *The Beginnings of Washington as Described in Books, Maps and Views* (Washington, 1917).
7. Henry Clay was speaker of the House of Representatives at this time.

110. To Peter Irving

New York, Dec. 30, 1812.

* * * I mentioned in former letters that I had undertaken to conduct the Select Reviews at a salary of 1,500 dollars.[1] It is an amusing occupation, without any mental responsibility of consequence. I felt very much the want of some such task in my idle hours; there is nothing so irksome as having nothing to do. You will, in future, send the periodical publications to me, and from time to time send an account of cost and charges, that I may settle with my bookseller. [I]² wish you also to forward, as soon as they can be procured, copies of new works that appear, that are not of a local or too expensive nature, fit for republication in this country. I suppose you can make arrangements with the principal booksellers to this effect, who would be attentive to so regular a customer. Any periodical work, besides those at present sent, which you may think of importance, I wish you to subscribe to.

We are all alive, at present, in consequence of our naval victories.³ God knows they were well-timed to save the national spirit from being depressed and humiliated by the paltry war on the frontiers. The impolicy of depending on militia and volunteers is now made glaringly apparent, particularly for offensive war, and the nation is incensed at having its character for bravery jeoparded by such short-sighted measures and such miserable military quacks as have been bolstered into command. Should this war continue, resort will be had to regular forces, a larger army will be raised by means of increased bounty and pay; and from the evidences given by our regular troops whenever they have' had an opportunity to grapple with the foe, I make no doubt that they will sustain the national character as gallantly on land as it has been on the ocean. * * *

The day before yesterday a public dinner was given in honor of Hull, Jones, and Decatur.⁴ It was the most splendid entertainment of the kind I ever witnessed. The City Assembly Room was decorated in a very tasteful manner with the colors and flags of the Macedonian. Five rows of tables were laid out lengthways in the room, and a table across the top of the room, elevated above the rest, where the gallant heroes were seated, in company with several of our highest civil and military officers. Upwards of four hundred citizens of both parties sat down to the dinner, which was really sumptuous. The room was decorated with transparencies representing the battles, &c. The tables were ornamented with various naval trophies, and the whole entertainment went off with a soul and spirit which I never before witnessed. I never in my life before felt the national feeling so strongly aroused, for I never before saw in this country so true a cause for national triumph. * * *

January 2, (1813.)—You will accept, my dear brother, my warmest wishes of a happy New Year, and give them also to the little household at Birmingham. It is idle to repeat the desire I constantly feel once more to see you all on this side of the Atlantic, enjoying these honest festivals together. * * *

January 12, (1813.)—The vessel having been detained for want of passports, I open this letter to add a few lines. Gen. Armstrong[5] has been nominated to the Senate as Secretary at War, and William Jones,[6] of Philadelphia, as Secretary of the Navy. I don't know whether I have mentioned in the preceding part of my letter that brother William was held up for Congress, and, owing to a coalition of the Clintonians and Feds, lost his election by about 200 votes.[7] * * *

P.S.—I had almost forgot to mention that Dunlap has nearly finished a Biography of Cooke.[8] He wishes to send a copy of the MSS. out to you and get you to dispose of it advantageously for him. He will write to you particularly on the subject, and, as he is an old friend and a very worthy man, I make no doubt you will do every thing in your power to benefit him. * * *

Send me out a handsome coat, but not with a waist as long as a turnspit's. By Brevoort you can send me the coat, a waistcoat or two of fashionable kind, and any thing that your fancy may suggest. I am determined Brevoort sha'n't throw me too much in the background with his Bond street fashions.[9]

PUBLISHED: PMI, I, 291–94; F. L. Mott, *A History of American Magazines, 1741–1850* (Cambridge, Mass., 1930), pp. 279–80 (in part).

1. After purchasing the *Select Reviews and Spirit of Foreign Magazines*, Moses Thomas, a Philadelphia bookseller and publisher, asked WI to become editor. At this time the title was changed to *The Analectic Magazine, Containing Selections from Foreign Reviews and Magazines, Together with Original Miscellaneous Compositions.* See Frank Luther Mott, *A History of American Magazines, 1741–1850*, p. 279.

2. The printed text omits the "I."

3. The victories of the *Constitution,* the *Wasp,* and the *United States* in the last half of 1812 were humiliating to the British and encouraging to the Americans. For details of these engagements see Theodore Roosevelt, *The Naval War of 1812* ([New York, 1924], chaps. 4 and 5), for detailed accounts of American naval activities in 1812. See also Horsman, *War of 1812,* pp. 58–66.

4. Isaac Hull (1773–1843), Jacob Jones (1768–1850), and Stephen Decatur (1779–1820) were honored at the dinner, though Captain Jones did not arrive in New York in time for the occasion. For other details see the NYEP, December 30, 1812.

5. John Armstrong, with a long record of public service, became secretary of war in February, 1813.

6. William Jones (1760–1831), a Revolutionary soldier of distinction, served as secretary of the navy from January 12, 1813, to December 2, 1814.

7. William Irving apparently lost to Egbert Benson, who resigned on August 2, 1813. Irving won the special election and served from January 22, 1814, to March 3, 1819.

8. William Dunlap, dramatist, artist, and theater manager, completed the *Memoirs of George Fred. Cook, Esq., Late of the Theatre Royal Covent Garden* in February, 1813. The book was published by D. Longworth of New York shortly thereafter, and later in London by H. Colburn.

9. Henry Brevoort was touring in Europe at this time.

111. To Henry Brevoort

New York, ⟨Dec⟩ Jany 2d. 1813

Dear Brevoort,

The uncertainty of your movements and my own wanderings have prevented me from keeping up any thing like a regular correspondence with you. Had I thought you would have wintered in England I should have written you before this⟨;⟩—but I will not spin out excuses.

I passed the early part of last Summer at a little retreat near hellgate, in the neighbourhood of the Gracies, Rhinelanders &c—and spent two months quietly and delightfully there. In august I sat off for the residence of the Highland Chieftain,[1] whither I was accompanied by James Renwick—we passed a few days very pleasantly there, during which time Renwick took a variety of sketches of the surrounding Scenery. The noble captain has completely failed in the matrimonial campaign—the lady shewing no symptoms of encrease.[2] I begin to despair of my coat. From the captain's I proceeded to the country seat of John R L——[3] where I remained for a week, in complete fairy Land. His seat is spacious and Elegant with fine grounds around it—and the neighbourhood is very gay and hospitable. I dined twice at the Chancellors[4] and once at old Mrs Montgomerys.[5] Our own household was numerous and charming—In addition to the ladies of the family there were Miss McEvers & Miss Hayward.[6] Dick McCall[7] also, was there; who was languishing at the feet of the fair Angelica[8]—He is engaged to be married to her. Had you but seen me, Happy rogue! up to my ears in "an ocean of peacocks feathers"—or rather like a "Strawberry smothered in cream."[9] The mode of living at the manor is exactly after my own heart—You have every variety of rural amusement within your reach, and are left to yourself to occupy your time as you please. We ⟨had⟩ made several charming excursions, ⟨such⟩ and you may suppose how delightful they were, ⟨how in su⟩ through such beautiful scenery, with such fine women to accompany you—They surpassed even our Sunday morning rambles among the groves on the Banks of the Hudson, when you and the divine Hen[10] were so tender & sentimental, and you displayed your Horsemanship so gallantly by leaping over a three barrd gate.

After returning from my Hudson excursion I was sent on an expedition to the eastward to ⟨secure our⟩ rescue our property from the hands of privateers men; who had carried in several vessels to eastern ports, having goods on board consignd to us.[11] This was a busy & hurried jaunt, in which I had no time for amusement. After my return I was sent on a mission to Washington, to carry a petition from the importing merchants praying for a remission of their Bonds.[12] This kept me for six weeks at Washington, from whence I have just returned, having happily Succeeded in the object of my journey[13]—There you have a brief sketch of my life for this six or seven months past—which has been a rather more busy one than common.

I am now once more at our old quarters[14] and am at this moment writing at my usual corner of the table before the fire which honest John[15] has just trimmed and replenished; would to heaven my dear fellow you were as formerly seated opposite to me. I cannot tell you my good Hal, how very much I miss you. I feel just as I did after the departure of my Brother peter, whose place you had in a manner grown into, and supplied. The Worthy Patroon[16] also has departed for Spain, to reside at Cadiz ⟨in the emp⟩ as an agent for LeRoy Bayard & McEvers,[17] and though I rejoice in his good prospects yet I cannot but deplore his departure. So we get scattered over this troubled world—this making of fortunes is the very bane of social life; but I trust when they are made we shall all gather together again and pas⟨t⟩s the rest of our lives with one another.

I have undertaken to conduct the Select Reviews,[18] for ⟨an⟩ the sake of pastime & employment of idle hours. I am handsomely paid & the work is no trouble—When you return we must determine on some new mode of living, for I am heartily tired of this Boarding house system. Perhaps it will be better to get a handsome set of appartments & furnish them. But of this we will talk further when we meet. I was at your fathers two or three days since. The old gentleman[19] ⟨had⟩ is highly tickled with the success of our Navy—He was so powerfully excited by the capture of the Macedonian,[20] that he actually performed a journey to the Brothers,[21] above Hellgate, where the frigates lay wind bound; and he brought away a piece of the Macedonian, which he seemed to treasure up with as much devotion as a pious Catholic does a piece of the True Cross. Your Mother is well, and is looking forward with the utmost impatience for your return.

A few days since we had a superb dinner given to the naval heroes,[22] at which all the great eaters and drinkers of the City were present. It was the noblest entertainment of the kind I ever witnessed. on New Years eve a grand Ball[23] was likewise given, where there was a vast display of great & little people. The Livingstons were there in all their glory. ⟨Mrs⟩ Little Rule Britannia made a gallant appearance at the head of a train of ⟨Beauty among which⟩ ↑beauties; among whom↓ were the divine Hen, who looked very inviting and little Taylor,[24] who looked still more so. Brittania was gorgeously dressed in a queer kind of hat of stiff purple & silver stuff, that had marvellously the appearance of Copper, and made us suppose that she had procured the real Mambrinos helmet.[25] Her dress was trimmed with what we simply mistook for scalps, and supposed it was in honour of the nation, but we blushed at our ignorance ↑on↓ discovering that it was a gorgeous trimming of Marten tips—would that some eminent furrier had been there to wonder & admire.

The little Taylor was as amusing and fascinating as ever. She is an arrant little Tory and ⟨amused?⟩ entertained me exceedingly with her sly jokes upon our navy. She looks uncommonly well and is as plump as a partridge.

I am sorry to inform you that Mrs Hoffman has been very alarmingly ill, and is still confined to her room though slowly recovering. Her complaint had symptoms of a pulmonary nature and gave great anxiety to her friends. I trust however that she will get the better of it. She bears her illness with all that gentleness & meekness that ever distinguish her, and appears more amiable & lovely under sickness than when in the full enjoyment of health and spirits.

Ann is passing the Winter at Mr Hoffmans. Charles has been unfortunate in business. I was always affraid that these huge ostentatious Book Establishments of Philadelphia would not answer. He has nearly ⟨most⟩ settled with his creditors and is expected here in a few days. They have lost their youngest child but the eldest[26] is one of the most beautiful little creatures I ever saw Ann is in good health & spirits and looks uncommonly well.

Our winter does not promise to be as gay even as the last; neither do I feel as much disposed to enter into dissipation. ⟨Some of my⟩ Mrs Renwicks family is in mourning for the death of Dr Kemp,[27] of course they do not go abroad so much, and their fire side is more quiet & pleasant. Young Bangup has gone to Charlestown with Mr Gray,[28] to get an insight into Southern commerce.

James[29] has been lecturing at Columbia College on natural philosophy, in place of Dr Kemp. He has gained great credit and is reappointed to the situation. The professors speak very highly of him, & are particularly pleased because he asks no compensation.

The Gracies[30] are likewise in mourning for the death of old Mrs Rogers,[31] Mrs Gracies mother. Mr Gracie has moved into his new house and I find a very warm reception at the fire side. Their countryseat was one of my strong holds last summer, as I lived in its vicinity. It is a charming warm hearted family, and the old gentleman has the soul of a prince. The fair Sally is soon to give her hand to James King.[32]

Goodhue is engaged to Miss Clarkson,[33] the sister to the pretty one. The engagement suddenly took place as they walked from church on christmas day, and report says the action was shorter than any of our naval victories, for the lady struck on the first Broadside.

This war has completely changed the face of things here. You would scarcely recognize our old peaceful city. Nothing is talked of but armies, Navies, Battles &c Men who had loitered about, the hangers on and encumbrances of society, have all at once risen to importance and been the only useful men of the day.

Had not the miserable accounts from our frontiers dampened in some measure the public zeal,³⁴ I believe half of our young men would have been military mad—As it is, if this war continues, & a regular army be raised instead of depending on volunteers & militia³⁵—I believe we shall have the Commissions sought after with avidity, ⟨you⟩ ↑by↓ young gentlemen of education and ⟨fo?⟩ good breeding, and our army will be infinitely more respectable and infinitely more successful.

I hope this letter may find you on the eve of your departure for this country, I do long most earnestly to see you here again. I suppose my brother will remain longer in Europe, and much as I wish to see him home once more, I feel content that he should stay until he can return with money in both pockets and the whole of us be able to live after our own hearts for the rest of our lives.

God bless you my dear fellow/Yours ever
W I.

Mr Henry Brevoort Jr.

Jany 12.³⁶

Dr Brevoort

I ⟨open⟩ add a few lines, by way of Memorandum. Get my brother Peter to have his likeness taken by some good painter & bring it out with you. *do not neglect this.*³⁷ Look for scarce and odd books & make up a collection of quaint & curious works. When at London visit the ⟨Tabard⟩ Talbot Inn Bourough high St. Southwork. It is the ancient Tabard Inn³⁸ where our old friend Jeffery Chaucer & his pilgrims lodged on their journey to Canterbury 1383 & they pretend to shew you the Chamber where he supped—vide Gents. Magazine for Sept 1812.³⁹ I happened to lay my hands on the passage this morning.

[I h]ave [*MS torn*] a likeness of little Booth⁴⁰—whom I love for Pete[rs] [*MS torn*] sake—⟨remember⟩ ↑commend↓ me heartily to her if you ever visit [her] [*MS torn*] after the receipt of this letter.

Mrs Hoffman is perfectly out of danger & almost well

God bless you my dear fellow
W I

Addressed: Mr Henry Brevoort Jr. / care of P & E Irving & Co / Liverpool [This is the address for the letter; after the postscript was added on a new sheet, another address was given on the recto of it as follows: Henry Brevoort Esqr. / Care of P Irving & Co / Liverpool / and it was readdressed as follows in another hand: at Mrs Nourse's Lodgings / No 14 George Street / Edinburgh]
Manuscript: NYPL—Seligman Collection.   Published: LIB, I, 71–80; PMI, I, 283–84, 294–97 (in part).

1. Captain Frederick Philipse.

2. See WI's letters of May 15, 1811, and July 8, 1812, where he mentions making a wager with John King that the recently married captain would have a child by spring.

3. John Robert Livingston (1755–1851), brother of Chancellor Robert R. Livingston, had an estate north of Poughkeepsie. For genealogical details, see the chart opposite page 516 in George Dangerfield, *Chancellor Robert R. Livingston of New York, 1746–1813* (New York, 1960).

4. Chancellor Livingston's estate was called "Clermont."

5. Probably Mrs. Janet Montgomery (1743–1828), the widow of General Richard Montgomery and the sister of Robert R. and John Robert Livingston.

6. Miss McEvers may be the daughter of Charles McEvers, president of the New York Insurance Company and a member of the older mercantile aristocracy, who lived in a mansion at 43 Wall Street. See Scoville, *Old Merchants of NYC,* I, 10, 302. Brevoort informed WI in 1827 that Miss Hayward had married Mr. Cutting, and that she is a daughter of old H. and Miss Cruger. See LBI, I, 160. Whether this is the same Miss Hayward is impossible to determine.

7. Richard McCall was one of the Lads of Kilkenny, with the nickname of "Oorombates."

8. Angelica Livingston, daughter of John R. Livingston, who died unmarried in 1815.

9. From George Peele's *The Old Wives Tale,* in *The Works of George Peele,* ed. A. H. Bullen (London, 1888), I, 307, line 80.

10. This person is mentioned earlier in WI to Brevoort, March 5, 1811.

11. No other details of this trip seem to have survived.

12. See WI's letter to James Renwick, November 24, 1812, for other details.

13. After being debated intermittently for a month the measure to remit fines and penalties on merchants' bonds, relating to imports of British goods, was finally passed on December 23, 1812. See *Annals of Congress,* 12th Cong., 2d sess., pp. 450–51, 198–443, passim, and 1315.

14. At Mrs. Ryckman's boarding house at 16 Broadway.

15. Presumably Mrs. Ryckman's handy man.

16. The name given to Gouverneur Kemble by the Lads of Kilkenny.

17. A New York commercial firm located at 66 Washington St. See Scoville, *Old Merchants of NYC,* I, 302–3.

18. See WI's letter of December 30, 1812–January 12, 1813, to Peter Irving for other details.

19. Henry Brevoort, Sr. (1747–1841).

20. The *United States* under the command of Captain Stephen Decatur, had captured the 38-gun British frigate *Macedonian.* See Roosevelt, *The Naval War of 1812,* pp. 103–11; Horsman, *War of 1812,* pp. 63–65.

21. Two small islands in the East River, lying between Riker's Island and Ward's Island.

22. On December 29, 1812. See WI's letter to Peter Irving, December 30, 1812–January 12, 1813, for more particulars. See also Guernsey, *Chronicles of NYC,* pp. 143–59.

23. "Splendid Naval Ball,—On Thursday evening a splendid naval ball was given at Gibson's Hotel in honor of the same occasion which had been celebrated by the naval dinner of Tuesday preceding . . ." (NYEP, January 2, 1813).

24. See the letter of WI to Henry Brevoort, July 8, 1812.

25. An allusion to the episode in *Don Quixote* (pt. I, chap. 3, 8), in which

the Don mistakes a basin for the helmet of Mambrino, the Moorish warrior.

26. The name of this child has not been determined. Two of the Nicholas children, Matilda and Emma, survived to adulthood, but their dates have not been recorded in the family genealogy. See [Eugene A. Hoffman], *Genealogy of the Hoffman Family—Descendants of Martin Hoffman*, p. 277.

27. Dr. John Kemp, professor of natural philosophy at Columbia College.

28. Perhaps Edward Gray, John Pendleton Kennedy's father-in-law, with whom WI spent much time in his home in Baltimore in the 1850's. The *New York Directory* for 1812 lists a John Gray, merchant, and a William Gray, attorney. In 1813, a Nicholas Gray, inspector general, is listed.

29. James Renwick.

30. The family of Archibald Gracie.

31. Mrs. Elizabeth Rogers had died on November 19, 1812, in her ninety-first year. See NYEP, November 21, 1812.

32. James King (1791–1853), the third son of Rufus King, married Sarah Rogers Gracie on February 4, 1813.

33. Jonathan Goodhue (1783–1848), a New York merchant, married Catherine Rutherford Clarkson (1794–1861) on April 24, 1813. See *The Clarksons of New York* (New York, 1876), II, chart facing p. 7.

34. The surrender of Forts Michilimackinac, Dearborn, and Detroit, coupled with the American setbacks on the Niagara frontier, caused concern among many Americans. See Horsman, *War of 1812*, pp. 34–49.

35. After extensive debate the House passed a bill to raise an additional military force on January 14, 1813. See *Annals of Congress*, 12th Cong., 2d sess., pp. 843–44, 1322–25.

36. This note, as PMI (I, 297) suggests, is probably a postscript to WI's letter of January 2, 1813. The manuscript of this part is preserved in NYPL—Seligman Collection.

37. Peter, however, was unwilling to have his portrait painted. See PMI, I, 297.

38. The Tabard Inn remained in existence until 1875.

39. A plate showing the courtyard of the Talbot Inn (originally the Tabard Inn) on Borough High Street, Southwork is to be found in the *Gentleman's Magazine* 82 (September, 1812), facing p. 216.

40. Sarah Booth (1793–1867), a diminutive English actress popular at this time.

112.   To Ebenezer Irving

New York, August 12, 1813.

Dear Brother:

I have just come from your house, where they are all well and in good order. ° ° ° The children are very hearty, and exceeding good boys. They were highly delighted with your letter,[1] received yesterday, in which you mention them all; and Pierre[2] assures me that Theodore[3] not only spells Ba-ba, but Di-al, which he intends informing you of under his own hand. He has been projecting a mighty letter to you for several days, but has been delayed by a great scarcity of pen, ink, and paper. The two latter, he informed me this morning, he had procured, but was in want of a pen. I have put him in the way of getting one, and trust he will find no further difficulty in accomplishing this great undertaking. I have told him to write on one page of a sheet, and I will fill up the letter. He said he supposed his mama would be able to tell his writing from mine; but to make him quite easy on that score I have agreed that we shall each put our names to our respective letters.

PUBLISHED: PMI, I, 308–9.

1. Ebenezer Irving was on tour with his wife and youngest child, Sanders (1813–1884). His letter apparently has not been preserved. See PMI, I, 308.

2. Pierre Paris Irving (1806–1876), Ebenezer's oldest child.

3. Theodore Irving (1809–1880), Ebenezer's third child.

113.   To Ebenezer Irving

New York, Augt. 13th. 1813

Dr Brother,

Annexed you have a very valuable epistle from Pierre[1] to his mamma; which is the result of many days meditation & preparation. Your family is all very well and the boys continue to conduct themselves like little noble men. I have nothing new to inform you of, and merely write to ⟨let⟩ make you feel easy about your home—

Your affectionate br
WI.

Mr Ebenr Irving

ADDRESSED: Mr Ebenr. Irving / Care of Mess. Davis & Brown / Merchts. / Boston
POSTMARKED: NEW YORK / [unrecovered]
MANUSCRIPT: SHR.

1. The letter of six-year-old Pierre Paris has been preserved:

Dear mother.   New York Augst 12
Mamma i forgot to speak to you for you went[.] i hope you are very well[.] i hope you are very glad that you did not take none of us[.] grandmamma said that i was a very good boy ever since you have been gone[.] theodore spells in dial et corn[.] we are all very well at home[.] i want to hear your letter red loud.
thurs day afternoon.
Pierre Irving.

114.   To Moses Thomas

N York Oct 13th. 1813

Dr Sir

By this mail you will receive Byrons Poem[.][1] Eastburn[2] has likewise a copy but I do not think he will publish. It is too small a poem to quarrel about & cannot be of any thing the value to him as to you—you having

published his former poem.[3] This copy was given me by Mr Chas
Wilkes.[4] There has been an Edition published subsequent to this in
England with additions.[5] The edinburgh review ⟨copies⟩ gives one extract
superior to any thing in this edition. It is of about 20 lines & will come
in page 2d. I will copy it off & send it to you when I have leisure[6]

Eastburn advtd. Mrs Opies Novel,[7] but recd. next day a letter from a
Printer in Boston mentioning that he had announced it 3 weeks since &
offring Eastburn terms for copies. It is a stupid novel I am told. Whatever Cap [*MS torn*] Haff may have said to Eastburns men about with-
holding my pamphlets, he made no difficulty with me, but inclosed
letters that came with the parcels, in a polite note, & left orders at the
public stores that the parcels should be delivered to me. He is a windy
fellow & may have vapoured to shew his importance, but is always
extremely civil to me. Indeed however *officious* I may be in politics (about
which by the bye⟨⟩) I trouble myself very little) I am on very good
terms with all our public officers—and if I were not, I feel very little
care for their hostility—*I am a pretty strong cock in my own barn yard.*

Yours truly
WI.

ADDRESSED: Mr Moses Thomas / Bookseller / Phila.   POSTMARKED: New York /
    13 / OCT
MANUSCRIPT: Yale.
    On another sheet of the letter WI had canceled the following: "New York.
Octr. 13th 1813. / D Sir / By the mail you will receive Byrons Poem / furnished
me by Mr Wilkin Eastburn has likewise / a copy"

1. *The Giaour*, which John Murray published on June 15, 1813. See Thomas
J. Wise, *A Bibliography of the Writings in Verse and Prose of George Gordon
Noel, Baron Byron* (London, 1963), I, 76–79.
    2. James Eastburn was a New York publisher.
    3. Moses Thomas had brought out the first American edition of *Childe Harold's
Pilgrimage* in 1812.
    4. See WI to Henry Brevoort, February 7, 1811, n. 12.
    5. A second edition, expanded from 685 to 816 lines, appeared in England
in early July. See Wise, *Bibliography of Byron*, I, 79–80.
    6. The first edition of *The Giaour* was discussed in the *Edinburgh Review* 21
(July, 1813), 299–309. WI's statement, however, is puzzling. He indicates that
one of the extracts printed in the magazine is not in the edition in his possession,
thereby suggesting that the copy of the poem used by the reviewer was an expanded
edition. However, the number of pages in the copy of *The Giaour* under review is
41, which corresponds to the first edition. (The second edition, published in July,
1813, had 47 pages.) Possibly WI had not checked his copy carefully against
the review.
    7. Probably *Tales of Real Life*, which was published by Bradford & Read of
Boston in two volumes. Mrs. Opie's *New Tales* in two volumes appeared with a
New York imprint in 1813 but without the name of the publisher. It has not been
ascertained if this is the same work as the Boston edition.

115. *To William Bainbridge*

New York, March 24th. 1814

Dear Sir,

I received your last letter[1] a few days Since and will be very much obliged to you for the additional documents you promise me respecting the Tripolitan Captivity.[2] The papers, journals &c[3] from Philadelphia came to hand some time since. I have not as yet commenced, and it is probable, from being a little hurried at present with various concerns, I shall not take the Subject in hand for some little time to come. I wish when I set about it, to be wholly at liberty to give my mind to it, and go through with it at one sitting, without interruption.

I thank you for your fourth of July invitation, and should be proud to take a launch in the first born American Ship of the line;[4] but I do not think I shall be able to give myself that gratification. I promise at all events to drink your health deeply on that day, and a "potation pottle deep"[5] to the success of your first cruise

I am, my dear Sir, in haste—/very truly yours

Washington Irving

William Bainbridge Esq.

ADDRESSED: Commander Wm Bainbridge / Navy Yard / Boston   POSTMARKED:
   NEW-YORK / MAR / 25   DOCKETED: Washington Irving March 23 1814
MANUSCRIPT: NYHS (Naval History Society Collection), mounted in James Fenimore
   Cooper, *History of the United States Navy* (New York, 1890), chap. II, pt. 2,
   p. 232; extra illustrated.
   William Bainbridge (1774–1833) commanded the *Constitution* when it captured
a British frigate in the South Atlantic during the War of 1812; he supervised the
construction of the 74-gun *Independence* at the Boston Navy Yard and was commander on her first cruise to the Mediterranean in 1814.

   1. This letter has not been located.
   2. On October 31, 1803, the *Philadelphia*, commanded by Captain Bainbridge,
was grounded on a reef off the shore from Tripoli and forced to surrender, with
the crew imprisoned by the Bashaw of Tripoli. See Maclay, *A History of U. S.
Navy*, I, 244–50.
   3. WI is probably referring to documents relating to the capture of the *Philadelphia* in 1803 which he intended to use for an article in the *Analectic Magazine*.
The capture of the *Philadelphia* is mentioned in J. K. Paulding's "Introductory
Essay" of *The Naval Chronicle, Analectic Magazine* 6 (September, 1815), 244–45.
   4. The *Independence*, which Bainbridge commanded after its completion.
   5. *Othello*, II, iii, 76.

116.   To Charles Prentiss

New York, April 4th. 1814

Dear Sir,

Your letter,[1] being directed to Philadelphia instead of this City, did not reach me until several days after the date. I am sorry that the nature of my engagements with the Analectic Magazine, does not enable me to give that encouragement to original productions which I could wish. The magazine is owned by Mr Moses Thomas Bookseller Philadelphia, I receive a Stipulated sum yearly for editing it; the original articles which I occasionally ⟨furnish⟩ ↑write for it↓ are entirely gratuitous, having engaged merely to select & arrange articles from foreign publications. Indeed the ⟨original⟩ plan of the work did not contemplate original matter, and though it has been in some measure departed from, yet we have rather chose to keep the original part, limited & subordinate. Mr Thomas has been applied to by various persons offering to write for the work, but has declined, alledging that the expenses are already heavy, and as much as he thinks he can afford. As the Port Folio is more exclusively devoted to American literature, and the proprietors are in the habit of paying for original writings I think it probable you would find them readily disposed to embrace your offers.

The anecdotes you have communicated to me of your mode of life, and prospects are peculiar and interesting. The perseverance with which you have devoted yourself to the muses,[2] and ⟨the⟩ your early determination, so steadily adhered to ⟨of⟩ through a long course of years, of attempting an epic at forty,[3] do certainly bespeak no ordinary zeal and enterprize in literature. I hope your success may be equal to your exertions & your wishes. at any rate it is no ways disgraceful to fail in a great attempt; the magnitude and difficulty of the enterprize gives a dignity even to defeat.

Should I hear of any opportunity of rendering you a Service in the way you propose you may be assured of my disposition to promote your interests & persuits—in the mean while with the best wishes for your welfare & Success

I am respectfully/Your hbe St

Washington Irving

Charles Prentiss Esq.

MANUSCRIPT: American Antiquarian Society.

Charles Prentiss (1774–1820), who studied at Harvard, was a poet, biographer, and editor working mostly in Washington, D.C., and the Middle Eastern States.

1. This letter has not been located.

2. Prentiss brought out *A Collection of Fugitive Essays, in Prose and Verse* in 1797 and edited a literary paper, *The Child of Pallas,* in Baltimore a few years later.

3. This project apparently never came to fruition, for publishers' lists and library records do not include an epic poem by Prentiss.

117. To Moses Thomas

New York. July 16th. 1814

Dear Sir,

I recd yours of 15th.[1] inclosing the Dft on Howe & Deforest for 180 93/—I think it worth your while to get Porters likeness[2] without delay; and likewise to get a biographical sketch drawn out by some person who can write a neat article.[3] I wish to begin upon Bainbridges[4] & therefore will not be able to do Porters before it would be anticipated & made stale by other writers. His ⟨ad⟩ life has been adventurous & would abound with romantic particulars. I would dress up any article that should be furnished; but can not at present hunt up facts & do the dead colouring. I think it worth Your while to pay some job writer for the occasion, as it would be a very *taking* article at the present moment.

I am waiting with some impatience to hear from Mr Verplanck & to receive his biography of Trumbull.[5] The work is at a stand for want of it.

Yours truly

W I.[6]

MANUSCRIPT: SHR.

In the left margin, written lengthwise on the paper, is a comment by Moses Thomas: "This being a *business* Letter, has no interest except from the fact of its ↑being↓ the *handwriting* of Washington Irving—I send it, not having an autograph except on one or two recent letters which it could not be taken from. M T." Thomas was the Philadelphia bookseller and publisher who had bought *Select Reviews* in 1812 and persuaded WI to become its editor. See STW, I, 136–37.

1. This letter has not been located.

2. A portrait of David Porter painted by Joseph Wood (ca. 1778–1852) and engraved by David Edwin (1776–1841) appeared in the *Analectic Magazine*, n.s. 4 (September, 1814), opposite p. 225. Irving's article on Porter is found on pages 225–43.

3. At this point Thomas placed a circle with a plus sign in it, indicating a note at the bottom of the sheet which states: "These articles were intended for the Analectic Magazine of which Mr Irving was then the Editor and I the publisher. M.T."

4. WI apparently never wrote a sketch of Bainbridge, probably because of his involvement in the activities of the volunteers of the New York State Militia who had been activated to protect New York City during its blockade by the British. See Guernsey, *Chronicles of NYC*, II, 149ff.

5. Gulian Verplanck, who along with James K. Paulding, was a regular contributor to the *Analectic* during WI's editorship, never contributed a biography of Trumbull to the magazine.

6. Below the complimentary close and initials Thomas wrote "W.I. was Washington Irving."

118.   To Joseph Delaplaine

New York, August 10th. 1814

Dear Sir,

I am much obliged to you for the compliment you pay my vanity, in requesting the loan of my portrait to be engraved, but do not think myself entitled to a distinction of the kind. I am already a little too much in the glare of notoriety for my own comfort & advantage, and have an utter repugnance to being obtruded more conspiciously on public notice. ⟨Had I even the⟩ Were I even vain enough to think myself worthy a place in the biographical work[1] you propose, I should decline the hazardous honour for I would rather that ninety nine should ask why I was *not* there, than incur the possibility of one persons asking why I *was*. With the best wishes for your success in your laudable undertaking I am respectfully

Your hbl st.
Washington Irving

Mr. Joseph Delaplaine.

ADDRESSED: Mr Joseph Delaplaine / Bookseller / Philadelphia   POSTMARKED: NEW YORK / AUG / 11   DOCKETED: Washington Irving / New York August 1st. 1814 / ansd. 19 Do. *Note*: On the same docket line with "Washington Irving," past a fold in the sheet is written "((B))."
MANUSCRIPT: Tulane University.

Joseph Delaplaine (1777–1825) operated a bookstore and publishing business in Philadelphia.

1. Delaplaine was collecting material for his *Repository of the Lives and Portraits of Distinguished Americans*, which was published in Philadelphia in three parts in 1815 and 1816.

119.   General Order

G.O.:   Headquarters, New York, August 30th, 1814.

The Reverend Mr. Westbrook[1] having been selected by Brigadier General Heermance[2] for Chaplain of his Brigade of Detached Militia, is hereby assigned and brevetted accordingly, and the Commandants of Regiments of that Detachment are to dispense with the appointment of Regimental Chaplains.

By order of the Commander in Chief:
Washington Irving, Aid-De-Camp.

PUBLISHED: *Public Papers of Daniel D. Tompkins, Governor of New York, 1807–1817* (New York, 1898–1902), I, 509.

The manuscripts of this and subsequent orders prepared by WI were destroyed in the fire of the state capitol in Albany in 1911.

1. The Reverend Cornelius D. Westbrook (1782–1858) was pastor of the Reformed Dutch Church of Fishkill, New York, from 1806 to 1830. Later he was a minister in Peekskill and Cortlandt. See Francis M. Kip, *A Discourse Delivered on the 12th of September, 1866, at the Celebration of the 150th Anniversary of the First Reformed Dutch Church, Fishkill, New York* (Fishkill, 1866), pp. 40–42.

2. General Martin Heermance (1765–1824) a descendant of one of the original settlers of Rhinebeck, New York, was brigadier general of the 20th Brigade. See Edward M. Smith, *Documentary History of Rhinebeck* (Rhinebeck, 1881), pp. 84, 183; Hugh Hastings, comp., *Military Minutes of the Council of Appointment of the State of New York, 1783–1821* (Albany, 1901), pp. 99, 123.

120. To Henry Brevoort

[New York, August? 1814?]

Dear Brevoort,

Dennis[1] has come home laden with ⟨news⟩ anecdotes of your Expedition, and yourself. According to his account you landed safely on your head at Benny Cornwalls[2] at seven in the evening & flourished your heels in the air for Joy. He relates long conversations which he has had with you about the fair Julia, besides several tender things which you said in your sleep, ⟨and⟩ from all that I can learn, you must have rehearsed some of the capers that the renowned hero of LaMancha cut in the mountains, and sent Dennis, as your discreet & faithful Squire, to report them to your Dulcinea. Dennis[3] has fairly knocked Marches[4] Brains out with a Quotation; and turned our house perfectly upside down with laughter at his good speeches. I question whether the sage Panza ever occasioned more jollity in the Dukes household than Dennis did this afternoon ⟨before her Grace the Dutchess, her maids of honor at⟩↑among↓ the gentlemen of the Supper Room. Poor Mrs Bradish[5] was nearly annihilated by the Shouts of able bodied laughter from that fat Varlet March. Dennis ⟨h⟩ informs us that he and you keep a Journal ⟨and?⟩ which is so exquisitely humorous that ⟨the⟩ Mrs Cooper[6] on only looking at the first word fell into a fit of laughing that lasted half an hour. We look forward with vast expectations to the perusal of this manuscript.

We all sent an Invitation in form to the Commodore & his lady[7] to dine with us this afternoon but they declined on account of the heat of the day—invited us to tea & gin in the evening. We went over there in full force & passed a very pleasant evening. They dine with us tomorrow. Monday Morning. I have laid out your *Spy glass*, Boots, *Chess* men &c. & *had thoughts of sending* all the other Nicknacks I could find in your Drawers; but have thought it best to reserve the rest until you have tired yourself with these — The flute is not in the Draw; for which I am very glad—I do not think it would be an innocent amusement for you;

as no man has a right to entertain himself at the expense of others (persons feelings & comfort.) Dennis is full of business He has to bustle out to your sisters—then to Mrs Coopers then home & then the lord knows where—It is a proud day for Dennis.

He mentioned as a great mark of Mrs Coopers politeness that she told him on their ride up, "Dennis ⟨if⟩ don't be bashful or constraind, if you feel sleepy take a nap whenever you please." We all assured him that such vast indulgence could only be in consequence of his having made himself wonderfully agreeable. I beg if you make any stay you would contrive to dispatch Dennis up to town from time to time to report progress: he has given the household a good months laughter in the course of a handful of hours. Dont omit to keep him at his studies of Shakespeare—he hints that Cooper begins to be a little jealous of his dramatic powers.

I should like to pay Rockaway a visit this Week, but ⟨the⟩ I have allowed the little major[8] to take holliday ⟨with⟩ & go to the country with his wife & little trudgens[9] & must play merchant[10] for a few days.

My horse is doing well & according to Patricks[11] account eats his oats like a Jontleman[12]

Yrs truly
W I

ADDRESSED: Mr Henry Brevoort Jr / Rockaway / Mr D Sampeyo
MANUSCRIPT: NYPL—WI Papers.   PUBLISHED: LIB, I, 50–53; PMI, I, 306–8.
    In an unidentified hand is written "August. 1814" upside down at the fold of the address side of the MS. In pencil "1814" is canceled and "1811" substituted—a penciled note under the dateline at the head of the letter reads: "Brevoort absent from March 1812 to Dec 1813—& not at Mrs Bradish's in 1811"—then "August 1814" is inserted—the dateline, not in WI's hand reads "N York 1811–(August?)"

    1. Dennis Sampayo, a Portuguese who was staying at Mrs. Bradish's boarding house at the corner of Rector and Greenwich Streets. See LIB, I, xxv; PMI, I, 306–8.
    2. A Benjamin Cornwall, a butcher in Brooklyn, is listed in the 1814 New York City Directory.
    3. Over this word in another hand is "Sampayo a portuguese."
    4. March was a wine merchant. See LIB, I, xxv. The firm of March & Benson, merchants, 47 South, is listed in Longworth's Directory for 1813 and 1814, but no person named March is included.
    5. The mistress of the boarding house at 124 Broadway.
    6. The former Mary Fairlie, who had married T. A. Cooper.
    7. Stephen Decatur, acclaimed for his daring feats during the Tripolitan War (1801–1805), had married Susan Wheeler, daughter of a wealthy Norfolk merchant, on March 8, 1806. Decatur was killed in a duel with Commodore James Barron on March 22, 1820.
    8. The little major refers to Ebenezer Irving who was first major of the 10th Regiment of Infantry in New York County. See Hastings, Military Minutes ... 1783–1821, p. 1462.

9. Litttle Trudgens was WI's familiar name for one of Ebenezer's children, probably Sanders, born on February 9, 1813, who would be toddling at this time. Or WI may have been referring to the latest arrival, Eliza, who was born on May 27, 1814.

10. WI was apparently assisting in the family business.

11. Probably the stableman.

12. This spelling is probably WI's jocular attempt to approximate Patrick's pronunciation.

121. General Order

G.O.:   Headquarters, New York, 2d Sep'r, 1814.

The Commander in Chief[1] has witnessed with high satisfaction the alacrity with which the division under the command of Major Genl. Stevens[2] has entered into actual service. The equipment and soldierlike appearance of the troops, and the large number of Volunteers that has joined the Division give honorable testimony of the military and patriotic spirit, which at this interesting crisis animates all ranks and conditions. It is such generous zeal, such unanimity· of feeling and action that constitutes the real strength of a free community.

The Division being now transferred to the command of Major General Lewis[3] for a term of service, the Commander in Chief, while he expresses the pride he feels in being able to[4] the national demand so fine and formidable a body of men, exhorts them to persevere in the punctual performance of their duties as citizens and soldiers; to exert themselves to the utmost to deserve the approbation of their present commandant, and never for a moment to forget, that to their courage and good conduct are confided the safety of their firesides, the protection of their families, the welfare and reputation of their cities, and the honor of the nation.

By order of the Commander in Chief:
Washington Irving, Aid-De-Camp.

PUBLISHED: *Public Papers of Daniel D. Tompkins*, I, 510; Guernsey, *Chronicles of NYC*, II, 252–53; NYEP, September 5, 1814.

1. General Daniel D. Tompkins.

2. Ebenezer Stevens (1752–1823), a participant in the Boston Tea Party and various campaigns in the Revolutionary War, had amassed a large fortune as a merchant in New York City in his later years. See *Public Papers of Daniel D. Tompkins*, I, 504–5; Guernsey, *Chronicles of NYC*, I, 105–6.

3. Morgan Lewis (1754–1844), governor of New York from 1804 to 1807, served on the Niagara frontier in 1813 before becoming commander of the region around New York City.

4. A note indicates that a word or words are missing. The transcription in Guernsey has added "furnish to" after "to."

122. General Order

G.O.:   Headquarters, New York, 8th Sept., 1814

The Division of Quartermasters of the Militia ordered into service in the 3d Military District are severally required to execute bonds to the United States with satisfactory sureties in the penalty of $15,000 each. The Brigade Quartermasters and Assistant Dep. Quartermaster Generals will execute bonds with sureties in the penalty of 10,000 Dollars each, and Regimental Quartermasters will execute bonds with sureties in the penalty of 5,000 Dollars each, the sureties to be approved by the Quartermaster General of the District. The Regimental Paymasters will execute bonds with such sureties and in such penalties as Samuel Edmunds[1] Esquire, Principal Paymaster of Militia, shall approve and direct. The Militia Quartermasters of every grade in this district are required to report themselves immediately to the Quartermaster General of the District and will make no contracts, payments or requisitions otherwise than through the head of the Department. The paymasters will report themselves to Mr. Edmunds at Tammany Hall and will act under his orders.

By order of the Commander in Chief:

Washington Irving, Aid-de-Camp.

PUBLISHED: *Public Papers of Daniel D. Tompkins*, I, 510–11; NYEP, September 9, 1814.

1. Samuel Edmunds (1760–1826) of Hudson, Columbia County, New York, was sheriff in 1801, state assemblyman in 1803, and judge of the Columbia County court of common pleas from 1810 to 1812. See F. Ellis, *History of Columbia County, New York* (Philadelphia, 1878), pp. 47, 103, 109; William Raymond, *Biographical Sketches of Distinguished Men of Columbia County* (Albany, 1851), p. 79.

123. To Henry Brevoort

N York Sept 9th. 1814.

Dear Brevoort,

I have nothing new to tell you and write in great haste. Judge Van Ness desires me to inform you that should there be any difficulty in your ⟨whi⟩ way;[1] which his assistance would be important in removing, to write him word and he will do every thing in his power to assist you, and even come up to Vermont if necessary—He appears to be very sincerely interested for your success. I inclose you a letter recd by the Saratoga; which I presume is from L Herbette.[2] The household are all well

God bless & prosper you,/Your friend

W I.[3]

ADDRESSED: Mr Henry Brevoort Junr / Burlington. / Vt. DOCKETED: Sept 9. 1814 / W Irving.

MANUSCRIPT: NYPL—Seligman Collection. PUBLISHED: LIB, I, 81.

There is a faint profile sketch of a head in pencil, presumably by WI, on the address sheet.

1. Henry Brevoort was apparently in Vermont on business, presumably connected with Astor's fur-trading activities. On September 6, 1814, Brevoort had been commissioned a first lieutenant in the "Iron Greys" artillery company. See the facsimile of that commission in LBI, I, facing p. xviii.

2. One of the fur traders in John Jacob Astor's employ. See letters of September 22, 1810, and June 8, 1811. See Porter, *Astor*, I, 568.

3. On the blank sheet which is the verso of the address leaf someone (probably Brevoort) has listed the following names with the comment, "All failed within 2 or 3 weeks": "A. R & W T Laurence, Abm. Riker & Co, Ben. Huntington, J & P Rapelye, Penfold & Stevenson, Thoms. Carpenter, Carpenter & Fowler, Ketchum & Carpenter, Pratt & Smith, Henry Hyman, Gabriel Havens, Minturn & Champlin, A & N Brown, W & Jonas Minturn, Post & Minturn, Robert Bowne, John L Bowne; Smith, Taylor & Co, H King & Co, L L Whitney." With the exception of Smith, Taylor & Co., all of these firms or individuals are listed in the *New York City Directory* for 1814.

124. General Order

G.O.:   Headquarters, 15th Sept'r, 1814.

The Battalion under the command of Lieut. Col'l Smith[1] of Orange, and that under the command of Lieut. Coll. Woodward[2] of the same County, are organized into a Regiment. to be Commanded by Coll. Smith, with the following field and Staff: Major, Barnabas Many;[3] _____ James Faulkner;[4] Adjutant _____ Brewster;[5] Quartermaster John Miller;[6] Paymaster James Grant Junior; Surgeon Robert C. Hunter;[7] Surgeon's Mates William H. Newkirk[8] and Charles Douglass.

Lieut. Col. Woodward and Adjutant James Bingham[9] will be discharged from service so soon as the consolidation shall be completed; the first, to enable him to attend the Legislature of which he is a member; and the second, on account of his being a supernumerary Officer.

Lieut. Col'l Bevier's[10] Battalion and Lieut. Colonel Connors'[11] of Richmond County, are likewise to form a Regiment, to be commanded by the Senior Lieut. Coll. The Regimental Staff will be assigned in a future Order. The two Regiments mentioned in this Order and a detachment of Horse Artillery from the Richmond troop, form one Brigade to be commanded by Brigadier Genl. John Swartwout.[12]

By order of the Commander in Chief:

Washington Irving, Aid-de-Camp.

PUBLISHED: *Public Papers of Daniel D. Tompkins*, I, 513–14.

1. Leonard Smith (1752–1840) of Newburgh, New York, had been commandant of the militia in Orange County since 1804. He was made major general of the 5th

Division (19th and 34th Brigades) in 1818. See E. Shepard, *Orange County, N. Y. Deaths (1829–1857)* (Goshen, N.Y., 1967), p. 3; Hastings, *Military Minutes ... 1783–1821*, pp. 719, 1974.

2. Benjamin Woodward (b. 1780), who founded the village of Mt. Hope, near Wallkill, in 1807, served several sessions in the New York Assembly and was a state senator from 1827 to 1830. He was promoted to lieutenant colonel in 1814 and resigned in 1816. See Charles E. Stickney, *A History of the Minisink Region* (Middletown, N.Y., 1867), p. 153; E. Ruttenber and L. Clark, *History of Orange County, N.Y.* (Philadelphia, 1881), p. 510; Russel Headley, *The History of Orange County, N. Y.* (Middletown, N.Y., 1908), p. 327; Hastings, *Military Minutes ... 1783–1821*, pp. 610, 1447, 1742.

3. Barnabas Many lived in Blooming Grove in 1775. Numerous members of the Many family resided in Hamptonburgh, Goshen, and Blooming Grove in the early nineteenth century. See Samuel Eager, *An Outline History of Orange County* (Newburgh, 1846–1847), p. 530; Headley, *The History of Orange County*, p. 892.

4. James Faulkner was an ensign in the state militia in 1806 and a second major in 1814. See Eager, *An Outline History of Orange County*, pp. 230, 622; Hastings, *Military Minutes ... 1783–1821*, pp. 845, 1447, 1742.

5. Edward Brewster of Blooming Grove served at various times as school commissioner and school inspector. See Ruttenber and Clark, *History of Orange County, N. Y.*, pp. 630, 637.

6. John Miller (1777–1861) of Montgomery was made brigade quartermaster of the 34th Brigade in 1815. See Gertrude A. Barber, *Graveyard Inscriptions of Orange County, New York* (New York, 1930), IV, 40; Ruttenber and Clark, *History of Orange County, N. Y.*, p. 379; Hastings, *Military Minutes ... 1783–1821*, p. 1559.

7. Dr. Robert C. Hunter (1793–1843) practiced medicine in Hamptonburgh from 1815 until his death. See E. Shepard, *Orange County, N. Y. Deaths (1829–1857)*, p. 17; Ruttenber and Clark, *History of Orange County, N. Y.*, p. 180.

8. Dr. William H. Newkirk practiced medicine at Unionville in 1816. In 1822 he was surgeon's mate in the 148th Regiment of Infantry. See Hastings, *Military Minutes ... 1783–1821*, p. 2358.

9. James Bingham (d. 1844) of Wallkill became an ensign in 1809 and captain of the 5th Regiment in 1815. Apparently he was not discharged by this order. See Ruttenber and Clark, *History of Orange County, N. Y.*, p. 436; Hastings, *Military Minutes ... 1783–1821*, pp. 1547, 1901.

10. Benjamin Bevier (1762–1822), a resident of Ulster County who served in the state assembly, later became brigadier general of the 23rd Brigade of Infantry. See Katherine Bevier, *The Bevier Family* (New York, 1916), pp. 119–20; Hastings, *Military Minutes ... 1783–1821*, pp. 69, 1660, 1820.

11. Richard Connor, Jr. (1763–1853), a wealthy Staten Island surveyor, farmer, and tanner, became commandant of the 146th Regiment in 1812, a post he resigned in 1818. See Richard Bayles, *History of Richmond County* (New York, 1887), p. 517; C. Leng and W. Davis, *Staten Island and Its People* (New York, 1933), V, 72; Hastings, *Military Minutes ... 1783–1821*, pp. 137, 1403, 1912.

12. John Swartwout (1770–1823), brother of WI's crony, Samuel Swartwout, was an ardent supporter of Aaron Burr and a Tammany politician who served in the state assembly in 1798–1799, 1800–1801, and 1820–1821. See Arthur Weise, *The Swartwout Chronicles* (New York, 1889), pp. 262, 276–80, 282, 608.

125. General Order

G.O.:   Headquarters, Albany, 15th Sept., 1814.

Truman Hicks[1] is brevetted and assigned as Adjutant, Jonathan Kellogg[2] as Quartermaster, and Burr Hendrick[3] as Paymaster of a Regiment of detached Militia whereof John Prior[4] is Lieut.-Colonel Commandant, and they are to be obeyed and respected accordingly.

By order of the Commander in Chief:

W. Irving, Aid-de-Camp.

PUBLISHED: *Public Papers of Daniel D. Tompkins,* I, 514.

1. Truman B. Hicks lived in Hadley, Saratoga County, New York, where he was coroner from 1818 to 1820. See G. Anderson, *Our County and Its People* (Boston, 1899), p. 463.

2. Jonathan Kellogg of Ballston, Saratoga County, had served as county treasurer in 1800, county supervisor from 1802 to 1811, and as county jailer in 1811. See G. Anderson, *Our County and Its People,* pp. 463–64.

3. Burr Hendrick (1786–1829) lived in Greenfield, Saratoga County, most of his life and died in Saratoga Springs.

4. John Prior of Greenfield was made commandant of the 59th Regiment of Infantry in 1810 and brigadier general of the 9th Brigade in 1816. He later served as judge of the common pleas court of Saratoga County. See N. Sylvester, *History of Saratoga County, N. Y.* (Philadelphia, 1878), p. 182; G. Anderson, *Our County and Its People,* pp. 413, 459, 467–68; Hastings, *Military Minutes . . . 1783–1821,* pp. 1143, 1749, 1815.

126. To Henry Brevoort

Albany Sept 26th. 1814

Dear Brevoort,

I have just arrived here in the Suite of the Governor.[1] How long I shall remain here I know not. Perhaps a week or more: though, if ⟨the⟩ affairs remain tranquil at New York I shall endeavour to be sent with some business to ⟨?some?⟩ one or other of the Armies on the lines.

The Iron Greys[2] go on very well. They are attached to a regiment commanded by Lt Col Cadwallader D Colden, and will be encamped in a few days in the vicinity of Greenwich. I have been incessantly occupied since I saw you by the duties of my station;[3] and feel more pleased than ever with it. I am very anxious to hear how matters go with you. I think there is no prospect of immediate peace and am of opinion, that should the British wait the results of the present campaign,[4] they will rather be disposed to continue ⟨the⟩ hostilities; to wipe out the stains of late defeats. This Scourging Campaign[5] has on the whole been thus far a degrading one to them & the ⟨?Voy?⟩ Victory on Champlain[6] will be a pill not easily swallowed. I wish you would treasure up all the striking

particulars you may hear concerning it, as I must give McDonough[7]
a dash.

In great haste/Yours truly
W I.

P.S. The Commercial world is aghast at New York in consequence of
recent failures. Minturn & Champlin, Post & Minturn, Robert Bowne,
& Thos Eddy have gone by the board & others are tottering.[8]

ADDRESSED: Mr Henry Brevoort Junr. / Burlington / Vermont. DOCKETED: Sept
25. 1814 / W Irving
MANUSCRIPT: NYPL—Seligman Collection. PUBLISHED: LIB, I, 82–83; PMI, I,
314–15.

1. Daniel D. Tompkins, governor of New York, was also major general of the
New York militia.

2. A volunteer company of 112 men of the New York State Militia, to which
WI was attached. It was so named because of the color of their uniforms. Captain
Samuel Swartwout, a long-time friend of WI's, was its commanding officer, with
Henry Brevoort, Jr. as first lieutenant; Henry Carey, second lieutenant; Philip
Rhinelander, third lieutenant; and Gouverneur S. Bibby, fourth lieutenant. Among
the privates was Fitz-Greene Halleck, who wrote a poem honoring the group.
One version of the poem was sung to the tune of "Adams and Liberty." See *The
Poetical Writings of Fitz-Greene Halleck,* ed. James Grant Wilson (New York,
1869), pp. 145–55; Guernsey, comp., *Chronicles of NYC,* II, 304–5; Nelson Fred-
erick Adkins, *Fitz-Greene Halleck: An Early Knickerbocker Wit and Poet* (New
Haven, 1930), pp. 38–40.

3. WI served as General Tompkins's aide-de-camp.

4. The British had been attacking on various fronts, with a blockade of New
York and the burning of Washington as major achievements.

5. The British had sailed up the Potomac River and landed near Baltimore. Their
land attack was unsuccessful, as was their bombardment of Fort McHenry.

6. British ships on Lake Champlain were defeated by American vessels, with
the result that Americans gained control of the lake and forced the British to
withdraw to Canada.

7. Thomas MacDonough (1783–1825) was the victorious American commander
who defeated the British at Plattsburgh on Lake Champlain on September 11, 1814.

8. These firms failed financially at this time. Minturn and Champlin, owned by
Nat, Jonas, and Edward Minturn and John Champlin, had subscribed $18,000 to
the United States during the war mobilization. Post and Minturn, operated by Henry
Post, Jr., who had married a Minturn, had lent $50,000 to the United States gov-
ernment during the war. Bowne and Eddy were Quaker businessmen. See Scoville,
Old Merchants of NYC, I, 98–99, 331; II, 342–45; III, 57, 103, 111–13.

127. *To Ebenezer Irving*

[Albany, September 28, 1814]

I leave this at four o'clock in the morning for Sackett's Harbor.[1]
Affairs, I am afraid, are about to look squally on our Canada frontier.
Drummond[2] has fallen back to Fort George, and Brown[3] is not in

sufficient force to pursue him. Izard[4] has landed at Genesee River; and by the time he forms a junction with Brown, or advances on Fort George, Drummond, I apprehend, will be able to get to the head of the lake, so that I think he has escaped from our clutches. In the meanwhile, we hear that Chauncey[5] is at Sackett's Harbor. If the enemy takes the lake with his large ship, Chauncey is dished; he dare not come out, and may be attacked in the harbor by land and sea. It is said he does not mean to remain in the harbor; but to put out again immediately. As there is no regular force there of any consequence, I shall be empowered, if on consulting the officers there it is deemed necessary, to order out a requisite militia force. Should matters be safe there, and the lake be unmolested by the enemy, I think it probable I shall sail to the upper part of it, and visit Brown's army; having powers to transact business there, if necessary.

The travelling, at present, is rough; but the expedition will be a very interesting one.

PUBLISHED: PMI, I, 315–16.

1. WI carried two letters from General Tompkins to Sackett's Harbor. Since these letters suggest the nature of WI's responsibilities, they are quoted in full.

To Colonel Irving

Albany, September 28, 1814.
Dr. Sir: You are required to proceed without delay to Sackett's harbour & deliver the enclosed communications. Should the recent emergencies demand a more extended authority to Major Genl. Widrig[a] & to Brigadiers Genl. Hale,[b] of Fairfield, Herkimer County, Brig. Genl. Dodge,[c] Montgomery County, Brig. Gen. Walter Martin[d] of Lewis, or to the Commandant of the Jefferson Brigade,[e] you are authorized to issue such general order to those Commandants, as, upon consultation at the Harbour may be deemed essential to the security of that frontier. You will likewise please to ascertain & give me on your return, muster rolls & inspection returns of the Militia now in service at the Harbour, & will please to acquaint me with the situation & probable fate of the American squadron on Lake Ontario. The time of your return will be governed by your own discretion.

A. Oliver Collins,[f] Utica, Oneida County, [James] Stewart,[g] Otsego formerly Jabez N. M. Hurd,[h] Cazenovia, Madison County.

Lt. Col. W. Irving

P. S. In case you proceed from the Harbour to Niagara, you may do so, & upon reporting yourself to Major Genl. Brown,[i] obtain from him a return of the Militia of this State in service under his command, a return of the killed & wounded of Militia on the late occasion, & from Major Genl. Porter[j] a return of the officers entitled to Brevet on account of services & bravery in former actions. You will please to report to me as often as may be convenient, & practicable.

[PUBLISHED: *Public Papers of Daniel D. Tompkins*, III, 551–52.]
Identification of persons mentioned in this letter:

a. George Widrig of Frankfort, Herkimer County, a member of the state assembly from 1800 to 1807, was a major general in the 5th Division of the New York

Militia in 1812. He commanded the 13th Division in 1818 and resigned in 1819. See Hastings, *Military Minutes . . . 1783–1821*, pp. 151, 1302, 1974, 2069; N. Benton, *History of Herkimer County* (Albany, 1856), pp. 377–78.

b. James Haile, a resident of Fairfield, Herkimer County who had come from Massachusetts in 1790, was made brigadier general of the 21st Brigade in 1812, replacing George Widrig. He was a town supervisor in 1815 and a trustee of the Herkimer Manufacturing Company. See Benton, *History of Herkimer County*, p. 398; G. A. Hardin & F. H. Willard, *History of Herkimer County* (Syracuse, 1893), pp. 311, 315; Hastings, *Military Minutes . . . 1783–1821*, p. 1379.

c. Richard Dodge, WI's brother-in-law and a resident of Johnstown, Montgomery County, was brigadier general of the 11th Brigade in 1810 and major general of the 14th Division in 1818. See Hastings, *Military Minutes . . . 1783–1821*, pp. 583, 1116, 1974; W. Frothingham, *History of Fulton County* (Syracuse, 1892), pp. 248, 249.

d. Walter Martin (1764–1834), founder of Martinsburgh in 1802 and its postmaster from then until 1831, was lieutenant colonel commandant of a regiment in Oneida County in 1804 and was made brigadier general of the 26th Brigade in 1805. During his life Martin was assistant justice of the Oneida County court, loan commissioner, state road commissioner, and state senator. See Hastings, *Military Minutes . . . 1783–1821*, pp. 746, 808; F. Hough, *History of Lewis County, New York* (Albany, 1860), pp. 172–74.

e. The commandant of the Jefferson Brigade in 1814 was Brigadier General Thomas B. Benedict (1783–1829), a native of Woodbury, Connecticut who moved to DeKalb, St. Lawrence County, about 1803. Raising a volunteer company, he took them to Ogdensburg, where he fought in nearly every battle in the area. See H. Benedict, *Genealogy of the Benedicts in America* (Albany, 1970), I, 372.

f. Oliver Collins (1762–1838) was lieutenant colonel in command of the 13th Brigade in 1804 and brigadier general in 1811. While commanding officer at Sackett's Harbor, Collins court-martialed many of his troops who had deserted because of the bad accommodations there. See Hastings, *Military Minutes . . . 1783–1821*, pp. 746, 1250; William Cutter, *Genealogical and Family History of Northern New York* (New York, 1910), I, 294–95.

g. James Stewart of Worcester, Otsego County, was an ensign in 1798, lieutenant colonel commandant of the 7th Regiment in 1809, brigadier general of the 2d Brigade in 1814, and major general of the 16th Division in 1818. See Hastings, *Military Minutes . . . 1783–1821*, pp. 469, 1106, 1457, 1975.

h. Jabez N. M. Hurd (1778–1855), who settled in Cazenovia, Madison County, about 1800, was, variously, storekeeper, postmaster, coroner, treasurer, and president of the village in the next two decades, as well as county clerk from 1815 to 1821. He was brigadier general of the 35th Brigade in 1811 and major general of the 17th Division in 1820. See Gertrude A. Barber, *Deaths Taken from the New York Evening Post*, XXXI, 71; John E. Smith, *Our County and Its People* (Boston, 1899), pp. 81, 223; L. M. Hammond, *History of Madison County* (Syracuse, 1872), p. 219; and Hastings, *Military Minutes . . . 1783–1821*, pp. 1265, 2196.

i. Jacob Brown (1775–1828), who founded Brownsville in Jefferson County and developed a steamboat monopoly on Lake Ontario, was lieutenant colonel commandant of the New Jefferson County regiment in 1809 and in 1811 became brigadier general of the 4th Brigade. Because of his heroism in the war, the United States Congress in 1814 passed a resolution thanking him for his courage and valor and ordered a medal struck in his honor. In 1815 New York City gave him the freedom of the city. See F. Hough, *History of Jefferson County* (Albany, 1854), pp. 420–28; and Hastings, *Military Minutes . . . 1783–1821*, pp. 1079, 1201.

j. Peter Buell Porter (1773–1844), a Yale-educated lawyer who moved to upstate New York in 1793, was active in local and state politics before his election to Congress in 1809. During the War of 1812 he commanded "Porter's Volunteers" with distinction at the battles of Chippewa, Lundy's Lane, and Fort Erie. Subsequently he served as secretary of war under John Quincy Adams. See *Biographical Dictionary of the American Congress* (Washington, D.C., 1950), p. 1694.

To Major General George Izard

Albany, September 28, 1814.

Sir: The bearer is Col. Irving, one of my Aids de Camp. I beg leave to observe that by communication of the 16th of August last, you were informed of my instructions to Major General Widrig & the Brigadier Generals of Oneida, Herkimer, & Madison[a] to comply with any requisitions which might be made on them by the Commanding officer at the Harbour, without waiting for the orders to pass thro' me. Col. Irving is authorised to issue any further & more extensive orders which the emergencies may require & I pray you to advise him of any further measures which may require the interposition of my official authority to secure the frontier of Sackett's Harbour & its vicinity.

To the Commanding officer at Sackett's Harbour.

[PUBLISHED: *Public Papers of Daniel D. Tompkins*, III, 553.]

a. These brigadier generals were, respectively, Walter Martin, James Haile, and Jabez N. M. Hurd.

2. Lieutenant General Sir George Gordon Drummond (1772–1854) was the British commander whose troops had been driven away from American-held Fort Erie, in Canada across from Buffalo. See Horsman, *War of 1812*, pp. 120, 134, 182–84.

3. Major General Jacob Brown (1775–1828) checked Drummond's attack on September 17, 1814. See Horsman, *War of 1812*, p. 183.

4. Major General George Izard (1776–1828) brought reinforcements to the American troops at Fort Erie. See Horsman, *War of 1812*, p. 183.

5. Commodore Isaac Chauncey (1772–1840), who had commanded American naval forces on Lake Ontario since September, 1812, made his headquarters at Sackett's Harbor on the northeastern shore of Lake Ontario. He had retreated there following his blockade of Drummond's troops at Fort Erie. See Horsman, *War of 1812*, pp. 86, 184–85.

128. *General Order*

Head Quarters Albany Oct 3d. 1814

The Commanding Officer at Sacketts Harbor[1] having declared that post in imminent danger of invasion & attack, his excellency the Commander in Chief directs the Corps of Rifle men in the County of Madison, under the Command of Capt. Bennet Bicknell[2] and Capt. Eri Richardson,[3] to march without delay, properly armed and equipped,

to the defence of that post, on the receipt of orders to that effect from
Brigdr General Jabez Hurd[4]

By order of the Commander in Chief
Washigton Irving Aid de Camp

MANUSCRIPT: New York State Library. PUBLISHED: *Public Papers of Daniel D. Tompkins*, I, 514.

1. Major General George Izard, who had been commissioned a lieutenant
in 1792. See Guernsey, *Chronicles of NYC*, I, 181.

2. Bennett Bicknell, a prominent merchant, distiller, and hotel-keeper of
Morrisville, Madison County, was in command of a battalion of riflemen of the
35th Brigade of Infantry. See Hastings, *Military Minutes . . . 1783–1821*, p. 1417;
John E. Smith, *Our Country and Its People*, pp. 93, 209, 211, 234–35, 461.

3. Eri Richardson, who founded Erieville in Madison County, was in charge
of the 129th Regiment of Infantry. See Hastings, *Military Minutes . . . 1783–1821*,
p. 1496; John E. Smith, *Our County and Its People*, pp. 109, 113, 383; Mary K.
Mayer and Joyce C. Scott, *Cemetery Inscriptions of Madison County, N. Y.* (New
York, 1960), I, 73.

4. Hurd was the commander of the 35th Brigade. See Hastings, *Military
Minutes . . . 1783–1821*, p. 1265.

129. General Order

G.O.:   Headquarters, Albany, October 3rd, 1814.

The Commanding officer of the troops and post of Sackett's Harbor,
having declared that post and the neighboring frontier in immediate
danger of invasion, the following Brigades, or any specified parts thereof,
will march without delay to such rendezvous as shall be assigned them
by special orders from the commanding officer at the Harbour:

The thirteenth Brigade in the County of Oneida commanded by
Brig'r Genl. Oliver Collins;

The Herkimer Brigade under the command of Brig'r Genl. James
Haile;

The Brigade under the command of Brig'r Genl. Walter Martin, and
the remainder of the Militia of the County of Jefferson.

The officers will be particular in having the men armed and equipped,
comformably to law. Wilful delinquencies in this respect have become so
frequent, they will be henceforth noticed and the legal penalties
strictly enforced.

By order of the Commander in Chief:
Washington Irving, Aid-de-Camp.

PUBLISHED: *Public Papers of Daniel D. Tompkins*, I, 514–15.

130. To Ebenezer Irving

Sackett's Harbor, Oct. 3, 1814.

Dear Brother:

I arrived here this morning after incessant travelling through the mire for four or five days — the last three on horseback. The British have completed their large ship,[1] and she has dropped down to Snake Island, where she lays under the batteries.[2] Chauncey lays at anchor about six miles off the harbor. It is expected the British will immediately take the lake and Chauncey be obliged to come in. Preparations are making to resist an attack by land and sea, which is expected.[3] Breastworks are throwing up and pickets erected, which will enclose the whole place, and form protection for the militia. I have been constantly employed at the General's quarters all day, so that I have not been able to look about me. In compliance with the instructions of the Governor, I have ordered out a large reinforcement of militia,[4] and hope they may come in time; but there is a sad deficiency of arms and military munitions. I write in great haste, as the mail is on the point of departing. Give my love to mother and the family; I am in excellent health, and feel all the better for hard travelling. Should there be no business to detain me here, I shall leave this place in a day or two. I wish first to visit Chauncey's fleet, and should like to witness an action were there a prospect of an immediate one.

PUBLISHED: PMI, I, 318–19.

1. This was the *St. Lawrence*, which carried 112 guns and 1000 men. See Benson J. Lossing, *The Pictorial Field-Book of the War of 1812* (New York, 1868), pp. 885–87.

2. A mistake. She had not dropped down. The large ship was the *St. Lawrence*, of 90 guns. (P. M. Irving's note. See PMI, I, 318.)

3. This attack never materialized.

4. WI ordered the militia of four counties to be called up. See Lossing, *The Pictorial Field-Book of the War of 1812*, p. 887.

131. To William Irving, Jr.

[Sackett's Harbor, ca. October 4, 1814]

The Lady of the Lake[1] happening to come into the harbor, I went out in her to the fleet which lay at anchor off Stoney Island, about 11 miles distant, and remained on board with Chauncey for part of two days; during which time he took me around the little fleet,[2] and I had a fine opportunity of witnessing their admirable order and equipment. It is a gallant little squadron, and I could not but regret continually that it should be doomed to rot in a fresh-water pond. The Superior[3] is by great odds the finest frigate I was ever on board of. Her gun-deck shows a tremendous battery. I was in hopes of having an opportunity of looking into Kingston Harbor and getting a peep at that *big ship*,[4] which is the bug-bear of these seas; the Lady of the Lake, however, was not sent on a reconnoitring expedition while I was in the fleet, and I did not think proper to make any request.

PUBLISHED: PMI, I, 319–20.

1. The lookout boat in Chauncey's squadron. Benson J. Lossing, *The Pictorial Field-Book of the War of 1812*, p. 885.
2. Chauncey's squadron consisted of eight warships—*Superior, Mohawk, Pike, Madison, Jones, Jefferson, Sylph*, and *Oneida*—with a total of 228 guns. See Lossing, p. 885; and Theodore Roosevelt, *Naval War of 1812*, p. 330.
3. The *Superior*, of 1580 tons and with a crew of 500 men, carried 76 guns. See Roosevelt, *Naval War of 1812*, p. 330.
4. "The St. Lawrence, of 90 guns" (P. M. Irving's note, PMI, I, 320).

132. General Order

G.O.: Headquarters, Albany, October 5th, 1814.

Brigadier Genl. Collins, commanding the post of Sackett's Harbour, will make such requisitions on the Deputy Quartermaster General or such purchases of Camp equipage or hollow ware as may be deemed necessary for the Militia forces actually at the Harbour, and those that may rendezvous there and in its vicinity, conformably to General Orders of the 3rd instant.

By order of the Commander in Chief:
Washington Irving, Aid-de-Camp.

PUBLISHED: *Public Papers of Daniel D. Tompkins*, I, 514.

133. General Order

G.O.: Headquarters, Albany, October 7th, 1814.

The Commanding officer at Sackett's Harbour having declared that post in imminent danger of attack, you will lose no time in assembling the forces under your command and marching them to Watertown, where they will report themselves, either to Genl. Collins, or to such officer as he shall have appointed to receive the troops that shall arrive there. It is strictly enjoined that the men come armed and equipped according to law. Delinquencies will be noticed and the legal penalties enforced.

By order of the Commander in Chief:
Washington Irving, A-d-C.

PUBLISHED: *Public Papers of Daniel D. Tompkins*, I, 515–16.

134. To William Irving, Jr.

[October 14, 1814]

I feel more and more satisfied with my situation. It gives me a charming opportunity of seeing all that is going on, and Tompkins is absolutely one of the worthiest men I ever knew. I find him honest, candid, prompt, indefatigable, with a greater stock of practical good sense and ready talent than I had any idea he possessed, and of nerve to put into immediate execution any measure that he is satisfied is correct. I expect he will have the command here in a few days, in which case my situation will be every thing I could wish.

PUBLISHED: PMI, I, 320–21.

135. To Henry Brevoort

New York Octr. 16th. 1814.

Dear Brevoort,

I returned here some days since, after having made a rough but interesting journey to Sacketts Harbour. Military business goes on steadily here, and the progress that the militia have made is surprising. The Iron Greys have become very expert with their arms and correct in their evolutions; you will find yourself a complete Johnny Raw among them. By the bye, they are very much at a loss to conceive what you are about, & do not half like your long absence. The Gallant Sam[1] has fairly changed front, and instead of laying Siege to Douglas Castle has charged Sword in hand and carried little Coopers[2] intrenchments. In plain English, ⟨that⟩ he has abandoned the lady of the bleeding heart and has paid his addresses to Alice Ann Cooper & what is more, they *are actually engaged.* I could scarce credit the report; until I had it confirmed from his own mouth. Your old flame Maria Laight takes vast credit on herself for having been very potent in promoting the match: in honest secrecy, the old puss thought at first Sam was in love with herself. He used[3] to ask her to ride out to Coldens &c & she affected great confusion when ⟨he⟩ twitted about him; a little time served to Shew her the mistake, and I must do her the justice to say she turned it off very cleverly, and made a very faithful confidant. Sam & the company agree extremely well & matters go on smoothly.

The folks here are in the alarm again; expecting an attack. You will have heard before this of the force with which Lord Hill[4] is coming out; and it is certain th⟨is⟩e intention of his expedition was an attack on this place. ⟨Whether⟩ Circumstances may induce him to alter it; but I think it probable we shall have our mettle tried.

I am impatient to hear of your having effected your business[5] and that you are on your route homewards. You will of course be on the look out, and ⟨dis consider whether⟩ learn what is the situation of affairs here: should we be in immediate danger of attack; this will not be the place to bring goods: as business will be at a stand.

We had letters recently from the Doctor,[6] by the John Adams.[7] He was then at Amsterdam & had been to Paris, Ghent &c[.] he was about to return to Ghent & was waiting the result of our negociations,[8] to determine his mercantile proceedings—He had become acquainted with the Commissioners[9] and I make no doubt was on very good terms with them. He purposed afterwards to rejoin the Brummagen Family.[10]

You will see by the terms demanded by England that there is no chance for a Speedy peace—Goods must therefore sell well. Every body here & I trust throughout the country is indignant at the insulting proposition of the enemy & but one Spirit seems to animate all ranks & parties, a determination to bend every effort to ⟨p⟩ the prosecution of a vigorous war.

The household at Mrs Bradishes continues the same as usual. March[11] is aid to Little Morton,[12] and ⟨can⟩ has swelled so much on the occasion that he can hardly keep from bursting his Breeches. Cruger[13] is aid to Lewis[14] who has now a very formidable staff.— Hamilton[15] Little Lewis, Big Dom Lynch,[16] Montgomery Livingston,[17] and Cruger—what a sage council of War they could hold! I expect however, that Lewis will shortly be removed from the command of this post[18]—and when the Kite falls, the bobs in the tail must follow.

Yours truly
W I.

ADDRESSED: Mr Henry Brevoort Jr. / Burlington. / Vermont.   DOCKETED: Oct. 16 1814 / W Irving

MANUSCRIPT: NYPL–Seligman Collection.   PUBLISHED: PMI, I, 321–22 (in part); LIB, I, 84–87.

1. Samuel Swartwout.

2. Alice Ann Cooper, whom Swartwout married later in 1814, was the daughter of Dr. Charles Cooper of Albany.

3. WI wrote "used" over another word.

4. Lord Rowland Hill (1772–1842), a hero of the Peninsular War, had been suggested as head of a British expedition to North America in 1814, but the project was abandoned.

5. Brevoort presumably had been looking after his fur-trading interests.

6. Peter Irving, who was abroad handling the business affairs of the family firm.

7. The corvette John Adams arrived at New York on the evening of October 5, 1814, after a 36-day voyage from Ostend. See NYEP, October 6, 1814.

8. The negotiations included discussion of American rights to sail the seas unmolested, a point of vital interest to the Irving importing firm.

9. The American commissioners included John Quincy Adams, James A. Bayard, Henry Clay, Jonathan Russell, and Albert Gallatin. See Horsman, *War of 1812*, pp. 251–52.

10. The Henry Van Warts in Birmingham.

11. See WI's letter to Brevoort, [August ? 1814?], note 4.

12. General Jacob Morton (1761–1836), a short man with a large head, was commander of the 1st Brigade of Artillery. See Guernsey, *Chronicles of NYC*, I, 335–37; II, 182.

13. Henry Cruger, Jr. had been a lieutenant in the Third New York Militia as early as 1797. See Guernsey, *Chronicles of NYC*, I, 335 n.

14. Major General Morgan Lewis was commandant of the Third Military District with headquarters in New York City. See Guernsey, *Chronicles of NYC*, II, 90.

15. John C. Hamilton, who was first lieutenant in the Company of Riflemen organized in September, 1814. Guernsey, *Chronicles of NYC*, II, 306.

16. Dominick Lynch was a wine merchant. See Scoville, *Old Merchants of NYC*, I, 169–71.

17. Montgomery Livingston is listed in the *New York City Directory* for 1814 as living at 5 State Street.

18. President James Madison had assigned the command of the Third Military District to Governor Daniel D. Tompkins on October 14, 1814, and General Lewis actually transferred authority on October 27, 1814. See Guernsey, *Chronicles of NYC*, 363–65.

136. *To Moses Thomas*

New York, Oct. 21st. 1814

Dear Sir,

The duties of my situation as aid to the Commander in chief have so completely engrossed my time & attention that I have not been able to attend to my private concerns; which must be my excuse for not having answered your late letters.[1]

With respect to the Vignette—⟨Some⟩ I had thoughts that a head of Milton executed in a similar style to that of Homer, might be designed by Mr Sully[2]—I think the vignettes of Fairman[3] ⟨not of the⟩ rather insipid— but would not have him told I say so. They are very pretty & will answer for many works but are not masculine enough for the magazine.

⟨A S⟩ An engraving of Rodgers[4] might be given without the Biography. As to Randolph[5] I have a very good portrait of him in my possession, painted by Jarvis[6] from which an engraving might at any time be made. By the way, the Portrait of Commodore Perry[7] has never been returned to Mr Waldo,[8] nor have you answered his letters concerning it. This is inexcusable[.] he was promised that it should be returned in two or three weeks & it is now many months. He has spoken to me several times on the subject & appears to be very anxious. I beg you will have this attended to without delay.

I intend to draw on you (perhaps tomorrow) for 200 Dollars. My recent expences have been great & cash is necessary — I wish you would make a statement of our Account up to last July. I wish a settlement, that I may pay Paulding according to my agreement with him.[9] As I have not been able to attend to the work of late, I shall not insist on full pay for the Subsequent months; and am affraid that I shall have to give up all formal agency in the work after the close of the year;[10] though I shall always feel disposed to render it all the assistance in my power. My time is too much taken up with other matters to do justice to a literary undertaking of the kind.

Very truly yours &c
WI.

ADDRESSED: Mr Moses Thomas / Bookseller / Philadelphia   POSTMARKED: New
    York / Oct / [unrecovered]
MANUSCRIPT: Yale.

This letter is cataloged by the Beinecke Library, Yale, as addressed to Moses Thomas.

1. These letters to WI have not been located.
2. The title page for Volume IV (1814) included a vignette by Thomas Sully depicting the blind Milton listening to his daughters read to him. Sully settled in Philadelphia in 1808 for the rest of his life.
3. Gideon Fairman (1774–1827) was a member of a Philadelphia engraving firm.
4. John Rodgers, a hero of the Tripolitan War, who captured 23 British ships during the War of 1812.
5. John Randolph of Roanoke, whom WI had known for several years.
6. WI had visited John Wesley Jarvis in Baltimore in March, 1811, when he was painting Randolph's portrait. WI asked for a reproduction, which is alluded to in the letter. He gave it to the New-York Historical Society in 1858. See PMI, I, 274–75.
7. Oliver Hazard Perry (1785–1819), whose victory over the British in September, 1813, had prompted an article in the Analectic for December, 1813.
8. Samuel Lovett Waldo (1783–1861) painted the portrait of Commodore Perry which illustrated the article in the Analectic.
9. The details of the pay scale for Paulding's contributions to the Analectic are not known.
10. WI found the responsibilities of editorship onerous and did give up the post at the close of 1814. See STW, I, 141.

137. To William Irving, Jr.

[New York, October 27, 1814]

The Governor arrived in town yesterday, and this day will take command.[1] I expect and hope he will keep his staff stirring, and have been endeavoring as much as the little leisure I have would permit to prepare myself for the duties of my situation.

PUBLISHED: PMI, I, 322.

1. Daniel D. Tompkins replaced General Morgan Lewis as commandant of the Third Military District at New York. See Guernsey, *Chronicles of NYC*, II, 363–65.

138. To William Irving, Jr.

[New York, December 20, 1814]

As to the bill[1] on which you spoke, I consider it another of those skeleton measures, which, after having been stripped of flesh, and blood, and muscles, is sent forth to mock the country with a mere shaking of dry bones. We shall now have men for six months to drill and make soldiers of, and six months to feed and support in winter quarters. If it had been eighteen months we might have had two campaigns out of them, or if six months, we could have had one and no after trouble and expense of keeping them through a long winter: I think you were right, however, to support any show of defence, though I regret that you were not able to effect any thing more substantially efficient. I am really heartsick at the present wretched state of public affairs, and loathe that make-shift policy that has only aimed at scuffling through present embarrassments, and maintaining present popularity at the risk, or rather certainty, of future confusion and disaster.

PUBLISHED: PMI, I, 323–24.

1. The bill to which WI alludes provided for the calling up of 80,000 militiamen. It was passed by the House on December 14, 1814. See *Annals of Congress*, 13th Cong., 3d sess., pp. 928–29.

139. To William Dunlap

Head Quarters 3 Milty. Dist. U. S./Decr. 24th., 1814.

Sir,

You are appointed a Captain in the Militia of the State of New York, and ordered into the Service of the United States to act as assistant Pay Master to Samuel Edmonds Esquire,[1] Pay Master General of the Militia of the State of New York—

By order of H. E. D. D Tompkins/Commanding 3d Milty. Dist. U. S.

Washington Irving A D Camp.

Wm: Dunlap Esq

ADDRESSED: Wm Dunlap Esq.
MANUSCRIPT: Bibliothèque Municipale, Nantes, France.

William Dunlap (1766–1839) had a long association with the arts in New York City as a result of his playwriting and translations and adaptations from

German drama, his managing of the Park Theater, his painting, and his histories of American drama and the arts of design. Details about his appointment are found in a letter of Daniel D. Tompkins, February 28, 1815. See *Public Papers of Daniel D. Tompkins, Governor of New York*, III, 637. Dunlap held the post of paymaster until late 1817. See *The Diary of William Dunlap*, ed. Dorothy C. Barck, in *Collections of the New-York Historical Society* 62 (1929), xxii, xxvi.

1. Samuel Edmunds was appointed district paymaster of the northern area on September 12, 1812. See *Public Papers of Daniel D. Tompkins*, I, 400–401.

140.   To Major Henry Lee

Trenton, Jany 11th. 181⟨4⟩5

Dear Lee—

You forgot to give me a letter concerning the Horse,[1] I wish you would send it to me by return of Mail, ⟨directed⟩ or rather write an order at the end of a long letter. How is the fair Serena[2] her father informs me that her cold was bad & her face swoln, God bless her sweet countenance, & keep ⟨if⟩ ↑it↓ from all harm — !

In great haste/ Your friend
W Irving

P.S. I am in hopes of arriving ⟨in time⟩ at Philadelphia in time to have a laugh this evening with Mrs Camel.

ADDRESSED: Major Henry Lee / at Mrs Bradishes / Greenwich St / New York
    POSTMARKED: TREN: NJ / JAN/11   DOCKETED: January 1815 / W Irving
MANUSCRIPT: Va.–Barrett.

Henry Lee (1787–1837), a son of Light Horse Harry Lee and a half-brother to Robert E. Lee but twenty years older, had been a major in the 36th Infantry on the staffs of Generals James Wilkinson and George Izard during the War of 1812.

1. WI may be referring to the horse he used while in the army, an animal named Archy of which he was very fond (see PMI, I, 325). Possibly after WI resigned his commission he asked Lee to dispose of Archy for him. Or perhaps Lee agreed to buy the horse; hence WI's suggestion that Lee send a letter or write an order (i.e., a draft in payment for Archy). WI's later disillusionment with Lee may be foreshadowed in this incident. For other details concerning the WI-Lee relationship, see M. A. Weatherspoon, "1815–1819: Prelude to Irving's *Sketch Book*," *American Literature* 41 (January, 1970), 567–69.

2. Serena Livingston, daughter of John R. Livingston, was known to WI through their mutual friends, the Hoffmans. For other details about the relationship of WI and Serena, see Weatherspoon, "1815–1819: Prelude to Irving's *Sketch Book*," pp. 566–71.

141. To William Irving, Jr.

Philadelphia, Jan. 15, 1815.

Dear Brother:

On arriving in Philadelphia I find that Bradford and Inskeep have failed and ruined poor Moses Thomas, the bookseller, who publishes the Analectic.[1] This will detain me here some time to arrange my affairs with him and settle about the future fate of the Magazine. This circumstance, and the vileness of the roads, &c., have induced me to give up my intention of visiting Washington for the present. I shall, therefore, return to New York in about a week.

PUBLISHED: PMI, I, 326.

1. The difficulties of Moses Thomas and the *Analectic Magazine* are reflected in an advertisement by Van Winkle and Wiley in the NYEP on January 7, 1815, advising that they had undertaken the agency of the *Analectic Magazine,* replacing Abraham H. Inskeep, W. B. Gilley, and Prior and Dunning, all of New York: "Owing to untoward circumstances, the Magazine for January will not be ready for delivery till Monday or Tuesday next [January 9 or 10]." On January 9, W. B. Gilley advertises that, despite the announcement of Van Winkle and Wiley, he can supply the *Analectic Magazine* to his subscribers.

142. To Gulian C. Verplanck

Philadelphia, Jany 17th 1815.

Dear Sir,

On my arrival in this city I was much concerned to hear of the complete failure of Bradford and Inskeep, and to find they had dragged down poor Moses in their fall.[1] Their failure has occasioned great talk in this city and is considered a very shameful one. Bradfords character is deeply injured & many harsh things are said of him. I believe that Thomas failure is in consequence of theirs — and that he is not to be censured in the affair, otherwise than for having conducted his business in the same diffuse, ⟨un⟩ sprawling manner in which all our principal booksellers dash forward into difficulty. He is universally pitied as far as I have heard & is considered an industrious, obliging meritorious man. He wishes much that the magazine may be kept alive, ⟨& wan⟩ until he can get through his troubles & resume it on more regular and certain terms. If you have any thing prepared I think it would be as well to get out another number,[2] & in the mean time try to make some arrangements for its future existence. Its circulation is so extensive & the Subscription list so valuable that it is worth while to maintain such a channel of literary information. I shall as soon as I find liesure, write the biographies I have mentioned at all events.

These failures I am affraid will sensibly affect the interests of literature ⟨& deter[*unrecovered*]⟩ and deter all those from the exercise of
the pen who would ⟨be int⟩ take it up as a means of profit —

I understand your dash at the philosophers in the last number[3] has
drawn on us all the vengeance of some potent pamphleteer. I presume
some doctors apprentice, who for his dilligence in pounding the pestle,
has been regularly inducted into one of the learned societies. If you have
one of the pamphlets[4] by you send it on to me—it is good now & then to
hear a little disagreeable truth of ones self. I expect between you and
Jim[5] I shall regularly have my doublet dusted every month or two; as
I find I always am inculpated in ⟨all⟩ your iniquities. This comes of a
mans keeping bad company.

I shall remain in philadelphia some few days longer & should be glad
to hear from you relative to Thomas' Business—

Remember me affectionately to Eliza/Very truly Yours,
W Irving.

ADDRESSED: Gulian C Verplanck Esq / New York.   POSTMARKED: PHI / 17 / JA
MANUSCRIPT: NYPL—WI Papers.

1. The failure of these publishers and booksellers was one of the results
of the suspension of specie payments by banks in the United States. The official
statement is printed in NYEP, January 9, 1815.

2. None of the articles in the February or March issues of the *Analectic Magazine* has been identified as Verplanck's.

3. In a review of "The Universal Receipt Book . . ." in the *Analectic Magazine*
(5 [January, 1815], 42–53), Verplanck writes, "There is, then, in most of your
large towns a worthy set of philosophers, who, for the good of science, and the
honour of their country are willing to submit to the drudgery of dragging a long string
of unwieldy capital letters after their names, for instance, as LL.D, A.A.S., M.H.S.S.,
N.Y.H.S.S., F.L.P.S.N.Y., etc. and other like uncouth and cabalistic combinations
of capitals." (p. 43). WI or Verplanck had earlier made a similar jibing allusion
to the titles of DeWitt Clinton and his friends. See *Analectic Magazine* 4 (October,
1814), 349–50; July, *Verplanck*, pp. 46–47.

4. A reference to DeWitt Clinton's "An Account of Abimelech Coody and
Other Celebrated Writers of New York: In a Letter from a Traveller to His Friend
in South Carolina," which was published in early January, 1815. See July, *Verplanck*, p. 272.

5. James Kirke Paulding was also a regular contributor to the *Analectic*. For
the extent of his participation, see Ralph M. Aderman, "James Kirke Paulding's Contributions to American Magazines," *Studies in Bibliography* 17 (1964), 144–45.

143.   To Gulian C. Verplanck

Philadelphia, Jany. 21st. 1815.

Dear Sir,

I received your letter of the 17th.[1] and communicated the contents to
Thomas. He says he has forwarded a letter to Van Winkle & Wiley

signed by his Assignees ⟨which⟩ containing terms which he thinks will perfectly secure them. He has also written to you on the subject of the Magazine. As to my conduct towards him it has not been such as to call forth any particular expressions of gratitude. I promptly signed off whatever was due to me, because I thought him unfortunate & the victim of other peoples misconduct — and I told him that should he continue the magazine on his own account, I should cheerfully contribute to it gratuitously for the purpose of setting him a going again. I however would never again undertake the editorship of that or of any other periodical work.

I at the same time told him that I thought it probable you would be willing to continue the Editor[2] provided you were secured in a proper ⟨remun⟩ compensation for the irksome labour of the business; and indeed I believe you would find it greatly to your advantage to keep the work up, until some satisfactory arrangement can be made. The Subscription list is so large that it would take a long time to get any other work into so prosperous a circulation

For the sums which Thomas is indebted to you, You will have your chance with the other creditors

Should Van Winkle & Wiley find themselves encouraged to print ⟨anoth⟩ a Number for february, I think you had better get one ready, and prevent the impression that the work is likely to fall through —

I am very sorry to hear that Eliza[3] is again unwell — She should not, in her present delicate state of health run any risks at those dangerous night parties. Remember me affectionately to her.

Your friend
Washington Irving

P S I have not yet seen this bantling[4] which you suspected to have been begotten between those two Giants in Literature & Science the Mayor & the Doctor.[5] It must be a monstrous production to have warranted such a suspicion. Take care how you meddle another time with Philosophers: its well we've been let off with a mere pamphlet & not buried alive under those Spungy octavoes which these prolific varlets so readily spawn forth.

———————

Since writing the foregoing I have seen your letter to Thomas,[6] and concur entirely with you as to your propositions for the future conduct of the Work.

I shall remain here ⟨a few⟩ three or four days [MS torn] [yet] [MS torn] ⟨It⟩ if I can make any arrangements to promote the interests of poor Moses, will most assuredly do it.

By the Bye — I believe Van Winkle & Wiley have not sent on the Box of Magazines & reviews &c[.] if so I wish them to hold them in their possession for me — as I have many preceding & succeeding numbers & shall receive more by future arrivals to make up sets. I have not received any recompense for them nor indeed sent in any bill — As they are broken sets they can be of not one third the value to any one else that they can to me.

ADDRESSED: Gulian C Verplanck Esqr. / New York.   POSTMARKED: PHI 21 JA
    DOCKETED: Washington Irving.
MANUSCRIPT: SHR.

    1. This letter has not been located.
    2. Apparently Verplanck never assumed the role of editor of the *Analectic Magazine* because of his own domestic problems at this time.
    3. Mrs. Verplanck was pregnant; she gave birth to a child on April 19, 1815, following which she contracted tuberculosis, which eventually took her life in 1817. See July, *Verplanck*, p. 50.
    4. This is WI's epithet for DeWitt Clinton's "An Account of Abimelech Coody and Other Celebrated Writers of New York."
    5. WI is referring to DeWitt Clinton and Dr. Samuel L. Mitchill, for both of whom he had only contempt.
    6. This letter has not been located.

144. To Ebenezer Irving

[Philadelphia, January 26, 1815]

With respect to the pamphlet[1] that has appeared I had heard pretty much its contents; but there are matters of Course which men must expect who make themselves conspicuous in literary or indeed ⟨in⟩ any other pursuits—The immediate provocation, I believe, was an article that appeared in the last Magazine, satirizing our learned societies[2]—I had no part in it, though I think the satire well merited—I am sorry my friend Gill[3] suffered himself to get into a passion; if he cant bear a retort in kind he should never throw the first stone—One or two of the jokes that have been cracked on my fellow victims have amused me so much that I almost forgive the author for all his cruelties towards myself.

MANUSCRIPT: NYPL—Berg Collection (copy in P. M. Irving's handwriting).

    1. De Witt Clinton's *An Account of Abimilech Coody and Other Celebrated Writers of New York*. . . . For other details see WI to Gulian Verplanck, January 17, 1815.
    2. "The Universal Receipt Book . . . ," *Analectic Magazine* 5 (January, 1815), 42–53.
    3. WI's nickname for Gulian Verplanck. In his copy P. M. Irving inserted "[Verplanck]" after "Gill."

145. To Mrs. S. B. Ryckman

New York, Feby 13th. 1815.

Dear Madam,

Your letter[1] has not been answered sooner in consequence of my being absent, at Philadelphia, from whence I returned but three or four days since. I have written to the Governor[2] in behalf of Mr Ryckman[3] but as I am not ⟨in with⟩ of the Governors party[4] in politics, I do not know what influence any reccommendation of mine is likely to have in these party arrangements.

I congratulate you on the return of peace, which, by reviving all kinds of business, will I trust enable Mr Ryckman to get in some way of maintaining you both comfortably.

Give my sincere remembrances to Mr & Mrs Jarvis[5] and the family & believe me

Sincerely your friend
Washington Irving

Mrs S B Ryckman

ADDRESSED: To / Mrs S. B. Ryckman / Care of Saml Jarvis Esq. / Stamford / Connecticut
MANUSCRIPT: NYPL—WI Papers.

1. This letter has not been located.
2. Governor Daniel D. Tompkins, a Democratic Republican, who served as James Monroe's vice-president from 1817 to 1824.
3. Albert Ryckman (1769–1818) married Sally Burrall Jarvis (1774–1842) in 1792. They kept a boarding house on Broadway, at which WI and Brevoort had stayed. Apparently the Ryckmans ran into financial difficulty, for neither Albert nor the boardinghouse is listed in the New York Directory after 1815. Whether Governor Tompkins helped Ryckman is unknown. He died in Amelia Island, Florida, a stronghold of privateers and slave smugglers until December, 1817, when the president sent naval and military forces, which quietly took possession of the island. Ryckman, however, is not listed in either the army or the navy lists; he must have been there in some civilian capacity, and probably died of a tropical fever. See F. Spies, Stamford, Connecticut. Inscriptions Copied from the Graveyards (Mt. Vernon, N.Y., 1929), pp. 104, 123; E. B. Huntington, Stamford Registration of Births, Marriages, and Deaths (Stamford, 1874), p. 65; G. Jarvis, The Jarvis Family (Hartford, 1879), p. 29.
4. WI was a Federalist at this time.
5. Samuel Jarvis (1745–1838) and Elizabeth Marvin were Sally Ryckman's parents who lived in Stamford, Connecticut. See Spies, Stamford, Connecticut. Inscriptions Copied from the Graveyards, pp. 104, 123; Huntington, Stamford Registration of Births, Marriages, and Deaths, p. 65; Jarvis, The Jarvis Family, p. 29.

146. To Oliver Hazard Perry

New York, Feby. 21st. 1815.

Dear Sir,

Mr Smith,[1] whom you was kind enough to receive as a Midshipman Some time since, is extremely anxious to See a little Service, and to be in active employ. As he apprehends that the peace may put an end to the fitting out of your squadron, and as Capt Porter has orders to hold his in readiness for Sea & expects to be put to the Mediterranean,[2] he wishes, if it be agreeable to you, to be transferred to his command[.] I have mentioned the matter to Capt P. who is willing to give him a situation provided You have no objection.

He is a smart ambitious lad, and I should like that he should have a chance of improving himself. If you should think proper to gratify his wishes, I would thank You to drop me a line ⟨when⟩ as soon as Your liesure will permit.

I suppose this sudden news of peace[3] has taken You all aback. You however, of all men, have the least cause to regret it; having reaped a rich harvest of Laurels, and, I thank heaven, escaped from an expedition, which, however great your zeal for public Service might have reconciled You to it, I always looked upon with pain, as unworthy of Your dignified stand in public estimation

Our household are all in high spirits on this influx of good news, and I wish You were here to help us rejoice. Present my Sincere regards to Mrs Perry,[4] and my congratulations on this event which must set her heart at rest about your safety.

With my best wishes for Your happiness & prosperity

I am dear Sir,/Your friend

Washington Irving

Come. O. H Perry.

DOCKETED: Washington Irving / 21st. Feby 1815 / requesting that / Midshipman Smith / may be transferred / from his to Capt / Porter's Command / as he wishes to / see active / Service.

MANUSCRIPT: New York State Library.

1. Probably John H. Smith, who was appointed as midshipman on January 1, 1815. He was promoted to lieutenant on January 13, 1825, and died on November 30, 1836. See Edward W. Callahan, *List of the Officers of the Navy of the United States and of the Marine Corps from 1775 to 1900* (New York, 1969), p. 506.

2. Porter's expectations were not fulfilled. Passed over in favor of Stephen Decatur for the Mediterranean assignment, Porter was appointed to the Board of Navy Commissioners, where he remained from April, 1815, to December, 1822. See David F. Long, *Nothing Too Daring: A Biography of Commodore David Porter, 1780–1843* (Annapolis, 1970), pp. 172–73, 175, 203.

3. News of the signing of the Treaty of Ghent on December 24, 1814, which

ended hostilities with the British, reached the United States on February 11, 1815. The treaty was formally ratified by Congress on February 17, 1815.

4. Mrs. Perry was the former Elizabeth Champlin Mason, who married the naval officer on May 5, 1811, at Newport, Rhode Island.

147. *To Moses Thomas*

N York 8th. May. 1815

Dr Sir,

By the Eolus[1] I understand there are numerous periodical works arrived from my Brother.[2] I shall get them on shore this afternoon & leave them with Verplanck. By Same Vessel I have recd. Scotts New Poem "*The Lord of the Isles*"[3] but have not yet got it on shore. I shall advertise it for you in this afternoons papers[4] & you will do the same in the phila. Papers.

I have directed my brother,[5] who ⟨conduct⟩ is the acting partner of our house here, to send the Books &c which arrive, to Mr Verplanck—or any other person you may direct—& to forward the Accounts to you. You will be so good as to settle the latter as they are presented. ⟨They will⟩ Such simple arrangement will prevent the accumulation of large debts which are always inconvenient to discharge—and will be more agreeable to my Brother, who is a regular man of business. I shall visit England before my return to this country & shall be mindful of your interests while there.

Should I find any other works by the Eolus worthy of publication I will advertise them for you.

With sincere wishes for your welfare/I am/Your friend
W I.

P. S. When I have read Scotts poem I will leave it with Wiley[6]— subject to your order.

ADDRESSED: To / Mr Moses Thomas / Bookseller / Philadelphia   POSTMARKED: [*unrecovered*] / May / 8
MANUSCRIPT: Yale.

1. Listed among the arrivals in NYEP May 8, 1815: "The Russian brig AEolus, Grimmenga, 68 days from Liverpool, with dry goods and salt to Joseph Howland on board, and to the order of Andrew Ogden. . . ."
2. Peter Irving in Liverpool.
3. This book was published on January 15, 1815.
4. Not advertised in NYEP of May 8, 1815.
5. Ebenezer Irving.
6. Probably Charles Wiley, printer and bookseller at 3 Wall Street.

148.   To Moses Thomas

N York May 16th. 1815

Dear Sir,

I have changed my plan with respect to my tour abroad,[1] and shall
sail from this direct for Liverpool on sunday next in the Ship Mexico.[2]
Let me know how I can be of service to you in England & command me.

Yours very sincerely

Washington Irving

M. Moses Thomas

ADDRESSED: Mr Moses Thomas / Bookseller / Philadelphia   POSTMARKED:
    NEW.YORK / MAY / 16   DOCKETED: From W Irving / May 1814
MANUSCRIPT: NYPL—Berg Collection.

1. WI had originally planned to accompany Stephen Decatur on the *Guerrière*
sent to the Mediterranean to suppress the Algerian pirates.

2. The *Mexico*, commanded by Captain Wicks, cleared New York on May 23.
See the NYEP, May 23, 1815.

149.   To _____

[before May 25, 1815]

If you visit Bordeaux call on Monsr. Colk Ferrier, Rue du Serrurier,
Fauxbourg (I think of) St. Antoine Enquire after the health of his family
&c and write me every particular concerning them. I resided with them
five weeks, and as it was just after my launch into the great world, I
have always remembered that family with great interest. Ask after my
friend Little Zerbin, a pug dog, with whom I was very intimate, but who,
I fear, has long Since slept with his fathers.

Let me know how Jona Jones' family is, and his pretty daughter Sally,
who took an emetic one morning while I was visiting them. I believe
She is Since married. Be particular in visiting the Cathederal Church of
St André, it is a noble specimen of Gothic architecture. I ascended one
of the spires & would advise you to do the same—the ascent is curious,
in the ⟨thick⟩ & the prospect very fine. The Palais Galien is a fine remain
of an ancient ampitheater I used to pass thro it at all hours of the day
& night, on my route to & from my lodgings

On Your route to ↑Toulouse↓ take notice of the noble prospects from
the heights of Moissac

From Toulouse I went by the Canal to Bezier it is tedious however,
& the post road is preferable

At Montpellier I put up at Hotel du Midi. an excellent inn[.] I was
acquainted with a fine old fellow of the name of Walsh at Montpellier—

though my stay being but for three days I did not see very much of him. He is Irish by birth, but I believe is Consul for Cette, at present.

Stop at Nismes for two or three days, there are ruins will worthy attentive examination—The most perfect Ampitheater extant. The famous Maison Carrée &c. which last is an exquisite dainty in Architecture.

Avignon is worthy attention, if it were only for the romantic picturesqueness of its environs &c Visit Vaucluse by all means. I neglected it to my Sorrow. In the portico of the Church of *Notre dame de don* is a picture of St George & the dragon & before him a lady kneeling said to be likenesses of Petrarch & Laura.

At Marseilles I put up at the Hotel Franklin, kept by a good old widow lady.

You will find little Cathalin, the Consul, a *queer one.*

If you visit Nice, which I hardly think You will put up at the *Hotel des Etrangeres.* It was kept by a worthy Swiss, who was uncommonly kind to me, as was likewise, all his family during the time of my detention

At Genoa, should you visit there, Enquire particularly after the family of Mrs Bird, at whose house I have passed many a delightful day—She had a fine family of daughters, to whom God Send good husbands— Larry Lack Britches & his Wife Mrs Larn'd Damnable (I E) Mr & Mrs Walsh, were inmates of her family, with their daughters Wit almighty & Grim Dragon—Ask likewise after little Caffarena—he is lame of one leg Sings a fine Song & was clerk of Hale Storms—he is a worthy little fellow. I was likewise acquainted at Madame Gabriacs—who had a daughter that must be a Woman by this time—Ask likewise after the fair but frail Madame La fleche—whom I greatly admired, but who Sinned with Jerome Bonaparte.

John Carlo Di Negri, I was likewise acquainted with[.] he talks english well & is a fine fellow. But by this time all my Generous friends must be completely hidden under french & italian titles.

At Rome ask after Sigr. Carraciolo, an excellent landscape painter, with whom I was intimate.

We had rooms in the Piazza di Spagna.

MANUSCRIPT: NYPL—Seligman Collection.

This undated fragment in WI's hand is bound in a volume in the Seligman Collection containing the letters of WI to Henry Brevoort, Jr. The letter, which is not included in the printed texts of the WI-Brevoort letters edited by George S. Hellman, may not have been addressed to Brevoort but to another friend who, planning to travel in southern Europe, had asked WI for advice on his itinerary. Although tentatively dated by NYPL as 1840, the letter was probably written at least twenty-five years earlier. Stephen Cathalan, alluded to in the ninth paragraph, died in 1819; WI speaks of him as being alive at the time the letter was written (although he could have died, of course, without WI's being aware of it). Since

WI gives precise, accurate details about acquaintances and the cities he visited, it is possible that he had gleaned them from the thorough journals which he had kept on his trip. In all probability WI did not take these journals with him when he left for England on May 25, 1815, so the letter was written before that date. All of the persons mentioned in this letter have been identified in WI's letters or journals written during his travels in France and Italy.

150.   To Henry Brevoort, Jr.

Ship Mexico, Sandy Hook./Thursday Evening, May 25. 1815.

Dear Brevoort

I was extremely sorry to leave New York, without taking you by the hand. Unsettled and almost joyless as has been my life for some time past, yet when I came to the last moment of parting from home I confess it wrung my heart. But all is for the best and I am satisfied that a little absence will be greatly to my advantage.

I should have liked to have taken farewell of my worthy housemates,[1] of whom I shall retain a warm remembrance, and shall toast their memories whenever I can get a taste of the real beverage. Remember me to Mrs Bradish and Miss Claypoole, the unexpected hurry of my departure prevented my seeing them, in fact I was too much hurried and worried at the moment to think of any thing.

Give my farewell to William Kemble[2]–I shall write to you from England and beg you to let me hear from you whenever you have a scribbling fit & leisure moment to spare to an old and constant friend

God Bless you

W I.

Tell Lee[3] I shall open his dispat[c]hes in the morning; in the mean time I give him my hearty good wishes, & beg him to bid the L——s[4] adieu for me–I should have called there again had the vessel not sailed so abruptly.

The wind is springing up from the west and I trust we shall be clear at sea before morning. The ship gives much satisfaction & I am much pleased with my fellow passengers

ADDRESSED: To / Mr. Henry Brevoort Jr. / at Mrs Bradish's / New York
POSTMARKED: [unrecovered]   DOCKETED: W Irving 1815. / May 25.
MANUSCRIPT: NYPL–Seligman Collection.

1. At various times during WI's residence at Mrs. Bradish's boardinghouse at the corner of Greenwich and Rector Streets his fellow roomers included Miss Ellen Johnson, Commodore and Mrs. Stephen Decatur, March the wine merchant; Johnson, a Scotsman; Captain David Porter; and Dennis Sampayo, a Portuguese. See LIB, I, xxv.

2. William Kemble (b. 1795) was the son of Peter Kemble, Sr. and the brother of Peter, Jr., who had been one of the Lads of Kilkenny.

3. Major Henry Lee had announced his engagement to Serena Livingston. In the letter which WI had not yet opened Lee revealed that there was no engagement. See WI's letters to Brevoort, July 5 and August 19, 1815.

4. The family of John Livingston. WI may have had a romantic interest in Serena Livingston himself, and Major Lee's supposed betrothal to her may have encouraged WI's hasty departure from New York. See M. A. Weatherspoon, "1815–1819: Prelude to Irving's *Sketch Book*," *American Literature* 41 (January, 1970), 566–71.

151. *To Sarah Irving*

Birmingham July 4th 1815

My dear Mother

I arrived here the evening before last, after a very delightful ride from Liverpool,[1] which I left at six o'clock in the morning. The weather has been uncommonly fine since my arrival, and the country is in all its verdure and beauty. The journey from Liverpool to this place is through a perfect garden, so highly is the whole country cultivated. I found the family here in excellent health and spirits — as to Sally,[2] she never looked half so well in her life. She has grown plumper in figure and fresher in countenance than formerly. She says the change has chiefly taken place within a year; I was perfectly surprised at her appearance; she absolutely looks younger than when she left America, and five times as handsome. Harry[3] appears in good health at present and I do not see any alteration in his looks from his former indisposition. They have a remarkably fine family, of children, healthy and strong, with beautiful ruddy faces and always in fine spirits and good humour. Henry and Irving[4] have grown stout boys—little William[5] is a charming animated little fellow, with a countenance I think a little like his cousin James Dodge.[6] Matilda is a beautiful healthy child and Marianne[7] a little morsel of a creature, but promising to be very pretty & delicate. They are charmingly situated at a short distance from town within ten or fifteen minutes walk of the counting house; but yet completely in the country with a fine lawn for the children to play on. Sally makes an excellent housekeeper and her household is delightful. They are very much noticed and respected by the first people of Birmingham and have formed a very pleasing set of acquaintances. In short I am rejoiced to find them so comfortably and happily situated. I did not arrive at Birmingham until late in the evening. They had expected my arrival & Harry & a servant had gone different ways to look out for me. I missed them, however, and after wandering about for some time found my way to the house. Notwithstanding all this previous notice Sally was almost overcome at meeting me and it was sometime because[8] she could be composed enough to speak a word. The little folks had all retired to bed with great reluctance, but early in the morning I heard them about my door, consulting whether they should enter and very anxious that I should make my appearance, but very shy about making any approaches. I dressed myself & went out among them to their great delight and in a few minutes we became the most intimate friends imaginable. They spun their tops for me, and took me to see their Goat and their Peacock, and their rabbits and their cows for they own every thing on the place — and I was called as an umpire to determine which was the best dog, Henry's big black dog Nelson or Irving's dog Spot. They are fine manly well behaved little fellows and great favorites of their Uncle Peter — I find their nurse Peggy is still in the family superintending the Nursery. She is the same little queer woman as ever, but I have seen so many like her in England that her figure does not appear so old as formerly. We are in hopes that Peter will soon be sufficiently at leisure to come up here for a while. He has been at Liverpool ever since January last; and has been so completely over-whelmed by business and worried by indisposition that he requires a little relaxation & country air. He is on strict vegetable diet and writes to day that he continues to get the better of his complaint. I am in hopes of seeing my friend James Renwick[9] here to morrow or next day on his way from London to Liverpool, where he is going to attend to some business. He has visited the family here some weeks since shortly after his arrival.

I must conclude this letter that it may be in time to be sent to Liverpool. I shall write to you again to morrow or next day, as there will be several opportunities.

Give my love to the family and to my good friend Mary.[10]

Your affectionate Son
W. I.

MANUSCRIPT: NYPL–WI Papers (copy).

This copy, not in WI's handwriting, was probably made by PMI. At the top of the first page is written in the same hand "To Mrs Sarah Irving New York."

1. The distance between Liverpool and Birmingham is approximately 88 miles.
2. WI's sister Sarah, the wife of Henry Van Wart.
3. Henry Van Wart.
4. The two older Van Wart children, born in 1806 and 1808 respectively.
5. The third Van Wart child, whose birth date is unknown, died on May 14, 1868.
6. James Dodge (1795–1880) was the son of Ann Sarah Irving and Richard Dodge. WI is probably recalling how James looked when he was William's age.

7. The fourth and fifth Van Wart children, whose birth dates have not been discovered. Marianne died on August 20, 1887.

8. Probably an error by the copyist. The context suggests that "before" is the appropriate word here.

9. Renwick and WI set out later in the month on a visit to Kenilworth, Warwick, and Stratford-on-Avon, returned briefly to Birmingham, and then went on an excursion of Bath, Bristol, and Wales. See PMI, I, 336.

10. Probably a companion or servant attending Mrs. Irving.

152. To Henry Brevoort

Birmingham, July 5th. 1815.

Dear Brevoort,

You will see by the date of this letter, that I am safely housed under the hospitable roof of the Baron.[1] I found him & the Baroness and all the Young Van Tromps in excellent health & spirits and most delightfully situated in the vicinity of the town.[2] You would really be charmed with their establishment. My sister has altered very much since she left America; and particularly they tell me within the last year. Instead of an extremely slender figure she is now plump and healthful in her appearance, and far handsomer than ever she was. This England is certainly a most favourable country to the preservation of youth & youthful looks. I hope if I stay here a while I shall return quite a Younker again. My Brother Peter also seems quite unaltered though seven years has passed away since our parting — which you know is a fearful lapse of time to Gentlemen "of a certain age." At present, poor fellow, he is afflicted with a violent attack of the Erysipelas, which though yielding to strict regimen and prescriptions, confines him entirely to the house I passed a week with him in Liverpool, and found him the same identical being he was in America. I am in hopes he will be sufficiently well and disengaged in business to come up here soon, and to ⟨accompany⟩ take some little excursions about the country; which would be of great service to him after having been for months worn down by business, anxiety, & indisposition.

I saw Your friend Richards[3] at Liverpool & dined with him. He enquired about you & your affairs with much friendly interest. He has been a staunch and invaluable friend to both Van Wart & Peter, and behaved himself in the handsomest manner. He is very much grieved at present at the utter overthrow of poor Boney, whose cause and character he vindicates with great gallantry.

I ought to have mentioned before that my voyage, though a wintry one as to weather, was extremely pleasant from the good humour and good breeding that prevailed among my fellow passengers. I do not believe that the same number of passengers were ever mewed up together for thirty days in dirty cabins and with equal deficiency of comforts, that maintained more unvarying harmony and good will toward each other. I was particularly pleased with the British officers. Sir William Williams[4] is a cheerful, good hearted well bred gentleman, with fine animal spirits and great urbanity. Heckey[5] is one of the best temperd honest hearted fellows alive, but Major Hancock,[6] I found one of the most original entertaining and interesting characters that I have met with for a long time. A scholar, a man of reading & observation and of great humour and excentricity. I trust I shall meet with some of these gentlemen again at London, or in the course of my rambles in England.

I found honest Jack Wilkes[7] at Birmingham. He was on the hunt for me on the night of my arrival, ⟨but⟩ in company with Van Wart, but I got to the house without meeting them. ⟨Jack I am⟩ I regretted it, as I am told Jack was a little elevated, having dined out & got mellow on *Gooseberry* wine! We roasted him soundly for it the next day when he dined at Van Warts. He has gone to Liverpool but I hope to see him here soon again. I am happy to find that I shall be likely to meet his sister[8] in London. I am in daily expectation of James Renwicks arrival here, on his way to Liverpool where he is to be the day after tomorrow. I found from Mr. Davidson,[9] what were his movements & wrote to him to London to stop here on his way down, that⟨he⟩ we might concert future campaigning.

I am delighted with England. The country is enchanting and I have experienced as yet nothing but kindness and civility. I think it probable I shall go up to London for a few days before Parliament rises & the theatres close; after which I shall return to this place & from hence make excurisons about the country.

I have forborne making comments on the wonderful events that are taking place in the political world.[10] They are too vast and astonishing to be ⟨treated⟩ grasped in the narrow compass of a familiar letter — and indeed as yet I can do nothing but look on in stupid amazement — wondering with vacant conjecture—"what will take place next?" I am determind however to get a near view of the actors in this great Drama.

Just before I left N York, Lee put in my hands a note to be read when I should be out to sea. I read it according to the directions and found it to be a contradiction of the story which he told us about his declaration & engagement to Miss S L——[11] He said the story was merely got up to prevent Yourself, D Sampayo and me from quizzing him about her. A very paltry excuse, especially as I had for some time ceased to speak to him about her. He said his fabrication was known but to us three & if we said no more about it, the thing would go no further. He requested me to write to him from Europe—*Ill do no such thing.* I have not got over the disgust occasioned by this singular note, and still more strange fabrication. I consider his conduct as ⟨very⟩ totally irreconciliable to my ideas of honourable & delicate principle — I consider a man who can indulge in such an elaborate and systematic falsification of his word — involving too the character & interests of others, particularly of such a being as S. L——— as too dangerous↑a↓ man to be admitted freely & confidentially into domestic circles. I must say there was something about his pretended disclosure at which my feelings revolted — I felt pain at the prospect of a union so· dissimilar and discordant — and I even felt that delicate respect & admiration which I had long entertained for Miss L impaired & almost prostrated at the idea of her having so suddenly and strangely embibed an attachment which argued a coarse and gross taste, courted as she had been by glaring attentions and hyperbolical flattery. You will reccollect our conversations on this subject. ⟨I was rejoyced to find⟩ I do not know but that th⟨ese⟩is feeling⟨s⟩ of transient disgust made me less particular in seeking a particular⟨ly⟩ farewell from the ladies of the Palace than I should otherwise have been. I beg when you see them you will assure them of my unaltered friendship and most heartfelt good wishes. They have made many hours & days of my life pass happily and I shall always think of them with the most delightful reccollections.

I find Peter sent out a quantity of fashionable music to me, which was chosen by little Ellen Johnson,[12] who has become a Mistress of the art. I intended it for the Miss L——s and hope it has been delivered.

I cannot tell you how happy I feel at finding myself embosomed in my Sisters charming little family. I am like another being from what I was in that listless period of existence that preceded my departure from America. It seems as if my whole nature had changed — a thousand kind feelings and affections that had lain torpid, are aroused within me — my very blood seems to flow more warm and sprightly. Her children surpass my expectations. The boys are noble little fellows — full of innocent gaiety, buxom health and eternal good humour. My little god daughter Matilda is a sweet playful child, and even little Marianne though a mere mite of mortality, is full of pleasantness & good spirits. Every thing around me too, is so exactly to my taste. The House, the grounds, the Household establishment, the mode of living: never before did I find myself more completely at home. I wish to heavens you were here to enjoy all this with me — you would be most heartily welcomed.

I found on my arrival at Liverpool that Charles Kemble & his wife were acting there.[13] I called on them and renewed our acquaintance. Kemble tells me that in consequence of his being absent on the continent he did not get the letters from America until long after they were written. The terms offered by Mr Cooper[14] were not such as to tempt them across the Atlantic, as they could make as much by travelling ⟨about⟩ among the provincial Theatres of England. Besides they have a large & encreasing family which would be of itself a detriment. Kemble however talks as if he should like to make an excursion to America himself for a Year & leave Mrs K & the family in England. Such I think would be his best plan as Mrs K though an actress of undoubted talents has grown almost too large for many of the characters she plays — Particularly for the ⟨Ameri⟩ eyes of American audiences, who you know are accustomed to the more delicate figures of our American ladies. I should think a liberal offer might tempt Kemble to pay America a visit.

Give my kindest remembrances to Mrs Bradish, Miss Bradish, Miss Claypoole and all the household, especially my worthy friend Johnson, whose health I hope to drink in the true Beverage in his own brave country before long.

When you see Mrs Renwick remember me heartily to her and her family & tell her I shall keep a sharp look out upon that wild youth Jamie, who I fear is playing what Launce[15] calls "the prodigious Son" at London.

Remember me affectionately also to my good friends the Hoffmans, ⟨?and tell him for me before long?⟩ and let me know how they all do, and whether Charles Nicholas continues in public service — I shall write to you again soon & hope to receive some lines from you ín return.

Your friend
W I.

Mr H Brevoort Jr

ADDRESSED: Henry Brevoort Jr Esqr / At Mrs Bradishes. / New York   DOCKETED: July 5. 1815
MANUSCRIPT: NYPL—Seligman Collection; abridged copy, not in WI's hand, in Yale. PUBLISHED: PMI, I, 330–31, 339 (in part); LIB, I, 90–99.

1. WI facetiously referred to Henry Van Wart as Baron Van Tromp.

2. According to the Birmingham City directories, Van Wart lived on Newhall Street at this time.

3. Silas Richards, an American who first lived in Savannah, Georgia, and then in Liverpool, was one of the foremost cotton brokers and shippers of his age. The first packet ship out of New York was named the *Silas Richards*. With a counting house at Goree Piazza and a residence at 59 Duke Street, Richards was to become one of WI's closest friends in Liverpool. See A. Morse, *General Register of the Descendants of Several Ancient Puritans* (Boston, 1861), III, 219; *Gore's Directory of Liverpool* (1816), p. 222.

4. Sir William Williams was lieutenant colonel of the 13th Foot (1st Somerset), having joined the regiment in 1812. The 13th, with Williams as second in command, took part in the Battle of Plattsburg in 1813, and stayed at the frontier of lower Canada until the end of the war in 1815. The regiment embarked in transports for England on June 4, 1815, from Three Rivers (Canada). How WI

met the officers is puzzling, unless they did not sail with the troops and instead left from New York. For the history of the regiment see Sir Henry Everett, *The History of the Somerset Light Infantry* (London, 1934); T. Carter, *Historical Record of the 13th, 1st Somerset* (London, 1867). See also Great Britain War Office, *Monthly Army List*, July, 1815.

5. Heckey was not in the 13th Foot, nor does his name appear in the *Monthly Army List* in 1815.

6. Richard Butler Handcock joined the 13th in 1810 and was a major in 1814. He led the defense of a post on the La Cole River in 1814.

7. Jack Wilkes, son of John De Ponthieu and Mary Seton Wilkes, was the brother of Charles Wilkes, later a distinguished navy officer, and of Eliza Wilkes, whom WI was to meet later in London (see WI's letter of July 27, 1815). Jack Wilkes later became a banker in South Carolina and married Cecilia Lightwood. See Charles D. Wilkes, *The Wilkes Chronology*.

8. Eliza Wilkes was another child of John and Mary Seton Wilkes. See note 7.

9. This may be Andrew Davidson or Thomas Davidson, both of whom were merchants in Liverpool with places of business near the Irvings'. See *Gore's Directory of Liverpool* (1816), p. 89.

10. Although defeated at Waterloo in June, Napoleon had not yet been captured by the British. Public interest in Napoleon's fate ran high.

11. Another reference to Serena Livingston. See WI's letter of January 11, 1815.

12. Probably Ellen Johnson (1800–1837), daughter of Mr. and Mrs. John Johnson. She was an attractive, talented actress noted for her singing and harp playing. (See WI to Brevoort, December 9, 1816.)

13. WI met the Kembles on his earlier visit to England in 1805. See STW, I, 71.

14. T. A. Cooper was manager of the Park Theater.

15. Perhaps WI is thinking of Launcelot Langstaff, one of the characters in *Salmagundi*.

153. To Henry Brevoort

[Birmingham? July 16(?), 1815]

I must say I think the Cabinet[1] has acted with littleness towards him.[2] In spite of all his misdeeds, he is a noble fellow, and I am confident will eclipse, in the eyes of posterity, all the crowned wiseacres that have crushed him by their overwhelming confederacy.

If any thing could place the Prince Regent in a more ridiculous light, it is Bonaparte suing for his magnanimous protection.[3] Every compliment paid to this bloated sensualist, this inflation of sack and sugar,[4] turns to the keenest sarcasm; and nothing shows more completely the caprices of fortune, and how truly she delights in reversing the relative situations of persons, and baffling the flights of intellect and enterprise—than that, of all the monarchs of Europe, *Bonaparte* should be brought to the feet of the *Prince Regent*.

> "An eagle towering in his pride of place
> Was by a mousing owl hawked at and killed."[5]

PUBLISHED: PMI, I, 332

1. Lord Liverpool (1770–1828) was prime minister at this time, with Viscount Castlereagh (1769–1822) as foreign secretary and Henry Sidmouth (1757–1844) as house secretary.

2. Napoleon Bonaparte. For other reactions by WI to Napoleon, see his letter to Brevoort, August 19, 1815.

3. Napoleon surrendered and asked for the protection of English laws.

4. WI, echoing Prince Hal's phrase for Falstaff, seems to be reflecting the attitude toward the prince regent, George (1762–1830), who was to succeed his father to the throne in 1820.

5. *Macbeth,* II, iv, 12.

154. To Ebenezer Irving

[Birmingham, July 21, 1815]

Since I wrote you last I have made a short visit to London, where I was much gratified by seeing the House of Lords in full session, and the Prince Regent on the throne, on the proroguing of Parliament.[1] The spirits of this nation, as you may suppose, are wonderfully elated by their successes on the continent, and English pride is inflated to its full distention by the idea of having Paris at the mercy of Wellington and his army.[2] The only thing that annoys the honest mob is that old Louis[3] will not cut throats and lop off heads, and that Wellington will not blow up bridges and monuments, and plunder palaces and galleries.[4] As to Bonaparte, they have disposed of him in a thousand ways; every fat-sided John Bull has him dished up in a way to please his own palate, excepting that as yet they have not observed the first direction in the famous receipt to cook a Turbot—"first catch your Turbot."

The bells are ringing, and this moment news is brought that poor Boney is prisoner at Plymouth.[5] *John has caught the Turbot!*[6]

PUBLISHED: PMI, I, 331-32.

1. Parliament was officially closed on July 12, 1815. See London *Times,* July 13, 1815.

2. Paris surrendered to Wellington in early July, and Louis XVIII assumed power on July 8. See Thiers, *History of the Consulate,* XII, 249–83.

3. Louis XVIII (1755–1824), a man of almost sixty, was inclined to be temperate and patient in his political dealings. See J. Lucas-Dubreton, *The Restoration and the July Monarchy,* trans. E. F. Buckley (New York, 1929), pp. 3–9.

4. Field Marshal Blücher, commander of the Prussian troops allied with the British, had ordered the demolition of the Port d'Iéna, which commemorated a French victory over the Prussians. Blücher's orders were countermanded by Wellington. See Lucas-Dubreton, *The Restoration and the July Monarchy,* p. 9.

5. Napoleon surrendered to the British at Plymouth, England, on July 24. See Thiers, *History of the Consulate,* XII, 305.

6. The last paragraph is printed as a postscript.

155. *To William Irving, Jr.*

[London, July 21, 1815]

...I am extremely sorry that his[1] career has terminated so lamely; it's a thousand pities he had not fallen like a hero at the battle of Waterloo.

PUBLISHED: PMI, I, 332.

1. From the context of this printed excerpt it is clear that WI is referring to Napoleon.

156. *To Jean Renwick*

Birmingham, July 27th. 1815.

I promised you, my good friend, just before I left America to write to you from this side of the Atlantic, but I almost question whether ⟨I⟩ my dislike to letter writing would have suffered me to perform my promise, had I not a more interesting personage to write about ↑than myself↓ which is your Son James. Though a Bachelor I can easily fancy what must be the solicitude of a parent respecting the conduct and welfare of a darling child so far removed; and I can sympathize in the tender anxiety of a mother when she has first le⟨f⟩t flutter from under the maternal wing so wild & volatile a bird as the youthful professor.[1] I have thought proper therefore to lay before you a brief sketch of a tour of two days which I have just accomplished with the young gentleman, to view the beauties & wonders of Kenilworth & Warwick Castles;[2] in which my chief ⟨chagre⟩ care will be to keep your son in the foreground, with as much fidelity to truth and nature as he generally observes in those figures which stride with long staves & fishing ⟨poles⟩rods[3] in ⟨his landscapes⟩ ↑front of his landscapes.↓

While in London, & after my return to Birmingham I carried on a brisk correspondence[4] with the laird touching the place where we should meet to commence our Welsh tour; he urged very much a ⟨meeting⟩ that I should repair to Liverpool, or a[t][5] least that ⟨I⟩ we should form a congress at Shrewsbury; but by dint of perseverance I at length got him to come up to Birmingham. He arrived in the *Bang up*,[6] attracted no doubt by its dashing title. My Brotherinlaw had way laid the coach on the road and took him out of it—⟨while⟩ I was advancing with a footman as a corps de reserve, when at the other end of a lane I saw their two figures ⟨advancing⟩ ↑approaching↓ in the dusk & immediately recognized one to be the Laird from his turning out his toes, like Sir Christopher Hatton,[7] that great dancer of Yore.

That very evening (being Saturday) it was determined at Supper table that we should commence the campaign on Monday by a spirited dash to Kenilworth & Warwick. The next morning, therefore, like all true christian commanders, we went to church to invoke the smiles of providence on our adventurous enterprise. Here we found a "round, sleek oily man of God"[8] with a face that shone resplendent with roast beef & plumb pudding, holding forth on the late glorious battle of Waterloo & the surrender of Bonaparte. I was exceedingly amused with the awkward, goose like attempts of this full fed divine to get his imagination upon the wing. If you ever saw a gander, in a sudden fit of untoward volatility, endeavour to fly across a mill pond, ⟨and⟩ with his tail dragging in the water & his wings whipping the surface into froth and bubbles, you may form some idea of the soarings of this worthy preacher. There was a ⟨comical⟩ mixture of Poetry & prose, of figure & fact, of plain truth & slip shod heroics that was most delicately comic. The God of Battles, Lord Wellington, the destroying angel & several other military characters were jumbled to gether—& the ⟨destroyer⟩ ↑tyrant↓ was overthrown, the riegn of tyranny ⟨averted⟩ ended, the great fabric of delusion demolished and the standards of Waterloo brought express & laid at the feet of the prince regent, in the course of a single sentence. Such is a sample of the thousands of patriotic & triumphant sermons that are now droned forth, ⟨ever⟩ over velvet cushions, to honest fat headed hearers in every parish of this loyal little Kingdom. Every country curate & parish clerk now lords it over Bonaparte, whom but a short time since he looked upon with as much religious abhorrence and more real dread than he did Belzebub himself. I must do honest John Bull the justice however to say that now Bonaparte has thrown himself upon his honour & generosity, his feelings with respect to him seem very much to have changed; he still talks of keeping him safe — but you hear no more of hanging him or cutting off his head. I asked a staunch Englishman the other day, what the government would do were Louis the eighteenth or the allies to *demand* Bonaparte. He said he trusted the Government would refuse to give him up — that he was a fallen enemy who had thrown himself upon british magnanimity & he was sure the nation would stand by the government to a man rather than he should be given up to the demands of any foreign power. This feeling is no doubt occasioned in a great measure by the compliment which Bonaparte has artfully paid the nation in the mode of his surrender.

It being determined that we should depart *early* on monday morning, I repaired between seven & eight oclock to the chamber of the Laird, whom I found most surprisingly unwilling to rouse himself from a huge couch in which he was literally buried. We therefore held a council of war & finding that we had until Wednesday afternoon to spare, (when we were obliged to be back to dine out among some fair Brummagem ladies) we determined to do things soberly & rationally & by no means to travel on an empty stomach. I therefore retired again to bed until breakfast time — and after having taken a hearty meal, and made every preparation with maps, travelling books, sketch books &c we got under way about eleven oclock in a very comfortable post chaise.

Our first stage was to Stone Bridge, about nine & half miles — while the post chaise was preparing, I anticipated a proposition that the Laird was on the point of making, that we should take a Luncheon — an important precaution, as in the course of the next stage we were to attack Kenilworth castle; and I have experienced that these kind of researches are never carried on with ⟨patient⟩ industrious ⟨&⟩ animated, and persevering spirit, by a hungry tourist; whose fancy is too apt to be wandering away in impatient anticipation of the next meal. The laird therefore, who acted as ⟨steward⟩ Commissary and paymaster of the expedition summoned the Landlady, an old gentlewoman, whose figure and prominent nose & chin would have fitted her to play Punchinella;[9] ⟨without the result of their conference⟩ or, with the addition of a beard one of Macbeths witches.[10] The result of the conference, ⟨of⟩ & of the incantations of this weird Sister, was the sudden apparition of a cold duck & various accompanyments; which in spite of a very recent breakfast, were dispatched with incredible expedition. I must not omit to mention that in the midst of our repast a Barouche & four drove up to the inn, from which decended a very ugly old lady of fashion & several of he[r][11] waiting gentlewoman. This splendid arrival rather threw us into the shade; but we were much gratified by a visit from her ladyships coach dog — a very fine animal of the danish breed, who lounged into our room with the most civil, sociable air imaginable, and partook of our luncheon with a condescension & familiarity that delighted us. The Laird was particular in his attentions to the visitor, considering him as a sprig of nobility, & knowingly observing that a traveller in England should avail himself of every opportunity of making great acquaintances. By a collar on the dog we found his mistresses name was Lady Curtis[12] & I strongly suspect her to be the wife of a London Alderman of that name, though the Laird protests, with both hands up, against the remotest insinuation of the kind — bringing in support of the sterling nobility of his ⟨acquaint⟩ new acquaintance Certain Armorial bearings on the carriage, of which — I thank heaven, I am utterly ignorant —

⟨From⟩After[13] being thoroughly refreshed & rested we again set forth on our journey (by the bye I am getting on very slowly in my journal) and in the course of our stage stopped for a couple of hours to explore the ruins of Kenilworth Castle. As it is impossible to give a correct idea of ruins by description I must refer you to some sketches taken on the spot by the Laird, barely premising that you must make the usual allowances granted to all picturesque painters, who you know generally take about the same liberties with landscape that poets do with history. It is probable however, that when in this part of England you may have visited Kenilworth in which case description would be superfluous. Any one ⟨who⟩ that has once Seen this magnificent wreck of feudal grandeur can never forget it. It surpassed all my anticipations, and has a proud grandeur even in its ruins, that impresses you with the idea of opulence, and power and lordly superiority more than any of the splendid residences of living nobility which I have visited.

Our ride from this to Warwick was extremely beautiful We past the romantic old mansion called Guys cliff[14] which we were not able to visit, as the family was at home & most inhospitably excluded all inquisitive travellers. To put us in good humour, however, we shortly after passed a group of very pretty Warwick shire lassies at the Gateway of a very rural mansion, who kissed their fair hands to us in the true style of ancient chivalry. All the Gallant & romantic feelings of the professor were aroused by this charming salutation – in a sudden fit of enthusiasm he thrust his body out of the Post chaise window, waving his hand with the most impassioned gesticulation, and had I not providentially caught him by the skirts of the coat I verily believe he would have either flown back to these alluring Syrens – or have tumbled into the ditch. I felt for a moment exceedingly alarmed at this wild sally of youthful blood, but my apprehensions were ⟨dispelled quickly⟩ quickly quieted– ⟨the transport⟩ it was but a transient rapture⟨,⟩ and the next moment I saw the professor sink quietly into his corner of the chaise – elongate his face into its accustomed gravity, and as usual whistle a stave or two of false notes, which it would puzzle all the musicians in the world to assign to any existing tune.

Nothing further of any note happened to us on our ride to Warwick. On entering this comely little town our Post boy was about to stop at a hotel; when the professor ordered him to drive to the Warwick Arms,[15] which he observed was the best in the place, and as he had been there before he should feel quite at home. To the Warwick Arms therefore we drove, and by the way of giving us a flourish, the Post Boy rattled up to the door on a Gallop. The laird descended from the post chaise and entered the Inn with the lofty and protecting air of a Patron of the house. I followed him in perfect confidence of a distinguished reception. We were usherd up stairs with all due form and I stepped forward with chuckling anticipation of seeing the door of a magnificent saloon thrown open to receive us – a door indeed was thrown open – but ⟨i⟩alas! it opened to a little ⟨grue⟩ mean looking chamber, that appeared to have been sliced off of the end of a larger one – A Settee the chintz

covering of which had been taken off to wash stood in one corner of the
room and the whole furniture betokened that it was one of those appartments generally assigned to gentlemen of the Second table. ⟨On the
waiters⟩ On our being left in this room I looked around at the Laird
with, I suspect a very equivocal mixture of ruefulness and drollery; for
I had rather a stronger inclination to laugh than be vexed. The Laird
was whistling & rubbing his chin in evident perplexity of mind, how to
get out of the dilemma without committing his own importance or the
excellence of the Hotel. He understood my look, and immediately observed the Hotel must be extremely thronged with company, as all the
best rooms were evidently engaged — I did not feel disposed to press
the subject home, though I could not help incidentally observing in the
evening when the waiter brought in tallow candles, that the company
which had engaged the best rooms must have engaged all the wax lights —
a remark which the professor suffered to pass unnoticed. At night however, when I retired to my room I sat myself down on a chair, when to
my great consternation the crazy article gave way under me and I came
to the floor with the full force of an italian cadence. This was not to be
borne by flesh & blood. I flung into the professors room and upbraided
him bitterly with having brought ⟨t⟩ me to a hotel where I was treated
with all the indignity of ragged settees & tallow candles & where my
very chamber was beset with man traps instead of chairs. The poor
professor was completely at a loss how to account for this manifest want
of ⟨consideration⟩ respect to our rank & importance on the part of the
host — but in the course of our ⟨def⟩ conversation the true cause suddenly flashed upon me, which was that in an illstarred fit of thriftiness
the professor had *Economized* the post boy that brought us to the
house, out of *six pence* — to which I attribute all our subsequent indig-
nities. Giving him therefore a ⟨lecture⟩ ↑solemn↓ warning against all
future enormities of the kind I once more retired to my apartment and
extinguishing my tallow candle, soon sunk into an oblivion of all the
humiliations of the day —

The next morning, after the precaution of a hearty breakfast we
sallied forth, like two Giants refreshed with wine, to attack the Castle
of the redoubtable Guy of Warwick. As I do not profess to give you any
thing of the picturesque or descriptive in this letter I shall not enter
into a discussion of the lordly magnificence of this ⟨e⟩Enchanted castle,
or of the romantic beauties of the surrounding country. It is sufficient
to say that when loitering within its vast court, surrounded by immense
towers, long stretching battlements & lofty keeps, all mantled with ivy and
stained by time, you may almost realize the dreams of chivalry & romance, and fancy yourself transported back into the days of tilts &
tourneys. ⟨While I went⟩ While passing through the long halls & galleries

of the castle, ⟨through⟩ its Oriels, chapels, Armouries &c I was continually
thwarted in my attempts to forget the present in the past, and to identify
myself with the olden time of the castle, by the officious loquacity of the
attendant, ⟨an old⟩ ↑a gossipping female↓ who was forever pointing out
some painting by Titian, or Reubens, or some fine piece of china, or
some rich peice of furniture without seeming to think that the walls of
the Castle could be more interesting than any thing they contained. I had
once succeeded very tolerably in plunging myself head & ears into a
revery in the great court of the castle, while contemplating ⟨several of⟩
↑one of↓ its noblest features, called Caesars Tower[16] which one of the
old sybils of the castle informed us was built by *Caesar in the reign of
Oliver Cromwell.*[17] It is of vast magnitude & strength, rising to a great
height, crowned with battlements and turrets, pierced with loopholes,
and lighted by small narrow windows, where the daybeams have to
struggle through the immense thickness of the walls. While I was
gazing intently on this tower, I all at once descried at one of the high &
narrow windows ⟨of the Tower⟩ a female face, young &, of course, beautiful. I immediately conjured her into a damsel of romance immured in
this dark & dismal tower by some "Grim baron" and I believe in the
delusion of the moment, I should have proceeded to assail the tower
and deliver this distressed damsel from "durance vile["] had not the
professor dispelled the whole delicious dream by observing that he
supposed that pretty girl in the window was the gardeners daughter,
as his family inhabited the Tower — And now while I am speaking of
him I must not omit one anecdote, which shews at once the accurate
observation, and quick sagacity ⟨of⟩ at drawing conclusions, of my
worthy fellow traveller. While exploring the Donjon Keep of the castle
which ↑is↓ situated on a lofty mound, ⟨by⟩ ↑to↓ which you ascend by
winding labarynths and steep flights of steps, we encountered a party ⟨of⟩
consisting of three ladies & a Gentlemen — They were pretty and of
genteel appearance. Being all under convoy of the gardener we ↑were↓
for some time ⟨followed in the same track.⟩ ↑in company with them↓
The Professor — his hat a little on the back of his head, humming &
whistling with that air of nonchalance under cover of which he sees &
notices every thing, followed close on their track, until I saw that when
they came to ascend the winding steps of the turrets they were a little
embarrassed in their movements — upon which I hinted to the Professor
that on such occasions it was customary for the Gentlemen either to
precede, or to look at the surrounding scenery. I do not know whether
he took my hint — but some time after he observed to me, with a very
sagacious look, that the ladies were Scotch, and on my asking how he
could tell that, as he had not heard them say a word — he replied that
he knew it by the *neatness of their feet.*

I have little more to add of our adventures in this castle, excepting that my *observant* fellow traveller was detected under the shade of a tree taking a sketch of the Great gate of the castle and was ⟨suddenly⟩ ↑very discourteously↓ interrupted in his employment, no one being allowed to sketch in the grounds. This threw him into such a dudgeon that he absolutely refused to see Guys Porridge pot, and the Horns of the Great Cow[18] which he killed (which by the bye look wonderfully like the tusks of an Elephant)[.] I soothed his ire with some difficulty; but chiefly by the suggestion that he might revenge himself when outside of the castle grounds, by taking sketches of it from every part of the vicinity — I assisted him in this great scheme of vengeance & we took several of the most splenetic sketches of the castle you can imagine, and I have no doubt his portfolio will have several violent caricatures of it for the ⟨benefit of his⟩ amusement of his american friends.

On returning to the Hotel we as usual refreshed ⟨ourself⟩ ↑ourselves↓ from the fatigues of the morning by a hearty luncheon, & ordered a Post chaise for Stratford upon Avon. It was a matter of infinite gratification to the Laird that the Landlord at length seemed to recognize him & to entertain a proper opinion of his Guests — This the Laird proved to me by triumphantly ⟨bringing on⟩ ↑displaying↓ the bill, in which we certainly were charged like gentlemen of the first rank. He paid down the money with an air of great pride and satisfaction, and ostentatiously putting a double fee into the hands of the hostler stepped gaily into the Post chaise which rattled us off to Stratford.

The ride from Warwick to Stratford[19] is, I am told, not very interesting — this I give however, merely on heresay, for whether from the fatigues of the morning or the heartiness of the Luncheon, the Laird soon fell into a doze in one corner of the Post chaise, and I (considering myself bound to keep him company throughout the tour,) fell into a doze in the other.

I find my letter growing to such a length that I must exclaim, with the prosing Ghost of Hamlet "brief let me be."[20] Our reception at Stratford upon Avon, was very gratifying — for though the professor had not been there before & was not a patron of the house, we were shewn into the best rooms, and as no Barouches drove up to the door, we enjoyed without interruption the credit & cost of being ⟨amon⟩ the best company in the house.

As Every body knows every thing about Stratford upon Avon I shall not say any thing about it, nor have I time to tell the mingled & almost indescribable emotions with which one visits the chamber where Shakespear is said to have been born & the spot where he certainly lies buried.[21] The wall of Shakespears chamber is covered & literally blackened by the names of humble candidates for fame. Many of these as

usual have mischevious remarks scrawled after them by subsequent
scribblers — but I must mention one which stands as a worthy exception — While running my eye over these ⟨pen⟩ scrawlings I found the
name of *John King*.²² *1802*. after which some one had written with honest
& hearty brevity *"a good fellow"* — a true & pithy character to which every
one that knows him will readily subscribe —

From Stratford we returned the next morning, without accident or
mishap, to Birmingham, where we are now reposing from our toils &
adventures. We got back in time to dress & repair to a dinner party
a few miles off, in the charming family of Mr Bingham where we found
several very beauteous & agreeable damsels. In the evening we played
Loo with the ladies, who so dazzled the eyes & captivated the feelings
of the professor that he lost four or five shillings — he however consoled
himself under the loss with the boast that he had knowingly put off a bad
shilling — which had been refused at the toll gates!

I have thus, my dear Madam, at the expense of great labour and much
weariness of the pen, conducted you with us through this tour, as the best
mode of making you acquainted with the manner in which your son
comports himself during his foreign travel. You will no doubt be delighted with the continual instances of sagacity, observation & prudence
which it furnishes — and of that admirable thrift which saves a penny
though it should afterwards spend a pound. Your anxiety respecting his
personal welfare will also be at rest, when you perceive the sober considerate way in which he travels — ⟨eating⟩ by easy stages, and eating &
sleeping between every curious research or adventurous enterprize

We are now merely pausing at Birmingham to refresh ourselves for a
few days & to eat a few dinners — On Monday next we set forth on our
Grand Welsh tour — by the way of Bath & Bristol through south & north
Wales to Liverpool where I hope to find my Brother recoverd from a
long & irksome indisposition. The laird is diligently collecting works of
poetry & romance to elevate our imaginations on this tour — in the course
of which I ⟨think⟩ ↑have thoughts↓ without letting him know it, ⟨of being⟩
↑of passing↓ myself off for a young American nobleman travelling with my
tutor.

I had no idea when I began this letter of being betrayed into one of
such length — and I assure you it will be a long time before I write
such another — I have no great devotion to the art, and since my departure from America, my friends have treated me with such complete
neglect as to absolve me from all obligations to task myself in this way.
I have no wish to jog the reccollections of any that are disposed to forget
me, but I promise most faithfully to answer any letters that are written
to me, and to receive them with that joy & thankfulness with which a

traveller always receives tidings from that home where his dearest affections are centered.

James is seated at the table with me writing to Robert.[23] I ⟨leave⟩ ↑refer↓ you to hi⟨m⟩s letters for every thing I have left untold.

Remember me with affectionate regard to your family & believe me
Sincerely your friend
Washington Irving

Mrs Jane Renwick.

P S Tell Robert that we have discovered a little damsel at one of the Brummagem manufactures who spins fringe and looks amazingly like Mary Rhinelander[24] — If he wishes any of the article & will send out an order it shall be manufactured by her own fair hands.

I met with Charles King at London; he had just recoverd from a violent fall from the top of a mail coach which put one of his shoulders out. He looks uncommonly well and is in fine spirits, expecting his wife & children out.

I likewise ⟨met with⟩ called on Eliza Wilkes, who was staying with Mr & Mrs Simond[25] at Kensington house. I did not think she looked so well and animated as when in America, & told her so — but.she attributed it to having spent rather a dissipated week in the city.

———— Before I conclude my letter I must inform you, in great secrecy, that I think I have detected a flirtation between the professor and Miss Chirm, the fair daughter of a painstaking pump maker that lives opposite my Brotherinlaws warehouse. In fact I detected him in the very act of ogling her from the window, and he turned it off by a very paltry pun — observing that she was a very *chirming* girl!

ADDRESSED: Mrs Jane Renwick (Courtlandt St) New York.
MANUSCRIPT: Columbia.   PUBLISHED: *WI to the Renwicks*, pp. 22–32.

1. During the illness of Professor John Kemp in 1812 James Renwick had lectured on natural philosophy at Columbia College.

2. Kenilworth Castle, originally built in 1120 and later belonging to Simon de Montfort, John of Gaunt, and the earl of Leicester, was destroyed by some of Cromwell's officers during the Protectorate. About seven miles to the south stands Warwick Castle, which probably dates back to Saxon times. During the Civil War the Parliamentary forces successfully defended it against attacks from royalist supporters for Cromwell's forces.

3. "Rods" is written over "poles."

4. These letters have not been located.

5. Although WI wrote "a," he probably intended "at."

6. WI seems to use "Bang up" as the name for a coach or passenger vehicle, but such a usage does not seem to be recorded. One meaning for "Bang up" current at this time was heavy overcoat, but this hardly seems appropriate for July, even in England.

7. Sir Christopher Hatton (1540–1591), lord chancellor of England from 1587

to 1591, was known as a very good dancer, an accomplishment which made him a favorite of Elizabeth I.

8. WI's variant of "A little, round, fat, oily man of God" from James Thomson, *The Castle of Indolence*, canto I, stanza lxix, line 3.

9. A comic figure with exaggerated features found in the Punch and Judy pantomimes.

10. See *Macbeth*, I, iii, 46.

11. WI neglected to write the *r*.

12. Probably the wife of Sir William Curtis (1752–1829), a member of Parliament from 1790 to 1818. His brother was the Reverend Charles Curtis, rector of Solihull and St. Martin's, Birmingham, whom Lady Curtis may have been visiting at this time.

13. WI wrote "After" over "From."

14. The house at Guy's Cliff was built in 1751 in Palladian style onto a chapel of 1422. It is named after Guy of Warwick, a religious hermit of the tenth century, who lived his last years in a cave at the foot of the cliff. See Nikolaus Pevsner and Alexander Wedgwood, *The Buildings of England: Warwickshire* (Harmondsworth, 1966), pp. 301–3.

15. The chief inn in the town.

16. This section of the castle, with walls sixteen feet thick and rising to a height of 150 feet, was built shortly after the Norman Conquest.

17. Apparently as an afterthought WI inserted the words "which one . . . *Oliver Cromwell*" between the regular lines.

18. Guy of Warwick killed the monstrous dun cow of Dunsmore in the course of his adventures.

19. A distance of eight miles.

20. *Hamlet*, I, v, 59.

21. Shakespeare's birthplace on Henley Street and his tomb in the Church of the Holy Trinity.

22. John King was probably the brother of Charles King, the president of Columbia College. See the postscript to the letter.

23. Robert Renwick, the brother of James.

24. Mary Rhinelander (1795–1846), who was to marry Robert Renwick on December 6, 1815.

25. Mrs. Simond (née Frances Wilkes) was the aunt of Eliza and Charles Wilkes.

157. To Cadwallader Colden

Birmingham, July 29th 1815.

My dear Sir,

I received your letter[1] mentioning your conviction of the fallacy of your hydrostatic engine;[2] indeed the failure of the experiment previous to my leaving New York had destroyed my faith in the invention, and I consequently took no step in this Country, nor made any mention of the thing until I should hear further from you. I trust, however, you ⟨wi⟩have not suffered this disappointment to occasion any chagrin; or the sneers of the ignorant & dull, who are ever ready to triumph in the failures of the ingenious[?] [*rest of page missing*] friend Decatur[3] has had a successful rencontre with the Algerines. I rejoice most heartily in his success, and am extremely anxious to hear the particulars. He promised to write to me from the Mediterranean, but as yet I have received no letter, and the total ignorance in which I remain as to the situation of the Squadron, or its intended movements, prevents me from making any arrangements as to visiting it.[4] I am about to make a short tour in Wales with Mr Renwick,[5] and when affairs wear a more settled & certain aspect in Paris I think I shall pay it a Visit & see the conquering armies Encamped in the Champs Elysees [*rest of page missing*] hanging or beheading him, or even of exhibiting him in a cage. They think he ought to be sent to St Helena[6] where he would be perfectly secure and at the same time would have room for Exercise & air. "Damn the fellow" John[7] says — "let him have plenty of air."

Give my best regards to Mrs Colden and David and when you see the little household at Bergen give them my best wishes & reccollections

I am my dear Sir/Very truly Yours
Washington Irving

ADDRESSED: [C]adwallader [*MS torn*] D Colden Esq- / New York.   DOCKETED: 1815 July 19 / Washn. Irving / and. 15 Feby 1816
MANUSCRIPT: NYPL—Hellman Collection.
The bottom halves of the sheets are missing.

1. This letter has not been located.
2. On May 19 and June 2, 1815, Colden was issued patents for "Hydrostatic paradox, applied to move machinery." See *List of Patents for Inventions and Designs Issued by the United States from 1790 to 1847*, comp. Edmund Burke (Washington, 1847), p. 223.
3. Commodore Stephen Decatur, who had been WI's fellow boarder at Mrs. Bradish's, had accepted an assignment to fight against Algiers, partly to redeem himself for having been captured by the British early in 1815. See PMI, I, 326–29.
4. At one point WI had considered sailing to the Mediterranean with Decatur's squadron but decided against it at the last minute. See PMI, I, 328.
5. WI and James Renwick went from Birmingham to Liverpool via Bath, Bristol, and North and South Wales, joining Peter Irving in mid-August. See PMI, I, 336.
6. Napoleon had surrendered to the British on July 15, 1815, and the official decision to exile him on St. Helena was made on July 30, 1815.
7. John Bull (WI's facetious reference).

158.   To Henry Brevoort

Liverpool August 19th 1815.

My dear Brevoort.

I cannot tell you how much I have been gratified by your long letter of the 8th July.[1] I shall endeavour to repay it, when I have more leisure, by a letter of more length, if not more value, than ⟨this⟩ I am able to write at present. I have just returned from a delightful tour in Wales with Renwick, of which I have no time to furnish particulars. Our route was from Birmingingham[2] to the Leasowes, Hagley, Worcester, Tewkesbury, ⟨Glocester⟩ Cheltenham, Glocester, Bath, Bristol — Chepstow Tintern — Monmouth — Hereford, Leominster, Ludlow, Shrewsbury, Ellsmere, Langollen, Conway — Caernarvon, Bethgellert Llanrwst — Ruthin — Denbigh — Chester — Liverpool — As you know the country, you may judge what a charming tour it has been. As we had no letters to the Cloughs[3] I had not an opportunity of seeing your friend the little Apothecary, who had such a passion for Great lakes and mighty rivers; I had forgotten in fact whether he lived in Denbigh or one of the neighbouring villages. I found Renwick an excellent travelling Companion, and, from his uncommon memory, an exceeding good book of reference, so as to save me a vast deal of trouble in consulting my travelling books. The professor is now in Liverpool & will remain here until Smedburg[4] sails, when he intends paying Scotland a visit.

My Brother is still an invalid, but recovering from the flames of St. Anthony,[5] in which he has been almost consumed. He has been troubled for a few days past with rheumatic pains in one of his legs. I hope however that he will soon be well enough to make an excursion to Birmingham & that a visit to some watering place will completely restore him.

As to the subject of Lee's conduct,[6] I ⟨wrote⟩ gave you my opinion in a former letter, and am happy to find it accords so perfectly with your own. Indeed I was sure, from your correctness of mind, you could not but revolt from such a gross unnecessary imposition, such an elaborate tissue of fabrication. Above all, such an ⟨vile⟩ unwarrantable abuse of a ladys name, whose character & conduct ⟨should have⟩ would awe any being of the most ordinary delicacy into scrupulous respect. Upon my soul, the more I think of it, the more I am surprised at the hardihood of Lee in daring to treat with such licentious tongue, the name of such a pure and delicate creature as ⟨the⟩ S—— L——[7] But I need not dwell on this subject as I know you feel exactly as I do, and I think the manner in which you treated Lee exactly right. You may be assured I shall never mention the matter to any other being but yourself — though, as Dennis[8] was in some measure in Lee's wide spread confidence I question whether he has not proclaimed it on the house tops.

I received a very good, that is to say a very characteristic Letter yesterday from that worthy little tar Jack Nicholson, dated 7 July on Board the Flambeau off Algiers,[9] & giving a brief account of our affairs with Algiers. He mentions that "they fell in with & captured the Admirals[10] ship and *killed him*." As this is all that Jacks brevity will allow him to say on the subject I should be at a loss to know whether they killed the admiral *before* or *after* his capture. The well known humanity of our tars however, induces me to the former conclusion. He informs me that he had written to the Livingstons & sent them *Otto of Roses*, &c.

This triumph will completely fix Decaturs Reputation[11] — he may now repose on his Laurels & have wherewithal to solace himself under their shade. Give my hearty congratulations to Mrs Decatur,[12] & tell her that now I am willing she shall have the Commodo[re] [*MS torn*] [to her]self [*MS torn*], and wish her all comfort & happiness with him— [A gal]lanter [*MS torn*] fellow never stepped a quarter deck—God bless him

The Wiggins[13] family & Madame Bo⟨u⟩naparte[14] passed thro here while I was in Wales. I understand that they are at Cheltenham, but it is probable they will soon pass over to the continent, as the ladies are very anxious to visit Paris — though Wiggins wishes to stop a while in England. I think the poor man has his hands full with such a bevy of beautiful women under his charge, and all doubtless bent on pleasure & admiration.

Scott & Mercer[15] likewise passed thro' here while I was absent. What think you of Poor Boney in America — his fallen fortunes have awakend sympathy even in England. For my part I feel a kindness for him in his distresses, & think the cabinet here have acted with much littleness in their treatment of him.

I recd. a letter from Colden declaring the fallacy of ·his project.[16] I had long before lost all faith in it & had taken no steps concerning it in this country.

I beg you will remember me with great regard to Mrs & Miss Bradish & Miss Claypoole. I sent a ⟨number↑Vol⟩ No↓ of Byrons Hebrew Melodies to Miss B—— by Mr Clay[17] which I hope she received.

Give my hearty reccollections to those two worthies Walker and Johnson[18] and my good wishes to all the household — I shall write you more particularly soon.

Yours ever—
W.I.

P.S. Should you in the course of your journeyings see my fair friend Mrs Campbell[19] of Philadelphia give her my sincere regards. If you visit Philadelphia I am sure their house will be one of your favourite resorts —

I shall attend to your request concerning old Books, and shall peep into all the little stalls that I meet with.

ADDRESSED: To / Henry Brevoort Jr Esqr / New York. / *General Hamilton*   DOCK-
ETED: 1815 Aug 19
MANUSCRIPT: NYPL—Seligman Collection.   PUBLISHED: LIB, I, 100–105; PMI, I, 336, 338 (in part).

1. The holograph letter has not been located.
2. WI's misspelling.
3. The Cloughs of Wales were related to James Butler Clough (1784–1844), a Liverpoool cotton merchant and later father of Arthur Hugh Clough, the poet.

WI probably met James Clough through commercial contacts on the Liverpool wharfs.

4. Charles Gustavus Smedberg (1781–1845) was the fiancé of Isabella Renwick (1797–1862), James's sister. They were married on December 2, 1815. See Helen McIver, *Jaffrey-Jeffrey Family*, p. 6.

5. A popular name for erysipelas, Peter Irving's ailment.

6. See WI's letter of July 5, 1815, for other details.

7. For other details see WI's letter to Lee, January 11, 1815.

8. Dennis Sampayo, a boarder at Mrs. Bradish's.

9. Lieutenant John B. Nicholson, one of the Lads of Kilkenny, commanded the twelve-gun brig *Flambeau*, which was a part of the ten-ship American fleet which had left New York in May. See Maclay, *History of the U.S. Navy*, II, 88–89.

10. Rais Hammida, the Algerian admiral, was killed during the fight and his ship, *Mashouda*, captured on June 17, 1815. See Maclay, *History of the U.S. Navy*, II, 89–95.

11. In attempting to run the British blockade of New York in January, 1815, Decatur's ship, the *President*, was attacked and forced to surrender, with twenty-four men killed and fifty-six wounded. See Maclay, *History of U.S. Navy*, II, 64–71. This action discredited Decatur in the eyes of some Americans.

12. Mrs. Stephen Decatur (née Susan Wheeler) was living at Mrs. Bradish's boardinghouse.

13. This may be the family of Samuel Wiggins, a New York merchant with a store on Pearl Street. In a letter to her father Madame Bonaparte observes that "The family with whom I came over remain at a boarding-house," but she does not identify them further. See Eugene L. Didier, *The Life and Letters of Madame Bonaparte* (New York, 1879), p. 44.

14. Mrs. Jerome Bonaparte, with whom WI's name had been romantically associated in Washington in 1812. See WI's letter of December 18, 1812 to James Renwick.

15. Sir Walter Scott (1771–1832), the poet, antiquary, and author of the Waverley novels. Andrew Mercer (1775–1842), poet, man of letters, and editor of the *North British Magazine*.

16. See WI's fragmentary letter of July 29, 1815, to Cadwallader D. Colden concerning his hydrostatic engine. Colden's letter to WI has not been located.

17. Henry Clay was a member of the American mission which signed the peace treaty of Ghent. He left Liverpool for New York on July 15, 1815. See *The Papers of Henry Clay*, ed. James F. Hopkins (Lexington, Ky., 1961), II, 60.

18. Boarders at Mrs. Bradish's.

19. The wife of Archibald Campbell, brother of Thomas Campbell living in the United States.

159. To Henry Brevoort

Liverpool. August 23d. 1815.

Dear Brevoort,

I wrote you a hasty letter a few days since which you will receive pr the Genl Hamilton[1]—Since then I have recd. your letter by the Pacific,[2] and have again to express my sense of this attention. I had purposed writing you a long & particular letter; but have been so much engaged in scribbling to various persons, and in attending a little to our business here, on account of Peters indisposition, that I have no time to write leisurely & fully.

I am very glad to hear that you are likely to make an arrangement with the N. W. Company[3] on advantageous terms. I am satisfied that in Your hands it will turn to profitable account, though I think with You that nothing but a prospect of very considerable & certain gain should tempt You in any wise to link Your fortunes with others, or place Your independence of life & action in any wise in their controul.

I trust Your operations on this side the water will be successful, though you made rather a bad outset in remitting specie. Our business I trust will be very *good* — it certainly will be very *great*, this year, and will give us credit, if not profit. Notwithstanding that peter has been an invalid, and confined to the house almost continually since the Treaty of Ghent, yet he has managed to get through an immensity of business He is slowly getting over his complaint; but is very much afflicted at present with the rheumatism. ⟨Thomas⟩ He has very comfortable & handsome appartments in Bold St.[4] where I reside at present with him. Thomas,[5] that mirror of Silent & discreet domestics, still acts as his Squire; and retains the same immoveable solemnity of muscle that marked his countenance when you were here.

I do not know whether I mentioned to you my having become acquainted with little Booth,[6] during my short visit to London. I visited her several times and was very much charmed with her. She frequently mentioned you with great regard. Little Fidel[7] is still in full fire & vigour—and one of the most tyrannical little villains that ever existed. He ramps & roars & rages at his little mistress with such tremendous violence that I was more than once affraid that he would swallow her alive.

While at London I made an excursion to Sydenham to visit Mr Campbell[8] — unfortunately he was not at home. I spent an hour in conversation with Mrs Campbell[9] — who is a most engaging & interesting woman. Campbell was still engaged in getting his critical work through the press — and as he is a rigid censor of his own works — correcting is as laborious as composition to him. He alters & amends until the last moment. I am in hopes when he has this work off of his hands, he will attempt another poem. Mrs C gave me some anecdotes of Scott — but none so remarkable as to dwell in my memory. He has lost much by the failure of the Ballyntines,[10] but is as merry & unconcerned to all appearance as ever — one of the happiest fellows that ever wrote poetry. I find it is very much doubted whether he is the Author of Waverly & Guy Mannering — Brown,[11] one of the publishers, positively says he is not. It is reported that another novel will soon make its appearance from the same hand, called the antiquarian.[12]

I was agreeably surprised the other day by the arrival of long Peter Ogden[13] — the *hero* of New Orleans. (to use an American expression) He is likely to be a good deal in Liverpool and will have lodgings in our neighbourhood. Lawrence & his wife (late Fanny Ogden)[14] have likewise arrived. I saw them just after their landing. They have had a remarkably fine voyage. This place swarms with Americans — You never saw a more motley race of beings. Some seem as if just from the woods, and yet stalk about the streets & public places, with all the easy *nonchalance* that they would about their own villages — Nothing can surpass the dauntless independence of all form, ceremony, fashion or regulation of a downright, unsophisticated American. Since the war too, particularly, our lads seem to think they are the "salt of the earth,"[15] and the legitimate lords of creation. It would delight you to see some of them playing Indian when surrounded by the wonders & improvements of the old world — It is impossible to match these fellows with anything on this side of the water. Let an Englishman talk of the Battle of Waterloo & they will immediately bring up New Orleans & Plattsburgh[16] — A thorough bred — thougroughly appointed soldier, is nothing to a Kentucky Rifleman — As to British lakes & rivers, they are completely drowned in Lake Superior & the Mississippi The Welsh Mountains are molehills to the Alleghany — and as to all mechanical improvements they are totally eclipsed & annihilated by an American Steam boat.

I have had no letter from Thomas[17] since I have been in England — which rather surprises me, knowing his great propensity to write, even when he has nothing to say. How does the magazine come on. I shall continue to send out periodical works for it, until I can make some arrangement in London to take ⟨off⟩ the troublesome duty off our hands.

I should like to see the National Intelligencer now that Jim[18] is writing for it. These late triumphs on the continent will be sore blows to Jims plans — they will materially delay the great object of his life — the overthrow of the British Empire. His grand Coadjutor‾ Poor Boney has at length left the coast — for St Helena. I must say I think the Cabinet has acted with littleness towards him. In spite of all his misdeeds, he is a noble fellow, and I am confident will eclipse in the eyes of Posterity, all the Crowned wiseacres that have crushed him by their overwhelming confederacy.

If any thing could place the Prince Regent[19] in a more ridiculous light, it is Bonaparte suing for his magnanimous protection — Every compliment paid to this bloated sensualist, this inflation of sack & sugar, turns to the keenest sarcasm — and nothing shews more completely the caprices of fortune, and how truly she delights in reversing ⟨all⟩ the relative situations of persons & baffling the flights of intellect & enterprize — than that, ⟨Bonaparte should be⟩ of all the monarchs of Europe, *Bonaparte* should be brought to the feet of the *Prince Regent.*

> "An eagle towring in his pride of ⟨height⟩ ↑place↓[20]
> Was by a mousing owl hawked at & killed—"

In mentioning Mrs Campbell I ought to have told you that she spoke very particularly & very kindly of you. You were also ⟨mentione⟩ enquired after by various ⟨of the⟩ good people of Brummy, particularly the Binghams, where Renwick & myself dined. You may reccollect the family. The Old Gentleman is a hearty goodhumoured, right down John Bull, has very pretty & amiable daughters, one of them a little lame & a charming woman for a wife. It is a family where Peter is fond of visiting. During the short stays I have made at Birmingham I have found several very agreeable acquaintances among the neighbours

My only acquaintances as yet in this place are the families of Mr Richards & Mr Woolsey.[21] Mrs Richards is at present out of town. Mrs. Woolsey you must certainly reccollect. She is a perfect lady and a most amiable interesting woman — she likewise mentiond you in very flattering terms —

Remember me to Mrs Bradishes family & household —

Peter Ogden tells me that my old friend & quondam Vassal William[22] served him as *Valet de place* during his residence in N York. The good old man must feel much comfort in the restoration of the Bourbons.

Yours ever

W I.

P.S. If you can at any time send me pamphlets newspapers &c I should be very glad to receive them — you may leave them at our counting room to be forwarded by *private hand.* By a regulation of the last parliament all letters &c arriving from abroad are subject to full postage — and from a blunder in the Act, Newspapers &c are subject to equal postage with letters,[23] so that a parcel of Newspapers will come to perhaps a couple of Guineas. This prevents their being taken out of the post office & completely b⟨l⟩alks us in the reception of news in that way. It is expected that a provision will be made when parliament meets ⟨for their⟩ permitting the⟨ir⟩m to be delivered with light postage — Until then, however, the only mode of getting them to us is privately, by the ↑hands of↓ Captains or passengers.

ADDRESSED: Mr Henry Brevoort, Jr. / at Mrs Bradish's / New York. / p *Enterprize.*
    DOCKETED: 1815 Aug 23
MANUSCRIPT: NYPL—Seligman Collection.   PUBLISHED: LIB, I, 106–14.

1. The arrival of this ship does not appear in the marine list of NYEP. However WI's letter of August 19 sent by the *General Hamilton* does survive.

2. The departure of this ship does not appear in the marine list of NYEP. Brevoort's letter to WI has not been located.

3. Probably the Northwest Fur Company of John Jacob Astor and his associates. Brevoort had worked intermittently for Astor since December 1801. See Porter, *Astor*, I, 57.

4. This location was approximately one-half mile from the office of P. & E. Irving and Co. in the Goree Arcades along the Liverpool waterfront. See Henry S. and Harold E. Young, *Bygone Liverpool* (Liverpool, 1913), plate 15.

5. The surname of Peter Irving's servant has not been ascertained.

6. Probably Sarah Booth. See WI to Henry Brevoort, January 12, 1813.

7. Possibly a reference to Miss Booth's dog.

8. Thomas Campbell (1777–1844), an English poet whose *Gertrude of Wyoming* (1809) was very popular in the United States. WI had written a biographical sketch of Campbell for a collection of his poems published in 1810.

9. The former Matilda Sinclair (d. 1828), whom Campbell had married in 1803.

10. The failure of the John Ballantyne publishing firm had occurred in August, 1813. See Lockhart, *Life of Sir Walter Scott*, III, 72–77.

11. A member of the London publishing firm of Longman, Hurst, Rees, Orme, & Brown which brought out *Guy Mannering* in 1815.

12. *The Antiquary* appeared anonymously on May 4, 1816. See Edgar Johnson, *Sir Walter Scott, The Great Unknown* (New York, 1970), I, 518.

13. Captain Peter V. Ogden (1785–1820) commanded the first United States Dragoons at the battle of New Orleans. See Augustus C. Buell, *History of Andrew Jackson* (New York, 1904), II, 47. Ogden was later in merchandising in New Orleans with his brother George. See Wheeler, *Ogden Family*, p. 253.

14. Frances S. Ogden (1788–1824) married Nathaniel Lawrence (d. 1824) on June 1, 1815. Their trip across the Atlantic was probably a honeymoon. See Wheeler, *Ogden Family*, p. 194.

15. Matt. 5:13.

16. Scenes of decisive British defeats in the South and on Lake Champlain during the War of 1812.

17. Moses Thomas, for whom WI had edited the *Analectic Magazine*.

18. James Kirke Paulding, who had recently moved to Washington to become secretary of the board of navy commissioners, was contributing essays to the *National Intelligencer* under the name of "Parvus Homo." See Paulding, *Literary Life of J. K. Paulding*, p. 155.

19. George Augustus Frederick (1762–1830), who served as Regent from 1811 until the death of George III in 1820, ruled as George IV for a decade.

20. Adapted from *Macbeth*, II, iv, 12–13, "A falcon towering," etc.

21. Silas Richards and George Morrison Woolsey were Liverpool merchants with counting houses on Goree Street. (See Gore's *Directory of Liverpool* [Liverpool, 1816].) At the time of the bankruptcy of the Irving firm in 1818 Richards was designated as one of its assignees. See *Orders Made in Bankruptcy and Orders of the Lord Chancellor*, March 19, 1818 (Public Records Office, Order Book. B. 1. 148).

22. Presumably a serving man in New York City.

23. At the beginning of 1815 stamp duties were regulated by two acts of parliament—44 Geo. III, cap. 98 and 48 Geo. III, cap. 149. Later in 1815 these were

amended and recast by 55 Geo. III, caps. 184–85. See Elie Halévy, *A History of the English People in the Nineteenth Century* (London, 1949), I, 371, n.

160. To Ebenezer Irving

[Liverpool, August, 1815]

I found him[1] very comfortably situated, having handsome furnished rooms, and keeping a horse, gig, and servant, but not indulging in any extravagance or dash. He lives like a man of sense, who knows he can but enjoy his money while he is alive, and would not be a whit the better though he were buried under a mountain of it when dead.

PUBLISHED: PMI, I, 333.

1. Peter Irving was managing the family business in Liverpool.

161. To Henry Brevoort

Liverpool, Septr. 8th. 1815.

Dear Brevoort,

I have just returned from Accompanying Peter as far as Manchester, on his way to Harrowgate. He bore his journey so far very well, and yesterday I saw him off from Manchester, very comfortably stowed away in a chaise, loaded with as many conveniencies as the "Happy Man" whom you ⟨?pre?⟩ encountered of yore in Wales, and attended by his faithful, discreet, & taciturn man Thomas — or as we more currently call him "Solemn Silence." I trust the waters of Harrowgate will completely restore both skin & bone which is nearly all that remains of him. I shall remain here as long as the fall business requires my presence, & then join him at Harrowgate

I have not heard any thing ↑of↓ ⟨[*unrecovered*]⟩ Conger[1] since I saw him in London, except when in Bath, on my way to Wales. He had promised to meet me in Bath & accompany Renwick & myself on our Welsh Tour but on enquiring for him in that City I heard that he was at some Watering place & would not return in some days. I am in hopes of soon seeing Charles King in Liverpool to await the arrival of his family — I saw much of him while in London and, as you may suppose, found him a most desireable companion in the Metropolis. Charles is exactly what an American should be abroad — ⟨loyal⟩⟨Frank⟩[2] ↑frank↓, manly & unaffected in his habits & manners, liberal & independent in his opinions, generous & unprejudiced in his sentiments towards other nations, but most loyally attached to his own.

Peter received a letter some few days since, from Colin Robertson[3] —

dated on the Banks of the Superior — He was to return by the way of Hudsons Bay. He mentions having heard of your intention of ⟨jo⟩ doing Business with the NW — but hoped it was only Commission Business — as he thought that Compy on the Decline. He seems very sanguine as to the business in which he is engaged.

I have not heard any thing of Madame Bounaparte Since her arrival in this country, except that the News papers mention her being at Cheltenham. There are so many huge Stars & comets thrown out of their orbits & whirling about the world at present, that a little star like Madm B——— attracts but slight attention, even though she draw after her so sparkling a tail as the Wiggins family.

I regret very much that I was not in Liverpool when she arrived. I should have liked to have congratulated the little lady on the prospect of a speedy consummation of the great wish of her heart, a visit to Paris — and I should have delighted to bask in the sweet smiles of Mrs W. and her charming Sister.

We were ⟨much⟩ very uneasy some few days since from news from the family of the Van Tromps that little Irving had received a violent contusion in the head by a fall from a Poney — He however is now perfectly recovered, having inherited a solid dutch head from his father.

By mistake one of our Clerks has put a small parcel of Music for Miss Bradish, in the letter Bag of the Pacific — I had intended to have sent it by private hand. They are merely a few fashionable songs. I cant say much as to the selection[.] Liverpool is not the best place to get new music, & these were chosen by another hand — Give my regards to Mrs Bradish & her daughter — and my hearty remembrances to Johnson Walker & all the household.

In great haste/Yours ever
W I.

ADDRESSED: Mr Henry Brevoort Jr. / at Mrs Bradishs' / New York— / ⟨Pacific⟩ Saturn[?]   DOCKETED: Sept. 8. — 1815 / W Irving
MANUSCRIPT: NYPL—WI Papers.   PUBLISHED: LBI, I, 115–18; PMI, I, 337, 338–39 (in part).
In the address the name of the ship has been canceled and "Saturn[?]" added in another hand.

1. Probably a New York friend traveling in Europe. The *New York City Directory* for 1815 (pp. 168–69) lists six Congers, including Henry Conger, dry goods; James Conger, merchant; and John S. Conger, teacher.

2. "Frank" is written over "loyal," and then both are canceled.

3. Colin Robertson was a fur trader and factor for the Hudson's Bay Company. See E. A. Rich, *Hudson's Bay Company, 1670–1870* (New York, 1961), II, 288–90.

162. To Sarah Irving

[Liverpool, September 21, 1815]

I am leading a solitary bachelor's life in Peter's lodgings and perhaps should feel a little lonesome were I not kept so busy.

PUBLISHED: PMI, I, 337.

163. To Henry Brevoort

Liverpool, Septr. 26th. 1815.

My dear Brevoort,

I have at this moment so many things to attend to & letters to write, & the ship by which I send this is so immediately on the wing that I have barely time to scrawl a few lines ⟨My?⟩ I cannot lose a moment however in returning you a thousand thanks for your delightful letters[1] by the Minerva Smyth.[2] They were exactly such as a man wishes when away from home & if you knew how much they gratified me, I am sure you would think the trouble of them compensated a hundred fold.

The Minerva Smyth arrived the night before last. Yesterday morning I heard of her being in the river; & to my utter astonishment, that the worthy Governor[3] was on board. I was ready to exclaim "Stands Scotland where it did?"[4] for it really seemed as if one of the pillars of the earth had quit its base to take a ramble. ⟨I shall not be surprized now to⟩ The world is surely topsy-turvy and its inhabitants all shaken out of place—Emperors & kings, statesmen & philosophers, Bonaparte, Alexander, Johnson, & the Wiggins's all strolling about the face of the earth.

No sooner did I hear of the interesting group ⟨on Board⟩ that had come out in the Minerva Smyth than with my usual excitement, which is apt to put me in a fever, & make me overshoot my mark, I got a boat & set off for the ship, which lay about three miles off. the weather was boisterous, the Mersey rough, ⟨&⟩ I got well ducked & when I arrived on board, had the satisfaction to hear that my eagerness had as usual led me upon a wild goose chace & that had I made the least enquiry I should have found the passengers had all landed early in the morning. Away then I paddled across the river again & the tide being contrary was landed at the upper part of Liverpool—↑had to trudge two miles through dirty lanes and alleys↓ was two or three times entangled among the docks, & baulked by Draw Bridges ⟨in a⟩ thrown open—so that it was afternoon before I got to the Liverpool Arms, where I found the party all comfortably housed.

I cannot tell you how rejoyced I was to take the worthy Governor by the hand & to find myself in the delightful little circle—which brought

New York so completely home to my reccollection & feelings—Mrs King[5] has made an excellent sailor—and the children are in fine health & spirits. Little ⟨W⟩ Eliza is as wild as an Indian & delighted with every thing around her. Little Hetty is a beautiful creature and the Boy a noble animal![6] I never saw a nobler child—I dined with them & passed four hours most happily in talking over past scenes & distant friends

Charles King[7] has not arrived yet, but I expect he will be here tomorrow or next day. Mrs King is in better health than when I left New York & is in excellent spirits. The children have absolutely astonished the people at the Hotel. You know the great decorum of the English and the system of quiet & reserve by which their children are brought to behave like little men & women—whereas the little Kings, who are ⟨al⟩ full of spirits & health, ⟨h⟩ are just as noisy & frolicksome as if out at Hellgate— & racket about the Hotel just as they would at Papa Gracies in State St.[8] I was infinitely amused with their rantipole gambols—The little creatures are like birds let loose from a cage. Eliza King shewed me, with great pride, a certificate of ⟨g⟩ the good behaviour of herself & Hetty, ↑during the voyage↓ signed by the passengers—

Peter is at Harrowgate[9] taking the waters—He writes that he finds himself much better—though still troubled with the rheumatism. I am remaining in Liverpool to finish our fall business & get the establishment here in perfect order—after which I shall join Peter. I will write you more particularly when I have a moments time. Remember me to all the household & to your family

Yours truly
W I

I mentioned in a former Letter that little Booth had been Ill at Hereford during a Dramatic Tour. She is perfectly recovered & performs in London—She was so dangerously ill that at one time she was given over by the Physicians.

I have become acquainted with the Graemes[10] who speak of you with great kindness—I shall give you further account of them when I write particulars[.] I am very much pleased with them.

I have met them with a Mrs Donovan, a very young & beautiful woman—She looks something like Mrs Murphy—do you reccollect her? By the way I am glad to hear that Mrs Murphy is once more in New York—remember me to her with great regard. I hope she retains her beauty.

ADDRESSED: Henry Brevoort Jr Esqr. / At Mrs Bradish's / New York / Caroline Ann —   DOCKETED: Sept 26. 1815 / W Irving
MANUSCRIPT: NYPL—Seligman Collection.   PUBLISHED: LIB, I, 119–23; PMI, I, 339–40 (in part).

1. These letters have not been located.

2. The *Minerva Smyth* under the command of Captain James W. Allen cleared New York harbor on August 26, 1815. See NYEP, August 26, 1815.

3. WI and Brevoort used the name "Governor" for Alexander B. Johnson, their fellow boarder at Mrs. Bradish's, 9 State Street. *Longworth's Directory of New York* for 1815 lists Brevoort and Johnson as residing at this same address. Apparently Johnson, because of his dominating manner, was dubbed the "Governor," an epithet which WI also uses in his letter of December 28. On March 15, 1816, WI mentions that Johnson is about to sail for New York "to resume the Government of the Colony," presumably at Mrs. Bradish's, for in the same passage WI speaks of Mrs. Bradish and her daughter Eliza. George S. Hellman calls Johnson a Scotsman, a detail which the context here seems to corroborate. See LIB, I, xxv.

4. *Macbeth*, IV, iii, 164.

5. The former Eliza Gracie, daughter of Archibald Gracie, prominent New York merchant, married Charles King on March 16, 1810.

6. The King children were Eliza Gracie King (December 18, 1810–1883), Esther Rogers King (July 26, 1812–May 15, 1898), and Rufus King (January 26, 1814–October 13, 1876). See *American Families of Historic Lineage* (New York, n.d.), pp. 70–72; and Ralph M. Aderman, "Washington Irving and Rufus King," *Historical Messenger* (Milwaukee County Historical Society) 27 (March, 1971), 25–27.

7. Charles King had been traveling in England and Portugal on business since the spring of 1815. Upon his return to England he was asked to serve on a commission investigating conditions at Dartmoor Prison, where several thousand American prisoners of the War of 1812 were confined. When these prisoners attempted to break out on April 6, several were killed and many others injured. The report of the commission upheld the actions of the prison authorities as being justified, a judgment which provoked widespread criticism in the United States. Some of the repercussions of this report and pressing business concerns prevented King's meeting his family in Liverpool. See *The Life and Correspondence of Rufus King*, ed. Charles R. King (New York, 1894–1900), V, 484–85; *Annals of Congress*, 14th Cong., 1st sess., pp. 1506–1601; *American State Papers, Foreign Relations*, IV, 19–86.

8. Archibald Gracie (1755–1829), grandfather of the King children, lived at the corner of State and Bridge Streets, overlooking Battery Park.

9. Harrogate, in the Yorkshire moors about 20 miles north of Leeds, was famed for its spas. Peter Irving was taking baths at one of the medicinal springs there.

10. WI's spelling of Graham. Colonel George Graham lived at 6 Queen Square, Liverpool. See *Gore's Directory of Liverpool* (Liverpool, 1816), p. 122. In subsequent letters WI frequently mentions the Graham children, Lawrence and Grace.

164. To Henry Brevoort

Liverpool, Octr. 17th. 1815

Dear Brevoort,

I write merely to tell you that you must not think me negligent in my Correspondence. I will most certainly write to you amply when I have time; but for several weeks past I have been more *really* busy than I ever was in my life.[1] As I am a complete novice in business it of course takes up my whole time and completely occupies my mind, so that at present I am as dull commonplaced a fellow as ever figured upon Change. When I once more emerge from the mud of Liverpool, and shake off the sordid cares of the Counting House you shall hear from me. Indeed the present life I lead is utterly destitute of anecdote, or any thing that could furnish interest or embellishment to a letter—& my imagination is too much jaded by pounds shillings & pence to be able to invent facts or adorn realities.

By my last letter from Peter[2] I learn that he was about to leave Harrowgate & limp towards Birmingham His health was generally better, but his inveterate rheumatic complaint still torments him and renders him so much a cripple that he can scarcely walk about the room.

I am in hopes of being able to visit the good folks at Birmingham in a little while & shall feel right glad to turn my back upon Liverpool for a Season. I have been too much occupied here to think much of Society or amusement, otherwise I should have found the place rather *Triste*— As I did not expect to pass any time in Liverpool I brought out no letters for the place & of course know scarce any one except those with whom I have dealings in business. I have experienced very hospitable treatment from Mr Woolsey—Davidson & Macgregor & find honest Richards[3] house quite a home But there is a great lack of Companions of my own taste & turn

I have become very well acquainted with the Graemes and am very much pleased with them—Lawrence Graeme has lately ⟨had⟩ returned home on furlough. I am sorry he was not able to pass through N York on his return from Canada—he appears to be a very fine young man, Miss Grace is as blooming as hebe. She is very much given to write poetry, notwithstanding the severe criticisms of the old Colonel, who like honest Burchell, cries *fudge!* at the end of every stanza.

Renwick is still in Scotland figuring amongst the Caledonian Hunts. I have not had a letter from him since his departure for the North, but hear of him occasionally through Davidson. I expect he has mounted a pair of Leather Breeches and is playing off the knowing one [on th]e [MS torn] turf.[4]

I have not heard any thing of little Madame Bona[parte] [MS torn] for some time. My last accounts mentioned her as being still at Cheltenham enjoying herself greatly. The Wiggins were likewise there, honest Wiggins confined to his room by the rheumatism.

Johnson[5] is still in Liverpool. I occasionally meet him at Dinner & on Change—and we talk over old times and the many illustrious events that happened under his merciful & glorious government.

I hope you will accept this as *an apology* for a letter, I am writing in

real hurry—give my affectionate remembrances to Mrs & Miss Bradish
& Miss Claypoole if still with you & my hearty regards to the household.

Your friend
W I.

ADDRESSED: To / Henry Brevoort Jr Esqr. / at Mrs Bradish's / New York. / p
 Minerva Smyth} / Docketed: 1815 / Oct 17
MANUSCRIPT: NYPL—Seligman Collection. PUBLISHED: LIB, I, 124–27; PMI, I,
 340–41 (in part).
The name of the ship is not written in WI's handwriting.

1. With Peter's invalidism and the death of the chief clerk WI was left to
keep accounts and manage the business of P. & E. Irving Co. in Liverpool. He had
taken a quick course in bookkeeping in September to cope with the problem. See
STW, I, 150–51.
2. This letter has not been located.
3. These were Liverpool businessmen.
4. PMI has emended this lacuna in the same way. See PMI, I, 340.
5. Johnson, whom WI frequently mentions in his letters to Brevoort, was their
fellow boarder at Mrs. Bradish's.

165. To Ebenezer Irving

[October? 1815]

I could not help smiling at a passage in one of brother William's letters
to Van Wart, wherein he intimates that they should have to stop to take
breath from remitting; but in the mean time he must wait patiently and
do his best. This was something like the Irishman calling to his companion, whom he was hoisting out of the well, to hold on below while
he spit on his hands.

PUBLISHED: PMI, I, 341.

166. To Henry Brevoort

Liverpool, Nov. 2d. 1815.

Dear Brevoort,
   Mr Richards put in my hands some few days since a letter from you,
ordering a number of Books, as honest Richards seldom meddles with
any books beyond his counting house library he handed the order to me
requesting I would attend to it.
   I have put it in the hands of Mr Muncaster, a Bookseller of this place,[1]
who will gather together the works, and get as many of them as possible
in sheets, that they may be bound up here, according to my directions.
He has promised to put them at as favourable terms as they could be

procured from any of the trade. He is the Bookseller from whom Peter has been in the habit of procuring all the periodical & other publications sent out to me for two or three years past, and is very fair & reasonable in his dealings. As Murray is not the publisher of the greater part of the works, he would not be able to afford them cheaper than Mr Muncaster. They shall be forwarded to You as soon as possible.

I wish I had any thing interesting or agreeable to tell You, but I have been for some time past completely occupied in the concerns of our Liverpool establishment, and as I am a novice in business, they have engrossed my whole attention & rendered me good for nothing else. Peter is at Birmingham where I hope to join him next week, and have a little relaxation from my labours. I anticipate much gratification from the assemblage of our family forces in the redoubtable castle of the Van Tromps.

I was introduced a day or two since to Mrs Wood, lately returned from Scotland; one of the ladies of New Abbey, where you used to figure during your Scottish campaign. She appears to be a very frank pleasant little woman and I have no doubt I shall be still more pleased on further acquaintance.

The Graeme and his clan are all well. The fair Grace[2] continues most desperately poetical, in spite of the criticisms of the old Colonel and the rest of the family, who treat her poor Muse in the most unfeeling manner. I have unfortunately got entangled in an obstinate critical warfare with her on a passage in one of her poems, where she ⟨describes⟩ ↑compares↓ the eye of her hero to a sparkling gem *set in a pearly sea*— To this I objected most stoutly: inasmuch as I had never heard of any thing set in the Sea except the Sun. I would allow her hero a *pearly tear*, or what was more probably the case, a *drop in his eye*, or if she pleased a *cataract*, but as to having a Sea in his eye, it was altogether inadmissible — unless he was some aspiring dignitary of the church.

The Colonels son George[3] is home on furlough — He was wounded in the Battle of Waterloo — he is a fine animated handsome little fellow and extremely agreeable. The Colonels little family group is uncommonly pleasing & interesting.

Andrew Hamilton[4] arrived here about a fortnight since & has gone up to London, from whence, wh[en] [MS *torn*] [re]gularly [MS *torn*] equipped and fitted out he was to go to Cheltenham where Mrs O Berne has been passing the fashionable Season. I have heard nothing of Mad. Bonaparte, excepting that she was fashionable at Cheltenham & had taken lodgings seperate from the Wiggins'—Johnson is still in Liverpool & will remain here some time longer. Peter Ogden is likewise here & waxing very fat. James Renwick is playing the roaring blade in Scotland — I am told by good authority that he has fleeced all the old ladies in

Dumfries at cards — and has got the character among them of a perfect leg[5] —

Yours ever
WI.

ADDRESSED: To / Henry Brevoort Jr Esq. / at Mrs Bradish's / New York.   DOCKETED: 1815 Nov. 2 / W Irving
MANUSCRIPT: NYPL—Seligman Collection.   PUBLISHED: LIB, I, 128–31.

1. Thomas Muncaster had a bookshop at 1 Basnett Street. See *Gore's Directory of Liverpool and Its Environs,* p. 196.
2. Grace Graham was probably the daughter of Colonel Graham.
3. In 1816 a George Graham was listed as an officer in customs living at 27 Clement Street. Whether he is the Colonel's son is not clear. See *Gore's Directory of Liverpool,* p. 122.
4. Andrew Hamilton was a young Liverpool friend who provided the details incorporated into the story, "The Broken Heart." See PMI, I, 420.
5. WI is using the shortened form of "blackleg" in the sense of "a sharper."

167. To Henry Brevoort

Birmingham, Decr. 28th. 1815.

Dear Brevoort,

It is a long while since I have heard from you, and Since your last we have been very uneasy in consequence of hearing of your being dangerously ill. Subsequent accounts however have again put you on your legs & relieved us from our anxiety. I have lately been on a short visit to London; merely to see sights & visit public places. Our worthy friend Johnson and his Brother arrived in town while I was there, and we were frequently together. The Governor[1] enjoyed the amusements of London with high zest, & like myself, was a ⟨f⟩ great frequenter of the Theatres — particularly when Miss O Nealle[2] performed. We both agreed that were you in England you would infallibly fall in love with this "divine perfection of a woman."[3] She is, to my eyes, the most soul subduing actress I ever saw. I do not mean from her personal charms, which are great, but from the truth, force and pathos of her acting. I never have been so completely melted, moved and overcome at a theatre as by her performances. I do not think much of the other novelties of the day. Mrs Mardyn,[4] about whom much has been said & written, is vulgar without humour & hoydenish without real whim & vivacity. she is pretty, but a very bad actress. Kean[5] — the prodigy — is to me insufferable. He is vulgar — full of trick and a complete mannerist. This is merely my opinion — He is cried up as a second Garrick[6] — as a reformer of the stage &c &c — it may be so — He may be right & all other actors wrong — this is certain, he is either very good or very bad — I think decidedly the latter: & I find no medium opinions concerning him.

I am delighted with Young,[7] who acts with great judgement discrimination & feeling. I think him ↑much↓ the best actor ⟨I have seen⟩ at present on the English stage. His Hamlet is a very fine performance, as is likewise his Stranger, Pierre, Chamont,[8] &c I have not seen his Macbeth which I should not suppose could equal Coopers. ⟨but⟩ In fact in certain characters, such as may ⟨found classed⟩ be classed with Macbeth, I do not think that Cooper has his equal in England. Young is the only actor I have seen that can be compared with him[.] I cannot help thinking if Cooper had a fair chance, ⟨& would⟩ & the public were to see him in his principal characters, he would take the lead at one of the London theatres. But there is so much party work, managerial influence & such a widely spread & elaborate system of falsehood & misrepresentation connected with the London theatres, that a Stranger who is not peculiarly favoured by the managers, or assisted by the prepossessions of the public stands no chance. I shall never forget Coopers acting in Macbeth last spring,[9] when he was stimulated to exertion by the presence of a number of British officers. I have seen nothing equal to it in England. Cooper requires excitement, to arouse him from a monotonous, commonplaced manner he is apt to fall into — in consequence of acting so often before indifferent houses. I presume the ⟨return⟩ crowded ⟨theaters⟩ audiences which I am told have filled our theatres this season, must bring him out in full splendour.

While at London, I saw Campbell, who is busily employed printing his long promised work.[10] The publisher has been extremely dilatory, and have[11] kept poor Campbell lingering over the pages of this work for months ⟨rather⟩ longer than was necessary. He will in a little while get through with the printing of it, but it will not be published before spring. As usual he is busy correcting, altering & adding to it, to the last, & cannot turn his mind to any thing else, until this is out of hand.

I am writing this letter at the warehouse, while waiting for Van Wart to go home to dinner — he is nearly ready & I must conclude; but will write to you again soon & give you more chit chat.

Peter continues a cripple from the rheumatism, & is confined to the house; I do not think he will be able to go abroad before spring. He however is very chearful under his maladies. All the Van Tromps are well and in high spirits from the Christmas Holydays.

I saw Charles King & family ⟨just⟩ the very day I left London, where they had just arrived. They were in fine health & spirits. They tell me James Renwick was enjoying himself in Edinburgh. I have not heard from him for a long time. I had a long letter from Mrs Renwick[12] some time since & meant to have answered it before this, but have not been in the letter writing mood — I shall soon however pay off all debts of the kind. Remember me affectionately to Mrs & Miss Bradish and your family.— I rejoice to hear Gouv Kemble has returned safe & hope his voyage has been advantageous but the war was too short to yield much pickings

I am dear Brevoort/(in great *haste* & *hunger*)/Affectionately yours
WI.

ADDRESSED: To / Henry Brevoort Jr. Esqr / at Mrs Bradishs— / New York / p
    Catharine   DOCKETED: Birmingham Decr. 28 15 / W Irving.
MANUSCRIPT: NYPL—Seligman Collection.   PUBLISHED: LIB, I, 132–37; PMI, I,
    342–44 (in part).
    1. Alexander B. Johnson, their fellow boarder at Mrs. Bradish's. See WI's letters to Brevoort of September 26, 1815, and March 15, 1816.
    2. Eliza O'Neill (1791–1872) played Juliet at Covent Garden on October 2, 1815, Elwina in *Percy* on November 11 and three later times, and Monimia in *The Orphan* on December 2 and eleven other times. WI also saw her act in Birmingham. See Genest, *Some Account of the English Stage*, VIII, 539, 542, 543; PMI, I, 345.
    3. *Richard III*, I, ii, 75.
    4. Charlotte Mardyn (b. 1789) of Dublin made her first appearance at Drury Lane in London as Amelia in *The Lovers' Vows* on September 26, 1815, and played many roles during that season. See Genest, *Some Account of the English Stage*, VIII, 516–20, 524, 526, 531, 537.
    5. Edmund Kean (1787–1833) played at least nine roles at Drury Lane between October and the end of December, 1815, including five Shakespearean characters. See Genest, *Some Account of the English Stage*, VIII, 517–21.
    6. David Garrick (1717–1779), the great English actor who played many Shakespearean roles during the eighteenth century.
    7. Charles Mayne Young (1777–1856), who appeared at Covent Garden in the fall of 1815. See Genest, *Some Account of the English Stage*, VIII, 539, 543.
    8. WI is alluding to Young's roles in the English adaptation of Kotzebue's *Menschenhass und Rene* and Otway's *Venice Preserv'd* and *The Orphan.*
    9. T. A. Cooper appeared as Macbeth at the Park Theater on March 8, 1815. See NYEP, March 7, 1815.
    10. Probably Campbell's *Specimens of the English Poets,* which finally appeared in 1819.
    11. Although WI wrote "have," the context indicates that he should have written "has."
    12. This letter has not been located.

168. *To Ebenezer Irving*

[Liverpool, December, 1815]
    I have no intention for the present of visiting the continent. I wish to see business on a regular footing before I travel for pleasure. I should otherwise have a constant load of anxiety on my mind.

PUBLISHED: PMI, I, 346.

169. To _____

[Liverpool, January 9, 1816]

I would not again experience the anxious days and sleepless nights which have been my lot since I have taken hold of business to possess the wealth of Croesus.

PUBLISHED: PMI, I, 347.

170. To Henry Brevoort

Birmingham, March 15th. 1816.

My dear Brevoort.

I have received your most kind letter of Feby 10th[1] and also the Magazines & newspapers forwarded by Mr Selden.[2] I believe I am also still in your debt for your letter of the 1 Jany;[3] but indeed I have been so completely driven out of my usual track of thought and feeling by "stress of weather" in business, that I have not been able to pen a single line on any subject that was not connected with traffic. I have therefore a host of friendly letters by me, unanswered, but shall now endeavour to reply to them without further procrastination. We have, in common with most American houses here,[4] had a hard winter of it in money matters, owing to the cross purposes of last falls business, and have been harrassed to death to meet our engagements. I have never passed so anxious a time in my life — my rest has been broken & my health & spirits almost prostrated; but thank heavens we have weathered the storm & got into smooth water; and I begin to feel myself again. Brom[5] has done wonders, and proved himself an able financieur,[6] and, tho' a small man, a perfect giant in business. I cannot help mentioning that James Renwick[7] has behaved in the most gratifying manner. ⟨When⟩ At a time when we were exceedingly straightened I wrote to him begging to know if he could in any way assist us to a part of the amount we were deficient. He immediately opened a credit for us to the full amount, guaranteeing the payment of it, and asking no security from us than our bare words. But the manner in which ⟨all⟩ this was done heightened the merit of it — from the contrast it formed to the extreme distrust and ⟨niggardly?⟩ ↑tenfold↓ caution that universally prevails throughout the commercial world of England, in the present distressed times. I mention this because I know you will delight to hear any thing that tends to illustrate the worth of Renwick — whom, the more I know of him, the more I find reason to value & admire. You mention that Renwicks letters induce you to imagine that his spirits are depressed & harrassed. I have not observed this — you know he is not one of those mercurial beings that are readily excited or cast down; and whatever may be the state of his mind, it has no remarkable operation on the even tenor of his deportment. I believe he has been worried with Law business in England, which is not the most pleasant occupation; but he has been spending his winter very agreeably & advantageously in Edinburgh, and is now on a short tour in France, on his return he will embark ⟨from⟩ at Liverpool for New York, where he is very anxious to be—

I was delighted with your information that Gouvr. Kemble intended coming out to remain at Liverpool. Peter has since had a letter from him confirming it,[8] and it has occasioned great joy in the castle of the Van Tromps. What would I not give if you could likewise join us; but it would be selfish to wish it; as I am sure you[r][9] interest will be better consulted by remaining in New York; and eventually your happiness also. Whatever gratification you might derive from wandering for a while about Europe, the enjoyment would but be temporary; and dependant upon continual novelty & frequent change of place; but the solid, permanent happiness for life must spring from some settled *home*: and where would you find a home like N York.

I declare to you, now that I find myself likely to be detained in Europe by unexpected employment, I often feel my heart yearning towards N York & the dear circle of friends I have left there. I reccollect the thousand charms of existence which surrounded us there, and am astonished to think how insensible we were to them — but so it is, we are always regretting the past, or languishing for the distant — every spot is fresh & green but the one we stand on.

Your account of James Pauldings engagement & the probability of the marriage soon taking place somewhat surprised, but at the same time gratified me.[10] I am satisfied Pauldings talents will ⟨always⟩ secure his fortunes with the ruling party and he will make a good husband and be all the happier for the change of condition. It is what we must all come to at last. I see you are hankering after it, and I confess I have done so for a long time past. We are however ⟨at⟩↑past↓ that period when a man marries suddenly & inconsiderately — we may be longer making a choice, and consulting the convenience & concurrence of every circumstance, but we shall both come to it sooner or later. I therefore recommend you to marry without delay — you have sufficient means, connected with your knowledge & habits of business, to support a genteel establishment, and I am certain that as soon as you are married you will experience a change in your ideas. All those vagabond, roving propensities will cease. ⟨You⟩ They are the offspring of idleness of mind and a want of something to fix the feelings. You are like a bark without an anchor, that drifts about at the mercy of every vagrant breeze, or trifling eddy — get a wife & she'll anchor you. But dont marry a fool because ⟨she may⟩ she has a pretty face — and dont seek after a great Belle — get such a girl as Mary Baillie — or get her if you can; though I am affraid she has still an unlucky kindness at heart for poor Bibby,[11] which will stand in the way of her fortunes — I wish to god they were rich, and married, and happy —

By the bye, Bibby arrived in London while I was there and put up at the same Hotel with me, so that we were daily together. He is shortly to make his *debut* at Covent Garden in Sir Pertinax.[12] It is a most hazardous attempt. I feel very anxious for his success, but entertain strong apprehensions that the public may not take his imitations in the right way. In these matters it is all luck. I wished him to make his first appearance in some character suitable to his age, appearance & manner such as Belcour;[13] ⟨in⟩ which he would certainly play at least tolerably & prepossess by his personal advantages and appropriate deportment, & thus secure some foothold with the public — but he was determined to go for the whole, & perhaps he is right — ⟨the only st a⟩ but should he fail, he falls into utter d———n, whereas my plan would have given him a landing place in public opinion.

Before this you will have learnt the fate of poor Angelica Livingston[14]— I will not make any trite remarks on such an event — In my short experience I have seen so many lovely beings swept from the circle of my intimacy that I almost have grown callous to the shock — but the news of poor Angelicas death ⟨took⟩ reached me in a moment of loneliness and depression & affected me most deeply.

I have heard that Serenas health is likewise extremely delicate[15] — I hope she may take warning by the irreparable losses she has sustained, and take more care of her fragile frame — She always looked too delicate and spiritual for this rough, coarse world. You say she often enquires after me — give her assurances of my constant reccollection — she is the heroine of all my poetical thoughts where they would picture any thing very feminine and lovely — But where is the hero of romance worthy to bear away so peerless a face? — not among the worthy Young traders of New York most certainly.

I have had much gratification from the epistles of that worthy little Tar, Jack Nicholson;[16] who I find still sighs in the bottom of his ⟨belly⟩ ↑heart↓ for the fair Serena; though he declares that his hopes do not aspire to such perfection. Why did not the Varlet bring home the head of Rais Hammida[17] & lay it at her feet; that would have been a chivalric exploit few ladies could have withstood — and if Paulding had only dished him up in full *length* (if I may be allowed the word) in a wood cut in the Naval Chronicle,[18] like little David of yore with the head of Goliah in his fist, I think his suit would have been irrisistible.

In his last letter[19] Nicholson talks something of the possibility of his visiting England this year. I hope government will keep him better employed, though I should receive him with open arms and be more than glad at the meeting. But I want him to continue in the carear of honour and promotion and hope before many years to greet him as a Commodore.

You desire me in your letters to give you anecdotes of characters that I meet with and of any thing interesting or amusing that occurs in the course of my rovings. But in truth I have been so much engrossed by the cares of this world for some time past that I have not sought any society of the kind you are curious about. My last stay in London, which was for two months was a period of great anxiety and I felt in no mood to ⟨seek⟩ form new acquaintances, or even to enjoy scenes around me. I seemed to have lost my *cast*, and to have lost also all relish and aptitude for my usual pursuits — I hope to be able hereafter to give you more interesting letters — I think I shall visit Scotland this Summer, and if I can arrange matters, shall previously make a short excursion to Paris, in May or June. My movements must however depend on various circumstances connected with business and Peters health. He is still confined to the house; but more from extreme delicacy, in consequence of long nursing, than from any positive indisposition. When the Spring advances & the weather becomes settled & warm he will be able to take air & exercise. I long to have him reinstated, that he may accompany me in my out door rambles. I almost begin to lose all idea of him as a man of health & vigour.

During my last visit to London, as I was one day strolling in Bond Street whom should I encounter but little cousin John, alias Tophet. You may be sure I was astonished at the rencountre; and not less pleased. The surprise was equal on his part, as he knew nothing of my being in England, and indeed had heard at one time that I was dead. He gave me another Volume of his eventful history; which certainly rivals that of Gil Blas. He is in great favour with the Governor of Trinidad,[20] and has an office worth 1000$ per ann. besides other casual employments which assist to keep him comfortable — He has come to England in quest of a new office which it was expected would be made by Parliament the Session — but as it does not at present seem probable, he thinks of returning. I saw him almost daily during the remainder of my stay in Town. He is just the same honest, warm hearted, queer, amusing little fish — and is full of his reccollections of New York, which he thinks rather a preferable place to heaven.

⟨The Book⟩

When I was last in Liverpool (about 2 mos. since) your Books were in a state of great forwardness — I have not heard since about them but trust they must have been shipped — I shall write down on the subject & likewise ⟨hav⟩ attend to your request in purchasing & sending out others

You do not mention whether you are likely to make any arrangement with McTavish & the N W Company[21] — I really feel great interest in your temporal as well as spiritual concerns and should like to know how you are making out in the world & what are your plans — If you remain in N York I think you ought to have some regular employment that should occupy part of your time and claim your personal attention. ⟨and⟩ It would prevent that *ennui* of which you complain, and under which, in my days of Idleness I have so often suffered. Mere study will not do — it must be ⟨somethi⟩ employment for the hands, where no great intellect is required: so that it may be attended to in every mood of mind; and engage the attention when ↑too enfeebled or relaxed for↓ more intellectual pursuits.

By letters from Johnston,[22] at Liverpool, I find he is on the point of sailing for New York, to resume the Government of the Colony. I can fancy the great joy that will be diffused throughout the establishment on his return & would give more than I chuse to mention to be present on the occasion. He will give you some idea of the *gay dissipated* life we led in London; where he figured in great style in the west end of the town.

I am very happy to hear that Mrs Bradish and Eliza have recovered their health in a great degree, and hope to hear in my next letters of their perfect reestablishment. Give them my most affectionate regards and tell Mrs Bradish that often & often this winter in London, when I have been suffering in my solitary chamber from a cold & indisposition, have I wished myself under her fostering care, and partaking of her grand Specific, wine whey. By the mass, I look back with as much longing to her bounteous establishment, as ever the children of Israel did to the flesh pots of Egypt,[23] or Tom Philips, to Norton's kitchen.

I wish you would give me a particular account of the whole household, not forgetting old William, Fanny, and Flora & her offspring[24] — I hope the latter are cherished for my sake —

I shall endeavour in a day or two to pay off my arrearages to Mrs Renwick for her long & delightful letter received last November[25] — I have not been in the vein of writing since or it should have long since been answered. William Renwick[26] arrived in Liverpool during my absences so that I have not seen him.

I have had also a very agreeable letter from ↑Sam↓ Swartwout giving a promising account of his farm and his little wife,[27] both of which promise to be very productive. I hope he may have abundant cause of rejoicing from both.

And now I must bring this garrulous Scrawl to a conclusion, as I have many other letters to write now I am in the vein — What a skimble-skamble letter have I written! However, I have scribbled away just as I have been accustomed to talk to you — perfectly unstudied & unreserved, trusting to your friendship to excuse weaknesses and your discretion not to repeat confidings — Many parts of this letter I would not have trusted to any eye but yours, for though there are ⟨not⟩ no matters of great secrecy, yet they are foolish thoughts & feelings that I would not wish repeated — so keep them to yourself —

I wish you would send ↑to↓ me the numbers of the Analectic Mag. that have the traits of Indian character — & the story of King Philip[28] — likewise a copy of the History of New York[29] — send them by the first opportunity.

By the bye, I have never heard whether ⟨th⟩ a quantity of Music that peter sent out for me, & which must have arrived shortly after I left America, was ever delivered, according to my directions to the Miss Livingstons; and if so, how it pleased. I wish you would let me know —

And now, my dear fellow, with my best remembrances to your worthy parents and family I have only to give you the affectionate regards & hearty blessing of Your friend

WI.

P.S. I am highly pleased with the favourable accounts I have received from others as well as yourself, of ⟨the⟩ little Newman.[30] I have had no letter from him, at which I am disappointed, but suppose he did not know where I was exactly. I wish should his ship[31] come to New York you would be attentive to him & see if he wants any assistance in procuring Books; or any thing that may be of real service to him ↑in acquiring useful information.↓ ⟨I have taken care that he shall⟩ His other wants will be taken care of; and perhaps Decaturs[32] idea is correct, that young officers should be taught to live on their pay, as it makes them careful managers —

King Stephen[33] must have arrived long before this letter with his cargo of live stock. I have seen none of the folks act, that he has taken out; but should think that Barnes & his wife[34] would be acquisitions. He offered Miss O Neale[35] 6,000£ for one years engagement to perform in the American Theatres — But her engagements here would not permit her to accept the ⟨engagement⟩ offer. She continues in great currency & is shortly to appear in comedy.

Little Booth[36] is well & often speaks of you — she has lost Fidele, who died of the gout in his stomach from high living — thank God for this dispensation — he was a cursed noisy, nasty little cur — though his little mistress *took on* sadly for his loss.

Charles King & his family are all alive & merry in London, where I had frequently the pleasure of seeing them. It was like being in New York to get among his joyous household—

farewell.

W I.

ADDRESSED: To / Henry Brevoort Jr Esqr. / at Mrs Bradish's / New York / per Trident   DOCKETED: W Irving / March 15. 1816
MANUSCRIPT: NYPL—Seligman Collection.   PUBLISHED: LIB, I, 138–54; PMI, I, 347–51 (in part).

Upside down, opposite the second line of the address is written: "$50.50 May 3rd / 3 Mo. 40000$"

1. This letter has not been located.
2. David Selden (1785–1861) was a wealthy New York merchant who married Gertrude Richards, a relative of Silas Richards. On February 6, 1818, Selden filed and was discharged for bankruptcy. See *Indices to Insolvent Assignments to Dec. 31, 1855.*
3. This letter has not been located.
4. Another American firm in Liverpool at this time was Brown, Shipley, & Co. See Scoville, *Old Merchants of NYC*, V, 260.
5. A nickname for Ebenezer Irving. See PMI, I, 348.
6. WI added the extra *u* to the word.
7. WI's traveling companion in Warwickshire the previous summer.
8. In 1815 Kemble acted as a supply agent for American Navy vessels during the Algerine war. His letter to Peter Irving has not been located.
9. WI omitted the *r*.
10. Paulding's engagement to Gertrude Kemble, his long-time acquaintance and sister of Gouverneur and Peter Kemble, ended with their marriage on November 15, 1818.
11. In early February of 1815, Gouverneur Bibby (1790–1872), billed as "a Young Gentleman of this City," made his first appearance on the stage of the Park Theater by imitating George Frederick Cooke's performance as Richard III. Within two months he had imitated Cooke's roles as Sir Archy MacSarcasm, Sir Pertinax MacSycophant, and Shylock. As a result, he was invited in 1816 to perform in London, where WI met him. Sarah Booth, the actress, reports her favorable impression of Bibby's talents in a letter to Brevoort on June 2, 1816. See LBI, I, 206–7. See also Odell, *NY Stage*, II, 439; T. Allston Brown, *A History of the New York Stage* (New York, 1964), I, 18; Genest, *Some Account of the English Stage*, VIII, 550–52.
12. Bibby played the role of Sir Pertinax MacSycophant in Macklin's *Man of the World* on April 16, 1816, at Covent Garden Theater. See Genest, *Some Account of the English Stage*, VIII, 550–51.
13. A young orphan, a character in *The West Indian* (1771), a sentimental comedy by Richard Cumberland (1732–1811).
14. The unmarried daughter of John R. Livingston, Angelica had recently died.
15. It is possible that WI's continued solicitude for Serena was prompted by his romantic interest in her. See M. A. Weatherspoon, "1815–1819: Prelude to Irving's *Sketch Book*," *American Literature* 41 (January, 1970), 566–71.
16. Lieutenant John B. Nicholson, one of the Lads of Kilkenny, who had been commissioned on May 12, 1812, commanded the twelve-gun brig *Flambeau*, part

of the ten-vessel squadron which set out in May of 1815 either to arrange peace with the Barbary States or to wage war against them. See Maclay, *History of the U. S. Navy*, II, 88–89; *Analectic Magazine*, n.s. 6 (December, 1815), Appendix to *The Naval Chronicle*, p. 2. Nicholson's letters to WI have not been located.

17. The daring Algerian admiral who was fatally wounded in an exchange of gunfire between his flagship, the *Mashouda*, and the *Guerrière* and *Constellation*. See Maclay, *History of the U. S. Navy*, II, 94.

18. Paulding's "Account of Rais Hammida, The Late Algerine Admiral" appeared in the *Analectic Magazine*, n.s. 7 (January, 1816), 10–16.

19. This letter has not been located.

20. Sir Ralph Woodford was governor of Trinidad from 1813 to 1829. See Sir Alan Burns, *History of the British West Indies* (London, 1954), p. 608.

21. Probably WI is referring to an agreement made on February 6, 1815, and finally approved in October, 1815, between Astor and the partners of the North West Company, which included McTavish's firm. See Porter, *Astor*, II, 690.

22. In his letter of December 28, 1815, WI describes some of his activities in London with Alexander B. Johnson.

23. See Exod. 16:3.

24. Probably pets at Mrs. Bradish's. Flora was a dog there. See PMI, I, 350.

25. This letter has not been located. Her son, James Renwick, was to marry Brevoort's sister Margaret Ann on October 10, 1816.

26. William Renwick (1799–1847), son of Jean Jeffrey Renwick. See Helen McIver, *Jaffrey-Jeffrey Family*, p. 3.

27. This letter has not been located. Swartwout married the daughter of Charles Cooper of Albany. She was a niece of Cadwallader D. Colden. See WI's letter of October 16, 1814. Swartwout and his brothers owned the land between Hoboken and Weehawken and a tract between the Hackensack River and the approach to Newark.

28. "Traits of Indian Character" had appeared in the *Analectic Magazine*, n.s. 3 (February, 1814), 145–56, and "Philip of Pokanoket" in the June, 1814, issue, pp. 502–15.

29. Probably the second edition of 1812.

30. Presumably this is William D. Newman, a midshipman on the *Guerrière* who was commissioned on February 1, 1814. See *Analectic Magazine*, n.s. 6 (December, 1815), Appendix to *The Naval Chronicle*, p. 13.

31. The *Guerrière*.

32. Stephen Decatur was in command of the *Guerrière*.

33. Stephen Price, the manager of the Park Theater who frequently introduced foreign actors to New York audiences.

34. John Barnes (1761–1841) and his wife, Mary Greenhill Barnes (1780–1864), appeared at the Park Theater in April, 1816, with Mrs. Barnes in the role of Juliet on April 17, and as Angela in M. G. Lewis's *The Castle Spectre*, and also as Aladdin on April 19. Barnes first appeared as Sir Peter Teazel in Sheridan's *The School for Scandal* (1777) on April 22 with Mrs. Barnes as Lady Teazel. On April 26 he appeared in Sheridan's *The Rivals* (1775) and on the following night in Mrs. Centlivre's *The Busybody* (1709). See Odell, *NY Stage*, II, 453–55.

35. See WI's letter of December 28, 1815.

36. See WI's letters of August 23 and September 26, 1815.

171. To Mrs. Jean Renwick

Liverpool, April 5th. 1816.

My dear Mrs Renwick,

I cannot suffer any more time to elapse without at least sending you an apology for a letter in return for the ⟨f⟩ very kind and very charming one which I received from you last November.[1] I have been intending ever since to write you a very long reply; but the magnitude of the intention has prevented the performance; ⟨and⟩ ↑for↓ I am now so much a man of business, of mere pounds shillings and pence business, that I have little leisure for writing — and when liesure does come, I find every gay thought or genteel fancy has left my unhappy brain and nothing remains but the dry rubbish of accounts — Woe is me! how different a being am I from what I was last Summer, when the Laird and I went forth Castle hunting among the Welsh mountains —[2] Those days of chivalry when we emulated the deeds & adventures of Don Quixote.

The last I saw of James was in London about five or six weeks since, when he was on the eve of his departure for France; which fair country he meant to discuss in the course of six weeks — pretty much as he used to do a ⟨book⟩ novel in 5 vols, between tea time and Supper, napping into the bargain — In the mean time here am I, like a fowl with one wing clipped, making now and then a struggling flutter to Birmingham & London, but soon brought back again to this Barn yard — utterly incapable of flying across the channel

James and myself were together for more than a week in London; but both so much occupied by business as not to have much time to devote to matters of curiosity or amusement; added to which I was grievously tormented with a cold that made me a perfect invalid. ⟨I can⟩ The climate of England does not appear to agree with James[.] he says he has not been free from a cold ever since his arrival in Europe. I hope the air of France may prove more genial.

I ought at the very commencement of this letter to have congratulated you on the happy changes in your family;[3] but I suppose long before this ↑you↓ have ↑been↓ quite overwhelmed and sated with congratulations of the kind; which relish very flat & stale so long after the event. I hope Lady Jane[4] is not still disposed of or at least that Agnes[5] remains hand and heart free — really there threatens to be quite a scarcity against we youngsters arrive at marriageable years.

This is a sad silly scrawl, but I am writing with might and main, to fill up a sheet before [the?] [*MS torn*] letter bag of the vessel closes; which will be almost instantly. I mean this merely as an apology as I before said, for indeed I intend to write you a letter, which shall at least equal yours in length if it falls short in merit. I am just returned to Liverpool & at present hurried — I saw Mrs Davidson the day before yesterday and we talked, as usual, a great deal about you and your household—remember me most heartily to them all and believe me my dear madam

Most truly/Your friend

W I.

P.S. Gouvr. Bibby is to make his first appearance at Covent Garden on the 16 Inst. in Sir Pertinax.[6] The manager & performers are much pleased with his rehearsal. Payne (of America) appears the same night at Drury Lane in Zaphna.[7]

ADDRESSED: Mrs Jane Renwick / Courtlandt Street / New York. / per *Marcellus*
MANUSCRIPT: Columbia.   PUBLISHED: *WI to Renwicks*, pp. 33–34; PMI, I, 351–53.

1. This letter has not been located.
2. In July and August, 1815, WI and Renwick had traveled south and west of Birmingham and into Wales.
3. A reference to the marriage of Isabella Renwick to Charles G. Smedberg on December 2, 1815, and of Robert Renwick to Mary Hobart Rhinelander on December 16, 1815. See *WI to the Renwicks*, p. 34, n.
4. Jane Jeffrey Renwick (1801–1848), Mrs. Renwick's daughter.
5. Agnes Renwick (1807–1840), Jane's younger sister.
6. Apparently Bibby's name was unfamiliar, for he is called Beattie, an American, by a reviewer who praised his acting and said, "This gentleman . . . must be a considerable acquisition to the theatre." See London *Times*, April 17, 1816, and WI's letter of March 15, 1816.
7. A change in plans apparently eliminated Payne's performance. He is not mentioned in the advertisements or reviews of plays at Drury Lane during this period. Payne had played the role of Zaphna in *The Tragedy of Mahomet* as early as March 1, 1809. See NYEP, February 27, 1809, and March 6, 1809. He also appeared in the role in England. See Gabriel Harrison, *John Howard Payne* (Philadelphia, 1885), p. 75.

172. To Moses Thomas

Liverpool, April 27th. 1816.

Dear Sir,

I send you by this ship a small pamphlet containing the verses lately written by Lord Byron addressed to his wife,[1] which have been all the talk ⟨he⟩ in England ⟨of late⟩ for some time past & have been published in all the papers. The ⟨first⟩ lines beginning Fair thee well are addressed to the Wife[2] — the next, to her Governess[3] — Lord & Lady Byron have signed articles of separation[4] & it is said he has gone on his travels again.[5] You had better publish this pamphlet at once & sell off the edition as fast as possible — as various booksellers in London are vamping up similar pamphlets, and giving additions — which I will send when they come to hand⁶ — one I observe has a ⟨sk⟩ biographical sketch of his Lordship — I have recd. the 2 No of the Hebrew Melodies⁷ & will send it by a ship about to sail to Philadelphia⁸ —

The antiquary⁹ is not out yet —

Your friend
WI.

ADDRESSED: Mr Moses Thomas / Bookseller / Philadelphia / pr Ship Mexico
    POSTMARKED: NEW-YORK / JUN / 15   DOCKETED: W Irving / Liverpool /
    April 27th. 1816
MANUSCRIPT: Yale.

1. This pamphlet of four pages, containing "Fare Thee Well" and "A Sketch," is described in Wise, *Bibliography of Byron*, I, 110–11.

2. Anne Isabella Milbanke (b. 1792), whom Byron had married on January 2, 1815.

3. Mrs. Clermont, who had been Mrs. Byron's governess. See *The Works of Lord Byron: Letters and Journals*, ed. Rowland E. Prothero (London, 1904), III, 268 n.

4. On April 21, 1816. See Leslie A. Marchand, *Byron, A Biography* (New York, 1957), II, 605.

5. Byron left London April 23 for Geneva. See Marchand, *Byron, A Biography*, II, 607.

6. Moses Thomas published *Lord Byron's Farewell to England and Other Late Poems*, an edition of 96 pages. Also in 1816 Van Winkle & Wiley of New York brought out *Ode of the Star of the Legion of Hanover, Napoleon's Farewell, Fare Thee Well, and a Sketch, etc.* in a volume of 24 pages.

7. Two issues of *Hebrew Melodies* were published in 1815 by John Murray. See Wise, *Bibliography of Byron*, I, 103–4.

8. The publishing house of Moses Thomas, for whom WI had worked on the *Analectic Magazine*, was located in Philadelphia.

9. *The Antiquary* appeared in early May, 1816. See Lockhart, *Life of Sir Walter Scott*, IV, 5.

173. To Henry Brevoort

Liverpool, April 29th. 1816.

My dear Brevoort,

I wrote you a rigmarole letter some time since from Birmingham.¹ Since then I have been most of the time at Liverpool leading a most dreary life; for the hard times here make every body dismal. Peter is still at Birmingham, and the Spring has been so backward that he has not been able to trust his rheumatic limbs out of the house —

Your books were forwarded some time since by Ogden Richards & Selden. The[y] ought to have been sent out long before but the Bookseller sent the Box thro' mistake to our Warehouse instead of Richards, and our clerks had no directions concerning them. So they reposed quietly in a corner until my arrival. By this ⟨s⟩Opportunity I send you the last number of the Edinburgh Review,[2] which is just out — It will come in the Letter Bag. ⟨I have⟩ There is a Surtout, close Bodied coat & Waist-coat for you at our Counting House ⟨but⟩[.] I shall ⟨not be able to⟩ forward it by the Rosalie Capt Merry[3] to sail 8th. of next month —

I presume before this you have seen accounts from the London Papers of Bibby's first appearance in Sir Pertinax.[4] The criticisms are favourable beyond my hopes. Even that stern Critic the Examiner speaks in the highest terms of him. These favourable accounts are confirmed by a letter from Miss Booth to my Brother,[5] who says "He acted *excellently* well." She says the Boxes were uncommonly brilliant. That there was occasional disturbance from the Galleries which were crowded by holi-day people who had come to see a new afterpiece ⟨but⟩ and who, not being able to hear themselves, determined that no body else should — At length the pit rose, hats waved & pit & boxes united in applause *long & loud* after which the peice went admirably; and he made his exit amidst ["]the most general applause she ever heard." This is a very satisfactory account, as we may depend upon it — which we cannot do on news paper criticisms

She adds, "I dont know why the play has not yet been repeated, a few days I believe will decide the determination of the managers in his behalf. I hear they wish him to act some other character instead of Sir Pertx., which if he does he will be lost — for it will be the general opinion that he failed in that — and if he plays Shylock he brings Keans[6] friends upon him before he has sufficient hold of the town to crush any attempt of party" —————

You see poor Bibby has his hands full, and a very difficult card to play. These London managers are hard fellows to deal with. I should not be surprised if the real obstacle is their wish to make a three years engage-ment with Bibby — which they hinted at when he first applied, in case he should succeed; but which he told me he should not agree to on any account — One thing is certain, and it must do him great good with american audiences, that he has played on a London Theatre with success —

Having said thus much about Bibby I have little more to add; for I have nothing interesting [or a]musing [*MS torn*] in the present round of my existence to write about. Davidson had a letter from James Renwick some days since, ⟨wh⟩ dated at Paris, which he was about leaving for Holland on his way to England. I hope to see him here before long.

Give my affectionate regards to Mrs Bradish & the Girls, and if the

worthy Governor has returned shake him heartily by the hand for me
and give my good wishes to the rest of the household —

Your friend
W I.

ADDRESSED: To / Henry Brevoort Jr. Esq. / at Mrs Bradish's / New York. / p *Mexico*
    DOCKETED: Liverpool 29 Ap: 1816 /Wash: Irving
MANUSCRIPT: NYPL—Seligman Collection. PUBLISHED: LIB, I, 155–58.

1. March 15, 1816.
2. This issue (no. 51, February, 1816), contained ten articles, including reviews
of Schlegel's *Lectures on Dramatic Literature* and Sir Humphrey Davy's *Treatise
on fire damp in mines*.
3. The *Rosalie* arrived in New York on June 26, 42 days out of Liverpool. See
the Marine List of NYEP, June 26, 1816.
4. The review in the London *Times* (April 17, 1816) was very favorable:
"A new performer appeared at this theatre [Covent Garden] last night.... Beattie,
we have heard, is the gentleman's name. He is said to be a native of America, and
a pupil of Cooke in 'Sir Pertinax Macsycophant.'... we do not hesitate to say, that
the new actor...displayed, not only a perfect understanding of the character, but
an admirable general knowledge of the stage, on which we see no reason to doubt
that he is capable of attaining the very highest eminence. His style in showing off
the brilliant passages of the character was spirited, powerful, and characteristic....
This gentleman, we are of opinion, must be a considerable acquisition to the theatre."
5. This letter has not been located.
6. Bibby played Shylock at Covent Garden on May 10, 1816, thereby competing
with Kean, who had played the role at Drury Lane on April 1, 1816. See Genest,
Some Account of the English Stage, VIII, 531.

174. To Moses Thomas

Liverpool, ⟨April⟩ May 3d. 1816.

Mr Moses Thomas
Dear Sir,
    Inclosed you have a bill of lading of a Box and a paper parcel of
periodical works, forwarded by the ship Margaret,[1] (which brings this
Letter) The contents of these you will find in Bill of parcels inclosed
(No 4. & No 5). Nos. 1. 2. & 3 were sent by the Mercury.[2]
    By this opportunity I have sent likewise three different editions of
Lord Byrons last poems[3]—they have severally been thrown in the letter
bag as they came to hand—likewise his second set[?] of the Hebrew
Melodies.[4]

Yours truly
W Irving

P. S. In the last edition of these pamphlets of Lord Byron You will find
parts of a poem entitled "the Curse of Minerva"[5] Mr Geo Dallas[6] has the

whole poem in Mss. It was not published by Lord Byron, but as part of it has crept to light perhaps Mr Dallas may not object to letting the whole appear

ADDRESSED: Mr Moses Thomas / Bookseller / Philadelphia / pr Margaret.   POST-
     MARKED: [*small red stamp blurred and unrecovered*]   DOCKETED: W Irving /
     Liverpool / May 3rd. 1816
MANUSCRIPT: Pforzheimer Library.

1. The *Margaret*, under the command of Captain Kean, reached Philadelphia on July 16 but remained in quarantine until July 24, 1816. See NYEP, July 17 and 25, 1816.

2. The *Mercury*, commanded by Captain Yardsley, reached Philadelphia on June 13, 1816, after a voyage of fifty days from Liverpool. See NYEP, June 14 and 15, 1816.

3. WI is referring to "Fare Thee Well!" and "A Sketch from Private Life," which had been published in April of 1816. See Wise, *Bibliography of Byron*, I, 108–11. These and other poems were published in pirated editions under the title of *Poems on His Domestic Circumstances* (London, 1816).

4. WI is speaking of the second portion of *Hebrew Melodies* with music by I. Braham and I. Nathan and published by I. Nathan, No. 7 Poland Street, Oxford Street in 1816. See Thomas L. Ashton, *Byron's Hebrew Melodies* (Austin, 1972), pp. 216–17.

5. Among the poems in the pirated editions of *Poems on His Domestic Circumstances* is "The Curse of Minerva," based on the text printed as "The Malediction of Minerva; or, The Athenian Marble Merchant" in the *New Monthly Magazine*, 1st ser., 3 (April 1, 1815), 240–42. See *The Works of Lord Byron*, ed. Ernest Hartley Coleridge (London, 1898), I, 453; *Library of Congress Catalog of Printed Cards*, XXIII, 141. A privately printed edition of "The Curse of Minerva" had appeared in 1812. See Wise, *Bibliography of Byron*, I, 69.

6. George M. Dallas of Philadelphia was a friend of WI and other members of the Lads of Kilkenny coterie. For other details about him see WI to Henry Brevoort, July 8, 1812.

175. To John P. Van Ness

Liverpool, May 7th. 1816.

My dear Sir,
     After the many kind proofs I have received of your attention to my reccommendations I am encouraged to introduce to your civilities Mr Thomas Hulme, an English Gentleman, on a tour through the United States. Mr Hulme is a man of great worth and respectability. He has amassed a large fortune by his own industry & enterprise, and being strongly impressed with the advantages of our form of government, and the many blessings our country enjoys, is disposed to transfer his family & fortune across the Atlantic. His present visit is merely one of information, prior to his ultimate removal As I am sure you will appriciate the

value of Emigration of such men to our country, I am satisfied you will do every thing in your power to assist Mr Hulme in obtaining local information respecting our manufactories, lands &c &c in short such information as a capitalist is anxious to acquire who has funds to invest— & that a stranger is desirous of obtaining, who intends becoming a citizen.

Remember me in the most affectionate manner to Mrs Van Ness, Miss Burnes & your daughter,[1] who by this time I presume is almost a young woman

With great regard & good wishes/Your friend
Washington Irving

Col John P Van Ness.

MANUSCRIPT: Dr. Robert F. Loeb; copy at Columbia.

1. For details about the Van Ness family see WI's letter of February 26, 1810.

176. To Henry Brevoort

Liverpool, May 9th. 1816.

My dear Brevoort,

By the Rosalie,[1] under care of Capt Merry, I send a Trunk of clothes to my Brother Ebenr. In which are a Surtout, Blk Coat, and Blk cloth waistcoat for you. I have also directed a Bookseller to send some books, in a paper parcel, to Messrs Ogden Richards & Selden to be forwarded to you — they will probably come by this ship.

I have nothing new to tell you. I wrote to you recently, giving an ↑account↓ of Bibbys first appearance—He plays again tomorrow night in Shylock and Sir Archy—

I was in hopes of hearing from you by the Rosalie, but was disappointed — a letter from you is like a gleam of sunshine through the darkness that seems to lower upon my mind. I am here alone, attending to business — and the times are so hard that they sicken my very soul. Good god what would I give to be once more with you, and all this mortal coil shuffled off of my heart.[2] I must say however that I have received very kind attentions from some of the Liverpool families ⟨since my⟩ of late & could easily form a very polite and agreeable circle of acquaintances — but the cares of business, in these gloomy times harrass my mind & unfit me for society, and I have therefore avoided it as much as possible. There is one Lady here however, a Mrs Rathbone[3] with whom I am much pleased — She is amiable, intelligent, and has a charming simplicity of manners. She has the person and looks of our little friend Ann McMasters,[4] and a few evenings since I found her in a gown of a kind of mulberry coloured silk similar to that little Great-heart used to wear — All this made her look like an old acquaintance — and there were a thousand reccollections of home, and distant friends & past scenes, conjured up by this trifling circumstance, that almost made my heart overflow—

I met with a Mr Shepherd[5] at dinner some days since, he is a clergyman. a friend of Roscoes,[6] and one of the Literati of Liverpool. He is very excentric & facetious in conversation — He has since sent me a book of his editing[7] — accompanied with some civil compliments about my history of N York, and an invitation to dine with him at his residence in the country. I have evaded his invitation, for truly I am not in the vein just now — My dear Brevoort what would I ↑not↓ give to have you with me. In my lonely hours I think of the many many happy days we have passed together and feel that there is no friend in the world to whom my heart turns so completely as it does to you — For some time before I left New York I thought you had grown cold & indifferent to me — I felt too proud to speak frankly on the subject but it grieved me bitterly. Your letters have convinced me that I was mistaken, and they were like cordials to my feelings.

I am writing very weakly & very garrulously—but I have no restraint in writing to you—as I am convinced that what I write will be recd. with indulgence. You know all my failings & foolishnesses and regard them with a friendly eye; but do not let any one see my nonsense—

In the trunk which ⟨brings⟩ contains the clothes is a number of Lord Byrons Hebrew Melodies. It is for Eliza Bradish—will you see that she gets it — Let me know how she & her mother and all the family do —

Write to m⟨y⟩e, my dear fellow, as often as you have half an hour to bestow on an old friend—

I expect James Renwick here in eight or ten days. I suppose he will soon take passage for America Peter[8] is still at Birmingham but I hope his health will permit him to come to Liverpool in about a week—

Your friend
WI.

ADDRESSED: Henry Brevoort Jr Esq. / at Mrs Bradish's / New York. / pr Rosalie}
    DOCKETED: Liverpool May 9. 1816 / Washington Irving
MANUSCRIPT: NYPL—WI Papers. PUBLISHED: PMI, I, 353 (in part).

1. The *Rosalie* arrived in New York on June 26, 1816.
2. *Hamlet*, III, i, 67.
3. Possibly the wife of William Rathbone, a Liverpool merchant engaged in the North American trade. See B. Guiness Orchard, *Liverpool's Legion of Honour* (Liverpool, 1893), p. 581.
4. Ann McMasters may be the daughter of James McMasters, a grocer at 1 Rutgers in New York. See Longworth's *New York City Directory* for 1816.

5. William Shepherd (1768–1847), a dissenting minister and a student of Italian literature.

6. William Roscoe (1753–1831), historian, banker, scholar, and man of letters. WI was to give his impressions of Roscoe in the first number of *The Sketch Book*.

7. Probably *Systematic Education: or Elementary Instruction in the Various Departments of Literature and Science* (London, 1815).

8. This sentence is a kind of postscript which starts opposite the complimentary close.

177. *To Moses Thomas*

Liverpool, May 15th. 1816

Mr Moses Thomas

In the William Wise,[1] which brings this letter I have sent to the address of our NYork house "*The Antiquary*["][2] in 3 vols. by the author of Waverly &c you may advertize it immediately on receipt of this Letter —

I sent a copy some days since to the care of Mr Blake Boston by the Liverpool trader[3]— and a copy also of "The Poets pilgrimage to Waterloo"— a poem by R Southey[4]— you may therefore advertize the latter also if it has not yet come to hand.

Yours &c
WI.

ADDRESSED: Mr Moses Thomas / Bookseller / Philadelphia / pr William Wise
    POSTMARKED: New York / Jul / 1   DOCKETED: W Irving / Liverpool May 15 / 1816
MANUSCRIPT: Yale.

1. The British brig *William Wise* under the command of Captain Wise reached New York on June 30, 1816. See NYEP, July 1, 1816.

2. Scott's novel, *The Antiquary*, appeared early in May, 1816. See Lockhart, *Life of Sir Walter Scott*, IV, 5.

3. The *Liverpool Trader* arrived in Boston on July 1, 1816. See NYEP, July 5, 1816.

4. This poem was published by Longman in late April or early May of 1816. See *Poems of Robert Southey*, ed. Maurice H. Fitzgerald (London, 1909), p. 762.

178. *To Moses Thomas*

Liverpool, May 18th. 1816.

Mr Moses Thomas
Sir

By the ⟨?Brig Th?⟩ Commerce[1] via NYork. I have sent to Messr P & E Irving & Co. who will forward the same to you per Mail, "*Mador of the*

Moor"[2] a poem by James Hogg.— and *"Christabel"*[3] a poem by S T Coleridge —

Yours truly
WI.

ADDRESSED: Mr. Moses Thomas / Bookseller / Philadelphia / Commerce   POST-
    MARKED: New York / JUL / 4   DOCKETED: W. Irving / Liverpool May /
    18th 1816
MANUSCRIPT: Yale.

1. The *Commerce* arrived in New York on July 5, 1816, 43 days from Liverpool.
See NYEP, July 5, 1816.
    2. James Hogg (1770–1835) had published this long narrative poem in Spen-
serian stanzas in Edinburgh earlier in 1816.
    3. *Christabel* was published by John Murray in February, 1816.

179. To Henry Brevoort

Birmingham, July 16th. 1816

My dear Brevoort

I have tried repeatedly to arouse myself to the exertion of answering your long and delightful letter of May 18th.[1] but found as often, that I might as well attempt to raise spirits from "the vasty deep"[2] as to raise my own spirits to any thing like animation.

I have been so harrassed & hagridden by the cares & anxieties of business for a long time past, that I have at times felt almost broken down in health and spirits. This was particularly the case this spring, when I was for a long time alone at Liverpool, brooding over the hardships of these disordered times.[3] Peters return to Liverpool enabled me to crawl out of the turmoil for a while, and I have for some time past [been][4] endeavouring to renovate myself in the dear little circle of my sisters family.

I have attempted to divert my thoughts into other channels; to revive the literary feeling & ⟨if⟩ to employ myself with my pen; but at present it is impossible — My mind is in a sickly state and my imagination so blighted that it cannot put forth a blossom nor even a green leaf — Time & circumstances must restore them to their proper tone.

I thank you ⟨most⟩ in the most heartfelt manner for your assistance to my worthy brother Ebenezer[5] — The difficulties he must experience give me more uneasiness than any thing else. I hope he may be able to surmount them all, and that we may work through the present stormy season without any material injury.

I am happy to find from your letter that your own circumstances are so good — As to your not having added much to your fortune since I left you, it is not a matter of concern, I was only apprehensive lest you should have experienced heavy losses in these precarious times – and your silence↑on the subject↓for ⟨some?⟩ a considerable while filled me with uneasiness. I rejoice in the confidence you express of your future prospects, and in the intention you seem to entertain of forming a matrimonial connexion. I am sure it will be a worthy one; and though as a Bachelor, I might lament you as lost to the fraternity, and feel conscious that some of those links were broken which, as bachelors bound us together, yet I could not suffer myself to regret a change of situation which would give you so large an accession of domestic homefelt enjoyment. As to my return to America, to which you advert in terms that fill my heart, I must say ⟨it is quite uncertain in America?⟩ it partakes of that uncertainty which at this moment envellopes all my future prospects – I must wait here a while in a passive state, watching the turn of events, and how our affairs are likely to turn out – "My bread is indeed *cast upon the waters*" – and I can only say that I hope to *"find it after many days."*[6] It is not long since I felt myself quite sure of fortunes smiles, and began to entertain, what I thought, very sober and rational schemes for my future comfort & establishment – At present, I feel so temptest tossed and weather beaten that I shall be content to be quits with fortune for a very moderate portion, and give up all my sober schemes as the dreams of fairy land. But I will make no promises or resolutions at present, as I know they would be like those formed at Sea in a storm, which are forgotten as soon as we tread the shore, or the weather grows propitious – This you may be assured of – all my ideas of home and settled life centre in New York – and ⟨that⟩ I have had too little pleasure or even comfort in England to wean me from that delightful little spot of earth.

I have written this letter more to account for my not writing a better one – Indeed I have scarcely any thing to write about even if I were in the vein – I am merely vegetating for the present, and quite out of the way of interesting characters or interesting incidents. On my way up here from Liverpool, I came round by Shrewsbury & stopped for a couple of days with a young gentleman of my acquaintance, at his fathers seat a few miles beyond Chester on the border of Wales. In one of our morning strolls among the banks of the Alun, a beautiful little pastoral stream that rises among the welsh mountains & throws itself into the Dee, we encountered a Veteran angler of old Isaac Waltons school.[7] He was an old greenwich outdoor pensioner – had lost one leg in the battle at Camperdown,[8] had been in America in his youth & indeed had been quite a rover, but for many years past had settled himself down in his native village not far distant, where he lived very independently on his pension & some other small annual sums amount-

ing in all to about 40£ His great hobby & indeed the ⟨sma⟩ business of his
life was to angle — I found he had read Isaac Walton very attentively —
he seemed to have imbibed all his simplicity of heart, contentment of
mind and fluency of tongue. We kept company with him almost the
whole day — wandering along the beautiful banks of the river, admiring
the ease and elegant dexterity with which the old fellow managed his
angle, throwing the fly with unerring certainty at a great distance &
among overhanging bushes, & waving it gracefully in the air, to keep
it from entangling, as he stumped with his staff & wooden leg from one
bend of the river to another. He kept up a continual flow of cheerful
& entertaining talk, ⟨seemingly at⟩ and what I particularly liked him
for was, that though we tried every way to entrap him ⟨to⟩ into some
abuse of America & its inhabitants, there was no getting him to utter
an ill natured word concerning us. His whole conversation and ⟨this⟩
deportment ⟨was⟩ illustrated old Isaacs maxims as to the benign influence of angling over the human heart — ⟨This little ramble brought the⟩
I wished continually that you had been present, as I know you would
have enjoyed with exquisite relish, this genuine Angler, & the characteristic scenes through which we rambled with him. I ought to mention
that he had two companions — one, a ragged picturesque varlet, that
had all the air of a veteran poacher & I warrant could find any fish
pond in the neighbourhood in the darkest night — the other was a disciple
of the old philosophers, studying the art under him & was son & heir
apparant to the Landlady of the Village tavern.

This amusing rencontre brought all the beauties of old Isaac Walton
to my reccollection — and awakened so many pleasant associations and
rural feelings that I have had a hankering ever since to take a ramble
in Derbyshire, where I believe the scene of his book is laid — and if
I can only muster up spirits enough to take a solitary excursion for a week
or ten days I do not know but I shall go that way, as soon as the rainy
weather, which has prevailed for some *two months* past, has given
place to a little gleam of Summer and sunshine. Should that be the
case, I may pick up something in my rambles to scribble to you about
— But it is very possible that dismal letters from NYork may intervene
& take away all disposition from the excursion—

I cannot go into ⟨a⟩ notice of the many very interesting anecdotes
of my friends which your letter contains. I am much gratified by the
prospects of McT____s[9] setting[10] in N. Y. and making such an agreeable
matrimonial connexion The Catons[11] &c arrived at Liverpool since I left
there. Peter dined in company with them and was very much pleased
with them. I shall make a point of cultivating the acquaintance of Betsey
Caton should I meet with her & she be disposed to be sociable. As to
your concern in business with McT. I think it might prove a very

advantageous connexion — and he is ⟨doub?⟩ certainly a charming Companion — but beware of partnerships — they throw you at the mercy of another persons discretion, over whose judgement or inclination you may have no controul — You can make your fortune by yourself — without perplexing or thwarting yourself with any one — From the little I have seen of business I am satisfied there is nothing that a man should be more wary & considerate about, than entering into partnerships.

Long before this reaches you Renwick will have returned — and you will have had many a long talk with him about his travels. I have not been able to enjoy his society in Europe as I expected. We made a charming tour in Wales together last summer — ⟨It was about the only last gleaming?⟩ and I had anticipated a delightful journey to Scotland; but I had to halt in Liverpool to attend to business, and then began my troubles —

Remember me affectionately to Mrs Renwick and her family, I envy you the happy hours you will pass at their summer retreat.[12] I reccollect the place, it is a beautiful one — but Mrs Renwick has the talent of diffusing happiness around her wherever she is.

I must also beg you to remember me most heartily to my worthy inmates at Mrs Bradishs, particularly ⟨Mr?⟩ that good man & true Govr. Johnston, who I ⟨at?⟩ hope will never have need to break the Guinea he got from me in London — I trust his worthy compeer Walker is yet with you, as usual *on the wing for Virginia,* I hope to find him unflown on my return —

I wrote some time since to Eliza Bradish[13] and hope the letter reached her in safety, as I would not have all the secrets it contained, known to the world on any account. Give my warmest remembrances to her and her mother, and entreat the latter to refrain from further purchases, lest she ruin herself with good bargains —

I am extremely pained to hear from you of the continued ill health of Serena L—— if her father wishes to preserve her from following the lovely beings that have been swept from her side — he should send her at once to the South of france — were she to go out there in the early part of the Autumn and remain in those climates until next summer she might be fully restored — but the misfortune is, that these expeditions are always taken too late — I beg you to give my particular remembrances to her and her sisters —

This is a sad, lackadaisical scrawl — but I had no idea, when I began this I should have been able to scrawl so much — Do not let the meagreness of my letters ⟨prevent you⟩ discourage you from writing. In my present listless & uncomfortable state of mind your letters are inexpressibly gratifying — and the last I received I have kept by me as a cordial against low spirits.

Give my sincere regards to your worthy parents and your sister and believe me my dear fellow

Most truly yours
WI.

If that worthy little Tar Jack Nicholson is with you tell him I return him a thousand thanks for his letter[14] and will answer it ⟨as⟩ soon—

I am affraid that we must give up all expectation of seeing Gouv Kemble out here — The disappointment will be great to us all; but I hope his present scheme[15] may be a profitable one, in which case I shall not repine — I would write to him but he is such a bird of passage that it is like shooting flying; there is no knowing when a letter would reach him.

I shall be happy to hear that James K P. is married to G____ and divorced from the Analectic. I think James is in the way of fortune & preferment, if he has spirit & judgement to manage his opportunities, & I think he will make a good husband & she certainly will make an excellent wife. But his connexion with the magazine, tho' it yields present profit, is I am affraid of no advantage to his literary reputation, for his Naval Chronicle is, in every respect, executed in his worst style—[16]

MANUSCRIPT: NYPL—Seligman Collection.   PUBLISHED: LIB, I, 163–74; PMI, I, 357 (in part).

1. This letter has not been located.
2. See *Henry IV*, Part I, III, i, 52.
3. WI refers to the financial collapse which followed the peace at the conclusion of the Napoleonic wars and affected agriculture, industry, and trade.
4. WI inadvertently omitted this word.
5. Brevoort had presumably lent money to the Irving importing firm in New York which was managed by Ebenezer Irving. Peter had overcommitted the firm's capital as a result of some of his agreements with English manufacturers. See PMI, I, 341.
6. Eccles. 11:1.
7. WI drew upon this episode for his essay, "The Angler," in *The Sketch Book.*
8. A town in Holland on the North Sea, near which the British defeated the Dutch navy in 1797.
9. Probably McTavish, who had been associated with Brevoort in fur trading.
10. WI may have intended to write "settling."
11. Richard Caton (1763–1845) was a wealthy cotton manufacturer from Baltimore. His daughters Mary, Elizabeth, and Louisa, who were known as the three "American Graces," all married into English aristocracy. WI had probably met them during his visits to Baltimore a few years earlier.
12. The location of this retreat has not been ascertained.
13. This letter has not been located.
14. This letter has not been located.

15. Probably a reference to Kemble's plan to cast cannon, a venture which was carried out when Kemble established the West Point Foundry in Cold Spring, New York.

16. Between January and September, 1816, Paulding contributed to the *Analectic Magazine* twelve articles and a poem on topics related to the United States Navy. See Ralph M. Aderman, "James Kirke Paulding's Contributions to American Magazines," *Studies in Bibliography* 17 (1964), 145.

180. To Sarah Irving

Birmingham, August 31st. 1816

My dear Mother,

Since last I wrote to you Peter and myself have made an excursion of about a fortnight, into Derbyshire. By great good luck the weather was tolerably fair during our jaunt; for this has been the most rainy year I ever experienced. ⟨We had⟩ Our little tour was very interesting; the valleys or rather glens of Derbyshire are beautifully romantic and there are many wonderful caverns and mines, several of which we explored; particularly the great cavern at the peak, which goes by a name so wicked and abominable that I would not repeat it for the world.[1] We also visited the splendid seat of the Duke of Devonshire at Chatsworth[2] and were shewn the apartments where poor Mary Queen of Scots was confined for a considerable time. They still retain the same bed & furniture that they had at the time of her imprisonment; which though old fashioned are still rich and magnificent. Previous to this Excursion Peter had been a little unwell, and I was fearful he might have a return of his old complaint; the journey however put him in full health and spirits and I was delighted to find him quite himself again. After our Derbyshire jaunt Peter remained at Liverpool to attend to business and I returned to Birmingham along the border of Wales, passing through Chester, Wrexham, Shrewsbury &c.

On my return I received your letter written in July[3] and was greatly gratified to hear of your good good health; your letter was a long one and written to us all; I hope you do not task yourself too much in writing such long letters. I know it must be a matter of trouble and weariness at your age. and beg you will not think it necessary to write often to me, and when you do, let your letters be very short — Ebenezer always mentions how you are in his letters, and will write any thing you tell him. Though I am delighted to receive letters from you, yet I cannot but think of the trouble they may cost you in the writing; a few lines therefore will be sufficient at a time. I hope you will not find yourself lonely now Ebenezer has removed from your neighborhood.[4] I am sure he will visit you whenever it is in his power, for he is as good a son as he is a brother; and indeed it is the constant wish of all your children to make you as comfortable and happy as possible.

The family here are all in usual health. M[r?] [*MS torn*] Van Wart is not very hearty and intends going to Cheltenham⁵ next week, to drink the waters for a week or ten days[.] I have promised to accompany him. Lewis⁶ is in London and fully occupied with the wonders of that Great City; I suppose he will return to Birmingham in about a fortnight. He is very observant of every thing he sees, and I have no doubt will profit greatly by his visit to Europe. Give my love to the family in which I of course include Miss Benedict⁷ who ⟨I know⟩ I trust keeps a good eye upon you & takes care that you behave yourself well

Your affectionate son
W. I.

ADDRESSED: Mrs Sarah Irving / Care of P & E Irving & Co / New York. / ⟨South Carolina⟩ Packet
MANUSCRIPT: Yale.

1. The hilly area in Derbyshire known as the Peak is about thirty miles long and twenty-two miles wide. The highest points are Kinderscout (2080 feet), Axe Edge (1810 feet), and Marn Tor (1710 feet). The Peak Cavern near Castleton, with a forty-two foot arch at its entrances, extends nearly 2000 feet into the mountains and includes a river called the Styx. Daniel Defoe reported that the name given to the arched entrance was "The Devil's A____e in the Peak." See *A Tour Through England and Wales* (London, 1928), II, 172.

2. Built in 1687–1706 in Palladian style, this edifice was 560 feet long and contains the State Apartment, State Dressing Room, State Drawing and Dining Room as well as the Sketch, Picture, and Sculpture galleries. Mary Stuart was once a prisoner in an earlier building on the same site.

3. This letter has not been located.

4. At the time of her death Mrs. Irving was living at 41 Ann Street. Ebenezer lived at 58 Beekman and later on Bridge Street. See *New York City Directory* for 1815–1816 and 1816–1817.

5. Cheltenham is a watering-place about fifty miles southwest of Birmingham. According to Baedeker, "The waters are chalybeate and saline, and are considered efficacious for dyspepsia and affections of the liver." *Great Britain* (Leipsic, 1890), p. 181.

6. Probably Lewis Irving (1795–1879), the eldest son of William Irving.

7. Miss Benedict was apparently a companion or servant for Mrs. Irving.

181. To Sarah Irving

Birmingham, Octr 18th. 1816.

My dear Mother,

I have suffered some little time to elapse without writing to you, having nothing particular to write about. But I know you are anxious to hear frequently from us and are fond of receiving letters. Mr Van Wart has had a severe attack of the Quinzey sore throat, which confined him to the house for a fortnight, and part of the time to his bed. His throat was so much swelled and inflamed that he could not swallow any thing but fluids, and even spoke with some difficulty. He sufferd much pain and uneasiness and we felt quite anxious, until the gathering broke and relieved him. He is now well again, and his physician thinks this attack will have a favourable effect on his general health. Sally and the children are well. The two eldest boys are under the care of a young clergyman of Birmingham[1] and are coming on very well in their education. Little William does not yet go to school. He is a most engaging little fellow and extremely amusing. Matilda and Marianne are beautiful children and as good as they are handsome

Lewis left us a few days since for Scotland, where he intends making a short tour. He has been to London and Seen all the Lions, of which ⟨he has⟩ I believe he has written home accounts to his brothers. He is a worthy amiable lad, and conducts himself with great discretion and propriety[.] I make no doubt that his visit to Europe will be of advantage to him and that he will give great satisfaction to his father when he returns.

Peter remains at Liverpool. I have intended for some time past to join him there but one circumstance or other has prevented me.—I think I shall join him shortly. He is in good health at present, though I think he is more delicate in Constitution than he used to be. For myself I never was heartier and am only affraid of growing *too fat*. I am in hopes Peter may be able to leave Liverpool soon and come up to Birmingham for a time. It would be quite a treat for him to escape from the cares of business and pass a little while with the family.

I had a letter from Mrs Paris[2] lately and am happy to find that Isaac[3] is growing out of his complaint. I shall answer her letter by the next opportunity. I hope something has been done to put Mr Dodge[4] in profitable employment, and that his little girls[5] are well taken care of. I have written on this subject some time since to my Brothers and they know my wishes and disposition in this respect. Richard has been very unfortunate; but we are all liable to misfortunes & should Stand by one another. It ⟨was⟩ is a great satisfaction to me to think that his sons are in a way to get well acquainted with business and to be able hereafter to make their own way in the world and assist him should he stand in need of their aid.

Remember me affectionately to the family and to my good friend Mary;[6] whose constant attention and kindness to you I shall never forget

Mr Van Wart is at my elbow and desires me to give his love to you. I am my dear Mother

Your affectionate son
W. Irving

ADDRESSED: Mrs Sarah Irving / Care of Mess: P & E Irving & Co. / New York
MANUSCRIPT: SHR—Collection of Mrs. Margaret Gracie Paris.

1. Probably the Reverend Rann Kennedy (1772–1857), a clergyman of the Church of England, who was master of King Edward's School in Birmingham. For a description of Kennedy, see WI's letter to Henry Brevoort, December 9, 1816.

2. This letter has not been located.

3. Isaac Paris, born April 19, 1799, was the oldest son of Daniel and Catharine Paris.

4. Richard Dodge, WI's brother-in-law, was left with a large family when his wife died in 1808.

5. WI is referring to Jane Ann Dodge (1799–1875), Eliza Dodge (1801–1887), and Helen Dodge (1802–1885).

6. Probably Mrs. Irving's companion.

182. To William Irving, Jr.

[Liverpool, fall?, 1816]

My heart is torn every way by anxiety for my relatives. My own individual interests are nothing. The merest pittance would content me if I could crawl out from among these troubles and see my connections safe around me.

PUBLISHED: PMI, I, 357.

183. To Henry Brevoort

Birmingham. 6th. Nov. 1816.

My dear Brevoort,

I received some time since your letter of Sept 8th[1] and feel most grateful for these repeated proofs of kind reccollections, especially when I consider the poor returns I make. You threaten to charge me with something more than want of punctuality if I do not write oftener and I am sensible my silence exposes me to many hard imputations, but I cannot help it — I can only say it is not for ↑want of↓ having you continually in my thoughts and near my heart, nor for want of the constant desire and frequent resolve to write. But some how or other there has been such a throng of worldly cares hurrying backward & forward through my mind for a long time past, that it is even as bare as a market place: and when I do take hold of my pen, I feel so poverty struck, such mental sterility, that I throw it down again in despair of writing any thing that should give you gratification. In fact I was always a poor precarious animal — but am just now worse than ever. So bear with my present delinquency & perhaps at some future moment, when the fit is on me and I am fresh of thought & ready of word (as I sometimes am when I least expect it) I will repay you tenfold.

In my last letter, which I am ashamed to say was written so long ago as July last, I talked of an excursion into Derbyshire and promised you particulars, if any thing presented worth writing about. Not having been in a narrative mood since my return, I have sufferd so long a time to elapse, that impressions made on my mind have been effaced — incidents have lost the freshness of novelty and all the little associations of thought, & feeling & fancy that constitute the enjoyment of a ramble and the charm of its recital have completely evaporated. To attempt to give you a detail therefore would be useless, though I cannot help talking a little about it, as I have scarcely any thing else to furnish out a letter, and as I know it will bring up a thousand agreeable reccollections to your mind of similar rambles you have taken in this country.

According to arrangements made by letter with Peter[2] I met him at Buxton,[3] to which place he travelled from Liverpool, in the identical Tilbury[4] in which you and he performed your Scottish peregrinations.[5] I arrived ⟨a lit?⟩ rather late in the evening so that he had dined & gone out; but as I knew his old haunts I ⟨repair⟩ asked the way to the theatre & was shewn to what had once been a barn, but was now converted to the seat of Empire & the epitome of all the Kingdoms of the earth. Here I found Peter enjoying with the most perfect complacency & satisfaction, some old stock play,[6] which he had seen performed a hundred times by the best actors in the world, & which was now undergoing murder and profanation from the very worst. You know of old his accommodating palate in this particular; and ⟨how⟩ with what relishing appetite he will either "feed on the mountain" or "batten on the moor"[7] — the worst of the matter, however is, that in his unbounded good will towards the vagrant race, he takes the whole company under his protection and wont allow you to laugh at any of them. This troop seemed almost an establishment — the Manager, his wife & daughter performed in the play and four of his children danced a garland dance. I understood the ⟨[unrecovered]⟩ ↑establishment↓ was somewhat on the plan of ⟨Twait⟩ poor Twait's theatrical commonwealth[8] — & the company divided on an average about 7/6 each pr Week.

At the hotel where we put up we had a most singular & whimsical assemblage of beings. I dont know whether you were ever at an English watering place, but if you have not been, you have missed the best opportunity at studying english oddities, both moral and physical—I no longer wonder at the english being such excellent caricaturists, they have such an inexhaustable number & variety of subjects to study from. The only care should be not ↑to↓ follow fact too closely for Ill swear I have met with characters & figures that would be condemned as extravagant, if faithfully delineated by pen or pencil. At a watering place like Buxton, where people really resort for health, you see the great tendency of the English to run into excrescences and bloat out into grotesque deformities. As to noses I say nothing of them, though we had every variety, ⟨from the pug to the brick handled, and from that to the⟩ some snubbed and turned up, with distended nostrils, like a dormant[9] window on the roof of a house — others convex & twisted like a Buck handled knife & others magnificently efflorescent like a full blown cauliflower — But as to the persons ⟨of⟩ that were attached to these noses, fancy every distortion, ⟨and⟩ protuberance ↑& pompous embellishment↓ that can be produced in the human form by high & gross feeding, by the bloating operations of malt liquors, by the rheumy influence of a damp, foggy, vapourish climate. One old fellow ⟨whose⟩ was an exception to this, for instead of acquiring that expansion and spunginess to which old people are prone in this country from the long course of internal & external soaking ↑they experience,↓ he had grown dry & stiff in the process of years. The skin of his face had so shrunk away that he could ⟨mouth⟩ not close eyes or mouth — the latter therefore stood on a perpetual ghastly grin; and the ⟨latter⟩ former on an incessant stare. He had but one ↑serviceable↓ joint in his body which was at the bottom of the back bone, and that creaked & grated whenever he bent. He could not raise his feet from the ground, but skated along the drawing room carpet, whenever he wished to ring the bell — The only signs of moisture in his whole body was a pellucid drop that I occasionally noticed on the end of a long dry nose. He used generally to shuffle about in company with a little fellow who was fat on one side and lean on the other. That is to say, he was warped on one side as if he had been scorched before the fire, he had a wry neck, which made his head lean on one shoulder—his hair was snugly powdered and he had a round, smirky smiling ⟨face with⟩ apple face with a bloom on it like that of a frost bitten leaf in autumn. We had an old ↑fat↓ general by the name of Trotter who had, I suspect, been promoted to his high rank to get him out of the way of more able and active officers, being an instance that a man may occasionally rise in the world through absolute lack of merit. I could not help watching the movements of this redoubtable old Hero, who, I'll warrant has ⟨gua⟩ been the champion & safe guard of half the garrison towns ↑in↓ England, and fancying to myself how ⟨such a gentleman⟩ Bonaparte would have delighted in having such toast & butter generals to deal with. This old lad is doubtless a sample of those generals that flourished in the old military school — when armies would manouvre & watch each other for months; now and then have a desparate skirmish and after ⟨so a?⟩ marching & countermarching about the "low countries" through a glorious campaign, retire on the first pinch of cold weather, into snug winter quarters in some fat flemish town, and eat & drink and fiddle through the winter. Boney must have sadly disconcerted the comfortable system of these old warriors by the harrassing restless cut & slash mode of warfare that he introduced. He has put an end to all the old *carte and tierce* system[10] in which the cavaliers of the old school fought so decorously, as it were with a small sword in one hand and a chapeau Bras in the other. During his career there has been a sad laying on the shelf of old generals who could not keep up with the hurry, the fierceness and dashing of the new system; and among the number I presume has been my worthy housemate old Trotter. The old gentleman, in spight of his warlike title, had a most pacific appearance. He was large and fat — with a broad hazy muffin face, a sleepy eye and a full double chin. He had a deep ravine from each corner of his mouth, not occasioned by any irascible contraction of the muscles, but apparently the deep worn channels of two rivulets of gravy that oozed out from the huge mouthfuls that he masticated. But I forbear to dwell on the odd beings that were congregated together in our Hotel. I have ⟨merely?⟩ been thus prolix about the old general because you desired me in one of your letters to give you ample details whenever I happened to be in company with the "great & glorious" and old Trotter is more deserving of the epithets ⟨of any of my⟩ than any of the personages I have lately encountered—

Nov. 13th. From the foregoing scribbling you will perceive that after setting out with many apologies for having nothing to say, I had absolutely got into a most garrulous vein, and had I not been interrupted I believe I should have scribbled off a very long & very flippant letter. I was obliged however to break off to attend to some other matter and have not been able since to get into the narrative vein again. As I hear the Pacific[11] is about sailing from Liverpool I must een hurry off this letter as it is, lest another long ⟨interval⟩ period elapse before you get a line from me. Should I at any time feel in the mood to give you some more Derbyshire sketches I will not fail to take pen in hand.

I must now say a word or two in reply to your letter of the 8th Septr. I rejoice to find that Mac[12] is absolutely linked to Miss Caton, and wish all happiness to their union. ⟨I am also glad to find by their intention of residing in Canada, that the idea of settling yourself in business with McTavish & Co I do not think it would hold from either to your comfort or advantage—You had better avoid all partnerships—your own knowledge of business and means of conducting it will be sufficient for all your reasonable wants & wishes⟩

I have not met with the Catons in England, though I have heard of them. They were greatly admired & noticed at Cheltenham. The Duke of Wellington[13] paid them particular attention to the great annoyance of many dowagers who had daughters anxious for fashion & notoriety.

Your account of the brevity of the old ladys[14] nether garments really
distresses me — what will become of the world when these land marks
of primitive decorum and staid discretion are carried away by the tide
of fashion. If she does not return to her former sobriety of apparel and
demean herself like a most grave & reverend young gentlewoman, I
insist that you take Flora[15] from under her guardianship. By the way,
I cannot help observing that this fashion of short skirts must have been
invented by the french ladies as a complete trick upon ⟨Lady⟩ John Bulls
"womenfolk." It was introduced just at the time the English flocked in
such crowds to paris. The French women you know are remarkable for
pretty feet and ankles and can display them ⟨with⟩ in perfect serenity.
↑The English are remarkable for the contrary.↓ Seeing the proness of
the English women to follow french fashions, they therefore led them into
this disastrous one: and sent them home with their petticoats up to their
knees ⟨sh⟩ exhibiting such a variety of sturdy little legs, as would have
afforded Hogarth an ample choice to match one of his assemblages of
queer heads.[16] It is really a great source of curiosity & amusement ⟨to
walk⟩ on the promenade of a watering place, to observe the little sturdy
English women, trudging about ⟨with⟩ ↑in their↓ stout leather shoes,
⟨ankles & red knees?⟩ and ↑to↓ study the various *understandings* brought
to view by this mischivious fashion.

I must conclude or this scrawl will be too long. When you write next
let me know something about the movements of that great Scavenger S
Swartwout & how his peat marshes[17] came on. How are Mr & Mrs Cooper
making out, where he is acting &c — What is Charles Nicholas doing — &c.

Remember me most affectionately to Mrs Renwick and her family &
let me know when the worthy professor quits this transitory state — of
celibacy—

Give my warmest regards to your good lady Hostess, and also the ladies
of the little parlour — I wrote to the old gentlewoman[18] a long while since,
when I sent her Moores Sacred Melodies.[19] I expect an answer from her —
Remember me to Johnson & the rest of the household —

Yours most heartily
WI.

DOCKETED: [*on page 8 of holograph letter*] Nov 6. 181⟨5⟩6 / Watering place
    characters [*in another hand*].
MANUSCRIPT: NYPL–Seligman Collection. PUBLISHED: LIB, I, 175–87; PMI, I,
    354–55 (in part).

1. This letter has not been located.
2. This letter has not been located.
3. One of the chief spas in England, Buxton had hot springs with a temperature of 82 degrees F.
4. A giglike two-wheeled carriage named after its builder.

5. Brevoort and Peter Irving had been in Edinburgh together during the late fall of 1812 and the winter of 1812–1813. At this time Brevoort gave Walter Scott a copy of *Knickerbocker's History of New York*. See LBI, I, 64, 72, 99.

6. This play has not been identified.

7. A variation of *Hamlet*, III, iv, 66–67.

8. In 1813 a group of disgruntled actors organized themselves into a company and began to perform in November at the New Theatre in Broadway, with William Twaits (d. 1814) as one of the directors. See Odell, *NY Stage*, II, 413.

9. Someone has written *er* above the *ant* of "dormant."

10. With this reference to thrusts in fencing WI suggests that Bonaparte used unconventional methods in his fighting.

11. The *Pacific* left Liverpool on November 17 and arrived in New York thirty-three days later. See NYEP, December 30, 1816.

12. This is probably the McTavish who was Brevoort's partner in the fur trade. He was mentioned in WI to Brevoort, July 16, 1816.

13. Arthur Wellesley, Duke of Wellington (1769–1852), who defeated Napoleon at Waterloo.

14. WI is apparently referring to one of the boarders at Mrs. Bradish's.

15. A dog at Mrs. Bradish's boardinghouse. See PMI, I, 350.

16. WI is probably alluding to Hogarth's engraving, "Group of Heads, Intending to Display the Difference Betwixt Character and Caricature." See *The Complete Works of William Hogarth*, intro. James Hannay (London, n.d.), p. 181.

17. In 1815 Samuel Swartwout bought tracts of salt marsh between Hoboken and Weehawken, built embankments, drained the land, and by 1819 was cutting 400 tons of hay from it annually.

18. Probably another reference to the old lady with the short skirts.

19. Thomas Moore's *Sacred Songs* was published in the spring of 1816.

184. To Henry Brevoort

Birmingham. Decr. 9th. 1816.

My dear Brevoort,

Since I last wrote I have received your letter of Octr 16th.[1] I congratulate you with all my soul on the marriage of your Sister with our invaluable friend Renwick.[2] It cannot but prove a happy union, and must add largely to your means of domestic happiness. I trust my dear fellow providence is laying a solid foundation for the welfare of yourself and your relatives and that you will all go on to flourish in well merited and honourable prosperity.

I feel deeply sensible of the sympathy you evince in my cares and troubles. I assure you however that they were chiefly occasiond by my apprehensions for my connexions, and being now ⟨assured⟩ ↑confident↓ that my Brothers in NYork will be able to weather the storm & spread their sails cheerily on the return of fair weather I shall not let present ⟨un⟩ difficulties give me any uneasiness. I thank you again & again for your kind assistance to my worthy Brother the Major.[3] He is one of the most excellent little men living and I feel any good office done to him ten times more than if it were rendered to myself. I beg you will continue to give him an occasional call. Your advice will often be of service to him as you have a better idea of general business than he probably has, from his being exclusively occupied by one branch of trade.

Frank Ogden[4] and his Brother Peter passed a couple of days in Birmingham not long since. Frank gave me a great many entertaining anecdotes about the establishment at the Battery[5] & its dependent Colony, and made me completely homesick. Your letters also, have frequently the same effect. They contain so many allusions to old jokes that have passed between us — so many characteristic ⟨touches⟩ sketches of persons and scenes about which we have so often gossipped and laughed in our little chamber councils, that they awaken a thousand reccollections and delightful associations. After all, it is the charm of existence to have some crony who exactly jumps with our humour; ⟨with whom we can⟩ in whose company we can completely unbutton and throw loose the garb of cautious reserve in which our minds are generally so straightly clad — and can give every thought and whim free scope. ⟨How⟩ I do delight in these snug confidings, wherein we canvas the events of the day—and amuse ourselves with the odd characters and circumstances we have witnessed. It is really doubling existence, and living over past moments with encreased enjoyment; for there Seems to be more brightness in the reflected gleams of gay hours, than there was in their original sunshine.

You will smile when I tell you that, after all the grave advice I once gave you about getting married, I really felt regret on fancying, from the purport of one of your letters, that you had some serious thoughts of the kind; and that I have indulged in selfish congratulation on finding nothing in your subsequent letters to warrant such an idea. All this too, notwithstanding that I wish you ⟨every⟩ happiness, and am certain that the married state is most likely to insure it. But we are all selfish beings. Fortune by her tardy favours and capricious freaks seems to discourage all my matrimonial resolves, and, if I am doomed to live an old Bachelor, I am anxious to have good company. I cannot bear that all my old companions should launch away into the married state and leave me alone to tread this desolate & sterile shore, and it is a consoling and a cherished thought with me, ⟨that⟩ under every vicissitude; that I shall still be able to return home, nestle comfortably down beside you, and have wherewithal to shelter me from the storms and buffetings of this uncertain world. Thank heaven I was brought up in simple and inexpensive habits, and I have satisfied myself that, if need be, I can resume them without repining or inconvenience. Though I am willing therefore that fortune should shower her blessings upon me, and think I can enjoy them as well as most men, yet I shall not make myself unhappy if she chuses to be scanty, and shall take the portion allotted to me with a cheerful and contented mind.

I am writing you a queer rigmarole letter containing no news ⟨and scribbled?⟩ in return for your delightful letters which are perfect chronicles of domestic events. You have the best knack of writing domestic letters of any one I know — every sentence presents me a picture, or gives me ↑a↓ bulletin about some one or other of my friends. and the very careless, ready manner in which they are dashed off gives them ⟨the⟩ truth & spirit. I wish I had something to give you in exchange, but just ⟨know⟩ ↑now↓ I am sterile. Brummagem anecdotes would give you little entertainment. Yet I must say I have found many good people here, and some few that are really choice. Among these I must especially mention my particular friend the Revd. Rann Kennedy, of whom I may some day or other give you a more full account. He is a most excentric character, and is both my admiration and amusement. He is a man of real *genius*—preaches admirable sermons—and has ⟨his head full of poetry being⟩ for a long time past been on the *point* of producing two or three poetic works, though he has not as yet *committed any of* his *poetry* to paper. He however says he has it all in his brain — and indeed has occasionally ⟨reported⟩ ↑recited↓ some passages of it to Peter & myself that have absolutely delighted us. With all this he has the ⟨naivity⟩ ↑naivete↓ of a child; is somewhat hypocondriacal and ⟨some think⟩ ↑in short is↓ one of the queerest mortals living. He is a great favourite of ⟨[*unrecovered*]⟩ Doctor Parr's,[6] and is very anxious to make me acquainted with that formidable old Grecian. He has two or three likenesses of ⟨old⟩ Parr hanging about his house & the old fellow is a great deal at Kennedys when in Birmingham to the great annoyance of Mrs Kennedy: For Parr is a great gourmand and epicure, & when he dines with any of his particular friends is very apt to extend his domineering spirit to the concerns of the Larder & the Kitchen, and order matters to his own palate; an assumption of privilege which no true housewife can tolerate

I have not seen Peter for four months past. In fact not since our little excursion into Derbyshire, which I delight to look back upon as a green spot in this barren year. — I should have joined him before this at Liverpool but he has been continually giving us hopes of his coming up here, and we now look confidently for him in a day or two to remain & eat his christmas dinner with us. You cannot think how heart felt the gratification is at those little family assemblages, particularly with us who are "strangers & sojourners in the land"[7] and see nothing but gloom and trouble around us. You have no idea of the distress and misery that prevails in this country: it is beyond the power of description: ⟨How? could⟩ In America you have financial difficulties, the embarrassments of trade & the distress of merchants ⟨all this is in some s?⟩ but here you

have what is far worse, the distress of the poor — not merely mental
sufferings — but the absolute miseries of nature — Hunger, nakedness,
wretchedness of all kinds that ⟨those are subject to⟩ ↑the labouring↓
people in this country are liable to.[8] In the best of times they do but
subsist, but in adverse times they starve. How this country is to extricate
itself from its present embarrassments, how it is to emerge from the
poverty that seems to be overwhelming ⟨about?⟩ it, and how the government is to quiet the multitudes that are already turbulent & clamorous,
and are yet but in the beginning of their real miseries, I cannot conceive
⟨[unrecovered]⟩—but I have some how or other rambled away into a
theme ⟨about⟩ which would neither edify nor amuse you, so we will not
pursue it.

I have ordered Mr Muncaster to forward the Books you wrote for
and shall occasionally send such new works as I think you may relish;
except it be such light popular works as are likely to be immediately
reprinted in America at a much cheaper rate.

The Books lent me by Col Gibbs[9] are at Liverpool & when I go down
there I will pack them up and take care that he shall receive them in
good order. You may⟨st b⟩ tell him I shall be happy to be of any service to
him in Europe.

I wish when next you see Mrs Renwick, you would give her my congratulations on the various changes & encreasings of her family. I think
I can see her, the centre of a happy domestic system, which is warmed
and gladdened by the emanations of her generous heart — God Bless her!
say I — and grant that the happiness she delights to shed around her
may all be reflected back upon herself — and then I'm sure she'll be the
happiest of mortals.

Remember me likewise to your worthy parents, who are enjoying the
greatest blessing of old age, that of seeing their children prosperous and
happy.

I feel greatly indebted to my good friend Mrs Bradish for dreaming
so often about me, and indeed I value it as no trifling instance of kindness & goodwill, that she who has so many domesticated with her occasionally, should bestow such particular reccollection upon me. I am glad
to hear such favourable accounts of Eliza's health, and that the dissipation
of Elizabethtown has agreed with her so well — How I should delight
to spend a cosey hour in the little parlour! Well — well! We shall all get
together again by & bye [and ha]ve [MS torn] merry times once more.

You mention the prosperity of the Theatre. I wish you would interest
yourselves for the Johnsons,[10] they are old friends of mine and both
Peter & myself are very anxious for their success. Ellen Johnson[11] is a
charming girl and I think must prove a good actress. I have never seen her
perform. How is Bibby making out—I presume he is giving touches of

Kean as I perceive he acts some of Keans characters — How does his affair with Mary Bailly go on.

Give my best regards to the worthy Governor & the rest of the household — I am

my dear Brevoort/yours ever

WI.

ADDRESSED: To / Henry Brevoort Jr. Esqr. / at Mrs Bradish's / New York. Minerva
    DOCKETED: Birmingham Dec. 9, 1816 / W Irving
MANUSCRIPT: NYPL—Seligman Collection.   PUBLISHED: LIB, I, 188–98; PMI, I,
    357–58 (in part).

Upside down at the top of the address sheet is written "To yr Mrs regards." It does not seem to be WI's handwriting.
    1. Brevoort's letter has not been located.
    2. Margaret Ann Brevoort married James Renwick on October 10, 1816.
    3. Ebenezer Irving.
    4. Francis Ogden (1783–1857), a New York business man who later became United States consul in Liverpool.
    5. During the War of 1812 a battery was built at the foot of Manhattan Island. The structure was later called Castle Clinton, and then Castle Garden when its rooms were used for public meetings. Wilson, NY, Old and New, II, 17–18.
    6. Samuel Parr (1747–1825) was a cleric and classical scholar widely known for his strong Whig views.
    7. WI is probably misquoting Gen. 23:4.
    8. WI was apparently more aware of the plight of the poor than most visitors to England, at this time beset with depression, inflation, and business failures. See W. O. Henderson, Industrial Britain under the Regency (London, n.d.), pp. 1–2.
    9. George Gibbs (1776–1833), a wealthy merchant of Newport, Rhode Island, interested in science and letters.
    10. John Johnson and his wife were actors from England whom WI had seen perform at the Park Theater. See Ireland, NY Stage, I, 130.
    11. Ellen Johnson (1800–1837), daughter of Mr. and Mrs. John Johnson, was an attractive, talented actress noted for her singing and harp-playing. See Ireland, NY Stage, I, 320–22.

185. To Henry Brevoort

Birmingham, Jany 29th 1817.

My dear Brevoort,

I have your letter of the 21st Nov.[1] which as usual is full of interesting matter about those I most love and care for. How much am I indebted to you for these repeated and persevering acts of friendship. I wish I could give you details equally interesting in return; but in my present monotony of life and almost torpor of intellect it is a matter of difficulty to finish out a letter.

I have made an arrangement with Mess Longman Hurst & Co[2] to furnish me with books at the same rate they supplied Renwick. The

greater part of the old works you wrote for has been sold. They have
sent me such as remained on hand, and a few others that I ordered from
a Supplementary catalogue. They publish a new catalogue shortly which
I shall send you. I must beg your indulgence in retaining a few of these
works by me for a little while, as I wish very much to look over them
& presume you are not in immediate want of them, but only desire them
to complete your library. I shall be very careful of them. Longman & Co
have promised to look out for the other works you ordered, & to send
them to me as they come to hand.

⟨You are right in your idea⟩

Peter passed the Holydays with us and returned to Liverpool about
ten days since. He is in excellent health and we enjoyed ourselves
highly together; in spite of hard times. I am in hopes he will be enabled
to come up here again before long, if not I shall pay him a visit in
Liverpool. The Lady Baroness has enriched her husband with another
son, and both mother and child are doing well.[3] We shall have a famous
troop of Van Tromps. They are all uncommonly fine children and a
perpetual source of entertainment. We have generally a grand game
of romps in the evening, between dinner & tea time, in the course of
which I play the flute & the little girls dance. They are but pigmy
performers, yet they dance with inimitable grace, and vast good will,
and consider me as the divinest musician in the world; So thank
heaven I have at last found auditors who can appreciate my musical
talents.

You wish to know whether in visiting the banks of the Dove[4] I was
animated by the reccollections of honest old Isaak Walton. I assure you
I bless the memory of that illustrious old angler a thousand times,
for having suggested to me an excursion fraught with the most
pleasureable incidents. Among these our ramble thro' Dove dale was
peculiarly delightful. Peter & myself went over there from Matlock.
At the last place we had become slightly acquainted with old Bishop
Bathurst of Norwich & his family,[5] ⟨?the most?⟩ Sir Thomas Williams
(vice admiral of the Blue)[6] & his lady & a few others, ⟨?Heard?⟩ who
seemed disposed to be very civil. It was the good fortune of Peter
& myself just after entering dove Dale, to overtake a party consisting
of Sir Thos Williams & his Lady, the Miss Bathursts[7] (three lovely girls)
and Sir Francis ⟨ford⟩ Ford[8] who was paying attentions to one of the
young ladies. They were on a ramble of curiosity like ourselves and had
brought provisions with them to make a repast champêtre, that they
might be enabled to pass the day in the Dale and return in the evening.

We joined the party and in a few minutes we were all on the most
sociable terms. Sir Thomas ⟨married⟩ we found gentleman Sailor, good
humoured, social and entertaining — His lady, whom he had married

but a year or two before, was much younger than himself, well bred, well informed, with a tincture of Chemistry, Botany & other fashionable studies. The Miss Bathursts had ⟨a⟩↑that↓delightful frankness & simplicity of manners which I have so often remarked in the really fine women of this country, and Sir Francis Ford, though not the most polished Baronet I have met with, having been brought up at Barbadoes, ⟨yet?⟩ was amiable, unassuming, and as agreeable as a man utterly in love can be, in the presence of his Mistress. If a man could not be happy with such a party in such a place, he may give up all hopes of sublunary felicity. For my part I was in Elysium Nothing so soon banishes reserve and produces intimacy as a participation in difficulties. The path through the Dale was rugged and beset with petty hazards. We had to toil through thickets & Brambles — Sometimes to step cautiously from stone to stone in the margin of the little river where the pre-cipitous hills over hung its current — We had to scramble up into caverns and to climb rocks — all these were calculated to place both parties in those relative situations which endear the Sexes. I had a ⟨lovely⟩ woman, lovely woman! clinging to me for assistance & pro-tection — looking up with beseeching weakness & dependence in the midst of difficulties & Dangers — while I ⟨with⟩↑in↓all the swelling ⟨spirit⟩↑pride↓of a lord of the Creation, looked upon my feeble companion with an eye of infinite benevolence & fostering care — braved every ⟨danger⟩ peril of land & water — and sustained a scratched hand or a wet foot with a fortitude that called forth the admiration of the softer sex!

⟨But then Brevoort⟩

But all these dangers past — when we had descended from the last precipice, and come to where the Dove flowed musically through a verdant meadow — then — fancy me — oh thou "Sweetest of Poets" wandering by the course of this romantic stream — a lovely ⟨"object"⟩ ↑girl↓—who felt ⟨"emotions with ten times the force of common ordinary mortals"⟩ hanging on my arm — pointing the beauties of the[9] surrounding scenery—and repeating in the most dulcet voice tracts of heaven born poetry! If a Strawberry Smotherd in cream has any consciousness of its delicious situation, it must feel as I felt at that moment.

We had proceeded a great distance up the Dale when the day became overcast, and a slight shower or two admonished us to return. The showers grew more heavy so that we had to stop occasionally in the caverns of the hills, to shelter ourselves. At the last cavern, called St Marys cave,[10] the rain became heavy & continued and finding an old woman & her daughter there who had been employed partly as guides & partly ⟨as⟩ to carry the provisions for the ⟨of⟩ repast champetre, we determined to make our dinner in the cavern — A cloth was spread on the bottom of the cave, we seated ourselves around on fragments of rock and made a merry banquet. After dinner as the rain continued we had to resort to various amusements to pass away the afternoon. ⟨Some⟩ One of the Young ladies Sang. Sir Thomas Williams sang a whimsical medley — until the thought struck us to have a dance in the style of Macbeths witches[11] We got the girl that had carried the provisions, to sing a country dance which she did with an invincible gravity of countenance and a resounding nasal twang, while we danced a Boulangé.[12] We had after this a long dismal Ballad from the country girl, sang in admirable style; and a most frightful story of a Ghost by the old woman, who had seen it "with her own eyes!" together with several anecdotes of a gang of Gypsies that infested the neighbourhood.

The winding up of the adventures of the Dale was, that the rain continuing with unabating violence, and evening approaching we had to abandon the cavern. As the dale does not admit of the enterance of carriages, having nothing but a foot path winding thro' it we were obliged to trudge for a mile and half through a steady, pitiless, drenching rain, so that by the time we reached the carriages we might have been mistaken for a party of river deities just dripping from the Dove. All parties however were in such high good humour — that even the de⟨c⟩scending torrents could not extinguish or allay our gaiety. Peter was unutterably delighted with the occurrences of the Day and begged me to assure you that the ramble ⟨with⟩ about Loch Katrine was "a fool to it"— I rather think however you will not be able to comprehend the pleasures of this memorable ramble in any very lively manner from the brief sketch I have scrawled out. The delights of any party of pleasure of the kind ⟨?any?⟩ are occasioned by so many little ⟨imperceptible⟩↑indescribable↓circumstances, fugitive feelings and temporary excitements, that you may as well attempt to give a deaf man an idea of the ⟨delicate inflexions⟩ chromatic graces and delicate inflexions of a strain of music. I might have expanded my detail of this ramble over the scenes hallowed by honest Waltons simple muse,[13] through a sheet or two more — but I am always impatient & diffident of these narratives — lest I am only entertaining myself with[14] agreeable reccollections, which may be tedious & trifling to those in whom they do not awaken the same associations.

I must conclude this scrawl that it may be forwarded to Liverpool with other letters that are going. I shall write to you in a day or two & give you a list of the Books I have procured.

By the way I wish you to send me by the first private opportunity, or by some Captain of a vessel that knows our house in L'pool — a copy that you have in your possession of "*Styles Judges*"[15] it is a little, old book giving an account of the regicides Who took refuge in America.

I wish to shew it to an old gentleman here, who has a curiosity on the subject & will return it carefully to you.

I have recd a letter[16] & Barrel of apples from my good friend Mrs Bradish & will answer her letter in a day or two. Give my affectionate remembrances to her & Eliza & the Claypooles if still with you.

Remember me to the household/Yours ever

WI.

ADDRESSED: For / Henry Brevoort Jr. Esq / at Mrs Bradish's / New York. /
    Ann Marie}   DOCKETED: W Irving 1817 / Birmingham Jan: 29 1817
MANUSCRIPT: NYPL—Seligman Collection.   PUBLISHED: LIB, II, 3–13; PMI, I,
    359 (in part).

1. This letter has not been located.

2. Longman, Hurst & Co. was a publisher and bookseller on Paternoster Row, London.

3. WI, who facetiously refers to his sister Sarah as Baroness Van Tromp, is reporting the birth of his namesake, Washington Van Wart.

4. Izaak Walton lived on the Dove River near Mill Dale, which is about ten miles southwest of Mattack. Dovedale is a narrow limestone valley of the Dove, extending for about five miles.

5. Henry Bathurst (1744–1837), consecrated bishop of Norwich in 1805, was considered to be the only liberal bishop in the House of Lords at this time.

6. Sir Thomas Williams (1762?–1841), who was knighted in 1795, had served with distinction in North American stations and in encounters against the French.

7. The daughters of Bishop Bathurst, Henrietta (b. 1789), Tryphena, and Caroline (b. 1798). See Mrs. Thistlethwayte, Memoirs and Correspondence of Dr. Henry Bathurst, Lord Bishop of Norwich (London, 1853), pp. 50, 89.

8. Sir Francis Ford (1787–1839) was the eldest son of Sir Francis Ford, 1st baronet (1758–1801), who lived most of his life at Barbadoes in the West Indies. See Burke's Peerage, pp. 971–72.

9. Written over an unrecovered word.

10. WI's descriptions of the scenery of the River Dove are corroborated by J. Aikin in A Description of the Country ... Round Manchester (London, 1795), pp. 501–2.

11. See Macbeth, IV, i, 127–30.

12. The fifth figure of the quadrille.

13. As revealed in the descriptions of the River Dove in Part II of The Compleat Angler, or the Contemplative Man's Recreation (1653).

14. Above "with" is an ink spatter.

15. Probably a reference to Ezra Stiles, A History of the Three Judges of King Charles I (Hartford, 1794). This book was in WI's library at Sunnyside.

16. This letter has not been located.

186. *To Henry Brevoort*

Liverpool, March 10th 1817

Dear Brevoort,

By Mr Selden, who sails in the Nestor I forward you the following works

Sir Edward Barry on the Wines of the Ancients[1]	1 vol
The Simple Cobler of Aggawam in America &c.[2]	1 vol
Cumberland on the first plants of Nations[3]	1 vol
Conversations on political Economy[4]—	1 vol
Jeremy Taylors dissuasion from Popery[5]	1 vol
Hurds dissertations[6]	3 vols
La Hontans Voyages[7]	2 vols
Remains of Sir Walter Raleigh[8]	1 vol
Raleighs arts of Empires[9]	1 vol
History of Patient Grissel—(old pamphlet)[10]	
Virginia impartially examined[11]	1 vol
Longman & Cos New catalogue[12]	

Along with them I send the following works belonging to Col. Gibbs[13] which I wish you to return to him with my thanks, and offers of any services I can render him in Europe

Sonnini, Voyage dans L Egypte[14]—	3 vols
Voyage de la Propontide &c[15]	2 vols
Voyages En Syrie[16]	2 vols
Grece et Turquie	2 vols
a volume of plates and maps to ditto—	
Constantinople[17]	2 vols

Beside the books I have forwarded on your account I have likewise Ogilbys America,[18] Hennepins Voyage[19] and Stiths Hist. Virginia—[20] These three Peter and myself wish to read, and therefore have taken the liberty to detain them a little while. Many of the Books you wrote for had been sold by Longman & Co. previous to my application; but they have promised to look out for them for me — I expect to go up to London this Spring & will then look round for the books↑mentiond in your order↓that are deficient.

I have been in Liverpool a fortnight and have been continually on the point of writing but the wind, which has detained the shipping here for nearly two months, having still blown obstinately from the west, I have postponed the thing from day to day — The wind is now getting round and↓the ships↑will probably get away in a few hours — I am therefore all in a hurry & have not time to write but this scrawl.

Mercer & Leavenworth[21] are on the point of sailing & will give you all the news & gossip of the day — Mercer has been the very mirror of fashion in Liverpool

I wrote to you at some length about a month or six weeks since & believe the letter is now on board one of the ships in the [harbour] [*MS damaged*]

I am my dear Brevoort

Affectionately yours
WI.

P.S. I wish you to send out any good views either engravings or drawings that you can procure of *New York* — & the adjacent Scenery — Selden will hand you the last Nos of the Edinburgh & Quarterly Revs[22]

ADDRESSED: For / Henry Brevoort Jr. Esq. / New York / p. D Seldon Esqr   DOCK-
ETED: Liverpool 10 March 1817 / Washn. Irving
MANUSCRIPT: NYPL—WI Papers.   PUBLISHED: LIB, II, 14–17.

1. Sir Edward Barry, *Observations Historical, Critical, and Medical, on The Wines of the Ancients* . . . (London, 1775).

2. Nathaniel Ward, *The Simple Cobbler of Aggawam in America* (London, 1647; reprinted Boston, 1713).

3. Richard Cumberland, *Origines Gentium Antiquissimae; or Attempts for Discovering the Times of the First Planting of Nations* (London, 1724).

4. Jane Marcet, *Conversations on Political Economy* . . . (London, 1816). Apparently this was one of a series of simplified works written by this author for school children.

5. Jeremy Taylor, *A Dissuasion from Popery to the People of Ireland* (London, 1664; 4th ed., 1668).

6. Richard Hurd, *Moral and Political Dialogues with Letters on Chivalry and Romance*, 3d ed. (London, 1765). WI is apparently confusing "Dialogues" and "Dissertations."

7. La Hontan, *New Voyages to ·North America* . . . (London, 1703). A French edition appeared in the same year. Another edition was published in London in 1735.

8. *Remains of Sir Walter Raleigh* (London, 1657). Other editions were published in 1661, 1664, 1669, 1675, 1681, 1702, and 1726.

9. Sir Walter Raleigh, *The Cabinet-Council: Containing the Chief Arts of Empire, and Mysteries of State* . . . (London, 1658); another edition appeared in 1692.

10. Probably *The Ancient, True and Admirable History of Patient Grissel, A Poor Mans Daughter in France* . . . (London, 1619); reprinted in Percy Society Publications 3, no. 4 (1842).

11. William Bullock, *Virginia impartially examined, and left to publick view, to be considered by all judicious and honest men* (London, 1649).

12. Sale catalogs of Longman's Bookshop at 39 Paternoster Row for 1816 and 1817 are listed in the *British Museum General Catalogue of Printed Books*, CXLIV, 224.

13. This may be George Gibbs, who used the title of Colonel by courtesy. He is mentioned in *J&N*, I, 420.

14. Sonnini De Manoncourt (Charles Nicolas Sigisbert), *Voyage dans la Haute et Basse Egypte, fait par ordre de l'ancien Gouvernement* (Paris, an 7 [1799]).

15. Jean Baptiste Le Chevalier, *Voyage de la Propontide et du Pont-Euxin* (Paris, 1800), as listed in Alexandre Cioranescu, *Bibliographie de la Littérature Française du Dix-Huitième Siècle* (Paris, 1969), II, 1066.

16. Possibly Volney's *Voyage en Syrie et Égypte, pendant les Années 1783–1785* (Paris, 1787), or De la Roque's *Voyage de Syrie et du Mont-Liban* (Paris, 1722). See Cioranescu, III, 1768; II, 1037.

17. Probably Jacques Dallaway, *Constantinople Ancienne et Moderne et Description des Cotes et Isles de l'Archipel et de la Troade* (Paris, 1799).

18. John Ogilby, *America: being the latest and most accurate description of the New World . . .* (London, 1671).

19. WI is referring to one of the works by Louis Hennepin: *Voyage curieux du R.R.L. Hennepin . . .* (The Hague, 1704; other editions appeared in 1711, 1712, 1731); or *A Voyage to North America* (1705), or *Nouveau Voyage d'un pais plus grand l'Europe* (Utrecht, 1698; other editions 1715, 1720, 1731).

20. William Stith, *The history of the first discovery and settlement of Virginia* (Williamsburg, 1747).

21. These men have not been positively identified. The NYEP for April 24, 1817, reported that on the previous evening the *Ann Maria* commanded by Captain Waite had arrived in New York after a forty-day trip from Liverpool, with passengers A. Leavensworth and J. Mercen. WI's spelling of both surnames clearly differs from printed versions.

22. The final sentence is written between the texts of the second and third pages, running vertically from the bottom to the top of the page.

187. To Henry Brevoort

Liverpool, March 24th. 1817.

My dear Brevoort,

Richards informs me that he has written to you requesting your friendly assistance in the investigation and settlement of the concerns of the New York house (Andw. Ogden & Co)[1] He appears very anxious to secure your earnest attention to this business. It will no doubt be a very disagreeable task to you, but when you consider how completely poor Richards' fortunes are in jeopardy—how worthy a fellow he is, and how promptly and liberally he behaved towards yourself when your fortunes depended upon the turn of a die, and when ⟨t⟩ any backwardness on his part would have sufferd the golden moment to pass by, I am sure your own good heart will need no further impulse to do every thing that lies in your power to promote his interest. I will not therefore dwell on the subject. You will learn from Richards letters and from conversations with Selden all the particulars of the case. It is a most cruel one, and that intolerable *dolt* (for I hope he is no *worse*) Andw Ogden, has a vast deal to answer for. I feel most deeply anxious for Richards & Selden. Their acts of kindness to us have been many and momentous & independent of grateful considerations, the fairness, liberality and honourable disposition that have been manifested in all their dealings have won my strongest regard.

It seems a long time since I last heard from you. The singular perversity of the seasons interrupts the communications of friendship as well as the concerns of business—"the times are sadly out of joint—"[2] I am in hopes as the wind is favourable, there will be an arrival in a day or two that will bring me some intelligence from home. I have been for a month ⟨at⟩ in Liverpool—and count the days as they lag heavily by. Nothing but my wish to be with Peter & relieve the loneliness of his life would induce me to remain an hour in this place. It is a bustling busy town, but to me a very uninteresting one. I have received attentions from some people who seem both amiable & intelligent; but the ⟨people⟩ good folks here are both too busy & too dissipated to be social, and a Stranger who has not business to employ his time will find it a dead weight on his hands.

I have become rather sociable with some of the officers the 85th. part of which regiment is quartered here,[3] and am highly pleased with them. Among them are Lt Col Warburton,[4] who you may reccollect in New York immediately after the peace and Lt Col Brown,[5] who was at the capture of Washington & ↑was↓ left there among the wounded. Warburton bears honourable testimony to the hospitable treatment he received in New York, And Brown speaks with unaffected warmth & gratitude of the extreme kindness of the people of Washington, who, notwithstanding he was one of a band that had laid waste their homes & spread barbarous destruction around, vied with each other in bestowing the tenderest & most soothing attentions to his sufferings. He expresses the strongest disapprobation of the excesses committed at the capitol.

There is in this regiment also a very fine young fellow Charles Fox,[6] a Son of Lord Holland, he has a noble frankness & ingenuousness of disposition & a degree of enthusiasm that I do not often find in the English character. He has been particularly civil to me & has repeatedly expressed a wish that I would take introductory letters to his father & friends when I go to London.

I hope Peter will get through the occupations & entanglements of business sufficiently in the course of a few weeks so as to be enabled to accompany me in some excursion that will enliven & refresh us both & be like turning over a new page in existence—for life has been but a dull and tedious task to us both for some time past. I am now and then most heartily home sick, and once in a great while I feel as if I could almost be sick of the world, if I chose to give way to such weakness of the spirit; but these fits are but transient and the result of the life of inactive suspence I have been compelled of late to lead. I never suffer them to get a lodgement in my mind, but shake them resolutely out. In a little while the stream of events will again resume a lively & animating current[.] in the mean time I shall live on patiently & calmly, being most truly and solemnly convinced that there is a wise & good providence that over rules our destinies and directs every thing for the best.

Remember me affectionately to those whom you know I love and believe me my dear Brevoort

ever most truly yours
W I.

ADDRESSED: To / Henry Brevoort Jr Esqr. / at Mrs. Bradish's / New York / Pacific.

DOCKETED: Liverpool 24 March 1817 / W Irving

MANUSCRIPT: NYPL–Seligman Collection. PUBLISHED: LIB, II, 18–22.

1. Andrew Ogden (1771–1819), the main partner of Andrew Ogden & Co., was a well-to-do New York merchant whose name appears frequently in records of city affairs, such as members of merchants' committees and donors to charity. He was remotely related to Josiah Ogden Hoffman (probably about a tenth cousin); their common ancestor was John Ogden (1610–1682). Andrew became partners with Jabez Harrison in 1815; the *New York Directory* lists Andrew Ogden & Co. at 192 Pearl Street until 1813–1814; in 1815–1816 Ogden & Harrison is listed at the same address. In 1816 the company moved to Spring Street. Ogden's twenty-year-old son died in 1817; business reverses swept away his property and undermined his health and reason. He died two years later. Jabez Harrison filed and was discharged for bankruptcy on August 8, 1818; Ogden apparently salvaged something, as he is not listed in the *Indices*, although almost all of the other New York Ogdens are (eight Ogdens went bankrupt between 1814 and 1829). See Anna Vermilye, *Ogden Family History* (Orange, N.J., 1906), p. 11; *Indices to Insolvent Assignments to Dec. 31, 1855* (New York, 1857).

2. WI's variation of *Hamlet*, I, v, 189.

3. The 85th Regiment was sent to America in 1814 after participation in the Peninsular Campaign. It joined other British units in the Chesapeake Bay area on August 15, 1814, and engaged with them in the battle of Bladensburg. See C. R. B. Barrett, *The 85th King's Light Infantry* (London, 1913), p. 131.

4. Augustus Warburton (d. May 22, 1836), who had been inspecting field officer of militia in Canada in 1811, was appointed to the 41st Regiment on September 3, 1813. He joined the 85th Regiment on May 11, 1815. See Barrett, *The 85th King's Light Infantry*, p. 534.

5. George Brown (1790–1865), who joined the British army in 1806, fought in America during the War of 1812 and was wounded at Bladensburg. He was made brevet lieutenant colonel on September 29, 1814. See Barrett, *The 85th King's Light Infantry*, p. 476.

6. Charles Richard Fox (1796–1873) served in the Royal Navy from 1809 to 1813 and was then appointed ensign in the 85th Regiment on June 29, 1815. He later joined the Grenadier Guards, in which he rose to the rank of general. See Barrett, *The 85th King's Light Infantry*, p. 492.

188. To Henry Brevoort

Liverpool, May 20th. 1817.

My dear Brevoort,

Mrs Schmidt[1] and her sister Helen Bache[2] are on the point of embarking for New York. I cannot let them depart without sending you a line though I have nothing worth communicating. They have revived a thousand reccollections of past scenes of innocent pleasure and light hearted enjoyment. Mrs Schmidt has given me several anecdotes of you while on a visit at Kinderhook, which ⟨has⟩ completely placed you before me. She has a pretty knack at narration, and indeed I have been delighted by the pleasing *naive* manner in which both these little lady travellers recount their adventures and the wonders they have seen. Mrs Schmidt looks pale & delicate; she is too tender a plant to bear much rough weather. Helen is greatly improved in every respect since I saw her in America. She will no doubt be a Belle on her return, and as you are a veteran in the fashionable world I commend her to your fostering countenance & protection. You cant think how my heart warms at the sight of these lovely little beings associated as they are with home feelings & home reccollections. Their sudden appearance in Liverpool has been like an "Angel visit" to me, and like angels they seem to ↑beckon↓ me away to a better world; but sinful mortal that I am, I must still linger behind on this dim spot of earth. I have assisted in shewing them the Lions of Liverpool, which they have regarded with the supreme *sang froid* of experienced travellers, intimating that they have seen vast deal better things in Germany. Helen Bache takes notes and threatens to eclipse Lady Morgans France[3]— I beg you will be particular in questioning her about Wrexham church, Windsor Castle and the rows at Chester.

I was greatly concerned some short time since at hearing of the death of ⟨Eliza⟩ ↑Mrs.↓ Verplanck.[4] I had previously received very discouraging accounts of the state of her health but had hoped the climate of France would have restored her. Verplanck was here about a fortnight since and has gone to Scotland. He seemed in good health and tolerable spirits, though thinner than usual. His conversation was quite enlivening to me. He talks of returning to the continent, & particularly of re-visiting Holland previously to his return home. I feel very anxious for Mrs Hoffmans health.[5] The repeated trials she is doomed to undergo, must, in spite of her habitual meekness and resignation, prey on her heart and render life utterly joyless. You tell me that Mr. H. suffers from the hardships of the times. I should have thought men in his profession rather likely to benefit by them. I wish he would give up political life[6]—it is a vile tissue of petty trick & intrigue in the State

of New York, & unaccompanied by either honour or real advantage —
His business would alway[s]⁷ ensure him high respectability and
abundant support.

Yesterday [I]⁸ dined ⟨with⟩↑at↓ Mr Davidsons for the first time
[this] [*MS torn*] season; for I have avoided all company as much as
possible. Mrs Davidson shewed me a letter from Mrs Renwick which
presented a perfect picture of her happy household, and also contained some kind remembrances to myself. I wish when you see Mrs
R. you would give her my most affectionate reccollections, and remember
me also to James and his Spouse and the rest of that charming family
circle. I hope I have yet some happy days in store to be passed among
them when the present storms & glooms of adversity have passed away.

God bless you my dear Brevoort/Your friend
W I.

PS. Peter desires to be commended heartily to you.

ADDRESSED: For / Henry Brevoort Jr. Esquire / at Mrs Bradish's / New York
    DOCKETED: Liver[pool] [*MS torn*] 20 May 1817 / W Irving
MANUSCRIPT: NYPL—Seligman Collection.   PUBLISHED: LIB, II, 23–26.

1. Mrs. Schmidt (née Eliza A. Bache, 1797–1874) married J. W. Schmidt in
1815. See [Oscar Egerton Schmidt], *Smaller New York and Family Reminiscences:
de Rham, Schmidt, Bache, Barclay, Paul Richard* (New York, 1899), p. 29.

2. Helen Bache (1799–1864) was the sister of Eliza Bache Schmidt and the
youngest child of William Bache (1773–1829). See Schmidt, *Smaller New York*,
p. 29.

3. Lady Morgan (Sydney Owenson) published *France* in London in 1817. A
French edition was published in Paris in the same year.

4. Eliza Fenno, whom Verplanck married in 1811, died in Paris on April 29.
1817, from consumption. See July, *Verplanck*, pp. 50–51.

5. Like her sister, Mrs. Verplanck, Mrs. Hoffman had a rather delicate constitution.

6. Although Hoffman was a justice of the New York Supreme Court, he was
probably involved behind the scenes in the special election for governor in April,
1817. See Dennis Tilden Lynch, "The Growth of Political Parties," in *History of
the State of New York*, ed. Alexander C. Flick (Port Washington, N.Y., 1962),
VI, 50–51.

7. WI omitted the *s* from the word.

8. WI inadvertently omitted the "I."

189.   To Washington Allston

Birmingham. May 21st. 1817.

My dear Alston,

Your letter of the 9th. inst and likewise the parcel containing the
pictures came safely to hand and should have been acknowledged
sooner, but I have been much discomposed since last I wrote to you,

by intelligence of the death of my mother.[1] Her extreme age made such an event constantly probable, but I had hoped to have seen her once more before she died, and was anxious to return home soon on that account. That hope is now at an end,—and with it my immediate wish to return, so that I think it probable I shall linger some time longer in Europe.

I have been much struck with your conception of the Warning of Belchazzar.[2] It is grand & poetical; affording scope for all the beauties & glories of the pencil, and if it is but executed in the spirit in which it is conceived, I am confident will ensure you both profit and renown. As to its future fate however, ⟨leave that to⟩ never let that occupy you[r][3] mind—unless it be to stimulate you to exertion. As to sending it to America, I would only observe, that unless I got very advantageous offers for my paintings I would rather do so—as it is infinitely preferable to stand foremost as one of the founders of a school of painting in an immense, & growing country like America, in fact to be an object of national pride and affection, than to fall into the ranks in the crowded galleries of Europe; or perhaps be regarded with an eye of national prejudice, as the production of an American pencil is likely to be in England. I will not pretend at this moment to discuss the merits of your design for the proposed painting; I do not feel in the vein; but if at a more cheerful moment any idea suggests itself, that I may think worth communicating, I will write to you —

I cannot express to you how much I have been pleased with the two designs for Knickerbocker[4] — The characters are admirably discriminated, the humour rich, but chaste, and the ⟨whole effect perfectly⟩ ↑expressions peculiarly↓natural and appropriate. I scarcely know which figure in your picture to prefer; the Constable is evidently drawn *Con Amore,* and derives additional spirit from standing in high relief opposed to the ineffable phlegm of old Wouter. Still however the leering exultation of the fortunate party is given to the very life, and is evident from top to toe — the bend of the knee, the play of the elbows, the swaying of the body are all eloquent; and are finely contrasted with the attitude and look of little Schoonhoven; By the way, I must say the last figure, has tickled me as much as any in the picture — But each has its peculiar merits, and is the *best* in its turn. The Sketch by Leslie is beautiful; ⟨He has⟩ The dutch girl is managed with great sweetness & naiveté — the expression of her chin and mouth shews that she is not likely to break her lovers heart. The devoted lear of the lovers eye and the phlegmatic character of the lower part of his countenance form a whimsical combination The very cat is an important figure in the groupe & touched off with proper expression. A delicate humour pervades the whole; the composition is graceful and there is a rural air about it that is peculiarly pleasing. I dwell on these little sketches, because they give me quite a new train of ideas in respect to my work: and I only wish I had it now to write, as I am sure I should conceive the scenes in a much purer style; having these pic[tures] [MS torn] before me as corrections of that *grossierté* into which the sent[iment of?] [MS torn] a work of humour is apt to run. At any rate it is an exquisite gratification to find that any thing I have written can present such pleasing images to imaginations like yours & Leslie's; and I shall regard the work with more complacency, as having in a manner, formed a link of association between our minds

The law suit[5] was [a]n[6] entirely imaginary incident, without any personal allusion, ⟨I believ⟩ though by a whimsical coincidence there was a Barent Bleecker at Albany[7] who had been comptroller; and his family at first suspected an intention to asperse his official character. The suspicion however was but transient, and is forgotten; so that the picture will awaken no hostility

I had no idea, when I began this letter that I should have filled the sheet; but words beget words; I shall write to you again before long and will then endeavour to direct my attention to topics more immediately interesting to you. In the mean while give my most friendly remembrances to Leslie & believe me truly Yours.

Washington Irving

ADDRESSED: For / Washington Allston Esqr / Buckingham place / Fitzroy Square / London   POSTMARKED: [unrecovered] / 22 MY 22 / 1817 / [unrecovered] 23 MY 23 / 1817   DOCKETED: Washn. Irving / 21 May 1817
MANUSCRIPT: Harvard.   PUBLISHED: PMI, I, 365–68; Waldron, WI and Cotemporaries, pp. 230–31.

1. Sarah Sanders Irving (b. April 14, 1738) died on April 9, 1817.
2. Allston's painting, measuring twelve by sixteen feet, was based on the account in Dan. 5. Later Allston started to change the perspective in the painting, a task left unfinished at the time of his death. See Flagg, *Washington Allston*, pp. 334–35.
3. WI omitted the *r* when he wrote the word.
4. These were sent by Allston and included his sketch of Wouter Van Twiller's decision in the case of Wandle Schoonhoven and Barent Bleecker (Book III, Chapter I) and a design by Charles Leslie on the Dutch courtship (Book III, Chapter IV).
5. This episode is recounted in Book III, Chapter I of *Knickerbocker's History*.
6. An ink blot obscures the *a*.
7. Barent Bleecker (b. June 9, 1760), a prominent businessman and financier in Albany, was never comptroller of the state of New York, though he was president of the Albany Bank from 1820 to 1840. Since Bleecker was childless, the protests about WI's treatment in *Knickerbocker's History* were probably made by Bleecker's brother Rutger and his sister Blandina and their families. See Jerome B. Holgate, *American Genealogy* (Albany, 1848), p. 93; and *Landmarks of Albany County, New York*, ed. Amasa J. Parker (Syracuse, 1897), pp. 363–64.

190.   To Henry Brevoort

Birmingham, May 26th. 1817.

My dear Brevoort,

I forward to you printed sheets of the greater part of the two first volumes of Campbells new Work,[1] which he had sent to me, understanding that I was about to sail for America. He wishes to try if something cannot be procured for them from an American Bookseller.[2] I am sure you will take a pleasure in promoting his interest in this particular; and any emolument that may arise from the experiment will be of importance to him for I believe his purse is rather light.

He does not seem very sanguine of the result and is willing to abide by any bargain that can be made. He says he is affraid the work will not appear very tempting to an American Bookseller on the first inspection of the sheets forwarded & that he may not be captivated by the selections from old & almost obsolete authors which take up the earlier part; but he says the last half of the publication is better than the present, and not so dry. The whole will be preceded by a dissertation giving an account of all the eminent poets ⟨od⟩ containing a conspectus of the history of English poetry.[3] This I make no doubt will be a most able and interesting article. This prefatory essay he can send in Mss but nothing else, as he makes continual alterations while the work is printing. He will however send out the sheets as fast as they are printed; so that if a Bookseller begins at once to reprint it he will be able to get the work out in America within a week or two of its appearance here. An advantage to any Bookseller taking this copy would be that should the work come to a second Edition Campbell, can supply him with additions that would prevent competition.

Eastburn[4] once agreed to share the profits of the first edition with Mr Campbell but I presume Eastburn is not publishing at present & not in circumstances to make a good bargain. If Campbell were to furnish additional matter for a second edition he ought likewise to share the profits of the latter. If you could sell the work out & out for a decent sum down it would be preferable — I have no doubt that Campbells name & reputation will give the work a run at first, and its merits will render it a *stock book* of regular demand & consequently *good property* It is therefore well worth the attention of some steady man in the trade. If you make a bargain to share profits take care that it is with some one of this description for the generality of ⟨Am⟩ our booksellers are so much on the grasp and the stretch that they ⟨can scarcely ever⟩ never know what their profits are; or if they do, they cannot command money to pay their debts punctually. Should you receive any money for campbell ⟨dir⟩ remit it direct to him at *Sydenham near London*[5] and you had better communicate direct with him as to any arrangements you may make. Excuse all this trouble which I am giving you my dear fellow but I know no other channel through which to promote poor Campbells wishes in America

I received some time⟨s⟩ since your kind letter[6] urging my return — I had even come to the resolution to do so immediately, but the news of my dear mothers death put an end to one strong inducement that was continually tugging at my heart, and other reasons have compelled me to relinquish the idea for the present. I have led a fitful miserable kind of life for a long time past — Now & then a little gleam of sunshine to rally up my spirits, but always sure to be followed by redoubled gloom. The cares & sorrows of the world seem thickening upon me and though I battle with them to the utmost & keep up a steady front, yet they will sometimes drag me down — However I do not wish to trouble you with my complainings and if I do not write to you often believe me it is not for want of having you constantly in my thoughts, but because I have nothing pleasing to write about. Remember me affectionately to all such as take an interest in my welfare God Bless you my dear Brevoort and keep you prosperous & happy —

Yours ever
Washington Irving

ADDRESSED: For / Henry Brevoort Junr Esq / at Mrs Bradishes / State Street / New York. / p Betsey   DOCKETED: May 25, 1817
MANUSCRIPT: NYPL—WI Papers.   PUBLISHED: LIB, II, 27–31; PMI I, 365 (in part).

1. A reference to Thomas Campbell's *Specimens of the British Poets*, which was published in 1819 in seven volumes.

2. Apparently no American bookseller was willing to publish Campbell's selections, for the title is not listed in Ralph R. Shaw and Richard H. Shoemaker, *American Bibliography, A Preliminary Checklist for 1819* (New York, 1963).

3. This treatise was published as *An Essay on English Poetry* (Boston, 1819).

4. James Eastburn was a bookseller who had literary rooms at the corner of Wall and Broad Streets. See NYEP, January 6, 1817.

5. Campbell lived at Sydenham from 1804 to 1820.

6. This letter has not been located.

191. To Henry Brevoort

Liverpool, June 7th. 1817.

My dear Brevoort,

I have made repeated attempts to reply to your letter of 30th. April[1] but have torn the page to pieces before I had filled it; yet I cannot suffer that letter to lie unacknowledged, for it was a perfect cordial to my feelings.

I have felt the correctness of your advice that I should return home & had prepared to do so, but troubles have thickened upon us & I cannot leave Peter to buffet them alone.[2] I do not pretend to render any active assistance. I have long been utterly passive in respect to business; but my company is of importance to keep up his spirits in these trying times. Do not imagine I suffer myself to be broken down and unmanned by complicated evils. I have made up my mind to them & indeed grown familiar with them by dismal anticipation. As you observe it is useless to attempt to "patch up grief with musty proverbs,"[3] there is a nothing-ness in all verbal consolation & sympathy. The heart is competent to digest its own sorrows — Your letter gave the true kind of consolation; it filled my mind with agreeable ideas of distant friends, and home scenes, where I yet hope to find some pleasure in existence. You have furnished me with quite a train of pleasing meditations and diverted my thoughts from my own dreary situation.

I am happy to find, by the account you give of my lovely friend Mrs Campbell[4] that she had recovered from the shock her spirits must have received from her fathers death. It is singular that I had been dreaming of her the very night before I received your letter, and had fancied myself taking a long ramble with her in which she had said a thousand witty & agreeable things, not one of which, as usual, I could reccollect on waking. When next you see her, tell her I am infinitely gratified by her friendly reccollection. I do not remember the circumstances you allude to of her veto against the story of Jessy Marvin,[5] but it could not help being good as she was concerned in it. I dare say it was some joke at my expense, and I always take care to forget such jokes as soon as possible.

The marriage of Serena L——[6] is in the best style of modern romance. I hope the Colonel[7] is as amiable in the parlour as he is gallant in the field; if so, he is the very man for her. I should not have liked to hear of her marrying some common placed Counting house gentleman.

I have had a very friendly message from Jack Nicholson,[8] through one of his relations resident in Liverpool, & am glad to hear the worthy little Tar is promoted to a Captaincy. He writes that he does not despair of commanding a *seventy four* before he dies; but I rather think Jack was speaking in parables, as he must have been about that time opening his batteries upon the younger Miss Nevison[9] who Frank Ogden tells me is about *six feet high* — Jack had always too great a heart for his little body. Moores new poem[10] is just out. I have not sent it to you, for it is ⟨very⟩ dear and worthless. It is written in the most effeminate taste & fit only to delight boarding school girls & lads of nineteen just in their first loves. Moore should have kept to songs & epigramatic conceits. His stream of intellect is too small to bear expansion, it spreads into mere surface.[11]

Mr & Mrs Derby[12] have been two or three days in Liverpool but I have not seen them. Indeed I am living like a hermit, passing my time entirely at home, excepting now & then I take a walk out of ↑town↓ for exercise, or pay a visit to Peter Ogden[13] who is in our neighbourhood, & is confined to the house by indisposition This is a singular contrast to the life I once led, but one gets accustomed to every thing, and I feel perfectly contented to keep out of sight of the world & indeed have at present no relish for so[ciety.] [*MS torn*]

Such a mode of life affords scanty material for letter writing, and you must excuse me for being very dull. Indeed I had no idea of getting through this letter as well as I have when I commenced.

Remember me affectionately to Mrs Renwick & her family, to Mrs Bradish & the girls and to my worthy friend the Governor who I hope still reigns undisturbed over the Colony.

God bless you my dear Brevoort/Affectionately yours

WI.

ADDRESSED: For / Henry Brevoort Junr Esq— / at Mrs Bradish's / New York / p Favorite   DOCKETED: Liverpool 7 June 1817 / Washington Irving
MANUSCRIPT: NYPL—Seligman Collection.   PUBLISHED: LIB, II, 32–36.

1. This letter has not been located.

2. The troubles resulted from Peter Irving's overpurchase of English goods for shipment to America at a time when the demand for such imports was declining. See STW, I, 149–54; PMI, I, 341.

3. Probably a variant of *Much Ado About Nothing*, V, i, 341.

4. Mrs. Archibald Campbell, the wife of Thomas Campbell's brother living in the United States, had moved in the same social circles in New York and Philadelphia as had WI. See WI's letter to Brevoort, August 19, 1815.

5. WI may be referring to Jesse Merwin.

6. For a summary of WI's feelings toward Serena Livingston, see M. A. Weatherspoon, "1815–1819: Prelude to Irving's *Sketch Book*," *American Literature* 41 (January, 1970), 566–71.

7. Colonel George Croghan (1791–1849), a nephew of George Rogers Clark, had distinguished himself in the War of 1812 in the fighting in the Maumee River valley.

8. This letter has not been located.

9. Nicholson's romance with Miss Louisa Nevison apparently captured the interest of his bachelor friends. Paulding speaks of Nicholson's being "sorely handled" by Miss Nevison at Norfolk. See *Letters of J. K. Paulding*, p. 51.

10. Thomas Moore's poem, "Lalla Rookh," which was published in May, 1817, became, despite WI's strictures, very popular.

11. Although WI was a severe critic of Thomas Moore at this time, they later became fast friends when WI met the Irish poet in England and France.

12. Elias Haskett Derby (1766–1826), a New England merchant engaged in

overseas trading, was married to Lucy Brown. See WI's letter of May 13, 1807, to Mary Fairlie.

13. Peter Ogden (1785–1820), a merchant in New Orleans, died there of yellow fever. He was in partnership with his brother George (1779–1824). See Wheeler, *Ogden Family*, p. 253.

192. To Henry Brevoort

Liverpool, June 11th. 1817.

My dear Brevoort,

I have forwarded you ↑to collect↓ on behalf of Mr Muncaster, Bookseller, a set of Exchg. drawn by our house in his favour, on Moses Thomas ↑for books sent the latter.↓ It was the only mode that presented of closing this a/c with the Bookseller; as we did not wish such a petty a/c to ⟨remain⟩ be unpaid — I wish you would be accommodating to Thomas in settling it; but he has been remiss in remitting to us in advance, or such an a/c would not have accumulated. It is thus one always gets in petty scrapes by trying to serve others.

Van Wart has called a meeting of his creditors on the 23d inst.[1] They are friendly in their dispositions towards him & I hope he will get favourable terms.

I write in haste — Peter is well and so am I, which is as much as can be expected in these hard times —

Your friend
W I.

ADDRESSED: Henry Brevoort Jr. Eqr— / at Mrs Bradishs / New York. / pr. *Favourite*⟩ DOCKETED: Livep: June 11. 1817 / W Irving
MANUSCRIPT: NYPL—Seligman Collection. PUBLISHED: LIB, II, 37.

WI sent two letters to Brevoort on the same day dealing with the same subject, possibly by different ships to insure the safe arrival of at least one of them.

1. The Birmingham Public Library has three circulars relating to Henry Van Wart's financial difficulties in 1817. The first, dated June 23, 1817, reports a meeting of Van Wart's creditors, chaired by Thomas Attwood, at which they agreed to accept settlement from Van Wart of nine shillings on each pound of indebtedness. On July 3, 1817, William Wallis, a disgruntled creditor, issued another circular denying that he had called Van Wart a swindler. Wallis also describes a meeting with Van Wart on the street during which Van Wart threatened to pull Wallis's nose. This dialogue led to an exchange of blows between the two men. A third circular of July 31, 1817, tells of Wallis's son's going to Van Wart's house and horsewhipping him. In a concluding note Wallis observes that Van Wart, "after residing in Birmingham about seven years, had obtained credit for near £100,000 sterling, and had offered a composition of 9s. in the pound, by *his* acceptance. And the creditors were also told that, on *certain conditions*, if any should object to so long a period, and prefer a guarantee in this country, at 12 months after date, for *five* shillings in the pound, responsible purchasers would be found." Appar-

ently Van Wart's financial problems were not resolved in 1817, for he declared himself bankrupt and surrendered to the commissioners for hearings on February 13, 14, and 28, 1818. Probably his failure is related to that of Peter and Washington Irving, for the notice of all three bankruptcies appeared in *Aris's Birmingham Gazette* on February 9, 1818. Since Van Wart's hearings were held in Birmingham, notice of them also appeared in the two following issues of the weekly newspaper.

193. To Henry Brevoort

Liverpool June 11th 1817.

Dear Brevoort,

We have drawn on Mr Moses Thomas of Philadelphia, in favour of *Mr Thomas Muncaster Bookseller, Church Street, Liverpool,* for Books forwarded at various times to Mr Thomas. As Mr Muncaster has no correspondent in ⟨N York⟩ America, you will do me a favour in collecting the amount of the Bill for him, & forwarding it to h⟨im⟩is address as above

Your friend[1]

Washington Irving

P S. Mr Muncaster has ⟨forwarded⟩ procured most of the works I formerly sent to you & should you have any further commands of the kind I would reccommend him to a continuance of your favours.

ADDRESSED: Henry Brevoort Jr. Esqr. / at Mrs Bradish's / New York / p Golconda
    DOCKETED: Liverpool Jun 11. 1817 / W *Irving*
MANUSCRIPT: NYPL—WI Papers & Seligman.   PUBLISHED: LIB, II, 38.

WI sent two copies of this letter to Brevoort, the second by the *Favourite*. The second version is identical to the first, but without the cancellations and with "(2d)" at the top of the sheet. The endorsement to the left of the signature is also different: "Bill £70 St.g / favor Thos. Muncaster / 2nd of Exchg." This copy is in NYPL—Seligman Collection.

1. Along the left side, opposite the complimentary close and the signature is written "lt of Exc £ / favor Thos. Muncaster."

194. To Henry Brevoort

Liverpool, June 21st. 1817.

My dear Brevoort

Mr Coles,[1] late Secretary of Mr Madison, is passenger in the Tea plant[2] & has a number of the Edinburgh Review for you. I believe you are acquainted with him, If not I hope you will become so as he is a very worthy fellow —

Peter and myself are in good health

God Bless you —

WI.

P.S. I believe I some time since requested you to procure me some Books &c but you need not do so, as I shall not have money to repay you — I hope however you have sent me Styles Judges.[3]

MANUSCRIPT: NYPL—Seligman Collection.   PUBLISHED: LIB, II, 39.

1. Edward Coles (1786–1868), a cousin of Mrs. Madison, was returning from a diplomatic mission to Russia at this time.

2. According to NYEP, August 7, 1817, the ship *Tea Plant,* commanded by Captain Brown, arrived in New York on August 6, 1817, after a journey of 43 days.

3. Also mentioned in WI's letter of January 29, 1817.

195. *To Henry Brevoort*

Liverpool July 11th. 1817.

My dear Brevoort,

Your letter of June 11th.[1] has remained for several days unanswered, though I have made many attempts at a reply. I find it almost impossible under the present circumstances to write letters; but your kind inquiries spring from too friendly a feeling to be disregarded.

I have no intention of returning home for a year at least. I am waiting here to ⟨[*unrecovered*]⟩ extricate myself from the ruins of our unfortunate concern after which I shall turn my back upon this scene of care & distress, and shall ⟨henceforth for⟩ pass ⟨the⟩ a considerable part of my time in London. I have a plan[2] which, with very little trouble, will yield me for the present a scanty but sufficient means of support, and leave me leisure to look round for something better. I cannot at present explain to you what it is — you would probably consider it precarious, & inadequate to my subsistence — but a small matter will float a drowning man and I have dwelt so much of late on the prospect of being cast homeless & pennyless upon the world; that I feel relieved in having even a straw to catch at.

I have weighed every thing *pro and con* on the subject of returning home & have for the present abandoned the idea. My affections would at once prompt me to return but in doing so, would they insure me any happiness? Would they not on the contrary be productive of misery? I should find those I love, & whom I had left prosperous — struggling with adversity without my being able to yield them comfort or assistance. Every scene of past enjoyment would be a cause of regret & discontent. I should have no immediate mode of support & should be ⟨?au?⟩ perhaps a burthen to my friends who have claims enough on their sympathy & exertions. No — no — if I must scuffle with poverty let me do it out of sight — where I am but little known — where I cannot even myself contrast present penury with former affluence. In this country I have a plan for immediate support — it may lead to something better — at any rate it places me for the time above the horrors of destitution or the more galling mortifications of dependence —

Besides I am accustomed & reconciled to ⟨adversity in the⟩ the features of adversity in this country; but were I to return to America I should find it under a new face and have to go through something of what I have already experienced before I could get on similar terms of familiarity.

I hope I have now given you sufficient reasons for my remaining abroad. My mind is made up to it: & though now and then, when I get letters from home, particularly yours which paint home scenes so vividly, I feel my heart yearning towards New York with almost a sickly longing, yet I am convinced I am acting for the best. ⟨Let me for a time depend upon my self & endeavour to ?slip from? out my [*unrecovered*]⟩

I wish circumstances would induce you to come out to Europe. You talk of visiting Canada — why not cross the Atlantic. The obstacles are merely ideal — Three weeks would land you in England — Profit might be combined with the visit. But I dont wish to hold out temptations that may lead to evil —

Remember me affectionately to such of my friends as enquire after me, and if any complain of my not writing ↑to them↓ tell them I have lost the art —

God Bless you my dear Brevoort/Your friend

WI.

ADDRESSED: To / Henry Brevoort Jr Esq— / at Mrs Bradish's / New York. / p
    Illinois}   DOCKETED: Lipl: July 11 1817 / W Irving
MANUSCRIPT: NYPL—Seligman Collection.   PUBLISHED: LIB, II, 40–43; PMI, I,
    368–69 (in part).

1. This letter has not been located.
2. WI had apparently begun note-taking for essays in *The Sketch Book* by early summer of 1817; by August he had already drafted several sketches. See STW, I, 166, 168.

196. To Henry Brevoort

Liverpool, July 21st 1817.

Dear Brevoort,

Sometime since[1] I forwarded to you our Bill on Moses Thomas for 70£ Stg. in favour of Mr Thomas Muncaster,[2] with a request that you would collect it & forward the proceeds to Muncaster. This was for the purpose of securing a debt to the latter for books purchased for Thomas. We have lately received a remittance from Thomas of 100£. Should therefore our Draft on him have been presented & accepted, you need not present it for payt. but cancel it & return it to us.

By Mr McEvers,[3] who sails in the Anna Maria[4] I send you a collection of discoveries &c in Africa.[5]

I write in haste as the bag is about to be taken away in which this letter goes —

Your friend

WI.

ADDRESSED: To / Henry Brevoort Jr Esquire / at Mrs Bradish's / New York. / p
    Ann Maria}   DOCKETED: Liverpool 21 July 1817 W Irving / W Irving
MANUSCRIPT: NYPL–Seligman Collection.   PUBLISHED: LIB, II, 44.

1. See WI's letter of June 11, 1817.
2. Thomas Muncaster ran a bookshop at the corner of Church and Basnett Streets across from St. Peter's Church. See Picton, *Memorials of Liverpool*, II, 158.
3. This may be Charles McEvers (1764–1841), whom WI knew through his acquaintance with John Robert Livingston. Livingston's son later married McEvers' daughter. See *Bayard Genealogy and Bayard Family Notes* (unpaged) at NYHS.
4. The *Anna Maria*, commanded by Captain Wait, arrived in New York on August 13, 1817.
5. This is probably James Riley, *An Authentic Narrative of the Loss of the American Brig Commerce, Wrecked on the Western Coast of Africa, in the Month of August, 1815 . . . With An Account of the Sufferings of the Surviving Officers and Crew, Who Were Enslaved by Wandering Arabs* . . . (London, 1817).

197.   To Peter Irving

London, Aug. 19, 1817.

My dear Brother:

I have yours of the 17th. I received likewise the parcel, which contained a letter from Brevoort, and one from Mrs. Bradish. I enclose Brevoort's to you.[1]

I had a very pleasant dinner at Murray's.[2] I met there with D'Israeli,[3] and an artist,[4] just returned from Italy with an immense number of beautiful sketches of Italian scenery and architecture.

D'Israeli's wife[5] and daughter[6] came in, in the course of the evening, and we did not adjourn until twelve o'clock. I had a long tête-á-tête with old D'Israeli in a corner. He is a very pleasant[7] cheerful old fellow; curious about America, and evidently tickled at the circulation his works have had there; though, like most authors just now, he groans at not being able to participate in the profits. Murray was very merry and loquacious. He showed me a long letter from Lord Byron,[8] who is in Italy. It is written with some flippancy, and is an odd jumble. His lordship has written 104 stanzas of the 4th canto. He says it will be less metaphysical than the last canto, but thinks it will be at least equal to either of the preceding. Murray left town yesterday for some watering-place, so that I had no further talk with him; but am to keep my eye on his advertisements, and write to him when any thing offers that I may think worth republishing in America. I shall find him a most valuable acquaintance on my return to London.

I called at Longman & Co.'s,[9] according to appointment, and saw Mr. Orme.[10] They are not disposed, however, to make any arrangement.[11] They have been repeatedly disappointed in experiments of the kind, and are determined not to trouble their thoughts any more on the subject. They had just received letters from America on the subject of Moore's poem Lalla Rookh, which they had sent out either in MSS. or sheets; but there were two or three rival editions in the market,[12] which would prevent any profits of consequence.

They intimated that they would be willing to give an advantage in respect to the republication of new works, for any moderate price in cash; but they would not perplex and worry themselves with any further arrangements, which were only troublesome and profitless. They intimated, for instance, a disposition to sell an early copy of *Rob Roy* for a small sum in hand. But as I knew they had not yet received the MSS. of that work, I did not make any offer. It will be time enough by-and-bye. I find it is pretty generally believed that Scott is the author of those novels, and Verplanck[13] tells me he is now travelling about, collecting materials for Rob Roy. I see that there will be a great advantage in being here on the spot during the literary seasons, with funds to make purchases from either authors or booksellers. They consider the chance of participation in American republication so very slender and contingent, that they will accept any sum in hand, as so much money found. I have written to Thomas, advising him to remit funds to me for the purpose; if he does so, I will be able to throw many choice works into his hands.

Mishter Miller[14] is full of the project of going out to New York, to set up an establishment there. He thinks he will have an advantage in publishing plays, from his interest with the theatres here, which will enable him to get MS. copies, and the countenance of King Stephen,[15] which has been promised him. He talks of embarking in September or October, should he be able to make his arrangements in time. He must beware the "Dusky Davy."[16]

PUBLISHED: PMI, I, 373–75.

1. These letters have not been located.

2. John Murray (1778–1843) carried on the publishing business started by his father at 50 Albemarle Street. Murray's drawing room was renowned as a gathering place for writers, especially those whose books he published. See James K.

Paulding, *A Sketch of Old England, by a New England Man* (New York, 1822),
II, 135 (cited by STW, I, 433). For other details, see WIHM, pp. 3–9.

3. Isaac D'Israeli (1766–1848), who was independently wealthy, devoted himself to writing. By 1817 three volumes of his *Curiosities of Literature* had appeared.

4. William Brockedon (1787–1854) was a painter and inventor who exhibited
regularly in the Royal Academy and British Institution shows.

5. D'Israeli married Maria Basevi (1775–1847) in 1802.

6. Sarah D'Israeli (1802–1859), who never married, helped her father, after
his blindness, to complete the *Amenities of Literature* (1841).

7. The three-volume abridgement of PMI (ca. 1869) has a comma following
"pleasant," an addition probably made by an editor at Putnam's. For the four-
volume edition PMI probably followed WI's holograph, presumably without the
comma, for his transcription.

8. Byron's letter written from Venice on July 15, 1817, reports that he had
written 104 stanzas of Canto IV of *Childe Harold's Pilgrimage*. See *The Works
of Lord Byron. Letters and Journals*, vol. IV, ed. Rowland E. Prothero (London,
1904), 153.

9. Longman was a bookseller located on Paternoster Row.

10. Orme was one of the partners of Longman & Company. By 1826, through
the successive introduction of partners, the firm was known as Longman, Hurst,
Rees, Orme, Brown, & Green.

11. WI had sounded out Mr. Orme about the possibility of reprinting some good
American books, as he was to approach Murray two months later. See WI to Murray,
October 16, 1817; WIHM, p. 13; STW, I, 157.

12. Thomas Moore's *Lalla Rookh, An Oriental Romance* was published by Longman, Hurst, Rees, Orme, and Brown in 1817; an American edition by Moses Thomas
also appeared in 1817.

13. WI's former collaborator on the *Analectic Magazine*, Gulian Verplanck, had
recently come from Paris after the death of his wife Eliza (the sister of Maria
Fenno Hoffman) of consumption. See July, *Verplanck*, p. 53.

14. John Miller, an English publisher who specialized in American authors,
brought out the first volume of WI's *Sketch Book*. See WIHM, pp. 6–9, 10, 19. PMI
(I, 375) places *"sic"* after "Mishter."

15. Stephen Price was the manager of the Park Theater in New York.

16. David Longworth, the publisher of *Salmagundi*.

198.   To Peter Irving

[Edinburgh, August 26, 1817]

The first two days of our voyage[1] were unfavorable; we had rain and
head wind, and had to anchor whenever the tide turned. But Saturday,
though calm, was beautiful, with a bright sunny afternoon and a bright
moon at night. On Sunday we had a glorious breeze, and dashed bravely
through the water. I have always fine health and fine spirits at sea,
and enjoyed the latter part of this little voyage excessively. On Monday morning we came in sight of the coast of Northumberland, which at
first was wrapped in mist; but as it cleared away, we saw Dunstanborough

Castle[2] at a distance; and some time after, we passed in full view of
Bamborough Castle,[3] which stands in bleak and savage grandeur on the
sea-coast. You may recollect these places, mentioned in the course of
the Abbess of Hilda's voyage in Marmion:[4]

> "And next they crossed themselves to hear
> The whitening breakers sound so near,
> Where boiling through the rocks they roar
> On Dunstanborough's caverned shore.
> Thy tower, proud Bamborough, marked they there;
> King Ida's castle, huge and square,
> From its tall rock look grimly down
> And on the swelling ocean frown."

We next skirted the Holy Isle,[5] which was the scene of Constance
de Beverly's trial;[6] and where the remains of the Monastery of St. Cuthbert[7] are still visible; though apparently converted into some humbler
purposes, as a residence of people that attend the beacons. To make a
long story short, however, about twelve o'clock I landed at Berwick.
I had intended proceeding from thence to Kelso, and so to Melrose,[8]
&c.; but I found there would be no coach in that direction until Wednesday; so I determined to come to Edinburgh direct, and visit Melrose
from thence. After walking about Berwick, therefore, and surveying
its old bridge, walls, &c., I mounted a coach and rattled off through the
rich scenes of Lothian to this place, where I arrived late last night.

I got the parcel from you this morning; but neither Mrs. Fletcher[9]
nor Mr. Erskine[10] are in town. I left a card for Jeffrey,[11] whose family
is three miles out of town. His brother[12] called on me about an hour
afterwards, but I was not at home. Edinburgh is perfectly deserted, so
that I shall merely have to look at the buildings, streets, &c., and then
be off. I am enchanted with the general appearance of the place. It
far surpasses all my expectations; and, except Naples, is, I think, the
most picturesque place I have ever seen.

I dined to-day with Mr. Jeffrey, Mrs. Renwick's[13] brother. He informs
me that Mrs. Fletcher is in Selkirkshire, but that the family is rather
secluded, having lost one of the young ladies about three months since
by a typhus fever. I did not learn which it was. Mrs. Grant[14] is likewise
in the Highlands.

Walter Scott[15] is at Abbotsford;[16] busy, it is supposed, about Rob
Roy, having lately been travelling for scenery, &c. They told me at
Constable's[17] that it will be out in October, though others say not until
towards Christmas.[18] As it will probably be some days before Preston[19]
reaches here, I do not know but I shall make an excursion to Melrose, and

make an attempt on Walter Scott's quarters, so as to be back in time to accompany Preston to the Highlands. I have a very particular letter to Scott from Campbell.[20] * * *

August 27th.—A gloomy morning, with a steady pitiless rain. What a contrast to the splendor of yesterday, which was a warm day, with now and then a very light shower, and an atmosphere loaded with rich clouds through which the sunshine fell in broad masses; giving an endless diversity of light and shadow to the grand romantic features of this town. It seemed as if the rock and castle assumed a new aspect every time I looked at them; and Arthur's seat was perfect witchcraft. I don't wonder that any one residing in Edinburgh should write poetically; I rambled about the bridges and on Calton height yesterday, in a perfect intoxication of the mind. I did not visit a single public building; but merely gazed and revelled on the romantic scenery around me. The enjoyment of yesterday alone would be a sufficient compensation for the whole journey.

But I must bring this rambling letter to a close. I am delighted with the idea of your Welsh excursion. What a charming party you have! One of the Miss Mathers I have seen two or three times at Mrs. Bolton's,[21] and was very much pleased with her; the Boltons, Jays, and Woolseys,[22] are lovely beings. I wish I could despatch one-half of me to accompany you. Oh! for a little of Townshend ubiquity.[23] I trust you will have that embryo nabob back to Liverpool before long. I made two or three rambles with him in London. He is the very man for a ramble of the kind. I feel really sorry that he is going to India, for he is truly a worthy, good fellow. * * *

There is nobody in Edinburgh, and I shall merely remain here as a head-quarters from whence to make two or three excursions about the neighborhood. I think it probable I shall leave this by the 4th of next month.

Your affectionate brother[24]

W. I.

Half-past one.—Jeffrey has just called on me. I am to dine with him to-day *en famille,* and also to-morrow, when I shall meet Dugald Stewart[25] and Madame La Voissier, whilom the Countess De Rumford.[26] Jeffrey tells me I am lucky in meeting with Dugald Stewart, as he does not come to Edinburgh above once in a month.

P. S. — As I was too late for the mail yesterday, I have reopened this letter, merely to add a word or two more.

I walked out to Jeffrey's castle yesterday with his brother, John Jeffrey, and had a very pleasant dinner. I found Jeffrey extremely friendly and agreeable; indeed, I could not have wished a more cordial reception and treatment. He has taken an ancient castellated mansion on a lease of thirty-two years, and has made alterations and additions, so that it is quite comfortable, and even elegant within, and is highly picturesque without. Jeffrey inquired particularly after you. He offered me a letter to Scott; but as Campbell's is very particular, I thought it would be sufficient.[27] He is to mark out a route for me in the Highlands. I expect to be much gratified by my dinner there to-day. I find in addition to the persons already mentioned, we are to have Sir Humphrey Davy's lady,[28] who was formerly Miss Apreece, and a *belle esprit*. * * *

The weather is still sulky and threatening. If it is fine tomorrow, I shall probably be off for Melrose.

PUBLISHED: PMI, I, 376–80; Waldron, *WI & Cotemporaries*, p. 214 (in part).

1. WI had left London on August 21, sailing along the eastern coast of England and landing at Berwick on the Tweed River on August 25. See *Notes While Preparing the Sketch Book, etc., 1817*, ed. Stanley T. Williams (New Haven, 1927), p. 44.

2. The ruins of this castle lie along the shore about 20 miles south of Berwick.

3. It is located about ten miles south of Berwick.

4. Canto II, part VIII, lines 17–24, in *The Poetical Works of Sir Walter Scott*, ed. J. Logie Robertson (London, 1926), p. 106.

5. Also called Lindisfarne, located about 1½ miles from the mainland, four or five miles from Berwick.

6. One of the episodes in Canto II of *Marmion* dealt with Constance de Beverly, a Benedictine nun who, after falling in love with Marmion and living with him as a page, was tried by her order for violation of her vows, found guilty, and immured in the walls of a local convent, together with a monk who was condemned at the same time.

7. This monastery was established by Bishop Cuthbert while he was abbott at Lindisfarne from 685 to 687.

8. WI took the coastal route, from Berwick to Edinburgh, a distance of about 45 miles, rather than the longer inland route through the Berwick Hills. Melrose is about 37 miles from Edinburgh, with Kelso ten miles farther east and Berwick an additional 24 miles.

9. The former Eliza Dawson (1770–1858), Mrs. Archibald Fletcher was married to a lawyer and reformer who was a good friend of Sir Walter Scott.

10. William Erskine (1769–1822), Lord Kinnider, was a friend whom Scott consulted on literary matters.

11. Francis Jeffrey (1773–1858), lawyer and editor of the *Edinburgh Review*, was one of the dominating figures in the literary scene in Edinburgh at this time.

12. John Jeffrey was a merchant who had lived for a number of years in Boston, Massachusetts. He returned to Scotland and married a sister of John Wilkie.

13. Jean Jeffrey, who had married William Renwick and moved to America, was the daughter of the Reverend Andrew Jeffrey of Lochmaben, Scotland. Irving refers to one of her brothers who remained in Scotland.

14. Mrs. Anne Grant (1775–1838), who had lived in America before the Revolution, was a member of the circle of Scott, Jeffrey, and Lockhart.

15. Walter Scott, well known as a poet and a folklorist, had been given a copy of *Knickerbocker's History* when Brevoort had visited him in 1813. See PMI, I, 239–40.

16. In 1812 Scott had bought a farm along the Tweed River about three miles from Melrose. Here he built Abbotsford, a mansion in which he lived the rest of his life.

17. Archibald Constable (1774-1821) gained prominence as the publisher of the *Edinburgh Review*.

18. *Rob Roy* was published on December 31, 1817. See Lockhart, *Life of Sir Walter Scott*, IV, 106.

19. William Campbell Preston (1794-1860), a South Carolinian who had gone to Europe for his health and was studying law at the University of Edinburgh, accompanied WI on several walking tours.

20. This letter has not been located.

21. Probably Mrs. John Bolton, the wife of a Liverpool merchant. See WI to Peter Irving, September 22, 1817, for other details.

22. The Jays have not been identified. Woolsey may be George Muirison Woolsey (b. 1762), an American merchant who went to England to protect his property from confiscation after the Embargo. He married Abby Howland (d. 1833) in 1797 and lived in Liverpool for several years, where WI may have first met him.

23. Possibly a reference to Chauncey Hare Townshend (1798-1868), who, as the context suggests, was an energetic traveler. He published a volume of poems in 1821.

24. The word "brother" was apparently omitted in the four-volume edition. In the three-volume abridgement (ca. 1869) it was added, and for purposes of clarity it has been adopted.

25. Dugald Stewart (1753-1828), a popular philosopher who had taught at the University of Edinburgh, now lived in retirement at Kinneil House, Linlithgow.

26. Marie Anne Pierret Paulze (b. 1757), widow of Antoine Lavoisier (1743-1794), had married Sir Benjamin Thompson, Count Rumford (1753-1814) in 1805, but by mutual agreement they separated on June 30, 1809.

27. Campbell's letter enabled WI to gain entry into Scott's family. For details of WI's reception, see Lockhart, *Life of Sir Walter Scott*, IV, 88-95. In a letter to John Richardson, dated September 28, 1817, Scott gives his reaction on meeting WI: "When you see Tom Campbell, tell him, with my best love, that I have to thank him for making me known to Mr. Washington Irving, who is one of the best and pleasantest acquaintances I have made this many a day. He stayed two or three days with me, and I hope to see him again" (*Familiar Letters of Sir Walter Scott* [Boston, 1894], I, 440).

28. Lady Davy (1780-1855), daughter of Charles Kerr of Kelso, had married Sir Humphrey Davy (1778-1829) in 1812, after the death of her husband, Shuckburgh Ashley Apreece in 1807.

199. To Henry Brevoort

Edinburgh, Aug 28th. 1817.

My dear Brevoort,

I received your letter of July 2d.[1] a few days since, while in London, but had not time to answer it from thence, and I now am in such a hurry of mind & body that I can scarce collect my thoughts & settle myself down long enough to write.

I was in London for about three weeks,[2] when the town was quite deserted. I found however sufficient objects of curiosity & interest to keep me in a worry; and amused myself by exploring various parts of the city; which in the dirt & gloom of winter, would be almost inaccessable.

I passed a day with Campbell at Sydenham.³ He is still simmering over his biographical & critical labours and has promised to forward more letter press to you. He says he will bring it out th⟨is⟩e ⟨Sum⟩ coming Autumn. He has now been teasing his brain with this cursed work⁴ about seven years, a most lamentable waste of time & poetic talent.

Camp⟨all⟩bell seems to have an inclination to pay America a visit,⁵ having a great desire to see the country, and to visit his Brother⁶ whom he has not seen for many years. The expence however is a complete obstacle. I think he might easily be induced to cross the Seas; and his visit made a very advantageous one to our Country He has twelve lectures written out, on Poetry & Belles Lettres which he has delivered with great applause to the most brilliant London Audiences.⁷ I believe you have heard one or two of them They are highly spoken of by the best judges. Now could not subscription lists be set on foot in NYork & philadelphia, among the first classes of people, for a course of Lectures ↑in each city,↓ and when a sufficient number of names are ↑is↓⁸ procured to make it an object, the lists sent to Campbell with an invitation to come over and deliver the lectures. It would be highly complimentary to him — would at once ⟨improve⟩ remove all pecuniary difficulties — and if he accepted the invitation his lectures would have a great effect in giving an impulse ⟨and a proper direction⟩ to American literature and a proper direction to the public taste. Say the Subscription Was 10$ for the course of Lectures — I should think it an easy matter to fill up a large list at that rate for how many are there in N. York who would give that sum to hear a course of lectures on Belles lettres from one of the first Poets of Great Britain. I sounded Campbell on the subject and have no doubt that he would accept such an invitation. Speak to Renwick on the Subject and if you will take it in hand I am sure it will succeed. Charles King would no doubt promote a ⟨f⟩ thing of the Kind; and Dr Hosack⁹ would be delighted to give his assistance, and would be a most efficient aid —

While at London I ⟨ha⟩ made the acquaintance of Murray the Bookseller, who you know is a most valuable acquaintance to a stranger, as by his means considerable access is gained to the literary world. I dined with him and met, among two or three rather interesting characters Old D'Israeli with whom I was much entertained. He is a cheerful, sociable old gentleman full of talk & anecdote. He was very curious about America and seemed much pleased with the idea of his works being reprinted and circulated there. I saw two or three of the Lions of the Quarterly Review in Murrays Den: but almost all the literary people

are out of town; and those that have not the means of travelling, lurk
in their garrets, and affect to be in the country; for you know these poor
devils have a great desire to be thought fashionable. I have no doubt
I shall find Murray's den a great source of gratification when I return
to London.

Ogilvie[10] was at London and had just finished a short course of his
exhibitions. He had lectured at Freemasons Hall. His lectures had been
very well attended considering the season: his audiences applauded and
the papers speak well of him. I did not hear any of his orations in London
and cannot tell how far his success was prompted by the exertions of
American & Scotch friends. He however seems to be very well satisfied
and has gone to Cheltenham — He means to ⟨orat⟩ deliver orations at
a few of the provincial towns and return to London towards winter.

I have not time to detail any more particulars of London Gossip. I
left there on the 21st. inst. in a packet for Berwick on Tweed, having
some occasion to visit Edinburgh, & intending to make a short excursion
into the Highlands.[11] I found ⟨th⟩ myself ⟨in⟩ ↑among↓ a motley, but
characteristic assemblage of passengers. All Scotch and ⟨many⟩ ↑some↓
of them fat studies for Walter Scott. The first part of the voyage
was tedious: head winds & Bad weather. The latter part however was
delightful. I am always in high health & spirits at Sea and I cannot
express to you how much I was excited when we came on the coast of
Northumberland; so gloriously sketched off in the Second canto of
Marmion.[12] We had a smacking breeze and dashed gallantly through the
waves. We passed ⟨in sit⟩ by "Dunstanboroughs caverned shore"[13] and
saw the old castle of that name seated on a rocky eminence, but half
shrowded in morning mist. The day brightend up as we ⟨came in⟩
approached Bamborough castle; which stands ⟨sternly and⟩ in stern and
lordly solitude on the Sea coast — Scotts discription of it is very poetical,
but accurate

> Thy tower proud Bamborough, marked they there,
> King Ida's castle, huge & square,
> From its tall rock looks grimly down
> And on the Swelling ocean frown—

We sailed close by this old ruin and then skirted the Holy isle, where
Scott lays the Scene of Constance de Beverlys trial and where the remains
of St Cuthberts monastery are still visible. You may imagine the excitement of my feelings in this romantic part of my voyage. I landed at
Berwick after being four days on the water, and ⟨af⟩ having satisfied
my curiosity with this old & celebrated place, I took coach & rattled off
for Edinburgh — and here I am —

This place surpasses my utmost expectations, in regard to its situation and appearance. I think it the most picturesque romantic place I have ever seen except Naples. ⟨The⟩ I had several letters of introduction, but ↑almost↓ every body is out of town. Mrs Fletcher and her family are in the highlands and rather secluded — about four months since she had the misfortune to lose her finest daughter, (Grace) by a Typhus fever.

The day before yesterday I dined with Mrs Renwicks brother Mr Jeffrey, who has been extremely attentive to me. I was very much pleased with him and his family; Mrs. Jeffrey is a very pleasant woman & they have a fine family of children. I left a card the same day at Mr Francis Jeffreys ⟨house⟩ (the Reviewer) house. His family are about 3 miles off in the country. He called on me yesterday and invited me to dine with him *en famille*. I accordingly footed it out to his little castle yesterday in company with his brother John Jeffrey. He has leased for thirty two years, an old castellated mansion, situated ⟨at the [*unrecovered*]⟩ at the foot of a beautifully romantic range of hills, and in a perfect seclusion though but three miles from Edinburgh. He has made considerable additions & alterations, is ornamenting his grounds with great taste, and has altogether one of the most picturesque, poetical little domains that the heart of an author could desire. I ⟨had⟩ passed a most agreeable afternoon; my reception ⟨& entertainment⟩ was frank, cordial & hospitable and I found Jeffrey an amiable & pleasant man in his own house. I never saw him to such advantage before. Mrs Jeffrey looks thin & is nervous; but is in good spirits, and seems happy, and I think has reason to be so. They have a charming little daughter of whom Jeffrey seems both fond & proud.

I am to dine there again today — when I am to meet ⟨Prof⟩ Dugald Stewart, who, most luckily for me, happens just now on a visit to Edinburgh. I shall also meet Madame LaVoisier, late Comtesse de Rumford and the Lady of Sir Humphry Davy formerly ⟨Miss⟩ ↑Mrs↓ Apreece Sept 6th. I must scrawl a conclusion to this letter as fast as possible: as I am very much pressed for time. I dined at Jeffreys the day mentioned; but was disappointed in meeting Mr Stewart; he was detained home by indisposition. His wife & daughter[14]—were there and we had a large party, among whom were ⟨beside them⟩ also Lord Webb Seymour,[15] whom you may have met as he resides almost continually at Edinburgh. He is brother to the Duke of Somerset,[16] and is a very agreeable, unaffected well informed man — Also Mr Murray[17] an advocate of Edinburgh and one of the writers for the review & several others. — Lady Davy talked at a great rate and in charming style — I was very much pleased with her. — But *allons* —

The next ⟨morning at⟩ day I set off for Melrose — and reached Selkirk that evening from whence on Saturday morning early I took chaise for the abbey. On my way I stopped at the gate of Abbotsford & sent in my letter of introduction to Walter Scott, with a card & request to know whether it would be agreeable for him to receive a visit from me in the course of the day. ⟨In a few minutes I came⟩ Mr Scott himself came out to see me and welcomed me to his house with the genuine hospitality of the olden times. In a moment I found myself at his breakfast table, and felt as if I was at the social board of an old friend. Instead of a visit of a few hours I was kept there several days — and such days! You know the charms of Scotts conversation but you have not lived with him in the country — you have not rambled with him about his favourite hills and glens and burns. You have not seen him dispensing happiness around him in this little rural domain. I came prepared to admire him; but he completely won my heart and made me love him. He has a charming family around him — Sophia Scott[18] who must have been quite a little girl when you were here is now grown up, and is a sweet little ⟨highland⟩ mountain lassie. She partakes a great deal of her fathers character—is light hearted, ingenuous, intelligent and amiable — can tell a whimsical story and sing a border song with the most captivating naivete. ⟨I dont know any thing more delightful then a family scene ↑party↓.⟩ Scott was very attentive in shewing me the neighbouring country. I was with him from morning to night and was constantly astonished and delighted by the perpetual & varied flow of his conversation. It is just as entertaining as one of his novels, and exactly like them in style, point, humour, character & picturesqueness. I parted with him with the utmost regret, but received a cordial invitation to repeat my visit on my ⟨return⟩ ↑way↓ back to England, which I think I shall ⟨accept⟩ do — I should not forget to mention that he spoke of you in the most friendly terms; and reproached himself for not having written to you; but says he is ⟨a⟩ extremely remiss in letter writing.

Since my return to Edinburgh I have dined with Constable the Bookseller, where I met with Professor Leslie—[19]

Little Blackwood the Bookseller[20] speaks of you with great regard — He says he shall send you the numbers of a new monthly magazine which he is publishing and which possesses considerable merit.

I must conclude, as I have to hurry to court to hear Jeffrey plead — and must make preparations for a short excursion to the highlands.

God Bless you/Your friend
WI.[21]

P.S. I have recd. a letter from Carey[22] informing me of the arrangement with Eastburn[23] for Campbells work;[24] which is very satisfactory — Remember me to all friends — I have heard you repeatedly spoken of in Edinburgh with the highest regard —

ADDRESSED: Henry Brevoort Junr. Esqr. / New York. / P. Aurora}   DOCKETED:
Edinb: Augt. 28. 1817 / Washingn. Irving / visit to W. Scott.
MANUSCRIPT: NYPL—Berg Collection.   PUBLISHED: LIB, II, 45–56; PMI, I,
371–72 (in part).

This letter repeats many of the same details found in WI's letter of August 26
to his brother Peter.

1. This letter has not been located.

2. WI arrived in London about August 1 and lodged at Mrs. Halloway's in
Cockspur Lane. He departed for Berwick on August 21. See PMI, I, 370; STW, I,
156–58, 421.

3. The existing records do not indicate which day WI made his visit to Thomas
Campbell.

4. *The Specimens of English Poets*, which appeared in 1819 in seven volumes,
received widespread popular acclaim.

5. Apparently this plan did not materialize.

6. Archibald Campbell (1760–1830), the poet's oldest brother, went to America
at the age of seventeen and remained there for the rest of his life. See William Beattie,
Life and Letters of Thomas Campbell (London, 1849), I, 24–25, 27.

7. Campbell had originally delivered his lectures on poetry in 1812, but he
was unsuccessful in persuading John Murray to publish them. By April, 1816, their
publication had been postponed indefinitely. See Beattie, II, 210–11, 320–22.
Campbell's lectures are also discussed in Cyrus Redding, *Literary Reminiscences
and Memoirs of Thomas Campbell* (London, 1860), I, 97–120.

8. The "is" written above "was" seems not to be in WI's hand.

9. Dr. David Hosack (1769–1835) was a prominent New York physician interested in promoting culture and the arts.

10. WI had known James Ogilvie in New York in 1809. See WI's letters of
May 11 and October 23, 1809.

11. Many of these same details are given in the letter to Peter Irving on August
26, 1817.

12. For a similar enthusiastic response to *Marmion*, see WI's letter to his
brother Peter, August 26, 1817.

13. *Marmion*, canto II, pt. 8, line 147.

14. In July, 1790, Helen D'Arcy (1765–1838) married Stewart as his second
wife. His daughter Maria (d. 1846) remained unmarried and served her father
as secretary and editor.

15. Webb John Seymour (1777–1819) was one of the editorial associates of the
Edinburgh Review. See John Clive, *Scotch Reviewers: The Edinburgh Review,
1802–1815* (Cambridge, 1957), pp. 189, 195.

16. Edward Adolphus Seymour (1775–1855), eleventh duke of Somerset, eldest
child of Webb Seymour (1718–1793).

17. Probably John Archibald Murray (1779–1859), a friend of Scott and a
contributor to the *Edinburgh Review*.

18. Sophia Scott (1799–1837) was the oldest child. The other children included
Walter (1801–1847), Anne (1803–1833), and Charles (1805–1841).

19. Probably Sir John Leslie (1766–1832), who held the chair of mathematics
at the University of Edinburgh and wrote articles on mathematics and science
for the *Edinburgh Review*.

20. William Blackwood (1776–1834), an antiquarian bookseller and agent for

John Murray, founded *Blackwood's Magazine* to compete with the *Edinburgh Review.*

21. Diagonally to the right of the initials is written *"Washington Irving"* in another hand.

22. Mathew Carey (1760–1839) was a Philadelphia bookseller who was later to publish WI's books.

23. James Eastburn was a New York publisher.

24. Probably Campbell's *Specimens of British Poets,* which finally appeared in 1819.

200.   To Peter Irving

To P Irving

Abbots ford, Septr 1t. 1817.

My dear Brother,

I have barely time to scrawl a line before the gossoon[1] goes off with the letters to the neighbouring post office.

I was disappointed in my expectation of meeting with Dugald Stewart at Mr Jeffreys; Some circumstance prevented his coming; though we had Mrs & Miss Stewart The party however was very agreeable & interesting. Lady Davy was in excellent spirits and talked like an angel. In the evening when we collected in the drawing room she held forth for upwards of an hour; the company drew round her and seemed to listen in mute pleasure[2] – even Jeffrey seemed to keep his colloquial powers in ⟨[unrecovered]⟩ check to give her full chance – She reminded me of the picture of the Minister Bird with all the birds of the forest perched on the surrounding branches in listening attitudes. I met there with Lord Webb Seymour, ⟨who⟩ brother to the Duke of Somerset. He is almost a constant resident of Edinburgh – He was very attentive to me: wrote down a route for me in the highlands and called on me the next morning when he detailed the route more particularly. I have promised to see him when I return to Edinburgh – which promise I shall keep as I like him very much –

On Friday in spite of Sullen, gloomy weather; I mount[ed?][3] the top of the mail coach, and rattled off to Selkirk. It rained heavily in the course of the afternoon & drove me inside – On Saturday morning ↑early↓ I took chaise for Melrose; and on the way stopped at the gate of Abbots Ford, & sent in my letter of introduction, with a request to know whether it would be agreeable for Mr Scott to receive a visit from me in the course of the day. The glorious old minstrel himself came limping[4] to the gate; took me by the hand in a way that made me feel as if we were old friends: in a moment I was seated at his hospitable board among his charming little family and here have I been ever since – I had intended

certainly bein[g] [*MS torn*] back to Edinburgh today ↑(Monday)↓—
but Mr Scott wishes me to stay until Wednesday; that we may make
excursions to Dryburgh Abbey[5] Yarrow[6] &c as the weather has held up
& the Sun begins to shine. I cannot tell you how truly I have enjoyed
the ⟨time⟩ hours I have passed here — They fly by too Quick, yet each
is loaded with ⟨,⟩ story, incident or song, and when I consider the world
of ideas, images and impressions that have been crowded upon my mind
since I have been here it seems incredible that I should only have been
two days, at abbots ford — I have rambled about the hills with Scott;
visited ⟨st⟩ the haunts of Thomas the Rhymer[7] — and other spots renderd
classic by border tale and witching song — and have been in a kind of
dream or delirium.

As to Scott, I cannot express my delight at his character & manners —
He is a sterling golden hearted old worthy — Full of the joyousness of
⟨a youthful & [*unrecovered*]⟩ youth, with an imagination continually fur-
nishing forth picture—and a charming simplicity of manner that puts you
at ease with him in a moment. It has been a constant source of pleasure
to me to remark his ⟨kindness⟩ deportment towards his family, his neighbours, his domestics, his very ⟨cat⟩ dogs & cats — every thing that comes
within his influence seems to catch a beam of that sunshine that plays
round his heart — but I shall say more of him hereafter, for he is a
them[e] [*MS torn*] on which I shall love to dwell—

Before I left Edinburgh I saw Blackwood in his shop — It was accidental my conversing with him — He found out who I was — is extremely
anxious to make an ↑american↓ arrangement — Wishes to get me to write
for his magazine — (the Edinburgh Monthly) wishes to introduce me
to ⟨Wilson⟩ Mackenzie[8] — Wilson[9] &c in short I am quite sure of him —
Constable called on me just before I left town — he had been in the
country & just returned — He was very friendly in his manner — Lord
Webb Seymour coming in interrupted us & Constable took leave[.] I
promised to see him on my return to Edinburgh. He is about regenerating
the old Edinburgh magazine, & has got Blackwoods editors away from
him in consequence of some feud they had with him. This makes Blackwood very anxious to get assistance from me, and he intimated he was
affraid Constable would endeavour to secure me for his work — Thus
you see I am likely to make my visit to Edinburgh turn to more account
tha⟨t⟩n I anticipated — besides its being delightful from the attentions
I received — ⟨For⟩ Commend me to Hamilton — I hope to hear from
him soon & shall write to him again —

Your aff Br.
WI.

PS This morning we ride to Dryburgh Abbey — and see also the old
Lord of Buchan,[10] who you know is a queer one—

ADDRESSED: P Irving Esquire / Liverpool.   POSTMARKED: GALLASHIELS / 381 – B
   DOCKETED: Washington Irving / Abbotsford Sept 1st. 1817 / Visit to
   Walter Scott:
MANUSCRIPT: Va.–Barrett.   PUBLISHED: PMI, I, 380–82 (in part); Waldron,
   WI & Cotemporaries, pp. 178–79 (in part).

1. A servant-boy.
2. See also the passage dated September 6 which was added to WI's letter
to Henry Brevoort, begun on August 28.
3. WI's pen apparently ran off the page.
4. Scott's lameness resulted from an attack of poliomyelitis during a period
of teething when he was about eighteen months old. See Lockhart, *Life of Sir
Walter Scott,* I, 14–15; and Thomas Crawford, *Scott* (Edinburgh, 1965), p. 2.
5. Dryburgh Abbey, founded in 1150, was destroyed in the sixteenth century.
Scott and John Gibson Lockhart, his son-in-law, are buried in the ruins of the
Abbey.
6. It is not clear whether WI means Yarrow Water, the stream starting at
St. Mary's Lock and running for about 12 miles until it joins with Ettrick Water,
or Yarrow Kirk, a church built in 1640, about midway on the stream. See W. S.
Crockett, *The Scott Country* (London, 1902), pp. 372, and passim.
7. Thomas of Erceldoune (fl. 1220?–1297?), seer and poet in Scottish folklore, is associated with the area around Earlston, a village 4½ miles from Melrose.
See Crockett, *The Scott Country,* pp. 312, and passim.
8. Henry Mackenzie (1745–1831), member of Edinburgh literary circles known
for his periodical essays, *The Mirror* (1770) and *The Lounger* (1785–1786) and
for his sentimental novels, *The Man of Feeling* (1771) and *The Man of the
World* (1773).
9. John Wilson (1785–1854), professor of moral philosophy at the University
of Edinburgh, contributed articles to *Blackwood's Magazine* under the pseudonym
of Christopher North.
10. David Stewart Erskine (1742–1829), 11th earl of Buchan, had purchased,
in 1786, the estate of Dryburgh, with its ruined abbey, from an impoverished
granduncle of Scott's. See Crockett, *The Scott Country,* p. 492. For other comments
about the earl of Buchan, see WI's essays on Abbotsford in *The Crayon Miscellany*
(Philadelphia, 1835), pp. 71–72.

201. To Peter Irving

To P Irving

Edinburgh, Sept 6th. 1817.

My dear Brother,

I received your letter dated from some place on your Welsh excursion,
and also a letter from NYork,[1] and one from Mr Woolley[2] inclosing a
twenty pound note the receipt of which you will inform him. Tell him
also that I did not subscribe to the work he mentions in his letter.

I left abbots ford on Wednesday morning, and never left any place with
more regret. The few days that I passed there were among the most

delightful of my life, and worth as many years of ordinary existence. We made a charming excursion to Dryburgh abbey but were prevented making our visit to Yarrow by the arrival of company. I was with Scott from morning to night; rambling about the hills and streams, every one of which would bring to his mind some old tale or picturesque remark. ⟨it⟩ I was charmed with his family. He has two sons and two daughters. Sophia Scott, the eldest is between seventeen and eighteen, a fine little mountain lassie with a great deal of h⟨i⟩er fathers character and the most engaging frankness and naivete. Ann the second daughter is about sixteen; a pleasing girl, but her manners not so formed as her sister. The eldest lad — Walter is about fifteen, but surprizingly tall of his age having the appearance of nineteen. He is quite a sportsman — Scott says he has taught him to Ride to shoot and to tell the truth — The younger boy Charles however is the inheritor of his fathers genius[.] he is about twelve, and an uncommonly sprightly amusing little fellow. It is a perfect picture to see Scott & his household assembled of an evening — The dogs stretched before the fire — The cat perched on a chair — ⟨The⟩ Mrs Scott and the girls sewing, and Scott either reading out of some old romance, or telling border stories — Our amusements were occasionally diversified by a border song from Sophia — who is as well versed in border minstrelsy as her father —

I am in too great a hurry however to ⟨make dwell on the⟩ make details — I took the most friendly farewell of them all on Wednesday morning, and had a cordial invitation from Scott to give him another visit on my return from the highlands; which I think it probable I shall do.

I found Preston here on my arrival — he had been in Edinburgh for three days. We shall ⟨go to⟩ ↑set off for↓ the Highlands tomorrow — Scott has given me a letter to Hector Macdonald Buchanan[3] of Ross Priory Loch Lomond, with a request for him to give me a day on the Lake. This Macdonald is a fine fellow, I understand & a particular friend of Scotts — He took Scott up the Lake lately in his barge when Scott visited Loch Lomond so I shall be able to trace Scott in his Rob Roy scenery —

We dined yesterday with Constable, and met Professor Leslie there; with whom I was somewhat pleased, and more amused —

I have arranged with Constable greatly to my satisfaction in respect to Books &c and shall be enabled to forward Rob Roy in time to secure the first publication to Thomas.

I have also made an arrangement with Blackwood —

I shall return to Edinburgh after my visit to the Highlands, and stop here a day or two: so you may address letters to me here ⟨care of⟩ MacGregors Ho[tel.] [MS torn]

I received a very pleasant letter from Hamilton for which give him my
thanks and assure him I will answer it the first leisure moment

Affectionately your br.

WI.

ADDRESSED: P Irving Esquire / Liverpool.   DOCKETED: Washington Irving /
Edinburgh Sept 6th 1817.
MANUSCRIPT: Va.–Barrett.   PUBLISHED: PMI, I, 383–84 (in part); Waldron,
WI & Cotemporaries, pp. 182–83 (in part).

1. These letters have not been located.
2. Jeremiah Wooley was a New York merchant with a business at 33 Chatham.
See *New York City Directory* for 1817, p. 459.
3. One of Scott's colleagues during his clerkship who now lived at Ross Priory
and whom Scott visited nearly every year. See Lockhart, *Life of Sir Walter Scott,*
II, 105, 270. Scott's warm letter to Buchanan introducing WI is reproduced in
George S. Hellman, *Washington Irving Esquire* (New York, 1925), facing page 100.

202.   To Peter Irving

To P Irving

Edinburgh. Sept 20th. 1817.

My dear Brother.

I arrived here late last evening after one of the most delightful excursions I ever made — We have had continual good weather, and weather
of the most remarkable kind for the season. Warm, genial, serene sunshine. We have journied in every variety of mode — by chaize, by coach,
by gig, by boat, on foot and in a cart — and have visited some of the
most remarkable and beautiful scenes in Scotland. The journey has been
a complete trial of Prestons indolent habits. I had at first to tow him
along by main strength for he has as much alacrity at coming to anchor
and is as slow getting under way as a Dutch Lugger — The grand difficulty was to get him up in the morning, however by dint of perseverance
I at last succeeded in rousing him from his lair at 6 oclock — and making
him pad the hoof often from morning till night. The early part of the
route he complained sadly and fretted occasionally — but as he proceeded
he grew into condition and spirits, went through the latter part in fine
style and I brought him into Edinburgh in perfect order for the turf.
I found here your letter of Septr. 6th.[1] acknowledging my letter from
Abbots ford. I afterwards wrote you one from this place which I sent
⟨within⟩ in a parcel, with other letters for M Thomas & Brevoort[2] — I hope
they get safe to hand. I recd. the 20£ post note in due order —

I found also a most kind and friendly letter from Townshend, which I
answerd last night.[3] I feel greatly indebted to him for his many attentions

to me, and the desire he expresses in this letter that I should cultivate
the acquaintance of his Brother & family. I really feel deep regret at
Townshends departure on such a distant expedition which makes it uncertain whether we shall ever meet again. My heart warms towards him
at the prospect of parting and all his worthy, good fellow qualities seem
to throng upon my mind. I shall miss him sadly if I have to pass much time
at Liverpool — however God bless and prosper him wherever he goes —
⟨I must⟩

I am delighted with your account of your Welsh excursion — it must
have been charming with such a party. I wish when you see the Woolleys
& the Boltons[4] you would remember me most cordially to them.

I must hasten to conclude this letter — this is Saturday—and I wish to
arrange what I have to do in this place this morning that I may leave it
if possible on Monday morning. I intend to pay another visit to Abbots
Ford — I could not leave Scotland with a quiet conscience if I did not
have one more *crack* with the prince of minstrels, and pass a few more
happy hours with his charming family. I want to set out another evening there — Scott reading occasionally from Prince Arthur[5] — telling
border stories or characteristic anecdotes — Sophy Scott singing with
charming naiveté a little border song — the rest of the family disposed in
listening groups, while grey hounds, spaniels and cats bask in unbounded
indulgence before the fire. Every thing aroun[d] [*MS torn*] Scott is perfect character and picture—

On my return to Edinburgh I found a most friend[ly] [*MS torn*] note
from Jeffrey[6] dated sometime back inviting me to dinner on the day after
to meet again Lady Davy & Sir Humphrey — or three days after to meet
Dr Mason[7] of N York. I am too late for either party; but there is a kindness
in these repeated attentions and in the style of the note that is very
gratifying to me —

I should have written to Hamilton, but from your letter I should judge
he is in London — Remember me to Kernan

Your aff Br.
W I.

ADDRESSED: P Irving Esquire / Mess P Irving & Co / Liverpool   POSTMARKED:
SEP / W 20 A / 1817   DOCKETED: Washington Irving / Edinburgh Sept
20th. 1817.
MANUSCRIPT: Va.–Barrett.   PUBLISHED: PMI, I, 384–86 (in part); Waldron,
WI & Cotemporaries, pp. 182–83 (in part).

1. This letter has not been located.
2. These letters have not been located.
3. This letter has not been located.
4. Probably John Bolton (b. 1756) and his wife. Bolton, a wealthy Liverpool
merchant living on Duke Street, was a close friend and supporter of George Canning. See Josceline Bagot, *George Canning and His Friends* (New York, 1969),

II, 287 n.; J. A. Picton, *Memorials of Liverpool Historical and Topographical* (London, 1875), I, 245, 263, 342.

5. WI recorded his impressions of Scott's reading in "Abbotsford": "The evening passed away delightfully in this quaint-looking apartment, half study, half drawing room. Scott read several passages from the old romance of Arthur, with a fine· deep sonorous voice, and a gravity of tone that seemed to suit the antiquated, black-letter volume. It was a rich treat to hear such a work, read by such a person, and in such a place . . ." ("Abbotsford," in *The Crayon Miscellany,* p. 37).

6. This letter has not been located.

7. Dr. John M. Mason (1770–1829), pastor of the Associate Reformed Church in New York from 1792 to 1810, had gone to Europe for his health in 1816. Mason, who had studied theology in Edinburgh in 1791, later became president of Dickinson College.

203. *To Peter Irving*

To P Irving

Edinburgh, ↑Sunday↓ Sept 22d. 1817.

Dear Brother,

I leave Edinburgh in about half an hour on my way to England. I have been induced to hasten my departure a little for the purpose of having Prestons Company, who I think it probable I shall bring to Liverpool & then send him on by ⟨the⟩ South Wales &c to London — I have arranged matters entirely with Constable and Blackwood and have nothing further to detain me here.

I dined yesterday with Jeffrey, and found a very agreeable party of Edinburgh gentlemen there — I cannot but repeat how much I feel obliged to Jeffrey for his particular attentions, ⟨to me⟩ and the very friendly manner in which he has deported towards me. He has made his house like a home to me. I have had many kind invitations to return and pass part of the winter in Edinburgh when the fashionable world will be here — and indeed I have met with nothing but agreeable people & agreeable incidents ever since I have been in Scotland.

Mr Constable will send by coach a parcel for me containing an engraving from a fine painting which he has of Walter Scott — I wish you to take care of it. There were but a limited number of impressions taken, ⟨so⟩ I feel much obliged to Mr Constable for the present & great value for the engraving —

I forgot to mention that I did not visit Inchbracken as the coach to Perth did not go in that direction & we could not conveniently bring it into our route —

—We go to Selkirk tonight and tomorrow shall pay Scott a visit — I do not mean to stop with him however, as I understand he has been run down with company lately and ⟨I can perceive Constable is uneasy about lest he should be⟩ must require all his leisure to get Rob Roy through the Press in time —

I can perceive Constable is a little uneasy ⟨about⟩ lest Scott's time should be too much taken up by company —

Remember me to Townshend who I think I shall certainly see before he sails

Your aff Br.
W I.

ADDRESSED: *Single* / P Irving Esqr. / Liverpool   POSTMARKED: SEP / W (21) A / 1817   DOCKETED: Washington Irving / Edinburgh Sept 22th 1817 MANUSCRIPT: Va.–Barrett. PUBLISHED: PMI, I, 386–87.

204. To Walter Scott

Hawick, Sept. 23d. 1817.

My dear Sir,

I have been excessively disappointed in not meeting with you yesterday. It was not my intention to have intruded again on your hospitality for I had heard in Edinburgh how much your time has been engrossed by company of late, but I could not feel satisfied to leave Scotland without once more seeing you. I had hoped to have had that pleasure at Jedburgh, but was most provokingly detained all day at Melrose for want of a chaise so as not to reach Jedburgh until after your departure. I can only then take farewell of you by letter, which I do with a heart full of the warmest sentiments of regard. Surrounded as you are by friends among the most intelligent & illustrious, the goodwill of an individual like myself cannot be a matter of much importance yet I feel a gratification in expressing it, and in assuring you that I shall ever consider the few days I passed with you and your amiable family as among the choicest of my life.

My tour in the Highlands was delightful — The weather was as fine as could be desired, and the scenery beyond my expectations. Indeed every thing has conduced to make my scottish excursion, one of the most ⟨agreeable⟩↑charming↓I ever made; I have met with nothing but agreeable people and agreeable incidents, and I return with a heart stored with golden reccollections for after years.

Mr MacDonald Buchanan[1] was not at home when we came Down Loch Lomond so that I did not call at Ross Priory, but I had the satisfaction of meeting with him at Mr Jeffreys a few days since.

I cannot but express my satisfaction, on calling at your house yesterday, at being welcomed by my old friend Hamlet,[2] and at learning that he and his fellow culprit Hector[3] had been reprieved from the "Tyburn tree" and a pony bought for their amusement & reformation. I felt so much interested by every moving thing in your establishment that I should have grieved had any of them met with disaster

Whether I shall ever have the pleasure of again seeing you is a matter of extreme uncertainty, f[or] [*MS torn*] when once seperated in this wide world, who can tell if they will ever be jostled together again; but wherever I go I shall bear with me the warmest wishes for the happiness of yourself & your family.

Present my sincere remembrances to Mrs Scott and the young people & believe me my dear Sir

Very faithfully/Your friend
Washington Irving

Walter Scott Esq—

ADDRESSED: Walter Scott Esqr. / Abbots Ford / Melrose. /   POSTMARKED: HAWICK / [*unrecovered*]   DOCKETED: Mr. W. Irving / 23 Sept 1817
MANUSCRIPT: National Library of Scotland.   PUBLISHED: *Familiar Letters of Sir Walter Scott* (Boston, 1894), I, 441–42.

1. Scott had given WI a letter of introduction to Buchanan. See WI's letter to Peter Irving, September 6, 1817.
2. Scott's pet greyhound. See Lockhart's *Life of Sir Walter Scott*, IV, 100 n. See also WI's "Abbotsford" (*The Crayon Miscellany*, 1835), pp. 15, 56–57.
3. Probably another of Scott's pet dogs.

205.   *To Henry Brevoort*

Liverpool, Octr. 10th. 1817.

My dear Brevoort,

I have received your letter of Aug. 20th.[1] and congratulate you most heartily on the happy change you are about to make in your situation.[2] I had heard rumours of the affair before I received your letters, and my account represented the lady of your choice exactly such an one as your best friends could have wished for you. I am almost ashamed to say that at first the news ⟨almost?⟩ had rather the effect of making me feel melancholy than glad. It seemed in a manner to divorce us forever; for marriage is the grave of Bachelors intimacy and after having lived & grown together for many years, so that our habits thoughts & feelings were quite blended & intertwined, a seperation of this kind is a serious matter—not so much to you, who are transplanted into the garden of matrimony, to flourish & fructify and be caressed into prosperity—but for poor me, left lonely & forlorn, and blasted by every wind of heaven— However ⟨hea⟩ I dont mean to indulge in lamentations on the occasion.

Though this unknown piece of perfection has completely usurped my place, I bear her no jealousy or ill will; but hope you may long live happily together, and that she may prove as constant & faithful to you as I have been—Indeed, I already feel a regard for her, on your account, and have no doubt I shall at some future day feel a still stronger one on her own—

I am writing hastily, with a mind occupied by various concerns, and in a hurried moment, which must account for the insufficiency of this scrawl. I have written to Campbell on the subject of his work[3]—I had expected long since to have received further portions from him, but he is a dilatory being and is simmering over this work like an old woman over a pipkin. I am glad Eastburn did not begin to print; as I perceive there is no depending on Campbells promptness—I shall ⟨take occasion⟩ transmit the work as fast as I receive it.

I feel gratified by the exertions my friends are making to get me the situation in London,[4] though I doubt their success. These places are generally given to political favourites. I merely wanted such a situation for a little while. I have no desire to remain long in Europe, still while I am here, I should like to be placed on good ground, and look around me advantageously. A situation of the kind would have that effect, and would enable me to return home at a proper season, and under favourable circumstances: not to be driven to my native shores like a mere wreck—

⟨You⟩ The letter inclosed from Smedberg & Co.[5] to Acct[?] Irving & Co. has been forwarded to them and acknowledged & I have drawn on them for 60£ of which P & E I & Co are regularly advised—

I must again apologize to you my dear Brevoort for this miserable scrawl but I am excessively hurried.

Give my love to all the good beings around you—and to your *wife* too, if by this time you are married and believe me, as ever—

affectionately yours
W. I.

ADDRESSED: To / Henry Brevoort Jr. Esqr. / at Mrs Bradish's / New York / p Stafford} DOCKETED: Liverp: 10 Oct 1817 / W Irving
MANUSCRIPT: NYPL—Seligman Collection. PUBLISHED: LIB, II, 57–60; PMI, I, 388 (in part).
WI wrote "congratulations &c" in very small handwriting above the address.

1. This letter has not been located.

2. Brevoort married Laura Elizabeth Carson of Charleston, South Carolina on September 20, 1817.

3. WI had discussed the possibility of the publication of Campbell's lectures in a letter to Brevoort on August 28, 1817.

4. WI is alluding to the efforts of his family and friends to secure for him the

appointment as secretary of the United States Legation in London. See WI's letter to William Irving, December 23, 1817, for other details.

5. Charles G. Smedberg (1781–1845) was a New York merchant located at 68 Washington Street. On December 2, 1815, he had married Isabella Renwick, the sister of WI's traveling companion in England two years earlier. See Helen H. McIver, comp., *Genealogy of the Jaffrey-Jeffrey Family*, p. 6.

206. To Walter Scott

Liverpool Oct. 15th. 1817.

My dear Sir,

The parcel which accompanies this contains American editions of Some of your poems.[1] Miss Scott seemed pleased with their appearance and their lilliputian size, and perhaps a little struck with the "nigromancy" by which a quart of wine was thus conjured into a pint bottle

I told her I would send them to her when I had made my tour, and beg you will present them to her as a very poor return for the pleasure I have received from her little border songs, which still dwell on my ear. I regret that some of the volumes are rather the worse for their journey among the Scotch mountains, but I had no fairer copies at hand.

With my best remembrances to Mrs Scott and the rest of the family I am my dear Sir

very faithfully/Yours—
Washington Irving.

Walter Scott Esq.

MANUSCRIPT: Pierpont Morgan Library.

1. Among the possible small-sized editions which Irving may have given Sophia Scott are *Ballads and Lyrical Pieces* (New York, 1811; 13½ cm.); *The Field of Waterloo* (Philadelphia, 1815; 14 cm.); *The Lady of the Lake* (Baltimore, 1811; 13 cm.); *The Lay of the Last Minstrel* (Baltimore, 1812; 13½ cm.); *The Lord of the Isles* (Philadelphia, 1815; 13½ cm.); and *Marmion* (Baltimore, 1812; 13 cm.).

207. To John Murray II

Liverpool, Octr. 16th. 1817.

Dear Sir,

I perceive by the papers that the fourth Canto of Child Harold[1] is received and I understand that Tuckeys narrative[2] is in the press. If it is your wish to Secure a participation in the profits of American republication in the way I suggested when I had the pleasure of seeing you in London, I would advise you not to lose time, as ships sometimes loiter in port & days may be lost here even after the work is sent. As the poem cannot be very voluminous it might be worth while to have it transcribed — Tuckeys Narrative can be sent in sheets — or the first half of it forwarded as soon as the sheets are printed & the remainder by a Subsequent opportunity. I regret I did not See the advertisement of Lord Amhersts embassy[3] in time to forward it for you, as I think something might have been done with it in America.

I wrote to Mr Thomas when I was in London, on the subject — desiring him to send you whatever was interesting from the American press & think it probable you will receive the works in a few weeks. I have no doubt you will find an understanding of the kind a Source of considerable and encreasing advantage, & that you will be able to make arrangements ⟨by which you will⟩ for profiting materially by the American market —

It has occurred to me that if you could afford to strike off copies of the Quarterly Review at a cheap rate so as to deliver them in America as low, or lower than the American Editions, you might authorize Mr Thomas to take subscriptions They would have the advantage of being put in the hands of subscribers earlier than the republished copies could be. Should you forward the copies of Childe Harold &c. Direct them care of *Messr P. Irving & Co. Liverpool,* and they will be ⟨forw⟩ transmitted to America by the earliest opportunity.

I have recently returned from a very pleasant tour in Scotland. A very few days after I dined with you I was at Constables table & afterwards at Jeffreys, and I assure you I found great gratification in thus visiting the adversar[y] [*MS torn*] camps in so short a space of time, and having a peep at the two great powers that divide the world of criticism.

When you See Mr Walter Hamilton[4] I beg you will remember me to him; in the mean while if I can be of [any?] [*MS torn*] service to you I shall be happy of your commands

I am dear Sir/Yours faithfully
Washington Irving.

ADDRESSED: John Murray Esqr — / Albemarle Street / London —   POSTMARKED: Liverpool Oct 16 1817; London Sep 18   DOCKETED: 17 Oct 16 / Irving W. MANUSCRIPT: John Murrray.   PUBLISHED: WIHM, pp. 11–13.

1. Although Byron had completed Canto IV of *Childe Harold's Pilgrimage* on July 29, 1817, Murray did not publish it until April 28, 1818. See Wise, *Bibliography of Byron*, I, 64.

2. John Kingston Tuckey, *Narrative of an Expedition to Explore the River Zaire, Usually Called the Congo, in South Africa, in 1816, under the Direction of Captain J. K. Tuckey, R. N. To Which Is Added, The Journal of Professor Smith; and Some General Observations on the Country and Its Inhabitants,* which Murray

published in 1818 in an edition of 498 pages. Two New York editions, each of
410 pages, also appeared in 1818.

3. This was the account prepared by Henry Ellis, *Journal of the Proceedings of
the Late Embassy to China*, which Murray published on October 6, 1817. For
other details, see WIHM, p. 12.

4. Walter Hamilton, a member of the Royal Asiatic Society and author of
The East India Gazetteer, was "an old and intimate friend of Mr. Murray" and
one of the coterie which gathered at John Murray's drawing room. See Samuel
Smiles, *A Publisher and His Friends: Memoir and Correspondence of the Late
John Murray . . .* (London, 1891), II, 85.

208.   *To Mrs. Josiah Ogden Hoffman*

Liverpool, Nov. 23, 1817.

My dear Mrs. Hoffman:

It is with the utmost concern that I have heard of the accident that
has happened to Charles,[1] not merely on his account, but on account
of the shock it must have given to your feelings, already so much harassed
by repeated afflictions. I hope the poor little fellow has recovered his
health, and that you have been enabled to sustain this new trial with
your accustomed resignation.

It is a long time since I heard from you, but I am conscious this is
my own fault, as you wrote the last letter.[2] I have, however, been so
beaten down by cares and troubles, that I have almost abandoned letter
writing, and, indeed, would do so altogether, but that I am fearful
those whose affection I most value would either forget me or think I
had forgotten them. I would offer you consolation under your various
afflictions, but I know how futile all verbal consolation is. The heart
must battle with its own sorrows, and subdue them in silence; and
there are some minds, as there are bodies, of such pure and healthful
temperament, that they have within their natures a healing balm to
medicine their own wounds and bruises. To the soothing influence of
such a spirit, my dear friend, I trust for your once more recovering tranquillity after all the sorrows and bereavements you have suffered.

I met with Mr. Verplanck[3] both in Liverpool and London, in the
course of the present year. We were frequently together while in London,
where I parted with him about three months since; he to go to the continent, and I to Scotland. The sight of him brought a thousand melancholy
recollections of past times and scenes, of friends that are distant,
and of others that are gone to a better world. When I look back for
a few short years, what changes of all kinds have taken place! Is this
a period of time peculiar for its vicissitudes? or has the circle in
which I have moved been particularly subject to calamities? or is it
indeed but the common lot of man, as he advances in life, to find the

blows of fate and fortune thickening around him? These questions continually spring up in my mind, as I cast a painful eye on the wrecks
and ruins that a few short years have produced. It seems as if sorrow
and misfortune had gone the rounds of my intimacy, and penetrated into
my household; and when I see how many of the best of beings have suffered under heavy visitations, I feel that such a one as I have no
right to repine at what has fallen to my share.

It has given me great satisfaction to hear that Ogden[4] is doing
well at the bar, and is in a fair way to acquire both business and
reputation. I am heartily glad that he has been able to wean himself
from the navy,[5] and so far to conquer the roving propensities and unsettled habits incident to it, as to apply himself to the technical routine
of legal business. It argues sound qualities of head. Young men must
"sow their wild oats" some way or other, and it is not often a young man
does it in so gallant and generous a manner. Now, that his thoughts and
ambition have taken such a regular and valuable direction, his late
cruisings about the world will have an advantageous effect. They will
serve to enlarge his knowledge of mankind, increase his stock of ideas,
and give a dash of spirit and *mercurialness* to his character that will
counteract the sordid effects of commonplace business. He had always
a fine aspiring spirit, from the time he was a boy and used to scramble
on my back to storm the office window and enact Alexander. I look
forward to his being the pride and comfort of his father at that period
of life when a man begins to live again in his children.

* * * The whole country here is in mourning for Princess Charlotte;[6]
and never did I see public grief so unusual and unaffected. Indeed,
it is impossible for any one of common feeling not to be touched by
the circumstances of her story; for it is not often in the rank of royalty
that we find so much frank heartedness; such strength of all the natural
affections, such simplicity of honest enjoyment, such conjugal tenderness and devotion, so much, in short, of all that is excellent and endearing
in common life. And all this to be suddenly withered at a blow, and
two such loving and noble hearts to be torn asunder at the very
moment when they were looking for a new link of attachment and an
increase of domestic felicity; but such is human life.

I hear that Mary[7] is well satisfied with her residence in the woods.
* * I trust she and her husband will live to see the whole wilderness
blossoming like the rose around them; and themselves prospering
and multiplying with the country. I have had also some very satisfactory rumors about Murray;[8] of which, however, I shall say nothing,
but that I wish him prompt success in all his suits, whether in the
court of law or of Hymen.

I long to see you all once more; but when it will be my lot, I cannot tell. My future prospects are somewhat dark and uncertain; but I hope for the best, and that I may yet find wholesome fruit springing out of trouble and adversity.

Give Mr. Hoffman my faithful and affectionate recollections; tell Charles I am glad to hear that he has stood his sufferings like a man. Kiss my little goddaughter for me, and believe me, my dear friend,

Yours as ever,

Washington Irving.

PUBLISHED: PMI, I, 389–91; Waldron, *WI & Cotemporaries*, pp. 239–41 (in part); Homer S. Barnes, *Charles Fenno Hoffman* (New York, 1966), p. 23.

1. On October 24, 1817, Charles Fenno Hoffman had an accident in which his leg was crushed between a boat and a pier on Courtlandt Street. As a result, his right leg was amputated above the knee. See Homer F. Barnes, *Charles Fenno Hoffman*, p. 21.

2. This letter has not ben located.

3. Verplanck was Mrs. Hoffman's brother-in-law. His wife had died in Paris in the spring of 1817. See WI's letter of May 20, 1817.

4. A son by J. O. Hoffman's first wife, he studied law in Goshen, Orange County, New York, where he was admitted to the bar.

5. Ogden Hoffman, upon graduation from Columbia College in 1812, joined the navy and served with Commodore Decatur in the Algerian war.

6. Princess Charlotte (1796–1817), only child of the prince of Wales (later George IV), died on November 6 after giving birth to a stillborn child. The mourning period extended from then until the funeral on November 19. See the London *Times*, November 8–20, 1817.

7. Probably Mary Hoffman, wife of Philip Rhinelander. She died on September 7, 1818.

8. David Murray Hoffman (1791–1878), nephew of J. O. Hoffman, married Frances Amelia Burrall on December 16, 1817. See William Wickham Hoffman, *Eleven Generations of Hoffmans in New York: Descendants of Martin Hoffman, 1657–1957*, p. 12.

209.   To William Irving, Jr.

Liverpool, Dec. 23, 1817.

* * * Ebenezer tells me you have been exerting yourself to get me appointed to the Secretaryship of Legation at the Court of St. James, but without success; but that you hoped to get some other appointment for me.[1] I feel in this as in many other things deeply indebted to your affectionate care for my interests; but I do not anticipate any favors from Government, which has so many zealous and active partisans to serve; and I should not like to have my name hackneyed about among the office-seekers and office-givers at Washington. Indeed, for the present I would rather that all consideration should be given to helping up poor Ebenezer and Peter, and let me take care of myself. I feel excessive anxiety on Ebenezer's account, with such a numerous family to support, and I scarcely feel less on Peter's, who is brought down at a period of life when a man begins to crave ease and comfort in the world.

For my own part, I require very little for my support, and hope to be able to make that little by my own exertions. I have led comparatively such a lonely life for the greater part of the time that I have been in England, that my habits and notions are very much changed. For a long while past, I have lived almost entirely at home; sometimes not leaving the house for two or three days, and yet I have not had an hour pass heavily; so that if I could but see my brothers around me prospering, and be relieved from this cloud that hangs over us all, I feel as if I would be contented to give up all the gaieties of life. I certainly think that no hope of gain, however flattering, would tempt me again into the cares and sordid concerns of traffic. * * *

I have been urged by several of my friends to return home immediately; their advice is given on vague and general ideas that it would be to my advantage. My mind is made up to remain a little longer in Europe, for definite, and, I trust, advantageous purposes, and such as ultimately point to my return to America, where all my views and wishes, my ambition and my affections are centred. I give you this general assurance, which, I trust, will be received with confidence, and save the necessity of particular explanations, which it would be irksome for me to make. I feel that my future career must depend very much upon myself, and therefore every step I take at present, is done with proper consideration.[2] In protracting my stay in Europe I certainly do not contemplate pleasure, for I look forward to a life of loneliness and of parsimonious and almost painful economy.

PUBLISHED: PMI, I, 392–93.

1. A search of the letters received by the state department in the National Archives does not reveal William Irving's letter, so it is not possible to ascertain what other appointments William was soliciting for his brother.

2. In view of the impending bankruptcy of the importing house, WI was already thinking of the literary project which finally materialized as *The Sketch Book*.

210. To the Reverend Rann Kennedy

[Springfield, December 29, 1817]

My dear Sir,—

I cannot refuse myself the satisfaction of expressing to you, while my feelings are still warm on the subject, the great delight which I have received from your Poem.[1] It was just put into my hands yesterday morning, and I read it through three times in the course of the day, and each time with increased gratification. It both excited and affected me: some of your periods seemed to roll through my mind with all the deep intonations and proud swells of Milton's verse—they have the same density of thought and affluence of language. Your varied descriptions of popular feelings are pictured off with a graphic touch that reminds me of Shakespeare's descriptions; they fill your Poem with imagery, and make it in a manner to swarm with population. It is like one of those little mirrors on which we see concentered, in a wonderfully small space, all the throng and bustle of a surrounding world. . . .

I am, dear Sir/With great respect, Your Friend,

Washington Irving.

Springfield, December 29th, 1817

Published: The Reverend Rann Kennedy, *A Poem on the Death of Her Royal Highness The Princess Charlotte of Wales and Saxe Cobourg*, 3d ed. (London, n.d.), p. [3]; Birmingham *Weekly Mercury*, 1900 (clipping in file of Birmingham Public Library).

The Reverend Rann Kennedy (1772–1851) was a classical scholar, poet, and clergyman, associated for more than fifty years with St. Paul's Chapel, Birmingham. For details about him, see J. A. Langford, *Notes and Queries*, 4th ser. 10 (December 28, 1872), 528–29.

1. The poem, the full title of which is cited above, is a blank verse tribute to the granddaughter of George III, who died on November 6, 1817.

211. To Henry Brevoort

Liverpool, Jany 28th. 1818.

My dear Brevoort,

I have not written to you for·some time past for in fact the monotonous life I lead; being passed almost continually within doors, leaves me little to communicate[.] I have just written to Campbell,[1] stating the contents of your letter of Decr 4th.[2] and shall let you know his reply the moment I receive it.

I inclose a reply to the kind letter of Mrs B.[3] but it expresses nothing of what I feel. How happy a period of my life it will be when I can once more return home and feel myself among true friends. But I cannot ⟨bear⟩ bring myself to think of returning home under present circumstances

We are now in "train" to pass through the Bankrupt act.[4] it is a humiliating alternative but my mind is made up to any thing that will extricate me from this loathsome entanglement in which I have so long been involved — I am eager to get from under this murky cloud before it completely withers & blights me. For upwards of two years have

I been bowed down in spirit and harrassed by the most sordid cares —
a much longer continuance of such a situation would indeed be my
ruin. As yet I trust my mind has not lost its elasticity, and I hope ⟨yet⟩
to recover some cheerful standing in the world. Indeed I feel very
little solicitude about my own prospects — I trust something will turn
up to procure me subsistence & am convinced, however scanty &
precarious may be my lot I can bring myself to be content. But I feel
harrassed in mind at times on behalf of my brothers. It is a dismal
thing to look round on the wrecks of such a family connexion. This is
what, in spite of every exertion, will sometimes steep my very soul
in bitterness. Above all, the situation of my poor Brother Ebenezer
and his family distresses me.[5] My dear Brevoort, whatever friendship
you feel for me, never trouble yourself on my account, but lend a
helping hand, when he is extricated from present difficulties, once
more to put him in a way to get forward. He is a capable & indefatigable
man of business & in a regular line, cannot but make out well. His
ruin has been occasioned by circumstances over which he had no
controul. Do not suppose I am wishing you to jeopard⟨y⟩ your own
interests in the least — but the mere advice and countenance of two or
three prosperous men to one in his situation have the most reviving
effects. Once get him under way, and he has a cheerful perseverance
& steady application that will carry him regularly forward.

Excuse me writing on these irksome subjects — I had determined not
to do so any more, but they are uppermost in my thoughts and will
sometimes find their way to my pen.

In the course of two or three months I hope to have finally
got through difficulties here, and to close this gloomy page of existence
— what the next will be that I shall turn over, is all uncertainty; but I
trust in a kind providence that shapes all things for the best, and
I yet hope to find future good springing out of these present adversities.

I am my dear Brevoort/Affectionately yours
W. I.

ADDRESSED: For / Henry Brevoort Jr. Esq — /Mrs Bradish's / New York
    DOCKETED: Liverp: Jan: 28 — 1818 / Wash: Irving
MANUSCRIPT: NYPL—Seligman Collection.   PUBLISHED: LIB, II, 61–64; PMI, I,
    394–95 (in part).

1. WI's letter to Campbell and Campbell's reply have not been located.
2. Brevoort's letter has not been located.
3. Mrs. Brevoort's letter to WI and his reply have not been located.
4. The official notice of bankruptcy of P. & E. Irving and Company appeared
in the London *Times*, February 2, 1818; in *Billinge's Liverpool Advertiser*, February 2, 1818; in *Gore's General Advertiser* (Liverpool), February 5, 1818; and in
Liverpool *Mercury*, February 6, 1818.

5. As the New York partner in the importing firm Ebenezer Irving also went bankrupt at this time.

212. *To Charles R. Leslie*

Liverpool, Febry. 8th. 1818.

My dear Sir,

I have this moment received your letter dated the 5th.[1] and answer it on the spot, to shew you that I am not as inattentive as you imagine. Whether I am heartless or not, it is not for me to say. my friends must read my heart and judge of it—A mans own word is never taken in these matters. But if I am to be judged, ⟨by⟩ with respect to yourself, by the circumstance of not answering the two letters you have written to me I can only plead *that I have never received them.* What mode you took of sending them I am at a loss to imagine, as a letter thrown into any post office, ⟨ho⟩ would ⟨ultimately if⟩ however misdirected, ultimately find its way to the general post office at London; from whence it would certainly be forwarded to me. ⟨I am⟩ I have been continually anxious to hear from you & to know where you were that I might write to you; but had no clue by which to find you. Preston wrote to me from London in October last,[2] mentioning some turn of good fortune which had befallen you; and that you were gone to Scotland. I immediately wrote to him for particulars and enquired after your address; but I received no reply from him; until a very few days since I had a letter from him dated Paris;[3] wherein he referred to some preceding letter dated at Callais (which never came to hand) He gave me no information therefore concerning you—and I again wrote to him in reply,[4] repeating my enquiries—I am minute and and tedious on this point — because I cannot rest comfortable while any such impression with respect to me exists in your mind—At the happy prospects which have brightened around you I rejoice most heartily—they are refreshing & enlivening ⟨they have⟩ I feel as if daylight were reflected back upon me from some ⟨object⟩ neighbouring object that before was dark—Yet, whatever you may think, I'll assure you that never did I take so strong an interest in your concerns as when I imagined you cast down and surrounded with danger and uncertainty. If I ⟨had⟩↑did↓ not manifest⟨ed⟩ it to your satisfaction, it ⟨is⟩↑was↓ because ⟨I⟩ my means of rendering aid and encouragement were dried up—my mind was harrassed and exhausted and worn bare by perplexities to which it was unaccustomed and by the daily & nightly meditation on the distress & ruin of my dearest relatives.[5]

As you are desirous of hearing something about myself I can only say that I have been here for several months, waiting in hopes that the concerns of the house might be quietly adjusted; but finding the attempt useless, or likely to consume life & spirits in the ⟨sl⟩ tedious process, we have submitted to the ordeal of the Bankrupt law & thus struggle through the thickest of the slough—anything to get extricated from these loathsome entanglements. I am rightly served for ever suffering myself to get within their reach.

My tour in Scotland was a delightful one and had a most happy effect on me. I shall ever love that country & its inhabitants. It seemed as if I drew in animation, cheerfulness, & hope with the blessed air of the Scotch mountains. I ⟨have⟩ passed through some of the noblest Scenery lighted up by an italian sunshine—for I never saw finer weather in any part of the world. I was lifted up in spirit too by the kind reception I met with from some men whose notice would flatter a man of far loftier pretensions than myself. Jeffrey shewed me repeated attentions, and that too with a frankness and friendliness which I shall never forget. I have always felt admiration of his talents; but I never knew what his heart was until I saw him under his own roof. Walter Scott too, took me into the bosom of his family & kept me with him several days; these days are counted among the happiest of my life[.] I cannot think of Scott but my heart warms. Little did these gentlemen think that they were then pouring the sweetest balm upon a bruised spirit and binding up a broken reed.

My time for some months past has been spent almost exclusively within doors. I have declined all invitations and scarcely go over the threshold for days together—My Brother is constantly with me, and by a variety of ⟨occupation⟩ mental occupations we get through the day without a moment hanging heavy on our hands. I feel perfectly contented and in fact I do not think my time ever passed away more completely to my satisfaction.

⟨The chief⟩ I only regret that in a couple of months my brother & myself seperate—he returns to America & I remain in England—when our fortunes will permit us to come together again I cannot tell, but this is one of the real stings of adversity. However I am determined if possible to let nothing ⟨shake⟩ disturb the composure of mind which I have happily attained, and I look forward to an uncertain futurity with a confidence that all the dispensations of providence will work out for the best.

Preston had determined at one time to pass his winter in Edinburgh, to which I had strongly advised him—Some sudden impulse however took him to Paris and he writes me that he intends on the 15t of this month to set out for Italy by the way of Marseilles, to return through Switzerland next spring—Go down the Rhine and come over to ⟨It⟩ England again in the Summer. He appears delighted with Paris. He wishes to knew your address that he may write to you. If you write to him address to the care of *Messrs. La fitte Perigeaux & Co. Paris.*[6] and take care to pay the postage of the letter, or it will not be forwarded.

And now my dear Sir, let me again repeat how happy I am to find you ⟨once more⟩ so delightfully situated and Surrounded with such a family connexion as you describe. I hope you have managed the good fortune that has befallen you[7] in such manner as to secure some annual income, that will make you independent of the vicissitudes of a popular life—And I hope more especially that you have formed some scheme of life connected with ⟨the⟩ your amiable family, rather than resting on the uncertainty of public applause: for depend upon it the sweet waters of contentment flow steadily though quietly from the retired well springs of domestic endearment, but he who depends upon the torrent of popular applause will often, like poor Ostogral[?] ↑of Bazra↓,"find the channel dry & dusty"

My Brother desires to be remembered to you in the most particular manner; and feels truly gratified in hearing [*MS ends here.*]

MANUSCRIPT: NYPL—Berg Collection.

The name "Mr Ogilvie" is written vertically on the left margin of the last MS page. The sheet with the conclusion, signature, and address is missing.

1. This letter has not been located.
2. This letter has not been located.
3. This letter has not been located.
4. This letter has not been located.
5. WI alludes to the business failure of his brother Ebenezer and his brother-in-law Henry Van Wart.
6. This firm also served as WI's banker when he lived in Paris.
7. The nature of Leslie's good fortune has not been ascertained.

213. To Moses Thomas

[March 3, 1818]

I notice what you say on the subject of getting up an original work; but I am very squeamish on that point. Whatever my literary reputation may be worth, it is very dear to me, and I cannot bring myself to risk it by making up books for mere profit.

PUBLISHED: PMI, IV, 200.

214. To Henry Brevoort

Liverpool, March 22d. 1818.

My dear Brevoort.

If you have not already done it I wish you by the first opportunity to remit to Messr A & S Richards[1] Liverpool the amount of the Draft on Mr Thomas paid into your hands some time since. It was for books purchased for Mr Thomas and I have had to borrow money from Richards to settle the Booksellers A/C. Mention to Richards that the money is on my account & to be subject to my orders[2]—

I now inclose the second of a set of Exchg on M Thomas for five hundred Dollars which I will thank you to collect[.] I shall draw on you when I have occasion for money for my current expenses, as I can I think dispose of drafts on you to A & S Richards — I shall always take care to replace ⟨such⟩ the amount of such drafts by drafts on M Thomas or in some other manner. This appears just at the moment to be the most convenient channel of getting at such slender pecuniary resources as I have at my command. I wish you ⟨to⟩ not to put the drafts on Mr Thomas into ⟨[unrecovered]⟩ circulation but collect them privately—; that is to say not to put them in the Bank; but make the matter as convenient to Thomas as possible.[3]

I shall write to you particularly in reply to your letter from Charlestown[4]— This is a mere letter of Business[5]—

Yours ever

W Irving

Henry Brevoort Jr Esqr

ADDRESSED: Henry Brevoort Jr. Esq. / New York.   DOCKETED: Liverpool 28 March 1818 / Wash: Irving
MANUSCRIPT: NYPL—WI Papers.   PUBLISHED: PMI, I, 396 (in part).

Two manuscript versions of this letter exist in WI's handwriting, suggesting that he probably sent both of them to Brevoort by different boats. The other version (no. 215) is printed in LIB, II, 65–66.

1. A. & S. Richards was a large importing firm in Liverpool. In 1820 the Richards firm imported 17,632 bales of cotton, more than any other house in Liverpool. See D. M. Williams, "Liverpool Merchants and the Cotton Trade, 1820–1850," in *Liverpool and Merseyside*, ed. J. R. Harris (London, 1969), pp. 190, 202.

2. The sense of this paragraph is the same in the other version, where WI wrote "If you have not already done so I wish you to remit by the first opportunity to Mess A & S Richards the amount of the Draft ⟨collecte⟩ paid you by Moses Thomas some time since, I think it was about 70£ Sterling. It was to pay for Books purchased for him, and I have had to borrow money of Richards for that purpose. You can tell A & S Richards that the money is to be on my account subject to my orders."

3. In the second paragraph WI also changed the wording somewhat from the other version, when he wrote "I now inclose you a draft on M Thomas for

⟨immediate?⟩ five hundred Dollars, which I will thank you to collect You need not put it in circulation, but account privately with M Thomas for it. I shall draw on you, (probably in favour of A & S Richards) as my current expenses require and you may depend on my putting you in funds either by drafts on M Thomas, or in some other way."

4. This letter has not been located.

5. WI's other version of this paragraph was somewhat different: "I will write in reply to your Letter from Charlestown at a moment of more leisure This is merely on business—"

215. To Henry Brevoort

Liverpool March 22d. 1818.

My dear Brevoort,

If you have not already done so I wish you to remit by the first opportunity to Mess A & S Richards the amount of the Draft ⟨collecte⟩ paid you by Moses Thomas some time since, I think it was about 70 £ Sterling. It was to pay for Books purchased for him, and I have had to borrow money of Richards for that purpose. You can tell A & S Richards that the money is to be on my account subject to my orders.

I now inclose you a draft on M Thomas for ⟨immediate?⟩ five hundred Dollars, which I will thank you to collect You need not put it in circulation, but account privately with M Thomas for it. I shall draw on you, (probably in favour of A & S Richards) as my current expenses require and you may depend on my putting you in funds either by drafts on M Thomas, or in some other way.

I will write in reply to your letter from Charlestown at a moment of more leisure—this is merely on business—

Yours ever

W Irving—

H Brevoort Jr Eqr

ADDRESSED: Henry Brevoort Jr. Esqr. / at Mrs Bradish's / New York — / Atlantic
    DOCKETED: Liverpool 22 March 1818 / Wash: Irving
MANUSCRIPT: NYPL—WI Papers.

Above the address WI wrote in a small hand "1st."

216. To Ebenezer Irving

[Liverpool, April 24, 1818]

I feel confident that I shall be able to rub along with my present means of support; and in the mean time am passing my time advantageously by attending to some studies that will be of future service to me; so you need give yourself no solicitude on my account.

PUBLISHED: PMI, I, 396.

217. *To Henry Brevoort*

Liverpool, April ⟨2⟩30th. 1818.

My dear Brevoort

Your letter of the 8th. March was handed me by the Messrs Gibbes,[1] with whom I was very much pleased They have just left this for London, and gone direct, as fast as coach can carry them; though I urged them almost with tears in my eyes to go by the way of Chester, Shrewsbury, &c &c and to travel leisurely. The weather is heavenly and the country is just breaking out into all the loveliness of Spring — but they were bitten with the travellers most fatal malady, the eagerness to *get on*— and so away they have gone pell mell for London, where I should almost rejoice to hear they were well besmoked and befogged for ⟨their the⟩ ↑their↓flight of the charms of ⟨genial?⟩ dame nature.

Your letter most unluckily reached me the very afternoon of the day on which McGillivray[2] sailed for New York; I did not see him while he was here; and am at a loss to know whether he purchased the Harp for Mrs Brevoort or not. I shall make inquiry when I go to London; but wish you would write me word at all events whether he has or not — and whether I shall from time to time send Mrs Brevoort some *choice Musick*, for the musick that is generally sent out to America is ⟨Si⟩commonplace Sing Song. I hope McGillivray has not got the harp, for I think I have means of getting her a very choice one, through the judgement of one of the first Harpplayers in England There is great choice in the article. You will smile to find me talking knowingly of musick — but I have become a little of a dabbler. As one mode of battling with the foulfiend during the long and gloomy trial I have undergone I took hold of my flute again and put myself under the tuition of a master; and now begin to know one end of the instrument from the other — I found the prescription excellent at times when I could not read and dared not think; and thus have extracted some little sweet out of the bitterness of adversity. An application from Mrs B for Music therefore is not more out of my way than yours for Books, and I shall be glad at any time to execute a commission for either of you to the best of my powers.

I shall go to London before long and shall then attend to your request about books — prints &c.

A few days since Peter & myself attended the wedding of Joseph Curwen[3] whom you may reccollect as one of the Club of Philadelphia, and who has married Miss Selina Gadsden of Charleston— a lady acquainted with your wife and who has given me many interesting particulars concerning her — She is a charming woman & will be quite an addition to the American society in Liverpool.

We are waiting here for the final settlement of our concerns;[4] our certificates are going the round for Signature after which Peter will sail for New York — I intend remaining some time longer in England. I have received no answer from Campbell in reply to ⟨the⟩ ↑a↓letter I wrote him on the receipt of yours. I am surprised at his silence, but it is possible he ⟨defer⟩ is a little perplexed, and defers talking on the subject until he comes to Liverpool, which will be shortly, to deliver a course of Lectures at the Liverpool Institution[5]—

I have several letters to write by this opportunity and must be brief: Give my best remembrances to Mrs B and believe me my dear Brevoort

affectionately yours.

W I

ADDRESSED: Henry Brevoort Junr / Esqr. / *New York.* / Courier   DOCKETED:
    Liverpool 30 Apl. 1818 / Washington Irving
MANUSCRIPT: NYPL—Seligman Collection.   PUBLISHED: LIB, II, 67–70.

1. Thomas S. and Morgan Gibbs were New York merchants. See Scoville, *Old Merchants of NYC,* V, 41. George Gibbs had a mercantile establishment at 70 South Street. See *New York City Directory* for 1817–1818.
    2. William McGillivray of Montreal was head of the North West Company and an associate of Brevoort's in the fur trade.
    3. Joseph Curwen (b. ca. 1783) emigrated to Philadelphia in 1784 with his father, John Curwen.
    4. The bankruptcy of P. & E. Irving and Company.
    5. Campbell did not begin his lectures at Liverpool until late October, 1818. See William Beattie, *Life and Letters of Thomas Campbell,* II, 340–41.

218. To Henry Brevoort

Liverpool, ⟨April 30th⟩↑May 1st.↓1818

Dear Brevoort

I some time since inclosed you a draft on Mr Thomas for five hundred Dollars; I have this day drawn on you↑at⟨60 days sight⟩ three months after date↓ for a like amount favour of Messr A & S Richards—I may hereafter draw on you in same way, as it is the most convenient ⟨form⟩↑way↓ for me to draw funds from America. I shall always take care to replace ⟨such⟩↑any↓funds I may draw out of your hands without delay—if I do not have them placed there in advance.

I wrote to you some time since likewise to remit to A & S Richards the money paid to you by Mr Thomas last year for his draft. I have had to borrow money of Richards on the presumption that ⟨the⟩ such amount was on the way.

Yours truly
WI

MANUSCRIPT: John Winslow Collection.   PUBLISHED: LIB, II, 71.

219. To Henry Brevoort

Liverpool, May 19th. 1818.

Dear Brevoort,

I have before written to you on the subject of the amount of a draft on Moses Thomas, paid to you some time last year. I find this unlucky little lump of money is undergoing detention in your hands in consequence of some over caution of my brother Ebenr. who is either affraid I will be extravagant on the receipt of such a sum or that the ship will sink under the weight of it. If you have not remitted it before the receipt of this, to Silas Richards, do so at once. I have had to borrow ↑from Richards↓ the amount of it to pay for Books sent to M Thomas. ⟨and⟩

I am happy to inform you that we have had our Certificates duly signed and they have only now to go through the Lord Chancellors hands.[1] It has been a tedious business owing to the scattered ⟨situation⟩ residences of our Creditors, and to the wrong headedness of some of them—and as is often the case in matters of the kind—we have almost invariably met with delay and perversity when we had every reason to ⟨respect t⟩ expect the reverse[2]—

It will take a little while to settle all matters here and get the necessary papers for my brother Ebenrs. discharge, after which Peter will set sail for New York—I hardly think he will get away before the first of July.

⟨I hear that you are in⟩

The last letters from home mention you as being in New York *En Garçon!* I presume you are building your nest like other happy birds, in the Spring time.

I have already acknowledged your letter containing the request about the Harp &c The departure of Mr McGillivray on the very morning of the day whence I received the letter, without my seeing him has left me completely in the dark whether he has bought the Harp or not.

I had a long letter from James Paulding[3] some days since—He appears to be delightfully and happily situated at Washington: but mentions that his health is very delicate. I declare the receipt of this letter has been one of the most pleasing circumstances that I have met with [in][4] a long time. It brought back so many reccollections of our ⟨l⟩ old literary communions and was written in one of ⟨t⟩ James' most warm hearted moments. ⟨However⟩

I received a letter from Campbell[5] a few days since wherein he apologizes for not having ⟨writ⟩ answered my letter before on the subject of a visit to America ↑in consequence of a severe fit of illness↓. I am sorry

[to] [*MS torn*] say he relinquishes the thing altogether, alledging that he is "too old." I must confess I had lost almost all expectation of his going out, for he seems to ⟨be⟩ want nerve and enterprize

I have nothing further to tell you of news. I have little to say of myself, my time passing with great uniformity, being spent chiefly within doors. I have been some time past engaged in the study of the German Language,[6] and have got on so far as to be able to read and *splutter* a little. It is a severe task, and has required hard study; but the rich mine of German Literature holds forth abundant reward. Give my best regards to Mrs B and believe me my dear fellow

Yours Ever—
WI.

ADDRESSED: Henry Brevoort Jr. Esqr. / New York. / Marsha   DOCKETED: Liverpool
    9 May 1818 / Wash: Irving
MANUSCRIPT: NYPL—Seligman Collection.   PUBLISHED: LIB, II, 72–75.

1. According to the Enrolment Books of the lord chancellor's office, the certificates were filed on May 25, 1818, by the Irvings' attorneys and finally delivered out on June 22, 1818, thus completing the case. See PRO, Enrolment Books.

2. Among the documents preserved in the Certificates of Conformity of the lord chancellor's office was one from George Austin of Liverpool who wished to file his claim for indebtedness against the personal estates of Peter and Washington rather than against the company which had filed for bankruptcy. See PRO, Certificates of Conformity (1817–1819), pp. 202–3.

3. Paulding wrote to WI on April 5, 1818. See *Letters of J. K. Paulding*, pp. 56–57.

4. Apparently through inadvertence WI neglected to write the bracketed word.

5. This letter has not been located.

6. In their conversations the preceding September Scott had probably suggested the importance of German literature to WI. See STW, I, 154.

220.   To Henry Brevoort

Liverpool, May 23d. 1818.

My dear Brevoort,

I enclose you a draft at sixty days sight for Five hundred Dollars on Moses Thomas Philadelphia which I will thank you to present for acceptance. I have this day likewise drawn on you for a like Amount at four months date in favour of Silas Richards Esqr.

I would observe that no draft I have drawn on you has any relation to a bill drawn on you for Mr Muncaster on M Thomas and collected by you last year. I have already desired you to remit the proceeds of that bill to Mr Richards for my account, as I had to borrow the amount from him

Affectionately yours
Washington Irving

Henry Brevoort Jr. Esq/New York.

ADDRESSED: Henry Brevoort Jr. Eqr. / New York.   DOCKETED: W Irving / Liverp: 28 May 1818
MANUSCRIPT: NYPL—Seligman Collection.

The figure "1" followed by a superscript period appears near the top of the address sheet, apparently in WI's hand.

221. To John? Bolton

[June 18, 1818]

Dear Sir,
Inclosed is the letter of Walter Scotts, which I have just found in looking over my papers. Likewise one from Mr Jeffrey and one from Mr Campbell the poet, which may be of some value to your collection

With great regard/Yours truly
Washington Irving

June 18th. 1818

ADDRESSED: Mr Bolton
MANUSCRIPT: Andrew B. Myers.

Probably John Bolton, a merchant whom WI knew in Liverpool. See WI to Peter Irving, September 20, 1817, for other details.

222. To Henry Brevoort

Leamington July 7th. 1818.

My dear Brevoort,
It is a long while since I have heard from you, and though I know you must be taken up with the cares and comforts and enjoyments of Matrimony, and the novelties of housekeeping and domestic establishments yet I cannot consent to be so completely forgotten—I dont mean to complain for I know it is the nature of things and ⟨the reason that⟩ what we poor Bachelors must make our minds up to—but only do the thing decently and let me down as easy as possible. I wrote to you some time last winter enclosing a reply to Mrs Bs kind letter[1]— you have never acknowledged the receipt of that letter. I hope it arrived safe and that you did not, in some sudden *fit of jealousy* suppress our correspondence. I am delighted to hear that you have established

yourself in the country adjoining to Mrs. Renwicks—how charmingly you must live, with such a delightful family circle—

I wrote to Gouverneur Kemble[2] a long time since but have received no reply. I hope he is doing well at the Foundery

I am here with my sister Mrs Van Wart, whose health has suffered of late, but she is now getting quite well again[.] Van Wart has resumed business in a prosperous style—and I have no doubt of his going on well and ultimately building up a fortune—

I drew two sets of Exchg on you for 500$ sometime since against similar drafts on M Thomas forwarded to you for collection. I have heard nothing on the subject but hope they have been honoured— as I depend upon them for my ways & means. I shall not trouble you again in that way—as it must be a little out of your way of business— but at the time I drew the bills there was no other convenient mode presented itself.

I wish I had something to write about or was in a mood to write something worth reading—but—wretched as this scrawl is, it is the best my intellect can furnish out—accept it therefore as a mere testimony of constant reccollection. Give my sincere regards to Mrs B and to such of our friends as still think or care about me and believe me as ever

affectionately yours,

W I.

ADDRESSED: Henry Brevoort Jr. Esqr. / New York.   DOCKETED: Lemington—7 July 1818 / *Wash: Irving*
MANUSCRIPT: NYPL—Seligman Collection.   PUBLISHED: LIB, II, 77–79; PMI, I, 400–401 (in part).

1. See WI's letter of January 28, 1818.
2. This letter has not been located.

223. *To Silas Richards*

Birmingham July 17th. 1818.

My dear Sir,

I have recd. no advice of the acceptance of either of the drafts on Brevoort; and was on the point of writing to you, to know if you had. I will thank you to let me know when you receive advice, as I shall want to draw against them. Should any Box or parcel arrive to your address for me, from America, I wish it to be sent to the care of H Van Wart.

I am happy to say that Van is full of *business and business of the right kind,* and is in high spirits. I hope you are not melted down or

turned blue and yellow by this hot weather: and that your correspondents in America will allow you sufficient liesure to turn yourself inside out at Cheltenham.

The country is completely parched up.[1] The *Bread stuffs* will be all
ready baked before they leave the fields so that American flour will
be in great demand. I have heard of several oxen roasted whole of
late — but whether by the heat of the sun while grazing — or by the
successful candidates for Parliament I have not been able to ascertain

It is whisperd in the Brummagem smokeshops that the Admiralty
are thinking of employing the navy to tow the ice back to the north
pole, lest this should be turned into a tropical climate — this however is between ourselves —

Give my sincere regards to Mrs Richards and all the young folk
& believe me

Very truly yours
Washington Irving

Silas Richards Esqr.

MANUSCRIPT: Rush Rees Library, University of Rochester.

1. The Maidstone *Gazette* comments about the drought in England at this
time: "The weather in this part of the country has lately been excessively hot. The
thermometer during the last week several times stood at 89, and in the sun at
116" (quoted in the London *Times*, July 30, 1818).

224. To Charles R. Leslie

Birmingham, July 29th. 1818.

My dear Leslie,

I thank you for your letter and the information it contains. I have
since recd. one from Allston,[1] but as he will probably be out of town
about this time, I must trouble you instead of him.

I wish the plates[2] put in the printers hands as soon as possible, and
to be executed on the best paper.[3] *Two thousand of each.* I should
like also to have three hundred ↑*proof impressions*↓ of each struck
off in such manner that they would do to frame should any persons like
to have them in that manner — if not they can hereafter be cut down
to the size of the volume. You & Allston will have as many struck off
for yourselves as you please — Let me know the whole expense and
I will find the money immediately.

I have had my trunk packed to come to London — and should have
attended to all this myself — but one circumstance or other continually
occurs to ⟨f⟩ baffle my plans, and I am at this moment in a little
uncertainty when I shall get there. I shall try hard to see Allston

before he sails — had he been going to Embark at Liverpool the thing would have been certain. I regret excessively that he goes to America now that his prospects are opening so promisingly in this country — but perhaps it is all for the best —

His *Jacobs Dream*[4] was a particular favourite of mine. I have gazed on it again & again and the more I gazed the more I was delighted with it — I believe if I was a painter I could at this moment take ⟨the p⟩ a pencil & delineate the whole with the attitude & expression of every figure.

Allston gives me a charming account of your picture of Ann Page & Master Slender[5] — I hope you will[6] take frequent opportunities to steal away from the painting of portraits to give full scope to your taste and imagination.

ADDRESSED: Charles R. Leslie [Esq.] / Buckingham [Place] / Fitzroy [Square] / Londo[n]   POSTMARKED: D / 31 JY 31 / 1818
MANUSCRIPT: NYPL—Berg Collection.   PUBLISHED: PMI, I, 403–4; Leslie, *Autobiographical Recollections*, p. 207 (in part).
Because the signature was cut away, the final sentence and the complimentary close, as well as part of the address on the verso, are missing. Those missing elements have been supplied conjecturally in brackets.

1. Written from London on July 24, 1818. See PMI, I, 401–3.
2. The plates are engravings prepared for the third edition of *Knickerbocker's History of New York*. Leslie's "Dutch Courtship" was the frontispiece to volume I, and Allston's "A Schepen Laughing at a Burgomaster's Joke" was the frontispiece to volume II. See Langfeld & Blackburn, *WI Bibliography*, p. 12. See also Allston's comments about Leslie's "Dutch Courtship" in a letter of May 9, 1817 (PMI, I, 363) and WI's reactions in his letter of May 21, 1817 to Allston.
3. In his letter of July 24 Allston had stated that "the price of printing your plates would be five pounds a thousand—and that on French paper, which is the best; this includes the paper" (PMI, I, 403).
4. This biblical painting, executed in 1817, was sold to Lord Egremont. See PMI, I, 402; Flagg, *Washington Allston*, pp. 132–33.
5. See PMI, I, 402–3.
6. The manuscript ends here; the remainder of the text is taken from the printed version in PMI, I, 404.

225. *To Henry Brevoort*

London, Sept. 23d. 1818.

My dear Brevoort,

Permit me to introduce to you Mr Bartley,[1] late of Drury Lane Theatre, who with Mrs Bartley[2] is about to make a Tour in the United States[3] — As you have seen the performances of Mrs Bartley I need say nothing on the subject — except that I consider her visit to America as a most gratifying event to the Lovers of the Drama. The private character & deportment of Mr & Mrs Bartley have been such as to secure them the most flattering reception in the best circles of this country, and I feel very solicitous that they should receive similar advantages in America. Permit me therefore to commend them to your attentions and to request that you will interest yourself to make their stay among you both agreeable & advantageous

Your friend
Washington Irving

Henry Brevoort Jr Esqr

ADDRESSED: For / Henry Brevoort Jr. Esq / New York. / Bartley Esq   DOCKETED: W Irving / London 23d.. Septr / 1818
MANUSCRIPT: NYPL—Seligman Collection.   PUBLISHED: LIB, II, 80.

    At the upper part of the address leaf above "For/" in pencil are the words "5 Pearl Street" not in WI's hand. Between "Henry Brevoort Jr. Esq" and "New York." appears in ink "Sandy Hill" in still another hand.

    1. George Bartley (1782?–1858), an English actor who specialized in comic roles, began his dramatic career at Drury Lane Theatre in 1802.

    2. Sarah Smith Bartley (1783–1850) was a tragic actress whose talents and reputation overshadowed her husband's.

    3. The Bartleys played various roles at the Park Theater from November 18, 1818, to December 23, 1818. Their final appearance at the Park Theater was on May 5, 1819, in *The Winter's Tale*. See Odell, *NY Stage*, II, 524–26, 561.

226. To George Bartley

London, Sept 24th. 1818.

My dear Sir,

    Very particular occupations and engagements prevented my calling at the Theatre[1] for several days, and when I did call I found that you had left town. I had intended forwarding the letters to Mr Cape but I have this morning recd. — a letter from him telling me that you are at Liverpool & to sail the 1st Octr. I am busy writing the letters and will forward them in time ⟨care⟩ by coach to save postage[.] they will be directed to the Care of Mr William Grassel Bookseller — next door but one to the Atheneum where you will please to enquire for them. I shall send them by tomorrow evenings coach — or at farthest the next day so that they will be sure to be on time.

In great haste/Your friend & St.
Washington Irving

Bartley Esqr[2]

ADDRESSED: For / —— Bartley Esqr. / of Drury Lane Theatre. / Liverpool. POST-MARKED: SEP / 24 / 18
MANUSCRIPT: SHR.

1. The Bartleys were associated with the Drury Lane Theater.

2. WI apparently did not know Bartley's first name. In his letter to Joseph Hopkinson he refers to the actor as "Mr. Bartley." See WI's letter of September 26, 1818, to Bartley.

227. To Joseph Hopkinson

London, Sept 24th. 1818.

Dear Sir

This letter will be handed to you by Mr Bartley late of Drury Lane Theatre who with his lady is about to Embark for America — to make a professional tour through our country.

Mrs Bartley has for several years supported the principal line in Drury Lane theatre and is considered one of the best performers in the Kingdom. The eminence of her talents as well as the amiableness and correctness of her private character have procured her the attentions of the first circles in this country.

I know you to be an ardent and critical admirer of Shakespeares; and I would ⟨[unrecovered]⟩ observe that Mrs Bartley has been much sought after in the fashionable world, for Private readings and recitations of her plays. Might not such an ⟨select & ele⟩ elegant amusement be introduced into our country —

Of Mr Bartley I can speak in the highest terms as a gentleman of amiable character and great respectability. Permit me to commend them to your attention & kind offices —

With my best remembrances to Mrs Hopkinson[1]

I am my dear Sir/Very truly yours

Washington Irving

Joseph Hopkinson Esqr/&c &c &c

ADDRESSED: For / Joseph Hopkinson Esqr / &c &c &c / Philadelphia / [( )]Bartley Esqr.)

MANUSCRIPT: Va.–Barrett.

Joseph Hopkinson (1770–1842), congressman and jurist, was well known as the author of "Hail Columbia" (1798).

1. Mrs. Hopkinson was a friend in Philadelphia whom WI had met on his visits to the Nicholases, Gratzes, and Merediths.

228. To Nicholas G. Biddle

London Septr. 26th. 1818

Dear Sir,

This will be handed to you by Mr Bartley late of Drury Lane Theatre, who with Mrs Bartley are about to make a Tour through the United States You must be aware of Mrs Bartleys dramatic reputation, having for several years supported the principal line at Drury lane and been considered one of the most eminent performers in England She has also received particular attentions from the best society and been received into the first circles. I look upon her visit to America as likely to be of great benefit to public taste, and wish her reception to be such as to encourage persons of equal talent & eminence in the elegant arts to turn their attentions to America —

Mr Bartley is a gentleman highly respected here for the amiableness & correctness of his private character as well as for his professional merits. As a man of letters and one who I know has the improvement of his country in every thing that is polite and elegant at heart I have made free to commend Mr & Mrs Bartley to your good offices and shall be happy of any opportunity to reciprocate civilities and to prove⟨to you⟩ the very great respect and regard I entertain for you.

Very truly/Your friend

Washington Irving

Nicholas G Biddle Esqr.

DOCKETED: W Irving [upper right corner of MS page 1]
MANUSCRIPT: LC.

229. To George Bartley

London Sept 26th. 1818.

Dear Sir,

Herewith you will receive several letters of Introduction for my friends in America

I could have wished to have furnished you with more; but during the ⟨few⟩ three years that I have been absent from America fate and misfortune seem to have been particularly busy in the circle of my intimacies. Such changes have taken place by deaths, removals, disasters &c and I have myself been so beaten down by fortune that when I take pen in hand for the purpose I feel at a loss whom to address —

Accept my best wishes for your prosperity and happiness & believe me

Yours very truly

Washington Irving

———————— Bartley Esqr.

ADDRESSED: For / —— Bartley Esqr / Liverpool.
MANUSCRIPT: Va.–Barrett.

230. To Henry Brevoort

London Sept 27th. 1818.

My dear Brevoort

It is some time since I received your letter of July 21: but I am so little in the vein of letter writing now adays that I find myself continually procrastinating. Your letter cheered a dull & lonely hour and made me feel for a little while quite at home and among friends again. I wish you joy of your son[1] and hope and trust he will add greatly to the stock of domestic enjoyments that seem continually augmenting around you. Give my congratulations to Mrs Brevoort on the occasion, if it has not grown too old a story by the time this letter arrives.

I have been in London for about Six weeks, and shall make it most probably my head quarters while I remain in England. My health has been but indifferent this summer, having been nervous and debilitated which produced ⟨great⟩ at times great depression of Spirits.[2] As the weather grows cool however I feel myself reviving and hope soon to be myself again.

I believe I mentioned to you in a former letter that ⟨Ogilvie⟩ I had met with Ogilvie[3] in England—He is now in London and is preparing for another attempt at oratorical display in the Metropolis. He was very Successful in Scotland, but has never had a fair chance at the London folks—I think his success here very problematical, though men vastly his inferiors have succeeded; but there is great caprice in public taste in London. By the death of a relative he has fallen heir to a little family estate called Dunnydeen, which is sufficient for all his moderate wants. I see him frequently, and am more convinced than ever of the pureness of his intentions and goodness of his heart. He is quite a visionary but a most interesting one.

You mention that the Booksellers are wanting a new Edition of Knickerbocker—I have been preparing one and am only waiting to get two plates printed to send it out ⟨for⟩ to Moses Thomas for publication.[4] The two plates are excellent engravings from two ⟨pl p⟩ drawings by Leslie and Allston—The pictures have great merit. I have ordered two or three hundred proofs of each to be struck off in case any persons ⟨wan⟩ might be inclined to purchase them for framing as specimens of Allstons & Leslies Abilities[.] I wish to cover the expenses as far as possible—They have cost a considerable sum—at least ⟨a⟩ considerable to my slender purse. I hope this new Edition will bring me in a little money soon ⟨to⟩ or my purse will soon run d[ry] [MS torn]

I have drawn on Moses Thomas for three hundred [dollars] [MS torn] ↑in your favour↓ to pay off a Booksellers account for Books sent him—I had not intended to trouble you again in this way—but I did not know whether my Brother William would be in town

Can I be of any service to you in buying Books as I shall probably be for some time in London —

Remember me to such of my friends as seem to care any thing about me and give my sincere regards to your better half—

I am my dear Brevoort—as ever

affectionately yours
W I.

P. S. I have given Mr Bartley of Drury lane a letter of introduction to you—Mrs Bartley I am told is a fine intelligent woman and I thought you would feel an interest in knowing her.

Inclosed, first of Exchg on Moses Thomas, at 60 days sight for 300$ favour of H Brevoort Jr[5]

ADDRESSED: For / Henry Brevoort Jr. Esqr / New York / Pacific   DOCKETED: W. Irving. / London Septr. 27 / 1818.

MANUSCRIPT: NYPL—Seligman Collection.   PUBLISHED: LIB, II, 81–84.

1. James Carson Brevoort (July 10, 1818–December 7, 1887), who later served as WI's secretary while he was minister to Spain.

2. WI had been depressed by the bankruptcy of P. & E. Irving Company and by his inability to write creatively again.

3. James Ogilvie, the orator whom WI had met in America more than a decade earlier. See WI's letter of May 11, 1809.

4. A third edition of *Knickerbocker's History of New York* appeared in two volumes in 1819 with engravings by Charles Leslie and Washington Allston. See Langfeld & Blackburn, *WI Bibliography*, pp. 11–12.

5. The passage, "Inclosed . . . Jr" is written along the lower left margin of the sheet.

231. To Ebenezer Irving

[London, October 13, 1818]

I have forwarded to your care a parcel containing plates for the new edition of the History of New York, which I will thank you to forward safely and without delay to Mr. Thomas, as I wish the work to be printed as soon as possible. There are but two plates, one for each volume; but they are charming little things by Allston and Leslie, and are engraved in the best style. The engraving and printing of them has cost me about one hundred pounds sterling.

As to the sealed packet, which I left with you, it may be destroyed. I have nothing now to leave my brothers but a blessing, and that they have whenever I think of them.

PUBLISHED: PMI, I, 408.

232. To Henry Brevoort

London, Oct. 16th. 1818.

My dear Brevoort,

I have this day drawn on you at ninety days date in favour of Mess. A. & S. Richards for Three Hundred Dollars. It is against a draft which I lately sent you, on Moses Thomas for a like amount at sixty days sight.

I am writing in extreme haste that my letter may go by a parcel which is making up.

Yours affectionately
W. I.

PUBLISHED: LIB, II, 85.

233. To Ebenezer Irving

[London, late November, 1818]

Flattering as the prospect undoubtedly is, which your letters hold out,[1] I have concluded to decline it for various reasons, some of which I have stated to William.[2] The principal one is, that I do not wish to undertake any situation that must involve me in such a routine of duties as to prevent my attending to literary pursuits.

PUBLISHED: PMI, I, 409.

1. On October 24, 1818, William Irving had written about an arrangement for Washington to take the post of first clerk in the navy department. See PMI, I, 408–9.

2. PMI (I, 409) notes: "This letter never came to hand, or has been lost."

234. To John Howard Payne

[December, 1818?]

Dear Payne,

I find you have many applications for orders,[1] and should feel delicate about applying for any — but I know they cost you nothing & that you are anxious to have your friends present. I mean to get Newton[2] & Leslie to accompany me & make a party to persuade the folks not to hiss. If you can furnish us with orders—so: if not we will go at our own expense & consider ourselves at liberty to hiss as much as we please.

We will call at your lodgings on our way to the theater, if you have spare orders leave them for us. I wish to hold out no menace; but I have in my possession a cat-call; that has been of potent service in helping to damn half a score of new tragedies—

Yours truly
W Irving

ADDRESSED: John H Payne Esqr

MANUSCRIPT: Va.–Barrett. PUBLISHED: *Scribner's Magazine* 47 (October, 1910), 465–66; Grace Overmyer, *America's First Hamlet* (New York, 1957), pp. 168–69.

WI apparently wrote this note on part of the blank verso of a letter to Payne. On the address side of the sheet, written upside down from WI's "John H Payne Esqr" is "honour I shall be much obliged of & remain Dear Payne / Yours most sincerely / James OLeary / 4 Queens Square / Westr."

Although this letter is undated, the context suggests that it was written as *Brutus* was about to open at Drury Lane Theatre on December 3, 1818. WI. Newton, and Leslie, as well as Payne, were all in London at this time. See STW, I, 170; Overmyer, *America's First Hamlet*, pp. 168–69.

1. Orders were free passes to theaters or other places of entertainment. An early playbill for *Brutus* indicates that orders could not be admitted. See Overmyer, *America's First Hamlet*, p. 169.

2. Gilbert Stuart Newton (1794–1835), a nephew of the painter Gilbert Stuart and a close friend of Charles Leslie, established himself as a successful portrait painter.

235. *To Moses Thomas*

[Liverpool, 1818]

. . . able to keep on quietly & regularly in the path I have marked out for myself, without the danger of being overtaken by want on the way. *In the mean time continue to have faith in me.*

I may have occasion before long to draw on you, but shall do it at such dates as not to inconvenience you. I have had to pay 25 *guineas* for ⟨a plate⟩ the engraving of a drawing by Leslie for Knickerbocker.[1] I shall have as much more to pay for one by Allston,[2] which however will not be done these two ↑or three↓ months: this delay is very inconvenient as I want to ⟨get⟩ have a new Edition published as soon as possible.[3] The engravings will be in the very best style—

I see there are two volumes of tales in prose by Hogg[4] coming out: I shall endeavour to secure them for you. Have you published all his poems; if not I think it worth your while for they have great merit. His *Kilmeny* in the *Queens Wake*[5] is one of the most beautiful little tales in modern poetry. You will find biographical ⟨th⟩ anecdotes of Hogg in the late Scots Magazine[6] which are very interesting—he is an extraordinary genius of Natures own production.

Yours truly
W I.

MANUSCRIPT: Andrew B. Myers.   PUBLISHED: *Autograph Catalog No. 5* of Robert
   F. Batchelder, Ambler, Pennsylvania [September, 1973], p. 13.
   The allusions to the drawings of Charles R. Leslie and Washington Allston suggest that the letter was written in 1818 in connection with the planning of the
third edition of *Knickerbocker's History of New York*, which Moses Thomas published in 1819.

   1. On December 20, 1817, Leslie wrote to WI: "I have put the sketch of the
'Dutch Courtship' into the hands of a very excellent engraver. It will be done in
two months; the price will be twenty-five guineas, which is not high for the style
in which he will do it." See Leslie, *Autobiographical Recollections*, p. 205.
   2. The cost of Allston's engraving was thirty-five to forty guineas. See Allston
to WI, March 13, 1818; PMI, I, 398.
   3. The engraving for Allston's drawing was not completed until late July, 1818.
WI then asked Leslie in London to arrange for 2000 copies of each sketch to be
made for use in the edition which Moses Thomas was about to undertake. See
Allston to WI, July 24, 1818 (PMI, I, 401–2); WI to Leslie, July 29, 1818.
   4. *The Brownie of Bodsbeck; and Other Tales* (Edinburgh, 1818).
   5. "Kilmeny" was published as "The Thirteenth Bard's Song" in *The Queen's
Wake*, which first appeared in 1813. See Edith C. Batho, *The Ettrick Shepherd*
(New York, 1969), p. 193.
   6. Probably "Tales and Anecdotes of the Pastoral Life," also published in
Blackwood's Magazine 1 (April, 1817), 22–25; (May, 1817), 143–47; (June, 1817),
247–50.

236.   To Samuel Rogers

[January 12, (1819)]

My dear Sir,
   I find to my great joy that I have been under a mistake as to the
day of the week, and that I have no engagement for tomorrow. So if my
Chair at your table is still vacant I shall be most happy to fill it

                                             Very truly yours
                                             Washington Irving
Tuesday, Jan. 12th.

MANUSCRIPT: SHR.

   At the top of the letter is printed in capital letters "WASHINGTON IRVING TO SAM-
UEL ROGERS.—G. S. H." The initials are probably those of George S. Hellman. As
determined by the perpetual calendar, the date is 1819.
   Samuel Rogers (1763–1855), son of a wealthy banker and author of *The Pleasures
of Memory* (1792), was well known for his famous breakfasts and other social
activities.

237. To Ebenezer Irving

London, March 1 1819.

My dear Brother

This letter is accompanied by a small parcel containing some manuscript for publication. It will form the first number of a work[1] to be continued occasionally should this specimen meet with sufficient success. I have no time to explain myself particularly on the subject as it is now almost one oclock at night and the parcel must go away early in the morning. I will write more fully by the same ship that brings this.

I wish Mr Thomas[2] to have the publication of this work, and that you should make arrangements with him accordingly. His conduct towards me has uniformly been of a kind that entitles him to ⟨the⟩ friendship and confidence ⟨whoever takes out the copy right⟩ The copy right must be taken out by the booksellers, but privately secured to me. A large edition should be struck off — three or four thousand[3] — ⟨were I on the spot I should say *five* thousand⟩ and the price must be pretty high. ⟨I know⟩ If it is known to be my work I presume it will have quick sale, and large editions make good profits. I want to to recieve ⟨pro⟩ the profit from it as soon as possible as my purse is slender.

Do not show the Mss. to any one, nor say any thing about it. Write to Thomas *confidentially.* It is better to awaken no expectations. I shall feel very anxious to hear of the success of this first re-appearance on the literary stage — Should it be successful, I trust I shall be able henceforth to keep up an occasional fire. It has cost me much coaxing up of my mind to get it in training again.

The work must be advertized in the papers some time beforehand, so as to give time for Booksellers to order it from the publisher.

I must now to bed, but will write to you as I said before, at more length by this same opportunity

Give my love to Eliza[4] and the family —

Your affectionate Brother
WI.

ADDRESSED: Mr Ebenr Irving / New York. / Rosalie}   DOCKETED: March 1. 1819
MANUSCRIPT: NYPL—Seligman Collection.

This letter was sent to Ebenezer Irving. For corroboration see WI's letter to Brevoort, March 3, 1819.

1. The first part of *The Sketch Book* containing "The Author's Account of Himself," "The Voyage," "Roscoe," "The Wife," and "Rip Van Winkle," appeared in New York on June 23, 1819, printed by C. S. Van Winkle, and priced at 75 cents. See Langfeld & Blackburn, *WI Bibliography*, pp. 15–16.

2. Owing to Thomas's financial difficulties, this arrangement did not materialize. See WI's letter to Brevoort, March 3, 1819.

3. The first issue was 2000 copies. See STW, I, 173.
4. Elizabeth Kip Irving (1779–1827), Ebenezer's wife.

238. To Ebenezer Irving

[London, March 3, 1819]

I have sent by Capt. Merry, of the Rosalie,[1] the first number of a work which I hope to be able to continue from time to time. I send it more for the purpose of showing you what I am about, as I find my declining the situation at Washington has given you chagrin. The fact is, that situation would have given me barely a genteel subsistence. It would have led to no higher situations, for I am quite unfitted for political life. My talents are merely literary, and all my habits of thinking, reading, &c., have been in a different direction from that required for the active politician. It is a mistake also to suppose I would fill an office there, and devote myself at the same time to literature. I require much leisure and a mind entirely abstracted from other cares and occupations, if I would write much or write well. I should therefore at Washington be completely out of my element, and instead of adding to my reputation, stand a chance of impairing that which I already possess. If I ever get any solid credit with the public, it must be in the quiet and assiduous operations of my pen, under the mere guidance of fancy or feeling.

I have been for some time past nursing my mind up for literary operations, and collecting materials for the purpose. I shall be able, I trust, now to produce articles from time to time that will be sufficient for my present support, and form a stock of copyright property, that may be a little capital for me hereafter. To carry this into better effect it is important for me to remain a little longer in Europe, where there is so much food for observation, and objects of taste on which to meditate and improve. I feel myself completely committed in literary reputation by what I have already written; and I feel by no means satisfied to rest my reputation on my preceding writings. I have suffered several precious years of youth and lively imagination to pass by unimproved, and it behooves me to make the most of what is left. If I indeed have the means within me of establishing a legitimate literary reputation, this is the very period of life most auspicious for it, and I am resolved to devote a few years exclusively to the attempt. Should I succeed, besides the literary property I shall amass in copyright, I trust it will not be difficult to obtain some official situation of a moderate, unpretending kind, in which I may make my bread. But as to reputation I can only look for it through the exertions of my pen. * * *

In fact, I consider myself at present as making a literary experiment, in the course of which I only care to be kept in bread and cheese. Should it not succeed — should my writings not acquire critical applause, I am content to throw up the pen and take to any commonplace employment. But if they should succeed, it would repay me for a world of care and privation to be placed among the established authors of my country, and to win the affections of my countrymen.

* * * I have but one thing to add. I have now given you the leading motive of my actions — it may be a weak one, but it has full possession of me, and therefore the attainment of it is necessary to my comfort. I now wish to be left for a little while entirely to the bent of my own inclination, and not agitated by new plans for subsistence, or by entreaties to come home. My spirits are very unequal, and my mind depends upon them; and I am easily thrown into such a state of perplexity and such depression as to incapacitate me for any mental exertion. Do not, I beseech you, impute my lingering in Europe to any indifference to my own country or my friends. My greatest desire is to make myself worthy of the good-will of my country, and my greatest anticipation of happiness is the return to my friends. I am living here in a retired and solitary way, and partaking in little of the gaiety of life, but I am determined not to return home until I have sent some writings before me that shall, if they have merit, make me return to the smiles, rather than skulk back to the pity of my friends.

PUBLISHED: PMI, I, 412–14 (in part); STW, I, 172–74 (in part).

1. The *Rosalie* left London on March 11, 1819. See NYEP, April 16, 1819.

239. To Ebenezer Irving

[March 3(?) 1819]

I have seen what Verplanck said of my work.[1] He did me more than justice in what he said of my mental qualifications; and he said nothing of my work that I have not long thought of it myself. * * He is one of the honestest men I know of, in speaking his opinion. There is a determined candor about him, which will not allow him to be blinded by passion. I am sure he wishes me well, and his own talents and acquirements are too great to suffer him to entertain jealousy; but were I his bitterest enemy, such an opinion have I of his integrity of mind, that I would refer any one to him for an honest account of me, sooner than to almost any one else.

PUBLISHED: PMI, I, 241 (in part).

This excerpt may be a part of the preceding letter which WI wrote to Ebenezer on March 3, 1819. PMI quotes the passage out of chronological order, but the context suggests that it belongs to 1819.

1. On December 7, 1818, Gulian C. Verplanck spoke to the New-York Historical Society on American nationalism. In the course of his remarks he commented on WI's "burlesque history of New-York, in which it is painful to see a mind, as admirable for its exquisite perception of the beautiful, as it is for its quick sense of the ridiculous, wasting the riches of its fancy on an ungrateful theme, and its exuberant humor in a coarse caricature.

"This writer has not yet fulfilled all the promise he has given to his country. It is his duty, because it is in his power, to brush away the pretenders who may at any time infest her society, her science, or her politics: or if he aspires, as I trust he does, to strains of a higher mood, the deeds of his countrymen, and the undescribed beauties of his native land afford him many a rich subject, and he may deck the altar of his country's glory with the garlands of his taste and fancy" (Gulian C. Verplanck, "An Anniversary Discourse Delivered before the New-York Historical Society, Dec. 7, 1818," in *Discourses and Addresses* [New York, 1833], p. 63). See also PMI, I, 241.

240. To Henry Brevoort

London, March 3d. 1819.

My dear Brevoort.

I have this moment received your letter of Feby 2d.[1] which came most opportunely, ⟨for I was⟩ as it shewed the impossibility of my relying further on poor Thomas in literary matters, and I was on the point of commencing ⟨?an enquiry of?⟩ further operations with him. He is a worthy honest fellow, but apt to entangle himself. Were I a rich man I would give him my writings for nothing — as I am a very poor one, I must take care of myself.

I have just sent to my brother Ebenr.[2] Mss: for the first number of a work which if successful I hope to continue occasionally. I had wished him to send it to Thomas for publication; but I now must have it published by some one else. Will you, as you are a literary man and a man of liesure, take it under your care. I wish the copy right secured for me, and the work printed, and then sold to one or more ⟨p⟩ booksellers, who will take the whole impression at a fair discount. & give cash or good notes for it. This makes short work of it — and is more profitable to the author than selling the copy right. I should like Thomas to have the first offer — as he has been and is a true friend to me & I wish him to have any advantage that may arise from the publication of it.

⟨If you are in N York⟩

If the work is printed in NYork will you correct the proof sheets, as I fear the Mss: will be obscure & occasionally incorrect, & you are well acquainted with my handwriting.

I feel great diffidence about this re-appearance in literature. I am conscious of my imperfections — and my mind has been for a long time past ⟨bur⟩ so preyed upon and agitated by various cares and anxieties, that I fear it has lost much of its cheerfulness and some of its activity.

I have attempted no lofty theme nor sought to look wise and learned, which appears to be very much the ⟨?tone?⟩ fashion among our American writers at present — I have preferred addressing myself to the feeling⟨s⟩ & fancy of the reader, more than to his judgement — My writings may appear therefore ⟨as⟩ light & trifling in our Country of philosophers & politicians — but if ⟨as such⟩, they possess merit ⟨it is all I aspire at in the work⟩ in the class of literature to which they belong it is all to which I aspire in the work. I seek only to blow a flute accompaniment in the national concert, and leave others to ↑play↓ the fiddle & frenchhorn.
⟨I wish the v⟩

I shall endeavour to follow this first number by a second as soon as possible, but some time may intervene — for my writing moods are very precarious, and I have been ↑renderd↓ excessively ⟨wearied and⟩ nervous by the kind of life I have led for some time past.

Your request that I should draw on you when in want of money is one of the many gratifying proofs of friendship which I have received from you. Indeed the offer is a most acceptable one: for I have been much annoyed by the idea of running short of funds, and was determined not to ask for any ⟨lo⟩ ↑in↓ advance. I can draw on you with confidence, as you will receive the proceeds of my writings, which I hope will more than cover my drafts. The supply of cash will enable me to go over to the continent by & bye, where I wish to visit a few places before I return to America. I may therefore draw on you in the course of a few weeks for *1000$* — especially if I feel confidence in the prosecution of my work — If I can get my mind into full play, and dash off a set of writings that may do me credit; I shall return home with alacrity, and it will hasten my return — but I cannot bear the thoughts of limping home broken down & spiritless, to be received kindly in remembrance of former services.

I wish you to keep the contents of this letter to yourself — say nothing of my Mss: ⟨or my plans concerning it I⟩ and dont let any one see it before printed — I dread awakening expectations

Give my most affectionate regards to your wife, who I love for your sake as well as her own. The misfortunes of the Renwicks[3] gave me some dismal feelings — it seemed as if another little region of ⟨affe⟩ my happiness was laid waste — and thus piece by piece the whole home scene I had left behind was becoming desolate. Give them my best wishes & remembrances.

I read your statement of the affair with Strong[4] with feelings of indignation and surprise — Indignation that so worthless a wretch could have it so much in his power to molest the peace of the worthy — and surprize that you should have sufferd it to annoy you to such a degree — or to fancy that your fair, generous and immaculate character needed any statement to vindicate it.

God bless you my dear Brevoort — Your friend

WI.

P.S. I wish a pretty high price to be put on my work; and that the Booksellers should be brought to moderate terms. ⟨If⟩ Do not press poor Thomas about the 300$ if still unpaid — let him have time — I fear I shall be sadly disappointed in the receipt of funds from the new edition of the Hist of NYork — I had depended upon it for current expenses; but must now look forward to the future exertions of my pen.

ADDRESSED: Henry Brevoort Jr. Eqr. / New York. / Rosalie: DOCKETED: London
    March 3. 1819 / Washington Irving.
MANUSCRIPT: NYPL—Seligman Collection.   PUBLISHED: LIB, II, 86–91; PMI, I,
    414–16 (in part).

1. This letter has not been located.

2. See WI's letter of March 1, 1819.

3. Apparently an allusion to the failure of James Renwick's business, brought about by the collapse of his British correspondents. See *DAB*, XV, 506. Brevoort mentions the Renwicks in a letter to WI on September 9, 1819. See LBI, I, 114.

4. In his letter of October 2, 1818, Brevoort tells of his difficulties with Harvey Strong: "I send you a minute statement of a disgusting dispute & its consequences forced upon me by a person named Harvey Strong — You will perceive it to have been one of these unavoidable occurences incident to men of the most unoffending dispositions.— I wish you to set the affair in its true light to any who may have noticed the filthy advertisements of Strong in our Newspapers — The statement is enclosed to Mr. Richards, who will peruse it, & transmit it to you.— Possibly you may think I have treated this vile brawl with disproportionate importance — but I cannot rest until the calumny is effectually refuted.— The sentence of the Court & Jury in distinctly acquitting me from every imputation of Strong, was decisive as to public opinion in New York & elsewhere — but I am happy to say that without this formality, those who had the slightest knowledge of me, regarded Mr. Strong's advertisement as the libels of a miscreant who had been chastised in the manner he deserved.—

"The fine of 250$ imposed by Mr. Colden exclusively for a breach of the peace, was considered by every person who attended to the trial, as exorbitant & unwarranted by the offence, (notwithstanding the very handsome concessions &c., &c. made to me in delivering the sentence of the Court.) —

"The affair derived its sole importance from the base conduct of our editors, especially Mr. Noah, of the Advocate, whose apology was not a sufficient atonement for his misconduct.— If every blackguard who can pay for the insertion of an advertisement, may be permitted to calumniate any person in the community, the peace of society is at an end — The laws of the land, as expounded by Mr. Colden, inflict 250$ penalty for chastising a person with every circumstance of justification — Yet these laws yield no adequate redress for the defilement of a mans reputation in the public prints—But I will not add another word to a subject which has terminated so entirely as I could have wished, and which has already sunk into oblivion—" (see LBI, I, 101–3).

241. To Henry Brevoort

London. April 1st. 1819.

My dear Brevoort,

I send a second No. of the Sketch Book It is not so large as the first but I have not been able to get more matter ready for publication;[1] and indeed I am not particular about the work being regular in any way. The price of this number of course must be less than the first

I have read your article in the Feby number of the Analectic[2] with great pleasure. I am glad you are occupying your abundant leisure in this way It will give you an object to excite your mind & give a Seasoning to existence — and I think you may both do yourself great credit and american literature service by writing occasionally.

I have been delighted with Verplancks oration—It does him honour and shews of what he is capable[.] I hope he will not put our old dutch burghers into the notion that they must feel affronted with poor Diedrich Knickerbocker just as he is about creeping out in a new edition[.] I could not help laughing at this burst of filial feeling ⟨o⟩in ⟨the⟩ Verplanck, on the jokes put upon his ancestors Though I honour the feeling & admire the manner in which it is expressed — It met my eyes just as I had finished the little story of Rip Van Winkle and I could not help noticing it in the introduction to that Bagatelle — I hope Verplanck will not think the article was written in defiance of his Vituperation. ⟨Tell⟩ Remember me heartily to him, and tell him I mean to grow wiser and better and older every day and to lay the castigation he has given me seriously to heart—

Give my best regards to Mrs Brevoort, and believe me my dear Brevoort —

Yours affectionately
W I.

PS. I hope you have been able to make arrangements with Thomas for the publication of my writings[.] I should greatly prefer its ⟨appearing⟩ being published by him.

If you can suggest any hints that will be of service to me in the work — and any thing that will cheer & excite me, do so I beg of you. Let me know what themes &c would be popular and striking in America; for I have been so long in England that ⟨I begin to⟩ things cease to strike me here as novelties &³ ↓begin↑ to wear a common place⟨d⟩ aspect —

ADDRESSED: Henry Brevoort Junr Esqr. / New York. / p *Tom Hazard*   DOCKETED: London Ap. 1. 1819 / W. Irving
MANUSCRIPT: Va.–Barrett.   PUBLISHED: LIB, II, 92–94; PMI, I, 420 (in part); *The American Writer in England*, intro. C. Waller Barrett (Charlottesville, 1969), p. 20 (in part).

1. The second number of *The Sketch Book* contained "English Writers on America," "Rural Life in England," "The Broken Heart," and "The Art of Book Making."
2. Brevoort may have written the unsigned review of Verplanck's "Anniversary Discourse Delivered Before the New-York Historical Society, December 7, 1818," appearing in the *Analectic Magazine* 13 (February, 1819), 138–55. Most of the article is excerpts from Verplanck's address.
3. In different handwriting "begin" is written after "&."

242. *To Henry Brevoort*

London, April 25th. 1819.

My dear Brevoort,
It is with the greatest pleasure that I make you acquainted with my friend Mr. Ticknor,¹ who is just returning from a residence in Europe and will probably pass a few days in New York. I reccommend you to see as much of him as you can for your own sake.
With best regards to Mrs Brevoort I am

Yours affectionately
W Irving

ADDRESSED: Henry Brevoort Jr. Esqr. / New York. / Geo Ticknor Esqr.   DOCKETED: W. Irving
MANUSCRIPT: Harvard.

1. George Ticknor (1791–1871), a graduate of Dartmouth College who had gone to Europe in 1815 to study and travel before accepting a professorship at Harvard.

243. *To James A. Hillhouse*

[London, May 11, 1819]

My dear Sir,
I have called to talk with you about the Mss:¹ and am sorry you are not at home. I have read it with great satisfaction and feel quite of Mr Trumbulls² opinion. I did not bring it with me as you might not

be at home & I did not like to leave it open. When I see you I will talk more explicitly — at present I can only say that I should think you might safely follow the bent of your inclination as to the mode of ushering it to the world. I will leave the work sealed up and directed to you, at my lodgings should you think proper to call ⟨f⟩ or send for it — I am so uncertain a being at this moment that I can make no appointment, but am generally at home throughout the day —

with great regard/Yours truly
WI.

Norfolk St. May 11. [1819]

ADDRESSED: Hillhouse Esqr.   DOCKETED: W. Irving / 11th May. 1819
MANUSCRIPT: Va.–Barrett

The American poet, James A. Hillhouse (1789–1841), visited England in 1819 and published *Percy's Masque* during his visit. WI apparently did not remember Hillhouse's first name.

1. Probably of *Percy's Masque*.
2. John Trumbull (1750–1831), author of *The Progress of Dulness* (1772–1773) and *M'Fingal* (1775–1782) and later a Connecticut jurist, had probably encouraged Hillhouse's publication of the work.

244.   To John Treat Irving

London May. 13th. 1819.

My dear Brother,

By the ship[1] which takes this I forward some Mss. for publication, being the third number of an occasional work[2]—As I did not know whether Ebenr. would be in NYork I have inclosed the pacquet to Messrs. Irving & Smith[3] and directed it to be handed in case E. I. was absent, either to Wm I. Yourself—or Brevoort. Should it be put in your hands have it published in the same way as the preceding[4]—I drew on you some time since for, I believe 300$. I presume the draft was accepted and that I can now get the proceeds from Richards[5] in Lpool. I shall write to him on the subject—as I am out of money. I drew because I apprehended I should be out of cash before I could get my writings in course of publication. I hope by th⟨is⟩e time this arrives some of them may be in print & the question settled whether they are profitable.[6] Should they be so, I wish you to refund yourself for the draft out of the proceeds—as I do not ⟨w⟩ consider that I have any possible claim on the estate—at any rate I do not wish to receive any thing from it.

I am writing in extreme haste and have only time to add my love to Abby[7] and the family and believe me in all fortunes and situations

Your affectionate Brother
Washington Irving

P. S. Should there be any objection to Peters Draft for 300$ drawn at the same time with mine—I wish you to ⟨ref⟩ get the payment of it also, out of the proceeds of the work, ⟨as⟩ though as he has been actively employed in settling the affairs of the house—he may have a claim on the estate. do not say any thing to him on the subject—but let him suppose the draft is disposed of according to his expectations. ⟨by⟩

Should my writings pay well—I hope to be able to keep up occasional publications—and thus keep ahead of my expenses—

ADDRESSED: John T Irving Esqr. / New York. / p Juno   DOCKETED: W Irving to Jno T Irving / May 19th 1819
MANUSCRIPT: Va.–Barrett.   PUBLISHED: *The American Writer in England*, intro. C. Waller Barrett, p. 20 (in part).

1. According to the address leaf, the ship was the *Juno*, which arrived in New York on June 29, 1819, according to NYEP for June 30, 1819.
2. The third number of *The Sketch Book* contained "A Royal Poet," "The Country Church," "The Widow and Her Son," and "The Boar's Head Tavern."
3. Their firm was located   at 142 Pearl Street.
4. Each part was published in separate wrappers. The first two numbers appeared on June 23 and July 31, while the one under discussion in this letter appeared on September 13, 1819. See Langfeld & Blackburn, *WI Bibliography*, p. 15.
5. Messrs. A. & S. Richards were associated with P. & E. Irving in Liverpool.
6. WI, of course, had been left without any means of support as a result of the failure of the family importing firm.
7. John Treat Irving married Abigail Spicer Furman on April 27, 1806.

245.   To Henry Brevoort

London, May 13th. 1819.

My dear Brevoort,

By the ship which brings this I forward a third number of the Sketch Book, and if you have interested yourself in the fate of the preceding I will thank you to extend your kindness to this also. I am extremely anxious to hear from you what you think of the first number — & am looking anxiously for the arrival of the next ship from N York — My fate hangs on it — for I am now at the end of my *fortune* — ⟨Should the⟩ I am writing in excessive haste for the parcel by which this goes is ⟨cl⟩ about to be closed —

Give my sincere regards to Mrs Brevoort and believe me my dear fellow

ever yours,
WI.

The Mss: has gone under cover to Mess Irving & Smith.

ADDRESSED: Henry Brevoort Jr Esqr / New York. / p Juno   DOCKETED: London
     May 13, 1819 / *Washington Irving*
MANUSCRIPT: NYPL—Seligman Collection.   PUBLISHED: LIB, II, 95; PMI, I, 422–23
     (in part).

246. To John Howard Payne

[London, June 4, 1819]

Dear Payne.

The Mss.[1] was not returned until yesterday and I have not had time
to look over it. I shall be very anxious to hear what Young[2] thinks of it.
and what your prospects are of having it represented. Drop me a line
when you have leisure

Yours truly
W I.

Friday Morng. June 4th. [1819]

ADDRESSED: J H Payne Esqr—   DOCKETED: Washington Irving / London June 4. 1819
MANUSCRIPT: Columbia.

1. WI is probably referring to a draft version of Payne's play *Virginius; or,
the Patrician's Perfidy.* See Grace Overmyer, *America's First Hamlet*, p. 172.
    2. Charles M. Young (1777–1856), regarded by many at the time as the most
important English tragedian, played regularly at Covent Garden, with which
Payne had been associated as publicist and actor before his break with the manager,
Henry Harris.

247. To Henry Brevoort

London July 10th. 1819.

My dear Brevoort,

I recd. a few days since your letter of the 9th. June and a day or
two afterwards yours of 2d. & 8th. May[1] which had been detained in
Liverpool. This last gave me your opinion of my first Number. I had felt
extremely anxious to ascertain it, and your apparent silence had discouraged me.

I am not sorry for the delay that has taken place in the ⟨work⟩
publication — ⟨I⟩ as it will give me ⟨lies⟩ more time to prepare my next
number. Various circumstances have concurred to render me very
nervous & subject to fits of depression that incapacitate me for literary
exertion. All that I do at present is in transient gleams of Sunshine
which are soon overclouded and I have to struggle against continual
damps and chills. I hold on patiently to my purpose however — in

hopes of more genial weather hereafter, when I will be able to exert myself more effectively.

It is a long while since I have heard from my Brother William and I am apt to attribute his silence to dissatisfaction at my not accepting the situation at Washington. A circumstance which I apprehend has disappointed others of my friends. In these matters however great weight should be given to a mans tastes & inclinations. The value of a situation is only as it contributes to a mans happiness — and I should have been perfectly out of my element and uncomfortable in Washington. The place could merely have supported me, and ⟨I⟩ instead of rising, ⟨I should have⟩ as my friends appeared to anticipate, I should have sunk even in my own opinion. My mode of life has unfortunately been such as to render me unfit for almost any useful purpose. I have not the kind of knowledge or the habits that are ⟨fitted f⟩ necessary for business or regular official duty. My acquirements, tastes & habits are just such as to adapt me for the kind of literary exertions I contemplate. It is only in this way I have any chance of acquiring real reputation, and I am desirous of giving it a fair trial — I have long since been committed in print — & when once launched a man has no alternative — he must either do better or be judged by what he has done. My only regret is that my pecuniary wants have forced me to take the field before I felt myself sufficiently prepared, or my mind in a sufficient state of ⟨system? and⟩ freedom from other cares, and fullness of literary excitement. Had I been able to save but a pittance from the wrecks of our concerns, so as to keep me above the fear of a positively empty purse, I should have felt more ease of mind and been able the better to have matured my plans. At present my efforts must all be precarious, subject to delays & imperfections.

I feel perfectly satisfied with your arrangements respecting the work, & more than ever indebted to you for these offices of friendship. I have delayed drawing on you until I should hear further about the work; but shall have to do so soon.

I am sorry that Paulding has undertaken to continue Salmagundi[2] without consulting me — He should have done so as I am implicated in the first Series. I think it a very injudicious thing. ⟨and one that will⟩ The work was pardonable as a juvenile production and has been indulgently received by the public — But it is full of errors, puerilities & impertinencies which James should have had more judgement than to guarantee at his maturer age. I was in hopes it would gradually have gone down into oblivion: but it is now dragged once more before the public & subject to a more rigorous criticism. I am glad however that ⟨the⟩ James is not writing another large poem[3] as I understood he was. He is too eager to get into print and too impatient of the labour of

.correction to write large poems though he has poetical thoughts in abundance.

Peter is well & desires to be heartily remembered to you. Letters have been written home in his behalf for the situation of Consul at Marseilles — vacant by the death of the late occupant.[4] I hope our friends & connexions will push the matter promptly & effectually — if they cannot ⟨get this⟩ do this for him they can do nothing.

Give my sincere regards to Mrs Brevoort & speak a good word for me now & then to your little boy who I hope some day or other to have for a playmate.

Remember me to the rest of your domestic circle and believe me as ever

Affectionately yours
WI.

ADDRESSED: To / Henry Brevoort Jun: Esqr. / New York. / per Martha   DOCKETED: London 10 July 1819 / Washington Irving
MANUSCRIPT: NYPL—Seligman Collection.   PUBLISHED: LIB, II, 96–100; PMI, I, 423–25 (in part).
The name of the ship is written in another ink and in another hand.

1. These three letters by Brevoort have not been located.
2. Paulding's first number in *Salmagundi; Second Series* appeared on May 30, 1819; the series continued until September, 1820.
3. WI is alluding to *The Backwoodsman*, which had appeared in 1818.
4. The United States consul at Marseille had been Stephen Cathalan, a Frenchman who had represented official American interests in various capacities since 1790. He was succeeded by J. Dodge of Massachusetts, whose appointment was consented to by the United States Senate on January 31, 1820. See *J&N*, I, 81; A. R. Hasse, ed., *Index to United States Documents Relating to Foreign Affairs, 1828–1861* (Washington, D.C., 1914–1921), III, 1722.

248.   To Henry Brevoort

London July 28th. 1819.

My dear Brevoort —

As usual I have but a few moments left to scribble a line before the opportunity departs by which I write. I have seen ⟨th⟩ a copy of the first number of the Sketch book, which was sent out to a Gentleman of my acquaintance. I cannot but express how much more than ever I feel myself indebted to you for the manner in which you have attended to my concerns. The work is got up in a beautiful style; I should scarcely have ventured to have made so elegant an *entreé* had it been left to myself, for I had lost confidence in my writings. I have not discovered an error in the printing, and indeed have felt delighted at my genteel appearance in print. I would observe that the work appears to be a little too *highly pointed*. I dont know whether my manuscript was so, or whether it is the scrupulous precision of the printer — High pointing is apt to injure the fluency of the style if the reader attends to all the stops —

I am quite pleased that the work has experienced delay, as it gives me time to get up materials to keep ⟨up this⟩ the Series going. I have been rather *aflat* for a considerable time past, and able to do nothing with my pen & was fearful of a great *hiatus* in the early part of my work which would have been a disadvantage. My spirits have revived recently and I trust, if I recieve favourable accounts of the works taking in America, that I shall be able to go on with more animation.

I had intended to dispatch a number[1] by this ship — it is all written out, & stitched up—but as I find you will not stand in immediate need of it, I will keep it by me for a few days ⟨to⟩ as there is some trivial finishing necessary — You may calculate upon recieving it however by one of the first ships that sails after this.

I do not wish any given time to elapse between the numbers — but that they should appear irregualarly — indeed the precariousness & inequality of my own fits of composition will prevent that.

Should the first number come to a second edition I have noticed two trivial errors in Grammar, which I would have corrected — There are doubtless other inaccuracies — but these only have caught my eye in hastily running over the number

Page IV of the prospectus line *third*— for — "those high honours *that* are"
read—"those high honours *which* are"
Page 45. line 8. for — "and true love *will not brook* reserve"
read — and true love *never brooks* reserve"
I would wish an alteration also in a passage which is rather strongly expressed viz: Page 21. line 6. for. "I *question whether columbus*" &c [rea]d — [MS torn] "*no one that has not felt them can concieve the delicious thro*[ng] [MS torn] [of] [MS torn] sensations &c"

I ⟨shall⟩ look anxiously for your letter[2] by the packet, which must come to hand in a few days — and trust at the same time to hear something of the reception of my work — until then I shall continue a little nervous.

Give my sincere regards to Mrs Brevoort, and do let me hear more about your domestic establishment — I am continually picturing you to myself in your character of a husband & father —

Remember me also to your worthy parents and to the Renwick circle and believe me my dear Brevoort in all moods & fortunes most affectionately yours—

WI.

ADDRESSED: Henry Brevoort Junr. Esqr / New York / p Amity   DOCKETED: London.
    July 28th. 1819 / Washington Irving
MANUSCRIPT: NYPL—Seligman Collection.   PUBLISHED: LIB, II, 101–4; PMI, I,
    425–26 (in part).

1. The contents for the fourth number of *The Sketch Book*, which when published included "The Mutability of Literature," "Rural Funerals," "The Inn Kitchen," and "The Spectre Bridegroom," were sent to New York on August 2.

2. This letter has not been located.

249. To Henry Brevoort

London, Aug. 2d. 1819.

My dear Brevoort:—

I forward Sketch Book No. 4 to my Brother E. Irving. I find in the printed copy of No. 1 three or four inaccuracies in language in addition to those already pointed out, but I have not the number by me to correct them. These errors will take place whenever an author has not the advantage of correcting the proofs where he sees his sentiments fairly printed and brought out in a final compass under his eye. I wish you would keep an eye to see that grammatical inaccuracies do not occur. I often alter my sentiments after they are written out, which is apt to make these errors.

I send the present number with reluctance for it has grown exceeding stale with me, part of it laid out by me during a time that I was out of spirits and could not complete.

I am in great haste, and am as ever

Affectionately yours
W. I.

PUBLISHED: LIB, II, 105; PMI, I, 428 (in part).

250. To Henry Brevoort

London, Aug. 12th. 1819.

My dear Brevoort,

I have recd. your letter of July 9th.[1] which has given me infinite gratification; but I have not time to reply to it as I could wish. I wrote to you lately expressing how much I was delighted by the manner in which you got up my work: the favourable reception it has met with is extremely encouraging, and repays me for much doubt & anxiety. I

am glad to hear from you and my brother Ebenr., that you think my
second number better than the first. The manner in which you have
spoken of several of the articles is also very serviceable; it lets me
know where I make a right hit and will serve to govern ⟨al⟩ future
exertions.

I regret that you did not send me at least half a dozen copies of the
work, I am sadly tantalized having but barely the single copy — I have
not made any determination about republishing in this country, and shall
ask advice, if I can meet with any one here who can give it me: but
my literary acquaintance is very limited at present. I wish you would
enquire & let me know how the history of New York[2] sells, ⟨as I have
not heard it⟩ as Thomas is rather negligent in giving me information
about it. Let him have his own time in settling for it, as I believe
the poor fellow is straightened in these hard times.

You observe that the public complains of the price of my work[3] —
this is the disadvantage of coming in competition with ⟨those⟩↑repub-
lished English↓works for which the Booksellers have not to pay any
thing to the authors. If the American public wish to have literature of
their own they must consent to pay for the support of authors. A work
of the same size & got up in the same way as — my first number would
sell for *more* in England and the cost of printing &c would be *less*.
The Booksellers have required a large discount from you, such as is
allowed on all heavy stock books — Periodical works in this country
only ⟨pay⟩↑allow↓25 pr Cent and popular works that promise ready
sale only 20 pr Ct. When I published the first Edition of Knickerbocker
I only allowed Bradford & Inskeep 20 pr ct and they took all the risk
of the works not selling — I am however perfectly satisfied with the
allowance you have made if it induces the Booksellers to be attentive
to the work—⟨but⟩ I only mention this to shew that the terms on which
you have published the work are fair & reasonable as literature goes.
For my part if ⟨my⟩ I can succeed in writing so as deservedly to please
the public and gain the good will of my countrymen it is all I care
about — I only want money enough to enable me to keep on my own
way and follow my own taste and inclination — and as my habits are
not expensive, a very little money will enable me to do that.

I drew on you lately in favour of Mr Saml Williams[4] at 30 days sight
for *1000$*. Genl Boyd[5] bought the draft and I have the money.

I have sent a few days since my 4th. number. I forgot to obliterate
a sentence in an article headed John Bull. It is as follows — *"He is like
the man who would not have a wart taken off of his nose because it had
always been there &c &c*[.]*"* as I do not like the simile & question whether
it is a good & pleasant one you had better run a pen through it and let
the paragraph end with the words *"family abuses"*

I have mentioned several errata in the first number which ⟨require⟩ were caused by ⟨my ne⟩ negligence or alterations — I have since seen↑two or three↓others but I cannot at this moment ⟨di⟩ point them out — should ⟨the⟩ another edition be published I will thank you to look over it narrowly — ⟨No⟩ Page 80. line 4. for "The dogs too—*not one of* which he recognized for *his* old *acquaintances*" — read "not one of which he recognized for *an* old *acquaintance* —"

Page 29.   no garden of thought *or* elysium of fancy
                      read   *nor* elysium &c
      30.   not on the exclusive devotion of time & wealth *or*
            the quickening &c
            read—*nor* the quickening &c
   41. line fifteen —they are monarchs
                read they are *the* monarchs—perhaps the
whole sentence would be better by making it in the singular — viz. *"I have observed that a married man falling into misfortunes is more apt to retrieve his situation in the world than a single man*

—But I will not plague you with these petty troubles. These are all such corrections as an author makes when he has proof sheets to look over — and for want of that final revision I must expect to appear ungrammatical & awkward occasionally[.] I feel very much obliged by Verplancks notice of my work in the Analectic[6]— and very much encouraged to find it meets with his approbation. I know no ones taste to whom I would more thoroughly defer —

You suppose me to be on the continent, but I shall not go for some time yet — and you may presume on letters &c finding me in England.

I have looked through James P.s first Number of Salmagundi[7] & am pleased with some parts of it — but cannot but regret he had not suffered the old work to die a natural death. He ⟨has⟩ is not necessitated to publish for bread & should now take time to produce something finished and corrected to the best of his ability on which he might safely rest his reputation — He will only write himself below his real value by hasty effusions:

I must conclude for my letter is called for — Accept my dear Brevoort a thousand and a thousand thanks for all your kindnesses — I will not apologize to you for all the trouble I give you for there is something delightful to me in the idea that my writings are coming out under your eye and that you in a manner stand godfather to all my children. I feel as if it is a new tie that binds us together.

Give my most affectionate regards to your wife ⟨and⟩ ⟨the little⟩

                                        and believe me ever/Yours &c
                                                               W.I.

ADDRESSED: Henry Brevoort Junr. Esqr. / New York. / p Robert / [?Sad.?] 14 Augt.}
    DOCKETED: London Aug: 12. 1819 / Washington Irving
MANUSCRIPT: NYPL—Seligman Collection.   PUBLISHED: LIB, II, 106–11; PMI, I,
    429–30 (in part).
The name of the ship is in another ink and hand.

1. This letter has not been located.
2. A new edition of the *History of New York*, published by Charles Wiley, was
advertised in NYEP for July 7, 1819.
3. The price was three dollars.
4. Samuel Williams was an American banker in London who assisted his fellow
countrymen with their financial affairs. See WIHM, pp. 36–37.
5. Probably John Parker Boyd (1764–1830), an American soldier in the War
of 1812 who had earlier served as a soldier of fortune in India.
6. See 6 (July, 1819), 78–79. Verplanck mentions WI's "rich, and sometimes
extravagant humour, his gay and graceful fancy, his peculiar choice and felicity of
original expression," and his "pure and fine moral feelings which imperceptably
pervade every thought and image."
7. This was dated May 30, 1819.

251.   To [*William Sotheby*]

[August 13, 1819]

My dear Sir,

    Will you have the goodness to thank Miss Baillie[1] for me for her
very kind & acceptable present of the book. I had hoped to have seen
you, and expressed my thanks in person; but I have been so unsettled,
and so hurried by a thousand things that I have been obliged to leave
this with many other agreeable things unaccomplished.

    I return you a silk handkerchief which came with the book by
mistake, having been sent to you by Miss Baillie! with my kindest
regards to Mrs & the Misses Sotheby

believe me dear Sir/Ever very faithfully/Your obliged friend
Washington Irving

Friday Morng./Aug. 13th. [1819]

MANUSCRIPT: Va.–Barrett.

    The date is determined by the perpetual calendar and the fact that WI was in
London at this time in 1819.

    From WI's close to the letter it is clear that the addressee is William Sotheby
(1757–1833), a popular literary figure in London known for his poems, plays,
and translations. Moreover he was a friend of Joanna Baillie.

    1. Joanna Baillie (1762–1851) was a Scottish poetess and dramatist, to whom
Sotheby had dedicated a volume of dramas in 1814. See Margaret S. Carhart, *The
Life and Work of Joanna Baillie*, Yale Studies in English, vol. 64 (New Haven,
1923), p. 41.

252. *To Ebenezer Irving*

London, Aug. 16th. 1819.

My dear Brother,

By the ship which brings this is a small parcel which I will thank you to hand as usual to Brevoort

In great haste/Your aff. B.
WI.

I am writing at the last possible moment, or should be more particular —

DOCKETED: Washn. Irving. London Augt. 16. 1819 / advises of small parcel for
 Sketch Book / per Cincinnatus. to be given to Brevoort
MANUSCRIPT: NYPL—Seligman Collection.
 Beneath the docketing appears a penciled notation: *"Ebenezer* Irving."

253. *To Henry Brevoort*

London. Aug. 16 1819

Dear Brevoort,

In great haste I enclose you an essay[1] which I have just scribbled—and which I wish inserted in the fourth number in place of one of the articles — as I am affraid the number has too great a predominance of the humourous. You may insert it in the place of John Bull:[2] and keep that article for the fifth number—I have not had time to ⟨look⟩ give this article a proper finishing, and wish you to look sharp that there are not blunders and tautologies in it. It has been scribbled off hastily and part of it actually in a church yard on a recent ramble into the country — The part beginning at Page 21 must commence on a separate page with a line above it such as I have marked to shew that it is a kind of note or codicil; though if you think best you may omit the codicil altogether.

Should this Essay come too late for the fourth number ⟨you⟩ keep it by you for the fifth—Do not shew any of my Mss: ⟨until they appear in⟩ but let every thing appear ⟨unperceived⟩ in print unanticipated.

In great haste/Yours affectionately
W I.

ADDRESSED: Henry Brevoort Junr Esqr. / New York. / Cincinnatus DOCKETED:
 London Aug 16. 1819 / Wash: Irving
MANUSCRIPT: Va.–Barrett. PUBLISHED: LIB, II, 112–13; PMI, I, 430–31 (in
 part); *The American Writer in England*, intro. by C. Waller Barrett, p. 20
 (in part).

 1. "Rural Funerals."
 2. "John Bull" was subsequently published in the sixth number.

254.   To John G. Lockhart [?][1]

[August 20, 1819]

My dear Sir:

I send you herewith a copy of Knickerbockers New York.[2] It is a raw juvenile production and I hope will be read with great indulgence — Indeed I feel extremely and I may say painfully diffident in handing my writings to one who is in daily intercourse with the *Great Spirits* of the earth.

With great regard believe me/Yours faithfully

Washington Irving

21 Edward St Portland Place/Aug. 20th. [1819][3]

MANUSCRIPT: NYPL–Seligman Collection.

1. It is quite probable that John G. Lockhart (1794–1854), who married Walter Scott's daughter Sophia on April 29, 1820, is the recipient of this letter. Already a critic feared for his fierce strictures, Lockhart noticed *Knickerbocker's History* favorably in *Blackwood's Magazine* for February, 1820.

2. The third edition of *Knickerbocker's History*, published in two volumes in the spring of 1819 by Moses Thomas. See WI to Henry Brevoort, April 1, 1819.

3. In view of the time necessary for the new edition of *Knickerbocker's History* to reach London and in view of Lockhart's notice early in 1820, 1819 seems to be the proper year.

255.   To Richard Rush

Aug. 27. 1819./Edward Street.

My dear Sir,

It will give me great pleasure to dine with you on Sunday. I regret that my brothers absence from town will prevent his availing himself of your invitation

With great respect,/I am, very truly yours —

W Irving

His Excellency,/R Rush.

MANUSCRIPT: Princeton.

Richard Rush (1780–1859), who had been attorney general and secretary of state under Madison, was appointed United States minister to Great Britain in 1817, a post which he filled with distinction until 1825.

256. To Richard Rush

Sept 3d. 1819./21 Edward St.

Dear Sir,

I shall be very happy to dine with you on Sunday—I regret that my Brother will not be in town at this time

With great respect/Yours truly
Washington Irving

His Excellency/Richard Rush.

MANUSCRIPT: Princeton.

257. To Henry Brevoort

London Septr. 9th. 1819.

My dear Brevoort,

I have recd. this morning a parcel from Liverpool containing two ⟨pap⟩ parcels from you — one of four of the first number, and the other, five of the 2d. number of the Sketch Book — with Your letter[1] pr Courier. The Second number is got up still more beautifully than the first, I cannot express to you how much I am delighted with the very tasteful manner in which it is executed. You may tell Mr Van Winkle[2] that it does him great credit and has been much admired here as a Specimen of American typography — and among the admirers is Murray,[3] the "prince of Booksellers," so famous for his elegant publications. Indeed the manner in which you have managed the whole matter gives me infinite gratification — You have put my writings into circulation, and arranged the pecuniary concerns in such a way as to save future trouble and petty chafferings about accounts, and to give the whole an independent and gentleman like air. I would rather sacrafice fifty per cent than have to keep accounts, and dun booksellers for payment.

The manner in which the work has been recieved and the eulogiums that have been passed upon it in the American papers and periodical works[4] have completely overwhelmed me. They go far, *far* beyond my most sanguine expectations and indeed are expressed with such peculiar warmth and kindness as to affect me in the tenderest manner. The receipt of your letter and the reading of some of these criticisms this morning have renderd me nervous for the whole day[.] I feel almost appalled by such success, and fearful that it cannot be real — or that it is not fully merited, or that I shall not act up to the expectations that may be formed — We are whimsically constituted beings — I had got out of conceit of all that I had written, and considered it very questionable stuff — and now that it is so extravagantly bepraised I begin to feel affraid that I shall not do as well again. ⟨How You⟩ However we shall see as we get on — As yet I am extremely irregular & precarious in my fits of composition — The least thing puts me out of the vein, and even applause flurries me and prevents my writing, though of course it will ultimately be a stimulus. I have done very little for some time past — The warm weather is against me, and I have been anxious and a little restless in mind. I shall endeavour to dispatch the fifth number[5] soon.

By the bye — I break off in the middle of my letter, lest I should again forget a matter on which I have intended to speak for these two years — You once sent me a Mss: copy of my article about Philip of Pokanoket[6] — copied by Miss Goodrich[7] and I have been ungallant enough never to acknowledge so very marked a kindness. It has perpetually slipped my memory when I have been writing and has now in an unaccountable way popped into my brain — Will you make her my very best acknowledgements — and apologize for the tardiness with which they are made — and at the same time present her with a copy of the Sketch book, & continue to send her the numbers, as the only return a poor devil of an author can make. I feel the more obliged to Miss Goodrich for the trouble we[8] took as I had no claim on the score of acquaintanceship to such an act of civility.

I have been somewhat touched by the manner in which my writings have been noticed in the evening post.[9] I had considered Coleman[10] as cherishing an ill will towards me, and to tell the truth have not always been the most courteous in my opinions concerning him. It is a painful thing either to dislike others or to fancy they dislike us, and ↑I↓ have felt both pleasure and selfreproach at finding myself so mistaken with respect to Mr Coleman. I like to out with a good feeling as soon as it rises, and so I have dropt Coleman[11] a line on the subject.

I hope you will not attribute all this sensibility to the kind reception I have met with to an authors vanity — I am sure it proceeds from very different sources. Vanity ⟨I am⟩ could not bring the tears into my eyes— as they have been brought by the kindness of my countrymen. I have felt cast down, blighted and broken spirited and these sudden rays of sunshine agitate even more than they revive me.

I hope — I hope I may yet do something more worthy of the approbation lavished on me —

I unexpectedly a day or two since met with William Renwick[12]—I did not immediately recognize him[.] he has grown so much and looks so manly. He resembles James very much in countenance — He was just from Paris & was to set off for Edinburgh the next morning — via Liverpool. I had a couple of hours conversation with him and was highly pleased with him — He seems to have spent his time in Europe to advantage —

Give my best regards to your wife and remember me heartily to ⟨your⟩ ↑the↓ little circle of our peculiar intimacy — I am my dear Brevoort

Yours affectionately

W I.

P.S. In looking over this letter I find it is all about myself — but I have no time to add any more & write about anything else

ADDRESSED: For / Henry Brevoort Jr. Esqr. / New York. / p *Atlantic*   POSTMARKED: Ship. Atlantic / Sailed Oct. 3. / W. Matlock   DOCKETED: 1819 Sept 9 ↑Sept 9↓ W Irving

MANUSCRIPT: NYPL—Seligman Collection.   PUBLISHED: LIB, II, 114–19; PMI, I, 432–33 (in part).

The name of the ship is in another ink and another hand.

1. Brevoort's letter has not been located.

2. C. S. Van Winkle was the American printer of *The Sketch Book*.

3. In 1820 John Murray became WI's English publisher.

4. *The Sketch Book*, Number I received a half-column notice in NYEP of June 26, 1819. The reviewer, who was Henry Brevoort, noted the "graces of style; the rich, warm tone of benevolent feeling; the freely-flowing vein of hearty and happy humour, and the fine-eyed spirit of observation, sustained by an enlightened understanding, and regulated by a perception of fitness—a tact — wonderfully quick and sure, for which Mr. Irving has been heretofore so much distinguished." (For the identification of Brevoort as the reviewer, see LBI, I, xxiv.) On August 3, 1819, NYEP devoted a full column to a summary of the selections of *The Sketch Book*, Number II, together with numerous favorable critical comments. The *Analectic Magazine* 14 (July, 1819), 78–79, noticed the first number of *The Sketch Book*. The second number was reviewed in the *Ladies Literary Cabinet* 1 (August 7, 1819), 101; and the *New England Galaxy* 2 (July 2, 1819), 151, reprinted favorable comments from NYEP for June 26.

5. Actually the copy for the fifth number was not sent until late October.

6. In a letter to Brevoort on March 15, 1816, WI had requested a copy of the *Analectic Magazine* for June, 1814, containing his sketch of King Philip.

7. Miss Goodrich may have been related to A. T. Goodrich, who operated a bookstore and lending library at 124 Broadway.

8. WI doubtless meant to write "she."

9. See note 4 above.

10. William Coleman, editor of NYEP.

11. This letter has not been located. Apparently Coleman did not print it in his newspaper.

12. The third son of Jean Jeffrey Renwick.

258. To Gideon Fairman

[September 10, 1819]

My dear Sir,

This will be handed by Robert Craig.[1] I would suggest to you again the importance of getting him quarterd in the house as soon as pos-

sible[.] London is a sad place for a lad to be travelling to & fro in the
evening —

With great regard/Yours truly

W Irving

Septr. 10th. [1819]

ADDRESSED: G. Fairman Esqr. / Austin Friars / Enquire at the New England
    Coffee / house. Thread needle St.   DOCKETED: Wn Irving Esqr. / 21
    Edward / Street[?] / Portland Place / R Irving — / Sept. 10. / 1819
MANUSCRIPT: SHR.

This letter is addressed to Gideon Fairman, an engraver whom WI knew during
his editorship of the *Analectic Magazine*. Fairman lived in England from 1819
to 1822.

1. The context suggests that Robert Craig was possibly about to become an
apprentice or a helper in Fairman's engraving business.

259.   To Charles R. Leslie

London, Septr. 13th. 1819.

You Leslie!

What's the reason you have not let us hear from you since you set out
on your travels.[1] We have been in great anxiety lest you should have
started from London on some other route of that Six inch square map of
the world which you consulted, and through the mistake of a hairs
breadth, may have wanderd—the lord knows where. Here have been
sad evolutions & revolutions since you left us. Newton had his three
shirts and six collars packed up in a half of a saddle bag for several days
⟨f⟩ with the intention of accompanying Lyman, Everett & Chas Williams[2]
to Liverpool & returning ⟨throu⟩ with the latter through Wales, in which
case they intended beating up your quarters and endeavouring to surprize you with your Mallstick[3] turned into a shepherds crook. Sighing at
the feet of Miss Maine,[4] Newton ⟨but scamper up & down⟩ did nothing
for two or three days but scamper up & down between Finsbury Square
and Sloan Street like a cat in a panic, taking leave of every body in the
morning, and calling upon them again in the evening, ⟨until t⟩ when to
his astonishment he found charles Williams had the private intention
of ⟨sail⟩ embarking for America — Charles has actually sailed, and Newton
instead of his Welsh tour accompanied me in a tour to Depthford and
Eltham.[5] He has now resumed his station at the head of Sloane Street —
Jones has taken possession of the bottom, and between them both I
expect they will tie the two ends of the street into a true lovers knot.

For my part I have almost been good for nothing since your departure,
and would not pass another Summer in London if they would make me
Lord Mayor.

I have recd. the Second number of the Sketch Book — and ⟨am⟩ shall be quite satisfied if I deserve half the praise they give me in the american Journals — but they always overdo these matters in America[.] I am glad to find the Second number pleases more than the first — The sale is very rapid & altogether the success exceeds my most sanguine expectation. Now you suppose I am all on the alert — and full of spirit and excitement — no such thing. I am just as good for nothing as ever I was & indeed have been flurried and put out of my way by these puffings. I feel something as I suppose you did when your Picture[6] met with success — anxious to do something better— and at a loss what to do —

But enough of egotism — Let me know how you find yourself — how you like wales — what you are doing and especially when you intend to return. I hope you wi[ll] [MS torn] not remain away much longer. Have you seen Mi[ss] [MS torn] Maine — I presume not — as you went away without calling or sending for Miss Bollmans[7] Letter, for which you will have to do penance on your return.

My Brother is still absent — he desired me to remember him to you should I write — Newtons Manikin has at length arrived, and he is to have it home in a few days when it is to be hoped he will give up rambling abroad & stay home and ⟨make⟩ drink tea and play the flute to the lady — Mrs Macdougall means to give her a tea party and it is expected she will be introduced in to company with as much *eclat* as Peregrine Pickles protegeé.[8]

I have now fairly filled my sheet with nonsense and craving a speedy reply am ever

Yours
WI.

ADDRESSED: For / Charles R. Leslie Esqr / care of J W Dillwyn[?] Esqr / Penller-gare / Swansea POSTMARKED: SE 14 1819
MANUSCRIPT: NYPL—Berg Collection. PUBLISHED: PMI, I, 434–35 (in part); Leslie, *Autobiographical Recollections*, pp. 213–15.

1. Leslie was visiting some Quaker friends in Wales. See PMI, I, 433.
2. These are American friends of Leslie's with whom he had planned to visit Wales. See Leslie, *Autobiographical Recollections*, p. 213. But Charles Williams is also identified as a member of an English banking firm in Paris, Welles et Williams. See J&N, III, 221. Everett may be Alexander Hill Everett (1790–1847), who was chargé d'affaires in the Netherlands at this time.
3. A painter used the mahlstick, a staff about one yard long with a wooden or leather ball on one end, to support and steady his hand as it held the brush.
4. Although Newton was interested in Miss Maine, she married someone else in October, 1820. See Leslie, *Autobiographical Recollections*, p. 220.
5. These are communities south of the Thames in the vicinity of Greenwich.
6. Probably a reference to Leslie's painting of "Sir Roger de Coverley Going to Church," which he sold to Mr. Dunlop, a rich tobacco importer. See Leslie, *Autobiographical Recollections*, p. 213.

7. Apparently a friend of Miss Maine's.

8. WI is probably alluding to Peregrine Pickle's taking of Emelia Gauntlet to various social affairs in London. See Tobias Smollett, *The Adventures of Peregrine Pickle,* chaps. 74–76.

260. To Henry Brevoort

London Sept 21t 1819.

My dear Brevoort,

By the Atlantic, Capt Matlock¹ you will receive ↑a parcel containing↓ corrected copies of the 1 and 2d. Nos of the Sketch Book, from which I wish the Second editions − (if ⟨any⟩ ↑they↓ should go to 2d. editions) to be printed

I am at work on the 5th. Number,² and hope to ⟨get it⟩ send it in time to have it published ⟨about⟩ ↑before↓ Christmas³—My mind gets running away from me now & then and breaking into subjects which are not fitted for the number in hand, ↑and sometimes I have long intervals of literary incapacity↓ which mean ⟨s m⟩ delays −

In great haste/Yours affectionately
WI.—

ADDRESSED: Henry Brevoort Junr. Esqr. / New York. / p ⟨Atlantic⟩ Courier
  POSTMARKED: American Packet / Courier / [*unrecovered*] / Ship (6)   DOCK-
ETED: Sep: 1819 / W Irving
MANUSCRIPT: NYPL—Seligman Collection.   PUBLISHED: LIB, II, 209.
The name of the ship, including the cancellation, is written in another hand.

1. *The Atlantic,* commanded by Captain Matlock, reached New York on November 9, 1819, after a thirty-six-day voyage from Liverpool. See NYEP, November 9, 1819.

2. The fifth number of *The Sketch Book* included "Christmas," "The Stage Coach," "Christmas Eve," and "Christmas Day."

3. It was deposited for copyright on December 16, 1819, and placed on sale on January 1, 1820. See Langfeld & Blackburn, *WI Bibliography,* p. 15.

261. To Henry Brevoort

[September, 1819]

My dear Brevoort,

Should the first two numbers go to a second edition let it be printed from the ⟨enc⟩ accompanying copies. I have made many trivial, perhaps unimportant corrections, but ⟨it must be expected when⟩ these errors will occur when the writer has not an opportunity of giving his work a last revision in the proofsheets. Do not let these corrected copies be seen by others or they will imagine my writings abominably faulty; whereas it may be I am too fastidious —

Yours affectionately
W I.

ADDRESSED: Henry Brevoort Jr Esqr   DOCKETED: London Sep: 1819 / W Irving /—
MANUSCRIPT: Va.–Barrett.

262. To Henry Van Wart

[September? 1819][1]

My dear Brother,

Your invitation to Brummy[2] to the christning came quite unexpected, and has quite perplexed me. I am expecting every day and I may say every hour, a copy of the first number of my work from America — and it is important I should be here at the time to see if any arrangement can be made here for republishing it — as I am fearful some Bookseller in the American trade may get hold of it, & think it worth republication; and so run out an edition of it without my ⟨correctin⟩ adapting it for the London public — or participating in the profits. Had I my choice I would rather it should not be republished here until more numbers appear & enough could be given at once to stamp its character. I am also busy just now preparing more Mss: to send out. It is therefore peculiarly [important that][3] the article arrive between this & tuesday so that I can see it & speak with a Bookseller,[4] I may be able to come down for a few days, but I very much doubt it. If I am not there you must get someone to stand godfather for me.[5]

I do not wish you to mention the reason for my not coming down; for though these small concerns are very important to a man in my situation — they may appear very trivial to others —

I long to see you all once more and to have a peep at my namesake who I understand is a miracle.

Give my love to Sally and the young folks—

Your affectionate Br.
W I.[6]

MANUSCRIPT: SHR. PUBLISHED: Robert E. Spiller, *The American in England* (New York, 1926), p. 281.

1. Although Robert E. Spiller in *The American in England*, p. 281, dates the letter as early December, it is evident from WI's letter to Brevoort, dated September 9, 1819, that he has just received copies of the first number of *The Sketch Book*. Therefore early September is a more likely date.
2. Birmingham.
3. WI omitted these or similar words when he switched to another sheet.

4. John Murray of 50 Albemarle Street, London, who had recently attracted widespread attention as publisher of Byron's *Don Juan.* After considerable deliberation Murray declined the proposal. For WI's retrospective account of this event see the preface to *The Sketch Book,* Author's Revised Edition (New York, 1848), vii–viii.

5. WI had apparently been invited to participate in the christening ceremonies for Washington Irving Van Wart (1819–May 10, 1823), his nephew, the youngest child of Henry and Sarah Van Wart.

6. About an inch below the initials is written "Washington Irving" in another hand.

263. To Ebenezer Irving

[London, October 28, 1819]

Whether No. V. will please or not I cannot say, but it has cost me more trouble and more odd research than any of the others.

PUBLISHED: PMI, I, 447.

264. To Henry Brevoort

London, Octr. 28th. 1819

My dear Brevoort

This will introduce you to my friend Col. Aspinwall,[1] Consul for the UStates at London, whom I reccommend to your particular attention as ⟨I⟩ a gentleman for whom I entertain the highest friendship and esteem.

Yours ever
Washington Irving

Henry Brevoort Jr Esqr.

ADDRESSED: Henry Brevoort Jr. Esqr. / New York. / Col. Aspinwall.
MANUSCRIPT: Huntington.

1. Colonel Thomas Aspinwall (1786–1876), who was United States consul in London from 1815 to 1853, served as WI's literary agent in England after 1824. For other details see Charles C. Smith, "Memoir of Col. Thomas Aspinwall," *Massachusetts Historical Society Proceedings,* 2d ser. 7 (November, 1891), 32–38.

265. To John Murray II

Edward Street/Octr 28th. 1819.

My dear Sir,

I feel much obliged by your very kind note of yesterday.[1] I am perfectly conscious of the force of your objection[2] to the work I offered, and that my writings have that deficiency in scope and fullness, which results from some degree of self diffidence, and a want of practice and experience. I may improve as I proceed and shall feel proud and happy if on some future occasion I may have any thing to offer that may be deemed worthy of your attention

With great respect/Yours truly
W Irving

J Murray Esqr.

DOCKETED: 1819 Oct: 28 / Irving, W
MANUSCRIPT: NYPL—Berg Collection. PUBLISHED: WIHM, pp. 18–19.

1. John Murray's letter of October 27 is quoted in WIHM, p. 18.
2. Apparently Murray was influenced by some of his critic-friends as well as by business reasons to reject WI's proposal to publish *The Sketch Book.*

266.   To Walter Scott

London Octr 30th. 1819.

My dear Sir,

By one of the Leith Packets I have sent you ↑(to the care of Mr John Ballantyne)¹↓ three numbers of a miscellaneous work of mine called the Sketch Book, which is published occasionally at New York. The copies are not as neat & new as they ought to be, but they are the only ones I can lay my hands on not having received a proper Supply. They have many errors, which result from my not being at hand to give the ↑authors↓ last corrections, of the Proofsheets. I am conscious also of their being deficient in many respects, in consequence of my not having sufficient practice and experience in composition, I know however that you are an indulgent reader, and look for merits rather than faults.

My friends advise me to republish in this country but I am so much of a stranger here and so unacquainted with the mode of dealing with Booksellers that I am quite at a loss how to proceed. Should my writings meet with your approbation may I ask for your kind word in the business. ⟨The E⟩ Copious extracts have been made from the work in Mr Constables Magazine,² with flattering encomiums[.] perhaps he may be disposed to make an offer for a volume comprising what has already been published—corrected & altered, and several articles of similar nature. Should this take I can furnish him with another volume, and as success will give confidence & spirit I may hereafter have something of more interest to offer him. I should like to hear his answer as soon as possible should you think proper to mention the thing to him—as I want to have the work published immediately. ⟨[*Four or five words unrecovered*]⟩

I feel that I am taking a great liberty in making this request; but indeed my situation here is so peculiarly insulated that I do not know to whom else I can apply: and the reverses of fortune I have experienced since I had the pleasure of Seeing You, make my literary success a matter of Serious importance to me. But the best apology I can offer is the character you have acquired of being prompt and happy to befriend and oblige; which must often subject you to similiar taxes.

I sent, about two years since, just—after my return from Scotland, a set of the American editions of your poems for Miss Scott,[3] they were directed to You & put in a parcel going to Mr Constable—I am apprehensive they never reached you, and may be in some corner of Mr Constables ware[house] [*MS torn*] to this day —

Present my sincere remembrances to Mrs Scott and the family —To pass four days as delightfully as those I spent under your roof at Abbotsford I would willingly undertake a pilgrimage to the Banks of the Tweed.

With the greatest respect & regard/I am my dear Sir/Yours truly
Washington Irving

Walter Scott Esqr

ADDRESSED: Walter Scott Esqr. / ⟨Edinburgh⟩ / Melrose.   POSTMARKED: OCT / 30 / 1819.   DOCKETED: W Irving
MANUSCRIPT: National Library of Scotland.

WI wrote "Edinburgh," which is canceled. "Melrose" is written in another hand, probably by a post office employee.

1. John Ballantyne and Company of Edinburgh was Scott's publisher.
2. The *Edinburgh Magazine and Literary Miscellany* for September and October, 1819 reprinted two sketches in each number. See William B. Cairns, *British Criticisms of American Writings, 1815-1833* (Madison, Wisc., 1922), p. 62.
3. Sophia Scott, who married John Gibson Lockart on April 29, 1820.

267.   To Ebenezer Irving

[London, October 31, 1819]

I intend republishing in this country, the work[1] having been favorably received by such as have seen it here, and extracts having been made from it with encomiums in some of the periodical works.

PUBLISHED: PMI, I, 438.

1. *The Sketch Book.*

268. To Walter Scott

21 Edward St. Portland Place London/Novr. 3d. 1819.

My dear Sir,

I wrote to you a few days since[1] requesting your kind word with Mr Constable on the Subject of a work I am scribbling, but as I neglected to give my address Mr Constable will not know where to write to me, should he feel so disposed. I am obliged therefore to trouble you again which I do with great reluctance — and have given my address at the top of the letter.

It is with great concern I have heard lately of the death of that worthy wight Lockie Longlegs,[2] whose appearance I shall never forget striding along the profile of [the][3] knoll in his red night cap, with his flimsy garments fluttering about him — I trust he will not be lost to history in this biographical age —

With sincere remembrances to your family I am my dear Sir with great regard

Yours faithfully
Washington Irving

Walter Scott Esq.

MANUSCRIPT: National Library of Scotland.   PUBLISHED: *Studies in Scottish Literature* 3 (October, 1965), 116.

1. On October 30, 1819.
2. When WI visited Scott at Abbotsford, they encountered Lauchie Long Legs living on an adjoining farm. A year or two after WI saw him he died of apoplexy during an argument. See Lockhart, *Life of Sir Walter Scott*, IV, 305; *Crayon Miscellany*, pp. 51–54.
3. WI omitted "the."

269. To Walter Scott

London, 20th. Novr. 1819.

My dear Sir,

I cannot express how much I am gratified by your letter[.][1] I had begun to feel as if I had taken an unwarrantable liberty, but some how or other there is a genial sunshine about you that warms every creeping thing into heart and confidence. Your literary proposal[2] both surprises and flatters me as it evinces a much higher opinion of my talents & capacity than I possess myself. I am peculiarly unfitted for the post proposed. I have no strong political prejudices, for though born and brought up under a republican government, and thoroughly convinced that it is the best for my own country, yet I have a deep *poetical* veneration for the old institutions of this country and should feel as sorry to see them injured or subverted as to see Windsor Castle or Westminster Abbey demolished to make way for snug brick tenements. But I have a general dislike to politics[.] I have always shunned them in my own country, and have lately declined a lucrative post under my own government[3] & one that opened the door to promotion, merely because I was averse to political life or to being subjected to regular application or local confinement.

My whole course of life has been desultory and I am unfitted for any periodically recurring task, or any stipulated labour of body or mind. I have no command over my talents such as they are; am apt to be deserted by them when I most want their assistance & have to watch the veerings of my mind as I would those of a weather cock. Practice & training may bring me more into rule, but at present I am as unfit for Service in the ranks as one of my own country Indians or a Don Cossack. I must therefore keep on pretty much as I have begun, writing when I can & not when I would. I shall occasionally shift my residence, and trust to the excitement of various scenes & objects to furnish me with materials; though I hope as I gain ⟨practice⟩ experience & confidence to be more copious & methodical. I am playing the Egotist, but I know no better mode of answering your very kind proposal, ⟨but⟩ than by shewing what a very good for nothing kind of being I am.

Should Mr Constable feel inclined to make a bargain for the wares I have at present on hand[4] he may encourage me to further enterprize and it will be something like bargaining with a gypsy who, if you at one time buy of him a wooden bowl, may at another time bring you a Silver tankard.—At any rate I should like to have his reply soon, as in case he declines I shall immediately make some other arrangement.

It may be a gratification to the friendly feeling you have evinced towards me to know that the success & sale of the work in America is beyond the most sanguine anticipations I could have ⟨[unrecovered]⟩ [MS torn] though I by no means feel a confidence from that circumstance of its success with the more critical public of this country.

And now my dear Sir I will finish this egotistical scrawl by again expressing my heartfelt gratification at the interest you have taken in my concerns—and believe me I feel more joy and rejoycing in your good opinion than I should in all the Gold & Silver in friend Constables ↑breeches↓ pockets—albeit his pockets are none of the shallowest.

Present my Sincere regards to Mrs Scott and the family & believe me most faithfully

Your friend
Washington Irving.

P. S. It gives me the greatest pleasure to hear that friend Lauckie died game.

ADDRESSED: Walter Scott Esqr. / Castle Street / Edinburgh.   POSTMARKED: NO 20
    1819   DOCKETED: Washington Irving
MANUSCRIPT: National Library of Scotland.   PUBLISHED: PMI, I, 441–42 (in part);
    Waldron, *WI & Cotemporaries*, p. 34 (in part); *Familiar Letters of Sir Walter Scott*, II, 60–61 (in part).

1. Scott wrote to WI on November 17, 1819. See PMI, I, 439–40.

2. Scott had asked WI to consider editing an anti-Jacobin magazine appearing weekly in Edinburgh at a stipend of £500 per year. See PMI, I, 439.

3. WI's brothers had arranged for his appointment to a clerkship in the navy department in Washington. See William Irving's letter of October 24, 1818 to WI (printed in STW, I, 170–71) and WI's reply of March 3, 1819, to Ebenezer Irving.

4. WI had hoped that Constable might be persuaded to bring out an edition of *The Sketch Book*. See WI to Scott, October 30, 1819.

270.   To Mrs. Josiah Ogden Hoffman

[London, November 26, 1819]

My especial intimates are our young countrymen, Leslie and Newton, who have lodgings not far from mine, so that we see each other almost every day. You have no doubt heard of Leslie's rapidly increasing reputation. He has done himself vast credit lately, by a beautiful picture of Sir Roger de Coverley going to church.[1] He bids fair to take the lead in that most captivating line of painting, which consists in the delineation of familiar life. I make no doubt, in the course of a little while, he will be one of the most celebrated and most popular painters in Great Britain. He has all the materials within him for excelling in the walk he has chosen — A deep sense of moral feeling; an exquisite idea of beauty; a quick eye for character, and for external nature: a rich vein of humour, chastened and sweetened by the purest benevolence of heart: add to these a perfect devotion to his art, and an intimate knowledge of every thing in it that depends upon study and diligent practice, and I think you will agree with me in forming the highest anticipations of his future celebrity.

Newton is the nephew of Stewart,[2] our great portrait painter. He is not so experienced in his art as Leslie, but has uncommon requisites for it. There is a native elegance about every thing he does; a delicate taste, a playful fancy, and an extraordinary facility at atchieving, without apparent labour or study, what other painters, with the labour and study of years, cannot attain. His eye for colouring is almost unrivalled, and produces beautiful effects, which have surprised experienced painters, who have been aiming at colouring all their lives. The only danger is, that his uncommon natural advantages may make him remiss in cultivating the more mechanical parts of his art; and he may thus fall short of that pre-eminent stand in his profession which is completely within his reach, though he cannot fail at all events to become a highly distinguished painter. He is yet but a student in his art, but has produced several admirable portraits, a little fancy piece, of Falstaff's escape in the Buck-basket,[3] of great merit, and is now engaged on a little cabinet picture for the next exhibition of the British Gallery, which will be quite a *gem*. I have been rather prolix about these two intimates of mine — but I thought an account of them would be interesting to you, as being young men of whom our nation will hereafter have reason to be proud.

PUBLISHED: NYEP, January 12, 1820; PMI, I, 406–7.

This extract was printed in NYEP for January 12, 1820, from a copy provided by Mrs. Hoffman. P. M. Irving, who also printed the letter, assigned the date and stated that the original was lost. See PMI, I, 407. The present text follows that printed in NYEP.

1. Leslie painted the picture of Sir Roger for his friend Mr. Dunlop, a wealthy merchant, and later made a copy for Lord Lansdowne. See Leslie, *Autobiographical Recollections*, p. 213.

2. Gilbert Stuart (1755–1828), who studied with Benjamin West in London and became a fashionable painter there, returned to America in the early 1790's and established himself as a brilliant painter of the portraits of Americans in public life.

3. Charles Leslie, in a letter to Washington Allston on February 6, 1819, states that Newton sent this picture of Falstaff to the British Gallery, where it received high praise. See Flagg, *Washington Allston*, p. 146.

271. To Ebenezer Irving

[London? December 29, 1819]

The article you object to, about Christmas,[1] is written for peculiar tastes — those who are fond of what is quaint in literature and customs. The scenes there depicted are formed upon humors and customs peculiar to the English, and illustrative of their greatest holyday. The old rhymes which are interspersed are but selections from many which I found among old works in the British Museum, little read even by Englishmen, and which will have a value with some literary men who relish these morsels of antiquated humor. When an article is studied out in this manner, it cannot have that free flowing spirit and humor that one written off-hand has; but then it compensates to some peculiar minds by the points of character or manners which it illustrates. Had

I not thought so, I certainly would not have taken the trouble which the article cost me. If it possesses the kind of merit I mention, and pleases the peculiar, though perhaps few tastes to which I have alluded, my purpose in writing the article is satisfied, and it will go to keep up the variety which is essential to a work of the kind. . . .

I send you MS. for No. VI[2] There is a Knickerbocker story[3] which may please from its representation of American scenes. It is a random thing, suggested by recollections of scenes and stories about Tarrytown. The story is a mere whimsical band to connect descriptions of scenery, customs, manners, &c.

PUBLISHED: PMI, I, 447–48.

Although the two paragraphs to Ebenezer were not printed as part of the same letter by PMI (I, 447–48), they both deal with *The Sketch Book* and probably are WI's response to Ebenezer's answer to WI's letter of October 28.

1. This essay was to be an item in the fifth part of *The Sketch Book*.

2. At this time WI sent "The Legend of Sleepy Hollow" to be added to "The Pride of the Village" and "John Bull," which had been sent to New York on August 4, 1819. See PMI, I, 428, 430–31.

3. WI had drafted the outline of the story of Ichabod Crane and Brom Bones during a visit to the Henry Van Warts in the summer of 1818. See PMI, I, 448–49.

272. To Gilbert Stuart Newton

[1819–1820]

Dear Newton.

I have so many engagements for this evening that I have to give up what I fancy would be far the most agreeable. I enclose you therefore a ticket for Lapis's concert, which I have no doubt will be an excellent one. If ⟨p⟩ however you are otherwise engaged, or do not feel disposed to go, send the ticket back to me that I may give it some one else

Yours truly
W Irving.

Friday —

ADDRESSED: G S Newton Esqr.
MANUSCRIPT: Va.–Barrett.

273. To Ebenezer Irving

[London, January 13, 1820]

I have just made arrangements to have a volume of the Sketch Book published here. I expect the first proof-sheet to-day, and the volume will be published in about a month. If the experiment succeeds I shall follow it up by another volume.

PUBLISHED: PMI, I, 445.

274. *To John Howard Payne*

21 Edward St. Portland Place/Jany 28th, 1820.

My dear Payne,

I am gratified by the receipt of your letter[1] for more reasons than one. It enables me to explain the circumstances of my not sending the loan you requested last summer; it also lets me know that you are still alive and in good heart, and it gives me an opportunity of removing the idea you entertain of my being prejudiced against you by the gossip of dining-out gentlemen. The fact is, though my purse was rather short you should have had the sum you requested to borrow immediately but I was not at home when your messenger arrived. I put the sum in a note for you, expecting he would call again, but he did not. I did not like to send it to your old lodgings in Southampton Street,[2] as I supposed from various circumstances you might have some difficulties with your Landlord there and the note might only occasion cross purposes. I was part of the time out of town & so from these causes joined to some negligence of disposition Wednesday slipped by and the thing passed out of my mind. I have made various enquiries after you of Leslie & others who I thought might know something of you but never could find what was your address.

As to the idea of your pursuing a system of *financiering*, I confess I once did think you were acting inconsiderately and unjustifiably, in depending upon the casual assistance of others, without having any laudable object or definite pursuit—⟨and this⟩ but this opinion was at once and completely destroyed by your telling me of your having a Tragedy[3] in preparation. You have no idea what an agreeable revolution took place at that moment in my feelings with[4] [MS *mutilated*] Had your play been unsuccessful it could not have affected [MS *mutilated*] it was enough for me that you [MS *mutilated*]—ambition and steadfastly [MS *mutilated*] The letter to Mr Harris[5] which you read to me completely confirmed my renovated esteem for you. It gave me the whole story of your struggles here, & shewed that you had been busily employed when others considered you idle, & that your difficulties had been occasioned by the faithlessness of others, not by your own imprudence. Instead therefore of suffering others to prejudice me against you, I have ever since taken pains, whenever your name was mentioned, to put your conduct & situation in a proper & favourable light. I had hoped before this to hear of your tragedy coming out ⟨act at one of the theatres, & hope you have not abandoned the vein o⟩ dramatic ⟨success⟩ ↑authorship↓ which you so successfully opened.

I feel much obliged to you for your offer concerning my work[6]—⟨ however mean to let it take its own chance with the critics — It ⟨is

↑will be↓ published at my own expense, as an experiment — or rather because I found that if I did not publish it others would, and I wished it to come out correct & in a favourable form.

I do not wish to intrude into your concerns or trouble you with any enquiries about your plans & therefore shall ask no questions. If you are a *sedentary man during the week,* perhaps you are at leisure on Sundays, and if ever you feel disposed to give a call at 21 Edward St. and take some Sunday breakfast at 9 ⟨or ½ past⟩ you will find my Brother & myself most happy to see you and we will talk over matters and things at large —

My Brother desires to be particularly remembered to you/Believe me[7]

[*Signature cut out*]

John Howard Payne Eqr—

P. S I find your play[8] has been very successful at the American Theatres — What a Pity you did not secure the property of it in America. ⟨By⟩ A letter from Phila. mentions that Cooper is great in the part of Brutus[9]—

MANUSCRIPT: Columbia University Library.

1. Payne had written to WI on the preceding day.
2. A few months earlier Payne had been forced out of his lodgings for non-payment of rent, but it is not clear if they were on Southampton Street. See Grace Overmyer, *America's First Hamlet,* p. 176.
3. *Virginius; or, the Patrician's Perfidy,* for which Payne could not find a producer. See Overmyer, *America's First Hamlet,* p. 189.
4. At this point a piece of the page with WI's signature on it has been cut away, removing at the same time the left half of the first five lines on page 3 of the manuscript.
5. Henry Harris (d. 1839), manager of Covent Garden Theatre, for whom Payne had worked from 1816 to 1818. Payne felt that Harris had not adequately compensated him for his writing and translation and had not followed his promise of helping Payne's acting career. See Overmyer, *America's First Hamlet,* pp. 154–60.
6. In his letter of January 27, 1820, Payne had offered to review the *Sketch Book* favorably. See STW, I, 436, n. 63.
7. The remainder of the complimentary close and the signature have been cut away.
8. *The Tragedy of Brutus; or, The Fall of Tarquin.*
9. T. A. Cooper played the role of Brutus in New York on November 1, 1819, and in Philadelphia on November 15 and 27, 1819. See Overmyer, *America's First Hamlet,* p. 398; James, *Old Drury of Philadelphia,* p. 292.

275. To Ebenezer Irving [?]

[late January, 1820]

enquiries on the subject, and found that Mr Williams[1] had received letters from his brother Charles,[2] who had conversed with Irving & Smith;[3] What had been the purport of their conversation I do not know, but its effect was to chill the confidence of the Williams' in Van Wart;[4] and thus to take from him the plank on which he was swimming for life. I beg you will mention this to William:[5] that he may see how necessary it is to be guarded in conversation respecting a friend even at three thousand miles distance.

Whatever may have been poor Vans past indiscretions he has suffered enough for them—heaven knows; and the *least* his friends can do to get him going again, is to give him the cheapest of all earthly gifts to the giver—a good word. But I have done with all remonstrances on this subject⟨;⟩:. According to the common maxim "trade must be left to regulate itself"

Give my love to Eliza[6] and the family and believe me my dear brother

Affectionately Yours

WI.

P.S. In publishing a second edition of No 5.[7] ⟨T⟩the Manuscript addition may be got onto the same quantity of paper by omitting the blank leaves or rather half titles between the articles—They are not necessary where the number is made up of one general article, such as Christmas. P.S. In page 429. of No. 5. I have restored the passage relating to the peacock pie but I cannot find the note belonging to it, ⟨You must have⟩ among my copies of the Mss. You of course must have it among the Mss scraps which were omitted—I wish it to be restored—& put at the bottom of the page as in the original Mss:

MANUSCRIPT: Irving Kingsford.

The first portion of this letter is missing.

If WI was sent a copy of No. 5 of *The Sketch Book* immediately upon publication and responded at once upon receipt of the reply from New York three and one-half to four weeks later, he probably wrote this letter in late January, 1820. See note 7.

1. Samuel Williams of the Welles and Williams firm. He was an American banker in London.

2. Charles Williams represented Welles and Williams in Paris. The context suggests that he was visiting in New York.

3. Irving and Smith were auctioneers in New York. William Irving was a partner in the firm. See Scoville, *Old Merchants of NYC*, I, 349.

4. For a time after his bankruptcy in 1818 Henry Van Wart had disagreements with various Birmingham businessmen who had been his creditors. Possibly the discussion related to some of these matters.

5. William Irving.

6. Ebenezer Irving's wife, Elizabeth Kip.

7. WI is referring to *The Sketch Book*, the fifth number of which had appeared on December 31, 1819. See NYEP, December 31, 1819.

276. To Walter Scott

21 Edward St. Portland Place/London, Feby 9th. 1820.

My dear Sir,

I am ashamed that I have suffered so long a time to elapse without replying to your last very kind letter,[1] wherein you gave me some information respecting the mode of treating with Booksellers. As I felt a little perplexed, I determined to wait until your intended arrival in London[2] & then take your advice. I found afterwards that circumstances had induced you to alter your intention, and that you would not be in town for some months. Averse therefore to give you any further trouble on what must appear so trifling a subject; and in fact very doubtful whether my work would be of sufficient merit or consequence in Mr Constables[3] eyes, I took the readiest mode that presented itself and employed a Bookseller,[4] whom I happened to know from his being in the American trade, to publish the Book for me at my own risk & expense. I am aware that as he is not rich, nor of the first class, the work stands but a poor chance, but at any rate I shall come correctly before the public; which is some consideration with me, as I have percieved my writings inserted occasionally in periodical works, with all the errors of the American edition

I have mentioned all this to account for my having committed what in most mens eyes would be deemed a grevious offence: asked advice, and then neglected to pursue it: but I trust you are forgiving. The volume I am publishing will form a neat octavo and will be out in about ten days or a fortnight.[5]

I am ashamed my dear Sir to gossip to you so much about myself and my trivial concerns; but you have inspired me with a confidence in your kindness; and though I have been so long in England I yet feel so much of a stranger here that I naturally turn to any quarter in which I am confident of good will.

Present my respectful remembrances to [Mrs. Scott] [MS torn] and the rest of your family. Should you put your [plan?] [MS torn] in practice of passing through London on your way to the continent with my friend Charles,[6] I hope I may know when you are in town that I may have the pleasure of waiting on you.

with great regard/I am very faithfully yours
Washington Irving.

Walter Scott Esqr.[7]

ADDRESSED: Walter Scott Esqr. / Edinburgh   POSTMARKED: FEB / [unrecovered] / 1820 DOCKETED: Washington / Irving.
MANUSCRIPT: National Library of Scotland.

1. On December 4, 1819, Scott had written to WI with details of procedures in English publishing. See PMI, I, 442–44.

2. Although Scott had indicated on December 4, 1819, that he would be "in London in the course of a month," he actually did not arrive until March 30, 1820, to receive his baronetcy. See PMI, I, 444.

3. Archibald Constable, the Scottish publisher who was long associated with the publication of Scott's Waverley novels.

4. John Miller of Burlington Arcade.

5. The volume containing the first four numbers of *The Sketch Book* appeared on February 23. See WI's letter to Ebenezer Irving, February 24, 1820.

6. Scott's son, born in 1805.

7. WI had placed the name of the addressee at the lower left corner of the first page of the manuscript.

277. *To John Howard Payne*

7 Oclock/[London] Feby. 23d. 1820

My dear Payne

I have just got home, or you should have had an answer sooner. I inclose you the 5£ you request. Drop me a line by twopenny post if you receive it: as there may be some blunder of the servants. I think under all circumstances you will be right to return in the Cincinnatus[1]—and will be more likely to turn both your dramatic and literary talents to account in America than you will be here. I would suggest to you the idea of connecting yourself with one of the many magazines publishing in America—Your knowledge of Europe & european topics would be of great value to any publication of the kind.

With great regard/Yours truly—
W.I.

ADDRESSED: J. H Payne Esqr. / care of Mrs Potez / 29. Arundel St / Strand.
MANUSCRIPT: Columbia.

1. The *Cincinnatus* left England on May 5, 1820, and arrived in New York on June 16, after a trip of 41 days. See NYEP, June 16, 1820.

278. *To Ebenezer Irving*

[London, February 24, 1820]

The volume containing the first four numbers of the Sketch Book was published on Monday[1] last by John Miller, Burlington Arcades. I shall not publish any more, and should not have done this, had there not been a likelihood of these works being republished here from incorrect American numbers.

PUBLISHED: PMI, I, 449.

1. February 16, 1820.

279. *To Henry Brevoort*

London, March 27th 1820.

My dear Brevoo⟨r⟩tt,

As I hear you have once more got back to New York I cannot let the packet depart without addressing you a line, though to write at this moment is to tear ideas up by the roots. I wish to heaven when you determined to unsettle yourself for a season and to venture on the salt seas, you had made England a visit instead of Charleston. The trouble would have been about the same, and you might have shewn Mrs B all the wonders of London. I have just returned from a Visit to Van Warts. I had not seen the family for more than a year and a half during which time I had been leading a solitary life in London. I passed about ten days with them, and it was a wr⟨i⟩etched struggle to part from them again; it almost unmanned me, and I have scarcely been myself since. Their children have grown finely; and the⟨y⟩ir youngest,[1] who was born since my residence in London, is called after me, which ↑perhaps↓ ⟨makes me Th?⟩ is The reason I think him a remarkably fine little fellow.

I lately sent E. I. a copy of the London Edition of the Sketch Book which I presume he will shew you. I found some delay and difficulty in making arrangements with any popular Bookseller, so I threw it into the hands of little Miller to be published on my own account, & let it take its chance. In spite of the disadvantages of such a mode of publication it is getting on, and is well spoken of by such of the Reviews as have noticed it. There is a strong Article in its favour in Blackwoods Magazine which is by Mr Lockart,[2] the author of Peters letters to his Kinsfolk.[3] He is shortly to be married to Walter Scotts eldest daughter— and by a letter which I lately recd. from Scott,[4] I find the article was written at his instigation—So much for an authors egotism; ⟨I⟩ any other but yourself would think I was writing from vanity—I wish I did possess more of it—but it seems my curse at present, to have any thing but confidence in myself or pleasure in any thing I have written—

Leslie's pictures of "Master Slender & anne Page"—and "Sir Roger de Coverly going to church"[5] are getting engraved. I will put down your name for proof copies, as I am sure you will like to have them

I had a delightful letter from James Paulding[6] lately, dated from Washington; it brought so many reccollections of early times and scenes and companions and pursuits to my memory, that my heart was filled to overflowing. What I would give to live over a few of the happy hours we ha[ve] [p]assed [*MS torn*] together! I am happy to find from Paulding's[7] [*MS torn*] he is pleasantly situated at Washington, and comfortable in his circumstances. There seems to be a pitiful and illiberal spirit indulged towards him by the writers in our reviews & news-papers.[8] What is the state of our literature that it can afford to treat with slight & contumely such a writer as Paulding—There is no one that has ever pourtrayed American scenery and characters with greater truth and beauty. ⟨It seems to me that there is a great deal of caprice in the public humour in putting me and [*unrecovered*] in the⟩ It is an ungenerous and unkind thing to put him & me in contrast, as some have done, and to praise me at his expense. It is excessively painful to me, and unjust to him[9]—I neither deserve, nor desire distinction of that kind and those that make it, do not understand our distinct and com-parative merits—

But I find I am scribbling again about myself—I am in a miserable mood for letter writing and will ⟨not⟩ write ⟨to⟩ you more fully when in a writing humour. Give my sincerest regards to Mrs Brevoort, and to our little knot of intimates & believe me ever

Affectionately yours,
W I.

ADDRESSED: Henry Brevoort Junr Esqr. / New York. / pr Amity   DOCKETED: Wn: Irving / March 27th. / 1820.
MANUSCRIPT: NYPL—Seligman Collection.   PUBLISHED: LIB, II, 120–23; PMI, I, 457 (in part).

1. Washington Irving Van Wart.
2. Lockhart's article appeared in *Blackwood's Magazine* 6 (February, 1820), 554–61.
3. This book, which appeared in 1819 under the pseudonym of Peter Morris the Odontist, contained descriptions of Edinburgh society which offended the Whigs.
4. Written on March 1, 1820. See PMI, I, 450–51.
5. In his letter to Leslie on July 29, 1818, WI had commented on three sketches.
6. Written on January 20, 1820. See *Letters of J. K. Paulding*, pp. 60–62. WI alludes to it again in a letter of August 15, 1820.
7. The words "letters that" are written above the line by another hand.
8. WI is repeating details from Paulding's letter concerning Fitz-Greene Halleck's attack in *The Croaker Papers*. See *Letters of J. K. Paulding*, p. 60.
9. In 1819 Paulding alone had revived *Salmagundi*, a venture which taxed his imagination and ingenuity to the limit. Many of the critical reactions contrasted him with WI, his partner in the earlier *Salmagundi* of 1807–1808.

280. To Henry Brevoort

London, May 13 1820.

My dear Brevoort:—

I send this letter by my friend Delafield,[1] whom I presume, you know; if not, you ought to know him, for he is a right worthy fellow. He has in charge a portrait of me,[2] painted by Newton, the nephew of

Mr. Stuart. It is considered an excellent likeness, and I am willing that it should be thought so—though between ourselves, I think myself a much better-looking fellow on canvas than in the looking-glass. I beg you to accept it as a testimony of my affection; and my deep sense of your true brotherly kindness towards me on all occasions. Do not let the likeness be seen much until it is framed. I ask this on Newton's account, who is a young artist and anxious that his works should appear to advantage, and paintings without frames have an unfinished appearance. Newton is an elegant young man and an artist of great promise. He is already noted for his fine eye for colouring, and his extraordinary tact and facility of pencil.

I recd yesterday your letter of the beginning of April[3] to which I will reply more at length by another opportunity. The Sketch Book is doing very well here. It has been checked for a time by the failure of Miller; but Murray has taken it in hand,[4] and it will now have a fair chance. I shall put a complete edition to press next week, in two volumes; and at the same time print a separate edition of the second volume,[5] to match the editions of the first already published. I have recd very flattering compliments from several of the literati,[6] and find my circle of acquaintance extending faster than I could wish. Murray's drawing-room[7] is now a frequent resort of mine, where I have been introduced to several interesting characters, and have been most courteously received by Gifford.[8] Old D'Israeli is a staunch friend of mine also; and I have met with some very interesting people at his house.[9] This evening I go to the Countess of Besborough's,[10] where there is to be quite a collection of characters, among whom I shall see Lord Wellington, whom I have never yet had the good luck to meet with.—Do apples swim!

Scott, or rather Sir Walter Scott, passed some time in town when he came up to get his Baronetcy.[11] I saw him repeatedly and was treated by him with all the hearty cordiality of an old friend. I believe the interest he took in the Sketch Book and his good word for it have been of great service to it. He inquired particularly after you.[12] He is still the same right true honest, hearty, unaffected, unassuming boy as when you knew him. Popularity has no effect on his sound head and worthy heart. He has given me repeated invitations to come down to Scotland and pass some time with him. Sophy Scott is by this time married to Lockhart.

I shall not send any more manuscript to America, until I put it to press here, as the second volume might be delayed, and the number come out here from America. The manner in which the work has been received here, instead of giving me spirit to write, has rather daunted me for the time. I feel uneasy about the second volume, and cannot write any fresh matter for it.

I was at the Anniversary Dinner of the Royal Institution[13] a few days since, where to my surprise I met with Brandram[14]—you recollect him as the *companion de voyage* of Dan Reidy[15] on the Canada tour about sixteen years since. We renewed our acquaintance and he left his card for me this morning.

Campbell is residing in town for the present, as he is lecturing at the Royal Institution.[16] He leaves London in three or four weeks for Tuscany where he means to pass a year.[17]

A new poem is coming out by Lord Byron called the Prophecy of Dante[18]—I presume it is a ghost one. He sent likewise the third & fourth cantos of Don Juan[19] which Murray has returned to him and begged him to reconsider & revise them. The third canto I am told is miserable in every way. The fourth possesses much beauty.

The death of our gallant friend Decatur[20] is indeed a heavy blow. I regret extremely that the correspondence is published.[21] It is an ill judged thing and not calculated to raise the character of either of the parties. I feel deeply for poor Mrs. Decatur, whose situation must be wretched in the extreme.

I must conclude this scrawl as Miss Delafield[22] has entered the drawing room where I am scribbling it. Remember me to Mrs. Brevoort and to the rest of our friends, and believe me, most affectionately

Yours

W. I.

PUBLISHED: LIB, II, 124–28; PMI, I, 453–54 (in part).

1. John Delafield (1786–1853), an American banker in London who was not permitted to leave England during the War of 1812. He married WI's English cousin, Mary Roberts, and, after suffering great losses in 1819, returned to New York.

2. The Gilbert Stuart Newton portrait of WI at 37 is reproduced as the frontispiece to Volume I of STW.

3. Dated April, 1820; printed in LBI, I, 121–27.

4. With failure of John Miller, Murray, probably at the suggestion of Sir Walter Scott, took over the publication of *The Sketch Book*. See the preface to *The Sketch Book*.

5. On the title page of the first volume is the imprint of John Miller; in the second volume, that of John Murray. See Jacob Blanck, *Bibliography of American Literature*, V, 19.

6. Lockhart reviewed the first volume favorably in *Blackwood's Magazine* 6 (February, 1820), 554–61. On March 1, 1820, Scott observed that "you have only to be known to the British public to be admired by them; and I would not say so unless I was really of that opinion" (PMI, I, 450–51).

7. For background concerning Murray's literary salon see WIHM, pp. xl–xlv, 3–20.

8. William Gifford (1756–1826) was the influential editor of the *Quarterly Review* which Murray published.

9. Isaac D'Israeli lived at Bloomsbury Square at this time.

10. Lady Henrietta Frances Spencer, wife of Frederic Ponsonby, third earl of Bessborough.

11. Scott received this honor on April 9, 1820.

12. On a visit to Scott in 1813 Brevoort had presented him with a copy of *Knickerbocker's History of New York*. See *Familiar Letters of Sir Walter Scott* (Boston, 1894), I, 296; PMI, I, 240, 300.

13. The Royal Institution received its charter in 1800; so WI probably attended the twentieth anniversary observance.

14. Thomas Bandram (1782–1855) was an English merchant. See *J&N*, I, 4. Hellman mistakenly transcribes the name as "Brandsam."

15. Miss Wright tentatively identifies Reidy as David Reedy, a New York insurance broker. See *J&N*, I, 4.

16. Campbell was repeating the lectures on poetry which he had previously given at Liverpool and Birmingham.

17. Campbell spent six months (May to October, 1820) on the Continent, visiting Rotterdam, Bonn, and Vienna. He returned to London in November, 1820.

18. Although Murray had received this poem by Byron in March, 1820, it was not published until April 21, 1821, with *Marino Faliero*. See Wise, *Bibliography of Byron*, II, 31.

19. These cantos, plus the fifth, were published in 1821. See Wise, *Bibliography of Byron*, II, 4.

20. While serving on the Board of Navy Commissioners, Commodore Stephen Decatur made and refused to retract remarks which offended Commodore James Barron. They met in a duel in Bladensburg, Maryland on March 22, 1820, and Decatur died of his wounds.

21. Shortly after the tragic duel Gales and Seaton, printers in Washington, D.C., published a twenty-six-page pamphlet entitled *Correspondence, between the late Commodore Stephen Decatur and Commodore James Barron, which led to the unfortunate meeting of the twenty second of March.*

22. Probably Susan Maria Delafield, sister of John Delafield, who later married Henry Parish. See Scoville, *Old Merchants of NYC*, IV, 140.

281. To James K. Paulding

London, May 27, 1820.

My dear James:

It is some time since I received your very interesting and gratifying letter of January 20th,[1] and I have ever since been on the point of answering it, but been prevented by those thousand petty obstacles that are always in the way of letter writing.

I feel very much indebted to you for the interest you have taken in Peter's welfare;[2] but I think it vain to expect any appointment for him under Government. I had hoped while William Irving was in Congress,[3] that he might have interest enough to get Peter some situation without any trouble or importunity, but since he has withdrawn from public life I give up all hopes of the kind. * * *

You have taken the trouble to make some explanations as to your literary concerns which were quite unnecessary. I have no idea of rivalship or competition in our writings,[4] and never could have suspected you of any thing of the kind. I have no feeling toward you than that of the old fellowship of the pen with which we started together, heaven knows how carelessly and vagrantly; and am only solicitous that you should maintain your stand in Literature. . . .[5]

As I am launched upon the literary world here,[6] I find my opportunities of observation extending. Murray's drawing-room is a great resort of first-rate literary characters; whenever I have a leisure hour I go there, and seldom fail to meet with some interesting personages. The hours of access are from two to five. It is understood to be a matter of privilege, and that you must have a general invitation from Murray. Here I frequently meet with such personages as Gifford, Campbell, Foscolo,[7] Hallam, (author of a work on the Middle Ages.)[8] Southey,[9] Milman,[10] Scott, Belzoni,[11] &c., &c. The visitors are men of different politics, though most frequently ministerialists. Gifford, of whom, as an old adversary, you may be curious to know something, is a small, shrivelled, deformed man of about sixty, with something of a humped back, eyes that diverge, and a large mouth. He is generally reclining on one of the sofas, and supporting himself by the cushions, being very much debilitated. He is mild and courteous in his manners, without any of the petulance that you would be apt to expect, and is quite simple, unaffected, and unassuming. Murray tells me that Gifford does not write any full articles for the Review, but revises, modifies, prunes, and prepares whatever is offered; and is very apt to extract the sting from articles that are rather virulent. Scott, or Sir Walter Scott, as he is now called, passed some few weeks in town lately, on coming up for his baronetcy. I saw him repeatedly, having formed an acquaintance with him two or three years since at his country retreat on the Tweed. He is a man that, if you knew, you would love; a right honest-hearted, generous-spirited being; without vanity, affectation, or assumption of any kind. He enters into every passing scene or passing pleasure with the interest and simple enjoyment of a child; nothing seems too high or remote for the grasp of his mind, and nothing too trivial or low for the kindness and pleasantry of his spirit. When I was in want of literary counsel and assistance, Scott was the only literary man to whom I felt I could talk about myself and my petty concerns with the confidence and freedom that I would to an old friend—nor was I deceived—from the first moment that I mentioned my work to him in a letter, he took a decided and effective interest in it, and has been to me an invaluable friend. It is only astonishing how he finds the time, with such ample exercise of the pen, to attend so much to the interests and concerns of others; but no one ever applied to Scott for any aid, counsel, or service that would cost time and trouble, that was not most cheerfully and thoroughly assisted. Life passes away with him in a round of good offices and social enjoyments. Literature seems his sport rather than his labor or his ambition, and I never met with an author so completely void of all the petulance, egotism, and peculiarities of the craft; but I am running into prolixity about Scott, who I confess has completely won my heart, even more as a man than as an author; so, praying God to bless him, we will change the subject.

Your picture of domestic enjoyment indeed raises my envy. With all my wandering habits, which are the result of circumstances rather than of disposition, I think I was formed for an honest, domestic, uxorious man, and I cannot hear of my old cronies snugly nestled down with good wives and fine children round them, but I feel for the moment desolate and forlorn. Heavens! what a haphazard, schemeless life mine has been, that here I should be, at this time of life, youth slipping away, and scribbling month after month and year after year, far from home, without any means or prospect of entering into matrimony, which I absolutely believe indispensable to the happiness and even comfort of the after part of existence. When I fell into misfortunes and saw all the means of domestic establishment pass away like a dream, I used to comfort myself with the idea that if I was indeed doomed to remain single, you and Brevoort and Gouv. Kemble would also do the same, and that we should form a knot of queer, rum old bachelors, at some future day to meet at the corner of Wall street or walk the sunny side of Broadway and kill time together. But you and Brevoort have given me the slip, and now that Gouv. has turned Vulcan and is forging thunderbolts so successfully in the Highlands,[12] I expect nothing more than to hear of his conveying some blooming bride up to the smithy. But Heaven prosper you all, and grant that I may find you all thriving and happy when I return.

I cannot close my letter without adverting to the sad story of our gallant friend Decatur; though my heart rises to my throat the moment his idea comes across my mind. He was a friend "faithful and just"[13] to me, and I have gone through such scenes of life as make a man feel the value of friendship. I can never forget how generously he stepped forth in my behalf, when I felt beaten down and brokenspirited; I can never forget him as the companion of some of my happiest hours, and as mingled with some of the last scenes of home and its enjoyments; these recollections bring him closer to my feelings than all the brilliancy of his public career. But he has lived through a life of animation and enjoyment, and died in the fulness of fame and prosperity; his cup was always full to the brim, and he has not lingered

to drain it to the dregs and taste of the bitterness. I feel most for
her he has left behind, and from all that I recollect of her devoted
affection, her disconsolateness even during his temporary absence and
jeopardy, I shrink from picturing to myself what must now be her
absolute wretchedness. If she is still near you give her my most affectionate remembrances; to speak of sympathy to her would be intrusion.

And now, my dear James, with a full heart I take my leave of you.
Let me hear from you just when it is convenient; no matter how long
or how short the letter, nor think any apologies necessary for delays,
only let me hear from you. I may suffer time to elapse myself, being
unsettled, and often perplexed and occupied; but believe me always
the same in my feelings, however irregular in my conduct, and that no
new acquaintances that a traveller makes in his casual sojournings
are apt to wear out the deep recollections of his early friends. Give my
love to Gertrude,[14] who I have no doubt is a perfect pattern for wives,
and when your boy grows large enough to understand tough stories,
tell him some of our early frolics, that he may have some kind of
acquaintance with me against we meet.

Affectionately your friend,
W. Irving.

Peter, who is sitting by me, desires me to remember him most heartily
to you and Gertrude.

PUBLISHED: PMI, I, 455–59; W. I. Paulding, *Literary Life of James K. Paulding*,
  p. 120; Samuel Smiles, *A Publisher and His Friends*, II, 130.

1. Paulding's letter told of his literary activities and his domestic arrangements
in Washington, where he was serving as secretary to the Board of Navy Commissioners. See *Letters of J. K. Paulding*, pp. 60–62.

2. Apparently Paulding had tried to use his influence to obtain a position in
one of the departments or bureaus for Peter Irving.

3. William Irving served in Congress from January 22, 1814, to March 3, 1819.

4. Unaware of WI's venture, Paulding had revived *Salmagundi* at about the
same time as the first number of *The Sketch Book* appeared.

5. This paragraph was printed only in Paulding, *Literary Life of J. K. Paulding*,
p. 120.

6. WI is referring to the publication of the first volume of *The Sketch Book* in
England in February, 1820.

7. Ugo Foscolo (1778–1827) was an Italian writer who had fled to England
in 1816 after his refusal to take an oath of loyalty to the Austrian government.

8. Henry Hallam (1777–1859) had published *A View of the State of Europe
during the Middle Ages* in 1818.

9. Robert Southey (1774–1843), a prolific writer in poetry and prose, had been
named poet laureate in 1813.

10. Henry Hart Milman (1791–1868), a poet and playwright who was professor
of poetry at Oxford from 1821 to 1831, became dean of St. Paul's in 1849.

11. Giovanni Battista Belzoni (1778–1823), who had recently excavated Egyptian
temples, was now preparing exhibits of his findings at the British Museum.

12. In 1818 Gouverneur Kemble had established the West Point Foundry Association at Cold Spring, on the Hudson opposite the United States Military Academy, to manufacture cannons for the army.

13. *Julius Caesar*, III, ii, 90.

14. Gertrude Kemble, whom Paulding had married on November 15, 1818.

282. To Ebenezer Irving

[London, June 28, 1820]

It is a sketch[1] drawn almost entirely from the life; and, therefore, if it has no other merit, it has that of truth and nature.

It is not likely that I shall publish another number soon. I have had so much muddling work with the Sketch Book from publishing in both countries, that I have grown tired of it, and have lost all excitement. I shall feel relieved from a cloud, when I get this volume printed and out of my sight. * * *

PUBLISHED: PMI, I, 459.

1. "The Angler." WI describes the fisherman who served as the basis for the sketch in his letters of July 16, 1816, and January 29, 1817, to Brevoort.

283. To Henry Van Wart

London, Ju⟨ly⟩ne 29th /20

My dear Brother

I want fifty Pounds. ⟨which⟩ As you may have a parcel to forward when you receive the letters by the packet, You can send the money at the same time

Yours affectionately
W I.

We have put a small book and a pamphlet in this parcel, by way of making it worth ↑the⟨cut⟩cost of↓carriage

ADDRESSED: Henry Van Wart Esqr. /Birmingham   DOCKETED: Washington Irving June 29/20

MANUSCRIPT: Bodleian Library, Oxford.

284. To William S. Cardell

London Aug 14th. 1820

My dear Sir

I have received your letter of July 9th.[1] in a moment of great hurry, when on the point of setting off for the Continent. I have not therefore been able to give the plan of the proposed Institution[2] that calm and full consideration which is necessary to understand ⟨fully⟩ thoroughly its extent and bearings. Still, from the cursory glance which I have taken it appears to me to promise the most important advantages to our national Literature. The circumstance of choosing the officers and members from among the most distinguished men of Letters of various and widely separated parts of the union³ is well calculated to obviate local jealousies, and to give universal currency and weight to the opinions of the Institution. It appears to me to be the surest way of protecting our paternal language from useless and vulgar innovation, and⟨of⟩forming a kind of ordeal, through which all those *new words* must pass, which are absolutely requisite to express—⟨any⟩↑those↓*new things* originating in our Country. It will be in fact a representative body of learning & talents of the Union.

I cannot but be deeply sensible of the honour done me by the Committee in offering to enroll me among the Counsellors; indeed under all circumstances there is something very affecting to me to be thus remembered and esteemed by some of the most worthy and distinguished of my Townsmen; but I am too conscious of my wants and imperfections to aspire to any situation of the kind You require men of method; of business; of varied and accurate knowledge, and of sound practical judgement; and I should but be usurping a place for which I was not fitted, and which would be much more advantageously and meritoriously conferred on some other man. Permit me therefore most respectfully to decline a distinction to which I do not feel myself entitled; and for which, in my present unsettled & wandering state, I could make no ⟨adequate⟩ returns even in common place services. Should there be any ⟨thing⟩↑way↓however in which I could promote the views of the Institution I shall be most happy to exert myself to the utmost, through mere love of the cause, and beg I may be considered perfectly at ⟨the⟩↑its↓command. I shall communicate ⟨the⟩ these intentions of the Committee to Mr Linley Murray,⁴ and shall request him to direct his answer to you. I believe he resides in the Country and that I shall have to write to him, I should otherwise see him personally.

Will you present to the Committee my most heartfelt acknowledge-ments for the good opinion they have testified of me, and my zealous wishes for the success of their undertaking.

With great respect—I am Sir/Very truly yours—

Washington Irving

ADDRESSED: To, / William S Cardell Esqr. / &c &c &c / New York. / pr Albion
    DOCKETED: Washington Irvings / Letter—London— / Aug. 1820
MANUSCRIPT: Yale.

William S. Cardell (1780–1828) was an educator in New York City who published several spelling books and grammars for school children, including *Analytical Spelling Book . . .* (1823); *Essay on Language* (1825); and *Philosophical Grammar of the English Language* (1827).

1. This letter has not been located.

2. Cardell established the American Academy of Language and Belles Lettres in 1820 to collect and interchange literary intelligence, to guard against local and foreign corruptions in the language, to adjudicate on the use of doubtful words and phrases, to establish the approved orthography among variant forms, and to set and maintain the British standard of writing throughout the United States. For a full statement on the purpose of the Academy, see *Literary and Scientific Repository* 2 (January, 1821), 69–83.

3. At NYHS are letters to Cardell from John Marshall (June 25, 1821), accepting membership, and from John C. Calhoun (April 24, 1821), refusing membership on the grounds that he did not have time and energy, apart from his public commitments, to devote to it.

4. Lindley Murray (1745–1826), born in Pennsylvania, settled in England in 1784 and established himself as an authority on English language and grammar.

285. To Ebenezer Irving

London, Aug. 15, 1820.

The Sketch Book has been very successful in England. The first volume is out of print, which is doing very well, considering that it is but four or five months since it was published; that it has had to make its own way; against many disadvantages; being written by an author the public knew nothing of, and published by a bookseller, who was going to ruin.[1] The second volume, of which a thousand were printed, is going off briskly; and Murray proposes putting to press immediately a uniform edition of the two volumes at his own expense. I have offered, however, to dispose of the work to him entirely, and am to know his answer tomorrow.[2] He wishes likewise to publish an edition of Knickerbocker, which has been repeatedly spoken well of in the British publications, and particularly in Blackwood's Magazine, in which I have received the highest eulogium that has ever been passed upon me.[3] It is written by Lockhart, author of Peter's Letters to his Kinsfolk, and son-in-law to Sir Walter Scott. You will perceive that I have dedicated my second volume to Scott; but this dedication had not been seen by Lockhart, at the time he wrote the eulogium. Should a new and complete edition of the work be published in America, I wish the dedication to be placed in the first volume. I cannot sufficiently express how sensible I feel of the warm and affectionate interest which Scott has taken in me and my writings. My second volume has been noticed by two or three periodical publications,[4] and in the same favorable way with the first. I have received abundance of private marks of approbation from literary people here; and upon the whole, have reason to be highly gratified with the success of my literary enterprise in this country. After all I value success here chiefly as tending to confirm my standing in my own country; for it is to popularity at home that I look as the sweetest source of enjoyment.

Published: PMI, I, 460–61.

1. John Miller of Burlington Arcade.
2. Murray bought the copyright for two hundred pounds (note in PMI, I, 460).
3. Lockhart's review appeared in *Blackwood's Magazine* 6 (February, 1820), 554–61.
4. See *Literary Gazette* 2 (July 25, 1820), 465; *Edinburgh Review* 34 (August, 1820), 160; *Literary Chronicle and Weekly Review* 2 (August, 1820), 546.

286.   To Walter Scott

London, August 15th. 1820

My dear Sir,

In consequence of the favourable reception of the first volume of the Sketch Book, and the encouragement you were so kind as to give me, I have been induced to bring out a Second,[1] ⟨which I⟩ a copy of which I trust you have before this received. I wish the work were better, and under other circumstances I think I could have made it better; but I have been so new to the ground which I was treading, and so daunted by the idea of writing absolutely for a British public, that my powers, such as they are, have been almost paralyzed.

I write this letter cheifly to apologize for the liberty I have taken in dedicating the work to you[2] without previously ascertaining from you whether it would be agreeable; but in fact the last sheet was going to the press, and I could not resist the impulse to express simply but honestly the feelings of my heart. I had no idea that you could be honoured or flattered by so poor a tribute from so inconsiderable a peisonage, but I felt as if it would do me good and ease a certain fullness of the heart just to say what I have said.

In the last number of Blackwood I perceive a very flattering notice of my Knickerbocker,[3] which I presume is from the pen of Mr Lockart.[4] I feel very sensible of the warm and friendly feeling that shines through his writing, and which induces him to give me more praise than even my vanity as an author can admit. These Eulogiums will oblige me to publish an edition of the work in this country; Murray has repeatedly mentioned the thing; but I have always felt affraid of the work as being local, crude and juvenile. I find however that the notices in Blackwood have put one of the Booksellers in the American trade on the scent;[5] and I shall, I fear, be obliged to publish in my own defence, to prevent a spurious & incorrect republication.[6]

I shall leave London the day after tomorrow for the continent, and shall probably remain for some time at Paris. Could I render you any service while there it would give me the greatest pleasure, and a letter addressed to the care of[7]

Present my particular remembrances to Lady Scott and the family and I beg you will assure Mr Lockart that I shall be happy at some future day to acknowledge to him personally how much I have been flattered and gratified by his literary friendship.

With the highest regard/I am my dear Sir/truly yours
Washington Irving

Sir Walter Scott Bart.

ADDRESSED: Sir Walter Scott / ⟨Edinburgh⟩ / Melrose   POSTMARKED: AUG / [*unrecovered*]/ 1820 / POSTAGE TO / ? DATE AUG 31 ? / NOT PAID DOCKETED: Washington / Irving

MANUSCRIPT: National Library of Scotland.   PUBLISHED: *Studies in Scottish Literature* 3 (October, 1965), 117–18.

WI wrote "Edinburgh," which is canceled. "Melrose" is written in another hand, probably by a post office employee.

1. On August 10, 1820, John Murray had registered *The Sketch Book* for copyright at Stationers' Hall, and on August 16 Murray paid WI 250 guineas for the copyright. See WIHM, pp. 220, 25.

2. In the second volume was WI's dedication: "To Sir Walter Scott, Bart. this work is dedicated, in testimony of the admiration and affection of the author."

3. See *Blackwood's Magazine* 6 (February, 1820), 554–61.

4. WI mentions this same point in his letter to Ebenezer Irving on August 15, 1820.

5. William Wright, a bookseller at 46 Fleet Street, brought out a pirated edition of *Knickerbocker's History* about this time.

6. Ironically, Murray's edition, which WI authorized, followed the text of the 1812 edition rather than that of the 1819 edition of Moses Thomas.

7. A blank space one inch deep intervenes at this point on the page before WI starts the next paragraph. In a letter to Brevoort on this same day WI suggests that mail to him be sent to Reuben Beasley, United States consul at Le Havre. Probably WI had intended to give the same information to Scott.

287. *To Henry Brevoort*

London, Aug 15th. 1820.

My dear Brevoort,

I wrote to you not very long since—and I sent sometime since by Delafield[1] a portrait which I trust you have received before this. I am now in all the hurry and bustle of breaking up my encampment, and moving off for the Continent.[2] After remaining so long in one place it is painful to cast loose again and turn oneself adrift: but I do not wish to remain long enough in any place in Europe to make it a home.

Since I have published with Murray I have had continual opportunities of seeing something of the literary world, and have formed some very agreeable acquaintances. You know Murrays drawing room is a complete rendezvous of men of talent; where you meet with the first characters of the day;³ and it has been for some time past ⟨m⟩ an almost daily resort of mine. There have been several literary Coteries set on foot lately by some Blue Stockings of fashion, at which I have been much amused. Lady Caroline Lamb⁴ is a great promoter of them. You may have read some of her writings, particularly her Glenarvon,⁵ in which she has woven many anecdotes of fashionable life & fashionable characters, and hinted at particulars of her own story and that of Lord Byron. She is a strange being—a compound of contradictions, with much to admire, much to stare at and much to condemn. Among the most pleasant acquaintances I have met with at Murrays is a young man by the name of Mitchell;⁶ who has recently published the first volume of a translation of Aristophanes and writes those very clever & very amusing articles in the Quarterly Review on the manners of the Athenians ⟨[unrecovered]⟩ Greek cookery &c.⁷ He is an excellent scholar, and possesses withal a very ⟨delicate⟩ genuine vein of delicate humour, that gives a ⟨spiciness⟩ freedom and sportiveness to his writings not frequently found among Scholastic men. I have been very much pleased also with Belzoni, the traveller, who is just bringing out a personal narrative of his researches,⁸ ⟨with a⟩ illustrated with very extraordinary plates There is the interior of a temple, excavated in a hill, which he discovered & opened; which had the effect on me of an arabian tale. There are rows of Gigantic statues, Thirty feet high, cut out of the Calcarious rock, in perfect preservation. I have been as much delighted in conversing with him & getting from him an account of his adventures & feelings, as was ever one of Sindbads auditors. Belzoni is about six feet four or five inches high; of a large frame, but ↑a↓ small and I think a very fine head; ⟨and at times has the [unrecovered] very fine expression of countenance⟩ and a countenance which at times is very expressive & intelligent. I have likewise been very much pleased with a young man by the name of Cohen,⁹ who writes for the Quarterly Review—particularly those articles on the Superstitions & mithology of the middle ages, on which subject, by the bye, he has undertaken to write a quarto work.¹⁰ He is remarkable for the extent & diversity of his knowledge, and particularly for ⟨knowing⟩ being informed on all kinds of odd & out of the way subjects.

I have also frequently met with Mr Hallam, whose able & interesting work on the middle ages you have no doubt seen and most probably have in your library. Like all other men of real talent & unquestionable merit, he is ⟨easy⟩ affable & unpretending—He is a copious talker and you are sure when he is present to have ⟨the⟩ conversation briskly kept up.—But it is useless merely to mention names in this manner;

and is too much like entertaining one with a description of a banquet, by merely naming the dishes. One thing I have found invariably, that the greater the merit, the less has been the pretension; and that there is no being so modest, ⟨and⟩ natural, unaffected and unassuming as a first rate genius.

I lately received a few lines from Henry Cary[11] by Mr. Wallack[12] the Actor. It gave me the greatest pleasure to recognize his handwriting, and to receive this proof of reccollection. I had received some account of him a short time before from Col Perkins,[13] whose daughter I find is married to a ⟨sister of⟩ Brother of Carys. I am rejoiced to find that Cary is prospering in the world. No man better deserves prosperity and none I am sure will make a better use of it. I wish you would remember me to him heartily—I should write to him; but I have several to write to; and to tell the honest truth I find it hard work to bring myself to the task of letter writing.

I am delighted also to hear that our worthy Patroon[14] is doing well with his foundery—God bless & prosper him and make him as rich and as happy as he deserves to be—I believe I told you in my last of a long letter which I received from James Paulding[15]—it was a most gratifying one to me; and it gave me a picture of quiet prosperity and domestic enjoyment which it is delightful for a wandering, unsettled being like myself to contemplate—Oh my dear Brevoort how my heart warms towards you all, when I get talking and thinking of past times and past scenes. What would I not give for a few days among the highlands of the Hudson with the little knot that was once assembled there. But I shall return home and find all changed, and shall be made sensible how much I have changed myself. It is this idea which continually comes across my mind when I think of home, and I am continually picturing to myself the dreary state of a poor devil like myself who after wandering about the world ⟨returns⟩ among strangers returns to find himself a still greater stranger in his native place

> He feels like one that treads alone
> From Banquet hall deserted,
> Whose lights are fled, whose garlands dead,
> And all but he departed.[16]

When you write to me next direct to the care of Beazley[17] our consul at ⟨Bord⟩ Havre—who will forward the letter to me wherever I may be. And now my dear fellow I must take my leave—for it is midnight and I am wearied with packing trunks and making other preparations for my departure. The next you will hear from me will be from France, and after passing five years in England among genuine John Bulls it will be like entering into a New World to cross the Channel

Remember me particularly to Mrs Brevoort, and to our intimate
friends and believe me most truly & affectionately

Yours W.I.

ADDRESSED: Henry Brevoort Junr Esqr / New York / Per *"Albion"* / J M
    DOCKETED: London Aug 15, 1820 / Washington Irving
MANUSCRIPT: LC.   PUBLISHED: LIB, II, 129–35; PMI, I, 461–63 (in part).

1. John Delafield, an American in the banking business in London, mentioned
in WI's letter of May 13, 1820.

2. WI and his brother Peter started for Paris on August 17.

3. Among the people WI met at Murray's were Isaac Disraeli; William Brockedon, an artist; John Miller; Walter Hamilton, a writer; Lady Caroline Lamb; Giovanni Belzoni; Henry Hallam; William Gifford; Thomas Campbell; Henry Milman;
and Robert Southey.

4. Lady Caroline Lamb (1785–1828), who attained notoriety as a result of her
infatuation with Lord Byron.

5. *Glenarvon* was published in three volumes in 1816.

6. Thomas Mitchell (1783–1845), a graduate in classics from Cambridge,
brought out a two-volume translation of Aristophanes's comedies earlier in 1820.

7. WI is probably alluding to Mitchell's essay-review of Henry David Hill's
*Essays on the Institutions, Government, and Manners of the States of Ancient
Greece,* which appeared in the *Quarterly Review* 22 (July, 1819), 163–203. Mitchell
also contributed articles to the *Quarterly Review* in March, 1813; April, 1819; and
May, 1820.

8. Giovanni Battista Belzoni, whom WI met at Murray's, published *Narrative
of the Operations and Recent Discoveries within the Pyramids, Temples, Tombs,
and Excavations in Egypt and Nubia* . . . under the John Murray imprint in 1820.

9. Probably Francis Cohen (1788–1861), who later changed his name to
Palgrave. From 1814 to 1820 he was a steady contributor to the *Edinburgh* and
Quarterly Reviews.

10. Cohen's early books on the Middle Ages included a translation of Wace's
Le Romant des Ducs de Normandie (1818 and 1828), *History of England,* vol. I,
The Anglo-Saxon Period (1831) and *Truths and Fictions of the Middle Ages:
The Merchant and the Friar* (1837).

11. Henry Carey (1785–1857) was a New York merchant, born in Chelsea, Massachusetts, who lived in New York from 1810 to 1856. He died in Florence, Italy.

12. Probably James William Wallack (1791?–1864), who had just returned from an
American tour.

13. Thomas H. Perkins (1764–1854) was a wealthy Boston merchant, philan-
thropist, and statesman. In 1819 his daughter Mary married Thomas G. Carey
(1791–1859), a lawyer and merchant who moved from Massachusetts to New
York in 1821.

14. Gouverneur Kemble.

15. WI mentions Paulding's letter of January 20, 1820 (printed in *Letters of
J. K. Paulding,* pp. 60–62) in a letter to Brevoort on March 27, 1820.

16. From Thomas Moore's "Oft, in the Stilly Night."

17. Reuben Beasley, who was American consul in Le Havre from 1818 to 1848,
was also active in various business enterprises there.

288. *To Henry Brevoort*

Paris, Septr. 22d. 1820.

My dear Brevoort,

Peter and myself have taken a part in an enterprize for navigating the Seine by steam.[1] It will require a little capital on our part, and peter will enter actively into the concern—I shall put into it 5000$ which I apprehend is all that I am worth in the world. I shall take no further share; nor suffer my mind to be occupied by it; as I wish to turn my attention entirely to literature. I have engaged thus far, chiefly for the purpose of promoting Peters views. The project will require an advance of pecuniary assistance from our friends in N York—I have just drawn on William Irving for 2000$ and have written to him at some length on the subject. I must refer you to my letter to him & letters from Peter to him & John T.[2] for further explanations, as I am at this moment pressed for time & very much indisposed with a head ache. The purport of this letter is that you will use your exertions to prevent my brothers from disappointing us in this business. I do not doubt their good will; but they are apt to hang fire; and delay would completely frustrate the whole enterprize as far as we are concerned; as there are men of capital here extremely desirous of entering into the scheme. If my brothers are unable to furnish the money required in time I wish you would assist them as far as your convenience will permit—at any rate do not let them delay, & postpone, & demur until the time is gone by. ⟨for that⟩ ⟨with many⟩ Peter has now been living on hopes, and very feeble ones, for two or three years; it is pretty evident they are not likely to strike out any thing for him in america; and now that he has struck out something for himself it behoves them to back him like true brothers — But it is needless for me to multiply words to you on this subject — I know you will do all that is right and friendly in the business.

I wish you would write to me by the way of Havre, care of R. G. Beasley American Consul at Havre—it is a long time since I have heard from you.

I have been about a month in Paris; but having been a little restless in mind I have not enjoyed it as much as I should otherwise have done — I shall write to you again when more composed and in better mood—

Remember me with great regard to Mrs Brevoort & believe me my dear Brevoort

Most affectionately yours
W. I.

Henry Brevoort Jr Esqr.

ADDRESSED: Henry Brevoort Junr. Esqr / New York.   POSTMARKED: Received &
    Forwarded / by / [?Bonnay?] & Cie   DOCKETED: Pa[ris] [MS torn] Sep.
    22. 1820 / Washington Irving
MANUSCRIPT: NYPL–Seligman Collection.   PUBLISHED: LIB, II, 136–38.

1. For other details, see WI's letter to William Irving, September 22, 1820.
    2. Peter's letters have not been located. WI is referring to his brother John
Treat Irving as well.

289.   To William Irving, Jr.

Paris, Sept. 22, 1820.

My Dear Brother:

I have just drawn two sets of Exchange on you, one at 60 and another
at 90 days for $1, 000 each. I presume Peter has written at large[1] about
the project to promote which these bills are drawn. I will, however, give
a few particulars. On our way from England here we stopped at Havre,
where we unexpectedly found Mr. Edward Church,[2] who had just put
a steamboat on the Seine, to run between Havre and Rouen.[3] It had made
but one trip; but the prospects were so favorable that Mr. Beasley, our
consul, who is well acquainted with the river and its localities, had
entered warmly into the enterprise.[4] We took passage in the steamboat
for Rouen, and were struck with the populousness of the banks of the
river, the quantity of traffic carried on upon its waters, and the magnificence of the scenery. It appeared to be one of the most advantageous
places possible for steam navigation, both as to procuring freight and
passengers; and we both at the same time conceived the idea that a
share in a new enterprise of the kind would be a most promising mode
of turning a small amount of money and some activity of talent and
exertion to large account. It was not like a mere random experiment,
for Mr. Church, the conductor of the enterprise, had already proved
his capacity by his very successful attempts on the Garonne. The
circumstance, too, of the parties owning the boat being such intimate
friends was greatly in favor of a participation in the concern. After our
arrival in Paris, we talked the matter over with one another and with
Mr. Church, and Peter wrote to Beasley. He has since been at Rouen
and is at present at Havre, where, after making minute examinations,
all which tend to confirm us more and more in our anticipations, he
has made arrangements for taking a share in the general concern
(which will include two other boats about to be built) to the amount
of ten thousand dollars. I have agreed to embark one-half of the
amount, ($5,000,) which I trust is not more than the value of my
literary property in the hands of E. I., and shall draw on you to that
amount. As it will no doubt be in advance of the proceeds of my

writings, you must avail yourself of them as they come in; or, if it is necessary to your convenience, you may dispose of the copyrights.

I am induced to take this share in the enterprise, not from a desire of making money for myself, but to enable Peter to lay hold of what I consider the *best*, and indeed what is the *only* chance for getting into fortune's way again, that has presented since our disasters. It will once more give him employment, and employment to which he is particularly adapted by the turn of his mind and his personal activity; and I think it will pay him largely for his trouble. I shall not enter any further into the scheme myself, nor shall I take any active part. The part we take will be entirely in his name. I shall turn my attention entirely to literary pursuits; and I think I shall pursue them with more cheerfulness when I see prosperity once more dawning around us. . . .

I trust you will all exert yourselves to launch him fairly in this enterprise, which he seems to look upon as his last cast. . . .

If Peter would have accepted the money and lived on it, until something turned up; if he would have shared my morsel with me as I made it, it was at his service. I have repeatedly told him so. I have urged it upon him in a variety of ways. I have endeavored to foist a loan of money on him, but it has all been in vain. He has a tenacious, and, as I think, a false and squeamish delicacy on that head; and will not take a farthing from me. Were I in his situation and he had the fullest purse, I would share it without hesitation. I would think I did not do him justice in declining to share his better luck. I have therefore done the best I could to serve him; and if the steamboat business fails and all that I advance is lost, my only regret will be on his account.

I have been about a month in Paris, and begin to feel a little more at home. Mr. Gallatin[5] has been extremely attentive to me. I have dined with him repeatedly. Either Paris or myself has changed very much since I was here before. It is by no means so gay as formerly; that is to say, the populace have a more grave and triste appearance. You see but little of the sprightliness and gaiety of manner for which the French are proverbial. However, as I have been here but a little time I will not begin to give opinions; and as I wish my letter to go safe, I will not interlard it with any speculations on national character or concerns. . . .

Published: PMI, II, 14–16, 19.

1. Peter Irving had written to his brothers William and John in New York, asking for a loan of $5000. See PMI, II, 16.

2. Edward Church, the American Consul at Lorient in Brittany, had started a steamboat service in the Bordeaux area in 1818. In August, 1820, Church had just begun operating a similar service from Le Havre to Rouen. See Young, *WI-Bordeaux*, pp. 62–63.

3. On September 21, 1820, the *Journal du Havre* (no. 223) announced: "Le bateau à vapeur Le Triton partira demain matin, à six heures; il prendra du fret et des passagers pour Rouen à tous autres ports de la Seine."

4. Beasley, in fact, is credited by students of the subject with starting ferry service by steamboat between Le Havre and Honfleur in 1819: "C'est un Américain, M. Beasley, Consul des Etats-Unis dans notre ville, qui organisa, en 1819, le premier service à vapeur sur Honfleur. Ce service—assez irrégulier, d'ailleurs, dans les premières années—eut pour pionnier le vapeur le Triton, capitaine Toutaine, achète à Bordeaux." Louis Brindeau, *Les Premiers Bateaux à Vapeur au Havre* (Le Havre, 1901), p. 10.

5. Albert Gallatin served as American minister to France from 1816 to 1823.

290. To John Murray II

Paris. Octr. 26th. 1820.

My dear Sir,

On taking up a London paper this morning[1] I found my name given at full length in an advertizement of Cawthorns as author of a poem ⟨j⟩ he has just published intitld *"The Lay of a Scottish Fiddle."*[2] As I wish to be answerable for no ones sins but my own I would take it as a particular favour if you would contradict it in your next advertizement of the Sketch Book &c.[3] The work in question was written by a Mr Paulding.[4] What particularly annoys me is that th[is] [*MS torn*] poem was a burlesque on the writings of Sir Walter Scott for whom I have so perfect an esteem & affection, and besides it contained political and national reflections of a different nature from those I have entertained.

I see that you have published The History of N York and understand you hurried it out to prevent a spurious edition[5] from being thrown into ⟨the⟩ circulation: for which I am glad though I should have liked to have made some corrections and alterations.[6]

I see you are all yet occupied with the queens pilgrimage to Jerusalem; and have a famous array of Crusaders who have all been with her to the Holy Land.[7] I expect Bergamis[8] effigy will figure cross legged at some future day in Westminster abbey. By the way I was lately taking care of a young friend who lay very ill of a fever, and was obliged to have a female attendant or *garde* as they are called here, to watch with him at nights. She was a very decent french woman. By mere accident I was enquiring one day about her circumstances when she told me that her husband was Coachman to Bergamis daughter — I felt a little surprize, as you may suppose, and on questioning her further I found that Victorine, the child of five years of age, is at a boarding school in the vicinity of Paris, where she has a carriage, and male & female attendants to the number of five, ↑for her particular service↓!—This you may depend on as a fact: for the honest woman told it with the utmost simplicity & frankness— Truly this Bergami is a fellow of most princely notions!

Present my sincere regards to Mrs Murray &/believe me dear Sir,

[*Signature clipped from letter*]

John Murray Esqr.

ADDRESSED: To / John Murra[y] / A[lbermarle Street?] / [London?]   POSTMARKED: FPO OC. 31 1820   DOCKETED: Irving Esqr / Oct 26. 1820
MANUSCRIPT: John Murray.   PUBLISHED: Smiles, *A Publisher and His Friends*, II, 132; WIHM, pp. 28–30.
Because the complimentary close and signature have been clipped from the letter, part of the address is missing.

1. Probably the *Morning Chronicle* of October 21, 1820. The London *Times* carried the ad for the first time on October 30. For the full text of the advertisement, see WIHM, p. 29, n. 10.

2. This work, first advertised in the *Morning Chronicle* for October 21, 1820, was a pirated edition of James Kirke Paulding's parody which had originally been published in August, 1813. See Ralph M. Aderman, "Publication Dates of Three Early Works by James Kirke Paulding," *Papers of the Bibliographical Society of America* 59 (first quarter, 1965), 49.

3. Murray's subsequent ads in the *Morning Chronicle* did not call attention to the mistake in identity.

4. WI's aloof attitude toward his former collaborator probably stemmed from the fact that he wished to dissociate himself from adverse criticism of the British and especially, as he suggests, of his new friend, Walter Scott.

5. Earlier in 1820, Walter Wright, an English publisher, had printed an unauthorized edition of *Knickerbocker's History*. Murray also probably wished to capitalize on the current favorable interest in WI which *The Sketch Book* had stimulated.

6. WI eventually made some of these changes in the Author's Revised Edition of 1848.

7. Amelia Elizabeth Caroline of Brunswick-Wolfenbüttel (1768–1821) had married George Augustus Frederick, the son of George III, presently prince regent and later George IV, in April, 1795. In the following March they were formally separated, after the birth of a daughter, with the queen returning to Blackheath. On July 12, 1816, the queen, who had been living in various places on the Continent since 1814, entered Jerusalem with an entourage of 200. See Roger Fulford, *The Trial of Queen Caroline* (New York, 1968), pp. 29–34.

8. Bartolomos Bergamis or Bergami or Pergami (d. 1841), an Italian military officer who became Caroline's courier, was grand master of the Knights of the Order of St. Caroline, an order of chivalry instituted by Queen Caroline. She later bought him a villa near Milan. See Joanna Richardson, *George the Magnificent* (New York, 1966), pp. 172–76.

291. To Richard Rush

Paris, Oct. 28, 1820./4 Rue Mont Thabor.

My Dear Sir:

I feel very much obliged by your letter of the 20th,[1] and am highly flattered by the letter of Lady Lyttleton,[2] which you were so good as to enclose, and which I herewith return. It is indeed delightful to receive applause from such a quarter. As her ladyship seems desirous of full and explicit information as to the authorship of the Sketch Book, you may assure her that it was entirely written by myself; that the revisions and corrections were my own, and that I have had no literary assistance either in the beginning or the finishing of it. I speak fully to this point, not from any anxiety of authorship, but because the doubts which her ladyship has heard on the subject seem to have arisen from the old notion that it is impossible for an *American to write decent English.* If I have indeed been fortunate enough to do any thing, however trifling, to stagger this prejudice, I am too good a patriot to give up even the little ground I have gained. As to the article on Rural Life in England, which appears to have pleased her ladyship, it may give it some additional interest in her eyes to know that though the result of general impressions received in various excursions about the country, yet it was sketched in the vicinity of Hagley[3] just after I had been rambling about its grounds, and whilst its beautiful scenery, with that of the neighborhood, were fresh in my recollection.

I cannot help smiling at the idea that any thing I have written should be deemed worthy of being attributed to Sir Walter Scott, and that I should be called upon to vindicate my weak pen from the honor of such a parentage. He could tenant half a hundred scribblers like myself on the mere skirts of his literary reputation. He never saw my writings until in print; but though he has not assisted me with his pen, yet the interest which he took in my success; the praises which he bestowed on some of the first American numbers forwarded to him; the encouragement he gave to me to go on and do more, and the countenance he gave to the first volume when republished in England have, perhaps, been more effectually serviceable than if he had revised and corrected my work page by page. He has always been to me a frank, generous, warm-hearted friend, and it is one of my greatest gratifications to be able to call him such. Indeed, it is the delight of his noble and liberal nature to do good and to dispense happiness; those who only know him through his writings know not a tithe of his excellence.

Present my sincere remembrances to Mrs. Rush, and believe me, dear sir,

With very great respect,/Yours faithfully,

Washington Irving.

PUBLISHED: PMI, II, 21–23.
This letter is based on a draft of WI's reply. See PMI, II, 23.

1. Part of Rush's letter to WI is printed in PMI, I, 20.
2. Lady Sarah Spencer (d. 1870) who married William Henry Lyttleton (1782–1837) in 1813, subsequently served as governess of the children of Queen Victoria. In her letter to Rush, Lady Lyttleton asks for proof and assurance that *The Sketch Book* was written by an American and not by Sir Walter Scott. She calls "the style and nature of the work ... new and peculiar," remarks about "the admirably just descriptions of English *rural* life," and calls it "The prettiest and *most amiable* book we have read for a long time." See PMI, II, 20–21.
3. The coincidence here is interesting. Hagley was the home of Lord and Lady Lyttleton in Staffordshire, about thirty miles from Birmingham, where WI often visited the Van Warts. At Hagley Lord Lyttleton observed the old-fashioned Christmas customs described in *The Sketch Book*. See PMI, II, 22, n.

292. To John Murray II

Paris, Octr. 31st. 1820.

My dear Sir,

I have just received your letter of the 26th. which has almost over-powered me with the encomiums it contains.[1] I am astonished at the success of my writings in England, and can hardly persuade myself that it is not all a dream. Had any one told me a few years since in America, that any thing I could write would interest such men as Gifford and Byron[2] I should have as readily believed a fairy tale. If Mr Gifford will be so good as to suggest what parts of Knickerbocker might be curtailed with advantage[3] I shall endeavour to modify the work accordingly. I am sensible that it is full of faults, and would almost require rewriting, to make it what it should be — but I find it very difficult to touch it now; it is so stale with me. I shall write to Mr Leslie on the subject of the Sketches.[4] I am very glad you have seen him, and have taken an interest in him. He is deserving of the highest en-couragement and patronage; he is full of talent, and full of merit. You can be of great service to him, and I think with advantage to yourself. It is one of the enviable circumstances of your lot, that you are enabled to do so much good to a variety of the most interesting and valuable people and to surround yourself with agreeable talent of every kind.

The specimen you have sent me of the new edition of the Sketch Book is very handsome — I like the size. I will look over the work and send you any corrections that may occur, and when I have a spare copy, will interline the *passages* first published in England. The *articles* that were first published there were "Westminister Abbey — Stratford-on-Avon — Little Britain — The Angler — & L'Envoy." — Gagliani[5] says that You can Send any parcel for me to their correspondent Baldwin & Co[6]—but that it must be mentioned to the Baldwins that it is with Gaglianis permission — otherwise the parcel may be refused—They have a parcel sent from London the first of every month, but it is likely they will have one the middle of November—I am much obliged to you for what you say about my drawing on you; as in the state of my finances it will be a matter of some convenience.

I have been rather an idle man since my arrival in Paris; and indeed have been so flattered by the circumstance of republishing in England, and the attention that has been so liberally shew⟨ed⟩n to my writings and myself there, that I must take a little time to let my mind get calm and collected. I feel a little too anxious just now.

I have just received a Letter from a Bookseller in New York[7] who is publishing a poem written by a son of his lately deceased; a young clergyman of great promise.[8] The ⟨poem is⟩ subject of the poem is taken from the story of King Philip the celebrated Indian chief[9]— (on which by the way Southey is writing a poem)[10] It is in ⟨Six pa⟩ Six cantos & forms ⟨300?⟩ about 300 pp. 12 Mo. It is entitled "Yamoyden: a tale of the Wars of King Philip, with notes & a preface ⟨The⟩ *by the late Rev. James Wallis Eastburn M.A. and his friend."*

The friend is a young gentleman[11] who at the age of 18 produced a poem entitled "The Bridal of Vaumond," which shewed great poetical promise. These young gentlemen had visited all the scenes of King Philips exploits: noticd the scenery & collected all the historical and traditional facts that were extant. The poem is very highly spoken of, by various persons of cultivated taste that have seen it—and the novelty of an Indian poem, written on the spot and by persons familiar with Indian manners may give it additional interest. The object of all this, is, to reccommend the work to your attention. I am requested by the authors father to do so. He writes that he will send the sheets as they are printed to my correspondents in Liverpool and a complete copy when finished. I will write to have them submitted to you for ⟨com⟩ your perusal, and you will determine whether the work will be desireable for republication, and what terms you can afford to offer. I have not seen the work, and only speak from the representations of others, which are very strong in its favour. ⟨I have seen⟩

Present my best regards to Mrs Murray, and likewise to my friends the D'Israelis; by whose kind enquiries I am very much obliged.

I am my dear Sir/With very great regard/Yours faithfully

Washington Irving

John Murray Esqr.[12]

P. S. As you are printing the Sketch Book I just reccollect an error I observed this morning in Vol II P. 50. line 6 for "*grazing*" read "*dozing.*"[13]

DOCKETED: W Irving. Esq / Oct 30. 1820
MANUSCRIPT: John Murray.   PUBLISHED: Samuel Smiles, *A Publisher and His Friends* ..., II, 131–32 (in part); WIHM, pp. 31–34.

1. Murray's letter is printed in PMI, II, 24–26.
2. Gifford and Byron responded favorably to *The Sketch Book*. See WIHM, p. 31, n. 16.
3. Gifford's comments were probably made to Murray in a conversation. No reviews of *Knickerbocker's History* appeared in the *Quarterly Review* at this time.
4. See WI's letter of this date to Leslie.
5. In 1800 G. A. Galignani established a bookshop specializing in English books. His sons followed him in the business, which still continues at 224 Rue de Rivoli. For details about the firm, see *A Famous Bookstore* (Paris, 1920); Giles Barber, "Galignani's and the Publication of English Books in France from 1800 to 1852," *The Library*, 5th ser. 16 (December, 1961), 267–86. WI spelled the name as "Gagliani."
6. Probably the London bookseller, Baldwyn & Co., 122 Newgate Street, Cheapside. See WIHM, p. 32, n. 21.
7. James Eastburn.
8. James Wallis Eastburn (1797–1819), a graduate of Columbia College and an ordained Protestant Episcopal deacon, had died en route to the Canary Islands for his health. McClary (WIHM, p. 33) transcribes his name as "Eastman."
9. Philip (d. 1676), son of Massassoit and sachem of the Wampanoag Indians, started a war against the New England colonists after the beheading of three of his warriors in 1675.
10. Southey's "Oliver Newman: A New-England Tale" was never finished. First published in 1845, it also appears in *The Poetical Works of Robert Southey* (London, 1873), pp. 788–809. For other details about the Irving-Southey relationship, see WIHM, p. 33, n. 22.
11. Robert Charles Sands (1799–1832), a sociable young journalist, later assisted William Cullen Bryant in editing the *New York Review and Athenaeum Magazine* (1825–1826) and by himself edited the *Commercial Advertiser* (1826–1832). He also contributed essays and poetry to *The Talisman*, a literary annual. *The Bridal of Vaumond*, with a dedication to WI, had appeared under the imprint of James Eastburn & Company in 1817.
12. WI placed the name of the addressee at the bottom of the first manuscript page. His practice has been regularized.
13. This correction was made in Murray's second edition of 1821 (II, 20, line 3). See WIHM, p. 34, n. 25. This variant is not noted in Langfeld & Blackburn, *WI Bibliography*, p. 12.

293.   To Charles R. Leslie

Paris, Octr 31st. 1820.

My dear Leslie

I have recd. two letters from you,[1] and ought to have replied long before this but I have been out of the mood for Letter writing and so have deferred it from day to day and so—time has run on. I now write in great haste, to avail myself of an opportunity free of expense

—I have just recd. a very long and very friendly letter from Mr Murray,[2] who in fact has over whelmed me with eulogiums. It appears that my writings are selling well, and he is multiplying editions. I am very glad to find that he has made your acquaintance, and still more that he has taken a great liking to you. He speaks of you in the most gratifying terms. He has it in his power to be of service to you, and I trust he will be. He tells me that he has requested you to look over Knicker-bocker for subjects for ⟨E⟩eight or ten Sketches—and the Sketch Book for a couple,[3] & he wishes me to assist you with my opinion on the subject. I will look over the books and write to you in a day or two[.] Murray is going to make me so fine in print that I shall hardly know myself. Could not Allstons design[4] be reduced without losing the characteristic humour of it? I am delighted to find that your labours are to be thus interwoven with mine; so that we shall have a kind of joint interest & pride in every volume. My dear Boy it is a grevious thing to be separated from you; and I feel it more and more. I wish to heaven this world was not so wide; and that we could manage to keep more together in it. This continual separating from those we like is one of the curses of an unsettled life; and with all my vagrant habits I cannot get accustomed to it.—I have seen the Doctors ↑(Bollman's)↓[5] son, and Miss Foote, and have had many anecdotes of you all—How delighted I should have been to have partaken of your revels at Winkfield. I was amused by your earnest reasoning to convince me that I should not shrink with horror from the young Bollman,[6] because he came into the world without a licence—No one can help how he ⟨is born⟩ comes into the world, he is only answerable for his conduct after he gets there. I was very much pleased with the lad; he has much of the Doctors ↑his father's↓[7] countenance.

I am glad to hear that you are getting on well with your picture;[8] and that you grew more & more pleased with it. Depend upon it, it is one of those pictures that will do you very essential service. It will give you a standing with men whose opinions have great weight in society—Men curious in literature and in antiquities The picture will please them as shewing not merely technical skill, and the ordinary eye for the picturesque; but as displaying research; mind, and strong literary feeling. It is a highly classical *english subject*—I hope you will follow it up by some thing in the same line; the researches you have made for this picture will make you feel more at home in another. I feel a continual want to be with you and Newton, to see how you both get on.

I had a very acceptable letter from Willis[9] a few days since Tell him I will write to him soon—but I must first write to Peter Powell,[10] to whom I am in debt—I have so so many persons to write to in England

and America that, being a very lazy letter writer, it is but ⟨[*unrecovered*]⟩ now & then I can bring a letter to bear upon each—

Mr. Tappan,[11] who bears this letter, told me that it was the wish of Fairman[12] & yourself that an engraving should be made from the likeness you have of me. It is a matter I do not feel so much objection to as I did formerly, having been so *much upon the town* lately as to have lost much of my modesty. And as I understand that there has been some spurious print of my phiz in america, I do not care if another is made ⟨if⟩ to push it out of sight. You will only be careful to finish the picture[13] so as not give it too fixed & precise a fashion of dress. I preferred the costume of Newtons likeness of me,[14] which was trimmed with fur. These modern dresses are apt to give a paltry common placed air.

Give my love to all the lads[15] and believe me

Most affectionately yours
WI.

P S. I can give you no idea when I shall return to England. I have no plan on the subject—

ADDRESSED: Charles. R. Leslie Esqr. / 8 Buckingham Place / Fitzroy Square / London

MANUSCRIPT: NYPL—Berg Collection.   PUBLISHED: PMI, II, 26–28; Leslie, *Autobiographical Recollections*, pp. 222–23.

1. Dated London, September 15, 1820, and London, October 18, 1820. Excerpts from them are printed in Leslie, *Autobiographical Recollections*, pp. 220–22.

2. Written from London on October 25, 1820.

3. These sketches are discussed in several subsequent letters exchanged between WI and Leslie. See WI's letters of December 3 and December 24, 1820, printed in Leslie, *Autobiographical Recollections*, pp. 226–27, 230–31. Leslie provided nine illustrations for the new editions of *Knickerbocker's History* and *The Sketch Book* which Murray published in 1823. See Leslie, *Autobiographical Recollections*, p. 215.

4. For *Knickerbocker's History* Allston prepared a single illustration, Wouter Van Twiller deciding a law suit. See Leslie, *Autobiographical Recollections*, pp. 215–16.

5. The word in parentheses has been added in pencil above the line by another hand. The Bollmans are probably the family of Dr. Justus Erich Bollman (1769–1821), a Hanoverian physician who helped to rescue the Marquis de Lafayette from an Austrian prison in November, 1794. Later Bollman engaged in speculations on both sides of the Atlantic, participated in Aaron Burr's conspiracy to establish an empire in the Southwest, lived for a time at George Logan's home in Philadelphia, and contributed to the *Port-Folio* in 1809. A restless person, Dr. Bollman changed his residence frequently. It is possible that WI had met him in Philadelphia and later renewed his acquaintance in England in 1820. See Andreas Latzko, *Lafayette* (Garden City, 1936), pp. 248–65; F. B. Tolles, *George Logan of Philadelphia* (New York, 1953), p. 148; R. C. Randall, "Authors of the *Port-Folio* Revealed by the Hall Files," *American Literature* 11 (January, 1940), 388;

and Thomas Perkins Abernethy, *The Burr Conspiracy* (New York, 1954), pp. 57–58, 175–79, and passim. Miss Foote is apparently the fiancée of Dr. Bollman's son. (See WI's letter to Leslie, November 30, 1820.) In his letter of September 15, Leslie indicates that he, Gilbert Stuart Newton, and William Willes ("Father Luke") (see note 9 below) had visited Dr. Bollman's at Winkfield, a village in Berkshire, five miles southwest of Windsor. Leslie writes: "We have all three spent a most delightful week there with the Bollmans, Miss Maine (who is to be married the 4th of October), and Miss Foote." See Leslie, *Autobiographical Recollections*, p. 220.

6. The word "Bollman" has been crossed out in pencil, presumably by someone other than WI.

7. Two words above the line are written by another hand.

8. "May Day Revels in the Time of Queen Elizabeth," which was exhibited at the Royal Academy in 1821. See Leslie, *Autobiographical Recollections*, pp. 231–32.

9. William Willes (d. 1851), a native of Cork, was a painter studying at the Royal Academy and one of WI's intimates in London at this time. Sometimes called "Father Luke," he occasionally exhibited at the Royal Academy and British Institution. In 1849 he was appointed headmaster of the School of Design at Cork on its founding. After a prolonged illness he died in January, 1851. Among his paintings are "A Serenade," "A River Scene," "A Midsummer Night's Dream," and "The Mock Funeral." See Bryan's *Dictionary of Painters and Engravers,* ed. George C. Williamson (New York, 1905), V, 376; Walter G. Strickland, *A Dictionary of Irish Artists* (Dublin, 1913), II, 531–32; Ben Harris McClary, "Two of Washington Irving's Friends Identified," *American Literature* 37 (January, 1966), 471–72.

10. Peter Powell (b. 1792), a witty artist who compensated for his short height by excessive activity, exhibited marine and landscape paintings between 1826 and 1854. See E. Benezit, *Dictionnaire Critique et Documentaire des Peintres, Sculpteurs, Dessinateurs et Graveurs* (1954), VII, 2; G. K. Nagler, *Neues allgemeines Kunstler-Lexikon* (Munich, 1941), XI, 575–76.

11. Perhaps this is Arthur Tappan (1786–1865), a New York merchant who had visited England in connection with his cloth importing business. Or it may be one of his brothers, Benjamin (1773–1857) or Lewis (1788–1873), who were later active in abolition activities.

12. Probably Gideon Fairman, a Philadelphia engraver with whom WI had dealt during his editorship of the *Analectic Magazine*. See WI's letter to Moses Thomas, October 21, 1814.

13. Leslie's painting, now in the NYPL, portrays WI wearing a high-collared white shirt and a dark coat with a fur-trimmed collar.

14. Newton's painting is owned by John Murray, 50 Albemarle Street, London. The fur collar in this portrait is more noticeable than the one in Leslie's painting.

15. This name was given to the circle which included WI, Leslie, Newton, Willes, and Powell. See WIHM, pp. 22–23.

294. To Henry Brevoort

[October? 1820]

... They have acted as they thought for my interest, and were no doubt persuaded that by refusing my drafts they would prevent my engaging in what they thought an injudicious enterprise....[1]

I am confident they do it out of zeal for my interest, but a man may be killed even by kindness.

PUBLISHED: PMI, II, 17.

1. WI alludes to the refusal of his brothers in New York to honor his drafts on them so that he and Peter Irving might invest in the Seine River steamboat venture. For other details, see WI's letters of September 22, 1820, to William Irving and to Henry Brevoort.

295.   To Charles R. Leslie

Paris, Novr. 30th. 1820

My dear Leslie,

I cannot let Mr Marx[1] depart without scrawling you a line. I hear you are getting on with the Sketches for Knickerbocker &c and that you have executed one on the same subject that Alston once chose; viz P Stuyvesant⟨s lecture⟩ rebuking the Cobler.[2] I wish you would drop me a line and let me know what subjects you excute, and how You & Murray make out together. I hear that you have taken 'the childe'[3] to Murrays; you have only to make him acquainted with ⟨Little⟩ Willis & Peter Powell, and he will then be able to make one at your teakettle debauches.

I have just made a brief but very pleasant and interesting excursion into Lower Normandy in company with Mr Ritchie.— I must refer you to a letter Scribbled to Peter Powell[4] for a full and faithful narrative of this tour. I have never been more pleased with any tour that I have made. The little towns of Lower Normandy seem to have been built and peopled with an eye to the picturesque. The fine Gothic churches; the old quaint architecture of the private houses — the beauty of the common people particularly the peasantry — Their peculiar costumes, all form continual pictures — But I believe you will get a better idea of them from the sketches of the Lewis's[5] than from any description that I can furnish—By the bye I saw the Card of one of the Lewis's in the hands of a young man of the college at Falaise, who accompanied me about the beautiful ruin of the castle where William the Conqueror was born.[6] He told me that Lewis had taken several sketches of the castle — it certainly is a most ⟨romantic⟩ picturesque morsel of antiquity. I anticipate great pleasure at some future day; in looking over Lewis sketches again & recalling some of the curious old ⟨towns &⟩ buildings & streets of the Norman towns.

I received a letter a few days since from Newton[7] by Miss Peat.[8] She had been some time on the way to Paris & the letter was of an old date – I shall write to Newton the next opportunity & likewise to Willis to whom I am indebted for a most agreeable letter.[9]

I find by the Lymans[10] that the sloan Street Romance[11] ⟨has been⟩ is still unfinished, and that materials are daily springing up for another volume. That young MacDougal[12] has come back piping hot from the West Indies. That Ann[13] has cut the dancing master and consented to elope with the old lady – That Jones[14] has retired to either a convent or a nailery in the neighbourhood of Birmingham—and that Newton is busy, with a brush in each hand, and his hair standing on end turning Ann's ⟨pictures into⟩ portraits into likenesses of Mary Queen of Scotts, General Washington and the lord knows who[15] – "there never was such times!"

I have seen Miss Foote, who is at the same establishment with Miss Texier[16] – It was before my excursion to Normandy for I have not had time since. I got a whole budget of news ⟨fr⟩ of you all. Marx tells me that the Doctor[17] is certainly to be married to Miss Foote on her return to England in the Spring.

My Brother is now in Paris & will probably pass the Winter here. I wish to heavens you & Newton were here with us. Mr Lyman tells me that Charles Williams[18] talks of visiting Paris this winter for a short time. I think he had better bring Newton with him by way of Interpreter.

I shall send you the Sketches you require by Mr Marx When you see Willis tell him I will answer his letter soon. Let me hear from you often and dont wait for my replies as I am if possible more averse to letter writing ↑even↓ than ⟨?ever?⟩ Alston. This letter is scrawled in bed, which must account for its defects.

Yours most affectionately

W Irving.

ADDRESSED: C R Leslie Esqr. / 8· Buckingham Place / Fitzroy Sqr. / London
MANUSCRIPT: NYPL–Berg Collection. PUBLISHED: Leslie, *Autobiographical Recollections*, pp. 223–25; PMI, II, 30–31 (in part).

1. Probably Asher Marx (d. 1824) of the New York firm of Marx and Linsley, 74 Queen Street. See Scoville, *Old Merchants of NYC*, IV, 32–33.

2. This picture was included in Murray's edition of 1823. See Leslie, *Autobiographical Recollections*, p. 215.

3. This was WI's epithet for Gilbert Stuart Newton. See Leslie, *Autobiographical Recollections*, p. 220.

4. This letter has not been located.

5. WI has not clearly indicated which members of this English family of artists he is talking about. Frederick Christian Lewis (1779–1856) was an engraver and landscape painter; his brother George Robert (1782–1871), was a portrait and landscape painter; another brother, William (fl. 1804–1838), exhibited at the Royal Academy from 1815 to 1838. See *Bryant's Dictionary of Painters and Engravers*, III, 219; *Thieme-Becker Allgemeines Lexikon der Bildenden Künstler*, XXIII, 162.

6. According to tradition, William the Conqueror, the natural son of Count Robert and Arleth, was born in the castle of Falaise in late 1027 or early 1028. See Aristide Guilbert, *Histoire de Villes de France* (Paris, 1848), V, 639–40; Karl Baedeker, *Northern France* (Leipzig, 1894), p. 181.

7. This letter has not been located.

8. Miss Peat was a member of the group which socialized with WI, Newton, Leslie, Powell, and Willes in London. She has not been precisely identified.

9. This letter has not been located.

10. Theodore Lyman (1792–1849), author of *The Political State of Italy* (1820), who married Mary Elizabeth Henderson of New York on May 8, 1821. See LBI, I, 141; *DAB*, XI, 518.

11. The Sloane Street romance probably involved Gilbert Stuart Newton. See WI to Charles R. Leslie, September 11, 1819, and December 19, 1820.

12. Probably William Macdougall, to whom WI alluded in his letter to Leslie, September 13, 1819.

13. Ann was a beautiful girl with whom Newton had been in love. See Leslie, *Autobiographical Recollections*, p. 224.

14. This may be George Jones (1786–1869), an artist whose pictures of Waterloo won a prize from the British Institution in 1820.

15. As far as is known, Newton did not paint portraits of Queen Mary or George Washington. WI is probably merely suggesting that Newton was eliminating from his paintings any traces of his former love.

16. This may be Florentine Texier, daughter of Pierre Texier, whose sister Jenny (1765–1829) had married Jonathan Jones, an American businessman in Bordeaux. WI had a letter of introduction to Jones in 1804 and met members of the Jones family when he visited Bordeaux in 1825. See Young, *WI-Bordeaux*, pp. 53–58; *J&N*, III, 206–7, 306.

17. Probably Dr. Bollman. See WI's letter to Leslie, October 31, 1820.

18. Charles Williams was an American businessman associated with his brother Samuel, whose firm was located at 13 Finsbury Square. On April 13, 1821, WI sent a letter to Charles Williams at this address. See Edgar P. Richardson, *Washington Allston: A Study of the Romantic Artist in America* (Chicago, 1948), p. 116.

296. To Richard Rush

Paris, Dec. 6, 1820.

My Dear Sir:

I feel very much indebted to you for your letter of the 27th,[1] and hardly know how to express myself as to the very flattering communication from Mr. Lyttleton.[2] It is enough to excite the vanity of a soberer man than myself. Nothing would give me greater gratification than to avail myself of the hospitable invitation of Lord and Lady Spencer,[3] but at present it is out of my power to leave Paris, and would be deranging all my plans to return immediately to England. Will you be kind enough to convey to Mr. Lyttleton my sincere acknowledgments of his politeness, and also of the honor done me by Lord and Lady Spencer; but above all, my heartfelt sense of the interest evinced in my behalf by Lady Lyttleton, which I frankly declare is one of the most gratifying circumstances that have befallen me in the whole course of my literary errantry.

Excuse all this trouble which circumstances oblige me to give you Excellency, and believe me, with my best remembrances to Mrs. Rush,

Yours very faithfully,

Washington Irving.

PUBLISHED: PMI, II, 23–24.

1. This letter has not been located.

2. William Henry Lyttleton was an accomplished scholar of Greek. He printed a *Catalogue of Pictures at Hagley* and *An Account of Napoleon Bonaparte's Coming on Board HMS Northumberland, 7 Aug. 1815.*

3. George John, second earl of Spencer (1758–1834) and Lavinia Bingham (d. 1831) were the parents of Mrs. Lyttleton. Spencer had been first lord of the admiralty until 1800 and home secretary in 1806 and 1807. He later engaged himself in administrative work in Northampton County.

297. To Charles R. Leslie

Paris Decr. 19th. 1820.

My dear Leslie,

I have just received yours of the 3d. I like all the subjects that you have chosen for the designs except that of Wm the Testy suspending the vagabond by the Breeches.[1] The circumstance is not of sufficient point or character in the ⟨Story⟩ history, to be illustrated—⟨Sket⟩ still it may have struck you in a difft manner, and have afforded scope for humorous sketching. I had hoped to hear from Mr Murray before this & to have recd. a copy of Knickerbocker & of the Sketch book for correction—I pointed him out a mode of forwarding books to me, but I presume he has been too much hurried to attend to it. When you hear of a private opportunity I wish you would ask Mr Murray for ⟨p⟩ copies of the works, & send them to me.

I received a letter from Peter Powell,[2] in which he speaks of my portraits being in the engravers hands, and that it is painted in the old venetian costume—⟨now⟩ I hope you have not misunderstood my meaning when I spoke ⟨[unrecovered]⟩ about the costume in which I should like it to be painted. I believe I spoke something about the costume of Newton's Portrait—I meant Newton's portrait of *me*, not of *himself*[3]—If you reccollect he painted me as if in some kind of overcoat, with a fur cape—a dress that had nothing in it remarkable, but which merely avoided any present fashion that might in a few years appear ⟨so?⟩ stupid. The venetian dress such as Newton painted himself in, would have a fantastic appearance, and savour of affectation. If it is not too late I should like to have the thing altered—let the costume be simple & picturesque, but such a one as a gentleman might be supposed to wear occasionally at the present day. I only wanted you to avoid the capes & corners & angles with which a modern coat is so oddly & formally clipped out at the present day.

I have not the Sketch Book at hand to refer to; ⟨but⟩ so as to see that the measure & melody of the sentence is ⟨not altered⟩ not injured by the omission you mention in the story of the Widow & her son[4]—I am very much obliged to you for the correction.

When I look over Knickerbocker, to prepare the new edition, I will attend to your hint about pruning any indelicate parts.[5]

As I have no plan fixed that points immediately to England it is needless to say any thing on the subject. Indeed my chief care as yet must be to keep quiet, and endeavor to write something more, for publication; if I move about & shift my situation, I disturb my thoughts unsettle my habits and lose a great deal of time; and if I lose much more time I shall have the spectre of an empty purse haunting me. I am obliged therefore to pitch my tent for a time until I can make ⟨a little⟩ money enough to secure me from want for two or three years—The change from London to Paris deranged me completely ⟨and⟩ I am now getting into train again; but a return to England would unsettle me again for a long time. I received not long since a most flattering invitation from Earl Spenser & his Lady to pass the Christmas Holydays at their Seat at Althorp—The invitation was forwarded by Mr Rush, and was given in a manner peculiarly gratifying. If I were in England now, an invitation or two of this kind would make me a goodfornothing gentlemanly fellow for a month [?or two?] [MS torn] I understand you have introduced Newt[on] [MS torn] to Mur[ray and I ho]pe [MS torn] he & the Childe like each other—

Tell peter Powell I cannot answer his letter until I have answered one which I received from Willes an age ago[6]—

I hope Newton will commence another picture soon, otherwise he will stand a chance of falling into the hands of the Rowleys or some other pretty girls and paint himself into a scrape again—Powell speaks of some fine portrait which he has painted of a Gentleman & which is considered his *chef d'ouvre*, but does not say whose portrait it is—I hope it is some one of consequence that may get him into notice.

By the bye—I ⟨just⟩ have just ascertained a mode of forwarding books to me. Direct the ⟨boo⟩ parcel to me to the care of R. G. Beasley Esquire, Consul of the United States, Havre—put this in an Envellope directed to *Thomas Shaw Esqr. Southampton—for R. G. Beasley Esqr. American Consul. Havre—*⟨The⟩ Send the parcel by coach from the White Bar ⟨in⟩ Piccadilly—and pay the postage to Southampton—

Whatever expense you are at I will reimburse you and for your trouble
I give you my love—which is better than silver & gold—Give the same
address to Mr Murray if he has any thing to send.

I am very glad that you & Newton have found out the Otiss's—& I
hope you will be able to make some agreeable acquaintances for them
in London Remember me to them most affectionately. They are often
mentioned by the friends they made in Paris, in terms of the greatest
esteem and affection.

Give my hearty regards to Newton, Willes—Powell—the Bollmans
the Hoffmans and all our little circle of intimates—My Brother desires
likewise to be particularly remembered—

Yours ever
W I.

Addressed: Charles R Leslie. Esqr / Buckingham Place / Fitzroy Square / London
    PORT · PAYÉ / 20[?] / P. P. / P.   Postmarked: FPO / DE 23 / 1820
Manuscript: NYPL—Berg Collection.   Published: Leslie, *Autobiographical Recol-*
    lections, pp. 228–29 (in part); PMI, II, 29, 31 (in part); *Harper's Magazine*
    24 (February, 1862), 356 (in part).

   1. In his letter of December 3, 1820, Leslie writes: "The subjects I have
chosen are, a Dutch fire-side, with an old negro telling stories to the children;
William the Testy, suspending a vagrant by the breeches on his patent gallows;
Peter Stuyvesant confronting the Cobbler; and Anthony Van Corlear taking leave
of the young vrows" (printed in Leslie, *Autobiographical Recollections*, p. 226).
   2. This letter has not been located.
   3. WI had mentioned this subject in his letter of October 31 to Leslie.
   4. WI is replying to the following remarks in Leslie's letter of December 3:
"I do not know whether you will be angry with me or approve what I am going
to tell you. Collins, to whom I had lent the 'Sketch Book,' observed that in the
article of the 'Widow's Son' a passage runs thus, 'The service *being ended*, they
proceeded to lower the coffin into the grave.' Now he remarked that the coffin is
always lowered into the grave *during* the service or previous to it, for at the words
'ashes to ashes, and dust to dust' some earth is thrown in upon it. When he came to
this passage he said it destroyed the illusion, for the story had taken the strongest
hold of his feelings, and he had been convinced that he was reading an account of
a real scene. I took the liberty therefore of suggesting to Mr. Murray to leave out
these few words 'the service being ended,' which without any other alteration does
away with the objection to the passage. I am afraid you will be displeased with
my meddling, which I should on no account have dared to do had not the alteration been so very small. There was not time to write and hear from you, as the
volume is in press, and it is probable after all that the suggestion was too late
for the forthcoming edition" (Leslie, *Autobiographical Recollections*, pp. 226–27).
   5. In speaking of Diedrich Knickerbocker, Leslie had observed, "I must say
that in some of *his jokes* he goes near to be thought a little indelicate. Now these
jokes of the old gentleman being *very few* and not among his best, I really think
he would not suffer by dispensing with them in future" (Leslie, *Autobiographical
Recollections*, p. 227).
   6. These letters from Peter Powell and William Willes have not been located.

298. *To David B. Warden*

[December 30, 1820]

My dear Sir,

I am sorry that I have not a copy of the Second volume of the Sketch book by me. My copy is lent out, but when I get it back I will send it to you. I am glad to hear of your being once more in good health & able to go about as usual. Your note by Mr McCay made me acquainted with a very agreeable & estimable man, for which I thank you

With great regard./Yours truly
W Irving.

Rue Mont Thabor/Decr. 30th. 1820.

ADDRESSED: a Monsr. / Monsieur D. B. Warden / Rue du Pot de Fer. St Sulpice No 12   POSTMARKED: December 30 1820
MANUSCRIPT: Maryland Historical Society.
At the top of the first page, as a kind of docket, is written "from W. Irving—"

299. *To Henry Brevoort*

Paris March 10th. 1821.

My dear Brevoort,

I have this moment heard of a vessel which sails from Havre tomorrow afternoon,[1] and have barely time to Scrawl a line, to be sent off immediately with a letter Peter is sending by the Estafette.[2]

I received your letter of Novr. 24[3] and also letters from my Brothers[4] on the same subject — viz. their declining to honour my Drafts. I have no doubt they were influenced by the best motives, wishing to throw impediments in the way of my entering into what they considered an injudicious enterprise; but I had already committed myself; the Drafts were for an interest actually purchased in the ⟨en⟩ concern, and the dishonoring the drafts only ⟨sub?⟩ prevents my fulfilling my engagements punctually, and obliges me to do it by hook & by crook, and at some loss. I have however written to them on the subject. ⟨I have entered into the⟩ I was actuated merely by a wish to see Peter embarked in some thing that might turn out advantageous — and as he seems fully persuaded that the steamboat project[5] will do so, I will leave the whole share that I have taken in it to him—I have not turned my mind much to the subject, but have left him to investigate and manage it. I hope it may open the way to something profitable for him

You must not take amiss any little peevishness on the part of my Brothers; they have been so much worried and disheartened by the troubles of the world for some years past, that any new perplexity may fret them — You know them well, and know how worthy they are in heart & mind, and how truly they esteem you; ⟨leave⟩ excuse therefore any little impatience they may evince in my affairs; which I am affraid give them a great deal of anxiety and trouble from the very affection which they bear me.

You urge me to return to New York — and say many ask whether I mean to renounce my country? For this last question I have no reply to make—⟨I can⟩ and yet I will make a reply— As far as my precarious and imperfect abilities enable me, I am endeavouring to serve my country— Whatever I have written has been written with the feelings and published as the writing of an American — Is that renouncing my Country? How else am I to serve my country — by coming home and begging an office of it; which I should not have the kind of talent or the business habits requisite to fill?— If I can do any good in this world it is with my pen — I feel that even with that I can do very little, but if I do that little, and do it as an american I think my exertions ought to guarantee me from so unkind a question as that which you say is generally made—

As to coming home — I should at this moment be abandoning my literary plans, such as they are. I should lose my labour on various literary materials which I have in hand, and ⟨↑work up parts↓which⟩ ↑to work up which↓I must be among the scenes where they were conceived[6]— I should arrive at home at a time when my slender finances require ⟨an active exer⟩ an immediate exercise of my talents; but should be so agitated & discomposed in my feelings, by the meetings with my friends — the revival of many distressing ⟨for⟩ circumstances & trains of thought — and I should be so hurried by the mere attentions of society that months would elapse before I could take pen in hand & then I would have to strike out some entirely new plan & begin ab. ovo. As to the idea you hold out of being provided for *sooner or later* in our *fortunate* city — I can only say that I see no way in which I could be provided for, not being a man of business, a man of Science, or in fact any thing but a mere belles lettres writer — And as to the fortunate character of our city—To me & mine it has been a very disasterous one—I have written on this point at some length as I wish to have done with it.—My return home must depend upon circumstances, not upon inclinations. I have, by patient & persevering labour of my most uncertain pen, & by catching the gleams of sunshine in my cloudy mind, managed to open to myself an avenue to ⟨a⟩ some degree of profit & reputation—I value it the more highly because it is entirely independent and self created; and I must use my best endeavours to turn it to account. In remaining therefore abroad, I do it with the idea that I can best exert my talents, for the present, where I am—⟨Should

I however, find that I am⟩ and that I trust will be admitted as a sufficient reply, from a man who has but his talents to feed & clothe him.

I have not been able to call on L'herbette[7] — the fact is, I am harrassed by company & engagements which it is impossible to avoid, & which take up more of my time than I like to spare—as well as dissipating my thoughts — I shall be obliged to quit Paris on that very account— though I intend to see L'herbette before I leave this. I have become very intimate with Anacreon Moore,[8] who is living here with his family — Scarce a day passes without our seeing each other & he has made me acquainted with many of his friends here. He is a charming joyous fellow — full of frank, generous, manly feeling. I am happy to say he expresses himself in the fullest and strongest manner on the subject of his writings on America; which he pronounces the great sin of his early life— He is busy upon the life of Sheridan, & upon a poem[9]— His acquaintance is one of the most gratifying things I have met with for some time; as he takes the warm interest of an old friend in me & my concerns.

Canning[10] is likewise here with his family and has been very polite in his attentions to me — He has expressed a very flattering opinion of my writings both here & in England; and his opinion is of great weight & value in the critical world. I had a very agreeable dinner at his house a few days since, at which I met Moore, Sir Sydney Smith[11] & several other interesting characters.

You mention Jack Nicholson being appointed to the Franklin 74[.][12] I presume it is as Flag Captain — Does he still wear that queer Cockade like a star fish in front of his hat. How I should delight to see the honest round little rogue again, and shake his little bare hand.

I have neglected to get the music you request,[13] and am ashamed of myself for so doing, but I will get it & send it by the first opportunity

My letter is called for & I must conclude[.] remember me sincerely to Mrs Brevoort & to the rest [of the] [MS torn] family connexion & believe me my dear Brevoort

Ever affectionately yours
WI.

PS — I understand that you have completely withdrawn from business — Why dont you undertake some work — an historical work — a tract of Am: history — something to occupy your time & mind & keep off ennui — You ought to make yourself an active member of all the public institutions of our city—⟨In your⟩ Situated as you are, with your abilities & advantages it is your duty — and it would be a source of reputation and enjoyment to you — I have repeatedly intended to write to you at some length on this subject — You are indolent ↑& diffident↓ & would

find the first outset difficult — but every step would lessen the difficulty
until it became mere pleasure

ADDRESSED: To /Henry Brevoort Jr. Esqr. / New York. / Havre, March 12, 1821 /
    forwarded by y: o.dt / R G Beasley   DOCKETED: Paris, March 10, 1821 /
    Washington Irving
MANUSCRIPT: NYPL–Seligman Collection.   PUBLISHED: LIB, II, 139–46; PMI, II,
    36–38 (in part).

1. Possibly the *Dolphin,* with Captain Burgess, which reached New York on
May 4, or the *Dalmarnock,* with Captain Cummings, which arrived on May 5.
See NYEP, May 4 and 5, 1821.

2. The estafette was a mounted courier or messenger service used in France
at this time.

3. Printed in LBI, I, 128–31. Some of WI's comments are in response to Brevoort's letter of January 8, 1821. See LBI, I, 132–36.

4. These letters from William and Ebenezer Irving have not been located.

5. See WI's letter of September 22, 1820, for details about the steamboat
project. Peter had taken $10,000 worth of shares, expecting Washington to con-
tribute one-fourth of the capital from his income from *The Sketch Book* and
Ebenezer and William also to pass along funds to him. See STW, I, 196, and
WIHM, p. 26.

6. WI was working on the sketches which became *Bracebridge Hall.*

7. Brevoort's friend from his fur-trading days. See WI's letters of September
22, 1810; June 8, 1811; September 9, 1814.

8. Thomas Moore (1779–1852), whose *Lalla Rookh* (1817) was still very
popular, had gone to Paris because of difficulties arising from the defalcation of his
deputy in Bermuda. (Moore had been made admiralty registrar in Bermuda in
1803.) As a result, Moore was liable for £6000. In 1820 the debt to the admiralty
was reduced and paid with the help of Lord Lansdowne. See Howard Mumford
Jones, *The Harp That Once—* (New York, 1937), pp. 206–8, 215–16.

9. While in Paris, Moore wrote "The Loves of the Angels." His life of Sheridan
was published in 1825.

10. George Canning (1770–1827), who had retired from the government after
the trial of Queen Caroline in 1820, was traveling in Europe at this time. In 1822
he became foreign minister of Great Britain. Canning was a close friend of Sir
Walter Scott, whose praise of WI he had heard.

11. Sydney Smith (1771–1845), a regular contributor to the *Edinburgh Review*
for over twenty-five years, had expressed his anti-American views in that journal
in January, 1820, when he asked, "In the four quarters of the globe, who reads
an American book?" By this time WI had provided *The Sketch Book,* which was
acclaimed internationally.

12. The *Franklin,* a 74-gun warship built under the direction of Samuel Humph-
reys at the Philadelphia Navy Yard in 1815, served as flagship of the Mediterranean
Squadron until March, 1820, and then as flagship of the Pacific Squadron from
October, 1821, to August, 1824. See *American Sea Power Since 1775,* ed. Allan
Westcott (Philadelphia, 1947), p. 99; *Dictionary of American Naval Fighting Ships*
(Washington, 1963), II, 443.

13. In November, 1820, Brevoort had asked WI to procure for his wife "a
dozen popular airs, waltzes & dances, simple or with variations, for the Harp. The
music of Bochsa is always good, but not so well adapted for society as the com-

positions of less scientific or polished composers. She would prefer you would select any agreeable lively music of the above named description by fashionable composers" (LBI, I, 130).

300. To Charles R. Leslie

[March or spring, 1821]

My dear Leslie,

I have been intending this long time past to write to you, and a good intention, of long standing, is a matter to boast of in this naughty world—How comes on your picture[1] — I presume it is nearly finished — Did you call on Sir Walter Scott while he was in town[2] & ask him to look at it — if not, you ⟨ought⟩ have behaved shabbily — I presume before this you have seen Miss Foote, I intended to have written by her but was occupied at the time and let the opportunity slip unimproved. I find the Doctor is going on a distant Journey, and the Damsels of Sloane Street are to take care of themselves during his absence — I trust you & Newton will keep an eye on them — I think Jones ought to be drummed to his duty there again, as I understand he has grown rather delinquent for some time past.

I have heard that you are to pass some months at Windsor, to copy several of Sir Peter Lelys pictures[3] for some Lord or other — Is this the case, and if so, when do you go there — it will be a charming situation for you during the Summer Months. Let me know who this Lord is that has taken you into favor — I find by Newtons Letter[4] that he and the old Euphuist, the *ci devant Jeune Homme* that haunts exhibitions, have become sworn friends. I presume the childes[5] new-fledged reputation will introduce him into a great deal of dilletanti society — and that good company will come nigh to be the ruin of him — I have been sadly bothered with the same evil of late, and have had to fight shy of invitations that would exhaust time and spirits. ⟨My most agreeable acquaintance?⟩ The most interesting acquaintance I have made in Paris is Moore the Poet,—who is very much to my taste — I see him almost every day & feel as if I had known him for a life time. He is a noble hearted, manly spirited little fellow, with a mind as generous as his fancy is brilliant.

I hope you have better weather in London than we have in Paris — Such a Spring! nothing but rain in torrents; and cold boisterous winds. They may say what they please of London weather; I never passed a more dirty, rainy Season in London than this last winter has been in Paris; and then the Streets are so detestable in dirty weather, that there is no walking in them — my only consolation at such times is the vicinity of the Garden of the Tuilleries; which is but a short distance from my lodgings; and which I consider as a park attached to my mansion — though I must own I prefer my Park of St James and Kensington Gardens — the latter particularly as it has glorious lawns of green grass that I can roll on, whereas in the Tuilleries there is no place to rest except one Sits on a cursed cold stone bench; or pays two sous for a vile Straw bottomed chair—

I am Scrawling as fast as my pen can go for I find it is near the hour of ↑closing the↓ post office and I am determined this letter shall go by mail though it cost me fifteen sous — I wish you would take pen [in] [*MS torn*] hand at once and let me know how you are getting on with your picture — what else you are about — when you go to Windsor — How Long you stay there — who you are to paint the pictures for — what subject you have in view for your next painting — what Newton is doing — what Luke⁶ is doing & what Peter Powell is doing — Answer these questions, and then you may add what you please — I have given you a scheme for a letter — When it is done ⟨send it⟩ do not wait for private hand but send it per Post. never mind the postage for once. I want exceedingly to hear from You — the sooner the better

[*complimentary close and signature clipped*]

ADDRESSED: Charles. R. Leslie Esqr. / Buckingham Place / Fitzroy Square / London. DOCKETED: from W. Irving 8.
MANUSCRIPT: NYPL—Berg Collection. PUBLISHED: Leslie, *Autobiographical Recollections*, pp. 225–26; PMI, II, 44–45 (in part).
Although WI did not date this letter, "Dec" and "1820" have been written at the top of the page by two different hands. Tom Taylor (Leslie, *Autobiographical Recollections*, p. 225) dates the letter as 1820, but PMI correctly observes (II, 44) that it belongs to the spring of 1821. In the third paragraph WI alludes to spring in Paris, and a few lines earlier he mentions his acquaintance with Thomas Moore which was also alluded to in his letter to Brevoort of March 10, 1821. A reasonably precise date for this letter would be March or spring, 1821.

1. "May Day Revels in the Time of Queen Elizabeth." See WI's letter to Leslie, October 31, 1820.
2. Scott did not come to London as early as WI had anticipated. As late as January 17, 1821, he is writing letters from Edinburgh. See Lockhart, *Life of Sir Walter Scott*, V, 47.
3. Sir Peter Lely (1618–1680), painter of many English courtiers, nobles, and statesmen, executed a series of "Beauties" at Windsor Castle for the duchess of York. The collection is now at Hampton Court.
4. Newton's letter has not been located.
5. WI's epithet for Gilbert Stuart Newton.
6. The name given by WI and his cronies to William Willes. See WI's letter of October 31, 1820.

301. To Henry Brevoort

Paris, April 5th. 1821.

My dear Brevoort,

I am extremely sorry to be again under the necessity of tasking your friendship in money matters. I have drawn on you this day at Sixty days sight, in favour of Ezra Weeks Esqr.[1] for one thousand Dollars. It is to ⟨meet⟩ provide for one of the Bills which my Brothers dishonored & which must come back in a few days. It would be useless to draw on my Brothers again, as they do not seem to consider it a matter of any moment or delicacy to refuse my drafts; you I am confident will think otherwise.[2] They have acted as they thought for my interest, & were no doubt persuaded that by refusing my drafts they would prevent my engaging in what they thought an injudicious enterprize – They should have known that it was too late – that I was committed – and that to refuse my drafts was to oblige me to take them up as well as I could, in a strange country, and to pay damages into the bargain—But ⟨L⟩ enough of this—had I had any other means of extricating myself from an irksome predicament I would not have again intruded on your kindness – I have tried to manage the matter in other modes & have only met with disappointment & mortification – I determined therefore to resort again to you, who, I say it in fullness & sincerity of heart, have always acted like a true Brother to me—

I ⟨wrote⟩ have written by the Cadmus[3] – via Havre, to my brother E.I. to replace in your hands the amount of the Draft: he having ample means of mine in his hands for the purpose. ⟨This is the only way I have of getting⟩ At a moment of more leisure and pleasanter feelings I will reply to your very interesting letter of Jany 8th.[4] at present I am out of tune – These money matters always play the mischief with me.[5]

Give my sincere regards to Mrs Brevoort & believe me/
Most affectionately yours
W Irving—

H Brevoort Jr Esqr.

ADDRESSED: Single. / To – / Henry Brevoort Junr Esqr / New York. / ⟨per Messrs A & S Richards / Liverpool.⟩   POSTMARKED: C. AP / 10 / 1821 / FPO / AP. 10 / 1821   DOCKETED: Paris 5 Apl. 1821 / Washn. Irving
MANUSCRIPT: NYPL—Seligman Collection.   PUBLISHED: LIB, II, 147–48.

1. Ezra Weeks was a New York builder whom WI presumably met in Paris. Weeks saw the coronation of George IV; and, according to Brevoort, "His adventures in high life are the amusement of Gotham" (LBI, I, 147).

2. Brevoort helped WI during his current financial difficulties. On June 15, 1821, Brevoort wrote: "I have recd. your Letters dated the 5, 14, & 21 April. The two dfts for $1000 each have been accepted; and should your brother E be unable

to make up the remittance of $1000 to Mr. Beasley, I have promised to assist him with the residue, but it is probable that he will not stand in need of help.— I am happy to understand that by this arrangement your mind will be disengaged from pecuniary matters and exclusively devoted to literature.—

"The explanation you have given of your future ability to discharge these advances, is perfectly satisfactory; I can, without inconvenience, wait until your means will enable you to do so at your leisure. Meanwhile, it affords me real pleasure to be of use to you, and I beg you will not burthen your mind with any weight of obligation" (LBI, I, 143).

3. The *Cadmus*, under the command of Captain Whitlock, arrived in New York on May 26, 1821. See NYEP, May 26, 1821.

4. Printed in LBI, I, 132–36.

5. Another version of this letter (no. 302) was sent to Brevoort by a different route.

302. To Henry Brevoort

Paris, April 5th. 1821.

My dear Brevoort,

It is with great regret that I am compelled by circumstances again to task your friendship in money matters[.] I have this day drawn on you at sixty days sight, in favour of Mr Ezra Weeks for One thousand Dollars. It is to meet the return of one of my Drafts which my Brothers dishonoured. To draw on them would be idle, notwithstanding that they might have funds of mine in their hands — they have shewn that they will not hesitate to refuse my drafts, whatever may be the situation in which their refusal may place me in a strange country. I am confident they do it out of a zeal for my interest — but a man may be killed even by kindness. You I feel confident regard matters of this kind in another light than that of mere interest, and know how much a mans feelings & delicacy are involved in his engagements — I know therefore that in drawing on you my bills will be properly honoured ⟨and my⟩ and that you will feel a punctilious scruple in protecting my credit. ⟨My Brothers⟩ I shall write to my brothers to refund you the amount of the draft in due time.

I should not, as you must be well convinced, have drawn this draft were I not fully satisfied that you would not be kept out of the money — I hope and trust that I shall in a little time be able to drag myself out of these detestable ⟨dependencies⟩ pecuniary difficulties and these eternal cross purposes in money matters, which I have been trammeled with for some years past & which play the very vengeance with me — ⟨My Brothers⟩ It has been my doom to ⟨be shewn⟩ contend incessantly with chills & damps which destroy all the sunshine of my mind; ⟨I can and⟩ I can scarce get my imagination in train and feel it warming up & expanding, but some cursed worldly care ⟨and⟩ or sordid mercenary entanglement, ⟨misunderstanding⟩ comes creeping over me and wraps me all in fog — Had my mind been free and my feelings unharrassed ⟨and⟩ by petty cross purposes I think I should have done a great deal more & a great deal better than I have done — and should at this moment been free of all pecuniary difficulties — However — it is not to be helped — Every man has his difficulties & cares with which he must contend—

I have recd. your letter of Jany 8th. to which I will reply at more leisure — it is full of interesting matter — I must conclude this letter that it may be sent off to be in time for the Ship —

Remember me very sincerely to Mrs Brevoort and believe me my Dear Brevoort with constant reccollection

Affectionately yours —
Washington Irving

Henry Brevoort Jr Esqr./New York—

ADDRESSED: Henry Brevoo[rt] [*MS torn*] Junr. Esq. / New York. / Cadmus
     DOCKETED: Paris 5 Apl. 1821 / Washington Irving
MANUSCRIPT: NYPL—WI Papers.   PUBLISHED: LIB, II, 149–51.
     Under Brevoort's docketing and written upside down is "Havre, April 8th, 1821 / forwarded by yr. ob. St. / R G Beasley"
This letter repeats the same ideas as the other one of this date to Brevoort. Because of the urgency of his request, WI probably sent it to New York by a different route.

303.   To Charles Williams

Paris April 13th. 1821.

My dear Sir

Whilst I was in London you ⟨und⟩once undertook to forward a draft of mine to New York for Collection & the next day surprized me by the proceeds of it in ready money.[1] As I doubt whether my name ⟨i⟩ on paper can work equal Miracles in Paris I want to avail myself again of your friendly alchymy. In plain words I have present occasion for one thousand Dollars, & wish to draw on my friend Mr Henry Brevoort of New York for that amount. You know best how such a Bill is to be disposed of: can you manage it for me, and in the mean time put me in possission of five thousand francs, or authorize me to draw on you for such amount as will produce that sum. If so, I will thank you to let me know whether I shall send the Bill to you, or what disposition I shall make of it here — I feel loth to trouble you in this manner, *but* I am a very inexpert financier & not in the way of negociating paper — If ever you should turn scribbler and I should wax rich & become a Banker I shall be happy to return your friendly offices in Kind.

I am delighted with Newtons success.² I always said the boy had the stuff in him if it could only be worked out — He has now nothing to do but to work like a beaver; study hard; keep to his eazel and *avoid good company,* and he may yet come to some good; to the great joy & infinite relief of his friends — You need not tell him I say so however — we must not turn his head by too great praise.

With my best remembrances to your Brother & my hearty good wishes to the worthy Knights of the round table³ who assemble at your house on Sundays I am very truly

Your friend
Washington Irving

No 4 Rue Mont Thabor/à Paris.
Charles Williams Esqr.

ADDRESSED: To / Charles Williams Esqr. / corner of Finsbury Square / London.
POSTMARKED: FPO / Ap. 17 / 1821   DOCKETED: 1821. / Washington Irving—
13 April / — 17 — / — 17 —
MANUSCRIPT: NYPL—Berg Collection.
In the upper right corner of address fold is written "S. *Williams.*" Apparently the letter was franked and the postage on it paid by Samuel Williams.

1. Earlier letters do not mention this kindness by Charles Williams. Probably as the brother of Samuel Williams, the London banker, he had access to financial agents not available to most Americans abroad.

2. In a letter of April 2, 1821, Charles R. Leslie had told WI that Newton had "made a very brilliant little sketch from Moliere of a genteel love quarrel. A lady and gentleman returning miniatures, letters, &c, &c.—the lady's maid tittering behind the chair of her mistress. It promises to be his best picture" (Leslie, *Autobiographical Recollections,* p. 233).

3. An allusion to the group of artistic cronies which included Leslie, Newton, Peter Powell, and William Willes ("Father Luke").

304. *To Henry Brevoort*

Paris April 14th. 1821

My dear Brevoort,

I wrote you a hasty line a few days since¹ advising you of a draft which I had drawn on you on the 5th inst for one thousand dollars, to provide for my first bill on William Irving, returned—I shall have to draw on you again in a few days for a like sum of 1000$ to pay my Second Bill on W Irving which I expect back presently. ⟨When I lately drew on you⟩ In the advice of my draft of the 5th inst, I mentioned that I should write to E I to refund you the amount in due time. I did write to that effect²—but I think I must now request you to remain in advance to me for some little time, for reasons which will be explained to you in the course of this letter—The Simple State of the case is this—

The amount for which I engaged last year in the Steam Boat concern was *5000$*. Of this I paid one thousand Dolls from money due me in London—for the remaining I gave four Bills on W.I. for 1000$ each—three of which were forwarded; the fourth remains in Mr Beasleys hands—Of the three which were forwarded, ⟨I have recd intel-⟩ one has already come back dishonoured—to meet this I drew on you on the 5th. another is shortly expected, to meet that I shall have to draw on you in a few days—The third bill went out by the Syren³ and is payable in May, I trust that will be ⟨paid⟩ ↑taken up↓ by E. I. as he wrote in December last that he would be in the receipt of 1000$ in May from former sales of my works. There then remains one thousand Dollars to be remitted to R G Beasley to make up the amount of my engagement. I trust E. I. will be able to furnish a part of that from other sales which he may have made since December— I wish you to make up ⟨the⟩ ↑any↓ deficiency there may be, and remit the same to R G Beasley. You will then be in advance to me the amount of two Bills on you for 1000$ each and such part of another 1000$ as E. I. may not be able to furnish. I trust I have made myself clearly understood—I wish you to see that ⟨I am put in⟩ the 4000$ is fully made up—I shall not draw on you any further than the two bills of 1000$ each: trusting that my third draft dated in last year on Wm Irving, will be honoured at maturity—or that at any rate you will take care that whatever may be deficient, is remitted—

I am asking this favour, my dear fellow, in very plain and direct terms, but in fact I depend on you to ⟨deb⟩ disembarrass me from these paltry difficulties which are teazing & perplexing me—and doing me more than their pecuniary amount in positive injury. I ask this pecuniary assistance from you with confidence—*first* because you have repeatedly given me the most gratifying proofs of your readiness to befriend me in this way—and *secondly,* because I am certain you will not incur the loss of a farthing by it. The ⟨reason⟩ *first* reason is due to you & the generous & affectionate interest you have ever taken in my concerns—the *second* is due to myself, for if I did not feel the certainty of being able to reimburse, I must come to bread & water & sleep on a board before I would ask pecuniary favours from any one.

I have said that it is likely you may be some little time in advance of such part of the 4000$ as you may furnish: as literary property is not immediately available. I do not however depend solely on the proceeds of the property in my brothers hands to reimburse you. I have a Mass of writings by me which, so soon as I can bring them into ⟨arrange⟩ form and prepare them for publication, will I trust produce me something very handsome in *cash down* in England;[4] besides augmenting my copy right property in America. I do not speak this from any conceit of the writings themselves, but from a mere knowledge of ⟨the⟩ *literary trade.*—The success of the Sketch Book in England has been ↑far↓ beyond my most sanguine expectation & any book I should now offer for sale, *good or bad*, would be sure to find a ready purchaser at a high price among the Booksellers—As I am anxious however to get reputation rather than money, I do not wish to hurry into print & it will take me some time yet to arrange and complete the writings I have in hand. I do not wish this circumstance to be mentioned to any one—as I never like to have anticipations of my literary appearances; I merely tell it to you, to shew you the grounds on which I feel ⟨encouraged to ask for⟩ ↑justified↓ in asking your pecuniary aid. I trust my next work will fairly relieve me from all further embarrassment of the kind—and ⟨that⟩ I shall thenceforth be able to keep ahead of my resources.

I am particular in wishing *you* to make these advances, because my Brother Peter has renewed his request to John T. Irving for a loan; and I do not wish his request to be interfered with, by any necessity for J.T.I. or any other of my connexions to advance money on my account. Peter is more anxious than ever to secure an interest in the Steam boat concern, & I am very solicitous that he should have every facility. A situation in the concern is ⟨bound?⟩ ↑open↓ to him by which he will be able, with strict economy to clear his ⟨wants?⟩ support; ↑independent of the profits that may arise from his share in the property;↓ and there is every prospect of the business being lucrative. To give plain demonstration that this is not merely chimerical I inclose you a statement of the receipts & expenditures of the Steam boat since its establishment as a passage boat between Havre & Honfleur.[5] It has had every possible disadvantage to contend with; ⟨being⟩ having to establish its character; overcome the prejudices of the public, contend with long established packetboats; to run at high wages, ⟨which⟩ & expenses which it took some time to systamatize & reduce—& the whole experiment has been made during the winter months and the early part of an uncommonly inclement & stormy spring—during which season ⟨the travelling is⟩ there is comparatively but little travelling. In spite of all these things it has to my great surprize made money—for it was calculated that there would certainly be a pecuniary loss, & the only gain would be experience & an established reputation—The fine season is now commencing when the traversing is very great; and at times⟨,⟩ (from the frequency of fairs on both side of the Seine) immense. It is a matter of course therefore that the profits must ⟨be⟩ increase in proportion—A new boat, adapted to the navigation of the river is also about to run between Havre & Rouen, through a country full of population and studded with populous little towns—I think the anticipations of profit from such a navigation are perfectly reasonable—⟨My⟩ Peter has given the whole concern the most Scrupulous examination and is convinced that it holds out a prospect of advantage and ultimate independence to him; which it would be difficult to find at present in any other quarter— I trust my Brothers will not rashly a second time decide from their presumptions in opposition to his investigations and shrink back from rendering such temporary aid as may place him in a path to comfortable & creditable independence for the rest of his days. I do not question for a moment their disposition to to do every thing to promote both our interests; I should feel outraged by such a suggestion; but they ⟨are⟩ ↑have grown↓ morbid & timid in money matters, from past misfortunes & they are apt to hesitate & doubt, and talk together & do nothing: and by doing nothing, play the very vengeance with those who rely on their active assistance. You hinted in one of your former letters[6] about being hurt by some observations of my Brothers, in the course of your conversations with them on the subject of my affairs. I am at a loss to think what ⟨they⟩ cause they could find for any captious observation, in the kind & affectionate zeal you have manifested in my poor & paltry concerns. I should be loth to subject you to any thing further of the kind; but bear with them my dear Brevoort for my sake; and be assured they are only activated by brotherly anxiety for my interests; which unluckily they have a little marred by their very anxiety.—So much for these "weary" money matters—

I have now been about eight months in Paris, living an odd sort of life—shut up in my room a great part of my time and seeing scarcely any thing of french society—circumstances having thrown me almost entirely among the americans & the English. In fact the anxiety I have to do something more in literature, ⟨&⟩ the petty involvements of myself & friends, and the wish to put an end to these also, have so agitated & perplexed my mind, that I have neither been able to enjoy society fully, nor to profit by liesure & abstraction. I have advances made ⟨f⟩ me by society, that, were I a mere seeker of society, would be invaluable; but I dread so much ⟨getting⟩ being put out in my pursuits & distracted by the mere hurry of fashionable engagements, that I keep aloof, and neglect opportunities ⟨that⟩ ↑which↓ I may perhaps at some future day ⟨be sorry for⟩ look back to with regret. When I have launched another work, and a successful one,

I trust I shall feel more completely at ease both in mind & circumstances.—One of my greatest sources of gratification here is ⟨f⟩ the intimacy of Moore, the poet,[7] whom I see almost every day, and who is one of the worthiest and most delightful fellows I have ever known. Mr. Astor has been passing the Winter here with his Son and Daughter[8] The former is in ⟨a⟩ very bad health, and seems in a state of mental Stupor—His Situation ⟨give⟩ causes great anxiety & distress to his father & sister; and there appears but little prospect of his recovery. Miss Astor is quite a clever, agreeable girl—I have been quite gratified by meeting again with Mr Astors Nephew George Eningher[9] whom I had not seen for several years. He has given me a world of anecdote about New York, and particularly about yourself.—He will be in New York again almost as soon as this letter—

You have given me much interesting information in your last;[10] which unluckily I cannot lay my hand on—to reply to—I am heartily glad that James Renwick is snugly nestled in the old College,[11] which is a safe harbour for life; and a very comfortable & honourable one. The other appointments[12] contemplated will be of great Service to the College & to the literary character of the State—Verplanck is just where he should be[13] & I hope he will cut politicks and devote himself to his pen, which will make a greater man of him than the highest political preferment ⟨in the⟩ to which he could fight & scramble.—

I am delighted with the North American Review:[14] it is the best work of the Kind we have ever had, and will be an interesting work to Europeans; as it is divested of national hostilities & political prejudices—

Your account of Keans success[15] is very interesting and I was amused with the odd assemblage at John R L's festival:[16] ⟨a⟩ Kean is a strange compound of merits & defects—His excellence consists in sudden & brilliant touches—in vivid exhibitions of passion & emotion— I do not think him a *discriminating* actor; or ⟨a⟩ critical either at understanding· or delineating *character*—but he produces effects which no other actor does. He has completely bothered the multitude; and is praised without being understood. I have seen him guilty of the grossest & coarsest pieces of false acting, and most "tyranically clapped"[17] withal; while some of his most exquisite touches passed unnoticed—

I must bring this letter to a close, that it may be in time. Give my sincere regards to Mrs Brevoort, and my hearty remembrances to Your father & mother and the re[st of] [MS torn] your family connexion, and believe me my dea[r] B[revoor]t [MS torn]

Ever yours affectionately
W Irving.

P.S. I am uncertain about my continuance in Paris, and not having fixed exactly on my summer residence I wish you to direct to me after the receipt of this care of Henry Van Wart Esqr Birmingham—

ADDRESSED: To / Henry Brevoort Jr. Esqr. / New York. / ⟨care of Messrs A & S Richards / p Liverpool⟩ / p Albion   POSTMARKED: Forwarded by Y. O. St. / Harvey V Latham of Liverpool   DOCKETED: Paris Ap[ri]l [MS torn] 14. 1821 / Washington Irving
MANUSCRIPT: NYPL–Seligman Collection.   PUBLISHED: LIB, II, 153–65; PMI, I, 344; II, 48 (in part).

1. On April 5, 1821.
2. This letter has not been located.
3. The *Syren* had reached New York on February 4, 1821. WI had probably sent his bill on this voyage. See NYEP, February 5, 1821.
4. By mid-May WI had completed 130 pages of the manuscript of *Bracebridge Hall*. See WIHM, pp. 35–36.
5. As early as November 7, 1820, the *Triton* was making daily round trips between Le Havre and Honfleur, with departures from Le Havre at 10:00 A.M. and from Honfleur at 1:30 P.M. at fares of two francs for first class and one franc for second class for one way. See *Journal du Havre*, no. 262, November 7, 1820.
6. See Brevoort's letter of November, 1820 (LBI, I, 129).
7. The letters and diary of Thomas Moore from this period indicate that WI mingled extensively with the English-speaking colony in Paris.
8. John Jacob Astor, who had been traveling in Europe since June, 1819, was joined in Paris by his son John Jacob, Jr. (1791–1867) and his daughter Eliza (1801–1838). The son was mentally incompetent. See Porter, *John Jacob Astor*, II, 1036.
9. Son of Astor's sister Catherine (b. 1757 or 1758) and George Ehninger, a German distiller. George, Jr. (b. 1792) did not get along with his uncle, who considered him a poor merchant. Porter, *John Jacob Astor*, II, 1030.
10. See Brevoort's letter of January 8, 1821 (LBI, I, 132–36).
11. In 1820 Renwick became professor of natural philosophy and experimental chemistry at Columbia College, a post he held for thirty-three years.
12. Brevoort had reported that "When the funds are adequate, VerPlanck is to be appointed Prof: of Rhetoric" (LBI, I, 132).
13. Verplanck, who had written for the *Analectic Magazine* during WI's editorship, had been elected to the New York legislature the preceding November, after a running battle against the Clintonian faction of the Federalists. Verplanck had published satiric verses in the New York *American* under the title of "The Bucktail Bards." They were later collected and published as *The State Triumvirate, A Political Tale: And the Epistles of Brevet Major Pindar Puff* (1819). See July, *Verplanck*, pp. 60–71.
14. This journal, begun by William Tudor in 1815 and edited by Edward Everett from 1820 to 1823, defended and promoted a national literature for the United States.
15. As Brevoort explains in his letter, Edmund Kean (1787–1833) had arrived in New York on November 24, 1820, playing "sixteen nights in the Anthony St. Theatre to crowded audiences & enthusiastic applause" (LBI, I, 133). Subsequently Kean performed in Philadelphia, Boston, Baltimore, and New York again before

leaving the United States on June 6, 1821. See Harold N. Hillebrand, *Edmund Kean* (New York, 1966), pp. 200–223.

16. According to Brevoort, "On New Year's day, he [Kean] had dined at Jno. R. Livingstons with a party of forty persons. . . . Everything went left handed & a score of absurdities were committed" (see LBI, I, 135).

17. *Hamlet*, II, ii, 356.

305. *To Colonel Gideon Fairman*

Paris, April 19th. 1821.

My dear Fairman,

I received lately your letter by Mr Carpenter[1] and was very happy to hear from you & to see him — He has gone to Orleans some days since. I hope you are making money by the *Ream* as fast as your machines can work[2] —

The main purpose of this letter is concerning the son of Mrs Holloway[3] whom I introduced to you some time since, and who you promised to take into your establishment. I find Mrs H is obliged to take him from school in June next, not being able at present to afford the expense. It would be injurious to the lad and a source of anxiety to her should he remain id⟨d⟩le at his present time of life: I want you therefore to take him under your wing as soon as you possibly can. The little fellow is extremely anxious & ambitious of getting forward and making himself of service to others and a source of comfort to his family, and from what I have seen & known of him I am sure you will find him one who will grow in your favour & confidence. I feel very strongly interested in this matter. I became acquainted with Mrs Holloway by mere chance, having accidentally taken lodgings at her house; but I discovered excellent natural traits of character in her which won my respect and friendship, and I felt strong sympathy for the fortitude & perseverance with which she struggled against many troubles and afflictions. I also feel great regard for others of her connexions whom I have seen. In taking her child under your care therefore and treating him with that kindness, which in fact is inseparable from your nature; in attending to his instruction & improvement, and ↑in↓ fitting him to be the staff and support of the family that may possibly be one day leaning on him; you will be gratifying me in a most especial manner and at the same time laying up a source of future gratification for your own good heart. Take charge of him therefore, my dear Fairman, as soon as you conveniently can, *for my sake*, and I trust he will act so that you ⟨shall⟩ will hereafter keep him by you *for his own* — Excuse the earnestness with which I press this matter; but indeed I am very solicitous to see this little fellow well placed; and I do not know any one with whom I would so gladly see him fixed as with you —

Tell Mrs. Fairman I am much flattered by her treasuring up my old purse. I wish it was Fortunatus's purse⁴ for her sake; but as it is, it's a bad relique & carries no good luck with it; for my purse is sadly afflicted with the curse of Emptiness. Give her my best regards, and also to Col Perkins,⁵ to Mr & Mrs Miller⁶ and the rest of your circle —

With great regard/Yours faithfully
Washington Irving

P.S—I shall write to Mrs Holloway to call on you with her son Marseilles: when he returns home from school.

ADDRESSED: Col: Fairman / Fleet Street. / London / 69   POSTMARKED: ⟨[unre-covered]⟩ Post / Unpaid / 22 Ap[?] Holborn
MANUSCRIPT: Va.–Barrett.

1. Probably WI is referring to John Carpenter, an English landscape painter who exhibited in the late 1820's or to G. Carpenter, who exhibited at the Royal Academy and at the British Institution in 1831 and 1832. Another possibility is J. Carpenter, a painter of miniature portraits whose work was shown at the Royal Academy between 1837 and 1855. See *Dictionnaire des Peintres, Sculpteurs, Dessinateurs et Graveurs,* ed. E. Benezit, II, 331.

2. WI is alluding to Fairman's engraving business in London.

3. WI had lived at her home in Cockspur Lane, London, in August, 1817. Here, according to Marseilles Holloway, WI wrote part of *The Sketch Book* and probably "Mountjoy" in 1818. See STW, I, 421.

4. The purse of Fortunatus had magical properties which enabled its owner to draw ten pieces of gold from it at any time.

5. Probably Colonel Thomas H. Perkins (1764–1854), a Boston merchant who spent part of his time looking after his business interests in England. See Robert E. Spiller, *The American in England* (New York, 1926), p. 160.

6. John Miller was the English publisher of the first volume of *The Sketch Book.* WI had met him at the home of John Murray in 1817. See STW, I, 156; WIHM, pp. 6–9.

306. To Henry Brevoort

Paris, April 21st. 1821.

My dear Brevoort,

I wrote to you lately at considerable length,¹ explaining my reasons for drawing on you for one thousand Dollars on the 5th. inst. and telling you that I should draw for a like sum in a few days—I have this day drawn a Second sett of Exchange on ⟨for⟩ you for 1000$— it is in favour of Saml Williams Esqr. of London, and is at thirty days sight. I had intended to have drawn it *Sixty* days; but had neglected to specify that date in a letter which I wrote to Charles Williams requesting to know whether their house ⟨could⟩ ↑would↓ cash a draft ⟨to that amount⟩ ↑for 1000$↓ on you; and in reply he gave me permission to draw on them & sent me a form of a draft on you; supposing I did not know the exact form—It was at thirty days sight—so I thought best to sign the form they sent me; and I hope the shortness of the time will not put you to inconvenience —

I shall not draw on you any more — I trust ⟨my⟩ the third draft which I drew on my Brothers last year will be taken up by my brother E.I. as he will have cash of mine to more than the amount in his hands, when it ⟨falls⟩ comes to maturity — I have however explained myself fully on these points in a former letter[2] — I trust I shall not have to trouble you any more in this way; and I should not now have done so, but I did not know how else to extricate myself from a pecuniary embarrassment, which has occasioned me loss of time, loss of money & loss of spirits. Peter has set off this morning for Havre to attend to the Steamboat concern. He seems very confident of its becoming a lucrative enterprize & he is by no means a Sanguine man at present — I hope to God it may: and that he may be enabled once more to get his head above water. —

I have mentioned in my former letter that I wished you to remain in Advance of the two thousand Dollars; and if necessary to assist my brother E.I. in making up a remittance of a thousand dollars, to be paid to Mr Beasley to take up a fourth bill which he did not send for collection last year — I do not want my brothers to advance money on account of my engagement in the concern, lest it should prevent their complying with Peters request, lately renewed, that they would make him a loan — I expect the proceeds from my literary property in E I's hands will soon be sufficient to reimburse you—but if not, I have some [MSS.][3] [MS torn] which as soon as I can prepare for publicat[ion] [will just?] [MS torn] put me in cash from their sale in London to make up whatever may be deficient. It may take me some time however to complete & to arrange what I am about, my writing moods are so irregular & uncertain & I am so liable to be put out, by circumstances — I do not wish ⟨you to⟩ it to be known that I have any thing positively in preparation, as I do not like to awaken any expectations —

I shall write to you shortly — a good, sociable, hearty letter; without any of these cursed money matters in it which always wither me Soul & body, when I have to meddle with them — Remember me sincerely to Mrs Brevoort & believe me

Yours ever & affectionately
W.I.

ADDRESSED: Henry Brevoort Junr Esqr. / New York.   DOCKETED: Apl. 21 – 1821 /
Washington Irving
MANUSCRIPT: NYPL–Seligman Collection.   PUBLISHED: LIB, II, 166–69.

1. See WI's letter of April 14, 1821.
2. WI's letter mentioned above.
3. WI is alluding to materials that became part of *Bracebridge Hall.*

307.   To John Howard Payne

[April 30, 1821]

My dear Payne,

I did not get to the Panorama Dramatique[1] on Saturday evening;
but I saw Moore & others of the party who were there, and were highly
pleased. Moore seems to have been quite struck with the piece –
he thinks the story very interesting & affecting, and the getting up of
the piece ⟨very⟩ quite singular & ingenious & very picturesque. He
thinks it would appear to much greater advantage & effect in one of
the large London Theatres where the ⟨Scen⟩ machinery decorations &c
are so superior. He was very much delighted with the last scene
(the apotheosis) though it seemed to have shocked one of the ladies
a little. That scene it appears to me will be a critical one – it may
mar the piece, or it may give it an extraordinary attraction. Moore
says the Sand scene was rather defective – it seemed to be beyond
the scope of their art; excepting ⟨that⟩ the representation of the sand
thickening in the atmosphere – I presume the whole ↑scene↓ could
be better managed on the London boards—

Yours very truly
W Irving

Rue Mont Thabor No 4/April 30th. 1821.

ADDRESSED: à Monsieur / Monsieur Payne / Petite Rue de St Pierre No 16 / Pont
aux Choux   POSTMARKED: Mai 1 1821   DOCKETED: Washington Irving /
Paris, May 1. 1821.
MANUSCRIPT: Va.–Barrett.   PUBLISHED: Gabriel Harrison, *John Howard Payne,*
pp. 103–4.

According to Gabriel Harrison, this letter by WI was copied off and included in
a letter which Payne sent to R. W. Ellison on May 1, 1821. See *John Howard Payne,
His Life and Writings,* pp. 103–4.

1. The Panorama Dramatique opened on the Boulevard du Temple on April
14 with a three-act melodrama, *Ismayl et Maryam, ou l'Arabe et la Chrétienne* by
Dupetit-Méré and Taylor and with *Monsieur Boulevard* by Balisson de Rougemont
and Carmouche. See Henri d'Almeras, *La Vie Parisienne sous la Restauration* (Paris,
n.d.), pp. 137–39; Charles Beaumont Wicks, *The Parisian Stage, Part II (1816–
1830)* (University, Ala., 1953), pp. 41, 52. WI's subsequent reference to sand
probably refers to a scene in *Ismayl et Maryam.*

308. *To Mrs. Story*

[May 4, 1821]

Mr Irving is engaged to dine at two, at a charboniers—Rue de deux Ecus—Halle au blé—to attend a concert at five, at a Tinmans rue plat d'etain and to go to a ⟨concert⟩ ball at eight at a Marchand de Modes—Rue des Rats—but he will break all these engagements and give up the charms of the Dames de la Halle for the pleasure of waiting on Mrs Story—
⟨Apr⟩ May 4th. 1821

MANUSCRIPT: NYPL—Berg Collection.   PUBLISHED: STW, I, 199 (in part).

Mrs. Story, an Englishwoman who was a close friend of the Thomas Moores, with whom WI was intimate at this time, was also living in Paris. WI had met her at Moore's as early as February 3, 1821. See *Memoirs, Journal, and Correspondence of Thomas Moore*, ed. Lord John Russell (London, 1853), III, 196.

Despite its outward formality, the note suggests by its tone that WI was on very familiar terms with Mrs. Story.

309. *To Henry Brevoort*

Paris, May 15th. 1821.

My dear Brevoort,
    I send you a parcel of music for the Harp,[1] which I hope may please Mrs Brevoort. It was selected by a french Lady who plays admirably on that instrument. She says the musick is simple, and good, and by some of the best composers—
    I wrote a long letter to you a short time since,[2] and have not at this moment any thing very particular to add, especially as I have to dispatch this letter in a few moments by Mr Ehninger — who is on his way to Havre. I am looking impatiently for the arrival of Wm Gracie,[3] who will be able to give me a world of news about my friends in New York. I see that the Estephania[4] has arrived at Antwerp and Gracie must be by this time in Paris[.] I hope the dispatches he brings to Mr Gallatin[5] will be such as to produce a satisfactory arrangement between the two Countries.
    Mr Ehninger is waiting for my letters and I have yet to write one to Peter who is at Havre —
    Give my best regards to Mrs Brevoort and believe me
                                                    Yours affectionately
                                                    Washington Irving
Henry Brevoort Junr. Esq

ADDRESSED: Henry Brevoort Junr. Esqr / New York.   DOCKETED: Paris May 15–
    1821 / Washn. Irving   ENDORSED: Havre. / [M]ay [*MS torn*] 17, 1821 /
    Recd. & for[war]ded [*MS torn*] by / yr. ob. St. / R G Beasley
MANUSCRIPT: NYPL–WI Papers.   PUBLISHED: LIB, II, 170–71.

Brevoort's docket is written upside down at the bottom; Beasley's endorsement
is written upside down at the top. At the right margin on a level with his docketing Brevoort wrote the following figures: 193 09 79

$$\overline{8:13:10}:18.7$$

1. In his letter of November 24, 1820, to WI, Brevoort had asked for this
music, and WI apologized for his delay and neglect on March 21, 1821.

2. Probably WI's letter of April 21, 1821.

3. The eldest son of Archibald Gracie and a member of his father's commercial
house.

4. On April 11, 1821, NYEP reported that the *Stephania* sailed for Antwerp
the preceding day with William Gracie and sixteen other passengers aboard.

5. At this time Albert Gallatin was the United States minister to France.

310.   To John Murray II

[July 6, 1821]

My dear Sir,

I write in very great haste, to acknowledge the receipt of your Letter
of the 29th. ult[1]–I am extremely happy to hear that the Sketch Book
has been favourably noticed in the Quarterly.[2] I have not seen the
review, but I doubt whether any criticism in it can be so emphatic
as that in your Letter[3] — You were certainly intended for a critick —
I never knew any one convey so much meaning in so concise and
agreeable a manner — In compliance with your request I have drawn
on you for ⟨the⟩ an hundred pounds — in favour of Mr Saml Williams
of London — The supply came opportunely — I am on the point of
leaving Paris for Bruxelles, and where I shall go from thence is at
present undetermined; but I shall write to you from the Netherlands,
should I make any stop there. I have been leading a "miscellaneous"
kind of life at Paris — if I may use a literary phraze. I have been rather
distracted by engagements, in spite of all my efforts to keep out of
Society. ⟨I have not⟩ Anacreon Moore is living here: and has made
me a gayer fellow than I could have wished; but I found it impossible
to resist the charm of his society. Paris is like an English watering
place, with the advantage of the best kind of amusements, and excellent
society.

I have scribbled at intervals, and have a mass of writings by me;[4]
rather desultory, as must be the case when one is so much interrupted;
but I hope, in the fullness of time, to get them into some order —

I write in extreme haste, having to pack up and make other preparations for departure —

With my best regards to Mrs Murray & the rest of your family I am my dear Sir

Very faithfully yours,
Washington Irving

Paris July 6th 1821
John Murray Esqr.

ADDRESED: John Murray Esqr. / Albemarle St / London.   POSTMARKED: FPO JY.10
1821   DOCKETED: *6 July 1821* / W. Irving Esq / for Bracebridge / Hall
MANUSCRIPT: John Murray.   PUBLISHED: PMI, II, 48–49; WIHM, pp. 36–37;
Smiles, *Memoir of John Murray,* II, 130 (in part).

1. Printed in PMI, II, 48, and in WIHM, pp. 36.

2. By Henry Matthew in *Quarterly Review* 25 (April, 1821), 50–67. He regards *The Sketch Book* as the best American writing since the Revolution and singles out "The Legend of Sleepy Hollow" and "The Spectre Bridegroom" for special attention.

3. Apparently WI is being facetious, for Murray merely directs him to draw £100 and calls attention to the article in the *Quarterly Review.*

4. Another allusion to *Bracebridge Hall.*

311. To John Howard Payne

[July 9, 1821]

My dear Payne,

I leave Paris on Wednesday morning for Bruxelles—and shall in all probability go from thence to Engd. My resolution has been taken rather Suddenly—I shall be at home all tomorrow morning, packing & you will find me if you will call

I should like very much to see you before I go & to know what I can do for you in London

Yours truly
W I.

Monday Morng—

ADDRESSED: Monsieur / Monsr. Payne / Petit Rue de St Pierre No 16 / Pont aux
Choux   POSTMARKED: July 9, 1821   DOCKETED: W Irving / Paris / July
9, 1821
MANUSCRIPT: Va.–Barrett.

312. To John Howard Payne

London, 41 Gr. Marlboro' St./ Augt. 1, 1821.

My dear Payne:

I recd your letter of 16th July[1] about 23d or 24th but have been looking out in vain for the personal parcel containing the dramatic piece.[2]

It has not as yet come to hand. I had intended before this to have gone to my sisters, in the country but have remained in town in daily expectation of the arrival of the parcel. I wish you would enquire after it, and forward it without delay, to the above address. I called on Hazlitt[3] a day or two after my arrival. He is not the Editor of the Magazine,[4] but writes for it at the rate of 16 guineas a sheet. (I. E. a guinea a page) The Mag: is at present owned by Taylor & Hessey.[5] He told me he would speak to them on the subject, and thought it probable they would be induced to take writings from you, on experiment, at the same rate. Though of course they would not want above half a sheet, say 8 pages from one author per month, as they like to have a variety of styles and authors. He told me he would either call on me or write me after he had seen Taylor & Hessey. I have heard nothing from him as yet.

As to your wish respecting Mr. Rush[6] I do not know whether I shall ever have an opportunity of talking freely enough with him to make the suggestion. I called on him a day or two after my arrival but he suffered ten or twelve days to elapse before he returned my call; and then talked a few minutes with Mr. Newton, at whose lodgings I am, and took leave before I could come down stairs; making some apology that he had to go to call on some one at Dicks coffee house.[7] He is rather whimsical in his arrangements about visitors and I had not seen him for many months before I left London last year for Paris. I do not care on my own account; having no inclination just now for any society — but I felt chagrined as I wanted to speak on your concerns.

Price[8] is here beating up for recruits. Philips[9] will go out on a regular engagement. Charles Kemble[10] seems inclined to pay America a visit. Price has offered Braham[11] 10,000£ for one year. Braham lends a listening ear and I should not be surprised if he should be tempted to go a year or so hence. Kean having behaved like a fool and a jackanapes in America,[12] and completely quarrelled with his own bread and butter, has come back post haste to London, and resumed his throne at Drury Lane with a flourish of trumpets from Elliston.[13] Both manager and actor have been completely baulked. Kean has failed to draw houses, and in consequence of sudden indisposition, and the advice of his physician, has resolved not to appear again until next winter!

The Coronation Piece at Covent Garden[14] draws bumpers. A show of the kind is now acting at Drury Lane,[15] but I have not heard with what success.

I have heard nothing of the Solitaire[16] — it certainly has not yet been published; but may possibly be in hand. I see that the Surrey Theatre has got hold of the pretty little piece "L'auberge de grand Frederick,"[17] which pleased me so much just before leaving Paris.

Let me hear from you, what you are about. I stay almost entirely at home, and have been but twice out of doors for five days past; yet I am in a dreadfully idle vein. The closeness and the thickness of the London air seems to have got into my brain. I wish my self back again at Paris a dozen times a day.

Do not fail to enquire about the Mss. and forward it immediately; as I want to go into the country.

Yours most truly,
W. Irving

ADDRESSED: Monsr. J. H. Payne / Petite Rue de St. Pierre No. 16, / Pont aux Choux / a Paris

PUBLISHED: *Scribner's Magazine* 47 (October, 1910), 466–67.

Although the Thatcher T. Payne Luquer collection of Payne manuscripts is now in the Columbia University Library, the holograph of this letter has not been located. The editors have been obliged to use the printed version in *Scribner's Magazine* as copy-text, with the realization that Luquer omitted passages and regularized WI's spelling and punctuation.

1. This letter has not been located.

2. In his letter of August 23, 1821, WI identifies the work as *The Borrower*.

3. William Hazlitt (1778–1830) was writing for the *Edinburgh Review,* the *Edinburgh Magazine,* and the *London Magazine* in 1821. See Herschel Baker, *William Hazlitt* (Cambridge, 1962), pp. 321, 328.

4. After Hazlitt had been approached to become editor of the *London Magazine* and had declined, John Taylor assumed the editorship. See Baker, *William Hazlitt,* p. 408; Tim Chilcott, *A Publisher and His Circle: The Life and Works of John Taylor, Keats's Publisher* (London, 1972), pp. 132–34.

5. James Hessey and John Taylor (1781–1864), who on April 26, 1821, had purchased the *London Magazine* from Robert Baldwin, continued as owners until 1825. See Baker, *William Hazlitt,* p. 408; Josephine Bauer, *The London Magazine 1820–1829* in *Anglistica* 1 (1953), 144; Chilcott, *A Publisher and His Circle,* p. 132.

6. Richard Rush was the United States minister to Great Britain.

7. Located at No. 8 Fleet Street, South. See Walter Thornbury, *Old and New London: A Narrative of its History, its People, and its Places* (London, n.d.), I, 44.

8. Stephen Price, manager of the Park Theater, whom WI had known in New York.

9. Henry Philips (1801–1876), a bass singer just beginning his career. In 1823 he joined the troupe at Covent Garden.

10. Charles Kemble did not visit America until 1832, when he made his debut on September 19 as Hamlet. See Odell, *NY Stage,* II, 603.

11. John Braham (1774?–1856), the outstanding tenor of the day, made his first appearance on the American stage at the Park Theater on December 21, 1840. See Ireland, *NY Stage,* II, 341; Odell, *NY Stage,* IV, 450.

12. For details about Kean's tour see WI's letter of April 14, 1821.

13. Robert W. Elliston (1774–1831) was manager-director of the Drury Lane Theatre from 1819 to 1826.

14. In connection with the coronation of George IV on July 19, 1821, the king commanded a performance of Shakespeare's *Henry IV*, Part II, with its coronation pageant of Henry V in the last act. Macready played the king and Kemble the prince of Wales in twenty-seven performances up to August 17. See Henry Saxe Wyndham, *The Annals of Covent Garden Theatre from 1732 to 1897* (London, 1906), II, 13; John Genest, *Some Account of the English Stage*, IX, 114.

15. On its bill for August the Drury Lane Theatre included *Coronation* with Frederic Reynolds's *The Dramatist*. See Genest, *Some Account of the English Stage*, IX, 94; London *Times*, August 1, 1821. "At Drury Lane . . . Robert Elliston had achieved a theatrical miracle. He had recreated the pageant of the Coronation. Determined that every detail should be perfectly reproduced, he had enlisted the help of Court officials. His designers had inspected the royal robes in advance; he himself, superbly regal on and off the stage, had rehearsed his cast of hundreds with the *Morning Herald* in his hand, and he had become so lost in the part of the King that he soon believed he was George IV in person." See Joanna Richardson, *George IV, A Portrait*, pp. 225–26.

16. Having left Paris on July 11, WI may be referring to a production he heard about but did not see. *Le Solitaire, ou l'Exilé du Mont Sauvage*, a three-act melodrama by Crosnier and A. V. de St.-Hilaire, was performed at the Théâtre de la Porte-Sainte Martin on July 12, 1821. See Charles Beaumont Wickes, *The Parisian Stage: Part II (1816–1830)*, 74; PMI, II, 51.

17. *L'Auberge du Grand Frédéric*, a one-act comedy in prose by W. Lafontaine and Theaulon, was performed at the Théâtre des Variétés on June 16, 1821. See Wickes, *The Parisian Stage*, p. 6. Although the listings in the London *Times* for the Surrey Theatre are incomplete, it is possible that "an entirely new Comic Burletta, founded on an historical fact, called Frederick and Voltaire; or The King and the Poet[,] [with] [t]he overture and music by Mr. Erskine, [and] with selections from eminent composers," may be an adaptation of *L'Auberge du Grand Frédéric*. See London *Times*, July 24, 1821.

313. To William Harris

[London, August 6, 1821]

Dear Sir

I have just received your letter[1] accompanying a Diploma of Master of Arts, which the Trustees of Columbia College have done me the Honor of conferring on me. If any thing could add to this distinguished mark of approbation and esteem, it would be the very flattering manner in which it has been bestowed. I beg you will communicate to the board of Trustees my deep sense of their unexpected, and, I must say, unmerited kindness; I feel that it is far, far beyond my deserts.

Nothing is nearer to my heart than the desire of meriting the good opinion of my countrymen; and, above all of my Townsmen; but their good will has outstripped all my efforts; and I despair of ever doing enough to prove myself worthy of the rewards already lavished upon me.

Accept my thanks for the good wishes you are so kind as to express, on your own part, and which I most heartily reciprocate. Hoping that you may long continue to fill with dignity and ability the distinguished situation in which you are placed,

I remain,/Dear Sir,/With great respect,/
Your friend & very humble servt–
Washington Irving

London. Aug 6th. 1821.
The Revd. William Harris/&c. &c. &c.

MANUSCRIPT: Columbia.   PUBLISHED: *Columbia Library Columns* 9 (February, 1960), 28–29.

The Reverend William Harris (1765–1829), an Episcopal clergyman and graduate of Harvard College (1786), was rector of St. Mark's-in-the-Bowery from 1802 to 1816 and president of Columbia College from 1811 to 1829.

1. This letter is printed together with a description and reproduction of the diploma in Andrew B. Myers, "Washington Irving's First Academic Laurels," *Columbia Library Columns* 14 (May, 1965), 21–25.

314. To George Joy

[August 10, 1821]

My dear Sir,

I handed the Book to Murray some days since, and he promised to look over it, and give me an answer. He has gone to cheltenham without doing so; and indeed, I question, whether, in the hurry of preparation for departure & the multiplicity of his concern, he has had time even to look at the Book. It generally takes some time to get an answer from him on matters of business–I think it probable he has handed the work to some body to read & give him an opinion of it. When I hear from him on this subject I will let you know–

Very truly yours
Washington Irving.

Friday Aug ⟨9⟩ 10th.

ADDRESSED: George Joy Esqr. / New Ormond Street / 24   POSTMARKED: [*unre-covered*] / Unpaid / Berners 8 [?] & [?]   DOCKETED: London / Wn. Irving to G. Joy / Augst 10th 1821.
MANUSCRIPT: Va.–Barrett.

315. To John Howard Payne

London, Aug. 23d. 1821.

My dear Payne

I have recd. your letter of Aug 12th.[1] Your piece "(The Borrower")[2] came to hand the day after I last wrote to you; having been lying at the office where the Ambassadors Bag is opened, the packet being considered

too large to send by the twopenny post. I am sorry to say that I have not
been able to do any thing with it. I saw Elliston the morning after I
received it. He read the piece that same day, and got George Lamb³
to read it. I saw him by appointment the same evening behind the
Scenes; but he said it would not do. It ⟨was⟩ would be considered an
imitation of Diddler.⁴ He regretted the thing extremely, as he wished
to serve you, and he was particularly in want of a small piece, just at
that time, to precede his coronation spectacle. The latter I know to be
the case, as to the former you are the best judge. He was extremely civil
and put me in his free list. I find by his talk that he has an agent in
Paris at a weekly salary. I forget his name.

I then got Miller⁵ to offer the piece at the Haymarket (⟨th⟩ Covent
Garden theatre being closed)[.] I should have offered it myself in person,
but Terry⁶ has never had the civility to respond to some advances I once
made to his acquaintance. I told Miller however to use my name as
sending and reccommending the piece. I heard nothing further until
last evening, though I wrote in the interim, urging a prompt reply. Last
evening I recd. the piece with a note from Little Miller who says "I
received the Farce from Mr Terry yesterday. He had previously written
to me to say that he had read it very carefully, but that his opinion was
that it would not be successful on representation. He regretted this, because they want *one act* pieces at the Haymarket theatre, & I regret
it because I should have been glad to have been serviceable to the
author."

I know, from other sources, that they are much in want of attractive
novelties at the Haymarket.

Hazlitt has gone out of town without letting me hear from him on the
subject of the Magazine; though he had positively promised to do so.

I feel extremely chagrined at not being able to give you more profitable
reports; but I hope that the pieces which you have sent to Mrs Glover⁷
may be more successful. Should she be out of town, and the pieces be
sent to me I will try to do something with them. I intend leaving town
myself however, in the course of four or five days, as I am anxious to
see my Sister & her family. When I return to town I will let you know;
and I hope I may then be able to render you more effectual service.
I am terribly hampered and tied up at present;—⟨having⟩ being anxious
to get something ready for the press,⁸ but not being able to command
my time & my mind sufficiently to do any thing. I am therefore in that
uncomfortable state of being, neither able to employ my time for myself,
nor to spare it for others. Staying home to write, but not being able to
get my thoughts home enough for the purpose.

You suggested in your ⟨lette⟩ first letter that I should wri[te] [*obscured
by seal*] something about N.B.⁹ in my next work. I have no intention of

the kind; but could you not get some interesting anecdotes concerning him, and swell them out, either for a Pamphlet or for a magazine — for the latter I think it would certainly command cash. Talma[10] could give you many curious anecdotes. Those relative to his private life, familiar habits, manners, talk, dress &c &c would be most interesting — all the world knows him as a public character & every scribbler scribbles about him as a politician — Facts are what are most interesting — and the less comments the better — collect all kind of anecdotes, good bad or indifferent — from all kinds of people — ⟨Say⟩ tell every thing that you have ever heard or seen — You are on the spot. to collect facts — So long as you tell anecdotes no matter how much you tell — Send the mss. to me, care of Newton — 41. Gt Marlboro St. and I am sure I can get something for it — if only a guinea a sheet from a magazine —

Let the whole appear candid & good humoured, without leaning to either side — ⟨I would then⟩

[Unsigned]

P.S. I shall leave "the Borrower" sealed up, in the hands of Mr Newton —[11]

ADDRESSED: a Monsieur / Mons. J H. Payne / Petite rue St Pierre No 16. / Pont aux Choux / à Paris   POSTMARKED: August 26 1821 [other postmark unrecovered] DOCKETED: London Aug 23. 1821 / W Irving
MANUSCRIPT: Columbia.   PUBLISHED: Scribner's Magazine 48 (October, 1910), 467–68.

1. This letter has not been located.
2. Apparently this work was never produced.
3. George Lamb (1784–1834), amateur actor, lawyer, writer, and politician who had been a member of the committee of management of Drury Lane Theatre in 1815, after which he adapted Timon of Athens, translated Catullus, and served in Parliament.
4. Jeremy Diddler, a character in James Kenney's Raising the Wind (1803), "lives by his wits, and borrows small sums of money of everybody that he meets." See Genest, Some Account of the English Stage, IX, 613.
5. John Miller, who had gone into bankruptcy after publishing the first volume of The Sketch Book, had resumed publication of literary works, very often those by Americans.
6. Daniel Terry (1780?–1829), an actor-playwright and friend of Scott's who had adapted The Heart of Midlothian in 1819, was associated with Covent Garden from 1813 to 1822.
7. Mrs. Glover (née Butterton) (1779–1850) began her stage career in Bath in 1795 and by 1797 had gone to Covent Garden, where she was a member of the company for many years. She married Samuel Glover in 1800.
8. This was Bracebridge Hall, on which Murray had advanced WI £100 on June 29, 1821. See WIHM, p. 36.
9. Probably Napoleon Bonaparte, who had died on May 5, 1821.
10. François Joseph Talma, who spent his early years in England and acted

in both English and French roles. WI had seen him play at the Théâtre Française on
May 29, 1805, during his first visit to Europe. See *J&N*, I, 424.
   11. Written upside down at the bottom of the sheet.

316. *To Mrs. Thomas W. Storrow*

London, Aug. 26th. 1821.

My dear Mrs Storrow,
   I cannot let Bancroft[1] depart without scribbling you a line, if it is only
to ask how you all do, and to let you know that I often think of you all,
and wish myself back again among my playmates in Rue Thevenot.[2] I
have regretted leaving Paris ever since I arrived in England. The thick
atmosphere of this country, or rather of London, has befogged my brains
and beclouded my spirits, and I have been almost good for nothing. I
have been detained in town by various circumstances and have not been
able to go to my Sisters; but hope to do so before long. London appears
very monotonous and commonplaced after Paris, and is quite a different
place to me from what it was formerly; though indeed, it is a season of
the year when London is always particularly dull and uncomfortable. I
miss my Sunday parties sadly. The people here are all too old for me. I
know no one that will tell stories and play at pawns with me.
   I was quite surprised by the appearance of Mr Bancroft; who I had
supposed on his way for Italy. He lives at such a distance from me that
I have not been able to see him as often as I could wish; and I presume
his time is very much taken up with "Seeing The Lions." He told me
Susan[3] was thinking of writing a letter to me by him; but put it off;
until ↑after↓ the 25th. when she would be able to give me an account of
the Concourse.[4] I shall look for it with great impatience, and hope Minny[5]
will write a line too; and if Charles[6] will do the same, I shall be too
happy. I beg they will let me know all about Sarah;[7] and that young lady
at School that was rather cool for a time with Susan; but who had a
good heart; and whether *Petite* still continues her *Soirees,* and whether
Monsieur Jacques and the big bass voice attend—and how the little cat
comes on, and whether Justine has yet put her in corsets—in a word, to
give me an account of the whole circle of our intimates. What I would
↑not↓ give to be this moment on the Sopha in the little room, talking
over these interesting matters, instead of sitting here, in smoky London,
scribbling to the tolling of church bells, on a rainy Sunday. I have
no home here in London to dine at on Sundays, with a family circle to
make me feel as if I were among my own.
   I have kept out of company almost entirely since my arrival here, and
am chiefly with Newton and Leslie—I have a room at Newtons lodgings,

⟨which⟩ in a very quiet and pleasant part of the town. The Astors[8] passed a few Days in London lately but have gone off on a tour. Bayard[9] and his family are about to return to Paris, and from thence to go by the way of Havre to America—I have seen but little of them, and have not visited Mrs Harman & little Miss Muss[10] since I have been in London; I am ashamed to say it—but ⟨then⟩ I cannot help it; this is such a vast wilderness of a place that it is next to impossible to pay visits and ⟨kee⟩ follow [a]ny [*MS torn*] literary pursuits at the same time.

I hope friend Wilder[11] and family are all well, ⟨I hope⟩ and that the peace Society[12] has been able to determine upon a name and proceed to business, as they are terribly wanted among the Greeks; They should send two or three old gentlemen in cocked hats with all the speed to America, also, to put out the war among the Spaniards — I think the worthy little old good for nothing gentleman that breaks into such raptures about Wilders wine & his wife (quelle femme!) might be of the number.

But my paper is full, and I have talked nonsense enough — I should be ashamed to send it to you, if I was not aware that you know already how much nonsense there is in my nature.

Remember me most heartily to the *Bon homme*,[13] I hope he wont be jealous at my writing to you instead of him — give my love to the dear little girls, and to that *brave homme* Charles and give me a little family gossip when you have a leisure moment.

Affectionately your friend,
Washington Irving

P.S. I have just seen Bancroft & he says that You and Mr Storrow are coming to London in a few days. I hope I may be in town when you arrive — if not Mr Storrow must write me a line to Birmingham

Tell Susan I shall be looking out for her account of the *Concourse*, and will be sadly disappointed if she does not write soon — Tell Minny I always think of her when I pull out my purse; and the thought of her takes away from the ⟨sadness of⟩ ill humour with which one always pays money.

ADDRESSED: Mrs. Sarah Storrow / Rue Thevenot / a Paris
MANUSCRIPT: Harvard.   PUBLISHED: WIS, pp. 3–6.

Sarah Phipps Brown (1783–1837) married Thomas Wentworth Storrow (1779–1862) in 1804. They lived in Paris from about 1815 to 1830. See Henry Greenleaf Pearson, *Son of New England, James Jackson Storrow, 1864–1926* (Boston, 1932), genealogical table; WIS, p. vii.

1. George Bancroft (1800–1891), who had taken his doctorate at the University of Göttingen in 1820, was touring Europe before returning to his home in New England.

2. The location of the Storrows' house in Paris.

3. Susan Clark Storrow (1807–1843), who married WI's nephew, Henry Van Wart (b. 1806).

4. Probably WI is referring to the *concours général entre lycées et collèges de Paris et de Versailles*, a competitive examination recently instituted for students who wished to continue their schooling. According to *La Grande Encyclopédie* (XII, 316), "Il a lieu an mois juillet entre des meilleurs élèves des certaines classes déterminées, selon des conditions d'âge et de scolarité fixées par divers règlements, entre autres par celui de juin 1820."

5. "Minny" is Ann Louisa Storrow (1811–1837), another of the Storrow children.

6. Charles Storer Storrow (1809–1904), brother of Susan and Minny.

7. Sarah and the other persons mentioned in this sentence are apparently schoolmates of the Storrow children.

8. John Jacob Astor, who was touring in Europe in 1821. See WI's letter of April 14, 1821, for other details.

9. Probably William Bayard (1761–1826) of the New York shipping firm of LeRoy, Bayard, & Co., or one of his sons, Robert or William, Jr. See Scoville, *Old Merchants of NYC*, I, 162, 302; II, 57, 133, 168, 172–84, 320, 324.

10. Mrs. Harman and Miss Muss are not identified.

11. Samson V. S. Wilder (1780–1865), merchant, banker, and author of numerous religious tracts, who was actively promoting Greek independence in Paris at this time. He gave a Greek printing press to American missionaries for the publication of tracts for Greek soldiers and civilians. See Stephen A. Larrabee, *Hellas Observed: The American Experience in Greece, 1775–1865* (New York, 1957), p. 110.

12. This was probably the Société des Amis de la Morale Chrétienne et de la Paix, which the London Peace Society and American advocates of peace helped to form. See Merle Curti, *The American Peace Crusade, 1815–1860* (Durham, 1929), pp. 38–39.

13. WI's facetious name for Thomas Wentworth Storrow.

317. To Thomas Moore

[London, August? 1821]

My dear Moore,

I have been intending to write to you ever since I have been in London; and as good intentions are next to good acts I beg you will give me credit for them. I send this by a young gentleman[1] to whom I have also given a letter of introduction to you; and whom I introduced to Mrs Moore[2] when she was in London. He is a Young Countryman of mine, of excellent connexions and one of the most amiable and agreeable beings that I have ever known. His parents were English[3] and he was intended for the British Army, but took a decided turn for Painting. For a time he confined himself to portrait painting and shewed great talent, and a remarkable eye for colour. He was sent to Italy, from whence he found his way to England, where I first met with him about three years since, and have ever since made him my own.[4] He has taken up a beautiful department of his art, painting of cabinet pictures, and ⟨has⟩

the few paintings which he has produced have attracted great attention & been purchased by the first amateurs. I think he will take the lead in a little while, in the line of fancy subjects in elegant life. Of his companionable qualities you will be able to judge yourself, if you see as much of him as I wish you to do, both for his sake & your own. He is well bred, intelligent, lively and full of entertaining anecdote & observation — I have given him a letter to Villamil,[5] also. He sings and has good taste in music, and may be a pleasant acquaintance for Mrs Villamil.[6] I regret extremely that he is going away just now; for I have kept out of society since I have been in town & he has been one of my great resources, at companionable hours.

I was delighted to see Mrs. Moore in London, with those two lovely girls[7] which she had just brought fresh from the groves. Heavens what charming creatures they will be for rural parties in Kinneys garden of Eden.[8] I think I already see them under the "greenwood tree"[9] at the famous grotto. The two days that I passed in company with this travelling groupe have made a bright Spot in my dull sojourn in London; for to tell the truth ⟨my Lon [*unrecovered*]⟩ London appears terribly monotonous to me after residing in Paris. Had it not been for the half a dozen reasons that forever stand in the way of a mans doing what he likes, I should have put my knapsack on my back and have gone off at once with the party to Paris

I have regretted Paris ever since I left it;[10] and have wished myself back a thousand times. I have led a dogged life here, having shut myself up and kept clear of all Society; yet after all I have ⟨been⟩ not been able to do much, and feel as far ↑off↓ as ever from finishing any thing for the press.[11] "The Murray" is very anxious to have some thing more. He has grown amazing fond of me, and his fondness encreases with every edition.[12]

I presume you have read the Second part of Don Juan.[13] I am delighted with many parts of it, and I dont know but upon the whole I prefer it to the first part. ⟨Ther⟩ It does not dwell so much on ⟨its⟩ libidinous scenes; the licentiousness is less naked and offensive. There are some things in it that are exquisite. Murray has two Tragedies, Sardanapalus & The Foscari.[14] He does not seem to anticipate much effect from them; but I do not think Murray the best of Judges; for all that he is So fond of me.

⟨I presume⟩ I understand Kenney has written you some account of our journey to England. I enjoyed it very much, and had several very pleasant Scenes with Kenney; whom I have found more and more cause to like and respect, the more I have known him. I have not seen him for some time past, and presume that he is shut up, ↑and occupied in↓ the miserable labour of writing some pleasant farce.

I understand that you have been passing some time very pleasantly between Holland House and Lord Rancliffes,[15] during Mrs Moores absence. I am glad I made the visit at Lord Hollands[.][16] I was delighted with my dinner there; ⟨and very and⟩ and with the opportunity it gave me of seeing Lady H.[17] to advantage. She is a very different Woman from what I had imagined, with very Singular traits of character. ⟨She is quite different from what I⟩ ⟨expected.⟩ I think she is a woman that on further acquaintance I should like very much, and should not fear at all. I had imagined her very sarcastic, and I have a horror of sarcastic women, they have one so much at their mercy; unless a man will be brutal and cut back again; which I could no more do than I could strike a woman. She charmed me by the manner in which she spoke of poor Bonaparte—it shewed kind & generous feelings.

How does that little "lady bird" Miss Story come on. Is she as great a Blue Stocking as ever? I have her now before me, with that little considering cap on; and that little head hanging on one side, and that eye fixed on the table, musing on some piece of small mischief.—Ah well a day! I wish I was once more among you all; revelling among the groves of Belleveu.[18] What a pity it is that we can never know when we are precisely in the greenest spot of the landscape; and that we only find it out when we look back upon it. When I sit here in a dingy room of this dingy metropolis, and think of the times when I had but to mount a cuckoo and for fifteen sous be whisked out in Style to your cottage at La Butte, I wonder that I could keep for a day out of your company. I feel like an Englishman, returned to Port & Porter in London who looks back with sorrowing to the days when he revelled in Champaign at Paris, and wonders that he did not value it ten times as much, and get drunk on it ten times as often.

Farewell my dear Moore. Give my best regards to your good wife; I will not send a Stronger message, for fear of making you jealous. I have thought a great deal upon the matter and have come to the conclusion that she is about as good a woman as I know; and so God bless you both—and little Tom into the bargain

Yours ever
Washington Irving

MANUSCRIPT: NYPL—Seligman Collection.

S. T. Williams dates this letter as [July 1821?]. (See STW, I, 436, n. 56.) It was probably written in August, 1821, because WI refers to the second part of *Don Juan*, which appeared in August; it is probably before September 4 because WI mentions seeing Mrs. Thomas Moore, who was in England from July 24 to September 4, 1821. Moore himself came to England in late September, after his wife had returned to Paris. See *The Journal of Thomas Moore, 1818–1841*, ed. Peter Quennell (New York, 1964), pp. 60–62.

1. Probably Gilbert Stuart Newton, who went to France in September, 1821, and by November was painting a portrait of Moore. See Leslie, *Autobiographical Recollections,* pp. 236, 241, 243.

2. Elizabeth "Bessy" Dyke (ca. 1794–1865), an Irish actress and dancer, had married Moore on March 25, 1811.

3. After leaving Boston with the evacuation of the British troops in 1776, Henry Newton (d. 1803) became collector of British customs at Halifax, Nova Scotia. His wife Anne was the sister of Gilbert Stuart, the painter, who became the art instructor of Gilbert Stuart Newton.

4. WI alludes frequently to Newton in his letters written in the fall of 1820.

5. A Spaniard who rented a cottage near Moore's at Sèvres. See *The Letters of Thomas Moore,* ed. Wilfred S. Dowden (Oxford, 1964), II, 954.

6. Mrs. Villamil was an excellent singer. See *The Letters of Thomas Moore,* I, 493.

7. The daughters of the Reverend Mr. Belcher, vicar at Ashbourne, Derbyshire. See *The Letters of Thomas Moore,* II, 920.

8. James Kenney (1780–1849), a dramatist who adapted French plays for the English stage. By his "garden of Eden" WI was referring to the garden and fixtures overlooking the Chateau Bellerie, where Kenney was living. See STW, I, 436, n. 56; Findlay Muirhead and Marcel Monmarché, *Paris and Its Environs* (London, 1922), pp. 310–11.

9. *As You Like It,* II, v, 1.

10. WI, in the company of Kenney, left Paris on July 11, 1821. See STW, I, 203.

11. WI had been working intermittently on the sketches that were to make up *Bracebridge Hall.*

12. On June 29, 1821, Murray had written: "Draw upon me for a hundred pounds, of which I beg thy acceptance, and pray tell me how you are and what you are about. . . . There is a review of the Sketch Book in the Quarterly, which you will like." See PMI, II, 48.

13. Cantos III, IV, and V appeared on August 8. See Truman Guy Steffan, *Byron's Don Juan: The Making of a Masterpiece* (Austin, 1957), p. 36.

14. Murray published these plays, together with *Cain, A Mystery,* on December 11, 1821. See Truman Guy Steffan, *Lord Byron's Cain* (Austin, 1968), p. 6.

15. George Augustus Parkyns, second Baron Rancliffe (1785–1850).

16. Henry Richard Vassall Fox, third Baron Holland (1773–1840), member of the cabinet in 1807 and a scholar of modern and classical languages.

17. Elizabeth Vassall Webster, Lady Holland (1770–1845), who married Baron Holland in 1797, attracted attention with her fashionable gatherings of intellectuals, wits, and people of social and political prominence at her home in London. See Derek Hudson, *Holland House in Kensington* (London, 1967), passim.

18. Bellevue is a village on the bank of the Seine southwest of Paris, near Sèvres.

318. To Peter Irving

[September 6, 1821]

I received your letter giving an account of the steamboat concerns. I am sorry they are not more productive; not on my own account, but on yours, but I hope they will grow better and better. I do not calculate on any proceeds from that quarter, so that you need not feel solicitous for me; but only manage that you may do something for yourself.* *

I have a mass of writings by me which I am endeavoring to bring into shape for publication, but question whether I shall get any ready in time for the fall season. I have been kept in town by a correspondence with Payne, and an ineffectual attempt to get a little piece of his played at one or other of the theatres. I shall go to Birmingham in a few days and take Leslie with me. Had I been there, I would go off at once with Newton for France. I could finish my writings as well in France as here, and there is no comparison between the countries as a residence. London is terribly dull and monotonous after Paris.

When I have been a little while at Birmingham, unless I am detained by literary concerns, I shall return to Paris by the way of Havre; but if I should have a prospect of getting any thing ready for the press, I will do it first.

I have a variety of writings in hand, some I think superior to what I have already published; my only anxiety is to get them into shape and order.

* * * * *

I have fagged hard to get another work under way, as I felt that a great deal depended upon it, both as to reputation and profit. I feel my system a little affected now and then by these sedentary fits to which, until two or three years past, I have not been accustomed. When I get my present manuscript finished and off of hands, I think I will give myself holiday.

PUBLISHED: PMI, II, 53–54.

319. To Ebenezer Irving

[September 28, 1821]

I have been upwards of two months in England. I came over in hopes of getting some manuscript ready for the press this autumn, but ever since my arrival in England I have been so much out of health as to prevent my doing any thing of consequence with my pen. I have been troubled with bilious attacks, to which I had never before been subject. It is the consequence of being too much within doors, and not taking exercise enough. I am now dieting myself and taking medicine, and I trust I shall, with a little care and attention, get myself in fine order again. I am very anxious to get something into print, but find it next to impossible, in my present state of health, to do any thing material. Murray is also extremely desirous; and indeed the success of my former writings would ensure a run to any thing I should now bring forward. * * * * *

You have wished for an additional number of the Sketch Book, but

I have not been able to prepare one, being occupied with other writings. If you could clear off the stock of odd numbers that remain, even though it should be at considerable sacrifice, I wish you would do it. We could then publish a complete and corrected edition in two volumes.[1]

PUBLISHED: PMI, II, 57–58.

   1. C. S. Van Winkle printed a third edition of *The Sketch Book* in two volumes in 1822–1823, presumably binding together parts which appeared in these years. See Stanley T. Williams and Mary Allen Edge, *A Bibliography of the Writings of Washington Irving*, p. 103; Langfeld & Blackburn, *WI Bibliography*, p. 22.

320.   *To Charles R. Leslie*

Edgbaston Castle, Octr 7th. 1821.

My dear Leslie,

   I have been looking for a letter from you every day. Why dont you drop me a line? It would be particularly cheering just now. I have not been out of the house since you left here, having been much indisposed by a cold—I seem at the mercy of every breath of air that blows. I have had pains in my head, my face swoln, and yesterday passed the greater part of the day in bed; which is a very extraordinary thing for me. To day I feel better; but I am Sadly out of order; and what especially annoys me is that I See day after day & week after week passing away without being able to do any thing —

   The little folks lament your departure[1] extremely. George[2] has made his appearance in a new pair of Grimaldi Breeches,[3] with pockets full as deep as the former. To ballance his ball and marbles he has the opposite pocket fitted with a peg top and a prodigious quantity of dry pease; so that he can only lie comfortably on his back or his belly. The ↑three eldest↓ boys[4] kept the house in misery for two or three days by pea blowers, which they had bought at an enormous price of a Tinman. They at last broke the blowers, and George pocketed the peas. — He says he means to take care of them till his brothers come home at Christmas.

   Have you began any picture yet; or have you any immediately in ⟨view⟩ contemplation?

   ⟨I said⟩ I recd. a letter from Newton,[5] which I presume was forwarded from Mr Wms.[6] by your direction—Why did not you open it. It was dated the 15 Sept. He had arrived but two or three days—Had sailed up the Seine from Havre to Rouen with my Brother in the Steam Boat.[7] He had dined with Moore — Had passed a morning in the Louvre, where he met Wilkie;[8] and strolled the Gallery with him. He speaks in raptures of the Louvre. He says it strikes him in quite a different way from what it did when he was there before. He intended to go to work a day or two afterwards & expected to pass the greater part of his time there. He does not say when he will return; but I should think he must be about setting off at present.

Friday. Octr. 14th. I have walked out to day for the first time since You left here. I have been completely knocked up with serious ailments. My legs continue as much inflamed as ever, though I have been drenched with draughts and loaded to the very muzzle with pills. I have a physician to attend me; who attributes my complaints to an obstruction of the liver, and is proceeding accordingly — God send him success and me patience.

Have you seen Murray. When you see him you need not say where I am. I want to be quiet & not to be bothered ⟨by⟩ in any way. Tell him I am in a country doctors hands at Edgbaston[9] somewhere in Warwick-shire — I think that w[ill] [MS torn] puzzle any one, as Edgbaston has been built only within a year or two — Get me all the pleasant news you can, & then set down in the evening & scribble a letter; without minding points or fine turns. My Sister is very anxious to hear of you — You have quite won her heart, not so much by your merits, as by your attention to the children —

By the way the little girls have become very fond of the pencil since you were here: and are continually taking their Dolls likenesses.[10]

ADDRESSED: Charles R. Leslie Esqr. / Buckingham Place / Fitzroy Square / London.
  POSTMARKED: 13 OC 13 / 1821
MANUSCRIPT: NYPL—Berg Collection.   PUBLISHED: Leslie, *Autobiographical Recol-
  lections*, pp. 235–37 (in part); *Home Journal*, July 28, 1860, p. 3 (in part);
  PMI, II, 58–60 (in part).

1. Leslie had accompanied WI to Birmingham, visiting Oxford, Stratford-on-Avon, Warwick, and Kenilworth en route. WI's sketch of "The Stout Gentleman" grew out of experiences on this trip. See Leslie, *Autobiographical Recollections*, pp. 43–44. Leslie was a guest of the Van Warts before returning to London.

2. George Van Wart, a younger child of Henry and Sarah Van Wart.

3. Joseph Grimaldi (1779–1831), an English pantomimist, often played the role of a clown, dressed in large, baggy pants that were attached to his jacket. WI probably saw him perform at Covent Garden. See R. J. Broadbent, *A History of Pantomime* (New York, 1964), p. 169; David Mayer, III, *The Harlequin in His Element: English Pantomime, 1806–1836* (Cambridge, Mass., 1969), p. 63.

4. The older Van Wart boys were Henry, Irving, and William.

5. The manuscript of this letter has not been located. The postscript dated September 17 is printed in PMI, II, 60–61.

6. Probably Samuel Williams, American banker in London whose offices served as a clearing house for the mail of Americans in England.

7. At this time Peter Irving was involved in the steamboat venture in Le Havre with Reuben Beasley and Edward Church.

8. David Wilkie (1785–1841), whom WI met in Paris and Seville. Wilkie was to make a drawing of WI in Seville in 1828.

9. Edgbaston was a suburb a short distance southwest of Birmingham. Today it is completely developed and surrounded by outlying suburbs. Van Wart's house was near what is now 13 Calthorpe Road, Edgbaston, where the Birmingham Civic Society has erected a plaque in WI's honor. See Birmingham *Post*, June 8, 1957.

10. The manuscript ends here; the complimentary close and signature appear to have been cut away.

321. To Charles R. Leslie

Edgbaston. Octr. 25th. 1821.

My dear Leslie

I thank you a thousand times for your letter.[1] I had intended to have answered your preceding one before; but I was not in mood or condition to write, and had nothing to say worth writing. I am still in the hands of the Physician[2] — I have taken draughts and pills enough to kill a horse; yet I cannot determine whether I am not rather worse off than when I began. The inflamation has ⟨spread to⟩ encreased on my left leg, and appeared likewise on my right, and I have had biles[3] on my right hand that have nearly crippled me. ⟨These⟩ I have been obliged to keep within doors almost continually since you left here; and have grown so tender that I take cold if I venture out even in fine weather. ⟨I fear I shall have⟩ I fear it will take time and trouble to ferret this villainous malady out of my system and make me my own man again.

On one favourable day of my complaint, I rode over to Solihull[4] in a gig, to see the Boys.[5] I went in a gig with Van Wart and our worthy little friend George. I wished you with us a dozen times. You would have been delighted with the School house, and the village, and the beautiful old church and the surrounding landscape. It is all picture. When you come here again you must by all means visit the boys at School —

The young rogues are as hearty and happy as ever school boys were. They took us about their walks and the scenes of their enterprizes & expeditions. The neighbouring park, and several charming fields & green lanes. The morning ramble ended at the Shop of one of the best old women in the world, who sells cakes and tarts to all the Schoolboys. Here they all spoiled their dinners and nearly ruined their Papa; and George, with a citizenlike munificence, having eaten till he was fairly tired, distributed sundry cakes at the door, to some of the poor children of the village. I have no doubt that he has left a most excellent name behind him. The little girls[6] talk of you very often and wish you here. They always want to know whether you do not mention them in your letters; and beg that I will give their loves to you and Mrs Timson.[7] — I am babbling about nothing but children; but in truth, they are my chief company and amusement at present and I have little else to talk about.

I do not know any thing about your book of extracts. I laid it out for you before I left town & thought you took it with you one day. It may be among some books & papers that I left at Mr Perkins[8] — if so it must remain till I return to town. I cannot, at this moment, suggest any thing for your Christmas piece — I do not know your general plan. Is it to be a daylight piece — or an Evening round a Hall fire—? Is there no news of Newton? If I had thought he would remain so long at Paris I would have written to him. I am glad to hear that you are so snugly fixed with friend Powell[9] for the winter — though I should have been much better pleased to have heard that you were turned neck and heels into the street Recconcile it to yourself as you may, I shall ever look upon your present residence as a most serious detriment to you; and were you to lose six or even twelve months in looking for another I should think you a gainer upon the whole.

What prospects are there of the plates being finished for Knickerbocker and the Sketch Book?[10] When do you begin a large picture, and what subject do you attack first?[11] It is time that you had something unde[r] [*MS torn*] way. I must leave a space to reply to friend Peter, so fare[well] [*MS torn*] for the present — Mr & Mrs Van Wart desire to be particularly remembered to you. They often talk of you & hope you will pay them another visit. By the bye their house is an excellent central spot from which to make excursions when you are in quest of materials —

Yours ever,
WI.

My dear Powell,[12]

I have not much paper to spare, so must be brief. I am sorry you are treating Leslie as the drunken Irishman did his friend in the Kennel — he could not draw him out, but faith he'd come and lie by him. I beg you will exert your omniscience with respect to London, and find some better place where you may both move to in the Spring. If you live much longer where you are I shall expect to hear of your both being taken up by the Botherall of the parish and sent to the house of correction ⟨[*three unrecovered words*]⟩ for some Row in the neighbourhood. I was in hopes that Leslies eyes were gradually opening to the horrors of his situation; but your companionship confirms him in his evil ways, and I now look upon his case as desperate as that of any confirmed woman of the town. Did he know what a universal subject of sorrow & shaking of the head it is among his friends, I think he might yet be rescued from the clutches of the Bridgens.[13]

I am Scrawling this letter in bed & it is time to get up so farewell[.]
I hope your pupils in Sloane Street[14] improve under your tuition.

Yours truly
WI.

ADDRESSED: Charles R Leslie Esqr. / Buckingham Place / Fitzroy Square   POST-
MARKED: [Birmingham] / 25 OC 25 / 1821
MANUSCRIPT: NYPL–Berg Collection.   PUBLISHED: Leslie, *Autobiographical Recol-
lections*, pp. 239–40 (in part); PMI, II, 63–64 (in part).

1. Leslie's letter of October 22, 1821, to WI is printed in Leslie, *Autobiographical
Recollections*, pp. 237–38.

2. WI's physician was Dr. Samuel Dickenson (1769–1821), an eminent surgeon
of Birmingham, who died on November 9, 1821. See Aris's *Birmingham Gazette*,
November 12, 1821; and WI's letter of December 8, 1821, to Leslie.

3. Probably WI's spelling for "boils."

4. A village about 7½ miles southeast of Birmingham on the Stratford road.

5. The three older Van Wart boys were in boarding school at Solihull.

6. Marianne and Matilda Van Wart. Newton had written that he was "at present
painting the portraits of the two little girls." See Leslie, *Auobiographical Recollections*, p. 237.

7. Mrs. Timson is not identified.

8. Perkins was G. S. Newton's landlord in London. See Leslie, *Autobiographical
Recollections*, p. 220.

9. Peter Powell. See WI's letters of October 31, November 30, and December
19, 1820.

10. During the previous spring Leslie had written to WI, "Most of the drawings
from 'Knickerbocker' are with the engravers. There is little hope of their being
done however before Christmas" (April 2, 1821); "The plates for your works are
all in the hands of the engravers" (May 25, 1821). See Leslie, *Autobiographical
Recollections*, pp. 233, 235. WI, planning for new illustrated editions, had probably
forgotten Leslie's remarks.

11. On December 5 Leslie admitted that he had not yet started a large picture,
owing to the distracting demands on his time caused by his election to the Royal
Academy in November, 1821. See Leslie, *Autobiographical Recollections*, pp. 44, 246.

12. In his letter of October 22, Leslie describes his arrangement with Peter
Powell: "Powell and I commenced housekeeping a week ago. . . . During breakfast
Powell gives me a lesson in French. At five we both study carving. After tea I
teach him to draw the figures, and at odd times he instructs himself in German
and the pianoforte, and once a week he unfolds to me the mysteries of political
economy according to Cobbett" (Leslie, *Autobiographical Recollections*, p. 237).

13. The Bridgens were friends of the Irving-Leslie circle. Mrs. Bridgen is mentioned in a letter of August 20, 1821, from Leslie to Washington Allston. See
Flagg, *Washington Allston*, pp. 170–71.

14. Apparently Leslie and Powell, together with G. S. Newton, had been involved with some young ladies from Sloane Street socially or professionally. WI
alluded to Newton's Sloane Street romance in a letter of November 30, 1820. In
his letter of October 22 to WI, Leslie states that Powell was delivering weekly
lectures on perspectives in Sloane Street. See Leslie, *Autobiographical Recollections*,
pp. 224, 237. WI's observation to Powell may be construed as being archly ironical.

322.   To Ebenezer Irving

Birmingham, Nov. 1, 1821.

My Dear Brother:

I have but a few minutes to reply to your letter of the 8th October,[1] which I received this afternoon, but indeed I have little to say; the letter has taken away all spirit to write.

The calamities in poor sister Catherine's family[2] are dreadful. She has had her cup of bitterness filled to the brim, and I fear will suffer seriously in health by these repeated trials. They must have a severe effect upon her nerves, and I fear the composure and resignation which she expresses in her letter to Isaac are but the temporary effects of the stimulus which even severe affliction will sometimes give during the first stages of sudden misfortune. It is the after-sorrow that preys upon and undermines the health. I wish she could be got away from Johnstown for a time, and cheered by the society of friends and the variety of the city.

Brother William's situation,[3] I perceive, is hopeless. I had been persuading myself that there was reaction in his system, and that he might be induced to make a voyage to France in time to produce a complete renovation; but the tenor of all the letters from New York puts an end to all hopes of the kind. I cannot reconcile myself to the thought.

*   *   *   *   *

Give my most affectionate remembrances to Brother William. I would write to him, but cannot trust my feelings, whenever the thought of him comes over my mind, I feel my heart and eyes overflow.

PUBLISHED: PMI, II, 65–66.

1. This letter has not been located.
2. As WI indicates in his letter to Leslie on November 2, 1821, Catharine Paris lost two daughters suddenly. See also PMI, II, 65.
3. William Irving died of tuberculosis on November 9, 1821. See PMI, II, 65, and genealogy chart in STW, II, opposite 254.

323.   To Charles R. Leslie

Edgbaston, Nov 2d. 1821.

My dear Leslie

I wish to heaven you would drop me a line now & then and give me all the chit chat that you can, to cheer & interest me. It would be charity just now, when I am shut up from the world and suffering in health & spirits. I have dismal letters from America. My Sister has lost two of her daughters, by sudden & brief illness, the last her eldest a fine girl of seventeen — Their distresses have affected her own health. There are no hopes entertained of my Brother Williams recovery.[1] I received letters yesterday that gave these accounts and have quenched every spark. of animation or cheerfulness in me[.] I am still preyed upon by this tedious complaint, and find the eruptions on my legs worse than ever, while ⟨my⟩ the general tone of my system is relaxed and en-nervated by this nursing and confinement.

I have now given you reasons enough why I cannot write often to you; but why you should write occasionally to me. I have no news to give & no cheerful feelings to write from — you are in ⟨the abo⟩ London where every thing is news—and can tell me of your own occu-pations which are always interesting to me. I want you therefore to give me a mere gossipping letter. Tell me what news there is of Newton & when he is expected back. I am surprised at his remaining so long at Paris, since he says he is tired of it. What pictures are you about—what one do you intend to paint for the exhibition—Have you done any thing to Sir Roger—Do you intend to attack the Christmas piece & what is your plan—is it to be a fire side piece or not? Do you think of the Shakespeare subject.[2] One of these ought to be your choice in preference to the Heiress,[3] for your next subject I do not think the Heiress would be striking enough, at least it has never struck me as being calculated to bring out your powers in any force. How do the Bollmans? — Jones?[4] &c &c What is Luke[5] doing, has he any promising subject in hand?

I hope you and Peter[6] are getting comfortably through the Honey Moon, and find housekeeping pleasant. I only fear that your not being obliged to go out for your dinner will make you take less exercise than before,[7] and your health will suffer. My own case is a proof of how ⟨bil⟩ one really loses by over working ⟨and keeping too much⟩ ↑oneself↓ keeping too intent upon a sedentary occupation — I attribute all my present indisposition, which is losing me time, spirit, every thing, to two fits of close application, and neglect of all exercise, while I was at Paris.—I am convinced that he who devotes two hours each day to vigorous exercise, will eventually gain those two and a couple more into the bargain.[8]
[what] state are the [engrav]ings in, for the [ne]w Editions?[9]

ADDRESSED: Charles R. Leslie Esqr / Buckingham Place / Fitzroy Square /London
    POSTMARKED: [Birmingham?] / NOV 2 / D // 3 NO 3 / 1821
MANUSCRIPT: NYPL—Berg Collection.   PUBLISHED: Leslie, *Autobiographical Recol-lections*, pp. 240–41.

1. On the preceding day WI had received word about these family misfortunes in a letter of October 8 from his brother Ebenezer.
2. In his response of November 5, Leslie indicated that he had recently painted

two portraits (not specified) and "made a drawing from the 'Royal Poet' which I shall show Murray in a day or two." He did not respond to WI's other questions. See Leslie, *Autobiographical Recollections*, p. 242.

    3. Regarding this picture, Leslie responded that "Notwithstanding your objections to my 'Heiress,' I *must* paint it.... Don't dissuade me from painting the 'Heiress,' for you will only damp me and prevent my doing it as well as I otherwise should. I do not expect to make a very important picture of it, but it is a commission, and will not take me very long. Besides, I mean to make it pay well." Apparently, however, Leslie was dissuaded, for a note adds that "He *did* paint it, but not till 1845, for E. Bricknell, Esq., in whose gallery at Hearne Hill, it now hangs." See Leslie, *Autobiographical Recollections*, p. 242.

    4. These are acquaintances mentioned in earlier letters.

    5. William Willes, called "Father Luke" by WI and Leslie.

    6. Peter Powell. See WI's letter of October 25, 1821. After "Peter" is an asterisk. Running vertically in the left margin opposite the word in another hand is "°Peter Powell."

    7. Leslie protested in his letter of November 5 that "I do not find that I take less exercise than I used to." See Leslie, *Autobiographical Recollections*, p. 242.

    8. The MS ends here, without closing, the signature having been clipped off.

    9. These words are written sideways along the left margin of the third and last MS page. Several words were apparently clipped off along with the signature.

324. To Charles R. Leslie

Edgbaston — Novr. 8th. 1821

My dear Leslie

I congratulate you with all my soul on your admission to the Royal Academy,[1] of which friend Luke has just given me the tidings. It is no more than what you have long deserved; but it is not always that a man gets what he deserves.

I did not mean to undervalue your study of the Heiress, only in comparison with the other Subjects you had in contemplation. The others are uncommonly *Rich and Striking* and fitted to draw out your peculiar powers, in delineating character, costume &c &c—I have no doubt but you will make a very excellent thing of the Heiress — and the landscape that you sketched ⟨in Derb⟩ at Haddon Hall[2] will enrich it & give it architectural interest and picturesque associations. By the bye, whenever you want to gather a little information about Haddon Hall you will find a description of it, with a plate or two, in the 6th. vol of the Archaeologia[3]—⟨by the bye⟩ you will find that work a mine of antiquarian knowledge, and curious facts—as to customs, architecture, dress &c — It is in many quarto vols. by the antiquarian Society. In the 9th & 10th vols of the "Censura Literaria" are elaborate disquisitions on Hawking & Hunting by Hazlewood[4] —

Your letter of the 5th.[5] was most acceptable & gratifying — and I thank you for ⟨the⟩ a vast deal of amusement afforded me by the description of the "Milling School."[6]

I think Willis has pitched upon a famous good thing in his contemplated picture. Depend upon it he will ⟨do⟩ ↑gain↓ himself both honour & profit by it. If he succeeds, as I am convinced he will, I would advise him to make a companion to it, in a view of Paris, from one of the ⟨Hills in the distance⟩ Neighbouring Hills —

As to medical advices I have had the advice of ↑one of↓ the best surgeons here, a Skillful man. I fear however I shall be a long time getting rid of this complaint. It seems to gain ground in spite of all efforts to dislodge it. It is unaccompanied by pain, but it is irksome & troublesome, and the confinement it necessarily causes, is at times depressing —

The Citizen[7] has been unwell from a cold, but is getting better — He has lately become something of a theologian, and has taken a great notion to talk about the deity, and asks very many odd questions. I heard him instructing his little sisters the other day on the subject and assuring them, among other things, that nothing could hurt God — "a horse could not bite him." He tells me long stories every evening as we lie on the Sopha together. They however, all turn upon the same things — the adventures of two little girls — who ⟨wh⟩ walk in a woods, where they are chased by a "Savage Cart horse," until they run into a gentlemans house, where they have a fine supper, and in setting out the supper table the Citizen generally exhausts his fancy and the ⟨intervening⟩ residue of his short evening.

All the children talk about you continually, and Marianne begs her Mamma, when she writes to you to tell you that if you dont come to Birmingham she'll come after you to London —

I must conclude or I shall lose the post. Give my thanks to Willis for his kind letter. I will answer it soon. He talks something of an intention on the part of Newton to come here. I need not say how rejoiced I should be to see him — God bless you my dear Boy

Yours ever

WI.

ADDRESSED: Charles R Leslie Esqr. R. A. / Buckingham Place / Fitzroy Square / London— POSTMARKED: BIRMINGHAM / NOV 9/ [D?] // 10 NO 10 / 1821 MANUSCRIPT: NYPL—Berg Collection. PUBLISHED: Leslie, *Autobiographical Recollections,* pp. 244–45 (in part).

1. Leslie had just been made an associate of the Royal Academy. See Leslie, *Autobiographical Recollections,* p. 44.

2. In September, 1821, WI and Leslie had visited Haddon Hall, owned by the duke of Rutland, on the banks of the River Wye in Derbyshire.

3. *Archaeologia,* Volume VI, was published by the Society of Antiquaries of

London in 1782. Edward King's "Sequel to the Observations on Ancient Castles" covers pages 231–375, of which pages 346–59 deal with Haddon Hall. Plates XLIX and L relate to this building.

4. *Censura Literaria* 10, no. 39 (1809), pp. 225–65 contains Samuel Egerton Brydges's discussion of *A Collection of Writings on Hunting in Verse and Prose, with Notes and Cohering Commentary* by Joseph Haslewood.

5. Printed in Leslie's *Autobiographical Recollections*, pp. 242–44.

6. WI is apparently referring to Leslie's description of several sparring matches at Five Court which involved the milling groups of partisans supporting the various fighters.

7. WI's facetious name for his young nephew, George Van Wart. A marginal note in another hand states "One of his nephews by marriage."

325. To Charles R. Leslie

Edgbaston, Decr. 8th. 1821.

My dear Leslie,

I feel most sensibly the kindness of your letter,[1] which however is just like yourself, full of goodness.

I should feel tempted to come to London at once, and to try how I could make out at Newtons Quarters, which upon the whole I think would best suit me; but at present it is out of my power. I have changed my Physician and the present one has put me on an entirely different course. The applications that he has prescribed for my legs have produced such an effect that I cannot walk without pain and difficulty and have to lie down, or else to sit with my feet in a horizontal position the whole time. They are in a wretched plight. To travel in such a situation is out of the question. I hope some good effect will result from this severe treatment, and I shall seize the first favourable turn in my complaint to come to town, though I doubt whether I shall get there before christmas. The Surgeon[2] that first prescribed for me was one that had tended my Sisters family ever since they have been here: He was a man of talents in his profession. The poor fellow died rather suddenly and I was afterwards in the care of his partner — a young surgeon,[3] who however pursued pretty nearly the same course with me that had been prescribed — My present Physician is Dr John Johnstone,[4] who is reckoned one of the first Physicians in Birmingham and who is unquestionably a man of abilities and learned in his profession. So that I believe I have very good advice. I have however an obstinate complaint to deal with, and fear I shall have much more trouble before I get clear of it. Every thing is done here to make me comfortable; my good sister almost makes a child of me.

I hope to hear of your getting under way with another Painting soon; and trust that the good spirits and good health you have picked up will enable you to despatch the thing with spirit & expedition. You do not say how the engravings are coming on for the new Editions of my works, ⟨or⟩ nor whether you have shewn Murray your last Sketch.

Give my hearty thanks to our worthy friend Powell for his kind offer of his room. I long to be among you all once more — I think a few tea drinkings with the old set would be of great service to me — But the physicians have got hold of me and I am no longer my own man. I have kept clear of them all my life till now, and now they have got me in their clutches I fear they will make "worms meat" of me before they let me go again.

God bless you my dear Boy—

[*Signature cut out*]

Sunday, 9th. I received last night your letter of the 7th.[5] and have again to thank you for ⟨the⟩ ⟨very⟩ your goodness in taking such trouble on my account. My present predicament renders it impossible to say when I shall be able to come to town; and if I were to come I fear Martins[6] would be too far out of the way. I want something more central. I think I wont trouble Newton until I can look out for some other place if I find I cannot be comfortably accommodated there. I had a dismal day yesterday. I could Scarcely put a foot to the ground & lay from two oclock until eleven at night without Stirring from the Sopha. I am now writing in bed before day light; and am in hopes from the looks of my unlucky limbs that I have passed through a kind of fiery ordeal, and will be more comfortable. Let me hear from you now and then, for your letters are better than medicine to me —How does Newton come on. I suppose he has nearly finished his Lovers Quarrels[7] — and is ready for some thing else. He must have his mind in good tone for Composition after his visit to Paris. I will write to him when next I write. I feel very deeply his kindness with respect to his rooms. Indeed I feel towards you all more than it is necessary to express —

Mr & Mrs Van Wart desire to be very particularly remembered to you. You are often the theme of conversation with them and the children and I can assure you that ⟨your⟩ a visit from you at any time would be quite a jubilee in the household —

ADDRESSED: Charles R. Leslie Esqr / 8. Buckingham Place / Fitzroy Sqr. / London—
    POSTMARKED: DEC 9 / D / 10 DE 1[0] / 1821
MANUSCRIPT: NYPL—Berg Collection.   PUBLISHED: Leslie, *Autobiographical Recol-lections*, pp. 246–47 (in part).

    1. Dated December 5, 1821. See Leslie, *Autobiographical Recollections*, pp. 245–46.
    2. Dr. Samuel Dickenson. See WI's letter of October 25, 1821.
    3. This may be Dr. George Freer, whose office was located on New Street as was Dr. Dickenson's. See *The Triennial Directory of Birmingham* ... (Birmingham, 1821), pp. 38, 48.

4. Dr. John Johnston had an office in Temple Row. See *The Commercial Directory for 1818–19–20* ... (Manchester, 1818), p. 49.

5. This letter has not been located.

6. WI is probably referring to the lodgings of John Martin (1789–1854), a painter whose *Belshazzar's Feast* was exhibited at the British Institution in 1821. He was a friend of Leslie, Newton, and their circle.

7. WI must have forgotten that Leslie had written to him on December 3, 1820, that Newton's *The Lover's Quarrel* from Molière's *Le Dépit Amoureux* had been finished for some time. This picture was engraved for the *Literary Souvenir* of 1826. See Leslie, *Autobiographical Recollections*, p. 228; *Bryan's Dictionary of Painters and Engravers*, IV, 17.

326.   To Mrs. Thomas W. Storrow

Birmingham. Decr. 10th. 1821.

My dear Mrs Storrow,

I am affraid you will be all out of patience with me for not answering your delightful little family pacquet of last summer. I have been waiting for an opportunity of sending a pacquet in return, but am so out of the way of opportunities that I must give it up, and write to you by post. I will answer the letters of the dear little girls by the first private hand that presents. Indeed I have been in no mood for letter writing for a long time past. I have been sadly out of health ever since my return to England. I felt out of order when in London without knowing what ailed me. I made a little tour about the beginning of September, and came to my Sisters at Birmingham; where I have been laid up ever since — I was troubled with what I considered a slight bilious attack; and had an inflammation on the skin of my left foot—The inflammation increased, accompanied by feverishness and I was induced to take medical advice. When a man once gets into the Doctors hands it is a long while before he gets out again. They have made a complete job ⟨of⟩ and I may say *Job* of me; excepting that I have not his patience. The physician attributed my indisposition to an obstruction of the liver and proceeded accordingly. I have taken medicine enough to set up a country apothecary, but to no effect — The inflammation extended to both legs and became intolerable. The confinement I underwent & the medicines I took rendered me tender & liable to colds; and I have had a sad feverish time of it—I have changed my Physician within a few days and am under a totally different course of treatment. It is severe in its effects as yet — and I cannot stand or move without pain & difficulty. I hope however this is an ordeal that will be attended with salutary consequences; and will enable me to get about again

It is fortunate that I am at my Sisters, where I am well nursed, and have that tender and affectionate treatment which is more efficacious with me than all the medicine in the world. I often wish that you and my sister lived near each other: I know no two beings that would suit each other better. She is one of the most amiable, excellent beings in the world. She has a fine family of children; among whom I am a most important personage from my invaluable talent at telling nonsensical stories. There are two charming little girls, one nearly seven the other about 8. They now and then invite some of their little friends to see them ⟨and⟩ with the promise that "Uncle shall tell Some of his stories." It would amuse you to see me, with my crippled limbs stretched on a Sopha, Surrounded by a little fairy circle, all listening with breathless attention to some harum-Scarum tale that sets all sense and probability at defiance.

I was very much delighted with the letters from the dear little girls.[1] Susans account of domestic concerns and of the School was very amusing and very charmingly written. She will be a good letter writer. And my dear little Minny deserves my thanks for her pleasant little note. Nor must I forget that *brave Homme* Charles, whose transcript of the telegraphic intelligence was highly gratifying. How much I wish to see you all again — I think we should have fine times now that the Bon Homme has treated the young Ladies to a Piano. I little thought when I parted with you in Paris that I should be at this time passing a dismal sick winter in England. I shall get out of this country as soon as possible for I think the climate of the continent will have a good effect in restoring my health.

I have had affecting news from America which has in some measure ⟨an assisted to⟩ contributed to encrease the virulence of my malady. There have been two or three deaths among my relatives, and the most distressing is that of my eldest Brother—one who was like a father to the family, and whose worth in every respect was such as to make his loss one of the dismallest events that ever happened to me.

By the time this letter reaches you the young folks will be home for the Holydays. Give my love to them all and tell them not to forget me. I wish they would write to me again without waiting for my reply. I give them my word that I will reply; and their letters would be extremely gratifying. I want another letter from Susan about her school, and to hear how she and Minny make out in their classes.

Give my hearty regards to the Bon Homme — and to Pere Wilder & family and believe me truly & affectionately: your friend

Washington Irving.

ADDRESSED: à Madame / Madame Storrow / Rue Thevenot / (Rue Petit Carreau) / à Paris   POSTMARKED: 272 / F 21 / D/ PAID / 11DE11 / 1821 // BIRMINGHAM / DEC 10 / Decembre / 11 / 1821
MANUSCRIPT: Harvard.   PUBLISHED: WIS, pp. 7–10.

1. These letters have not been located.

327. To Ebenezer Irving

London, Jan. 29, 1822.

My Dear Brother:

By the packet from Liverpool which brings this letter I forward you a parcel, containing the first volume of Bracebridge Hall, or The Humourists, a Medley in two volumes.[1] I had hoped to have sent both volumes, but I have not been able to get the second volume ready in time for this opportunity, though I have tried until the last moment. You will receive it, however, by the next opportunity, and very probably before you can have made the necessary arrangements for printing. At any rate, put the first volume to press *immediately* and publish it *as soon as possible*, with or without the second volume. As it is not like a novel, but rather a connected series of tales and essays, it is of no great importance that they should be published together; but it is of the greatest importance that some part of the work should appear as early as possible, to give me some chance of securing copyright. I shall have to put it to press here in a very short time, as the season is advancing, and my publisher is very impatient; besides, the public has been expecting something from me for some time past, and it will not do to let expectation get too high. If the work is not got out very soon therefore in America, there will be a chance of an English copy getting out beforehand, and thus throwing me at the mercy of American publishers. Should the number of copies make any material difference in the time of getting out the work, you had better let the first edition be rather small;[2] and put another to press the moment I furnish you with proof sheets of the English edition, in which there will doubtless be many alterations, as I have not had time to revise some parts of the work sufficiently, and am apt to make alterations to the last moment.[3]

The work had better be printed in duodecimo; and to save time in binding, let the volumes be put up in lettered covers like the Sketch Book. The second edition can be got up in better style. The first volume runs, as near as I can guess, between 340 and 350 pages of the American edition of the Sketch Book. The second volume will be about the same size. You can make your estimates accordingly. Put what price you think proper. I do not care about its being a very high one. *I wish, expressly, Moses Thomas to have the preference over every other publisher.*[4] I impress this upon you, and beg you to attend to it as earnestly as if I had written three sheets full on the subject. Whatever may have been his embarrassments and consequent want of punctuality, he is one who shewed a disposition to serve me, and who did serve me in the time of my necessity, and I should despise myself could I for a moment forget it.

Let him have the work on better terms than other publishers, and do
not be deterred by the risk of loss.

I have not had time to page the work, but must beg you to do it.
I have given a table of contents in the order in which the papers are to
be put, and have numbered each with a pencil for *your* direction. These
numbers are *not* to be printed over the papers. Perhaps it will be best
to advertise the work as in the press, to secure orders in time.

I have no time left to say any thing further. I have fagged until the
last moment, and am now fit to go to bed. My health is still unrestored.
This work has kept me from getting well, and my indisposition on the
other hand has retarded the work. I have now been about five weeks
in London, and have only once been out of doors, about a month since,
and that made me worse.

Published: PMI, II, 71–73.

1. Apparently this was a manuscript copy with which WI hoped to start production of the American edition.

2. The first American edition was issued in 1000 copies on May 21, 1822. See
Langfeld & Blackburn, *WI Bibliography*, p. 24.

3. WI followed the plan he outlined here, issuing the altered first English
edition as the basis for the second American edition. See Langfeld & Blackburn,
WI Bibliography, p. 24.

4. Since Moses Thomas of Philadelphia was not in a position to undertake the
publication, C. S. Van Winkle of 101 Greenwich Street in New York City published
the work.

328. *To Thomas W. Storrow*

57. Russell Square. London/Feby 1st. 1822.

My dear Storrow,

I have suffered an enormous time to elapse without answering your
very kind letter;[1] and what is worse I have no other excuse to offer but
that I have postponed replying to that, as I have to a number of other
letters from my friends in the steady determination of writing the next
day, and the next, until the lapse of time has at length frightened me
into exertion

I thank you and all your amiable household for the anxiety you
express about my health, and your wish for me to come to paris. My
health still continues bad. I managed to get to town the day after
Christmas and have been quartered ever since in the hospitable mansion
of my friends the Messrs Hoffman[2] of Baltimore; where I have every
kindness and attention shewn me. I have been confined to the house
ever since my arrival until these two days past; when I have felt so
much better as to drive out and take a little fresh air in the middle of

the day—but my malady has seemed to return with renewed virulence today, and I feel in consequence quite downhearted. There seems to be no conquering it—I have had the advice of several skillful Physicians & Surgeons and have pursued a course of diet and taken the most powerful alterative medicines for several months but all in vain.

I should like extremely to be able to come to Paris for I think the change of air would do me good and the change of scene still more. But I cannot leave London for the present. I must remain here for a time to try and do something in the literary way; in which I have been sadly retarded by my indisposition. Indeed I question whether I could bear the journey in my present state of health.

I wish Mrs Storrow would write me a letter and tell me all about the little household in Rue Thevenot. I should be sure of getting from her all that domestic chit chat which is so interesting and delightful, and which women only can write. I want to know how Susan and Minny that[3] that *brave Homme* Charles come on. And how all our little circle of intimates are employing and amusing themselves this winter— I would give any thing to be stretched on that Sopha you talk of, and to have the "historical Society" collected round me. I could tell them *Such Stories!* Since I left them I have fallen in with another old woman and have got from her a whole budget of tales. If ever I escape from the Doctors hands and get safe to Paris again I shall have some wonderful histories to relate when we young folk gather together in the little parlour. I speak with confidence of my new stock of stories for I have tried them upon several convocations of the most experienced little story mongers in all Birmingham & have come off with unbounded applause.

Does Susan ⟨get⟩ go to school still or has Mamma put a large bunch of Keys to her girdle and made her House-Keeper. I thought she was getting a little of a matronly housekeeping air before I left Paris. As to Minny I suppose she as usual is studying hard, and preparing to carry off some of the best prizes at the next concourse. As soon as I get well enough I mean to go to the Admiralty and consult the telegraph which I understand is in active correspondence with that in Mont Martre, and I make no doubt, can procure me all the news of the School—

How do our good friends the Wilders—I suppose the Wednesday evenings are kept up as usual. I look to have this letter answered by Mrs Storrow, and beg she will give me all the news she can of all our circle of acquaintance, down to Petite and the cat.

Give my most affectionate regards to Mrs Storrow — Susan, Minny & Charles, and remember me particularly to the Wilders

I am my dear Storrow/Very truly yours
W Irving

ADDRESSED: a Monsieur. / Monsr. Thomas W Storrow / Rue Thevenot / (Pres Rue
    Petit Carreau) / à Paris. POSTMARKED: F 22 / 218 / Fevrier 8 1822
MANUSCRIPT: Harvard. PUBLISHED: WIS, pp. 10–12.

    1. This letter has not been located.

    2. Hoffman was WI's "friend and countryman," "from whom he had received
repeated and urgent invitations" and with whom "he was most comfortably
accommodated for more than six weeks, experiencing from Mr. Hoffman and his
family the most hospitable and delicate attentions, and being made to feel completely at home." See PMI, II, 70.

    3. STW transcribes this word as "thot," apparently assuming that WI was using
a shortened form of "thought." However the conformation of the vowel in this
word is the same as in the succeeding one, so it is rendered "that," even though WI
may have intended "thot." Perhaps he intended to write "and that" but anticipated
and repeated the "that."

329. *To Henry Colburn*

Russell Square,[1] Feby 12th. 1822

Dear Sir,

    A friend of mine in Paris[2] is occupied in the translation of a new work,
of which he writes as follows, under date of January 24th. "Yesterday
a new work of *L'Abbé de Pradt* in two volumes, entitled like the former,
"Europe and America,"[3] a sort of political and historical retrospect of
1821 came out here, and is greatly sought after. I glancd through it
last night, it treats of all the high events of the past year; and it appears
to me likely to have a great sale; for the only two articles I read, viz,
England and Napoleon are powerful and most interesting. I shall begin
a translation of it on Monday and shall get through about 30 pages ⟨in⟩
a day. There are (say) 800 pages 8. vo. in all." According to this statement he must have translated the greater part by this time ⟨and the
whole⟩ which could be obtained by return of post if written for and the
residue in the course of a very few days.

    Should you think proper to make any proposals for the work ↑Mr
Miller↓ is authorized to receive them, and to make a definite arrangement. From my knowledge of the abilities of the translator, I think I
can safely say the work will be ⟨rendered⟩ well executed. He has a
ready & rapid pen and commands a pure, fluent and graceful english
Style. He speaks of other works, "rich in interest," which have recently
appeared, and which he has thoughts of translating should he be encouraged by the Success of this; and I think you would find him a
valuable correspondent — At present I am not authorized to mention his
name; though it would of course be made known to you hereafter—

    In giving this reccommendation I do it frankly & conscientiously; for no motives of private friendship should ever induce me to mislead a man of business in matters of this kind.

I am Sir, with very sincere regard

Yours truly
Washington Irving

ADDRESSED: Henry Colburn Esqr. / Conduit Street
MANUSCRIPT: Va.–Barrett.

Henry Colburn (d. 1855), who founded several magazines, including the *New Monthly Magazine, Literary Gazette,* and *Court Journal,* made a fortune as a publisher and a journalist.

1. In another hand below "Russell Square" is written "(London)."
2. John Howard Payne. See WI's letter of March 17, 1822, for other allusions to this project.
3. WI uses double quotation marks for the title. Dominique de Fourt de Pradt (1759–1837) was sent to Poland as ambassador in 1812. His earlier book which WI refers to is *L'Europe et l'Amérique depuis le congrès d'Aix-la-Chapelle* (Paris, 1821); the second is *L'Europe et l'Amérique en 1821* (Paris, 1822). See *La Grand Encyclopédie,* XXVII, 534; *Catalogue Général des livres imprimés de la Bibliothèque Nationale,* CXLII.

330. To Susan Storrow

London. Feby 28th. 1822.

My dear little lady,

I have owed you a letter for a long time and fancy you have given up the debt as a bad one; if so you will be the better pleased at having it paid at last—and thats the best excuse I can offer for the delay. I have ⟨been⟩ wished myself back to Paris a thousand times since I left there; for I have been out of health ever since I ⟨have⟩ arrived in England. My time has been passed amost entirely at home, I have seen very little therefore of gaiety, and look back with many a Sigh to the balls and routs we use to have in *Rue Thevenot.*

It is true I had some little amusement of the kind when at Birmingham, where my nieces introduced me to some young ladies of their acquaintance, and we used to have a quadrille now and then; but they do not dance as well as the young ladies in France, and indeed some of them had not as yet begun dancing lessons.

I arrived here just in time for the Coronation;[1] which was a very grand sight. There was a magnificent procession of all the nobility in their robes and jewels and coronets; and the judges in their gowns and wigs; and all the other functionaries in their proper costumes. All the world was there; holyday was given to all the Schools; the Servants were permitted to look out of the garret windows in the streets where the procession did not pass; in those where it did, every window was hired out for several golden guineas; You have no idea what sums of money were expended ⟨on the occasion⟩ ↑By the nobility and gentry;↓ even my Landlady[2] had an old silk gown made quite new for the occasion, and her two daughters had red morocco shoes and coronation ribbands on their hats. The King looked amazing grand; dressed in a huge robe of ermine and velvet, with a splendid crown, and long ringlets hanging down his back. I was quite surprized to see the old gentleman with such a fine head of hair, until I was told it was all false; but that it was the rule for the King to have long flowing ringlets on his coronation day; because the kings wore them in old times. He had so much clothes on that ⟨they⟩ he had to employ Six lads to help him carry it. He is considered a very great king by some of his subjects, particularly those in office, who have the best chance of knowing him; others speak very scandalously of him; for my part as I am a stranger in the country I take no part with either side; but this I will say I do not think him so great a King as Louis the 18th.[3] by at least a hundred weight. It is certain, however, that before he grew very fat he was one of the most graceful Kings of the day, and even now it is said there is no monarch can equal him for the grace with which he takes off his travelling cap[4]—

But these are dangerous matters to be meddling with — keep all this part of my letter to yourself — the lord knows what would become of us both, if it were found we were corresponding about politics.

I hope when the gentleman returns who takes this letter (Mr Loomis) that you will let me hear from you in reply; and let me know how every thing goes on at school and at home; how you and the young lady with a good heart make out; and whether you have gained any more prizes.

Has our friend Petite given any *Soirées* this winter, or are her parties confined merely to the Summer.

I had thought long before this to have been back at Paris; but here I am still and here I must remain a little longer, and then I fear I shall have to make for Aix La Chapelle or some other watering place to endeavour to regain my health. However, some day or other we will I trust be all assembled together again, and have some more parties either at Montmorenci, or in the Rue Thevenot — and the Sooner the better, say I.

I must now finish my letter that I may have time to write one to my dear little Minny before Mr Loomis calls. You must let her know all the news contained in this excepting what relates to politics — as she is too young yet to have her head perplexed with such matters.

Adieu my dear Susan — keep as good a girl as you were when I left you and you will be as good as need be.

Your affectionate friend
Washington Irving

ADDRESSED: Miss Susan Storrow / Paris.
MANUSCRIPT: Harvard.   PUBLISHED: WIS, pp. 13–15.

1. George IV (1762–1830) was crowned at Westminster Abbey on July 19, 1821.

2. WI's landlady has not been identified.

3. Louis XVIII (1755–1824) was restored to the French throne in 1814. At that time he "had commanding features and an agreeable voice, but though only fifty-nine years of age was already an infirm old man. His unwieldy bulk, and the frequent attacks of gout from which he suffered, rendered him almost incapable of moving without assistance." See Major John R. Hall, *The Bourbon Restoration* (London, 1909), p. 7.

4. George IV was described at his coronation: "He held in his unwieldy body with a broad belt, he hid the lower part of his face in a large black neckcloth, he covered his uniform with tags and frogging, embroidery and orders. He was trying to conceal his age, his ill-health, his apprehension, his perpetual emotional insecurity. And yet, somehow, he contrived to charm, as he had always done." See Joanna Richardson, *George IV, A Portrait*, p. 216.

331.   To Charles Wiley

London, March 6th 1822.

My dear Sir,

I have mislaid your letter[1] on the subject of "the Spy," which prevents my replying to the particulars of it, though I may to the general purport. I received your letter at a time when I was confined to my room ⟨that⟩ by an indisposition that has afflicted me for many months, and has rendered me incapable of attending to any business. I did not see Mr Murray until some time afterwards, when he informed me that he had shewn the novel to Mr Gifford, who, however, did not give a sufficiently favourable report to induce him to publish it. I procured the Novel from him and offered it to Mr Colburn. He told me he had published the previous novel[2] by the same author, and had been promised to have the publication of this one; a copy of which he had been expecting. It was now, he said, too late, as another Bookseller (Mr Whitaker)[3] has got hold of a copy and put it to press—and in fact the work appeared a few days afterwards.

I regret extremely that the work had not been sent to Colburn in the first instance. He is a fashionable publisher; liberal in his prices and anxious to get american works of merit; whereas Murray is precisely the worst man that an American work can be sent to. He has the offer of ↑almost↓ every thing that is choice, and is extremely fastidious and he is surrounded by literary advisers, who are prejudiced against any thing american. I have more than once been requested to offer american works to him such as Jameydon[?],[4] Mr Tudors work[5] &c but he has always declined them after causing a considerable loss of time ⟨and⟩

by neglecting ⟨to⟩ or forgetting to answer my applications, I happening
to be absent from London at the time.

The best course for Authors in America to take would be to send
⟨their works in⟩ Manuscript copies of their works to Mr John Miller
Bookseller Fleet Street & request him to dispose of them to the best
advantage. He is a worthy & obliging man & to be depended upon in
every way. He is in the American business, and disposed to do every
thing to serve Americans A book should not be sent printed, if the
author wishes to get a price for it, as the Booksellers know they cannot
[MS torn] a copyright & may be printed upon by other publisher[s]

I have not heard what sale the work has had. It has been out but
a very few days and I have been confined to the house by indisposition.
I have read it with great interest, and think it ought to have success
on both sides of the water

With best wishes I am my dear Si[r]–/Very truly yours

Washington Irving

ADDRESSED: Mr Wiley/ Bookseller / Wall Street / New York
MANUSCRIPT: Fenimore Cooper Family Papers.   PUBLISHED: *Correspondence of
James Fenimore Cooper*, I, 89–90.

Charles Wiley (1782–1826) started a bookstore in 1807 which developed into
a publishing firm by 1814. His store was a gathering place for the literati of New
York City. See Charles A. Madison, *Book Publishing in America* (New York,
1966), pp. 15–16.

1. This letter has not been located. It is mentioned but not printed in PMI,
II, 73.
2. *Precaution*, published in 1820.
3. George B. Whittaker (1793–1847), a London bookseller who later published
Mary Russell Mitford and Anthony Trollope.
4. Probably *Yamoyden* by Robert C. Sands and James W. Eastburn. See WI's
letter of October 31, 1820.
5. William Tudor (1779–1830), founder and first editor of the *North American
Review*, who had published *Letters on the Eastern States* (1820) and *Miscellanies*
(1821).

332. To John Howard Payne

No 35 Maddox Street. Hanover Square/London, March 17th. 1822.

My dear Payne,

It is a long while since I have heard from you. Miller shewed me a
letter from you some short time since, which related to a translation you
were making of a work of De Pradts. I wrote a letter on the subject
to Colburn,[1] but was sorry to find that he did not consider a work of
DiPradts likely to pay for republication — As I see by the papers the
work is advertised by some other publisher[.][2] I hope you have been

able to make a bargain elsewhere. I have been out of health ever since I wrote to you last summer. I went ⟨the⟩ into the country on a tour, but was laid up at my Sisters at Birmingham until after Christmas, when I got up to town but was confined to the house here for above a couple of months. I have lately been able to get abroad again & am now in a fair way of recovery. It has deranged all my plans and put ⟨them⟩ me sadly behind hand in my literary concerns. Since I have been able to get out of doors I have made acquaintance with some of the Booksellers; ⟨I⟩ and particularly with Taylor & Hessey,[3] the proprieters of the London Magazine. These are the persons to whom Hazlitt promised me to speak about you last summer—I find from them that he never mentioned the subject. I have talked with them twice about you. They would be glad to receive communications from you. Their terms are ten guineas a sheet for any thing admitted into the Magazine; but they will give more, in proportion to the merits of the writings; and I really believe they may be depended upon for fair candid judgement & honourable dealing. Their wish is to make their Magazine good, & they feel that to do so they must pay for good writing. You can see ⟨sp⟩ their work at Gallgnani[4] and I am much mistaken in my judgement of your style & abilities if you cannot write in a better vien than most of the correspondents to that work. I told them that you proposed to give notices of the public amusements of Paris & accounts of the new pieces; dished up ⟨into⟩ ↑in↓ a more narrative & picturesque manner than the usual jogtrot critical notices — In fact your true way is to ⟨send make little stories⟩ ↑tell↓ the stories of any striking piece, in something of a storytelling manner. I would reccommend to you also to make articles out of any new work, instead of translating the whole work. Thus, for instance, with respect to the Abby de Pradts work, you might have taken out all that struck your fancy relative to Bonaparte; mixed it up with personal anecdotes that you might have gathered concerning him at Paris, and so have made at small expence of thought or labour a very curious article that would have been highly acceptable to one of the Magazines. I should think for such articles you might get fifteen guineas a sheet.

There is another work about starting here, to be published quarterly, by Andrews[5] in Bond Street, to be called *The Album*.[6] Andrews has been very anxious to get me to edit it but I totally declined. He wishes me to write for it; but I would make no promise, indeed I have other plans that will engross me. I spoke to him of you, and made such a representation that he expressed a great ⟨disposition⟩ ↑wish↓ to have you among his correspondents. I think he may be likely to answer your purpose even better than Taylor & Hessey. His work will not have so crowded a page & of course an authors matter will go mu[ch] [*MS torn*] further. He will have much fashionable custom & support & so w[ill] [*MS torn*] be enabled to pay well. He comes ⟨last⟩ into the field when several magazines have got the start of him; he is therefore at a loss for writers, and has his corps of correspondents entirely to form. I think therefore you may make yourself very valuable in his eyes. I told him you could furnish him with the literary & Dramatic news of Paris; and miscellaneous articles of a literary & amusing nature. ⟨and⟩

I think, therefore, that one or other, or both, of these periodical works will furnish you with ready money for any current articles you may get up — ⟨and⟩ they seem both inclined to be liberal; but of course they wait to have a specimin of what You can do, before they make terms. ⟨If you think Th⟩ Periodical works of this kind have lately taken a very important hand in English literature & are daily engrossing more & more, the pens of miscellaneous writers of talent. They enable authors to get cash down for fugitive & careless writing that would otherwise lay unpublished in their portfolios. I shall be in London for some few weeks longer & should be glad to hear from you & to be of Service to you if in my power; though I apprehend my few forays last summer will give you but a bad opinion of my efficiency. I can only say that I most honestly have the will. When I am not here you had best send any Mss. to Miller & let him make the bargain with Taylor & Hessey or Andrews — mentioning the circumstance of the Mss: having been forwarded at my request. For it is the disposition of both those publishers to be on very friendly terms with me & my name may be of service until your own gets it due weight with them. When you have once become known to each other & established a correspondence, you will be able to send your Mss. to them direct.

I want to see you embarked in Miscellaneous literature; for I think you will get more credit & eventually more profit from it than from the Drama. I think you have an ease & gracefulness in your style which will ⟨put⟩ be enough to make your way. The public here know nothing of you as a miscellaneous writer; and indeed you seem yourself for many years to have ⟨abandoned⟩ lost all idea of the kind; and to have forgotten that it was your early talents as an essayist that first gained you notoriety

Do try your hand again my dear Payne, and dont depend so exclusively on the drama for reputation & support. I again repeat that the late encrease and improvement of periodical Works, has opened a new field of profit to authors, especially to authors who are not currently known in literature.

Yours truly
W Irving.

ADDRESSED: A Monsieur / Monsr. J. H. Payne / No 25 Rue du Columbier / Hotel de la Louisiane / Faubourg St Germaine / Paris   POSTMARKED: [unrecovered]

22 / Mars? 29 1822   DOCKETED: au pa Suis No [*unrecovered*] /No 136 — /
[*unrecovered*]
MANUSCRIPT: Va.–Barrett.

1. See WI's letter of February 12, 1822.
2. G. Cowie and Company.
3. See WI's letter of August 1, 1821.
4. Galignani's bookstore in Paris was the center for books published in English, even as it is today.
5. John Andrews was a gourmand and bibliophile who frequented Murray's drawing room. See WIHM, p. 44.
6. Andrews launched *The Album* in April, 1822, with F. B. B. St. Leger as editor. It continued until April, 1825.

332a. To ———

[March 23, 1822]

Learned men are fond of being admired for things in which they do not excel; but are apt to grow indifferent to the real sources of their celebrity. Cuvier[1] is impatient of ⟨being⟩ talking about natural history and comparative anatomy, and delights in political conversation. He says he only studied natural history for his amusement, but that political economy is his forte — He is a very indifferent politician and the best comparative anatomist in the world.

Washington Irving
London, March 23/1822.

MANUSCRIPT: Newberry Library.
From this single sheet it is not possible to ascertain whether it is the last page of a letter or merely a quotation which WI prepared for an autograph seeker.

1. Baron Georges Léopold Chrétien Frédéric Dagobert Cuvier (1769–1832) is remembered for *Leçons d'anatomie comparée* (1801–1805), *L'Anatomie des mollusques* (1816), and *La Règne animal distribué d'après son organisation* (1817), works which served as the foundation of the discipline of comparative anatomy.

333. To Peter Irving

35 Maddox Street, Hanover Square/London, March 24, 1822.

My Dear Brother:
I have been looking for a letter from you for some time past. I suppose the steamboat must have resumed its voyages during the present month, and I want to know how it operates and whether it holds out better prospects.
I have sold my new work to Murray, and it is in the press.[1] It will form two volumes nearly about the size of the Sketch Book, to be entitled Bracebridge Hall, or the Humourists, being of a miscellaneous

nature like the Sketch Book, but connected by a set of characters and incidents. Murray gives me a thousand guineas for it, in his notes at three and six months.[2] My friends thought I ought to have had more for it, but I am content. I am glad to find that Gifford thinks it superior to the Sketch Book, as to composition, and calculated to increase my reputation.

As the steamboat may continue as dry as the bull that the Irishman undertook to milk,[3] I send you a couple of hundred pounds to keep you in pocket money until the boat begins to pay better. I beg you won't be squeamish about the thing. If you don't want the money, it may as well lie idle in your hands as in mine; and if you do want it, why you must get it from some source or other, and I don't know any one more unexceptionable than from one who has been a great part of his life under such pecuniary obligations to you. But the best way is not to say any thing pro or con about the matter, but let it be as it should be, a matter of course between us. I hope and trust to get more writings ready for the press long before I shall exhaust my funds in Europe, independent of what will be accumulating in America.

PUBLISHED: PMI, II, 77–78.

1. The English edition of *Bracebridge Hall* appeared on May 23, 1822. See Langfeld & Blackburn, *WI Bibliography*, p. 23.
2. Other accounts of the amount of Murray's payment are given in PMI, II, 76–77 and STW (I, 207). For a convenient summary of the matter, see WIHM, pp. 41–42.
3. Not identified.

334.   To Miss Rebecca Bond

[April 6, 1822][1]

My dear Madam,

It will give me very great pleasure to meet Sir Robert & Lady Liston,[2] and if you please I will breakfast with you on Tuesday, as on Monday I am engaged. Should that day not suit let me know and I will come any other that you may appoint — If I receive no message from you to the contrary I shall consider Tuesday as the day fixed.

With compliments to Miss Travis/believe me very truly/
Yours friend &c
Washington Irving

Maddox Street/Saturday. April 6.

ADDRESSED: Miss Bond / Orchard Street / Portman Square   DOCKETED: 1822 / Washington Irving / to Miss Rebecca Bond
MANUSCRIPT: National Library of Scotland.

Miss Rebecca Bond has not been identified, but it is apparent from the tone of WI's note that she is someone with whom he was on familiar terms.

1. The year, ascertained by the perpetual calendar, is corroborated by WI's address on Maddox Street at this time.

2. Sir Robert Liston (1742–1836), a diplomat who served in Madrid, Stockholm, Constantinople, and Washington, was an accomplished linguist in ten languages. He married Henrietta Marchant (d. 1828) of Jamaica in 1796.

335. To ———

[London, May 11, 1822]

My dear Sir,

It will give me great pleasure to meet the party at the Exhibition[1] on Thursday next. I shall be waiting for them there at 11 oclock.

Present my best regards to your family and believe me

Very truly yours,
Washington Irving

Maddox Street/May 11th.

MANUSCRIPT: Va.–Barrett.

WI lived on Maddox Street between March and July of 1822, so this letter can be dated as 1822.

1. Probably the exhibition of John Martin's painting of *Belshazzar's Feast*, which was on display at 80½ Pall Mall. See London *Times*, May 11, 1822.

336. To Lady Holland

Maddox Street. June 3d. 1822.

I cannot but feel extremely flattered by the favourable opinion which your Ladyship is so kind to express of my late work; more especially as I was very much guided and encouraged in the plan and executions of it by some remarks on the Sketch Book that incidentally fell from you when I had the pleasure of seeing you at Paris. Believe me there is no tribunal of taste for which I have a more implicit deference than that which exists at Holland house,[1] and there is no person in whose good opinion I shall ever feel more proud to enjoy a place than in that of your Ladyship.

I regret extremely that prior engagements prevent my having the Honor of dining at Holland House on Thursday next —

With great respect/I am your Ladyships/Most obliged & faithful Servt

Washington Irving

MANUSCRIPT: Va.–Barrett.

1. Holland House, a Tudor mansion in Kensington Road, was a center of fashionable London society. For details, see Derek Hudson, *Holland House in Kensington* (London, 1967).

337. To Richard Rush

[June 5, 1822][1]

My dear Sir,

I shall be very happy to accompany Mrs Rush[2] to the Marchioness of Staffords,[3] and will make a point of being at home tomorrow at two for that purpose. I mention this hour, as you specify it in your note; and I should like to make the visit as early as would be convenient to Mrs Rush as I have an appointment with a gentleman in the city at four oclock *precisely*—With my best compliments to Mrs Rush I am

Dear Sir/very respectfully/Yours &c
Washington Irving

Maddox Street./Wednesday. June 5th.

DOCKETED: Mr ↑Washington↓ Irving. — / ⟨Mr Irving B⟩ / June 5. 1822. / To go
    with / Mrs R to the / Marchioness of / Stafford's.
MANUSCRIPT: Princeton.

1. The year was established by the perpetual calendar and by WI's residence on Maddox Street.

2. Mrs. Rush, the former Catherine E. Murray of Annapolis, Maryland, was married on August 29, 1809, to Richard Rush, United States minister to Great Britain.

3. Elizabeth, countess of Sutherland, who had married George Granville Leveson-Gower, second marquis of Stafford, on September 4, 1785, was a skilled water colorist and a leader in literary and artistic circles.

338. To Richard Rush

[June 8, 1822][1]

My dear Sir,

I regret that I was absent from home when your Servant called with the messages[2] yesterday; ⟨&⟩ I did not receive them until late at night—I have sent an acceptance to Chorland[3] house this morning & shall feel much obliged to you if you will call for me on Tuesday as you proposed.

With great respect/Very truly yours
Washington Irving

Maddox Street./Saturday June 8th.

ADDRESSED: His Excellency / Richard Rush / &c &c &c / 51 Baker Street /
    Portman Square
MANUSCRIPT: Princeton.

1. The date was determined by the perpetual calendar and by WI's address in Maddox Street.

2. These messages have not been located.

3. Not identified.

339. *To John Howard Payne*

London, June 8th. 1822.

My dear Payne:

I have suffered an enormous time to elapse without writing to you;[1] but in truth I am behindhand with all my friends and have suffered such an amount of epistolary debts to accumulate that I am almost in despair of paying even the interest. Miller has no doubt told you long since of the success or rather want of success with Elliston. I called on him twice without seeing him, and being unwell & lame at the time I had to commit the matter to Miller. Elliston did not pretend to dispute your claims but plead poverty and incapacity to pay. The last time I saw him he told me he had been paying you off in weekly sums to Mrs. Glover,[2] so I suppose the debt is liquidated before this. He appeared to be rather sore at your having dunned him through others; & thought it was rather exposing the nakedness of the Land. I do not think it worth your while to deal with him hereafter. As Covent Garden is in new hands you might be able to get your pieces brought out there; & Charles Kemble who is at the head of the management is a gentleman and a man to be depended upon.

The manuscript[3] you sent me I could not get any thing for at the London Magazines to which I applied. They thought the stories had not sufficient interest & point & would prefer something not so merely translation.

Hessey one of the proprietors of the London Mag: would like to have something from you entirely original & would then judge how much he could afford to give per sheet. I could do nothing with the plan you proposed about republishing lithographic plates of Bonapartes history with accompanying details. There has been so much published about Bonaparte that the public is rather sated with the subject; & the expense of the prints &c. would not be paid, by the additional sale.

I have hoped to have received from you the theatrical essay which you promised to send by Kenney;[4] but Kenney has never arrived and whether or no the manuscript is sleeping in his pocket at Paris I cannot say. I should think you might do something very good in that line. I want to see you *swimming without corks* — throwing by translations and reconstructions and writing something from your own brain. A set of essays, tales &c. taken from your own dramatic experience & invention would be more likely to succeed than any thing you could translate.

I have published a couple of volumes lately, which seem to be well received. The getting them ready for the press has been a grievous task for me, as I have been out of health ever since my return to England. The confinement of body & tasking of mind necessary for composition have retarded my recovery and I am still subject to lameness & to inflammation in my legs. I shall leave London in the course of a week or two, for a watering place on the continent probably Aix La Chappelle, and shall see you in Paris towards the latter part of the autumn.

Before I go out of town I will have a talk with Charles Kemble about you, as I am on very good terms with him, and I will endeavour to secure a favourable reception for any thing you may send to his theatre.

With best wishes I am my dear Payne

Yours truly
W. Irving

P.S. I have this moment heard that Stephen Price is just arrived in London—22 days from n. york. Of course on a recruiting expedition[5] — Price means to visit Paris soon.

ADDRESSED: a monsieur / Monsr. John H Payne / ⟨No 25 Rue de la Colombier Faubourg St Germaine / Paris⟩ / [readdressed in another hand] [unrecovered] du Salon Literaire / No 156 [Palais?] Royal / Paris
MANUSCRIPT: Columbia. PUBLISHED: Scribner's Magazine 48 (October, 1910), 469–70.

1. WI's last letter to Payne was written on March 17, 1822.
2. Mrs. Julia Betterton Glover had played in Payne's Brutus.
3. Probably Abbé de Pradt's Europe and America, which WI discussed in his letter of February 12, 1822, to Henry Colburn.
4. James Kenney, an English dramatist with whom Payne had collaborated on The Portfolio (1817).
5. Stephen Price of the Park Theater had also sought English actors for the American stage the previous summer. See WI's letter to Payne, August 21, 1821.

340. To Henry Brevoort

London, June 11th. 1822.

My dear Brevoort,

It is a long time since I have heard from you, ⟨the⟩ Your visits to Charleston[1] seem always to interrupt our correspondence. For my part, between ill health; ⟨the omnipoten⟩ hard scribbling to make up for lost time and get another work into the press; and the many engagements and interruptions that consume ⟨tim⟩ my time and distract my mind since my return to England, I find it impossible to keep up punctual correspondences, & and am now overwhelmed with epistolary debts. About three weeks since I launched a new work ⟨upon⟩ which you have doubtless seen long since in America. The English edition has many alterations & additions, as I got into better health & spirits after I sent my Mss: to America, and was enabled to improve the work while printing. It seems to give satisfaction here, and I am nearly killed with kindness, for I have not a moment to myself, and am so fatigued with company and dinner & evening parties, that I find it impossible to regain ⟨my⟩ ↑a↓ perfect state of health, but am still troubled with lameness & inflammation in the ancles, the lingering of my tedious malady. I shall, however, soon leave this scene of bustle & dissapation & go to a watering place on the continent (aix La Chapelle) where I hope thoroughly to reinstate my health. Within these two months past I have given myself up to society more than I have at any time since I have been in Europe, having for the last four or five years been very much shut up, & at home. I was determined this spring to give myself a holiday & make use of the opportunity presented me of seeing fashionable life. I have done this to a considerable degree, though I have suffered much drawback on account of the indifferent state of my health.

The success of my writings ha⟨ve⟩s given me ready access to all kinds of Society. And I have ⟨seen⟩ been the rounds of routs, dinners, operas, balls & blue stocking ⟨?evening?⟩ coteries. I have been much pleased with those parties in which rank & fashion and talent are blended: and where you find the most distinguished people of the day in various departments of literature art & science brought into familiar communion with leading statesmen and ancient nobility. By the bye I had many inquiries made after you by Sir James Mackintosh,[2] who retains a most friendly reccollection of you. ⟨fashionable⟩

John Randolph[3] is here, and has attracted much attention—He has been sought after by people of the first distinction. I have met him repeatedly in company, and his excentricity of appearance & manners makes him the more current and interesting. For in high life here, they are always eager after every thing strange and peculiar. There is a vast deal, too, of the old school in Randolphs manners, ⟨and⟩ the turn of his thoughts and the style of his conversation, which seems to please very much. Young Hammond[4] was also much liked here and I only regretted that he did not stay a little longer—He is one of the ⟨most⟩ best bred young men that I have met with from our country, and one who I think will be distinguished in the Society of New York for good manners & good sense. There seems a strong disposition to be pleased with any thing american just now, among the better classes in England; and a great curiosity awakened respecting our literature &c. Among other interesting acquaintances that I have made is Mrs Siddons.[5] She is now near Seventy and yet a magnificent looking woman. It is surprising how little time has been able to impair the dignity of her carriage or the noble expression of her countenance. I heard her read the part of Constance[6] at her own house one evening; and I think it the greatest dramatic treat I have had for a longtime past.

I shall leave this letter open, that I may add some thing more before I send it off. I have many to write to, and must portion the brief time I have, among several letters. I have written to my Brother E. I. to settle the balance I am owing to you; though the debt of gratitude & affection that I owe you for all your kindness & friendship I can never repay; and indeed I feel a gratification in being in this respect your debtor. I hope you will keep a friendly eye upon my brother E. I. who poor fellow, has again to toil his way up hill in life, with a numerous family to weigh him down.[7] Do him all the kind offices in your power & believe me I shall ever feel them more sensibly than if they were done to myself. I shall leave London in two or three weeks for the continent & so soon as I have reinstated my health I shall make a hasty tour, that I have been contemplating for several years past—When that is accomplished, I shall have one grand obstacle removed ⟨that⟩ to my return home; and will endeavour to arrange my concerns so as once more to see my native land; which is daily becoming dearer & dearer to my imagination, as ⟨time gives it all⟩ the lapse of time gives it all the charms of distance—

June 30th. I had thought to have been off to the continent before this; but yet here I am—However I am resolved to go in the course of a week. I have made so many very interesting and agreeable acquaintances of late that I find it hard to get away from them. Indeed I have got on sociable terms with most of the men of letters & the leading artists of the day, that are in London and am continually meeting with curious & entertaining characters

A few.days since I was made acquainted with old Lady Jones, widow of Sir William Jones.[8] I had no idea of her being yet alive. She is lively & cheerful & in full possession of her faculties & animal spirits. She is the daughter of the Bishop of St. Asaph[9] who voted against the American War. She remembers Dr Franklin who was a friend of her fathers; and relates two or three anecdotes of him. She has always been a very strong friend of America.

I lately passed a few days at the Country seat of Mr Thomas Hope, author of Anastasius.[10] You have read his work I presume; which I think one of the most extraordinary productions of the day—He is an extremely interesting man. Somewhat shy & reserved to Strangers but full of knowledge & talent, and most amiable in his manners, when you become acquainted with him. He has written a vast deal, that he has never published; and is now busy upon a Metaphysical work. He has voluminous travels in manuscript, and is a masterly draughtsman. It is a thousand pities that he cannot be persuaded to publish more. His travels must be full of interesting incident & observation.

Rogers[11] the poet returned not long since from the Continent and I breakfast occasionally with him, & meet Crabbe[12] & others of his literary friends. He has one of the completest & most elegant little Bachelor establishments that I have ever seen. It is as neat, & elegant, and finished, and small, as his own principal poem.

July 1st. I have scrawled this letter at intervals; for I have many to write to, & am so distracted by engagements & occupied by making preparations to go to the continent, that I have hardly a moment of leisure time, or quiet thought[.] Matthews,[13] the comedian is coming out to make a tour in America, which I have no doubt will be a successful one. His powers of entertainment are wonderful. By his talents at imitation he in a manner raises the dead and makes them walk & talk for your amusement; for his specimens of Tate Wilkinson—Macklin, Wilkes[14] &c &c are among the best of his imitations. He is a very correct, gentlemanlike man in private life, and at times the life of a dinner table by his specimens of characters of the day. I shall give him letters to America & among others to yourself.

I have written a letter to that honest tar Jack Nicholson[15] & am ashamed that I have not done so before—but really I have no time to write often—and find myself more and more getting into habits of procrastination.

I wish you would make interest, through James Renwick—to get the College ⟨[unrecovered] to by⟩ to employ John Miller Bookseller Fleet Street, as a literary agent in London. He is a most deserving & meritorious little man—indefatigable in the discharge of any commission entrusted to him; and moderate & conscientious in his charges. He devotes himself almost exclusively to American business. I would strongly reccommend him to yourself should you at any time want books from London—He could hunt up any rare works; and I believe you would save money by employing him.

Give my Sincere regards to Mrs Brevoort and remember me affectionately to the Renwicks and to your fathers family

I am my dear Brevoort,/Ever most truly yours

Washington Irving

ADDRESSED: Henry Brevoort Junr. Esq / New York. / Meteor   DOCKETED: London [June 11] 1822 / Washington Irving

MANUSCRIPT: NYPL–Seligman Collection.   PUBLISHED: LIB, II, 172–81; PMI, II, 80–82, 86–88, 107–8 (in part).

1. Mrs. Brevoort, the former Laura Carson, was a native of Charleston, South Carolina. On October 9, 1821, Brevoort had written to WI: "We are to take our departure for Charleston . . . on the 21st inst. . . . My wife & sons will remain with Mrs Carson until May" (LBI, I, 150).

2. Sir James Mackintosh (1765–1832), doctor, lawyer, philosopher, and author, was a member of Parliament at this time. Brevoort had probably met him on his visit to London a decade earlier.

3. John Randolph, the Virginia politician whom WI had known for many years, had taken a leave of absence from the House of Representatives in March, 1822, to try to recover his health. He had arrived in England on April 6. See Hugh A. Garland, *The Life of John Randolph of Roanoke* (New York, 1850), p. 171.

4. Not identified.

5. Mrs. Sarah Siddons, a member of the Kemble family of actors, had a successful stage career which extended from 1775 to 1812. After her retirement she gave large parties at her house on Upper Baker Street and readings from Shakespeare.

6. One of Mrs. Siddons's greatest roles was that of Constance in Shakespeare's *King John.*

7. By this time Ebenezer Irving had had twelve children, eleven living, with the newest arrival, Washington Ebenezer, having been born on March 14, 1822.

8. Lady Jones, the former Anna Maria Shipley, had married Sir William Jones, linguist and orientalist, in 1783.

9. Jonathan Shipley (1714–1788), a liberal clergyman who was canon of Christ Church and dean of Winchester before becoming bishop of St. Asaph in 1769.

10. Thomas Hope (1770?–1831), a writer and collector who was a member of the Royal Society and the Society of Antiquaries, had brought out *Household Furniture and Interior Decoration* in 1807 and *Costume of the Ancients* in 1809. *Anastasius: or, Memoirs of a Greek, Written at the Close of the Eighteenth Century* was published in three volumes by John Murray in 1819.

11. Samuel Rogers (1763–1855), poet and connoisseur of art whose house on St. James Street was the scene of gatherings of eminent social and literary figures. His famous breakfasts were the talk of London. His reputation as a poet rested on his *Pleasures of Memory* (1792), which had gone to fifteen editions by 1806.

12. George Crabbe (1754–1832), a poet and cleric whose best known writings were *The Village* (1783), *The Parish Register* (1807), and *The Borough* (1810). He was on a visit to London when WI met him.

13. Charles Mathews (1776–1835), a character actor of nervous temperament who played at the Haymarket, Covent Garden, and Drury Lane Theaters. He appeared in Baltimore in September, 1822, and at the Park Theater in New York in November, 1822. See T. Allston Brown, *History of the American Stage* (New York, 1870), p. 238.

14. Tate Wilkinson (1739–1803) was an eccentric actor and provincial stage manager. Charles Macklin (1700–1797) was an Irish actor well known for his portrayal of Shylock. John Wilkes (1727–1797), a member of Parliament and Lord Chamberlain from December, 1779, until his death, was a man with irregular features and a squint which lent themselves to Mathews' imitations. In March, 1822, Mathews presented *Mr. Mathews at Home* at the Theatre Royal, English Opera House, Strand, a performance which featured vignettes from his youth, including

interviews with Wilkes, Macklin, and Wilkinson. See Mrs. Ann Mathews, *A Continuation of the Memoirs of Charles Mathews, Comedian* (Philadelphia, 1839), I, 165–66.

15. This letter has not been located.

341. To Mr. and Mrs. Richard Rush

[June 14, 1822][1]

Mr Washington Irving will have the Honor of dining with Mr & Mrs Rush on Sunday the 16th.

Maddox Street/—Friday June 14th. [1822]

ADDRESSED: Mrs Rush / Baker Street / 51.
MANUSCRIPT: Princeton.

1. The date was determined by the perpetual calendar.

342. To Catharine Paris

The Deepdene, Surry,/June 21st. 1822.

My dear Sister;

I have for a long time been intending to write to you, but I find there are few good intentions more liable to be procrastinated than those about letter writing. And indeed I have now adays, so much to do with my pen in literary occupations that I find it difficult to keep up any thing like correspondence. It is with the greatest pleasure that I learnt by my last letters from home that you were again restored to health and to composure of mind. You have had Severe trials, my dear Sister, which make all the misfortunes which others of us have undergone shrink to nothing in comparison. It has excited both my pride and admiration to hear how well you have sustained your heavy calamities; shewing a strength of mind ⟨superior?⟩ that was not to be broken down even by the feebleness & infirmities of the body. But I do not intend to dwell upon melancholy themes: the past is full of sorrows for us all, let us hope that we are to have better times to compensate us for what we have undergone. It has been a load of sadness taken off of my mind that Ebenezer has at length extricated himself from his difficulties and is again launched in business.[1] With his steady & industrious habits and his excellent character he cannot but do well, and I trust he has friends about him whose disposition to assist him will be equal to their means. Van Wart is doing excellent business[2] and his prospects are extremely promising — our dear Sister though delicate in her frame is once more in good health. She has an uncommonly fine family of children who are all growing up charmingly and are the pride and joy of their mother.

Poor Sally — her character is strengthened and improved by the trials she has undergone and I feel more and more cause to love her, every time I visit her. I cannot express to you how deeply I have felt her affectionate kindness to me during a long and painful indisposition that I suffered at her house. The unobstrusive, the quiet, yet ⟨the steady⟩ the watchful and unremitting attention with which she administered to all my ailments and consulted all my habits and wishes. And then the fond interest she takes in my literary Success — I really believe she felt as anxious about the fate of my new work, as she did about her husbands business.

I am still very much troubled by a lingering cutaneous complaint, which I have long been endeavouring to cure, and had almost succeeded; but I have been so much occupied in preparing my new work for the press, and since its publication have been So harrassed by society; and by continual invitations out, which I found it in vain to withstand; that my recovery has been impeded; and I am frequently quite lame with the inflammation of my ancles. Literary success, if it has its charms has likewise its disadvantages: and in so huge a place as London, where there is such a world of idle people living at their ease, with nothing to consult but amusement & society, the least notoriety takes away from a man all command of his time or person; unless he becomes absolutely rude & churlish. If I remain any time in England when I return from the Continent, I shall pass it almost entirely in the country; where I can be more to myself and have my mind undistracted by visitors & invitations. I cannot, however, but feel sensible of the extreme kindness & hospitality that is lavished on me by all ranks; though it is apt to be a little too engrossing. I am now writing from a Country Seat in a beautiful part of the country where I am passing a few days. It is the residence of Mr Thomas Hope, one of the richest & most extraordinary men in England — not more famous for his wealth & magnificence than for being the author of *Anastasius*; a work of great merit & curious character. His wife, the Hon. Mrs Hope,[3] is one of the loveliest women in the Kingdom, and one of the reigning deities of fashion. Their country Seat is furnished in a style of taste & magnificence of which I can give you no idea — Yet with all this they are delightfully frank, simple and unpretending in their manners — especially in their country retreat; which is the true place to see English people to advantage. There are several persons on a visit ⟨to them⟩ here, besides myself, and time passes away very pleasantly. Shall I give you an idea of English fashionable country⟨life⟩↑hours↓ in a few words — I am sure it will make you stare, as contrasted with your own quiet sober hours—

We breakfast at ten, excepting such as choose to breakfast in their own rooms; which is at every ones option — The Breakfast is tea, coffee,

Eggs, hot rolls, bread &c—. After Breakfast the company lounge about either in their room—the library — the drawing room, grounds or garden—At one Oclock, the bell rings again for *Lunch* (I E the Luncheon) this is a meal of some importance — There are several hot dishes; such as poultry — light dishes of cutlets &c — with cold meats — tarts, fruits, wines &c—after Lunch there are several hours to get rid of by reading, lounging about the appartments — retiring to your room to read, write &c — Strolling about the grounds, driving or riding about the neighborhood — at Half past Six the bell rings to give warning that dinner is at hand; when the company retire to their rooms to dress for dinner — as dinner is a meal at which the fashionable world in England always appear in full dress. At seven Oclock the second dinner bell rings, when the company assemble in the drawing room and in a little while the dinner is announced as served, when all repair to the dining room. After the Ladies retire from table & the gentlemen have sat some time over their wine (which they do not ⟨sit⟩ by any means so long at as formerly) coffee is anounced, when the gentlemen join the ladies in the drawing room, or library which are adjoining, and take coffee — this is generally between nine and ten — tea is served up shortly after, at which one of the ladies presides, and the evening is passed in conversation; music; and lively little games which the English have learnt from the french, and which task the ingenuity and call out the invention & agreeable talents of the company. Some Cool beverage such as lemonade &c is brought in towards the latter part of the evening and about twelve oclock, the company breaks up for the night

Such is the course of a days avocations at the Deepdene; and it is a pretty fair specimen of the general mode of passing a day at a fashionable English Country Seat at this season. In the sporting seasons, especially during the winter months the mode of life is very different. as then the gentlemen are very much occupied in hunting; shooting &c but just now there is no sport of the kind and indeed, no sportsmen in the party at the Deepdene

June 28th. I was betrayed into a gossipping account of my sojourn in the country a few days since; but perhaps it will be amusing to you — So I will let it go. I have just received your letter of the 13th. of May.[4] It was as unlooked for as it was most welcome— and I have wept over it, my dear Sister, like a very child. Not that there is any thing positively unhappy in it; but I have grown very soft and weakhearted on some points, and am easily affected on them — As to poor Isaacs[5] unlucky outset; it is one of those little rubs which a young man must look for on his outset in life & which are wholesome, ina[s]- [*MS torn*] much as they put him on his guard against greater evils. I am glad to hear of Ebenezers recovery and that he is again started in the world. You talk of *misgivings*— you must not yield to them. We have as great a right to anticipate good as evil; for one happens in just as haphazard a way as the other. Ebenr begins the world again with friends more able and willing to help him than when he first started. As to his family; some of his boys will in a very few years be able to take care of themselves and to help him; and then his family will be an advantage instead of an incumbrance. I have great confidence in his doing well; and I trust that we have all weathered the roughest times and are gradually getting into smooth water again

You cannot think how much you have gratified me by expressing the satisfaction derived from my writings & ↑from↓ the public sentiments expressed about them. One of the purest pleasures which literary Success can yield me, is the satisfaction it may give my relatives My life has been, for the greater part, a desultory & unprofitable one, owing ↑perhaps↓ to the great ascendancy of my imagination, over the more valuable faculties of the mind — I have often felt humiliated & distressed by the idea that I must be an ⟨source⟩↑object↓ of censure ⟨to⟩ among my friends; you may judge then how heartfelt is my gratification at finding you & my dear Sister Sally expressing a pride in what I have done & what others say of me. Believe me, my dear Sister, the fondest wish of my heart will be gratified, ⟨I⟩ if I can act so as to enjoy the affection of my relatives while living & to leave a name that may be cherished by the family, when my poor wandering life is at an end. If I do not act up to this wish more fully, it is because that [despite all] [*MS torn*] my good intentions, I am yet a weak irregular being, full of imperfections.

⟨Give my⟩ I hear that Jane Ann[6] has called one of her children after me. Tell her I feel very deeply this mark of her affection. I hope she & her husband are living happily & prosperously. Give my love to your husband and family, and also to Richard Dodge and his household. I hope it will not be long my dear Sister before I shall have the happiness of seeing you all once more.

In the meantime be assured of my constant remembrance and tender affection.

God bless you/Your Brother
Washington Irving

MANUSCRIPT: Yale.   PUBLISHED: PMI, II, 83–85 (in part).

1. Ebenezer's business was located on Pearl Street, first at No. 142 and later at No. 145. See *New York City Directory* for 1821 and for 1822–1823.

2. In 1821 Henry Van Wart was listed in the directory as a merchant; apparently he had recovered completely following his bankruptcy in 1818. See *Triennial Directory of Birmingham* (Birmingham, 1821), p. 135.

3. Louisa Beresford, daughter of the archbishop of Tuam who married Thomas Hope in 1806.

4. This letter has not been located.

5. Isaac Paris (b. April 19, 1799) was the son of Daniel and Catharine Paris. The nature of his "unlucky outset" has not been ascertained.

6. Jane Ann Dodge (1799–1875), fourth child of Richard and Ann Dodge, had married John Frothingham in December, 1816. She named her third child after her uncle.

343. To William Harness

[June 26, 1822][1]

My dear Harness,

I arrived in town early this morning, having posted all night[.][2] of course I am rather fagged. I should like to have a gossip with you, but you live so far off & I am so lame & hurried, that I cannot make the expedition ⟨at⟩ with the uncertainty of finding you at home. Why cannot you call & breakfast with me tomorrow morning. I generally breakfast before nine; but will keep back my breakfast tomorrow morning until ten at a venture—so that you may come either by or before that hour as may best suit your conveniences

Yours truly
Washington Irving

Maddox Street/Wednesday. 26 June.

ADDRESSED: Revd. William Harness / King Street / Portman Square   POSTMARKED: 7 o'Cloc[k] 26 JU 1822 N. T   DOCKETED: Washington Irving. MANUSCRIPT: SHR.

William Harness (1790–1869), a curate who later edited Shakespeare's plays and wrote his biography, was a close friend of Lord Byron's.

1. The year was determined by the postmark on the address leaf.

2. WI had spent several days with Thomas Hope at the Deep Dene, Surrey. See WI's letters to Brevoort, June 11 and June 30–July 1, 1822; and to Mrs. Paris, June 21, 1822.

344. To Moses Thomas

London, June 29th. 1822.

My dear Sir,

I have recd. your letter[1] concerning the first Edition of Bracebridge Hall.[2] I have written to my Brother[3] respecting the various points of your letter and have requested him to make some arrangement by which you should be saved harmless from any premature publication of a second edition; though I should think you would be able to put off an edition of one thousand in the course of three months. Your offer for the American edition is certainly a very fair one; but I have long since determined to retain the American copy right of my works as long as possible—as I wish to have complete controul over them.

As to my Brothers terms & arrangements they are matters which I must leave to himself. I always give him general directions, and express my own inclinations; but ⟨it would⟩ I have too much confidence in his correct, honourable & amiable nature, ⟨to⟩ and his sound judgement, to clog him with petty stipulations; unable as I am from the distance at which I am placed, to judge of what is proper & expedient; and intrusive as I already am upon his obliging disposition.

With respect to yourself it has always been, and still is, my uniform wish to reciprocate with you all kind of friendly offices—My Brother knows such to be my wish, and I am sure will act conformably wherever circumstances will permit.

I am sorry that any malarrangement between you should mar the circulation of my new work; and hope it may be remedied in future a⁴ editions. Thirty percent appears to me to be a very ⟨foreign?⟩ fair discount on a work that is pretty sure to be of ready sale—I have given no directions in the case however, & do not care how much discount is allowed—I leave all that to my friends in N York to arrange; & my only wish is, that the terms should be liberal & satisfactory—

I have not your letter by me, but I believe I have answered the main points of it, and am at the moment so much hurried by various letters that I have to write, previous to setting off for the Continent, that I have no time to enter more into detail; and indeed there is no need of it. I have written to my brother all that it is necessary & proper that I should write, and I hope you will be able to carry on your dealings pleasantly & advantageously with each other

I am, as ever,

Your sincere friend
Washington Irving

ADDRESSED: Mr Moses Thomas / Bookseller / Philadelphia / Lancaster
MANUSCRIPT: University of Rochester Library.

1. This letter has not been located.
2. Thomas published 1000 sets of the two-volume edition on May 21, 1822. Volumes I and II had been deposited for copyright in New York on April 5 and May 9, 1822, respectively. The second American edition used as copy text the first English edition (published by John Murray on May 23, 1822), which incorporated WI's revisions and changes. See Jacob Blanck, comp., *Bibliography of*

American Literature (New Haven and London, 1969), V, 19; and Langfeld & Blackburn, *WI Bibliography*, p. 24. For other details about the American publication of *Bracebridge Hall*, see WI to Ebenezer Irving, January 29, 1822.

3. Ebenezer Irving, who was acting as WI's agent.

4. WI probably intended to cancel this letter.

345. *To John E. Hall*

London, June 30th. 1822.

My dear Sir,

I have received your letter of April 29th. The previous letter to which you allude came to hand when I was in France, and I replied to it at some length; but it appears my reply[1] never reached you. The Situation in which I was at the time, so far from London; put it out of my power to render ⟨the⟩ you the Services you required. The proofsheets of the life of Anacreon[2] which you say you transmitted me, were never received.

I have talked with Carpenter[3] about your proposed work. He says that the translation by Moore[4] could not be ⟨collected⟩↑published↓in the work without an infringement of his copy right, which of course he could not permit. He says, however, that if the life were well executed, so as to be entertaining & attractive, he should have no objection to treat with you about it; but↑that↓at the present day, ⟨h⟩ it is necessary that a work of the kind should be executed in a very, masterly manner, as the age is extremely erudite & critical in such matters.

I think, if you have the Mss: or printed sheets you had better transmit them to Mr Miller and let him act as your agent either with Carpenter, or any other Bookseller that may be disposed to undertake the thing. Of course, if Carpenter is not the man you will have to substitute other translations instead of Moores; which would be a disadvantage to the work.

As to Well written articles concerning America, there are various magazines that would be glad to receive contributions of the kind; as a lively interest exists on the subject of America & American literature. Your best way is to send your Mss: to Miller & get him to dispose of them to the best advantage ⟨alowed⟩ allo[wing him a percentage][5] both to repay him for his trouble & to make it worth his while to take pains. He is fully to be depended upon. The terms with the most popular magazines is from ten to 15 & 20 Guineas a sheet, according to the merit of the article or the reputation of the Author. The Editors always require to See Some of the Authors Writings before they make any offer.

I have handed the Conversations on the Bible[6] to a young clergyman,[7] a literary character, to read them & report on them; I will then see if I can do any thing with the printers about them. There is such an inundation of works for the press, however, that you have no idea of the difficulty there is in getting any thing even looked at, by a publisher, unless the Author has an established name.

The Spy is extremely well spoken of by the best circles[8] & has a very fair circulation; not a bit better than it dese[rves] [*MS torn*] for it does the author great credit. The Selections of "Amer[ican] [*MS torn*] poets"[9] is I believe, by one of the Roscoe family.[10] The poets Selected from are Paulding, the authors of Yamoyden[11] — The author of "Fanny"[12] Pierpoint,[13] Bryant[14] & one or two others whose names do not at this moment occur to me.

I shall leave London in the course of next week, for Aix La Chapelle, where I propose remaining some time to take the waters; having been ⟨?rather?⟩ out of health ⟨for⟩ nearly a year past — Any thing you wish done at London, however, you may be sure of having faithfully done by Mr Miller. In sending proofsheets &c do not send through the post office or Letter bag, for the postage would then amount to *pounds Sterling* & the letters &c remain unclaimed — Send large pacquets by private Hand —

I wish when you see Mr Ewing[15] you would remember me to him as an old friend who would not willingly be forgotten by him — Tell him Anacrean Moore holds him in honoured remembrance

I am my dear Sir —

Very sincerely your friend
Washington Irving.

ADDRESSED: John E Hall Esqr. / Office of the Portfolio / Philadelphia / Lancaster
    DOCKETED: 30 June 1822 / Washington Irving [*In another hand*]: Presented
    by / Harrison Hall
MANUSCRIPT: NYPL—Berg Collection; NYPL—Duyckinck Papers (copy). PUB-
    LISHED: *Irvingiana*, pp. lxiii–lxiv.

John Elihu Hall, whom WI had met in Baltimore in 1811, edited the *Port Folio* in Philadelphia from 1816 until its demise in 1827.

1. These letters to WI and WI's reply have not been located.

2. In 1806 Hall had written a life of Anacreon for the *Port Folio* which was expanded and printed in the magazine from 1819 to 1821. He had apparently sent proof sheets to WI in an attempt to have the memoir published in England.

3. William Hookham Carpenter (1792–1866) was a bookseller and publisher on Lower Brook Street in London.

4. Thomas Moore's translation of Anacreon had been published in Philadelphia in 1804. In his biography of Anacreon Hall had used quotations from Moore's translation.

5. Part of the bottom of the page is missing. The text is restored here and elsewhere from a copy of the letter preserved in the Duyckinck Papers in NYPL.

6. *Conversations on the Bible* by Hall's mother, Sarah Ewing Hall (1761–1830), had been published anonymously in 1818.

7. Probably William Harness, who was thirty-two years old. See WI's letter to Harness, June 26, 1822.

8. Notices of Cooper's *The Spy* had appeared in *Colburn's New Monthly Magazine* 6 (April, 1822), 173; *Monthly Censor* 1 (June, 1822); *Monthly Literary Register* 1 (June, 1822); and *Literary Chronicle and Weekly Review* 4 (July 6, 1822).

9. *Specimens of the American Poets* was published in London by T. & J. Allman in 1822.

10. Possibly a member of the family whom WI knew in Liverpool: William Roscoe or his children—Thomas (1791–1871), Henry (1800–1836), or Mary Anne (1795–1845). Neither the Library of Congress *Catalog of Books* nor the British Museum *General Catalogue* lists a collection of American poetry edited by a member of the Roscoe family.

11. Robert C. Sands and James W. Eastburn.

12. Fitz-Greene Halleck (1790–1867), who with Joseph Rodman Drake in 1819 had written a series of satiric poems called the *Croaker Papers*, also brought out *Fanny*, a burlesque of New York society written in imitation of Byron's *Beppo* and *Don Juan*. WI closed the title with a single quotation mark.

13. John Pierpont (1785–1866), author of *Airs of Palestine*, a poem in heroic couplets praising sacred music.

14. William Cullen Bryant (1794–1878), whose early poems were collected and published in 1821.

15. Probably Samuel Ewing, whom WI had known in Philadelphia a decade earlier. See his letter of November 24, 1812.

346. To Peter Irving

June 30, 1822

I have been leading a sad life lately, burning the candle at both ends, and seeing the fashionable world through one of its seasons. The success of my writings gave me an opportunity, and I thought it worth while to embrace it if it were only for curiosity's sake. I have therefore been tossed about "hither and thither and whither I would not;" have been at the levee and the drawing-room, been at routs, and balls, and dinners, and country-seats; been hand-and-glove with nobility and mobility, until like Trim[1] I have satisfied the sentiment, and am now preparing to make my escape from all this splendid confusion.

PUBLISHED: PMI, II, 88–89.

1. Corporal Trim in Laurence Sterne's *Tristram Shandy.*

347. To William Wood

London, July 5th. 1822.

My dear Wood,

You will of course become acquainted with my friend Mr Charles
Matthews, in the way of business; let me also ask for him your most
⟨frien⟩ kind attentions in the way of friendship. He is a gentleman for
whom I have a great respect and regard & feel a confidence in reccommending him in the strongest terms to the good offices of my friends.

With great regard / Your friend

Wm Wood Esq.   Washington Irving

ADDRESSED: William Wood Esqr. / Theater / Philadelphia   DOCKETED: Washn.
Irving London 5th July 1822 / fm Mr Matthews / His Complemt of hyslop / on
his Last Visit to America
MANUSCRIPT: HSP.
William B. Wood was an actor known for his playing of comic roles. With Wil-
liam Warren (1767–1832) he managed the Chestnut Street Theater in Philadelphia.

348. To Gilbert Stuart Newton

[London, July 5, 1822]

Dear Newton,

I expect to leave London tomorrow morning, in a Steamboat for
Holland[1] — So if you want to see any thing more of me, before I am
blown up, or boiled down, come & breakfast with me

Yours ever

July 5th   W Irving.

MANUSCRIPT: Va.–Barrett.

1. The steamboat *Rapid*, commanded by Alex Smith, was scheduled to sail for
Rotterdam from Irongate Stairs at the east corner of the Tower on July 6. See
London *Times*, July 4, 1822.

349. To John P. Van Ness

London, July 6th./22

My dear Sir,

Should my friend Mr Charles Matthews[1] make any stay in Washington
permit me to ask for him your kind attentions. He proposes making
a dramatic tour in America, and I can assure you, that great as are his

professional talents, they are not exceeded by his private worth & social qualities.

With my most affectionate remembrances to Mrs Vanness I am ever
Your sincere friend
Washington Irving

ADDRESSED: Genl. John P. Van Ness / City of Washington
MANUSCRIPT: University of Rochester Library.

The address is written on a piece of paper two inches high. Although the same width as the sheet on which WI has written his message, it is less than one-third as long. Probably the address has been clipped from the full sheet.

1. Charles Mathews had been recruited by Stephen Price to tour in the United States in the fall of 1822. On October 19, 1822, Mathews wrote to his wife: "I am going back to Baltimore to-day, and thence to-morrow to Washington, where I perform by myself for two nights...." Presumably Mathews presented his letter of introduction from WI to General Van Ness at this time. See Mrs. Ann Mathews, *A Continuation of the Memoirs of Charles Mathews, Comedian* (London, 1839), I, 199.

350. To Charles Williams

[July 6, 1822]

not man of business enough to express myself technically, but will request my Brother in Law Mr Van Wart, to drop a line to Mr Williams on the Subject; and only mention this, to shew that the thing originates entirely with myself, and is not ↑mentioned↓ at the request or with the knowledge of any one else.

I had hoped to have seen you & talked with you on the subject: but your absence from town prevented me & now I am on the Wing for Holland.

Farewell, my dear Sir, and believe me with Sincere regard
Your faithful & often obliged friend
Washington Irving.

ADDRESSED: Charles Williams Esqr / 13. Finsbury Square   POSTMARKED: 12 o'Clock / 6 • JY / 1822   DOCKETED: 1822 / Washington Irving — 6 — / to / C. W. Recd. 15 — / Ansd. 15 — / [*four additional lines of docketing unrecovered*]
MANUSCRIPT: NYPL—WI Papers.

Only the last sheet of this letter has been located. WI had also written to Charles Williams, probably the brother of an American banker in London, on April 21, 1821.

351. *To Thomas W. Storrow*

Haerlem, July 11th. 1822

My dear Storrow,

I scribble you a hasty line to let you know that I am again in this side of the Channel, which is a great point gained towards our once more meeting. I left London on Saturday the 6th.[1] in a Steam Boat which landed me safely at Rotterdam after a very pleasant voyage of about thirty hours; but which would have been shorter, had the wind not been directly ahead. ⟨[unrecovered]⟩ I am making a solitary, but pleasant tour among the Mynheers; I wait today to hear the celebrated Organ[2] of this place, after which I go to Amsterdam. I shall remain there a couple of days and then journey on to Aix La Chapelle,[3] to take the waters; being still troubled with the cutaneous complaint that has so long worried me. I had nearly conquered it, in London, by the aid of dry fumigating baths of Sulphur;[4] but a little neglect, and going too much into company[5] has ⟨[unrecovered]⟩ caused something of a return; and I am now rather ⟨crippled⟩ shakled by it. I hope however to get entirely clear of it this Summer, and to come to you all at Paris in the latter part of the Autumn,[6] quite a hearty man again.

I sent Mrs Storrow a copy of my last work[7] sometime since, by a Major Warburton, who was going to Paris, I hope she received it safe.

How do you all do? & what are you all doing. I long to be again installed in my presidential chair in the Rue Thevenot. I mean to get into the confidence of every old woman I meet with in Germany and get from her, her budget of wonderful stories.[8] The time must be near at hand when the little princesses[9] are to be released from that enchanted castle where they remain shut up & guarded by two ferocious dogs. I presume they will set up for little women of course,[10] the moment they leave school, and that I shall have to approach them with my hat in my hand. Mrs Storrow will no doubt surrender the Keys to Susan at once, and Minny will be entitled to sit up one hour later of an evening—Dear! Dear! what changes are continually taking place in this world!

Charles[11] I trust does not participate in this domestic revolution, but remains sometime longer a school boy. It cannot be expected that he should get on so rapi[dly as] [MS torn] his sisters; for boys you know do not grow men [as young?] [MS torn] [a]s little girls do women. The young ladies ho[wever do?] [MS torn] [o]f course continued to play with him occasionally [and] [MS torn] admit him into their circle—It will be their [duty to?] [MS torn] have an eye to him, and bring him forward as much as they may think proper. The young women must without fail, make their appearance at Neighbor Wilders Conversaziones on Wednesday Evenings.

I dined & past a pleasant evening at Mr Everetts at the Hague the day before yesterday; ⟨I sin⟩ which is the only fair chance I have had of opening my lips since I have been in Holland. I do not know whether you have ever been in this part of the world; you would be much pleased with it. The towns are extremely clean & well built; ⟨and⟩ The old fantastic buildings, have a ⟨picturesque effect agreeable⟩ picturesque look, and the canals bordered by fine trees have a beauty of effect that you would not expect ⟨from ca⟩ on canals.

Give my love to Mrs Storrow and the young people and let me hear from some one or other of you, though I should frankly prefer any of the family to yourself as a correspondent; for they all write longer & more interesting domestic letters than you do — Direct. to me, if you write pretty soon—poste restante *Aix La Chapelle* — if you defer it for any time then direct *post restante Heidelberg*—God bless you all

Yours ever
W I.

ADDRESSED: a Monsieur / Monsr. Thoma[s W] Storrow / Rue Thevenot. No 24 / à Paris   POSTMARKED: [J]uillet 16 [182]2 / PAYS·BAS / PAR / VALEN-CIENNES / HAARLEM / F.15

MANUSCRIPT: Harvard.   PUBLISHED: WIS, pp. 16–18.

1. S. T. Williams (WIS, p. 16) gives the date as July 8, but he misread WI's figure. The perpetual calendar indicates that July 6 is the date on which Saturday fell in 1822.

2. The organ in the Groote Kerk, built by Christ. Müller in 1735–1738, with its three keyboards, sixty stops, and 5000 pipes, was one of the largest and most powerful instruments in the world. See Karl Baedeker, *Belgium and Holland* (Leipzig, 1897), p. 297.

3. WI was in Aix-la-Chapelle by July 19. He remained there for "between two and three weeks." See WI to Thomas W. Storrow, August 20, 1822.

4. WI described the nature of these baths to Thomas W. Storrow in a letter of August 20, 1822, and asked about their availability in Paris.

5. WI also alluded to these social activities in a letter to Henry Brevoort on June 11, 1822.

6. Actually WI did not reach Paris until a year later.

7. *Bracebridge Hall*, which had appeared in England on May 23, 1822.

8. This remark forecasts, perhaps, *Tales of a Traveller*.

9. The Storrows' daughters, Susan (b. 1807) and Minny (Ann Louisa, born in 1811).

10. S. T. Williams had transcribed this as "courts." See WIS, p. 17.

11. Charles Storer Storrow (b. 1809).

352. *To Sarah Van Wart*

Aix-La-Chapelle, August 2, 1822.

My Dear Sister:

I have now been here for upward of two weeks, and have had rather a lonely, uncomfortable time of it. For a greater part of the time I have been almost confined to my room, and have suffered extremely from the inflammation in my legs. I have been without any acquaintance and even without a disposition to make any; for my lameness and suffering almost unfit me for society. I am at times quite dispirited by this returning virulence of my complaint; it is so tedious of cure; it so completely alters all my habits of living and subjects me to such continual baths of a powerful kind, that I sometimes fear it may effect some injury to my constitution, and prepare the way for other maladies. As yet, however, my general health is good, and if I could only get unfettered from this cruel malady, I should have nothing to complain of. I am disappointed in Aix-la-Chapelle.[1] To me it is a very dull place, and I do not find that others seem more pleased with it. The environs of the town are beautiful. There are public gardens that almost surround the walls, and very lovely country in every direction, but I have been unable to avail myself of the delightful walks, and have only once taken a drive in a carriage in the vicinity.

This is the birthplace, and was once the seat of empire of Charlemagne, that monarch so renowned in history and song. His tomb is in the cathedral,[2] and is only marked by a broad slab of black marble, on which is the inscription, *Carolo Magno*. The Cathedral is an extremely ancient, venerable-looking pile. Every night I hear the hours chimed on its bells; and the midnight hours announced by the watchman from its tower. The Germans are full of old customs and usages, which are obsolete in other parts of the world. At eleven, twelve, and one o'clock the watchman on the tower of the Cathedral, when the clock strikes, blows as many blasts of a horn as there are strokes of the clock; and the sound of these warning notes of time in the stillness of the night, has to me something extremely solemn.

The people have an antiquated look, particularly the lower orders. The women dress in peculiar costumes. As to the company at the hotels and public saloons, it is composed of all nations, but particularly northern nations: Russians, Prussians, Germans, Dutch, &c. Everywhere you see military characters, in fierce moustaches and jingling spurs, with ribbons and various orders at their button-holes. Still, though there are many personages of rank here, the place is not considered the most fashionable, and there are many rough characters in the crowds that throng the saloons. Indeed it is somewhat difficult to distinguish a gentleman from a common man among these northern people; there is great slovenliness of dress and coarseness of appearance among them; they all smoke; and I have often been surprised to hear a coarse-looking man, whom I had set down for some common tradesman, addressed as Monsieur the Count or the Baron.

The weather has been very bad for several days past. As soon as it gets more settled, and I feel well enough to venture the journey, I think I shall make another push, and ascend the Rhine to Wisbaden, which is a more pleasant and fashionable watering-place; and where, from all I can learn, I think the waters will be more efficacious than here. At any rate, I shall then have seen the most beautiful part of the Rhine, and if I do not amend pretty readily in my health, I shall make for Paris at once, get in the neighborhood of a dry vapor bath, and then lay by until I make a perfect cure. It is extremely tantalizing to be here just on the frontiers of Germany, in the vicinity of some of the most beautiful and romantic scenery in Europe, and to be thus fettered and disabled. * * *

PUBLISHED: PMI, II, 91–93.

1. Site of an old Roman town, Aix-la-Chapelle (German Aachen) was the capital of Charlemagne's kingdom north of the Alps as well as location of baths dating from the first century A.D. See Karl Baedeker, *The Rhine from Rotterdam to Constance* (New York, 1906), pp. 4–12.

2. Charlemagne built part of the cathedral in the period from 796 to 804 in Byzantine style.

353. *To Sarah Van Wart*

Wisbaden, Aug. 19, 1822.

My Dear Sister:

I have just received the letter from you and Mr. Van Wart,[1] crammed full of very agreeable and interesting matter. How it has cheered and gratified me in my present solitude, for I am here solitary amidst a crowd. My worthy friend[2] with whom I came on here left me last Monday, and I have been without a companion through the week; for at these watering-places the people are all continually going and coming, making but transient stay, and are too much taken up with their own parties and companions to trouble themselves with a stranger and an invalid, who cannot speak their language. Perhaps the fault rests with myself, for my present indisposition takes away from my spirits, and from that alacrity in conversation which is necessary to make the most of society in travelling.

*   *   *   *   *

Though I have no acquaintances here, yet I contrive to get through my days very tolerably. There are fine public walks and shrubberies immediately opposite my hotel,[3] and a beautiful public garden within five minutes' walk. My windows command a prospect of it, and I limp to it, and pass part of my days there. I have not been able to apply myself to literary labor since the publication of my last work. It seems as if my mind took holiday the moment it was out of the traces, like a horse turned loose in the pasture; and as I am anxious to restore my health perfectly, I have not attempted to task myself in the least. I wish you were here with me to enjoy some of the fine scenery of this neighborhood, and to take a day's tour among the woody glens and charming little valleys that lie among the Taunus mountains,[4] or to coast along the lovely borders of the Rhine[5] where the hills are covered with woods and vineyards, and crowned with mouldering old castles. I am very much pleased with the Germans; they are a frank, kind, well-meaning people, and I make no doubt were I in a place where I could become intimate, I should enjoy myself very much among them. The mode of living here is quite primitive in some respects, particularly as to hours. I am now in a very fine fashionable hotel. I find the house in a bustle between six and seven in the morning, when the company bathe and then breakfast in their rooms. At one o'clock dinner is served in the grand saloon at a table d'hôte. Some hotels dine at two o'clock, but this is considered rather late. *After* dinner, generally, the toilette is made for the evening promenade, the theatre, the ball, or concert, or whatever may be the amusement of the evening. At some hotels there is a table d'hôte again for supper at about eight o'clock, which is as hearty a meal as the dinner; but at the hotel where I stay the guests order supper according to their inclination. The play goes in at six o'clock and comes out at nine. The balls begin at seven or at most eight o'clock, and are generally over between ten and eleven. Most commonly the good folks are all quiet and in bed by ten o'clock—after all, there is something very sensible and comfortable in this old fashioned style of living, and it seems to be healthy too, for the Germans, in general, are very hearty-looking people. * * *

Aug. 20th.—I have had a restless, sleepless night from this tormenting malady. I believe I walked a little too much yesterday, it being Sunday, and the public gardens full of people of all ranks. I think I shall quit Wisbaden in a day or two, and go to the old city of Mayence, or Mentz,[6] about six miles from hence, on the banks of the Rhine. There is a bath there of the kind I require, and I shall have the resource of a large town to interest me, besides being able to make excursions on water among the beautiful scenery of the Rheingau, and up the Mayne to Frankfort, for the river Mayne empties into the Rhine just at Mayence.

By-the-bye, the fair at Frankfort[7] commences in a few days, which is one of the greatest fairs in Europe. * * *

8 o'clock, evening.—I am just returned from a delightful drive among the mountains, and up to a place called Du Platte,[8] where the Duke of Nassau[9] (in whose territories I now am) had a hunting lodge. I set off about five o'clock, that I might enjoy the sunset among the mountains. I cannot express to you how charming these drives are among beautiful woody mountains, with every now and then prospects over an immense tract of country, with the Mayne and Rhine winding through it. The weather is temperate and serene, especially in the evenings. The landscape is dotted with villages. Mayence is a striking object in every view, and far off to the south the prospect is bounded by the blue heights of the Odenwald. It is in this latter region you may recollect that I laid the scene of my little story of the Spectre Bridegroom.[10] It would amuse you to see me in a crazy, clumsy open carriage, drawn by two ragged, bony, long-tailed horses, and harnessed with old ropes and rotten strips, which are the kind of hackney vehicles in German towns. Here I sit with my legs coiled up something like a Turkish bashaw, and hold a mongrel conversation, made up of English, French, and German, with the driver. The one that drove me this afternoon was full of admiration of the Kerzog[11] von Nassau, (the Duke of Nassau,) whom he seemed to regard as the greatest potentate on earth. He was continually breaking out into eulogies of the forests, the hills, the vineyards, all which belonged to the Kerzog; and then the vast number of deer and wild boars in these forests, all belonging to the Kerzog; and then the fine hunting seat, where the Kerzog came in the autumn to hear the belling of the deer; all his raptures were expressed in bad and broken German to enable me the better to understand him, and accompanied by great grimace and gesticulation. * * *

I have determined to shift my head-quarters after dinner to-day to Mayence on the banks of the Rhine, about five or six miles from this, and I will continue my letter from that place.

Aug. 21, Evening.—Here I am safely quartered at Mayence; and though I felt some regret at leaving the splendid hotel and pleasant environs of Wisbaden, yet I find much to compensate me at this place. The bath here is a kind of private property of an old gentleman, a kind of half philosopher and Jack-of-all-trades, who constructed it for his own cure. He knows, therefore, how to administer it, which is a great advantage; for I suffered much pain from the ignorance of the attendants at Wisbaden, who make the baths too hot, which nearly occasioned fainting, and produced severe pain in my ankles. This place is remarkably well situated for enjoying the scenery of the Rhine. From the bridge of boats which crosses the river in front of the town, there

is a beautiful view down the Rheingau with several little islands covered with trees, while along the opposite side of the river lie the warm
sunny hills which produce the finest Rhine wines. They lie exposed to
the south, and sheltered by the range of Taunus mountains from the
north winds, so that their grapes have the choicest influence of sun
and weather. Nothing can be more charming than this look down the
river, with the fine range of mountains closing the view; and then, on
looking up, there is the little chateau and village of Hockheimer, famous
for its wine; the confluence of the Mayne, and the purple heights of the
Odenwald away in the distance.

Mayence is one of those old battered warrior towns that enjoy the
advantage of being knocked about, and battered, and taken, and
retaken in every war. The old cathedral[12] bears marks of the last siege,[13]
some of the towers being in ruins, and the traces of a bombshell in the
interior. The town has two or three fine streets, and several huge
rambling old German palaces; some turned into hospitals, some into
barracks for soldiers, and some shut up and inhabited, I presume, by
ghosts and hobgoblins. Many parts of the town are very old with time-
worn and war-worn towers. The place is now garrisoned by German
confederates, so that there are troops of different powers here. At the
inn[14] where I put up, and which is kept by a fat, jolly, waggish old
Frenchman,[15] a great Bonapartist in his heart, there is a table d'hôte
frequented by several officers, Russian, Austrian, Prussian, &c. I have
dined here on a visit I made some days since to Mayence, and was very
much pleased with the motley group, who were all acquainted with
each other, and full of conversation. One of the pleasantest things in
travelling on the continent is to meet with table-d'hôtes of this kind
in garrisoned towns. You find at them always a variety of strongly
marked characters; men who have led a rambling campaigning life,
and seen a great deal of the world.

Aug. 22d.—I have taken a bath at the old philosopher's, who is quite
an original; an author, a lawyer, a chemist, and for aught I know, an
alchemist, for he is poor and fanciful enough to be one. He lives in a
huge old mansion, that has once had some claims to magnificence, but
it is now rather *rattish*, and stands in a silent, grass-grown street. Had
I known the old gentleman a little earlier, he would have given me
some excellent hints for my alchemist; as it is, I shall turn him to account
some way or other, and mean to study him attentively.

I am quite pleased with my quarters. The hotel is quite a specimen
of one of these frontier hotels, and abounds with characters. * * * *

PUBLISHED: PMI, II, 94–100.

1. This letter has not been located.
2. Thomas Brandram, an English merchant whom WI had first met in 1803

on his trip to upstate New York and Canada and later in London. See PMI, II, 93–94; J&N, I, 4; J&N, III, 6.

3. Hotel in Wiesbaden.

4. The Taunus Mountains lay north and east of Wiesbaden, extending toward Frankfurt, though somewhat north of it.

5. The Rhine River was four miles south of Wiesbaden.

6. WI uses the French spelling for Mainz, located at the confluence of the Rhine and Main Rivers.

7. The autumn fair, sanctioned as early as 1240 by Frederick II, enhanced Frankfurt's reputation as a trade center.

8. A hill north of Wiesbaden noteworthy for its spectacular view of the area.

9. WI probably means Duke Frederick-Auguste, who died on March 24, 1816. The duke in 1822 was Frederick-William, who was born on January 9, 1816. See La Grande Encyclopédie, XXIV, 820.

10. This gothic tale was included in The Sketch Book.

11. Probably PMI's mistaken transcription, here and elsewhere in the letter of "Herzog."

12. A cathedral had existed at Mainz as early as 406 A.D., but it was destroyed by fire several times. Although the French had used the church as a barracks and powder magazine, it was restored to sacred uses in 1814. See Baedeker, The Rhine from Rotterdam to Constance, p. 159.

13. The siege occurred between January 2 and May 4, 1814. See La Grande Encyclopédie, XXIII, 449.

14. Hotel de Darmstadt.

15. Johann Adnot. See J&N, III, 10–12.

354. To Thomas W. Storrow

Wisbaden,[1] Aug 20th. 1822

My dear Storrow,

As I suppose you must by this time have got safe back to your Strong hold in Rue Thévenot, I will trouble you with another despatch. The sudden migration in the Storrow family did certainly throw me into great surprize, and must have caused quite a sensation in your neighborhood. I hope La Dame Storrow, enjoyed her visit to England and that her health is all the better for it; if not the best thing you can next do is to bring her to the Rhine, and try what fine air, fine roads & fine scenery will do for her. I have had a mingled time of suffering & enjoyment since I wrote to you. I grew very lame in trudging about the dutch towns, and unluckily as a make shift, I applied to my legs a recipe given me by old Lady Liston[2] (may God bless her, and preserve her from her own prescriptions!) — it played the vengeance with me — between that & the heat of travelling my malady returned with all its virulence—I could scarcely put my feet to the ground & bear my weight upon them — In this way I had to travel for three or four days in a State of Suffering that I cannot express, until I got to

Aix la Chapelle where I lay by for between two & three weeks. The baths alleviated the severity of my complaint but appeared to make slow progress towards a cure. I was very much confined to my room and very lonely & dispirited; when luckily an English Gentleman,[3] an old acquaintance arrived there; and I was induced, lame as I was, to accept a seat in his carriage & come on to Wisbaden to try the waters here. I made the journey more comfortably than I had anticipated; and being able to loll full length in the carriage I enjoyed the beautiful Scenery of the Rhine, which we saw in full perfection, in most delightful weather. I have now been here about eleven days, and find myself considerably benefited by ↑a↓ dry vapour bath of Sulphur, which I found here. I shall endeavour to see a little more of Germany, by going from place to place where baths of the kind I require are to be found; and then, if I find this complaint still lingers about me, I will hasten to Paris and lay by until I am perfectly cured. I understand there are very good Sulphur baths at Tivoli; I wish you would enquire whether there are dry fumigating Sulphur baths there; or in what part of Paris a bath of the kind is to be met with — I know there are such at the Hospital St Louis, for ⟨it is near⟩ they are considered sovreign remedies in cutaneous complaints. Take care to be correctly informed — It is not a vapour bath from hot water; but a dry air bath, from the Smoke of Sulphur. ⟨Wherever such baths are to be met with in Paris⟩ I should like to know where such baths are situated and where quiet & convenient appartments are to be met with in the vicinity; that I may know where to pitch my tent in case I have to repair to Paris; without being obliged to limp about from house to house in my disabled condition. I do not think however that I shall come to Paris for some weeks yet; & if I get on with the baths in Germany I shall not quit this country until late in the Autumn.

I wish I could meet with Coolidge,[4] for I am sadly in want of a companion, now that I am so much crippled & confined to the house without the disposition to Study or Scribble—Has he given no directions where letters might find him?

This letter I presume will find you with your little family assembled around you — I long to see you all again — it seems an age since we parted; and a great part of the time has been sad and uncomfortable with me. I am affraid I shall not be in a state to lead off in the dance with the young princesses, but at any rate I can lie on the Sopha and tell Stories; having met with several very wonderful and true ones in the course of my travels. I beg in particular they will put me in mind of "the Governors daughter and the prince of Fairy land,"[5] a story, the authenticity of which, is not to be doubted.

When next you write I beg the Madame may help out the letter;

you write admirably to the point my dear Sir, but terribly brief; a ladys pen is always more communicative — I want to hear all about your journey to London & what ⟨wa⟩ and whom you saw there — and I want to know something of family affairs in Rue Thevenot —

Give my love to all the household—/Your friend,

W Irving.

P.S. I have changed my quarters to *Mayence,* where there is a vapour bath[.] I shall probably remain here for some little time and if you can fill a letter for me ⟨and will forward⟩ among you & will send it here post restant I cannot tell you how much good it will do me

Mayence, Aug 22d.

P.S. *encore* — I have encountered at my present lodgings a Russian Colonel,[6] who has suffered from the same malady that I am at present tormented with—He ⟨has⟩ is able to give me all the information necessary about the Baths at Paris; so you need not trouble yourself on that account. If you should know where Coolidge is, and should be writing to him, let him know that I am at Mayence at the Hotel De Darmstadt[.] I think it very probable that I shall remain at this place or in the vicinity for Some time, as I find I can have very good advices here—and good remedies —

ADDRESSED: A Monsieur / Monsr Thomas W Storrow / Rue Thévenot / à Paris
POSTMARKED: Août 25 1822
MANUSCRIPT: Harvard.   PUBLISHED: WIS, pp. 18–22.
    In the upper left corner of page 1 "*26 augt*" is written in another hand; it is probably Storrow's notation or docket.

    1. WI consistently spelled Wiesbaden in this manner.
    2. Harriet Marchant (d. 1828) of Jamaica who married Sir Robert Liston, a diplomat, in 1796. For details about Liston see WI's letter of April 6, 1822.
    3. Thomas Brandram. See *J&N,* I, 4; III, 6.
    4. Joseph Coolidge (1798–1879), who was making a tour of Europe after taking his M.A. degree at Harvard in 1820. See Ellen M. Oldham, "Lord Byron and Mr. Coolidge of Boston," *The Book Collector* 13 (Summer, 1964), 211–12.
    5. Not identified.
    6. Not identified. In his journal of August 21, 1822, WI notes that "Col. [*blank*] a Russian has his room opposite to mine. Malade imaginaire — a room litterd with books. Col in robe de chambre." See *J&N,* III, 12.

355.   *To Peter Irving*

[August, 1822]

Away then we rolled; he[1] had a charming light open carriage in which I could loll at full length; he was a capital traveller, took the management of every thing upon himself; had an excellent servant who was all attention to me, and in spite of my malady I made one of the pleasantest excursions possible. Though too lame to explore the curious old towns and the romantic ruins which we passed, yet I lolled in the carriage, and banquetted on fine scenery in Brevoort's favorite style. After all that I had heard and read, the Rhine far surpassed my expectations. Indeed, I am perfectly delighted with Germany. After posting thus for four days *en prince*, we arrived at Wisbaden.[2]

✿   ✿   ✿   ✿   ✿   ✿

I am glad to find that you are in good spirits. Never fear about the future. Our means will be gradually accumulating, and when a man has a little money in hand, he can hold up his head and command fortune. Opportunities of profit always increase in proportion to means. One good thing is in your favor; you know how to enjoy life on a little, and I'll engage that that little at least shall not be wanting. Whatever I can do towards your comfort or prosperity is but a scanty return for the favors and obligations you have heaped upon me since childhood. Yours has been a life of practical generosity, of active benevolence and kindness, and it would be hard indeed if you did not reap some trifling harvest from the good seed you have so liberally sown. All that I can do is feebly to follow the generous example you have set. When you were in prosperity, you made it a common lot between us; so it shall remain as far as our situations and pursuits permit. Let there be one main end in view, which I trust we shall accomplish before any great length of time—the securing for each of us a little annual certainty wherewith to buy *bread* and *cheese*, then we can trust to fortune for the *oil* and *wine*.

PUBLISHED: PMI, II, 94, 143.

Although these passages are printed separately by P. M. Irving, they appear to be parts of the same letter.

1. Thomas Brandram. See PMI, II, 93.

2. WI and Brandram met on August 3 and probably left for Wiesbaden on August 5, reaching that town on August 9.

356.   *To Sarah Van Wart*

Mayence, Sept. 2, 1822.

My Dear Sister:

I despatched a very well-filled letter[1] to you from this place about ten days since. I have now been here nearly a fortnight, but do not yet find myself in condition to travel. I have been obliged to abandon the dry vapor baths, at least for the present. I found myself nearly overcome by them two or three times, and that they were followed by severe pains in the legs for several hours, as if the muscles were contracted.

*   *   *   *   *   *

I am now convinced, though reluctantly, that this malady has an internal origin, and arises from the derangement of the system, and particularly of the stomach. The anxieties that I suffered for three or four years in England used frequently to affect my stomach, and the fits of study and literary application, and the disuse of exercise to which I frequently subjected myself, and to which I had not previously been accustomed, all gradually prepared the way for some malady, and perhaps the one under which I at present suffer has prevented one of the more dangerous nature. I now foresee that it will take me some time, and patience, and care to restore my system to a healthful tone; all these external applications are but palliative; they relieve me from present pain and inconvenience, but it must be by diet, by gentle and slowly operating remedies, by easy recreation and tranquillity, and moderate exercise of mind, that I must gradually bring my constitution once more into vigorous activity, and eradicate every lurking evil.

I feel the value of life and health now in a degree that I never did before. I have always looked upon myself as a useless being, whose existence was of little moment. I now think, if I live and enjoy my health, I may be of some use to those who are most dear to me.

Notwithstanding the continuance of my complaint, I think the change of country and climate has been of service to me. The beautiful scenery among which I have lived of late, the fine weather and the pure and healthful air of these parts have had a most genial effect upon mind and body. I do not know when I have been more alive to the influence of lovely landscapes. * * I am most kindly attended by every one belonging to the hotel; am quite one of the family of mine host,[2] and have daily lessons in French and German from one of his daughters, la belle Katrina, a pretty little girl of sixteen who has been educated in a convent.

I am leading a very idle life. I read considerably, but I do not pretend to write; and my mind has complete holiday, so that it will be some time before I get another work under way.

Sept. 9th.—I returned last night from a delightful tour of three days. The weather was so fine and I felt so comfortable that I was tempted to visit some of the beautiful scenery of the Rhine. Accordingly I set off early one morning in company with a young English officer[3] in one of the passage boats of the river, and made a voyage to Coblentz, about sixty miles down the river, where we arrived late in the evening. This took me through some of the finest scenery through which I had passed in my journey up the Rhine; I then saw it from the land; I now had an opportunity of seeing it from the water. I cannot express to you how much I am delighted with these beautiful and romantic scenes. Fancy some of the finest parts of the Hudson embellished with old towns, castles and convents, and seen under the advantage of the loveliest weather, and you may have some idea of the magnificence and beauty of the Rhine. * * *

PUBLISHED: PMI, II, 100–102.

1. See WI's letter of August 19.
2. Johann Adnot, who had two sons and two daughters. See J&N, III, 10–12.
3. Captain James Wemyss of the 2nd Regiment of Dragoons. See J&N, III, 13.

357. To Sarah Van Wart

Heidelberg, Sept. 18, 1822.

My Dear Sister:

I despatched a long letter to you[1] just as I was leaving Mayence. I broke up my encampment there on the 13th, and set off for Frankfort about twenty miles distant, in company with Captain Wemyss, a young English officer of the dragoons. We reached Frankfort in the evening, but found some difficulty in getting lodgings, for though the town is large, with enormous inns, yet the place is so crowded during the fair that every house is full. At one inn where we applied, we could not get admittance; another which made up one hundred and eighty beds, had but one room vacant—at length the servant at the inn procured us two neat rooms at a shoemaker's, which we took for three days at the rate of two Brabant crowns a day; a huge price for Germany. This fair of Frankfort is held twice a year, in spring and autumn, and lasts several weeks each time. You must not judge of it, however, from your fairs. It is an assemblage of merchants and traders from all parts of Germany, Holland, France, &c., who meet here to transact business, and trade on a large scale, while the public squares and the quay along the river are built up with streets of little wooden booths, shops of small traders, where all kinds of wares and merchandise are exhibited. In one of the squares are a few shows and a temporary circus, but business seems to be much more attended to than pleasure. The whole city swarms like a beehive, and the streets are like moving pictures, for the various dresses, the peculiar costumes of the peasants, the antique German buildings, and the intermingling of soldiery strolling about, continually put one in mind of the scenes depicted in the works of the old painters. In Frankfort, as usual, every one dined at a table-d'hôte about one o'clock, and supped about nine in the evening. The saloon of the hotel where I ate, was very large, with a gallery for musicians, who played during the repast. Throughout Germany the table-d'hôtes are always attended by strolling musicians, singers, &c., who perform several tunes and then make a collection from the gentlemen at the table (the ladies are always excepted), who pay each a piece of six kreutzers (i.e. about a penny halfpenny); sometimes the music is very good. I like the custom. * * * *

Frankfort is a beautiful town, and the only one that I have seen in Germany that appears to be thriving and increasing. In most of the German towns, in consequence of the breaking up of the little German principalities and courts during the time of Bonaparte, and the merging of these petty governments into large states, you see continually the traces of former splendor; the ruins of petty aristocracies; old palaces deserted and falling into ruin; or turned into barracks, hospitals, &c. Frankfort, on the contrary, is an independent commercial town; its palaces are built by bankers and merchants, and are continually increasing. Some of the new streets are superb; but as I have a taste for the antique, particularly for the antique of the middle (or gothic) ages, I was more interested by the old parts of the town, particularly the part that faces along the river Maine, with the old bridge, the ancient towers, and the mountains of the Odenwald in the distance. I met with great civility at Frankfort from Mr. Kock, one of the first bankers of the place, to whom I happened to have a letter of introduction. I was a little indisposed, however, during my stay, and could not walk about much, or I should have enjoyed highly this scene of bustle and throng. After staying about three days, I left Frankfort in company with Captain Wemyss, and we came on leisurely in a voiture through Darmstadt to this place, which is in the Duchy of Baden. We came by what is called the Berg Strasse,[2] or mountain road, a route famous for its beauty of scenery. Our road lay along the foot of the mountains of the Odenwald, which rose to our left, with vineyards about their skirts, and their summits covered with forests, from which every now and then peeped out the crumbling towers of some old castle, famous in German song and story; to our right spread out a rich plain as far as the eye could reach; with a faint line of blue hills marking the course of the distant Rhine. It is all in vain to attempt to describe the beauty of these scenes—the continual variety of romantic scenery that delights the eye and excites the imagination, and the happy abundance that fills the heart. The exuberant quantity of fine fruit that I see around me, reminds me of our own country. The roads are bordered by orchards of apples and pears, where the trees are so loaded that the branches have to be supported by stakes, lest they should break. In some parts of the country, through which we passed, they were getting in the vintage, which will be a memorable one. Men, women, and children, were busy in the vineyards on the side of the hills; the road was alive with peasants laden with baskets of fruit, or tubs in which the grapes were pressed. Some were pressing the grapes in great tubs or vats, on the roadside. In the afternoon there was continual firing of guns, and shouting of the peasants on the vine hills, making merry after their labor, for the vintage is the season when labor and jollity go hand in hand. We bought clusters of delicious grapes for almost nothing, as we travelled along, and I drank of the newly pressed wine, which has the sweetness of new cider. The farther we advanced into the Duchy of Baden, the richer the scenery became; for this is a most fertile territory, and one where the peasantry are remarkably well off. The comfortable villages are buried in orchards and surrounded by vineyards, and the country people are healthy, well clad, good-looking and cheerful.

With all my ailments and my lameness, I never have enjoyed travelling more than through these lovely countries. I do not know whether it is the peculiar fineness of the season, or the general character of the climate, but I never was more sensible to the delicious effect of atmosphere: perhaps my very malady has made me more susceptible to influences of the kind. I feel a kind of intoxication of the heart, as I draw in the pure air of the mountains; and the clear, transparent atmosphere, the steady, serene, golden sunshine, seems to enter into my very soul. There seem to be no caprices in this weather. Day succeeds to day of glorious sunshine. The sun rises bright and clear, rolls all day through a deep blue sky, and sets all night without a cloud. There are no chills, no damps; no sulky mist to take one by surprise, or mar the enjoyment of the open air.

Sept. 20th.[3] — I have been three days at Heidelberg, and have passed the time very pleasantly. This is a famous little old town, situated just at the entrance of a narrow valley, between steep mountains. The Neckar, a clear, beautiful river, flows by it, and between the mountains you look out over a vast, rich plain, through which the Neckar winds its course to the Rhine; and the distant horizon is bounded by Mont Tonnere, and the high Vosges mountains that wave along the frontiers of France. On a hill which rises immediately above Heidelberg, are the ruins of the old castle,[4] one of the most splendid and extensive ruins in Germany. There is a public garden and fine shady walks laid out along the brow of the hill, all about the old castle, from whence you have charming views over the plain of the Rhine, and up the valley of the Neckar. I have received the most hospitable attentions from Count Jennison,[5] who resides at this place, to whom I brought letters from his friends in England. He is a very elegant and agreeable man, and speaks English as perfectly as an Englishman. He was Grand Chamberlain to the late King of Wurtemberg,[6] and was once minister to the Court of St. James,[7] where he married an English lady of rank.[8] His daughters speak English, and the family is very amiable and agreeable. As it is the fashion here to dine at one o'clock, we have long afternoons, which in this serene golden season, are delightful. Count Jennison has taken us out each afternoon in an open carriage, and shown us some of the loveliest prospects in this enchanting neighborhood. We have likewise made the acquaintance of a young Silesian prince, and Count Shoenberg,[9] a young Saxon noble-man, who both reside in the same hotel with us, so that we have plenty of society and amusement. As this neighborhood abounds with old castles, famous in legend and goblin tale, and the country is wonder-fully diversified by wild and rich scenery, you may imagine how delight-ful every little excursion must be. I am now so much recovered from my lameness, as to be able to take long walks among the hills, and to scramble among the ruins of old castles, and I find the exercise has a fine effect upon my general health. There is a good bathing house opposite the hotel, where I take a tepid bath every morning, medicated with sulphuret of potasse, which I find to be extremely efficacious.

PUBLISHED: PMI, II, 103–6, 109–10.

1. Written between September 2 and 9.

2. This road was originally built by the Romans along the western slopes of the Odenwald between Frankfurt and Heidelberg.

3. Although PMI prints this passage separately, it probably belongs to the letter started on September 18. WI frequently resumed interrupted letters by placing the new date at the beginning of the paragraph.

4. The castle, situated on the edge of the Konigstuhl overlooking the town and the Neckar River, was probably built by Count Palatinate Lewis I, with additions by Rupert III and others. In 1689 it was blown up by the French; later restorations came to nought when the castle was struck by lightning in 1764, leaving the remains as they survive today. Still preserved in the cellar is the Heidelberg Tun, a huge wine cask holding about 49,000 gallons.

5. Francis Jenison (1764–1824), an expatriate Englishman born in Durham, served as a diplomat and functionary for various German states. From 1797 to 1816 he was high chamberlain to the royal household of Charlotte Augusta, daugh-ter of George III, and Prince Frederick at Stuttgart.

6. Frederick (d. 1816) was king of Wurtemberg from 1798 to 1816.

7. In 1793.

8. Jenison's second wife was Mary Beauclerk, whose mother, Diana (1734–1808), was the eldest daughter of the second duke of Marlborough.

9. Count Schoenberg may be the son of August von Schönberg, who lived near Meissen and whom WI met later in Dresden. See J&N, III, 125.

358. *To Sarah Van Wart*

Hansack (Black Forest), Oct. 3, 1822

My dear Sister:

My last letter was written from Heidelberg,[1] which place I left on the 30th September in company with Capt. Wemyss, the same young officer of dragoons that has travelled with me from Mayence to Frankfort, &c. Our first day's journey brought us to Carlsruhe,[2] the capital of the duchy of Baden, a very pleasant, well-built little place, mostly new, with a fine palace, public buildings, gardens, theatre, &c. These little German potentates have fine times of it, living on the fat of the land in the midst of beautiful scenery. They seem to have all the sweets of sovereignty, without its cares and troubles. From thence we went to Baden,[3] one of the most romantically situated watering-places I have ever seen. It is in a small picturesque valley that runs like an inlet from the broad plain of the Rhine into the bosom of the mountains. Among the pine-covered mountains that overlook the town are the ruins of a grim old castle,[4] and another protecting castle[5] crests the hill on which the upper part of the town is built. In this last old castle there are long galleries of pictures of all the Electors of Baden, and the heroes of its reigning family for several centuries back, that have a most martial appearance, clad to the teeth in glistening steel. Underneath the castle we were shown subterraneous apartments that equalled the fabrications of novelists. They were chambers where the secret tribunal[6] held its sittings, and where its victims were confined, and if convicted, tortured and executed. This was a mysterious association that, some centuries since, held all Germany in awe. It was a kind of Inquisition that took cognizance of all kinds of offences. Its sittings were held in secret; all its movements were wrapped in mystery. Its members consisted of all ranks, from the highest to the lowest; all sworn to secrecy; all forbidden to make known their being members; and all sworn by the most imposing oaths to inflict the punishments decreed by the tribunal, without regard to any tie of kindred or affection. A man, therefore, once condemned by the tribunal had no chance of escape. He knew not where to fly, or in whom to confide; his bosom friend, his very brother might be a member of the terrible tribunal, and, of course, obliged to be his executioner. The subterraneous apartments of the old castle of Baden was one of the places were the secret tribunal was held. The place was worthy of the institution. You can imagine nothing more dismal than the cells and dungeons of which it was composed. There was one vaulted room, black with the smoke of tapers, in which the judges of the tribunal had held their sittings. Narrow winding passages through walls of prodigious thickness led to the dungeons of the prisoners and the places of torture.

All these were completely shut up from the light of day, and the doors were formed of immense blocks of stone that turned heavily on their pivots, groaning as they moved. There was one great pitfall, down which, we were told, prisoners were precipitated after execution; but enough of this gloomy picture.

From Baden we continued on up the rich valley, or rather plain of the Rhine; away to our right, at a great distance, waved the Vosges mountains on the frontier of France, while near by on our left were the mountains of the Black Forest, with now and then the ruins of an old castle among the woods of birch and pine. The road, as usual throughout the Rhine country, ran along a level at the foot of the mountains. The landscape became more fertile even than those parts of the Rhine through which we had already passed. We had entered into that part of Suabia called the pays d'or (*i.e.* the golden country) on account of its happy fertility. The road was bordered by fruit trees, and ran through fields of grain, or along vine-covered hills. The peasants were all busy in the fields, getting in their stock of potatoes and other vegetables. The vintage was over, and every now and then we passed wagons bearing great pipes of new wine, with bunches of flowers and streamers of ribbons stuck in the bung. The weather was serene and delightful, and nothing could be more gratifying than the picture of cheerful industry rewarded by abundance, which presented itself on every side.

We stopped at Kehl,[7] a small village on the German side of the Rhine, where we passed the night and left our carriage and trunks, that we might not be incommoded by custom house officers. In the morning we took a hired carriage and drove to Strasbourg, about a league off. This is an important old town on the frontiers of France and on the banks of the Rhine; I assure you, I felt a kindly throb in finding myself in territories of the gay nation; and I had several strong tugs of feeling that pulled me towards Paris. However, I resisted them all, and having looked at the noble cathedral of Strasbourg,[8] and from its tower looked out over a magnificent reach of country, watered by the Rhine, I turned my back upon Strasbourg and France, and ordering post-horses at Kehl, bade a long and reluctant adieu to my summer friend and companion, the Rhine. It was really like parting with an old friend when I took the last look at this majestic stream about which I had passed so many weeks; our road now lay up the narrow valley of Kenseg[9] that runs into the bosom of the Black Forest. I had bidden adieu to the gay borders of Germany that divide it from France, and was now about to penetrate into its interior. The valley of Kenseg is one of the most romantic and beautiful of the Black Forest; but unluckily for its verdant beauties, we entered it just before dusk. What we wanted in beauty of scenery, however, was made up in wildness and romance. The uncertain effect of partial moonlight now and then breaking from among clouds, was admirable among these wild scenes. Our road lay sometimes under steep hills with overhanging forests of black pines; sometimes it crossed and re-crossed the narrow valley over wooden bridges with streams rushing under them, and it was not until late that we arrived at the village where I am now writing this letter.

I am now scribbling late at night in a little village[10] in the valley of Kenseg, in the heart of the Black Forest. The inn is such an one as is sometimes shewn on the stage, where benighted travellers arrive and meet with fearful adventures. We were shewn into a great public room, wainscotted with wood, blackened by smoke, in which were waggoners and rustic travellers supping and smoking; a huge, rambling staircase led up to a number of old-fashioned wainscotted apartments. The hostess is dressed in one of the antique costumes of the country, and we are waited upon by a servant man in a dress that would figure to advantage in a melodrama; and a servant maid that is a Patagonian in size, and looks, as to costume, as if she had come out of the ark. This little village is composed of houses of wood and plaster. It is in a narrow part of the valley, with mountains about it covered with the black forests of pine that have given the forest its name. The Kenseg, a wild mountain stream, runs through the valley. The ruins of an old castle[11] are perched upon a hill that rises just above the village, and may be seen from my window while I am writing. I can hear the owl hoot from the ruins of the castle, and the reply of some of his companions from the neighboring wood. Good-night.

Ulm, Oct. 6th.—We arrived here last night. After passing through the mountains of the Black Forest, we came down into broad open plains, watered by the early windings of the Danube, which we have traced from its source among the mountains. The country became more completely German. We found few, comparatively, that could speak French. The towns were antiquated in fashion; the people peculiar in costume. At length we left the Duchy of Baden, and crossing the little principality of Hohenzollern, we entered the kingdom of Wurtemberg, and, late at night, or rather toward morning, arrived at Ulm.[12] Here we are in a huge, old-fashioned German hotel,[13] with long galleries, or corridors, decorated with paintings, portraits, and stags' horns, and the windows looking out upon the Danube. To-morrow we resume our route, intending to make a bend through the kingdom of Bavaria, and so to travel on to Vienna, where I shall make some stay.

Munich, Oct. 14th.—After leaving Ulm we continued along the Danube for the purpose of visiting the field of Blenheim,[14] where the great battle was fought in 1704, that gave such splendor to the British arms, and reflected such glory upon Marlborough.[15] You know it was this battle that gave the name to Blenheim House, built by government for the Duke. We had fine weather as usual; and I had an excellent opportunity of examining this famous battle-ground. From Donanworth, a village beyond Blenheim,[16] we made a sudden bend, taking our leave of the Danube for a season. I must observe that this river already began to exhibit some beautiful scenery, rambling through very beautiful country, particularly between Blenheim and Donanworth. It was as yet but a moderate stream. However, I shall be on its banks again before arriving at Vienna, and shall then find it wonderfully improved in size. From Donanworth we made a bend into the heart of the kingdom of Bavaria, and the second day arrived at this place,[17] which is the capital, where we have been nearly a week. This is a most charming little capital. With a population of only about fifty thousand people, it combines more advantages than are to be met with in cities of three times its size. One of the finest libraries in Europe, a magnificent theatre, an Italian opera, a smaller theatre, splendid galleries of paintings, and princely palaces.[18] There has been a grand fête on the king's birth-day, which gave me a fine opportunity of seeing both the court and the populace. The king[19] is a most amiable, worthy man, and extremely beloved by his people. It was quite an affecting sight to see him in public, surrounded by the multitude, without any guards to keep them off, and followed with acclamations and blessings. The royal family is very handsome; there are several princesses. I had a good view also of Eugene Beauharnois,[20] the stepson of Bonaparte. He married a daughter of the King of Bavaria, and is one of the most fortunate of Bonaparte's relatives and followers; for he has ever maintained a character for honor and bravery, and now lives in opulence and ease, with a superb palace, a charming wife and family, beloved by his father-in-law, the old king, and esteemed by the public.

This place is quite remarkable for its musical resources. Mozart composed several of his best operas at Munich,[21] and ever since the place has had a musical turn. The orchestra of the theatre is admirable. There is a female singer here,[22] that to my taste is preferable even to Catalani.[23] We have music, morning, noon, and night, for there are three of the best military bands that I have ever heard, and one or other of them seems to be continually parading the streets. * * * This place is rather more subject to changes and chills than other of the southern parts of Germany, owing to its vicinity to the mountains of the Tyrol, which stretch along the horizon to the south, and have their cragged summits already covered with snow. To-morrow we shall resume our route for Vienna, going round by the way of Salzburg to visit the salt mines. We shall strike the Danube again at Lintz, and then continue along it, through a most beautiful and interesting country, to Vienna. * * I am happy to say that my health continues to improve, and that I am gradually getting the better of my malady. At present I can walk about without any inconvenience, and indeed am on my legs almost the whole day.

When at Strasbourg, I saw in a bookshop a French translation of the Sketch Book,[24] different from that I had in England, and much superior, ornamented with plates. I find that it has likewise been translated into German, and selections published from it in various German periodical works.[25] A translation of Bracebridge Hall is also about to be published at Berlin.[26] * * *

Give my love to all the young folks and to the neighbors. What lots of stories I shall have to tell when I get to Brummy again. * * *

PUBLISHED: PMI, II, 110–17.

1. Dated September 18–20, 1822.

2. A town about 34 miles southwest of Heidelberg. The palace was built between 1750 and 1782.

3. Lying at the entrance to the Black Forest, Baden is almost 23 miles southwest of Karlsruhe.

4. The old castle was first occupied by Margrave Hermann II (d. 1130). See Baedeker, *The Rhine from Rotterdam to Constance*, p. 369.

5. The Neue Schloss on the hill north of the town of Baden was founded in 1479, enlarged in 1530 and 1570 to 1580, and seriously damaged in 1689, after which it was partially restored. See Baedeker, *The Rhine from Rotterdam to Constance*, p. 371.

6. The Vehmgericht or Femgericht of fourteenth- and fifteenth-century Germany.

7. A village about 31 miles from Baden, across the Rhine River from Strasbourg.

8. The cathedral was founded about 600 and was rebuilt in Romanesque style beginning in 1176, with Gothic elements added between 1250 and 1290. WI probably ascended the Minster Tower, which is 465 feet high. See Baekeder, *The Rhine from Rotterdam to Constance*, p. 312.

9. The Kinzig River, flowing in a northwesterly direction, enters the Rhine near Kehl.

10. Hausach, about 30 miles southeast of Kehl. See J&N, III, 26.

11. This castle of the Princes of Fürstenberg was destroyed in 1643 by the French.

12. According to his journal, WI proceeded to Engen, via Villengen and Donaueschingen on October 4; on the next day he viewed Lake Constance at Stockach and traveled hard to reach Ulm. See J&N, III, 26–27.

13. The Black Ox. See J&N, III, 27.

14. The site of the defeat of the Bavarians and French by the duke of Marlborough and Prince Eugene of Savoy on August 13, 1704.

15. John Churchill, first duke of Marlborough (1650–1722).

16. About 45 miles northeast of Ulm.

17. Munich is about 65 miles from Donauwörth.

18. WI is probably referring to the Staatsbibliothek, Prinzregententheater, Nationaltheater, Residenztheater, Nymphenburg Palace, Glyptothek, Stadtmuseum, and the Archbishop's Palace, among other buildings.

19. Maximilian I (1756–1825) was king of Bavaria from 1806 to 1825.

20. Eugène de Beauharnais (1781–1824) married Amelia Augusta, daughter of Maximilian, in 1806.

21. WI may be indulging in hyperbole here. Mozart probably composed parts of *La Finta Giardiniera* (K. 196) in December, 1774, and some passages of *Idomeneo* in late 1780 or early 1781. See Otto Erich Deutsch, *Mozart, A Documentary Biography* (Stanford, 1966), pp. 149–51, 189–93; Louis Biancolli, *The Mozart Handbook* (New York, 1962), p. 590.

22. WI heard Madame Clara Vespermann (1799–1827) sing in Weber's *Der Freischütz* on October 13. See *J&N*, III, 43.

23. Angelica Catalani (1780–1849), popular Italian singer on a European tour at this time.

24. Two French translations of *The Sketch Book* appeared in 1822, one published in Paris by C. Le Telliers Fils, and the other by Ponthieu of Paris. It is not clear which one WI had seen in London. See Williams and Edge, *A Bibliography of the Writings of Washington Irving*, pp. 135–36.

25. Five pieces from *The Sketch Book* were translated into German by W. A. Lindau and published in September, 1822, as *Erzählungen von Washington Irving* by Arnoldische Buchhandlung of Dresden. Earlier translations which included "The Voyage" and "Rural Life in England" appeared in the *Morgenblatt für gebildete Stände* (Stuttgart, 1819, issues Number 269–270 and 283–284). The same paper printed Francis Jeffrey's laudatory comments about *The Sketch Book* from the *Edinburgh Review* (supplement *Literaturblatt*, no. 5 [1821], p. 20) and "The Stout Gentleman" ("Ein Reiseabenteuer") (no. 152–54 [June 26–28, 1822]). See Reichart, *WI and Germany*, pp. 70–71, 176.

26. WI is probably referring to the translation of S. H. Spiker published in 1823 in two volumes by Duncker and Humblot. See Williams and Edge, *A Bibliography of the Writings of Washington Irving*, p. 48.

359. To Thomas Moore

Munich, Octr. 16th. 1822.

My dear Moore

I received some three or four weeks since, your letter[1] at Heidelberg, where it was lying amidst a heap of misshapen German epistles and smelt villainously of tobacco smoke from the company it had kept. I am very glad to hear that your muse has been more propitious at Passy than she was at Sev[r]es.[2] I shall look with impatience for the publication. I like the Size of the poem,[3] it is sufficiently large to give you scope, and yet not so large but that you can touch up every part with the magic tints of your pencil. Tell Mrs Moore she is one of the best criticks in the world;[4] or, which to me is the same thing, one of the best natured. In return for ↑her↓ gratifying encomium which you were so good as to transcribe, I must inform you, that, in visiting the royal palace here, I found in a small bookcase of the Queen of Bavarias[5] Boudoir, an edition in English of your poems,[6] apparently very much used—which makes me think her majesty has almost as good a taste for poetry as Mrs Moore has for prose.

I had hoped to have been in Paris this autumn, but here I am travelling towards Winter quarters, either in Vienna or Dresden. Shortly after I wrote to you from Holland I had a violent return of my complaint and was rendered so lame as to be unable to walk about. I got with some difficulty to Aix La Chapelle where I was laid up for three weeks. From thence I got up the Rhine and passed almost all the Season at Wisbaden and Mayence; slowly recovering from my indisposition, and often confined to the house. Still I was enabled at times to enjoy drives about the fine scenery of those parts, and became very intimate with some of the finest parts of the Rhine. I was so much delighted with what I had seen of Germany, that on recovering sufficiently to venture again on long journeys, I set out ⟨to⟩ in quest of adventures; like a true knight Errant, hardly knowing whither I should direct my course. In this way I travelled and travelled from Mayence to Frankfort, from Frankfort to Heidelberg; from Heidelberg about the Neckar & the Odenwald — then to Karlsruhe & Baden — then to Strasbourg and then through the Black forest to Ulm; intending to visit the field of Battle of Blenheim & afterwards to push for Dresden; but from Blenheim I turned off in another direction, came to Munich,[7] and having passed ten or twelve days here, seeing fetes, operas and picture galleries, I am on the point of starting for Salzbourg, then to the banks of the Danube and so to Vienna, where I shall repose some time ⟨from⟩ ↑after↓ my ramblings[.] I do not know when I have enjoyed travelling more; the weather has been uncommonly fine; the countries through which I have passed abound with ⟨fin⟩ noble Scenery and are full of story; and this desultry mode of wandering just suits my humour. The only drawback on all this pleasure is that I am burning the candle at both ends all this time. I am spending money, and my pen is idle — If I could only turn Pegasus into a posthorse, ye Gods! how I should travel —

I wish when either you or Mrs Moore write to Mrs Story[8] You would tell her that I should have written to her myself long since, but I never knew her address in the country. I had expected to See Mr Story in town in June as he had appointed; but either he ⟨never came⟩ ↑did not come↓ to town at that time, or he neglected to call on me. Let her know however that I am still alive and daily remember her & Miss Morris in my prayers.

I am writing in great haste, for I am on the point of Starting. Give my most affectionate remembrances to Mrs Moore, and my blessing to little Tom Bull[9]—

God bless you my dear Moore/Yours ever
Washington Irving.

ADDRESSED: a Monsieur /⟨Monsr⟩ / Monsr. Thomas Moore / à Passy / aux Soins des Messieurs ⟨Galignani⟩ / ⟨[unrecovered]⟩ / Rue Vivienne / ⟨à Paris⟩ / a Passy /

No 19 — / a Passy No 19   POSTMARKED: ⟨[unrecovered]⟩ München / 17 OCT
1822. / BAVIERE / PAR / STRASBOURG
MANUSCRIPT: HSP.

1. Moore wrote to WI on August 5, 1822. See PMI, II, 106–7.

2. WI omitted the r in his spelling. During Moore's residence in France he had lived at Sèvres and Passy in the vicinity of Paris.

3. *Loves of the Angels,* an oriental poem which was published in 1823.

4. Moore quotes his wife as saying, "I have just finished Bracebridge Hall, and am more than ever delighted with the author. How often he touches the heart! at least mine." See PMI, II, 107.

5. Caroline of Baden (1776–1841) had married Maximilian I (1756–1825) in 1796.

6. One-volume editions of Moore's poems up to this time include *Epistles, Odes, and Other Poems* (London, 1806), *Lalla Rookh* (London, 1817), and *Irish Melodies* (London, 1821).

7. For a detailed account of this trip, see Reichart, *WI and Germany,* pp. 50–53; WI's letters to Mrs. Van Wart, dated August 2, 19, September 2, 9, 18, 20, and October 3–14, 1822.

8. The Storys were friends of Thomas Moore in Paris. WI probably became acquainted with them through Moore. See WI to Mrs. Story, May 4, 1821.

9. Moore's son Tom was calling himself "John Bull." See PMI, II, 106.

360.   To Sarah Van Wart

Vienna, Oct. 27, 1822.

My Dear Sister:

 * * * I left Munich, in company with Captain Wemyss, on the 17th, for Salzburg. We travelled as before, in an open carriage of Captain Wemyss, with a caleche top,[1] which we could put up in case of bad weather. We had thus a fine view of the country on all sides, with the benefit of riding in the open air, which I think has had an excellent effect on my health. * * * *

It took us a day and a half to get to Salzburg. The latter part of the road was very interesting. We passed along a beautiful lake, called the Chiem Zee,[2] or as they pronounce it Kem See, which lies just at the feet of high and picturesque mountains, some of them already tipped with snow. In this part of Bavaria the country people live on their farms, as in England, which gives the country a much more cheerful and populous look than in other parts of the continent, where the country is all naked plain, and the peasantry huddled together in villages. The peasantry, however, are very ugly; indeed, since I have passed the Black Forest, I have seen nothing of the comeliness among the country people that I saw on the Rhine, particularly the lower part of the Rhine, from Mayence downwards. Before reaching Salzburg, we passed the frontier barrier of Bavaria, and entered the Austrian dominions.

Salzburg is one of the most romantic places, as to its situation and scenery, that I have ever beheld. It is a little old Archiepiscopal city,[3] in a narrow but beautiful valley; surrounded by high mountains, a branch of the Tyrolean Alps, many of which are tipped with snow. The Saal, a rapid clear stream, rushes by the town. A huge old castle[4] frowns down upon it, from a craggy height that rises immediately from the town, while on a height on the opposite side of the river stands a venerable convent of Capuchins.[5] As Austria is a country in which the Catholic religion holds still a powerful sway, the little city of Salzburg is well supplied with convents, and the bells of these and the churches are ringing to prayers almost every hour in the day. The only variety to this solemn steeple music, is a chime of bells in one of the towers, which play a waltz three times a day, and I presume all the street devotees are expected to dance to it. The season was not yet so far advanced as to destroy the beauty of the landscape; indeed it seemed to me as if the rich yellow tints of autumn increased the effect of this wild mountain scenery, by mingling a hue of melancholy with its grandeur. The heavy mists, too, that prevail among the mountains early in the mornings at this season, produced splendid effects, as they gradually broke up and rolled away; revealing crag after crag, mountain after mountain; and for a long time involving the remote vistas of the mountains in obscurity. The sun always shone out toward midday with extreme warmth, as if to revenge himself on the mist that had tried to obscure him. * * * *

In one of the mountains near by Salzburg, there are famous salines or salt works,[6] which we visited. The whole mountain is perforated and wrought into as many galleries and passages as an ant-hill. We were for a long time under ground, descending great shafts, or being wheeled along subterranean passages on a kind of hand-wagon. These mountain regions are full of fable and elfin story; and I had some wonderful tales told me which I shall keep in mind against I have another match at story-telling with the children. There is one great mountain that towers into the clouds close by Salzburg, which is called the Untersberg,[7] which the common people believe to be quite hollow, with churches and palaces inside; where the Emperor Charles V. and all his army remain spell-bound.

After remaining between two or three days at Salzburg, we resumed our journey, * * * * travelled all night, and the next day[8] about four o'clock, arrived safe at Vienna.

* * * * * *

Vienna, Nov. 10th. —This letter has been lying by me unfinished for a fortnight; for I have been so much occupied in looking about, that I have had no time to write. This is one of the most perplexing cities that I was ever in.[9] It is extensive, irregular, crowded, dusty, dissipated, magnificent, and to me disagreeable. It has immense palaces, superb galleries of paintings, several theatres, public walks, and drives crowded with equipages; in short, every thing bears the stamp of luxury and ostentation; for here is assembled and concentrated all the wealth, fashion, and nobility of the Austrian empire, and every one strives to eclipse his neighbor. The gentlemen all dress in the English fashion, and in walking the fashionable lounges you would imagine yourself surrounded by Bond street dandies. The ladies dress in the Parisian mode; the equipages are in the English style, though more gaudy; with all this, however, there is a mixture of foreign costumes, that gives a very motley look to the population in the streets. You meet here with Greeks, Turks, Polonaise, Jews, Sclavonians, Croats, Hungarians, Tyroleans; all in the dress of their several countries; and you hear all kinds of languages spoken around you. The Emperor is at present in Italy, attending the Congress at Verona.[10] I have seen the other members of the Imperial family several times at the theatre, where they appear in the Imperial box, without any show, nor any sensation on the part of the audience, as it seems quite a common occurrence. The most interesting member of the family, however, was the young Napoleon, son of poor Boney. His mother, now called the Archduchess Marie Louise, was, as you may recollect, daughter of the Emperor of Austria.[11] She is now at Verona. The young Napoleon, or the Duke of Reichstadt, as he is called, is a very fine boy, full of life and spirit, of most engaging manners and appearance, and universally popular. He has something of Bonaparte in the shape of his head and the lower part of his countenance; his eyes are like his mother's. I have seen him once in an open carriage, with his tutor. Every one took off his hat as the little fellow passed. I have since seen him at the theatre, where he appeared to enjoy the play with boyish delight; laughing out loud, and continually turning to speak to his more phlegmatic uncles, the other young princes.

A few days since, I made a most interesting tour of two days to visit some of the scenery of the Danube, and particularly the ruins of the Castle of Durnstein, where Richard Coeur de lion was confined.[12] You may remember the story of his captivity, which is one of the most romantic in English history, and has been the theme of novels, poems, and operas. He was one of the bravest monarchs that ever sat on the English throne. In returning from a crusade in the Holy Land, he was cast away in the gulf of Venice, and fearful of falling into the hands of the King of France, he attempted to travel across Germany in the disguise of a pilgrim. He was discovered at Vienna by Leopold, Duke of Austria, who sold him to the Emperor of Germany. He was confined in the Castle of Durnstein between one and two years; tantalized with hopes of being released, on paying an enormous ransom, and with fears of being delivered captive to his bitter enemy, the King of France[13]—but I am wandering into a string of ill-told historical anecdotes which you will find much better related in any English history; though the great charm of his story has been given by poetry and romance. He is the same monarch who figures so gallantly in Walter Scott's romance of Ivanhoe.

I was accompanied in my little tour by an agreeable young Irish gentleman of the name of Brooke. Though it was in the month of November, yet the weather was serene and beautiful. We had that steady golden sunshine which is peculiar to autumn. The country, though nearly stripped of foliage, had still enough of the lingering tints of autumn to render it pleasing. Our route for the first day lay through rather lonely scenes, where there was no high road; among woods and high hills. We visited the chateau of an Austrian nobleman, situated on a hill, with its dependent village gathered round its skirts, and looking over a great extent of sunny valley. It had quite an air of solitary pride and dominion; there being not another residence of any consequence within sight. As the family were absent, we had an opportunity of ranging over the whole castle, which was of great extent, with billiard rooms, and a saloon fitted up for private theatricals. The next morning we started before daylight, and in a fog; after travelling for some time, day dawned, but we were still involved in obscurity, and ascending and descending hills and valleys, without being able to see a hundred yards before us. About seven o'clock, the sound of a matin bell gave us warning that we were in the neighborhood of the convent of Gottwick, or Gottwied;[14] one of the most interesting objects in the course of our route. It is situated on the summit of a mountain that commands one of the grandest prospects of the Danube. We left the carriage at the foot of a steep ascent that forms the highest part of the mountain, and set off for the convent on foot. The fog was still so thick that we could not see any thing of the convent until we got close to it, when it seemed suddenly to loom upon us out of the mist; its vast buildings and lofty towers looking dim and shadowy, like a great palace of enchantment, just rising into existence. As we approached we heard the sound of the organ, and that mass was performing in the chapel. We found our way there, and entered a magnificent church,[15] with a remarkably rich altar-piece. After mass, we entered the convent, and requested permission to see the interior. The superior, a round, sleek, jolly looking friar, received us with great politeness, and being obliged to attend to the duties of the convent, requested one of the young monks to attend us, who showed us the library, which is very valuable, with many rare manuscripts. He also showed us the cabinet of natural history, &c. The convent is of vast extent; superbly built, very wealthy, and very hospitable, with cellars as well stored with old wine as the library with old books.

From hence we descended to the Danube, and crossing it on a long bridge, we continued on to the old castle of Durnstein. Here we passed some time exploring the ruins. The castle stands on the summit of a rocky height, among stern mountains. The Danube winds below it, and you have a long view up and down the river. The scenery is grand and melancholy, and the story of the Lion-hearted Richard has given a peculiarly romantic interest to the place. Our return from hence was through very beautiful country, frequently in view of the Danube, and we did not reach Vienna until late at night, highly satisfied with our tour.

I must not omit to mention that I lately received a packet from Mr. Storrow, containing three letters from you, dated Sept. 1, Sept. 21, and October 7.[16] You must imagine how gratifying they were to me. They brought me at once into your dear little family circle, and made me forget for awhile that I was so far adrift from any home. These little tidings of the fireside, to a man that is wandering, are like the breezes that now and then bring to the sea-beaten sailor the fragrance of the land. I feel most sensibly your affectionate solicitude about my health. I am happy to say I am daily improving; and in a little while I trust I shall have no more remains of my complaint. It no longer gives me any trouble; but I continue my foot-baths night and morning, while any traces of it remain, for fear of a relapse; as I am conscious that my constitution is not yet actually what it should be. * * *

I am beginning to think of leaving Vienna. I shall probably stay a week longer and then take my departure for Dresden, which will be my winter quarters. It is a more quiet and intellectual city than this; for here the people think only of sensual gratifications. There is scarcely any such thing as literary society, or I may say literary taste in Vienna. Dresden, on the contrary, is a place of taste, intellect, and literary feeling; and it is the best place to acquire the German language, which is nowhere so purely spoken as in Saxony. Dresden is about three hundred miles from here by the shortest road, which lies through Moravia and Bohemia. I think it very probable that I shall make the journey alone, as there are few persons travelling for pleasure so late in the season; and I prefer travelling alone unless I can find a companion exactly to my mind.

PUBLISHED: PMI, II, 117–24.

1. This was a roof which folded back in pleasant weather but could be raised in bad weather.

2. About 50 miles southeast of Munich, midway between Munich and Salzburg.

3. Prior to 1802, when it was secularized, Salzburg was the richest and the strongest ecclesiastical principality in southern Germany.

4. The fortress of Hohensalzburg is located on the southeastern corner of the Monchsberg, a wooded hill along the western side of Salzburg.

5. The Capuchin monastery is situated on the Kapuzinberg, a height on the east bank of the Salzach River.

6. WI refers to the salt mines on the Durrnberg near Hallstein, about eleven miles south of Salzburg on the Salzach River.

7. Lying southwest of Salzburg, the Untersberg, consisting of the Geiereck (5910 feet), the Salzburger Hochthron (6080 feet), and the Berchtesgadner Hochthron (6470 feet), dominates the region. A cavern with unusual ice formations, the Kolowrats-Hohle, is to be found in the Untersberg. See Karl Baedeker, *The Eastern Alps* (Leipzig, 1907), pp. 103–4.

8. October 23.

9. WI probably had this reaction because he had no letters of introduction and was left almost entirely to himself in a strange city.

10. From October to December of 1822 Franz I (1768–1835) represented Austria in the meeting of the Quintuple Alliance (including Great Britain, Prussia, Russia, and France) to discuss the means of suppressing the revolutionary movement in Spain and of dealing with the growing tension between Russia and Turkey over the Greek struggle for independence.

11. Napoleon Francis Charles Joseph Bonaparte (1811–1832), son of Napoleon I and Marie Louise (1791–1847), who was the daughter of Franz I of Austria. Young Napoleon's titles—king of Rome, prince of Parma, Napoleon II—were replaced by that of the duke of Reichstadt.

12. Richard I (1157–1199) was captured on December 21, 1192, in an inn near Vienna by Duke Leopold of Austria while returning through Germany from the Third Crusade, and he was imprisoned in the castle of Dürnstein overlooking the Danube until March, 1194, when negotiations for his ransom of 150,000 marks were completed with Henry VI, emperor of Germany (1165–1197).

13. Philip Augustus (1165–1223), who had quarreled with Richard I during the Third Crusade.

14. Established in 1072, the Benedictine monastery of Gottweig was situated on a hill on the south bank of the Danube across from Krems. A description of the plan of the monastery is to be found in Eugene Susini, *Austria* (New York, 1961), pp. 106–7.

15. This church was built between 1719 and 1783, but its twin steeple towers were never completed.

16. These letters have not been located.

361. To Susan Storrow, Minny Storrow, Charles Storrow, and Thomas W. Storrow

To Miss Susan Storrow

Vienna, Novr. 10th. 1822.

My dear and excellent little lady,

I ought long since to have acknowledged and answered your charming letter;[1] but I have been so much occupied in travelling and travelling, like the heroes in story books, and have been so much taken up with seeing haunted castles and Kings pallaces that I have had no time to write letters; so as I know you are very considerate and very indulgent I am sure you will excuse me. I have just returned from a two days excursion up the banks of the Danube to the ruins of the old Castle of Dürnstein where Richard Coeur de leon was confined.[2] I presume you know the romantic story of his captivity; if not, you will find it in the History of England — or rather, you will pick it up from the novels and operas that have been founded on it—as poets and dramatists are always the best relaters of historical facts. As I presume you have a proper lady-like taste for ruined castles I wish you could have been with me to see this one; it would do any young ladys heart good to look at it. It is built round the very peak of a high craggy rock, among stern dark mountains, and gloomy forests; with the Danube sweeping along below it. In one part of the ruins is the sweetest dark dungeon you can imagine; cut out of the Solid rock; in which I'll warrant Richard was often put on bread & water, when he happened to be a little restive. I never saw a finer castle for a heroine to be confined in, or a ghost to haunt; though after the most diligent enquiry I could not find that the old ruins were haunted by a single goblin; which rather surprized me. The castles in Germany are generally very well off in that particular; and I have met with some that have had half a dozen ghosts to garrison them. What stories I shall have to tell you when I get once more to Rue Thevenot![3] — By the way, put me in mind, when I see you, of the Emperor and his army shut up in the enchanted mountain — which mountain I have absolutely seen with my own eyes — put me in mind of the little dwarf woman, with twenty rings on her fingers, who came nobody knew whence, and who went, nobody knew whither — Put me in mind of the Black Huntsman and the enchanted Bullets.[4] Put me in mind — but no matter, only let me get back once more to the historical society of Rue Thevenot, and we'll have fine times I'll warrant you.

I was extremely sorry that I could not join your little rural community at Nanterre;[5] what pleasant walks we should have had in the fields; and then Charles's kite and ninepins and Minnys Swing and Chaumiere — really I never had such a captivating picture of country delights set before me. I could hardly help turning ⟨to⟩ my back upon Germany and all its haunted castles, and making the best of my way to Paris. However, I hope we shall all have some merry times together when I get back; and that your papa will hire some other Country Seat in the suburbs for you all to ruralize in. I am heartily glad you have got safe out of the clutches of that school mistress and her two big dogs; though I hope you do not fail to keep up some friendly communications with Miss Sarah and that young lady that had such a "good heart." Commend me to them both when you see them.

How do our friends in the Court yard come on — does Petite give evening parties still; and is the big bass voice still to be heard? I have a thousand questions to ask you, and a thousand things to tell you; but as I must write in this letter to Minny and Charles, I must defer them all until some other time. ⟨I have⟩ I hope the cares and duties of house-keeping do not so entirely engross your time as to prevent your still taking lessons. I anticipate much pleasure from that piano which has lately been introduced into the house, and trust that at the next ball I dance at in the Rue Thevenot it will save me the trouble of playing the Quadrilles upon the bellows.

Farewell my dear little woman; let me have another family letter from you all soon, and do not forget, amidst the dissipations of Rue Thevenot

Your affectionate friend
Washington Irving.

To Miss Louisa Ann Storrow—/These.

My dear Minny,

I have already told Susan how sorry I was that I could not enjoy the pleasures of the Cottage at Nanterre last Summer, and how I should have been delighted to have had my turn at the Swing and a ride on the Donkeys; but all that *pour une autre fois.* You have said nothing in your letters about our friends the Miss Wilders;[6] nor whether you have any more tea parties; and what beau you have in my place. I am affraid those young ladies have quite forgotten me. By the bye, talking of young folks, I have just seen little Napoleon,[7] who you know lives in Vienna. A fine boy he is let me tell you; full of life and spirit—very handsome, and very much liked by every body — Folks tell me —— but however it wont do to talk politics, as I may get you into difficulties should this letter be Seen — yet they do say that there is not a boy of his age in all paris that can dance better than him — but this you must keep to yourself, as it might cause some uneasiness, should it get to the ears of the french Government. I hope that, though you have left school, you have not given up your studies; and that Susan helps you on in the highway to learning as much as lies in her power. I regret very much that I should never have been able to attend any of the concours of your Pension[8] as I should have liked to see You and Susan receive the applause of the audience for your merits. I shall, however, be able to judge of your application when I return, when I trust I shall find you two very sensible, accomplished, conversible little Gentlewomen.

Adieu, My dear Minny,/believe me your sincere friend
WI.

à Monsr. Charles Storrow,

My dear Sir,

This letter I trust will find You safe at School, enjoying the Soupe Maigre and lentilles, of which you talk; and which I think admirable diet for Scholar; keeping both body and soul light and active. I wish you could see some of the Military schools here; where little gentlemen of ten years old ⟨and⟩ are dressed out *a la militaire* with cocked hats; regimentals, long sabres, and now & then a military blue cloak; so that they begin by being little men and I presume grow up to be boys. I am glad to hear from Minny that You gained a wreath of Laurels at the Lycee. I hope Mamma has treasured it up, and that you wear it on all family fetes. I have been ⟨making continually⟩ looking out continually of late for our friends Mr Ritchie & Mr Coolidge,[9] whom your papa said were coming to Vienna; but I hear nothing of them, and I am now about setting off for Dresden so that I fear there will be but little chance of our meeting. ⟨Tell Mr Coolidge⟩ You must make Mr Coolidge take the presidential chair of the historical society when he arrives; and tell you all the wonderful adventures he has met with in his travels; though, between ourselves, the world has terribly fallen off in latter days; men meet with nothing of the adventures that they did in old times — I have travelled and travelled a vast deal this summer, but have not met with a single Giant, or a fiery dragon. Still, however, I have picked up some strange matters to discuss when next we meet, and have yet several parts of Germany to see, which abound with wonders. Of these, hereafter, in the mean time believe me ever

Yours very faithfully
W. I.

Thos. W Storrow Esqr

Vienna, Novr. 16th. 1822.

My dear Storrow,

I received your letter of the 14th. Octr.[10] with the letters it enclosed and which were quite a treat to me. I have had so much to say to the young folks that I can only scrawl you a line in a Corner of my letter. I have been disappointed in not meeting with Coolidge & Ritchie and now give them up. I leave this [place][11] the day after tomorrow for Dresden, where I think of going into winter quarters and studying German. I am glad to hear my friend Charles is about the same thing— what fine times we shall have when we meet spluttering high dutch ⟨to the⟩ together, to the admiration and the confusion of the whole household. I hope dame Storrow will take good care of herself this winter;

which I am assured on good authority is going to be a Severe one. I wish I could pass it with you; but my fate seems to be to wander; or rather, it is my vocation. Your mention of the *boild beef* the Sopha wheeled to the fireside, the new Cat, all brought such a picture of household enjoyments before me, that for a moment I sighed, even among the splendours and revels of Vienna. Should any more letters arrive for me forward them *Poste restante* — to Dresden and do let me hear from you all — consider me as one of your family absent, and believe me every most truly Yours

W.I.

ADDRESSED: à Monsieur / Monsieur Thomas W Storrow / Rue Thèvenot No 24. / à Paris   POSTMARKED: WIEN / Novemb[re] 27 182[2]
MANUSCRIPT: Harvard.   PUBLISHED: WIS, pp. 22–28.
   WI included letters to several members of the Storrow family on the same sheets by writing them in sequence.

   1. This letter has not been located.
   2. For other details about this trip see WI's letter to Mrs. Van Wart, October 27–November 10, 1822.
   3. The Paris address of the Storrows.
   4. WI heard these stories while he was in the Salzburg area. Professor Reichart has noted that they have not been preserved in Dr. Franz Ziller, *Mittheilungen der Gesellschaft für Salzburger Landeskunde, 1860–61.* See Reichart, *WI and Germany,* p. 173, n. 47.
   5. A village on the outskirts of Paris, northwest of the Bois de Bologne, where the Storrows had a cottage.
   6. Presumably the daughters of Samson Wilder.
   7. The son of Napoleon Bonaparte, who resided with his grandfather, Franz I. See WI's letter to Sarah Van Wart, October 27–November 10, 1822.
   8. WI alludes to the girls' studies and examinations in the concours in his letters of February 1 and 28, 1822.
   9. Thomas Ritchie and Joseph Coolidge were American friends, mentioned in earlier letters.
   10. This letter has not been located.
   11. WI inadvertently omitted the bracketed word.

362.   To Charles R. Leslie

Dresden, Decr 2d. 1822.

My dear Leslie
   I drop you this line chiefly to introduce to you Lieutenant Montagu, of the Royal Artillery, who has just been my travelling companion through Bohemia; and⟨,⟩ who, I hope, will be able to give Satisfactory accounts of me. I wrote to Newton from Munich, and had hoped before this to have had a reply; but have been disappointed. I am very anxious to hear from you all, and to know what you are all doing. For my part, my whole

Summer has been devoted to travelling: gazing about, and endeavouring to regain a good State of health; in which latter I am happy to say I have in a great measure Succeeded. By dint of bathing and a little attention to diet I have conquered the malady that so long rendered me almost a cripple; and the exercise, change of air, and refreshment of Spirits incident to travelling have operated more favorably on my general health. Since I wrote to Newton[1] I have [travelled][2] among the Salzbourg mountains; then by the way of Linz to Vienna, where I remained nearly a month; then through part of Moravia and Bohemia, Stopping a few days at the fine old city of Prague, to this place; where I mean to winter How ⟨much⟩ I should have liked to have had you as a travelling companion throughout my Summers tour. You would have found continual exercise for the pencil, and objects of gratification & improvement in the noble galleries that abound in the principal German Cities.

I shall now take a master and go to work to study German If I can get my pen to work so much the better; but it has been so long idle that I fear it will take some time to get it in a working mood. I hope you have made some more designs for my works and that the engravings are finished of those that were in hands. Take care to get for me Alstons design for the judgement of Wouter Van Twiller;[3] and endeavour, if possible, to get all the originals into your hands. How do you come on in housekeeping Have you got to new & comfortable quarters. How often have I thought of you in exploring some of these old German towns where you might have a wing of a deserted palace almost for nothing. Such glorious painting rooms, that might be blocked up or pulled to pieces to your humour. The living is in fact wonderfully cheap in many of the finest cities of Germany. In Dresden, for example, I have a very neat, comfortable and prettily furnished appartment on the first floor of a Hotel; it consists of a cabinet with a bed in it, and a cheerful Sitting room that looks on the finest Square[4]—I am offered this appartment for the winter at the rate of *thirty Six Shillings* a month!—would to heavens I could get such quarters in London for any thing like the money. I shall probably remain here until the Spring opens, as this is one of the pleasantest winter residences and peculiarly favourable for the study of the German Language, which is here spoken in its purity. Which way I shall direct my wanderings when I leave this I cannot say. I find it is all useless to project plans of tours, as I seldom follow them, but am apt to be driven completely out of my course by whim or circumstance. Do write to me, & direct your letters, *poste restante, Dresde*. Let me know all the news you can collect of our acquaintances and tell me what you are all doing. Have the Bollmans[5] left Paris and returned to America? — How goes on Lukes picture of Greenwich; I presume it is nearly finished. What Subjects have you in hand or what is in view &c &c.

I sent you word in my letter to Newton that I wished you, when the plates illustrating my works were published, to get some setts f[rom] [MS torn] Murray for me & Send them to Mr Van Wart — to be forwarded to my brother in America. One sett to be given to Mr Brevoort of New York —

I find by a letter from my Brother that he met with that worthy personage Mr Peter Powell at Rouen, and that they had a world of pleasant conversation together — I have been writing to my Brother[6] endeavouring to persuade him to pay England a winters visit, but I doubt whether my persuasions will be Successfull.

Farewell, my dear Boy, for further particulars concerning myself: if you wish any I must refer you to Mr Montagu; you may take his word freely for any thing he says good of me; but should ⟨you⟩ he say anything to the contrary I entreat you to be exceeding cautious how you yield credence —

Give my hearty remembrances to "the childe." Father Luke and all the rest of the fraternity; not forgetting my excellent & worthy friend Peter Powell — Yours ever

W I.

ADDRESSED: Charles. R. Leslie Esqr. / 8 Buckingham Place / Fitzroy Square / W. Montagu Esqr
MANUSCRIPT: NYPL—Berg Collection. PUBLISHED: Leslie, *Autobiographical Recollections*, pp. 248–49 (in part); PMI, II, 129–32 (in part).

1. This letter has not been located.
2. WI omitted the past participle of the verb. Both Taylor (Leslie, *Autobiographical Recollections*, p. 248) and PMI (II, 129) have silently added "been" at this point.
3. For other details see WI to Washington Allston, May 21, 1817.
4. WI lived at the Hôtel de Saxe on the New Market Place. See Reichart, *WI and Germany*, p. 70.
5. A family with whom WI and his artist friends were intimate in London before he left for the Continent.
6. This letter has not been located.

363. *To Gilbert Stuart Newton*

Dresden Decr. 2d. 1822.

My dear Newton,

I write this merely to make you acquainted with my friend & fellow Traveller Lieutenant Montagu[1] of the R. Artillery who has ⟨just⟩ been my Compagnon du Voyage through Bohemia. As I have just written a long letter to Leslie[2] giving him a most minute and circumstantial account of all my travels I must refer you to him for further particulars —

I wrote to you from Munich and had hoped long before this to have recd. your reply — why are you so tardy. Mr Montagu will tell you all about me should you wish to know anything —

Yours ever —
W Irving.

MANUSCRIPT: Va.–Barrett.

1. Willoughby Montagu, a first lieutenant in the British Royal Artillery, accompanied WI from Vienna through Bohemia to Dresden on a trip which lasted from November 18 until November 28, including a four-day stop at Prague.

2. See WI's letter to Leslie, dated December 2, 1822.

364. *To Thomas W. Storrow*

Dresden Decr 22d. 1822.

My dear Storrow,

I received a letter a few days since from my Brother in law Mr Van Wart requesting my advice about sending his eldest son, a lad of about fifteen,[1] to France for Several months, to initiate him in the French Language. ⟨I have reccom⟩ He did not know whether to send him to a Public School, or to board him in a French Family. As I knew no family to reccommend him to, & doubted much whether any could be found, where a boy of his age would be properly looked after, I advised him to Send him to a public School, and mentioned the one where my friend Charles[2] goes — and I took the liberty further of saying that, should he send him to that school, ⟨I was su⟩ he might reccommend him to your care, and that I was sure you and Mrs Storrow would keep a friendly eye upon him for my sake — I hope I have not over rated your good will for me; I have judged only from my own feelings towards you & yours. ⟨H?⟩ The lad in question is an uncommonly fine boy and one in whom I feel uncommon interest; as he is the eldest of the family and will be his fathers main stay. He is of a fine disposition, remarkably apt at his studies and a great reader. I think he & charles will like one another much. I have scribbled this merely on the *possibility* of his being sent to paris; as it may be thought best to send him to some place in the country; though I know my Sister so well that I am sure it would be a consideration that would outweigh almost every other, the having her boy under the kind eye of Mrs Storrow.

The last time I wrote to you was, I think, from Vienna,[3] and the greater part of my letter was to the Young folks — Since then I have made a tour, or rather a straight course, through Bohemia, Stopping about four days at its old Capital Prague;[4] a very interesting old city. I have now been here about three weeks, and am settled for the Winter. This place pleases me very much. It is cheerful, yet quiet — The Society very agreeable and on an easy footing. The city itself very neat and convinent — from its moderate Size;[5] and the environs beautiful. I came here without any letters, but Mr Morier[6] the English Ambassador has been uncommonly attentive to me. He has made his house almost like a home to me; has introduced me to all the foreign ministers, who form the gayest & most agreeable circle here, has made me acquainted with some of the first characters of the place, and this day he is to introduce me to court[7]— I have therefore every opportunity of seeing society to advantage, and am greeted with civilities from all quarters. The only drawback is that there are german translations of my works just appearing, and my writings & myself are topicks in the little literary papers which abound in Germany. This has made me an object of blue Stocking curiosity and ⟨I h⟩ instead of quietly taking a post of observer in society I have to talk — and to fight my way through tough conversations with the aid of bad french and worse german. Theres no such thing as lounging about *mum chance,* or stealing a comfortable nap in a corner of a Sopha.

The mode of living here is somewhat old fashioned as to hours; but still very pleasant. The royal family & the old nobility and people about court, dine at *One* oclock. the Younger part of the Nobility, who like more fashionable hours dine at two. The foreign ministers, & the English resident here, dine about four — visits of ceremony are sometimes paid at twelve oclock, but more commonly between five and Six. At Six oclock the fashionable world go to the theatre, where the performance lasts commonly until half past eight or at most nine — After the theatre you pay sociable visits to families with whom you are acquainted, and before eleven you are at home, & ready for bed—Such is fashionable life at Dresden. It is true this routine is broken in upon by evening parties, Balls &c — particularly during Carnival. ⟨at⟩ You go to Balls & routs about eight oclock — and they rarely last later than twelve — I like the ⟨privilege⟩ ↑custom↓ of paying visits in the evening particularly — it always puts society upon an easy social footing.

I must now leave off to dress for court. The levee is held at twelve oclock; just after morning ⟨ch⟩ Service of the Chapel — I shall write my opinion of the King, queen & the rest of the royal family, in some future letter, to the young princesses, as I know they take particular interest in topicks of the Kind. Give my love to your household — I shall be extremely disappointed if I do not receive a letter soon from Susan, Minny & Charles

Yours ever —

W Irving.

ADDRESSED: à Monsieur / Monsr. Thomas W Storrow / Rue Thevenot / à Paris.
    POSTMARKED: DRESDEN / 22 DE 22 / Decembre 30 1822
MANUSCRIPT: Harvard.   PUBLISHED: WIS, pp. 29–32.

1. Henry Van Wart, Jr., who was born in 1806.
2. Charles Storrow, the thirteen-year-old son of Thomas Storrow.
3. On November 10, 1822.
4. WI arrived in Prague on the evening of November 22 and left on the morning of November 26.
·5. Dresden had a population of about 50,000 people at this time. See Reichart, *WI and Germany*, p. 68.
6. John Philip Morier (1776–1853) was British envoy extraordinary to the court of Saxony from 1816 to 1825.
7. At noon on Sunday, December 22, WI was presented to Princes Anton (1755–1836) and Max (1759–1838), who were brothers of the king, to Prince Johann (1801–1873) and his wife, Amelia Augusta, and to Princess Maria Amelia (1794–1870). WI then proceeded to the royal apartments where he met the king, Friedrich August (1750–1827). See *J&N*, III, 98–99.

365.   To Karl August Böttiger

[January 6, 1823]

My dear Sir,
    Will you have the kindness to forward the enclosed note to Messrs Duncker and Humbolt,[1] and add to the many obligations which you have already conferred upon,
    Dear Sir,/Very respectfully and gratefully/Your sincere friend & Servt
                                                    Washington Irving
Hotel de Saxe/Jany 6th 182⟨2⟩3

MANUSCRIPT: Nürnberg Museum.

Karl August Böttiger (1760–1835), director of the Dresden Museum of Classical Art whom WI met at the home of the British envoy extraordinary, John P. Morier, has been called "perhaps the most influential – though not the most important – figure in the cultural life of Dresden." See Reichart, *WI and Germany*, p. 75.

1. These were the Berlin publishers of a translation of *Bracebridge Hall*, which appeared in 1823 in two volumes. WI used the spelling "Humbolt" for "Humblot." See also *J&N*, III, 54.

366.   To Sarah Van Wart

Dresden, March 7, 1823.

My Dear Sister:
    * * * My winter in Dresden has been extremely agreeable. I have become quite at home among the good people, and am invited to every thing that is going on in the world of fashion and gaiety. The old court has particularly pleased me from its stiff old fashioned formalities, and buckram ceremonies. I have been treated uniformly with the most marked attention, by all the members of the royal family, and am in

great favor with the old queen.[1] There is a singular mixture of state and familarity in some of the court fêtes. There have been,[2] for instance, several court balls given by the royal family. At those given by the king, the common people are admitted as spectators, and rows of seats are erected for them on each side of the great saloon in which the company dance. Here then you see the nobility and visitors of the court, in full court dresses, dancing in the centre of the saloon, while on each side are long banks of burly faces wedged together, men, women, and children, and gazing and curtseying as at a theatre. As the court dances are not always the most dignified, one would think this opportunity of seeing royalty cutting capers, would be enough to destroy the illusion with which it is surrounded. There is one romping dance called "the Grandfather," something in the style of *Sir Roger de Coverly*,[3] which generally winds up the balls, and of which the princes and princesses are extremely fond. In this I have seen the courtiers of all ages capering up and down the saloon to the infinite amusement of the populace, and in conformity to the vagaries of the dance, I have been obliged to romp about with one of the princesses as if she had been a boarding school girl. * * * *

I wish I could give you a good account of my literary labors, but I have nothing to report. I am merely seeing and hearing, and my mind seems in too crowded and confused a state to produce any thing. I am getting very familiar with the German language; and there is a lady[4] here who is so kind as to give me lessons every day in Italian, which language I had nearly forgotten, but which I am fast regaining. Another lady[5] is superintending my French, so that if I am not acquiring ideas, I am at least acquiring a variety of modes of expressing them when they do come. * * * *

Give my love to Mr. Van Wart and to all the dear young folks. How I long to see them all once more. I shall have a world to talk about, when I once more resume my corner on the sofa. * * * *

PUBLISHED: PMI, II, 136–38 (in part).

1. Queen Maria Amelia (1752–1828).
2. The three-volume abridgement (ca. 1869) has a comma after "been." That punctuation has been adopted for the present text.
3. WI mentions this dance in his journal entry for December 31, 1822. See *J&N*, III, 104.
4. Identified as Mrs. Foster in PMI, II, 137. Mrs. Amelia Foster was the third wife of John Foster (1765–1831), of the Bogue Estate, Jamaica, and of Buckhill House, and Lord of the Manor of Marston, Bedfordshire. She had come to Dresden in late summer or early fall of 1820 with her five children: Mary Amelia (Emily) (1804–1885), Flora (1806–1876), Algernon (1811–1821), Arthur Fitzjohn (1813–1842), and Morgan Hugh (1815–1891).
5. Emily Foster, according to PMI, II, 137.

367.   To Peter Irving

Dresden, March 10, 1823.

My Dear Brother:

What a time have I suffered to pass by without writing to you. I can give no excuse for it but the wretched and unsatisfactory one, of continual procrastination, and too much distraction and dissipation of mind; but I know you to be indulgent in these cases, and not to consider a casual career of dissipation among the *crying* sins. I have been passing a very agreeable, a very idle, but I trust after all, a very profitable winter in Dresden; for though I have done nothing with my pen, and have been tossed about on the stream of society, yet I console myself with the idea that I have *lived into* a great deal of amusing and characteristic information; which after all, is perhaps the best way of studying the world. I have been most hospitably received and even caressed in this litttle capital, and have experienced nothing but the most marked kindness from the king downwards. My reception, indeed, at court has been peculiarly flattering, and every branch of the royal family has taken occasion to show me particular attention, whenever I made my appearance. I wish you were here with me to study this little court; it is just the thing that would delight you. It is one of the most formal and ceremonious in Europe, keeping up all the old observances that have been laid aside in other courts. The king is an excellent old gentleman, between seventy and eighty,[1] but a staunch stickler for the old school. He has two brothers, Prince Max and Prince Antoine, and the trio are such figures as you see in the prints of Frederick the Great. Prince Max is one of the most amiable old gentlemen I have ever met with; his countenance and manners peculiarly benevolent; he has two sons, Frederick and John (the former will one day inherit the throne), and two daughters, the youngest of whom is the present Queen of Spain.[2] Prince Antoine, the other brother of the king, is a brisk, lively little gentleman; very religious, but withal as great a hunter as Nimrod,[3] and as fond of dancing as King David. He married a sister of the Emperor of Austria,[4] an old lady that is a complete picture of the dames of the old school. Prince Antoine has always shown a great fancy for me, and I believe I owe much of my standing in the old gentleman's favor, from dancing French quadrilles. I have dined with the king, and been at a number of balls and soirées given by the different members of the royal family; as at these balls every one must be in uniform or court dress, they are very showy.

Among the other institutions which the king keeps up, is a grand hunting establishment in the old style. As this is the only place in Europe where any thing of the kind is maintained in the ancient manner, I have been very much interested by it. The king has his forest masters; his chasseurs, piqueurs, jägers, &c., &c. There are large forests appropriated to the chase, where deer and boars are preserved; and the country abounds with game. I have followed the king twice to the boar hunt;[5] the last time we had a fine run of upwards of two hours. The king was followed by a numerous hunting retinue, all clad in hunting costumes of green. The *chasse* was in a forest which is traversed by roads, lanes, and paths in every direction; and the noise of the hounds and horns, the sight of huntsmen dashing about through the forest in every direction, and of the old king and his retinue galloping along the alleys of the forest, formed altogether one of the most animating scenes I have ever witnessed. The boar was not overpowered until he had killed one dog and wounded several.

Finding how much I was interested in their *chasse*, the old queen (who has always shown me great kindness) was so obliging as to order another kind of *chasse*, that I might see how the wild boars were taken in nets; which was very amusing, but by no means so animating and interesting as the *chasse* on horseback.

Among the other amusements of the winter, we have had a little attempt at private theatricals. These have been at the house of Mrs. Foster, an English lady of rank, who has been residing here for a couple of years. She has two daughters, most accomplished and charming girls. They occupy part of a palace,[6] and in a large saloon a little theatre was fitted up, the scenery being hired from a small theatre; and the dresses from a masquerade warehouse.[7] It was very prettily arranged, I assure you. We first tried Tom Thumb,[8] which, however, went no further than a dressed rehearsal, in which I played the part of King Arthur, to Mrs. Foster's Dollalolla; and the other parts were supported by some of the English who were wintering in Dresden.[9] There was then an attempt to get up a little opera,[10] altered from the French by Colonel Livius,[11] a cousin of Mrs. Foster, and some such a character as I have described in Master Simon[12] in my last work. The colonel, however, who is a green-room veteran, and has written for the London theatres, was so much of a martinet in his managerial discipline, that the piece absolutely fell through from being too much managed. In the mean time a few of the colonel's theatrical subjects conspired to play him a trick, and get up a piece without his knowledge. We pitched upon the little comedy of *Three Weeks after Marriage*,[13] which I altered and arranged so as to leave out two or three superfluous characters. I played the part of Sir Charles Rackett; Miss Foster, Lady Rackett; Miss Flora Foster, Dimity; Mrs. Foster, Mrs. Druggett; and a young officer by the name of Corkran,[14] the part of Mr. Druggett. You cannot imagine the amusement this little theatrical plot furnished us. We rehearsed in Mrs. Foster's drawing-room, and as the whole was to be kept a profound secret, and as Mrs. Foster's drawing-room is a great place of resort, and as especially our dramatic sovereign, Colonel Livius, was almost an inmate of the family, we were in continued risk of discovery, and had to gather together like a set of conspirators. We, however, carried our plot into execution more successfully than commonly falls to the lot of conspirators. The colonel had ordered a dress rehearsal of his little opera; the scenery was all prepared, the theatre lighted up, a few amateurs admitted: the colonel took his seat before the curtain, to direct the rehearsal. The curtain rose, and out walked Mr. and Mrs. Druggett in proper costume. The little colonel was perfectly astonished, and did not recover himself before the first act was finished; it was a perfect explosion to him.[15] We afterwards performed the little comedy before a full audience of the English resident in Dresden, and of several of the nobility that understood English, and it went off with great spirit and success. We are now on the point of playing *The Wonder*,[16] which I have altered and shortened to suit the strength of the company, and to prune off objectionable parts. In this, I play the part of Don Felix, to Miss Foster's Violante. She plays charmingly; the part of Colonel Briton I have had to alter into a British captain of a man-of-war, to adapt it to the turn of the actor who is to play it, viz: Captain Morier, of the Navy, brother of the British Minister.[17] I have dwelt rather long on this subject because I know you relish matters of the kind.

I enclose you a first and second of exchange for one hundred pounds sterling, which I beg you to use as frankly as I should do. I am sorry to find the steamboat does not answer, and I really think it is losing time and trouble to prosecute the matter any further. * * *

At all events, don't suffer yourself to be discouraged. I will join you some time in the course of this year, and then between us we will make the pot boil briskly.

PUBLISHED: PMI, II, 138–43.

1. Friedrich August I was born in 1750.

2. Prince Max's daughters were Princess Maria Amelia and Maria Josepha, who married Ferdinand VII of Spain in 1819.

3. "A mighty hunter before the Lord" (Gen. 10:9).

4. In 1787 Max married Maria Therese of Austria.

5. WI went boar-hunting with the King's party on January 10 and 21. See *J&N*, III, 109–10, 118–19.

6. The Fosters were living at Courland Palace, located two blocks from WI's hotel on Neumarkt Square. See *The Journal of Emily Foster*, ed. Stanley T. Williams and Leonard B. Beach (New York, 1938), pp. 33–34, 109.

7. In his notebook for January 8, 1823, WI indicates that he was "Busy in the Morng getting dresses for private theatricals—found a Warehouse of Dresses kept by a Jew—ascended a narrow dark staircase to get to it—chose dresses—" See *J&N*, III, 108.

8. *The Tragedy of Tragedies; or, The Life and Death of Tom Thumb the Great* (1730-1731) by Henry Fielding.

9. WI lists the entire cast in his notebook entry for January 8, 1823. See *J&N*, III, 108.

10. This was *Maid or Wife: or, The Deceiver Deceived*, based on *Frontin Mari Garçon* by Scribe and Mélesville. For details about this work by Livius see Walter A. Reichart, "Washington Irving's Friend and Collaborator: Barham John Livius, Esq.," *PMLA*, 56 (June, 1941), 517-18.

11. Barham John Livius (1787-1854) of Bedford, England, who had adapted French plays for the English stage, was now working in Dresden with German dramatic materials. For other details see Reichart, "Washington Irving's Friend and Collaborator: Barham John Livius, Esq.," pp. 513-31; Percy R. Kirby, "Washington Irving, Barham Livius and Weber," *Music and Letters* 31 (April, 1950), 133-47; George R. Price, "Washington Irving's Librettos," *Music and Letters* 29 (October, 1948), 348-55.

12. In *Bracebridge Hall* Master Simon, a relative of Squire Bracebridge, occupied himself with details relating to the past and genealogy.

13. *Three Weeks After Marriage* (1764) was a comedy by Arthur Murphy (1727-1805).

14. Carl Cochrane had come to Dresden with his sister, Mrs. Williams, in late September, 1822. WI does not refer to him as an officer in his notebooks.

15. WI does not record these details in his notebooks.

16. *The Wonder; a Woman Keeps a Secret* (1714) by Susanna Centlivre (1667?-1723). This play was performed before a group of notables on April 4, 1823. See *J&N*, III, 135.

17. William Morier (1790-1864), who later became an admiral in the British navy.

368.   To Charles R. Leslie

Dresden, March 15th. 1823.

My dear Leslie,

I have just been siezed with a fit of letter writing after having nearly forgotten how to use my pen; so I take the earliest stage of the complaint to scribble to you.   I ha⟨ve⟩d hoped to ⟨hav⟩ receive a gratuitous letter from you before this; but you are one of those close codgers that never pay more than the law compells you. I am extremely sorry to hear from Newton[1] that he has been so ill — tho' I am by no means surprized at it; as he played all kinds of vagaries with a constitution naturally delicate. I trust this fit of illness will teach him the necessity of daily and regular attention to exercise & diet; which all the advice in the world will not beat into a young mans head. There is more time lost by these daily attempts to gain time than by any thing else; and he who will endeavour to cheat his health out of an hour or two a day in extra fasting or extra application will in the end have to pay days & weeks for those hours.

How often I have wished for you and Newton during the last

eight or nine months ⟨during⟩ in the course of which I have been continually mingling in scenes ⟨and⟩ full of character and picture. The place where I am now passing my time is a complete study. The court of this little Kingdom o[f] Saxony ⟨one of the⟩ perhaps the most ceremonious and old fashioned in Europe, and one finds here customs and observances in full vigour that have long since faded away in other courts. The King is a capital character himself — a complete old gentleman of the ancient school and very tenacious in keeping up the old Style. He has treated me with the most marked kindness and every member of the royal family has shewn me great civility. What would greatly delight you is the Royal hunting establishment, which the king maintains at a vast expense, being his hobby. He has vast forests stocked with game — ⟨Forest⟩ and a complete Forest police — Forest masters; chasseurs—piqueurs Yagers &c &c — Several hunting lodges — packs of hounds — horses &c &c. The charm of the thing is that all this is kept up in the old style — and to go out hunting with him you might fancy yourself in the midst of one of those Scenes of old times which we read of in poetry & romance

I have followed him twice to the Boar hunt — the last we had extremely good Sport — the Boar gave us a chace of upward of two hours, and was not overpowered until it had killed one dog and desperately wounded several others. It was a very cold winter day with much snow on the ground — but as the hunting was in a thick pine forest, and the day was sunny, we did not feel the cold.

The King and all his hunting retinue were clad in an old fashioned hunting ⟨dress⟩ ↑uniform↓ of green, with green caps — The Sight of the old Monarch and his retinue gallopping through the alleys of the forest — the yagers dashing singly about in all directions cheering the hounds — the Shouts — the blasts of hòrns, the cry of hounds ringing through the forest altogether made ⟨of⟩ one of the most animating Scenes I ever beheld. I have become very intimate with one of the Kings Forest Masters, who lives in a picturesque old hunting lodge with towers — formerly a convent — and who has undertaken to shew me all the economy of the hunting establishment What glorious groupings, and what admirable studies for figures & faces I have seen among these hunters —

By this time your painting of Autolycus[2] must be nearly finished— I love to hear a description of it from Newton. Do tell me something about it yourself—Have you thought of a subject for your next — and have you entirely abandoned the ⟨Shakespeare⟩ Scene of Shakespeare brought up for Deer stealing — I think it would be a subject that you would treat with peculiar felicity and you could not have one of a more general nature since Shakespeare and his scanty biography are known in all parts of the world. Upon my soul the more & more I think of it the more I am convinced it is a subject that you might make a masterpiece of — it is one you should paint at least as large as your May Day[3] — and introduce a great number of figures. Do think of it — You might make a great impression by such a picture.

I have done nothing with my pen since I have left you! absolutely nothing! I have been gazing about; rather idly perhaps — but yet among fine Scenes & striking characters and I can only hope that some of them may stick to my mind, and furnish me with materials in some future fit of scribbling — I have been fighting my way into the German language & I am regaining my italian and for want of more profitable employment have turned *play actor!* We have been getting up private theatricals here at the house of an English lady — I have already enacted Sir Charles Rackett, in three weeks after marr[iage][4] with great applause, and am on the point of playing Don Felix i[n] The wonder[5] — I had no idea of this fund of Dramatic talent lurking wit[hin] me; and I now console myself that if the worst comes to the worst I can turn stroller & pick up a decent maintenance among the barns in England. I verily believe Nature intended me for a vagabond.

Do write to me on the receipt of this; and give your letter to Newton who will forward it by the British Ambassadors bag—Let me know what you are all doing, and what are your views & intentions. How does Peter Powell & how does Father Luke. Newton in his last letter gave me unfavourable intelligence of poor Luke—Can you tell me anything of my good friend Mrs [?Lotteway?][6] and how she is getting on. She talked of taking a new house, if she has so, I might be able to render her some service by reccommending friends to her.

I must write to Newton & to several others[7] by this opportunity and so I will bring my letter to a close that I may have time and ideas left. Give my kindest remembrances to your sister and believ[e] me dear Leslie ever yours truly

Washington Irving.

P.S. I hope you intend to make some designs for Bracebridge Hall — I would rather have the work illustrated by you than by any one else.

Addressed: Charles R Leslie Esqr. / Historical Painter / London.
Manuscript: NYPL—Berg Collection.   Published: Leslie, *Autobiographical Recollections*, pp. 250–52 (in part); PMI, II, 144–47 (in part).

1. This letter of Newton's has not been located.

2. Tom Taylor suggests that this character from *The Winter's Tale* was painted for Mr. J. Sheepshanks in 1836 and later hung in the National Gallery. See Leslie, *Autobiographical Recollections*, pp. 249, 359.

3. *May Day in the Time of Queen Elizabeth* was exhibited at the Royal Academy in 1821. See Leslie, *Autobiographical Recollections*, p. 357.

4. *Three Weeks After Marriage* by Arthur Murphy. The paper is torn along
the edge, and portions of three missing words have been supplied in brackets.
   5. *The Wonder; a Woman Keeps a Secret* by Susannah Centlivre.
   6. WI's writing is obscured at this point.
   7. These letters have not been located.

369.   To Mrs. Amelia Foster

[April–May, 1823]

letters of¹
a gloomy nature. I read [*two or three words unrecovered*] time ↑kept↓²
in anxiety about a sister³ [whose?] constitution [was?] [*MS faded*]
[de]licate,⁴ who was dangerously ill, and whose [life was?] [*MS faded*]
all important to a numerous & lively family. I [*unrecovered*] [*unrecovered*] had a letter from her just after leaving her [*unrecovered*] when
she had been confined for weeks: but I [had?] heard no further from
her, in consequence of the delitaraness of diplomatic conveyances.⁵ I
had distressing news of the illness & mental malady of my brothers
widow⁶ in america; which for some time occasioned great anguish &
alarm in her family. I heard of the failure of schemes⁷ in which I had
ventured as much as I could afford, in the hopes of benefiting others
that were dear to me. But I will not pursue these dismal details—I have
said enough to shew you that I do not torment myself without a cause.
   You wonder why I am not married. I have shewn you why I was
not long since—when I had sufficiently recovered from that loss, I
became involved in ruin. It was not for a man broken down in the
world to ⟨make⟩ drag down any woman to his paltry circumstances, and
I was too proud to tolerate the idea of ever mending my circumstances
by matrimony. My time has now gone by; and I have growing claims
upon my thoughts, and upon my means [slender?] [*MS torn*] & precarious as they are. I feel as if I had [already?] [*MS torn*] a family to
think & provide for, and. . . . Such are some of the ⟨cares & clouds⟩
↑dark shadows↓ that [*unrecovered*] [*MS torn*] obtrude themselves
upon my brightest momen[ts and] [*MS torn*] haunt me in places where
I ought to be full of en[joy]ment, [*MS torn*] and suddenly check me
in the midst [of] [*MS torn*] my vivacity. I am too apt to be absor[bed in]
[*MS torn*] the delights of intimate & social intercourse and to lose all
thought and relish for these pursuits on which I depend, and which
require complete abstraction & devotion of the mind. And then ⟨the⟩
I am seized with compunction at my selfish indulgence, reccollect how
much good I could & ought to do for others, and that while I am idly
amusing myself the useful purposes of life are neglected. You want to

know some of the *fancies* that distress me; I will mention one as a
specimen of many others. I was one evening going to a Ball at the
Countess de Hohenthals.[8] I had not slept well the night before & after
dressing myself I lay down on the Sopha & fell asleep. I dreamt of my
poor Brother[9] whom I had lost about eighteen months before, & whom
I had not seen for years. We walked & talked together. The dream was
most vivid and consistent & affecting. When I went to the Ball I was
engaged to dance, I think with both Emily & Flora, I tried to dance but
could not; my heart sank at the very sound of the music and I had to
give up the attempt & go home. Do you want some of the real causes.
While at Dresden I had repeated feelings since I entered upon the
world, which like severe wounds and maims in the body, leave forever
after a morbid sensitiveness, and a quick susceptibility to any new
injury. ⟨I was neither⟩ Still there was always a reaction in my spirits;
they rose readily of themselves when the immediate pressure was
removed; ⟨I had always a⟩ I never soured under sufferings; my disposition which was ⟨not⟩ originally rather impatient, seemed to soften
under trials, and I had always a great facility at receiving pleasurable
impressions.

When I was very young I had an irrepressible flow of spirits that
often went beyond my strength Every thing was fairy land to me. As
I had some quickness of parts I was intended for the Law which with
us in America is the path to honour and preferment—to every thing that
is distinguished in public life. I read law with a Gentleman[10] distinguished both in legal and political concerns, one who took a great
part in public affairs & was eminent for his talents. He took a fancy
to me, though a very heedless student, and made me almost an inmate
of his house. He had lately married for the second time; a woman[11]
much younger than himself, one of the most amiable and gentle of human
beings. She was like a sister to me. By his first wife[12] he had two
daughters Ann & Matilda.[13] They were little more than children, the
eldest was about fourteen. They were two lovely little beings. Ann
was brilliant both as to beauty and natural talent. Matilda was a timid,
shy, silent little being, and always kept by the side of her step mother;
who indeed looked more like an elder sister, and acted like a most tender
one. I saw a great deal of them. I was a mere stripling, and we were
all shy and awkward at first, but we soon grew sociable and ↑I↓ began
to take a great interest in Matilda, though little more at the time
than a mere boyish fancy.—I am growing perhaps too minute—I dont
want to make any romantic story. After a time the delicate state of
my health induced my friends to send me to Europe. I was absent
nearly two years. On my return I resumed my legal studies. My meeting
with my little female friends was a delightful one. Ann was encreased

in beauty, indeed there was an effulgence in the beauty of her countenance that struck every one. I reccollect my meeting with Matilda as if it was yesterday. She came home from school to see me, she entered full of eagerness, yet shy from her natural timidity, from the time that had elaps[ed] [MS torn] since we parted, and from the idea of my being a *travelled man*, instead of a stripling student—Heavens what a difference the interval had made She was but between fifteen & sixteen, just growing up, there was a softness and delicacy in her form and look, a countenance of that eloquent expression, yet that mantling modesty—I thought I had never beheld any thing so lovely—

We saw each other every day and I became excessively attached to her. Her shyness wore off by degrees. The more I saw of her the more I had reason to admire her. Her mind seemed to unfold itself leaf by leaf, and every time to discover new sweetness—No body knew her so well as I for she was generally timid & [unrecovered] [MS torn] [yet] [MS damaged] I in a manner studied her excellence. Never did I meet with more intuitive rectitude of mind[,] more native delicacy, more exquisite propriety in thought word & action than in this young creature. I am not exaggerating—what I say was acknowledg[ed] [MS torn] by all that knew her. Her brilliant little sister used to say that people began by admiring her but ended by loving Matilda. For my part I idolized her. I felt at times rebuked by her superior delicacy & purity and as if I were a coarse unworthy being in comparison.

This passion was terribly against my studies. I passed an examination, however, and was admitted to the bar, ⟨though more⟩ more through courtesy than desert, for I scarcely answered a single question correctly; but the examiners were prepossessed in my favour. I felt my own deficiency and despaired of ever succeeding at the Bar. I could study any thing else rather than Law, and had a fatal propensity to Belles lettres. I had gone on blindly, like a boy in Love, but now I began to open my eyes and be miserable. I had nothing in purse nor in expectation. I anticipated nothing from my legal pursuits, ⟨and the⟩ and had done nothing to make me hope for public employment or political elevation. I had begun a Satirical & humorous work (the History of N York) in company with one of my brothers[14] but he had gone to Europe shortly after commencing it, and my feelings had run into so different [a] [MS torn] vein that I could not go on with it. I became low spirited & disheartned and did not know what was to become of me. I made frequent attempts to apply myself to the law; but it is a slow & tedious undertaking for a young man to get into practise; and I had unluckily no turn for business. The Gentleman with whom I had studied saw the state of my mind. He had an affectionate regard for me—a paternal one I may say. He had a better opinion of my legal capacity tha[n] [*MS torn*] it merited. He urged me to return to my studies t[o] [*MS torn*] ↑apply↓ myself to become well acquainted with the law—and that in case I could make myself capable of undertaking legal concerns he would take me into partnership with him & give me his daughter. Nothing could be more generous. I set to work with zeal to study anew, and I considered myself bound in honour not to make further advances with the daughter until I should feel satisfied with my proficiency in the Law—It was all in vain. I had an insuperable repugnance to the study—my mind would not take hold of it; or rather by long despondency had become for the time incapable of dry application. I was in a wretched state of doubt and self distrust. I tried to finish the work which I was secretly writing, hoping it would give me reputation and gain me Some public appointment. In the mean time I saw Matilda every day and that helped to distract me.

In the midst of this struggle and anxiety she was taken ill with a cold. Nothing was thought of it at first, but she grew rapidly worse, and ⟨was? ↑the illness↓ formed itself into a consumption⟩ fell into a consumption. I cannot tell you what I suffered. The ills that I have undergone in this life have been dealt out to me, drop by drop, and I have tasted all their bitterness. I saw her fade rapidly away beautiful and more beautiful and more angelical to the very last. I was often by her bed side and in her wandring state of mind she would talk to me with a sweet natural and affecting eloquence that was overpowering—I saw more of the beauty of her mind in that delirious state than I had ever known before. Her malady was rapid in its course, ⟨yet⟩ and hurried her off in two months. Her dying struggles were painful & protracted. For three day[s] & nights I did not leave the house & scarcely slept. I was by her when she died—all the family were assembled round her, some praying others weeping, for she was adored by them all—I was the last one she looked upon—I have told you as briefly as I could what if I were to tell with all the incidents & feelings that accompanied it would fill volumes. She was but about seventeen years old when she died.—

I cannot tell you what a horrid state of mind I was in for a long time—I seemed to care for nothing—the world was a blank to me—I abandoned all thoughts of the Law—I went into the country, but could not bear ⟨to be alone⟩ ↑solitude↓ yet could not enjoy society—There was a dismal horror continually in my mind that made me fear to be alone—I had often to get up in the night & seek the bedroom of ⟨some?⟩ my brother, as if the having a human being by me would relieve me from the frightful gloom of my own thoughts.

Months elapsed before my mind resumed any tone; but the despondency I had suffered for a long time in the course of this attachment, and the anguish that attended its catastrophe seemed to give a turn to my whole character, and ⟨produced⟩ threw some clouds into my disposition which have ever since hung about it. When I ⟨could⟩ ↑became↓ ⟨get⟩ ↑more↓ calm & collected I applied myself, by way of occupation, to the finishing my work.[15] I brought it to a close, as well as I could, and published it but the time & circumstances in which it was produced rendered me always unable to look upon it with satisfaction. Still it took with the public & gave me celebrity, as an original work was something remarkable & uncommon in America. I was noticed caressed & for a time elated by the popularity I gained. I found myself uncomfortable in my feelings in N York & travelled about a little. Wherever I went I was overwhelmed with attentions; I was full of youth and animation, far different from the being I now am, and I was quite flushed with this early taste of public favour. Still however the career of gaiety & notoriety soon palled upon me. I seemed to drift about without aim or object, at the mercy of every breeze; my heart wanted anchorage. I was naturally susceptible and tried to form other attachments, but my heart would not hold on; it would continually recur to what it had lost; and whenever there was a pause in the hurry of novelty & excitement I would sink into dismal dejection. For years I could not talk on the subject of this hopeless regret; I could not even mention her name; but her image was continually before me, and I dreamt of her incessantly.

My Brothers saw that there was no likelihood of my succeeding in the Law; and they wished me to cultivate my general talents and devote myself to literature. Indeed they were all indulgence to me. ⟨so⟩ Two of them had engaged in various speculations, for at that time every thing was a matter of Speculation, from the unsettled state of affairs. They gave me an interest in their concerns on condition that I should never appear or take any active part in business, but pursue my literary avocations. They were successful in their Enterprizes; wealth flowed in upon us, I was little elated by it. I cared nothing for money it seemed to ⟨ar?⟩ come too late to do me good. I read a good deal at times, but I could not bring myself to write, I had grown indifferent to literary reputation. I felt a degree of apathy growing upon me, which was dismal. We were threatened by invasion and every one had to take some part in Military concerns. I went with the Governor as Military Secretary & then as Aid de Camp. This was the first thing that roused and stimulated me, but it did not last long; for peace took place, the forces were disbanded & I had nothing to do. My literary notoriety had made me an object of attention, I was continually drawn into Society, my time & thoughts dissipated and my spirits jaded. I became weary of every thing and of myself. While in this mood a squadron was fitted out against the Algerines. The Commodore[16] was a particular friend & invited me to accompany him on the enterprize. I determined to do so: to break off in this way from idle habits and idle associates & fashionable dissipation, and when I returned to settle myself down to useful and honourable application. The Squadron delayed sailing so long that I got out of patience. Napoleon had returned from Elba, and all Europe was again in agitation—I resolved to sail at once to England & get over to the Continent to see the armies. I had a hard parting with my good old mother. I was her favorite child & could not bear to leave her in her old days; but I trusted to return after a short absence, quite another being & then to settle down quietly beside her for the rest of ⟨my⟩ her life.

When I arrived in England I found my Brother[17] ill. I stopped to be with him as his illness was tedious. Just then, great reverses took place in affairs of all kind. My Brothers had entered into large speculations and were completely involved in the difficulties of the ⟨kind⟩ times. I was involved with them, for ⟨they⟩ my name had been implicated in their transactions. Every struggle and Sacrafice to avoid ruin was in vain. It approached in its most overwhelming form. I saw it coming from a distance, and that it was unavoidable. I was no man of business; I knew nothing about it & disliked the very name; to such a one the horrors of commercial embarrassments and ruin are strange and frightful and humiliating. This new calamity seemed more intolerable even than that which had before overcome me. That was solemn and sanctifying, it seemed while it prostrated my spirits, to purify & elevate my soul. But this was vile and sordid and humiliated me to the dust. Good heavens what I suffered for Months and months and months—I lost all appetite[.] I scarcely slept—I went to my bed every night as to a grave—I saw the Detestable ordeal of Bankruptcy in the distance and that it was in-evitable, for my name stood committed in a commercial form. I would not live over the dreadful term of trial to be sure of a long life of felicity. In the midst of my distress I heard of my poor Mothers death.[18] She died without a pang she talked of me to the last, and would not part with a letter which she had received a few days before from me. I loved her with all the affection of a son, and one of my most poignant griefs wa[s] [*Edge obscured by binding*] that her latter days should be embittered by my reverses. Shall I say it then, I heard of her death with a momentary satisfaction; for she died ignorant of my misfortunes and escaped the pang of seeing the child she was so fond & proud of ⟨har?⟩ ruined and degraded.

I underwent ruin in all its bitterness & humiliation—in a strange land —among strangers. I went through the horrible ordeal of Bankruptcy.[19] It is true I was treated with indulgence—even with courtesy; for they percieved that I was a mere nominal party in the concern—But to me it was a cruel blow—I felt cast down—abased—I had lost my *cast*—I had always been proud of Spirit, and in my own country had been, as it were, a being of the air—I ⟨would not⟩ felt the force of the ⟨?question?⟩⟩↑text↓ "a wounded spirit who can bear?" I shut myself up from society—and would See no one. For months I studied German day & night by way of driving off horrid thoughts—The idea suddenly came to return to my pen. not so much for support, for bread & water had no terrors for me, but to reinstate myself in the worlds thoughts—To raise myself from the degradation into which I considered myself fallen. I took my resolution—threw myself a stranger into London, shut myself up and went to work—The terrible ⟨flashings⟩ vicissitudes of feelings I had suffered for nearly two years, while involved in ⟨the⟩ ruin⟨s⟩ ⟨of⟩ & bankruptcy, had ⟨terribly⟩ shattered my nerves & it took a long time to get my mind into operation—At length I succeeded. Just as I was getting my pen into activity I received a letter from America offering me an honourable place under Government.[20] I declined it— my pride was up—I would receive nothing as a boon granted to a ruined man—I was resolved if ⟨forget⟩ possible to raise myself once more by my talents, and owe nothing to compassion. In this way I produced the Sketch Book—You know its success—You think no doubt I ought to be elated & made happy by it—But you have no knowledge of the many counter checks to this enjoyment, in the misfortunes of my once flourishing family—nor do I intend to enter into them. It is not two years Since I lost my elder Brother—a man whom I loved better than any other man on the face of the earth—a man full of worth & talents, ⟨and⟩ beloved in private and honoured in public life—He died of a rapid decline brought on ⟨b⟩ I am convinced by the acute anxiety and distress of mind he had suffered.

I have mentioned to you in a brief manner Some of the leading circumstances which have distressed me Since my entering upon life. ⟨They may be⟩↑There were many minor & collateral ones on which I have not touched. ⟨They may be⟩ All these may be↓ ⟨such as man?⟩ events of ordinary occurrence, but they have cut my spirit to the quick, and left behind a morbid sensitiveness that it is difficult always to overcome. Still I have enough of the original elasticity of my nature to rise again from under severe pressures, and there is an activity in my imagination, which though it sometimes plays me false & paints every thing black, yet is more apt to soften and tint up the harshest realities. Indeed I often reproach myself with my cheerfulness and even gaiety at times when I have real cause to grieve. ⟨but wh⟩ Whatever you may think of me, the natural inclination of my mind is to be cheerful; but I have had so many shadows thrown across my path; I see so much doubt before & sorrow behind me; I see every enjoyment hanging on so transient and precarious a tenure, that I cannot help sometimes falling into dejection.

If I seem at times over anxious about my literary labours, it is in some measure because literary occupation is the only one that really interests & absorbs my mind and furnishes me with an end & object in existence, but it is in a great measure because my literary success has enabled le[21] to be of important service in a variety of ways, to those that are dearest to me; and has been a source of pride and satisfaction to my family in the midst of gloom & misfortune

I have now talked to you on subjects that I recur to with excessive pain, and on which I am apt to be silent, for there is little gained by the confiding of grievances. It only overclouds other minds witho[ut] [Edge obscured by binding] brightning ones own. ⟨You have⟩ I prefer summon[ing] [Edge obscured by binding] up the bright pictures of life that I have witnessed and dwelling as much as possible on the agreeable You have more than once spoken to me about my family; I could not talk of my relatives without recalling continually circumstances acutely painful. I never can think of any of them without love and respect, for I dont know one that I ought not be proud of; but they have met with their troubles and trials. Why should I trouble you with the cares & clouds that pass across my mind[.] they pass away of themselves if imaginary, if otherwise sympathy is of no avail. I do not live merely for myself. I have others to think for, and am ⟨full of⟩ at times full of cares & projects, and involved in responsibilities, for I was brought up in the habit of ⟨thinking⟩ considering the interests and welfare of my relations as my own. The Death of my Elder Brother who was every thing to the family, has encreased my cares and duties; ⟨to and⟩↑though↓ I feel how apt I am to be negligent of them, and how incompetent I am at best to fulfill them. ⟨I ought to return to⟩ [end of MS]

Manuscript: Yale. Published: STW, II, 255–62; PMI, I, 224–27 (in part).

In his transcription S. T. Williams has placed the first two paragraphs at the end of the letter.

WI wrote this autobiographical sketch for Mrs. Foster and her daughters. According to Flora Foster Dawson's testimony (PMI, IV, 361), written many years later, WI produced the account of his romance with Matilda Hoffman during an absence of a day or two following an excursion to Wesenstein castle with them on May 17. However, S. T. Williams and L. B. Beach in their notes to *The Journal of Emily Foster* ([New York, 1938], pp. 129–30) suggest that WI's two-day absence from the Fosters occurred on April 29 and 30 following Emily's displeasure at the gossip linking her name romantically with WI's. His avoidance of the Fosters on these days is corroborated by his journal. (See J&N, III, 144–46.) When WI resumed his visits to the Fosters in early May, he presumably gave them the autobiographical memoir. It is possible that Mrs. Dawson, in recalling the episode nearly forty years later, inadvertently confused or telescoped the chronology of events. In any case, it is certain that WI wrote the account before he left for Prague on May 20. As Mrs. Dawson observes, "It was left with us under a sacred promise that it should be returned to him; that no copy should be taken; and that no eyes but ours should ever rest upon it. The promise was faithfully kept, though great was the temptation to keep this history of his early love" (PMI, IV, 361). According to PMI (I, 223), WI in later years kept this letter in a locked repository in a package marked "Private Mems."

1. These words are written in another hand.
2. This word is written in another hand.
3. Ann Sarah Dodge.
4. Much of this page, particularly along the left margin, is damaged, and the writing faded or destroyed.
5. WI is probably alluding to his anxiety about his sister during his first trip to Europe from 1804 to 1806.
6. Julia Paulding Irving (b. 1768), wife of William Irving, died on January 24, 1823. The nature of her illness has not been ascertained.
7. WI is probably referring to the failure of the Seine River steamboat venture.
8. The Countess Hohenthal held a ball on January 25, 1823. See J&N, III, 121.
9. William Irving had died on November 9, 1821.
10. Josiah Ogden Hoffman.
11. Maria Fenno Hoffman was fourteen years younger than her husband.
12. Mary Colden Hoffman, who died on February 19, 1797.
13. Actually there was another daughter, Mary, who was born on June 15, 1796, plus a son, Ogden (1794–1856).
14. Dr. Peter Irving.
15. *Knickerbocker's History of New York.*
16. Stephen Decatur.
17. Peter Irving.
18. Mrs. Sarah Irving died on April 9, 1817.
19. The bankruptcy papers of the Irving brothers were filed in early February, 1818. See WI to Henry Brevoort, January 28, 1818.
20. William Irving had spoken to Henry Clay in Congress about the possibility of a government appointment for WI. See PMI, I, 392.
21. WI probably intended to write "me" instead of "le."

370. To Mrs. Amelia Foster

Dresden–May 4 1823

My dear Mrs. Foster

I will be with you at two today to be ready for dinner at whatever time it may be served – I had declined an invitation[1] that I might dine with you as I recollected it was Miss Foster's birthday – I send you a few lines[2] which I have scribbled on the occasion[.] if you think them in any way worthy of the subject and that they would give her any pleasure — Slip them into her scrap book, if not slip them into the stove that convenient altar, and sacrifice them as a burnt offering to appease the muses—I have no confidence in my rhymes ———— I shall say nothing about Prince Frederick's party for I have no idea of letting my wishes interfere with your family arrangements — God bless you —

Yours truly
Washington Irving

MANUSCRIPT: Va.–Barrett.   PUBLISHED: PMI, II, 151–52.

This letter and the poem alluded to in it are preserved in a copy probably made by Mrs. Foster. On the same page as the letter are excerpts from a letter which WI wrote from Bordeaux on May 7, 1826. On April 27, WI wrote in his journal: "write verses to E on birthday." See J&N, III, 143.

1. As WI indicates at the end of this note, he had been invited to a party at Prince Frederick's.

2. WI's poem was copied and preserved (at Va.–Barrett). It is also printed in PMI, II, 152–53.

To Miss Emily Foster on her birthday—

'Twas now the freshness of the year
When fields were green and groves were gay
When airs were soft, and skies were clear
And all things bloomed in lovely May

Blest month when Nature in her prime
Bestows her fairest gifts on earth
This was the time—the genial time
She destined for her favourite's birth

and emblems delicate she chose
Thy gentle virtues to bespeak
The lily and the pale pale rose
She faintly mingled in thy cheek.

The azure of her noontide sky
With dewy gleams of morn combining
She took to form thy speaking eye
With heaven's own blue serenely shining

She bade the dawning's transient blush
The light and warmth of day revealing
At times thy pallid beauty flush
With sudden glows of thought and feeling

But oh, the innate worth refined
She treasured in thy gentle breast.
The generous gifts of heart and mind
They best can tell, who know thee best.

    Bloom on bloom on frank Nature's child
    Her favourite flower, her spotless one,
    Still may she keep thee pure, unsoiled,
    Still fresh though ever shone upon—

371. To Mrs. Amelia Foster

[May 21, 1823]

content[1] to appear as I have too often appeared, with all my imperfections —trusting to that intelligence & toleration of faults which should always accompany intimate friendship.

    I was delighted to see the two boys once more before I ⟨sat⟩ set out— The dear little fellows—in some respects they put me so much in mind of their two sisters—You cant think how much I was gratified by the good will shewn by the little rogues at parting. I like to be liked by children for there's no stuff nor hollowness in their manifestations of attachment—No [*unrecovered*] [*Top two-thirds of verso of page is cut away.*] The trees are dressed out in their young leaves and gay blossoms, the birds are in full song—neither have yet entered upon the cares of the year—the former as yet ⟨have no fruit nor the latter⟩ has not begun to bear fruit nor the latter to lay eggs—

    I am very much pleased with my travelling companion[2]— He is full of feeling for his profession and for his favourite amusement of drawing —An old fortress a field of battle, or a fine landscape puts him into an extacy; such is ⟨th⟩ just the companion to have in travelling through these old campaigning countries—& among beautiful scenery. He had made a military plan of the battle of Bautzen[3] and from a tower of the town he ⟨pointed out the whole⟩ explained the whole, very clearly, as I thought, even to my inexperienced apprehension. This morning ⟨we⟩ our road lay through the Scenes of the severest fighting, and as Cockburn was fighting the battle over again with all the enthusiasm of a young soldier, and placing the scene vividly before my imagination, I could not but contrast it with the Scene actually before my eyes. The quiet beauty & serenity of the landscape. The fields all in verdure; enamelld with flowers, the *Hearts ease* & *Forget me not*, springing as if purposely ⟨plante⟩ Sown, from the turf under which so many brave fellows lie buried. and thousands of larks hovering in the Air and filling it with melody. What demi-devils we are to mar such Scenes of quiet & loveliness with our passions—Shakespeare, I think it is, says if mortals had the power of Jove we should have continual thunder *"nothing but thunder"*[4] As it is, how infinitely more mischief & misery does man inflict with his pigmy imitations than the Deity with all his tremendous power of Lightning & thunderbolt—What is the amount of all the evil inflicted by lightning, tempest, earthquake and volcano, to the over-whelming and widespreading miseries of war—

I do not reccollect whether you mentioned having been at the ruind convent[5] where I am scrawling this—though as you are all such explorers of glens and visitors of ruins you can hardly have missed it—The whole way from Zittau[6] hither is full of fine Scenery. We came thro it after five Oclock. I dont know when I have been more delighted with fine Scenery excepting perhaps at Tharand[7]—but then I had Such companions to help me enjoy it. The valley that leads up to the ruin put me in mind of English Scenery—as indeed many of the places in this part of Saxony do—The cottages are so surrounded by garden and grass plat—so buried in Trees, and the moss coverd roofs almost mingling & blending with the surrounding vegetation—The whole Landscape is completely rustic. ⟨and⟩ The orchards were all in bloom—and as the day was very warm the good people were seated in the shade of the trees, spinning ⟨with⟩ near the rills of water that tinkled along thro the green sward—But I must stop scribbling for I see Cockburn is finishing his sketching. He has made a couple of very pretty ⟨doing?⟩ sketches; one of a part of this noble old ruin—another a peep from it; between the rocky defiles of the valley to the fine plain that stretches beyond; sprinkled with cottages—with Zittau glittering in the centre—[8]

Zittau—We have had a lovely walk back from Oëwien; We stopped So long on the way for Cockburn to sketch a cottage Scene and a groupe of peasant Girls, that the Moon was out in all her splendour long before we reached Zittau; So I sauntered along pursuing that chain of speculations we were all amusing ourselves [End of holograph]

with[9] the other evening, when leaning over the balcony that looks into your garden and gazing at the stars. I like to enter a strange town by moonlight; if the houses are high and spacious it makes every thing look splendid and stately. The fine white light it sheds freshens up the colors of the buildings and makes them all look clean, and then the broad masses of light, the deep shadows, throw every thing into such grand proportions, that you seem to be wandering among palaces. Such was the case even with little Zittau, as I strolled under its arched gate-way and up the principal street.

Friedland, May 22, 1823.

We have ransacked the castle of Wallenstein,[10] and I have seen his sword, and a drum with his name on it, and his portrait.[11] I was all in a glow while looking at these things and thought it was with the recollec-tion of this great man; but it was with the recollection of the glowing poetry in which Schiller has embalmed him. I'd rather have conceived and written that noble poem than have achieved Wallenstein's greatest victory.[12] I have been to the spot from which I presume Emily took her sketch of the castle. I hope she will excuse my apparent familiarity in using her beautiful name instead of the formal one of Miss Foster. Were I writing to any one but yourself I should not do it; I would have given any thing at the time to have heard her in her own delightful way talk about Schiller's play and the scenes she preferred. Cockburn has just finished a very slight and hasty, but very pretty and correct sketch. . . .

MANUSCRIPT: Illinois—Bentley Papers.   PUBLISHED: PMI, II, 153–55 (in part); PMI, IV, 398–400 (in part).

The holographs of this and subsequent letters from WI to the Fosters (numbers 371, 372, 373, 375, 378, 380), written during his trip to Prague in May and June of 1823, are in the Richard Bentley Papers in the University of Illinois Library. Since some pages or portions of some of these letters are missing, the printed text will be used as copy-text to fill in the gaps. Even with these additions, some of WI's letters to the Fosters remain incomplete.

The history of the publication of these letters is unusual and deserving of notice. When Pierre M. Irving was gathering materials for his uncle's biography, he wrote to Emily Foster Fuller and requested copies of WI's letters to her mother. The material which she sent him was included in Volume II of *Life and Letters of Washington Irving* between pages 157 and 160. When Richard Bentley published these letters in the second volume of his English edition of the *Life and Letters of Washington Irving*, they provoked responses from Mrs. Fuller and her sister, Flora Foster Dawson. In particular, Mrs. Dawson was distressed that Pierre Irving had omitted any mention of WI's deep interest in Emily Foster during his stay in Dresden. Bentley apparently encouraged Mrs. Dawson, so she prepared an account of the relations of WI and the Foster family. When Mrs. Fuller heard of her sister's action, she supplied Bentley with her version of the family relationship with WI. Since her account was only one-fifth as long as her sister's, she sent Bentley the originals of the letters which WI had written to her mother and herself to expand and clarify her version of the story. Whether Mrs. Fuller is responsible for clipping away two-thirds of one of the leaves in the letter of [May 21, 1823] and cutting out half a line in the letter of May 28, 1823 has not been determined by the editors. The narratives of the two Foster sisters—Chapter XXIII by Flora Dawson and Chapter XXIV by Emily Fuller—represent Bentley's unauthorized additions to Pierre M. Irving's biography of his uncle.

The letters supplied by Mrs. Fuller and preserved in the Bentley Papers at the University of Illinois provide the copy-text for WI's letters to the Fosters. As copy-text for those printed portions for which the holographs have not been found, the present editors employ the source which seems most nearly to approximate WI's holograph, on the basis of available evidence. Since a collation of pages 395–413 of Volume III of the Bentley (or English) edition of the *Life and Letters* with the Appendix to Volume IV of the Putnam (or American) edition (pp. 387–403) reveals no substantive changes and since Putnam's house-styling is closer to WI's practice than Bentley's house-styling, the American edition is here used for copy-text for the sections for which WI's holograph has not been found.

The date has been established by WI's references in his journal for May 21 to the battlefield at Bautzen being "enameld with hearts ease & forgetmenots" and to Zittau and the ruined convent at Oybin. See *J&N*, III, 163–64.

1. The top two-thirds of the first page have been clipped away.

2. John Cockburn (1801–1837), a lieutenant in the artillery, accompanied WI on a tour of Bohemia and Silesia.

3. The battle of Bautzen, fought on May 20–21, 1813, brought victory to Napoleon over the Prussians and Russians.

4. *Measure for Measure*, II, ii, 110–13.

5. Oybin, or Ouwein, about 7½ miles southwest of Zittau, was a rock 1680 feet high, site of the ruins of a church and convent established in 1639 by Emperor Charles IV. See PMI, II, 153; J&N, III, 164; Baedeker, *Northern Germany*, p. 195.

6. Zittau is a town east and south of Dresden. WI's route from Dresden to Zittau via Bischofswerda and Bautzen was about 63 miles.

7. Tharandt is a town between Dresden and Freiberg at the junction of three valleys.

8. To this point WI wrote in pencil; hereafter he used ink.

9. The remainder of the letter is taken from the text printed in PMI, II, 154–55.

10. Albrecht Eusebius Wenzel von Wallenstein (1583–1634), an Austrian general during the Thirty Years' War, purchased Friedland Castle in 1622. After his death at the hands of four English mercenaries the castle reverted to the crown.

11. WI is referring to a portrait painted in 1626 by Kauelfersch and regarded as the best likeness of Wallenstein.

12. WI's deep interest in Wallenstein is mirrored in the extensive quotations from Schiller's *Wallensteins Lager* and *Wallensteins Tod* which he copied into his commonplace books. See J&N, III, 594–95, 597–602.

372. To Mrs. Amelia Foster

Hirschberg.[1] May 23. [1823]

We arrived here late last evening after a very rugged journey across the country by roads only fit for country Waggons. We passed through much beautiful Scenery, and the Riesen gebirge[2] were in sight, though mantled in clouds. In th⟨is⟩e afternoon the wind and the weather ⟨has⟩ changed and we had an occasional shower. Still the mountains looked grand in their dark covering of mist, and as the clouds detached themselves and rolled off in great piles into the blue sky they were finely lit up by the sunshine.

On entering Hirschberg we found the public Square and some of the streets partially illuminated and Mine host of the White horse where we put up, usherd us into rooms brilliantly lit up by half a dozen tallow candles in each window. He informed us that it was the *Pfingster fest*[3] whe⟨re⟩n the townsmen shot at the target, and that the procession would soon come by escorting home the King of the Year. The grand pageant passed shortly after with full band playing the Jager chorus from| the Frei schütz[4]—and all the Burgerschaft in military array, with the King of sharpshooters in the midst of them The tag, rag & Bobtail of the place shouting in the rear. Mine host of the White horse, a jolly round fellow, had stuffed hi⟨s⟩m ⟨[*unrecovered*]⟩ ↑self↓ into an old Hussar Jacket on the occasion, informing us that in his Younger days he had belonged to one of the volunteer corps. He kindled up, like a⟨n⟩ veteran warrior at this military parade of his townsmen, and pointed out the uniform of each company that marched by, telling us the name, character, atchievements and *craft* of every leader—

This is an overcast rainy morning and we are confined to the house. My companion is making an excellent sketch, from the window, of the public Square which lies before our Hotel— After an early dinner we start for Schmiedeberg.[5] I ought to have mentioned that Hirschberg is the Scene of Some of my friend Rübezahls[6] gambols, which gives it an interest to me.

Schmiedeberg—afternoon. We arrived here about four oclock after driving through Some beautiful valley Scenery. We are now at the foot of the Riesen gebirge, and the weather promises to be fair tomorrow—So that we shall be able to explore Some of the Scenery. The mountains, ⟨like every thing else⟩ do not equal my expectations; but that is the case with every thing in this world, of which we hear a great deal before hand. The valley in which Schmiedeberg is situated is soft and verdant, and when it is seen with the advantage of sunshine, must be lovely My fellow traveller is already in the field, landscape hunting; but I am obliged to keep to the house—I have unluckily taken cold in the sudden change of weather yesterday, and am threatened with a pain in one side of my head. I hope I may escape any Serious attack; I sufferd acutely from an attack [*MS ends here*]

Perhaps[7] a good deal of mountain scrambling to-morrow will drive it off, or may overpower the feeling of pain, by mental excitement. I love mountains; the soul seems lifted up by them, as well as the body, and one breathes a purer and freer atmosphere. The evening is now coming on. You are all seated, I suppose, in the little Pavilion. I shall lie down on the sofa, and drive away this pain by picturing you all at your occupations, and recalling the many evenings of homefelt enjoyment I have passed among you. They were the sweetest moments that I have passed in Dresden, though I fear I often trespassed on the patience of others. We fancy others feel the sunshine that is only in our own bosoms, and, while full of good humor and good will, the idea never enters one's mind that even one's good humor may be irksome.

I shall never forget poor Miss W., who, wrapped up in ecstasy with her own music, did not perceive that all the company were either yawning, or laughing at her.

Still those were sweet moments, for they made me know and prize you all. I would not give up one such evening for all the fashionable parties we were at together. Perhaps there is some selfishness in this.

I felt of some consequence in those little domestic scenes; but when we entered the great maze of fashion, I was like the poor little duck[8] in the Grossen Garten,[9] and was fain to draw off to a corner. But I always like such domestic scenes and full-flowing conversations the best. When I consider how I have trifled with my time, suffered painful vicissitudes of feeling, which for a time damaged both mind and body— when I consider all this, I reproach myself that I did not listen to the first impulse of my mind, and abandon Dresden long since. And yet I think of returning! Why should I come back to Dresden? The very inclination that draws me thither should furnish reasons for my staying away. Well, well, I must leave off scribbling, for I am writing at random. Good-night.

Manuscript: Illinois—Bentley Papers.   Published: PMI, IV, 391–92, 388–90.

The pages of this holograph have "9" and "10" in the upper outside corners, suggesting that they are part of a longer letter started earlier.

1. Hirschberg is a picturesque town located at the confluence of the Bober and Zacken Rivers.

2. The Riesengeberge, or Giant Mountains, composed chiefly of granite and covered with a variety of plants, flowers, and trees, run in a northeasterly direction from the source of the Oder River. These mountains are the most Alpine of any in Germany. See Baedeker, *Northern Germany*, p. 198.

3. WI regularly wrote "Pfingsterfest" for "Pfingstenfest." This celebration of Pentecost on Whitsunday in commemoration of the descent of the Holy Spirit on the disciples of Christ was accompanied by contests, pageants, and other festivities.

4. *Der Freischütz*, with music by Carl Maria von Weber and libretto by Friedrich Kind, was first performed in Berlin at the Royal Opera on June 18, 1821. The Huntsmen's Chorus, "Was gleich wohl auf Erden" ("The joy of the hunter on earth"), is in Act III, preceding the finale.

5. The distance from Hirschberg to Schmiedeberg is about 15 miles.

6. Rübezahl was a kindly spirit living in the Riesengeberge. WI had drawn upon the Rübezahl legend preserved in Otmar's *Deutsche Sagen* as related in Büsching's *Volk-Sagen, Märchen und Legenden* for some of the details in "The Legend of Sleepy Hollow" in *The Sketch Book*. See Reichart, *WI and Germany*, pp. 26, 28.

7. The copy-text for this portion of the letter is PMI, IV, 388–90. It is unquestionably a part of WI's letter begun at Schmiedeberg on the afternoon of May 23. Probably WI wrote it just before he retired for the night. The reference in this sentence to his pain seems to relate to the pain in his head mentioned in the preceding paragraph. In his journal for May 23 WI writes: "Have a pain in my face & as the ⟨evening is⟩ weather is unsettled I do not go out—but finish letter to Mrs F" (*J&N*, III, 166).

8. The following note was added in PMI, IV, 389: " 'In a neglected part of the Grossen Garten was a lonely little lake, near a deserted palace. The only vestige left of the gayety once there, was a melancholy swan, pining alone, until a wild duck took pity on its forlorn estate, and kept it company. There, cheered by his gay little friend, they used to sport and play, until, in an evil hour, three more swans were brought to the place. When the little wild duck came, as usual, to seek his old companion, ungrateful as he was, he turned against him, and, puffing out with

pride, joined his new acquaintances to drive off his former friend, who still hung about in corners, and tried to follow, with love stronger than life. But if he dared approach, they all united to attack him, till at last, with blows from their beaks, they killed him, faithful to the last.' This is the duck Mr. Irving refers to."

9. "Mr. Irving was in this, as in some other modest fancies, quite mistaken; he was a great deal too much sought after to be suffered to remain in a corner. Besides that, when he was in spirits, and when a few of the friends he valued were with him, he was lively and brilliant even in general society; although, no doubt, a little jar against his feelings threw him back into reserve" (P. M. Irving's note; PMI, IV, 389).

373. To Mrs. Amelia Foster

Prague, Wednesday May 28th 1823

My dear Mrs Foster,

We arrived here late last evening and I received your letter early this morning—The one which you sent to Herrnhuth I never received, as I never thought of enquiring for a letter there—Should it be returned to you, remember I claim it as my property. I ⟨wrote⟩ sent you a long, rambling letter from Schmiedeberg[1]—written at various times & places, and finished in a very feverish mood and I apprehend a very feverish style; for I was suffering extremely from a violent pain in my face & throat. My indisposition continued for two or three days, accompanied by great pain & fever.[2] I was really affraid at one time I should be laid up among the mountains; but luckily I kept clear of the Doctors, and ⟨by⟩ through the good nursing of a kind hearted chambermaid, I was once more enabled to put my head out of doors—Should Livius have another attack of his complaint[3] I advise him to send forthwith to Schmiedeberg for my *Stube madchen* who is worth all his Doctors & apothecaries put together. As soon as I could bear travelling we set off, and crossed a part of the Riesengebirge to Landshut & So on to Konig-gratz & to this place[4]—where I am scrawling this letter under a tree in a garden of some Bohemian Prince, while my companion is at his usual work of sketching.

Your letter of Sunday[5] only makes me regret that I did not get your other which you say contained your journal up to Friday but how in heavens name could you suppose that it could find me at Herrnhut.[6] Did you suppose I was likely to linger among those meagre sould people? I am quite annoyed at the idea that the letter should lie in the office of that joyless community.[7]

——I write my letters at haphazard moments, which will account for their being written sometimes with pen, sometimes with pencil, as either is at hand. We had a tedious, irksome journey after entering

Bohemia—I was not perfectly recovered; and such roads⟨,⟩—and such delays⟨,⟩—and such impassive phlegm and absolute stupidity! Yesterday we were in constant exertion to get on from four oclock in the morning until eleven at night and accomplished what in England would have been a half days journey. Really it requires all the *menschliche tugend* and *Empfindsamkeit* of a German to bear with these people.[8] Bohemia is a tedious monotonous country. Yet I am glad to have seen it at this favourable season—to it the most favourable. Last November when I passd through it was all brown; the fields newly plowd & sown—partly wrapped in fogg—destitute of foliage or herbage & altogether dreary. At present it is coverd with verdure—the wide fields waving with grain, like the Green billows of a lake—The houses surrounded by orchards in full leaf and blossom. and though the country is still monotonous from its want of hills, yet it has a look of fertility and abundance that is always gratifying. When the Summer is advanced & the crops are gathered it will again be arid and dismal.

I have not been able to enjoy the Riesen Gebirge as much as I had expected. My unlucky indisposition deterred me from venturing to their Snowy summits, or lingering long among their uncertain valleys. Even now I feel myself languid and almost good for nothing, after so severe an attack of pain and fever and such a rough course of travelling as succeeded it.

Mr Cockburn is delighted with Prague and is determined to fill his sketchbook from it. He certainly possesses a most happy talent for taking sketches either of landscapes, streets or groups; quite masterly I think. Indeed he is a young man of peculiar & strong traits of character and indications of talent; though encrusted, if I may use the word, with almost unconquerable diffidence as it respects society. I have been more & more pleased with him the more I have seen & known of him; though I fancy he is a man *you* would know much longer before he would give you an opportunity of knowing what he was worth ↑he is so diffident among Ladies—↓ I always like to meet with these naturally gifted men, of ⟨[*unrecovered*]⟩ natural good Sense & natural good feeling, and I prize them the more from being very much *ennuied* by the polished and passable and universally current men of society.

I must finish this letter and send it to the post; and yet what a letter it is! Still it may procure me a reply, and for that purpose I let it go. I am in truth quite spiritless and listless. My mind has been in a restless state of strife & indiscision and has sunk into almost apathy, from its exhaustion. I hope to hear from you again—I do not know when I shall leave this—I have fifty ⟨though⟩ plans of what I ought to do & only one of what I should really like to do. My ideas have been flying to all points of the compass, and what I shall do in the end, whether go north, south, east or west—stay where I am,—or tamely come back to Dresden [*one-third of line cut from sheet*] is what perplexes me. It is very ridiculous to talk in this way, and I feel that it is so; yet how can I write frankly & not speak from what is uppermost in my mind. If I come back to Dresden I ought to be ready to start at once with Lutzerode[9]— and if I start with him I only come back to take a farewell that would be a ⟨very un⟩ more uncomfortable one than I will choose to ⟨take⟩ acknowledge—I am now away and have in a manner cheated myself into a parting, for when I bid you all adieu I thought I should most certainly see you all again in twelve days or a fortnight—Why then not keep away now I am here—I like Prague—there are bold, proud features about it. I like these old war worn, warrior towns—and the vast, silent, deserted palaces of the Bohemian ⟨princes⟩ ↑nobility↓ that one meets with, frowning in heavy magnificence, give a poetical character to the place. Thank heaven I know no body here and during the short stay I have to make I am not obliged to go to Evening parties or to pay formal visits. I feel as if I could be for a long time without any desire to see another evening gathering—I want to be either quite alone, with my mind in full exercise, or quite in motion; with my imagination kept in excitement by the rapid change of objects—a partial pause at this moment throws me into a state of inquietude, and suffers a thousand fruitless & uncomfortable feelings to come thronging upon me— ——I must conclude this scrawl for I see the time is nearly expired within which I can throw it in to the post—I hope to hear from you tomorrow or next day & will write to you again—It is a goodfornothing scrawl, but it must go—

Give my remembrances to the young ladies and to the boys—I think of them all continually and if they really think & care for me half as much, they do, twice as much as I hope for—

Yours ever most truly

W I.

MANUSCRIPT: Illinois—Bentley Papers.   PUBLISHED: PMI, IV, 392–96.

1. This letter has not been located.

2. See WI's letter of May 23. WI had arrived in Schmiedeberg at 4:00 P.M. on that date.

3. From these symptoms it is possible that WI may have had a case of scarlet fever, somewhat milder than the one Cockburn contracted in Prague a few days later.

4. The nature of Barham John Livius's ailment is not known.

5. The distance from Schmiedeberg to Prague is about 122 miles.

6. This letter has not been located.

7. Herrnhut, a town between Lobau and Zittau, had been founded by members of the Moravian Brethren in 1722 on land donated by Count Nikolas Ludwig von

Zinzendorf (1700–1760). See Baedeker, *Northern Germany*, p. 264. To this point WI wrote in pencil; hereafter he used ink.

8. The German words WI uses do not quite suggest the idea of patience and endurance implied by the sense of this sentence.

9. Carl August, Freiherr von Lützerode (1794–1864) at this time was aide-de-camp to Prince Johann of Saxony. WI was on friendly terms with him during his stay in Dresden. See *J&N*, III, 93, 115, 136.

374. To Mrs. Amelia Foster

May 28, 1823.

I ought to say something of Herrnhuth, which is one of the great objects of curiosity in this part of the world. We passed three or four hours there, and went through the institutions, churchyard, &c. It is all very excellent in its way, but I would rather live in a wilderness than there. I have no relish for this *triste* simplicity, that consists in negatives. It seems the study of these worthy people to divest life and nature of everything that Heaven intended should embellish this short existence. I am not, it is true, the one to judge impartially in this instance, having been accustomed to dress everything too much with the illusions of the fancy, but surely we were not gifted with the delightful powers of the imagination thus to combat with them and quench them. Nature is simple herself, but then she is varied and beautiful in her simplicity. If the Herrnhuthers were right in their notions, the world would have been laid out in squares and angles and right lines, and everything would have been white, and black, and snuff-color, as they have been clipped by these merciless retrenchers of beauty and enjoyment. And then their dormitories[1]—think of between one and two hundred of these simple gentlemen cooped up at night in one great chamber! What a concert of barrel-organs in this great resounding saloon! And then their plan of marriage! The very birds of the air choose their mates from preference and inclination—but this detestable system of *lot*![2] The sentiment of love may be, and is, in a great measure, a fostered growth of poetry and romance, and balderdashed with false sentiment; but, with all its vitiations, it is the beauty and charm, the flavor and fragrance of all intercourse between man and woman; it is the rosy cloud in the morning of life; and if it does too often resolve itself into the shower, yet to my mind, it only makes our nature more fruitful in what is excellent and amiable. But I forget—you sent me to bless, and not to curse the Herrn-huthers, and I will not curse them. May they be blessed here and here-after! but, in the mean time, preserve me from their heaven upon earth. I know nothing more dismal, more quenching to heart and mind, than this sterile, monotonous simplicity. The quaint German song says:

"Ich habe viel gelitten
In dieser schöner[3] Welt;"

but give me the world, the "naughty world," with all its cares and
crosses, but with all its natural charms, its innocent pleasures, and the
fantastic embellishments that poetry has thrown about it, in preference
to the regular, right-angled, whitewashed world of a Herrnhuther——
And so, good-night!

PUBLISHED: PMI, IV, 390–91.
This letter, for which no holograph has been located, was probably started by
WI in the evening after he had posted his earlier letter of this same date
(number 373).

1. For the single men and women the Moravian Brethren provided choirs,
or segregated dwellings, in which they lived until they were married. See Gillian
Lindt Gollin, *Moravians in Two Communities* (New York, 1967), pp. 67–75.
2. The Moravian Brethren used the lot, which they regarded as a manifestation
of Christ's will to the religious group, as a means of determining policy and of
placing persons in various positions in the community. Included in this latter
function was the practice of submitting the name of the marriage partner to the
lot. See Gollin, *Moravians in Two Communities*, pp. 50–52.
3. It is impossible to determine whether WI or someone else is responsible for
writing "schöner" instead of "schönen."

375. To Mrs. Amelia Foster

Prague, June 1st 1823.

I thank you a thousand times, my dear Mrs Foster for your letter of
Wednesday.[1] I cannot tell You how interesting it was to me, placing the
dear little circle of the pavillion So completely before my eyes. I was
so impatient to read it that I would not wait till I got to my Lodgings
which were distant from the post office—yet I would not read it in
the bustle & confusion of the Street. I tried to get admitted to Wallensteins garden[2]—it was closed—So I scrambled up to the grassy
ramparts, and read it in quiet, with old Prague & the Moldau at my
feet. I have since read it over half a dozen times, for whenever I read
it, it seems to bring me among you all again.

I am scribbling in poor Cockburns room, who is quite ill with a
fever and Sore throat—It appears to be a bilious attack brought on
by a cold. We have called in a physician, who appears to be rather one
of the *langsams*,[3] he has prescribed a variety of doses and applications,
but I trust nature will fight her own battle against both the disease
and the Doctor.

All Prague is in an uproar with a religious fete[4] The great street below

my window is Swarming with crowds of Priests, Burgerschaft in regimentals, the different trades, crafts & mysteries, with Banners &
garlands of flowers, and peasant men & women in every variety of colour
& costume until the whole Street looks like one great moving flower
bed—Just opposite the Hotel is a temporary altar erected, to which
there is a grand procession, and the air resounds with music from a
variety of bands attending the different Corps—which, mingling with
the ringing of bells ⟨makes the oddest⟩ and the chaunting of priests
& school children, makes the oddest confusion of sounds you can
imagine—A few days since we had a grand ceremony of the Kind at
which all the artillery assisted, and there was a procession on the fine
Bridge which bestrides the Wolga— It had a noble effect, and looked
like a conquering army entering old Prague.

There is something very striking and interesting to me about this
old city. It has more of a continental look than Dresden—The latter in
fact seems to have been altered, and repaired, and pulled down, and
built up, until it has become quite a decent, good looking common
place town; like a disbanded soldier, tamed down into a sober respectable citizen. But Old Prague still keeps its warrior look,[5] and
Swaggers about with its rusty corslet & helm, though both sadly bat-
terd. There seems to me to be an air of style & fashion about the
first people of Prague, and a good deal of beauty in the fashionable
circle—This perhaps is owing to my contemplating it from a distance,
and my imagination lending its tints occasionally—Both actors and
audience contemplated from the pit of a theatre look better than when
seen from the Boxes and behind the Scenes. I like to contemplate
society in this way occasionally, and to dress it up by the help of
fancy, to my own taste. When I get ⟨among⟩ in the midst of it, it is
too apt to lose its charm—and then there is the trouble and ennui of
being obliged to take an active part in the farce—but to be a mere
spectator is amusing. I am glad therefore that I brought no letters
to Prague. I shall leave it with a favourable idea of its society and
manners, from knowing nothing accurate of either; and with a firm
belief that every pretty woman I have seen is an angel; as I am apt
to think ↑every↓ pretty woman—until I have found her out.
Monday 2d. I have passed the night on a sopha in Cockburns room,
who has had a very restless night, with a high fever; and complains of
his throat this morning. ———

The physician has just been here, and pronounces Cockburns malady
to be the Scarlet fever, and indeed it appears to be so from the colour
of his skin; leeches are to be applied to his throat which is much
inflamed. You need not tell his Brothers the nature of his malady, as
they might write home and make his family uneasy. I have a better

opinion of the Doctor than I had at first—The people of the house are very attentive—there is an excellent *Stubemadchen* who nurses him with a true womans kindness—and for my own part I shall do my best; So I hope among us all we shall set him up again before long— This has been an unlucky journey for us both, ⟨but⟩ and both have paid the penalty for invading Rübezahls dominions.

I wish You would have the kindness to send to Mr Moriers & enquire if any letters have arrived for me, & if So send them ⟨by⟩ here by return of post—also if there are any letters for me or *for Mr Cockburn* at the Post office, let them be forwarded here. Should little Montucci[6] ever call, or send his artist,[7] about my likeness, tell him not to wait for my return, but to do what he pleases, So he does not caricature me. I am very indifferent about it, and am sorry I referred him to you, but at the time I thought of having impressions struck for America—it was a mere transient thought, and not worth the trouble—

You charge me with tormenting myself almost into a nervous fever because I cannot write—Do you really think me so anxious about literary reputation; or so nervous about the fleeting and fallacious popularity of a day? I have not been able to write it is true, because I have been harrassed in mind—but I have not been harrassed [*End of MS*]

MANUSCRIPT: Illinois–Bentley Papers; Va.–Barrett (copy).   PUBLISHED: PMI, II, 155–57; PMI, IV, 396–98.

WI's holograph (Illinois–Bentley Papers) has been used as copy-text.

1. This letter has not been located.

2. The Wallenstein (or Valdstejn) Palace, constructed in baroque style, and the formal gardens in front of it were commissioned by General Albrecht Wallenstein. Included in the gardens are replicas of the sculptures by Adrian de Vries done in 1626–1627, the originals having been carried off by the Swedes in 1648.

3. German idiom for "slow ones."

4. This was the feast of Corpus Christi, which began on the Thursday following Holy Trinity Sunday (eighth Sunday after Easter) and continued on to the ninth Sunday after Easter. (Easter occurred on March 30 in 1823.) It was a joyous celebration in which all social levels of the community participated. See *New Catholic Encyclopedia* (1967), IV, 347.

5. WI is alluding to the barricades erected in the western part of the city to protect it from Swedish invasion and to the fortifications and moat surrounding the old town.

6. Dr. Antonio Montucci, a professor of English and Italian, supervised the publication of *The Sketch Book* in an English version in Dresden at this time. WI had conferred with him before setting out for Prague. See *J&N*, III, 137, 147, 148, 150, 153.

7. On May 18, 1823, an unnamed artist had prepared a drawing of WI for an engraving in Montucci's edition of *The Sketch Book*. See *J&N*, III, 153.

376. To Henry Brevoort

Prague, June 6th. 1823.

My dear Brevoort,

It is a long long time since I have heard from you; and if I mistake not you are two or three letters in my debt. To my last I certainly have never received a reply. It was written just before my departure from England.[1] It is singular, I have received no reply to that nor to several letters that I sent off about the same time. Whether they all went in one vessel and that vessel was lost or whether they have miscarried in any other way I know not, but I never have hea[r]d[2] of one of them being received; and had they been I think I should have had some reply or other. One was to Mrs Cooper—(our old friend Mary Fairlie) one to Jack Nicholson[3] &c &c—Do write to me my dear fellow when you receive this and let me know how you are, what you are doing, and all about you—Do not forget me because I am so long absent, and do no[t] [*MS torn*] think I forget you, because I do not write oftener. The movi[ng] [*MS torn*] from place to place, the remoteness of places for the transmission of letters; the time taken in studying languages, and the thousand other impediments and distractions incident to such a wandering, miscellaneous, half vagrant, half literary life as I have been leading for some time past, totally put all regular or frequent correspondence out of the question. I postpone writing from day to day and week to week, until I look back with compunction and find that months have elapsed; and then the very length of time that has gone by makes the sitting down to write a formidable undertaking.

I have been passing ten or eleven months in various parts of Germany. In the course of this time I have visited the Rhine, and some of the principal places in Wurtemburg, Bavaria been at Vienna—& through Bohemia to Dresden—where I wintered. My residence at Dresden was very pleasant—I became acquainted with every body, and was most kindly and hospitably recieved. The Old King & Queen & the whole of the Royal family were uncommonly gracious and I [found] their court a very curious and entertaining one; being kept up in all the formalities of the old school, which have been laid aside in other courts.

I left Dresden between two and three weeks since on a tour in Silesia & to the Riesen Gebirge or Giant Mountains—in company with a young English Officer. We passed through some of the scenes of fighting of Frederick the Great and of Bonaparte, and found the traces of their exploits still existing. I was very much pleased with Silesia, particularly the valleys near the mountains which in verdure, fertility and rural beauty rival some of the finest scenery in England. Among the mountains I was laid up for two or three days with a cold and a rheumatic pain in one side of my head which deterred me from climbing to the Snowy heights; besides I am apt to admire mountain scenery more from the foot than the top of the mountain. Having crossed this chain of mountains we entered Bohemia and ⟨f⟩ after two days travelling through wretched cross roads arrived at this place. This is my second visit to old Prague, having been here last November on my way from Vienna [to] [MS torn] Dresden. It is a fine proud old warrior city, carrying about it marks of former splendour and hard fighting. The Bohemian nobility, however, do not live in any thing like their former magnificence, especially in Prague—If they make any display it is when resident at Vienna. I had intended passing only two or three days here and then returning to Dresden, but unfortunately my travelling companion Mr Cockburn has fallen ill of the Scarlet Fever, so for a week past I have had to play the part of nurse to him—He is not yet able to leave his bed, but I hope to set him on end again in the course of two or three days more.

Dresden July 5th. I began this letter about a month since, but was interrupted in writing it by the [MS torn] of a sick room. My companion was confined to his chamber for about three weeks—As soon as he was able to bear the fatigue of travelling we set out on our return to this place by the way of Toeplitz; passing by Culm the scene of Van Dammes defeat; and crossing the Erz mountains.[4] I am now making my farewell visits in Dresden and shall leave it in the course of a week to make a tour in the centre of Germany among ⟨the Harz⟩ some of the Small States, & to visit the Harz Mountain[s][5] [MS torn] af[ter] [MS torn] which I think I shall shape my course towards Franc[e.] [and] [MS torn] pass some little time at Paris. My unsettled life for some t[ime] [MS torn] past and the attention I have paid to ⟨for⟩ the Study of foreign languages has prevented me from ⟨any⟩ preparing any thing further for the press, nor shall I be able to do so until I get through my tour and pitch my tent quietly for a season. How do you employ your time? You must have abundance of leisure, which, if not employed, is the most insupportable of all earthly blessings. I wrote to you long since that I wished you to commence some work, by way of having an object in view to trav[el] [MS torn] up to in ⟨the⟩ such a straightforward path of life as that which you are enabled to pursue. I think you could execute some historical tract with great ability and not only give yourself occupation & amusement, but gain high reputation, and leave something valuable to the country. ⟨I would not⟩ As you ⟨are⟩ do not like perhaps the task of a regular work you might make it more easy to yo[ursel]f [MS torn] & more agreeable to reader[s] [MS torn] in general by ⟨making⟩ writing it in the form of essays or letters—which would give an opportunity for familiar illustration and philosophical remark—of course it ought to be on some branch of our own history.

I have just heard that a work has appeared entitled Old England by a New England man, containing some very severe but also some very excellent strictures on English politics, manners, literature &c. I suspect by the very title and air of the thing that it is from Paulding.[6] I hope he has digested his matter well and executed something that will do him lasting credit. He is generally to[o][7] hasty in ⟨wanting⟩ publishing and suffers his works to be disfigured by faults & blemishes, which the purblind critics in our country sieze on and exaggerate, without percieving the admirable merits that lie close beside them.

I wish when you write you would give me an account of the state, condition and occupation of our old cronies. Harry Ogden[8] I find is at length married and of course poor & happy. How does Gouv[9] come on at the foundry, is your brother still with [him?] where is Uncle Nick—still voyaging between New York & Canton?—Where is Jack Nicholson—still making love unsuccessfully? Do give me a word or two of all the old set. And now my dear fellow God bless you—I will not suffer so long a time to elapse again, without writing—& dont you let me be so long again without a letter. Remember me most kindly to your wife—teach your boys to like me. and believe me in all times & circumstances most truly & affectionately yours—

WI.

ADDRESSED: Henry Brevoort Junr. Esqr. / New York. / *Marmion.* POSTMARKED:
    Forwarded by / H[*unrecovered*] & Co. / Havre
MANUSCRIPT: Yale.

1. Dated London, June 11 to July 1, 1822.
2. WI wrote "head."
3. These letters have not been located.
4. WI's northwesterly route from Prague to Dresden covered about 75 miles. General Dominique Vandamme (1770–1830), Napoleon's leader of the Westphalian army, was defeated and captured at Kulm in northwestern Bohemia in August, 1813.
5. These mountains, west of Dresden, extended about 60 miles between the Elbe and Weser Rivers.
6. WI's suspicion was correct. James Kirke Paulding's *A Sketch of Old England by a New England Man* (New York, 1822) satirized the misrepresentations of the United States made by English travelers.
7. WI wrote "to."
8. One of the Lads of Kilkenny.
9. Gouverneur Kemble.

377. To Mrs. Amelia Foster

Prague [June] 8. 182[3]¹ [*MS torn*]

I am sadly disappointed in receiving no letter through Mr. M.² The
packet that I sent by his hand must certainly have miscarried or been
retarded. I ought to have had answers long since & I certainly should
had my letters been received[.] I am impatient to hear from you my
friend. How glad I shall be when I have seen what I want to see of Strange
lands & strange places & begin to tread back my steps in the traces of
old friendships; I am tired of being among strangers[.] my eye begins
to be sated with seeing & my ear with hearing, but I have prescribed
to myself certain places to see as certain books are prescribed to study
& I see them as we often read for information but not for entertainment.
It seems to me at times as if I am the least fitted being for this wandering life into which chance & circumstance has thrown me. I have strong
domestic feelings & inclinations & feel sometimes quite dreary &
desolate when they get uppermost. The excitement of ⟨a⟩ varying &
gay society soon subside with me & leaves a sad vacancy & feel as
if I could exclaim in the words of Schiller "Das Herz ist gestorben die
Welt ist leer"[.]³ at such times my only consolation is that in a little
while more I shall have seen enough of the world & then I will have
done with strange sights, strange faces & all the phantasonagoria of
society & give myself up to the society of those I like & those that care
for me. But I am writing in a sad humdrum vein though you must not
expect anything better from one shut up in a sick room, ...⁴ I
think your idea for the picture by Arnold⁵ is very good. Let Emily for
instance have a book & be looking up to Flora & pointing out a passage
while Flora is leaning over her & looking down at the book[.] I do
not think Flora has a down look but I think some of her looks down
are very becoming & if Emily while sitting to Mr. Arnold could but
cast up her eyes in the act of recollecting & repeating⁶ some favourite
passage of poetry. I think the painter could not well conceive any thing
better—Take care however that he does not infuse any German
Empfindsamkeit & *Gefühl* in the picture. Let it be as unaffected &
natural as the beings it represents. Perhaps when you think more on
the subject, or that they come to sit to the painter, some other & better
attitude may suggest itself. I have merely given my idea with respect
to the one you suggested.

Do not I beg of you give yourself any more trouble about Montucci
& the sketch. It is really—really of no importance to me—particularly as
I do not intend to have it engraved for America. At first I did feel a
little solicitous as I wished it to supplant the likeness already engraved
for my country—In which I am made to look like such a noodle that if

I really thought I looked so I would kick myself out of doors. But I was quite well satisfied with the sketch of the young artist—So let Montucci do as he pleases with it.

I can give you nothing in return for the ⟨little⟩ interesting little pictures you draw in your letters of your family circle—do let me have as many of them as you can—and yet they only play the fool with me, and make me wish myself back—and——well—well—well!

I wish to heaven I could get these wandering thoughts of mine to settle down upon paper. I think if I could get my mind fully employed upon some work it would be a wonderful relief to me—at present I am all discomposed—

I must finish this letter that it may be in time for the Post. Mr Cockburn desires me to thank You most heartily for your kindness in sending him the letters and for your attention to his brothers[7]—

Give my warmest remembrances to Your little family circle—

Yours truly
W I.

P. S. The continued illness of Cockburn puts the journey with Lutzerode[8] out of the question—I never made any fixed engagement to go with him & hope he is not calculating upon it, have you heard whether he is or no? I can say nothing about my future movements, for as yet my mind is in confusion on the subject, and I do not like to confess all the wild ideas & impulses that flit across it.

MANUSCRIPT: Va.–Barrett (Mrs. Fuller's copy); Illinois—Bentley Papers (WI's holograph). PUBLISHED: PMI, II, 157–58 (in part); PMI, IV, 400–401.

The copy-text for this letter is based on two manuscripts, as indicated above. Copy-text for the first part of the letter is Mrs. Fuller's copy.

1. Over *"Prague"* in Mrs. Fuller's copy is written "Paris," which has been canceled by another hand. "Nov." has a line through it, and a word, presumably "June," has been written above it. Most of this latter word has been lost because the brittle paper has broken from the margin of the sheet. The context indicates that the letter was written in Prague. WI's journal mentions his writing a letter to Mrs. Foster on June 8, 1823. See *J&N*, III, 171.

2. John Philip Morier, the British envoy in Dresden. WI mentions him in the letter of June 1, 1823, as a person to whom some of his mail may have been addressed.

3. *Die Piccolimini*, III, vii, 1765, in *Schillers Werke*, ed. Ludwig Bellermann (Leipzig, [1895]), IV.

4. At this point the version in PMI (II) skips to the last paragraph. The MS copy indicates an elipsis by seven periods but continues with "I think your idea . . ."

5. Heinrich Gotthold Arnold (1785–1854), a portrait and genre painter trained at Dresden, was a professor at the Academy there.

6. The surviving portion of WI's holograph, which begins with this word, serves as copy-text for the rest of the letter.

7. In his journal for April 16, 1823, WI noted that he "visited Cockburn who

with his 2 brothers are at board & lodging at the parsons" (*J&N*, III, 139). Presumably Mrs. Foster called upon or in some way noticed Cockburn's brothers in Dresden during his absence.

8. In his letter of May 28 WI had mentioned the possibility of traveling with Count Lützerode.

378. To Mrs. Amelia Foster

Prague, Saturday. June 13th. [1823]

I have just got your letter of Tuesday,[1] my dear Mrs Foster; Your kindness really overpowers me. How stupid I was not to have written earlier last week; and how intolerable are those tedious Germans with their post horses and post offices, that letters when they are written are so slow in coming to hand. really I grow heartily weary of this *langsam* country. Your letter which I have just received I ought to have received yesterday morning; and I began to wonder at your silence and to conjecture whether the Measles had really got into the family.

I thank you a thousand and a thousand times for the kind, the very kind solicitude you express about me; You who have so many dear delightful beings at home to occupy heart and soul, to trouble yourself about a wanderer like me. I am happy to be able to give you a good account both of my companion and myself. Mr Cockburn is entirely free from fever; nothing ails him now but weakness and he is daily gaining strength. He sits up the greater part of the day, in defiance of the doctors advice, and finds both strength and spirits recruited by it; both of which had been in a ⟨la⟩ very languid state while lying in bed. As to myself I believe I may consider myself as out of all danger of contagion—My health is as usual, and ⟨I⟩ now that my companion can sit up & amuse himself I go out a good deal in the open air. There are really delightful walks in the vicinity of this place. I often wish for you all here that I might shew you some charming strolls. There are several islands in the Moldau that are laid out in walks. One that particularly delights me is called, I think, der Grosser Venedig[2]—It is covered with trees and has the most beautiful shady ⟨paths and⟩ avenues and rambling footpaths, that wind among Groves and thickets along the banks of the Moldau. I spend hours there in the mornings before the Germans come to poison the air with themselves and their tobacco pipes. As to pure air, its too insipid for a German—Indeed he knows as little ⟨of⟩ what pure air is as a drunkard does of pure water, they both must qualify the element to their palates. I dont know a better punishment for German delinquents than to deprive them of their pipes and banish them to Buenos Ayres—theyd die of the purity of the atmosphere—But enough of the Germans—how came I to talk of them—

I am delighted to hear such good accounts of Troppeneger[3]—those dear little boys, I am glad they have got a worthy fellow to take care of them, who feels the value and importance of the trust confided to him. I like his schemes, and projects and theories and enterprizes— they shew zeal and interest in what he is about, and bespeak a simplicity of heart, which, when it is combined with good mental qualities, is I think invaluable. I like a man of Sense that now and then in the fullness of his heart, does things to make one smile. He is worth a dozen of those cool headed wary fellows that never do a foolish thing— they as seldom do a kind one.

I must finish this letter to get it to the post office (which is nearly a mile off) before a gathering storm of rain & thunder cuts off all communication. Will you tell Emily and Flora that their kind wishes are more gratifying to me than I can express. Good heavens what would I give to be with you this evening at the strawberry supper you talk ⟨off⟩ of.

Mr Cockburn desires me to express to you his very great sense of your kindness to his Brothers & to himself—

God bless you all/Yours truly
W I.

Will you remember me kindly to the Rumigny's[4] and tell them I thank them heartily for their enquiries.

MANUSCRIPT: Illinois—Bentley Papers.   PUBLISHED: PMI, IV, 401–3; PMI, II, 158–59 (in part).

1. This letter has not been located.
2. This picturesque park is on the island of Hetz, which was often called the Venice of Prague.
3. Troppeneger was the German tutor of Mrs. Foster's sons. He was to accompany them back to England when they left Dresden in July, 1823.
4. Count Marie Hypolite de Rumigny (1784–1871) was the French minister in Dresden.

379. To Mrs. Amelia Foster

[Prague, June 19(?) 1823]

Thank you my dear Mrs Foster for your kind attention in sending me the plan for my route[1] & still more for your kind note accompanying it. You talk of my coming back[.] I am ashamed to say it I am almost wishing myself back already[.] I ought to be off like your bird but I feel I shall not be able to keep clear of the cage. I wish I liked you all only half as much as I do.

Yours Ever
W. I.

MANUSCRIPT: Va.–Barrett.   PUBLISHED: PMI, II, 158 (in part).

This passage was copied by Mrs. Fuller onto the same sheet as excerpts from WI's letter of [June] 8 and separated by a line drawn across the middle of the page. The arrangement on the sheet of the text of WI's holograph of [June] 8 suggests that this passage is from a different letter, probably that of June 19, which WI wrote in response to letters he had received from Mrs. Foster on June 15, 18, and 19. See *J&N*, III, 173–74.

1. Apparently Mrs. Foster had suggested that WI and Cockburn take a different route back to Dresden and that she and her family would meet them at Schandau. See WI's letter of [June 23? 1823] for WI's reactions to these plans.

380. To Emily Foster

[Prague, June 23(?) 1823]

Mr. [Pigott][1] arrived here two or three days since, with his two sons. How often I have recollected your anecdotes of the embarrassments and cross purposes of the [Pigott] family last summer! They have had nothing but a tissue of *anlegenheit* since they have been here. At one time they lost their portmanteau; then they lost part of their clothes[2] at the Laundresses' which they have not as yet recovered, and so they go on from one petty scrape to another; and always manage to be *too late* for every thing—

I scribble this in a great hurry for I am busy making arrangements for breaking up our encampment.[3] You will complain of this letter no doubt—Take it however for what it is, as good as I can at this moment write⟨;⟩—and however brief I write and however little it may appear to you to come "from the heart" as you hint in one of your letters—believe me my sentiments towards you all ⟨does⟩ ↑do↓ not shift with my style nor depend upon the tone and turn of a period—

If you knew what I felt at the idea of one[4] more seeing You all You would not require any aid of rhetorick in the matter

At Töplitz I ⟨look to⟩ expect to hear when You go to Schandau[5]—or whether the unsettled state of the weather does not deter You from making the excursion.

& now God bless you all/Yours Truly

W I.

MANUSCRIPT: Illinois–Bentley Papers.   PUBLISHED: PMI, IV, 387–88.

The copy-text of the first three and one-half sentences is the printed text in PMI, IV, 387. WI's holograph is used for the remainder. PMI gives Emily Foster as the addressee.

Pigott, an English businessman living in Dresden, and his two sons reached Prague on June 20, 1823. (See *J&N*, III, 174.) From this fact and WI's allusion to packing in preparation to leave Prague this letter is tentatively dated June 23.

1. In the printed text here and in the next sentence there is a dash instead of the surname. The entry in WI's journal for June 20 makes the identification unmistakable.

2. WI's holograph begins with this word.

3. WI and Cockburn left Prague on June 24. See *J&N*, III, 175.

4. WI probably intended to write "once."

5. An attractive mountain town on the Elbe River, well known as a summer resort, Schandau is about 25 miles southeast of Dresden on the way to Prague via Bodenbach.

381. *To Annette Löwenstern*

[July 12, 1823]

I regret extremely my dear Miss Lowenstern that I am obliged to leave Dresden without taking leave personally of your family. I had intended coming out yesterday, but from some mistake in the directions yesterday I could not find your fathers Lodgings;[1] and was indeed so unwell, from a cold Which I caught at Schandau, that I was obliged to give up all idea of making my farewell visits to any one. Will you present my most kind & grateful farewell to your father and family and be assured of the deep sense I entertain of the friendship and kindness with which you all have honoured me—

with sincere regard and esteem

I am truly/Yours
Washington Irving

Dresden—July 12th. 1823

ADDRESSED: a Madmoiselle / Madmoiselle Loewenstern / Laubergast
MANUSCRIPT: Va.–Barrett.

Annette von Löwenstern was the daughter of Count Otto von Löwenstern, "a Livonian who held the title of Imperial Russian Councilor" in the diplomatic corps at the court in Dresden. On one occasion she made a sketch of WI in her notebook. Often the Löwensterns invited WI to share their box at the theater. See Reichart, *WI and Germany*, p. 78; *J&N*, III, 105, 180. Apparently WI dashed off this note just before his departure from Dresden with the Foster family.

1. Count Löwenstern maintained lodgings in Dresden, together with a country house at Laubergast, to which WI's letter was addressed.

382. *To Peter Irving*

[July(?) 1823]

They had made their house absolutely a home to me during my residence in Dresden. I travelled in an open carriage with Mrs. Foster;

the two Miss Fosters and her two little boys followed on in a post chaise with their German tutor.

The commencement of our tour was most auspicious, but after leaving Leipsic, as we approached the Hartz regions, we met with one of the most tremendous squalls of wind, dust, rain, hail, thunder and lightning I ever experienced.

PUBLISHED: PMI, II, 160.

INDEX